A DICTIONARY OF SYMBOLS

D1338935

A DICTIONARY OF SYMBOLS

Second Edition

by

J. E. CIRLOT

Translated from the Spanish by

JACK SAGE

Foreword by Herbert Read

Routledge & Kegan Paul

LONDON AND HENLEY

Translated from the Spanish
DICCIONARIO DE SIMBOLOS TRADICIONALES

English Translation
© Routledge & Kegan Paul Ltd 1962
14 Leicester Square,
London WC2H 7PH and
Broadway House, Newtown Road
Henley-on-Thames
Oxon. RG9 1EN

Second impression 1967
Second edition 1971
Reprinted 1973, 1976, 1978, and 1981
Reprinted as paperback 1983, 1984 and 1985

Printed in Great Britain by
Redwood Burn Ltd, Trowbridge

No part of this book may be reproduced
in any form without permission from the
publisher, except for the quotation of
brief passages in criticism

ISBN 0 7102 0017 X

CONTENTS

PLATES

FOREWORD

IN THE INTRODUCTION to this volume Señor Cirlot shows his wide and learned conception of the subject-matter of this dictionary, and the only task left to me is to present the author himself, who has been familiar to me for some years as the leading protagonist of a very vital group of painters and poets in Barcelona. Juan Eduardo Cirlot was born in Barcelona in 1916, and after matriculating from the College of the Jesuits there, studied music. From 1943 onwards he was active as a poet, and published four volumes of verse between 1946 and 1953. Meanwhile the group of painters and poets already mentioned had been formed (*Dau al Set*), and Cirlot became its leading theoretician. For historical or political reasons, Spain had been slow to develop a contemporary movement in the arts comparable to those in other European countries; its greatest artists, Picasso and Miró, had identified themselves with the School of Paris. But now a vigorous and independent 'School of Barcelona' was to emerge, with Antonio Tapies and Modesto Cuixart as its outstanding representatives. In a series of books and brochures Cirlot not only presented the individual artists of this group, but also instructed the Spanish public in the history and theoretical foundations of the modern movement as a whole.

In the course of this critical activity Señor Cirlot inevitably became aware of the 'symbolist ethos' of modern art. A symbolic element is present in all art, in so far as art is subject to psychological interpretation. But in so far as art has evolved in our time away from the representation of an objective reality towards the expression of subjective states of feeling, to that extent it has become a wholly symbolic art, and it was perhaps the necessity for a clarification of this function in art which led Señor Cirlot to his profound study of symbolism in all its aspects.

The result is a volume which can either be used as a work of reference, or simply read for pleasure and instruction. There are many entries in this dictionary—those on Architecture, Colour, Cross, Graphics, Mandala, Numbers, Serpent, Water, Zodiac, to give a few examples—which can be read as independent essays.

But in general the greatest use of the volume will be for the elucidation of those many symbols which we encounter in the arts and in the history of ideas. Man, it has been said, is a symbolizing animal; it is evident that at no stage in the development of civilization has man been able to dispense with symbols. Science and technology have not freed man from his dependence on symbols: indeed, it might be argued that they have increased his need for them. In any case, symbology itself is now a science, and this volume is a necessary instrument in its study.

HERBERT READ

INTRODUCTION

ACTUALITY OF THE SYMBOL

Delimitation of the Symbolic On entering the realms of symbolism, whether by way of systematized artistic forms or the living, dynamic forms of dreams and visions, we have constantly kept in mind the essential need to mark out the field of symbolic action, in order to prevent confusion between phenomena which might appear to be identical when they are merely similar or externally related. The temptation to over-substantiate an argument is one which is difficult to resist. It is necessary to be on one's guard against this danger, even if full compliance with the ideals of scholarship is not always feasible; for we believe with Marius Schneider that there is no such thing as 'ideas *or* beliefs', only 'ideas *and* beliefs', that is to say that in the one there is always at least something of the other—quite apart from the fact that, as far as symbolism is concerned, other phenomena of a spiritual kind play an important part.

When a critic such as Caro Baroja (10) declares himself against any symbolic interpretation of myth, he doubtless has his reasons for so doing, although one reason may be that nothing approaching a complete evaluation of symbolism has yet appeared. He says: 'When they seek to convince us that Mars is the symbol of War, and Hercules of Strength, we can roundly refute them. All this may once have been true for rhetoricians, for idealist philosophers or for a group of more or less pedantic *graeculi*. But, for those who really believed in ancient deities and heroes, Mars had an objective reality, even if this reality was quite different from that which we are groping for today. Symbolism occurs when natural religions are degenerating.' In point of fact, the mere equation of Mars with War and of Hercules with Labour has never been characteristic of the symbolist ethos, which always eschews the categorical and restrictive. This comes about through allegory, a mechanical and restricting derivative of the symbol, whereas the symbol proper is a dynamic and polysymbolic reality, imbued with emotive and conceptual values: in other words, with true life.

However, the above quotation is extremely helpful in enabling us to mark out the limits of the symbolic. If there is or if there may be a symbolic function in everything, a 'communicating tension', nevertheless this fleeting possession of the being or the object by the symbolic does not wholly transform it into a symbol. The error of symbolist artists and writers has always been precisely this: that they sought to turn the entire sphere of reality into a vehicle for impalpable 'correspondences', into an obsessive conjunction of analogies, without being aware that the symbolic is opposed to the existential and instrumental and without realizing that the laws of symbolism hold good only within its own particular sphere. This distinction is one which we would also apply to the Pythagorean thesis that 'everything is disposed according to numbers', as well as to microbiological theory. Neither the assertion of the Greek philosopher on the one hand, nor the vital pullulation subjected invisibly to the science of Weights and Measures on the other, is false; but all life and all reality cannot be forced to conform with either one theory or the other, simply because of its certitude, for it is certain only within the limits of theory. In the same way, the symbolic is true and active on one plane of reality, but it is almost unthinkable to apply it systematically and consistently on the plane of existence. The consequent scepticism concerning this plane of reality—the magnetic life-source of symbols and their concomitants—explains the widespread reluctance to admit symbolical values; but such an attitude is lacking in any scientific justification.

Carl Gustav Jung, to whom present-day symbology owes so much, points out in defence of this branch of human thought that: 'For the modern mind, analogies—even when they are analogies with the most unexpected symbolic meanings—are nothing but self-evident absurdities. This worthy judgement does not, however, in any way alter the fact that such affinities of thought do exist and that they have been playing an important rôle for centuries. Psychology has a duty to recognize these facts; it should léave it to the profane to denigrate them as absurdities or as obscurantism' (32). Elsewhere Jung observes that all the energy and interest devoted today by western Man to science and technology were, by ancient Man, once dedicated to mythology (31). And not only his energy and interest but also his speculative and theorizing propensities, creating the immeasurable wealth of Hindu, Chinese and Islamic philosophy, the Cabbala itself and the painstaking investigations of alchemy and similar studies. The view that both ancient and oriental man possessed a technique of speculative thought which assured them of some success in prophecy is affirmed by, for example, the archaeologist and historian, Contenau, who maintains that the schools of soothsayers and magicians of Mesopotamia could not have continued to flourish without a definite proportion of correct prognostications; and again by Gaston Bachelard (1), posing the question: 'How could a legend be kept alive and perpetuated if each generation had not "intimate reasons" for believing in it?' The symbolist meaning of a phenomenon helps to explain these 'intimate reasons', since it links the instrumental with the spiritual, the human with the cosmic, the casual with the causal, disorder with order, and since it justifies a word like *universe* which, without these wider implications, would be meaningless, a dismembered and chaotic pluralism; and finally, because it always points to the transcendental.

To revert to the question of the limits of the symbolic and to fix more precisely the aims of this work, let us consider how, on the façade of a monastery, for example, we may note: (*a*) the beauty of the whole; (*b*) the constructional technique; (*c*) its period-styling, bearing in mind the geographical and historical implications; (*d*) the implicit or explicit cultural and religious values, etc.; and also (*x*) the symbolic meaning of the forms. In this instance, the appreciation of the symbolical implications of an ogival arch beneath a rose window could constitute an item of knowledge different in kind from the other items we have enumerated. To facilitate analyses of this kind without, let us repeat, confusing the symbolic essence of an object—the transitory symbolic function which heightens it at any given moment—with its total significance as a real object in the world—that is our main aim. The fact that a Romanesque cloister corresponds exactly to the concept of *temenos* (sacred precinct) and to the images of the soul, the fountain and the central fount—like *sutratma* (silver thread), linking a phenomenon by way of its centre to its origin—does not invalidate or even modify the architectural and utilitarian reality of this cloister; it enriches its significance by identifying it with an 'inner form'.

SYMBOLISM AND HISTORICITY

One of the most deplorable errors of symbolist theory, in its 'spontaneous' as well as in its occult and even its dogmatic interpretations, lies in opposing the symbolical to the historical. Arguing from the premise that there are symbols—and, indeed, there are many—which exist only within their own symbolic structure, the false conclusion is then drawn that all or almost all transcendental events which appear to be both historical and symbolic at once —in other words, to be significant once and for all time—may be seen simply as symbolic matter transformed into legend and thence into history.

The most authoritative students of religion, orientalists and even esoteric scholars have recently raised their voices in protest against this error. Mircea Eliade asserts that 'the two points of view are only superficially irreconcilable . . ., for it must not be thought that a symbolic connotation annuls the material and specific validity of an object or action. Symbolism *adds* a new value to an object or an act, without thereby violating its immediate or "historical" validity. Once it is brought to bear, it turns the object or action into an "open" event: symbolic thought opens the door on to immediate reality for us, but without weakening or invalidating it; seen in this light the universe is no longer sealed off, nothing is isolated inside its own existence: everything is linked by a system of correspondences and assimilations. Man in early society became aware of himself in a world wide open and rich in meaning. It remains to be seen whether these "openings" are just another means of escape or whether, on the other hand, they offer the only possible way of accepting the true reality of the world' (18).

In this quotation we can see clearly formulated the distinction between the historical and the symbolic. We can also see the ever-present possibility of a bridge linking both forms of reality in a cosmic synthesis. The hint of scepticism in the concluding words of this Rumanian scholar should be ascribed to his predominantly scientific training at a time when science, with its emphasis upon the analytical approach, has achieved admirable results in every sphere of reality without showing itself capable of grasping the overall organic pattern, that is: as 'multiplicity in unity'. This scientific disaffection has been well defined by Martin Buber: *Imago mundi nova, imago nulla*. In other words, the world today lacks its own image, because this image can be formulated only by means of a universal synthesis of knowledge—a synthesis which, since the Renaissance and the *de omni re scibili* of Pico della Mirandola, has daily become more difficult.

In connexion with this question of the relationship between the historical and the symbolic, René Guénon has observed: 'There is indeed over-eager acceptance of the belief that to allow a symbolic meaning must imply the rejection of the literal or historical meaning; such a view shows an ignorance of the law of correspondences. This law is the foundation of all symbolism and by virtue of it every thing proceeding essentially from a metaphysical principle, which is the source of its reality, translates and expresses this principle in its own way and according to its own level of existence, so that all things are related and joined together in total, universal harmony which is, in its many guises, a reflection, as it were, of its own fundamental unity . . . One result of this is the range of meaning contained in every symbol: any one thing may, indeed, be regarded as an illustration not only of metaphysical principles but also of higher levels of reality' (25).

The above considerations make it clear that the symbolic in no way excludes the historical, since both forms may be seen—from the ideological point of view—as functional aspects of a third: the metaphysical principle, the platonic 'idea'; or all three may be seen as reciprocal expressions of one meaning on different levels. Going to the kernel of the problem, religion—which naturally absorbs so much of his attention—Jung agrees with Eliade and Guénon in his belief that 'the psychic fact "God" is a collective archetype, a psychic existent, which must not in itself be confused with the concept of a metaphysical God'. The existence of the archetype (that is, of the symbol) 'neither postulates a God, nor does it deny that he exists' (31); yet although this is, strictly speaking, unquestionable, it must surely be agreed—if only in theory—that the universality of an archetype affirms rather than denies the reality of the principle in question. Consequently the symbolic, being independent of the historical, not only does not exclude it but, on the contrary, tends to root it firmly in reality, because of the parallelism between the collective or individual world and the cosmic. And because of the great depth of the hidden roots of all systems of meanings, a further consequence is our tendency to espouse the theory that all symbolist traditions, both western and oriental, spring from one common source. Whether this one source once appeared in time and space as a primeval focal point, or whether it stems from the 'collective unconscious', is quite another matter.

We should like to emphasize that when we refer, in the various passages quoted and paraphrased, to 'tradition' or 'traditional doctrine', we are referring only to the continuity—conscious or unconscious—and the coherence of a system, as much in the dimension of space as in that of time. Some writers favour the doctrine of a spontaneous growth of historically unrelated ideas, while others believe only in the spread of ideas through culture. Loeffler, for example, comments upon the importance of proving that the creation of the storm-myth belongs neither to race nor tribe, since it occurred simultaneously in Asia, Europe, Oceania and America (38); this is akin to the contention of Rank that: 'The myth is the collective dream of the people', a concept substantiated by Rudolf Steiner. Bayley, following Max Müller, believes in the common origin of the human race, which he contends is proved by the universal themes of folklore, legend and superstition. Orientalism, the study of comparative religion, mythology, cultural anthropology, the history of civilization and art, esoterism, psychoanalysis, and symbological research have all combined to provide us with ample material to substantiate 'psychological truth', and this 'essential oneness';

further evidence has been forthcoming from the psychic and also from physiological bases common to us all on account of the importance of the human body—its shape as well as its postures—in relation to the simplest elements of symbolist dialectic.

ORIGIN AND CONTINUITY OF THE SYMBOL

The Development of Symbolism   Diel rightly asserts that the symbol is a vehicle at once universal and particular. Universal, since it transcends history; particular, because it relates to a definite period of history. Without going into questions of 'origin', we shall show that most writers agree in tracing the beginnings of symbolist thought to prehistoric times—to the latter part of the Palaeolithic Age. Our present knowledge of primitive thought and the deductions which can justifiably be drawn concerning the art and the belongings of early man substantiate this hypothesis, but substantiation has been forthcoming particularly from research upon epigraphic engravings. The constellations, animals and plants, stones and the countryside were the tutors of primitive man. It was St. Paul who formulated the basic notion of the immediate consequence of this contact with the visible, when he said: '*Per visibilia ad invisibilia*' (Romans i, 20). The process whereby the beings of this world are ordered according to their properties, so that the words of action and of spiritual and moral facts may be explored by analogy, is one which can also be seen, with the dawning of history, in the transition of the pictograph into the ideograph, as well as in the origins of art.

We could adduce an immense weight of testimony offered by human faith and wisdom proving that the invisible or spiritual order is analogous to the material order. We shall come back to this later when we define 'analogy'. Let us recall the saying of Plato, taken up later by the pseudo-Dionysius the Areopagite: 'What is perceptible to the senses is the reflection of what is intelligible to the mind'; and echoed in the *Tabula Smaragdina*: 'What is below is like what is above; what is above is like what is below', and also in the remark of Goethe: 'What is within is also without.' However it may be, śymbolism is organized in its vast explanatory and creative function as a system of highly complex relations, one in which the dominant factor is always a polarity, linking the physical and metaphysical worlds. What palaeolithic Man evolved out of this process is impossible to know except through indirect deductions. Our knowledge about the latter part of the Neolithic Age is considerably wider. Schneider and Berthelot both consider that this was the period (that is: possibly the fourth millenary before history) when man underwent that great transformation which endowed him with the gifts of creation and organization, qualities which distinguish him from the merely natural world. Berthelot, who has studied this process in the Near East, has given the name of 'astrobiology' to the religious and intellectual cultures of that epoch. The evolution of Man up to this point in history must have passed through the following stages: animism; totemism; and megalithic, lunar and solar cultures. The subsequent stages must have been: cosmic ritualism; polytheism; monotheism; and, finally, moral philosophy. Berthelot considers astrology, astronomy, arithmetic and alchemy of Chaldean origin, a contention which points conclusively to a single focal point in time and space.

He defines the value and significance of astrobiology in the following terms: 'Between on the one hand the world-vision—in many other respects variable and complex—of primitive races, and the vision of modern science and Western Europe on the other, an intermediary view has long held sway in Asia and the Mediterranean. It is what may be termed "astrobiology" or the interplay of astronomic law (the mathematical order) and vegetable and animal life (the biological order). All things form at one and the same time an organic whole and a precise order. The domestication of animals and the care of plants (agriculture) had become a reality long before history began, both in Chaldaea and in Egypt—that is, before 3,000 B.C. Agriculture ensures the regular production of precisely determined species of vegetable, and also ensures an appreciation of their annual "rhythm" of growth, flowering, fructifying, sowing and harvesting, a rhythm which is in direct and constant relation to the calendar, in other words, the position of the heavenly bodies. Time and natural phenomena were measured by reference to the moon before they came to be measured by the sun . . . . Astrobiology hovers between a biology of the heavenly bodies and an astronomy of human beings; beginning with the former, it tends towards the latter' (7). During the neolithic era the geometric idea of space was formulated; so also were the significance of the number seven (derived from this concept of space), the relation between heaven and earth, the cardinal points, and the relations between the various elements of the septenary (the planetary gods, the days of the week) and between those of the quaternary (the seasons, the colours, the cardinal points, the elements). Berthelot believes in the slow spread of these ideas, rather than in their spontaneous and independent appearance. He points to their probable dissemination through either the northern or southern areas of the Pacific, mentioning in passing that America may well have been, in spirit, a colony of Asia before that of Europe (7); and another stream may have been flowing in the opposite direction: from the Near East into Central Europe.

The argument about whether European megalithic culture came before or after the great oriental civilizations is far from settled. Here questions of symbolism arise. The importance of the Franco-Cantabrian zone in the Palaeolithic Age is well known; it is also known that the art forms of this district spread across Europe in the direction of Siberia and southwards across North Africa to the southernmost part of the continent. There was, no doubt, a period of transition between this early flowering and the great megalithic monuments. However that may be, Schneider specifically says in connexion with the symbolic forms studied by him (50): 'In the sixth chapter I shall try to summarize this esoteric doctrine, the systemization of which seems to have been originally the work of megalithic cultures.' And his attitude towards the zone of origin leaves little room for doubt for he states that 'the megalithic must have spread from Europe to India via Danubian culture, a new stage of development beginning with the Age of Metals'. He points out that there are marked similarities between the ideas of regions as far apart as America, New Guinea, Indonesia, Western Europe, Central Asia and the Far East, that is to say, of areas in all parts of the world.

Let us consider now the similarity between the discoveries attributed by Schneider to megalithic European culture and those ascribed by Berthelot to the Far East. In Schneider's opinion the final stage of neolithic development differed from the earlier stage 'in the preference it showed for static and geometric forms, in its organizing and creative genius (evolving fabulous animals, musical instruments, mathematical proportions, number-ideas, astronomy and a tonal system with truly musical sounds). The carrying over of totemistic mystical elements into a more advanced, pastoral civilization explains some of the fundamental characteristics of the new mystique. . . . The entire cosmos comes to be conceived after the human pattern. As the essence of all phenomena is, in the last resort, a vibrant rhythm, the intimate nature of phenomena is directly perceptible by polyrhythmic human consciousness. For this reason, imitating is knowing. The echo is the paradigmatic form of imitation. Language, geometric symbols and number-ideas are a cruder form of imitation.' Schneider then observes that according to Speiser and Heine-Geldern, 'the outstanding cultural elements of megalithic culture are: cyclopean buildings, commemorative stones, stones as the dwelling-places of souls, cultural stone-circles, *palafittes*, head-hunting, the sacrifice of oxen, eye-shaped ornaments, death-ships, family-trees, signal-drums, the sacrificial stake, and labyrinths' (50).

It is precisely these elements that have most successfully preserved their symbolic form down the ages. And did not these express, even in megalithic times, the very essence of human life, bursting from the unconscious in the shape of a constructive and configurating longing? Or was it, rather, the ever-present, primary forms of life, sacrifice and intellection of the world which found everlasting expression in these cultural creations, making an ineradicable impression on the mind of Man? One may unhesitatingly answer in the affirmative to both questions, for they refer to the different but parallel phenomena of culture and psychology.

SYMBOLISM IN THE WEST

It was Egypt who gave shape, in her religion and hieroglyphics, to Man's awareness of the material and spiritual, natural and cultural duality of the world. Either independently or together, the various civilizations of Mesopotamia developed their own particular systems; yet these systems were but outward variations of the one true, innermost, universal pattern. There are differences of opinion about dating the first appearance—or at any rate the final crystallization—of some of the most important and complex symbols. Some writers argue strongly in favour of remote origins. Krappe (35) holds that the scientific study of the planets and their identification with the gods of the Babylonian pantheon date only from the 7th century B.C.; but others trace these beginnings as far back as the age of Hammurabi (2000 B.C.) or earlier. Father Heras, for example, says: 'The early Indians, as has been revealed by inscriptions, were the discoverers of the movements of the sun across the sky—the basis of the zodiacal system. Their Zodiac had only eight constellations and each constellation was supposed to be a "form of God". All these "forms of God" in the end became deities, each one presiding over one particular constellation; this is what happened in Rome, for example. The eight Indian signs of the Zodiac are: Edu (ram), Yal (harp), Nand (crab), Amma (mother), Tuk (balance), Kani (arrow), Kuda (pitcher), Min (fish).' The dodecatemorian system of the Zodiac first appears in the form in which we know it as late as the 6th century B.C. Egyptian and Chaldean science was partly assimilated by the Syrians, Phoenicians and Greeks, reaching the latter largely through secret societies. Herodotus points out, in writing of the Pythagoreans, that they were obliged to wear linen clothes 'in accordance with the Orphic ceremonies, which are the same as the Egyptian . . .'.

The mythologies of the Mediterranean peoples were characterized by a vivid, dramatic vitality which came to be expressed both in their art and in their myths, legends and dramatic poetry. These myths enshrined the moral principles, the natural laws, the great contrasts and the transformations which determine the course of cosmic and human life. Frazer points out that 'under the names of Osiris, Tammuz, Adonis and Attis, the peoples of Egypt and Western Asia represented the yearly decay and revival of life, especially of vegetable life' (21). The tasks of Hercules, the legend of Jason, the 'histories' of the heroic age of Greece which provided the inspiration for the classical tragedies, have such great archetypal power that they constitute timeless lessons for mankind. But beneath this mythological and literary symbolism and allegory, a subterranean stream of oriental influence was beginning to flow in from the East.

Principally during the Lower Roman Empire, when the cohesion of the classical world was beginning to dissolve, Hebraic, Chaldean and Egyptian elements began to ferment. Dualist Manichaeism and Gnosticism began to threaten the position of early Christianity. Among the Gnostics, the emblem and the graphic symbol were used for the propagation of initiatory truths. Many of the innumerable images were not of their own creation but were compiled from various sources, mainly Semitic. Symbolism veers towards the Unitarian doctrine of reality and comes to be a specialized branch of speculation. Diodorus Siculus, Pliny, Tacitus, Plutarch, Apuleius all reveal some familiarity with oriental symbolism. Aristotelian thought also contained a strong element of symbolism. In Syria, Mesopotamia, Transcaucasia and Egypt, oriental Christianity had absorbed a vast symbological inheritance. Similarly, those Roman colonies in the West that survived the Nordic invasions retained many attributes of ancient times, including traditional symbols. But, according to the Rev. Fr. Festugière, in *La Révélation d'Hermès Trismégiste*, one of the currents which were most able to contribute to the formation of the symbolist and alchemic 'corpus' was that of the literature of the 'Mirabilia'. This was apparently founded by Bolus the Democritean during the 3rd–2nd centuries B.C. and was continued for centuries in a virtually unbroken tradition by Pseudo-Manetho, Nigidius Figulus, Demetrius, Apollodorus, etc., culminating in the *Book of the Things of Nature*, a Syrian work of the 7th century A.D.

The concept of the analogy between the visible and the invisible world is, then, held jointly by the pagan religions of the Lower Empire, by neoplatonic and Christian doctrines, except that each one of these three systems uses this concept for its own ends. According to Eliade, Theophilus of Antioch would point out, to those who denied the resurrection of the dead, the signs which God places in reach of Man in the realm of natural phenomena: the cycle of the seasons, of the days and nights. He would even go further and say: 'May there not perhaps be resurrection for the seeds and the fruits?' (18). In his *Letter* number LV, St. Augustine shows that teaching carried out with the help of symbols feeds and stirs

Title-page of book of emblems by Joachim Camerario
(Nuremberg, 1590) with symbolic tree, circle,
precinct and grotesques.

the fires of love, enabling Man to excel himself; he also alludes to the
value of all things in nature—organic and inorganic—as bearers of
spiritual messages by virtue of their distinctive forms and characteristics. All the mediaeval lapidaries, herbals and bestiaries owe their
origin to this concept. Most of the classical Fathers of the Church
have something to say about symbolism and since they enjoyed
such a high reputation in Roman times, one can see why this was the
period when the symbol came to be so deeply experienced, loved
and understood, as Davy emphasizes (14). Pinedo mentions the
immense cultural value, particularly during the Middle Ages,
of the *Clavis Melitoniae*—an orthodox version of ancient symbolism.
According to Cardinal Pitra—quoted by Pinedo—an awareness
of this 'Key' is to be found in most mediaeval authors. This is not
the place to give a summary of their ideas or works, but we should like
to mention in passing the important works of: Alan of Lille, *De
Planctu Naturae;* Herrad of Landsberg, *Hortus Deliciarum;* Hildegard of Bingen, *Scivias Domini, Liber Divinorum Operum Simplicis
Hominis;* Bernard Silvestris, *De Re Mundi Universitate;* Hugh of
St. Victor, *Didascalion, Commentarium in Hierarchiam Coelestem,*
etc. The *Key* of St. Melito, bishop of Sardis, dates from the 2nd
century A.D. Some other sources of Christian symbolism are:
Rabanus Maurus, *Allegoriae in Sacram Scripturam;* Odo, bishop of
Tusculum; Isidore of Seville, *Etymologiarum;* Johannes Scotus
Erigena, John of Salisbury, William of St. Thierry, etc. St. Thomas
Aquinas himself speaks of the pagan philosophers as sources of
external and demonstrable proofs of Christian truths. Concerning
the intimate nature of mediaeval symbolism, Jung observes that, in
those days 'analogy was not so much a logical figure as a secret
identity', that is to say, a continuation of primitive, animistic
thought (32).

The Renaissance also showed great interest in symbolism, although
in a manner more individualistic and cultured, more profane,
literary and aesthetic. Dante had fashioned his *Commedia* upon
a basis of oriental symbols. In the 15th century particular use
was made of two Greek writers of the 2nd and 3rd centuries A.D.
They are Horapollo, with his *Hieroglyphica*; and the anonymous
compiler of the *Physiologus*. Horapollo, inspired by the Egyptian
hieroglyphic system, the key to which had been lost by his time,
tried to reconstruct its meaning upon the basis of its configuration
and elemental symbolism. In 1467, an Italian writer, Francesco
Colonna, wrote a work, *Hypnerotomachia Poliphili* (published in
Venice in 1499), which enjoyed widespread success and in which
the symbol had now acquired the particular, mobile significance
which has come to characterize it in modern times. In 1505,
Colonna's editor published Horapollo's work, which in turn in-

fluenced two other important writers at the same time: Andrea Alciati, author of *Emblemata* (1531), which was to arouse a disproportionate taste for profane symbolism throughout Europe (Henry Green in his *Andrea Alciati and his Books of Emblems,* London, 1872, names more than three thousand titles of books dealing with emblems); and Giampietro Valeriano, author of the compendious *Hieroglyphica* (1556). In 15th-century painting there is abundant evidence of this interest in symbolism: Botticelli, Mantegna, Pinturicchio, Giovanni Bellini, Leonardo, for example; later, during the 16th, 17th and 18th centuries, this interest tended towards the allegorical. One may say that, from the latter part of the Middle Ages onwards, the West lost that sense of unity which characterized the symbol and symbolist tradition. Yet proof of its continued existence is offered by the occasional revelation of diverse aspects in the work of poets, artists and writers, from Giovanni da Udine to Antonio Gaudi, from Bosch to Max Ernst. In German Romanticism, the interest in the deeper layers of psychic life—in dreams and their meaning, in the unconscious—is the fount which has given rise to the present-day interest in symbology, which, although still partially repressed, again dwells in the deep wells of the spirit, as it did before being circumscribed by a system with a rigid cosmic pattern. Thus, Schubert, in his *Symbolik des Traumes* (1837), says: 'The prototypes of the images and forms utilized by the oneirocritic, poetic and prophetic idioms, can be found around us in Nature, revealing herself as a world of materialized dream, as a prophetic language whose hieroglyphics are beings and forms.' Most of the literature of the first half of the 19th century, especially the Nordic, presupposes a feeling for the symbolic, for the significant. Thus, Ludwig Tieck, in *Runenburg*, says of his protagonist: 'Insensitive from that moment to the beauty of flowers, in which he believes he can see "the gaping wound of Nature" throbbing' (the theme of Philoctetes as well as of Amfortas in *Parsifal*), 'he finds himself drawn towards the mineral world.'

Innumerable *genera* still conserve symbols in semeiotic form, ossified and sometimes degraded from the universal plane to the particular. We have already referred to literary emblems. In a similar class are the distinctive marks used by mediaeval and Renaissance paper-manufacturers. In this connexion, Bayley says that, from their first appearance in 1282 up to the second half of the 18th century, they had an esoteric meaning; and that in them, as in fossils, we can see the crystallization of the ideals of numerous mystic sects of mediaeval Europe (4). The popular art of all European peoples is another inexhaustable mine of symbols. One only has to glance through a work like that of Helmuth Th. Bossert in order to find amongst the images such well-known subjects as the cosmic tree, the snake, the phoenix, the ship of death, the bird on the rooftop, the two-headed eagle, the planetary division into two groups of three and of four, grotesques, rhomboids, lines and zigzags, etc. Furthermore, legends and folktales, when their editors have been faithful, as in the case of Perrault and the Grimm brothers, have retained their mythical and archetypal structure (38). In the same way, in lyrical poetry, alongside works created within the canons of explicit symbolism—best illustrated in the works of René Ghil—there are frequent flowerings of symbolic motifs springing spontaneously out of the creative spirit.

THE SYMBOLIC MEANING OF DREAMS

What a myth represents for a people, for any one culture, or for any given moment of history, is represented for the individual by the symbolic images of dreams, by visions and by fantasy or lyricism. This distinction does not imply dichotomy: many dreams have been known to express premonitions. But when the symbol—or the premonition—goes beyond the particular and the subjective, we find ourselves in the realm of augury and prophecy; symbolic laws can explain both phenomena, but the latter may be a revelation of the supernatural.

Given our contemporary psychoanalytic concept of the 'unconscious', we must accept the placing within it of all those dynamic forms which give rise to symbols; for, according to Jung's way of thinking, the unconscious is 'the matrix of the human mind and its inventions' (33). The unconscious was 'discovered' theoretically by Carus, Schopenhauer and Hartmann, and experimentally by Charcot, Bernheim, Janet, Freud and other psychologists. But this newly acquired knowledge merely showed to be internal what had formerly been thought to be external to Man. For example, Greek seers believed that dreams came from 'without', that is, from the domain of the gods. Now, esoteric tradition, in accordance with the Hindu doctrine of the three planes of consciousness, had always been aware that the vertical division of thought could also be seen on three levels: the subconscious (instinctive and affective thought); consciousness (ideological and reflexive thought); and superconsciousness (intuitive thought and the higher truths). Hence, by way of simplification, we shall adopt the Jungian term 'unconscious' instead of 'subconscious', since one rightly asks oneself when dealing with many authors: 'How can they be so certain that the unconscious is "lower" and not "higher" than the conscious?' (31).

The interest in dreams and their symbolic content goes back to Antiquity, when, although the theory was never consciously formulated, it was implied that the phenomenon could be considered as a kind of personal mythology, even though the manner of its expression was the objective, collective myth. The famous dreams of the Bible; the book of Artemidorus Daldianus; the interpretative dictionaries of Chaldean, Egyptian and Arabic origin bear witness to the attention paid to dreams as harbingers of hidden truths about the submerged life of the psyche and, more rarely, about external and objective facts. The mechanism of oneiromancy, like that of other divinatory or prophetic techniques, is a universal phenomenon; for such techniques are based upon the higher activity of the unconscious in response to certain stimuli, and upon the automatic acquisition of unconscious stores of knowledge remaining unperceived until 'read' in accordance with the principles of numbers, orientation, form and space. We must again underline the way in which Jung approaches this universal phenomenon. He says that the fact of 'an opinion being held for so long and so widely necessarily demonstrates that in some way it must be true, that is, *psychologically true*'. He explains psychological truth as a fact, not as a judgement or an opinion, and he considers that careful demonstration and corroboration are evidence enough for this (31).

Since an extensive bibliography of dreams is already available, it is here intended only to recall that they afford Man another means of making contact with his deepest aspirations, with the geometric or moral laws of the universe, and also with the muted stirrings of the submerged unconscious. Teillard points out that in dreams all layers of the psyche are revealed, including the deepest. And just as the embryo passes through the evolutionary animal stages, so we carry with us archaic 'memories' which can be brought to light (56). On the other hand, Carus believed that the soul was in communion with the cosmic, and that, oneirocritically speaking, the soul was susceptible to truths different from those which rule the waking life; in this way he associated dreams with those rituals which enabled Man to enter into the great secrets of Nature. It is usually accepted that modern ways of thinking differ from primitive thought-processes only with regard to consciousness, and that the unconscious has hardly changed since the Upper Palaeolithic Stage.

Oneirocritic symbols, then, are not strictly different from mythical, religious, lyrical or primitive symbols. Except that, with the primary archetypes, one finds intermixed a kind of subworld consisting of the remains of existential images drawn from reality, which may be lacking in symbolic meaning, which may be expressions of the physiological—merely memories—or which may also possess a symbolism related to the material and primary forms from which they originate. In this dictionary we have kept to traditional symbols only, but it is evident that other more 'recent' symbols must derive from the older—as the motor-car from the carriage—or else must be related through the symbolism of form, although this must always be a question of *similar* symbols, not of the *same* symbol nor of the same order of meaning.

There is another problem which we cannot ignore: not all human beings are on the same level. Even if we do not accept the idea of radical differences, or the concept of spiritual growth—a concept which always has a touch of the oriental and esoteric about it— it is undeniable that differences of intensity (emotion, inner life, richness of thought and feeling) and of quality (intellectual and authentically moral education) bring about essentially different levels of thought, whether it be logical or magical thought, rational speculation or oneirocritic elaboration. Havelock Ellis has pointed out that extraordinary dreams are confined to people of genius, and according to Jung even primitive races make a similar distinction; the Elgonyi tribe in the Elgon jungle explained to him that they recognized two types of dream: the ordinary dream of the unimportant man, and the 'great vision', generally the exclusive privilege of outstanding men (34). Hence interpretative theories of symbolic material must vary according to whether they are drawn from the analysis of the dreams of more or less pathological individuals, from the dreams of normal people, from those of outstanding men, or from collective myths. The materialistic tone pervading the symbolic classifications of many psychoanalysts is accounted for by the nature of their sources of information. On the other hand, the symbology of philosophers, founders of religions and poets is wholly idealist and cosmic in direction, embracing all objects, seeking after the infinite and pointing to the mysteries of the mystical 'centre'. This is verified by Jung, who shows that accounts of fantasy or of dreams always contain not only what is most peremptory for the narrator but also what for the moment is most painful (i.e. most important) for him (31). It is this 'importance' which fixes the plane upon which any system of interpretation must exist. Freud's definition ('Every dream is a repressed desire') points to the same conclusion, for our desires are the index of our aspirations and our potentialities.

THE SYMBOLISM OF ALCHEMY

In his *On Psychic Energy*, Jung has asserted that: 'The spiritual appears in the psyche as an instinct, indeed as a real passion. . . It is not derived from any other instinct, but is a principle *sui generis*, that is, a specific and necessary form of instinctual power.' Apart from the fact that this asseveration would seem to put an end to the assumption that science is necessarily materialistic, its importance lies in that it takes up the essential platonic doctrine of the soul, which we here equate with the Jungian principle of spirituality, even though at times it may be necessary to treat the two principles separately. Plato in *Timaeus*, Plotinus in the *Enneads*, elaborate the idea that the soul is a stranger on earth, that it has descended from the spaceless and timeless universe, or that it has 'fallen' on account of sin into matter, that it initiates a process of life-giving growth corresponding to the period of involution.

At any given moment, the inverse of this downward and inward movement can be produced: the soul recalls that its origin is beyond space and time, beyond living creatures and the world of objects, even beyond images; it then tends towards the annihilation of the corporeal and begins to ascend towards its Origin. Iamblichus explains this as follows: 'A principle of the soul is that it is superior to all Nature, and that through it we can rise above the order and the systems of the world. When the soul is thus separated from all subordinate natures, it exchanges this life for another and abandons this order of things to bind itself inseparably with another.' The idea of rotation is the keystone of most transcendent symbols: of the mediaeval *Rota*; of the Wheel of Buddhist transformations; of the zodiacal cycle; of the myth of the Gemini; and of the *opus* of the alchemists. The idea of the world as a labyrinth or of life as a pilgrimage leads to the idea of the 'centre' as a symbol of the absolute goal of Man—Paradise regained, heavenly Jerusalem. Pictorially, this central point is sometimes identified with the geometric centre of the symbolic circle; sometimes it is placed above it; and at other times, as in the oriental *Shri Yantra*, it is not portrayed at all, so that the contemplator has to imagine it.

But constantly we find a given theme reappearing under the guise of a new symbol: the lost object, the impossible or very difficult enterprise; or else it comes to be equated with a variety of qualities: knowledge, love, obtaining a desired object, etc. Alchemy was developed in two fairly well-defined stages: the mediaeval and the Renaissance, the latter terminating by the 18th century, when it split once again into its two original components: mysticism and chemistry. Alchemy is a symbolic technique which, together with the desire for positive discoveries in the field of the natural sciences, sought to materialize spiritual truths. Instead of confronting the mythical dragon in their search for 'treasure', like Cadmus, Jason and Siegfried, the alchemists sought to *produce* it by means of hard work and virtue. Their work was not aimed at a simple revelation of esoteric truths, nor was it materialistic: both purposes coalesced, however, to achieve something which for them had the significance of the absolute. Each operation, each detail, every subject, every instrument was a source of intellectual and spiritual life: they were authentic symbols. After being forgotten for a period, alchemy was reassessed as 'the origin of modern chemistry', and recently Bachelard, Silberer, Jung and others have come to see the true completeness of its meaning, at once poetic, religious and scientific.

Bachelard points out that alchemy 'possesses a quality of psychological precision' (33) and that, far from being a description of objective phenomena, it is an attempt to project human love into the 'heart' of things (1). Jung insists that the experiments of the alchemists had the sole purpose—like the ancient techniques of divination, though the former was more ambitious and persistent— of stimulating the deepest layers of the psyche and of facilitating psychic projections in material things, or in other words, of experiencing material phenomena as symbols which point to a complete theory of the universe and the destiny of the soul. For this reason, he says that 'the investigator had certain psychic experiences which appeared to him as the particular behaviour of the chemical process'. Elsewhere he defines this as 'chemical research which, through projection, incorporated unconscious psychic material', a remark which he rounds off by affirming that 'the real nature of matter was unknown to the alchemist. He knew it only by allusion. Searching for a solution, he projected the unconscious into the obscurity of matter in order to illuminate it. To explain the mystery of matter, he projected another mystery into what was to be explained' (32). The *summa* of this mystery, the deepest of secret aspirations, was the *coincidentia oppositorum*, of which 'the alchemists are as it were the empiricists, whereas Nicholas of Cusa is its philosopher' (33). But the alchemist did not merely pretend to carry out his experiments; he was, indeed, profoundly and pathetically engrossed in his search for gold. It was this interest, together with his sense of dedication that—as in the search for the Holy Grail— was the guarantee of final success, by dint of the virtuous practice which his unceasing labour demanded. To discover the secret of making gold was the mark of divine favour. Jung interprets the process psychologically as the gradual elimination of the impure factors of the spirit in the progress towards the immutable values of eternity. But this interpretation had been fully grasped by the alchemists themselves: Michael Maier, in *Symbola Aureae Mensae* (1617), says that 'chemistry encourages the investigator to meditate upon celestial blessings'. Dorn, in *Physica* (1661), alludes to the relationship which must exist between the worker and his research when he asserts: 'You will never make Oneness out of Otherness until you yourself have become Oneness.' Oneness was achieved by annihilating the desire for what is different or transitory and by fixing the mind upon what is 'higher' and eternal. Famous indeed is the maxim of the alchemists: *Aurum nostrum non est aurum vulgi.* This assertion—that their gold was not ordinary gold—seems to indicate that their symbolism excluded the material reality of the symbol, in favour of the spiritual. But, of course, it is hazardous to talk as if the varied work of so many researchers with such differing backgrounds was all of a piece. The demand for actual gold could be interpreted as being the same as the longing of the doubting St. Thomas. The chosen few were well content with the dream of the 'subterranean Sun' shining at the bottom of the alchemist's oven like the light of salvation within the depths of the soul, no matter whether this salvation is considered to be the product of religious faith or of that hypothetical 'process of individuation' into which Jung seems to have poured his finest thoughts and sentiments about Man. Of course, beneath this concept there lie hidden none other than the three supreme longings which seem to lead to felicity: first, the alchemic Rebis, or the androgynous being, signifying the conjunction of opposites and the cessation of the torment caused by the separation of the sexes, beginning with the time when the 'spherical man' of Plato was split into two halves; second, the establishing of the 'volatile' principle, that is, the annihilation of all change or transition, once the essence has been obtained; and, finally, the concentrating into one central point, as a symbol of the mystical centre of the universe—that is, of the irradiant origin (32) and of immortality.

DEFINITIONS OF THE SYMBOL

Definitions and analyses of the nature of symbols and of symbolism are all too frequent. But we should like to study some of the more thoughtful suggestions, keeping, as always in this work, within the limits of comparative analysis. For the Hindu philosopher Ananda K. Coomaraswamy, symbolism is 'the art of thinking in images', an art now lost to civilized Man, notably in the last three hundred years, perhaps in consequence of the 'catastrophic theories of Descartes', to quote Schneider. Coomaraswamy, then, shares the views of Fromm and of Bayley, explicit in the titles of their respective works: *The Forgotten Language* and *The Lost Language of Symbolism.* However, this loss—as anthropology and psychoanalysis have shown —is limited to consciousness and not to the 'unconscious', which, to compensate, is perhaps now overloaded with symbolic material.

   Diel considers the symbol to be 'a precise and crystallized means of expression', corresponding in essence to the inner life (intensive and qualitative) in opposition to the external world (extensive and quantitative) (15). In this, he agrees with Goethe, who asserted: 'In the symbol, the particular represents the general, *not* as a dream, *not* as a shadow, but as a living and momentary revelation of the inscrutable.' We suggest that the distinction made by Diel between the inner and the outer worlds is a general truth, applicable not only to the Cartesian method: the world of *res cogitans* is one which recognizes extension. How is it possible, then, for it to ignore the quantitative if the qualitative arises from 'groups' of quantity?

Marc Saunier, in his literary and pseudomystical style, points to an important characteristic of symbols when he states that they are 'the synthesizing expression of a marvellous science, now forgotten by men', but that 'they show us all that has been and will be, in one immutable form' (49). He thereby assigns to symbols—or recognizes, rather—their didactic function as timeless objects *per se*, at least in their intimate structure, for the other factors are cultural or personal variants.

The connexion between created and Creator is also apparent in the symbol. Jules Le Bêle recalls that 'every created object is, as it were, a reflection of divine-perfection, a *natural and perceptible sign* of a supernatural truth', thus echoing the Pauline proposition *Per visibilia ad invisibilia*, as well as the assertion of Sallust that 'The world is a symbolic object.' Landrit insists that 'symbolism is the science of the relations which unite the created world with God, the material world with the supernatural; the science of the harmonies existing between the diverse parts of the universe (correspondences and analogies)', operating within the process of involution, that is, of the materiality of all things.

Here we must interpose a distinction and a clarification. Erich Fromm (23), steering his course along the normal channels of symbolic knowledge, lays down three kinds of symbol which are different in degree: (*a*) the *conventional*, (*b*) the *accidental*, (*c*) the *universal*. The first kind comprises simple acceptance of a constant affinity stripped of any optical or natural basis: for example, many signs used in industry, in mathematics and in other fields. The second type springs from strictly transitory conditions and is due to associations made through casual contact. The third kind is that which we are now studying and is defined, according to Fromm, as the existence of the *intrinsic relation* between the symbol and what it represents. It is obvious that this relation does not always have the same vitality. For this reason, as we have already pointed out, it is difficult to classify symbols with exactitude.

This language of images and emotions is based, then, upon a precise and crystallized means of expression, revealing transcendent truths, external to Man (cosmic order) as well as within him (thought, the moral order of things, psychic evolution, the destiny of the soul); furthermore, it possesses a quality which, according to Schneider, increases its dynamism and gives it a truly dramatic character. This quality, the essence of the symbol, is its ability to express simultaneously the various aspects (thesis and antithesis) of the idea it represents (51). Let us give a provisional explanation of this: the unconscious, or 'place' where symbols live, does not recognize the inherent distinctions of contraposition; or again, the 'symbolic function' appears at the precise moment when a state of tension is set up between opposites which the consciousness cannot resolve by itself.

For psychologists, the symbol exists almost wholly in the mind, and is then projected outwards upon Nature, either accepting language as its being and its form or converting being and form into dramatic characters, but it is not seen in this way by orientalists and esoteric thinkers, who base symbolism upon the incontrovertible equation macrocosm=microcosm. For this reason René Guénon points out that: 'The true basis of symbolism is, as we have said, the correspondence linking together all orders of reality, binding them one to the other, and consequently extending from the natural order as a whole to the supernatural order. By virtue of this correspondence, the whole of Nature is but a symbol, that is, its true significance becomes apparent only when it is seen as a pointer which can make us aware of supernatural or "metaphysical" truths—metaphysical in the proper and true sense of the word, which is nothing less than the *essential function of symbolism*. . . . The symbol must always be inferior to the thing symbolized, which destroys all naturalist concepts of symbolism' (29). This latter idea is repeatedly stressed by Guénon, declaring that 'what is superior can never symbolize what is inferior, although the converse is true' (25) (provided, we must add, that one is dealing with a specific symbol of inversion). On the other hand, what is superior can remind us of what is inferior.

The observations of Mircea Eliade are very interesting in this respect. He assigns to the symbol the mission of going beyond the limitations of this 'fragment' which is Man (or any one of his concerns) and of integrating this 'fragment' into entities of wider scope: society, culture, the universe. Even if, within these limitations, 'an object transmuted into a symbol—as a result of its being possessed by the symbolic function—tends to unite with the All . . . this union is not the same as a confusion, for the symbol does not restrict movement or circulation from one level to another, and integrates all these levels and planes (of reality), but without fusing them—that is, without destroying them', integrating them, in short, within a system. On the other hand, Eliade believes that if the All can appear contained within a significant fragment, it is because each fragment restates the All: 'A tree, by virtue of the power it manifests, may become a blessed haven, without ceasing to be a tree; and if it becomes a cosmic tree it is because *what it manifests* restates, point by point, what the totality manifests' (17). Here we have the explanation of the 'intrinsic relation' mentioned by Erich Fromm. Though transmuted to another plane of reality, it consists of the essential relationship between one process and another, between one object and another, an intimate relationship which has been defined as rhythm.

THE 'COMMON RHYTHM' OF SCHNEIDER

The analogy between two planes of reality is founded upon the existence in both of a 'common rhythm'. By rhythm we mean here not 'perceptible order in time', but the coherent, determinate and dynamic factor which a character or figure possesses and which is transmitted to the object over which it presides or from which it emanates. This rhythm is fundamentally a movement resulting from a certain vitality or from a given 'number'. It shows itself as a characteristic expression or formal crystallization. Thus, between the live snake, with its sinuous movement, and the snake appearing in inanimate relief, there may be an analogy which is not only formal (in the design, disposition, or in the specific shape of the animal) but also rhythmic—that is, of tone, of modality, of accent, and of expression.

Martin Buber, in his study of natural, primitive poetry, points out that Man—whether it be megalithic Man, our contemporary Primitive, or 'romantic' Man seeking natural spontaneity in his relations with the cosmos—'does not think about the moon as such, which he sees every night; for what he retains is not the image of a wandering, luminous disc, nor that of an associated demonic being, but that of the immediate emotive image, the lunar fluid flowing through bodies' (quoted by Gaston Bachelard, 2). This is exactly the view of Schneider also, pointing to the aptitude for symbolic and rhythmic thought of Primitive Man, who could identify the movement of a wave with that of the backs of a moving flock of sheep (51). Davy recalls that Boethius had alluded earlier to a 'common rhythm' when he asserted that only those things which have the same matter in common—meaning, in this context, the same 'vital aspect'—can mutually transform and interchange themselves (14). Rhythm may be understood as a grouping of distances, of quantitative values, but also as a formal pattern determined by rhythmic numbers, that is, as spatial, formal and positional similitude.

But there is a deeper meaning to the concept of rhythm, which is precisely that expounded by Schneider upon the basis of Primitive

Man's identification of one 'living, dynamic cell' with two or more different aspects of reality. For this reason, he points out that: 'The definition of the common rhythm varies considerably according to the culture in question. Primitive beings found related rhythms particularly in the timbre of the voice, the rhythm of walking, motion, colour and material. More advanced cultures preserve these criteria, but they give more importance to form and material (the visual) than to the criteria of the voice and the rhythm of walking. Instead of conceiving these related rhythms dynamically and artistically as primitive people did, higher cultures think of them as abstract values and order them according to a reasoned classification of a static and geometric kind. . . . Whereas Primitive Man saw that forms and phenomena are essentially fluid, more advanced civilizations have given pride of place to the static aspect of forms and the purely geometric outlines of shape' (50).

Rhythms and modes, then, allow relationships to be established between different planes of reality. While natural science establishes relationships only between 'horizontal' groups of beings after the classification of Linnaeus, mystic or symbolic science erects 'vertical bridges' between those objects which are within the same cosmic rhythm, that is, objects whose position 'corresponds' to that of another 'analogous' object on another plane of reality: for example, an animal, a plant or a colour. According to Schneider, this idea of correspondences comes from belief in the indissoluble unity of the universe. Thus, in megalithic and astrobiological cultures, the most disparate phenomena are brought together, by virtue of their having a 'common rhythm'; 'hence one finds that such elements as the following are correlated: musical or cultural instruments and implements of work; animals, gods, and heavenly bodies; the seasons, the points of the compass, and material symbols; rites, colours and offices; parts of the human body and phases in human life' (51). Symbolism is what might be called a magnetic force, drawing together phenomena which have the same rhythm and even allowing them to interchange. Schneider deduces some important ontological conclusions from this: 'The apparent multiplicity of outward forms spreading out over concentric planes is deceptive, for, in the last resort, all the phenomena of the universe can be reduced to a few basic rhythmic forms, grouped and ordered by the passage of time' (51). He also draws gnostical conclusions: 'The symbol is the ideological manifestation of the mystic rhythm of creation and the degree of truth attributed to the symbol is an expression of the respect Man is able to accord to this mystical rhythm' (50). The rhythmic link between the world outside Man and the physiology of Man is demonstrated by Schneider's affirming that Primitive Man and his animal-totem—though different beings

—are joined in a common rhythm, whose basic element is the *cry-symbol* (51). Jung has amplified the psychological implications of this concept, demonstrating the deep and constant relationship between rhythm and emotion (31).

At this point we must comment upon the conclusion implicit in Schneider's thesis that, in spite of the multiplicity of forms which phenomena seem to take on, there is a lack of clearly independent forms in the universe. Indeed, morphology in its systematic analysis of forms has found that only a few are fundamental: this is particularly true of biology, in which the ovoid is a basic form from which the sphere, its segment and many intermediate forms are derived. In fact, symbological analyses often seem to offset a certain narrowing of scope by an added richness in depth, for the few basic situations that do exist appear under varying, though secondary, guises. Similarly, the only 'original' numbers are the first decade of the Greek system or the numbers up to twelve in the oriental system. The rest come under the rule of 'multiplicity', which is merely a reordering of the basic series. Besides, the place of symbolism is within the archetypal pattern of each being, each form, each rhythm. Within this archetypal pattern, thanks to the principle of concentration, all like beings can be presented as one being. And in addition, by virtue of this oneness, the predominant rhythm transmutes all that might appear to be separate; so that, to give an example, not only do all dragons stand for The Dragon, but any symbolic daub resembling a dragon is also The Dragon. And we shall see that this is a consequence of the principle of 'sufficient identity'.

JUNG'S ARCHETYPE

In the equation macrocosm=microcosm there is the implied possibility of explaining the former by the latter, or vice versa. The 'common rhythm' of Schneider belongs rather to the tendency to explain Man by reference to the world, while Jung's 'archetype' tends to explain the world by reference to Man. This is logical, since the archetype does not stem from forms or from figures or objective beings, but from images within the human spirit, within the turbulent depths of the unconscious. The archetype is, in the first place, an epiphany, that is, the revelation of the latent by way of the recondite: vision, dream, fantasy, myth. These spiritual manifestations are not, for Jung, substitutes for living things—are not lifeless effigies; they are the fruits of the inner life perpetually flowing out from the unconscious, in a way which can be compared with the gradual unfolding of creation. Just as creation determines the burgeoning of beings and objects, so psychic energy flowers into an image, an entity marking the true borders between the informal and the conceptual, between darkness and light.

Jung uses the word 'archetype' to designate those universal symbols which possess the greatest constancy and efficiency, the greatest potentiality for psychic evolution, and which point away from the inferior towards the superior. In *On Psychic Energy*, he specifically says: 'The psychological mechanism that transforms energy is the symbol.' But, in addition, he appears to give a different meaning to the archetype, linking it strictly with the structure of the psyche, when he distinguishes it from the symbol in so far as its ontic significance goes. To clarify this, let us quote some of Jung's own observations: 'The archetypes are the numinous, structural elements of the psyche and possess a certain autonomy and specific energy which enables them to attract, out of the conscious mind, those contents which are best suited to themselves. The symbols act as transformers, their function being to convert libido from a "lower" into a "higher" form. . . . It was manifestly not a question of inherited ideas, but of an inborn disposition to produce parallel images, or rather of identical psychic structures common to all men, which I later called the archetypes of the collective unconscious. They correspond to the concept of the "pattern of behaviour" in biology' (31). 'The archetypes do not represent anything external, non-psychic, although they do of course owe the concreteness of their imagery to impressions received from without. Rather, independently of, and sometimes in direct contrast to, the outward forms they may take, they represent the life and essence of a non-individual psyche' (33). That is to say, there is an intermediate realm between the oneness of the individual soul and its solitude, and the variety of the universe: between the *res cogitans* and the *res extensa* of Descartes, and that realm is the image of the world in the soul and of the soul in the world, in other words, the 'place' of symbolism 'working' in areas prepared by the archetypes— eternally present, the 'problem being whether the consciousness perceives them or not' (32).

In his *Essais de psychologie analytique*, Jung again defines the nature of the archetypes as the ready-made systems of both images and emotions (that is, of rhythms). They are inherited with the brain-structure—indeed, they are its psychic aspect. They are, on the one hand, the most powerful of instinctive prejudices, and on the other, the most efficient aids imaginable towards instinctive adaptations. Jung points out that the idea of such 'image-guides' of ancestral origin had already appeared in Freud, who called them 'primitive fantasies'. Jolan de Jacobi, in her work on Jung's psychology (30), says that Jung took the expression from St. Augustine, who used it in a sense which is very similar to the platonic 'idea', that is, the primordial reality from which the realities of existence arise as echoes and fragments. Archetypes are like all-embracing parables:

their meaning is only partially accessible; their deepest significance remains a secret which existed long before Man himself and which reaches out far beyond Man. Jolan de Jacobi identifies symbols for practical purposes with the archetypes, mentioning as examples of the latter: the 'night sea-crossing', the 'whale-dragon', figures such as the prince, the child, the magician or the unknown damsel. We cannot further debate Jung's concepts without going more deeply into his psychological and anthropological theory, which would be beyond the scope of this work. To return to the relationship between, or identity of, the symbol and the archetype, we might say that the latter is the mythical and merely human aspect of the former, whereas a strict system of symbols could exist even without human consciousness, since it is founded upon a cosmic order determined by those 'vertical' relationships which we mentioned when commenting upon the 'common rhythm' of Schneider. In short, it is a synthesis which transmutes systems of vibrations, echoing one basic' and original 'model', into a spiritual idiom expressed usually in the numerical series.

ANALYSIS OF THE SYMBOL

The basic ideas and suppositions which allow us to conceive of 'symbolism', together with the creation and vitality of each symbol, are the following:

(a) Nothing is meaningless or neutral: everything is significant. (b) Nothing is independent, everything is in some way related to something else. (c) The quantitative becomes the qualitative in certain essentials which, in fact, precisely constitute the meaning of the quantity. (d) Everything is serial. (e) Series are related one to another as to position, and the components of each series are related as to meaning. This serial characteristic is a basic phenomenon which is as true of the physical world (in its range of colours, of sounds, of textures, of landscapes, etc.) as of the spiritual world (in its virtues, vices, humours, feelings, etc.). Factors which account for serial arrangement are: limitation; the integration of discontinuity and continuity; proper order; graduation; numbering; the inner dynamism of the component elements; polarity; symmetrical or asymmetrical equilibrium; and the concept as a whole.

If we take any 'symbol'—for example, the sword, or the colour red—and analyse its structure, we shall see that it can be split up into both its real and its symbolic components. First, we find the object in itself, in isolation; in the second place we find the object linked to its utilitarian function, to its concrete or factual reality in the three-dimensional world—directly, in the case of the sword; or indirectly, giving colour, for example to a cloak, in the case of the colour red; in the third place, we find what enables the object to be considered as a symbol: that structure which we have termed 'symbolic function', or the dynamic tendency of the object to link up with its corresponding equivalents in all analogous series, nevertheless principally tending to show the particular metaphysical meaning. In this symbolic function we can still distinguish between the symbolic meaning and the general meaning, the latter being

Engraving in the *Historiarum liber* of Herodotus (Paris, 1510) with the important symbols of the primordial waters, ship, woman, bees and phoenix.

frequently ambivalent and charged with allusions whose variety, however, is never chaotic, for it is marshalled along the co-ordinate line of a 'common rhythm'.

Thus, the sword, iron, fire, the colour red, the god Mars, the rocky mountain, are all interrelated because they are oriented along one 'symbolic line'. They all imply the longing for 'spiritual determination and physical annihilation', which is the profoundest meaning of their symbolic functions; but in addition they are joined together —they beckon to each other, one might say—by virtue of the inner affinity that binds all these phenomena, which are, in truth, concomitants of one essential cosmic modality.

In consequence, apart from this network of relations linking up every kind of object (physical, metaphysical, mental, real and unreal in so far as they have 'psychological reality'), the symbolic order is established by a general correlation between the material and the spiritual (the visible and the invisible) and by the unfolding of their meanings. These components, which account for the 'mode of being' of the object, may be complementary or disparate; in the case of the latter an ambivalent symbol is produced. Schneider mentions the flute as an example (50). The flute in form is phallic and masculine, whereas its sound is feminine. It is an instrument which stands in curious, inverse relation to the drum, with its deep masculine tones and its rounded, feminine shapes. One indispensable aspect of the relationship between abstract forms (geometric or biomorphic, intellectual or artistic) and objects is the mutual influence they have upon each other. Let us analyse another symbol: water, for example. Its predominant characteristics are: (i) it fertilizes; (ii) it purifies; (iii) it dissolves. These three qualities have so much in common that their relationship can be expressed in a variety of ways, although one constant factor always emerges: the suspension of form—that is, the lack of any fixed form (fluidity) —is bound up with the functions of fertilization or regeneration of the material, living world on the one hand, and with the purification or regeneration of the spiritual world on the other. It is this bond which helps to explain the vast symbolism of water, appearing in the midst of solid areas of the cosmos, with the power of destroying the corrupt and of initiating a new cycle of life—the latter meaning is one that extends to the zodiacal signs of Aquarius and Pisces, and confirms the words of the Psalm: 'I am poured out like water, and all my bones are out of joint' (Psalm xxii, 14).

These basic concepts, then, are the justification and the fundament of the symbolic order of things. Jung, however, working within the framework of his symbolic logic, does not accord them the same priority. Speaking of the libido, or vital energy, he says that we have the following possibilities of symbolization: (i) *Analogous comparison* (that is, a comparison between two objects or forces on the same co-ordinate of a 'common rhythm'), as, for example, fire and the sun. (ii) *The objective, causative comparison* (which is based upon the properties of the symbolic object itself), as, for example, the sun as life-giver. (iii) *The subjective, causative comparison* (which functions like the second group, except that it immediately identifies the inner force with some symbol or some object possessing a relevant symbolic function), as, for example, the phallus or snake. (iv) *The functional comparison*, based not upon symbolic objects themselves but upon their activity, informing the image with dynamism and drama; for example, the libido fecundates like the bull, is dangerous like the boar, etc. The relevance to myth of this last group is self-evident (31).

SYMBOLIC ANALOGY

According to the *Tabula Smaragdina*, the threefold principle of the analogy between the outer and the inner world is: (i) the common source of both worlds; (ii) the influence of the psychic upon the physical; (iii) the influence of the physical world upon the spiritual. But the analogy lies not only in the relation between the inner and the outer world, but also in the relation between the various phenomena of the physical world. Material or formal resemblance is only one of the many possible analogies, for analogy can also exist in connexion with function. At times, the act of choosing reveals a basic analogy between the inner motives and the ultimate goal. Let us quote some examples of analogy by way of clarification. From religious literature we learn that the Order of St. Bruno preferred precipitous and remote places for their communities; the Benedictines would choose mountain-heights; the Cistercians, pleasant valleys; and the Jesuits of St. Ignatius, the cities. For those conversant with the character of these foundations it is almost unnecessary to point out that their very choice of situation implies a landscape-symbolism, or that, looked at in another way, the places selected are eloquent proof of the guiding spirit behind each of these communities.

The Pigmies of Equatorial Africa believe that, in the rainbow, God expresses His desire to communicate with them. This is why, as soon as the rainbow appears, they take up their bows and shoot at it. . . . (17). The incomparable beauty of this striking image tells us more about analogy than any analysis can. Other aspects of the same kind of thing may be seen in certain superstitions, such as the belief of many races that by undoing the bolts, locks and latches of the home during the birth of an infant, they can facilitate its coming into the world (21). One more analogy: the process of creation—which oriental theogonies explain as both progressive multiplication and as division, since all things derive from unity—has its analogous counterpart in the related myths of the carving up of the body of Osiris in Egypt, of Prajapati in India and of Dionysos in Greece (40).

As examples of formal analogy or resemblance, we quote four symbolic ways of referring to the Centre: the Hindu Wheel of Transformations in the centre of which is a space which is either quite unadorned or else filled with just the symbol or image of a deity; or the Chinese *Pi*, a disc of jade with a hole in the centre; or the idea that the Pole star, piercing the sky, points the way along which the merely temporal world must move in order to rid itself of the restrictions of time and space; or, finally, in the West, the Round Table with the Holy Grail standing at its centre point. We can see in all these very different objects an almost obsessive repetition of the image of a duality: the centre contrasted with the circumference, as a twofold image of the ineffable origin of the world of phenomena. But there is one legend which opens up great possibilities in analogy, for it contains both formal analogy (resemblance) and functional analogy. It is the myth of the cursed hunter, who leaves the Mass just when the Consecrated Form is being raised aloft, to go hunting. One can see delineated here a spiral movement which 'repeats' the creation of the physical world. The soul abandons the centre (the circular form of the Host) and leaves for the outer part of the wheel, where movement is swifter (symbolized by the endless chase after an unattainable quarry).

Analogy, as a unifying and ordering process, appears continuously in art, myth and poetry. Its presence always betrays a mystic force at work, the need to reunite what has been dispersed. Let us quote two cases—one of art criticism, the other literary but bearing upon the first—which have analogy as their sole foundation. Cohn-Wiener says 'Reliefs enable us to appreciate that there (in Babylon) clothes do not emphasize the shape of the body, as in Egypt: they hide it, in the way that murals conceal the rough marks of a building.' Théophile Gautier characterized Burgos cathedral as: 'Vast as a stone pyramid and delicate as a woman's curl', and Verlaine called the Middle Ages (which had created this cathedral): 'Vast and delicate'.

We have to persist in our study of analogy, for it is perhaps the corner-stone of the whole symbolic edifice. If we take two parallel actions, as expressed in the phrases: 'The sun overcomes the darkness', and 'The hero slays the monster', there is a correspondence between the two phrases (and the two actions). We have to conceive of each one as a three-part series: subject, verb, predicate. There is an analogy in function: both subjects, both verbs, both predicates are interrelated. In addition, as we have chosen two actions with a 'common rhythm', the parts of the series could be replaced or interchanged without causing any break or confusion in the system: we could equally well say 'The sun slays the monster' or 'The hero overcomes the darkness'. To take another example, in the parallel expressions: 'The sun shines with golden brilliance' and 'Gold shines with golden brilliance', the common predicate allows not only the interchange but also the identical equation of subject. From the intermediate phrase: 'The sun shines like gold' or 'Gold shines like the sun', comes the irrefutable conclusion: 'The sun—in so far as its brilliance is golden—is gold.' This equation occurs not because of the intrinsic value of its components but because of the significance of their position, for the relationship is concerned only with the dynamic or, in other words, symbolic, position of objects. This identical equation, then, is what we have called 'the principle of sufficient identity' and what we consider to be the core of symbolism. Clearly, this identity is 'sufficient' (that is, sufficient for symbolic purposes) from the very moment it is created in the very heart of the dynamic potential of the symbol. When their functions coincide and reveal their allegiance to one essence, both objects, although different on the existential plane, become one on the symbolic plane and therefore interchangeable; they are now—to use the scholastic terms—the *coniunctio* (integrating conjunction) of what was formerly *distinctio*. This is why symbolic technique is a matter of progressively ordering such identities within genuine common rhythms. Also, for the above reasons, the symbolic image is not an 'example' (an external and hypothetical relation between two objects or two correspondences) but an internal analogy (a necessary and constant relationship).

SYMBOL AND ALLEGORY—SYMBOL AND ARTISTIC EXPRESSION

As a general rule, writers on the subject distinguish in essence between the symbol and the allegory. Bachelard (3) defines the latter as 'a lifeless image, a concept which has become over-rationalized'. For Jung (30), allegory is a limited kind of symbol reduced to the rôle of a pointer, designating only one of the many potential series of dynamic meanings. Again, the difference between allegory and symbol may be understood by reference to the hypothesis of Wirth, for whom the essential function of the symbol is to explore the unknown and—paradoxically—to communicate with the incommunicable, the partial discovery of these unfathomable truths being achieved through symbols (59). Diel illustrates the difference between allegory and symbol with a vivid example: 'Zeus hurls a thunderbolt, which on the meteorological plane is a straightforward allegory. This allegory is transmuted into a symbol when the act acquires a psychological meaning, Zeus becoming the symbol of the spirit and the thunderbolt symbolizing the sudden appearance of an illuminating thought (intuition) which is supposed to come from the god himself' (15). This cipher is a semeiotic expression, a conventional abbreviation for a known constant. Allegory is seen therefore as the mechanism of the symbol, in which the chief characteristic of the latter is devitalized and turned into a mere cipher which, because it is dressed up in traditional, symbolic garb, may even appear to be alive.

Allegories have often been created quite consciously with theatrical or literary ends in mind. Cesare Ripa's *Iconologia* is a vast thesaurus of personifications and allegories. Mythological dictionaries provide many examples in which realistic portrayal deprives them of symbolic value. Thus, according to Cochin, Cruelty is depicted as a fearful hag smothering a child in its cradle and laughing in the firelight; and Dusk as a youth with a star on his forehead and the black wings of a bat, fleeing beneath a veil representing night. Even more mechanical are the allegories representing science, the arts or industry. Cosmography is usually shown as an old woman; she wears a blue cape studded with stars while her dress is earth-coloured. In one hand she holds an astrolabe, in the other a compass. At her feet are the globes of the earth and the heavens. These examples prove that the elements of allegory are symbols which are in no way distinguishable from true symbols. Their function alone is modified and inverted, for, instead of indicating metaphysical and spiritual principles—instead of possessing an emotional content—they are artificial creations designating physical realities and nothing else.

But in certain circumstances the components of allegory can revert to their symbolic state, that is, if the unconscious seizes upon them as such, overlooking their semeiotic and representational ends. Hence we may speak of an intermediate zone of images consciously created, even if calling upon ancestral memories, perhaps through the medium of dreams or visions. We find an example of this in the playing-cards of the Tarot, the compositions of which seem to be carried out according to a criterion analogous to that of many allegories or mythical figures. The only difference is that their mysteriousness places them beyond the reach of reason and enables them to act as stimuli to the unconscious. The same thing frequently happens in art: symbols have come to be placed within conscious, traditional and dogmatic systems, but their inner life still pulses beneath this rationalized order, even becoming audible from time to time. In ornamentation, strict rhythm rather than symbolic rhythm is at work. The inner force of the rhythm is conveyed to the observer who is moved by it according to his nature, but it is rare for even the suspicion of a psychological or cosmic significance to rise to the surface of his consciousness, although he may perceive its dynamic essence. We have read with interest René Alleau's recent work, *De la Nature des symboles*, and find the distinctions he draws between symbol and *synthema* interesting from a formalistic standpoint but of less help than hindrance towards the proper understanding of the spiritual and psychological meaning of symbols.

The same thing occurs with artistic expression, which may be related to symbolization but must not be confused with it. Artistic expression is a continuous, flowing, causal and direct relation between the inspiration and the final representation, which is both the means and the end of the expressive process. Symbolization is discontinuous, static, indirect, transcending the object in which it is enshrined. In music and in painting, one can easily distinguish between the expressive and the symbolic factors. But since we cannot here go into such particulars, we shall confine ourselves to determining the parts played by these factors in some general artistic tendencies. Thus expressionism, confronted with the material world of objects, tends to destroy them and to submerge them in a swirling stream of psychic forces, overwhelming the expressive figures and, with its power, obliging them to become part of a system of free rhythms. Symbolism, on the other hand, while isolating each form and each figure, attracts, as if with magnetic lines of force, all that has 'common rhythm', that is, all that has natural affinity. It thus reveals that the profound meaning behind all series of symbolic objects is the very cause of their appearance in the world of phenomena. Concerning the relationship of the art-form with the author, let us refer again to the concept of endopathy, anticipated by Dante in his *Canzoniere*: 'He who would paint a figure, if he cannot become that figure, cannot portray it.' This is a further affirmation of 'common rhythm', like the earlier observation of Plotinus that the eye could not see the sun unless it became to some degree a sun itself and vice versa. In symbolist doctrine, there is never any question of mere relation between cause and effect but rather of 'mutual causality'. In symbolism, everything has some meaning, everything has a purpose which at times is obvious, and at others less so, and everything leaves some trace or 'signature' which is open to investigation and interpretation.

Perhaps a deeper conception than the scientific ones is that of Sufic mysticism. Henry Corbin, in *Creative Imagination in the Sufism of Ibn 'Arabi* (London, 1969), referring to the idea of the *ta'wil* professed in Sufism, states that it is essentially a method of symbolic understanding of the world, based on the transmutation of everything visible into symbols. He adds that this is practicable through the 'intuition of an essence or person in an Image which partakes neither of universal logic nor of sense perception, and which is the only means of signifying what is to be signified'. Sufism admits an intermediate kingdom (an 'interworld', as it is called) between phenomenic reality and logical or ideal reality. This interworld is the pure truth of all things, but elevated to a magicomystic, angelic position. In other words, according to this doctrine, the Oneness, before reaching material realities, multiplies itself into other realities, which must perforce be objects of amazed contemplation. (These other realities are material realities which have been transformed and appear in the function of their dominant quality, their spiritual 'office'.) Asín Palacios, in his *Escatología musulmana en la Divina Commedia*, proved the connexion between Dantean idealism and the Islamic study of the contemplative life.

APPRECIATION AND INTERPRETATION

The Problem of Interpretation   In the 19th century, mythology and symbolism were much discussed, particularly in connexion with the problem of interpretation. Max Müller derived the majority of myths from solar phenomena, in particular Dawn representing victory over Darkness, while Schwartz and his school gave pride of place to the storm (35). Soon another interpretative approach came into being, in which all celestial and meteorological images came to be considered as secondary to mental and spiritual symbols. So, for example, Karl O. Müller, in his *Kleine deutsche Schriften*, remarked that, essentially, the myth of Orion had nothing astral about it, and that only subsequently did it come to be placed in the heavens. This process of projecting the worldly into the celestial sphere, in particular into the astral, is known as catasterism. The arrival of the psychological thesis, however, did not invalidate the arguments for celestial provenance—such as those put forward by Dupuis in his *L'Origine de tous les cultes*—and this is yet a further proof that the symbol is plurisignal, a term first used by Philip Wheelwright. Basically, all these problems of 'origin' are of very secondary importance. From the point of view of symbolist tradition, there is no question of priority, only of simultaneity: all phenomena are parallel and related. Interpretations only indicate the starting-point of the interpreter, not the causal or prior condition within the system itself.

These inevitable qualifications inherent in symbolic interpretation are underlined by Gaston Bachelard in his prologue to Diel (15), when he says, not without irony: 'Are you a rationalist historian? You will find in myth an account of famous dynasties. Are you a linguist? Words tell all, and all legends are formed around sayings. One more corrupted word—one more god! Olympus is a grammar controlling the functions of the gods. Are you a sociologist? Then in myth you will find the means by which, in primitive society, the leader is turned into a god.' The only all-embracing interpretation which would seem to fit the original meaning of myths and symbols is the one that takes this meaning right back to the metaphysical source, to the dialectic of creation. Louis Renou praises Zimmer's 'intuitive appreciation of the metaphysical approach to the myth', which is to say, his fidelity to his subject, an approach embracing both the philosophical and the religious aspects (60). But argument about all the possible interpretations dates not from our times, nor from recent times, but from Antiquity. Seznec recalls that the ancients evolved theories about the origins of the gods, based upon interpretations which can be summed up as expressions of three essential attitudes: (a) myths are more or less modified accounts of historical facts, of people raised to the rank of gods, as happened in historical time with Alexander the Great; (b) myths express the conflicts inherent in the natural world, for which reason gods had to be supernatural, cosmic symbols; (c) myths are the fabulous expression of philosophical or moral ideas. We would rather say that myths, and a great number of other archetypal symbols, are all three things at once. Or better still, that they are concrete, historical realities, that they are at once cosmic and natural; moral and psychological realities are merely restatements on three planes (history, the physical world, the psychic world) of the same basic ideas. Euhemerism, a system which gives preference to historical interpretation, does not, however, in any way affect the nature of symbol or myth, because, as we have already said, the simultaneous occurrence of an abstract and general manifestation with its materialization in a moment of space-time not only implies no contradiction, but actually is a proof of their true existence on both planes.

In the world of symbols, totemistic interpretation does no more than demonstrate relationships, without elucidating meanings: it forges connecting-links between beings endowed with 'common rhythm', but it does not indicate the meaning of these beings. To say that Athena was the nocturnal owl, the Magna Mater a lioness or Artemis a she-bear, is to say nothing about the meaning of the gods nor about their respective animal-symbols. The analysis of meaning is the only thing which can lead to the reconstruction of the inner structure of each symbol. Similarly, realism, which sees in a fable merely a different version of the original event or an amalgam of varied elements, offers only a secondary explanation of the problem of 'origins' without attempting to go deeply into the *raison d'être* of the entity. To say that the image of the bat gave birth to the idea of the hippogryph, the chimaera and the dragon, is to give the minimal idea of the expressive and symbolic value of such fabulous animals; only an analysis of their context, their behaviour and their purpose can bring us close to the myth of the symbol with its considerable capacity for dynamic transfiguration. Krappe is speaking in terms of realism when he says that the well-known tradition of associating the tree with the serpent can be traced 'quite simply to the fact (easily verifiable in all countries where snakes live) that these reptiles generally make their holes at the foot of a tree' (35). Even if we grant the accuracy of this explanation, what could it tell us about the intensity of this myth, with its powerful symbolism expressing Biblical temptation? Clearly, symbolism is something *quite different*. It is the magnetism which reality—whether it be simple (the object) or complex (the relationship)—is seen to exert by virtue of its spiritual potential within the cosmic system. The snake and the tree are related analogously in their outlines, in the resemblance of the reptile to the roots of a tree, and in the relationship between the tree and the erect snake on the one hand, and the columns of Boaz and Jachin on the other: a binary image of the essential paradox of life— the paradox of Good and Evil. While the tree raises its branches to the sun as if in an ecstasy of adoration, the snake is poised ready to strike. This is the essence of the symbol and not the fact that snakes nest at the foot of a tree. What is more, applying the traditional law that facts never explain anything but are the mere consequence of principle, we can say that if the snake makes its nest beneath trees, this is precisely because of this inner relationship.

PSYCHOLOGICAL INTERPRETATION

Given that every symbol 'echoes' throughout every plane of reality and that the spiritual ambience of a person is essentially one of these planes because of the relationship traditionally established between the macrocosm and the microcosm, a relationship which philosophy has verified by presenting Man as the 'messenger of being' (Heidegger): given this, then it follows that every symbol can be interpreted psychologically. So, for example, the secret room of Bluebeard, which he forbids his wife to enter, is his mind. The dead wives which she encounters in defying his orders are the wives whom he has once loved, that is, who are now dead to his love. Jung emphasizes the twofold value of psychological interpretation; it has thrown new light upon dreams, daydreams, fantasies and works of art, while on the other hand it provides confirmation of the collective character of myths and legends (31). He also points out that there are two aspects of the interpretation of the unconscious: what the symbol represents in itself (objective interpretation), and what it signifies as a projection or as an individualized 'case' (subjective interpretation). For our part, objective interpretation is nothing more nor less than understanding. Subjective interpretation is true interpretation: it takes the widest and profoundest meaning of a symbol in any one given moment and applies it to certain given examples.

Psychological interpretation points the middle way between the objective truth of the symbol and the particular circumstances influencing the individual who experiences the symbol. The prejudices of the interpreter must, in varying degrees, also be taken into account, for it will often be difficult to wean him from his particular likes and dislikes. It is here that symbols acquire secondary, accidental and transitory meanings, quite apart from their universal quality. The sword, without ever losing its objective meaning (which we explained earlier) comes to acquire various secondary meanings —which may even, because of its vital potential, appear momentarily as the primary sense—according to whether the symbol occurs in the mind of a soldier, a priest, a collector of swords or a poet. And this is to mention only one limiting factor, in itself extensive enough, embracing, as it does, character-study. The symbol, then, like water, finds its own level, which is the level of the interpreting mind. The difficulties of interpretation are therefore enormous, whereas the difficulties in the way of appreciating the symbol are almost elementary. Much scepticism about symbolism—especially among psychologists—arises because of the confusion of two quite different aspects of the function of symbolism: (i) the manifestation of the true meaning of the symbolic object, and (ii) the manifestation of a distorted meaning superimposed by an individual mind prejudiced by circumstantial or psychological factors. The difficulties of psychological interpretation concern not so much the series of 'multivalencies' of the symbol (common rhythm), as the variety of outlook of the interpreting mind, influenced either unconsciously by the power of the symbol or consciously by his own *Weltanschauung*.

One example of this kind of prejudiced interpretation can be seen in the Freudians, who claimed to unveil the universal sexuality of all objects and forms because they demonstrably belonged to one or the other of two broadly opposed groups: the masculine and the feminine. But the Chinese, with their Yang-Yin symbol, and the Hindus, and the Hebrews had long ago established the essential polarity of the world of phenomena according to generic principles, including the sexual division. Nevertheless, no matter how an object might be classified, it would never lose its potential significance; for its grouping constitutes only one of its symbolic representations and not, of course, the most important. The Talmud, furthermore, had discovered the interesting method of interpreting sexual dreams not always as immediately meaningful but often as indirectly significant or portentous (Fromm, 23). To dream of sexual relations with, for example, one's mother signified the attainment of the highest degree of wisdom. That Roman divines were also aware of this is proved by the interpretation given to a similar dream of Julius Caesar, to whom it was prophesied that he would inherit the world. But on the other hand one cannot deny those psychological interpretations which point to sexual ends. When a man, in the Talmud, 'sprinkles an olive tree with olive oil', he betrays symbolically an incestuous desire. The distortion of symbols inherent in any method of psychological interpretation derived from abnormal minds and applied to abnormal conditions may be seen in the patterns of meaning evolved by Volmat in his *L'Art psychopathologique*. For him, the symbol 'grows around a dynamic system, that is, around a structure within the dimensions of time and personality'. Such distortion of the true meaning of symbols arises from an over-restriction of their function, from over-identification with the psychological mechanism which construes it and with the *alter ego*, although it makes up for this restriction by its added intensity. Everything is made as subjective as possible: the tree is no longer the cosmic tree, but a projection of the self; and similarly with mountains. Water and fire present only their negative and destructive connotations, not the positive ones of purification and regeneration. By associations, only the tragic and mournful connotations are investigated: such is the construction put upon flowers and animals, for example. In the same way, this kind of interpretation overruns the object, altering it wherever necessary to fit abnormal symbols. Houses lose their doors and windows (symbols of openings, outlets, hopes of salvation); trees lose their leaves and never bear fruit. Catastrophes, which in traditional symbolism have the ambivalent meaning of both destruction and of fecundation and regeneration, are here limited to negative and destructive functions. One can understand that symbology built upon interpretation at this level can lay no claim to objectivity: it is no longer metaphysical but psychological.

On the other hand, to limit symbolic interpretation to the analysis of meaning, or to enumerating the qualities of the thing and its spiritual counterparts, is not enough. Not because the method is inherently deficient, but because in practice no one can see clearly and wholly what the object in question is.

A confrontation with symbolist tradition therefore becomes necessary, a tradition with secular associations and interpretations of undoubted value and universality; it is, then, essential to apply the comparative method whenever possible.

LEVELS OF MEANING

Corresponding to the multiplicity of symbolic objects linked by a 'common rhythm' is the multivalency of their meanings, each one distributed analogously on a separate level of reality. This power of the symbol to evince a meaning not only on one level but at all levels is borne out by all those who have written about symbology, notwithstanding their scientific outlook. Mircea Eliade stresses this essential characteristic of the symbol, emphasizing the simultaneity of its different meanings (17)—although, strictly, instead of 'different meanings' one ought to speak of the different values and particular aspects assumed by the basic meaning. Schneider gives a vivid example of this kind of progressive ordering of meaning, with its separate patterns on each plane of reality. He notes that if we take three fundamental planes: (i) vegetable and meteorological life; (ii) natural human life; and (iii) spiritual growth; then the concepts of death and rebirth—respectively symbolized by the moon in its waning and waxing phases—signify on these three levels: (i) drought and rain; (ii) illness and cure; and (iii) fossilization and flux (51).

Schneider goes on to suggest that the symbol is the inner link between all that is analogous or associated, rather than the dynamic potential of each separate object. He suggests that 'every symbol is a rhythmic whole embracing the essential, common rhythms of a series of phenomena, which are scattered over different planes by virtue of their secondary rhythms. They spread out from a spiritual centre and their clarity and intensity decrease as they approach the periphery. The reality of the symbol is founded upon the idea that the ultimate reality of an object lies in its spiritual rhythm—which it incarnates—and not in its material aspect' (50), or its functional aspect. Diel shares this view, applying it to myths, such as that of Demeter and her daughter Persephone, where he points out that the Eleusinian Mysteries imply three levels of meaning: the agrarian, the psychological and the metaphysical, the mystery lying in the integration of these three levels of reality; and these three levels correspond to the levels of all forms of sense-perception and knowledge. Hence, interpretation becomes the selection of one level as predominant, leaving aside the question of interaction, symbolic degradation and over-restriction within the particular. It is quite legitimate to see Medusa as a cloud, Chrysaor the golden sword as lightning, the galloping hoof beats of Pegasus as the thunder. But by limiting the upwards-tending dynamism of the symbol within these meteorological concepts, the unbounded potential significance of the symbol becomes confined within the limits of allegory.

From the Freudian school onwards, the level of a great many symbolic interpretations has been that of sexual activity. The swan, for example, has come to be seen simply as a symbol of hermaphroditism; yet on the mystical plane it has always alluded to the androgynous god of many primitive and astrobiological religions, as well as to the *rebis* of the alchemists and to the bisexual Man of Plato. Confining the symbol in this way within the narrow limits of allegory, restricting it to a lower plane in the pattern of the universe, is known in symbology as the 'degradation of the symbol'. And this degraded meaning may not only affect the interpretation it receives, but also the symbol itself. At times, degradation is brought about by trivial vulgarization: thus, arising from the myth of Mercury and Perseus flying through space with the aid of their winged sandals, we have the more modest journeyings of those who wear the seven-league boots (38); out of the myth of the 'Islands of the Blessed', which is connected with the mystical 'centre', there has arisen the urge for 'ocean paradises' which even Gauguin sought to turn into reality; out of the mythical battles between Osiris and Set, and Ormuzd and Ahriman, come the struggles between the 'good' and the 'bad' in literature (17). Lévy-Bruhl, in *L'Expérience mystique et les symboles chez les primitifs*, adduces some similar examples of fairy-story deformation of the symbol. Other forms of degradation are: over-particularized interpretation, leading to lengthy and arbitrary descriptions of 'the language of flowers' and so on. Over-intellectualized, allegorical interpretations are another aspect of the same thing—for example, asserting that 'the union of Leda and the swan signifies the pairing of Power and Injustice'; similarly, 'identifications' through so-called analogy. This dangerous tendency is what led to the decadence of symbolist movements during the Renaissance. In all the examples of deformation we have given, one finds the same basic falsification: the creative drive of the symbol—its tendency to revert to its Origin—is restricted, and it is made to bear labels which are over-concrete, too materialized or inferior. Its metaphysical function is arrested, and consequently a single plane of reality comes to be mistaken for the sum of all possible levels of symbolic meaning. If this use of symbols is recognized as deformation, then—as we suggested earlier when commenting upon Caro Baroja—a general distrust of ready-made symbolic meanings and the attempt to use them to explain myth, would seem to be justified. The influence of the symbol must be allowed to pervade all levels of reality; only then can it be seen in all its spiritual grandeur and fecundity.

THE SYMBOLIZING AGENT AND THE SYMBOLIC OBJECT

In accordance with our usual practice of using the comparative rather than the deductive method and avoiding over-classification, we have not drawn rigid dividing-lines between the separate meanings of each particular symbol on its various levels of reality. We have not done so because our sources have been very varied and we have preferred to reproduce their content with a minimum of editorial comment. Another reason for not stating clear-cut conclusions is that in our opinion it is not always possible to accept the particular views of some writers, however estimable they may be as compilers or even as interpreters of symbols. For example, Loeffler says that in oriental and Nordic mythology, each symbol, myth or legend contains 'four superimposed moral lessons: (i) an historical lesson, that is, an epic narration dealing with real facts and people and serving as a kind of "material backing" for the symbolic teaching involved; (ii) a psychological lesson, depicting the struggle between spirit and matter on the human plane; (iii) a lesson bearing upon life on our planet; and (iv) a lesson upon the constitution of matter and cosmic order' (38). This schematic division is surely misleading, for we must remember that, for any given level of meaning, it is not the meaning itself which changes but the way it is adapted or applied. Finally, we have not favoured this kind of classification—despite its serial 'multivalency'—for the reason that symbols, traditionally at least, seem to have an inborn tendency to settle upon one particular plane. Thus, some symbols are primarily concerned with psychology, others with the cosmological or natural orders. There are those too, we must point out, which exist in order to reconcile different levels of reality, particularly the psychic with the spatial. The best example of this is that of the mandala, and all those symbols of conjunction or those uniting the three worlds. Thus, for example, steps are symbolic of the connexion between the conscious and the unconscious, just as they are a connexion between the upper, the terrestrial and the nether worlds. The idea of order is an essential one in symbolism and is expressed through the ordering of space, geometric forms, and numbers, and by the disposition of living beings as symbols in positions determined by the law of correspondences. Another essential idea of symbolist doctrine is that of the cycle, either as a series of possibles—expressed particularly through the septenary and all its associated or derived symbolic forms—or as a process which closes up some of the possibilities once the cycle is completed. Zodiacal symbolism is a perfect illustration of this cosmic structure. The relation of destiny with the cyclic process is implied in the figures of the legendary Tarot pack; the wealth of symbolic knowledge which is contained in each and every one of its cards is not to be despised, even if their symbolic significance is open to debate. For the illustrations of the Tarot afford clear examples of the signs, the dangers and the paths leading towards the infinite which Man may discover in the course of his existence.

The great themes of death and resurrection, related respectively with the cycle of involution (progressive materialization) and evolution (spiritualization or the return to the point of origin), gave rise to many myths and legends. The struggle to come to grips with truth and the spiritual centre appears in the form of battles and trials of strength, while those instincts which shackle Man and hold him down appear as monsters. According to Diel, 'the symbols most typical of the spirit and of intuition are the sun and the sunlit sky; those of the imagination and the darker side of the unconscious, are the moon and night. The sea symbolizes the mysterious immensity from which everything comes and to which everything returns' (15). All natural and cultural objects may be invested with a symbolic function which emphasizes their essential qualities in such a way that they lend themselves to spiritual interpretation. So, for example, rocks, mountains and all topographical features; trees and vegetables, flowers and fruit, animals, works of architecture and the utilities, the members of the body and the four elements. But it should be remembered that this catalogue of objects becomes much shorter when the objects become possessed of certain symbolic potentials, when they are strung together, as it were, along one line of meaning. For example, within the symbolism of levels and of the relation between heaven and earth, the mountain, the tree, the temple and steps can often be equated. On occasions, such a relationship appears to be created by or at least to bear the imprint of one principal symbol. It is for this reason that Mircea Eliade can say that 'the intuitive awareness of the moon as the source of rhythm as well as the source of energy, life and regeneration (of material things) has built up a veritable network between all the different cosmic planes, creating symmetries, analogies and communion between phenomena of infinite variety. . . . We have, for example, the series: Moon, rain, fertility, woman, snake, death, periodic regeneration; but at times only a part of the series is apparent: Snake, woman, fecundity; snake, rain, fecundity; or woman, snake, eroticism, etc. A complete mythology has been built up around these smaller, secondary groups' (17), especially around the principal symbol.

The symbolic object appears as a quality or a higher form, and also as an essence justifying and explaining the existence of the symbolizing agent. The most straightforward of symbological analyses based upon simple enumeration of the qualitative meanings of the object, sometimes, while the 'mode of existence' is being investigated, will reveal a sudden opening which illuminates its meaning through an association of ideas. This association should never be thought of as a mere external idea in the mind of the investigator, outside the symbol itself, but rather as a revelation of the inner link—the 'common rhythm'—joining two realities to the mutual benefit of both. For this reason, when one reads in Picinelli's work: 'Sapphire:—Arouses pity. In colour similar to the sky: it shares its colour. It gladdens the heart. A symbol of heavenly reward. Contemplative', then one must agree that, within the limits of his implicit analysis, the writer is right as far as he goes, although the terms implying anticipation ('arouses pity') and moral effect ('it gladdens the heart'), are not strictly explanations of the symbol but of a reaction arising from its contemplation.

SYMBOLIC SYNTAX

Symbols, in whatever form they may appear, are not usually isolated; they appear in clusters, giving rise to symbolic compositions which may be evolved in time (as in the case of story-telling), in space (works of art, emblems, graphic designs), or in both space and time (dreams, drama). It is necessary to recall that, in symbolism, each detail invariably has some particular meaning (4), and that the way a symbol is oriented also calls for attention: for example, fire pointing downwards represents erotic life; while, pointing towards the sky, it expresses purification. Schneider mentions also the importance of the location of the object: a basket changes its meaning when placed on the head, for 'any given object changes in significance according to the "common rhythm" it is made to respond to' (50). Combinations of symbols evidence a cumulative meaning. Thus, a crowned snake signifies the crowning of instinctive or telluric forces. Emblems are very often based upon a conjunction of various simple symbols in any given sphere. At times they are concordant symbols, at times discordant. An example of the former is the frequent mediaeval emblem of the heart enclosed within a circle from which tongues of flame radiate. The three constituent parts of this emblem refer to the Trinity: the heart represents Love and the mystic centre, the circle represents eternity and the flames, irradiation and purification. On other occasions the symbol is formally simple yet structurally it is made up from two or more sources: thus, the tree is given the form of a cross, or the cross the form of a leafless tree—a symbol which also occurs in mediaeval emblematic designs. An example cited by Bachelard falls within this class of confederate symbol: appearing in a dream of Jean-Paul are 'white swans with wings outspread like arms' (2). This kind of symbolic syntax is found most frequently in allegories and attributes. If the globe, the symbol of the world, has an eagle above it (8), it expresses the consecration of power. Medusa's head—with its negative, destructive character—placed in the centre of a symbolic space, signifies destructiveness (15). Very important, too, is the vertical positioning of the symbol. Higher elevation along a given vertical axis always indicates spiritual superiority—by analogy of physical with metaphysical 'height'. For this reason, the *uraeus* of Egyptian sovereigns expressed the spiritualization of the inner force (symbolized by the snake) when it was positioned on the forehead, on a spot the importance of which is well known to Tantrist Yoga.

Symbolic syntax, in respect of the relationship between its individual elements, may function in four different ways: (a) *the successive manner*, one symbol being placed alongside another; their meanings, however, do not combine and are not even interrelated; (b) *the progressive manner*, in which the meanings of the symbols do not interact but represent different stages in the symbolic process; (c) *the composite manner*, in which the proximity of the symbols brings about change and creates complex meanings: a synthesis, that is, and not merely a mixture of their meanings; (d) *the dramatic manner*, in which there is an interaction between the groups and all the potentialities of the preceding groups are synthesized. We have followed the practice of Enel—who would appear to have settled the problems which preoccupied Horapollo and Athanasius Kircher—and taken several examples from the Egyptian system of hieroglyphics, which well illustrates the last group. Further ideas upon the 'de-ciphering' of complex symbols can be drawn from what we have suggested when dealing with spatial and pictorial symbolism. Moreover, we note that the meaning of any symbol can be enriched by the application of the law of correspondences and its corollaries. In other words, objects possessing 'common rhythm' barter some of their properties. But we must also recall that the Scylla and Charybdis of symbolism are (firstly) devitalization through allegorical over-simplification, and (secondly) ambiguity arising from exaggeration of either its meaning or its ultimate implications; for in truth, its deepest meaning is unequivocal since, in the infinite, the apparent diversity of meaning merges into Oneness.

If we take all the possible applications of an analytical method founded upon the symbolism of space or of lineal direction, or of determinate or indeterminate, regular or irregular forms, or of the gamut of texture and colour, we can see that they are indeed very numerous; one in particular is the comprehension of those works of art which portray the immediate projection of inner forces and fantasies not in the figurative world but in the material. It could here be objected that abstract—geometric, biomorphic or textural —painting, or surrealist visions, do not call for conscious discrimination, since the aim of the creator—as Richard Wagner said of his music—is to forget all about the psychological mechanism and let the unconscious speak to the unconscious. This is as true as it is to note that the implications of symbology are sometimes disturbing and even sinister. For this reason, and others already mentioned, we have not given analytical descriptions of paintings, dreams or literature. This is not the place to discuss the implications of symbolist theory; anyone who wishes is free to make use of the mystic bonds to which we allude or to ignore them as he sees fit. We only wish to add that we regard our work less as a reference-book than a book to be read at leisure. And that only by seeing all the symbols compiled as a whole can the reader learn anything about any one of them; for symbolic meanings are often surprising, such as that implied in the relationship between the *retiarius* and *mirmillo* gladiators and the zodiacal signs of *Pisces* (aquatic forces of dissolution, its attributes being the net and the trident) and *Cancer* (the solar force, its attributes being fire, the shell of the crab and the sword)—a relationship which explains and justifies the gladiators' unceasing struggle in the gilded amphitheatres of Rome. Then again, dynamism plays an important rôle. The sun, for example, may rule over or be ruled by the moon. In the latter case, we are faced with the law of becoming; in the former, with the law of being, as defined by Evola. One last observation: We have on occasion added to the symbolic meaning those allegorical meanings which we have thought might prove of some interest.

Abandonment The symbolism of abandonment has a similar range of reference to that of the 'lost object', and they are both parallel to the symbolism of death and resurrection (31). To feel abandoned is, essentially, to feel forsaken by the 'god within us', that is, to lose sight of the eternal light in the human spirit. This imparts to the individual's existence a sense of estrangement—to which the labyrinth theme is also related.

Ablution To quote Oswald Wirth: 'In alchemy, the subject, having undergone *nigredo* (blackness) followed by death and putre-faction, is subjected to ablution, an operation which makes use of the slow dripping of condensation from the vapours that rise from the carcass when a moderate flame applied externally is alternately raised and lowered in intensity. These continual drops serve to bring about the progressive washing of the material, which changes from black to grey and then gradually to white. The whiteness is an indication of the success of the first part of the *Magnum Opus*. The adept worker achieves this only by purifying his soul of all that commonly agitates it' (59). Washing, then, symbolizes the purification not so much of objective and external evil as of subjective and inner evils, which we might call 'private'. It is hardly necessary to add that the latter kind of purification is much more difficult and painful than the former, since what it sets out to destroy is something which is bonded to existence itself with all its vital urges. The principle involved in this alchemic process is that implied in the maxim 'Deny thyself . . .', and an indispensable precept for true moral progress.

Abnormality In primitive cultures, maimed beings, as well as madmen, were believed to possess supernatural powers—the shamans, for example. In primitive magico-religious thinking, the outstanding ability of physically abnormal individuals is not regarded, as it is in modern psychology, as having been developed in compensa-tion for the abnormality, but rather the other way round: the maiming, the abnormality, the tragic destiny were the price the individual had to pay for some inborn extraordinary gift—often the gift of prophecy. This belief was universal (9). In some mythologies, maimed beings are connected with the moon and its phases; there are mythic lunar beings, with only one hand or one foot, who have the magic power to cure disease, bring rain, and so on (17). This conception of abnormality is not restricted to animate beings, but applies equally to objects. According to Cola Alberich, abnormal objects have always been considered as particularly useful in warding off malignant influences. Such objects are: stones with embedded fossils; amulets shaped like a six-fingered or a four-fingered hand; double almonds in one shell; unusually shaped grains of corn, etc. (12). There is an interesting parallel to be drawn between the spontaneous interest evinced by Primitive Man in strange or abnormal objects, and the more deliberate, 'poetic' treatment bestowed by surrealists upon such objects as elements in the symbolic process. The belief in the magic powers of abnormal objects is connected with the symbolism of the jester (that is, the inverted king, the sacrificial victim) and with the symbolism of the moon.

Abracadabra Many words and phrases relating to rituals, talismans and pentacles have a symbolic meaning, either in themselves or in the way they are used, which is expressed either phonetically or, more frequently, graphically. This word was in frequent use during the Middle Ages as a magic formula. It is derived from the Hebrew phrase *abreq ad hâbra*, meaning 'hurl your thunderbolt even unto death'. It was usually inscribed inside an inverted triangle, or was set out so that it formed a triangle (39) thus:

```
A B R A C A D A B R A
A B R A C A D A B R
A B R A C A D A B
A B R A C A D A
A B R A C A D
A B R A C A
A B R A C
A B R A
A B R
A B
A
```

This magic word has also been related to the Abracax (Abraxas, Abrasax) of the Gnostics. It is in reality one of the names of the sun-god, Mithras (4).

Abyss The abyss in any form has a fascinating dual significance. On the one hand, it is a symbol of depth in general; on the other, a symbol of inferiority. The attraction of the abyss lies in the fact that these two aspects are inextricably linked together. Most ancient or primitive peoples have at one time or another identified certain breaks in the earth's surface or marine depths with the abyss. Among the Celts and other peoples, the abyss was inside mountains; in Ireland, Japan and the South Sea islands, it was at the bottom of seas and lakes; among Mediterranean peoples it was just beyond the horizon; for the Australian aborigines, the Milky Way is the abyss *par excellence*. The abyss is usually identified with the 'land of the dead', the underworld, and is hence, though not always, associated with the Great Mother and earth-god cults (35). The association between the nether world and the bottom of seas or lakes explains many aspects of legends in which palaces or beings emerge from an abyss of water. After King Arthur's death, his sword, thrown into the lake by his command, is caught as it falls and, before being drawn down to the bottom, flourished by a hand which emerges from the waters.

Acacia This shrub, which bears white or pink blooms, was considered sacred by the Egyptians, partly, no doubt, because of its dual coloration and also because of the great mystic importance of the white-red principle (8). In Hermetic doctrine, according to Gérard de Nerval in his *Voyage en Orient* (9), it symbolizes the testament of Hiram which teaches that 'one must know how to die in order to live again in eternity'. It occurs with this particular symbolic meaning (that is, the soul and immortality) in Christian art, especially the Romanesque (20).

Acanthus The acanthus leaf, a very common ornamental motif in architecture, was, during the Middle Ages, invested with a definite symbolism derived from its two essential characteristics: its growth, and its thorns. The latter is a symbol of solicitude about lowly things. According to Bishop Melito of Sardis, they signify the awareness and the pain of sin. We may mention here that in the *Diary* of Weininger, there is no difference between guilt and punishment. A more generalized symbolism, alluding perhaps to natural life itself, with its tendency towards regression or at least towards stunting, appears in the Gospels in the parable of the sower (Luke viii, 7), where we read that some of the seed (of spiritual principles and of salvation) fell amongst thorns and was choked. And in the Old Testament (Genesis iii, 18) the Lord tells man that the earth will yield to him thorns and thistles (46).

Acrobat Because of his acrobatics, which often involve reversing the normal position of the human body by standing on his hands, the acrobat is a living symbol of inversion or reversal, that is to say, of that need which always arises in time of crisis (personal, social or collective historical crises) to upset and reverse the established order: idealism turns into materialism; meekness into aggressiveness; serenity into tragedy; order into disorder, or vice versa. Acrobats are related to other aspects of the circus and, in particular, to the mystery of the Hanged Man in the Tarot pack, which has a similar significance.

Activity In the mystic sense, there is no activity other than spiritual movement towards evolution and salvation; any other form of activity is merely agitation and not true activity. On this point, the West is in full accord with the East, for, according to the doctrine of Yoga, the highest state (*sattva*), characterized by outward calm, is that of greatest activity (the activé subjugation of the lower impulses and their subsequent sublimation). Thus, it is not surprising that Cesare Ripa, in his *Iconologia*, through a process of assimilation with the exalted images of the Archangel St. Michael and of St. George, represents 'Virtuous Action' as a warrior armed in a gilt cuirass, holding a book in one hand and in the other a lance poised ready to be thrust into the head of a huge serpent which he has just vanquished. The head of Vice, crushed under his left foot, completes the allegory. Hence, every struggle or victory on the material plane has its counterpart in the realm of the spirit. Thus, according to Islamic tradition, the 'Holy War' (the struggle against the infidel, depicted with weapons held at the ready) is simply an image of the 'Great Holy War' (the struggle of the faithful against the Powers of Evil).

Adam Primordial Man. The name is derived from the Hebrew *adama* (= earth). G. G. Scholem, in *On the Kabbalah and its Symbolism* (London, 1965), states that, initially, Adam is conceived as 'a vast representation of the power of the universe', which is concentrated in him. Hence the equation macrocosm = microcosm. In both the Bible and the platonic doctrine of the androgyne, Eve appears as an excision of the first being, which integrated sexual duality. Do the tree and the serpent reproduce the same duality on another symbolic plane? Or do they express a different duality to that contained in the first human couple, which is the symbol of the internal and external excision of the living being? Eve, in the rôle of persuader, appears as a mediator between the serpent (the source of evil, which William Blake likened to energy) and man, who would have been free and indifferent, and who would have 'fallen' only under pressure.

Aerolite A symbol of spiritual life which has descended upon earth. A symbol of revelation; of the 'other world' made accessible; and of the heavenly fire in its creative aspect, i.e. as seed. Tradition has it that, just as there are 'upper waters', there is also 'upper fire'. The stars symbolize the unattainable aspect of this fire; aerolites and meteorites are its messengers, and hence they are sometimes associated with angels and other heavenly hierarchies (37). It must be remembered that the iron first used by man was meteoric (which may account for the common root of the word *sidereal* and other words beginning with the prefix *sidero-*). The belief in a symbiotic relationship between the heavenly and the terrestrial worlds lies at the root of the idea of the 'cosmic marriage', a concept with which primitive astrobiological thought sought to explain the analogy, as

well as the tangential relationship, between the antithetical worlds
of heaven and earth.

Ages, The For the purposes of the morphology of symbols, an age
is exactly the same as a phase. The lunar 'model' of the four phases
(of waxing, fullness, waning and disappearance) has sometimes
been reduced to two or three phases, and sometimes increased to
five. The phases in the span of human life have undergone similar
fluctuations, but in general they are four, with death either omitted
or combined with the final phase of old age. The division into four
parts—quite apart from the importance of its relationship with the
four phases of the moon—coincides with the solar process and the
annual cycle of the seasons as well as with the spatial arrangement
of the four points of the compass on the conceptual plane. The
cosmic ages have been applied to the era of human existence, and
also to the life of a race or an empire. In Hindu tradition, the
Manvantara, also called *Mahâ-Yuga* (or the Great Cycle), comprises
four *yuga* or secondary periods, which were said to be the same as
the four ages in Greco-Roman antiquity. In India, these same ages
are called after four throws in the game of dice: *krita*, *tretâ*, *dvâpara*
and *kali*. In classical times, the ages are associated with the symbolism of metals, giving the 'golden age', 'silver age', 'bronze age' and
'iron age'. The same symbolic pattern—which in itself is an interpretation—is found in the famous dream of Nebuchadnezzar
(Daniel ii) as well as in the figure of the 'Old Man of Crete' in
Dante's *Commedia* (*Inferno*, XIV, ll. 94-120) (60, 27). Progress
from the purest metal to the most malleable—from gold to iron—
implies involution. For this reason René Guénon comments that
the successive ages, as they 'moved away from the Beginning', have
brought about a gradual materialization (28). And for this reason,
too, William Blake observed that 'Progress is the punishment of
God'. So that progress in life—in an individual's existence—is
tantamount to gradual surrender of the golden values of childhood,
up to the point in which the process of growing old is terminated by
death. The myths concerning the 'Golden Age' find their origin,
according to Jung, in an analogy with childhood—that period
when nature heaps gifts upon the child without any effort on his
part, for he gets all he wants. But in addition, and in a deeper sense,
the Golden Age stands for life in unconsciousness, for unawareness
of death and of all the problems of existence, for the 'Centre' which
precedes time, or which, within the limitations of existence, seems
to bear the closest resemblance to paradise. Ignorance of the world
of existence creates a kind of golden haze, but with the growing
understanding of concepts of duty, the father-principle and rational
thinking, the world can again be apprehended (31). The aims of surrealism are nothing short of reintegrating, as far as is practicable, this

state of emotional irrationality characteristic of primigenial peoples.

Agriculture Its allegorical representation is the figure of a goddess, like Ceres in appearance (with whom it may be identified), but with a plough and a plant bearing its first blossom. Sometimes, the allegorical figure carries a cornucopia full of fruits and flowers, or has both hands leaning on a spade or a hoe. The Zodiac is also included, to indicate the importance of the yearly cycle and the sequence of the seasons and the work that each season implies (8).

Air Of the four Elements, air and fire are regarded as active and male; water and earth as passive and female. In some elemental cosmogonies, fire is given pride of place and considered the origin of all things, but the more general belief is that air is the primary element. Compression or concentration of air creates heat or fire, from which all forms of life are then derived. Air is essentially related to three sets of ideas: the creative breath of life, and, hence, speech; the stormy wind, connected in many mythologies with the idea of creation; and, finally, space as a medium for movement and for the emergence of life-processes. Light, flight, lightness, as well as scent and smell, are all related to the general symbolism of air (3). Gaston Bachelard says that for one of its eminent worshippers, Nietzsche, air was a kind of higher, subtler matter, the very stuff of human freedom. And he adds that the distinguishing characteristic of aerial nature is that it is based on the dynamics of dematerialization. Thoughts, feelings and memories concerning heat and cold, dryness and humidity and, in general, all aspects of climate and atmosphere, are also closely related to the concept of air. According to Nietzsche, air should be cold and aggressive like the air of mountain tops. Bachelard relates scent to memory, and by way of example points to Shelley's characteristic lingering over reminiscences of smell.

Alchemy The real beginnings of alchemy date back to the first centuries A.D., when it was practised mainly by Greeks and Arabs. Elements from various traditions, including Christian mysticism, were later incorporated. It was essentially a symbolic process involving the endeavour to make gold, regarded as the symbol of illumination and salvation. The four stages of the process were signified by different colours, as follows: black (guilt, origin, latent forces) for 'prime matter' (a symbol of the soul in its original condition); white (minor work, first transmutation, quicksilver); red (sulphur, passion); and, finally, gold. Piobb analyses the symbolic meaning of the various operations. The first, known as *calcination*, stood for the 'death of the profane', i.e. the extinction of all interest in life and in the manifest world; the second, *putrefaction*, was a consequence of the first, consisting of the separation of the destroyed remains; *solution*, the third, denoted the purification of matter;

Athanor, the alchemists' oven (after an old engraving).

distillation, the fourth, was the 'rain' of purified matter, i.e. of the elements of salvation isolated by the preceding operations; fifthly, *conjunction* symbolized the joining of opposites (the *coincidentia oppositorum*, identified by Jung with the close union, in Man, of the male principle of consciousness with the female principle of the unconscious); *sublimation*, the sixth stage, symbolized the suffering resulting from the mystic detachment from the world and the dedication to spiritual striving. In emblematic designs, this stage is depicted by a wingless creature borne away by a winged being, or sometimes it is represented by the Prometheus myth. The final stage is *philosophic congelation*, i.e. the binding together inseparably of the fixed and the volatile principles (the male/invariable with the female/'saved' variable). Alchemical evolution is epitomized, then, in the formula *Solve et Coagula* (that is to say: 'analyse all the elements in yourself, dissolve all that is inferior in you, even though you may break in doing so; then, with the strength acquired from the preceding operation, congeal') (48). In addition to this specific symbolism, alchemy may be seen as the pattern of all other work. It shows that virtues are exercised in every kind of activity, even the humblest, and that the soul is strengthened, and the individual develops. Evola (*Tradizione Ermetica*) writes: 'Our Work is the conversion and change of one being into another being, one thing into another thing, weakness into strength, bodily into spiritual nature. . . .' On the subject of the hermaphrodite, Eugenio d'Ors (*Introducción a la vida angélica*) writes: 'That which failed to "become two in one flesh" (love) will succeed in "becoming two in one spirit" (individuation).'

Alcohol   Alcohol, or life-water (*aqua vitae*) is fire-water, i.e. a symbol of the *coincidentia oppositorum*, the conjunction of opposites, where two principles, one of them active, the other passive, come together in a fluid and shifting, creative/destructive relationship. Particularly when burning, alcohol symbolizes one of the great mysteries of Nature; Bachelard aptly says that, when alcohol burns, 'it seems as if the "female" water, losing all shame, frenziedly gives herself to her master, fire' (1, 2).

Almond Tree   Traditionally, a symbol of sweetness and delicacy. As it is one of the first trees to blossom, late frosts can destroy its flowers. The precise observation of Nature, constantly practised by primitive man, is the source of this symbolic analogy, as of so many others which might at first seem merely artificial allegories.

Alpha and Omega   The first and last letters of the Greek alphabet, standing, therefore, for the beginning and end of all things. They are very frequently used in this sense in Romanesque art. Because of its shape, alpha is related to the pair of compasses, an attribute of god the creator; while omega is similar to a torch, i.e. to the fire of apocalyptic destruction. Animal figures have also been associated with this symbolism. In the frontispiece of a 12th-century manuscript of Paulus Orosius (Bibl. Laon, 137) alpha and omega appear respectively as a bird and a fish, i.e. the upper and the lower abyss.

Amphisbaena A fabulous animal, keeper of the 'Great Secret', according to a 16th-century Italian manuscript which belonged to Count Pierre V. Piobb. It is a symbol which occurs with some frequency in heraldic images, marks and signs. It was known to the Greeks, and it owes its name to the belief that, having a head at both ends, it could move forward or backward with equal ease. Sometimes it is depicted with the claws of a bird and the pointed wings of a bat (48). According to Diel (15), it was probably intended to express the horror and anguish associated with ambivalent situations. Like all fabulous animals, it instances the ability of the human mind to reorder aspects of the real world, according to supra-logical laws, blending them into patterns expressive of man's motivating psychic forces.

Anchor In the emblems, signs and graphic representations of the early Christians, the anchor always signified salvation and hope. It was often shown upside down, with a star, cross or crescent to denote its mystic nature. The Epistle to the Hebrews says: 'Which hope we have as the anchor of our soul' (4).

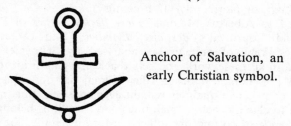

Anchor of Salvation, an
early Christian symbol.

Angel A symbol of invisible forces, of the powers ascending and descending between the Source-of-Life and the world of phenomena (50). Here, as in other cases (such as the Cross), the symbolic fact does not modify the real fact. In alchemy, the angel symbolizes sublimation, i.e. the ascension of a volatile (spiritual) principle, as in the figures of the *Viatorium spagyricum*. The parallelism between angelic orders and astral worlds has been traced with singular precision by Rudolf Steiner in *Les Hiérarchies spirituelles*, following the treatise on the celestial hierarchies by the Pseudo-Dionysius. From the earliest days of culture, angels figure in artistic iconography, and by the 4th millennium B.C. little or no distinction is made between angels and winged deities. Gothic art, in many remarkable images, expresses the protective and sublime aspects of the angel-figure, while the Romanesque tends rather to stress its other-worldly nature.

Animals Of the utmost importance in symbolism, both in connexion with their distinguishing features, their movement, shapes and colours, and because of their relationship with man. The origins of animal symbolism are closely linked with totemism and animal worship. The symbolism of any given animal varies according to its position in the symbolic pattern, and to the attitude and context in which it is depicted. Thus the frequent symbol of the 'tamed animal' can signify the reversal of those symbolic meanings associated with the same animal when wild. In the struggle between a knight and a wild or fabulous animal—one of the most frequent themes in symbolism—the knight's victory can consist either in the death or in the taming of the animal. In Chrétien de Troyes' mediaeval romance, Yvain, the hero is assisted by a lion. In the legend of St. George, the conquered dragon serves its conqueror. In the West, some of the earliest references to animal symbolism are found in Aristotle and in Pliny, but the most important source is the treatise *Physiologus*, written in Alexandria in the 2nd century A.D. Another important contribution was made one or two centuries later by Horapollo, with his two treatises on *Hieroglyphica*, based on Egyptian symbolism. From these sources flows a stream of mediaeval animal symbolism which produced such notable bestiaries as that of Philip of Thaun (A.D. 1121), Peter of Picardy and William of Normandy (13th century); or the *De Animalibus*, attributed to Albertus Magnus; *Libre de les besties* of Raymond Lull; and Fournival's *Bestiaire d'Amour* (14th century). The primitives' view of animals, as analysed by Schneider (50), is mirrored in all these works, namely that while man is an equivocal, 'masked' or complex being, the animal is univocal, for its positive or negative qualities remain ever constant, thus making it possible to classify each animal, once and for all, as belonging to a specific *mode* of cosmic phenomena. More generally, the different stages of animal evolution, as manifested by the varying degrees of biological complexity, ranging from the insect and the reptile to the mammal, reflect the hierarchy of the instincts. In Assyrian and Persian bas-reliefs, the victory of a higher over a lower animal always stands for the victory of the higher life over the lower instincts. A similar case is in the characteristic struggle of the eagle with the snake as found in pre-Columbian America. The victory of the lion over the bull usually signifies the victory of Day over Night and, by analogy, Light triumphing over Darkness and Good over Evil. The symbolic classification of animals is often related to that of the four Elements. Animals such as the duck, the frog and the fish, however much they may differ one from the other, are all connected with the idea of water and hence with the concept of the 'primal waters'; consequently, they can stand as symbols of the origin of things and of the powers of rebirth (37, 9). On the other hand, some animals, such as dragons and snakes, are sometimes assigned to water, sometimes to earth and sometimes even to fire (17). However, the most generally accepted classification—which is also the most fundamentally correct—associates aquatic and amphibious animals with water; reptiles with earth; birds with air; and mammals (because they are warm-blooded) with fire. For the purposes of symbolic art, animals are subdivided into two categories: *natural* (often in antithetical pairs: toad/frog, owl/eagle, etc.) and *fabulous*. Within the cosmic order, the latter occupy an intermediate position between the world of fully differentiated beings and the world of formless matter (50). They may have been suggested by the discovery of skeletons of antediluvian animals, and also by certain beings which, though natural, are ambiguous in appearance (carnivorous plants, sea urchins, flying fish, bats), and thus stand for flux and transformism, and also for purposeful evolution towards new forms. In any event, fabulous animals are powerful instruments of psychological projection. The most important fabulous animals are: chimaera, sphinx, lamia, minotaur, siren, triton, hydra, unicorn, griffin, harpy, winged horse, hippogryph, dragon, etc. In some of these the transmutation is a simple one, and clearly positive in character—such as Pegasus' wings (the spiritualization of a lower force)—but more often the symbol is a consequence of a more complex and ambiguous process of the imagination. The result is a range of highly ambivalent symbols, whose significance is heightened by the ingrained belief in the great powers exercised by such beings as well as in the magic importance of abnormality and deformity. In addition, there are animals which, while hardly or not at all fabulous in appearance, are credited with non-existential or supernatural qualities as the result of a symbolic projection (for example, the pelican, phoenix, salamander). There is a fragment by Callimachus on the Age of Saturn, in which animals have the power of speech (this being a symbol of the Golden Age which preceded the emergence of the intellect—Man—when the blind forces of Nature, not yet subject to the *logos*, were endowed with all sorts of extraordinary and exalted qualities). Hebrew and Islamic traditions also include references to 'speaking animals' (35). Another interesting classification is that of 'lunar animals', embracing all those animals whose life-span includes some kind of cyclic alternation, with periodic appearances and disappearances (18). The symbolism of such animals includes, in addition to the animal's specific symbolic significance, a whole range of lunar meanings. Schneider also mentions a very curious primitive belief: namely, that the voice of those animals which can be said to serve as symbols of heaven is high-pitched if the animal is large (the elephant, for example), but low-pitched if the animal is small (as the bee); while the converse is true of earth-symbol animals. Some animals, in particular the eagle and the lion, seem to embody certain qualities, such as beauty and the fighting spirit, to such an extent that they have come to be universally accepted as the allegorical representations of these qualities. The emblematic animals of Roman *signa* were: eagle, wolf, bull, horse and wild boar. In symbolism, whenever animals (or any other symbolic elements) are brought together in a system, the order of arrangement is always highly significant, implying either hierarchical precedence or relative position in space. In alchemy, the descending order of precedence is symbolized by different animals, thus: the phoenix (the culmination of the alchemical *opus*), the unicorn, the lion (the necessary qualities), the dragon (prime matter) (32). Symbolic groups of animals are usually based on analogical and numerical patterns: the tetramorphs of Western tradition, as found in the Bible, are a fundamental example; another example would be the Chinese series of the four benevolent animals: the unicorn, phoenix, turtle and dragon. The following animals occur particularly in Romanesque art: the peacock, ox, eagle, hare, lion, cock, crane, locust and partridge (50). Their symbolic meaning is mainly derived from the Scriptures or from patristic tradition, though some meanings, arising from analogy, such as that between cruelty and the leopard, are immediately obvious (20). The importance in Christianity of the symbols of the dove, the lamb and the fish is well known. The significance of the attitudes in which symbolic animals are depicted is usually self-evident: the counterbalancing of two identical—or two different—animals, so common in heraldry, stands for balance (i.e. justice and order, as symbolized for instance by the two snakes of the caduceus); the animals are usually shown supporting a shield or surmounting the crest of a helmet. Jung supports this interpretation with his observation that the counterbalancing of the lion and the unicorn in Britain's coat of arms stands for the inner stress of balanced opposites finding their equilibrium in the centre (32). In alchemy, the counter-balancing of the male and the female of the same species (lion/lioness, dog/bitch) signifies the essential contrast between sulphur and mercury, the fixed and the volatile elements. This is also the case when a winged animal is opposed to a wingless one. The ancient interest in animals as vehicles of cosmic meanings, over and above the mere fact of their physical existence, persisted from the earliest beginnings of the Neolithic Age up to as late as 1767, with the publication of such works as *Jubile van den Heyligen Macarius*. This treatise describes processions in which each symbolic chariot has a characteristic animal (the peacock, phoenix, pelican, unicorn, lion, eagle, stag, ostrich, dragon, crocodile, wild boar, goat, swan, winged horse, rhinoceros, tiger and elephant). These same animals, together with many others (such as the duck, donkey, ox, owl, horse, camel, ram, pig, deer, stork, cat, griffin, ibis, leopard, wolf, fly, bear, bird, dove, panther, fish, snake and fox) are those mainly used also as watermarks in papermaking. The use of watermarks, undoubtedly mystical and symbolic in origin, spread throughout the Western world from the end of the 13th century onwards. All the above particular symbolic uses rest on a general symbolism of animals, in which they are related to three main ideas: the animal as a mount (i.e. as a means of transport); as an object of sacrifice; and as an inferior form of life (4). The appearance of animals in dreams or visions, as in Fuseli's famous painting, expresses an energy still undifferentiated and not yet rationalized, nor yet mastered by the will (in the sense of that which controls the instincts) (31). According to Jung, the animal stands for the non-human psyche, for the world of subhuman instincts, and for the unconscious areas of the psyche. The more primitive the animal, the deeper the stratum of which it is an expression. As in all symbolism, the greater the number of objects depicted, the baser and the more primitive is the meaning (56). Identifying oneself with animals represents integration of the unconscious and sometimes—like immersion in the primal waters—rejuvenation through bathing in the sources of life itself (32). It is obvious that, for pre-Christian man (as well as in amoral cults), the animal signifies exaltation rather than opposition. This is clearly seen in the Roman *signa*, showing eagles and wolves symbolically placed on cubes (the earth) and spheres (heaven, the universe) in order to express the triumphant power of the force of an instinct. With regard to mythic animals, a more extensive treatment of this subject is to be found in the *Manual de zoología fantástica* of Borges y Guerrero (Mexico and Buenos Aires, 1957), in which such creatures are characterized as basically symbolic and, in most cases, expressive of 'cosmic terror'.

Anjana A type of witch in Hispanic folklore, the name perhaps being derived from Jana or Diana. These witches take on the form of old women to test out the charity of human beings. In their true form they are beautiful young women, fair haired and blue-eyed, clothed in tunics made of flowers and silver stars. They carry a gold staff and wear green stockings. They watch over animals and have underground palaces full of jewels and other treasure. The touch of their staff turns everything into riches (10). Symbolism of this kind reveals ancestral memories of druidesses; at a deeper level it also signifies the soul renewed by fusion with the 'mana personality'. The staff, a sigmoid symbol, is the emblem of those relationships linking apparently unrelated things. The green stockings allude to the primitive forces of virgin nature. The treasures and riches signify the spiritual powers harboured by the unconscious.

Antiquity The age of an object confers upon it an additional significance which eventually becomes more important than the original significance of the object itself. The significance of antiquity is derived from the following considerations: (i) Whatever is old is authentic, unadulterated, true, a link with the other world; old things do not deceive, therefore they stand for truth itself; (ii) Whatever is old is primitive, closer to that 'primigenial era' which boasted the 'Golden Age' of humanity; (iii) By analogy, whatever is old is related to the primitive stages in the individual's life, i.e. to the carefree life of the child, the 'paradise lost' of childhood.

Ants An attribute of Ceres, ants were utilized in soothsaying (8). There is an Indian myth in which they symbolize the pettiness of all things living—the fragile character and impotence of existence; but they also represent the life which is superior to human life (60). On account of their multiplicity, their symbolic significance is unfavourable.

Anvil A symbol of the earth and of matter. It corresponds to the passive and feminine principle, as opposed to the hammer, which denotes fecundation.

Apocalyptic Beast A symbol of matter in the process of involution: a snake or a dragon, for example, in so far as they are enemies of the spirit and a perversion of higher qualities (9). It has sometimes been equated with the feminine principle, in so far as this is a source of temptation and corruption, and particularly of stagnation in the process of evolution. Myths such as those of Calypso or the sirens are related to this theme.

Apollo In mythology and alchemy, his spiritual and symbolic significance is identical with that of the sun (15). The spreading golden hairs which crown the god's head have the same meaning as the bow and arrow (sunrays) (8). The Greek name for Apollo is, of course, Apollon, which means 'from the depths of the lion' and expresses the meaningful relationship of the sun with the fifth sign of the Zodiac, Leo (48).

Apple Being almost spherical in shape, the apple signifies totality. It is symbolic of earthly desires, or of indulgence in such desires. The warning not to eat the forbidden apple came, therefore, from the mouth of the supreme being, as a warning against the exaltation of materialistic desire (15). The intellect, the thirst for knowledge—as Nietzsche realized—is only an intermediate zone between earthly desire and pure spirituality.

Aquarius The eleventh archetypal sign of the Zodiac. Its allegorical representation is a figure of a man pouring water from an amphora. In the Egyptian Zodiac of Denderah, Aquarius carries two amphorae. This version merely affects the numerical symbolism;

it affords clearer proof of the dual force of the symbol (its active and passive aspects, evolution and involution), a duality which is of the essence in the important symbol of the Gemini. All Eastern and Western traditions relate this archetype to the symbolic flood which stands not only for the end of a formal universe but also for the completion of any cycle by the destruction of the power which held its components together. When this power ceases to function, the

 Zodiacal Sign of Aquarius

components return to the Akasha—the universal solvent—which is symbolized by Pisces. In these two signs of the Zodiac, then, the cosmic *pralaya*, or Brahma's night, runs its course. Its function, according to Hindu tradition, is to reabsorb into Oneness all those elements which originally seceded from it to lead separate individual existences. Thus, each end carries the seed of a new beginning (Ouroboros). The Egyptians identified Aquarius with their god Hapi, the personification of the Nile, whose floods were the source of the agricultural, economic and spiritual life of the country. Consequently, Aquarius symbolizes the dissolution and decomposition of the forms existing within any process, cycle or period; the loosening of bonds; the imminence of liberation through the destruction of the world of phenomena (40, 52).

Arabesque A type of ornamentation which appears to imply, apart from the cultural context of its proper name (Arabia, Islamic art), the idea of repetition, of turning back on oneself, of intertwining. To a certain extent, this idea relates it to Celto-Germanic ornamentalism and Irish and Viking art, but with profound differences. On the other hand, the arabesque has been associated by literati with the grotesque, because of its labyrinthine, sinuous form. There is more freedom in the Nordic plaits than in the oriental arabesques, which sometimes assume a circular shape, forming a kind of mandala.

Architecture The symbolism of architecture is, of course, complex and wide-ranging. It is founded upon 'correspondences' between various patterns of spatial organization, consequent upon the relationships, on the abstract plane, between architectural structures and the organized pattern of space. While the basic pattern of architectural relationships provides the primary symbolism, secondary symbolic meanings are derived from the appropriate selection of individual forms, colours and materials, and by the relative importance given to the various elements forming the architectural whole (function, height, etc.). The most profound and fundamental architectural symbol is the 'mountain-temple' (the Babylonian *ziggurat*, Egyptian pyramid, American *teocalli* or stepped pyramid, Buddhist *stupa*). It is based on a complex geometrical symbolism including both the pyramid and the ladder or staircase, as well as the mountain itself. Some of this symbolism can also be found in Western religious building, particularly Gothic cathedrals. Such temples often include essential elements from the *mandala* symbolism (that is, the squaring of the circle, through a geometrical diagram combining the square and the circle, usually linked through the octagon as an intermediate step) and from the symbolism of numbers (the significant figure standing for the number of essential factors: for example, 7 is very common in stepped pyramids; and, in the Temple of Heaven in Peking, 3—the number of floors—is the basic number, multiplied by itself because of the 3 platforms and the 3 roofs) (6). The figure 8, as we have seen, is of great importance as the link between 4 (or the square) and the circle. The Tower of the Winds, in Athens, was octagonal in plan. The eight pillars of the Temple of Heaven in Peking are another instance (6). As the cave inside the mountain is an essential element in mountain symbolism, it follows that the 'mountain-temple' would not be complete without some form of cave. In this sense, Indian rock-cut temples are a literal expression of the mountain-cave symbol: the temple actually *is* the cave cut into the side of the mountain. The cave stands for the spiritual Centre, the heart or the hearth (cf. the cave in Ithaca, or the Cave of the Nymphs in Porphyry). This symbolism implies a displacement of the symbolic centre, that is, the mountain peak of the world 'outside' is transferred to the 'inside' (of the mountain, and so of the world and of Man). The primary belief in the fundamental significance of an external form (such as the menhir, omphalos or pillar) is replaced by an interest in the space at the centre of things', identified as the ancient symbol of the 'world egg'. One of the specific symbols of this is the dome, symbolizing also the vault of heaven (which is why domes in ancient Persia were always painted blue or black). In this connexion, it is important to note that, in the geometrical symbolism of the cosmos, all circular forms relate to the sky or heaven, all squares to the earth, and all triangles (with the apex at the top) to fire and to the urge towards ascension inherent in human nature. Hence, the triangle also symbolizes the communication between earth (the material world) and heaven (the spiritual world). The square corresponds to the cross formed by the four Cardinal Points (6). And, of course, the pyramid is square in plan and triangular in section. This general symbolism, however, can be profoundly modified in certain directions by the addition of powerful secondary meanings or associations.

Thus, whereas Christianity comes to stress the importance of the human individual rather than the cosmos, temple-symbolism emphasizes the transcendence of the human figure rather than the contrast between heaven and earth—though the primary meaning can by no means be ignored. Already in Greek, Etruscan and Roman temple-building, this symbolic contrast, as well as the symbolism of gradual ascent (as in Babylonian *ziggurats*) had become subservient to the concept of a temple mirroring on earth the division of the heavens into an ordered pattern, and resting on supports (pillars, columns) which—since they originate from primitive lake-dwelling structures—relate the earth's surface to the 'primordial waters' of the ocean. The typical Romanesque church combines the symbolisms of the dome, and of the circle and the square, with two new elements of the greatest importance: the subdivision of the main body of the building into nave and two aisles (symbolic of the Trinity) and the cross-shaped plan, derived from the image of a man lying prostrate with his arms outstretched whereby the centre becomes not man's navel (a merely symmetrical division) but his heart (at the inter-section of nave and transept), while the main apse represents the head. As indicated above, each architectural element contributes to the general symbolism. Thus, in Gothic architecture, the symbol of the Trinity occurs repeatedly in triple doors, trefoiled, scalloped and pointed arches. The ogive in itself is nothing but a triangle with curved sides, with all the specific implications of triangle-symbolism outlined above (14, 46). The flammigerous arch, as the name indicates, is a symbol of fire, and it would be possible to see in the formal evolution of 15th-century Gothic a return to the apocalyptic meanings which were so important in Romanesque iconography (46). Jambs, pillars and side columns can be interpreted as 'guardians' of the doorway. Porches are the external counterpart of the altar-piece which, in its turn, is—as it were—the 'programme' set up in the heart of the temple. Cloisters also possess cosmic and spiritual implications. On the cosmic plane, and regarded as a spatial expression of a period of time, they stand for the cycle of the year, and by analogy, for the life-span of Man. The correlation is as follows: North-East side of the cloister—October December; North-West—January/March; South-West—April/June; South-East —July/September. The four divisions of the year (or of the human life-span of which it is an analogical image) are further correlated to the four phases of a ritual cycle of healing (or salvation): the first phase—death, danger and suffering; second phase—purifying fire; third—cure; fourth—convalescence (51). According to Pinedo, the South side, whence the warm winds blow, pertains to the Holy Spirit, inspiring the soul with the fire of charity and divine love; the North side, exposed to the cold winds, pertains to the devil and his insinuations that freeze the soul (46). As regards one of the most characteristic features of Gothic cathedrals—the twin frontal towers—Schneider points out that they are related to the two peaks of the Mountain of Mars (with its related symbols of the Gemini, Janus and the number 2), while the dome over the intersection of the nave and transepts stands for the Mountain of Jupiter (or unity). Paradise is above the platform and Hell (represented by the gargoyles) beneath. The four supports, pillars or piers which subdivide the façade and determine the location of the three doorways are the four rivers of Paradise. The three doors stand for faith, hope and charity. The central rosette is the Lake of Life, where heaven and earth meet (sometimes it also stands for heaven, towards which the apex of the triangular ogive points) (50). Attempts have also been made to define the probable allegorical significance of other parts of the architectural fabric of the cathedral. Thus, according to Lampérez, the church walls stand for humanity redeemed; the counterforts and flying buttresses for uplifting, moral strength; the roof for charity and shelter; the pillars, for the dogmas of the faith; the ribbing of the vaults, for the paths of salvation; the spires, for God's finger pointing to the ultimate goal of mankind. It will be seen that the special symbolic meanings here are obviously related to the appearance and functions of the various architectural elements. Two further facts should also be mentioned: the 'degraded' interpretation suggested by psychoanalysts whereby every building is seen as a human body (doors and windows—openings; pillars—forces) or spirit (cellars—subconscious; attics—mind, imagination)—an interpretation arrived at on an experimental basis; and the possibility of elaborating increasingly complex systems by combining a number of symbolic principles. Kubler, in his *Baroque Architecture*, analyses the case of Fr. Giovanni Ricci who, following the example of his mannerist forerunners Giacomo Soldati and Vincenzo Scamozzi, endeavoured to develop a new 'harmonic'—or ideal—architectural order, by integrating the existing systems (Tuscan, Doric, Ionic, etc.) into a scheme whereby each different mode was related to a specific temperament or to a certain degree of holiness (Plate III).

Aries   The Ram, a symbol of the creative impulse and of the spirit at the moment of its inception (4). The first sign of the Zodiac. In Hindu symbolism it stands for Parabrahman, that is, for the undifferentiated whole. Because the Zodiac is the symbol of the cycle of existence, Aries, its first sign, stands for the original cause or the thunderbolt which emerges from the Akasha of Pisces, that is, from the 'primordial waters'. Aries, because it stands for the initial impulse through which the potential becomes actual, is also related to the dawn and to Spring, and generally to the beginning of any cycle, process or creation. In Egypt the ram was the symbol of Amon-Ra, and the god was depicted with ram's horns. As regards human physiology, Aries controls the head and the brain, that is to say, the organs which are the centre of the individual's physical and spiritual energies, as Parabrahman is the centre of the cosmic forces (40).

Zodiacal sign of Aries.

Ark Both on the material and the spiritual planes the ark symbolizes the power to preserve all things and to ensure their rebirth (40). Biologically speaking, it can be regarded as a symbol of the womb (9) or of the heart (14), there being an obvious connexion between these two organs. The symbolism of Noah's ark has been the subject of much discussion beginning as early as St. Ambrose, *De Noe et Arca*, and Hugh of Saint Victor, *De arca Noe morali* and *De arca mystica*. The basic symbolism of the ark is the belief that the essences of the physical and spiritual life can be extracted and contained within a minute seed until such time as a rebirth creates the conditions necessary for the re-emergence of these essences into external life (14). Guénon has found subtle analogies, of great symbolic interest, between the ark and the rainbow. The ark, during the cosmic *pralaya*, floats on the waters of the lower ocean; the rainbow, in the realm of the 'upper waters', is a sign of the restoration of the order which is preserved below in the ark. Both figures together, being complementary, complete the circle of Oneness. They therefore correspond to the two halves of the ancient symbol of the 'world egg' (28). As a symbol of the heart (or of the mind, or of thought) the image of the ark is similar to that of the drinking-vessel, so frequent in mediaeval mysticism.

Arm In Egyptian hieroglyphs, the sign of the arm stands for activity in general. Other signs derived from this primary sign stand for special kinds of activity, such as working, offering, protecting, donating, etc. The hieroglyph depicting two raised arms is a symbol of invocation and of self-defence (19), a meaning which is universally recognized. A frequent motif in heraldic and emblematic devices is that of a weapon held by an arm emerging from a cloud, or from the surround of a picture. This is the avenging arm of the Lord of Hosts, or a call from the heavens for vengeance (39).

Arrow The weapon of Apollo and Diana, signifying the light of supreme power (4). In both Greece (8) and pre-Columbian America (39), it was used to designate the sun's rays. But, because of its shape, it has undeniable phallic significance, specially when it is shown in emblems balanced against the symbol of the 'mystic Centre', feminine in character, such as the heart. The heart pierced with an arrow is a symbol of 'Conjunction'.

Arthur, King The hero, king or penteyrn of the Silures of Caerleon in Wales. Around him are built the legends of the Round Table, the earliest known sources of which being the *Brut* (*c.* 1155) of the Norman, Wace, and the *Historia Regum Britanniae* (*c.* 1150) by Geoffrey of Monmouth, and the Welsh *Mabinogion* (or *Red Book*) containing the tale of Kuhlwch and Olwen (towards the end of the 9th century). Arthur appears to have been the son of the Breton leader, Uther Pendragon, whom he succeeded in 516. He is credited with deeds of mythic dimensions. For Rhys, he is an avatar of the Gallic god Mercurius Arterius, king of the fabled country Oberon. He is the archetype of the 'mythical king' who synthesizes the hopes of a race and who reflects 'primordial man'. Tradition refuses to accept his death and affirms that he will reappear in the specific shape of Arthur when the English have need of him to triumph over their enemies. Symbols closely connected with King Arthur are such as these: magic or miraculous swords and shields; the 'holy war' or the struggle between good and evil; the twelve knights with their implied relationship with the signs of the zodiac and the idea of totality.

Ascension The symbolism of ascension or ascent has two main aspects: externally a higher level in space signifies a higher value by virtue of its connexion with the symbolism of space and height; and, secondly, it pertains to the inner life, the symbolism of which concerns the 'upward impulse' rather than any actual ascent. As Mircea Eliade has observed: 'Whatever the religious context, and whatever the particular form they may take (shamanist or initiation rites, mystic ecstasy, dream-vision, heroic legend), ascensions of all kinds, such as climbing mountains or stairs or soaring upwards through the air, always signify that the human condition is being transcended and that higher cosmic levels are being attained. The mere fact of "levitation" is equivalent to a consecration. . . .' (17). But, according to a more straightforward interpretation based upon the concept of energy, the action of rising (as, in music, going from bass to treble, or from *piano* to *forte*) expresses an increase in intensity (38), whether it concerns domination or the lust for power, or any other urge whatsoever. All world-axis symbols (the mountain, ladder, tree, cross, liana, rope, the thread of the spider, spear) are connected with the symbolism of ascension (18).

Ashlar In the Egyptian system of hieroglyphs, the sign incor-

porating the ashlar (or squared stone) symbolizes material which has
been worked upon, or the results of creative activity. By analogy, it
refers to the trials necessitated by the spiritual evolution which Man
must undergo (19) before he can attain to the essential conditions of
regularity, order, coherence and continuity. The idea here is the
same as that expressed in the alchemic dialectic of the fixed and the
volatile principles. The connexion between the ashlar and the human
spirit arises from the general symbolism of the stone combined with
the notion of humanity as a perfect structure which ensures that
every 'saved' man is whole and firm as rock.

Ass This symbolic animal appears as an attribute of Saturn, in
his capacity as the 'second sun'. It is always on heat, and hated by
Isis (31). The significance of the mock crucifix, with an ass's head,
from the Palatine, must be related to the equation of Yahve with
Saturn (31), although it may be that it is related to the jester-symbol.
In connexion with the latter, the ass's head, frequently found in
mediaeval emblems, marks and signs, often stands for humility,
patience and courage. Sometimes there is a wheel or a solar symbol
between the ass's ears. This symbol, also found on the heads of oxen,
always denotes that the animal is a sacrificial victim (4). But the
symbolism of the ass involves still further complexities: Jung
defines it as *daemon triunus*—a chthonian trinity which in Latin
alchemy was depicted as a three-headed monster, one head representing mercury, the second salt and the third sulphur, or, in short, the
three material principles of matter (32). In Chaldaea, the goddess of
death is depicted kneeling on an ass which is being ferried across the
River of Hell in a boat. In dreams, the ass, especially when it appears
invested with a solemn and ritual aspect, is usually a messenger of
death or appears in connexion with a death, as destroyer of a life-
span.

Aureole A circular or oblong halo surrounding bodies in glory.
According to a 12th-century text, attributed to the abbey of St.
Victor, the oblong shape derives from the symbolism of the almond,
which is identified with Christ. This, however, does not change the
general sense of the aureole (6) as a relic of solar cults, and as a
fire-symbol expressive of irradiating, supernatural energy (31), or
as a manifestation of the emanation of spiritual light (which plays
such an important part in Hindu doctrine) (26). The almond-shaped
aureole, which usually surrounds the whole of the body, is usually
divided into three zones, as an active expression of the Trinity (6).

Axe A symbol of the power of light. The battle-axe has a
significance which is equivalent to that of the sword, the hammer
and the cross. But much more important and complex is the significance of the twin-bladed axe, related to the sign *tau* (4). This double-
headed axe is to be found in a host of works of art from India to

England, and specially in the Mediterranean countries—in Africa and Crete. Very often it is located over the head of an ox, just between its horns, when it comes to symbolize on the one hand the mandorla (related to horns because of its shape), and, on the other, the function of sacrifice in the relationship between the valley-symbol and the mountain-symbol (that is, between earth and heaven) (50). According to Luc Benoist, this twin-bladed axe is the same as the Hindu *vajra* and Jove's thunderbolt, becoming, therefore, a symbol of celestial illumination. Nowadays the double-bladed axe (the *labrys*) is associated with the labyrinth, both being symbols in the Cretan cult. The labyrinth denotes the world of existence—the pilgrimage in quest of the 'Centre' (6). In some paintings in Crete, such as that on a sarcophagus from Hagia Triada, we see a symbol made up of a cone, a double-bladed axe and a bird. The cone alludes to the deity; the axe, like all things dual, is an aspect of the Gemini, that is, of the focal-point of symbolic Inversion; the bird has been recognized as an image of the human soul ever since the time of the Egyptians (Waldemar Fenn). The axe is also symbolic of death ordered by a deity.

Babylon This is a symbol of considerable interest, even if cultural in concept rather than spontaneous or analogical. Like Carthage, Babylon is an image of a fallen and corrupt existence—the opposite of the Heavenly Jerusalem and of Paradise (37). In its esoteric sense, it symbolizes the solid or material world, in which the involution and evolution of the spirit takes place, or, in other words, the pervasion and desertion of matter by the spirit (37).

Balder A Nordic god killed by the mistletoe, which he himself personifies. Closely connected with various other symbols, such as fire, the sun and the oak (21); he is also related to Odin and the profound symbolism of the Hanged Man (in the Tarot pack).

Bandages Bandages, bands, sashes or swaddling-bands, in the Egyptian system of hieroglyphs, possess a double symbolism embracing both the swaddling-clothes of the newborn babe and the winding-sheet of the corpse in the tomb. They constitute a determinative sign corresponding to the letter S (a letter which has subsequently been construed as a snake) (19).

Basilisk A fabulous animal with a snake's body, pointed head and a three-pointed crest. In mediaeval descriptions it was said to be born of a yolkless egg laid by a cock and hatched by a toad on a bed of dung, and to have a three-pointed tail, glittering eyes and a crown on its head. Its glance was believed to be lethal, so that it could only be destroyed while its assailant was watching it in a mirror. This belief is related to the myth of the Gorgon's head. In the East, its body was supposed to be a mixture of cock, snake and toad. According to Diel, this projected image of the human psyche is clearly infernal in character, as is shown by its threefold attributes (its three-pointed crest and trifurcated tail) since they are an inversion of the qualities of the Trinity; and also by the predominance of evil components, such as the toad and the snake. It is one of the many 'keepers of treasure' mentioned in legend.

Basket For Jung, it stands for the maternal body (31). On Greek coins, the figure of a basket covered with ivy represents the Bacchanalian mysteries. It is said that Semele, while she was bearing Bacchus, was placed in a basket and thrown into the river (the symbolism of water being bound up with the idea of birth) (8).

Bat Because of its ambiguous nature, the bat is contradictory in implication. In China, for example, it is emblematic of happiness and long life (5). In Western alchemy it had a meaning which was not far removed from that of the dragon and that of the hermaphrodite. Its wings, nevertheless, are an infernal attribute (32).

Bath The symbolism of immersion in water derives from that of water itself, and signifies not only purification (a secondary symbolism taken from the general concept of water as a clear, cleansing liquid) but, more fundamentally, regeneration through the effect of the transitional powers (implying change, destruction and re-creation) of the 'primordial waters' (the fluid Element). In alchemy, this same meaning received a specialized application: the bath symbolizes the dissolution and also the purification of gold and silver.

Battering-Ram According to Fr. Heras, a symbol of penetration, that is, of an ambivalent force capable of either fertilizing or destroying.

Bear In alchemy, the bear corresponds to the *nigredo* of prime matter, and hence it is related to all initial stages and to the instincts. It has consequently been considered a symbol of the perilous aspect of the unconscious and as an attribute of the man who is cruel and crude. Since it is found in the company of Diana it is regarded as a lunar animal (31).

Bee In Egyptian hieroglyphic language, the sign of the bee was a determinative in royal nomenclature, partly by analogy with the monarchic organization of these insects, but more especially because of the ideas of industry, creative activity and wealth which are associated with the production of honey (19). In the parable of

Samson (Judges xiv, 8) the bee appears in this same sense. In Greece it was emblematic of work and obedience. According to a Delphic tradition, the second of the temples built in Delphi had been erected by bees. In Orphic teaching, souls were symbolized by bees, not only because of the association with honey but also because they migrate from the hive in swarms, since it was held that souls 'swarm' from the divine unity in a similar manner (40). In Christian symbolism, and particularly during the Romanesque period, bees were symbols of diligence and eloquence (20). In the Indo-Aryan and Moslem traditions they have the same purely spiritual significance as in Orphic teaching (50).

Bell Its sound is a symbol of creative power (4). Since it is in a hanging position, it partakes of the mystic significance of all objects which are suspended between heaven and earth. It is related, by its shape, to the vault and, consequently, to the heavens.

Belly The interior of the belly is invariably equated symbolically with the alchemic laboratory, or, in other words, with the place where transmutations are effected. Since these metamorphoses are entirely of a natural order, the belly-laboratory becomes, in a sense, the antithesis to the brain (57).

Belt The belt or girdle is a symbol of the protection of the body and, being an allegory of virginity, implies the 'defensive' (moral) virtues of the person. It is worth noting that the belt, together with gold spurs—doubtless sharing the same significance—was an attribute of the mediaeval knight. On the other hand, when the belt is associated with Venus, it takes on an erotic, fetishistic sense.

Binary Duality is a basic quality of all natural processes in so far as they comprise two opposite phases or aspects. When integrated within a higher context, this duality generates a binary system based on the counterbalanced forces of two opposite poles. The two phases or aspects can be either symmetrical (or in other words identical in extent and intensity) or asymmetrical, successive or simultaneous. Instances of a duality of successive phases would be phenomena such as: day and night; winter and summer; waxing and waning; life and death; systole and diastole; breathing in and out; youth and old age. Examples of duality which can be either successive or simultaneous: wet/dry; cold/hot; male/female; positive/negative; sun/moon; gold/silver; round/square; fire/water; volatile/fixed; spiritual/corporeal; brother/sister, etc. The right hand and left hand, corresponding to the two pillars Jachin and Boaz in Hebrew tradition, and to the gates of heaven and hell which the Latins associated with Janus, can be taken to symbolize a binary system. This is also the case with the King and Queen in alchemy (28). Whether the opposition is one of successive phases or of simultaneous movements of tension, does not affect the nature of the system, the ultimate expression of which is found in the myth of the Gemini; in the Manichean and Gnostic doctrines it takes the form of a moral duality in which evil is given an equal status with good. Evil and matter, according to Neo-Pythagorean doctrine, generate the *dyas* (duality), which is female in nature, and depicted in the Gnosis of Justin as a dual being, with a woman's torso and a snake's tail. Diel points out that this *dyas*, craving vengeance and locked in combat with the Pneuma, is the archetype of legendary figures such as Medea, Ariadne or Yseult (15). The mystery of duality, which is at the root of all action, is manifest in any opposition of forces, whether spatial, physical or spiritual. The primordial pairing of heaven and earth appears in most traditions as an image of primal opposition, the binary essence of natural life (17). As Schneider has observed, the eternal duality of Nature means that no phenomenon can ever represent a complete reality, but only one half of a reality. Each form has its analogous counterpart: man/ woman; movement/rest; evolution/involution; right/left—and total reality embraces both. A synthesis is the result of a thesis *and* an antithesis. And true reality resides only in the synthesis (50). This is why, in many individuals, there is a psychological tendency towards ambivalence, towards the breaking down of the unitary aspects of things, even though it may prove to be a source of most intense suffering. Before Freud, Eliphas Lévi had already suggested that 'Human equilibrium consists of two tendencies—an impulse towards death, and one towards life'. The death-wish is therefore as natural and as spiritual as the life or erotic impulse. The integration of these symbols within complex patterns of 'correspondences' reaches its highest pitch of perfection in the East, where cosmic allegories (such as the Wheel of Transformations, the *Yang-Yin* disk, the *Shri-Yantra*, etc.) provide a most intense, graphic expression of these notions of contradiction and synthesis. The basic elements of such antithesis are the positive principle (male, lucid, active), and, opposing it, the negative principle (female, obscure, passive); psychologically speaking, these correspond respectively to the conscious and unconscious components of the personality; and, from the point of view of Man's destiny, they correspond to involution and evolution (25). These symbolic figures are therefore not so much an expression of the duality of the forces involved, but rather of their *complementary* character within the binary system. Hindu doctrine asserts that Brahma is *sat* and non-*sat*, what-is and what-is-not: *satyam* and *asatyam* (reality and non-reality). In the Upanishads this synthesis is defined in dynamic terms as 'that which is in motion, yet nevertheless remains still'. Schneider explains these paradoxes with the suggestion that, in mystic systems, the antithesis is the complement, not the negation, of the thesis (50). It is in this sense that one should interpret the saying of Lao-Tse that 'he who knows his masculinity and preserves his femininity, is the abyss of the world' (58). Nevertheless, the tendency of opposites to unite in a synthesis is always characterized by stress and suffering, until and unless it is finally resolved by supernatural means. Thus, the step from thesis to ambivalence is painful, and the next step from ambivalence to ecstasy is difficult to achieve. The symbol of the 'Centre', the blue rose, the golden flower, the way out of the labyrinth—all these can allude to the meeting and 'conjunction' of the conscious and the unconscious, as of the union of the lover and the beloved. Metaphors such as 'The wolf also shall dwell with the lamb, and the leopard shall lie down with the kid; and the calf and the young lion and the fatling together; and a little child shall lead them' (Isaiah xi, 6), are references to the final coming of the Heavenly Jerusalem (25), where the binary synthesis is no longer dualistic severance or otherness, difference or separation, nor a balancing of opposing powers, but the assimilation of the lower by the higher, of darkness by light. The symbolism of ascension or ascent alludes not only to the possibility of a superior life for the privileged being, an initiate or saint, a hero or a thinker, but also to the primary and fundamental tendency of the cosmos to strive towards sublimation—to progress from mud to tears, from lead to gold. Rhythms vary, but movement is always in the same direction. Hindu doctrine refers not only to hope of Nirvana but also to the lessons to be learnt from *mâyâ*, or illusion. In the world of *mâyâ*—the world of phenomena—opposites cancel each other out, one opposite being balanced by another through the ceaseless interplay and transmutation of existence—the alternation of creation and destruction (60). The figure of the goddess Kâli, for instance, whose ritual required human sacrifice, is an example of symbolic counterpoise transcending the mere duality of opposing forces. The moral level reached by any religion can in fact be measured by its capacity to show, by means of dogma and imagery, how duality is transcended. One of the most powerfully poetic myths expressing the wish for cosmic unity is that in which it is said that the sun and the moon must be 'united' so that they are made to form a single being (17).

Bird Every winged being is symbolic of spiritualization. The bird, according to Jung, is a beneficent animal representing spirits or angels, supernatural aid (31), thoughts and flights of fancy (32). Hindu tradition has it that birds represent the higher states of being. To quote a passage from the Upanishads: 'Two birds, inseparable companions, inhabit the same tree; the first eats of the fruit of the tree, the second regards it but does not eat. The first bird is *Jivâtmâ*, and the second is *Atmâ* or pure knowledge, free and unconditioned; and when they are joined inseparably, then the one is indistinguishable from the other except in an illusory sense' (26). This interpretation of the bird as symbolic of the soul is very commonly found in folklore all over the world. There is a Hindu tale retold by Frazer in which an ogre explains to his daughter where he keeps his soul: 'Sixteen miles away from this place', he says, 'is a tree. Round the tree are tigers, and bears, and scorpions, and snakes; on the top of the tree is a very great fat snake; on his head is a little cage; in the cage is a bird; and my soul is in that bird' (21). This was given precise expression in ancient Egyptian symbolism by supplying the bird with a human head; in their system of hieroglyphs it was a sign corresponding to the determinative *Ba* (the soul), or the idea that the soul flies away from the body after death (19). This androcephalous bird appears also in Greek and Romanesque art, and always in this same sense (50). But the idea of the soul as a bird—the reverse of the symbolic notion—does not of itself imply that the soul is good. Hence the passage in Revelation (xvii, 2) describing Babylon as 'the hold of every foul spirit, and a cage of every unclean and hateful bird'. According to Loeffler, the bird, like the fish, was originally a phallic symbol, endowed however with the power of heightening—suggesting sublimation and spiritualization. In fairy stories there are many birds which talk and sing, symbolizing amorous yearning (and cognate with arrows and breezes). The bird may also stand for the metamorphosis of a lover. Loeffler adds that birds are universally recognized as intelligent collaborators with man in myths and folktales, and that they are derived from the great bird-demiurges of the primitives—bearers of celestial messages and creators of the nether world; this explains the further significance of birds as messengers (38). The particular colour of a bird is a factor which determines its secondary symbolisms. The blue bird is regarded by Bachelard (3) as 'the outcome of aerial motion', that is, as a pure association of ideas; but in our view, although this may well have been its origin, its ultimate aim is something quite different—to provide a symbol of the impossible (like the blue rose). In alchemy, birds stand for forces in process of activation; here the precise sense is determined by the location of the bird: soaring skywards it expresses volatilization or sublimation, and swooping earthwards it expresses precipitation and condensation; these two symbolic movements joined to form a single figure are expressive of distillation. Winged beings contrasted with others that are wingless constitute a symbol of air, of the volatile principle as opposed to the fixed. Nevertheless, as Diel has pointed out, birds, and particularly flocks of birds —for multiplicity is ever a sign of the negative—may take on evil implications; for example, swarms of insects symbolize forces in process of dissolution—forces which are teeming, restless, indeterminate, shattered. Thus, birds, in the Hercules legend, rising up from the lake Stymphalus (which stands for the stagnation of the soul and the paralysis of the spirit) denote manifold wicked desires (15). The 'giant bird' is always symbolic of a creative deity. The Hindus of Vedic times used to depict the sun in the form of a huge bird—an eagle or a swan. Germanic tradition affords further examples of a solar bird (35). It is also symbolic of storms; in Scandinavian mythology there are references to a gigantic bird called Hraesvelg (or Hraesveglur), which is supposed to create the wind by beating its wings (35). In North America, the supreme Being is often equated with the mythic personification of lightning and thunder as a great bird (17). The bird has a formidable antagonist in the snake or serpent. According to Zimmer, it is only in the West that this carries a moral implication; in India, the natural elements only are contrasted—the solar force as opposed to the fluid energy of the terrestrial oceans. The name of this solar bird is Garuda, the 'slayer of the *nâgas* or serpents' (60). Kühn, in *The Rock Pictures of Europe*, considers a Lascaux cave picture of a wounded bison, a man stricken to death and a bird on a pole, and suggests that, by the late Palaeolithic, the bird may have come to symbolize the soul or à trance-like state.

Birds Birds are very frequently used to symbolize human souls, some of the earliest examples being found in the art of ancient Egypt. Sometimes, they are depicted with human heads, as in Hellenic iconography. In the *Mirach* it is written that, when Mohammed went to heaven, he found, standing in the middle of a great square, the Tree of Life whose fruit restores youth to all those who eat of it. This Tree of Life is surrounded by groves and avenues of leafy trees on whose boughs perch many birds, brilliantly coloured and singing melodiously: these are the souls of the faithful. The souls of evildoers, on the other hand, are incarnated in birds of prey (46). Generally speaking, birds, like angels, are symbols of thought, of imagination and of the swiftness of spiritual processes and relationships. They pertain to the Element of air and, as noted in connexion with the eagle, they denote 'height' and—consequently—'loftiness' of spirit. This general symbolism has sometimes been narrowed down excessively to the particular, as often happens in traditional symbolism. Thus, Odo of Tusculum, in his sermon XCII, describes different kinds of spirituality in men in terms of the characteristics of different kinds of birds. Some birds, he says, are guileless, such as the dove; others, cunning like the partridge; some come to the hand, like the hawk, others flee from it, like the hen; some enjoy the company of men, like the swallow; others prefer solitude and the desert, like the turtle-dove. . . . Low-flying birds symbolize an earth-bound attitude; high-flying birds, spiritual longing (46).

Bite This, like the great majority of symbols, has a double meaning embracing both the mystic and the psychological planes. On the mystic level, the bite, or, rather, teeth-marks, are equivalent to the imprint or the seal of the spirit upon the flesh (since the teeth are the fortress-walls of the 'inner' or spiritual man). On the psychological level, and especially where animal-bites are concerned, it is symbolic, according to Jung, of the sudden and dangerous action of the instincts upon the psyche (32).

Blacksmith On some cultural levels, the position of blacksmith is considered to be held under the king's prerogative, and to be sacred (21). There is a close connexion between metallurgy and alchemy: According to Alleau, the blacksmith is equivalent to the accursed poet and the despised prophet. In the Rigveda, the creator of the world is a blacksmith (31); this may be accounted for by the associated symbolism of fire, but also by the fact that iron is associated with the astral world—the first iron known to man was meteoric—and with the planet Mars.

Blood From the standpoint of the chromatic or biological order, blood, since it corresponds to the colour red, represents the end of a series which begins with sunlight and the colour yellow, the intermediate stage being the colour green and vegetable life. The development from yellow to green and red appears in relation with a corresponding increase of iron. In cases of relationships as close as that between blood and the colour red, it is evident that both are reciprocally expressive: the passionate quality characteristic of red pervades the symbolism of blood, and the vital character of blood informs the significance of the colour red. In spilt blood we have a perfect symbol of sacrifice. All liquid substances (milk, honey and wine, that is to say) which were offered up in antiquity to the dead, to spirits and to gods, were images of blood, the most precious offering of all. Sacrificial blood was obtained from the sheep, the hog and the bull in classical times, and from human sacrifice among Asians, Africans and aboriginal Americans (as well as among the Europeans in prehistoric days). The Arabic saying, 'Blood has flowed, the danger is past', expresses succinctly the central idea of all sacrifice: that the offering appeases the powers and wards off the most severe chastisements which might otherwise befall. The driving-force behind the mechanism of sacrifice, the most characteristic of the symbolic inferences of blood, is the zodiacal symbol of Libra, representing divine legality, the inner conscience of man with its ability to inflict terrible self-chastisement. Wounds, by association, and for the same reason, have a similar function. Similarly with the colour red when its use appears irrational—when it mysteriously invades the object: for example, in alchemy, when matter passes from the white stage (*albedo*) to the red (*rubedo*); or the legendary 'red knight' who expresses the ever-passionate state of him who has mastered steed and monster. The Parsifal of Chrétien de Troyes is a red knight, wreathed in a pattern of images of such beauty and richness that we will quote the whole of the passage: 'A slab of red marble is floating on the water with a sword plunged into it. The knight who proves able to withdraw it will be a descendant of king David. He is clad in a coat of red silk and the aged man accompanying him hands him a cloak of scarlet lined with white ermine. . . . Parsifal meets a knight whose red armour turns all eyes that regard it red. His axe is red, his shield and his lance are redder than fire. In his hand he holds a cup of gold, his skin is white and his hair red.' Lévi, in his penetrating study of this symbol, quotes the following phrase: 'He was clothed in garments stained with blood,' for he had come through war and sacrifice (37). Of great interest, too, heightened by his discussion of the etymological sources, is the quotation supplied by Pinedo; the passage is taken from the commentary upon Isaiah lxiii, 1-2 ('Who is this that cometh from Edom, with dyed garments from Bozrah? . . . Wherefore art thou red in thine apparel?'). Pinedo comments: 'Edom and Bozrah—its capital—stand for all the nations of the Gentiles. The word Edom means "red" and Bozrah means "wine-press", which explains why the Holy Fathers say that he who comes "red" from the "wine-press" is none other than Our Lord Jesus Christ, for, according to them, this is the question which the angels put to him on the day of his triumphal ascension' (46).

Blow, To For primitives, blowing is a creative act which infuses or enlivens life, increases the force of something or changes its course. Shamans include the act of blowing in their rites.

Boar The symbolic significance of the boar, as of most other animals, is ambivalent. On the one hand it occurs as a symbol of intrepidness, and of the irrational urge towards suicide (8). On the other hand it stands for licentiousness (15). One of Vishnu's incarnations was in the form of a boar. In Babylonia and other Semitic cultures it was regarded as a sacred animal. In Celtic and Gallic legends there is always a note of distinction and positiveness about it (4). As a hostile force the boar ranks higher than the dragon or primordial monster, but below the lion.

Boat In the most general sense, a 'vehicle'. Bachelard notes that there are a great many references in literature testifying that the boat is the cradle rediscovered (and the mother's womb) (2). There is also a connexion between the boat and the human body.

Body For Gichtel, it is 'the seat of insatiable appetite, of illness and death'. In Mithraic thought (according to Evola) the soul, in order to free itself from the body, must cross seven spheres.

Bolt (or **Latch**) In Egyptian hieroglyphics, this sign represents

the link securing the two halves of a double-door, symbolizing by
analogy the will to resist any possibility of change (19).

Bone   A symbol of life as seen in the character of a seed. The
Hebrew word *luz* stands for the mandorla, embracing both the
tree and its inner, hidden and inviolable heart. But according to
Jewish tradition, it also refers to an indestructible, corporeal
particle, represented by a piece of very hard bone; it is, then,
symbolic of the belief in resurrection, and is comparable with the
symbol of the chrysalis from which the butterfly emerges (28).

Book   A book is one of the eight Chinese common emblems,
symbolizing the power to ward off evil spirits (5). The book
'written inside and out' is an allegory of the esoteric and exoteric,
cognate with the double-edged sword projecting from the mouth
(37). Broadly speaking, the book is related—as Guénon has
suggested—to the symbolism of weaving. The doctrine of Mohiddin
ibn Arabi in this respect may be summarized as follows: 'The
universe is an immense book; the characters of this book are written,
in principle, with the same ink and transcribed on to the eternal
tablet by the divine pen . . . and hence the essential divine phenomena
hidden in the "secret of secrets" took the name of "transcendent
letters". And these very transcendent letters, or, in other words,
all things created, after having been virtually crystallized within
divine omniscience, were brought down to lower levels by the
divine breath, where they gave birth to the manifest world' (25).

Bottle   According to Bayley, the bottle is one of the symbols of
salvation (4), probably because of the analogy (of function rather
than of shape) with the ark and the boat.

Bow   Shiva's bow is, like the *lingam*, the emblem of the god's
power (60). Basic to this symbolism is the concept of 'tension',
clearly defined by Heraclitus and closely related to the life-force and
to spiritual force. Benoist remarks that the bow and arrow, as
attributes of Apollo, stand for the sun's energy, its rays and its
fertilizing and purifying powers (6). The symbolism of the crossbow
is similar, but more complex, including, as it does, the 'conjunction'
of the bow and its stock.

Bower   Like the tower, the well and the door, it is a common
emblem of the Virgin Mary. That powerful painter of female
nature, John of Flanders (15th-16th centuries), frequently brings
these themes to bear upon his works. Generally speaking, the
bower is a feminine symbol (32).

Box   Like all receptacles whose basic use is keeping or containing,
the box is a feminine symbol which can refer both to the unconscious
(15) and to the maternal body itself (31). We do not here refer to
spherical objects, which are symbols of Oneness and of the spiritual
principle. The myth of 'Pandora's box' appears to allude to the

significance of the unconscious, particularly in the special sense of its unexpected, excessive, destructive potentialities. Diel relates this symbol to 'imaginative exaltation' (15). In addition, we would like to point out the analogy—the family resemblance—between Pandora's box and the 'third casket' which figures in so many legends. The first and second contain goods and riches; the third discharges storms, devastation, death. This is clearly an example of a symbol of human life (of the cycle of the year), which is divided into three stages, consisting of two favourable thirds and one adverse. A superb elaboration upon the Pandora theme is to be found in Dora and Erwin Panofsky's *Pandora's Box* (London, 1956). Particularly interesting is the authors' study of the literary heritage of a myth, and the ways in which it may be adapted to serve the visual arts.

Bramble A symbol of virginal purity consumed in its own flame (20). The Biblical burning bush, on the other hand, is symbolically related to the myth of Semele.

Branch When bearing blooms or fruit, it has the same significance as the garland. In the Egyptian system of hieroglyphs it means 'to give way' or 'bend' (19).

Branding or **Marking** The mark, especially when it takes the form of a painting or decoration (insignia) upon the body, is, like the seal, the sign or the signal, cognate with tattooing. Such brands may also have an incidental meaning occasioned by a particular circumstance (mourning, an initiation rite, etc.). But their deepest significance is connected with the symbolism of scars as the marks 'of the teeth of the spirit'. A brand is a distinguishing mark—and this is the original and predominating idea of each and every mark. The individual who wishes to 'belong' accepts the distinctive mark of the group he seeks to belong to; or if he wishes to express his own individuality, he can do so by means of determinative, unrevealed signs. Artistic or spiritual creation of any kind, the development of the personality, the mask, idiosyncrasies of dress or behaviour, are all derived from the essence of mark-symbolism.

Breathing Symbolically, to breathe is to assimilate spiritual power. Yoga exercises place particular emphasis upon breathing, since it enables man to absorb not only air but also the light of the sun. Concerning solar light, the alchemists had this to say: 'It is a fiery substance, a continuous emanation of solar corpuscles which, owing to the movement of the sun and the astral bodies, is in a perpetual state of flux and change, filling all the universe. . . . We breathe this astral gold continuously.' The two movements—positive and negative—of breathing are connected with the circulation of the blood and with the important symbolic paths of involution and evolution (3). Difficulty in breathing may therefore symbolize difficulty in assimilating the principles of the spirit and of the cosmos. The 'proper rhythm' of Yoga-breathing is associated with the 'proper voice' demanded by the Egyptians for the ritual reading of the sacred texts. Both are founded upon imitation of the rhythms of the universe.

Bridge According to Guénon, the Roman *pontifex* was literally a 'builder of bridges', that is, of that which bridges two separate worlds. St. Bernard has said that the Roman Pontiff, as the etymology of his name suggests, is a kind of bridge between God and Man (*Tractatus de Moribus et Officio Episcoporum*, III, 9). For this reason, the rainbow is a natural symbol of the pontificate. For the Israelites, it was the sign of the Covenant between the Creator and his people, and, in China, the sign denoting the union of heaven and earth. For the Greeks, it was Iris, a messenger of the gods. And there are a great many cultures where the bridge symbolizes the link between what can be perceived and what is beyond perception (28). Even when it lacks this mystic sense, the bridge is always symbolic of a transition from one state to another —of change or the desire for change.

Bucentaur A monster, half-man and half-ox or bull. In some monuments Hercules is shown fighting a bucentaur or smothering it in his arms. Like the centaur, this mythic animal is symbolic of the essential duality of man, but, in this case, stressing the baser— or animal—part. Hercules' struggle with the bucentaur is the archetype of all mythic combat: Theseus and the Minotaur, Siegfried and the dragon, etc. (8).

Buckle The buckle implies self-defence and protection, like the fibula on the one hand (which is the shield reduced to its minimal form), and the belt on the other (4). To undo one's belt is symbolically the same as 'letting one's hair down'.

Bucraneum A decorative motif deriving from the appearance of the remains of the head of the bull or ox, after it had been sacrificed by fire in ancient ritual (41).

Bull The bull is associated with the symbolism of Taurus (q.v.). It is a highly complex symbol, both from the historical and psychological point of view. In esoteric tradition it is an emblem used by the Hyperboreans as a totem against the dragon of the Negroes, and is equated with the god Thor, the son of heaven and of woodland (49). In principle, this emblematic use symbolizes the superiority of the mammal over the reptile, or of the Aryan over the Negro. The basic dilemma lies between the interpretation of the bull as a symbol of the earth, of the mother, and of the 'wetness' principle (11); and the view that it represents heaven and the father. Mithraic ritual seems to have been founded on the former: the sacrifice of the bull was expressive of the penetration of the feminine principle by the masculine, of the humid by·the igniferous (the rays of the sun, the origin and cause of all fecundity). Krappe, investigating these paradoxes, has pointed to the fact that the bull is the commonest tame animal of the Near East and relates this to the fact that bulls are depicted as lunar as often as solar (that is, they may be subject to either one or the other of the opposed principles we have just outlined). Sin was a Mesopotamian lunar god and he often took the form of a bull; Osiris, also a lunar god, was supposedly represented by the bull Apis. On the other hand, the Vedic god Sûrya is a solar bull. According to the Assyrians, the bull was born of the sun. Krappe explains this disparity not as an internal contradiction but as a consequence of the way in which the lunar and the solar cults succeed one another. The lunar bull becomes solar when the solar cult supplants the more ancient cult of the moon (35). But it may well be that the bull is first and foremost a lunar symbol because it is equated with the moon morphologically by virtue of the resemblance of the horns of the crescent moon, while it must take second place to the solar symbol of the lion. This is the view expressed by Eliade, for example, who suggests that the bull does not represent any of the astral bodies but rather the fecundating sky and that, from the year 2400 B.C. onwards, both the bull and the thunderbolt were symbols connected with the atmospheric deities, the bull's bellow being associated with the rolling of thunder. In all palaeo-oriental cultures, it was the bull which expressed the idea of power. In Accadian, 'to break the horn' signified 'to overpower' (17). According to Frobenius, the black bull is linked with the lower heaven, that is, with death. This belief prevailed in India; and in lands as remote as Java and Bali which fell under the influence of Indian culture, it was the custom to burn the bodies of princes in coffins shaped like bulls. There are Egyptian paintings of a black bull bearing the corpse of Osiris on its back (22). This interpretation is supported by Schneider's observation that, in so far as the bull corresponds to the intermediary zone between the Elements of Fire and Water, it seems to symbolize the communicating link between heaven and earth, a significance which could also apply to the bull of the royal tombs of Ur, which has a head of gold (representing fire) and a jowl of lapis lazuli (water). The ox symbolizes sacrifice, self-denial and chastity, and is also found in association with agricultural cults (50); it is, in other words, the symbolic antithesis of the bull, with its fecundating powers. If we accept that the bull is Uranian in implication, however, then the contradiction is resolved and the bull may be linked with the active, masculine principle, although only in so far as its maternal aspect has been superseded—supplanted, that is, by the son (the Sun or the lion).

This, at least, is what Jung has suggested, together with the idea that the bull, like the he-goat, is a symbol for the father (31).

Bunch   In Christian art, a bunch or cluster always symbolizes Christ and sacrifice. So, in the book of Numbers (xiii, 23), one reads: 'and (they) cut down from thence a branch with one cluster of grapes' (46).

Butterfly   Among the ancients, an emblem of the soul and of unconscious attraction towards the light (8). The purification of the soul by fire, represented in Romanesque art by the burning ember placed by the angel in the prophet's mouth, is visually portrayed on a small Mattei urn by means of an image of love holding a butterfly close to a flame (8). The Angel of Death was represented by the Gnostics as a winged foot crushing a butterfly, from which we may deduce that the butterfly was equated with life rather than with the soul in the sense of the spirit or transcendent being (36). This also explains why psychoanalysis regards the butterfly as a symbol of rebirth (56). In China, it has the secondary meanings of joy and conjugal bliss (5).

C

Cabiri   They are earth-god symbols, personified as little dwarfs, whose invisibility is implied by the hood covering their head. They were conceived to be deities watching over shipwrecked men. In all probability they are symbols of the extraordinary 'powers' held in reserve by the human spirit (32).

Caduceus   A wand with two serpents twined round it, surmounted by two small wings or a winged helmet. The rational and historical explanation is the supposed intervention of Mercury in a fight between two serpents who thereupon curled themselves round his wand. For the Romans, the caduceus served as a symbol of moral equilibrium and of good conduct. The wand represents power; the two snakes wisdom; the wings diligence (8); and the helmet is an emblem of lofty thoughts. To-day the caduceus is the insignia of the Catholic bishop in the Ukraine. The caduceus also signifies the integration of the four elements, the wand corresponding to earth, the wings to air, the serpents to fire and water (by analogy with the undulating movement of waves and flames) (56). This symbol is very ancient, and is to be found for example in India engraved upon stone tablets called *nâgakals*, a kind of votive offering placed at the entrance to temples. Heinrich Zimmer traces the caduceus back to Mesopotamia, detecting it in the design of the sacrificial cup of king Gudea of Lagash (2600 B.C.). Zimmer even goes so far as to state that the symbol probably dates back beyond this period, for the Mesopotamians considered the intertwining serpents as a symbol of the god who cures all illness, a meaning which passed into Greek culture and is still preserved in emblems of our day (60). According to esoteric Buddhism, the wand of the caduceus corresponds to the

Caduceus (Swiss, 1515).

axis of the world and the serpents refer to the force called Kundalini, which, in Tantrist teaching, sleeps coiled up at the base of the backbone—a symbol of the evolutive power of pure energy (40). Schneider maintains that the two S-shapes of the serpents correspond to illness and convalescence (51). In reality, what defines the essence of the caduceus is the nature and meaning not so much of its individual elements as of the composite whole. The precisely symmetrical and bilateral arrangement, as in the balance of Libra, or in the tri-unity of heraldry (a shield between two supporters), is always expressive of the same idea of active equilibrium, of opposing forces balancing one another in such a way as to create a higher, static form. In the caduceus, this balanced duality is twice stated:

Early Sumerian version of the caduceus.

in the serpents and in the wings, thereby emphasizing that supreme state of strength and self-control (and consequently of health) which can be achieved both on the lower plane of the instincts (symbolized by the serpents) and on the higher level of the spirit (represented by the wings).

Camel Traditionally considered in curious relation with the dragon and with winged serpents, for, according to the Zohar, the serpent in the Garden of Eden was a kind of 'flying camel'. Similar allusions are to be found in the Persian Zend-Avesta (9).

Cancer The fourth sign of the Zodiac. Orphic teaching sees it as the threshold through which the soul enters upon its incarnation. It is governed by the Moon in the performance of its symbolic rôle as mediator between the formal and the informal worlds (40).

Candelabra A symbol of spiritual light and of salvation. The number of its branches has always a cosmic or mystic significance. For example, the Hebraic seven-branched candelabra corresponds to the seven heavens and the seven planets (4).

Zodiacal sign of
Cancer.

Hebraic
seven-
branched
candelabra.

Candle, Lighted Like the lamp, it is a symbol of individuated light, and consequently of the life of an individual as opposed to the cosmic and universal life.

Canopy One of the eight emblems of good luck in Chinese Buddhism. It is also an allegory of regal dignity, and a symbol of protection (5). If it is square, it alludes to the earth; if it is circular, to the sky or the sun; in the latter case it is closely linked with the ritual parasol of so many primitive peoples and of the ancients.

Capricorn The tenth sign of the Zodiac. Its dual nature, expressed allegorically in the form of a goat whose body terminates in a fish's tail, refers to the dual tendencies of life towards the abyss (or water) on the one hand, and the heights (or mountains) on the other; these two currents also signify, in Hindu doctrine, the involutive and evolutive possibilities: the return to or the departure from the 'wheel of rebirth' (that is, the Zodiac).

Zodiacal sign of Capricorn.

Cask, Bottomless A famous Greek symbol which, as in the legend of the Danaides, symbolizes useless labour and, on another level, the apparent futility of all existence (8).

Castle This is a complex symbol, derived at once from that of the house and that of the enclosure or walled city. Walled cities figure in mediaeval art as a symbol of the transcendent soul and of the heavenly Jerusalem. Generally speaking, the castle is located on the top of a mountain or hill, which suggests an additional and important meaning derived from the symbolism of level. Its shape, form and colour, its dark and light shades, all play an important part in defining the symbolic meaning of the castle as a whole, which, in the broadest sense, is an embattled, spiritual power, ever on the watch. The 'black castle' has been interpreted as the alchemists' lair, as well as a rain cloud poised above a mountain-top (50). Its significance as the Mansion of the Beyond, or as the entrance to the Other World, would seem obvious enough. In a great many legends, the Castle of Darkness, inhabited by a 'Black Knight', is symbolic of the abode of Pluto; this is confirmed by Theseus' mythic journey into hell. Charon has his abode in a similar castle which is inaccessible to living men (the 'castle of no return' of folktales). In the legendary heaven of Nordic tradition, the same meaning is to be found. Melwas, the abducter of Guinevere, dwells in a castle surrounded by a deep moat, the only means of access being two bridges difficult to negotiate. According to Krappe, it is very possible that the underlying symbolism of all mediaeval tales and legends about a castle owned by a 'wicked knight' who holds captive all who approach his domain may well be that of the sinister castle of the Lord of the Underworld (35). On the other hand, the 'Castle of Light' is the 'redemption'-aspect of this same image. Piobb explains that the sudden appearance of a castle in the path of a wanderer is like the sudden awareness of a spiritual pattern. 'Before this fascinating vision, all fatigue disappears. One has the clear impression that treasure lies within. The splendid temple is the achieving of the inconceivable, the materialization of the unexpected' (48). The castle, in sum, together with the treasure (that is, the eternal essence of spiritual wealth), the damsel (that is, the anima in the Jungian sense) and the purified knight, make up a synthesis expressive of the will to salvation.

Cat The Egyptians associated the cat with the moon, and it was sacred to the goddesses Isis and Bast, the latter being the guardian of marriage (57). A secondary symbolism is derived from its colour; the black cat is associated with darkness and death.

Catastrophe A general symbol for a change wrought by mutation in a single process, and a frequent sign for the beginnings of psychic transformation (56). A secondary shade of meaning is added by the particular character of the catastrophe: that is, the predominant element, which will be air in the case of a hurricane, fire in the case of conflagrations, water in floods and deluges, and earth in earthquakes. Whether the catastrophe is, in the symbolic sense, positive or negative is, of course, entirely dependent upon the nature of the change wrought in the agent affected by it.

Cauldron Like the skull, a symbol of the receptacle of the forces of transmutation and germination. But whereas the skull, because of its vaulted shape, signifies the higher, sublimated and spiritual aspects of this process, the cauldron, being open at the top, has the opposite meaning of the baser forces of nature. Most of the mythic cauldrons which figure in Celtic tradition are located at the bottom of the sea or of lakes (indicating that the respective symbolisms of the cauldron and of water have coalesced, and that they both relate to the general symbolism of water, which is the vehicle of life and the medial element *par excellence*). We can see, then, that the skull is the receptacle for the 'upper ocean' or the reflection of it in Man, whereas the cauldron—the inversion of the skull—is the vessel for the 'lower ocean'. This is why pots and cauldrons figure so often in legends about magic and in folktales (17). The chalice is a sublimation and a consecration of the cauldron as well as of the cup, which is a pure symbol of containment (Plate IV).

Cave or **Cavern** Broadly speaking, its meaning is probably confined to that of the general symbolism of containment, of the enclosed or the concealed. It underlies certain images such as the mediaeval cave which symbolizes the human heart as the spiritual 'centre' (14). For Jung, it stands for the security and the impregnability of the unconscious. It appears fairly often in emblematic and mythological iconography as the meeting-place for figures of deities, forebears or archetypes, becoming therefore an objective image of Hades, although still expressive of the psychological unconscious (32). Cult sites in prehistory—some caves showing traces of the Ice Age were later made into Christian shrines. Lourdes is a religious cave of the Quaternary. Kühn has found traces of recent offerings in North African sites with prehistoric indications. Caves, with their darkness, are womb-symbols. That the German *Höhle* (cave) and *Holle* (hell) are related is not without significance. (See Herbert Kühn, *The Rock Pictures of Europe*.)

Centaur A fabulous being, half-man, half-horse, supposed by some to be the fruit of the union of Centaurus and the Magnesian mares. From a symbolic point of view the centaur is the antithesis of the knight, that is, it represents the complete domination of a being by the baser forces: in other words, it denotes cosmic force, the instincts, or the unconscious, uncontrolled by the spirit.

Centre To leave the circumference for the centre is equivalent to moving from the exterior to the interior, from form to contemplation, from multiplicity to unity, from space to spacelessness, from time to timelessness. In all symbols expressive of the mystic Centre, the intention is to reveal to Man the meaning of the primordial 'paradisal state' and to teach him to identify himself with the supreme principle of the universe (29). This centre is in effect Aristotle's 'unmoved mover' and Dante's 'L'Amore che muove il sole a l'altre stelle' (27). Similarly, Hindu doctrine declares that God resides in the centre, at that point where the radii of a wheel meet at its axis (51). In diagrams of the cosmos, the central space is always reserved for the Creator, so that he appears as if surrounded by a circular or almond-shaped halo (formed by the intersection of the circle of heaven with the circle of the earth), surrounded by concentric circles spreading outwards, and by the wheel of the Zodiac, the twelve-monthly cycle of labour upon the land, and a four-part division corresponding both to the seasons and to the tetramorph. Among the Chinese, the infinite being is frequently symbolized as a point of light with concentric circles spreading outwards from it. In Western emblems, an eagle's head sometimes carries the same significance (4). In some Hindu mandalas, such as the Shri-Yantra, the centre itself is not actually portrayed, but has to be supplied mentally by the contemplator; the Shri-Yantra is a 'form in expansion' (and a symbol, therefore, of the creation), composed of nine intersecting triangles circumscribed by a lotus flower and a square. A great many ritual acts have the sole purpose of finding out the spiritual 'Centre' of a locality, which then becomes the site, either in itself or by virtue of the temple built upon it, of an 'image of the world'. There are also many legends which tell of pilgrimages to places with character-istics which relate them to Paradise. This Chinese tale, for example, retold by the orientalist Wilhelm in his work on Lao-Tse: 'King Huangti had a dream. He crossed into the kingdom of the Hua Hsü. The kingdom of the Hua Hsü is west of the far West and north of the far North. It is not known how many hundreds of thousands of leagues it is from the Ch'i state. It can be reached neither by boat nor by carriage, nor on foot. It can be reached only by the spirit in flight. This country has no sovereign: everyone acts according to his own dictates; the people have no lawmakers: everyone acts according to his own dictates. The joys of life are not known, nor is the fear of death; so there is no premature death. Self-withdrawal is not known, nor is the shunning of one's fellows; so there is no love and no hate. Revulsion from what is distasteful is not known, nor is the search for pleasure; so there is no profit and no harm. No one has any preference, no one has any dislike. They enter the water and are not drowned, walk through fire and are not scorched. . . They rise up into the air as others walk on the face of the earth; they rest in space as others sleep in beds; clouds and mist do not veil their gaze. Claps of thunder do not deafen their ears. Neither beauty nor ugliness dazzles their hearts. Neither mountain nor ravine impedes their progress. They walk only in the spirit' (58). This concept of the Centre coincides, of course, with that of the 'Land of the Dead', in which the theme of the *coincidentia oppositorum* of mystic tradition comes to signify not so much 'opposition' as neutralization, in the characteristically oriental sense. The Centre is located at the point of intersection of the two arms of the superficial (or two-dimensional) cross, or of the three arms of the essential, three-dimensional cross. In this position it expresses the dimension of the 'infinite depth' of space, that is, the seed of the eternal cycle of the flux and flow of forms and beings, as well as the dimensions of space itself. In some liturgical crosses, as for example that of Cong in Ireland, the centre is marked by a precious stone.

Centre, Spiritual   In *Le Roi du Monde*, René Guénon speaks of the 'spiritual centre' which was established in the terrestrial world to conserve intact a treasure of 'non-human' knowledge. This, he suggests, is no less than the origin of the concept of 'tradition' from which are derived all the religious, mythical and philosophical customs and explanations of the world. Guénon points out that Saint-Yves d'Alveydre, in a posthumous work (*La Mission de l'Inde*, 1910), places *Agarttha* at the centre. The author connects this symbolic city with the Rosicrucians' 'solar citadel' and Campanella's *City of the Sun*.

Cerberus   A three-headed dog whose throat bristled with serpents. He was the guardian of the abode of Pluto on the banks of the Stygian lake. Neoplatonic doctrine saw in him a symbol of the evil genius. Later he came to be interpreted as the emblem of rotting in the grave, for if Hercules overcame him it was only because his tasks were directed towards the attainment of immortality (8). The three heads of Cerberus are—like the trident—the infernal replica of divine triunity. They are also related to the three Gorgons (40). In all threefold symbols of the baser forces of life, Diel, following his system of moral interpretation, sees the degradation of the three vital 'urges' (of conservation, reproduction and spiritualization), bringing about the death of the soul, which is why Cerberus, the guardian of dead souls in Tartarus, is charged with the task of preventing their return into the world above where atonement and salvation are still possible (15).

Chain   The Egyptian hieroglyphic sign in the shape of a vertical chain of three links formed by two lines intertwining (with a fourth link, left open, at the bottom) holds a dual symbolism: on the one hand, that of the caduceus of Mercury, standing for the dual streams —involution and evolution—of the universe (19); and on the other, implying the general symbolism of the chain, that is, bonds and communication. On the cosmic plane it is the symbol of the marriage of heaven and earth, similar to other symbols such as the cry of pain, the whistle of the stone hurled skywards by the sling, and the arrow (50). On the plane of earthly existence it is the symbol of matrimony: each link actually or potentially corresponding to a blood-relation-ship: father and mother, sons and daughters, brothers (51). In a wider sense related to the symbolism of bonds and cords, bands and twine, it is a symbol of social or psychic integration along with the secondary but very important characteristic of the toughness of its material. Amongst the Gauls there were comrades in arms who would enter into combat chained together in pairs so that if one

died, his companion was bound to fall too. A saying that is powerfully evocative of the spiritual significance of the chain symbol
is attributed to Louis XI of France: presenting a golden chain to
Raoul de Lannoi as an award for bravery, the king exclaimed:
'*Par le Pâque-Dieu*, my friend, thou art so ferocious in battle that
thou must be chained up, for I do not wish to lose thee lest I need
thy help once more'.

Chalice   The chalice of Christian liturgy is the transcendental
form of the cup. Related to the Grail, it frequently takes the form
of two halves of a sphere placed back to back. In this, the lower part
of the sphere becomes a receptacle open to the spiritual forces, while
the upper part closes over the earth, which it duplicates symbolically.
The chalice has a certain affinity with the Celtic symbolism of the
cauldron.

Chaos   Realistic philosophy sees chaos as the earliest state of
disorganized creation, blindly impelled towards the creation of a
new order of phenomena of hidden meanings (22). Blavatsky, for
example, asks: 'What is primordial chaos but the ether containing
within itself all forms and all beings, all the seeds of universal
creation?' Plato and the Pythagoreans maintained that this 'primordial substance' was the soul of the world, called *protohyle* by the
alchemists. Thus, chaos is seen as that which embraces all opposing
forces in a state of undifferentiated dissolution. In primordial
chaos, according to Hindu tradition, one also meets Amrita—
immortality—and Visha—evil and death (9). In alchemy, chaos was
identified with prime matter and thought to be a *massa confusa*
from which the *lapis* would arise (32); it was related to the colour
black. It has also been identified with the unconscious. But it is
better to regard chaos as the state preceding the condition of the
unconscious.

Chariot   One of the basic analogies in the universal tradition of
symbolism is that of the chariot in relation to the human being.
The charioteer represents the *self* of Jungian psychology; the
chariot the human body and also thought in its transitory aspects
relative to things terrestrial; the horses are the life-force; and the
reins denote intelligence and will-power. This is a meaning which
also appears in Cabalistic writing, where it is given the name
ascribed to the chariot itself—*Merkabah* (40, 55). The 'Sun Chariot'
is the Great Vehicle of esoteric Buddhism (4); the 'Chariot of
Fire', according to René Guénon, may be a symbol of the dynamic
and overriding power of the subtle mind (26). Be that as it may,
tales about gods or fairies travelling in chariots across land, sea
or sky are very frequent and of obvious symbolic interest. The
exact details of the vehicle and of the animals drawing it always
contribute something to the symbolism of the chariot as a whole.

So Perrault in his literary version of the folktale *La Biche au Bois*, says: 'Each fairy had a chariot of a different material: one was made of ebony drawn by white pigeons; others were of ivory drawn by crows; and others were made of cedarwood. . . . When the fairies became angry, their chariots would be harnessed only to winged dragons or serpents breathing fire out of their mouth and eyes.' The Sun Chariot (or the Chariot of Fire) is, in Loeffler's view, so powerful an archetype that it has found its way into most of the mythologies of the world. When it bears a hero, it becomes the emblem of the hero's body consumed in the service of the soul. The appearance, nature and colour of the team of animals drawing it represent the qualities, good or bad, of the motives driving the chariot onwards in fulfilment of its mission. Hence (for example) the horses of Arjuna (in the Vedic epic) are white, signifying the purity of the driver. A regional Polish tale has it that the Sun Chariot is drawn by three horses, one silver, one gold and one made of diamonds (38). This threefold aspect comes from the well-known significance of the number 3, as in the triple mandorlas and other comparable symbols and emblems.

Chariot, The   The seventh enigma of the Tarot pack. It depicts a youth clad in a cuirass, bearing a sceptre, and riding in a symbolic chariot. He incarnates the higher principles of Man's nature. In the chariot there can be seen an emblem of the Egyptian winged globe, representing the sublimation of matter and its evolutive motion. Furthermore, the chariot has red wheels, which are to be related to the whirlwinds of fire in the vision of Ezekiel. These wheels stand out in contrast to the blue canopy or pallium which covers the chariot, signifying the difference between the absolute and the relative. The allegory of this image is reflected in its smallest details. So, for example, the cuirass of the charioteer represents his defence against the baser forces of life; it is secured with five gold studs, denoting the four elements and the quintessence. On his shoulders there are two crescent moons representing the world of forms. The chariot is drawn by what at first seems to be a pair of sphinxes but which is in fact a two-headed amphisbaena, symbolizing the hostile forces which one must subjugate in order to go forward (in the same way as the two serpents counterbalance one another in the caduceus). Basil Valentine, in his *L'Azoth des Philosophes* (Paris, 1660), illustrates this principle of duality with a serpent coiled round the sun and moon, its extremities bearing the likeness of a lion and an eagle. This Tarot mystery, then, is associated with concepts of self-control, progress and victory (59).

Chequers   Any pattern consisting of squares, lozenges or rectangles, in alternating white and black colours (that is, positive and negative), or, for that matter, in other pairs of colours, stands in symbolic relation to the duality of elements inherent in the extension of time and hence in destiny. Thus, the Romans would mark a happy or an unhappy day with a white or a black stone respectively. The colour of chequer-work changes its meaning according to the particular symbolism of the colours. The significance of chequers, then, embraces concepts of combination, demonstration, chance or potentiality (48), as well as the effort to control irrational impulses by containing them within a given order. All orthogonal forms are symbols of the reason and the intellect, but not of the spirit, because the latter is content *par excellence*, whereas the rational never manages to be more than a system of apprehending things, that is, a container. The heraldic lozenge is a development of the chequer-board, the form of which is such that it represents the dynamic interaction of the two elements which, in all forms of chequer, are opposed and counterpoised one against the other in a pattern of duality. It is significant that the costume of the harlequin (a chthonian deity) is actually chequered or made up of lozenges, which proves beyond doubt that the harlequin is related to the gods of destiny.

Cherubim The cherubim or Kirubi (or Kherebu) which stood at the entrance to Assyrian temples and palaces were, according to Marques-Rivière, nothing less than gigantic pentacles placed there by the priests as 'keepers of the threshold'—a function which in China was fulfilled by griffins and dragons (39). The Egyptian cherub was a figure with many wings, and covered with eyes; it was an emblem of the night sky, of religion and vigilance (8).

Child A symbol of the future, as opposed to the old man who signifies the past (49); but the child is also symbolic of that stage of life when the old man, transformed, acquires a new simplicity—as Nietzsche implied in *Thus Spake Zarathustra* when dealing with the 'three transformations'. Hence the conception of the child as symbolic of the 'mystic Centre' and as the 'youthful, re-awakening force' (56). In Christian iconography, children often appear as angels; on the aesthetic plane they are found as *putti* in Baroque grotesque and ornamentations; and in traditional symbology they are dwarfs or Cabiri. In every case, Jung argues, they symbolize formative forces of the unconscious of a beneficent and protective kind (32). Psychologically speaking, the child is of the soul—the product of the *coniunctio* between the unconscious and consciousness: one dreams of a child when some great spiritual change is about to take place under favourable circumstances (33). The mystic child who solves riddles and teaches wisdom is an archetypal figure having the same significance, but on the mythic plane of the general and collective, and is an aspect of the heroic child who liberates the world from monsters (60). In alchemy, the child wearing a crown or regal garments is a symbol of the philosopher's stone, that is, of the supreme realization of mystic identification with the 'god within us' and with the eternal.

Chimaera A monster born of Typhon and Echidna. It is represented as having a lion's head, the body of a goat and the tail of a dragon. Flames flicker from out of its mouth. Like other teratological beings, the chimaera is a symbol of complex evil (8).

Choice The symbols for choice usually take the form of a cross-roads or a balanced symmetry of two opposing principles. The best-known allegory of choice shows a woman dressed in violet (signifying indecision, according to Otto Weininger, because as a colour it is neither blue nor red), standing at a cross-roads, with a snake crawling along one of the paths; and she is pointing to a verdant tree growing in the other path (8).

Chrism The signographic emblem of Christ, based on the combination of the first two letters of the word Χριστος, X and P. Attention has been drawn to the similarity between this sign, which figured on the Roman labarum (banner) from the time of Constantine, and the Egyptian anserated cross.

Chrysalis In the words of Wang Chung: 'The chrysalis precedes the cicada; simply by changing its shape, it becomes the cicada. When the soul leaves the body, it resembles a cicada which leaves its chrysalis in order to become an insect.' In Schneider's view, the mystic function of such a transformation presupposes qualities of balance, regeneration and valour (51). The ritual mask, as well as the theatre-mask, is probably closely connected with the idea of the chrysalis and metamorphosis. For, behind this mask, the transformation of an individual's personality is hidden from view.

Chthonian Demons Various beings mentioned in mythologies come under this heading, such as the Greek harpies and Erinyes, the Hindu Rakshasas, the Arabic djinns, the Germanic elves and valkyries, etc. They are symbols of thanatic forces, of the death-wish in various guises: the subtle fascination of dreams, or the heroic thrill experienced by the man who answers the call to battle (35). The quest for death—extremes meet (because of the curve of the conceptual line)—is apparent in limit-situations, not only in the negative aspect but also—and principally—at the peak of the affirmative. That is, vital optimism and perfect happiness of necessity imply the other extreme, that is, the presence of death.

Circle At times it is synonymous with the circumference, just as the circumference is often equated with circular movement. But although its general meaning embraces both aspects, there are some further details which it is important to emphasize. The circle or disk is, very frequently, an emblem of the sun (and indisputably so when it is surrounded by rays). It also bears a certain relationship to the number ten (symbolizing the return to unity from multiplicity)

(49), when it comes to stand for heaven and perfection (4) and sometimes eternity as well (20). There are profound psychological implications in this particular concept of perfection. As Jung observes, the square, representing the lowest of the composite and factorial numbers, symbolizes the pluralist state of man who has not achieved inner unity (perfection) whilst the circle would correspond to this ultimate state of Oneness. The octagon is the intermediate state between the square and the circle. Representations of the relationship between the circle and the square are very common in

Chinese Yang-Yin, surrounded by the eight trigrams.

the universal and spiritual world of morphology, notably in the mandalas of India and Tibet and in Chinese emblems. Indeed, according to Chochod, in China, activity, or the masculine principle (*Yang*), is represented by a white circle (depicting heaven), whereas passivity, the feminine principle (*Yin*) is denoted by a black square (portraying earth). The white circle stands for energy and celestial influences and the black square for telluric forces. The interaction implicit in dualism is represented by the famous symbol of the Yang-Yin, a circle divided into two equal sections by a sigmoid line across the diameter, the white section (*Yang*) having a black spot within it, and the black (*Yin*) a white spot. These two spots signify that there is always something of the feminine in the masculine and something of the masculine in the feminine. The sigmoid line is a symbol of the movement of communication and serves the purpose of implying—like the swastika—the idea of rotation, so imparting a dynamic and complementary character to this bipartite symbol. The law of polarity has been the subject of much thought among

Chinese philosophers, who have deduced from this bipolar symbol a series of principles of unquestionable value, which we here transcribe: (a) the quantity of energy distributed throughout the universe is invariable; (b) it consists of the sum of two equal amounts of energy, one positive and active in kind and the other negative and passive; (c) the nature of cosmic phenomena is characterized by the varying proportions of the two modes of energy involved in their creation. In the twelve months of the year, for example, there is a given quantity of energy drawn from six parts of *Yang* and six of *Yin*, in varying proportions (13). We must also point to the relationship between the circle and the sphere, which is a symbol of the All.

Circumference   A symbol of adequate limitation, of the manifest world, of the precise and the regular (25), as well as of the inner unity of all matter and all universal harmony, as understood by the alchemists. Enclosing beings, objects or figures within a circumference has a double meaning: from within, it implies limitation and definition; from without, it is seen to represent the defence of the physical and psychic contents themselves against the perils of the soul threatening it from without, these dangers being, in a way, tantamount to chaos, but more particularly to illimitation and disintegration (32). Circumferential movement, which the Gnostics turned into one of their basic emblems by means of the figure of the dragon, the serpent or the fish biting its tail, is a representation of time. The Ouroboros (the circle formed by a dragon biting its own tail) is to be found in the *Codex Marcianus* (of the 2nd century A.D.) and also in the Greek legend *Hen to Pan* (The One, The All), which explains how its meaning embraces all cyclic systems (unity, multiplicity and the return to unity; evolution and involution; birth, growth, decrease, death, etc.). The alchemists took up this Gnostic symbol and applied it to the processes of their symbolic *opus* of human destiny (32). Now, by virtue of its movement as much as by its shape, circular motion carries the further significance of that which brings into being, activates and animates all the forces involved in any given process, sweeping them along with it, including those forces which would otherwise act against each other. As we have seen, this meaning is basic in the Chinese *Yang-Yin* emblem (30). Almost all representations of time have some bearing upon the circle, as for example the mediaeval representations of the year.

Cithara (or **Cithern**)   A symbol of the cosmos, its strings corresponding to the levels of the universe. Being rounded on one side and flat on the other (like the turtle), it comes to signify the synthesis of heaven and earth (14, 50).

City   Up to a certain point it corresponds to landscape-symbolism in general, of which it forms one representational aspect, embracing the important symbols of level and space, that is, height and situation. With the dawning of history there arose, according to René Guénon, a true, 'sacred geography' and the position, shape, doors and gates, and general disposition of a city with its temples and acropolis were never arbitrary or fortuitous, or merely utilitarian. In fact, cities were planned in strict accord with the dictates of a particular doctrine; hence the city became a symbol of that doctrine and of the society which upheld it (28). The city walls had magic powers since they were the outward signs of dogma, which explains and justifies Romulus's fratricide. Ornamental reliefs on capitals, lintels, and tympana of the Middle Ages often depict the outlines of a walled city, although in a way which is more emblematic than symbolic. These ornaments are a kind of prefiguration of the heavenly Jerusalem. An angel armed with a sword is sometimes to be seen at the city gate (46). Jung sees the city as a mother-symbol and as a symbol of the feminine principle in general: that is, he interprets the City as a woman who shelters her inhabitants as if they were her children; that is why the two mother-gods Rhea and Cybele—as well as other allegorical figures derived from them— wear a crown after the pattern of a wall. The Old Testament speaks of cities as women (31).

Climate   The analogy between a state of mind and a given climate, as expressed by the interplay between space, situation, the elements and temperature, as well as level-symbolism, is one of the most frequent of all analogies in literature. Nietzsche, for example, embarked upon a passionate quest for the true climate—for the exact geographic location—corresponding to the inner 'climate' of the thinker (3). The universal value of pairs of opposites, such as high/low, dry/wet, clear/dark, is demonstrated in their continued use not only in physical and material but also in psychological, intellectual and spiritual matters.

Cloak   Within the symbolism of garments, the cloak is, on the one hand, the sign of superior dignity, and, on the other, of a veil cutting off a person from the world (48). The cloak of Apollonius is an expression of the complete self-possession of the sage, isolating him from the instinctive currents that move the generality of mankind (37). The actual position of the cloak is of great importance in determining the secondary symbolic meanings. For example, the Heddernheim relief of Mithras slaying the bull has a cloak flying out in the wind like wings, thereby equating the hero and the victim with the celebrated alchemic marriage of the volatile with the fixed (31). The material, adornments, colour and shape of the cloak add further shades of meaning. The two colours of the outside and the inside always correspond to a dual significance arising directly out of the symbolism of colours.

Clock Like all circular forms incorporating a number of internal elements, the clock may be interpreted as a kind of mandala. Since the essence of the clock is to tell the time, the predominant symbolism is that of number. As a machine, the clock is related to the notions of 'perpetual motion', automata, mechanism and to the magical creation of beings that pursue their own autonomous existence.

Clothes The wearing of skins by the Roman eagle-bearers appears to be of totemic origin. Without attempting to establish any theoretical connexion between a Sacher-Masoch's concept of 'skins' and their habitual use by women, this possibility must not be forgotten. The spotted skin of an animal (such as a panther) or a multicoloured or shot fabric are symbols of the Whole (the god Pan). In *Aurélia*, which abounds in symbols, Nerval says: 'and the goddess of my dreams appeared before me, smiling, dressed in Indian-style garments. . . . She began to walk among us, and the meadows grew green again and the flowers and plants sprang up over the earth at the touch of her feet.' In another passage, Nerval causes the drapery and designs of his beloved's dress to become so confused with the flowers and plants in a garden that they grow indistinguishable.

Clouds There are two principal aspects to cloud-symbolism: on the one hand they are related to the symbolism of mist, signifying the intermediate world between the formal and the non-formal; and on the other hand they are associated with the 'Upper Waters'— the realm of the antique Neptune. The former aspect of the cloud is symbolic of forms as phenomena and appearance, always in a state of metamorphosis, which obscure the immutable quality of higher truth (37). The second aspect of clouds reveals their family connexion with fertility-symbolism and their analogous relationship with all that is destined to bring fecundity. Hence the fact that ancient Christian symbolism interprets the cloud as synonymous with the prophet, since prophecies are an occult source of fertilization, celestial in origin (46). Hence also the conclusion of Bachelard that the cloud should be taken as a symbolic messenger (3).

Trefoil.

Clover (or **Trefoil**) An emblem of the Trinity. When it is located upon a mountain it comes to signify knowledge of the divine essence gained by hard endeavour, through sacrifice or study (equivalent to ascension) (4). Trifoliate forms, such as the Gothic three-lobed arch, bear the same significance; and, broadly speaking, so do all tripartite forms. In the Middle Ages, triple time in music was regarded in the same light, and it is so used by Scriabin in *Prometheus*.

Clown Like the buffoon, the clown is a mythic figure, and the inversion of the king—the inversion, that is to say, of the possessor of supreme powers; hence the clown is the victim chosen as a substitute for the king, in accord with the familiar astrobiological and primitive ideas of the ritual assassination of the king. The clown is the last, whereas the king is the first, but in the essential order of things the last comes second. This is confirmed by the folklore custom, mentioned by Frazer, in which village youths, during Spring festivals, would race on horseback up to the tallest mast (symbolizing the world-axis); he who came first was elected Easter king, and the last to arrive was made a clown and beaten (21).

Coal Like charred wood, the symbolism of coal is closely linked with that of fire. There is a certain ambivalence about it, since it sometimes appears as a concentrated expression of fire, and sometimes as the negative (black, repressed or occult) side of energy. The chromatic relationship between black and red—between coal and flames—can be seen in myths and legends as recounted by Krappe. According to an Australian tradition, the fire-bearing bird (the demiurge) had a red spot on its black back. Similar beliefs existed amongst the Celts, and in America and Asia (35).

Cobweb Apart from its association with the spider, the symbolism of the spider's web is identical with that of fabric. Because of its spiral shape, it also embraces the idea of creation and development —of the wheel and its centre. But in this case death and destruction lurk at the centre, so that the web with the spider in the middle comes to symbolize what Medusa the Gorgon represents when located in the centre of certain mosaics: the consuming whirlwind. It is probably a symbol of the negative aspect of the universe, representing the Gnostic view that evil is not only on the periphery of the Wheel of Transformations but in its very centre—that is, in its Origin.

Cock As the bird of dawn, the cock is a sun-symbol (4), and an emblem of vigilance and activity. Immolated to Priapus and Aesculapius, it was supposed to cure the sick (8). During the Middle Ages it became a highly important Christian image, nearly always appearing on the highest weathervane, on cathedral towers and domes, and was regarded as an allegory of vigilance and resurrection. Davy comments that vigilance in this context must be taken in the sense of 'tending towards eternity and taking care to grant first place to the things of the spirit, to be wakeful and to greet the Sun—Christ—even before it rises in the East'—illumination (14).

Coffer Like all objects whose essential quality is that of containing, it sometimes acquires the symbolic character of a heart, the brain or the maternal womb. The heart, the first of these meanings, is a figure characteristic of the symbolism of Romanesque art (14). In a broader sense, receptacles which can be closed up have, from the earliest times, represented all things that may hold secrets, such as the Ark of the Covenant of the Hebrews, or Pandora's box (48).

Cold In Bachelard's opinion, supported by literary analysis, cold corresponds symbolically to being in the situation of, or longing for, solitude or exaltation. Nietzsche, in his *Human, All Too Human*, makes a call for 'the cold, wild Alpine lands scarce warmed by the Autumn sun and *loveless*'. 'Thanks to the cold, the air gains in attacking virtues, it becomes spiritualized and dehumanized. In the frozen atmosphere, at higher altitudes, one finds another Nietzschean quality: silence' (1).

Colour Colour symbolism is one of the most universal of all types of symbolism, and has been consciously used in the liturgy, in heraldry, alchemy, art and literature. There are a great many considerations bearing upon the meaning of colour which we can here do little more than summarize. To begin with, there is the superficial classification suggested by optics and experimental psychology. The first group embraces warm 'advancing' colours, corresponding to processes of assimilation, activity and intensity (red, orange, yellow and, by extension, white), and the second covers cold, 'retreating' colours, corresponding to processes of dissimilation, passivity and debilitation (blue, indigo, violet and, by extension, black), green being an intermediate, transitional colour spanning the two groups. Then there are the subtle uses to which colour may be put in emblematic designs. The serial order of the colour-range is basic, comprising as it does (though in a somewhat abstract sense) a kind of limited set of definitive, distinct and ordered colours. The formal affinity between, on the one hand, this series of six or seven shades of colour—for sometimes it is difficult to tell blue from indigo, or azure from ultramarine—and, on the other hand, the vowel-series—there being seven vowels in Greek—as well as the notes of the musical scale, points to a basic analogy between these three scales and also between them and the division of the heavens, according to ancient astrobiological thought, into seven parts (although in fact there were sometimes said to be nine). Colour-symbolism usually derives from one of the following sources: (1) the inherent characteristic of each colour, perceived intuitively as objective fact; (2) the relationship between a colour and the planetary symbol traditionally linked with it; or (3) the relationship which elementary, primitive logic perceives. Modern psychology and psychoanalysis seem to place more weight upon the third of these formulas than even upon the first (the second formula acting as a bridge between the other two). Thus, Jolan de Jacobi, in her study of Jungian psychology, says in so many words: 'The correspondence of the colours to the respective functions varies with different cultures and groups and even among individuals; as a general rule, however, . . . blue, the colour of the rarefied atmosphere, of the clear sky, stands for thinking; yellow, the colour of the far-seeing sun, which appears bringing light out of an inscrutable darkness only to disappear again into the darkness, for intuition, the function which grasps as in a flash of illumination the origins and tendencies of happenings; red, the colour of the pulsing blood and of fire, for the surging and tearing emotions; while green, the colour of earthly, tangible, immediately perceptible growing things, represents the function of sensation' (30). The most important of the symbols derived from the foregoing principles are these: red is associated with blood, wounds, death-throes and sublimation; orange with fire and flames; yellow with the light of the sun, illumination, dissemination and comprehensive generalization; green with vegetation, but also with death and lividness (green is therefore the connecting-link between black—mineral life—and red—blood and animal life—as well as between animal life and discomposition and death); light blue with the sky and the day, and with the calm sea; dark blue with the sky and the night, and with the stormy sea; brown and ochre with the earth; and black with the fertilized land. Gold corresponds to the mystic aspect of the sun; silver to that of the moon. The different conclusions reached by psychologists and by traditional, esoteric thinkers, apparent in the above summaries, can be explained by the fact that in the psychologists' view, symbolic impressions formed in the mind may be merely fortuitous, whereas according to esoteric theory, the three series (of shades of colour, of component elements and natural appearances, and of feelings and reactions) are the outcome of a single, simultaneous cause working at the deepest levels of reality. It is for this reason that Ely Star, and others, maintains that the seven colours are severally analogous to the seven faculties of the soul, to the seven virtues (from a positive point of view), to the seven vices (from a negative viewpoint), to the geometric forms, the days of the week and the seven planets (55). Actually this is a concept which pertains more to the 'theory of correspondences' than to the symbolism of colour proper. Many primitive peoples intuitively sense that close links exist between all the different aspects of the real world: the Zuni Indians of Western America, for example, make a yearly offering to their priests of 'corn of seven colours', each colour pertaining to a planetary god. Nevertheless, it is worth while bearing in mind the most essential of these correspondences. For example: fire is represented by red and orange; air by yellow; both green and violet represent water; and black or ochre represent earth. Time is usually symbolized by a sheen as of shot silk. About the various shades of blue, ranging from near black to clear sapphire, there has been a great deal of speculation. The most relevant comments in our opinion are the following: 'Blue, standing for the vertical'—and the spatial, or the symbolism of levels—'means height and depth (the blue sky above, the blue sea below)' (32). 'Colour symbolizes an upward-tending force in the pattern of dark (or gloom and evil) and light (or illumination, glory and good). Thus, dark blue is grouped with black, and azure, like pure yellow, is coupled with white' (14). 'Blue is darkness made visible.' Blue, between white and black (that is, day and night) indicates an equilibrium which 'varies with the tone' (3). The belief that colours may be grouped in respect of their basic essentials, and within the general tendency to place phenomena in antithetical groups, according to whether they are of positive value (associated with light) or of negative (linked with darkness), is echoed even in present-day aesthetics, which bases the colour-system not upon the three primary colours of red, yellow and blue but upon the implied antithesis of yellow (or white) and blue (or black), taking red as the indirect transition between these two colours (the stages being: yellow, orange, red, violet, blue) and green as the direct (or summational) transition, this being the view of Kandinsky and Herbin. To sum up, those interpretations of colour symbolism which in our view have most importance: blue (the attribute of Jupiter and Juno as god and goddess of heaven) (56) stands for religious feeling, devotion and innocence (59); green (the colour pertaining to Venus and Nature) betokens the fertility of the fields (56), sympathy and adaptability (59); violet represents nostalgia and memories, because it is made up from blue (signifying devotion) and red (passion) (59); yellow (the attribute of Apollo, the sun-god) indicates magnanimity, intuition and intellect (56, 59); orange, pride and ambition (56, 59); red (the attribute of Mars), passion, sentiment and the life-giving principle (56, 59); grey, neutralization, egoism, depression, inertia and indifference—meanings derived from the colour of ashes (56, 59); purple (the colour of the imperial Roman paludament, as well as the Cardinal's) provides a synthesis comparable with, yet the inverse of, violet, representing power, spirituality and sublimation (56, 59); pink (the colour of the flesh), sensuality and the emotions (56, 59). One could go on with such interpretations *ad infinitum*, giving more and more exact meanings to more and more precise shades of colour, but to do so would be to fall into one of the traps of symbolism, that is, the temptation to evolve a hard-and-fast system of allegories. It is important, nevertheless, to bear in mind the analogy between the tone (that is, the intensity of a colour, or the degree of its brightness—its place on the scale between the opposite poles of black and white) and its corresponding level-symbolism. It must also be borne in mind that the purity of a colour will always have its counterpart in the purity of its symbolic meaning. Similarly, the primary colours will correspond to the primary emotions, whilst the secondary or tertiary colours will express symbols of like complexity. Children instinctively reject all mixed or impure colours, because they mean nothing to them. Conversely, the art of very advanced and refined cultures has always thrived upon subtle tones of yellowish mauve, near-violet pink, greenish ochres, etc. Let us now consider some of the practical applications of colour-symbolism, by way of clarification of the above. According to Beaumont, colour has a very special significance in Chinese symbolism, for it is emblematic of rank and authority; yellow for instance, because of its association with the sun, is considered the sacred privilege of the royal family (5). For the Egyptians, blue was used to represent truth (4). Green predominates in Christian art because of its value as a bridge between the two colour-groups (37). The mother goddess of India is represented as red in colour (contrary to the usual symbolism of white as the feminine colour), because she is associated with the principle of creation and red is the colour of activity *per se* (60). It is also the colour of blood, and for this reason prehistoric man would stain with blood any object which he wished to bring to life; and the Chinese use red pennons as talismans (39). It is for this reason too that when a Roman general was received in triumph he was carried in a chariot drawn by four white horses which were clad in gilt armour (as a symbol of the sun), and his face was painted red. Schneider, considering the essential bearing of the colour red upon alchemic processes, concludes that it is to be related to fire and purification (51). Interesting evidence of the ominous and tragic character of orange—a colour which in the view of Oswald Wirth is actually a symbol for flames, ferocity, cruelty and egoism—is forthcoming in the following passage taken from Heinrich Zimmer, the orientalist: 'After the Future Buddha had severed his hair and exchanged his royal garments for the orange-yellow robe of the ascetic beggar (those outside the pale of human society voluntarily adopt the orange-yellow garment that was originally the covering of condemned criminals being led to the place of execution) . . .' (60). To wind up these observations upon the psychic significance of colour, let us point to some correspondences with alchemy. The three main phases of the 'Great

Work' (a symbol of spiritual evolution) were (1) prime matter (corresponding to black), (2) mercury (white) and (3) sulphur (red), culminating in the production of the 'stone' (gold). Black pertains to the state of fermentation, putrefaction, occultation and penitence; white to that of illumination, ascension, revelation and pardon; red to that of suffering, sublimation and love. And gold is the state of glory. So that the series black—white—red—gold, denotes the path of spiritual ascension. The opposite or descending series can be seen in the scale beginning with yellow (that is, gold in the negative sense of the point of departure or emanation rather than the point of arrival), blue (or heaven), green (nature, or immediate natural life), black (that is, in the sense of the neoplatonic 'fall') (33). In some traditions, green and black are seen as a composite expression of vegetation manure. Hence, the ascending series of green—white—red, formed the favourite symbol of the Egyptians and the Celtic druids (54, 21). René Guénon also points to the significant fact that Dante, who knew his traditional symbology, has Beatrice appear in clothes coloured green, white and red, expressive of hope, faith and charity and corresponding to the three (alchemic) planes which we have already mentioned (27). The complex symbolism of mixed colours is derived from the primary colours of which they are composed. So, for example, greys and ochres are related to earth and vegetation. It is impossible to give any idea here of all the many notions which may be derived from a primal meaning. Thus, the Gnostics evolved the idea that, since pink was the colour of flesh-tints, it was also the colour of resurrection. To come back to the colour orange, the beautiful explanation of some allegorical figures in the alchemic *Abraham the Jew* contains a reference to orange as the 'colour of desperation', and goes on: 'A man and a woman coloured orange and seen against the background of a field coloured sky-blue, signifies that they must not place their hopes in this world, for orange denotes desperation and the blue background is a sign of hope in heaven.' And finally, to revert to green, this is a colour of antithetical tendencies: it is the colour of vegetation (or of life, in other words) and of corpses (or of death); hence, the Egyptians painted Osiris (the god of vegetation and of the dead) green. Similarly, green takes the middle place in the everyday scale of colours.

Colour (Positive/Negative) The conception of black and white as diametrically opposed symbols of the positive and the negative, either in simultaneous, in successive or alternating opposition, is very common. In our opinion it is of the utmost importance. Like all dual formulae in symbolism, it is related to the number two and the great myth of the Gemini. But some of its particular applications are of great interest; let us begin, for example, with the two sphinxes depicted in the seventh enigma of the Tarot pack. Here, one sphinx

is white and the other black (59). Again: there is a Catalan tale
which relates how some blackbirds which grew up near a magic
waterfall had snowy-white breasts, resembling the habits of Sisters
of Charity (10). In many primitive rites—medicinal dances, for
example—the dancers dress up in white clothes and blacken their
faces (51). The opposition of the two worlds (the subject of the
Gemini-symbol) finds its expression in Indo-Aryan mythology in
the portrayal of one white and one black horse (50). The 'water-
maidens' of Hispanic folklore wear white rings on the fingers of their
right hand and on their left wrist a gold, black-banded bracelet (10).
In Tibet, there are rites in which a man is chosen as the sacrificial
victim, and his face is painted half white and half black (21). Jung
recounts a dream of a man who saw himself as the pupil of a white
magician clothed in black who instructed him up to a certain point
beyond which—he was told in his dream—he would have to be
taught by a black magician dressed in white (34). Struggles between
black and white knights occur often in legends and folktales. There
is a Persian song which tells how a black knight defends a castle
against a white knight who fights valiantly to reach the treasure
within. Grimm has a myth of Lower Saxony which illustrates the
cosmic combat between the positive and the negative principles.
In Jung's version (31), it reads as follows: 'There was once a young
ash-tree that grew unnoticed in a wood. Each New Year's Eve a
white knight riding upon a white horse comes to cut down the
young shoot. At the same time a black knight arrives and engages
him in combat. After a lengthy battle the white knight overcomes
the black knight and cuts down the tree. But one day the white
knight will be unsuccessful, then the ash will grow, and when it is
big enough for a horse to be tethered under it, a mighty king will
come and a tremendous battle will begin' (implying the destruction of time and the world). Black, in fairly generalized terms, seems
to represent the initial, germinal stage of all processes, as it does in
alchemy. In this connexion, Blavatsky points out that Noah released
a black crow from the ark before he sent out the white dove. Black
crows, black doves and black flames figure in a great many legends.
They are all symbols closely related to the primal (black, occult or
unconscious) wisdom which stems from the Hidden Source (9).
Here, Jung points to the relevance of the 'dark night' of St. John
of the Cross and the 'germination in darkness' of the alchemists'
nigredo. Let us remember too that darkness for both Victor Hugo
and Richard Wagner signifies the maternal, and that light appearing
out of the gloom represents a kind of crystallization (33). Jung also
points out in this connexion that carbon—the predominant chemical
component in Man's organism—is black in so far as it is charcoal or
graphite, but that, in so far as it is a diamond (that is, crystallized

carbon), it is 'crystal-clear water' (32), thus underlining the fact that the profoundest meaning of black is occultation and germination in darkness (32). In this he is supported by Guénon, who maintains that black stands for all preliminary stages, representing the 'descent into hell', which is a recapitulation of (or an atonement for) all the preceding phases (29). Thus, the dark earth-mother—the Diana of Ephesus—was depicted with black hands and face, recalling the black openings of caves and grottos (56). This may also, of course, be concerned with a black woman, such as the one who appears in the Welsh tale of *Peredur* (Parsifal), implying the same sense of inferiority as in the case of the black man or the 'ethiops'. Amongst primitive peoples, black is the colour associated with inner or sub-terranean zones (9, 21). Black also sometimes comes to symbolize time (60), in contrast to white which represents timelessness and ecstasy. The function of white is derived from that of the sun: from mystic illumination—symbolically of the East; when it is regarded as purified yellow (that is, when it stands in the same relation to yellow as does black to the blue of the deep sea), it comes to signify in-tuition in general, and, in its affirmative and spiritual aspect, intuition of the Beyond. That is why the sacred horses of Greek, Roman, Celtic and Germanic cultures were white. Even today, in Dithmarschen in the south of Jutland, some people still recall the *Schimmelreiter*, a knight who would ride up on a white horse when the sea-dykes burst and a catastrophe threatened. Most of the words containing the root *alb*—Alberich, the alb-king or elf-king, the river Elbe, the Alps—allude to this shining light of the supernatural (16). According to Guénon, in *Le Roi du Monde*, the colour white represents the spiritual centre, Tula (Thule), the so-called 'white island', which, in India, is identified with the 'land of the living' or paradise. This is the same as mount Meru. Guénon believes that it also explains the etymology of the many geographical names containing *albo* (Alba Longa, the original city of Rome; Albion, Albano, Albany, Albania, etc.). In Greek, Argos has a similar meaning; and from it is derived *argentum*, silver-white. Nevertheless, the colour white, symbolically, does not relate to silver but to gold. Conversely, white, in so far as its negative quality of lividness goes, is (like green and greenish yellow) symbolic also of death (50) and the moon, the latter being the symbolic source of a number of rites and customs. Eliade men-tions moonlight dances performed by women with faces painted white (17). This principle of antithetical dualism is illustrated in a great number of allegories and symbols. The night, as the mother of all things, has been portrayed with a veil of stars, carrying two children in her arms, one white and the other black (4). Very common in Slavonic myth were Bielbog and Chernobog, the white and the black god respectively (35), closely related to the Gemini. The Ouroboros of the *Codex Marcianus* (of the 2nd century A.D.) has its top half black and the lower white; this inversion of the expected order imparts a sense of cyclic movement to the figure, further emphasized by the circular impulse suggested by the fact of its biting its tail. It is easy to recognize the bearing this has upon the binary symbol of the Chinese *Yang-Yin*, and indeed upon every system of graphic symbolism based upon opposites (32). This, then, is a question of an inversion-symbol—one of the basic strands in traditional symbolism—which helps to explain the ceaseless alternations of life/death, light/darkness and appearance/disappearance which make possible the continued existence of phenomena. There is a beautiful, double, complex symbol in the Rigveda (III, 7, 3) which well illustrates this dynamic, alternating dualism: fire, although clear and bright in the sky (or the air), leaves black traces on earth (that is a charred object). Rain, although black in the sky (as rain-clouds), becomes clear on earth (50). This weaving and unravelling of the strands of all the pairs of opposites is precisely the import of the positive/negative aspects of white/black, which we have sought to explain above. The Gemini, a symbol of the necessity of nature to transmute itself into binary and contradictory aspects, is represented by both white and black (51). But mankind has groped towards a way out of the terrible circle divided into two sections by a sigmoid line (such as that symbolized by the *Yang-Yin*) and this way is that indicated by the axis white/red or red/gold. Here we would again recall that the ascending scale of colours is black—white—red. Loeffler, in his examination of mythic birds in legend, links those which are black with inspiration of the mind, those which are white with eroticism and those which are red with the supernatural. We would also emphasize that in symbolism of mediaeval Christian art, black stands for penitence, white for purity and red for charity and love. Through love, then, man can find the way out of the closed, double circle. Pinedo recounts that St. Bernard's mother, while she was pregnant, dreamed of a white dog with a red back. A similar case to this is that of Blessed Juana of Aza, the mother of St. Dominic Guzman, who went on a pilgrimage to the tomb of St. Dominic of Silos to beg of him the favour of a son. The saint appeared to her and promised her that her wish would be granted, and she looked down and saw at her feet a white dog with a flaming torch in its mouth (46). In alchemy, white/red is the conjunction of opposites, or the *coniunctio solis et lunae*. Two-headed eagles and representations of the Rebis (a human-being with two heads) are usually coloured white and red, signifying the sublimation of the black/white antithesis. Also characteristic of alchemy is the curious white and red rose, symbolizing the union of water with fire. 'My beloved is white and ruddy', so sings the *Song of Songs* (v. 10), and the lily and the rose are essential symbols of white and red implicit in all mystic thought (46). When two colours are contrasted in a given symbolic field, the inferior colour is feminine in character ánd the superior is masculine. By 'inferior' we mean that which is lower within the alchemic order or series, which runs as follows: yellow, blue, green, black, white, red, gold. So, to take the black/white relationship, black is inferior and feminine; or, in the case of red/gold, gold is superior and masculine (or celestial, as against the terrestrial implications of the feminine principle). Any symbolic composition that, spatially, does not conform with this order presents us with a clear-cut example of Symbolic Inversion (q.v.). For example, in the normal symbolic pattern, white will be placed above black, red above white, and so on.

Column The single column pertains to the cosmic group of symbols representing the 'world-axis' (such as the tree, the ladder, the sacrificial stake, the mast, the cross), but also it may have a merely endopathic sense deriving from its vertical nature, implying an upward impulse of self-affirmation. Of course, there is a phallic implication too; for this reason, the ancients ascribed a column and a dolphin to Ceres as emblems of love and the sea respectively (8). The isolated column is, in short, as closely related to the symbolic tree as to the ritual erection of the megalithic stone or menhir. In allegories and graphic symbols there are nearly always two columns, not one. When they are situated on either side of a shield, they are equivalent to supporters, representing the balanced tension of opposing forces. They have a similar significance when they act as the supports of a lintel. In a cosmic sense, the two pillars or columns are symbolic of eternal stability, and the space between them is the entrance to eternity. They also allude to Solomon's temple (the image of the absolute and essential principles of building) (4). Variants of this symbol—or rather of its significance—are to be found in esoteric thought; nearly all of them are the result of applying the symbolism of the number two to the dual columns. Taking them as separate symbols, the two units making up the number two are different in kind. For the first unit corresponds to the masculine, affirmative and evolutive principle, whereas the second represents the feminine, negative, passive or involutive. It is for this reason that Saunier gives the particular significance of the two columns rising up at the entrance to temples as that of evolution and involution, or of good and evil (comparable with the Tree of Life and the Tree of Death—or Knowledge—in the Garden of Eden). On occasion, this abstract duality goes hand in hand with the physical duality of the material; thus, in the legendary temple of

Hercules at Tyre, one of the columns was made of gold and the
other of a semi-precious stone (49). In Hebrew tradition, the two
columns are known as Mercy and Severity (9). To return now to the
single column, we cannot fail to see in it a projection of—or an
analogous correspondence with—the spinal column; the same kind
of correspondence is to be seen in all forms of bilateral symmetry in
art, as well as in such organs of the human body as the kidneys or the
lungs. The vertebral column may be equated also with the world-
axis, in the same way as the skull-image is equated with the sky,
within the general relationship of the microcosm and the macrocosm.

Comb According to Schneider the relationship between the
comb and the (rowing-) boat is so close that both symbols seem to
merge in a way that is suggestive of the reconciliation of fire and
water (19). Since the comb is the attribute of some fabulous, female
beings, such as lamias and sirens, there is in consequence a relationship between it and the fleshless tail of the fish, in turn signifying
burials (or the symbolism of sacrificial remains—for instance the
bucraneum—or of devouring).

Compasses An emblematic representation of the act of creation
(37), found in allegories of geometry, architecture and equity (8).
By its shape, it is related to the letter A, signifying the beginning of
all things (4). It also symbolizes the power of measurement, of
delimitation.

Concord Concord expresses conformity, reconciliation and
harmony in diversity, or the state of peace reached between beings
or between the various forces and urges of being; its symbol is the
linking of hands or arms, an embrace, or interlacing lines. It is an
essential concept in the *Psychomachia* (the Struggle of the Soul) by
the Hispanic Latin poet Aurelius Prudentius Clemens (348-410),
author also of the *Peristephanon* (the Book of Crowns). On the other
hand, the analogy between the pairs: consonance—dissonance and
concord—discord, is evident. For that reason, dissonance intensifies
all warlike expressions in music, as in Varèse's *Arcana*.

Cone The symbolic significance of the cone is very complex and
may be derived from the association of the circle with the triangle.
In Byblus it was a symbol of Astarte, but in various parts of Syria,
according to Frazer, it was symbolic of the sun—further indication
that it can be given no precise meaning. It can also be taken as a
symbol deriving from the pyramid (21); it would then signify
psychic Oneness.

Conjunction A great many symbols touch upon the great myth
of *coniunctio* or unification, representing the *coincidentia oppositorum*
and, more particularly, the reconciliation of the separate sexes in
an eternal synthesis, after the platonic legend. In Jungian psychology,
this conjunction has a purely psychological meaning within the

psyche of one individual, as a counterpart of and a substitute for
the synthesis achieved through platonic love between two different
beings. Mystic longing has its being in the profound yearning for
absolute unity of all that is particularized and separate. In conjunction, then, lies the only possibility of supreme peace and rest.
The union of heaven and earth in primitive, astrobiological religions
is a symbol of conjunction, as is also the legendary marriage of the
princess with the prince who has rescued her (33, 38).

Constellation In Chinese symbolism, it is the third Element.
The first is the active, bright force called *Yang*, and the second the
passive, dark force called *Yin*. The constellation signifies the connexion between the Upper and the Lower Worlds, or what binds
together all that is different. It is one of the imperial emblems (5).

Coral Coral is the aquatic tree. It therefore partakes of and
blends together the symbolism on the one hand of the tree as the
world-axis, and on the other that of the (lower) ocean or abyss.
Hence, it may be equated with the roots of the terrestrial tree. On
the other hand, being red in colour, it is also related to blood; hence
it has, besides its abyssal connotation, a visceral significance which
is well captured in alchemic symbolism (8). According to Greek
legend, coral grew out of the drops of blood of the Gorgon
Medusa.

Cornucopia In mythology, it was the goat Amalthea who fed
the infant Jupiter with milk. Given that the general symbolism of
the horn is strength, and that the goat has maternal implications,
and in addition that the shape of the horn (phallic outside and hollow
inside) endows it with a complex symbolism (including that of the
lingam, or symbol of generation), it is easy to understand its allegorical use as the horn of abundance. Piobb points out also that the
cornucopia is an expression of prosperity deriving from its association with the zodiacal sign of Capricorn (48).

Correspondences The theory of 'correspondences' is basic to
symbolist tradition. The implications and scope of this theory are
beyond measure, and any valid study into the ultimate nature of the
universe must take it into account. But here we can give little more
than a brief idea of its scope, with some particular instances. It is
founded upon the assumption that all cosmic phenomena are limited
and serial and that they appear as scales or series on separate planes;
but this condition is neither chaotic nor neutral, for the components
of one series are linked with those of another in their essence and
in their ultimate significance. It is possible to marshal correspondences by forcing the components of any given scale or scales into
a common numerical pattern: for example, it is not difficult to
adapt the colour-scale from seven to eight colours, should one wish
to equate it with the scale of temperaments laid down by modern

character-study, or, for that matter, to reduce it from seven to six colours for some other comparable reason. But it is always preferable to make sure of the correspondences which exist (apparently) only in part between different patterns, rather than to force them into unnatural moulds. The attributes of the ancient gods were really nothing less than unformulated correspondences: Venus, for example, was felt to correspond with the rose, the shell, the dove, the apple, the girdle and the myrtle. There is also a psychological basis for the theory of correspondences, related to synaesthesia. Louis-Claude de St. Martin comments in his *L'Homme du désir*: 'Things were not as they are in our gloomy dwelling, where sounds can be likened only to other sounds, colours to other colours, one substance to another; there everything was of a kind. Light gave out sounds, melody brought forth light, colours had movement because they were alive; objects were at once sonorous, diaphanous and mobile enough to intermix and flow in a line through all space' (3). In Schneider's view, the key to all systems of correspondences is music. He points to a treatise by Sârngadeva in the Indian *Samgîta Ratnâkara* (I, iii, 48) of the 13th century which expounds the mystic relationship between music and animals. He comments that nothing similar is to be found in the West, although he suggests that the capitals of San Cugat del Vallés and those at Gerona (of the 12th century) portray a series of animals which, being disposed in a kind of scale, are somewhat comparable. He points likewise to Jakob Böhme and Athanasius Kircher, both of whom sought to incorporate all these ideas into their systems of mystic correspondences (*Musurgia universalis*) (50). Ely Star offers a somewhat crude explanation of correspondences: 'Each of the colours of the prism is analogous to one of the seven faculties of the human soul, to the seven virtues and the seven vices, to geometric forms and to the planets, etc.' (55). Clearly there are certain correspondences of meaning and situation in the physical world itself. For example, sound is the more shrill (or higher) the faster it moves, and vice versa; hence, speed corresponds to height and slowness to lowness, within a binary system. If cold colours are retrogressive, then coldness corresponds to distance, and warmth to nearness; here, then, we have another scientifically demonstrable correspondence. Taking the septenary system, Star suggests some correspondences between colours and musical notes, which we find exact enough: violet (the leading-note); red (the tonic); orange (the super-tonic); yellow (the mediant); green (the sub-dominant); blue (the dominant); indigo (the sub-mediant) (54). The Greeks, the Cabbalists and the Gnostics founded a great deal of their philosophy upon the theory of correspondences. Porphyry mentions the following, between the Greek vowels and the planets: alpha corresponding to the moon; epsilon to Mercury; eta to Venus; iota to the sun; omicron to Mars; upsilon to Jupiter; and omega to Saturn. Again: within the novenary system, he underlines the significance of the Hindu theory of 'modes', that is: the erotic, heroic, odious, furious, terrible, pathetic, marvellous, agreeable, humorous. The symbolism of plants, scents and animals is often based upon the theory of correspondences or derivations of it. To mention a few: the oak (by association with the sun), the walnut (with the moon), the olive tree (with Mercury), the pine (with Saturn); the correspondence may range from the most obvious (such as that of the oak allied with strength, or the palm tree with victory) to the less obvious (47). Among the most important of systems of correspondences is the Zodiac; corresponding to the twelve signs of the Zodiac, one finds the months of the year, the tribes of Israel, the labours of Hercules, and the colour-scale adapted to include twelve colours. Vital also is that relating to the parts of the human body: Aries (corresponding to the head), Taurus (the neck and throat), the Gemini (the shoulders and arms), Cancer (the chest and stomach), Leo (the heart, lungs and liver), Virgo (the belly and intestines), Libra (the backbone and marrow), Scorpio (the kidneys and genitals), Sagittarius (the thighs), Capricorn (the knees), Aquarius (the legs) and Pisces (the feet) (54). The first six signs form an involutive series which corresponds to the 'descending' colour-series of the alchemists, that is, from yellow, through blue and green, down to black. The evolutive series corresponds to the 'ascending' metamorphosis from black, through white and red, up to gold. Schneider, who has made a very useful study of correspondences, refers to Alberuni's *The Book of Instructions in the Elements of the Art of Astrology*, 1934, where the author relates the signs of the Zodiac with the principal elements of landscape: Aries corresponds to the desert, Taurus to the plains, the Gemini to twin mountain-peaks, Cancer to parks, rivers and trees, Leo to a mountain with castles and palaces, Virgo to the homestead, Scorpio to prisons and caves, Sagittarius to quicksands and centres of magic, Capricorn to fortresses and castles, Aquarius to caverns and sewers, Pisces to tombs (50). Piobb has also shown that there are correspondences between the signs of the Zodiac and the processes of the alchemists (48).

Cosmogony The basis of most cosmogonies is the 'cosmic sacrifice', expressing the idea that the creation of forms and matter can take place only by modifying primordial energy. Such a modification, so far as most primitive and protohistoric peoples are concerned, was seen to exist in such painful forms as mutilation, struggle or sacrifice. In Babylonian cosmogony it assumed the form of the killing of the original mother Tiamat (the dragon), whose body was used in the creation of heaven and earth (31). Hindu tradition links the struggle of the gods with a tribe of devils called Asuras, or with monsters of some other kind. According to the Rigveda, the gods would sacrifice a primeval being—the giant Purusha. In Persia it was a bull which was sacrificed by Ahriman or Mithras. In Scandinavia it was the giant Ymir who was dismembered by the Aesir gods and then used as the material for the creation of the world (35). Clearly, then, these cosmogonies have a psychological implication because they express the central idea that there is no creation without sacrifice, no life without death (this being the basis of all inversion-symbolisms and of the Gemini). Here we have the origin of all the bloody sacrifices of the world's religions. It is to the Chinese writer Huai-nan-tzǔ that we owe a more advanced cosmogony which, while incorporating certain of the above ideas, takes its inspiration mainly from the conception of the cosmos as a new order imposed upon primigenial chaos. Here is Wilhelm's version of this interesting passage of Huai-nan-tzǔ (58): 'The collapse of heaven had still taken no definite form. It was floating and swimming and was known as the great light. When the Sense began in the empty chaos of clouds, the cloud-chaos engendered space and time. Space and time engendered force. Force had fixed limits. The pure and clear floated upwards and formed heaven. The heavy and the muddy coagulated below to form earth. . . . The seed of heaven and earth is the union of the clear and the obscure. The concentrated seeds of the obscure and the clear are the four seasons. The scattered seeds of the four seasons is the quantity of things. The heat-force of the clear, when concentrated, engenders fire. The seed of fiery force is the sun. The cold strength of the dark, when concentrated, is water. The seed of water is the moon. . . . The path of heaven is round. The path of the earth is square. The essence of the round is the clear.' Every eschatological process is a partial regeneration of the universe, partaking of the cosmogonic and hence of the sacrificial. Similarly, it is not possible to transform the human soul in any way, except through sacrifice.

Cow Associated with the earth and with the moon. A great many lunar goddesses wear the horns of a cow on their head. When linked with the primigenial goddess Neith, the cow is a mother-symbol, representing the primal principle of humidity and endowed with certain androgynous—or gynandrous, rather—characteristics (31). In Egypt it was linked with the idea of vital heat (39). *Vac*, the feminine aspect of Brahma, is known as the 'melodious Cow' and as the 'Cow of abundance', the first description stemming from the idea of the world's creation out of sound, while the second—as hardly needs be said—comes from its function of nourishing the world with its milk, the fine dust of the Milky Way. In this we can see also the idea of heaven as a fecundating bull, with its sex inverted; in Hindu belief, the bull and the cow represent the active and the passive aspects of the generating forces of the universe (40).

Crane In cultures ranging from the Chinese to those of the Mediterranean, the crane is an allegory of justice, longevity and the good and diligent soul (51).

Creation In the Egyptian system of hieroglyphics, the whole process of creation is expressed by four signs: the spiral, as the symbol of cosmic energy; the squared spiral, as the symbol of the workings of this energy within the heart of matter; a formless mass, of self-evident meaning; and the square, as a symbol of organized matter (19). There is, then, a duality of the greatest theoretical importance—two paths: that by which abstract energy develops towards energy as an organizing force, and that followed by pure matter towards a state of matter ruled by a given order. Here lies the explanation of the process of all creation in its two most essential aspects: that of energy-content, and that of material form.

Cremation Death at the stake, the consummation of sacrifice through fire, and, from the mystic point of view, any kind of cremation, are all symbols of sublimation, that is, of the destruction of what is base to make way for what is superior; or, in other words, salvation of and through the spirit. This is the significance of the self-sacrifice of Hercules. It was a very common symbol among the alchemists. For example, the 24th emblem in Michael Maier's *Scrutinium Chymicum* (1687) shows a wolf—representing prime matter—burning in the furnace (32).

Crescent There is a dual significance to this symbol. In so far as it pertains to the moon, it stands for the world of changing forms or of phenomena, for the passive, feminine principle, and for things aquatic. Secondly, in mediaeval emblems of the Western world, and especially when associated with a star, it is a symbolic image of paradise (4).

Crest Because of its position on the helmet (linked symbolically with the head), the crest clearly stands for thought, and comes to be a symbol of the predominating theme—the *leitmotiv*—of the knight, which he displays as a token of his beloved (that is, his anima) and so giving tangible expression to his adventures and his combats. The encaged bird of Walter von der Vogelweide (of the 13th century) is probably an emblem of a soul yearning to fly away in freedom.

Crisis Man tends to question his destiny mostly in moments of crisis, that is, when the stream of life (either the stream within him of his feelings and passions, his abnormal urges or sense of inadequacy, or that flowing outside him—the flood of obstacles and failures in communication) goes against him or carries him along farther than he would wish. There is, then, a primordial desire in Man to experience 'inversion', that is, to find the technique whereby everything of a kind can be transmuted into its opposite. So, for example, illness inverted becomes health, hate becomes love, loneliness company, ignorance wisdom, dissension solidarity, rancour forgiveness, sadness happiness, the enemy's victory turns to rout and drought to fertility. Such inversion at first appears as a cross-roads, that is, as a potentiality. Then it takes the form of symbols of sacrifice, expressing the latent—and valid—idea that in every negative situation there is a direct or an indirect sense of guilt. Then, finally, come the symbols of Inversion proper and of rebirth.

Crocodile Two basically different aspects of the crocodile are blended in its symbolic meaning, representing the influence upon the animal of two of the four Elements. In the first place, because of its viciousness and destructive power, the crocodile came to signify fury and evil in Egyptian hieroglyphics (19); in the second place, since it inhabits a realm intermediate between earth and water, and is associated with mud and vegetation, it came to be thought of as an emblem of fecundity and power (50). In the opinion of Mertens Stienon there is a third aspect, deriving from its resemblance to the dragon and the serpent, as a symbol of knowledge. In Egypt, the dead used to be portrayed transformed into crocodiles of knowledge, an idea which is linked with that of the zodiacal sign of Capricorn. Blavatsky compares the crocodile with the Kumara of India (40). Then, finally, come the symbols of Inversion proper and of rebirth.

Cromlech It corresponds to the general symbolism of stone-monuments and is related to fertility cults. Eliade mentions that, in popular European beliefs even today, there are remnants of the ancient faith in the powers of large stones. The space between these rocks or stones, or the holes in the stones themselves, played an important part in fertility and health rites. The cromlech is regarded as a symbol of the Great Mother, whereas the menhir is clearly masculine (17).

Cronos By Cronos we mean here not so much the general symbolism of Saturn as those images of time which originated in oriental thought, and which were so common in the Lower Roman Empire. He is sometimes portrayed with four wings, two of which are outspread as if he were about to take flight, and two are lowered as if he were resting; this is an allusion to the dualism of time: the passage of time, and ecstasy (or transport beyond time). Sometimes he was also depicted with four eyes, two in front and two behind; this is a representation of simultaneity and of the position of the Present between the Past and the Future, a symbolism comparable with the two faces of Janus (8). More characteristic of the general symbolic meaning is the 'Mithraic Cronos', a deity representing infinite time, derived from the Zervan Akarana of the Persians. He has a rigid, human figure, and sometimes is bi-somatic:

a human body with the head of a lion. But when the head is human, then the lion's head is located on the breast. The trunk is enclosed in the five folds of an enormous snake—again denoting the duality of time: the passage of time intertwining with eternity—which, according to Macrobius, represents the path of the god along the celestial ecliptic. The lion, which is generally associated with sun-cults, is here a particular emblem of destructive and all-consuming time. It occurs in this sense in many representations of Roman as well as mediaeval funerals.

Crook The hooked staff is a pastoral attribute in the Church and a symbol of faith (4). By virtue of the sigmoid significance of the hook, it stands for divine power, communication and connexion (50); because of its spiral form it is a symbol of creative power.

Cross The complex symbolism of the cross neither denies nor supplants the historical meaning in Christianity. But in addition to

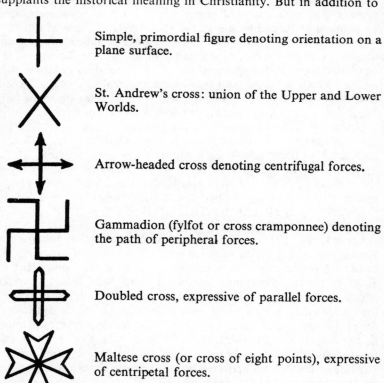

Simple, primordial figure denoting orientation on a plane surface.

St. Andrew's cross: union of the Upper and Lower Worlds.

Arrow-headed cross denoting centrifugal forces.

Gammadion (fylfot or cross cramponnee) denoting the path of peripheral forces.

Doubled cross, expressive of parallel forces.

Maltese cross (or cross of eight points), expressive of centripetal forces.

the realities of Christianity there are two other essential factors: that of the symbolism of the cross as such and that of the crucifixion or of 'suffering upon the cross'. In the first place, the cross is dramatic in derivation, an inversion, as it were, of the Tree of Paradise. Hence, the cross is often represented in mediaeval allegory as a Y-shaped tree, depicted with knots and even with branches, and sometimes with thorns. Like the Tree of Life, the cross stands for the 'world-axis'. Placed in the mystic Centre of the cosmos, it becomes the bridge or ladder by means of which the soul may reach God. There are some versions which depict the cross with seven steps, comparable with the cosmic trees which symbolize the seven heavens (17). The cross, consequently, affirms the primary relationship between the two worlds of the celestial and the earthly (14). But, in addition, because of the cross-piece which cuts cleanly across the upright (in turn implying the symbols of level and of the axis of the world), it stands for the conjunction of opposites, wedding

Cross of the Templars: forces disposed around a circumference.

Teutonic cross: four triangles denoting a centripetal tendency.

Cross of ovals, composed of one continuous line representative of the direction of movement of forces.

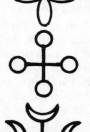

Cross with knobbed extremities representing the four Cardinal Points of space.

Lunate cross, representing (according to Piobb) the four tangential circumferences and the phases of the moon.

the spiritual (or vertical) principle with the principle of the world of phenomena. Hence its significance as a symbol for agony, struggle and martyrdom (14). Sometimes the cross is T-shaped, further emphasizing the near-equilibrium of the opposing principles. Jung comments that in some traditions the cross is a symbol of fire and of the sufferings of existence, and that this may be due to the fact that the two arms were associated with the kindling sticks which primitive man rubbed together to produce fire and which he thought of as masculine and feminine. But the predominant meaning of the cross is that of 'Conjunction'. Plato, in *Timaeus*, tells how the demiurge joins up the broken parts of the world-soul by means of two sutures shaped like St. Andrew's cross (31). Bayley stresses the fire-symbolism of the cross, and explains that all the words for 'cross' (crux, cruz, crowz, croaz, krois, krouz) have a common etymological basis in -*ak*, -*ur* or -*os*, signifying 'light of the Great Fire' (4). The cross has been widely used as a graphic emblem, very largely as a result of Christian influence but equally on account of the basic significance of the sign; for it is clear that all basic notions, whether they are ideas or signs, have come about without the prompting of any cultural influence. Hundreds of different shapes of crosses have been summarized in works such as Lehner's *Symbols, Signs and Signets*, and it has been found possible, by the study of graphic symbolism, to elucidate the particular meaning of each one. Many of them take the form of insignias of military orders, medals, etc. The swastika is a very common type of cross (q.v. *Swastika*). The Egyptian, anserated cross is particularly interesting in view of its antiquity. In Egyptian hieroglyphics it stands for life or living (*Nem Ankh*) and forms part of such words as 'health' and 'happiness'. Its upper arm is a curve, sometimes almost closed to form a circle. Enel analyses this hieroglyphic as follows: 'The phonetic significance of this sign is a combination of the signs for activity and passivity and of a mixture of the two, and conforms with the symbolism of the cross in general as the synthesis of the active and the passive principle.' The very shape of the anserated cross expresses a profound idea: that of the circle of life spreading outwards from the Origin and falling upon the surface (that is, upon the passivity of existence which it then animates) as well as soaring up towards the infinite. It may also be seen as a magic knot binding together some particular combination of elements to form one individual, a view which would confirm its characteristic life-symbolism. It may also signify destiny. Judged from the macrocosmic point of view, that is of its analogy with the world, the *Ankh*-cross may represent the sun, the sky and the earth (by reference to the circle, the upright and the horizontal lines). As a microcosmic sign, that is by analogy with man, the circle would represent the human head or reason (or the 'sun' which gives him life), the horizontal arm his arms, and the upright his body (19). In sum, the most general significance of the cross is that of the conjunction of opposites: the positive (or the vertical) with the negative (or horizontal), the superior with the inferior, life with death. The basic idea behind the symbolism of crucifixion is that of experiencing the essence of antagonism, an idea which lies at the root of existence, expressing as it does life's agonizing pain, its cross-roads of possibilities and impossibilities, of construction and destruction. Evola suggests that the cross is a synthesis of the seven aspects of space and time, because its form is such that it both maintains and destroys free movement; hence, the cross is the antithesis of the Ouroboros, the serpent or dragon denoting the primeval, anarchic dynamism which preceded the creation of the cosmos and the emergence of order. There is, thus, a close relationship between the cross and the sword, since both of them are wielded against the primordial monster (Plate V).

Cross-roads According to Jung, it is a mother-symbol. He comments: 'Where the roads cross and enter into one another, thereby symbolizing the union of opposites, there is the "mother", the object and epitome of all union.' Amongst the Ancients, cross-roads were symbols of an ambivalent theophany, since the joining up of three elements always presupposes the existence of the three principles of the active (or beneficent), the neutral (or resultant or instrumental) and the passive (or hurtful). Hence, cross-roads were sacred to the 'triform' Hecate. It was at the crossways that dogs were sacrificed to her, and the bodies of hanged men dumped (31).

Crow Because of its black colour, the crow is associated with the idea of beginning (as expressed in such symbols as the maternal night, primigenial darkness, the fertilizing earth). Because it is also associated with the atmosphere, it is a symbol for creative, demiurgic power and for spiritual strength. Because of its flight, it is considered a messenger. And, in sum, the crow has been invested by many primitive peoples with far-reaching cosmic significance. Indeed, for the Red Indians of North America it is the great civilizer and the creator of the visible world. It has a similar meaning for the Celts and the Germanic tribes, as well as in Siberia (35). In the classical cultures it no longer possesses such wide implications, but it does still retain certain mystic powers and in particular the ability to foresee the future; hence its caw played a special part in rites of divination (8). In Christian symbolism it is an allegory of solitude. Amongst the alchemists it recovers some of the original characteristics ascribed to it by the primitives, standing in particular for *nigredo*, or the initial state which is both the inherent characteristic of prime matter and the condition produced by separating out the Elements (*putrefactio*) (32). An interesting development of crow-symbolism is the representation of it with three legs drawn within a solar disk. In this form it is the first of the Chinese imperial emblems, and represents *Yang* or the active life of the Emperor. The three legs correspond to the sun-symbolism of the tripod: first light or rising sun, zenith or midday sun, and sunset or setting sun. In Beaumont's view, the crow in itself signifies the isolation of him who lives on a superior plane (5), this being the symbolism in general of all solitary birds.

Crowd   The idea of the 'crowd' is symbolically superior to that of 'multiplicity', since it implies a new concept of the numerous as a totality, or of Oneness as a fragmented whole. Thus, Jung's interpretation of the multitude or crowd is well judged; he asserts that, especially when moving or restless, it corresponds to an analogous movement in the unconscious (31). Homer has a well-known simile in which he likens a crowd of warriors in the *agora* (or in battle) to the ocean swell (constituting another symbol of the unconscious).

Crown   The essential meaning of the crown is derived from that of the head, with which it is linked—unlike the hat—not in a utilitarian but in a strictly emblematic manner. By reference to level-symbolism, we may conclude that the crown does not merely surmount the top of the body (and of the human being as a whole), but rises above it and therefore symbolizes, in the broadest and deepest sense, the very idea of pre-eminence. That is why a superlatively successful achievement is spoken of as a 'crowning achievement'. Hence, the crown is the visible sign of success, of 'crowning', whose significance reaches beyond the act to the person who performed it. At first, crowns were made out of the limbs of various trees, hence they are still connected with the symbolism of trees in general and of some trees in particular. They were the attributes of the gods; and they also were once a funeral-symbol (8). The metal crown, the diadem and the crown of rays of light, are symbols of light and of spiritual enlightenment (4). In some books of alchemy there are illustrations showing the planetary spirits receiving their crown—that is, their light—from the hands of their king—that is, the sun (32). The light they received from him is not equal in intensity but graded, as it were, in hierarchies, corresponding to the grades of nobility ranging from the king down to the baron (32). Books on alchemy also stress the affirmative and sublimating sense of the crown. In *Margarita pretiosa*, the six base metals are first shown as slaves, with their uncovered heads bowed low towards the feet of the 'king' (that is, gold); but, after their transmutation, they are depicted wearing crowns on their heads. This 'transmutation' is a symbol of spiritual evolution whose decisive characteristic is the victory of the higher principle over the base principle of the instincts. That is why Jung concludes that the radiant crown is the symbol *par excellence* of reaching the highest goal in evolution: for he who conquers himself wins the crown of eternal life (31). Secondary or more particular meanings sometimes arise from the shape or the material of the crown, on occasion differing considerably from the basic meaning outlined above. The ancient crown of the Egyptian pharaohs is a typical example of unusually shaped crowns with exceptional meanings. Marqués-Rivière here points to the emblematic and near-figurative source of its two basic components: a white and a red crown. The former is similar to the mitre-like bonnets worn in the East through the ages. The latter 'according to de Rochemonteix, is probably a pattern evolved from adapted hieroglyphs. The coif is probably a glass, the curved stem of which represents vegetation and the upright stem the ideogram of the earth. . . . M. E. Soldi sees the curved stem as a "projection of the solar disk, a spiralling flame which fertilizes the seeds" ' (39).

Crucifixion The symbolic meaning of the crucifixion—which does not oppose nor alter the historic fact, but provides further explanations of it—seems to be related to the suffering which is at the root of all contradiction and ambivalence, especially if one bears in mind the practice in mediaeval iconography of showing Jesus on the cross surrounded by symmetrical pairs of objects or beings. These paired items are sometimes, but not always, based upon the actual witnesses of the scene. Thus, the cross may be shown between the sun and the moon, between the Virgin and St. John, the good and the bad thief, the lance and the cup or chalice (or sometimes a stick and the sponge soaked in vinegar), and, of course, between heaven and earth. On occasion, there is the added symbol of the Holy Spirit balancing Adam's skull. These pairs of opposites, then, only serve to emphasize the essential binary system underlying the cross itself. The horizontal limb corresponds to the passive principle, that is, to the world of phenomena. The vertical limb denotes the active principle, that is, the transcendent world or spiritual evolution. The sun and moon are the cosmic representatives of this dualism, echoed also in the symmetrical placing of the Beloved Disciple and the Holy Mother (of opposite sexes) who stand also, respectively, for the outcome and the antecedent of the life and work of Jesus, and hence for the future and the past. The two thieves represent binary symmetry on the moral plane, that is, the two potential attitudes between which Man must choose: penitence leading to salvation and prevarication leading to damnation.

Crutch The symbolic meaning of the crutch derives directly from its literal sense: the invisible, moral or economic means of supporting any other form of existence that may 'lean' upon it. In this sense it has often appeared in Salvador Dali's paintings. It forms one of the Chinese emblems, again with the same significance (5). Frequently the crutch stands for an immoral, hidden or shameful support; this is because the foot is a symbol of the soul (15), and an infirmity or mutilation of the foot is the counterpart of an incurable defect of the spirit. Hence, in legends and adventure-stories, the common appearance of sinister characters, pirates, thieves and immoral hypocrites with crutches that bespeak their symbolic lameness. For a man to seek to revenge himself upon the cause of his mutilation shows that in his spirit he still retains some of his moral strength and that he will endure until he has been vindicated. This is the symbolic background to the famous novel *Moby Dick*, in which the protagonist has his leg torn off by the monster of the deeps, but pursues it dauntlessly to the end.

Crystal   Like precious stones, it is a symbol of the spirit and of the intellect associated with the spirit (56). It is interesting to note that mystic and surrealist alike share the same veneration for crystal. The 'state of transparency' is defined as one of the most effective and beautiful conjunctions of opposites: matter 'exists' but it is as if it did not exist, because one can see through it. As an object of contemplation, it offers neither hardness nor resistance nor suffering.

Cube   Among solid forms, it is the equivalent of the square. Hence it stands for earth, or the material world of the four Elements. Denis the Carthusian pointed out that cubic objects are not capable of rotation as are spheres, and that therefore they represent stability (14). This explains why the cube frequently forms part of allegories illustrating the solidity and the persistence of the virtues (8). It also explains why, in symbols and emblems, thrones or chariots are sometimes given cubical form.

Curl (or **Loop**)   In the Egyptian system of hieroglyphs, the loop is a determinative sign defining the ideas of either binding or unbinding, depending upon the position of the loose ends (19). It corresponds to the general symbolism of bonds and knots. The hair-curl takes its meaning from the symbolism of the hair.

Curtain   A symbol of separation, as in the 'veil of the Temple' in Jerusalem. According to Gershom Scholem, 'curtains hanging before the celestial realms of the worlds of the aeons play an important rôle in the Gnostic *Pistis Sophia*, apparently as a result of Jewish influence'. The succession of curtains is related to that of cloaks or veils, or even elements of dress and adornment, as they appear in the Mesopotamic poem of *Ishtar's Descent into Hell*. The action of parting curtains, rending veils or clothing, stripping off diadems, cloaks or bracelets, signifies a move towards an *arcanum* or the penetration of a mystery. Scholem, in *Les Origines de la Kabbale*, says that, among the emanations, similar curtains appear personified in the fountains of Isaac Cohen.

Cybele   This goddess, the wife of Saturn, is the personification of the energy animating the earth. The lions drawing her chariot represent the controlled energies necessary for evolution; the chariot in which she is riding is cubic in shape, the cube being a symbol of the earth. Her crown is shaped like a battlemented wall, and this, like the cube, also conveys a sense of building. Associated on occasions with this allegory, is a seven-pointed star (a symbol of cyclic progression) and a lunar crescent (a symbol of the world of phenomena, of the appearance and disappearance of earthly forms in the sublunary world).

Cycle The cyclic character of phenomena—cyclic, that is, because of the tendency of the final stage to curve back towards the initial stage of the process in question—leads to its being symbolized by figures such as the circle, the spiral and the ellipse. All processes are cyclic in this way, embracing movement in space, passage through time, and any change in form or condition, whether they are cycles pertaining to the year, the month, the week, the day, or the span of life of a man, a culture or a race. The symbolism of the Zodiac and the division into twelve (four times three and vice versa) are inextricably linked with the symbolic meaning of the cycle (40, 51). Graphically, the completed cycle is represented by two signs or images facing in opposite directions, symbolic of the acts of going and coming. This can be seen for example in Roman steles, having footprints pointing in opposite directions.

Cyclops A mythological giant, commonly portrayed as having a single eye in the middle of his forehead. This eye does not have the usual symbolism of the 'third' eye, but in this case, appears to symbolize the primary forces of nature.

Cydippe A man with one leg and one foot, found in Romanesque decoration. It is the antithesis of the figure of the two-tailed siren. If the latter is a symbol of femininity, arising out of the number two, the cydippe is symbolic of masculinity arising out of the uneven number one. It may also have some connexion with the figures of Hermes, and perhaps has a phallic significance.

Cypress A tree dedicated by the Greeks to their infernal deity. The Romans confirmed this emblem in their cult of Pluto, adding the name 'funeral' to it, a significance which still clings to it today (8).

Dactyls Mythic dactyls or fingers are related to the Cabiri (q.v.), and correspond to chthonian cults, their function being to link the nether world with the terrestrial (31). Symbolically they may be seen as those forces of the psyche which ordinarily go unheeded but which help as much as hinder the conscious projects of the reason. For Jung they figure among the symbols of 'multiplicity' which form around the essential elements of the psychic structure.

Daena In the ancient Iranian religion, the Daena symbolized the feminine principle (*Anima*) of the human spirit, while at the same time identifying it with the sum of the actions—good and bad—that man performs during his life. On the third day after his death, the just man is greeted on the bridge of Çinvat by a wondrously beautiful young girl, the Daena, who becomes united with him for eternity, thus reconstituting the primordial Androgyne. On a higher plane, the Cabbala needed to give reality to the principle of the eternal feminine and gave the name of Shekhinah to the 'feminine aspect of God'. The Shekhinah is a complex entity—possibly one of Jehovah's angels or Jehovah himself; in every case it is the Loved One referred to in the Song of Solomon. A. E. Waite, in *Secret Doctrine in Israel* (1913), points out that this spiritual principle bears no relation to that represented by the Virgin Mary of Christianity, but is related rather to the Holy Spirit of the Trinity. He observes that the Shekhinah is the angel who comes to the aid of those just men who are suffering, above all if they are suffering for love, and that her work in the soul is analogous to that of the soul in the body. The Daena, as has been stated, does not attain such an elevated position in the hierarchy and should rather be identified with the Jungian *anima*.

Dance   The corporeal image of a given process, or of becoming, or of the passage of time. In Hindu doctrine, the dance of Shiva in his rôle as Natarâjâ (the King of the Cosmic Dance, symbolizing the union of space and time within evolution) clearly has this meaning (6). There is a universal belief that, in so far as it is a rhythmic art-form, it is a symbol of the act of creation (56). This is why the dance is one of the most ancient forms of magic. Every dance is a pantomime of metamorphosis (and so calls for a mask to facilitate and conceal the transformation), which seeks to change the dancer into a god, a demon or some other chosen form of existence. Its function is, in consequence, cosmogonic. The dance is the incarnation of eternal energy: this is the meaning of the circle of flames surrounding the 'dancing Shiva' (60). Dances performed by people with linked arms symbolize cosmic matrimony, or the union of heaven and earth—the chain-symbol—and in this way they facilitate the union of man and wife (51).

Darkness   Equated with matter, with the maternal and germinant, but it pre-exists the differentiation of matter (9). The dualism of light/darkness does not arise as a symbolic formula of morality until primordial darkness has been split up into light and dark. Hence, the pure concept of darkness is not, in symbolic tradition, identified with gloom—on the contrary, it corresponds to primigenial chaos. It is also related to mystic nothingness, and, in consequence, Hermetic language is an *obscurum per obscurius*, a path leading back to the profound mystery of the Origin. According to Guénon, light is the basic principle behind differentiation and hierarchical order. The gloom which preceded the *Fiat Lux* always, in traditional symbolism, represents the state of undeveloped potentialities which give rise to chaos (29). Hence, the darkness introduced into the world, after the advent of light, is regressive; hence, too, the fact that it is traditionally associated with the principle of evil and with the base, unsublimated forces.

Day of Rest Like so many other aspects of existence—both in customs and in utilitarian activities—the concept of the Day of Rest does not arise from material or empirical necessity (even leaving aside the religious implications). According to Erich Fromm, the observance of the Sabbath amongst the Hebrews does not denote mere repose for reasons of health, but rather something much more profound. In effect, because work implies a state of change—of war—between man and the world around him, it follows that rest designates peace between him and Nature. One day a week —a day which, by virtue of the analogy between time and cosmic space, corresponds to the idea of the centre implicit in the position of the sun among the planets or the location of the earth according to the geocentric system—must be set aside for experiencing the spontaneous, perfect harmony of man in Nature. By not working, the human being can break away from the order of change which gives rise to history, and thereby free himself from time and space to return to the state of paradise (23). This symbolism provides the explanation, furthermore, of what Bell called 'the fiery restlessness of the rebel': the instinctive hatred of all forms of rest characteristic of the man of warlike spirit who challenges all Nature and the world as it appears to the senses.

Death Symbolically, death represents the end of an epoch, particularly when it takes the form of sacrifice or the desire for self-destruction in the face of unendurable tension (as with Romeo and Juliet, or Tristan and Isolde). The hero dies young for this same reason: Siegfried, Achilles or Balder for example. The public necessity for a sacrifice of this kind was what lay behind the 'ritual assassination of the king' in which the possibility of his survival was sometimes left open, should he prove victor in combat. As an example of this rite, Frazer cites a festival called 'The Great Sacrifice' in which the king of Calicut was made to hazard his crown and his life. It took place every twelve years, at the time the planet Jupiter turns back towards the constellation of Cancer, since there was a supposed relationship between the planet and the king's destiny (21).

Death, The The thirteenth enigma of the Tarot pack. This playing-card shows the well-known allegory of the skeleton with the difference that here, contrary to custom, he wields his scythe towards the left. And the bones of the skeleton are not grey but pink. The ground is strewn with human remains, but these remains, like

those in legend and folklore, have the appearance of living beings
—heads, for instance, keep their living expression; hands emerging
from the ground seem ready for action. Everything in this enigma-
card tends to ambivalence, underlining the fact that if life is, in
itself, closely bound up with death (as Heraclitus pointed out and as
mediaevalists and modern scientists have corroborated), death is
also the source of life—and not only of spiritual life but of the
resurrection of matter as well. One must resign oneself to dying in a
dark prison in order to find rebirth in light and clarity. In the same
manner as Saturn pruned the tree in order to rejuvenate it, so Siva
(or Shiva) transforms beings by destroying their form without
annihilating their essence. On the other hand, death is the supreme
liberation. In the positive sense, then, this enigma symbolizes the
transformation of all things, the progress of evolution, dematerialization; in the negative, melancholy decomposition, or the end of
anything determinate and therefore comprehended within a period
of time (59). All allegories and images of death have the same
significance. In Greek mythology, death was envisaged as the
daughter of the night and the sister of sleep. Horace depicts death
with black wings and a net for snaring his victims (8), a net which is
identical with that of the Uranian gods as well as that of the Roman
gladiator. Death is related to the Element earth and to the range of
colours from black, through the earth-coloured shades, to green.
It is also associated with the symbolism of manure.

Decapitation Ritual decapitation arose from the discovery in
prehistoric times that the head is the receptacle of the spirit. The
preservation of heads, as practised by certain primitive peoples,
holds the same significance as the separate burial of that part of the
body. The same symbolic meaning is attached to the decorative
use of sculpted heads, set at particular vantage points in many
mediaeval temples, such as Clonfert Cathedral, in Ireland.

Decorations (or **Medals**) The inverse of wound-symbolism.
They denote sublimation and glorification, and are related to the
red/white principle of alchemy.

Defile (or **Gorge**) Within the symbolism of landscape as a whole,
the gorge corresponds to the lower regions and is therefore closely
related to the maternal, the unconscious and, ultimately, to the
forces of evil. If the cavern, or the hollow interior of a mountain,
are authentic illustrations of the unconscious, which remains unknown or enigmatic or is experienced indirectly, then the gorge—
and the fissure—is a symbol of a crack in the conscious life through
which the inner pattern of the individual psyche, or of the world-
soul, may be glimpsed (32). Because of its associations with strategy,
or with other derived ideas, the gorge also incorporates the notion
of danger. By its shape, it implies a sense of inferiority in the face of

overwhelming odds (suggested by the mountains or masses of
earth and rock which in effect constitute the gorge). On the other
hand, these negative considerations may themselves be negated by
the symbolism implicit in the fact that water often runs along the
bed of the gorge—and water is always related to birth, regeneration
and purification; this is further proof that the gorge has a maternal
symbolism.

Deluge The tradition of the deluge, or of several deluges, is to
be found in all parts of the world, with the exception of Africa (35).
Science appears to have verified its historical reality. Within the
symbolic relationship between the moon and water, the deluge,
according to Eliade, corresponds to the three days of the 'death of
the moon'. As a catastrophe, the deluge is never represented as
final, because it takes place under the sign of the lunar cycle and of
the regenerating properties of water. It destroys forms, in other
words, but not forces, thus leaving the way open for the re-emergence
of life (17). Consequently, apart from its material connotation, the
deluge always stands for the final stage of a cycle, coinciding with
the zodiacal sign Pisces (9). Torrential rains always retain some of
the great symbolic content of the deluge; every fall of rain is tantamount to purification and regeneration, which in turn imply the
basic idea of punishment and completion.

Desert It has a profound and clear-cut symbolism. Berthelot
observes that the Biblical prophets, in order to counter the agrarian
religions based on fertility rites (related, according to Eliade, to
orgies), never ceased to describe theirs as the purest religion of the
Israelites 'when they were in the wilderness'. This confirms the
specific symbolism of the desert as the most propitious place for
divine revelation, for which reason it has been said that 'monotheism is the religion of the desert' (7). This is because the desert, in so
far as it is in a way a negative landscape, is the "realm of abstraction'
located outside the sphere of existence (37), susceptible only to things
transcendent. Furthermore, the desert is the domain of the sun, not
as the creator of energy upon earth but as pure, celestial radiance,
blinding in its manifestation. Again: if water is associated with the
ideas of birth and physical fertility, it is also opposed to the concept
of the everlasting spirit; and, indeed, moisture has always been
regarded as a symbol of moral corruption. On the other hand,
burning drought is the climate *par excellence* of pure, ascetic
spirituality—of the consuming of the body for the salvation of the
soul. Tradition provides further corroboration of this symbolism:
for the Hebrews, captivity in Egypt was a life held in opprobium,
and to go out into the desert was 'to go out from Egypt' (48).
Finally, let us point to the emblematic relationship of the desert
with the lion, which is a sun-symbol, verifying what we have said
about the solar symbolism of the desert.

Destruction   The traditional symbols of destruction are always ambivalent, whether we take the thirteenth mystery of the Tarot, the twelfth sign of the Zodiac (Pisces), the symbolism of water or fire, or of any form of sacrifice. Every ending is a beginning, just as every beginning contains an end; this is the essential idea of the symbols of mystic 'Inversion' which Schneider has subjected to such careful study. All this, then, should be borne in mind when we read such observations as the following by Rudolf Steiner (taken from *La Philosophie de la Liberté*): 'To transform being into an infinitely superior non-being, that is the aim of the creation of the world. The process of the universe is a perpetual combat . . . which will end only with the annihilation of all existence. The moral life of man, then, consists in taking part in universal destruction.' This 'destruction'—like the alchemic process—concerns only phenomena, or what is separate in space (the disjunct or the remote) and in time (the transitory). This is why Steiner entitled a collection of his poems *Destruction or Love*.

Devil, The   The fifteenth mystery of the Tarot pack. It takes the form of Baphomet (of the Knights Templars) portrayed as having the head and feet of a he-goat and the bosom and arms of a woman. Like the Greek sphinx, it incorporates the four Elements: its black legs correspond to the earth and to the spirits of the nether world; the green scales on its flanks allude to water, the undines, and dissolution; its blue wings to sylphs and also to bats (because the wings are membranous); and the red head is related to fire and salamanders. The aim of the devil is regression or stagnation in what is fragmentary, inferior, diverse and discontinuous. Finally, this Tarot mystery-card is related to the instincts and to desire in all its passionate forms, the magic arts, disorder and perversion (59).

Devouring   This symbol, which finds its literal expression in the act, or the fear, of being devoured, is to be found in modified form in the notion of Entanglement, and also, according to Diel, in that of sinking into mud or a swamp. Jung, in connexion with this, quotes the Biblical passage about Jonah and the whale, but Jonah is really better associated with the 'Night Sea-Crossing'. Jung also thinks (31) that fear of incest becomes fear of being devoured by the mother, and that this is then disguised by the imagination in such forms as the witch who swallows up children, the wolf, the ogre, the dragon, etc. On the cosmic plane, the symbol doubtless relates to the final swallowing up by the earth of each human body after death, that is, to the dissolution of the body, so that the symbol may well be related to digestion. In consequence, all those stories which 'have a happy ending', in which children who have been swallowed whole still live inside the animal and eventually escape, refer no doubt to the Christian dogma of the hope of resurrection in the flesh.

Dew All that comes down from the heavens (the thunderbolt, the aerolite, the meteorite, rain or dew) has a sacred character. But dew has a double significance, alluding also to spiritual illumination, since it'is the true forerunner of dawn and of the approaching day (33). The clear, pure water of dew is, according to some traditions, closely connected with the idea of light. There are occasional references in the Far East to the 'tree of sweet dew' situated on mount Kuen-Lun, the equivalent of the Hindu Meru and other sacred mountains symbolizing the world-axis. Light spreads outwards from this tree (25), and, through the process of synaesthesia, it has come to be known as the 'singing tree' of legend and folklore.

Diamond Etymologically, it comes from the Sanskrit *dyu*, meaning 'luminous being'. It is a symbol of light and of brilliance. The word 'adamantine' is connected with the Greek *adamas*, meaning 'unconquerable' (4). In emblems, it often indicates the irradiant, mystic 'Centre' (56). Like all precious stones, it partakes of the general symbolism of treasures and riches, that is, moral and intellectual knowledge.

Diana The goddess of woods, related to nature in general and to fertility and wild animals (21). She bears the Greek name of *Hecate*, meaning 'She who succeeds from afar', and she is therefore linked with the 'Accursed Hunter' (such as Wotan). Accompanied by dogs, she becomes a night-huntress, in turn linked with the demons of chthonian cults (31). It has been pointed out that her characteristics vary with the phases of the moon: Diana, Jana, Janus. This is why some mythological and emblematic designs show her as Hecate with three heads, a famous, triform symbol which—like the trident or the three heads of Cerberus—is the infernal inversion of the trinitarian form of the upper world. According to Diel, these threefold symbolic forms of the underworld allude also to the perversion of the three essential 'urges' of man: conservation, reproduction and spiritual evolution. If this is so, then Diana emphasizes the terrible aspect of Woman's nature. Nevertheless, because of her vows of virginity, she was endowed with a morally good character as opposed to that of Venus, as can be seen in the *Hippolytus* of Euripides.

Digestion A symbol for swallowing, mastery, assimilation and dissolution. What is 'undigested' is what cannot be dissolved, that is, what cannot be conquered or assimilated. The alchemists identified digestion with the dragon and with the colour green (representing the irreducible element of nature, in contrast with those substances which could be sublimated or transformed into spirit, or, in other words, 'digested'). Romanesque iconography is characterized by an extraordinary number of monsters swallowing or carrying in their belly or vomiting up animals, both real and fabulous, which they have devoured whole. The symbolism here must be that which we have just outlined, that is, parallel with yet contrary to the belief of the cannibal that by devouring and digesting the vital organs of his enemy he finally vanquishes him, incorporating within himself the potentialities of his victim.

Dionysos An infernal deity, and a symbol of the uninhibited unleashing of desire, or of the lifting of any inhibition or repression (15). Nietzsche drew attention to the antithesis between Apollo and Dionysos as symbols of the extreme views of art and of life, drawing man, respectively, towards either order or chaos; or, in other words —in accordance with the Freudian death-wish—towards either existence and eternal life, or self-annihilation. The insatiable character of the Greek god—who is supposed to have come from Asia Minor or from Scythia—is apparent in the attributes commonly ascribed to him, such as the thyrsus surmounted by a phallic pine-cone, or the serpent, the horse, the bull, the panther, the he-goat and the hog. According to Jung, the Dionysos-myth signifies the abyss of the 'impassioned dissolution' of each individual, as a result of emotion carried to the extremes of paroxysm and in relation to the urge to escape from time into 'pre-time', characteristic of the orgy; the myth is therefore representative of an unconscious urge (32).

Disappearance In many folktales, mediaeval legends and myths, sudden 'disappearances' occur. Sometimes this is as a result of the translation of the vanished object to a distant place, and sometimes as a result of pure and simple annihilation or destruction. Psychologically, this is a symbol of repression, particularly if the vanished object is malign or dangerous. In reality, it is a form of enchantment.

Disk An emblem of the sun and also of the heavens. In China, the 'sacred disk' is a symbol of celestial perfection (5), and the disk that actually represents the sky (the jade disk called *Pi*) has a hole in the centre. The 'winged disk' is one of the most widespread of ancient symbols, which is still in use today in signs and emblems; in the profoundest sense, it represents matter in a state of sublimation and transfiguration. The two small serpents which are often to be seen next to the disk are those of the caduceus, alluding to the equipoise of opposing forces (59). But in a more esoteric sense, the winged disk signifies the disk in movement—in flight; it is therefore correctly used today in emblems created by an age which has learnt how to dominate the air and space.

Disguise Disguise—or rather, 'transvestism'—finds its basis in the wearing of clothes belonging to the opposite sex. According to Eliade, this is a rite which is analogous to the symbolism of the orgy and frequently practised in it. Its purport is to resuscitate the hypothetical, primordial, androgynous being referred to by Plato in his Dialogues (17). Zimmer corroborates this symbolism, despite certain discrepancies, pointing out that in India there is a rite carried out every year at the beginning of the rainy season, in which an elephant is escorted in procession by men dressed as women, who in this way pay homage to maternal nature (60).

Disjunction Its simplest symbol is the letter Y, just as the letter X is the simplest symbol of inversion. It corresponds to the idea of a cross-roads, of a duality or multiplicity of divergent paths. In ancient images (14th–18th centuries), the cross of certain crucifixes is sometimes represented in the form of a Y.

Dismemberment An important symbol lies beneath the act of tearing to pieces, or tearing limb from limb. Let us begin with some examples of the way the symbol is used. The best known is the myth of Osiris torn to pieces by Set, who scattered the fragments which Isis then diligently sought out and pieced together again, one piece excepted. There are a great many legends and folktales which tell much the same story: giants' bodies are cut to pieces and then magically put together again. Siegmund's sword, in the Niebelungen saga, is broken in various places beyond repair; only Siegfried, his son, is capable of reforging it. According to Heinrich Zimmer, the dismemberment of the formless dragon Vritra, in Indian mythology, reveals the process whereby multiplicity sprang out of primigenial unity. Indian mythology also maintains that the creation of multiplicity was the outcome of the sin of Indra, whose expiation implies the reintegration of all existence into unity. Coomaraswamy maintains that the meaning of sacrifice is actually this creative and destructive movement—the systole and diastole of reality; present-day theories of cosmogony support this view (60). From the viewpoint of the individual and his spiritual life, it is interesting to note that the Graeco-Russian philosopher Gurdjieff (according to Ouspensky in his *In Search of the Miraculous*) founded his 'Institute for the Harmonic Education of Man' upon the basis of the need to end all dispersal (or 'dismemberment') of the attention and of spiritual Oneness. In their time, the alchemists had already found a way of symbolizing the state of inner separation of the spiritual components by means of the stages of the *opus*, which they called *solutio, calcinatio, incineratio*, portraying them sometimes in such emblems as personal sacrifices or mutilations of the body, such as cutting off the hands of the mother, or the claws of the lion, etc. (33). For Origen, the goal of Christianity was nothing less than the transformation of man into a being of inner Oneness. Conversely, for Jung, to be possessed by the unconscious (that is, by whims, manias and obsessions) is nothing short of being torn up into chaotic multiplicity. He also points out that the idea of displacement or *disiunctio* is the counterfoil to the growth of the child in the maternal womb (as well as to mystic *coniunctio*). In this way, then, every symbol which stands for an involutive, degenerating or

destructive process is based upon the changing of unity into multiplicity, as, for example, the breaking of a rock into many
fragments. Mutilations of the body, the prising apart of what is
united, are so many symbols of analogous situations in the spirit.

Distaff   Like the spindle and the shuttle, the distaff symbolizes
time, the beginning and the continuance of creation. Distaffs also
have a sexual significance. They are the attributes of the Parcae,
who spin the thread of life, and cut it short (56, 38).

Dog   An emblem of faithfulness, and it is in this sense that it
appears so often at the feet of women in the engravings on mediaeval
tombs; in the same way the lion, an attribute of the male, symbolizes
valour (20). In Christian symbolism, the dog has another sense,
deriving from the function of the sheep-dog: that of guarding and
guiding the flocks, which at times becomes an allegory of the priest
(46). In a more profound sense, though still related to the foregoing,
the dog is—like the vulture—the companion of the dead on their
'Night Sea-Crossing', which is associated with the symbolisms of
the mother and of resurrection. It has a similar significance when it
appears in scenes depicting the Mithraic sacrifice of the bull (31). In
alchemy, it was used as a sign rather than as a symbol. A dog
devoured by a wolf represents the purification of gold by means of
antimony.

Doll or Puppet   The doll, as a symbol, appears more often in
psychopathology than in the main stream of traditional symbolism.
It is well known that in a number of mental diseases the patient
makes a doll which he keeps carefully hidden. According to J.-J.
Rousseau the personality of the sick person is projected into the
toy. In other cases it has been interpreted as a form of erotomania
or deviation of the maternal instinct: in short, a hangover from, or
regression to an infantile state. Recently, in so-called 'Pop-art',
dolls have been included in 'informal' pictorial images. In Spain
Modesto Cuixart has produced the most dramatic and profound
work of this kind, the obvious symbolism of which is related to the
'putti' of Renaissance art, but, by a reversal of meaning, these dolls
are made to appear maimed and soiled as if they were the corpses
of children annihilated by bombs and other forces of destruction.

Dolphin   The figure of the dolphin can be seen in many allegories
and emblems, sometimes duplicated. When the two dolphins—or
even figures representing an indeterminate fish—are pointing in the
same direction, the duplication may be obeying the dictates of the
law of bilateral symmetry for merely ornamental reasons, or it may
be a simple symbol of equipoise. But the inverted arrangement, that
is, with one dolphin pointing upwards and the other downwards,
always symbolizes the dual cosmic streams of involution and
evolution; this is what the 17th-century Spanish writer Saavedra

Fajardo meant by 'Either up or down'. The dolphin by itself is an allegory of salvation, inspired in the ancient legends which show it as the friend of man. Its figure is associated with that of the anchor (another symbol of salvation), with pagan, erotic deities and with other symbols (20). The ancients also held that the dolphin was the swiftest of marine animals, and hence, when, among the emblems of Francesco Colonna, it is shown twined round an anchor, it comes to signify arrested speed, that is, prudence.

Door A feminine symbol (32) which, notwithstanding, contains all the implications of the symbolic hole, since it is the door which gives access to the hole; its significance is therefore the antithesis of the wall. There is the same relationship between the temple-door and the altar as between the circumference and the centre: even though in each case the two component elements are the farthest apart, they are nonetheless, in a way, the closest since the one determines and reflects the other. This is well illustrated in the architectural ornamentation of cathedrals, where the façade is nearly always treated as if it were an altar-piece.

Double Every case of duplication concerns duality, balanced symmetry and the active equipoise of opposite forces. Double images, the symmetrical duplication of forms or figures—such as the supporters in heraldry—symbolize precisely that. But any case of duplication based upon a horizontal axis, in which the upper figure is the inverse of the lower, has a deeper meaning arising from the symbolism of level. A dual being is often found in cabbalistic emblems, the upper figure being known as Metatron and the lower Samael; it is said of them that they are inseparable companions for life (57). It may well be that beneath this image there lies a symbol of the essential ambivalence of all phenomena, or, rather, that it refers to the great myth of the Gemini.

Dove The Slavs believe that, at death, the soul turns into a dove (4). This bird partakes of the general symbolism of all winged animals, that is, of spirituality and the power of sublimation. It is also symbolic of souls, a motif which is common in Visigothic and Romanesque art (46). Christianity, inspired in the Scriptures, depicts the third person of the Trinity—the Holy Ghost—in the shape of a dove, although he is also represented by the image of a tongue of Pentecostal fire (4).

Dragon A fabulous animal and a universal, symbolic figure found in the majority of the cultures of the world—primitive and oriental as well as classical. A morphological study of the legendary dragon would lead to the conclusion that it is a kind of amalgam of elements taken from various animals that are particularly aggressive and dangerous, such as serpents, crocodiles, lions as well as pre-historic animals (38). Krappe believes that the amazement occasioned by the discovery of the remains of antediluvian monsters may have been a contributory factor in the genesis of the mythic dragon. The dragon, in consequence, stands for 'things animal' *par excellence*, and here we have a first glimpse of its symbolic meaning, related to the Sumerian concept of the animal as the 'adversary', a concept which later came to be attached to the devil. Nevertheless, the dragon—like all other symbols of the instincts in the non-moral religions of antiquity—sometimes appears enthroned and all but deified, as, for example, in the standards and pennons pertaining to the Chinese Manchu dynasty and to the Phoenicians and Saxons (4). In a great many legends, overlaying its deepest symbolic sense, the dragon appears with this very meaning of the primordial enemy with whom combat is the supreme test. Apollo, Cadmus, Perseus and Siegfried all conquer the dragon. In numerous masterpieces of hagiography, the patron saints of knighthood—St. George and St. Michael the Archangel—are depicted in the very act of slaying the monster; there is no need to recall others than the St. George of Carpaccio, or of Raphael, or the St. Michael of Tous by Bermejo. For Dontenville (16), who tends to favour an historicist and socio-logical approach to the symbolism of legends, dragons signify plagues which beset the country (or the individual if the symbol takes on a psychological implication). The worm, the snake and the crocodile are all closely linked with the concept of the dragon in their own particular way. In France, the dragon is also related to the ogre as well as to Gargantua and giants in general. In Schneider's view, the dragon is a symbol of sickness (51). But before going further into its meaning, let us quote some examples to show how wide-spread are the references to this monster. The classics and the Bible very frequently allude to it, providing us with detailed information about its appearance, its nature and habits. But their descriptions point to not one but several kinds of dragon, as Pinedo has noted: 'Some give it the form of a winged serpent; it lives in the air and the water, its jaws are immense, it swallows men and animals having first killed them with its enormous tail. Conversely, others make it a terrestrial animal, its jaws are quite small, its huge and powerful tail is an instrument of destruction, and it also flies and feeds upon the blood of the animals it kills; there are writers who consider it to be amphibious, in which case its head becomes that of a beautiful woman with long flowing hair and it is even more terrible than the previous versions.' In the Bible, there are the following references to the dragon: Daniel xiv, 22, 27; Micah i, 8; Jeremiah xiv, 6; Revelation xii, 3, 7; Isaiah xxxiv, 13, and xliii, 20. There are further mentions by Rabanus Maurus (*Opera*, III), Pliny (VIII, 12), Galen, Pascal (*De Coronis*, IX), and among other characteristics which these writers ascribe to the dragon are the following particu-

larly interesting points: that it is strong and vigilant, it has exceptionally keen eyesight, and it seems that its name comes from the Greek
word *derkein* ('seeing'). Hence it was given the function, in clear
opposition to its terrible implications, of guarding temples and
treasures (like the griffin), as well as being turned into an allegory of
prophecy and wisdom. In the Bible, it is the negative side of the
symbol which receives emphasis; it is interesting to note that the
anagram of Herod in Syrian—*ierud* and *es*—means 'flaming dragon'
(46). Sometimes the dragon is depicted with a number of heads and
its symbolism then becomes correspondingly unfavourable, given
the regressive and involutive sense of all numerical increase. 'And
behold a great red dragon, having seven heads and ten horns, and
seven crowns upon his heads', in the words of Revelation (xii, 3).
On other occasions, the dragon is used in emblems, in which case it
is the symbolism of the form or shape which takes precedence over
that of the animal, as for example, the dragon biting its tail—the
Gnostic *Ouroboros*, a symbol of all cyclic processes and of time in
particular. The dragon figured quite frequently in alchemy; for the
alchemists, a number of dragons fighting with each other illustrated
the state of *putrefactio* (separating out the Elements, or psychic
disintegration). And the winged dragon represented the volatile
element, while the wingless creature stood for the fixed element
(according to Albert Poison). It is perhaps in China that this monster
has been most utilized and has achieved its greatest degree of transfiguration. Here it becomes an emblem of imperial power. Whereas
the Emperor numbered the five-clawed dragon among his ornaments,
the officials of his court had the right to keep only the four-clawed (5).
According to Diel, the generic dragon of China symbolizes the
mastering and sublimation of wickedness (15), because the implication is that of a 'dragon conquered', like that which obeys St. George
once he has overcome it. Frazer tells how the Chinese, when they
wish for rain, make a huge dragon out of wood and paper and carry
it in procession; but if it does not rain, then they destroy the dragon
(21). Chuang-tzŭ maintains that this arises from the fact that the
dragon and the serpent, invested with the most profound and all-
embracing cosmic significance, are symbols for 'rhythmic life'. The
association of dragon/lightning/rain/fecundity is very common in
archaic Chinese texts (17), for which reason the fabulous animal
becomes the connecting-link between the Upper Waters and earth.
However, it is impossible to generalize about the dragon of Chinese
mythology, for there are subterranean, aerial and aquatic dragons.
'The earth joins up with the dragon' means that it is raining. It plays
an important part as an intermediary, then, between the two extremes
of the cosmic forces associated with the essential characteristics of
the three-level symbolism, that is: the highest level of spirituality;

the intermediary plane of the phenomenal life; and the lower level of inferior and telluric forces. A related and powerful part of its meaning is that of strength and speed. The oldest Chinese images of the dragon are very similar to those of the horse (13). In esoteric Chinese thought, there are dragons which are linked with colour-symbolism: the red dragon is the guardian of higher science, the white dragon is a lunar dragon. These colours derive from the planets and the signs of the Zodiac. In the Middle Ages in the Western world, dragons make their appearance with the throat and legs of an eagle, the body of a huge serpent, the wings of a bat and with a tail culminating in an arrow twisted back upon itself. This, according to Count Pierre Vincenti Piobb, signifies the fusion and confusion of the respective potentialities of the component parts: the eagle standing for its celestial potential, the serpent for its secret and subterranean characteristic, the wings for intellectual elevation, and the tail (because the form is that of the zodiacal sign for Leo) for submission to reason (48). But, broadly speaking, present-day psychology defines the dragon-symbol as 'something terrible to overcome', for only he who conquers the dragon becomes a hero (56). Jung goes as far as to say that the dragon is a mother-image (that is, a mirror of the maternal principle or of the unconscious) and that it expresses the individual's repugnance towards incest and the fear of committing it (31), although he also suggests that it quite simply represents evil (32). Esoteric Hebrew tradition insists that the deepest meaning of the mystery of the dragon must remain inviolate (according to the rabbi Simeon ben Yochai, quoted by Blavatsky) (9). The universal dragon (*Katholikos ophis*) of the Gnostics is the 'way through all things'. It is related to the concept of chaos ('our Chaos or Spirit is a fiery dragon which conquers all things'— Philaletha, *Introitus*) and of dissolution ('The dragon is the dissolu-tion of bodies'). (The quotations are taken from the Pseudo-Democritus.) Regarding symbols of dissolution, Hermetic doctrine uses the following terms: Poison, viper, universal solvent, philo-sophical vinegar=the potential of the undifferentiated (or the *Solve*), according to Evola. He adds that dragons and bulls are the animals fought by sun-heroes (such as Mithras, Siegfried, Hercules, Jason, Horus, or Apollo) and—bearing in mind the equations woman=dragon, mercury and water; and green='what is un-digested'—that 'if the dragon reappears in the centre of the "Citadel of Philosophers" of Khunrath, it is still a dragon which has to be conquered and slain: it is that which everlastingly devours its own self, it is Mercury as an image of burning thirst or hunger or the blind impulse towards gratification', or, in other words, Nature enthralled and conquered by Nature, or the mystery of the lunar world of change and becoming as opposed to the world of immutable being governed by Uranus. Böhme, in *De Signatura rerum*, defines a will which desires and yet has nothing capable of satisfying it except its own self, as 'the ability of hunger to feed itself' (Plate VI).

Drum   A symbol of primordial sound, and a vehicle for the word, for tradition and for magic (60). With the aid of drums, shamans can induce a state of ecstasy. It is not only the rhythm and the timbre which are important in the symbolism of the primitive drum, but, since it is made of the wood of 'the Tree of the World', the mystic sense of the latter also adheres to it (18). According to Schneider, the drum is, of all musical instruments, the most pregnant with mystic ideas. In Africa, it is associated with the heart. In the most primitive cultures, as in the most advanced, it is equated with the sacrificial altar and hence it acts as a mediator between heaven and earth. However, given its bowl-shape and its skin, it corresponds more properly to the symbolism of the Element of earth. A secondary meaning turns upon the shape of the instrument, and it should be noted that it is in this respect that there is most variation in significance. The three essential shapes are: the drum in the form of an hour-glass, symbolizing Inversion and the 'relationship between the two worlds' (the Upper and the Lower); the round drum, as an image of the world; and the barrel-shaped, associated with thunder and lightning (50).

Dryness   Dryness is the principle directly opposed to that of organic life. The latter is associated with the fertility of the soil—plants and animal life. Dryness, on the other hand, is an expression of the psychic 'climate'. It is a sign of virility, of passion, of the predominance of the Element of fire (2). The symbol of the 'sea king' as a spirit immersed in the deeps of the unconscious is a clear example, with his cry: 'The man who rescues me from the waters of the ocean and leads me to dry land will be rewarded with everlasting riches.' The waters here symbolize debased existence, subject to time and to things transitory, behaving in accordance with the feminine principle of 'wetness'. Dryness is an image of immortality (32); hence the tendency of individuals anxious to recover their strength of spirit—or to acquire it—to make for the desert, the 'dry landscape' *par excellence*; and hence the fact that a man with a 'dry' personality is, contrary to appearances and common belief, really intensely passionate. Eliade observes that to aspire to be dry is to express the longing for the fleshless, spiritual life, and he quotes Heraclitus' maxim that 'Death, for the soul, is to become as water'. And to quote a fragment of Orphic teaching: 'Water is the death of the soul' (Clement, *Strom.* VI, 2, 17, 1—Kern 226); and Porphyry (*De antro nymph.*, 10-11) explains that the souls of the dead tend towards water because of the desire for reincarnation (17).

Dualism   Dualism is defined as any system which implies a binary pattern, but which is characterized less by a complementary thesis and antithesis tending to resolve into a synthesis than by two opposed principles. The Manichean and Gnostic religions were moral dualisms. Some cosmic forms of division into two parts—such as the Chinese year split into two halves, one (*Yang*) in which the active and benign forces predominate, and the other (*Yin*) in which the passive and malign forces prevail—are binary systems rather than dualisms, because the double, contradictory aspects are synthesized within a system of wider scope. R. Bertrand, in *La Tradition secrète* (Paris 1943), speaking about this *Yang-Yin* symbol, observes: 'The dualism of religion (or of mystic or cosmic philosophy) is theoretical or superficial; in actual fact, there is always something extra—a third term which prevents the two opposing terms from cancelling each other out, forcing both these force-principles to yield, that is, to function alternately and not simultaneously. Thus, the black and white of the *Yin-Yang* bounded by the circle of stability, *t'ai-chi*, combine to form in effect a ternary system, the *Tao*.' However, this solution by means of the 'third term' serves less to 'resolve' the problem than to prolong it indefinitely, since it encourages the persistence of the dualist state by virtue of the inner equilibrium which it implies. It is as if, in the symbolism of alchemy, the twin currents—ascending and descending—of solution and coagulation were kept in perpetual rotation. But this is in fact not the case: the positive forces triumph in the end—they *transmute* matter (that is, the passive, negative or inferior principle), redeem it and bear it upwards. Dual symbols are extremely common. To mention a few: the lash and the crook of Egyptian pharaohs; emblems featuring cattle and agriculture, in which a straight and a curved sword symbolize the 'straight' and the 'oblique' path; the cabbalistic columns Jachin and Boaz; Mercy and Severity.

Duck See **Goose.**

Dumbness A symbol of the early stages of creation, and of the return to this pristine state. Hence legends often allude to someone struck dumb as a punishment for grave sins (which themselves imply just such a regression) (9).

Dummy Like the homuncule and the mandragora, the dummy is an image of the soul, in primitive belief. The same applies to the scarecrow, the doll and any figure that bears a human likeness. Hence the belief in its magic properties.

Duplication In symbolism, this is as common as Inversion. It may appear in the form of a double colour-image (standing for the positive/negative principles), or as a symmetrical pattern of dualism, or as a binary system based upon a common horizontal axis, in which case the symbolic meaning reflects the ambivalence of the form or being in question, since the symbol is able to indicate whether this form or being is located above or below the median level. Duplication is, furthermore, like the reflection in the mirror, a symbol of consciousness—an echo of reality. It corresponds to the symbolism of the number two (31).

Dwarf A symbol of ambivalent meaning. Like dactyls, elves and gnomes, the dwarf is the personification of those forces which remain virtually outside the orbit of consciousness. In folklore and mythology, the dwarf appears as a mischievous being, with certain childish characteristics befitting its small size, but also as a protector like the Cabiri—this being the case with the 'woodland dwarfs'in the tale of Sleeping Beauty. For Jung, they may be regarded as the guardians of the threshold of the unconscious (32). Now, smallness may be taken also as a sign of deformity, of the abnormal and inferior; this is the explanation, then, of the 'dancing Shiva' appearing as an image of a deity dancing upon the prostrate body of a demon-dwarf who symbolizes the 'blindness of life', or the ignorance of man (his 'pettiness'). Victory over this demon signifies true wisdom (60). It is probable that some such idea as this was in the mind of the Renaissance sculptor Leon Leoni when he fashioned the effigy of Charles I subduing Fury.

Eagle A symbol of height, of the spirit as the sun, and of the spiritual principle in general. In the Egyptian hieroglyphic system, the letter A is represented by the figure of an eagle, standing for the warmth of life, the Origin, the day. The eagle is a bird living in the full light of the sun and it is therefore considered to be luminous in its essence, and to share in the Elements of air and fire. Its opposite is the owl, the bird of darkness and death. Since it is identified with the sun and with the idea of male activity which fertilizes female nature, the eagle also symbolizes the father (19). It is further characterized by its daring flight, its speed, its close association with thunder and fire. It signifies, therefore, the 'rhythm' of heroic nobility. From the Far East to Northern Europe, the eagle is the bird associated with the gods of power and war. It is the equivalent in the air of the lion on earth; hence it is sometimes depicted with a lion's head (cf. the excavations at Tello). According to Vedic tradition, it is also important as a messenger, being the bearer of the soma from Indra. In Sarmatian art, the eagle is the emblem of the thunderbolt and of warlike endeavour. In all Oriental art it is often shown fighting; either as the bird Imdugud, who ties the terrestrial and the celestial deer together by their tails, or as Garuda attacking the serpent. In pre-Columbian America, the eagle had a similar symbolism, signifying the struggle between the spiritual and celestial principle and the lower world. This symbolism occurs also in Romanesque art. In ancient Syria, in an identification rite, the eagle with human arms symbolized sun-worship. It also conducted souls to immortality. Similarly, in Christianity, the eagle plays the rôle of a messenger from heaven. Theodoret compared the eagle to the spirit of prophecy; in general, it has also been identified (or, more exactly, the eagle's flight, because of its swiftness, rather than the bird itself) with prayer rising to the Lord, and grace descending upon mortal man. According to St. Jerome, the eagle is the emblem of the Ascension and of prayer (50). Among the Greeks it acquired a particular meaning, more allegorical than properly symbolic in nature, in connexion with the rape of Ganymede. More generally speaking, it was believed to fly higher than any other bird, and hence

Heraldic eagle.

was regarded as the most apt expression of divine majesty. The connexion between the eagle and the thunderbolt, already mentioned above, is confirmed in Macedonian coinage and in the Roman *signum*. The ability to fly and fulminate, to rise so as to dominate and destroy baser forces, is doubtless the essential characteristic of all eagle-symbolism. As Jupiter's bird it is the theriomorphic storm, the 'storm bird' of remotest antiquity, deriving from Mesopotamia and thence spreading throughout Asia Minor (35). On Roman coins it occurs as the emblem of imperial power and of the legions. Its fundamental significance does not vary in alchemy, it merely acquires a new set of terms applicable to the alchemic mystique: it becomes the symbol of volatilization. An eagle devouring a lion is the symbol of the volatilization of the fixed by the volatile (i.e. according to alchemical equations: wings = spirit; flight = imagination, or the victory of spiritualizing and sublimating activity over involutive, materializing tendencies). Like other animals, when in the sign of the Gemini, the eagle undergoes total or partial duplication. Thus arises the two-headed eagle (related to the Janus symbol) which is usually depicted in two colours of great mystical significance: red and white. In many emblems, symbols and allegories, the eagle is depicted carrying a victim. This is always an allusion to the sacrifice of lower beings, forces, instincts and to the victory of the higher powers (i.e. father principle, *logos*) (50). Dante even calls the eagle the bird of God (4). Jung, ignoring the multiple significance of its symbolism, defines it simply as 'height', with all the consequences that flow from a specific location in space. On the other hand the constellation of the Eagle is placed just above the man carrying the pitcher of Aquarius, who follows the bird's movement so closely that he seems to be drawn after it by unseen bonds. From this it has been inferred that Aquarius is to be identified with Ganymede, and also with 'the fact that even the gods themselves need the water of the Uranian forces of life' (40).

Ear of Corn   An emblem of fertility and an attribute of the sun (8). It also symbolizes the idea of germination and growth—of the development of any feasible potentiality. The sheaf has a symbolic significance which confirms that of the individual ear: it adds the ideas of integration and control inherent in the symbolism of a 'bunch' to that of fertility or increase implicit in the single ear. Generally speaking, all sheaves, bunches and sprays stand for psychic forces which are integrated and directed to a proper purpose (Plate VII).

Earth, The   The Northern hemisphere is regarded as that which represents light, corresponding to the positive principle *Yang*; the Southern is linked with that of darkness and corresponds to *Yin*. Hence, cultural movements pass from the Northern to the Southern hemispheres (40).

Earthquake   Most primitive and astrobiological cultures attribute the cause of the earthquake to a theriomorphic demon. In Japan, the earth is supposed to be supported by a huge fish; in Sanskrit literature by a turtle; in North America by a serpent. The earthquake partakes of the general significance of all catastrophes—the sudden change in a given process, which may be either for the better or for the worse. On occasion the earthquake is thought to promote fertility. Basically it is an application of the universal symbolism of sacrifice and of cosmic Inversion (35).

Effigy   Every effigy, as an image of a being, expresses the psychic aspect of that being. Hence, given Jung's contention that the magic and the psychic are practically the same thing, it becomes easy to understand the importance of effigies in magic. The burning of a person in effigy—an ancient practice that has still not been totally banished—does not, then, betoken merely the impotent spite of one who is unable to attack the real person—although this may well be a secondary consideration—but is an act against the image of that person, that is, against the impression that he has made in the minds of others—against his memory and his spiritual presence. One can explain keepsakes and portraits on a similar basis, for they are linked in the mind not so much with the real person they pertain to, as with the *imago* or projection of that person within us. The effigy, consequently, is a symbol of an image rather than of a being.

Effulgence According to Evola, is a symbol of the force of the undifferentiated, or of dissolution.

Egg A great many prehistoric tombs in Russia and Sweden have revealed clay eggs which had been left there as emblems of immortality (17). In the language of Egyptian hieroglyphs, the determinative sign of the egg represents potentiality, the seed of generation, the mystery of life (19). This meaning persisted among the alchemists, who added explicitly the idea that it was the container for matter and for thought (57). In this way was the transition effected from the concept of the egg to the Egg of the World, a cosmic symbol which can be found in most symbolic traditions— Indian, Druidic, etc. (26). The vault of space came to be known as an Egg, and this Egg consisted of seven enfolding layers—betokening the seven heavens or spheres of the Greeks (40). The Chinese believe that the first man had sprung from an egg dropped by Tien from heaven to float upon the primordial waters. The Easter egg is an emblem of immortality which conveys the essence of these beliefs. The golden egg from which Brahma burst forth is equivalent to the Pythagorean circle with a central point (or hole). But it was in Egypt that this symbol most frequently appeared. Egyptian naturalism— the natural curiosity of the Egyptians about the phenomena of life—must have been stimulated by the realization that a secret animal-growth comes about inside the closed shell, whence they derived the idea, by analogy, that hidden things (the occult, or what appears to be non-existent) may actively exist. In the *Egyptian Ritual*, the universe is termed the 'egg conceived in the hour of the Great One of the dual force'. The god Ra is displayed resplendent in his egg. An illustration on a papyrus, in the *Œdipus Ægyptiacus* of Kircher (III, 124), shows the image of an egg floating above a mummy, signifying hope of life hereafter. The winged globe and the beetle pushing its ball along have similar implications (9). The Easter-time custom of the 'dancing egg', which is placed in the jet of a fountain, owes its origin, according to Krappe (who refers only to the Slavs), to the belief that at that time of the year the sun is dancing in the heavens. The Lithuanians have a song which runs as follows: 'The sun dances over a mountain of silver; he is wearing silver boots on his feet'(35).

Egypt A traditional symbol of the animal in man (57). Hence, 'to go out of Egypt' is to abandon the sensual and the material and to progress towards the Promised Land across the Red Sea and the desert: to progress towards a superior, transcendent state (46). The symbol is a Gnostic one.

Elements, The   The four-part distribution of the Elements, which, strictly speaking, corresponds to the three states of matter plus the agent which, through them, brings about the transformation of matter, corresponds to the concept, so often illustrated in symbolism, of the stability of the number four and its derived laws. Earth (or solids), water (or liquids), air (or gas) and fire (the temperature which brings about the transformations of matter) have been conceived in the West from pre-Socratic days onwards as the 'Cardinal Points' of material existence, and, by a close parallel, also of spiritual life. It is for this reason that Gaston Bachelard observes (3): 'Earthly joy is riches and impediment; aquatic joy is softness and repose; fiery pleasure is desire and love; airy delight is liberty and movement.' Jung stresses the traditional aspects: 'Of the elements, two are active—fire and air, and two are passive—earth and water.' Hence the masculine, creative character of the first two, and the feminine, receptive and submissive nature of the second pair (33). The arrangement of the Elements in hierarchal order of importance or priority has varied from age to age and writer to writer; one of the factors influencing this has been the question of whether or not to admit a 'fifth Element', sometimes called 'ether', sometimes freely designated 'spirit' or 'quintessence' in the sense of 'the soul of things'. It will readily be understood that the hierarchical progression must proceed from the most spiritual down to the most material, since creation is involution or materialization. Beginning, then, with the fifth Element at the Origin, identifying it with the power of the demiurge, next comes air (or wind) and fire, next water and lastly earth; or, in other words, deriving from the igniferous or aerial state comes the liquid and finally the solid. The connexion of the fifth Element (considered simply as the beginning of life) with air and fire is self-evident. Schneider, commenting upon Hindu tradition, observes that: 'We can establish the equation: sound equals breath, wind, the principle of life, language and heat (or fire)' (50). Now, Schneider goes on to say—and his criterion is here mainly psychological—that the *orientation* of the Elements is an important factor always to be held in mind; for example, fire oriented towards earth (or towards water) is an erotic Element, yet pointed towards air it stands for purification. He mentions the four mystic beings of Chinese mythology who express the fusion of two Elements: the phoenix combining fire and air, the green dragon air and earth, the tortoise earth and water, and the white tiger water and fire (50). Bachelard suggests that, within the psychic life (or artistic inspiration), no image is capable of accommodating the four Elements, since such an amalgamation would be tantamount to neutralization or insufferable contradiction. True images, in his view, are unitary or binary; they can mirror monotones of one substance or the conjunction of two (2). By virtue of the theory of correspondences, the Elements may be associated, up to a certain point, with the four ages and the points of the compass.

Elephant   Elephant-symbolism is somewhat complex for it embraces certain secondary implications of a mythic character. In the broadest and universal sense, it is a symbol of strength and of the power of the libido (42). Indian tradition has it that elephants are the caryatids of the universe. In processions, they are the bearers of kings and queens. It is interesting to note that, because of their rounded shape and grey colour, they are regarded as symbols of clouds. By a twist of magic thought, there arose first the belief that the elephant can create clouds and then the mythic postulate of winged elephants. A mountain-top or a cloud, elephant-like in outline, could represent an axis of the universe (60), and this idea—clearly primitive in origin—is probably what lies behind the use of the elephant in the Middle Ages as an emblem of wisdom (49), of moderation, of eternity, and also of pity (8).

Emblems   When the use of emblems was at its most widespread (16th–18th centuries), it was sometimes the custom to create true variations on an emblem, usually religious, basing them on the symbolic syntax. We have given a few examples of emblems based on the Sacred Heart.

Emperor, The   The fourth mystery in the Tarot pack. Here it takes the allegorical form of a figure seated upon a throne which is a cube of gold. Above him is a black eagle. In his hands he holds a globe of the world and a sceptre surmounted by a fleur-de-lis. The crest of his helmet includes four triangles, emblems of the four Elements. The predominantly red colour of his garments signifies invigorating fire, or intense activity. This Tarot mystery is closely related to the image of Hercules holding his club and the golden apples which he has taken from the garden of the Hesperides. The golden cube of the throne represents the sublimation of the con-structive and material principle, and the fleur-de-lis on the sceptre, illumination. In sum, then, the symbolism of this card concerns magnificence, energy, power, law and severity; and, on the negative side, domination and subjection (59).

Empress, The   The third enigma of the Tarot. She is shown full face, drawing herself up with hieratic stiffness. A smile plays upon her face, framed by fair hair. Her attributes are the sceptre, the fleur-de-lis and a shield with a silver eagle upon a purple background (an emblem of the sublimated soul in the bosom of spirituality). In the positive sense, this playing-card denotes the ideal, sweetness, domination by affective persuasion. In the negative sense, it stands for vanity and seduction (59).

Emptiness This is an abstract idea, the antithesis to the mystic concept of 'Nothingness' (which is reality without objects and without forms yet nurturing the seed of all things). In the Egyptian system of hieroglyphs, the hollow is defined as 'that place which is created out of the loss of the substance required for the building of heaven', and is thus related to space. On the sarcophagus of Seti I, there is an image of emptiness consisting of the half-full vessel of Nu (or Nou) which forms an inverted semicircle completed by a second semicircle located towards one side of the first (19).

Enchantment 'Enchantment' is a reduction to an inferior state. It is a metamorphosis in a descending direction, appearing in myths, legends and stories as a punishment or as the work of a malign power. It may be the transformation of a person into an animal (as in the case of the story of Circe, related in the *Odyssey*), or into a plant or a stone, as occurs in many folktales. The enchantment of the earth takes the form of a loss of fertility, as in Eliot's *The Waste Land*, which reproduces the situation created by the sin and the wounding of Amfortas in the story of *Parsifal*. Enchantment can also take the form of disappearance, translation to a distant place, or illness (generally: paralysis, dumbness, blindness). In such cases, it represents self-punishment or a punishment from above, as we stated earlier. In 'traditional' tales, if the enchantment is the work of a malign power (necromancer, black magician, sorcerer, dragon, etc.), it will always be lifted by the action of a hero who providentially intervenes with his powers of salvation and liberation.

Enclosure The walled city is also an image of the 'spiritual centre'. It appears to have been portrayed thus by Domenico di Michelino in his image of Dante; and it also appears frequently in this guise in the Middle Ages as the 'celestial Jerusalem'.

Enigma In alchemy, the enigma alludes to the relationship between the macrocosm and the microcosm (57). This means that, so far as traditional symbolism goes, the enigmatic aspect of a thing is expressive of its transcendence. Eliade bears out this point with his comment that the surprising thing about kratophanies and theophanies is that they have their origins in primitive societies— and also, we might add, in the All (17). But, more than this, since the enigma is in a way synonymous with the symbol, it also confirms the metaphysical nature of all symbolism. The enigma is also a literary genre (frequently with an esoteric meaning), especially cultivated—along with hieroglyphics and emblems—in the 16th to 18th centuries. Some enigmas that enjoyed great standing in England and Ireland in the 7th and 8th centuries must be considered as antecedents, as Marguerite M. Dubois has shown in *La Littérature anglaise du Moyen Age* (Paris, 1962).

Entanglement A symbol which is related to that of the net and that of bonds. It has been used as an ornamental motif right from prehistoric times, either in the form of entanglement or of a bunch or knot of ribbons. Sometimes vegetable and animal forms appear to rise—like grotesques—out of a mass of abstract nerve-cords resembling vegetable stalks or animated cords in the form of volutes, or coils or knots or interlacing lines; or sometimes—and this is a more advanced motif—clearly formed beings are shown enmeshed, as it were, in a cage. Entanglement-symbolism takes its place in legends, folklore and myths alongside primitive and Romanesque art. Thus a giant is enmeshed in trees, or the castle in the Sleeping Beauty story is hidden under an inextricable mass of vegetation. Jung has studied the question of entanglement with special care, recalling that Osiris is brought up lying in the branches of a tree which completely cover him. There is also the Grimm tale of a girl imprisoned between the wood and the bark of a tree. Again: while he is travelling by night, Ra's ship is engulfed by the serpent of night, this giving rise to a number of later mediaeval miniatures and tales. Jung also observes that entanglement is often associated with the myth of the sun and its daily rebirth. However, this is nothing more than a variant of the devouring symbol mentioned by Frobenius in connexion with sun-heroes (31). In the key to dreams of the Hindu *Yagaddeva*, one reads: 'He who while dreaming twines round his body lianas, creepers, cords or snakeskins, string or fabrics, dies', or, in other words, he returns to the maternal bosom (31). According to Loeffler, a thing which, on the psychic plane, is entangled, represents the unconscious, the repressed, the forgotten, the past. On the plane of cosmic evolution, it is the collective dream which separates one cycle of life from the other (38) (Plate VIII).

Erinyes, The In the classical tragedies, the erinyes sometimes appear in the form of dogs or serpents, which is an indication of their infernal character as chthonian demons (31). They personify remorse; that is, they are symbols of guilt turned to destructiveness directed against the guilty one (15).

Eternity The coins of several Roman emperors bear an allegory of eternity depicted in the figure of a girl holding the sun and the moon in her hands. And, in alchemy, there are comparable images, alluding to the *opus* as a 'conjunction' or a 'marriage of opposites', which illustrate the essential principle that the eternal order can be achieved only with the abolition of antithesis, separateness and change. Eternity has also been represented as infinite time, both in the 'Mithraic Cronos' and in the Ouroboros (the serpent or dragon which bites its own tail). The phoenix is another symbol of eternity (8).

Ethiops An alchemic symbol representing the *nigredo* or the initial stage of the alchemists' work. It can be seen for example in one of the images of the *Splendor solis* of Solomon Trismosin (1582). The Jungian interpretation of the figures and images of Negroes, Indians, savages, etc—whom he considers as symbols for the shadow or the darker side of the personality—does not contradict the first meaning, for, within the moral approach of alchemy, the *nigredo* is a precise illustration of the initial state of the soul before embarking upon its path of evolution and self-perfection (32).

Euphrates Specific geographical features sometimes form part of traditional symbols; the river Euphrates is an example. It is the equivalent of the fluid cosmos passing across the material world (or Babylon) in the two directions of involution and evolution (57). In a broad sense, the river, and indeed every river in the opinion of Heraclitus—without going into esoteric doctrine—is a symbol of time or of the irreversible nature of processes as they move onward.

Eve A symbol of the material and formal aspect of life, of *Natura naturans*, or mother-of-all-things (57). From the spiritual point of view, Eve is the inversion of the Virgin Mary, or the mother-of-souls. Inversions of this order have sometimes found a parallel expression in the contrasting use of similar names, such as Eros (the god of love) balanced against Ares (war, destruction and hate). This antithesis between Eve and Our Lady has been examined by Antonio de Sousa de Macedo in his *Eva y Ave o Maria triunfante*.

Excrement Gubernatis in his research into folklore, and Freud in his work in experimental psychology, have observed that what is almost worthless is often associated with what is most valued. So, for example, we find in legends and folktales the surprising association between excrement and gold (31), a relationship which occurs also in alchemy, since the *nigredo* and the ultimate attainment of the *aurum philosophicum* form the beginning and the end of the process of transmutation. All this symbolism is contained within Nietzsche's phrase: 'Out of the lowest the highest reaches its peak.'

Eye The essence of the question involved here is contained in the saying of Plotinus that the eye would not be able to see the sun if, in a manner, it were not itself a sun. Given that the sun is the source of light and that light is symbolic of the intelligence and of the spirit, then the process of seeing represents a spiritual act and symbolizes understanding. Hence, the 'divine eye' of the Egyptians —a determinative sign in their hieroglyphics called *Wadza*— denotes 'He who feeds the sacred fire or the intelligence of Man' (28)—Osiris, in fact. Very interesting, too, is the way the Egyptians defined the eye—or, rather, the circle of the iris with the pupil as centre—as the 'sun in the mouth' (or the creative Word) (8). René Magritte, the surrealist painter, has illustrated this same relationship between the sun and the mouth in one of his most fascinating paintings. The possession of two eyes conveys physical normality and its spiritual equivalent, and it follows that the third eye is symbolic of the superhuman or the divine. As for the single eye, its significance is ambivalent: on the one hand it implies the subhuman because it is less than two (two eyes being equated with the norm); but on the other hand, given its location in the forehead, above the place designated for the eyes by nature, it seems to allude to extra-human powers which are in fact—in mythology—incarnated in the Cyclops. At the same time the eye in the forehead is linked up with the idea of destruction, for obvious reasons in the case of the single eye; but the same also applies when there is a third eye in the forehead, as with Siva (or Shiva). This is explained by reference to one of the facets of the symbolism of the number three: for if three can be said to correspond to the active, the passive and the neutral, it can also apply to creation, conservation and destruction. Hetero-topic eyes are the spiritual equivalent of sight, that is, of clairvoyance. (Heterotopic eyes are those which have been transferred anatomically to various parts of the body, such as the hands, wings, torso, arms, and different parts of the head, in figures of fantastic beings, angels, deities and so on.) When the eyes are situated in the hand, for example, by association with the symbolism of the hand they come to denote clairvoyant action. An excessive number of eyes has an ambivalent significance which it is important to note. In the first place, the eyes refer to night with its myriads of stars, in the second place, paradoxically yet necessarily, the possessor of so many eyes is left in darkness. Furthermore, by way of corroboration, let us recall that in symbolist theory multiplicity is always a sign of inferiority. Such ambivalences are common in the realm of the unconscious and its projected images. Instructive in this connexion is the example of Argus, who with all his eyes could not escape death. The Adversary (Satan, in Hebrew) has been represented in a variety of ways, among others, as a being with many eyes. A Tarot card in the *Cabinet des Estampes* in Paris (Kh. 34d), for instance, depicts the devil as Argus with many eyes all over his body. Another comparable symbolic device is also found commonly in demonic figures: it consists of taking some part of the body that possesses, as it were, a certain autonomy of character or which is directly associated with a definite function, and portraying it as a face. Multiple faces and eyes imply disintegration or psychic decomposition—a conception which lies at the root of the demoniacal idea of rending apart (59). Finally, to come back to the pure meaning of the eye in itself, Jung considers it to be the maternal bosom, and the pupil its 'child'.[1] Thus the great

---

[1] The Jungian idea is expressed as a pun. 'Niña' means both 'daughter' and 'pupil (of the eye)'. The phrase 'Niña de los ojos' is like the English 'apple of one's eye', which gives something of the feel of the pun.—*Translator.*

solar god becomes a child again, seeking renovation at his mother's bosom (a symbol, for the Egyptians, of the mouth) (31).

Fairies   Fairies probably symbolize the supra-normal powers of the human soul, at least in the forms in which they appear in esoteric works. Their nature is contradictory: they fulfil humble tasks, yet possess extraordinary powers. They bestow gifts upon the newly born; they can cause people, palaces and wonderful things to appear out of thin air; they dispense riches (as a symbol of wisdom). Their powers, however, are not simply magical, but are rather the sudden revelation of latent possibilities. Because of this, it has been possible to link the legendary 'forgotten fairy' with the Freudian 'frustrated act' (38). In a more traditional sense, fairies are, objectively, spinners of thread like the Parcae; they also appear as washerwomen. They have been variously called: White Ladies, Green Ladies, Black Ladies; these are terms which tie up with the epithets applied to mediaeval knights—and for the same reason. Fairies are, in short, personifications of stages in the development in the spiritual life or in the 'soul' of landscapes. Thus, in Mesopotamia, they take the form of the Lady of the Plains, the Lady of the Fountain and the Lady of the Water (or Damgalnunna). They are prone to sudden and complete transformations, and they bear a certain resemblance to other mystic beings such as sirens and lamias (in their evil aspects) (16).

Fall, The   The Fall signifies the incarnation of the spirit. 'Man', observes Jakob Böhme, in *De signatura*, 'died, in so far as he was purely divine essence, because his inner desires, bursting out from the inner fiery centre . . . tended towards external and temporary birth.' Thus (in Evola's transcription), the divine essence or 'inner corporeity' (which nevertheless persists within Man) suffers physical 'death'.

Fan   Its symbolic significance depends on the shape and size. The large flabellate fan is related to air and wind, and is the emblem of Chung-li Chuan, the first of the Eight Chinese Immortals, who is said to have used it to revive the spirits of the dead (5). A fan of this type is usually heart-shaped, and is sometimes decorated with feathers. The feathers stress the association with aerial and celestial symbolism as a whole. It is an attribute of rank among several Asian and African peoples, and is still so used—with a cosmic significance —by the Pope (41). The characteristic Western fan is of the folding type, and hence associated with the phases of the moon, so that its symbolism relates to imagination, change and femininity. The changing pattern of phenomena, as shown in the rhythm of moon-phases (non-being, appearance, increase, full being, decrease), is expressed in terms of erotic, allegorical fan-language. So is the Heraclitean conception of perpetual flux. A fan is used in this latter sense by Max Ernst in one of his paintings.

Farmer   Among basic occupations, farming has a very special significance, not only because its activities take place in the sacred world of seeds, buds, flowers and fruits, but also because it follows the cosmic order as illustrated in the calendar. Cyclic sequences of terrestrial events following the pattern of celestial motions express a correlation which is fundamental to astrobiological thought. The farmer is therefore the guardian of agricultural rites, seeing out the 'old year' and seeing in the 'new'. In spiritual terms, this means that the farmer appears as the catalyst of the forces of regeneration and salvation, forces which join every beginning to every end, forging links which bind time together, as well as the successive seasons and renascent vegetation. Farming was essential not only for the development of primitive economy but also for the emergence of a cosmic consciousness in Man. Mircea Eliade puts it most aptly: 'What Man *saw* in the grain, what he *learnt* in dealing with it, what he was *taught* by the example of seeds changing their form when they are in the ground, that was the decisive lesson. . . One of the main roots of soteriological optimism was the belief of prehistoric, agricultural mysticism that the dead, like seeds underground, can expect to return to life in a different form' (17).

Farming   See *Agriculture*.

Father   The father-image, closely linked with the symbolism of the masculine principle, corresponds to consciousness as opposed to the maternal implications of the unconscious. The symbolic representation of the father is based upon the Elements of air and fire, and also heaven, light, thunderbolts and weapons (56). Just as heroism is a spiritual activity proper to the son, so dominion is the power peculiar to the father (17). Because of this, and also because he stands for the force of tradition (32), he represents the world of moral commandments and prohibitions restraining the forces of the instincts (31) and subversion.

Feather   Whether singular or in groups, the feather symbolizes the wind and the creator-gods of the Egyptian pantheon: Ptah, Hathor, Osiris and Amon (41). Feathers correspond to the Element of air—to the realm of the birds (48). And, for the same reason, cultures in which aerial myths predominate, such as those of the American aborigines, make use of feathers as an essential feature of their personal adornment. The feather head-dress of the Indian

chief closely relates him to the demiurgic bird. As a determinative
sign in the Egyptian system of hieroglyphs, the feather enters into
the composition of such words as 'emptiness', 'dryness', 'lightness',
'height', 'flight' (19). According to St. Gregory, feathers symbolize
faith and contemplation, and the quill denotes the Word (50). The
Egyptian sign for the quill signifies 'delineator of all things' (19),
though it may be that this sign really represents a cane-leaf; however, the meaning turns upon the function rather than the material.

Fecundity   In allegories, fecundity is usually represented by the

Symbol of the fecundity of sacrifice: the cross bears fruit
(after an engraving dated 1512).

poppy plant, because of its prodigious number of seeds; but it is also symbolized by a grain of barley, and by the bull, the hare and the rabbit (8).

Fertility Symbols of fertility are: water, seeds, phallic shapes. Granet recounts that, in China, the conjugal bed used to be placed in the darkest corner of the room, where the seeds were kept and above the spot where the dead were buried. Eliade maintains that the respective rites pertaining to forebears, harvests and the erotic life are so closely related to each other that it is impossible to distinguish between them (17). In Indian ritual, grains of rice serve to represent the seed of fertility (17).

Fibula The fibula—or clasp—is a minimal form of shield, and, like the belt, a symbol of virginity. In this sense it has found its way into many legends, especially in the *Kalevala* (38).

Fields In the widest sense, they signify spaciousness or limitless potentialities. Into this category come the Uranian gods such as Mithras, called 'the Lord of the Plains'. As lord of the sky, he has the task of conducting souls on their return to heaven (11), like other psychopomps such as Mercury.

Fight All combats are the expression of a conflict of some sort. A great many fights, dances and simulacra are rites, or the vestiges of rites, which express situations of conflict. In Sweden, according to Eliade, combats are enacted on horseback by two sets of riders personifying winter and summer. Usener ascribed a similar meaning to the combat between Xanthos and Melanthos—the fair one and the dark one. On the other hand, the struggle may correspond to the primordial, cosmogonic sacrifice, such as the sacrifice of Tiamat (or Tiawath) by Marduk. Struggles between the gods of vegetation and of drought (such as Osiris and Set) or between good and evil (Ahuramazda and Ahriman or Angramainyu, for example) modify the plane of conflict accordingly. Broadly speaking, the struggle is that of generation or involves antithetically opposed elements (17). For our part, we would suggest that the combats of Roman gladiators reflected an ancestral, mythic and symbolic background with the retiarius (or net-fighter) as the counterpart of Neptune and Pisces (symbolic of the celestial ocean, and the all-embracing god armed with the trident, as a sign of triple power, and with the net); likewise, the *mirmillo* was Cancer (the sun, or the son armed with a sword).

Figures The representational shape of figures is always of a piece with the object, or being, to which they allude. Symbolically speaking, a cock is the same thing as its figure whether painted, engraved or sculpted. When the figure is that of a living being, this being provides the predominant sense, although secondary meanings may be derived from the colour, the form, etc. When the figures are geometric, or when they represent architectural masses, it is

I. Roman sculpture incorporating symbolic *motifs*, throne, lions and cornucopia.

II. Modesto Cuixart. Painting, 1958.

III. **Architecture.** Portal of the church of San Pablo del Campo, Barcelona
—two columns and tetramorphs.

IV. **Cauldron.** Silver chalice, from Ardagh, Co. Longford, Ireland.

V. **Cross.** 10th-century monument at Clonmacnois, Ireland.

VI. **Dragon.** Chinese version of the cosmic dragon (Pekin).

VII. **Eagle.** A renaissance relief, from the Doge's Palace at Venice,
inspired by Roman 'signs'.

VIII. **Entanglement.** This symbolic *motif* is often found in Romanesque art—capitals, monastery of Santo Domingo de Silos, Spain.

IX. **Fish.** Early Christian symbol—13th-century gravestone, Lérida Museum, Spain.

X. **Fountain.** Gothic fountain—Casa del Arcediano (Archdeacon's House), Barcelona.

XI. Fracture. Giorgione, *The Storm:* symbolic elements include shattered columns, lightning, bridge, road, etc.

XII. **Gemini.** Roman statue of the Twins (Prado, Madrid).

XIII. **Grail.** Apparition of the Holy Grail over the Round Table (after a Gothic miniature—detail).

XIV. **Harp.** Detail of *Garden of Delights* by Bosch, in which the dramatic symbolism of the harp may be intuited.

XV. **Head.** Portal of the Romanesque cathedral at Clonfert, Co. Galway, Ireland, decorated with geometric symbols and human heads.

XVI. **Heaven.** Chinese symbol of heaven: the hole in this circular image of space signifies the path of transcendence.

again the symbolism of *form* which comes into play. Schematic figures—marks, signs, tattoos, engravings, prehistoric or primitive inscriptions, magic alphabets, etc—are all related to graphic symbolism, which is founded in the main upon space, number and geometric form. Given the analogy, the possible similarity or inner connexion between Man's works and those of his Creator, invented figures—cultural symbols or instruments—are always related to the natural figures which resemble them. Symbolic or mythic ideas which reveal some influence, resemblance or reminiscence of a natural form or figure, acquire thereby powerful symbolic implications. So, for example, the head of Medusa and the octopus; the swastika and the starfish; the double-bladed axe and the hawk in flight.

Fire   The Chinese, in their solar rites, utilize a tablet of red jade, which they call *Chang*; it symbolizes the Element of fire (39). In Egyptian hieroglyphics, fire is also related to the solar-symbolism of the flame, and associated in particular with the concepts of life and health (deriving from the idea of body-heat). It is also allied with the concept of superiority and control (19), showing that the symbol had by this time developed into an expression of spiritual energy. The alchemists retained in particular the Heraclitean notion of fire as 'the agent of transmutation', since all things derive from, and return to, fire. It is the seed which is reproduced in each successive life (and is thereby linked with the libido and fecundity) (57). In this sense as a mediator between forms which vanish and forms in creation, fire is, like water, a symbol of transformation and regeneration. For most primitives, fire was a demiurge emanating from the sun, whose earthly representative it was; hence it is related on the one hand with the ray of light and the lightning (35), and, on the other, with gold. Frazer lists many rites in which torches, bonfires, burning embers and even ashes are considered capable of stimulating the growth of the cornfields and the well-being of man and of animals. However, anthropological research has furnished two explanations of the fire-festival (as it persists today in the Valencian bonfires on the night of St. John, fireworks and the illuminated Christmas tree): on the one hand, there is the opinion of Wilhelm Mannhardt, to the effect that it is imitative magic purporting to assure the supply of light and heat from the sun, and, on the other, the view of Eugene Mogk and Edward Westermarck that it has as its aim the purification or destruction of the forces of evil (21); however, these two hypotheses are not opposing but complementary. The triumphant power and the vitality of the sun—by analogy, the spirit of the shining Origin—is tantamount to victory over the power of evil (the forces of darkness); purification is the necessary sacrificial means of achieving the sun's triumph. Marius Schneider,

however, distinguishes between two kinds of fire, depending upon
their direction (or their function): fire as in the axis fire-earth
(representing eroticism, solar heat and physical energy), and fire of
the axis fire-air (linked with mysticism, purification or sublimation,
and spiritual energy). There is an exact parallel here with the
ambivalent symbolism of the sword (denoting both physical destruction and determination of spirit) (50). Fire, in consequence, is an
image of energy which may be found at the level of animal passion
as well as on the plane of spiritual strength (56). The Heraclitean
idea of fire as the agent of destruction and regeneration is reproduced
in the Indian Puranas and in the Apocalypse (27). Gaston Bachelard
recalls the alchemists' concept of fire as 'an Element which operates
in the centre of all things', as a unifying and stabilizing factor.
Paracelsus demonstrated the parallel between fire and life,
pointing out that both must feed upon other lives in order to keep
alive. To steal fire like Prometheus, or to give oneself up to fire like
Empedocles, are two concepts which point to the basic dualism of
the human predicament. The middle way lies in the comfortable
solution of simply making material use of the benefits of fire. But
fire is ultra-life. It embraces both good (vital heat) and bad (destruction and conflagration). It implies the desire to annihilate time and
to bring all things to their end. Fire is the archetypal image of
phenomena in themselves (1). To pass through fire is symbolic of
transcending the human condition, according to Eliade in *Myths,
Dreams and Mysteries* (London, 1960).

Fire-water   Fire-water, like other alcoholic liquors, is a *coincidentia oppositorum* (water and fire) and is therefore related to nou-
mena and to the hermaphrodite. Alcoholism, therefore, may be
reckoned an attempt at *conjunctio*.

Fish   In broad terms, the fish is a psychic being, or a 'penetrative
motion' endowed with a 'heightening' power concerning base
matters—that is, in the unconscious. Because of the close symbolic
relationship between the sea and the *Magna Mater*, some peoples
have held the fish to be sacred. There were some Asiatic rites that
embraced fish-worship, and priests were forbidden to eat it. As
Jung has pointed out, the son of Atargatis (Ashtart or Astarte) was
named Ichthys (31). Schneider notes that the fish is the mystic Ship
of Life, sometimes a whale, sometimes a bird, and at other times
simply a fish or a flying fish, 'but at all times it is the spindle spinning
out the cycle of life after the pattern of the lunar zodiac' (50). That
is to say, the fish incorporates a variety of meanings, reflecting the
many essential facets of its nature. Schneider also mentions that for
some people the fish has a phallic meaning, whereas for others it
has a purely spiritual symbolism. In essence, the character of the
fish is twofold: by reason of its bobbin-like shape, it becomes a

kind of 'bird of the nether regions', symbolic of sacrifice and of the relationship between heaven and earth. On the other hand, by virtue of the extraordinary number of its eggs, it becomes a symbol of fecundity, imparting a certain spiritual sense (50). In this last sense it is found among the Babylonians, the Phoenicians, the Assyrians (4) and the Chinese (5). There are some fish that have a secondary significance because of their peculiar characteristics: for instance, the sword-fish is associated with the unicorn (32). The Chaldaic peoples used to portray the figure of a fish with the head of a swallow, as a harbinger of cyclic regeneration, an idea directly related to the symbolism of Pisces, the last sign of the Zodiac (40) (Plate IX). The fish became a primitive Christian symbol, principally on the basis of the anagram drawn from the name for fish: ichthys, the initials standing for $'I$-$\eta\sigma\sigma\nu\varsigma$ X-$\rho\iota\sigma\tau\sigma\varsigma$ Θ-$\epsilon\sigma\nu$ Y-$\iota\sigma\varsigma$ Σ-$\omega\tau\eta\rho$. Then it came to be taken as a symbol of profound life, of the spiritual world that lies under the world of appearances, the fish representing the life-force surging up.

Fish, Cosmic   Like the whale and the primordial monster, the cosmic fish symbolizes the whole of the formal, physical universe. The most striking example of this symbol is afforded by the splendid Scythian fish, made of gold, which was part of the Vettersfelde treasure, and which is now in the Museum of Berlin. The cosmic fish can take two different but complementary symbolic forms: The first and more frequent is simply narrative and spatial, for on the upper part of its body, above a heavily marked horizontal line, are four beings of the 'superior stage'—mammals (apparently they are a stag, a horse, a boar and a leopard). Below this line are beings of the 'lower stage'—those of the deeps (fishes and sirens). The second symbolic aspect is the product of morphological collation, based upon paraidolias: so, for instance, the two branches of the tail, reminiscent of two necks, constitute two sheep's heads, while in the middle of the tail there is an eagle spreading out its wings to form an analogous shape. Its eye comes to resemble an octopus, as much in its shape as in the implied comparison between the 'grasping' tentacles and the potentiality for 'grasping' objects apparent in its gaze. This golden fish, then, is a symbol of the progress of the world across the sea of 'unformed' realities (or of worlds dissolved or yet unformed, or of the primordial seas).

Fisher King   He belongs to the legend of the Grail. According to Marx, in *Nouvelles Recherches sur la Littérature Arthurienne*, this rôle of the mythical monarch relates him to the apostles or fishermen of the Sea of Galilee. In Robert de Boron's work on this theme, the Fisher King becomes the Rich Fisherman, which Marx regards as confirmation of the thesis. Fishing, symbolically, is not just 'fishing for men' but casting the bait into the depths of one's own inmost nature in order to reach the gnosis.

Fishing 'The path of the Grail was marked by a number of miracles; one of the brothers was called Brous and was also known as "the rich fisherman" because he had succeeded in catching a fish with which he had satisfied the hunger of all round him. Peter is called "the fisher of men" and the fish becomes a symbol of Christ.' This fragment of legend, taken from Waldemar Vedel, affords a clear explanation of the mystic sense of fishing and the fisherman, a sense which has been corroborated by all students of mythology and anthropology, Schneider among them. Fishing amounts to extracting the unconscious elements from deep-lying sources—the 'elusive treasure' of legend, or, in other words, wisdom. To fish for souls is quite simply a matter of knowing how to fish *in* the soul. The fish is a mystic and psychic animal that lives in water (and water is symbolic of dissolution and, at the same time, of renovation and regeneration). The fisherman is able—like the doctor—to work upon the very sources of life because of his knowledge of these founts. This is how it comes about that Parsifal meets the King of the Grail as a fisherman.

Flag Historically speaking, the flag or banner derives from totemistic insignia as found in Egypt and, indeed, in most countries. The Persians carried gilded eagles with outstretched wings on top of long poles; the Medes, three crowns; the Parthians, a sword-blade; the Greeks and Romans had *signa*, standards and banners. The important point about all these symbols is not the kind of figure used, but the fact that it is always placed at the top of a pole or mast. This raised position is expressive of a kind of imperious exaltation, or the will to 'heighten' the spiritual significance of the figure or animal by raising it above the normal level. From this is derived the general symbolism of the banner as a sign of victory and self-assertion (22).

Flame There are certain significant points of contact between the flame and light. For Bachelard, the flame symbolizes transcendence itself (1), whereas light signifies the effect of the transcendental upon the environment. He adds that 'The alchemist attributed the value of gold to the fact of its being a receptacle for the Element of fire (the sun); the quintessence of gold is fire. The Greeks represented the spirit as a gust of incandescent air' (1).

Fleur-de-lis An heraldic flower, non-existent in nature, which has been a symbol of royalty from the earliest times (46). As an emblem, its base is an inverted triangle representing water; above it is a cross (expressing 'Conjunction' and spiritual achievement), with two additional and symmetrical leaves wrapped round the horizontal arm; the central arm is straight and reaches up heavenwards, the symbolism being self-evident (59). During the Middle

Ages the lis was regarded as an emblem of illumination and as an attribute of the Lord (4).

Flight   The symbolism of flight comprises a variety of elements. The most basic derives from the pleasurable sensation of movement in a medium that is more subtle than water and unfettered by gravity. But, this apart, flying implies raising oneself and is therefore closely connected with the symbolism of level, not only in connexion with moral values but also with the notion of superiority applied to other qualities, such as power or strength. Diel has pointed out that the importance of the 'rise and fall' image—as illustrated in the myth of Icarus in particular—is corroborated by a great many authors (15). And Bachelard has observed that 'of all metaphors, only those pertaining to height, ascent, depth, descent and fall are axiomatic. Nothing can explain them but they can explain everything.' Flight has also been conceived as the 'transcendence of growth'. According to Toussenel, in *Le Monde des oiseaux*, 'we envy the bird his good fortune and endow with wings the object of our love, for we know by instinct that, in the sphere of complete happiness, our bodies will enjoy the power to wheel through space as the bird flies through the air' (3). Flight is related to space and light; psychologically it is a symbol of thought and of imagination.

Flocks   A traditional symbol for the forces of the cosmos, expressive of a state which is neither chaotic nor yet completely ordered (the ordering of chaos is symbolized by the bundle or sheaf). Flocks bear an analogy with constellations and certain stellar groups, since the moon is symbolically a shepherd—at least, this is true of some mythologies. But, at the same time, a flock implies multiplicity—which is a negative quality (40)—and the collapse of a force or an objective.

Flogging   In ancient thought, blows, flogging and flagellation do not signify punishment (i.e. vengeance or deterrence) but purification and encouragement. The Arcadian custom of flogging the effigy of Pan when the hunters came back empty-handed was intended to cast out the inhibiting powers (21). In many rites all over the world, flogging is considered necessary to restore possessed or bewitched individuals and, in general, to deal with all situations implying physical or spiritual impotence (51).

Flower   Different flowers usually have separate meanings, but, as so often happens, flower-symbolism is broadly characterized by two essentially different considerations: the flower in its essence, and the flower in its shape. By its very nature it is symbolic of transitoriness, of Spring and of beauty. The sixth of the 'Eight Immortals' of China, Lan Ts'ai-ho, is generally depicted clad in blue and carrying a basket of flowers; it is said that he was given to singing of the brevity of life and the ephemeral nature of pleasure (5). The Greeks and Romans, at all their feasts, always wore crowns of flowers. And they would strew flowers over the corpses as they bore them to the funeral pyre and over their graves (not so much as an offering as an analogy) (8). We have, then, another example of an antithetical symbol, like the skeleton which the Egyptians would bring to their banquets, as a reminder of the reality of death and as a stimulus towards the enjoyment of life. Now, because of its shape, the flower is an image of the 'Centre', and hence an archetypal image of the soul (56). 'Celestial flower' is the name given to a meteorite or a shooting star by the alchemists (57), and the flower was, for them, symbolic of the work of the sun (32). The significance would be adapted according to the colour of the flower. So, for example, orange or yellow-coloured flowers represent a reinforcement of the basic sun-symbolism; red flowers emphasize the relationship with animal life, blood and passion. The 'blue flower' is a legendary symbol of the impossible, and is probably an allusion to the 'mystic Centre' as represented by the Grail and other such symbols. The 'golden flower' is a famous parallel in Chinese mysticism, a non-existent flower which is also spoken of in alchemy; in the *Epistola ad Hermannum Arch. Coloniensem* (*Theatr. Chem.* 1622) it is given the name of 'the sapphire-blue flower of the Hermaphrodite' (32).

Flute The basic meaning of the flute corresponds to erotic or funereal anguish. The complexity of its symbolism derives from the fact that, if, by virtue of its shape, it seems to have a phallic significance, its tone is nevertheless related to inner, feminine intuitive feeling (that is, to the anima) (50). It is also related to the cane and to water.

Fool, The The final enigma of the Tarot, distinguished from the others because it is un-numbered—all the rest are given numbers from 1 to 21; the significance of this is that the Fool is to be found on the fringe of all orders and systems in the same way as the Centre of the Wheel of Transformations is 'outside' movement, becoming and change. This very fact is in itself a pointer to the mystic symbolism of the Fool, as it is touched upon in the Parsifal legend and others. This figure on the Tarot card is dressed in a costume of many colours denoting the multiple or incoherent influences to which he is subject. The red colour tends to orange, indicating— and this is unequivocal—the colour of the essential fire within him. He carries a bag at the end of his staff, this being symbolic of the mind and its burden. A white lynx is shown in the act of biting his left calf (left being the unconscious side), signifying what remains of his lucidity—that is, his remorse. But this does not deter him, rather does it urge him onward towards the background where may be seen an overturned obelisk—a solar symbol and also symbolic of the Logos—and a crocodile about to devour what must be returned to chaos. There is nothing definite to suggest that the Fool cannot be saved: on the contrary, his predicament, as we have described it, is balanced by the presence of a small, purple-coloured tulip (expressive of active spirituality) and a gold belt adorned with twelve plaques alluding to the Zodiac. This Tarot enigma corresponds, in short, to the irrational, the active instinct capable of sublimation, but related at the same time to blind impulse and the unconscious (59). For Schneider, the mythic and legendary Fool is closely related to the clown. In their medicinal ceremonies and rites, doctor and patient 'act mad', and, through frenzied dancing and 'extravagances', they try to invert the prevailing evil order. The logic of the process is clear enough: when the normal or conscious appears to become infirm or perverted, in order to regain health and goodness it becomes necessary to turn to the dangerous, the unconscious and the abnormal (51). Further, the Fool and the clown, as Frazer has pointed out, play the part of 'scapegoats' in the ritual sacrifice of humans.

Foot   In all probability, the foot is to be taken as an ambivalent symbol. For Jung, it is what confirms Man's direct relationship with the reality of the earth, and he considers that it is frequently phallic in significance (31). Ania Teillard points out that, like the hand, it is an essential part of the body and the support of one's entire person; she recalls that in the mythology of a number of countries the rays of the sun are compared with the feet, as witness the figure of the swastika (56). But Diel makes the revolutionary assertion that the foot is a symbol of the soul, possibly because it serves as the support of the body in the sense of keeping man upright. He quotes examples which show that, in Greek legends, lameness usually symbolizes some defect of the spirit—some essential blemish. Jung corroborates this, observing that Hephaestus, Wieland the Blacksmith and Mani all had deformed feet (31). May it not be that certain talents are given to men to compensate for some physical defect? Schneider has indicated the heel as the 'area of vulnerability and of attack' in the foot. It is the heel that scotches the serpent or that is wounded by it (as with Achilles, Sigurd, Krishna) (50). According to Aigremont, 'the shoe, like the foot and the footprint, has also a funereal implication. In a sense, a dying man "is going away". There is no evidence of his going away save his last footmarks. This sombre symbolism is illustrated, possibly, in the monuments characteristic of the Roman Empire, and, beyond question, in primitive Christian art. . . .' (And also, we might add, in Gothic art. The passage is quoted by Stekel.)

Footprints   Footprints symbolize the way of gods, saints or demonic spirits, etc. There are footprints of Buddha and Vishnu all over India. Kühn, in *The Rock Pictures of Europe*, says that the footprints of the Virgin Mary may be seen in a chapel in Würzburg; and the footprints of Christ in a hermitage in Rosenstein, Swabia.

Footwear A sign of liberty amongst the ancients, since slaves walked barefoot (46). Its symbolic meaning is linked with that of the foot, from which it acquires its general symbolic characteristics. Given the triple symbolism of the foot—(1) phallic according to the Freudians, (2) symbolic of the soul according to Diel, and (3) signifying, in our opinion, the relationship as well as the point of contact between the body and the earth—it follows that footwear partakes of all three potentialities, together with the general symbolism of level.

Ford This is an aspect of threshold-symbolism (q.v.), denoting the dividing-line between two states or two forms of reality, such as consciousness and unconsciousness, or waking and sleeping. Jung has drawn attention to the highly interesting fact that, in the exploits of Hiawatha, his victims are nearly always in the water or close to it. Every animal that rises out of a ford is a representation of the forces of the unconscious, like some demonic being or metamorphosed magician (31).

Forest Within the general symbolism of landscape, forests occupy a notable place, and are often found in myths, legends and folktales. Forest-symbolism is complex, but it is connected at all levels with the symbolism of the female principle or of the Great Mother. The forest is the place where vegetable life thrives and luxuriates, free from any control or cultivation. And since its foliage obscures the light of the sun, it is therefore regarded as opposed to the sun's power and as a symbol of the earth. In Druid mythology, the forest was given to the sun in marriage (49). Since the female principle is identified with the unconscious in Man, it follows that the forest is also a symbol of the unconscious. It is for this reason that Jung maintains that the sylvan terrors that figure so prominently in children's tales symbolize the perilous aspects of the unconscious, that is, its tendency to devour or obscure the reason (31). Zimmer stresses that, in contrast with the city, the house and cultivated land, which are all safe areas, the forest harbours all kinds of dangers and demons, enemies and diseases (60). This is why forests were among the first places in nature to be dedicated to the cult of the gods, and why propitiatory offerings were suspended from trees (the tree being, in this case, the equivalent of a sacrificial stake) (8).

Fossil Broadly, its symbolic significance corresponds to that of the stone, but, because of its ambivalent character, it embraces the concepts of time and eternity, life and death, the evolution of species, and their petrification.

Fountain (or **Source**) In the image of the terrestrial Paradise, four rivers are shown emerging from the centre, that is, from the foot of the Tree of Life itself, to branch out in the four directions of the Cardinal Points. They well up, in other words, from a common source, which therefore becomes symbolic of the 'Centre' and of the 'Origin' in action. Tradition has it that this fount is the *fons juventutis* whose waters can be equated with the 'draught of immortality'— *amrita* in Hindu mythology (25). Hence it is said that water gushing forth is a symbol of the life-force of Man and of all things (57). For this reason, artistic iconography very frequently uses the motif of the mystic fount; it is also to be found in Mithraism—a Pannonian votive inscription reads: *fonti perenni* (31). There can be no doubt that its significance as the mystic 'Centre' is confirmed and reinforced when it is portrayed in architectural plans: whether in the cloister, the garden or the *patio*, the fountain occupies the centre position, at least in the majority of architectural works built during periods within the symbolist tradition, as in Romanesque or Gothic edifices. Furthermore, the four rivers of Paradise are denoted by four paths which radiate out from the region of the cloister towards a clear space, circular or octagonal in shape, which forms the basin of the fountain; this basin is usually shaped, again, like a circle or an octagon, and sometimes there is a double basin. Jung has devoted much time to the study of fountain-symbolism, specially in so far as it concerns alchemy, and, in view of how much lies behind it, he is inclined to the conclusion that it is an image of the soul as the source of inner life and of spiritual energy. He links it also with the 'land of infancy', the recipient of the precepts of the unconscious, pointing out that the need for this fount arises principally when the individual's life is inhibited and dried up (32). The Jungian interpretation is particularly apt when the symbol concerns a fountain centrally placed in a garden, the central area then being a representation of the *Selbst* or individuality. He mentions as examples: the 'fountain of life' of the Florentine *Codex Spherae*, and the *Garden of Delight* painted by Hieronymus van Aecken (Bosch). He observes that the fountain, in the enclosed garden in the *Ars Symbolica* of Bosch (1702), signifies strength in adversity, and that the central area may be regarded as a *temenos* (a hallowed area) (32) (Plate X).

Fox   A common symbol for the devil during the Middle Ages, expressive of base attitudes and of the wiles of the adversary (20).

Fracture   In general, any state of matter or of form carries a literal symbolism which simply transposes to the mental, spiritual or psychic world the corresponding physical phenomenon. One can see a clear illustration here of the parallel between the two realms of the visible and the invisible. Naturally, the symbolic significance of the object is broadened in consequence. So, for example, a broken column takes its significance from the idea of fracture rather than the notion of the column as such—symbolically, it is the precise equivalent of the stunted tree. Charred wood, rusty iron, lichen-covered rocks are repellent to people of a certain temperament while the same things are attractive to others of a romantic nature precisely because they symbolize the 'conjunction of opposites' or the interplay of positive and negative forces. A fracture may reach the stage of absolute destruction when it becomes symbolic of spiritual ruin or death, as in the case of *The Fall of the House of Usher* by Poe. Giorgione, in his mysterious painting of *The Storm*, portrays two broken columns on a pedestal, which, according to the Freudian interpretation, would signify a critical sexual conflict. But we would rather interpret the picture as an illustration of the break-up of a unified whole (as symbolized by the number two), and this interpretation would seem to be confirmed by the fact that the man is separated spatially from the woman: he is in the left fore-ground of the painting in an attitude expressive of wandering, with the woman on the right, a stream flowing between them, and a flash of lightning, together with two columns, above. Thus, all physical fragmentation is symbolic of destruction and disintegration. Never-theless, there are instances when the break-up may be positive in character in that it symbolizes a possible way of escape. The Roman *Flamen Dialis* was not permitted to wear knots in any part of his garments, nor any bangle that was not split (21). The knots and bangles, bands or necklaces would here symbolize the various kinds of bondage that the priest had to rise above (Plate XI).

Frog The frog represents the transition from the Element of earth to that of water, and vice versa. This connexion with natural fecundity is an attribute derived from its amphibious character (50), and for the same reason it is also a lunar animal; there are many legends which tell of a frog on the moon, and it figures in many rites invoking rainfall (17). In Egypt, it was an attribute of Herit, the goddess who assisted Isis in her ritual resurrection of Osiris. The little frogs which appeared in the Nile a few days before it overflowed its banks were, therefore, regarded as heralds of fertility (39). According to Blavatsky, the frog was one of the principal beings associated with the idea of creation and resurrection, not only because it was amphibious but because of its alternating periods of appearance and disappearance (phases which likewise characterise all lunar animals). Frog-gods were once placed upon mummies and the early Christians incorporated them into their symbolic system (9). The toad is the antithesis of the frog, as the wasp is of the bee. Jung rounds off all this with his comment that, given its anatomy, the frog, more than any other of the cold-blooded animals, anticipates Man. And Ania Teillard recalls that in the centre of his picture of *The Temptation of St. Anthony*, Bosch places a frog, with the head of a very aged human being, poised upon a platter held up by a Negress. Here it represents the highest stage of evolution. Hence, the frequency of the 'transformation of prince into frog' in legends and folktales (56).

Fruit Equivalent to the egg, in traditional symbolism, for in the centre of the fruit is the seed which represents the Origin (29). It is a symbol of earthly desires.

G

Garden The garden is the place where Nature is subdued, ordered, selected and enclosed. Hence, it is a symbol of consciousness as opposed to the forest, which is the unconscious, in the same way as the island is opposed to the ocean. At the same time, it is a feminine attribute because of its character as a precinct (32). A garden is often the scene of processes of 'Conjunction' or treasure-hunts—connotations which are clearly in accord with the general symbolic function we have outlined. A more subtle meaning, depending upon the shape and disposition, or the levels and orientation, of the garden, is one which corresponds to the basic symbolism of landscape (q.v.).

Gargoyles Fabulous animals and monsters make their appearance in mediaeval religious art as symbols of the forces of the cosmos, or as images of the demoniacal and dragon-infested underworld; in the latter case they are captive animals—prisoners under the sway of a superior spirituality. This is shown by their position in the hierarchy of the ornamentation: they are always subordinated to angelic, celestial images (16). They never occupy the centre.

Garland It has been said (37) that everything in the universe is linked as in a garland; the observation may serve as a pointer to the actual symbolic significance of the garland. It is related to the grotesque, to the rosette, to string and all other tokens of bonds or connexion. The uses to which the garland has been put provide us with further definitions of its symbolism. The ancients would hang them at the entrance to their temples on feast-days, as a symbol of fellowship; and they used also to crown their captives with them (8). Here, as also in the case of the crowns worn by the guests at Egyptian, Greek and Roman banquets, it is the symbolism of the flower which prevails (signifying ephemeral beauty and the dualism or life and death).

Gazelle This animal is an emblem of the soul. From Primitive times it has been depicted in iconography in flight from—or in the jaws of—a lion or a panther. It symbolizes the persecution of the passions and the aggressive, self-destructive aspect of the unconscious.

Gemini, The As the third sign of the Zodiac, these heavenly twins take on the general significance of all symbolic twins (in that they are both divine and mortal, black and white), but the Gemini acquire the additional significance of a characteristic phase of the cosmic process as symbolized in the Wheel of Transformations: the moment, that is to say, in which pure creative force (Aries and Taurus) is severed into two parts, in such a way that one side of the dualism is elevated but the other descends into the multiplicity characteristic of phenomena. The pillars of Hermes, or those of Hercules, or the so-called Jachin and Boaz columns of the Cabala, are all symbols deriving from the great myth of the Gemini. In the zodiacal symbolism, the third sign is that of the objectivized and reflected intellect (40). Marius Schneider has made a profound study of the Gemini-myth in megalithic culture, showing that it has two tendencies, one white and the other black; one creates, the other destroys; both these characteristics are indicated by the arms of

Zodiacal sign of
the Gemini.

each of the Twins, which, in landscape symbolism, are identical with the river of youth and the river of death. The Gemini represent creative Nature (*Natura naturans*) and created Nature (*Natura naturata*), and this duality is sometimes illustrated in tales by a being that wears a mask, or by a Protean being capable of turning into a giant, a man or an animal. In medicinal rites, the Gemini, by virtue of their double but constant nature, are both the doctor and—more particularly—the invalid, as is borne out in legend and in myth—the Parsifal story, for example (Jean Arthur Rimbaud unknowingly alluded to this duality when he remarked that the poet is both the great invalid and the seer) (51). At times, two different conceptions of the Gemini can be distinguished (as in the parallel myth of the primordial and androgynous being): the 'Heavenly Twin', expressive of opposites, fused together and integrated into Oneness (represented by the spherical or perfect being); and the 'Earthly Twin' displaying the break, the split (as in two-headed Janus, or triform Hecate, etc.), that is, opposites in conflict or at least in dissidence. There is a third aspect, which is that of the individuation or splitting of the 'double being', but this has to do with the existential order and not the mythic. As a result of the dynamic tendencies of all contradictions (white tends towards black, night seeks to become day, the evil man aspires to goodness, life leads to death), the world of phenomena becomes a system of perpetual inversions, illustrated, for example, in the hour-glass which turns upon its own axis in order to maintain its inner movement: that of the sand passing through the central aperture—the 'focal point' of its inversion. The Gemini, in essence a symbol of opposites, is, in its dynamic aspect, then, a symbol of Inversion. According to the megalithic conception—and here we are following Schneider—the mountain of Mars (or Janus) which rises up as a mandorla of the Gemini is the locale of Inversion—the mountain of death and resurrection; the mandorla is another sign of Inversion and of interlinking, for it is formed by the intersection of the circle of earth with the circle of heaven. This mountain has two peaks, and every symbol or sign alluding to this 'situation of Inversion' is marked by duality or by twin heads. Two-headed eagles and cocks are also to be found in this context, the general symbolism of which is that of alternating contradiction; positive/negative, or low/high-pitched. All these are symbols of the harmonious ambiguity of 'thesis and antithesis, paradise and inferno, love and hate, peace and war, birth and death, praise and insult, clarity and obscurity, scorching rocks and swamps, surrounding the fountains and waters of salvation. Here, gay matters are discussed in grave tones, and the most tragic events are joked about' (50). If this cosmic situation were worked out in psychological terms, it would mean that the 'zone of contradiction' would become the threshold of unifying and unified mysticism. This would explain the abundance of contradictory epithets in the most sublime poetry, and the extraordinary richness of paradox in the deepest thinkers, such as Lao-Tse. Also corresponding to the mystery of the Gemini is the morphological fact that in every individual object there are two formal components, one varying, the other unvarying. In other words, one of its faces bespeaks its individuality, the other links it with its species (Plate XII).

Giant The deepest and most ancient meaning of the myth of the giant alludes to the supposed existence of an immense, primordial being, by whose sacrifice creation was brought forth. This cosmogonic myth was very common among primitive and ancient peoples, and it shows how rites involving the sacrifice of humans are an attempt to revive the initial sacrifice and to resuscitate the cosmic forces or to reawaken, at least, their favourable proclivities (17). Now, the giant is, in himself, neither good nor bad, but merely a quantitative amplification of the ordinary; hence, as the case may be, there are some legendary giants who are protectors and others who are aggressive. This sense of the giant as 'that which surpasses' human stature (here symbolic of power and strength), is also indicative of the broad significance of the giant. He may be an image of the 'Terrible Father', arising from childhood memories—children see their parents as giants—or an image of the unconscious, the 'dark side' of the personality menacing the Jungian *Selbst* (21), etc. It is interesting to note that in folklore the giant is tutelar in character: he is usually the defender of the common people against the overlord, upholding their liberties and rights. Without generalizing, one implication of the giant may be said to be the personification of collective Man—as implied in the maxim 'united we stand'—or of the life of a community (16). But the general myth of the giant is far from being confined to this specialized meaning. In nearly all symbolic traditions, he tends to appear as an outcropping of the marvellous and the terrible, even though he always has a certain quality of the inferior or the subordinate about him. The Bible refers to Goliath and to Og, king of Bashan at the time of the exodus (46). Samson has certain characteristics of the giant. In the West, Bodo, Rübezahl, Geryon, Gargantua and Hercules are the most significant in gigantomachy; in Greek tradition, there are the Titans and the Cyclops. Christian tradition has often seen Satan as a giant (50). The tragic hero is intimately linked with the giant, although, at times, in inverse relation as his adversary (60). Frazer describes the numerous cases in which giant figures in wood or wickerwork were set fire to during midsummer festivals, comparable with the Valencian *fallas* (or bonfires). The ancients would fill these figures with animals and even live men, who were burnt with the effigy. They were considered as representatives of the spirit of vegetation, or of the god sacrificed to the world—which brings us back once again to our cosmogonic interpretation. The giant may be a symbol of 'everlasting rebellion', of the forces of dissatisfaction which grow within Man and determine his history and his destiny; it may, that is to say, be a symbol of the Universal Man (Adam Kadmon, 21). Now, according to Jungian psychology, the giant's essence—or his appearance, rather—seems to correspond to the father-symbol, representing the spirit that withstands the instincts, or as the guardian of the treasure (that is, the mother—the unconscious), in which case it is identical with the dragon-symbol. Reviewing all this, Jung quotes the example of Humbaba, the guardian of the garden of Ishtar in the Gilgamesh epic (31).

Globe The sphere is a whole, and hence it underlies the symbolic significance of all those images which partake of this wholeness, from the idea of the mystic 'Centre' (56) to that of the world and eternity (8), or, more particularly, of the world-soul (4). In neoplatonic philosophy, the soul is explicitly related to the shape of the sphere, and the substance of the soul is deposited as quintessence around the concentric spheres of the four Elements. The same is true of the primordial man of Plato's *Timaeus* (32). In alchemy, the globe, when it is black in colour, is a symbol of prime matter, or it may be depicted with wings to imply spiritual movement or evolution —as, for example, in the *Philosophia Reformata* of Mylius (1622) (32). Another important association is that of perfection and felicity. The absence of corners and edges is analogous to the absence of inconveniences, difficulties and obstacles.

Gloves   Gloves, since they are worn on the hands, derive their symbolism from them. Of special interest is the right-hand glove, on account of the ceremonial custom of removing it when one approaches a person of higher rank, or an altar, or the Lord. This custom has twin symbolic roots: in so far as it implies a glove of mail, it signifies disarming oneself before one's superior; at the same time, since the right hand pertains to the voice and to the rational side of Man, it is a custom which suggests candour and the frank disclosure of one's mind.

Goblet (or **Drinking-cup**)   In Romanesque times, and especially when, as a chalice, it was furnished with a lid, it was a symbol of the human heart (14). In a broader sense it is, like the coffer and the chest, a notable symbol of containing. To a certain extent it may be seen as a material expression of the surrounds of 'wrapping' around the mystic Centre. An important secondary meaning, in addition to the main symbolism of containing, is derived from the symbolism of the particular liquids which can be contained in goblets, glasses or chalices, and expressive of the non-formal world of possibilities (4). This is the explanation of the fact that hydromancy is practiced with crystal or glass vessels which are supposed to have the power of talismans (57).

Gog and Magog   They signify respectively the king and the people, as in Ezekiel, where the people of the North-East of Asia Minor are specifically called the enemies of God. This meaning still persists among the Moslems (46).

Gold   In Hindu doctrine, gold is the 'mineral light'. According to Guénon, the Latin word for gold—*aurum*—is the same as the Hebrew for light—*aor* (26). Jung quotes the delightful explanation offered by the alchemist Michael Maier in *De Circulo Physico Quadrato* to the effect that the sun, by virtue of millions of journeys round the earth (or conversely) has spun threads of gold all round it. Gold is the image of solar light and hence of the divine intelligence. If the heart is the image of the sun in man, in the earth it is gold (32). Consequently, gold is symbolic of all that is superior, the glorified or 'fourth state' after the first three stages of black (standing for sin and penitence), white (remission and innocence) and red (sub-limitation and passion). Everything golden or made of gold tends to pass on this quality of superiority to its utilitarian function. Chrysaor, the magic sword of gold, symbolizes supreme spiritual determination. Gold is also the essential element in the symbolism of the hidden or elusive treasure which is an illustration of the fruits of the spirit and of supreme illumination.

Golden Fleece   This is one of the symbols denoting the conquest of the impossible or the ultra-reasonable (32). Since the sheep is symbolic of innocence and gold represents supreme spirituality and glorification, the Golden Fleece signifies that the quest of the Argonauts was for supreme strength of spirit through purity of soul—that quality which distinguished Sir Galahad, the mediaeval Knight of the Holy Grail. It is, in consequence, one of the most advanced forms within the general symbolism of treasure (15).

Goose   Like the duck, gander or swan, the goose is a beneficent animal associated with the Great Mother and with the 'descent into hell'. It is very often found in folktales (Mother Goose, Grimm's tales, etc.). It is linked with destiny as is proven by the 'goose game', a profane offshoot of the symbol in space–time, representing the dangers and fortunes of existence, prior to the return to the maternal bosom.

Gorgon   According to Frobenius, the gorgon is a symbol of the fusion of opposites: the lion and the eagle, the bird and the serpent, mobility and immobility (as in the swastika), beauty and horror (22). Hence it is symbolic of conditions beyond the endurance of the conscious mind, slaying him who contemplates it. Like other fabulous entities, it is also symbolic of the infinite number of forms in which creation can manifest itself.

Grafting   A symbol for artificial interference in the realm of natural order (4). It also has a sexual significance.

Grail, The   The Grail is one of the most beautiful and complex of legendary symbols. Basically, it embraces two different symbols, but it involves others too. The two main symbols are that of the Grail proper, and that of the quest. According to the Western legend (the Fisher King), a mysterious illness (symbolic, like that of Philoctetes) has stricken down the ancient monarch, the keeper of the Grail's secret. And in this rhythm and on this level everything around him is wilting like the peccant King himself (this being the theme of Poe's *Fall of the House of Usher* and of Eliot's *Waste Land*). The animals are declining, the trees bear no fruit, the fountains have ceased to play. Day and night, physicians and knights tend the ailing monarch. Sir Parsifal questions the king forthrightly: Where is the Grail? Instantly, the king rises and Nature is regenerated (18). The Swiss Knight Templar, Wolfram von Eschenbach, the author of

Parsifal, locates the action in Gaul, on the borders of Spain, where the hero Titurel has founded a temple for the preservation of the chalice of the Last Supper (27). It is said that the Grail came from the East and there it must return (32), which is a clear allusion to its significance as the 'source of illumination'. The cup itself has its own symbolism, but there is a legend which tells how it was fashioned by angels from an emerald that dropped from Lucifer's forehead when he was hurled into the abyss. Thus, just as the Virgin Mary redeems the sin of Eve, so the blood of the Redeemer redeems through the Grail the sin of Lucifer. This emerald, as Guénon has shown, is reminiscent of the *urnâ*, the pearl fixed to the forehead which, in Hindu symbolism, is the third eye of Siva (or Shiva), representing the 'sense of eternity'. The loss of the Grail is tantamount to the loss of one's inner adhesions, whether they are religious ties or—in the degraded (that is, the psychological) forms of the mystery—some other 'source of happiness'. Hence, this lapse of memory entails the loss of the primordial or paradisical state, as well as the death and withering up of Nature (that is, of one's own spiritual life). The Grail signifies at once a vessel (*grasale*) and a book (*gradale*). The quest, on the other hand, concerns, broadly speaking, the 'treasure hunt', which is actually the inversion of the endless chase of the 'Accursed Hunter', since the latter pursues phenomenal forms in their constant interplay of being and non-being, whereas the Grail implies, above all, the quest for the mystic 'Centre'—the 'unmoved mover', of Aristotle, or the 'unvarying mean' in Far Eastern tradition (28). The appearance of the Grail in the centre of the Round Table, round which are seated the Knights, closely parallels, in the symbolism of its form, the Chinese image of heaven (*Pi*), which is shaped like a circle with a hole (analogous with cup or chalice) in the middle. Ms. Fr. 112 of the Bibliothèque Nationale in Paris, *Lancelot du Lac*, depicts the moment in which the Grail is placed by two angels in the centre of the mystic Round Table (Plate XIII). One of the most widespread legends relates the Grail to the cup or plate in which Joseph of Arimathea caught the blood of Christ nailed to the Cross. The ideas of sacrifice and of self-chastisement (and in part the idea of castration) are associated with the symbolism of the Grail, as A. E. Waite demonstrates in *The Holy Grail* (London, 1933). It is obvious that sublimation of such sacrifice is also connected with the Grail, as in the legends of Parsifal and Sir Galahad.

Grapes Grapes, frequently depicted in bunches, symbolize at once fertility (from their character as a fruit) and sacrifice (because they give wine—particularly when the wine is the colour of blood). In baroque allegories of the Lamb of God, the Lamb is often portrayed between thorns and bunches of grapes.

Graphics We could compile and catalogue an immense repertoire of graphic signs. There is perhaps greater symbolic significance in these signs than in any other aspect of symbolism, because of the clear intention behind them to express an explicit meaning. One

●   Unity: the Origin.

——————   Passive, static principle.

| Active, dynamic principle.

□   Quaternary—material and passive.

◇   Quaternary—material and active.

✦   Material generation through the interaction of two opposing principles.

△   Ternary—neutral and successive.

△   Ternary—evolutive, since the vertical axis is the greater.

▽   Ternary—involutive since it is inverted.

contemporary scholar, Ernst Lehner, tells us that he himself collected 60,000 symbols, signs and marks of different kinds, from varying sources, cultures and periods. The graphic symbol (whether engraved, etched or drawn, or contrived in the form of a diagram,

emblem or plan by any other means, such as that of papermakers'
watermarks) offers a clear illustration of the mystic doctrine of form,
such as it was developed by oriental civilizations in particular. As
Shukrâshârya has said with such lyric fervour: 'The character of the
image is determined by the relationship between the worshipper and

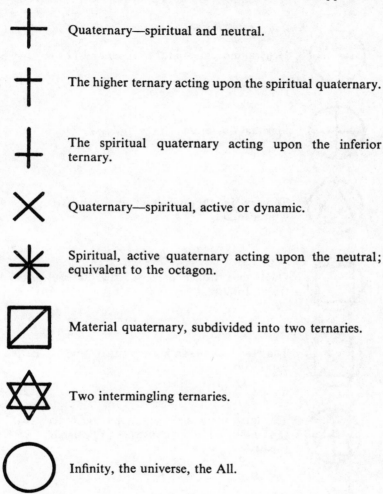

Quaternary—spiritual and neutral.

The higher ternary acting upon the spiritual quaternary.

The spiritual quaternary acting upon the inferior
ternary.

Quaternary—spiritual, active or dynamic.

Spiritual, active quaternary acting upon the neutral;
equivalent to the octagon.

Material quaternary, subdivided into two ternaries.

Two intermingling ternaries.

Infinity, the universe, the All.

the worshipped'; in this he is unconsciously echoing the biologist's
definition of form as 'the diagram between the inner urge of a body
and the resistance of the (physical) medium'. In Hindu doctrine,
beauty is the result not of external characteristics but of the emanation of a spiritual attitude; and the same is true of other aspects of

Centre of infinity: emanation or first cause.

 General movement in the Upper and Lower Worlds.

 Spiritual quaternary in the universe.

 Ternary in the universe: the spiritual principle within totality.

 Quaternary in the universe: the material principle within totality.

 The two quaternaries—spiritual and material—within totality.

 The quaternary acted upon by the ternary within the universe: the constructive principle within totality.

 Sensory, anthropomorphic principle (according to Piobb).

form, such as direction, order, arrangement, or the number of components. German mystics, as Luc Benoist recalls (6), have also applied themselves to shape (both in the round and diagrammatically) as a manifestation of the spirit. As Anna Katerina Emmerich observed: 'Nothing is pure form. Everything is substance and action, by virtue of signs.' The symbol as crystallized in creative art involves a high degree of condensation, deriving from its inherent economy of form and allusive power. This, then, is the psychological basis of the symbolism of graphics (the basis of the magical interpretation is to be sought in the literal interpretation of the theory of correspondences). It underlies the graphic symbolism of amulets, talismans, pentacles and divinatory signs from prehistoric times right up to the present day. Hence the strong and perfectly justified attraction exerted by certain shapes, emblems, flags, coats of arms, marks and medals, based not upon convention, as is usually suggested, but upon inner bonds of symbolic 'common rhythms' (30). Quite apart from their function as integrating or synoptic symbols, graphic symbols possess a singular mnemonic power, as Schneider has shown. He points to the fact that such figures as the spiral, the swastika, the circle with a central point, the lunar crescent, the double sigma, etc., were capable of conveying the most varied of philosophical, alchemical or astronomic data— a technique of interpretation capable of applying all the information supplied by these three disciplines to a single plane of significance. Any one given figure (with its series of multivalencies—that is, embracing several meanings which are not irrelevant or equivocal) varies in appearance and in significance with the 'rhythm-symbol' (that is, the idea and the intended direction) pervading it. Schneider adds, in connexion with Tanew's *Das Ornament die Elbetiza* (Ipek, 1942), that this constitutes one of the predominant features of ancient art, which 'is often unfortunately called decorative or ornamental art' (51). To enumerate some of the fields of activity which have been profoundly influenced by graphic symbolism: mythological attributes and figures, signs in astronomy and astrology, alchemy, magic and primitive mysticism, religions, heraldry, fabulous figures and monsters, ornaments, signs of diverse offices, numismatic signs, marks on porcelain, watermarks, etc. (36). If we pause to consider the prodigious variety offered by only one of these categories—ornaments, for example—it will become apparent that even a rough inventory of the symbolic ramifications would be impracticable here for material reasons. And we could add further headings: alphabets, for example, or ideographs, pictographs, metagraphs and mandalas, as well as graphic artistic compositions, embracing abstract painting for example, which—like Celtic, Anglo-Saxon and Nordic ornamental art—provides an unceasing flow of significant forms, expressed willy-nilly, for Man is quite incapable of creating anything which does not bear the marks of his subtle, urgent and all-embracing need for communication. To widen now the scope of this exposition, let us consider the lapidary signs to be found in the stones of many architectural edifices. A great many kinds of different marks have been catalogued, and, without doing violence to their esoteric meaning, we may group them, as follows, into: initial letters, anagrams, astrological, numerical, magic or mystico-Christian signs, or marks pertaining to associations or groups, or to building, or to nationality or race, or to benefactors, etc.

In ornamentation, Greek frets, wavy lines, series of spirals, coils of varying rhythms, sigmas, X-shapes, diamonds, circles, ovals, arrows, triangles, zigzags, triskeles and swastikas are all graphic shapes which, in symbolism, are grouped under the general heading of 'cosmic background', because they are all in effect symbols of the activity of natural forces and of the four Elements (41). In varying degrees, depending upon the period and personal or cultural prejudice, scholars researching into the history and pre-history of art—since few of them have taken any interest in the autonomous doctrine of symbolism—have either lumped these graphic symbols together as sun-symbols, or else as symbols of the hurricane and the heavens. J. Déchelette, for example, says in his *Manuel d'Archéologie préhistorique* that all the signs concerning dual, bilateral symmetry or the irradiating Centre 'were employed as images of the sun from the Bronze Age onwards'. We must not fail to mention one important fact, and that is the connexion of the symbolism of form with divination. The Chinese *Pa Kua*—whose system is described in the *I Ching* (*The Book of Changes*)—the random dots of geomancy, and the innumerable '-mancies' which have come down to us from Antiquity in a great many works upon the subject, are all founded for the most part upon the symbolism of form; this can be seen both in the identification of a given 'matrical shape' with the figure of a particular being (as happens in the case of Rorschach's tests with ink-blots) whose symbolic implications will determine the augury, and in the splitting up of a shape into its numerical components and its tendency towards a particular direction in space, in which case its symbolic sense is determined by the significance of the numbers and the space-zone associated with it. Frazer, for example, describes the Chinese belief that the life and destiny of a city is so influenced by its shape that its fortunes must vary according to the character of the thing which that shape most nearly resembles; and he relates that, long ago, the town of Tsuen-cheu-fu, the outlines of which were like those of a carp, frequently fell a prey to the depredations of the neighbouring city of Yung-chun, which was shaped like a fishing-net (21).

Jung has shown great interest in the question of graphic symbolism, geometric diagrams and numbers determined by the quantitative
factor of component elements, without, however, working up his
interesting—and valid—findings and conclusions into a comprehensive theory. He observes, for example, that the relationships
between number and shape depend not only upon the quantity
of the elements but also upon their individual shape and direction,
because the direction influences the quantitative factor in the same
way as fracture does. By way of illustration, he mentions that in the
ninth key of the *Duodecim Claves Fratris Basilii Valentini* (in
Museum Hermeticum, Frankfurt, 1678) there is an instance of
triunity appearing as unity, realized by splitting a Y-sign in the
centre, so that it becomes three strokes; and another of duality as a
quaternary, by forming a four-armed cross not with four lines but
with two independent but counterbalancing right angles, so that
they can be said to be two components by virtue of their continuity
but four from the point of view of their direction. He comments
also upon the fact that irregular quadrilaterals are expressive of
the tendency in the equilibrium of the symbolism of the number
four to adapt itself in conformity with the direction of the major
axis. If the horizontal line is predominant, then it reveals the
superiority of the merely rational intellect, whereas if the vertical
line prevails then it denotes spiritual non-rationalism. The sign of
the conjunction of the quaternary (the cross or the square) with
unity is expressed through the union of the numbers four and one,
that is, of the square (or the cross) and the circle. The relationship
between two intersecting diameters and the circumference is
emphasized by sometimes depicting the centre visibly as a small
circle symbolic of the mystic 'Centre'. The figure thus arrived at is of
great symbolic value: it expresses the original Oneness (symbolized
by the centre), the 'way out to the manifest world' (the four radii,
which are the same as the four rivers which well up from the *fons
vitae* or from the foot of the Cosmic Tree in Paradise), and the
return to Oneness (the outer circumference) through the circular
movement which 'smooths away' the corners of the square (these
corners implying the differentiation characteristic of the multiplicity
and the transitoriness of the world of phenomena). By adding a
further cross, shaped like an X, to this figure, the wheel is obtained;
and the wheel is the commonest symbol of the 'Centre' and of the
cycle of transformations. The importance of the relationship
between the circle and the square is quite extraordinary; religious
and symbolic art as well as profane works provide us with a great
variety of shapes incorporating both the circle and the square. But
to limit ourselves to religious symbolism, let us quote two instances
which are entirely unrelated yet produce the same result: first, the

so-called 'pentacle of Laos', a squared figure with a small square at its centre and four circles inside the angles, each divided into four internally; and secondly, the retable in the Cartuja de Miraflores (the Carthusian monastery near Burgos), which is arranged in a similar pattern, but incorporates figures of the Pantokrator and of tetramorphs. The underlying logico-symbolic force of such figures is so strong that, when one has recourse to an abstract image of a cosmic order, capable of expressing the intimate and intense relationship between the 'two worlds', one turns inevitably to this coniunctio joining the symbol for earth (the square) with that for heaven (the circle). The fact that figures incorporating the irradiant 'Centre' are cosmic symbols of the ultimate destiny of the spirit accounts for the fact that they are also psychological images of this same destiny, that is, of its presentiment and of the way of fulfilling it—in short, of the mystic idea of consummation (32). Hence, psychoanalysts have noted that the joining of the square with the circle (in such forms as the star, the rose, the lotus, concentric circles, the circle with a visible central point, etc.) is symbolic of the final stage in the process of individuation, or, in other words, of that phase of spiritual development when imperfections (irregular shapes) have been eliminated, as have all earthly desires (represented by malignant, biological symbols of monsters and wild beasts), for the sake of concentrating upon the achievement of Oneness and a vision of Paradise (such as that described by Dante at the end of his masterpiece) (56).

Other conclusions of Jung concerning the psychology of shapes are these: opposites are symbolized by a cross (signifying inner urges) and by a square (standing for the horizon); the process of rising above these urges is symbolized by the circle (33); exact duplication implies confirmation, but when the two symbols face in opposite directions they express the longing for wholeness, that is, the desire not only to explore the two spheres but to conquer all space; to go towards the left is to turn towards the unconscious and the past, to go to the right is to face consciousness and the future. Jung points, as an example, to an illustration in the Viatorium of Michael Maier (Rouen, 1651), showing two eagles flying in opposite directions (32).

Concerning graphic compositions proper, and their corresponding symbolic significance, we must not overlook the existence of the theory that they were originally ornamental, a thesis which is upheld by Baltrusaitis among others. He insists upon the a priori thesis that artists are faced with a certain area to fill up and the need to achieve certain artistic effects, proceeding from concepts of order, symmetry, logic and clarity. But man's aesthetic urges arose long after his need to express cosmic significances; and the contemporary concept of art as a sign and testimony of a state of mind, rather than as the creation of beauty or of aesthetic pleasure (which would seem automatically to preclude many modern works of art lacking in positive or loveable qualities), appears to favour the view that the primary impulse is to express a symbolic meaning. According to tradition, symmetrical forms in art spring from the same source (the Gemini) as the bilateral symmetry of the human figure, a symmetry which is echoed in the duplication of certain organs; such symmetrical forms include, for instance, the distribution of figures on a Romanesque or Gothic tympanum, or the arrangement of the supporters, the shield and helmet on an escutcheon. But if this idea of a common origin seems unacceptable, then the artistic preference for symmetry may be conceived as a simple anatomic projection, granted that the conviction of primordial rightness can only be experienced when the artificial is felt to be parallel, analogous or corresponding to the natural. A being with two arms at the sides of a body surmounted by a head must tend to formulate primarily an order or pattern in which one principal shape is located in the middle and two secondary shapes are placed at the sides. These elementary notions were first appreciated not—in all probability—in the Palaeolithic Age (an age about which our knowledge is scant, and when man was, in any case, living under constant pressure from the need to exert himself in utilitarian ways), but in the period of the dawning of history, from the latter part of the Neolithic up to the Bronze Age, or, in other words, from 5000 to 3000 B.C. This was the period, then, when cultural factors first appeared or when they reached a definitive stage of development. Ortiz is right to suggest that man not improbably, before arriving at a generic configuration of life, first created ideograms of the tangible realities of life, and specially of those entities, such as the wind, which have no concrete shape. Fire was seen as flame; water as a succession of waves; rain was likened to tears; lightning to the zigzag, and so on (41).

We do not wish to suggest that all pictographs or ideographs, let alone signs, of primitive or astrobiological cultures owe their origins to such motives as these, or that they disclose a similar, morphological process of development. We must here distinguish between: *realistic, imitative images* in the first place (properly, drawings or paintings); in the second place, *diagrammatic, imitative images* (which seek after the inner 'rhythmic' meaning of a given figure, as well as its outer form); and, in the third, *pure, rhythmic images* (such as signs for animals deriving from their tracks). Schneider observes that, in intermediary cultures, animal-symbols are not representations of physical shapes but rhythmic lines determined by the animals' movements. He adds that, in Malacca, the symbolism of a given animal may be applied to one of the four

Elements: so that, for example, the symbol for water is derived
from the rhythmic movements of the frog's legs (which, in any case,
are comparable with the rhythm of the waves); similarly, ants, as
well as centipedes, are signified by the rhythm of their movements (50).
This concept of 'rhythm' opens up enormous possibilities when
applied to the conception of the light of the spirit. Every man has
his own rhythm; and so has every culture. Style or personality are
in the last resort simply expressions of rhythm. Germain Bazin, in
his *Histoire de l'art* (Paris, 1953), suggests that abstract art is the
attempt to externalize the *essential rhythms* of the human, individual
and collective soul (the process being closely related to that of
endopathy as conceived by Aristotle, Vischer, Kant, Lipps, etc.).

Consequently, in order to decide upon the significance of any
graphic figure, we must bear in mind the following factors: (*a*) its
resemblance to figures of cosmic beings; (*b*) its shape, whether open
or closed, regular or irregular, geometric or biomorphic; (*c*) the
number of component elements making up the shape, together with
the significance of this number; (*d*) the dominant 'rhythms' as the
expression of its elemental, dynamic potential and its movement;
(*e*) the spatial arrangement, or the disposition of its different zones;
(*f*) its proportions; (*g*) its colours, if any. Factor (*a*)—its resemblance
to other figures—is so wide in scope and so obvious in its implications that comment would be superfluous. (*b*) The significance of
shape depends upon the relevant geometric symbolism, which we
have examined above. (*c*) The number of its components confers an
added symbolism to the secondary—though at times very important
—consideration of the shape (for example, the seven-pointed star
derives its significance as much from the septenary symbolism as
from the stellar shape). (*d*) Concerning the 'rhythms', we have
already pointed out the connexion with the number of component
elements and with animal-movements (Greek frets, and the broken
line fashioned after the trapeze are usually said to correspond to
earth-symbolism, the wavy line to air-symbolism, a succession of
incomplete spirals—or waves—as well as the broken line, to water-
symbolism, although fire is also associated with water because of the
triangular shape of the tongue of flame). (*e*) Regarding the spatial
arrangement: along the vertical axis, it is the symbolism of level
which matters most (implying qualities of morality and energy),
and on the horizontal axis, the left side is, as we have said, retro-
spective (for it is the zone of 'origin', linked with the unconscious
and with darkness), and the right side looks to the outcome. Hence,
the line running from the left downwards and then upwards towards
the right does not indicate a fall but an ascent, the converse also being
true. And for this reason, the St. Andrew's cross, with its two
intersecting and opposing lines standing for fall and ascent respec-

tively, is symbolic of the intermingling of the 'two worlds', and is therefore comparable with the mystic mandorla. In those figures which feature a centre together with dual, bilateral symmetry, we have two symbolic tendencies: first, that in which the rhythmic movements tend inwards, denoting concentration and also aggression (as, for example, in the classical symbol of the four winds blowing towards the centre); and secondly, that in which rhythms well up from the centre towards the four cardinal points, indicating the defence of 'wholeness" (the cross of St. Ferdinand is related to this) and bearing a certain relationship with the tetramorphs and the 'four archers' of megalithic culture. Irradiating figures denote dispersion, growth and involution. It must also be borne in mind that lines, in addition to their morphological properties, are also means of communication and of conjoining; this is why their significance must always be closely linked with the nature of the zones which they bring into contact. There are, it must be said, some theorists who carry the study of graphics to extremes of prolixity and detail. Ely Star, for example, examines the various shapes suggested by an upright line crossing a horizontal, simply by the process of linking the upright with the active principle and the horizontal with the passive. He comments that straight lines are always expressive of activity, compared with curves which denote passivity (54). To turn now to the way the first ideographic signs were associated with the constellations, it is very important to note that the modern view favours the theory that the constellations were the source of the alphabet. Gattefossé, Fenn and others are quite explicit upon this point. Zollinger shows how the Great Bear is the origin of the sign representing a bond, a link or an item of knowledge, how the Gemini gave rise to the number 8 and the letter H, how the eternal cyclic laws of the sun's orbit or the polar rotation of the earth gave rise to the swastika, the division of the increate into different forms inspired the Chinese *Yang-Yin* sign, the manifest world inspired the horizontal line, the 'Centre' the cross, and, finally, how the union of the three principles as represented by the signs for the Sun, the Moon and the cross originated the graphic symbol known as the emblem of Hermes. He goes on to mention the family resemblance between forms of bilateral symmetry such as the *Yang-Yin* sign, the *labrys* (the twin-bladed axe), the labarum and the cross (61). Bayley found that, among his collection of watermarks, were a large number of graphic signs with a precise meaning to them: three circles, or the clover-leaf and its derivatives stand for the trinitarian; the labyrinth shaped like a cross, denotes both inscrutability and close ties; wheels indicate the sun as the motivating force behind change and cycles (4). Concerning the symbolism of crosses, of which the varieties are numerous, we shall confine ourselves to indicating that they depend upon the shape of their arms and the 'rhythmic direction' which these arms suggest (as in centrifugal, centripetal, neutral or rotatory crosses) (47). The symbols for planets and many other marks which cannot be reduced to a simple geometric figure or explained as a combination of simple compónent elements, but which disclose a certain complexity of pattern, may nevertheless be interpreted with the help of the principles enumerated above. To give just one example: In alchemy, the sign for 'antimony', representing the intellectual 'soul' alive with all its virtues and faculties, is a cross placed upon a circle; the sign for 'green', denoting the vegetative 'soul' or the physiological world, is a cross inscribed within a circle; the sign for Venus, corresponding to instinctive behaviour or the base urges, is a cross placed below a circle. In short, there is nothing arbitrary about graphic symbolism (59): everything obeys a system which develops out of a single point and expands into more complex forms in which shape, rhythm, quantity, position, order and direction all help to explain and define the pattern.

Great Monarch, The   This is a term which is to be found in some Hermetic writings. According to Piobb, it owes its origin to an incorrect reading of the Greek, mistaking 'he who governs himself alone' for 'he who governs alone' (48). Be that as it may, the symbolism of the king refers, in any case, to him who triumphs over himself, that is, to the hero definitive and victorious (48).

Great Mother, The   The archetype of the Great Mother corresponds to certain feminine deities such as Ishtar in Babylonia, Isis in Egypt, Astarte in Phoenicia, Kâli-Durga in India, Ge and Demeter in Greece (56). It is usually considered to be a symbol of the fertilized earth (51), though the sea also appears in ancient cosmogonies with the same connotation (4). For Jung, the *Magna Mater* represents the objective truth of Nature, masquerading, or incarnate, in the figure of a maternal woman, a sybil, a goddess or a priestess, but sometimes taking the form of a church, for instance, or a city or district. This archetypal image he calls 'mana personality', corresponding to the 'Ancient of Days' who likewise takes such forms as the magician, sorcerer or sage (30).

Great Priest, The   The fifth enigma of the Tarot pack. The card shows him seated upon a throne between the two columns Jachin and Boaz (symbolic of intuition and reason). He wears white gloves to symbolize the purity of his hands. His sceptre terminates in a triple cross, the rounded ends of whose arms give rise to the septenary, alluding to the virtues necessary to combat the seven capital sins: Pride—the Sun; Sloth—the Moon; Envy—Mercury; Wrath—Mars; Lust—Venus; Greed—Jupiter; and Avarice—Saturn. Also depicted in this image are two disciples, both kneeling, one dressed in red (for activity) and the other in black (passivity). On the positive side, this enigma signifies the moral law, duty and conscience (59).

Great Priestess, The   The second enigma of the Tarot, representing Isis as the goddess of the night. She is seated, holding a half-opened book in her right hand and two keys in her left, one of which is golden (signifying the sun, the word, or reason) and the other silver (the moon or imagination). Her throne is situated between two columns—being two in number, they are an allegory denoting the feminine principle—which are in fact the columns called Jachin and Boaz in the Temple of Solomon, joined together by the veil which covers the entrance to the sanctuary. The first (the solar) column is red and corresponds to fire and to activity; the second (the lunar) is blue. The tiara which crowns the head of the Great Priestess has a lunar crescent—a symbol of cyclic phases and of the world of phenomena; this emphasizes the predominance of the passive, reflective and feminine qualities of the figure. She is leaning against the sphinx of the great cosmic questions, and the floor, being composed of alternate white and black tiles, denotes that everything in existence is subject to the laws of chance and of opposites. In the Besançon Tarot, this enigma takes the form of the figure of Juno. On the positive side, the Great Priestess signifies reflection and intuition; on the negative, intolerance (59).

Griffin   A fabulous animal, the front half of which is like an eagle and the rear half like a lion, with a long, serpentine tail. The blending of these two superior solar animals points to the generally beneficent character of this being; it was consecrated by the Greeks to Apollo and Nemesis (8). The griffin, like certain kinds of dragon, is always to be found as the guardian of the roads to salvation, standing beside the Tree of Life or some such symbol. From the psychological point of view it symbolizes the relationship between psychic energy and cosmic force (4). In mediaeval Christian art, from Mozarabic miniatures onwards, the griffin is very common, being associated with signs which tend towards ambivalence, representing, for instance, both the Saviour and Antichrist (20).

Grotesques   A type of ornament serving a largely decorative purpose. Favoured by the Romans, it became very common from the 15th century onwards, especially in the Plateresque style. Some of its characteristics owe their inspiration—like emblems—to Gnosticism which, as is well known, made wide use of the symbolic image in order to spread its doctrines. Bayley has collected a large number of grotesques and similar decorative motifs, among which the following figures predominate: the phoenix, swan, sheep, winged horses, serpents, dragons, gardens, diverse flowers, shrubs, sheaves, garlands, creepers, roses in jars, fruits, baskets of flowers and fruits, vines, pomegranates, trees (especially the evergreen sort), crosses, lilies, caducei, bolts, masks, steps, trophies, rosettes, bows, shields, brackets, swords, lances, cups and chalices, nude children, twins, sowers, fertility goddesses with multiple breasts, caryatids, damsels. All these items have their place in the world of symbolism as component parts of allegories, emblems, Romanesque and Gothic capitals, and so on. But the grotesque in itself, as a form and as a system, emphasizes the close bond between continuity and discontinuity—of ambivalence, that is to say, as expressed, for instance, in the myth of the Gemini. Hence, the grotesque is a general symbol for the world of phenomena and of the coherent unfolding of existence (4).

Guardian Just as the powers of the Earth·must be defended, so, by analogy, must all mythic, religious and spiritual wealth or power be protected against hostile forces or against possible intrusion by the unworthy. Hence the familiarity of the 'keeper of the treasure' in legends: almost invariably, this guardian is a griffin or dragon, or else a warrior endowed with superhuman powers. In temples, the idea of defence is implicit in the spatial organization and confirmed by the disposition of the walls, the doors and towers. In the Far East, the guardians are usually fabulous monsters. In Western countries, the same function may be performed by the figures inscribed on doorways. From the psychological point of view, guardians symbolize the forces gathered on the threshold of transition between different stages of evolution and spiritual progress or regression. The 'guardian of the threshold' must be overcome before Man can enter into the mastery of a higher realm.

Gum The term *Gummi arabicum* was one employed by the alchemists to denote the substance of transmutation, for they believed that, once spiritualized, it became endowed with analogous qualities of spiritual adhesion. It is a symbol for the seminal substance (32).

Hair (Body-Hair) Whereas hair on the head, because it grows on the top of the human body, symbolizes spiritual forces and can be equated, within the symbolism of water, with the 'Upper Ocean', body-hair is equivalent to the 'Lower Ocean', that is to say, it denotes the proliferation of the irrational power of the cosmos and of the instinctive life. This explains why the priests of many religions, the Egyptians among them, shaved off all their hair. And it also explains why the god Pan—a prefiguration of the devil—was depicted with hairy legs. Despite the above generalization, there are some traditions in which the hair of the head as well as on the body takes on a malign significance (8).

Hairs   In general, hairs represent energy, and are related to the symbolism of levels. That is, a head of hair, being located on the head, stands for higher forces, whereas abundant body-hair signifies the prevalence of the baser forces. Sometimes these two meanings have coalesced: on a Romanesque capital at Estibaliz, Adam is depicted beardless before the Fall and with long hair and bushy beard after he has fallen into sin (46). Hairs also signify fertility. Origen used to say: 'The Nazirites do not cut their hair because all that is done by just men prospers and their leaves to not fall' (46). In Hindu symbolism, hairs, like the threads of a fabric, symbolize the 'lines of force' of the universe (25). A full head of hair represents *élan vital* and *joie de vivre*, linked with the will to succeed (42). Again, hairs correspond to the element of fire, signifying the burgeoning of primitive forces (50). A highly important secondary meaning is derived from the colour of hair. Brown or black hair reinforces the symbolism of hair in general, that is, dark, terrestrial energy; golden hair is related to the sun's rays (31, 38) and to the whole vast sun-symbolism; copper-coloured hair implies a Venusian or demoniacal characteristic (32). Hairs, then, come to symbolize the concept of spiritualized energy. Phaldor, in his *Libro d'oro del sogno*, comments that they 'represent the spiritual assets of Man. Abundant, beautiful hair, for both man and woman, signifies spiritual development. To lose one's hair signifies failure and poverty' (56). Now, the reverse of loss brought about by forces outside Man's control is, in part, willing sacrifice. For this reason, Zimmer points out that all who renounce and defy the principles of procreation and multiplication of life, in order to embark upon the path of total asceticism, are bound on principle to cut their hair short. They must simulate the sterility of the aged and hairless who form the last link in the chain of generations. Some religions, as for example that of the ancient Egyptians, used to prescribe total depilation (60). Hair, wigs and beards were used by the Sumerians to ward off evil spirits (as was smoke).

Halo   The aureole, nimbus or halo is a luminous circle like a crown with which the ancients invested their deities and which Christians accord to the holy (8). It is a visual expression of irradiating, supernatural force, or, sometimes, more simply, of intellectual energy in its mystic aspect; the fact that the Ancients almost invariably equated intelligence with light is proof enough of this. Other kinds of halos are spherical in form: the Moslems, for example, often made use of the pearl to represent paradise and their belief was that the blessed, each one united with his houri, live in pearls. The halo is equated with the cage and, in particular, with the sphere itself (46). Jurgis Baltrusaitis, in *Le Moyen Age fantastique*, has collected a host of mediaeval drawings and paintings of beings enclosed in transparent spheres apparently made of glass. Many of the works of Hieronymus van Aecken (Bosch) contain examples of this. The halo, in this case, is a simple visual expression of a kind of determinism enveloping each man within his mode of being and his destiny, whether it is favourable and paradisiac, or adverse and infernal.

Hamlet Although literary myths do not normally enter into the scope of this work, we have decided to make an exception in the case of *Hamlet, Prince of Denmark*. This famous Shakespearian tragedy has its origins in a Nordic legend. Apart from the Renaissance dramatist's explanation of its 'obvious contents', it also lends itself to other explanations of latent contents, or, better, to disclosures on other planes. One of these interpretations, the psychoanalytic, would tend towards the belief that Hamlet really becomes mad, and that the assassination of his father by his uncle is mere fiction, an invention of his mind intended to help him to accept more easily the Oedipus complex which is so powerful in him. His satisfaction on killing Polonius, which foreshadows the moment when he kills his step-father, seems to bear out this explanation. So do his rejection of Ophelia (which may be interpreted in a different way), and his complete forgiveness of his mother, who in *Electra* (a Greek tragedy along similar lines) is implacably assassinated by her avenging offspring. A second explanation of *Hamlet*, which is more profound and symbolic, results from applying Gnostic doctrine to his story. Hamlet hates the world and considers it to be the work of the evil god, of the demiurge (the husband of his mother, who is the material and whom he pardons because he judges her to be the merely passive agent of Evil). He dreams of the good god, of the Father, who seems rather to be his own projection, his autodivination in a transcendent situation. The rejection of the world has a 'necrophiliac' explanation in the scene in the graveyard with Yorick's skull and an absolute manifestion in his spurning of Ophelia (woman = guilt). There is an angelism in Hamlet which causes us to consider him to be the symbol and archetype of Oedipal man, who suffers from being tied to the world, from being a material entity and from owning his existence to a being whom he would kill and by whom he might possibly be killed (cf. the slaying of the firstborn by the primitive father, according to Freud). As a case of anguish and repressions leading to a series of crimes which can only be resolved by his own self-destruction, Hamlet is a symbol of man in rebellion against the 'filial' situation, a humanized (and Christianized ?) symbol, successor to Aeschylus' 'Prometheus' and predecessor to Milton's 'Satan'. I owe these ideas to seeing the cinematographic *Hamlet*, directed and interpreted by Sir Laurence Olivier, whose intensity suggested to me all that I express here in the form of a hypothesis.

Hammer An instrument proper to the smith, endowed with the mystic power of creation (51). The two-headed hammer is, like the twin-bladed axe, an ambivalent symbol of the mountain of Mars and of sacrificial Inversion.

Hand In the Egyptian tongue, the term designating the hand was related to that for the pillar (or a support, or strength) and for the palm (4). In esoteric doctrine, the position of the hand in relation to the body, and the arrangement of the fingers, convey certain precise symbolic notions (48). According to the Egyptian system of hieroglyphs, the hand signifies manifestation, action, donating and husbandry. An eye in association with a hand—as for example in some oriental mythic beings—symbolize 'clairvoyant action' (19). Schneider concedes a major rôle to the hand 'because it is the corporeal manifestation of the inner state of the human being' and because 'it expresses an attitude of mind in terms other than the acoustic'—or, in other words, a gesture. It follows, then, that the raised hand is the symbol of the voice and of song; the hand placed on the breast indicates the attitude of the sage; placed on the neck it denotes sacrifice; two hands joined signifies mystic marriage— the Jungian individuation; the hand covering the eyes represents clairvoyance at the moment of death (50). Of great importance is the fact that the hand has five fingers, firstly, because of its broad analogy with the human figure (composed of four extremities plus the head), and, secondly, by reason of the symbolism of the number five (denoting love, health and humanity) (40). In Egyptian hiero- glyphics, the open hand signifies any specificially human task as well as magnetic force (19)—an idea also characteristic of pre- Columbian America. And a very similar belief lies behind the widespread use of the hand as an amulet in Islamic cultures. Accord- ing to Berber thought, the hand signifies protection, authority, power and strength; the *manus* had the same meaning for the Romans, symbolizing in particular the authority of the *pater familias* and of the emperor, and is sometimes to be seen surmounting the *signum* of the legions in place of the imperial eagle. In the Islamic amulets mentioned above, the figure of the hand undergoes various modifications or appears in association with other symbols, as, for instance, the star, the dove, the bird, the fan, the zigzag and the circle, forming emblems comparable with those of the Christian West (12). The familiar emblem of the 'linked hands' is expressive of a virile fraternity, or solidarity in the face of danger (49). In Jung's opinion, the hand is endowed with a generative significance (31). The difference between the right hand and the left is usually ignored, but when the distinction is made it appears merely to serve the purpose of enriching the basic significance with the additional implications of space-symbolism, the right side corresponding to the rational, the conscious, the logical and the virile; the left side representing the converse (33). There are alchemic images which represent a King clasping in his own left hand the left hand of the Queen. Jung suggests that this may refer to the unconscious character of their union but that it may also be indicative either of affection or of suspicion (33).

Hanged Man This figure has a profound and complex symbolism. It is enigma number twelve of the Tarot pack of cards, but its fundamental significance has wider implications. Frazer noted that primitive man endeavours to keep his deities alive by isolating them between heaven and earth, thereby placing them in a position which is immune to ordinary influences (21), especially terrestrial ones. This and every other kind of suspension in space implies, then, a mystical isolation which is doubtless related to the idea of levitation and to dream-flight. On the other hand, the inverted position is in itself a symbol of purification (because it inverts, analogically, the natural, terrestrial order) (50). Both the legend of the Hanged Man as a figure endowed with magic powers, and the Odin myth, belong to this symbolic system. Of Odin it was said that he had sacrificed himself by hanging. The relevant verses of *Havamal* read: 'I know that I have been hanging from the stormy tree for nine consecutive nights, wounded by the spear, as an offering to Odin: myself offered to myself.' Similar sacrifices are part of normal cult-practice in many parts of the world (21). Jung explains this symbolism in purely psychological terms, saying that 'hanging . . . has an unmistakable symbolic value, since swinging (hanging and suffering as one swings) is the symbol of unfulfilled longing or tense expectation' (31). The Tarot card mentioned above depicts a figure like the Minstrel hanging by one foot from a rope tied to a crossbar supported by two leafless trees. The interpretation is that the Hanged Man does not live the ordinary life of this earth, but, instead, lives in a dream of mystical idealism. The strange gallows from which he hangs is yellow in colour to indicate it consists of concentrated light, i.e. concentrated thought. Thus it is said that the Hanged Man hangs from his own doctrine, to which he is attached to such an extent that his entire being hangs upon it. The two trees between which he hangs are related—like anything that is connected with the numerical symbolism of 2—to the Boaz and Jachin pillars of the Cabala. They are coloured green tending to blue (natural or terrestrial nature tending towards heaven). The Hanged Man's clothing is red and white, these being the mystical colours of the two-headed eagle of the alchemists. His arms are tied together, and hold half-opened bags out of which gold coins are tumbling, this being an allegory of the spiritual treasures to be found in the being who performs this self-sacrifice. According to Wirth, the mythological hero closest to this symbolic character is Perseus, the personification of thought in action, who—in his flight—overcame the forces of evil in order to free Andromeda, who symbolizes the soul chained to the dull rock of matter, rising from the waves of the primeval ocean. In the positive sense, number twelve of the Tarot pack stands for mysticism, sacrifice, self-denial, continence. In the negative sense it denotes a Utopian dream-world (59).

Hare In the Egyptian series of hieroglyphs, the hare is a determinative sign defining the concept of being, and symbolic in consequence of elemental existence (19). Among the Algonquin Indians, the Great Hare is the animal-demiurge. The myth was also known to the Egyptians. In Greece, the lunar goddess, Hecate, was associated with hares. The German equivalent of Hecate, the goddess Harek, was accompanied by hares (35). In general, the hare is a symbol of procreation; it is ambivalent in that it may be considered as naturally amoral or moral. The Hebrews regarded it as an 'unclean' animal (Deuteronomy xiv, 7). For Rabanus Maurus, it symbolized lasciviousness and fecundity. However, it had also become, by Gothic times, an allegorical figure of fleetness and of diligent service, for it is to be found on many Gothic sepulchres as an emblem in this particular sense—a sense subsidiary to that outlined above (46). A feminine character is inseparable from the fundamental symbolization of the hare; hence it is not surprising to find that it was the second of the twelve emblems of the Emperor of China, symbolic of the *Yin* force in the life of the monarch (5). The Chinese conceived the hare as an animal of augury and it was said to live on the moon.

Harp Equated with the white horse (4) and the mystic ladder. It acts as a bridge between heaven and earth. This is why, in the Edda, heroes express their desire to have a harp buried with them in their grave, so as to facilitate their access to the other world. There is also a close connexion between the harp and the swan (50). It might also be regarded as a symbol of the tension inherent in the strings with its striving towards love and the supernatural world, a situation of stress which crucifies man in every moment of the anguished expectation of his earthly life. This would explain the detail of Bosch's *Garden of Delights*, where a human figure hangs crucified on the strings of a harp. Music being a symbol of pure manifestation of the Will (Schopenhauer), the harp would seem to be a particularly intense and characteristic embodiment of sound as the carrier of stress and suffering, of form and life-forces (Plate XIV).

Harpies Fabulous beings, daughters of Neptune and the sea, usually regarded as allegories or personifications of vice in its twin aspects of guilt and punishment (8). At a deeper level, they have been defined as a representation of the 'evil harmonies of cosmic energies' (48). Sometimes the emphasis is entirely on their dynamic nature, in which case they are depicted in the well-known attitude of 'swift movement', reminiscent of the swastika. This is also the case with the Erinyes and the Gorgons (41). In mediaeval decorative art they sometimes occur merely as emblems of the sign of Virgo in its musical aspects. In heraldry, the figure of the harpy has no sinister associations (48).

Harpist The symbolism of the harpist follows from that of his instrument. He frequently occurs in literature, one of the most famous examples being in Goethe's *Wilhelm Meister*. In a German poem—*Die Krone*—Guinevere arouses her husband's jealousy by telling him of a knight who rides past every night, singing. . . . Celtic folklore tells how Yseult was abducted by a harp-player. The tale of the Pied Piper describes how the children follow him as he plays a tune on his pipe. All these figures are personifications of the fascination of death, that is, Freud's death-wish. Also, in Greek mythology the psychopomp Hermes is the inventor of the lyre and the flute (35).

Hat According to Jung, the hat, since it covers the head, generally takes on the significance of what goes on inside it: thought. He recalls the German saying 'to put all ideas under one hat', and mentions that in Meyrink's novel *The Golem*, the protagonist thinks the thoughts and undergoes the experiences of another man whose hat he has put on by mistake (32). Jung also points out that, since the hat is the 'crown' and summit of an individual, it may therefore be said to cover him, an idea which carries a special symbolic significance. By its shape, the hat may be invested with specific significance; for example, that of the Minstrel in the Tarot pack (56). To change one's hat is equivalent to a change of mind or of ideas. The choice of a hat—associated with a particular social order —denotes the desire to be admitted to that set or to partake of its inherent characteristics. There are hats, like the Phrygian cap, that have a special phallic significance, and others that can confer invisibility (symbolic of repression).

Hawk An emblem of the soul in ancient Egypt, with the implication of solar transfiguration (57). Nevertheless, Pinedo maintains that it may have been a mediaeval allegory of the evil mind of the sinner. In the cloister at Silos there is an illustration of hawks tearing hares to pieces, and it appears to carry this significance (46), although, given the negative significance of the hare (it symbolizes fecundity, but also lasciviousness), the hawk might be taken as a symbol of victory over concupiscence (since it destroyed the lascivious hares). But this kind of struggle is better represented by the mythic and legendary motif—also frequent in folklore—of the griffin composed of various parts all struggling one against the other, so that it appears at once as executioner and victim.

Head In the Zohar, the 'magic head' stands for astral light (9); in mediaeval art it is a symbol for the mind (46) and for the spiritual life, which explains the frequency with which it appeared in decorative art. On the other hand, Plato in *Timaeus* asserts that 'the human head is the image of the world'. In corroboration of this, Leblant points out that the skull, the semi-spherical crown of the human body, signifies the heavens. Clearly, the head-symbol here coalesces with that of the sphere as a symbol of Oneness. It had the same significance in Egyptian hieroglyphics (19). The eagle's head has been used as a solar symbol and an emblem of the centre-point of emanation—that is, of the cosmic flame and the spiritual fire of the universe (4). Two, three or four heads shown in juxtaposition symbolize a corresponding intensification of a given aspect of head-symbolism. Thus, the Gemini, a symbol of the duality of Nature, or of the integrating (but not unifying) link between the two principles of creation, are represented by beings with two heads or two faces, like the Roman Janus for example. Hecate is depicted with three heads—she is called triform for this reason—a symbolism which may be related to the 'three levels' of heaven, earth and hell, as well as to Diel's three 'urges of life' (15). The juxtaposition of four heads or faces, as in the image of Brahma the Supreme Lord, stems from the same symbolism as that of the tetramorph (60). A factor of major importance bearing upon the symbolism of the head is mentioned by Herbert Kühn, in his *L'Ascension de l'humanité* (Paris, 1958). He makes the point that the decapitation of corpses in prehistoric times marked Man's discovery of the independence of the spiritual principle, residing in the head, as opposed to the vital principle represented by the body as a whole. Kühn adds that Neolithic thought was very close to the mediaeval in its conviction that an eternal and invisible essence underlies all appearances (Plate XV).

Head-dress and Throne In ancient, oriental cultures, and especially in Mesopotamia and India, there is always a formal and significant relationship between all the objects and edifices related to any one particular cult. For example, as Eliade notes, there is an inner and outer analogy between head-dress, thrones and palaces in Babylonian traditions: all three refer to the 'Centre' (17). And Luc Benoist has observed of Hindu cults that the altar, the temple, the throne, the palace, the city, the kingdom and the world are all by implication images of the 'Centre', their direct model being mount Meru (the centre of the world). The processional carriage is a temple-on-wheels (6), with all the 'correspondences' implied.

Heart In the vertical scheme of the human body, the focal points are three in number: the brain, the heart and the sexual organs. But the central point is the heart, and in consequence it comes to partake of the meanings of the other two. The heart was the only part of the viscera left by the Egyptians in the mummy, since it was regarded as the centre indispensable to the body in eternity; for all centres are symbols of eternity, since time is the motion of the periphery of the wheel of phenomena rotating around the Aristotelian 'unmoved mover'. In traditional ways of thought, the heart was taken as the true seat of intelligence, the brain being merely instrumental (25); hence, in ancient attempts to explain the profound and continuing analogies between concepts, the moon was said to correspond to the brain and the sun to the heart. All representations of the 'Centre' have been related in some way to the heart, either through correspondences or through substitution, as in the case of the goblet, the coffer and the cavern. For the alchemists, the heart was the image of the sun within man, just as gold was the image of the sun on earth (32). The importance of love in the mystic doctrine of unity explains how it is that love-symbolism came to be closely linked with heart-symbolism, for to love is only to experience a force which urges the lover towards a given centre. In emblems, then, the heart signifies love as the centre of illumination and happiness, and this is why it is surmounted by flames, or a cross, or a fleur-de-lis, or a crown (4).

Hearth A form of 'domestic sun', a symbol of the home, of the conjunction of the masculine principle (fire) with the feminine (the receptacle) and, consequently, of love (49).

Heat For Jung, heat is an image of the libido (31). Any representation—or even the mere mention—of heat always bears a symbolic relation to maturation, whether biological or spiritual (32). In emblems of the sun, it is portrayed as wavy lines alternating with the straight lines representing light. We should also bear in mind all the correspondences which exist between heat and tones, sounds, colours, the seasons, etc.

Heaven Here is Luc Benoist's version of a passage about heaven taken from the *Chândogya Upanishad*: 'In the beginning, all the universe was non-being. It became being. It grew and formed an egg, which remained unbroken for a year. Then it broke open. Of the two halves of the shell, one was of silver and the other of gold.' The latter was heaven, while the former became earth. In Hindu architecture, these two halves are represented by the altar and the *stupa* (6). One can clearly see in all this how the myth arose from converging formal analogies. Heaven has always been considered, except in Egypt, as part of the masculine or active principle, associated with things of the spirit and with the number three, whereas the earth is related to the feminine, passive or material principle, and the number four. Mircea Eliade has something to say about the. symbolism of heaven which is rather less abstract and therefore fails to be so cosmogonic: the azure of the sky, he suggests, is the veil which hides the divine face. The clouds are his garments. The light of heaven is the ointment with which he anoints his immense body. The stars are his eyes (17). Again: among oriental peoples, the dome of heaven is associated with the nomad's tent—quite apart from the usual heaven/earth association—as if they had a presentiment that three-dimensional space is only a kind of lid which prevents Man from penetrating into the mystery of the other world. Celestial space, then, ceases to be a container and becomes content of hyperspace, or rather, of trans-space. A terrible aspect of heaven can be seen in the myth of the cosmic catastrophe which William Blake appears to have had in mind when he wrote of 'the angry religion of the stars' (3). We must also remember that, from the earliest times, heaven has been thought of as consisting of several heavens, owing to the tendency of primitive logic to assign a separate, cellular space to each celestial body or group of bodies, a tendency which anticipates the theory of gravitation, the gravitational field and the laws of organic structures, and which illuminates the very essence of the relationship between the qualitative (the discontinuous) and the quantitative (the continuous) (Plate XVI).

Hecate A symbol of the Terrible Mother, appearing as the tutelar deity of Medea or as a lamia who devours men. She is a personification of the moon, or of the evil side of the feminine principle, responsible for madness, obsession and lunacy. Her attributes are the key, the lash, the dagger and the torch (31).

He-Goat The he-goat is a kind of scape-goat—a symbol of the projection of one's own guilt upon someone else, and of the consequent repression of one's conscience. Hence the traditional significance of the he-goat as an emissary, and its evil association with the devil (15). It is also, like the bull, a father-symbol (50).

Helios Helios signifies the sun in its astronomic aspect, just as Apollo symbolizes it in its spiritual aspect. In ancient cults, he appears as a god who presides over the seasons, vegetation, fecundity and the fruitfulness of the earth (15).

Helmet In heraldic symbolism, it is an emblem of lofty thoughts, or of hidden thoughts if the vizor is lowered. This latter aspect corresponds to the general symbolism of invisibility, which is thus equated with the hood and the hat (38), although this seems to be a clear case of undue emphasis upon one meaning at the expense of all the others. The inevitable and intimate association of the helmet with the head has an important bearing upon the relation between two symbols: thus, a helmet with a strange crest may be a symbol of highly imaginative or restless exhilaration. The hat, the hood and the mantilla have the same intimate, symbolic association with the head: their colour usually denotes the wearer's prevailing shade of thought.

Hemispheres In Egyptian hieroglyphics, the semicircle with the diameter as the base is a sign representing the sun's orbit and also the hemisphere. It symbolizes the Origin counterbalanced by the End—or birth counterbalanced by death. Grammatically, this hieroglyph expresses the feminine principle balancing the masculine (19).

Herald at Arms Like Egyptian and Chaldean scribes, heralds at arms are repositories of hermetic wisdom and, therefore, 'keepers of secrets', according to Alleau in *De la Nature des symboles* (Paris, 1958). Heralds at arms are related to shield-bearers and to the standard-bearers of ancient armies (e.g. the Roman *aquilifer*, or eagle-bearer).

Heraldic Symbols The outward components of heraldry (crowns, helmets, mantles, lambrequins, supporters, chains), like the inner elements (or arms: colours, metals, furs, parties, noble quarterings, figures), apart from their literal or anecdotal senses, have a symbolic significance, according to Cadet de Gassicourt and the Baron du Roure de Paulin, in *L'Hermétisme et l'art héraldique* (Paris, 1907). (Piobb supports their opinion in his review of the book in *L'Année occultiste et psychique*, 1907.) Metals and colours may be 'read' in terms of their own particular symbolism; parties and noble quarterings by spatial and graphic symbolism, as well as by their implicit 'correspondences'. Heraldic art recognizes five colours or enamels and two metals: gold (the Sun), silver (the Moon), gules (red—Mars), sinople (green—Venus), azure (Jupiter), purple (Mercury) and sable (Saturn). The symbolic meanings of colours, metals and parties are considered as products of the active (or spiritual) principle of the shield-of-arms working upon the passive, quaternary material symbolized by the surface of the shield. City coats-of-arms may be explained along similar lines, according to Gérard de Sède who, in *Les Templiers sont parmi nous* (Paris, 1962), suggests that the ship in the shield of the City of Paris may derive from the myth of the Argonauts, the quest for the Golden Fleece and the alchemical Work.

Herbs Herbs sometimes have the symbolic significance of human beings. This is suggested by the etymology of the Greek *neophytos* ('new herb') (17). They are also related to the idea of natural forces, both of good and evil. Because they can be both medicinal and poisonous, herbs are very commonly featured in legends and folktales, as well as in magic. The business of cataloguing the different characteristics of each herb or plant is clearly a matter for specialized study.

Hercules As a hero, Hercules became a symbol of the individual freeing himself in the quest for immortality, expiating his sins and errors through suffering and 'heroic striving'. In this way he was able, for his own sake and for that of his brother (whose existence relates Hercules to the Gemini-myth), to conquer, exterminate or master all monsters (symbolic of plagues, vices and the forces of evil) within the ordered and gradual process of the evolutionary struggle (15). His attributes are the club (a symbol of overwhelming force, of annihilation—not merely of victory) and the Nemean lion's skin (a solar symbol) (8). Hercules was unable to undertake a new task until after he had brought his previous trial to a successful con- clusion. Hence alchemists, from Antiquity to the Middle Ages, would interpret the myth of Hercules-the-hero as a configuration of the spiritual struggle which leads to the 'conquest of the golden apples in the Garden of the Hesperides'—or immortality. Piobb has linked the twelve trials of Hercules with the signs of the Zodiac—thus confirming his character as a solar hero recognized by mythologists —as follows: his victory over the giants such as Geryon and Cacus with Aries; the Cretan bull with Taurus; the pillars with the Gemini; the hydra of Lerna and the birds of lake Stymphalus with Cancer; the lion of Nemea with Leo; the Amazons with Virgo; the walls of Troy and the Augean stables with Libra; the boar of Erymanthus with Scorpio; the centaurs and the mares of Diomedes with Sagittarius; the stag of the golden horns with Capricorn; the eagle and Prometheus with Aquarius; and the monster which attacked Hesione with Pisces (48).

Hermaphrodite   Hermaphrodite deities, connected with the myth of birth (19), are found on many Egyptian monuments: for example, the pedestal of one of the colossi at Memnon. The hermaphrodite is a consequence of applying the symbolism of the number two to the human being, creating a personality which is integrated despite its duality. In India, this dual being—two sexes united in a single personality—was the primal force, the light from which life emanates (49), that is to say, the *lingam* (60). The myth of the hermaphrodite was also known in pre-Columbian Mexico, in the figure of Quetzalcoatl, the god in whom the laws of opposites and of the separate sexes are finally united. The hermaphrodite is, above all, a god of procreation (41), closely linked, and ultimately identified, with the Gemini archetype. Plato, in the *Symposium*, states that the Gods first created Man in the form of a sphere incorporating two bodies and both sexes. This shows to what extent he subjected reality to symbolic and conceptual patterns and how—in a characteristically Greek manner—he permitted mortals to partake of such qualities as hermaphroditism, which were generally regarded as exclusive to the more primitive gods (8). Psychologically, it must not be overlooked that the concept of hermaphroditism represents a formula (which, like most mythic formulas, is only an approxima- tion) of 'totality', of the 'integration of opposites' (17). In other words, it expresses in sexual—and hence very obvious—terms the essential idea that all pairs of opposites are integrated into Oneness. For Eliade, hermaphroditism is, therefore, simply an archaic form

ARDANARI ISWARA.

One of many representations of the Hermaphrodite, with symbolic coiling snake and lotus
(from C. J. W. Olliver, *An Analysis of Magic and Witchcraft*).

of divine bi-unity. Magic-religious thinking first stated this concept in biological terms, before clothing it in metaphysical (*esse non esse*) or theological language (the revealed or non-revealed world). The androgynous divinity was also known in China and in many other countries (Persia, Palestine, Australia, etc.) (17). In the androgynous myth we see, however, not only an expression of the cause but also of the controlling spiritual energy. This is very clearly brought out by Ely Star when he says that no happiness, unless it be one of the exceptions mentioned by St. Paul, can prove satisfying until it is made whole by marriage (which is an imperfect image of hermaphroditism), since the spirit always manifests itself as a segregated form in the world of existence, and this is a source of suffering and restlessness (54). Thus, the Hermaphrodite is not only linked to the remote Platonic past, but also projected into the future. In addition, it is clearly a symbol of an intellectual activity which is not in itself connected with the problem of the sexes. Blavatsky says that all peoples regarded their first god as androgynous, because Primitive humanity knew that he had sprung from 'the mind', as is shown by many traditions such as that of Minerva springing from the head of Jupiter (9). In alchemy, the Hermaphrodite plays an important rôle as Mercury; he is depicted as a two-headed figure, often accompanied by the word *Rebis* (double thing).

Hermit, The   The ninth enigma of the Tarot pack. It is an allegory of an old man carrying in his right hand a lantern partially covered by one of the folds of his cloak, which is dark outside (signifying withdrawal and austerity) but with a blue lining (representing aerial nature). If he finds the serpent of the instincts in his path, he does not destroy it but simply charms it into twining itself round his staff, as Aesculapius did. He is a master of the invisible. On the positive side, the hermit signifies tradition, study, reserve, patient and profound work. On the negative, he stands for all that is taciturn, tedious and meticulous (59).

Hero, The   The cult of the hero has been found necessary not only because of the exigencies of war, but because of the virtues inherent in heroism—virtues which have surely been apparent to Man from prehistoric times and which he has felt the need to exalt, emphasize and record. The magic, the apparatus and the splendour of the very appurtenances of the ancient warrior proclaim the truth of this, as does the custom of according an acclamation worthy of kings to the conquering hero. The relationship between the 'little holy war', that is the struggle with the material enemies outside, and the 'Great Holy War', or combat with the spiritual enemies inside the personality, inevitably gave rise to the same relationship being drawn between the hero of the 'little war' and the champion of the 'Great War'. Every heroic characteristic finds its analogy among the virtues necessary to vanquish chaos and overcome the temptations offered by the forces of darkness. This explains why, in many myths, the sun was identified with the hero *par excellence*. Hence, Alexander the Great is pictured on coins with the horns of Jupiter Ammon, that is, he is identified with the awakening sun of Spring under the sign of Aries. And this leads Jung to state that the most widely accepted of all the symbols of the libido—and he could equally well have said 'the spirit'—is the human figure as the hero— the subject of so many myths, legends and traditional tales. He adds that in the life destined for the hero, the historical and the symbolic are one and the same thing. The first object of the hero is to conquer himself; and this is the reason why the heroes of Germanic legends are usually portrayed with the eyes of a snake. The mythic hero, Cecrops, is half-man and half-serpent (31). A hero turned Christian is a hero turned knight, with the aid of the saintly warriors such as St. George and St. Michael (Plate XVII).

Heron Among the Egyptians, a symbol of the morning and of the generation of life. Together with the ibis and the stork, it carried a favourable significance (4).

Hesperides, The They are the daughters of Atlas and Hesperis. They lived in a garden with trees bearing golden apples, watched over by a dragon. Hercules took possession of these apples, following upon his victory over the guardian dragon. Vossius explained this myth by an astronomical analogy, whereby the Hesperides become eventide, the garden becomes the firmament, the golden apples the stars, the dragon the Zodiac and Hercules the sun (8). But this interpretation does not invalidate the psychology implicit in all the other symbols connected with this myth, in particular that of the hero and the treasure acquired only after great exertions.

Hieroglyphics Under this heading are grouped representative ideographs, i.e. comprising schematic images of objects, to which may be added others, more simple or more abstract. In itself, the basic concept of hieroglyphics is similar to that of the enigma. By antonomasia, hieroglyphics are confined to those of the Egyptian civilization (which recognized three forms of writing: hieroglyphic, hieratic and demotic). The hieroglyphic system attained a total of 900 signs (representative of ideas, syllables, words and letters, or their complements = determinatives). Because of its complexity, it was mastered only by the priestly caste, and, by Roman times, people were already beginning to forget how to decipher it. Horapollo Niliacus attempted to restore it in the 2nd and 3rd centuries of our era, taking symbolism as his basis. The subject was forgotten for centuries, until Father Athanasius Kircher revived it during the 17th century. Anybody interested in this subject should consult the work by Madeleine V.-David, *Le Débat sur les écritures et l'hiéroglyphe aux XVIIe. et XVIIIe. siècles* (Paris, 1965), which is a modern, symbolic, profound interpretation, based on that of Enel in *La langue sacrée*.

Hippalectryon A fabulous animal, half-horse and half-cock, and probably a sun-symbol.

Hippogryph A fabulous animal, half-horse and half-griffin, which Ariosto and other authors of books of chivalry gave to their heroes for a steed. It is a kind of supercharged Pegasus, a blend of the favourable aspects of the griffin and the winged horse in its character as the 'spiritual mount' (8).

Hippopotamus In the Egyptian system of hieroglyphs, it represents strength and vigour. It is also related to the ideas of fertility and water, and, consequently, to the mother-principle (19).

Hog A symbol of impure desires, of the transmutation of the higher into the lower and of the amoral plunge into corruption (15).

Hole A very important symbol, with two main aspects: on the biological level, it has fertilizing power and is related to fertility rites; on the spiritual plane, it stands for the 'opening' of this world on to the other world. Worship of 'perforated stones' in one form or another is very common all over the world. Eliade notes that, in the region of Amance, there is just such a stone in front of which women kneel to pray for the health of their children. To this day, in Paphos, barren women crawl through the hole of such a stone. Primitive Indian peoples were mainly concerned with its symbolism at the physical level, identifying the hole with the female sexual organs, although they too had an intuitive awareness of the fact that holes could stand for the 'gateway of the world', which the soul has to cross in order to be released from the cycle of *karma* (17). In the *Brihadaranyaka Upanishad* it is said that 'when a human being leaves this world, he makes his way through the air, and the air opens up for him as wide as a cartwheel' (50). The artistic expression of this symbol is found in the Chinese *Pi*, i.e. the representation of heaven. It is a jade disc with a hole in the middle; measurements vary from case to case, but according to the Chinese dictionary *Erh Ya*, the relation between the outside ring and the central hole remains constant. This hole is the Hindu 'gateway', also the Aristotelian 'unvarying mean' or 'unmoved mover'. The origins of the *Pi* are exceedingly remote, and carved and decorated *Pi* have also been found (39). As a symbol of heaven, the hole also stands specifically for the passage from spatial to non-spatial, from temporal to non-temporal existence, and corresponds to the zenith (52). The strange and roughly hewn door-openings of some neolithic stone-structures have been interpreted by some scholars as symbolic holes in the above sense; the laborious nature of these holes could otherwise have been avoided by means of the simple and well-known pillar-and-lintel method of construction. An outstanding example of this kind of door is that at Hagiar Kim (Malta). It is interesting to note, in this connexion, that the initiation ceremony among the Pomo Indians of Northern California includes a ritual blow from a grizzly bear paw, which is supposed to make a hole in the neophyte's back, on account of which he 'dies' and is reborn to a new stage of life. It is probable that, from the earliest times, the visual aspect of wounds helped to strengthen the association between the concept of the hole and that of passing into the other life. All this seems to be corroborated by the fact that in many symbolist pictures, e.g. in Gustave Moreau's *Orpheus*, the background landscape includes perforated rocks which are evidently invested with a transcendental significance. It is also worth recalling Salvador Dali's frequent practice, amounting almost to an obsession, of painting holes (regular in shape, like windows) on the backs of some of his figures.

Hollow A hollow is the abstract aspect of the cavern, and the inverse of the mountain. There are many symbolic significances superimposed upon the basic sense of the hollow, such as that of the Abode of the Dead, of Memories and of the Past, with further allusions to the mother and also to the unconscious (15), as the link between all these different aspects.

Honey In Orphic tradition, honey is a symbol of wisdom. The occult maxim 'the bees are born from the oxen' finds its explanation in the astrological relationship between Taurus and Cancer (40) and in the symbolic use of the ox as a sign for sacrifice, expressive of the idea that there is no higher knowledge without suffering. Honey was also credited with other meanings: rebirth or change of personality consequent upon initiation; and, in India, the superior self (comparable with fire). Given that honey is the product of a mysterious and elaborate process, it is easy to understand how it came by analogy to symbolize the spiritual exercise of self-improvement (56).

Hood The hood or cone-shaped hat often figures in ancient and mediaeval iconography. It is to be related with the Phrygian cap and other similar forms of headgear which are to be seen in Greek and Roman art. A relief of the 14th century shows Parsifal armed with two lances and wearing the cone-shaped cap characteristic of the Cabiri. It seems that the hood unites and blends together the two separate meanings of the cape and the hat; in addition, its shape and its colour contribute further to the symbolism as a whole (32). In Jung's view, the hood, since it envelopes practically the whole of the head and is almost spherical in shape, comes to symbolize the highest sphere, that is, the celestial world (represented symbolically by the bell, the vault, the upper part of the sand-bag and the double-pumpkin, as well as by the skull) (32). Furthermore, covering one's head signifies invisibility, that is, death. For this reason, the initiated appear in some scenes in ancient mystery plays with their heads covered by a cloak. Jung rounds off the presentation of his evidence with this piece of information: 'Among the Nandi, of East Africa, the newly-circumcised, the initiates, have to go about for a long time dressed in queer cone-shaped grass hats, which envelop them completely and reach to the ground. The circumcised have become invisible, i.e., spirits. The veil has the same significance among nuns' (31). Diel confirms this interpretation, taking the hood as a symbolic agent of repression or that which renders the psychic content invisible (15).

Horns Some of the unfavourable interpretations of horn-symbolism are due to the all-too-common association with the ancient symbol of the ox (standing for castration, sacrifice and persistent toil), or perhaps also as a result of 'symbolic inversion'. For, in fact, all primitive traditions prove that the horn is a symbol of strength and power. Hides and battle-helmets were adorned with horns from prehistoric times right up to the Middle Ages. The horn played its part in the decorative art of Asiatic temples; like the bucraneum (representing sacrificial remains), the horn was considered sacred. The precise meaning of the horn-symbol was understood as far back as Egyptian times. In their system of hieroglyphs, the sign of the horn indicates 'what is above the head' and, by extension, 'to open up a path for oneself' (in which it is comparable with the ram's head, Aries and the battering-ram). It is a striking fact that the signs which initiate the cycle of the Zodiac (Aries and Taurus) are both represented by horned animals (19). The relevant Egyptian hieroglyph also enters into composite words signifying elevation, prestige, glory, etc. (19). The single horn pertains in essence—apart from its employment in the emblem of the cornucopia or as a musical instrument—to the fabulous unicorn and the rhinoceros. The horn of the latter, carved out in the form of a cup, is one of the 'common emblems' of China, and stands for prosperity (and therefore for strength) (5). The same belief is found among the Gnostics, who expressly state that the horn symbolizes the 'principle which bestows maturity and beauty upon all things'. Jung offers the explanation that the horn is a dual symbol: from one point of view it is penetrating in shape, and therefore active and masculine in significance; and from the other, it is shaped like a receptacle, which is feminine in meaning (32). As a musical instrument, it figures in emblems symbolizing the spiritual call to join the Holy War. This particular meaning is corroborated by the crosses, trefoils, circles and fleurs-de-lis associated with the horn (4). Horns are the attributes of the Cilician god of agriculture. He holds handfuls of corn, symbolizing fertility.

Horse The symbolism of the horse is extremely complex, and beyond a certain point not very clearly defined. Eliade finds it an animal associated with burial-rites in chthonian cults (17), whereas Mertens Stienon considers it an ancient symbol of the cyclic movement of the world of phenomena; hence the horses, which Neptune with his trident lashes up out of the waves, symbolize the cosmic forces that surge out of the Akasha—the blind forces of primigenial chaos (39). Applying this latter concept to the biopsychological plane, Diel concludes that the horse stands for intense desires and instincts, in accordance with the general symbolism of the steed-and the vehicle (15). The horse plays an important part in a great number of ancient rites. The ancient Rhodians used to make an annual sacrifice to the sun of a four-horse quadriga, which they would hurl into the sea (21). The animal was also dedicated to Mars, and the sudden appearance of a horse was thought to be an omen of war (8). In Germany and England, to dream of a white horse was thought to be an omen of death (35). It is very interesting to note that the great myth and symbol of the Gemini, illustrated in pairs or twins, in two-headed beasts or in anthropomorphic figures with four eyes and four arms, etc., appears, too, in horse-symbolism, especially in the form of a pair of horses, one white and one black, representing life and death. The Indian Asvins—the probable source of Castor and Pollux—would depict themselves as horsemen. In mediaeval illustrations of the Zodiac, the sign for the Gemini is sometimes portrayed in this way, as for example in the Zodiac of Notre Dame de Paris (39). Considering that the horse pertains to the natural, unconscious, instinctive zone, it is not surprising that, in Antiquity, it should often have been endowed with certain powers of divination (8). In fable and legend, horses, being clairvoyant, are often assigned the task of giving a timely warning to their masters, as in the Grimms' fable, for example. Jung came to wonder if the horse might not be a symbol for the mother, and he does not hesitate to assert that it expresses the magic side of Man, 'the mother within us', that is, intuitive understanding. On the other hand, he recognizes that the horse is a symbol pertaining to Man's baser forces, and also to water, which explains why the horse is associated with Pluto and Neptune (56). Deriving from the magical nature of the horse, is the belief that the horse-shoe brings luck. On account of his fleetness, the horse can also signify the wind and sea-foam, as well as fire and light. In the *Brihadaranyaka Upanishad* (I, 1), the horse is actually a symbol of the cosmos (31) (Plate XVIII).

Hour-Glass A symbol denoting the inversion of the relations between the Upper and Lower Worlds—an inversion encompassed periodically by Shiva (or Siva), the lord of creation and destruction. Connected with it are the drum—similar in shape—and the cross of St. Andrew; the symbolic significance of all three is identical (51).

Hours, The   In the *Iliad*, the hours are personifications of the atmospheric moisture: they open and close the gates of Olympus, form and disperse the clouds, govern the seasons and human life. While they were performing these duties, they were regarded as daughters of Zeus and Themis, bearing such names as Eunomia, Dike and Irene, representing Law, Justice and Peace. All twelve constitute the retinue of Eos and are depicted ranged around the sun-throne or busily coupling the horses to the sun-chariot. We must observe, therefore: (*a*) that they are expressive of cosmic forces; (*b*) that they personify *moments* of these forces and therefore create the *opportunities* for human action. Their position, surrounding the sun, is analogous to the way angels (red and blue—positive and negative) are depicted encircling the mandorla of God in Christian iconography.

House   Mystics have always traditionally considered the feminine aspect of the universe as a chest, a house or a wall, as well as an enclosed garden. Another symbolic association is that which equates the house (and the above, related forms) with the repository of all wisdom, that is, tradition itself (4). In architectural symbolism, on the other hand, the house carries not only an overall symbolism but also particular associations attached to each of its component parts. Nevertheless, the house as a home arouses strong, spontaneous associations with the human body and human thought (or life, in other words), as has been confirmed empirically by psychoanalysts. Ania Teillard explains this by pointing out that, in dreams, we employ the image of the house as a representation of the different layers of the psyche. The outside of the house signifies the outward appearance of Man: his personality or his mask. The various floors are related to the vertical and spatial symbols. The roof and upper floor correspond to the head and the mind, as well as to the conscious exercise of self-control. Similarly, the basement corresponds to the unconscious and the instincts (just as sewers do, in symbols pertaining to the city). The kitchen, since this is where foodstuff is transformed, sometimes signifies the place or the moment of psychic transmutation in the alchemical sense. The intercommunicating rooms speak for themselves. The stairs are the link between the various planes of the psyche, but their particular significance depends upon whether they are seen as ascending or descending. Finally, there is, as we have said, the association of the house with the human body, especially regarding its openings, as was well understood by Artemidorus Daldianus (56).

Hunter In Ludovico Dolce's *Le Transformationi*, the following scene is described: In a clearing in a wood there is a small lake, with a man, kneeling, gazing into the surface of the water—a symbol of contemplation. In the background, a hunter on horseback, with a pack of dogs, is in pursuit of his prey—a symbol of action for its own sake, of repetition, of the pursuit of transitoriness, of the will to remain (as the Hindu phrase has it) on the 'wheel of reincarnations'. Lao-Tse (58) taught that racing and hunting only serve to madden the heart of Man, thus revealing that the enemy is within: that it is desire itself. Similarly, Zagreus—another name for Dionysos—means 'the Great Hunter' and stands for the insatiable incontinence of desire (15), according to the moral interpretation of Diel. For those who prefer a cosmic interpretation, the myth of the infernal hunt, in which colour and form are mixed together without rhyme or reason, alludes to the howling wind (3). The Arabs identify this wind with both the hunter and death (35). The figure of the accursed hunter is one which is to be found in a great many mythologies, traditions, legends and folktales. The following passage taken from Julio Caro Baroja will illuminate many aspects of the myth, and clarify what we have already said: 'A Basque tradition (*Abade chacurra*: the abbot's dogs) has it that an abbot or priest, much drawn to hunting, was saying Mass just as a hare happened to run past. The Abbot's dogs caught its scent and rushed out, howling, after it; the abbot deserted the Most Holy Sacrament, and hastened out of the temple after his dogs in pursuit of the prey. Henceforth, as a punishment, he was condemned to an endless chase, whirling across the plains behind his howling dogs, never to run down the quarry he so bootlessly pursues.' This is clearly a case of a symbol for a 'limiting situation', that is, of a falling away from the centre—or the tendency to do so—towards the endlessly turning periphery of the wheel of phenomena: unending because self-delusion is a perpetual incitement to the sterile urge of the pursuit of worldly things. In other versions the hare is the devil disguised. This theme of the accursed hunter is to be found called, variously. 'The Black Hunter', 'The Wicked Hunter' or 'The King's Dog'. It is derived from the myth of Odin, the god of souls. Amongst the so-called Celtic peoples, Odin has been replaced by King Arthur or Arthus, as is shown by the 'chasses du roi Arthus', traditional in Normandy. There are other similar traditions, such as the 'chasse Annequin' in Normandy, 'Manihennequin' in the Vosges, the 'chasse Saint Hubert' and 'du Grand Veneur' (10). In Dontenville's view, an important mythic precedent is to be found in Meleager and the boar (16).

Hurricane Anthropologists have found that many graphic symbols owe their origin to the hurricane—especially in America.

This is true, for instance, of the sigma, the double sigma and the swastika. But at the same time, the hurricane has a symbolic meaning of its own. Ortiz observes that the hurricane, like celestial bodies, has two characteristic motions: rotary and sideways. In its sidewise motion, there is an intermediary point of absolute calm: the so-called 'eye of the hurricane'. For American aborigines, the hurricane is cosmic synergy, since it contains three Elements within itself (fire or light-rays, air or wind, water or rain) and disturbs the fourth—earth. It was worshipped as a deity of the winds and waters, and also of the heavens (41). This latter aspect of its correspondences brings us once again to the celebrated and persistent celestial symbol of the 'hole' in the disc of Chinese jade, representing the concept of the zenith as a void through which one may pass out of the world of space and time into spacelessness and timelessness.

Hyle Hyle is protomatter, a symbol of the passive, feminine, primordial principle. According to Nicomachus of Gerasa, the pristine state of chaos of the hyle was fecundated by Number. Hildegard of Bingen (1098-1179), the abbess of Rupertsberg, in *Scivias*, describes cosmogonic visions in which *Nous* blends and harmonizes with the monster chaos (14).

Ibis The ibis is related to Thoth, the Egyptian god of wisdom. According to the Greek scholar Aelian, in his *De Natura Animalium*, this bird was chosen because it tucks its head under its wing when it sleeps, so that it comes to resemble the shape of the heart; and also because of the fact that the stride of the ibis measures exactly a cubit (which was the measure used in the building of temples), and because it destroyed harmful insects (19). There were two kinds of ibis: the white bird (associated with the moon) and the black. The belief was that Thoth hovered over the Egyptian people in the form of an *Ibis religiosa*, and that he taught them the occult arts and sciences (9).

Ice Given that water is the symbol of communication between the formal and the informal, the element of transition between different cycles, yielding by nature, and also related to the ideas of material, earthly fecundity and the Heraclitean 'death of the soul', it follows that ice represents principally two things: first, the change induced in water by the cold—that is, the 'congelation' of its symbolic significance; and, secondly, the stultification of the potentialities of water. Hence ice has been defined as the rigid dividing-line between consciousness and the unconscious (or between any other dynamic levels) (56). Although the negative sense is predominant, it is not lacking in a positive sense in so far as the solidification is tantamount to toughness, and the coldness implies resistance to all that is inferior; in this latter sense it corresponds to Nietzsche's freezing and 'hostile' air of mountain-peaks.

Identities Many symbols can, like the gods of old, be equated, relatively speaking, one with another. For example: the Ship of Fools and the Endless Chase (of the Accursed Hunter); or the 'centre' of the cross and the Holy Grail; or the centaur and the Gemini; or Pandora's box and effulgence. In the proper application of identities lies much of the true science of symbolism.

Image A pattern of forms and figures endowed with unity and significance. It is implied in the theory of form—and is true, also, of melody—that the whole is greater than the sum of its parts being, in a sense, their origin and justification. If for Sartre the image is a degraded awareness of knowing, for other psychologists the image is, in fact, the highest form that knowing can assume, for all knowledge tends towards a visual synthesis. Also to be borne in mind is the theory propounded by Sir Herbert Read in *Icon and Idea*, according to which every creation in the visual arts—and, in fact, every kind of pattern—is a form of thought and therefore corresponds to an intelligible mental concept. This leads us towards an intuition of the world as a vast repertoire of signs that await being 'read'. We may note here that some of the works of Trithemius and Athanasius Kircher tend towards this interpretation.

Image, Pictorial Every pictorial creation gives rise to an image, whether imitative or invented, with or without figuration. Alongside the symbolic meaning which subjects or figures may have, they possess, in a pictorial image, a symbolic background: spatial zones, colours, geometric or non-geometric forms, predominant axes, rhythms, composition and texture. In the most recent type of art, known as 'informalism', expression and symbolization are achieved through texture and lineal rhythm in particular, with colour taking a secondary rôle. To find the 'meaning' of a given work, one must think in terms of putting its elements in the order of their importance, assessing each kind of element within the pictorial system. Exactly the same thing occurs in architecture and sculpture.

Imago Ignota From about the middle of the last century, the tendency of poetry and the visual arts has been towards a mode of expression whose antecedents go back through the ages—but received a particular impetus, around the year 1800, from the works of William Blake—and which might, with justification, be termed hermetic. This movement was characterized by the quest for the obscure as a self-sufficient goal, and by the representation of 'harmonious wholes' whose fascination lies in their remoteness. There is an illuminating definition of poetry in this sense by the German poet Gottfried Benn: 'The writing of poetry is the elevation of things into the language of the incomprehensible.' It is this type of unfamiliar pattern that constitutes the 'unknown image'—a pattern of words, shapes or colours that has no correspondence with the normal, either in the world of exterior reality or in that of normal, human feelings. These 'unknown images' create their own kind of reality and express the spiritual need of particular individuals to live within this created reality. They symbolize, in sum, the unknown, the antecedents and the aftermath of man, or that which surrounds him and which his senses and his intelligence are incapable of apprehending or of appropriating. The scope of the unknown is immense, for it encompasses the Supreme Mystery or the Mystery of mysteries (the secret of the cosmos and of creation and the nature of Being), and also the psychological—and, indeed, existential —mystery of the 'unexplored'. What is unknown is that which is unformed. The 'unknown image' is also related to death and to the thread which connects death with life (Plate XIX).

Impossibilities This theme of the 'impossible' is one which appears very frequently in legends and folktales, embracing, for example, the life of the unborn, or the fruit of one tree growing upon another, etc. Some refrains reflect the same ideas, such as the well-known Spanish saying: 'Over the sea run the hares, over the mountain the sardines.' They may well be symbols of Inversion, but it seems clear that they are more likely to pertain to subversion. There is a possible relationship between such impossibilities, as well as errors or comedies of mistaken identity—likewise owing their origin to folklore—and the belief in the existence of beings, imps and goblins bent upon creating disorder. Father La Peña, in his work *El ente dilucidado*, has discussed the problem of whether men can live without eating, whether they can fly, and so on. In short, all these examples may be interpreted as a 'call to chaos': symbols of the regressive, orgiastic desire (10), comparable with certain aspects of surrealism.

Incest Whereas the union of analogous matter is a symbol of incest—in music, for example, the idea of a concerto for harp and piano—incest in itself symbolizes, according to Jung, the longing for union with the essence of one's own self, or, in other words, for individuation. This explains why the gods of antiquity very frequently engendered offspring through incestuous relationships (33).

Instruments Symbolically, they are objective portrayals of potentialities, actions and desires. Each instrument, therefore, possesses a purely literal meaning, as well as a further significance when it is applied to the psychological and spiritual plane.

Intersection The intersection of two lines, objects or paths is a sign of 'Conjunction' and communication, but also of symbolic Inversion, that is, of that point or zone where a transcendental change of direction is induced or sought. This is what lies behind the superstitious crossing of fingers or of objects. In medicinal dances, swords and iron bars are crossed in order to encourage a change (that is, a cure), or, to put it another way, to alter the course of a process so that it does not reach its ordinary or expected outcome (51).

Intestines An Egyptian determinative sign defining the concept of circulation (19). In a broader sense, intestines carry the same symbolism as the alembic. They are also connected with the labyrinth and with death (the return to the interior of the earth = mother, along the 'curved way' = Saturn's scythe).

Inversion According to Schneider, the continuity of life is assured by the mutual sacrifice which is consummated on the peak of the mystic mountain: death permits birth; all opposites are for an instant fused together and then inverted. What is constructive turns to destruction; love turns to hate; evil to good; unhappiness to happiness; martyrdom to ecstasy. Corresponding to this inner inversion of a process is an outer inversion of the symbol pertaining to it. This gives rise to a reversed arrangement of the symbolic structure. When the symbol has two aspects, the inversion of one determines that of the other. So, for example, if what is below is black and it seeks to ascend, it may do so by turning white. Or, conversely, if what is black is below and seeks to turn to white, then let it ascend and white it will be. This 'symbolic logic' of Inversion is, it hardly needs to be said, closely bound up with the myth of sacrifice. The more terrible the situation, the more urgent the need to transform and invert it (as in a public calamity or an unsuccessful war) and the greater must be the sacrifice; this explains the sacrifice of the Carthaginians and the pre-Columbian Mexicans. There is a psychological basis to this, since the mind, through the process of sublimation, is always promoting inversions and metamorphoses of this order. Ambivalence, contrast, paradox, or the *coincidentia oppositorum*, are capable, on account of their transcendent implications, of pointing the way to the other world, or of pointing, in a more practical way, to the focal point of Inversion. Jung observes that this is why the alchemists would express the unknowable by means of contrasts (33); and Schneider notes that, since the world is a duality, each phenomenon or thesis is denoted by its opposite. The closer phenomena come to the focal point of Inversion, the more they tend to collide with one another. The numerical expression of Inversion seems to be two and eleven. Symbols of Inversion are: the double-spiral, the hour-glass, the drum shaped like an hour-glass, St. Andrew's cross, the letter X, the quiver of arrows, and, in general, all that is X-shaped. Hence, the superstitious act of crossing the fingers is tantamount to tempting Fate; and, similarly, crime is a feature of many desperate rites, while primitives often insult the dead, because the insults, after passing through the focal point, are inverted—like rays of light—and changed into praise (50). Also symbolizing Inversion are all those beings or objects which are depicted upside down, such as the figure of the Hanged Man in the Tarot pack, the bat or vampire hanging from rock or branch, the acrobat on the trapeze, and so on. Still other examples of Inversion are those which tend to take the form of an antithesis; for example, according to L. Charbonneau Lassay in *Le Bestiaire du Christ* (Bruges, 1940), the malevolent animals—the toad, the scorpion, the rhinoceros and the basilisk— are the natural enemies respectively of the beneficent animals—the frog, the scarab, the unicorn and the cock. Similarly, the wasp is the antithesis of the bee, the he-goat of the crow. There are some inversions of symbols which owe their origins to racial or national factors, or to a change in the predominant caste: in Islam, politeness demands that the man should not remove his headgear, the opposite being the case in Christian countries. An instance of positive, historical sublimating inversion might be some humiliating situation —such as that in which the Roman army was made to pass under the yoke at Caudium—transformed into one of glory (with its characteristic expression of the triumphal arch, which was a particular obsession of the Romans). The custom among certain layers of society of turning the head of a saint downwards, or against a wall, is less an intended 'punishment' for the holy image than a consequence of the symbolism of Inversion: by inverting the physical position of the effigy, the faithful hope to invert his attitude towards them, and by virtue of the change in his attitude, to induce a change in their destiny.

Invisibility To become or to be invisible, psychologically corresponds to repression or to what is repressed. On the other hand, to become invisible is also, for the unconscious, an image of dissolution. Related to this symbol are the Night Sea-Crossing, Devouring and the *sol niger* of the alchemists (32).

Iopode A man with horse's hoofs, a feature of Romanesque decoration. It is undoubtedly related to the symbolism of the centaur, of which it may be a simplified version.

Ishtar Ishtar is pictured in many Western images and books of magic, as well as in esoteric thought, with a ring in her left hand and a cup or chalice in her right; or else armed like Minerva. These attributes denote the continuity of life, the power of invigorating liquids such as water, milk, blood and soma (related to the draught which Isolde gives to Tristan to drink), and the hardships of existence. Her weapons announce quite clearly that Ishtar loves the hero and despises the coward (59).

Island A complex symbol embracing several different meanings. According to Jung, the island is the refuge from the menacing assault of the 'sea' of the unconscious, or, in other words, it is the synthesis of the consciousness and the will (33). Here he is following the Hindu belief that—as Zimmer notes—the island is to be seen as the area of metaphysical force where the forces of the 'immense illogic' of the ocean are distilled (60). At the same time, the island is also a symbol of isolation, of solitude, of death. Most island-deities have something funereal about them—Calypso for instance. One could perhaps postulate an equation (of counterpoise and identity) between island and woman on the one hand, and monster and hero on the other.

Island, Accursed In the *Lai de Joseph d'Arimathie*, of the Romanesque period, the existence of an Accursed Island, which harboured infernal apparitions, enchantments, tortures and dangers, was postulated along with that of a Happy Island. This is the equivalent of the black castle in other legends. In both cases, it expresses the law of polarity which contrasts the Lower and the Upper Worlds, either on opposite sides of the earth, or above and below it.

Island of the Blessed Hindu doctrine tells of an 'essential island', golden and rounded, whose banks are made of pulverised gems, giving rise to its name of the 'island of the gems'. Sweet-smelling trees flourish on the land, and in the centre is a palace—the oriental equivalent of the *lapis philosophorum*. Inside the palace, in a jewelled pavilion, is the enthroned *Magna Mater* (60). According to Krappe, the 'Island of the Blessed' in its Greek version was the Land of the Dead (35), that is, a symbol, albeit a negative one, of the 'Centre' itself. Krappe goes on to speak of the perennial validity of the symbol, recalling how the Spanish nobleman Juan Ponce de León set off in search of Bimini and discovered Florida. The belief in the existence of the Island, or Islands, of the Blessed is something which one comes across in the most varied of sources. Blavatsky observes that 'Tradition says, and the records of the Book of Dzyan explain, that . . . where now are found but salt lakes and desolate barren deserts, there was a vast inland sea, which extended over middle Asia . . . (and) an island (of) unparalleled beauty' and this island was an exact copy of the island situated in the midst of the zodiacal wheel in the Upper Ocean (or the Ocean of the heavens). The signs of the Zodiac are themselves conceived as twelve islands (9). Finally, the Island of the Blessed (or the Happy Island) seems to be symbolic of earthly paradise for most classical writers. Schneider mentions the island visited by St. Brendan, according to mediaeval legend, where there was a huge tree growing near a fountain, and on its branches lived many birds. Two rivers flowed across the island: one was the river of youth and the other that of death (51). Here we have the clearest possible example of landscape-symbolism in which the terrestrial substance is integrated into a cosmic pattern by means of the essential elements of traditional symbolism.

Ivy Consecrated by the Phrygians to their god Attis. The eunuch-priests tattooed themselves with patterns of ivy leaves (21). It is a feminine symbol denoting a force in need of protection.

J

Jade The traditional Chinese symbolism of jade with its peculiar characteristics is derived from the broader universal symbolism of lithophanies. According to the Chinese tradition, jade possesses an essential quality of immortality as of right. Hence, it figured in rites and invocations from the 3rd millennium before our era: in figures of dragons and tigers, for example, which were intended to represent the cycle of decrease and increase in natural forces. This symbolism is dealt with in the *Chou Li*, dating from the 12th century B.C. It lists six ritual implements of jade: *Pi, Ts'ung, Hu, Huan, Kuei, Chang*. The *Pi*-symbol is a disk with a central hole signifying heaven, which is, as it were, a zone of perfect emptiness. *Hu* is a jade tiger. *Huan* is like a *Pi*, but is of black jade broken into two or three pieces; it is used in Chinese magic, particularly in the practices of necromancy. *Ts'ung* is the symbol of the earth; rounded inside and square outside, it is usually made of yellow jade (39). Generally speaking, jade corresponds to the masculine, *Yang* principle and to the dry Element.

Janus A Roman deity who is represented with two faces joined along the line from ear to jaw, the two faces looking in opposite directions. Like all symbols facing right and left at the same time, Janus is a symbol of wholeness—of the desire to master all things. Because of its duality, it may be taken to signify all pairs of opposites—that is, to be equivalent to the myth of the Gemini. It seems that the Romans associated Janus essentially with destiny, time and war. His faces were turned towards the past and the future, denoting both awareness of history and foreknowledge (the two-headed eagle has a comparable significance). But, as Guénon has rightly pointed out, two heads are, in fact, hindrances to the knowledge of true destiny, which lies in the 'eternal present' (25). This explains why many peoples (those of Northern Europe for example) invented similar symbols but with three heads arranged in the form of a rotating triangle, after the fashion of Janus, but with a third head facing forward. Triform Hecate is represented in this way (59). Janus also symbolizes the union of the powers of priest and monarch (28). Marius Schneider has suggested to us that Janus may also be identified with the two-peaked Mountain of Mars and, consequently, with all symbols of Inversion and mutual sacrifice.

Jerusalem, The Celestial 'And (the city) had a wall great and high, and had twelve gates, and at the gates twelve angels, and names written thereon, which are the names of the twelve tribes of the children of Israel. On the east three gates; on the north three gates; on the south three gates; and on the west three gates. And the wall of the city had twelve foundations, and in them the names of the twelve apostles of the Lamb' (Revelation xxi, 12-14). 'And he shewed me a pure river of water of life, clear as crystal, proceeding out of the throne of God and of the Lamb. In the midst of the street of it, and on either side of the river, was there the tree of life, which bare twelve manner of fruits, and yielded her fruit every month: and the leaves of the tree were for the healing of the nations' (Revelation xxii, 1-2). The celestial Jerusalem is usually described as a city in which the mineral element is predominant, whereas the lost Paradise is portrayed as a garden which is mostly vegetable in composition. Guénon, in noting this, has posed the question of whether we should 'say that the vegetation represents the proliferation of the seeds in the sphere of vital assimilation, whereas the minerals represent the results definitively "fixed"—"crystallized" as it were—at the close of a cyclic process of growth' (27). He links the twelve gates with the signs of the Zodiac, deducing that in this symbol a temporal cycle is transformed into a spatial one, upon the world's ceasing to rotate (28). St. John's apocalyptic vision, then, apart from its prophetic value, is a description, in terms of symbolic logic, of the all-embracing, unifying, 'saved' character of the paradise-to-be, seen as a 'new city'.

Jester The jester is the symbolic inversion of the king, and hence, in certain rites of the period immediately preceding history, it appears in association with the sacrificial victim. According to Schneider, he is the terrestrial counterpart of the Gemini, that is to say that the jester is an expression of duality and not a comic figure. The jester or clown says pleasant things harshly and terrible things jokingly (50). Certain deformed or abnormal beings, such as dwarfs, are closely related to, and even identical with, the figure of the jester.

Frazer relates of Asia Minor in the 6th century B.C. how 'when a
city suffered from plague, famine, or other public calamity, an ugly
or deformed person was chosen to take upon himself all the evils
which afflicted the community. He was brought to a suitable place,
where dried figs, a barley loaf and cheese were put into his hand.
These he ate. Then he was beaten seven times upon his genital
organs with squills and branches of the wild fig and other wild trees
while the flutes played a particular tune. Afterwards he was burned
on a pyre built of the wood of forest trees; and his ashes were cast
into the sea' (21). This passage illustrates the 'inverted' function of
the victim and shows how, by way of suffering and sacrifice, the
inferior creature could be sublimated into a superior being.

Jewels and Gems In most symbolic traditions, jewels signify
spiritual truths (4); the precious stones in the garments of princesses,
or in necklaces and bracelets, as well as gems shut away in hidden
rooms, are symbols of superior knowledge (38). In the case of
jewels belonging to princesses or ladies-in-waiting, they are clearly a
symbol closely connected with the Jungian 'anima'. Treasures guarded
by dragons allude to the difficulties of the struggle for knowledge—
knowledge not as science in the sense of an impersonal erudition,
but as the sum of experiences, and inextricably bound up with
living and with evolution. Gems hidden in caves refer to the intuitive
knowledge harboured in the unconscious. Another interesting
connotation sometimes appearing in mythic form and still alive
today in superstitions is that which associates the gem, symbolic of
knowledge as such, with the snake, representing energy which tends
towards a given end. The best example is the legend of the 'snake's
stone'. There are many folklore traditions which illustrate the belief
that precious stones once fell from the head of snakes or dragons.
This gave rise to the idea that the diamond is poisonous and that it
was once to be found in the jaws of serpents (according to the
Hindu, Hellenistic and Arabic belief), or that all precious stones
originated in their saliva (according to a belief widespread in
primitive cultures from the Far East to England). These myths
express the maximum degree of proximity possible between
'protector' and 'adversary'—between, that is, the guarding 'monster'
and the guarded 'treasure'. They constitute a synthesis of opposites,
an amalgam in which the antitheses become all but identical within
an ambivalent psychological zone marking out a common fund of
significance between the antithetical meanings. Eliade notes that
metaphysical emblems, watched over by serpents or dragons, come
to be represented by specific objects located in the forehead, the
eyes or mouth of these ophidia (17). At the same time, precious
stones incorporate the general symbolism of lithophanies, sublimated in the perfection and beauty of the gems. This is why

Gougenot des Mousseaux, in his *Dieu et les Dieux*, emphasizes the important part always played by stones. The aerolite, in particular, because of its connexion with the celestial sphere, represents the mansion and the vestments of a god descended upon earth. Shooting stars are related to angels. There is another tradition which imparts an infernal shade of meaning to the precious stone, by reason of the 'obscure' nature of the knowledge which it connotes. Plainly, in this case it is the feeling of aversion towards the material richness of the stone that prevails over—or is allied with—admiration for its hardness, colour and transparency. In this connexion, Baron Guiraud, in *La Philosophie de l'histoire*, comments that, when Lucifer fell, angelic light was given corporeal form in the shining stars and glittering gems. Jewels have also been equated with metals, as a kind of 'subterranean astronomy', and in fact, through the application of the theory of correspondences, with every other order of existence. All kinds of glistening specks of colour, too, may contain some of the symbolic sense of particular precious stones, but only as secondary meanings and by association with the essential symbolism of the stone itself. The Hebrews were well aware of the symbolic significance of jewels and made use of it in their liturgy. Lévi, in *Les Mystères du Rational d'Aaron*, recalls that 'The Rational, consisting of twelve precious stones (representing the twelve months of the year, and the signs of the Zodiac), was arranged as four lines with three stones in each, and the type and colour of the stones, from left to right and from top to bottom were: sardonyx (red), emerald (green), topaz (yellow), ruby (red tending to orange), jasper (deep green), sapphire (deep blue), jacinth (lilac), amethyst (violet), agate (milky), chrysolite (golden blue), beryl (darkish blue), and onyx (pink). Each one of these stones had a given magic ability. The order in which they appear is based upon their colour and luminosity, decreasing, as in a tongue of flame, from top to bottom and from the outside to the centre' (59).

Journey From the spiritual point of view, the journey is never merely a passage through space, but rather an expression of the urgent desire for discovery and change that underlies the actual movement and experience of travelling. Hence, to study, to inquire, to seek or to live with intensity through new and profound experiences are all modes of travelling or, to put it another way, spiritual and symbolic equivalents of the journey. Heroes are always travellers, in that they are restless. Travelling, Jung observes, is an image of aspiration, of an unsatisfied longing that never finds its goal, seek where it may (31). He goes on to point out that this goal is in fact the lost Mother; but this is a moot point, for we might equally well say that, on the contrary, its journey is a flight from the Mother. Flying, swimming and running are other activities which may be equated with travelling; and so also are dreaming, day-dreaming and imagining. Crossing a ford marks the decisive stage in the passage from one state to another (56). There is a connexion between the symbolism of the journey, in its cosmic sense, and the symbolism of the essential landscape of megalithic cults (or that seen by the shamans in their visions). Travelling may also be related to the complete cycle of the year or to the attempt to escape from it, depending upon certain secondary characteristics of the journey. But the true Journey is neither acquiescence nor escape—it is evolution. For this reason Guénon has suggested that ordeals of initiation frequently take the form of 'symbolic journeys' representing a quest that starts in the darkness of the profane world (or of the unconscious—the mother) and gropes towards the light. Such ordeals or trials—like the stages in a journey—are rites of purification (29). The archetype of the journey is the pilgrimage to the 'Centre' or the holy land—or the way out of the maze. The Night Sea-Crossing, equivalent to the Journey into Hell, illustrates certain basic aspects of journey-symbolism which still call for elucidation. Primarily, to travel is to seek. The Turkish Kalenderi sect require their initiates to travel ceaselessly, since, as we have suggested, travelling is often invested with a higher, sublimatory significance.

Journey into Hell Dante's descent into the inferno was anticipated by that of Aeneas in the *Aeneid* of Virgil, as well as by the journey of Orpheus. Asín Palacios, in his *Escatología musulmana de la Divina Comedia* (Madrid, 1919)—quoted by Guénon—has suggested that the Florentine poet based the path which he traced, as well as the pattern of the three worlds that he draws, upon the two works of Mohiddin ibn Arabi (who preceded him by more than eighty years), entitled *The Book of the Journey by Night* and *Revelations of Mecca* (27). From the symbolic point of view, and leaving aside the otherworldly implications of the two complementary universes—the 'central level of manifestation' and the terrestrial—the Journey into Hell symbolizes the descent into the unconscious, or the awareness of all the potentialities of being—cosmic and psychological—that are needed in order to reach the Paradisiac heights, except, that is, the divinely chosen few who attain to these heights by the path of innocence. Hell fuses together the ideas of 'crime and punishment', just as purgatory embraces the notions of penitence and forgiveness.

Journey of the Soul According to Hindu belief, the individual, upon freeing himself from the shackles of the manifest world, follows a route which is the inverse of that path which he took when entering into it. Within this system of thought there are two possible paths which he may take: either that of the liberated (*dêva-yâna* or the 'way of the gods') or else that followed by those who still have further states of individuation to pass through (*pitri-yâna* or the 'way of the ancestors'). As the *Bhagavad-Gitâ* observes: 'At this juncture, those who tend towards union, without having actually achieved it, leave manifest existence behind them, some to return to it later, others never to return. . . . Fire, light, day, the crescent moon, the half-year of the sun's ascendence and its northerly course—these are the luminous signs which lead to Brahma those who acknowledge Brahma. Smoke, night, the waning moon, the half-year when the sun descends towards the south—such are the signs that lead to lunar light and immediately to the return to states of manifestation' (26).

Judgement, The Day of   The twentieth enigma of the Tarot pack, representing the resurrection of the dead in the valley of Jehoshaphat, when the angel of the Apocalypse sounds the last trump. This angel has a sun-symbol on his forehead and his golden hair further emphasizes his sun-symbolism. Death, in the symbolic sense, is equivalent to the death of the soul—to ignoring the transcendental aim of Man. The tomb is the body and fleshly desires. The angel, by means both of his light and of his trumpet-call, 'awakens' the latent desire for resurrection in the man who has fallen into iniquity. The constellation which shows the closest affinity with this enigma is the Swan of Leda, the harbinger of the final 'Conjunction'. On the positive side, this card stands for illumination, regeneration, healing and resurrection. On the negative side, for hot-headedness and Dionysiac ecstasy (59).

Juice   Juice or sap represents life-giving liquid. It is a sacrificial symbol connected with blood and also with light as the distillation of igniferous bodies, suns and stars.

Jupiter   Among the Graeco-Roman gods, he corresponds to the supreme virtues of the judgement and the will. As the lord of the sky, his infernal counterparts are Pluto, the lord of the chthonian world, and Neptune as the lord of the deeps (symbolizing the unconscious). Jupiter's attributes are the thunderbolt, the crown, the eagle and the throne (8).

Justice   The eighth enigma of the Tarot, this is an allegory of the idea of justice personified as an image rather like that of the Empress, depicted full-face and symmetrical (this being symbolic of exact, bilateral equilibrium) with a red tunic and a blue cloak. In one hand, she holds up a pair of scales (symbolic of the equilibrium of good and evil), and in the other a sword (for psychic decisiveness, and the Word of God). Her throne is like the Emperor's, massively stable. A crown with fleurons shaped like iron lances surmounts the head-dress of this allegorical figure. The enigma is related to Libra, the sign of the Zodiac, and, like it, represents not so much external justice or social legality as inner judgement setting in motion the entire psychic (or psychosomatic) mechanism involved in the process of determining guilt; the idea behind this is basically the same as Weininger's concept of sin as intrinsically indistinct from punishment. Astronomically speaking, Justice is Astrea. In the positive sense, this enigma denotes harmony, a strict code of behaviour and firmness; in the negative sense, restriction, pettiness and craft (59).

K

Key   As an attribute, it pertains to several mythic characters, including Hecate (31). It is symbolic of mystery or enigma, or of a task to be performed, and the means of carrying it out. It sometimes refers to the threshold of the unconscious (32). The key to knowledge corresponds, within the cycle of the year, to the month of June (healing). The conjunction of the symbols of the male dove and the key signifies the spirit opening the gates of heaven (4). The emblem formed by two keys, sometimes placed over a heart, relates to Janus (4). In legend and folklore, three keys are often used to symbolize a like number of secret chambers full of precious objects. They are symbolic representations of initiation and knowledge. The first key, of silver, concerns what can be revealed by psychological understanding; the second is made of gold, and pertains to philosophical wisdom; the third and last, of diamond, confers the power to act (38). The finding of a key signifies the stage prior to the actual discovery of the treasure, found only after great difficulties. Clearly there is a morphological relationship between the key and the *Nem Ankh* sign (or 'Eternal Life')—the anserated cross of the Egyptians; their gods are sometimes shown holding this cross by the top as if it were a key, especially in ceremonies concerning the dead. But it should perhaps be pointed out that, in this case, it is the keys that derive from the anserated cross, the archetype of the key of Eternal Life that opens up the gates of death on to immortality.

King   In the broadest and most abstract sense, the king symbolizes universal and archetypal Man. As such, according to animistic and astrobiological ways of thought widespread from India to Ireland (21), he possesses magic and supernatural powers. He also expresses the ruling or governing principle, supreme consciousness, and the virtues of sound judgement and self-control (56). At the same time, a coronation is equivalent to achievement, victory and consummation (33). Hence any man may properly be called a king when he achieves the culminating point in the unfolding of his individual life. Deriving from, and equated with the king-symbolism are the symbols for gold, the sun and Jupiter. These symbols imply in essence the idea that the king is Man transposed to the solar plane, to the ideal or 'golden' situation—that is, 'saved' and made eternal. The idea of immortality was passed from god to monarch, and only later was it vouchsafed to the hero and later still to ordinary mortals in so far as they merited the 'crown' of success, having overcome certain obstacles (usually of a moral order). The king, quite apart from all this, may also symbolize the 'royalty'—'or grandeur—of Man. In this case, he may be subjected to a period of unfavourable or painful circumstances; when this is so, the particular symbol becomes that of the 'sick king' (like Amfortas in *Parsifal*), or of the 'sea-king' (signifying the negative aspect of humanity) (32). Love also plays a highly important part in the symbolism of royalty, since love is held to be one of the most obvious of culminating points in the life of Man. This is why the bride and bridegroom in the Greek marriage-ceremony wear crowns made of some precious metal. The king and queen together comprise the perfect image of the *hieros gamos*, of the union of heaven and earth, sun and moon, gold and silver, sulphur and mercury; and—according to Jung— they also signify the spiritual 'conjunction' that takes place when the process of individuation is complete, with the harmonious union of the unconscious and consciousness. The title of king is bestowed upon the most outstanding specimen in every species or type: so, the lion is the king of beasts, as is the eagle of birds or gold among the metals (57). To come back to the symbolism of the 'sick king', he— like such afflicted heroes as Philoctetes—signifies, on the one hand, the punishment which pursues sin as the shadow follows the body (given the existence of the light of consciousness), and, on the other, sterility of spirit. A particularly significant instance of the symbolic process is implied by the king's projecting his spiritual state on to nature around him, as happens with Amfortas in *Parsifal*, in the *Waste Land* of Eliot, and, to some extent, the *Fall of the House of Usher* by Poe. As for the 'sea-king', he is symbolic of the ocean (another version of Neptune) and therefore personifies the deeps of the unconscious in their regressive and evil form as opposed to the waters of the 'Upper Ocean' (the clouds, rain or fresh water) which are fecund (32). The 'aged king'—such as Dhritarashtra, the aged monarch of Vedic epics, or king Lear, or all those aged kings of legends and folktales—is symbolic of the world-memory, or the collective unconscious in its widest and most all-embracing sense (38). The king often exhibits, in concentrated form, the character- istics of the father and the hero, and there is a touch of the Messianic about him; by inversion of the temporal order of things, what is past becomes 'what is to pass' and the dead king is supposed by his subjects to be living a strange existence as a ghost, later to return to his country when it is in great danger. This legend tends to accrue to the names of historical monarchs who have fallen in strange or unhappy circumstances, as in the case of the Portuguese dom Sebastian or that of don Rodrigo, the last of the Gothic kings. The supreme example is the mythic king Arthur, called by Malory *Arthurus, rex quondam, rexque futurus* (q.v.) (16).

Knife   A symbol which is the inversion of sword-symbolism. It is associated with vengeance and death, but also with sacrifice (8). The short blade of the knife represents, by analogy, the primacy of the instinctive forces in the man wielding it, whereas the long blade of the sword illustrates the spiritual height of the swordsman.

Knight   A symbol which confirms what we have suggested concerning the steed. He is the master, the *logos*, the spirit which prevails over the mount (that is, over matter). But this is possible only after a lengthy period of apprenticeship, which may be seen, historically speaking, as a real attempt to create in the knight a human type superior to all others. As a consequence, the education of the knight was directed in part to strengthening him physically, but in particular to developing his soul and spirit, his affections (that is, his morals) and his mind (that is, his reason) in order to prepare him adequately for the task of directing and controlling the real world, so that he might take his proper place in the hierarchies of the universe (that is, in the feudal hierarchy, ordered after the celestial pattern, ranging from the baron up to the king). We also find mounted monks, priests and laymen skilfully controlling their steed, thereby demonstrating their allegiance to the spiritual (or symbolic) order of knighthood in deliberate competition with the historico-social order of knights. This is why in the bas-reliefs on the capitals in the cloister at Silos, knights are shown bestriding goats. Now, goats are symbolic of superiority, because of their association with high peaks, and Rabanus Maurus points out that knights mounted on goats must therefore be interpreted as saints (46). Of course, the purpose of the assimilation of saint with knight is to magnify the symbolic worth of the knight, as in the case of St. Ignatius Loyola. More profound examples of such assimilation are to be seen in that of the king and knight (King Arthur), or the king, knight and saint (St. Ferdinand III of Spain or St. Louis IX of France). This knight-symbolism is common in all symbolic traditions. Ananda Coomaraswamy observes that 'the "horse" is a symbol of the bodily vehicle, and the "rider" is the Spirit: when the latter has come to the end of its incarnations, the saddle is unoccupied, and the vehicle necessarily dies' (60). By taking account of certain other orders of things analogous with chivalry, including (particularly) alchemy (which was in fact a mediaeval technique of spiritual-

Knight Errant, after an early 16th-century engraving.

ization) and also certain aspects of colour-symbolism, we have been able to arrive at a system of analogies which we believe to be very helpful in explaining some of the more recondite aspects of the symbolism of knighthood. Mediaeval tales and legends often refer to a green, white or red knight, but most frequently of all to a black knight. Should we regard this as merely a matter of aesthetic appreciation of the colour in a literal and decorative sense? Or does the choice of colour proceed necessarily from a highly significant cause? The latter, we think. In alchemy, the rising scale of colours (the progressive, evolutive scale) is: black, white, red (corresponding to prime matter, mercury, sulphur), with gold representing the hypothetical, final stage. Conversely, it can be said that the descending scale would be from blue to green, that is, descending from heaven to earth. These two colours stand for the celestial, and the natural or terrestrial factors. Furthermore, black is associated with sin, penitence, the withdrawal of the recluse, the hidden, rebirth in seclusion, and sorrow; white with innocence (natural as well as that regained through expiation), illumination, openheartedness, gladness; and red with passion (moral or material—love or pain), blood, wounds, sublimation and ecstasy. We may therefore surmise that the Green Knight is the pre-knight, the squire, the apprentice sworn to knighthood; the Black Knight stands for him who undergoes the tribulations of sin, expiation and obscurity in order to attain to immortality by way of earthly glory and heavenly beatitude; the White Knight (Sir Galahad) is the natural conqueror, the 'chosen one' of the Evangelists, or the 'illuminated one' re-emerging from a period of *nigredo*; the Red Knight is the knight sublimated by every possible trial, bloodied from every possible sacrifice, supremely virile, the conqueror of all that is base, who, having completed his life's work, is fully deserving of gold in its ultimate transmutation—glorification. Knighthood should be seen, then, as a superior kind of pedagogy helping to bring about the transmutation of natural man (steedless) into spiritual man. An important part was played in this symbolic tradition by prototypes such as the famous, mythical knights of the court of King Arthur or patron saints such as St. George, Santiago of Compostela, or the archangel Michael. The practical means of achieving the knight's ultimate goal consisted of corporeal exertions, which were, in effect, not merely physical or material since the knight practised with *all* kinds of arms, and these arms stood for symbolic potentialities; these practical exertions, then, led eventually to the inversion of the world of desire through the ascetic denial of physical pleasure—the very essence of knighthood—and the almost mystic cult of the beloved. The knight's relative shortcomings while carrying out his sworn duties provide the explanation of the colour black which we have just examined. Nevertheless, other explanations have also been advanced, as for example that the knight is the 'guardian of the treasure', supplanting the monster he has conquered (the serpent or dragon). Clearly this symbolism is not opposed to that which we have proposed, rather does it support it by emphasizing the essential mission of the knight's service. Another interesting aspect of knight-symbolism—though, in a way, a negative one—can be seen in the use of the epithets 'wandering' and 'errant' in mediaeval tales, legends and folklore. At times, the adjective has a precise meaning, at other times it is much more imprecise. In every case, the wandering (or 'errantry') of the knight implies an intermediate position between the 'saved' knight and the accursed hunter, with the difference that the knight errant, so far from being caught up in the pursuit of his desires, is of course striving to master them—and this is what we had in mind when we observed that this aspect 'in a way, is a negative one'. Needless to say, this symbolism of one who takes the dark and lonely path of expiation, verifies our observation that the Black Knight is a symbol of withdrawal, penitence and sacrifice.

Heraldic knot.

Knot A complex symbol embracing several important meanings all of which are related to the central idea of a tightly closed link. It implies also the symbolism of the spiral and the sigmoid line (41). The sign for infinity—the horizontal figure 8—as well as the number 8 itself, are at once interlacing and also knotted, and this emphasizes the relationship of the knot with the idea of infinity—or, rather, with the manifestation of the infinite. It is comparable with the net, the loop and the plait, in that it expresses the concept of binding and fettering—a concept which is generally expressive of an unchanging psychic situation, however unaware of his predicament the individual may be: for example, that of the unliberated man who is 'tied down' by the Uranian god. This is why the *Flamen Dialis* of the ancient Romans could not wear knots in his habits; and this is also true of the Moslems on their pilgrimages to Mecca (21). These magic associations of binding, which form part of the symbolism of the knot, are sometimes given literal expression in magical practices, such as those of fishermen in the Shetland Islands who still believe that they can control the winds by the magic use of knots (21). A knotted cord forms a kind of closed ring, or a circumference, and hence it possesses the general significance of an enclosure, and of protection. The 'slip-knot' is a determinative sign in the Egyptian language, entering into the composition of words such as calumny, oaths, or a journey. The meaning must have originated in the idea of keeping in touch with someone who is far away, and there is unquestionably some connexion with the enigma of the Hanged

Man in the Tarot pack (19). The 'endless knot' is one of the eight
Emblems of Good Luck of Chinese Buddhism, representing
longevity (5); the symbolism here has taken one aspect of the
concept of the knot—that of pure connexion—and applied it to the
biological and phenomenal planes. Finally, the famous 'Gordian
knot' cut by Alexander the Great, by virtue of his determination
and his sword, is a long-standing symbol of the labyrinth, arising
out of the chaotic and inextricable tangle of the cords with which
it was tied. To undo the knot was equivalent to finding the 'Centre'
which forms such an important part of all mystic thought. And to
cut the knot was to transfer the pure idea of achievement and
victory to the plane of war and of existence.

Labyrinth An architectonic structure, apparently aimless, and
of a pattern so complex that, once inside, it is impossible or very
difficult to escape. Or it may take the form of a garden similarly
patterned. Ancient writings mention five great mazes: that of
Egypt, which Pliny located in lake Moeris; the two Cretan
labyrinths of Cnossus (or Gnossus) and Gortyna; the Greek maze
on the island of Lemnos; and the Etruscan at Clusium. It is likely
that certain initiatory temples were labyrinthine in construction for
doctrinal reasons. Ground-plans, sketches and emblems of mazes
appear fairly frequently over a very wide area, but principally in
Asia and Europe. Some are believed to have been conceived with
the purpose of luring devils into them so that they might never
escape. It is to be supposed, therefore, that, for the Primitive, the
maze had a certain fascination comparable with the abyss, the
whirlpool and other phenomena (8). Nevertheless, Waldemar
Fenn suggests that some circular or elliptical labyrinths in prehistoric
engravings—those at Peña de Mogor, for example—should be
interpreted as diagrams of heaven, that is, as images of the apparent
motions of the astral bodies. This notion is not opposed to the
previous one: it is independent of it and, up to a point, complementary, because the terrestrial maze, as a structure or a pattern, is
capable of reproducing the celestial, and because both allude to the
same basic idea—the loss of the spirit in the process of creation—
that is, the 'fall' in the neoplatonic sense—and the consequent need
to seek out the way through the 'Centre', back to the spirit. There is
an illustration in *De Groene Leeuw*, by Goosse van Wreeswyk

(Amsterdam, 1672), which depicts the sanctuary of the alchemists' *lapis*, encircled by the orbits of the planets, as walls, suggesting in this way a cosmic labyrinth (32). The emblem of the labyrinth was widely used by mediaeval architects. To trace through the labyrinthic

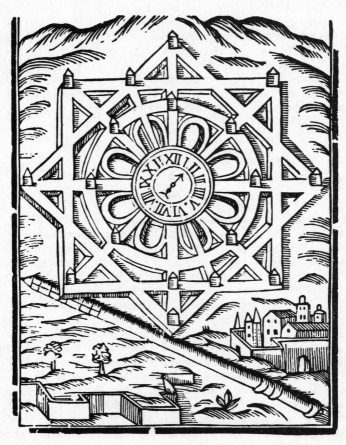

Labyrinth—the clock implies juxtaposition of time and space.
(After an old engraving.)

path of a mosaic patterned on the ground was once considered a symbolic substitute for a pilgrimage to the Holy Land (28). Some labyrinths shaped like a cross, known in Italy as 'Solomon's knot', and featured in Celtic, Germanic and Romanesque decoration, are a synthesis of the dual symbolism of the cross and the labyrinth; they are known, for this reason, as the 'emblem of divine inscrutability'. It is not difficult to make out, in the centre of the pattern, the figure of the swastika, which adds to the basic symbolism a suggestion of rotating, generating and unifying motion (4). For Diel, the maze signifies the unconscious, and also error and remoteness from the fount of life (15). Eliade notes that the essential mission of the maze was to defend the 'Centre'—that it was, in fact, an initiation into sanctity, immortality and absolute reality and, as such, equivalent to other 'trials' such as the fight with the dragon. At the same time, the labyrinth may be interpreted as an apprenticeship for the neophyte who would learn to distinguish the proper path leading to the Land of the Dead (17).

Lake In the Egyptian system of hieroglyphs, the schematic figure of a lake expresses the occult and the mysterious, probably by allusion to the underground lake which the sun has to pass over during its 'night-crossing' (but also simply by associating it with the symbolism of level, given that water always alludes to the 'connexion between the superficial and the profound'; a lake becomes, then, a fluid mass of transparency). In the temple of the god Amon, at Karnak, there was an artificial lake symbolizing *hyle*—or the 'lower waters' of protomatter. And, at certain times during the year, a procession of priests would cross the lake in boats, in this way re-enacting the 'night-crossing' of the sun mentioned above (19). The symbolism here is the same, broadly speaking, as that of the watery deeps. The Irish and Breton belief that the Land of the Dead is at the bottom of the ocean or of lakes may be derived from watching the sun setting over the water; and the death of human beings, and therefore by analogy the setting of the sun, was interpreted as passing over into the nether world. But, as we have suggested, the structure of lake-symbolism may have arisen directly out of the symbolism of level; for this latter symbolism, so deeply rooted in the psyche of man, equates all that is on a low level spatially with what is low in a spiritual, negative, destructive, and hence fatal, sense. The fact that water-symbolism is closely connected with the symbolism of the abyss serves to corroborate the fatal implications of the lake-symbol, for the part played by the liquid Element is to provide the transition between life and death, between the solid and the gaseous, the formal and the informal. At the same time, the lake—or, rather, its surface alone—holds the significance of a mirror, presenting an image of self-contemplation, consciousness and revelation.

Lamb The origins of the symbolism of the lamb are to be found in the Book of Enoch (32). It signifies purity, innocence, meekness (as well as unwarranted sacrifice). In allegories, it lies at the root of representations of either pure thought, or a just man, or the Lamb of God (4). Pinedo, however, points to the interesting relationship between the lamb and the lion, by inversion of their respective symbolic meanings. Examples of this are common in Christian symbolism, especially during the Romanesque period; a good instance is that of a tympanum in the church at Armentia, where the *Agnus Dei* is shown inside a circle (symbolizing the All, or perfection) accompanied by the epigraph: '*Mors ego sum mortis. Vocor Agnus, sum Leo fortis*' (I am the death of death. I am called a lamb, I am a strong lion) (46) (Plate XX). Its etymology suggests other symbolic meanings: Alleau, in *De la Nature des symboles* (Paris, 1958), proposes that *agnus* is related to the Greek *agnos* and therefore symbolizes the unknown; and that it is also related to *agni* (fire) and so is a sacrificial symbol of the periodic renovation of the world.

Lamia The mythic queen Lamia, celebrated for her beauty, was turned into a wild beast because of her cruelty. Ancient writings refer to lamias, in the plural, as beings similar to sirens, found in the company of dragons in caves and deserts. In 1577, Johann Wier published an entire treatise upon these beings, entitled *De Lamiis Liber*. According to Caro Baroja, this belief in lamias still persists in Gascony. Their attribute is the gold comb—a fish skeleton perhaps? —with which they comb their hair (10). Legend has it that lamias are devourers of children (8). Jung has pointed out that the fact that 'lamia' is also the word used for a huge and very voracious fish (from 'lamos'—an abyss) verifies the connexion between the devouring lamias and the dragon-whale of the kind studied by Frobenius in *Zeitalter des Sonnengottes* (31).

Lamp A symbol of intelligence and the spirit (56). It appears in this sense in the Greek myth of Psyche, in the legend of Diogenes and in the hermit (the ninth enigma) of the Tarot pack (40). The lamps of the ancients were shaped according to their function— profane, religious or funereal—and to suit the nature of the god to whom they were dedicated. There were lamps with twelve wicks, symbolizing the Wheel of the Zodiac. And there were perpetually burning lamps such as that kept alight by the vestal virgins, or that of the temple of Venus noted by St. Augustine (8).

Lance A symbol of war, and also a phallic symbol (8). It is a weapon of earthly character, in contrast to the celestial implications of the sword. It is connected with the symbolism of the cup or chalice. Generally speaking, the lance is comparable from the symbological point of view with the branch, the tree, the cross, and all symbols pertaining to the valley-mountain axis. In the *Libro del orden de caballería*, Raymond Lull expresses the belief that the lance is given to a knight as a symbol of rectitude. The 'bleeding lance', which appears in the legend of the Grail, has sometimes been interpreted as the lance of Longinus, relating it to that of the Passion. There are authors who reject this interpretation and see it rather as a general sacrificial symbol.

Landscape Logically speaking it may be deduced that the country-side—landscapes of all kinds—is the mundane manifestation of a dynamic complex which in origin was non-spatial. Inner forces are liberated to unfold as forms which disclose in themselves the qualitative and quantitative order of their inner tensions. Thus a mountain crest becomes a graphic sign. Let us take, by way of illustration, landscapes as they appear in dreams. Leaving aside the phenomenon of memory, reminiscence, or the complex association of various sense-data, the scenes and towns which figure in dreams are neither arbitrary and indeterminate nor objective: they are symbolic—that is, they well up in order to illuminate certain momentary experiences called forth by varying combinations of influences in varying degrees of intensity. Landscape-scenes arising in the imagination in this way are sustained solely by the validity, duration and intensity of the feelings which aroused them. Form—just as in physical morphology—is the diagram of force. Now, what we have said about landscapes in dreams can be applied also to an actual landscape, seen and selected by an automatic response of the unconscious, which detects in it an affinity that gives us pause and makes us return to it again and again. This, then, is a question not of a projection of the mind but of an analogy whereby the landscape is adopted by the spirit in consequence of the inner bond linking the character of the scene with the spirit of the observer himself. Subjecti-vism concerns only the act of choosing. The intellection of the significance of a landscape is, then, wholly objective, as is the grasping of the symbolic values of colours and numbers. The Chinese saw this with the utmost clarity: as Luc Benoist has observed, Chinese art has always placed more emphasis upon landscape than upon man (as a figure, that is to say), and upon the macrocosm rather than the microcosm. 'If the superior man loves the country-side,' to quote the words of Kuo Hsi, 'why is this so? Hills and gardens will always be the haunts of him who seeks to cultivate his original nature; fountains and rocks are a constant joy to him who wanders whistling among them. . .' (6). It is a well-established tradition of symbology that the different worlds (or zones) are strictly only different states of being. Hence the fact that the 'chosen site' is the enshrining image which arises out of it. The 'trysting place', when it truly possesses that character, and is not merely arbitrary or fortuitous, signifies a meeting or 'conjoining' in precisely this same sense—that is, transposed into topographical or spatial terms (26). However revolutionary these assertions may seem, they are nevertheless confirmed by the findings of the psychology of form and by isomorphism, since it has been shown that it is not possible to distinguish between psychic and physical formal pro-cesses—other than externally. In support of all this, there is the comment of Mircea Eliade that 'In point of fact, man never chooses a site, he simply "discovers it". . . . One of the means of discovering one's situation is by orientation' (17). Now, in order to grasp the symbolic sense of a landscape it is necessary to distinguish between the predominant elements and the merely incidental, and between the character of the whole and the character of the component elements. When the predominant element is a cosmic one, its effect is to bind all the other components together, and it is this cosmic ingredient which makes its influence felt over and above that of the individual features of the landscape. Instances of such cosmic features are the sea, the desert, the icy wastes, the mountain-peak, clouds and sky. It is when the ingredients of landscape-symbolism are varied and evenly balanced that symbolic interpretation is most needed. The interpreter must, then, look for the following: (a) a spatial pattern organized within particular limits which endow it with a structure after the manner of a building or a work of art. By spatial symbolism we mean, in the first place, the symbolism of level, that is, the disposition of the zones of the landscape according to the three levels of the normal, the lower and the higher; and secondly the symbolism of orientation, that is, the position of the accidental elements in relation to the north-south and the east-west axes. He must then bear in mind (b) the form—the pattern or the shape of the terrain, whether it is undulating or broken, steeply sloped or flat, soft or hard; (c) the positional relationship of the particular area chosen to the region as a whole or to the zone surrounding it—whether it is lower or higher, more open or more enclosed; and finally (d) the natural and artificial elements which make up the organized pattern: trees, shrubs, plants, lakes, springs, wells, rocks, sandy shores, houses, steps, benches, grottoes, gardens, fences, doors and gates. Also important is the predominating colour, or the clash of colours, or the general feeling of fecundity or barrenness, of brightness or gloom, of order or disorder. Roads and cross-roads are of great significance, and so are streams. About the objective meaning of each of the factors we have listed above there is much that we could say; however, since the more important factors—such as the symbolism of level—are dealt with under separate headings, we will here add no more than a few notes. Steepness indicates primitiveness and regression; flat country denotes the apocalyptic end, the longing for power and for death. There is a Persian tradition that, when the end of the world has come—when Ahriman is vanquished for ever, the mountains will be levelled and all the earth will become one great plain. Ideas cognate with this are to be found in certain traditions of Israel and France (35). It would not be hard to point to the history of architecture and town-planning as evidence of the subconscious application of these principles. Furthermore, there are some aspects of landscapes which have a symbolic air about them that is very difficult to analyse intellectually. For instance, the following descriptive passage from Dante's *Commedia* has always seemed to us to evoke an atmosphere of profound mystery: 'Around this little island, in its lowest reaches, there, where it is lashed by the waves, reeds grow in the soft mud' (*Purgatorio* I, 100). Independent of the cosmic significance of landscape, there may also be a sexual implication. It is also essential to bear in mind that this is not strictly a matter of symbols as such but of complex, symbolic functions. For instance, in scenes depicting low-lying topographical features, the following factors may be at work: (*a*) depth in the sense of what is base, comparable therefore with the wicked and infernal; (*b*) depth in the sense of what is symbolically profound; (*c*) depth as it pertains to the material earth itself, implying a chthonian and maternal symbolism. Only the context can help us to tell the essence from the accessory—as is true also of the vast majority of symbols. Here we must bear in mind the primitive concept of the archetypal 'ideal countryside'. Schneider has observed that the fact of there being so many identical names for rivers and mountains in different parts of the world, suggests that megalithic ways of thought must have led to the custom of naming the topographical features of different regions after some ideal model. This model, it may be argued, could be the product of the lasting impression made upon the mind of Primitive Man by a particular environment endowed with such unity and variety as to prevent him from ever wishing to leave it; but it could also be explained as the projection of a psychic order founded upon laws comparable with those governing quaternary patterns, or the mandala, etc. Man's attention was first drawn to the contraposition of heaven and earth by topographical features, and he gave expression to this in the struggle between gods and Titans, angels and demons, and in the opposition of mountain and valley. Next, he set out to explain the earth's surface by means of the laws of orientation, taking the four points of the compass from the apparent orbit of the sun as well as from the human anatomy, and identifying them as ambivalent forces—ambivalent because they are at once hostile to things external and the defenders of their limits. As Schneider adds: 'To preserve cosmic order, the gods fought with the giants and the monsters which had from the very beginning of creation sought to devour the sun. They stationed the heroic lion on the celestial mountain. Four archers'—the tetramorphs—'are continuously on guard day and night against anyone who attempts to disrupt the order of the cosmos' (50). The stockade, the wall or stone enclosure, comments Eliade, are among the oldest known parts of the structure of temples, appearing as early as in proto-Indian civilizations such

as that of Mohenjo-Daro and also in Crete (17). They owe their
origins to the same basic, primordial idea of the symbolism of
landscape—its representation of cosmic order. The mountain with
one peak is symbolic of the One—of transcendent purpose; the
two-peaked Mountain of Mars stands for the Gemini, the world of
appearances and the dualism of all forms of life. Both these symbolic
mountains find their symbolic complement in the general pattern
of archetypal landscape—also, incidentally, an image of the year;
this pattern is composed of the river of life (denoting the positive
phase) and the river of oblivion (the negative phase) which flow
through the sea of flames (expressing infirmity) and well up from a
single source (birth or the Origin). According to this scheme, every
landscape has a disastrous and a felicitous tendency, corresponding
on the temporal plane with the self-evident distinction between
'coming' and 'going' which in turn is analogous to the two halves of
human existence. But, quite apart from all this, the symbolic
interpretation of a landscape may be determined according to the
laws governing diverse and individual correspondences, as well as
the overall significance derived from the complex of meanings
afforded by its separate features. By way of an illustration of the
many possibilities of interpreting the significance of a landscape,
we will conclude with some comments on Vallcarca with its characteristic low-lying features. The gardens are at a lower level than the
city proper, and screened from it by the vegetation, which has
something of the archaic and oriental about it. The main street leads
north towards an open plain, signifying the process of disintegration.
On the other hand, those streets which lead towards the mountain
are on the favourable axis. In this case, the interpretation is obvious
enough, as it is in all instances of scenes where it is possible to
identify the essential features of archetypal landscape.

Lantern Like all 'lights' that are independent of the Light—
that which, in other words, is severed—the lantern symbolizes
individual life in the face of cosmic existence, transitory fact in the
face of eternal truth, 'distraction' in the face of essence. This explains
the magic use of lanterns. Because of its psychological interest, we
quote here a passage taken from a Chinese work of the Tang
dynasty: 'On the mid-Autumn feast-day, the devil turned himself
into a man, ingratiated himself with women and children and led
them off to secret places whence they could not escape (a death-
symbol). Seeing that this demon was greatly persecuting the people,
the jurisconsult Bao-Cong informed the king of the matter and
persuaded him to issue a decree to the effect that paper lanterns,
shaped like fishes, should be hung at the entrances of the houses.
In this fashion would the carp-demon, deceived by these images,
leave the Hundred Families in peace' (13).

Laurel　A tree sacred to Apollo and expressive of victory. Laurel leaves were used to weave festive garlands and crowns. The crowning of the poet, the artist or conqueror with laurel leaves was meant to represent not the external and visible consecration of an act, but the recognition that that act, by its very existence, presupposes a series of inner victories over the negative and dissipative influence of the base forces. There is no achievement without struggle and triumph. Hence the laurel expresses the progressive identification of the hero with the motives and aims of his victory. An associated idea is the generic implication of fecundity pertaining to all vegetation-symbols.

Lead　A metal associated with Saturn. The alchemists employed the image of a white dove contained in lead to express their central idea that matter was the receptacle of the spirit (32). The specific symbolism of lead is the transference of the idea of weight and density on to the spiritual plane.

Leaf　One of the eight 'common emblems' of Chinese symbolism, it is an allegory of happiness. When several leaves appear together as a motif, they represent people; in this sense it is closely related to the significance of herbs as symbols of human beings (5).

Leg　In the Egyptian system of hieroglyphs, the figure of a leg is symbolic of erecting, lifting and founding (19). The symbolic significance is related to that of the foot, and both symbols emphasize the fundamental difference, from the merely biological point of view, of the human form as compared with other animals, in that humans stand erect. The leg is also equivalent to the pedestal, and in Cabbalistic thought it denotes qualities of firmness and splendour.

Lemures　The Romans gave this name to disembodied spirits. According to Ovid, the festival of the Lemuralia was a commemoration of the dead. It is likely that the *umbra*—the ghost or apparition —is closely linked with the lemur, and that both are symbolic of certain states of psychic dissociation (47).

Zodiacal sign of Leo.

Leo　The fifth sign of the Zodiac. It corresponds to solar power, the will, fire, and the clear, penetrating light which passes from the threshold of the Gemini into the realm of Cancer. It is connected with feelings and emotions (40).

Leopard　An attribute of Dionysos, the leopard has been equated with Argus-of-the-thousand-eyes (4). It is a symbol of ferocity and of valour (5). The leopard, like the tiger and panther, expresses the aggressive and powerful aspects of the lion without his solar significance.

Letters of the Alphabet Letters, in all cultures, have a symbolic significance, sometimes in a twofold sense corresponding to both their shape and their sound. Letter-symbolism probably derives from Primitive pictograms and ideographs—quite apart, that is, from the theory of cosmic 'correspondences' which prescribes that each component of a series must correspond to another given component of a parallel series. Enel, in *La Langue sacrée*, has subjected the Egyptian alphabet to a profound and scrupulous study, selecting those that have a phonetic value from the vast repertory of syllabic and ideographic signs. He recalls that Horapollo Niliacus in antiquity, and Kircher and Valeriano in the Renaissance, tried unsuccessfully to analyse the meaning of these symbolic signs; it is only the work of Champollion, Maspero, Mariette, etc., which has made a true understanding possible. The significance of many Egyptian signs can best be understood by grasping the import of the so-called 'determinative' signs, governing groups of phonetic signs. We cannot here give any idea of this complex Egyptian system, which was a mixture of ideographic signs and phonetic signs, abstract allusions and concrete pictograms in the form of visual patterns, such as the sign for combat (two arms holding an axe and a shield) or figures denoting geographical places (Lower Egypt was represented by plants characteristic of the Delta). We must limit ourselves, then, to the so-called Egyptian alphabet, which Enel sees closely linked, in its development, with the idea of creation itself. Here is his explanation: 'Thus the divine principle, the essence of life and the reason for creation, is represented by the eagle, but, within the microcosm, this same sign expresses reason—the faculty which brings Man into proximity with the godhead, raising him above all other created beings. The creative manifestation of the reason-principle is action, depicted by an arm, a sign which is symbolic of activity in all its aspects, and is opposed to that for passivity—represented by a broken line as the image of the primary element. The nature of the action, and the vital movement, convey the divine word—represented as a schematic image of a mouth—as the first manifestation of the world's beginning. . . . The creative action irradiated by the word continues and develops into all the varied manifestations of life; its sign is a curving spiral—a pattern of the universe, representing the cosmic forces in action. From the point of view of the microcosm, as an expression, that is, of man's labours, the sign corresponding to the cosmic spiral is the squared spiral—a sign of construction. By his own efforts, and by utilizing the forces of nature susceptible to his will, Man can transform brute matter—denoted by a kind of irregularly formed rectangle—into organized matter: a rectangle, or a stone, with which he builds his home or a temple for his god (this being a schematic sign also pertaining to the temple). But the development of the creative forces of the macrocosmos, like that of human labour, is subject to the law of equilibrium (expressed by a semicircle based upon its diameter). There are two aspects to this equilibrium: (1) the swing of the needle of the scales through 180 degrees, and (2) the daily trajectory of the sun across the sky from East to West—the alpha and omega of St. John—represented by the bird of day (the eagle) and the night-bird (the owl), and corresponding respectively to life and death, dawn and sunset. . . . The connexion between the two opposite poles of these constant alternations is symbolized by the distinction between the "upper waters" and the "lower waters", and represented by a sign which is equivalent to the Hebrew *mem*. Through this connexion, day is transformed into night and life is born of death. This ceaseless flux forms the cycle of life which is symbolized by a snake which ceaselessly rears and undulates. The bonds uniting life with death, where man is concerned, are represented by swaddling clothes (echoed by the bandages that swaddle a corpse). . . . The forces which animate every manifestation of life are the dual streams of the evolutive/involutive principle, or descent and ascent, represented by the leg as a sign of upward movement. This hieroglyph has the same meaning, also, in relation to man's activities, since it is by means of his legs that he can go where he will: towards failure as well as towards success. The relationship between the dual streams is symbolized by a plaited cord. . . .' Other signs follow the same pattern: the tie or loop signifies the connexion between the Elements; the bolt, the fixed state of a mixture; the cane-leaf, human thought, etc. (19).

The letters of the Hebrew alphabet are characterized by a similar system with symbolic and semantic meanings; the system has two aspects: the Cabbalistic, and that which corresponds to figures on the cards of the Tarot. For example, the letter *aleph* denotes will-power, man, the magician; *beth*, science, the mouth, the temple door; *ghimel*, action, the grasping hand; etc. (48). In alchemy, too, letters are significant: A expresses the beginning of all things; B, the relation between the four Elements; C, calcination; G, putrefaction; M, the androgynous nature of water in its original state as the Great Abyss, etc. (57). But this is really a case of the fusing of true symbolism with purely conventional connotations—although the significance of the letter M is symbolic in the true sense. As Blavatsky observes, M is the most sacred of letters, for it is at once masculine and feminine and also symbolic of water in its original state (or the Great Abyss) (9). It is also interesting to note the relationship of the letter S with the moon by virtue of the symbolism of form; the S can be said to consist of a waxing and a waning moon counterbalancing each other.

Letters of the alphabet played a very important part among the Gnostics and in the mysteries of Mithraic cults; equivalents ascribed to them were taken from the symbolism of numbers, as well as from the signs of the Zodiac, the hours of the day, etc. One of the early Fathers of the church, Hippolytus, quotes the remark attributed to Marcus the Pythagorean that: 'The seven heavens . . . pronounced severally their vowels and all these vowels together formed a single doxology, the sound of which, transmitted below, became the creator. . .' (9). Similarly, each vowel was related to a colour (11). The seven letters also corresponded to the seven Directions of space (that is, the six extremities of the three-dimensional cross plus the centre) (39).

Among the Arabs, too, letters had a numerical value: the number of the letters in the alphabet was twenty-eight, like the days of the lunar month. Given the importance traditionally attached to the word—the Element of air—it is easy to understand why Man, in every system ever formulated, has always tried to prove the divine power of letters by making them dependent upon mystic and cosmic orders. Saint-Yves d'Alveydre, in *L'Archéometre* (1911), has made a broad study of letter-symbolism, although, in our opinion, he comes to somewhat arbitrary conclusions concerning the relationship between the alphabet, colour, sound, planets, the signs of the Zodiac, virtue, the element of nature, and so on. As an example, here is what he says about the letter M: 'It corresponds to the natural Origin, which gives rise to all temporal forms of existence. Its number is 40. Its colour, sea-green; its sign, Scorpio; its planet, Mars; its musical note, Re.' Of greater symbolic authenticity is the summary which Bayley makes, drawing upon a variety of sources of information to arrive at a synthesis of the intrinsic significance of the letters which now comprise our Western alphabet. Clearly, there are some letter-symbols of more obvious meaning than others. Here are some of the less obvious suggested by Bayley: A is related to the cone, the mountain, the pyramid, the first cause; B, (?); C, the crescent moon, the sea, the *Magna Mater*; D, the brilliant, the diamond, the day; E is a solar letter; F signifies the fire of life; G, the Creator; H, Gemini, the threshold; I, number one, the axis of the universe; L, power; M and N, the waves of the sea and the undulations of the snake; O is a solar disk, denoting perfection; P, R, the shepherd's crook, the staff; S, the snake or serpent; T, the hammer, the double-headed axe, the cross; U, the chain of Jupiter; V, a receptacle, convergence, twin radii; X, the cross of light, the union of the two worlds—the superior and the inferior; Y, three in one, the cross-ways; and Z, the zigzag of lightning (4). As an interesting sidelight, here are Bayley's conclusions concerning the ideas—merely conventional in this instance—related to initials most commonly figuring in mediaeval and 16th-century emblems: A (combined with V) signifies *Ave*; M is the initial letter of the Virgin Mary, and also a sign of the *Millennium*, that is, of the end of this world; R stands for *Regeneratio* or *Redemptio*; Z for *Zion*; S for *Spiritus*; SS for *Sanctus Spiritus*; T for *Theos*, etc.

Any study of letter-symbolism must be closely related to the examination of words. Loeffler recalls that, among the Aryans and also among the Semites, M has always been the initial letter of words related to water and to birth of beings and the worlds (Mantras, Manu, Maya, Madhava, Mahat, etc.) (38). Concerning the connexion between M and N, we believe that the latter is the antithesis of the former, that is: if M corresponds to the regenerating aspect of water, N pertains to its destructive side, or to the annihilation of forms. Letters, because of their associations, were one of the techniques used by the Cabbalists.

We cannot here do more than mention the study of the 'tifinars'; or prehistoric symbolic signs, made by R. M. Gattefossé in *Les Sages Ecritures* (Lyon, 1945). Also very interesting is the philosophy of letters—and of grammar—in their symbolic context worked out by M. Court de Gebelin in his *Du Génie allégorique et symbolique de l'antiquité* (Paris, 1777). Basing his study upon a primitive tongue, he draws conclusions concerning the mental attitudes which inspired the symbolism of proper names, linguistic roots, sacred fables, cosmogonies, symbolic pictures, escutcheons, hieroglyphs, etc., as well as of letters. For example, Λ, he suggests, can be: a cry, a verb, a preposition, an article, an initial letter—apart from its character in oriental tongues, etc. For a profound analysis of the Cabbalistic significance of the symbolism of letters, the work of Knorr de Rosenroth, *Le Symbolisme des lettres hébraïques . . . selon la Kabbala Denudata* (Paris, 1958), may be consulted. An important general review of the symbolism of letters and graphic signs is given by Alfred Kallir in his book, *Sign and Design* (London, 1961).

Level This is a term which refers to that aspect of the symbolism of space which is concerned with the simple moral pattern deriving from the notions of height and—ultimately—of centre. Hindu doctrine describes the three fundamental states of the human spirit as *sattva*, which is 'loftiness' of spirit; *rajas*—manifestation, struggle and dynamism; and *tamas*, or obscurity and brute instinct; and these three states are located on three vertical levels. Strictly speaking, there are five zones or levels: the absolute low level and the absolute high level, plus the central area divided into three zones merging into each other and at the same time bringing the outer extremes into progressive relationship. When the baser levels concern not the intellectual but the moral—which is in essence infinitely more complex and mysterious—then the precise significance of the symbolism is not nearly so hard-and-fast. There is always the possibility of symbolic Inversion, in which case the two opposing directions have something in common in that both partake of the idea of depth. Hence the saying: 'Deep calls to deep.' The temptations endured by the chosen few find their counterpart in the abysses of salvation which may be opened up for the reprobate. Dostoievski has spoken eloquently about this. Finally, here is a quotation from *L'Art chinois* by M. Paléologue, written in 1888: 'Under the Chinese Chou dynasty (11th century B.C.), the dead of the lower classes were buried in the plains; princes, on hills of moderate height; and emperors in tombs built on a mountain-top. The head of the corpse would be turned to face North.' In virtually every work of art whose composition is of an ideological rather than a naturalistic character, the vertical line locates the Three Worlds of the infernal, terrestrial (with its own, internal orders—the marine, the animal and the human) and celestial. Thus, in the Mesopotamian stele (or *Kudurru*), the illustrations are arranged on several levels, divided off by lines to suggest their relative values: the most primitive beings are placed at the lowest level (since they are closest to the 'primordial monster') while astral bodies and symbols of the godhead are situated on the highest plane. The same principles are true of Romanesque art.

Leviathan A huge, fabulous fish which bears the weight of the waters upon its back and which the Rabbis claimed was destined for the Supper of the Messiah (8). In Scandinavian mythology, the oceans are the creation of a great serpent or dragon which swallows the waters only to regurgitate them; this being is called Midgardorm (35). The Leviathan is an archetype of things inferior—of the primordial monster connected with the cosmogonic sacrifice, such as the Mesopotamian Tiamat (or Tiawath). Sometimes it is in all respects identical with the world—or, rather, with the force which preserves and vitalizes the world.

Liberation of the Damsel Of mythological origin (Siegfried waking Brunhild, the story of the Sleeping Beauty), it appears in pagan and Christian legends, and in books of knight-errantry. Perseus liberating Andromeda is possibly the archetype, though we must not forget St. George and the princess. In the 'matière de Bretagne', there are numerous instances of knights liberating damsels, and this could almost be regarded as their essential mission. As a symbol of the search for the *anima* and its liberation from the subjugation in which it is held by malign and inferior powers, it seems to be of mystical origin.

Libra The seventh sign of the Zodiac, Libra, is, like the cross and the sword, related to the symbolism of the number seven, and the sign for equilibrium, on both the cosmic and the psychic planes, and concerning both social and inward legality and justice. It is said, therefore, that the balance or scales designates the equilibrium between the solar world and planetary manifestation, or between the spiritual ego of Man (the *Selbst* of Jungian psychology) and the external ego (or the personality). It likewise indicates the equilibrium between good and evil; for, like Man, the scales has two tendencies, symbolized by the two symmetrically disposed pans, one tending towards the Scorpion (denoting the world of desires) and the other towards the sign of Virgo (sublimation). Man must, after the model of the scales, balance out his inner tendencies. According to traditional astrology, the sign of the balance rules the kidneys. The seventh sign pertains to human relations and to the union of the spirit within itself, that is to say, to spiritual and mental health. As an allegory of justice, it refers to the intimate and moderating influence of self-chastisement (40). As a symbol of inner harmony and of intercommunication between the left side (the unconscious, or matter) and the right (the consciousness or spirit), it represents 'Conjunction' (Plate XXI).

Zodiacal sign of Libra.

Life All things that flow and grow were regarded in early religions as a symbol of life: fire represented the vital craving for nourishment, water was chosen for its fertilizing powers, plants because of their verdure in spring-time. Now, all—or very nearly all—symbols of life are also symbolic of death. *Media vita in morte sumus*, observed the mediaeval monk, to which modern science has replied *La vie c'est la mort* (Claude Bernard). Thus, fire is the destroyer, while water in its various forms signifies dissolution, as suggested in the Psalms. In legend and folklore, the Origin of life —or the source of the renewal of the life forces—takes the form of caves and caverns where wondrous torrents and springs well up (38).

Light Light, traditionally, is equated with the spirit (9). Ely Star asserts that the superiority of the spirit is immediately recognizable by its luminous intensity. Light is the manifestation of morality, of the intellect and the seven virtues (54). Its whiteness alludes to just such a synthesis of the All. Light of any given colour possesses a symbolism corresponding to that colour, plus the significance of emanation from the 'Centre', for light is also the creative force, cosmic energy, irradiation (57). Symbolically, illumination comes from the East. Psychologically speaking, to become illuminated is to become aware of a source of light, and, in consequence, of spiritual strength (32).

Lightness The sonorous, the transparent and the mobile constitute a trilogy which is related to the sensation of lightness within (3). Air is the Element which corresponds primarily to this sensation. From the oneirocritic and literary points of view, the desire for lightness is depicted by the symbol of the dance—as in Nietzsche— rather than by flight. If the latter is in essence expressive of the will to rise above oneself and above others, the former concerns the urge to escape.

Lilith Lilith, in Hebrew legend, was the first wife of Adam. She was a night-phantom and the enemy of childbirth and of the newborn. In mythic tradition she was regarded as a satellite invisible from the earth (8). In Israelite tradition, she corresponds to the Greek and Roman Lamia. She may also be equated with Brunhild in the saga of the Niebelungen, in opposition to Kriemhild (or Grimhild, or Eve). She is symbolic of the Terrible Mother. All these characteristics relate her closely to the Greek figure of Hecate, with her demands for human sacrifice. Lilith personifies the maternal *imago* in so far as she denotes the vengeful mother who reappears in order to harry the son and his wife (a theme which, in some respects, is transferred to the Stepmother and to the Mother-in-Law). Lilith is not to be related literally to the Mother, but with the idea of the mother venerated (that is, loved and feared) during childhood. Sometimes she also takes the form of the despised mistress, or the 'long forgotten' mistress, as in the case of Brunhild mentioned above, or of the temptress who, in the name of the maternal *imago*, seeks and brings about the destruction of the son and his wife. There is a certain quality of the virile about her, as there is about Hecate, the 'accursed huntress'. The overcoming of the threat which Lilith constitutes finds its symbolic expression in the trial of Hercules in which he triumphs over the Amazons.

Ioannis da Sylveira, *Comentariorum in Textum Evangelicum.* Lugduni, 1670.

Lily An emblem of purity, used in Christian—and particularly mediaeval—iconography as a symbol and attribute of the Virgin Mary (46). It is often depicted standing in a vase or jar, which is, in its turn, a symbol of the female principle. Félix de Rosnay, in *Le Chrisme, les lys et le symbolisme de Paray* (Lyon, 1900), points to the connexion between the fleur-de-lis, in respect of the symbolism of its form, and the chrism or cross of St. Andrew intersected by the *rho*, and the ancient cross of the Aeduan Gauls (a cross with a vertical line traced through the centre), which is quite clearly a symbol of inversion; it was worn on the sword-guard. The lily, in Byzantium and among the Christianized Franks, was a sign of royalty.

Lingam The lingam is not just a sign for the phallus, but for the integration of both sexes, symbolizing the generating power of the universe (8). It is very commonly found in Hindu temples. A comparable symbol is that of the Tree of Life of the Persians whose seeds when mixed with water preserve the fertility of the earth (31). All symbols of 'conjunction' of this kind allude to the *hieros gamos*, without which the continuous process of creation and preservation of the universe would be inconceivable; hence they find their way into fecundity and fertility rites. In China, the lingam is called *Kuei*; it is an oblong piece of jade terminating in a triangle. The seven stars of the Great Bear are often engraved on the *Kuei* (39), probably symbolizing space and time (that is, the Seven Directions and the seven days of the week).

Lion The lion corresponds principally to gold or the 'subterranean sun', and to the sun itself, and hence it is found as a symbol of sun-gods such as Mithras. In Egypt, it used to be believed that the lion presided over the annual floods of the Nile, because they

Heraldic lion,
18th century.

coincided with the entry of the sun into the zodiacal sign of Leo during the dog-days. The lion-skin is a solar attribute (8). The equation of the sun and the lion, borne out by primitive and astro-biological cultures, persisted into the Middle Ages and found its way into Christian symbolism (14), although the significance of the lion is enriched by a variety of secondary symbolisms. In alchemy, it corresponds to the 'fixed' element—to sulphur. When counter-balanced by three other animals, it represents earth (although elsewhere it has been said that it stands for 'philosophical fire') (57), while gold is given the name of 'lion of metals'; the red-coloured lion is more strictly applicable to the latter (56). But, apart from these considerations, which lie more in the province of the theory of correspondences than in symbology proper, the lion, the 'king of beasts', symbolizes the earthly opponent of the eagle in the sky and the 'natural lord and master'—or the possessor of strength and of the masculine principle. As Frobenius notes, the motif of the solar lion which tears out the throat of the lunar bull is repeated interminably in Asiatic and African ornamentation (22). According to Schneider, the lion pertains to the Element of earth and the winged lion to the Element of fire. Both are symbolic of continual struggle, solar light, morning, regal dignity and victory. As a symbol of the Evangelists, the lion came to be associated with St. Mark in particular. Naturally, other meanings may be derived from the location or the context in which the lion appears. The young lion corresponds to the rising sun, the old or infirm lion to the setting sun. The lion victorious represents the exaltation of virility; the lion tamed carries, on the symbolic plane, the obvious significance which it has in real life (50). For Jung, the lion, in its wild state, is broadly speaking an index of latent passions; it may also take the form of a sign indicating the danger of being devoured by the unconscious (32). But this latter sense goes beyond lion-symbolism as such, being related to the general symbolism of devouring (which in turn is related to the symbolism of time). The wild lioness is a symbol of the *Magna Mater* (35).

Loaves of Bread   As with grains of corn, loaves are symbols of fecundity and perpetuation, which is why they sometimes take on forms that are sexual in implication.

Locusts   In Christian symbolism, locusts represent the forces of destruction (20), a symbolism which can be traced back to the Hebrew tradition of the 'plagues of Pharaoh'. To quote the words of the Bible (Revelation ix, 1-10): 'And the fifth angel sounded, and I saw a star fall from heaven unto the earth: and to him was given the key of the bottomless pit. And he opened the bottomless pit; and there arose a smoke out of the pit, as the smoke of a great furnace; and the sun and the air were darkened by reason of the smoke of the pit. And there came out of the smoke locusts upon the earth; and unto them was given power, as the scorpions of the earth have power. And it was commanded them that they should not hurt the grass of the earth, neither any green thing, neither any tree;

but only those men which have not the seal of God in their foreheads. And to them it was given that they should not kill them, but they should be tormented five months: and their torment was as the torment of a scorpion, when he striketh a man. And in those days shall men seek death, and shall not find it; and shall desire to die, and death shall flee from them. And the shapes of the locusts were like unto horses prepared unto battle; and on their heads were as it were crowns like gold, and their faces were as the faces of men. And they had hair as the hair of women, and their teeth were as the teeth of lions. And they had breastplates, as it were breastplates of iron; and the sound of their wings was as the sound of chariots of many horses running to battle. And they had tails like unto scorpions, and there were stings in their tails: and their power was to hurt men five months.'

Logos The Logos is the light and the life, at once spiritual and material, which combats both death and night (7). It is the antithesis of disorder and chaos, of evil and darkness. It is also cognate with the word and with thought.

Loops and **Bonds** In mythology and iconography, the symbolism of loops and knots has an endless number of variants, both as images of connexion and as forms of ornamental art, appearing as plaited links, rosettes, knots or ties, ribbons, cords or string, ligaments, nets and whips. In the broadest sense, loops and knots represent the idea of binding. It would seem that, if modern man —according to the 'existentialist' approach—feels himself to be 'thrown' into the world, the primitive, oriental and astrobiological man perceived that he was 'bound' to the world, to the creator, to the order and society of which he was part. Jurgis Baltrusaitis, in his *Etudes sur l'art mediéval en Géorgie et en Arménie*, distinguished the following types of rosette in Romanesque ornamentation: intersecting, intertwining, connecting and linking. He comments that intertwining plaits pertain to the most ancient of forms created by man, for they cannot be accounted a product of either barbarian art or of any particular Asiatic influence. Entangled in the knots, nets or cords, very commonly one finds monsters, animals or human figures. In the Egyptian system of hieroglyphs, the loop or tie was a sign corresponding to the letter T, and equivalent grammatically to the possessive (such as 'to bind', 'to dominate' or 'to possess') (19). A related symbol is that of Entanglement (q.v.). But there are particular aspects of this symbol which present it in a favourable light: the 'golden thread', for example, identical with the 'silver cord' in Hindu tradition, and with 'Ariadne's thread', and symbolic of the path leading to the creator. The mystic sense comes about by inversion: instead of the symbol representing external bonds, it comes to stand for inner links. The cordons which are such a constant feature of heraldry also pertain to these 'inner links', sometimes in the form of knots, or of ribbons bunched together to form the letter S or the number 8 (4), representing linkage or dependence in the feudal system of hierarchies (ratified in the oath of allegiance), or the sublimation of the idea of being 'in bondage' to one's superior (36). On the other hand, the external net which envelops and immobilizes should be related in significance to the words of the Bible (quoted by Pinedo): 'Upon the wicked he shall rain snares' (Psalms xi, 6) (46). Mircea Eliade has made a special study of the symbolism of knots and ties as they concern the tangle of thread which has to be unravelled in order to solve the essential basis of a problem. Some gods, such as Varuna or Uranus, are shown holding a length of rope, signifying their prerogative of supreme power. Eliade notes that there is a symbolic relationship between loops and bonds on the one hand and threads and labyrinths on the other. The labyrinth may be regarded as a knot to be untied, as in the mythic undertakings of Theseus and Alexander. The ultimate aim of mankind is to free himself from bonds. The same thing is to be found in Greek philosophy: in Plato's 'cave', men are fettered and unable to move (*Republic*, VII). For Plotinus, the soul 'after its fall, is imprisoned and fettered . . . but when it turns towards (the realm of) thought, it shakes off its bonds' (*Enneads* IV, 8). Eliade has also studied the morphology of bonds and knots in magic cults, distinguishing two broad divisions: (*a*) those which are beneficent and a protection against wild animals, illness and sorcery, and against demons and death; (*b*) those which are employed as a form of 'attack' against human enemies— symbolically the inverse of severing ropes or bonds (18). This latter practice is carried to the extent of tying up dead bodies to prevent them from performing the injurious acts which they were supposed to have indulged in (17, 18). Sometimes symbolic loops and ropes appear in vegetable form as foliage which inextricably envelops bodies that fall into it; this is a theme which is related to the symbolism of devouring, as well as to grotesques.

Lorelei A siren in Germanic mythology who appears on a rock bearing her name in the Rhine, and whose song is the perdition of mariners, for when they hear her singing they forget to watch out for the reefs and are dashed to pieces. The Lorelei is also related to the legend of the treasure of the Niebelungen.

Loss On the one hand, the sense of loss is bound up with the feeling of guilt together with a presentiment of ultimate purification or pilgrimage and journeying. On the other hand, the idea of losing and of rediscovering oneself, or the notion of the 'lost object' that is missed very painfully, are concepts parallel to that of death and resurrection (31). To feel lost or neglected is to feel dead, and hence, even though the blame for, or cause of, this feeling may be projected onto circumstantial matters, the true cause always lies in forgetfulness of the Origin and severance of the individual's attachment to it (as expressed in the thread of Ariadne). Within the twofold structure of the spirit (symbolized by the Gemini twins), loss corresponds to the equation of consciousness with the merely existential aspect of life, ignoring the eternal aspect of the spirit; and it is this which lies behind the 'lost feeling', or purposelessness, or the symbolic lost object.

Lotus   There is a certain parallel between the symbolism of the lotus and that of the rose in Western culture. In Egypt, the lotus symbolizes nascent life, or first appearance (19). Saunier regards it as a natural symbol for all forms of evolution (49). In the Middle Ages it was equated with the mystic 'Centre' and, consequently, with the heart (56, 14). As an artistic creation it is related to the mandala, its significance varying according to the number of its petals: the eight-petalled lotus- is considered in India as the Centre where Brahma dwells and as the visible manifestation of his occult activity (26). The figure eight is like the mandorla of Romanesque art, signifying the intersection of the earth (four, or the square) with heaven (the circle). The 'thousand-petalled' lotus symbolizes the final revelation; in the centre there is usually a triangle and inside the triangle is the 'great emptiness' symbolic cf formlessness. René Guénon has examined lotus-symbolism at great length, observing that 'The potentialities of being are realized by means of an activity which is always internal' (this is the 'growth' of Father Gratry) 'since it is exercised from the centre of each plane; furthermore, from the metaphysical point of view, it is impossible for external action to be brought to bear upon the total being, for such action is possible only on a relative and a particular plane. . . . This realization of potentialities is depicted in various symbolisms as the unfolding of a flower on the surface of the "waters"; generally, in oriental traditions, it is a lotus, and a rose or lis in the West. There is a further relationship between these flowers and the circumference as a symbol of the manifest world, as well as with the cosmic Wheel. This symbol finds other forms of expression in many different ways, but always related to the symbolism of numbers, that is, depending upon the number of petals' (25). From the remotest days of antiquity, the lotus was the unanimous choice of the Chinese, the Japanese, the Hindus, the Egyptians and the Aryans. The lotus flower growing out of the navel of Vishnu, symbolizes the universe growing out of the central sun—the central point or the 'unmoved mover'. It is the attribute of many deities (9). In lotus symbolism, the idea of emanation and of realization predominated over that of the hidden Centre, which is a Western accretion.

LOVE   194

Love Traditional symbols of love always express a duality in which the two antagonistic elements are, nevertheless, reconciled. Thus, the Indian *lingam*, the Chinese *Yang-Yin*, or even the 'Cross, where the upright beam is the world-axis and the cross-beam the world of phenomena. They are, in other words, symbols of a conjunction, or the expression of the ultimate goal of true love: the elimination of dualism and separation, uniting them in the mystic 'centre', the 'unvarying mean' of Far Eastern philosophy. The rose, the lotus flower, the heart, the irradiating point—these are the most frequent symbols of this hidden centre; 'hidden' because it does not exist in space, although it is imagined as doing so, but denotes the state achieved through the elimination of separation. The biological act of love itself expresses this desire to die in the object of the desire, to dissolve in that which is already dissolved. According to the *Book of Baruch*: 'Erotic desire and its satisfaction is the key to the origin of the world. Disappointment in love and the revenge which follows in its wake are the root of all the evil and the selfishness in this world. The whole of history is the work of love. Beings seek and find one another; separate and hurt one another; and in the end, comes acute suffering which leads to renunciation.' Or to put it another way: Maya as opposed to Lilith, illusion balanced by the serpent.

Loved One, The The woman loved, in the light of the Gnostic idea of the beloved as a mediator personified in Sophia (q.v.) and the Catharist view of human love as a form of mysticism, ceases to be a vessel for the perpetuation of the species and becomes a profoundly spiritual and spiritualizing entity, as in Dante, the paintings of Rossetti, the most exalted of the romantics, or in André Breton (*L'Amour fou*). The earliest and purest expression of this conception of the beloved seems to have occurred in Persia.

Lover, The The sixth enigma of the Tarot pack. It is related to the legend of Hercules which tells how he was given the choice of two women, the one personifying Virtue (or decisive activity, vocation, sense of purpose, and struggle) and the other Vice (passiveness, surrender to base impulses and to external pressures). The Lover, faced like Hercules with these two opposite modes of conduct, hesitates. He has parti-coloured clothes divided vertically: one half is red (for activity) and the other green (neutral—for indecision). On the positive side, this mystery-card implies the making of the right choice and represents moral beauty or integrity; on the negative side it alludes to uncertainty and temptation (59).

Lozenge One of the eight 'common emblems' of the Chinese, symbolic of victory. In graphics, the lozenge is simply a rhomb elongated along the vertical axis (5). The rhomb is a dynamic sign, as in St. Andrew's cross, and denotes the intercommunication between the inferior and the superior.

Luz The Hebrew word *luz* has a number of meanings: city-centre, like Agarttha; 'mandorla', or place of the apparition; and, according to Guénon (*Le Roi du Monde*), it also means 'an indestructible corporeal particle, symbolized by an extremely hard bone to which a part of the soul remains attached from the time of death to that of resurrection'. In *Le Mystère de la vie et de la mort d'après l'enseignement de l'ancienne Égypte*, Enel agrees with this interpretation.

Lycanthrope A legendary man whom the devil covers with a wolf's skin and forces to roam howling over the countryside (8), and symbolic of the irrationality latent in the baser part of man and the possibility of his awakening. Hence, it is similar in meaning to all evil monsters and fabulous beings.

Lyre A symbol of the harmonious union of the cosmic forces, a union which, in its chaotic aspect, is represented by a flock of sheep (40). The seven strings of the lyre correspond to the seven planets. Timotheus of Miletus raised the number of strings to twelve (corresponding to the signs of the Zodiac). A serial development of a similar kind is that effected by Arnold Schoenberg in our day by giving the same value to chromatic notes as to the notes of the diatonic scale, creating in place of the old scale of seven notes, a new one of twelve. Schneider draws a parallel between the lyre and the fire, recalling that in the temple of Jerusalem (according to Exodus xxxviii, 2) there was an altar with horns 'overlaid with brass' on either side, and the smoke of sacrifice rose up between them. The lyre, similarly, produces its sounds through the horns forming the sides of its structure, and representing the relationship between earth and heaven (50).

Mace A determinative sign in the Egyptian system of hieroglyphs, governing the ideas of the creative Word and achievement (19). It is related to the oar, the sceptre, the staff and the club, all of them symbolic instruments of one morphological family. In Egypt the oar was also linked with the idea of creating. As a weapon, the mace denotes a crushing blow or utter destruction and not simply victory over the adversary; it is therefore used as the insignia denoting the annihilation of the subjective, assertive tendency in Man, and also of the monsters symbolizing this tendency; for the same reason it is the attribute of Hercules (15).

Machines The symbolism of machines is founded upon the shape of their components and the rhythm and direction of their movement. Broadly speaking, this symbolism finds its inspiration in the obvious analogy with the physiological functions of ingestion, digestion and reproduction.

Macrocosm—Microcosm This relationship is symbolic of the situation in the universe of man as the 'measure of all things'. The basis of this relationship—which has occupied the minds of thinkers and mystics of all kinds in all ages—is the symbolism of man himself, particularly as the 'universal man' together with his 'correspondences' with the Zodiac, the planets and the Elements. As Origen observed: 'Understand that you are another world in miniature and that in you are the sun, the moon and also the stars' (33).

Maize One of the eight 'common emblems' of China, maize is symbolic of prosperity and is widely used in ornamental art (5). Almost all cereals have a common meaning in that they are spermatic images. Peruvians represent fertility by means of the figure of a woman made out of stalks of maize which they call 'the mother of the maize' (17).

Makara An Indian mythic monster, part-fish and part-crocodile. It is also to be found in the ornamental art of the Indonesians.

Man Man comes to see himself as a symbol in so far as he is conscious of his being. Hallstatt art, in Austria, shows fine examples of animal-heads with human figures appearing above them. In India, in New Guinea, in the West as well, the bull's or ox's head with a human form drawn between the horns is a very common motif. Since the bull is a symbol for the father-heaven, man comes to be seen as both his and the earth's son (22), also, as a third possibility, the son of the sun and the moon (49). The implications of Origen's remark: 'Understand that you are another world in miniature and that in you are the sun, the moon and also the stars', are to be found in all symbolic traditions. In Moslem esoteric thought, man is the symbol of universal existence (29), an idea which has found its way into contemporary philosophy in the definition of man as 'the messenger of being'; however, in symbolic theory, man is not defined by function alone (that of appropriating the consciousness of the cosmos), but rather by analogy, whereby he is seen as an image of the universe. This analogical relationship is sometimes expressed explicitly, as in some of the more ancient sections of the *Upanishads*—the *Brihadaranyaka* and the *Chandogya* for instance—where the analogy between the human organism and the macrocosmos is drawn step by step by means of correspondences with the organs of the body and the senses (7). So, for example, the components of the nervous system are derived from fiery substance, and blood from watery substance (26). These oriental concepts first appear in the West during the Romanesque period: Honorius of Autun, in his *Elucidarium* (12th century) states that the flesh (and the bones) of man are derived from the earth, blood from

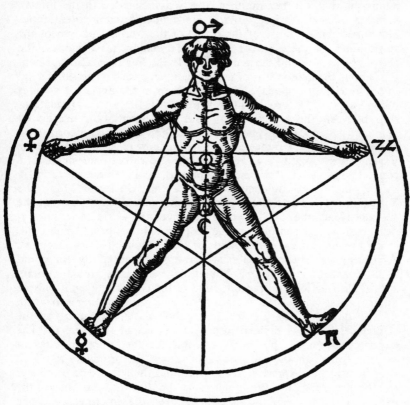

Man the microcosm (after Agrippa of Nettesheim).

water, his breath from air, and body-heat from fire. Each part of the body relates to a corresponding part of the universe: the head corresponds to the heavens, the breath to air, the belly to the sea, the lower extremities to earth. The five senses were given analogies in accordance with a system which came to Europe, perhaps, from the Hebrews and the Greeks (14). Thus, Hildegard of Bingen, living in the same period, states that man is disposed according to the number five: he is of five equal parts in height and five in girth; he has five senses, and five members, echoed in the hand as five fingers. Hence the pentagram is a sign of the microcosmos. Agrippa of Nettesheim represented this graphically, after Valeriano, who drew the analogy between the five-pointed star and the five wounds of Christ. There is a relationship, too, between the organic laws of Man and the Cistercian temple (14). Fabre d'Olivet, following the Cabala, maintains that another number closely associated with the human being is nine—the triple ternary. He divides human potentialities into three planes: those of the body, of the soul or life and of the spirit. Each of these planes is characterized by three modes: the active, the passive and the neutral (43). In the Far East, also, speculation about the symbolism of man began very early. The same kind of triple ternary organization is to be seen in the ancient teachings of the Taoists (13). It is also interesting to note that there is a relationship between the human being and the essential or archetypal animals (the turtle, the phoenix, the dragon and the unicorn) who appear to bear the same relation to man—who is central—as the tetramorphs do to the Pantokrator. Now, between man as a concrete individual and the universe there is a medial term—a mesocosmos. And this mesocosmos is the 'Universal Man', the King (*Wang*) in Far Eastern tradition, and the *Adam Kadmon* of the Cabala. He symbolizes the whole pattern of the world of manifestation, that is, the complete range of possibilities open to mankind. In a way, the concept corresponds to Jung's 'collective unconscious'. According to Guénon, Leibniz—perhaps influenced by Raymond Lull—conceded that every 'individual substance' must contain within itself an integral reproduction of the universe, even if only as an image, just as the seed contains the totality of the being into which it will develop (25). In Indian symbolism, *Vaishvânara*, or the 'Universal Man', is divided into seven principal sections: (1) The superior, luminous spheres as a whole, or the supreme states of being; (2) the sun and the moon—or rather, the principles to which they pertain—as expressed in the right and the left eye respectively; (3) the fire-principle—the mouth; (4) the directions of space—the ears; (5) the atmosphere—the lungs; (6) the intermediary zone between earth and heaven—the stomach; (7) the earth—the natural functions or the lower part of the body. The heart is not mentioned, because, being the 'centre' or dwelling-place of Brahma, it is regarded as being beyond the 'wheel' of things (26). Now, this concept of the 'Universal Man' implies hermaphroditism, though never specifically. For the concrete, existential human being, in so far as he is either a man or a woman, represents the dissected 'human' whole, not only in the physical sense but also spiritually. Thus, to quote the *Upanishads*: 'He was, in truth, as big as a man and a woman embracing. He divided this *atman* into two parts; from them sprang husband and wife.' In Western iconography one sometimes finds images which would seem to be echoes of this concept (32). A human couple, by their very nature, must always symbolize the urge to unite what is in fact discrete. Figures which are shown embracing one another, or joining hands, or growing out of roots which bind them together, and so on, symbolize 'conjunction', that is, *coincidentia oppositorum*. There is a Hindu image representing the 'joining of the unjoinable' (analogous to the marriage of fire and water) by the interlinking of Man and Woman, which may be taken to symbolize the joining of all opposites: good and bad, high and low, cold and hot, wet and dry, and so on (32). In alchemy, Man and Woman symbolize sulphur and mercury (the metal). In psychology, level-symbolism is often brought to bear upon the members of the body, so that the right side corresponds to the conscious level and the left to the unconscious. The shapes of the parts of the body, depending upon whether they are positive or negative—whether they are protuberances or cavities—should be seen not only as sex-symbols but also in the light of the symbolism of levels. The head is almost universally regarded as a symbol of virility (56). The attitudes which the body may take up are of great symbolic importance, because they are both the instrument and the expression of the human tendency towards ascendence and evolution. A position with the arms wide open pertains to the symbolism of the cross. And a posture in the form of the letter 'X' refers to the union of the two worlds, a symbol which is related to the hour-glass, the 'X' and all other symbols of intersection (50). Another important posture is that of Buddha in the traditional iconography of the Orient, a posture characteristic also of some Celtic gods such as the so-called 'Bouray god' or the famous Roquepertuse figure. This squatting position expresses the renunciation of the 'baser part' and of ambulatory movement and symbolizes identification with the mystic centre.

Mandala   This is a Hindu term for a circle. It is a kind of *yantra* (instrument, means or emblem), in the form of a ritual geometric diagram, sometimes corresponding to a specific, divine attribute or to some form of enchantment (*mantra*) which is thus given visual expression (6). Cammann suggests that mandalas were first brought to Tibet from India by the great guru Padma Sambhava in th' 8th century A.D. They are to be found all over the Orient, and always as a means towards contemplation and concentration—as an aid in inducing certain mental states and in encouraging the spirit to move forward along its path of evolution from the biological to the geometric, from the realm of corporeal forms to the spiritual. According to Heinrich Zimmer, mandalas are not only painted or drawn, but are also actually built in three dimensions for some festivals. One of the members of the Lamaist convent of Bhutia Busty, Lingdam Gomchen, described the mandala to Carl Gustav Jung as 'a mental image which may be built up in the imagination only by a trained lama'. He maintained that 'no one mandala is the same as another': all are different because each is a projected image of the psychic condition of its author, or in other words, an expression of the modification brought by this psychic content to the traditional idea of the mandala. Thus, the mandala is a synthesis of a traditional structure plus free interpretation. Its basic components are geometric figures, counterbalanced and concentric. Hence it has been said that 'the mandala is always a squaring of the circle'.

The expanding centre
—a concept exemplified in the Shri-Yantra mandala.

There are some works—the *Shri-Chakra-Sambhara-Tantra* is one—which prescribe rules for the better imagining of this image. Coinciding in essence with the mandala are such figures as the Wheel of the Universe, the Mexican 'Great Calendar Stone', the lotus flower, the mythic flower of gold, the rose, and so on. In

a purely psychological sense it is feasible to identify the mandala
with all figures composed of various elements enclosed in a square
or a circle—for instance, the horoscope, the labyrinth, the zodiacal
circle, figures representing 'The Year' and also the clock. Ground-
plans of circular, square or octagonal buildings are also mandalas.
As for the three-dimensional form, there are temples built after the
pattern of the mandala with its essential counterbalancing of
elements, its geometric form and significant number of component
elements. The stupa in India is the most characteristic of these
temples. Again, according to Cammann, there are some Chinese
shields and mirror-backs which are mandalas. In short, the mandala
is, above all, an image and a synthesis of the dualistic aspects of
differentiation and unification, of variety and unity, the external
and the internal, the diffuse and the concentrated (32). It excludes
disorder and all related symbolisms, because, by its very nature, it
must surmount disorder. It is, then, the visual, plastic expression of
the struggle to achieve order—even within diversity—and of the
longing to be reunited with the pristine, non-spatial and non-
temporal 'Centre', as it is conceived in all symbolic traditions.
However, since the preoccupation with ornamentation—that is,
with unconscious symbolism—is in effect a concern for ordering a
certain area—that is, for bringing order into chaos—it follows that
this struggle has two aspects: firstly, the possibility that some
would-be mandalas are the product of the simple (aesthetic or
utilitarian) desire for order, and secondly, the consideration that
the mandala proper takes its inspiration from the mystic longing
for supreme integration. In Jung's view, mandalas and all concomitant images—prior, parallel or consequent—of the kind
mentioned above, are derived from dreams and visions corresponding
to the most basic of religious symbols known to mankind—symbols
which are known to have existed as far back as the Palaeolithic Age
(as is proved, for example, by the Rhodesian rock engravings).
Many cultural, artistic or allegorical works, and many of the
images used in numismatics, must have sprung from this same
primordial interest in the psychic or inner structure (with its external
counterpart to which so many rites pertaining to the founding of
cities and temples, to the divisions of heavens, to orientation and the
space-time relationship, bear eloquent testimony). The juxtaposition
of the circle, the triangle and the square (numerically the equivalents
of the numbers one and ten; three; and four and seven) plays a
fundamental rôle in the most 'classic' and authentic of oriental
mandalas. Even though the mandala always alludes to the concept
of the Centre—never actually depicting it visually but suggesting it
by means of the concentricity of the figures—at the same time it
exemplifies the obstacles in the way of achieving and assimilating

the Centre. In this way, the mandala fulfils its function as an aid to man in his efforts to regroup all that is dispersed around a single axis—the Jungian *Selbst*. It is of interest to note that the same problem occupied the alchemists, except that a very different aspect of being was under investigation. Jung suggests that the mandala represents an autonomous psychic fact, or 'a kind of nucleus about whose intimate structure and ultimate meaning we have no direct knowledge' (32). Mircea Eliade, speaking as an historian of religions and not as a psychologist, sees the mandala chiefly as an objective symbol, an *imago mundi* rather than a projection of the mind, without, however, discrediting the latter interpretation. The structure of a temple—the Borobudur temple for instance—in the form of a mandala has as its aim the creation of a monumental image of life and the 'distortion' of the world to make it a suitable vehicle for the expression of the concept of supreme order which man—the neophyte or initiate—might then enter as he would enter into his own spirit. The same is true of the great mandalas traced on the ground with coloured threads or coloured dust. Here, rather than serving the purposes of contemplation, they have a ritual function in which a man may move gradually towards the inner area, identifying himself with each stage and each zone as he goes. This rite is analogous to that of entering into the labyrinth (denoting the quest for the Centre) (18), and the psychological and spiritual implications are self-evident. There are some mandalas which counterbalance not enclosed figures but numbers arranged in geometric discontinuity (for instance: four points, then five, then three), and are then identified with the Cardinal Points, the Elements, colours, and so on, the significance of the mandala being wonderfully enriched by these additional symbolisms. Mirrors of the Han dynasty depict the numbers four and eight balancing each other and disposed round the centre in five zones which correspond to the five Elements (that is, the four material Elements plus the spirit or quintessence). In the West, alchemy made quite frequent use of figures having a definite affinity with the mandala, composed of counterpoised circles, triangles and squares. According to Heinrich Khunrath, the triangle within the square produces the circle. There are, as Jung has pointed out, 'distorted' mandalas different in form from the above and based upon the numbers six, eight and twelve; but they are comparatively rare. In all mandalas in which numbers are the predominant element, it is number-symbolism which can best plumb its meaning. The interpretation should be such that the superior (or the principal) elements are always those nearest the centre. Thus, the circle within the square is a more developed structure than the square within the circle. And the same relationship to the square holds good for the triangle; the struggle between the number three and the number four seems to represent that between the central elements of the spirit (corresponding to three) and the peripheral components, that is, the Cardinal Points as the image of ordered externality (corresponding to four). The outer circle, on the other hand, always fulfils the unifying function of overriding the contradictions and the irregularities of angles and sides by means of its implicit movement. The characteristics of the Shri-Yantra, one of the finest mandala-instruments, have been explained by Luc Benoist. It is composed around a central point which is the metaphysical and irradiating point of primordial energy; however, this energy is not manifest and therefore the central point does not actually appear in the drawing, but has to be visualized. Surrounding it is a complex pattern of nine triangles—an image of the transcendent worlds; four of these triangles have the apex pointing upwards and the other five downwards. The intermediate—or subtle—world is suggested by a triple aureole surrounding the triangles. An eight-petalled lotus (signifying regeneration), together with others of sixteen petals, and a triple circle, complete this symbolic representation of the spiritual world. The fact that it exists within the material world is suggested by a triple-lined serrated surround, signifying orientation in space (6).

The mandorla symbolizes the intersection of the two spheres of heaven and earth.

Mandorla   Although the geometric symbol of the earth is the square (or the cube) and the symbol of heaven is the circle, two circles are sometimes used to symbolize the Upper and the Lower worlds, that is, heaven and earth. The union of the two worlds, or the zone of intersection and interpenetration (the world of appearances), is represented by the mandorla, an almond-shaped figure formed by two intersecting circles. In order that, for the purposes of iconography, the mandorla might be drawn vertically, the two circles have come to be regarded as the left (matter) and the right (spirit). The zone of existence symbolized by the mandorla, like the twin-peaked Mountain of Mars, embraces the opposing poles of all dualism (51). Hence it is a symbol also of the perpetual sacrifice that regenerates creative force through the dual streams of ascent and descent (appearance and disappearance, life and death, evolution and involution). Morphologically, it is cognate with the spindle of the *Magna Mater* and with the magical spinners of thread (50).

Mandragora (or **Mandrake**)   A plant which was supposed to have various magic properties, a belief arising out of the likeness of its roots to the human form. Mandragora was also the name of the ghost of a devil, who appeared as a tiny black man, beardless and with unkempt hair (8). For the primitive mind, the mandrake represented the soul in its negative and its minimal aspects.

Man-Eating Monster   A monster, dragon or sea-serpent with a human being in its jaws, symbolizes the danger of being devoured by the destructive forces of the unconscious, a fate to which only the most noble of man's faculties, such as his reason or his morals, are susceptible. In mediaeval iconography, this monster's head is an allegory of the gates of hell.

Manicora   A fabulous being which figures in Romanesque decoration, a quadruped covered in scales and with the head of a woman wearing a kind of Phrygian cap. Its significance may be compared with that of the siren; scales always allude to the ocean —to the primordial, Lower Waters.

Marriage   In alchemy, a symbol of 'Conjunction', represented symbolically also by the union of sulphur and mercury—of the King and the Queen. Jung has shown that there is a parallel between this alchemic significance and the intimate union or inner conciliation —within the process of individuation—of the unconscious, feminine side of man with his spirit.

Mars   The primitive and astrobiological conception of creation is that it can take place only through 'primordial sacrifice'; similarly, what has been created can only be preserved through sacrifice and war. The image of Janus, or the twin-peaked mountain of Mars, are symbols of inversion, that is, of the intercommunication between the Upper, non-formed World of future potentialities, and the Lower World of materialized forms. Schneider insists upon this principle as characteristic of the primordial order, commenting that 'its rigid law demands a death for each life, sublimates the criminal instinct to serve good and humanitarian ends, and fuses love and hate in the interests of the renewal of life. In order to preserve the order of existence, the gods struggled with the giants and monsters who from the beginning of creation sought to devour the sun'—the Logos (50). Mars is the perennial incarnation of this necessity for the shedding of blood, apparent in all orders of the cosmos. Hence, early cults of Mars embraced vegetation: it was to Mars that the Roman farmer appealed for the prosperity of his harvest (21). His attributes are weapons, and specially the sword.

Marsh   According to Schneider, marshlands are a symbol of the 'decomposition of the spirit'; that is, they are the place in which this occurs because of the lack of the two active elements (air and fire) and the fusion of the two passive elements (water and earth). Therefore, in legends, novels of chivalry, etc., marshes appear with this meaning. In the story of Gawain, knight of the Round Table, the protagonist finds himself in a marsh, and this implies his inability to bring his enterprise to a successful conclusion, just as when he is unable to mend the 'broken sword'. In *The Lovers*, by Leslie Stevens, the protagonist finds himself obliged to defend marshlands from a tower which has been profaned, premonitory signs of his downfall and death.

Mask All transformations are invested with something at once of profound mystery and of the shameful, since anything that is so modified as to become 'something else' while still remaining the thing that it was, must inevitably be productive of ambiguity and equivocation. Therefore, metamorphoses must be hidden from view —and hence the need for the mask. Secrecy tends towards transfiguration: it helps what-one-is to become what-one-would-like-to-be; and this is what constitutes its magic character, present in both the Greek theatrical mask and in the religious masks of Africa or Oceania. The mask is equivalent to the chrysalis. Frazer has noted some very peculiar types of masks used in the initiation ceremonies of some Oceanian peoples: the youths keep their eyes closed and

Mask of Mithras—Persian image of the Sun.

cover their faces with a mask of paste or fuller's earth, and pretend not to hear the orders shouted out by their elders. But they gradually recover, and on the following day they wash themselves clean of the crust which had covered their faces (as well as their bodies); and their initiation is then complete (21). Apart from this—the most essential—symbolic meaning, the mask also constitutes an image bearing another symbolic meaning which derives directly from it. The mask, simply as a face, comes to express the solar and energetic aspects of the life-process. According to Zimmer, Shiva created a lion-headed, slender-bodied monster, expressive of insatiable appetite. And when this creature demands of his creator a victim to devour, the god tells him to eat of his own body, which the monster does so that it is reduced to a mere mask itself (60). There is a Chinese symbol, T'ao T'ieh—the 'mask of the ogre'—which may well be similar in origin (5).

Matron A form of personification very common in all symbolic images bearing upon the feminine principle; she appears not as spirit but as mother-protector: the Night, the Earth, the Church or the Synagogue, for example. Cities too are very often personified as matrons wearing a mural crown. Their attributes and features add the finishing touches to the symbolic content of the image (32). Psychologically speaking, the matron seems to express the domineering side of the mother.

Matter According to Evola, matter is equivalent to the moon, and form to the sun.

Maya 'The lesson may be read psychologically, as applying to ourselves, who are not gods but limited beings. The constant projection and externalization of our specific shakti (vital energy) is our "little universe", our restricted sphere and immediate environment, whatever concerns and affects us. We people and colour the indifferent, neutral screen with the movie-figures and dramas of the inward dream of our soul, and fall prey then to its dramatic events, delights, and calamities. The world, not as it is in itself but as we perceive it and react upon it, is the product of our own maya or delusion. It can be described as our own more or less blind life-energy, producing and projecting demonic or beneficent shapes and appearances. Thus we are the captives of our own Maya-Shakti and of the motion picture that it incessantly produces. . . . The Highest Being is the lord and master of Maya. All the rest of us . . . are the victims of our own individual Maya. . . . To liberate man from such a spell . . . is the principal aim of all the great Indian philosophies.' (60)

Meadow Bachelard has pointed out that the meadow, being nourished by the waters of a river, is in itself a subject of sadness and that, in the true meadow of the soul, only asphodels grow. The winds find no melodious trees in the meadow—only the silent waves of uniform grass. Bachelard also mentions Empedocles' description of 'the meadow of ill fortune' (2).

Melusina A fairy occurring in legends, sometimes in the form of a siren. Jean d'Arras dealt specifically with this fabulous being in *La Noble Hystoire de Luzignen* (1393). When a great disaster was about to befall she would give voice to a scream thrice repeated. 'Melusina it was who caused mysterious buildings to be set up in a single night by swarms of workers who would disappear without trace once the work had been completed. When she marries, all her children have some physical abnormality; in the same way, her magic buildings all have some defect, like those bridges of the devil which always have one stone missing' (16). Melusina seems to be the archetype of intuitive genius, in so far as intuition is prophetic, constructive and wondrous, and yet at the same time is infirm and malign.

Menhir Like all stones, the menhir embraces the idea of lithophany. In particular, because it stands erect, it is symbolic of the masculine principle and vigilance. It is further related to the sacrificial stake and, in consequence, to the world-axis (with all its related symbols: the cosmic tree, the steps, the cross, etc.) (50). There are also phallic as well as protective implications, as Eliade has noted (17).

Mephistopheles He represents the negative, infernal aspect of the psychic function which has broken away from the All to acquire independence and an individual character of its own (32).

Mercury The planetary god and the metal bearing his name. In astronomy, he is the son of heaven and light; in mythology, he was engendered by Jupiter and Maia. In essence he is the messenger of heaven. His Greek name of Hermes signifies 'interpreter' or 'mediator'. Hence it is his task to conduct the souls of the dead to the Lower World. Like Hecate, he is often triform, that is, represented with three heads. He epitomizes the power of the spoken word— the emblem of the word; and for the Gnostics he was the *logos spermatikos* scattered about the universe, an idea which was taken up by the alchemists who equated Mercury with related concepts of fluency and transmutation (9). At the same time, he was seen as a god of roads (that is, of potentialities) (4). In astrology he is defined as 'intellectual energy'. The nervous system is controlled by him, for the nerves are messengers on the biological plane (40). Probably it was the alchemists, with their lofty speculations, who penetrated farthest into the archetypal structure of Mercury. In many cases they identified their transmutation-substance with the 'lively planet', that is, with the god whose metal is white and decidedly lunar. However, since Mercury is the planet nearest to the sun (related to gold), the resultant archetype has a double nature (of a chthonian god and a celestial god—a hermaphrodite) (32). Mercury (the metal) symbolizes the unconscious because of its fluid and dynamic character; it is essentially *duplex* for, in one way, it is an inferior being, a devil or monster, but in another sense it is the 'philosophers' child' (33). Hence, its unlimited capacity for transformation (as in the case of all liquids) came to be symbolic of the essential aim of the alchemist to transmute matter (and spirit) from the inferior to the superior, from the transitory to the stable. Mercury was also credited with an unlimited aptitude for penetration (32). Its synonyms of *Monstrum hermaphroditus* and *Rebis* ('something double') reveal its close connexion with the Gemini myth (Atma and Buddhi); its representation as a feminine figure and *Anima mundi* (32) is more frequent and significant than its absorption by the masculine principle alone. In this connexion René Alleau recalls that the essential stages of the alchemic process were: prime matter, Mercury, Sulphur, *Lapis*. The first phase corresponds to indifferentiation; the second to the lunar and feminine principle; the third to the masculine and solar, the fourth to absolute synthesis (which Jung identifies with the process of individuation). The attributes of Mercury are the winged hat and sandals, the caduceus, the club, the turtle and the lyre (which he invented and gave to Apollo) (8).

Metals   In astrology they are called 'terrestrial' or 'subterranean planets', because of the analogous correspondences between the planets and the metals (57). For this reason astrologers consider that there are only seven metals (influenced by the same number of spheres), which does not mean that mankind during the astro-biological period did not recognize more. As Piobb has pointed out, some engineers have noted that the seven planetary metals make up a series which is applicable to the system of the twelve polygons (48). But, apart from the theory of correspondences, the metals symbolize cosmic energy in solidified form and, in consequence, the libido. On this basis, Jung has asserted that the base metals are the desires and the lusts of the flesh. Extracting the quintessence from these metals, or transmuting them into higher metals, is equivalent to setting creative energy free from the fetters of the sense world (33), a process identical with what esoteric tradition and astrology regard as liberation from the 'planetary influences'. The metals can be grouped within a progressive 'series' in which each metal displays its hierarchical superiority over the one preceding it, with gold as the culminating point of the progression. This is why, in certain rites, the neophyte is required to divest himself of his 'metals'—coins, keys, trinkets—because they are symbolic of his habits, prejudices and characteristics, etc. (9). We, for our part, however, are inclined to believe that in each particular pairing of planet with metal (as Mars with iron) there is an essential element of the ambitendent, in that its positive quality tends one way and its negative defect tends the other. Molten metal is an alchemic symbol expressing the *coniunctio oppositorum* (the conjunction of fire and water), related to mercury, Mercury and Plato's primordial, androgynous being. And at the same time, the solid or 'closed' properties of matter emphasize its symbolism as a liberator—hence the connexion with Hermes the psychopomp mentioned under 'Mercury' above (32). The correspondences between the planets and the metals, from inferior to superior, are: Saturn—lead, Jupiter—tin, Mars—iron, Venus—copper, Mercury —mercury, Moon—silver, Sun—gold.

Metamorphosis The transformation of one being or of one species into another generally relates to the broad symbolism of Inversion, but also to the essential notion of the difference between primigenial, undifferentiated Oneness and the world of manifestation. Everything may be transformed into anything else, since nothing is really anything. Transmutation is quite another matter: it is metamorphosis in an ascending direction, carrying all appearances away from the moving rim of the Wheel of Transformations along the radial path to the 'Unmoved mover'—the non-spatial and timeless Centre. 'The duplicity of Mercurius', writes Jung, 'his simultaneously metallic and pneumatic nature, is a parallel to the symbolization of an extremely spiritual idea like the Anthropos by a corporeal, indeed metallic substance (gold). One can only conclude that the unconscious tends to regard spirit and matter not merely as equivalent but as actually identical, and this in flagrant contrast to the intellectual one-sidedness of consciousness, which would sometimes like to materialize matter and at other times to materialize spirit. . . .'

Minaret The minaret is a symbolic torch of spiritual illumination, since it embraces the symbols of the tower (on account of its height) and the belvedere or watch-tower (signifying the consciousness). Hence it appears as a figure emblematic of the city of the Sun—or Camelot, where King Arthur held his court. The same symbolic sense is sometimes represented by a skyline with towers and pinnacles (4).

Minotaur A fabulous monster the lower half of which was a man and the upper a bull. It was in order to contain the minotaur that the Cretan Labyrinth was constructed. The monster was carnivorous, and the vanquished Athenians were obliged every seven years to deliver up seven youths and seven maidens for it to eat. This tribute was paid three times, but on the fourth occasion Theseus slew the minotaur with the aid of Ariadne and her magic thread (8). Every myth and legend which alludes to tributes, monsters or victorious heroes illustrates at once a cosmic situation (embracing the Gnostic ideas of the evil demiurge and of redemption), a social implication (for example, of a state oppressed by a tyrant, or a plague, or by some other hostile force) and a psychological significance pertaining either to the collective or the individual (implying the predominance of the monster in man, and the tribute and sacrifice of his finer side: his ideas, sentiments and emotions). The minotaur all but represents the last degree in the scale of relations between the spiritual and the animal sides in man. The predominance of the spiritual is symbolized by the knight; the prevalence of the monstrous is denoted by the centaur with the body of a horse or bull. The inversion of this, where the head is animal-like and the body human, implies the dominance of base forces carried to its logical extreme. The symbolism of the number seven (as in seven-headed dragons, or a period of seven years, or the sacrifice of seven youths) always denotes a relationship with the essential series (namely: the days of the week, the planetary gods, the planets, and the Vices and Cardinal Sins together with their corresponding Virtues). To vanquish a seven-headed monster is to conquer the evil influences of the planets (in consequence of the equation of the planets with the instincts and the baser forces).

Minstrel, The   The first enigma of the Tarot pack, this figure of a minstrel is a symbol of the original activity and the creative power of Man. He is depicted on the Tarot card wearing a hat in the form of a horizontal eight (the mathematical sign for infinity); he holds up a magic wand ('clubs') in one hand, and the other three symbols of the card-pack are on the table facing him; these are the equivalent of diamonds, spades and hearts, which, together with the wand ('clubs'), correspond to the four Elements (as well as the points of the compass). These attributes symbolize mastery over a given situation. The minstrel's garb is multi-coloured, but the predominant colour is red—denoting activity. In its transcendental implications, the enigma is related to Mercury (59).

Mirabilia   During Antiquity and the Middle Ages, this name was given to strange and amazing incidents (the hidden powers of animals, plants and stones, natural phenomena, 'miracles', and the sympathies or antipathies which unite or separate such beings or incidents). The literature of the 'Mirabilia' obtained a great success, especially in Hellenistic Egypt, whence it passed to the mediaeval Western world via the Arabs. Strange or amazing incidents are frequently traditional symbols and were sometimes connected with magic and alchemy. According to the Rev. Fr. Festugière O.P. in *La Révélation d'Hermès Trismégiste*, Bolus the Democritean (c. 200 B.C.), Pseudo-Manetho (2nd–1st centuries B.C.), Nigidius Figulus (1st century B.C.), Demetrius and Apollodorus (1st century A.D.) greatly contributed to the upsurge of this literature. It continued to evolve, tinged with hermetism, and found its fullest expression in the *Book of the Things of Nature*, written in Syria at the beginning of the 7th century. The general symbolic meaning of the 'Mirabilia' doubtless corresponds to the equation orgy = chaos, established by Eliade. They express a nostalgia for the era of animist indifferentism, which, in part, can also be seen to take refuge in contemporary poetry, especially that of the symbolist movement. On the other hand, the belief in 'powers' and even in a personal psychology of all beings, their aspects and qualities, became well rooted in the Western world, down through the Lower Middle Ages, the Renaissance, and the baroque period. For example, Father J. E. Nieremberg's book, *Oculta filosofía de la Sympatia y antipatía de las cosas, Artificio de la Naturaleza y noticia naturel del mundo*, published in Barcelona in 1645, belongs to this ideological stream.

Mirror   As a symbol, it has the same characteristics as the mirror in fact; the temporal and existential variety of its function provides the explanation of its significance and at the same time the diversity of its meaningful associations. It has been said that it is a symbol of the imagination—or of consciousness—in its capacity to reflect the formal reality of the visible world. It has also been related to thought, in so far as thought—for Scheler and other philosophers—is the instrument of self-contemplation as well as the reflection of the universe. This links mirror-symbolism with water as a reflector and with the Narcissus myth: the cosmos appears as a huge Narcissus regarding his own reflections in the human consciousness. Now, the world, as a state of discontinuity affected by the laws of change and substitution, is the agent which projects this quasi-negative, kaleidoscopic image of appearance and disappearance reflected in the mirror. From the earliest times, the mirror has been thought of as ambivalent. It is a surface which reproduces images and in a way contains and absorbs them. In legend and folklore, it is frequently invested with a magic quality—a mere hypertrophic version of its fundamental meaning. In this way it serves to invoke apparitions by conjuring up again the images which it has received at some time in the past, or by annihilating distances when it reflects what was once an object facing it and now is far removed. This fluctuation between the 'absent' mirror and the 'peopled' mirror lends it a kind of phasing, feminine in implication, and hence —like the fan—it is related to moon-symbolism. Further evidence that the mirror is lunar is afforded by its reflecting and passive characteristics, for it receives images as the moon receives the light of the sun (8). Again, its close relationship to the moon is demonstrated by the fact that among the primitives it was seen as a symbol of the multiplicity of the soul: of its mobility and its ability to adapt itself to those objects which 'visit' it and retain its 'interest'. At times, it takes the mythic form of a door through which the soul may free itself 'passing' to the other side: this is an idea reproduced by Lewis Carroll in *Alice Through the Looking Glass*. This alone is sufficient explanation of the custom of covering up mirrors or turning them to face the wall on certain occasions, in particular when someone in the house dies (21). All that we have said so far by no means exhausts the complex symbolism of the mirror: like the echo, it stands for twins (thesis and antithesis), and specifically for the sea of flames (or life as an infirmity) (50, 51). For Loeffler, mirrors are magic symbols for unconscious memories (comparable with crystal palaces) (38). Hand-mirrors, in particular, are emblems of truth (4), and in China they are supposed to have an allegorical function as aids to conjugal happiness as well as a protection against diabolical influences (5). Some Chinese legends tell of 'the animals in the mirror'.

Mist Mist is symbolic of things indeterminate, or the fusing together of the Elements of air and water, and the inevitable obscuring of the outlines of each aspect and each particular phase of the evolutive process. The 'mist of fire' is that stage of cosmic life which follows upon the state of chaos (9) and corresponds to the three Elements which existed prior to the solid Element—earth.

Mistletoe A parasitic plant associated with the oak. Celtic druids once used to gather it to use in their fertility rites (8). It symbolizes regeneration and the restoration of family-life (49). Frazer has equated it with the 'golden bough', of which Virgil wrote: 'A wondrous tree shimmering with a golden light among the green foliage. Just as, throughout the cold winter, the mistletoe, guest of a tree that never engendered it, unfailingly displays its fresh greenery, flecking the sombre trunk with the yellow of its berries, just so do golden leaves show among the green foliage of the oak, and so would these golden leaves whisper to the gentle breeze' (*Aeneid*, VI). The yellow colour of the withered mistletoe-branch was thought—by a process of sympathetic magic—to be endowed with the power to discover buried treasure (21).

Monkey The simians generally symbolize the baser forces, darkness or unconscious activity, but this symbolism—like that of legendary fabulous beings—has two sides to it. If, on the one hand, this unconscious force may be dangerous, while it may degrade the individual, nevertheless it may also prove a boon—like all unconscious powers—when least expected. This is why, in China, the monkey is credited with the power of granting good health, success and protection, being related in this way to sprites, sorcerers and fairies (5).

Monolith In the Egyptian system of hieroglyphs, the monolith is a determinative sign associated with the name of the god Osiris and signifying 'to last'. In the myth, Osiris was slain by Set (or Typhon) and put together again by Isis. The ceremony performed in commemoration of this event included the erection of a monolith (a symbol of lithophanic unity) as a sign of resurrection and life

eternal (19), or of unity counterbalancing multiplicity, fragmentation and disintegration (this, in turn, being a symbol of the world
of phenomena 'fallen' into the multiplicity of the diverse—space—
and the transitory—time). The monolith, because of its shape and
position, possesses other secondary meanings alluding—as in the
case of the menhir—to the masculine, the solar and the procreative
principle.

Monsters   They are symbolic of the cosmic forces at a stage one
step removed from chaos—from the 'non-formal potentialities'. On
the psychological plane, they allude to the base powers which
constitute the deepest strata of spiritual geology, seething as in a
volcano until they erupt in the shape of some monstrous apparition
or activity. Diel suggests that they symbolize an unbalanced psychic
function: the affective whipping up of desire, paroxysms of the
indulged imagination, or improper intentions (15). They are, then,
par excellence, the antithesis—or the adversary—of the 'hero' and
of 'weapons'. For weapons are the positive powers granted to man
by the deity, and this is the explanation of the mysterious, miraculous
or magical context of weapons wielded by heroes in myth and
legend. Weapons, then, are the symbolic antithesis to monsters.
Diel has pointed out that, paradoxically, the chimerical enemy—
perversion, the fascination of madness or of evil *per se*—is the
fundamental adversary in the life of Man. On the social plane, the
motif of the monster ravaging a country is symbolic of the ill-fated
reign of a wicked, tyrannical or impotent monarch (15). The fight
against a monster signifies the struggle to free consciousness from the
grip of the unconscious. The hero's deliverance corresponds to the
sunrise, the triumph of light over darkness, of consciousness or the
spirit over the affective strata of the unconscious (31). In a less
negative sense, the monster may be equated with the libido (56).
Monsters are closely connected in symbolism with fabulous beings,
which afford a wider range of meanings embracing some that are
wholly favourable and positive such as Pegasus, the phoenix, etc.
Some of the principal monsters known to tradition and perpetuated
by art are the following: the sphinx, the griffin, the siren-fish, the
siren-bird, the lamia, the bird with the head of a quadruped, the
bird-serpent, the winged bull, the dragon, the giant fish, the giant
sea-serpent, the chimaera, the Gorgon, the minotaur, the triton,
the hydra, the salamander, the merman, the harpy, the hippogryph,
the sea-demon and the Fury (36). The head of a monster, dragon or
sea animal, with one or more human heads in its mouth, is a
mediaeval symbol of hell. Psychologically it represents the danger
of being devoured by the destructive forces of some species, a danger
which may affect only the more noble parts of the human being,
such as his moral sense or his reason. For Walter Abell, in *The*

Collective Dream in Art (Cambridge, 1957), monsters also symbolize the latent and dangerous forces, in a greater or lesser state of freedom, of the human unconscious in its aggressive and ugly aspect. He points out that monsters are the principal characters in the 7th-century Anglo-Saxon poem, *Beowulf*. He establishes an interesting comparison and asserts that, in later prehistory (the Neolithic Age, the Age of Metals), the monsters dominated the gods; between Antiquity and the Romanesque period, the gods succeeded in counterbalancing the monsters, who, nevertheless, still played an important rôle (as revealed, for example, in miniatures and capitals of the time); and in the Gothic period, the angelic spirits triumphed over the monsters. In more than one aspect, contemporary art, especially since Blake and Goya, might be taken as pointing to a certain 'resurrection of the monsters' and of the monstrous, as seen particularly in the surrealist movement.

Montsalvat In the legend of the Grail, it is the *mons salvationis*, the peak situated 'on distant shores which no mortal may approach', similar to the Hindu mount Meru, the polar mountain. It is the symbol of supreme spiritual fulfilment.

Montserrat There are some prehistoric paintings that depict a squatting man in such a way that his outline resembles the jagged or 'serrated' skyline of a mountain. And—although it is mere coincidence—the significance of Montserrat (the 'Serrated Mountain' near Barcelona) is precisely that it presents Man as occupying, through sacrifice, a marginal position at the point of intersection of the circles of heaven and earth (corresponding to the cross-symbolism). At the same time, some mediaeval representations of the siren are entitled *Serra*.

Moon The symbolism of the moon is wide in scope and very complex. The power of this satellite was noted by Cicero, when he observed that 'Every month the moon completes the same trajectory executed by the sun in a year. . . . It contributes in large measure to the maturation of shrubs and the growth of animals.' This helps to explain the important rôle of the lunar goddesses such as Ishtar, Hathor, Anaitis, Artemis. Man, from the earliest times, has been aware of the relationship between the moon and the tides, and of the more mysterious connexion between the lunar cycle and the physiological cycle of woman. Krappe believes—with Darwin—that this follows from the fact that animal life originated in the watery deeps and that this origin imparted a rhythm to life which has lasted for millions of years. As he observes, the moon thus becomes the 'Master of women'. Another essential fact in the 'psychology of the moon' is the apparent changes in its surface that accompany its periodic phases. He postulates that these phases—especially in their negative sense of partial and gradual disappearance—may have been the source of inspiration for the Dismemberment myth (Zagreus, Pentheus, Orpheus, Actaeon, and Osiris for example). The same might be said of the myths and legends of the 'spinners' (35). When patriarchy superseded matriarchy, a feminine character came to be attributed to the moon and a masculine to the sun. The *hieros gamos*, generally understood as the marriage of heaven and earth, may also be taken as the union of the sun and the moon. It is generally conceded nowadays that the lunar rhythms were utilized before the solar rhythms as measures of time, and there is also a possible equation with the resurrection—spring follows upon winter, flowers appear after the frost, the sun rises again after the gloom of night, and the crescent moon grows out of the 'new moon'. Eliade points to the connexion between these cosmic events and the myth of the periodic creation and recreation of the universe (17). The regulating function of the moon can also be seen in the distribution of the waters and the rains, and hence it made an early appearance as the mediator between earth and heaven. The moon not only measures and determines terrestrial phases but also unifies them through its activity: it unifies, that is, the waters and rain, the fecundity of women and of animals, and the fertility of vegetation. But above all it is the being which does not keep its identity but suffers 'painful' modifications to its shape as a clear and entirely visible circle. These phases are analogous to the seasons of the year and to the ages in the span of man's life, and are the reasons for the affinity of the moon with the biological order of things, since it is also subject to the laws of change, growth (from youth to maturity) and decline (from maturity to old age). This accounts for the mythic belief that the moon's invisible phase corresponds to death in man, and, in consequence, the idea that the dead go to the moon (and return from it—according to those traditions which accept reincarnation). 'Death', observes Eliade, 'is not therefore an extinction, but a temporal modification of the plan of life. For three nights the moon disappears from heaven, but on the fourth day it is reborn. . . . The idea of the journey to the moon after death is one which has been preserved in the more advanced cultures (in Greece, India and Iran). Pythagorean thought imparted a fresh impulse to astral theology: the "Islands of the Blessed" and all mythic geography came to be projected on to celestial planes—the sun, the moon, the Milky Way. It is not difficult to find, in these later formulas, the traditional themes of the moon as the Land of the Dead or as the regenerating receptacle of souls. (But) . . . lunar space was no more than one stage in the ascension; there were others: the sun, the Milky Way, the "supreme circle". This is the reason why the moon presides over the formation of organisms, and also over their decomposition (as the colour green). Its destiny consists of reabsorbing forms and of recreating them. Only that which is beyond the moon, or above it, can transcend becoming. Hence, for Plutarch, the souls of the just are purified in the moon, whilst their bodies return to earth and their spirit to the sun.' The lunar condition, then, is equivalent to the human condition. Our Lady is depicted above the moon, thereby denoting that eternity is above the mutable and transitory (17). René Guénon has confirmed that, in 'the sphere of the moon', forms are dissolved, so that the superior states are severed from the inferior; hence the dual rôle of the moon as Diana and Hecate—the celestial and the infernal. Diana or Jana is the feminine form of Janus (26, 17). Within the cosmic order, the moon is regarded as a duplication of the sun, but in diminished form, for, if the latter brings life to the entire planetary system, the moon influences only our own planet. Because of its passive character—in that it receives its light from the sun—it is equated with the symbolism of the number two and with the passive or feminine principle. It is also related to the Egg of the World, the matrix and the casket (9). The metal corresponding to the moon is silver (57). It is regarded as the guide to the occult side of nature, as opposed to the sun which is responsible for the life of the manifest world and for fiery activity. In alchemy, the moon represents the volatile (or mutable) and feminine principle, and also multiplicity because of the fragmentary nature of its phases. These two ideas have sometimes been confused, giving rise to literal interpretations which fall into the trap of superstition. The Greenlanders, for example, believe that all celestial bodies were at one time human beings, but the moon in particular they accuse of inciting their women to orgies and for this reason they are not permitted to contemplate it for long (8). In pre-Islamic Arabia, as in other Semitic cultures, the cult of the moon prevailed over sun-worship. Mohammed forbade the use of any metal in amulets except silver (39). Another significant aspect of the moon concerns its close association with the night (maternal, enveloping, unconscious and ambivalent because it is both protective and dangerous) and the pale quality of its light only half-illuminating objects. Because of this, the moon is associated with the imagination and the fancy as the intermediary realm between the self-denial of the spiritual life and the blazing sun of intuition. Schneider has drawn attention to a highly interesting morphological point with his observation that the progressive change in the shape of the moon—from disk-shape to a thin thread of light—seems to have given birth to a mystic theory of forms which has influenced, for example, the manner of constructing musical instruments (51). At the same time, Stuchen, Hommel and Dornseif have demonstrated the influence of the lunar shapes upon the characters of the Hebrew and Arabic alphabets, in addition to their profound effect upon the morphology of instruments. Eliade quotes Hentze's comment to the effect that all dualisms find in the moon's phases, if not their historical cause, at least a mythic and a symbolic model. 'The nether world—the world of darkness—is represented by a dying moon (horns = quarter moon; the sign of a double volute = two quarter moons facing in opposite directions; two quarters superimposed back to back = lunar change representing a decrepit, bony old man). The upper world— the world of life and of the nascent sun—is symbolized by a tiger (the monster of darkness and of the new moon) with the human being, represented by a child, emerging from its jaws' (17). Animals regarded as lunar are those which alternate between appearance and disappearance, like the amphibians; examples are the snail which leaves its shell and returns to it; or the bear which vanishes in winter and reappears in spring, and so on. Lunar objects may be taken as those of a passive or reflecting character, like the mirror; or those which can alter their surface-area, like the fan. An interesting point to note is that both objects are feminine in character.

Moon, The   The eighteenth enigma of the Tarot. It shows an image of the moon dimly lighting up the objects of the world with its uncertain light. Beneath the moon there is a huge, red crab resting upon the mud. The allegory also shows two watchdogs guarding the orbit of the sun and barking at the moon. Behind them, to the left and right, are two castles in the form of square towers, flesh-coloured and edged in gold. The moon is represented by a silvered disk bearing the outlines of a woman. Long, yellow rays stream out from this disk, intermixed with other shorter, reddish rays. Inverted drops of water are floating in the air, as if attracted by the moon. It is a scene which illustrates the strength and the dangers of the world of appearances and the imagination. The visionary sees things in a lunar light. The crab, like the Egyptian scarab, has as its function that of devouring what is transitory—the volatile element in alchemy —and of contributing to moral and physical regeneration. The watchdogs are a warning to the moon to stay away from the realm of the sun (the logos); the towers, on the other hand, rise up as a warning that the approach to the domain of the moon is beset by very real dangers (the 'perils of the soul' of primitive man). As Wirth describes it, behind the towers is a steppe-land, and behind that, a wood (the 'forest' as it appears in legends and folklore) full of ghosts. Beyond that there is a mountain (Schneider's 'twin-peaked mountain') and a precipice bordering a stream of purifying water. This seems to suggest the route followed by the shamans on their ecstatic journeys. There is another ancient Tarot card depicting a harpist singing, in the moonlight, to a young girl loosening her hair at a window. The image here alludes to the mortal characteristics of the moon, for the harpist is a widespread symbol of death (and of the death-wish), and the girl is unquestionably a symbol of the soul. This Tarot enigma, in sum, seeks to give instruction upon the 'lunar way' (of intuition, imagination and magic) as distinct from the 'solar way' (of reason, reflection, objectivity); but at the same time it is pregnant with negative and fatal significance. In the negative sense, it alludes to error, arbitrary fantasy, imaginative sensitivity, etc. (59).

Mother Mother-symbols are characterized by an interesting ambivalence: the mother sometimes appears as the image of nature, and vice-versa; but the Terrible Mother is a figure signifying death (31). For this reason, Hermetic doctrine held that to 'return to the mother' was equivalent to dying. For the Egyptians, the vulture was a mother-symbol, probably because it devours corpses (19); it also stood for the means whereby Hammamit (the universal soul) was split up into separate parts to form individual souls (19). For the same reason, the maternal sentiment has been said to be closely bound up with the nostalgic longing of the spirit for things material (18), or with the subjection of the spirit to the unformulated but implacable law of destiny. Jung mentions that in Jean Thenaud's *Traité de la Cabale* (of the 16th century) there is a mother-figure actually represented in the form of a god of destiny (32). He mentions further that the Terrible Mother is the counterpart of the *Pietà*, representing not only death but also the cruel side of nature—its indifference towards human suffering (31). Jung also notes that the mother is symbolic of the collective unconscious, of the left and nocturnal side of existence—the source of the Water of Life. It is the mother, he argues, who is the first to bear that image of the *anima* which the man must project upon Woman passing from the mother to the sister and finally to the beloved (32). A predominantly maternal social pattern—a matriarchal society—is characterized, according to Bachofen, by special emphasis upon blood relationships, telluric allegiances, and the passive acceptance of natural phenomena. Patriarchies are distinguished by a respect for man-made laws, the favouring of works of art and craft, and obedience to the hierarchy (23). Even now that matriarchal societies, sociologically speaking, no longer exist in the West, psychologically man is nevertheless passing through a phase when he is in all essentials dominated by the feminine principle. To come triumphantly through this stage and to reinstate the masculine principle as the guiding-rule of life—bringing to the fore the characteristically patriarchal qualities noted above—would signify an achievement of the kind that was once symbolized by the transformation of the 'lunar work' into the solar, or by the transmutation of mercury into sulphur. To quote Evola: 'Symbols of the earth-mother are: water, the mother of the waters, stone, the cave, the maternal home, night, the house of depth, and the house of strength or of wisdom.'

Mound of Earth A sign in the Egyptian system of hieroglyphs in the form of a rectangle with two sides incomplete. It symbolizes the intermediate stages of matter, and is related to the symbols of primordial waters and of slime (19).

Mountain The different meanings which have been attached to the symbolism of the mountain stem not so much from any inherent multiplicity as from the various implications of each of its component elements: its height, verticality, mass and shape. Deriving from the first idea (height) are interpretations such as that of Teillard, who equates the mountain with inner 'loftiness' of spirit (56), that is, transposing the notion of ascent to the realm of the spirit. In alchemy, on the other hand, the reference is nearly always to the hollow mountain, the hollow being a cavern which is the 'philosophers' oven'. The vertical axis of the mountain drawn from its peak down to its base links it with the world-axis, and, anatomically, with the spinal column. Because of its grandiose proportions, the mountain came to symbolize, for the Chinese, the greatness and generosity of the Emperor; it is the fourth of the twelve imperial emblems (5). But the profoundest symbolism is one that imparts a sacred character by uniting the concept of mass, as an expression of being, with the idea of verticality. As in the case of the cross or the Cosmic Tree, the location of this mountain is at the 'Centre' of the world. This same profound significance is common to almost all traditions: suffice it to recall mount Meru of the Hindus, the Haraberezaiti of the Iranians, Tabor of the Israelites, Himingbjör of the Germanic peoples, to mention only a few. Furthermore, the temple-mountains such as Borobudur, the Mesopotamian *ziggurats* or the pre-Columbian *teocallis* are all built after the pattern of this symbol. Seen from above, the mountain grows gradually wider, and in this respect it corresponds to the inverted tree whose roots grow up towards heaven while its foliage points downwards, thereby expressing multiplicity, the universe in expansion, involution and materialization. This is why Eliade says that 'the peak of the cosmic mountain is not only the highest point on earth, it is also the earth's navel, the point where creation had its beginning'—the root (18). The mystic sense of the peak also comes from the fact that it is the point of contact between heaven and earth, or the centre through which the world-axis passes, binding the three levels together. It is, incidentally, also the focal point of Inversion—the point of inter-section of the immense St. Andrew's cross, which expresses the relationship between the different worlds. Other sacred mountains are Sumeru of the Ural-Altaic peoples (17) and Caf in Moslem mythology—a huge mountain the base of which is formed by a single emerald called *Sakhrat* (8). Mount Meru is said to be of gold and located at the North Pole (8), thus underlining the idea of the Centre and, in particular, linking it with the Pole Star—the 'hole' through which all things temporal and spatial must pass in order to divest themselves of their worldly characteristics. This polar mountain is also to be found in other symbolic traditions, always bearing the same symbolism of the world-axis (25); its mythic characteristics were, in all probability, based upon the fixed position of the Pole Star. It is also called the 'white mountain', in which case it embraces both the basic mountain-symbolism with all the implications outlined above and that of the colour white (intelligence and purity). This was the predominating characteristic of Mount Olympus (49), the supreme, celestial mountain which Schneider sees as corresponding to Jupiter and equivalent to the principle of the number one. There is another mountain, relevant to the symbolism of the number two, and that is the mountain of Mars and Janus—that is, as the Gemini; basically, they represent two different aspects of the same mountain, but blending together the symbolism of the 'two worlds' of *Atma* and *Buddhi*, or the two essential, rhythmic aspects of manifest creation—light and darkness, life and death, immortality and mortality. This mountain has two peaks, in order to give visual expression to its dual or ambivalent meaning. It occurs constantly in traditional, megalithic culture, particularly in the form of a landscape, illustrating yet again the Protean myth of the Gemini, which bursts out in so many different forms in primitive thought and art. This mountain is also a form of mandorla consisting of the intersection of the circle of the heavens with that of the earth, and this mandorla is, as it were, the crucible of life, containing the opposite poles of life (good and bad, love and hate, fidelity and treachery, affirmation and negation, the numbers 2 and 11—both equal to one plus one—and finally construction and destruction). Incidentally, the animals which correspond to this all-embracing significance of the mandorla are the whale and the shark (51). In Hindu legend, the castle of Indra was built on this mountain; whereas in Roman legend it was the castle of Mars, and the home of the thunderbolt, the two-headed eagle and the Gemini. It has been called the 'mountain of stone' and is at once the abode of the living (the exterior of the mountain) and of the dead (the hollow interior) (50). Krappe has borne this out with the observation that 'The interior of a mountain has frequently been taken as the location of the Land of the Dead: the derivation of the Celtic and Irish fairy-hills, and of the legend, widespread in Asia and Europe, of a demiurge or hero asleep inside a mountain, one day to emerge and renew all things sublunar' (35). This myth has obvious connexions with the myth of Entanglement—of the castle inextricably entangled in a wood - and also with the story of the 'Sleeping Beauty'. All such myths are concerned with the mystery of a disappearance between appearance and reappearance. Schneider lists the following trades and professions as being associated with Mars: those of the king, physician, warrior and miner, as well as the martyr (51). In Western tradition, the mountain-symbol appears in the legend of the Grail, as Montsalvat (the 'mountain of salvation' or 'of health')—just as much a 'polar mountain' as it is a 'sacred island', according to Guénon; but always it is inaccessible or difficult to find (like the 'centre' of the labyrinth) (28). In general, the mountain, the hill and the mountain-top are all associated with the idea of meditation, spiritual elevation and the communion of the blessed. In mediaeval emblems, the symbolism of the 'mountain of salvation' is further defined by a complementary figure surmounting it, such as the fleur-de-lis, the star, the lunar crescent, the cross, steps, the crown, the circle, the triangle, or the number three. The letter Z sometimes occurs, standing for *Zion*; similarly, an R is short for *Regeneratio* (4). Some of these symbols have lent themselves to a poetic treatment that is well worth examination. From the moment when the mountain, so to speak, divests itself of its terrestrial and material character and becomes the image of an idea, the more numerous the component elements pertaining to this idea, the greater will be its clarity and force. Hence, mount Meru of India is considered to have the shape of a pure, seven-sided pyramid (corresponding to the seven planetary spheres, the seven essential virtues and the seven Directions of space) and each face has one of the colours of the rainbow. Seen as a whole, the mountain is a shining white, by which token it may be equated with the 'polar mountain' and the all-embracing image of totality (also symbolized by the pyramid-symbol), tending towards Oneness (symbolized by the peak)—to avail ourselves of the concepts of Nicholas of Cusa.

Mouth In the symbolism pertaining to the body, the most elementary association is the one between the organ or member and its function. It is, then, self-evident that, in Egyptian hieroglyphs, the mouth should stand for the power of speech and hence for the creative word. In this sense it stands for the pristine emanation of creative power. Very closely connected with this hieroglyph is another showing a mouth with a solar disk inside. This disk, primarily standing for the sun, is connected, but not identical, with the eye. (In hieroglyphs which are coloured, the eye is wholly blue, while the sign under discussion consists of a blue mouth with a little red circle inside) (19). Guénon supports this interpretation of the sign (29), pointing to the example of the *Mândûkya Upanishad* where, apropos the state of deep sleep, the mouth is said to represent integral consciousness (26). In the Old Testament, the concepts of mouth and fire are frequently associated; epithets such as 'devouring' or 'consuming', frequently applied to the latter, are descriptive of the functions of the former. Hence the fire-breathing animals of legend. Jung explains these associations by synaesthesia and suggests that they are connected with Apollo, the sun-god who is depicted with a lyre as his characteristic attribute. The common link between the symbolisms of sounding, speaking, shining and burning finds a physiological parallel in the phenomenon known as 'coloured hearing' whereby some individuals experience sounds as colours. Furthermore, it is hardly a coincidence that the two main characteristics that set Man apart from all other beings are the power of speech and the use of fire. Both are, in fact, the product of *mana* (psychic energy) (31). In consequence, mouth-symbolism, like fire-symbolism, has two aspects: creative (as in speech) and destructive (devouring). And, of course, the mouth is the point of convergence between the external and the inner worlds. This explains the frequent symbol of the 'monster's mouth', with sets of upper and lower teeth that are expressive of the 'interlocking' of the two worlds: heaven and earth or, more often, hell and earth (50). There are, in mediaeval iconography, abundant examples of the mouths of dragons or large fishes affording access to the inner world or to the underworld.

Mud   Mud signifies the union of the purely receptive principle (earth) with the power of transition and transformation (water). Mud is regarded as the typical medium for the emergence of matter of all kinds (17). Plasticity is therefore one of its essential characteristics, and it is related, by analogy, with biological processes and nascent states.

Multiplicity   Given the mystic and emanatistic character of the philosophy of symbolism whereby—as in Neoplatonism—the One is identified with the Creator, it follows that multiplicity must represent the farthest point from the Source of all things. If the image of the circle is taken to express the relationship between unity and multiplicity, then the centre corresponds to unity and the outer circumference or rim relates to multiplicity (as in the Buddhist Wheel of Transformations) (25). Jung has corroborated this principle from the psychologist's point of view, observing that multiplicity is always regressive in character, and recalling that when the protagonist of the *Hypnerotomachia Poliphili* appears surrounded by a bevy of women, this is an indication of the nature of the unconscious —but of the unconscious revealed as in a state of fragmentation. Hence the Greek maenads, Erinyes, Bacchantes, harpies and sirens all express a situation in which man's inner wholeness is torn to shreds (32). This is something which greatly concerned the alchemists, and one part of their work was directed to transforming the volatile (or the transitory and multiple) into the fixed (the stable, or the unified). Another way in which multiplicity is induced is by the creation of hierarchies. But, in addition to all this, we must note that multiplicity, and its consequence, diversity, may be products of division as well as of multiplication. For symbolic purposes, the essence of multiplication is division. As an example, we might suggest that in contrast to a unitary fruit like the apple, the pomegranate is a perfect illustration of multiplicity because it is internally subdivided into a multitude of cells. Hence the negative character of multiplicity, and hence the symbolic doctrine that the totality of the individual has no value until it has become transmuted—that is, until the individual has destroyed in himself the desire for dispersal in space (corresponding to multiplicity) and in time (corresponding to transitoriness) so that ultimately he may be transformed into an image of the One and so be assimilated into the eternal principle. This is a mystic tendency which does not fail to make its mark on the plane of existence, particularly where the moral issues of love are involved. Legends such as that of the Flying Dutchman afford a precise illustration of just such a pilgrimage of the spirit in its quest for the unique soul, searching through all those imperfect forms that lie in its path. The 'temptations' of Parsifal likewise correspond to this same symbolism. Symbolic jewels, when they come to lose their unitary significance as 'treasure' conceived as an integrated whole, and fall into multiplicity, acquire negative and distracting implications.

Multiplicity of a Common Element   A dream that occurs quite often among certain abnormal types of subjects involves a multitude —of objects or of people—all with the same characteristics, that is, the multitude comprises the multiplication of one single phenomenon instead of a collection of many different ones. This is a symbol alluding to the secret and, at root, terrible unity of all things. Now, the anguish which nearly always attends this symbol is a psychological consequence of 'repetition' (as studied by Kierkegaard) and of the fact that in this world it seems to be the law of diversification that prevails. Or, to put it another way, diversity justifies multiplicity. Multiple monsters imply the multiplicity of their own symbolism as images of disintegration, dissociation, dispersion and separation. For this reason it is a characteristically pathological symbol.

Music   The symbolism of music is of the greatest complexity and we cannot here do more than sketch out some general ideas. It pervades all the component elements of created sound: instruments, rhythm, tone or timbre, the notes of the natural scale, serial patterns, expressive devices, melodies, harmonies and forms. The symbolism of music may be approached from two basic standpoints: either by regarding it as part of the ordered pattern of the cosmos as understood by the ancient, megalithic and astrobiological cultures, or else by accepting it as a phenomenon of 'correspondence' linked with the

business of expression and communication. Another of the fundamental aspects of music-symbolism is its connexion with metre and
with number, arising out of the Pythagorean theory (27). The cosmic
significance of musical instruments—their allegiance to one particular
Element—was first studied by Curt Sachs in *Geist und Werden der
Musikinstrumente* (Berlin, 1929). In this symbolism, the characteristic shape of an instrument must be distinguished from the timbre,
and there are some common 'contradictions' between these two
aspects which might possibly be of significance as an expression of
the mediating rôle of the musical instrument and of music as a
whole (for an instrument is a form of relationship or communication,
substantially dynamic, as in the case of the voice or the spoken word).
For example, the flute is phallic and masculine in shape and feminine
in its shrill pitch and light, silvery (and therefore lunar) tone, while
the drum is feminine by virtue of its receptacle-like shape, yet
masculine in its deep tones (50). The connexion of music-symbolism
with self-expression (and even with graphic art) is well in evidence
in primitive music-making, which often amounted to almost literal
imitations of the rhythms and movements, the features and even the
shapes of animals. Schneider describes how, hearing some Senegalese
singing the 'Song of the Stork', he began to 'see as he was listening',
for the rhythm corresponded exactly to the movements of the bird.
When he asked the singers about this, their reply confirmed his
observation. Given the laws of analogy, we can also find cases of the
expressive transferred to the symbolic: that is, a melodic progression
as a whole expresses certain coherent emotions, and this progression corresponds to certain coherent, symbolic forms. On the
other hand, alternating deep and high-pitched tones express a
'leap', anguish and the need for Inversion; Schneider concludes
that this is an expression of the idea of conquering the space between
the valley and the mountain (corresponding to the earth and the
sky). He observes that in Europe the mystic designation of 'high
music' (that is, high-pitched) and 'low music' (low-pitched) persisted
right up to the Renaissance. The question of relating musical notes
to colours or to planets is far from being as certain as other symbolic
correspondences of music. Nevertheless, we cannot pass on without
giving some idea of the profound, serial relationship which exists
in phenomena: for instance, corresponding to the pentatonic scale
we usually find patterns grouped in fives; the diatonic and modal
scale, since it has seven notes, is related to most of the astrobiological systems, and is unquestionably the most important of all
the series; the present-day tendency towards the twelve-note series
could be compared to the signs of the Zodiac. But, so far, we have
not found sufficient evidence for this particular facet of music-
symbolism. All the same, here are the correspondences as set down

by Fabre d'Olivet, the French occultist: Mi—the Sun, fa—Mercury, sol—Venus, la—the Moon, ti—Saturn, do—Jupiter, re—Mars (26). A more valid series of relationships, at least in the expressive aspect, is that which links the Greek modes with the planets and with particular aspects of the *ethos*, as follows: the mi-mode (the Dorian) —Mars (who is severe or pathetic); the re-mode (the Phrygian)— Jupiter (ecstatic): the do-mode (the Lydian)—Saturn (pained and sad); the ti-mode (the Hypodorian)—the Sun (enthusiastic); the la-mode (the Hypophrygian)—Mercury (active); the sol-mode (the Hypolydian)—Venus (erotic); the fa-mode (the Mixolydian)—the Moon (melancholy) (50). Schneider's profound investigations into the symbolism of music seem to us well-founded. The tetrachord formed by the notes do, re, mi, fa, he considers, for instance, to be a mediator between heaven and earth, the four notes corresponding respectively to the lion (signifying valour and strength), the ox (sacrifice and duty), man (faith and incarnation) and the eagle (elevation and prayer). Conversely, the tetrachord formed by sol, la, ti, do, could represent a kind of divine duplicate of the previous tetrachord. Fa, do, sol, re are regarded as masculine elements corresponding to the Elements of fire and air and to the instruments of stone and metal, whereas la, mi, ti, are feminine, and pertain to the Elements of water and earth. The interval fa-ti, known to musicologists as a tritone (or augmented fourth), expresses with its dissonance the 'painful' clash between the Elements of fire and water —a clash occurring in death itself (50). We have been able to suggest here only a few outlines of the music-symbolism developed by Schneider in his work *The Musical Origin of Animal-Symbols*, the scope of which is so wide that, as he has privately intimated to us, he believes all symbolic meanings are at root musical or at least to do with sounds. This becomes easier to understand when we recall that singing, as the harmonization of successive, melodic elements, is an image of the natural connexion between all things, and, at the same time, the communication, the spreading and the exaltation of the inner relationship linking all things together. Hence Plato's remark that the character of a nation's music cannot be altered without changing the customs and institutions of the State (26).

Musician The musician is a common symbol of the fascination of death (personified by the Greeks as a youth). The Pied Piper of Hamelin in the well-known tale, the harpist and the citharist in legends and folktales, all allude to this one symbol. Music represents an intermediate zone between the differentiated or material world, and the undifferentiated realm of the 'pure will' of Schopenhauer. Hence its use in rites and liturgies (together with fire and smoke).

Names In esoteric thought, names are an integrating expression of the horoscope (49). There has been a great deal of speculation about the symbolic elements entering into the composition of names: letters in their graphic or phonetic aspects, similes, analogies, and so on. Piobb, for instance, has suggested that the name Napoleon is Apollo in the Corsican pronunciation of *O'N'Apolio* (48). The question of why a given name should determine the destiny of one individual but not of another is something which lies beyond the scope of this work. Here we must limit ourselves to describing the rational basis of the symbolism of names and its connexion with the Egyptian idea of the 'power of words' (as described in a poem by Edgar Allan Poe). Given the symbolic nature of the Egyptian language, it follows that a name could never be a product of chance but only of the study of the characteristics of a given thing, whether the name in question was common or proper. The name RN (signifying a mouth over the surface of water) represented the action of the 'word' upon passivity. Concerning personal nomenclature, the Egyptians believed that their names were a reflection of their souls. This gave rise to the belief that a name could have a magical effect upon some other person. The equation of name with character (and destiny) had its repercussions also in descriptive names, such as that of Osiris, which means 'he who is at the top of the steps' (the steps, that is, of evolution); or that of Arabia, signifying 'he who walks in silence'. Onomatopoeia was another highly important source in the genesis of language and its ideographic representation, whereby a given being is characterized by one of its essential aspects—as the lion by its roar, for example: or RW in Egyptian (19). Popular works on occultism which suggest symbolic implications for certain proper names, as in other cases of vulgarized interpretation, have some roots in authentic symbolism but they may also fall into the trap of being too hard-and-fast about the true scope of symbolism. Language has, in the last century or two, reached such a complex stage of development that the applied symbolism of etymology is subject to innumerable errors.

Narcissus Joachim Gasquet sees the Narcissus-myth as a primordial illustration not on the sexual but on the cosmic level, commenting that 'the world is an immense Narcissus in the act of contemplating itself', so that Narcissus becomes a symbol of this self-contemplative, introverted, and self-sufficient attitude (quoted by Bachelard, 2).

Nature The 12th-century writer Alan of Lille, in his *De planctu naturae*, describes Nature as an allegorical figure wearing a diadem set with jewels in imitation of the stars: twelve stones symbolize the signs of the Zodiac and seven stand for the Sun, the Moon and the five planets (14). This concept is wholly astrobiological in character, since it partakes of the tendency to bring the discipline of numbers to bear upon living things, and to infuse the astral, the mineral and the abstract with the vital forces of plant and animal life.

Necklace Broadly speaking, the threaded bead-necklace stands for the unifying of diversity, that is, it represents an intermediate state between the inherent disintegration of all multiplicity—always a negative state—and the state of unity inherent in continuity. Regarded as a string, the necklace becomes a cosmic and social symbol of ties and bonds. Because it is usually worn on the neck or breast, it acquires a symbolic relation with those parts of the body and with the signs of the Zodiac pertaining to them. Since the neck has an astrological association with sex, the necklace also betokens an erotic link.

Negro The image of the Negro always alludes to the baser part of man—to the substrata of the passions. This psychological fact, empirically proven by psychoanalysis, finds its parallel—or its origin—in traditional symbolic doctrine, according to which coloured people are the children of darkness and the white man is the child of the sun or of the white, polar mountain (49).

Neptune In primitive thought, he was the deity of heaven in its symbolic aspect of the 'Upper Waters', that is, the god of clouds and of rain. Later he became the god of fresh and fertilizing water. Finally, he was seen as the god of the sea. In this development we can trace not only a chronological and historical line of progress but, more especially, a spiritual projection of the myth of the 'fall', which finally became absorbed into the character of Neptune. The trident, seen from this point of view of 'descent'—of the 'fall'—can be equated with the thunderbolt. Charles Ploix, in *La Nature et les dieux*, on the other hand, identifies the trident with the magic wand used in water-divining (2). For the alchemists, Neptune was quite simply a symbol for water. Apart from the trident, his attributes are sea-horses (8), signifying the cosmic forces and the swelling rhythm of the foamy waves. The discovery of psychoanalysts that the ocean is a symbol of the unconscious has, at the same time, proved beyond question the relationship of Neptune with the deepest layers of the individual, and the universal, soul. Diel, therefore, is able to conclude that Neptune, like Pluto, symbolizes the negative aspect of the spirit. He is king of the deeps of the subconscious and of the turbulent waters of life; it is he who unleashes storms—representing the passions of the soul—particularly in his extreme rôle as the destroyer. Diel regards the trident as an emblem of the threefold sin arising from the corruption of the three 'vital impulses' of the spirit (conservation, reproduction and evolution), adding that the trident is also an attribute of Satan (15).

Net The net is the extreme form of expression of the symbolic bunch of ribbons, the bow and the bond, and hence it is closely bound up with the symbolisms of Entanglement and Devouring. It is the weapon of the Uranian gods, such as Varuna (18) and of those who fish in the waters of the unconscious. Ea, god of water and wisdom, did not fight the primordial monsters face to face but ensnared them by craft. The weapon of Marduk in his combat with Tiamat was again a net, a symbol of magic authority (17). The connexion between the net and heaven is explained in the following passage taken from the *Tao Te Ching*: 'The net of heaven', that is, the network of stars and constellations, 'is wide-meshed but lets nothing through' (58). The symbolism here strikingly illustrates the idea that it is not possible for the individual, by his own efforts (nor, of course, by suicide), to escape from the universe. God has bound us with his power and it is beyond our capacity to withdraw or leave.

Night Night is related to the passive principle, the feminine and the unconscious. Hesiod gave it the name of 'mother of the gods', for the Greeks believed that night and darkness preceded the creation of all things (8). Hence, night—like water—is expressive of fertility, potentiality and germination (17); for it is an anticipatory state in that, though not yet day, it is the promise of daylight. Within the tradition of symbology it has the same significance as death and the colour black.

Night-Sea Crossing This expression, frequent in works of symbology, originates in the ancient notion of the sun, in its nightly course through the lower abyss where it suffers death (which is sometimes conceived as a real death followed by resurrection, and at other times as purely figurative). This abyss was associated with the watery deeps of the third—or infernal—level, either in the sense of a lower ocean or of a subterranean lake. According to Leo Frobenius, in *Das Zeitalter des Sonnengottes*, all the sea-faring gods are solar symbols. For their passage they are shut up in a chest, hamper or trunk (symbolizing the maternal bosom) and exposed to a variety of perils. The direction of their journey is always contrary to the visible, daily course of the sun. Here is the account given by Frobenius of the archetypal avatars of this essential journey: 'A hero is swallowed by a sea-monster in the West. The animal journeys with him in its belly to the East. During the journey, the hero lights a fire in the belly of the monster and, feeling hungry, cuts off a slice of its heart. Shortly afterwards he observes that the fish has reached land; he then begins to cut away the flesh of the animal until he can slip out. In the belly of the fish it was so hot that his hair fell out. Often the hero sets free those who have been swallowed before him and they escape with 'him' (31). This basic situation takes on a variety of forms in a great many legends and folktales, but the essential features of devouring, confinement, enchantment and escape are always present. For Jung, this symbol is a kind of Journey into Hell comparable with the journeys described by Virgil and Dante, and also a sort of journey to the Land of Spirits, or, in other words, a plunge into the unconscious (33). But he goes on to add that darkness and watery deeps, in addition to being symbolic of the unconscious, also signify death—not in the sense of total negation but as the other side of life (or life in its latent state) and as the mystery which exerts its fascination over the consciousness from its abode in the abyss. The journey's end is expressive of resurrection and the overcoming of death (and the same applies to the end of a dream or of an illness). Related in symbolism to this is the story of Joseph cast into the pit by his brothers, and Jonah in the belly of the whale (32) (Plate XXX).

Nothingness The Upanishads laid down several different states of consciousness, ranging from wakefulness—peopled by objective forms—or daydreams—ordered in accordance with profound, subjective impulses—to the deepest state of consciousness experienced in dreams of the most intense character, devoid of images. This latter state is directly related to the mystic idea of nothingness. In order properly to grasp the notion of Nirvana, and to understand the ecstasy of self-annihilation, it is very important to recognize that this oriental 'nothingness' is not absolute negation—not the death of all things—but indifferentiation or, in other words, the absence of conflicts and contrasts and hence, the banishment of pain and dynamism. Guénon, in his explanation of this Hindu doctrine, comments: 'In this state the different objects of manifestation, including those of individual manifestation, external as well as internal, are not destroyed, but subsist in principal mode, being unified by the very fact that they are no longer conceived under the secondary or contingent aspect of distinction; of necessity they find themselves among the possibilities of the Self and the latter remains conscious in itself of all these possibilities, as "non-distinctively" beheld in integral Knowledge' (26). This concept of nothingness as 'non-objective reality'—and hence ineffable—probably reached the Hebrew mystics by way of the Middle East and Persia. According to Rabbi Joseph ben Shalom, living in Barcelona in the 13th century, more than to any other of the symbolic descriptions of the revelation of God, special attention should be devoted to that concerning the mystic nothingness, which is apparent in every abysmal crevice of existence. He suggests that in each transformation of reality, in each crisis, or moment of suffering, each metamorphosis or change of form, or on every occasion when the state of a thing is altered, then the abyss of Nothingness is spanned and made visible for a mystic instant, for nothing can change without making contact with that region of absolute being which the oriental mystics call Nothingness (the relevant passage is quoted by G. G. Scholem in *Major Trends in Jewish Mysticism*). There is a Cabbalistic anagram which serves to corroborate this by demonstrating that 'nothing' in Hebrew is *Ain*, and that the same letters form the word for 'I'—*Ani*.

Nudity The distinction between *nuditas virtualis* (purity and innocence) and *nuditas criminalis* (lasciviousness and vain exhibition) was already clearly established by Christians in the Middle Ages. Hence every nude must always have an ambivalent meaning and imply an ambiguous emotion: on the one hand, it lifts one's thoughts towards the pure peaks of mere physical beauty and (in a Platonic sense) towards the understanding of, and identification with, moral and spiritual beauty; but, on the other hand, it can never lose altogether its all too human ballast—its irrational attraction rooted in urges beyond the control of the conscious mind. Clearly, the human form revealed, whether in nature or in art, induces either one attitude or the other in the contemplator.

Numbers In symbolism, numbers are not merely the expressions of quantities, but idea-forces, each with a particular character of its own. The actual digits are, as it were, only the outer garments. All numbers are derived from the number one (which is equivalent to the mystic, non-manifest point of no magnitude). The farther a number is from unity, the more deeply it is involved in matter, in the involutive process, in the 'world'. The first ten numbers in the Greek system (or twelve in the oriental tradition) pertain to the spirit: they are entities, archetypes and symbols. The rest are the product of combinations of these basic numbers (44). The Greeks were much preoccupied with the symbolism of numbers. Pythagoras, for example, observed that 'Everything is disposed according to the numbers'. Plato regarded number as the essence of harmony, and harmony as the basis of the cosmos and of man, asserting that the movements of harmony 'are of the same kind as the regular revolutions of our soul' (24). The philosophy of numbers was further developed by the Hebrews, the Gnoptics and the Cabbalists, spreading to the alchemists as well. The same basic, universal notions are found in oriental thought—Lao-tse, for example: 'One becomes two; two becomes three; and from the ternary comes one'—the new unity or new order—'as four' (Maria Prophetissa) (32). Modern symbolic logic and the theory of groupings go back to the idea of the quantitative as the basis for the qualitative. Pierce suggests that the laws of nature and of the human spirit are based on these same principles, and that they can be ordered along these same lines (24). Apart from the basic symbols of unity and multiplicity, there is another general symbolism attached to the even numbers (expressing the negative and passive principle) and the uneven numbers (the positive and active). Furthermore, the numerical series possesses a symbolic dynamism which it is essential not to overlook. The idea that

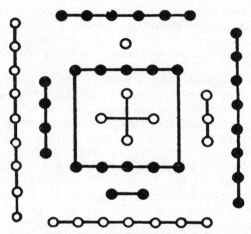

Oriental talisman based upon numbers.

one engenders two and two creates three is founded upon the premiss that every entity tends to surpass its limits, or to confront itself with its opposite. Where there are two elements, the third appears as the union of the first two and then as three, in turn giving rise·to the fourth number as the link between the first three, and so on (32). Next to unity and duality (expressing conflict, echo and primordial duplication), the ternary and the quaternary are the principal groupings; from their sum comes the septenary; and from their multiplication the dodecanary. Three is the more direct derivation of seven (since both are uneven) and four more closely related to twelve (both being even numbers). The usual symbolisms are as follows: The ternary represents the intellectual or spiritual order; the quaternary the terrestrial order; the septenary the planetary and moral order; the dodecanary the universal order. Here now are the most generally accepted symbolic meanings of each number, which will serve as a basis for a brief summary of the psychological theory of Paneth.

Zero Non-being, mysteriously connected with unity as its

opposite and its reflection; it is symbolic of the latent and potential and is the 'Orphic Egg'. From the viewpoint of man in existence, it symbolizes death as the state in which the life-forces are transformed (40, 55). Because of its circular form it signifies eternity.

One   Symbolic of being (40) and of the revelation to men of the spiritual essence. It is the active principle which, broken into fragments, gives rise to multiplicity (43), and is to be equated with the mystic Centre (7), the Irradiating Point and the Supreme Power (44). It also stands for spiritual unity—the common basis between all beings (55). Guénon draws a distinction between unity and one, after the Islamic mystic thinkers: unity differs from one in that it is absolute and complete in itself, admitting neither two nor dualism. Hence, unity is the symbol of divinity (26). One is also equated with light (49).

Two   Two stands for echo, reflection, conflict and counterpoise or contraposition; or the momentary stillness of forces in equilibrium (43); it also corresponds to the passage of time—the line which goes from behind forward (7); it is expressed geometrically by two points, two lines or an angle (44). It is also symbolic of the first nucleus of matter, of nature in opposition to the creator, of the moon as opposed to the sun (55). In all esoteric thought, two is regarded as ominous (9): it connotes shadow (49) and the bisexuality of all things, or dualism (represented by the basic myth of the Gemini) in the sense of the connecting-link between the immortal and the mortal, or of the unvarying and the varying (49). Within the mystic symbolism of landscape in megalithic culture, two is associated with the mandorla-shaped mountain, the focal point of symbolic Inversion, forming the crucible of life and comprising the two opposite poles of good and evil, life and death (51), Two, then, is the number associated with the *Magna Mater* (51).

Three   Three symbolizes spiritual synthesis, and is the formula for the creation of each of the worlds. It represents the solution of the conflict posed by dualism (43). It forms a half-circle comprising: birth, zenith and descent (7). Geometrically it is expressed by three points and by the triangle (44). It is the harmonic product of the action of unity upon duality (55). It is the number concerned with basic principles (41), and expresses sufficiency, or the growth of unity within itself (9). Finally, it is associated with the concepts of heaven (51) and the Trinity.

Four   Symbolic of the earth, of terrestrial space, of the human situation, of the external, natural limits of the 'minimum' awareness of totality, and, finally, of rational organization. It is equated with the square and the cube, and the cross representing the four seasons and the points of the compass. A great many material and spiritual forms are modelled after the quaternary (43). It is the number associated with tangible achievement (55) and with the Elements (41). In mystic thought, it represents the tetramorphs.

Five Symbolic of Man, health and love, and of the quintessence acting upon matter. It comprises the four limbs of the body plus the head which controls them, and likewise the four fingers plus the thumb (43) and the four cardinal points together with the centre (7). The *hieros gamos* is signified by the number five, since it represents the union of the principle of heaven (three) with that of the *Magna Mater* (two). Geometrically, it is the pentagram, or the five-pointed star (44). It corresponds to pentagonal symmetry, a common characteristic of organic nature, to the golden section (as noted by the Pythagoreans) (24), and to the five senses (55) representing the five 'forms' of matter.

Six Symbolic of ambivalence and equilibrium, six comprises the union of the two triangles (of fire and water) and hence signifies the human soul. The Greeks regarded it as a symbol of the hermaphrodite (33). It corresponds to the six Directions of Space (two for each dimension) (7), and to the cessation of movement (since the Creation took six days). Hence it is associated with trial and effort (37). It has also been shown to be related to virginity (50), and to the scales.

Seven Symbolic of perfect order, a complete period or cycle. It comprises the union of the ternary and the quaternary, and hence it is endowed with exceptional value (43). It corresponds to the seven Directions of Space (that is, the six existential dimensions plus the centre) (7), to the seven-pointed star, to the reconciliation of the square with the triangle by superimposing the latter upon the former (as the sky over the earth) or by inscribing it within. It is the number forming the basic series of musical notes, of colours and of the planetary spheres (55), as well as of the gods corresponding to them; and also of the capital sins and their opposing virtues (41). It also corresponds to the three-dimensional cross (38), and, finally, it is the symbol of pain (50).

Eight The octonary, related to two squares or the octagon (44), is the intermediate form between the square (or the terrestrial order) and the circle (the eternal order) and is, in consequence, a symbol of regeneration. By virtue of its shape, the numeral is associated with the two interlacing serpents of the caduceus, signifying the balancing out of opposing forces or the equivalence of the spiritual power to the natural (55). It also symbolizes—again because of its shape—the eternally spiralling movement of the heavens (shown also by the double sigmoid line—the sign of the infinite) (9). Because of its implications of regeneration, eight was in the Middle Ages an emblem of the waters of baptism. Furthermore, it corresponds in mediaeval mystic cosmogony to the fixed stars of the firmament, denoting that the planetary influences have been overcome.

Nine The triangle of the ternary, and the triplication of the triple. It is therefore a complete image of the three worlds. It is the end-limit of the numerical series before its return to unity (43). For the Hebrews, it was the symbol of truth, being characterized by the fact that when multiplied it reproduces itself (in mystic addition) (4). In medicinal rites, it is the symbolic number *par excellence*, for it represents triple synthesis, that is, the disposition on each plane of the corporal, the intellectual and the spiritual (51).

Ten Symbolic, in decimal systems, of the return to unity. In the *Tetractys* (whose triangle of points—four, three, two, one—adds up to ten) it is related to four. Symbolic also of spiritual achievement, as well as of unity in its function as an even (or ambivalent) number or as the beginning of a new, multiple series (44). According to some theories, ten symbolizes the totality of the universe—both metaphysical and material—since it raises all things to unity (9). From ancient oriental thought through the Pythagorean school and right up to St. Jerome, it was known as the number of perfection (50).

Eleven Symbolic of transition, excess and peril and of conflict and martyrdom (37). According to Schneider, there is an infernal character about it: since it is in excess of the number of perfection —ten—it therefore stands for incontinence (50); but at the same time it corresponds, like two, to the mandorla-shaped mountain, to the focal point of symbolic Inversion and antithesis, because it is made up of one plus one (comparable in a way with two) (51).

Twelve Symbolic of cosmic order and salvation. It corresponds to the number of the signs of the Zodiac, and is the basis of all dodecanary groups. Linked to it are the notions of space and time, and the wheel or circle.

Thirteen Symbolic of death and birth, of beginning afresh (37). Hence it has unfavourable implications.

Fourteen Stands for fusion and organization (37) and also for justice and temperance (59).

Fifteen is markedly erotic and is associated with the devil (59).

Other Numbers Each of the numbers from sixteen to twenty-two is related to the corresponding card of the Tarot pack; and sometimes the meaning is derived from the fusion of the symbols of the units composing it. There are two ways in which this fusion may occur: either by mystic addition (for example, $374=3+7+4=14=1+4=5$) or by succession, in which case the right-hand digit expresses the outcome of a situation denoted by the left-hand number (so 21 expresses the reduction of a conflict—two—to its solution—unity). These numbers also possess certain meanings drawn from traditional sources and remote from their intrinsic symbolism: 24, for example, is the sacred number in Sankhya philosophy, and 50 is very common in Greek mythology—there were fifty Danaides, fifty Argonauts, fifty sons of Priam and of Aegyptus, for example—as a symbol, we would suggest, of that powerful quality of the erotic and human which is so typical of Hellenic myths. The repetition of a given number stresses its quantitative power but detracts from its spiritual dignity. So, for example, 666 was the number of the Beast because 6 was regarded as inferior to seven (37). When several kinds of symbolic meaning are contained within a multiple number, the symbolism of that number is accordingly enriched and strengthened. Thus, 144 was considered very favourable because its sum was 9 $(1+4+4)$ and because it comprises multiples of 10 and 4 plus the quaternary itself (37). Dante, in the *Divine Comedy*, has frequent recourse to the symbolism of numbers (27).

The work of Ludwig Paneth upon numbers concerns not so much symbolism as such, but rather the normal interpretation of numbers from the psychologist's point of view as they appear in obsessions and dreams of average people. His conclusions are as follows:

One rarely appears, but where it does occur it alludes to the paradisiac state which preceded good and evil—which preceded, that is to say, dualism.

Two signifies counterpoise, or man's experience of separate existence, with its concomitant problems, inevitable analysis, dividing up, inner disintegration and struggle.

Three stands for biological synthesis, childbirth and the solution of a conflict.

Four, as a kind of double division (two and two), no longer signifies separation (like the number two) but the orderly arrangement of what is separate. Hence, it is a symbol of order in space and, by analogy, of every other well-ordered structure. As Simonides, the Greek poet, observed: 'It is difficult to become a superior man, tetragonal in hand, foot and spirit, forming a perfect whole.'

Five is a number which often occurs in animate nature, and hence its triumphant growth corresponds to the burgeoning of spring. It signifies the organic fullness of life as opposed to the rigidity of death. There is an erotic sense to it as well.

Six is, like two, a particularly ambiguous number: it is expressive of dualism $(2 \times 3$ or $3 \times 2)$. However, it is like four in that it has a normative value as opposed to the liberating tendencies of five and the mystic (or conflicting) character of seven.

Seven is, like all the prime numbers, an irreducible datum, and an expression of conflict or of a complex unity (the higher the prime number the greater the complexity). It is sometimes associated with the moon (since $7 \times 4 =$ the 28 days of the month).

Ten, in its graphic form as 10, is sometimes used to express marriage.

Nought, as the decimal multiplier, raises the quantitative power of a numerical symbol. A number of repeated noughts indicates a passion for grand things.

General Characteristics of Numbers Paneth draws a distinction between the arithmetical number and the symbolic number: the former defines an object by its quantity but says nothing about its nature, whereas the latter expresses an inner link with the object it defines by virtue of a mystic relationship between what is enumerated and the number itself. In arithmetic, the addition of 1 and 1 and 1 gives 3, but not triunity; in symbolism the second and third of these ones are intrinsically different from the first because they always function within ternary orders which establish the first term as an active element, the second as passive and the third as neuter or consequent. Aristotle spoke of the 'qualitative structure' of the numbers as opposed to the amorphous character of the arithmetical unity. Concerning the higher numbers, Paneth has this to say: 'The multiplication of a number simply increases its power: thus, 25 and 15 are both symbols of eroticism. Numbers composed of two digits express a mutual relationship between the individual digits (reading from left to right). For example, $23 = 2$ (conflict) and 3 (the outcome).' Numbers made up of more than two digits may be broken down and analysed in a number of different ways. For example, 338 may equal 300 plus 2×19, or else 3 and 3 and 8. The dynamism and symbolic richness of the number three is so exceptional that it cannot be over-emphasized. The reconciling function of the third element of the ternary, we would add, may appear in either a favourable or an adverse light. For instance, when in myths and legends there are three brothers or sisters, three suitors, three trials, three wishes, and so on (42), the first and second elements correspond broadly to what is already possessed, and the third element represents the magic or miraculous solution desired and sought after; but this third element may—as we have said—also be negative. Thus, just as there are legends where the first and the second fail and the third succeeds—sometimes it is the first six followed by the successful seventh—so there are others where the inversion of the symbolism produces the opposite result: the first two are favourable (and the second usually more so than the first) but then comes the third which is destructive or negative. The Three Kings, for example, offer the Infant Jesus gifts of gold, frankincense (both positive) and myrrh (negative). In almost all those myths and tales about three chalices, three chests or three rooms, the third element corresponds to death, because of the asymmetrical division of the cycle of man's life, composed of two parts which are ascending (infancy-adolescence, youth-maturity) and the third and last which is descending (old age-death). There is a Hebrew tale, called 'True Happiness', which exactly expresses the symbolic significance of this 'third element'. Here it is in Loeffler's exemplary version: 'A peasant and his wife, dissatisfied with their lot, envied those who dwelt in palaces, imagining their existence to be an unending flow of delights. While he was working in the fields, the man came across three iron chests. On the first was an inscription which said: "He who opens me will become rich." On the second he read: "If gold makes you happy, open me." On the third: "He who opens me, loses all that he possesses." The first chest was at once opened up and with the silver it contained the couple gave a sumptuous banquet, purchased splendid garments and slaves. The contents of the second chest enabled the couple to discover the luxury of refined living. But with the opening of the third, a terrible storm destroyed all their belongings' (38). The symbolism bears a relationship to the asymmetrical cycle of the year (Spring—Summer—Autumn followed by Winter) and to all symbols of the 'superior'—for superiority is always perilous.

Finally, there are also visual interpretations of number-symbols, derived from the shape of the digits; but such interpretations are of a specialized nature and are not always well-founded.

Numismatic Symbols   Coins have, from Antiquity, had a certain talismanic meaning, gradually lost with the passing of time: the power of a city, of a king, of a magistrate. Symbols, *signa* (ensigns), allegories and personifications have been stamped on them, clearly reflecting the cultural ethos of the day. Swastikas, tripods, tridents, labyrinths, chariots, winged horses, roses, tortoises, eagles, griffins, shields, crowns, bulls, cornucopias, etc., are frequently found on Greek coins. And on Roman coinage: military trophies, *signa* (standards) of the legions, ships' prows, heads of gods (especially double-headed Janus), eagles, votive crowns, chariots, temples, etc. It is worth noting that from the 4th to the 2nd centuries B.C. in the coinage of Luceria (Apulia) there appear geometric symbols such as ovals, triangles and series of dots, alongside Jupiter's thunderbolts, and also the cross-potent as it was later to appear in the Christian escutcheon of Jerusalem. Strictly speaking, mediaeval coinage dates from Carolingian times and displays crosses, anagrams, triple enclosures and very schematic temples. Byzantine coins are characterized above all by emperors' heads and figures of Christ, the Virgin and saints, as well as crosses and schematic ladders or steps. Mediaeval coinage in the West has a wide range of motifs, embracing various forms of cross, triple enclosures, roses, fleurs-de-lis, crowns, angels, armed knights, swords, hands raised in benediction, castles and shrines, lions, eagles, etc. On the reverse side of some coins there are veritable mandalas formed by the juxta-position of lobular enclosures, circles and crosses. From Renais-sance times onwards, money, by now secularized, takes on the standardized characteristics of Imperial Rome, with the face of a monarch on the obverse and heraldic shields on the reverse. But in many of the more imaginative stampings symbolic implications are still to be found in the form of 'wild men', solar symbols, religious or alchemical themes, etc. Islamic coins are usually based on calli-graphy, but they sometimes portray stars, figures and conjunctions of the square and the circle. Another topic, allegorical rather than symbolic, but nevertheless of great beauty, is found on mediaeval gold pieces and portrays the king standing, sword in hand, on a ship. A history of numismatic motifs in geography and in chronology has yet, we believe, to be written.

Nymphs The Greek word νύμφη means 'bride' and also 'doll'. The nymphs accompanying some of the mythic deities are symbolic of the concomitant ideas of those deities (48). According to Mircea Eliade, nymphs correspond in essence to running water, fountains, springs, torrents and waterfalls. The best known of the nymphs are the sisters of Thetis, the Nereides, who figure in the expedition of the Argonauts. By virtue of their association with the Element of water, their significance is ambivalent and they may preside equally over birth and fertility or dissolution and death (17). Jung, from the psychological standpoint of his theory of individuation, regards the nymph as an independent and fragmentary expression of the feminine character of the unconscious. He concludes, therefore, that what Paracelsus called the *regio nymphidica* corresponds to a relatively undeveloped stage of the process of individuation, a stage which he relates to the notions of temptation, transitoriness, multiplicity and dissolution (32).

Oak A tree sacred to Jupiter and Cybele, standing for strength and long life. Hercules' club, according to legend, was made of oak (8). Its consecration to Jupiter may derive from the ancient belief that the oak tree attracts the lightning more than any other. The oak had this symbolic and allegorical meaning throughout the Aryan cultures of Russia, Germany, Greece and Scandinavia (17). Like all trees, it represents a world-axis.

Oar In ancient rites connected with the founding of temples, the king would make the round of the site, an oar in his hand. Virgil mentions this ceremony in connexion with the rebuilding of Troy. It is a symbol of creative thought and the Word, the source of all action (19).

Obelisk A symbol of the sun-ray, by virtue of its shape. Because of its substance, it is bound up with the general symbolism of stone. It is further related to the myths of solar ascension and of light as the 'penetrating spirit', in consequence of its upright position and the pyramidal point in which it terminates.

Object The symbolism of objects varies with the kind of object in question. But, broadly speaking, every object consists of a material structure with certain unconscious elements adhering to it (31). The fact that these forgotten or repressed constituents should reappear in a new medium—the object—enables the spirit to accept them in a form different from the original. Utensils in particular are possessed of a mystic force which helps to strengthen the intensity and the rhythm of human volition. Thus, Schneider maintains that such instruments fulfil a triple rôle: they are cultural instruments, instruments of labour and finally reflections of the harmonious soul of the universe. The drinking-vessel, for instance, is a sacrificial vessel and also a drum. The blow-pipe is both a flute and a magic whistle, etc. (50). Such ideas as these, concerned with the primitive notion of an object, have lately been resuscitated by artistic movements such as Dadaism and surrealism. By depicting objects in common use as if they were works of art, Marcel Duchamp removed them from the context of their merely utilitarian function (their only function according to Western ways of thinking) and showed them in the light of their true essence, since that essence is revealed only in their uselessness (freed from the necessity to serve some useful purpose). He showed that it was possible to see in a bottle-stand, for instance, the very mystic structure that governed the Gothic spires rising in the form of a cage, or the lamps in Islamic mosques with their multiple, descending hoops; and that all the foregoing are related to the hollow pyramid of the Primitives (a symbol of the 'conjunction' of earth—or the mother—with fire— or the spirit), and also to the artificial mountain and the geometric temple. The form of the object, then, fulfils an essential rôle in determining the symbolism; thus, all those symbols which take the form of a twin bell, with the upper bell placed upside down on the lower—for example, the twin drum or the hour-glass—are closely related to the corresponding graphic symbol: the letter X, or the cross of St. Andrew (symbolic of the intercommunication between the Upper and the Lower Worlds). Objects that are simple in form and function usually correspond either to the active or to the passive groups; in other words, they represent either the contents or the receptacle. For instance: the lance (which is made to pierce) and the cup or chalice (whose sole function is to contain). The parallel between this classification and the division of the sexes is self-evident; but to limit the symbolic relevance of a given object to this sexual implication is to mutilate seriously its true symbolism. The 'conjunction' of the feminine and masculine principles within a complex object, specially if this object is—as in the case of a machine —endowed with movement, enables us to carry the sexual parallel a stage further and to characterize it as a kind of secularized lingam. The 'objects of symbolic function' of the surrealists were nothing but the practical illustration of this allusive reality, strengthened by the fetishistic character of the objects illustrated in their compositions. It was Lautréamont in *Les Chants de Maldoror* who best described this shifting of the symbolic significance of objects towards their generic grouping in his remark: 'beautiful as the chance-finding of an umbrella and a sewing-machine on a dissecting table'. As always, a symbol of integration such as this can be taken either on the cosmic plane or at the existential and sexual level. In the latter case, the umbrella would be a merely phallic representation, the machine would stand for the *cteis*, and the dissection-table would be an illustration of the bed. On the cosmic plane, the umbrella is the cosmic serpent, the machine is the jaguar, and the table is the universe. At the same time, objects owe part of their significance to their origins: objects fallen from heaven, such as aerolites and meteorites for example, partake of the sacred character of Uranus and constitute a symbol of the power of the celestial deities (17). Submarine objects, on the other hand, possess a viscous and abysmal quality betokening their irrational nature and their aptness for the expression of all that is base and unconscious. Sacred objects are so by virtue of their associations—as in the case of attributes or emblems for instance, or their origins—such as the legendary palladium of Troy, the Salian shields of Rome, the Hebrew Ark of the Covenant, etc. (28). To come back now to the broadest of generalizations, alongside their specific symbolism deriving from their form, function, character, origin, colour and so on, objects in themselves are always symbols of the world: that is, they are particular expressions of a material order which expounds both the blind irrational force of continuity and the structural pattern defining the object as opposed to the subject. Finally we would mention that an elaborate application of the theory of correspondences would demonstrate the serial structure of objects and suggest a way of reconciling their 'character' with the principles governing the two essential prototypes of the serial arrangement of the universe: that based upon the number seven, or the planetary prototype; and twelve, or the zodiacal model. The incomplete character of such forms of symbolic expression has been apparent to man since the earliest times, and for this reason the attempt was made to discover objects which could be invested with great symbolic power by means of the combination and juxtaposition of various ingredients, which were usually 'noble' in character, but were occasionally bizarre or even base—as was the case, for example, with the alchemic preparation known as 'prime matter'. The aim was to endow the object with all the powers inherent in the several planes of cosmic reality. An example of a 'complete object' of this kind is the sword in the Grail legend: its pommel was a precious stone of many colours, each colour representing a particular virtue; its haft was composed of the bones of strange beasts.

Objects, Marvellous Objects which are marvellous because of their rarity, beauty, splendour, or magical or miraculous qualities, frequently appear in myths, legends, folktales and books of knight-errantry. They are invincible weapons, talismans; on another plane, however, they are also purely and simply works of art, giving pleasure to their owner. The 'marvellous objects' *par excellence* are relics, or the ancestral symbols which sometimes become identified with them: the Grail, the bleeding lance, the Celtic cauldron, etc. Occasionally, the marvellous object is the motive for a symbolic 'test', such as the Sphinx's question to Oedipus; this is the case with the broken sword, which, in the legends of the Round Table, is given to Gawain and Parsifal for mending, and which Siegfried successfully achieves in the *Niebelungen*.

Ocean According to Piobb, the Graeco-Roman conception of the ocean encompassing the earth was a graphic representation of the current of energy induced by the terrestrial globe (48). Setting aside its grandeur, the two most essential aspects of the ocean are its ceaseless movement and the formlessness of its waters. It is a symbol, therefore, of dynamic forces and of transitional states between the stable (or solids) and the formless (air or gas). The ocean as a whole, as opposed to the concept of the drop of water, is a symbol of universal life as opposed to the particular (38). It is regarded traditionally as the source of the generation of all life (57), and science has confirmed that life did in fact begin in the sea (3). Zimmer observes that the ocean is 'immense illogic'—a vast expanse dreaming its own dreams and asleep in its own reality, yet containing within itself the seeds of its antitheses. The island is the opponent of the ocean and symbolic of the metaphysical point of irradiating force (60). In keeping with the general symbolism of water, both fresh and salt, the ocean stands for the sum of all the possibilities of one plane of existence. Having regard to its characteristics, one may deduce whether these potentialities are positive (or germinant) or negative (destructive) (26). The ocean, then, denotes an ambivalent situation. As the begetter of monsters, it is the abysmal abode *par excellence*, the chaotic source which still brings forth base entities ill-fitted to life in its aerial and superior forms. Consequently, aquatic monsters represent a cosmic or psychological situation at a lower level than land-monsters; this is why sirens and tritons denote a sub-animal order. The power of salt water to destroy the higher forms of land-life means that it is also a symbol of sterility, so confirming the ambivalent nature of the ocean—its contradictory dynamism (32). The ocean is also to be found as a symbol of woman or the mother (in both her benevolent and her terrible aspects) (56). As Frobenius comments in *Das Zeitalter des Sonnengottes*: 'If the blood-red sunrise is interpreted as the "birth" of an astral body, then two questions arise: Who is the father? And how did the mother come to conceive? And since she, like the fish, is a sea-symbol, and since our premiss is that the sun plunges into the sea and yet is born in it, the answer must be that the sea previously swallowed up the old sun and the appearance of a "new sun" confirms that she has been fecundated. The symbolism here coincides with that of Isis whose twin lunar horns embrace the sun.' This appearance of the sun and its disappearance back into the deeps of the ocean confirm that the 'Lower Waters' signify the abyss out of which forms arise to unfold their potentialities within existence. Thus, the ocean is equated also with the collective unconscious, out of which arises the sun of the spirit (32). The stormy sea, as a poetic image or a dream, is a sign of an analogous state in the lower depths of the affective unconscious. A translucent calm, on the other hand, denotes a state of contemplative serenity.

Octagon Embellishments, architectonic structures, and different dispositions based on the octagon (in ground-plan or elevation in the case of a building or structure such as a baptistry, fountain, etc.) symbolize spiritual regeneration, because the eight-sided figure is connected with this idea as the intermediary between the square and the circle. It is not surprising, therefore, that the majority of baptistries have a definite octagonal shape. However, twelve is sometimes used for baptismal fonts (the sum of the facets of the semi-polyhedron), because it symbolizes totality.

Octopus It has the same significance as the dragon-whale myth (31). As a decorative motif it appears most frequently in Cretan art. It is related to the spider's web and the spiral, both being symbolic of the mystic Centre and of the unfolding of creation. It has also been credited with a merely existential significance (41).

Ogre The origins of the ogre, a common feature in legend and folklore, go back to Saturn, who would devour his children as soon as Cybele gave them birth (38). If the core of the Saturn-myth is the idea that destruction is the inevitable outcome of creation (since creation takes place in time), then the ogre seems to be a personification of the 'Terrible Father'. Henri Dontenville derives the word 'ogre' from the definition of the Latin poet Ennius: *Pluto latine est Dis Pater, alii Orcum vocant.* Orcus was the lord of the underworld, with his mother Orca, and both are characterized by the Saturnian practice of eating little children (16). It is beyond doubt that these legends are also closely bound up with other ancient myths founded upon the most savage aspects of pre-human life and that, like other kinds of legend, they serve the cathartic function of issuing a warning.

Ojancanu   This is the name given to the Cyclops in the folklore of Northern Spain. According to Caro Baroja, the *Ojancanu* is regarded as a giant with red hair (and therefore Satanic), tall and stout, with one bright and evil-looking eye. If two eyes are an expression of normality, and three denote the superhuman (as in the case of Shiva), a single eye is a clear allusion to what is base. The Cyclops-myth appears in different versions throughout Europe and Asia Minor, but it is not known in the Far East (10). The *Ojancanu* is, in sum, a symbol of the evil and destructive forces behind the primary or regressive side of Man.

Old Man   In the Cabala, the Old Man is the symbol of the occult principle (like the holy or silver palace). In the modern study of symbols, the Old Man is regarded as the personification of the age-old wisdom of humanity, or of the collective unconscious. The Old Men (Elders) of the Apocalypse are the twelve prophets and the twelve apostles. The 'Ancient of Days' is a similar symbol, sometimes identified with the creative principle, the Cabbalistic *Ain-Soph* and the *Atum* of Egyptian religion (19). According to Jung, the Old Man, particularly when invested with special powers or prestige, is the symbol of the 'mana' personality, i.e. the spirituality of the personality which emerges when consciousness is overburdened with clarified, apprehended and assimilated matter welling up from the unconscious (30).

Olive Tree   A symbol of peace, consecrated by the Romans to Jupiter and Minerva. It carries the same symbolic significance in many oriental and European countries (8).

Omphalos   To quote Pausanias (X, 16, 2): 'What the inhabitants of Delphi call *omphalos* is made of white stone and is considered to be at the centre of the earth', and Pindar, in one of his odes, confirms this opinion. It is, then, one of the many symbols of the cosmic 'Centre' where intercommunication between the three worlds of man, of the dead, and of the gods, is effected (17). W. H. Roscher (according to René Guénon) collected a number of documents in a work entitled *Omphalos* (1913) which prove that this symbol was in existence among the most diverse of races. By locating it in one particular spot, man made of it a sacred zone around the 'centre of the world'. The material image of the *Omphalos* (the 'navel' in Greek) was known as the Bethel, which was made of stone and shaped like a pilaster. It has been suggested that the menhir may have had a similar significance. Another image of the omphalos may have been the ovoid stone as it sometimes appears in Greek designs encircled by a snake or serpent. In all these images we can descry the attempt to express the sexual principles of the cosmos: the pilaster is related to the masculine and active factor, the Egg of the World is connected with the feminine principle, and the egg encircled by the serpent suggests the synthesis of both principles in the *lingam*. More abstract and therefore spiritually superior ways of depicting this 'Centre' (at once cosmic, temporal and spatial, physical and metaphysical) are to be found in China: the hole in the middle of the disk of jade known as *Pi*, for instance, where the centre is identified as the non-being of mystic Nothingness, or the quadrangular pyramid rising up in the centre of each feudal domain where each face of the pyramid corresponds to one of the cardinal points and the summit represents the centre. These pyramids were also known in Ireland, according to J. Loth in his *Brehon Laws* (28).

One   The number one is equivalent to the 'Centre', to the non-manifest point, to the creative power or the 'unmoved mover'. Plotinus equates one with moral purpose, and multiplicity with evil—a distinction which is in complete accord with symbolist doctrine.

Orchestra   Symbolic of the activity of a corporate whole. This is the idea behind Schneider's remark that when the high and the low orchestras (that is, heaven and earth) perform the counterpoint of the cosmos, these two antithetical voices are 'descanting'. But when one of the voices imposes its own rhythm upon the other, then that voice is 'enchanting' its opponent (50).

Orgy   Orgies, characterized by drunkenness, sexual licence, excesses of all kinds and occasional transvestism, always correspond to a 'call to chaos' as a result of a weakening of the will to accept the norm in the ordinary way. Hence, as Eliade has pointed out, the orgy is a cosmogonic equivalent of Chaos and of supreme, ultimate fulfilment, as well as of the eternal moment and of timelessness. The Roman Saturnalia—whose origins go back to prehistoric times—or Carnival were expressions of the orgiastic urge. In these uninhibited festivities the tendency is to 'confuse forms' by means of the inversion of the social pattern, the juxtaposition of opposites and the unleashing of the passions—even in their destructive capacity. All this is a means not so much towards pleasure as to bring about the dissolution of the world in a momentary disruption—although the moment seems definitive while the orgy lasts—of the reality-principle, alongside the corresponding restoration of the primigenial *illud tempus* (17).

Orientation   In Islamic thought, orientation is the materialization of intent. The Orient, since it is the point where the sun rises, symbolizes illumination and the fount of life; to turn towards the east is to turn in spirit towards this spiritual focal point of light. Orientation plays its due part in rites and ceremonies all over the world, particularly in those to do with the founding of temples and cities. The orientation of Graeco-Latin temples and mediaeval churches was inspired by the same idea (28). However, not all mystic orientations take the east as their point of reference: there is an alternative point in the geography of the sky, symbolic of the 'hole' in space-time and of the 'unmoved mover'—and that is the North Star. The Etruscans located the abode of the gods in the north, and hence their soothsayers, when about to speak, would turn to face the south—that is, they would take up a position which identified them, ideologically, with the gods (7). To face the north is to pose a question. To turn westwards is to prepare to die, because it is in the watery deeps of the west that the sun ends its journey. The notion of orientation, taken in conjunction with the concept of space as a three-dimensional whole, plays a powerful part in the symbolic organization of space. The human anatomy itself, with its quasi-rectangular, symmetrical and bilateral pattern, in distinguishing between the front and the back thereby designates two corresponding points of orientation. The natural position of the arms and shoulders completes this quadrangular scheme—a symbolic pattern which, interpreted according to strictly anthropological and empirical criteria, would perhaps provide us with the key to the original conception of orientation as quaternary on the surface but septenary three-dimensionally (embracing north, south, east and west, together with the zenith, the nadir and the centre). Also closely linked with the symbolism of the cardinal points and orientation are the gestures and movements of the body, as symbolic expressions of the will applying itself in one direction or another. All attitudes of concentration denote the enshrining of the 'Centre' within the heart.

Ornamentation   This is a symbol of cosmic activity, of development in space and of the 'way out of chaos' (chaos being denoted by blind matter) (13). Ornamentation by virtue of graduated motifs—its progressive reconciliation with order—signifies the gradual stages in this evolutive development of the universe. The principal elements in ornamentation are the spiral, the sigma, the cross, waves, the zigzag; these are discussed in their appropriate place. Some of the basic principles behind these ornamental motifs concern graphic and spatial symbolisms. Negatively speaking, the art of ornamentation is opposed to figurative art, particularly when the ornaments are geometric forms or stylizations of plants. 'Beware of representation, whether it be of the Lord or of man, and paint nothing except trees, flowers and inanimate objects'; so spoke Mohammed according to the oral traditions or *Hadith*. For Moslems, consequently, art is a kind of aid to meditation, or a sort of mandala —indefinite and interminable and opening out onto the infinite, or a form of language composed of spiritual signs, or handwriting; but it can never be a mere reflection of the world of existence. In Islamic ornamentation—which we may regard as one of the basic prototypes—the essential constituents are as follows: plaits, foliage,

water

air

fire

earth

Ornamental symbols of the Elements.

polygons, arabesques, inscriptions, the twenty-eight letters of tne alphabet, five or six stylized flowers (such as the hyacinth, the tulip, the eglantine, the peach-blossom), certain of the fabulous animals and the seven smalts in heraldry. Patterns such as these are blended into a vast symbolic network reminiscent of polyphonic music and the aspiration towards the harmony of infinity (6). In figurative ornamentation—Romanesque for instance—every item represented possesses its own symbolic sense, while the pattern as a whole constitutes a veritable symbolic syntax.

Ouroboros This symbol appears principally among the Gnostics and is depicted as a dragon, snake or serpent biting its own tail. In the broadest sense, it is symbolic of time and of the continuity of life (57). It sometimes bears the caption *Hen to pan*—'The One, the

All', as in the *Codex Marcianus*, for instance, of the 2nd century A.D. It has also been explained as the union between the chthonian principle as represented by the serpent and the celestial principle as signified by the bird (a synthesis which can also be applied to the dragon). Ruland contends that this proves that it is a variant of the symbol for Mercury—the *duplex* god. In some versions of the Ouroboros, the body is half light and half dark, alluding in this way to the successive counterbalancing of opposing principles as illustrated in the Chinese *Yang-Yin* symbol for instance (32). Evola asserts that it represents the dissolution of the body, or the universal serpent which (to quote the Gnostic saying) 'passes through all things'. Poison, the viper and the universal solvent are all symbols of the undifferentiated—of the 'unchanging law' which moves through all things, linking them by a common bond. Both the dragon and the bull are symbolic antagonists of the solar hero. The ouroboros biting its own tail is symbolic of self-fecundation, or the primitive idea of a self-sufficient Nature—a Nature, that is, which, *à la* Nietzsche, continually returns, within a cyclic pattern, to its own beginning. There is a Venetian manuscript on alchemy which depicts the Ouroboros with its body half-black (symbolizing earth and night) and half-white (denoting heaven and light).

Oven or **Furnace** A mother-symbol. The alchemists' crucible is symbolic of the body, and the alembic is expressive of the *vas Hermetis* (31). But it has a further significance as a symbol of pure, spiritual gestation; it is in this sense that the glowing furnace makes its appearance in so many alchemic treatises, such as Michael Maier and the *Museum Hermeticum* (1678).

Oviparous Animals In India, birds, reptiles and all oviparous beings receive the name of 'twice born'. With this in mind we can conclude that the laying of the egg is equivalent to the birth of man, and the breaking out from the egg symbolizes his second birth or initiation (18).

Owl In the Egyptian system of hieroglyphs, the owl symbolizes death, night, cold and passivity. It also pertains to the realm of the dead sun, that is, of the sun which has set below the horizon and which is crossing the lake or sea of darkness (19).

Ox Broadly speaking, the ox is a symbol of the cosmic forces (40). In Egypt and in India, a more specialized symbolism was evolved for the ox, contrasting it with the lion on the one hand and with the bull on the other. For obvious reasons it became a symbol of sacrifice, suffering, patience and labour. In Greece and in Rome it was regarded as an attribute of agriculture and of foundation-laying (and so, by extension, was the yoke). Roman generals who had been granted the honour of a triumph would sacrifice white oxen to the Capitoline Jupiter as part of the ceremony (8). In

Herrad of Landsberg's *Hortus Deliciarum*, the moon's chariot is drawn by oxen (14), which points to the emasculated character of the animal (14). In mediaeval emblems, the ox is frequently found symbolizing patience, submissiveness and the spirit of self-sacrifice (20). Very often the ox-head, without its body, is shown with one of the following signs between its horns: a crown, a snake coiled round a staff, a chalice, a circle, a cross, a fleur-de-lis, a crescent moon or the Gothic 'R' (standing for *Regeneratio*) (4). The ox (because of its connexion with the moon) is also a symbol of darkness and night in contrast to the lion, which is a solar animal (50).

Palace In Cabbalistic symbolism, the sacred palace, or the 'inner palace', is located at the junction of the six Directions of Space which, together with this centre, form a septenary. It is, consequently, a symbol of the occult Centre—of the 'unmoved mover' (28). It is also known as the 'silver palace', the 'silver thread' being the hidden bond which joins man to his Origin and to his End (28). This concept of the Centre embraces the heart and the mind; hence, in legends and folktales, the palace of the old king contains secret chambers (representing the unconscious) which hold treasure (or spiritual truths). Loeffler suggests that palaces made of glass or of mirrors, and also those which suddenly appear as if by magic, are specially symbolic of the ancestral memories of mankind—of the basic, primitive awareness of the Golden Age (38).

Palafitte The architectural pillar and lintel owe their origin to the palafitte or lake-dwelling. Paul Sarrasin has shown that the classic Greek temple derives directly from lacustrine structures (22). The palafitte came about not just because of topographical necessity but as a consequence of motives of a mystic order: the urge to raise one's dwelling above the general level. Now, lake-dwellings acquire greater symbolic interest still by virtue of their connexion with three of the Elements: earth, since the lake-dwelling is a home—and the home is always associated in turn with the cave and the mountain; air, since it is elevated; and water, because the piles which support it are immersed in this Element. The palafitte is, then, a symbol of the world: it is both the Tree of Life and a mystic vessel, for its 'masts' touch the water, and its roof, sickle-shaped, is representative of the mandorla (q.v.) (50).

Palm   A classic emblem of fecundity and of victory (8). For Jung, it is also symbolic of the anima (32).

Pan   The god Pan is a symbol of nature, and is usually represented with horns (expressive of the sun's rays and of the aggressive force of Aries) and with legs covered with hair (denoting the vitality of base forces, earth, shrubs and the instincts) (8). In astrology, Pan is one aspect of Saturn, and is also equated with Satan and with life in its involutive, and, in particular, its base, aspects (39).

Pandora   According to Diel, Pandora is symbolic of the wicked temptations besetting humankind—the rebellious Promethean beings who have risen up against the divine order (15). She is also at times a representation of the irrational, wild tendencies of the imagination.

Pansy   In Spanish,[1] this flower is called 'thought' precisely because it is thought which it symbolizes by virtue of its clearly pentagonal pattern: five being the number that symbolizes man (48).

Papyri   In the Egyptian system of hieroglyphs, a rolled papyrus is a determinative sign defining the concept of knowledge. The fact that the papyrus is rolled signifies progress, efflorescence and omniscience. The unfolding of life itself is also symbolized by a roll of papyrus, though more frequently by a mat or carpet; in the words of Themistocles to Artaxerxes: 'Human life is like a rolled-up carpet slowly unfolding', an idea which Stefan George incorporated in one of his poems. In every case the symbolic significance corresponds not so much to the object or material in question as to the process of its manifestation (19).

Paradise Lost   Symbolic of the mystic 'Centre'—or, rather, of its manifestation in space. The Chinese locate it in central Asia, referring to it as a garden inhabited by 'dragons of wisdom', with the four essential rivers of the world—the Oxus, Indus, Ganges and Nile—rising out of a common source which is termed the 'lake of the dragons' (9). Leaving aside the Christian dogma, there are a host of Western and oriental legends dealing with the lost Paradise. It is found in symbolic traditions all over the world, and it is here that its true beginnings should be looked for. As a symbol of the spirit, it corresponds to that state which is above all queries and quibbles. The fall of man from the paradisiac state and his return to it find varied manners of symbolic expression, the most characteristic being the labyrinth. As Saunier has observed: 'When man comes to ponder this mysterious problem, he knows no more peace,

---

[1] *Pensamiento* in Spanish is the common name for 'thought' and the popular word for 'pansy'. The English word 'pansy' derives, of course, from the French *'pensée'*; and our synonym, 'heart's ease', is perhaps another pointer to the symbolic interpretation.—*Translator.*

for his mind, faced with a series of insurmountable obstacles, is shattered, filling his heart, his soul and his body with rage and despair. . . . Man, urged on by his desire . . . bent his mind to a rigorous investigation into the smallest particles of the cosmos, enshrined his intelligence in matter, and strove by hard and constant work to rediscover himself in the labyrinth of science. Only once he had grasped the worlds of the infinitely small and the infinitely large could man once again vibrate in sympathy with the cosmic harmonies and blend in ineffable communion with all the beings and things in earth and heaven' (49). The 'weekly day of rest' is a temporal image of Paradise, comparable with the Islands of the Blessed and El Dorado, etc., in geographical symbolism. The 'lost' characteristic, which gives the symbol of Paradise its particular symbolic direction, is connected with the general symbolism of the feeling of abandonment and fall, recognized by modern existentialism as an essential part of human make-up.

Parakeet Related to other members of the parrot family in its faculty for pronouncing words. Maurice Bouisson, in *Le Secret de Schéhérazade* (Paris, 1961), comments on the *Tuti nameh*, a Persian translation of Nakchabi's *Book of the Parrot*. He comes to the conclusion that it is a messenger-symbol, like the crow, and also a symbol of the soul (the Egyptian *ba*), like other birds. In *The Conference of the Birds*, by the 13th-century Persian poet Farid Ud-Din Attar, the parrot seeks the water of immortality.

Partridge The partridge is very common in Romanesque ornamentation—in the southern gallery of the cloister at Silos, for instance. Pinedo has noted how Aristotle, Theophrastus, Pliny and other ancient and mediaeval writers all have something to say about the characteristic habit of the partridge, succinctly expressed by St. Jerome as follows: 'Just as the partridge lays eggs and hatches young birds who will never follow it, so the impious man possesses wealth to which he is not entitled, and which he must leave behind when he is least inclined.' It is this idea that underlies the symbol of the partridge. Another symbolic function comes from the bird's capacity for deception. In the words of St. Ambrose: 'The partridge, taking its name from the word *perdendo* and in Hebrew called *kore* (to call and shout), is Satan tempting the multitudes with his voice' (46).

Paste According to Bachelard, the notion of matter is very closely related to that of paste. Water is here a predominant constituent, imparting cohesion. Hence it has been said that 'matter is the unconscious of form'. Mud is the 'dust' of water, just as ash is the 'dust' of fire. Bachelard goes on to suggest that mud, dust and smoke afford images which, in a changed and shadowy form, imply the matter from which they arise—they are the residue of the four Elements (2). They correspond to a quasi-aquatic state, and hence come into the symbolisms of dissolution and regeneration: ash and dust are expressive of an ending, but all ends are beginnings.

Peacock On Roman coins, the peacock designates the apotheosis of princesses, just as the eagle does of victors (8). The peacock's tail, in particular, appears in the eighty-fourth emblem of the *Ars Symbolica* of Bosch as a symbol for the blending together of all colours and for the idea of totality (32). This explains why, in Christian art, it appears as a symbol of immortality (20) and of the incorruptible soul (6). The common *motif* of the two peacocks symmetrically disposed on either side of the Cosmic Tree or *hom* —a feature which came to Islam from Persia and subsequently reached Spain and the West—denotes the psychic duality of man (related to the myth of the Gemini) drawing its life-force from the principle of unity (6). In the mystic horology, the peacock corresponds to dusk (50). In Hindu mythology, the patterns on its wings, resembling innumerable eyes, are taken to represent the starry firmament (50).

Pearl One of the eight 'common emblems' of Chinese tradition. It symbolizes 'genius in obscurity' (5), doubtless after the rather less categorical observation of Lao-tse that, 'Hence, the chosen one wears coarse garments, but in his breast he hides a precious stone' —by allusion to the pearl hidden inside its oyster. Because of all this, psychoanalysts have recognized that the function of the pearl is to represent the mystic Centre and sublimation (seen here as the transfiguration of an infirmity, or of some abnormality) (56). The Moslems often have recourse to the pearl as a symbol of heaven, since their belief is that the blessed are enclosed in a pearl, each one with his houri (46); there is an obvious connexion here with Plato's androgynous 'spherical man' who is both primordial and final. They also believe—and this confirms the parallel with the Platonic spherical man—that the pearl is the product of the 'conjunction' of fire and water. It has also been identified as the human soul (18). Pearls in large numbers take on a different character: despite their high value, they come to be mere beads: when joined they correspond to the symbol of the necklace, and when scattered they relate to the symbol of dismemberment, like all things that are dispersed.

Pegasus A winged horse which sprang from the blood of Medusa, the Gorgon, when Perseus cut off her head with the aid of the magic weapons given him by the gods. Bellerophon rode upon Pegasus in his fight with the chimaera. A similar being finds its way into mediaeval legends under the name of hippogryph. It symbolizes the heightening power of the natural forces—the innate capacity for spiritualization and for inverting evil into good.

Pelican An aquatic bird which, as legend has it, loved its young so dearly that it nourished them with its own blood, pecking open its breast to this end (8). It is one of the best-known allegories of Christ, and it is in this form that it figures as the seventieth emblem of the *Ars Symbolica* of Bosch (32)! Also one of the principal symbols in alchemy, it is to some extent the antithesis of the raven.

Perfume As Gaston Bachelard has shrewdly observed (3), scent or perfume in its association with the general symbolism of the air is tantamount to the wakes or tracks that mark the passage of solid bodies through the atmosphere, and consequently symbolic of memories or reminiscences. Whereas the pure, cold air of mountain heights is associated with heroic and solitary thought—in St. John of the Cross quite as much as in Nietzsche—a scent-laden atmosphere is expressive of the mind saturated with emotion and with nostalgia. The over-enthusiastic application of the laws of correspondences has led some people to lay down hard-and-fast symbolisms for every particular smell. It is feasible, however, to pick out some of the basic and characteristic significances attaching to particular smells and to arrange them in serial order so that they constitute a scale of values equivalent to those of colours, textures, shapes and all phenomena that are characterized by both continuity and discontinuity and that express the graduated differentiations of Oneness.

Persephone A personification of earth and of spring. The myth tells how the goddess was gathering flowers when the earth opened up and Pluto, the god of the underworld, appeared and carried her off to be his queen in hell. Her mother, Demeter, obtained this concession—that Persephone should spend two-thirds of the year with her (spring to autumn) and only one-third with her ravisher (winter). Folklore in many European countries preserves the archetypes of Persephone and Demeter in the figures of the 'Harvest Maiden' and the 'Mother of the Corn' (21).

Personification This may be defined as the attribution of human properties to an object, and as the embodying of an idea. The urge to personify objects or ideas is a peculiar characteristic of mythic thought, but it played a particularly important part during the period from the latter days of pre-history up to the rise of Christianity, which was the age of elaboration and crystallization of abstract ideas. Personification results from a synthesis of animism and of the anthropomorphic view of the world. The Ancients personified the great themes of destiny (life, death, good, evil), of the cosmic and elemental entities (heaven, earth, ocean, rivers, springs), man's emotions and impulses (fear, laughter, love and desire), the virtues (fortune, liberty, constancy, victory, fecundity), the collective entities (town or city) and the cultural fields (history and astronomy).

These themes came to constitute allegories once certain symbolic elements and attributes had accrued to them, so giving formal expression to their inherent reality or adapting irrational nature to more intelligible forms in which human conversation—the original form of analytic thought—was feasible. It hardly needs to be said that mythological deities can be explained, in part, as products of personification—apart, that is to say, from the fact that they correspond to the basic truths, to the basic 'series', and to the diversified meaning, of the universe.

Petrifaction   The myth of Deucalion, who made men out of stones, as well as lithophany, find their inversion in legends about petrifaction. This is clearly a question of the antithetical tendencies of evolution and involution. To petrify is to detain or to enclose. The glance of Medusa the Gorgon, so it was said, was sufficient to turn men to stone. There are many folktales and mediaeval legends which tell of similar cases of petrifaction or enchantment. Fairies, sometimes, instead of sending people to sleep—although the symbol is the same—turn them to stone and leave them looking like statues. In *Beauty and the Beast*, the two wicked sisters of the heroine are turned into statues. The words the author puts into the mouth of the good fairy illuminate the symbolic meaning: 'Become two statues, but retain your reason beneath the stone which envelops you. You shall stay by the door of your sister's palace and I shall inflict no other punishment upon you but to require you to witness her happiness. You may not return to your original state until you recognize the error of your ways' (38). Petrifaction, then, is the detention of moral progress—of the evolution of the soul. Sin forces this spiritual evolution from its proper course and, even if it does not plunge into the abyss, at least it arrests ('petrifies') and stagnates it. This is what happens in the case of Lot's wife, and this is the peril which Ulysses resolutely surmounts in his journey back to Ithaca (a symbol of the celestial homeland—of eternity assuming the aspect of temporal existence).

Phallus   A symbol for the perpetuation of life, of active power and of the propagation of cosmic forces (57).

Pheasant   Similar in symbolism to the cock. In China, it was the allegorical animal of light and of day (17).

Phoenix   A mythical bird about the size of an eagle, graced with certain features of the pheasant. Legend has it that when it saw death draw near, it would make a nest of sweet-smelling wood and resins, which it would expose to the full force of the sun's rays, until it burnt itself to ashes in the flames. Another phoenix would then arise from the marrow of its bones (8). Turkish tradition gives it the name of *Kerkés*, and Persian *Simurgh*. In every respect it symbolizes periodic destruction and re-creation (38). Wirth suggests a psychological interpretation of the fabulous bird as a symbol of the 'phoenix' which we all keep within ourselves, enabling us to live out every moment and to overcome each and every partial death which we call a 'dream' (59) or 'change'. In China, the phoenix is the emperor of birds and a sun-symbol (5). In the Christian world, it signifies the triumph of eternal life over death (20). In alchemy, it corresponds to the colour red, to the regeneration of universal life (57) and to the successful completion of a process.

Phonetics We quote the definition of phonetic symbolism as it appears in the *Rituale mitriaco*, bearing the stamp of traditional Egyptian ideas mentioned in the Book of the Dead: 'And the word, which is fundamentally an acoustic phenomenon, has greater value as a sound than as an expression of an idea, since the sound contained in it, and emanating from it as certain given vibrations, is the modulation of the cosmic breath; to sound a word, tuning it in, as it were, to the varied rhythms of the cosmos, is tantamount to restoring its elemental power' (11). Hindu tradition often alludes to the meaning, as sound, of letters, syllables and words. So, for example, the sound of each letter of the words *Makara* and *Kumara* is given a precise value as part of the general meaning of the word: the trilled 'r' is onomatopoeic, alluding to thunder as the symbol of creative power (it is for this reason that most verbs in almost all languages contain the letter 'r'), and the syllable '*Ma*' refers to matter, etc. (40). The tradition is that the entire essence of the universe is contained in the syllable '*Om*' (or *Aum*) of the Hindu or Tibetan languages: A=the beginning, U=transition, M=the end, or deep sleep. This mystic belief in the power of phonetics *per se* led the Gnostics and the followers of Mithras to insert passages entirely devoid of any literal sense into parts of their ritual chants, as a kind of symbolic music effective only by virtue of the power of their phonetic significance.

Phrygian Cap In part it is a phallic symbol. The fact that, being an item of headgear, it corresponds in symbolism to the head, ensures that its significance will embrace eroticism in its superior and sublimated—and at times obsessive—form. Hence, the Trojan Paris, being a pure type of Venusian man, who is destined in times of fortune and misfortune always to be at the mercy of Eros, is depicted with a Phrygian cap. Its red colour may also imply a sacrificial significance—either of self-immolation (as in the case of Cybele's priests) or of the immolation of others (as in the case of the French revolutionaries in 1789). In principle, every red bonnet has a similar meaning. The cap worn by the Venetian Doge (*il corno*) is a stylized version of the fisherman's bonnet—for the dignitary and the fisherman are symbolically alike—and, like the Phrygian cap, ends in a point.

Physical Processes Changes or transformations in matter may afford a symbolic significance comparable with the marks used by Rorschach in his tests. It was, in fact, upon the symbolism pertaining to processes of elaboration of 'prime matter' that the alchemists founded their entire practice, since they aspired to pass beyond the stages of combination of mercury with sulphur in order to produce, not the *aurum vulgi*, but the philosophers' gold; all of which is a clear indication of the spiritual nature of alchemy or, in other words, of its affinity with symbolism. As René Alleau has said, 'the material technique was only an apprenticeship, preparing the neophyte for the understanding of truths'. If we were to take works of art and ignore the material result, we would then see the genesis of the artist's work as a long process of self-education and of groping towards the ideals of truth and beauty.

Pictorial Image Every pictorial creation gives rise to an image, either imitated or invented, figurative or non-figurative. In any such image, alongside the symbolic significance attached to the subject or figure, there are also implications arising from the spatial distribution, the colours, the inclusion or absence of geometric shapes, the signs, predominant axes, rhythms, composition and texture. In the most recent, so-called 'informalist' style of art, the expression and symbolization is realized primarily by means of texture and line-rhythm, colour being of secondary significance. In order to grasp the 'meaning' of any particular work, it is first necessary to classify its component elements and to estimate the significance of each class of such components according to their prominence within the pictorial whole. Exactly the same is true of architecture and sculpture.

Pilgrim The concept of man as a pilgrim and of life as a pilgrimage is common to a great many peoples and traditions (4), for it accords with the great myth of the celestial origin of man, of his 'fall' and his hopes of being restored to the celestial realm, since the effect of all this is to make him something of a stranger during his stay on earth and to imprint the mark of the transitory upon his every step. Man leaves and returns to his place of origin—*exitus* and *reditus*. It is precisely this view of life as a pilgrimage that lends the Christian pilgrimage its special value (14). The following are the attributes associated with the symbolism of the pilgrim: the shell, the crook or staff, the well of the water-of-salvation which he finds in his path, the road, the cloak, etc. The idea is cognate with that of the labyrinth: to go on a pilgrimage is to come to understand the nature of the labyrinth, and to move towards the mastery of it as a means to the 'Centre'.

Pillar The solitary pillar is related to the world-axis, as are the post, the mast and the tree. The Egyptian hieroglyphic sign *zed* is interpreted both as a pillar and as the spinal column (there is no symbolic contradiction here) (39). Frobenius says that Africans interpret pillars as caryatids shorn of their human likeness, that is, as indirect images of man (21). When there are two pillars, the symbolism corresponds to that of the cabbalistic columns of Jachin and Boaz.

Pine-tree Like other evergreen trees, the pine is a symbol of immortality. Conifers, by virtue of their shape, also partake of the symbolism corresponds to that of the Cabbalistic columns of Jachin sacred tree, associating it with the cult of Attis. Pine-cones were regarded as symbols of fertility (4, 21).

Zodiacal sign
of Pisces.

Pisces The last sign of the Zodiac, closely bound up with the symbolism of water and of the 'dissolution of forms' which takes place in the Akasha. Neptune whipping up the waves with his trident, and calling forth bulls and horses out of them, is a symbolic expression of the resurgence of cosmic energy from the watery deeps of the primordial ocean. If Capricorn marks the beginning of the process of dissolution, Pisces denotes the final moment which, for this very reason, contains within itself the beginning of the new cycle. Related to Pisces are the avatar in the form of the fish of Vishnu in India, and the Chaldean myth of Oannes the man-fish. This twelfth house of the Zodiac, when transposed, by analogy, to the existential and psychic plane, denotes defeat and failure, exile or seclusion, and also mysticism and the denial of the self and its passions (40). The dual aspect of this symbol is well expressed by the zodiacal sign itself, composed of two fishes arranged parallel to one another but facing in different directions: the left-hand fish indicates the direction of involution or the beginning of a new cycle in the world of manifestation, while the fish that faces the right points to the direction of evolution—the way out of the cycle (52).

Plait Like bunches of ribbons, rosettes, ties and knots, the plait is symbolic of intimate relationship, intermingling streams and interdependence (19).

Planetary Gods They are personifications of idealized qualities of Man: 'modes' of existence and the range of the essential possibilities in behaviour and knowledge. Since these gods are endowed with enviable powers and disport themselves upon a delectable field of action, they have come to symbolize the triumph of the particular principle pertaining to each one of them; hence they frequently appear in mythology in association with ideas of justice and the underlying laws governing life (15). Through the process of catasterism, the major gods were projected into the heavens and identified with the sun, the moon and the five nearest planets. This can be clearly seen in the beginnings of astrobiological thought (7) in Mesopotamia. For the Chaldeans, the astral bodies were living but divine beings, an idea which persists in clear though fragmentary form in Aristotle and throughout the Middle Ages in the Western world, as Seznec has shown (53). The respective names of the gods among the Chaldeans, the Greeks and the Romans were these: *Shamash*, the Sun, Helios, Apollo; *Sin*, the Moon, Artemis, Diana; *Marduk*, Zeus, Jupiter; *Ishtar*, Aphrodite, Venus; *Nabu*, Hermes, Mercury; *Nergal*, Ares, Mars; *Ninib*, Cronos, Saturn. By virtue of the theory of correspondences, the relationships stemming from these gods embrace the whole—or almost the whole—of the pattern of the universe.

Planets   The planets constitute a particular order within the cosmos. It is the business of the science of astronomy to study them from a naturalistic and mathematical point of view, upon the basis of the system which Copernicus established with his *De Revolutionibus Orbium Coelestium* of 1543, according to which the sun is the centre around which are set the orbits of the planets: Mercury, the nearest, followed by Venus, Earth, Mars, the Asteroids, Jupiter, Saturn, Uranus, Neptune (and Pluto). But astrology and traditional symbolism owe their inspiration not to the Copernican system but to that which had been accepted by the Ancients. Since the validity of the symbolism here depends exclusively upon a process of catasterism (that is, the projection of a given mental order into the celestial order, or the interpretation of a 'series' capable of explaining phenomena in the psychological and spiritual world) it is unnecessary for us to examine the complex question of how far the Ptolemaic system (in part confirmed by the Theory of Relativity) can be reconciled with the Copernican. At the same time, the fact of there being seven planets responds to the idea of the seven planetary heavens, which in turn tallies with that of the seven Directions or areas in space (which in turn, when transposed into terms of time, becomes the origin of the seven days of the week). The relationship of the planets to the seven points in space is as follows: Sun—the zenith, Moon—the nadir, Mercury—the centre, Venus—the West, Mars—the South, Jupiter—the East, and Saturn—the North (54). The order in which astrology places the planets—counting the Sun and the Moon also as planets—is as follows, taking the Earth as the centre and then proceeding from the nearest to the farthest: Moon,

Mercury, Venus, the Sun, Mars, Jupiter, Saturn (Uranus and Neptune, although these two are not generally counted). The sex of these entities is clearly established so far as Venus, Mars, Jupiter and Saturn are concerned. Mercury appears as both masculine and androgynous. The Sun and the Moon have interchanged their sex through the ages, according to the culture of the period. The mystic basis of the planetary myth is to be sought in the generalization of Varro to the effect that the planets are celestial bodies and, at the same time, generators of life (7). Each of these generating powers has a characteristic sphere of action, which is its 'heaven', and the influence of this 'heaven' spreads out through the interpenetrating zones of space. Planetary symbolism reaches its highest degree of complexity in its relationship to the Zodiac; whereas the Zodiac symbolizes the grades and phases of a given cycle of creation, the planetary 'series' expresses rather the pattern of the moral world. The theory of 'correspondences', applied to the planets, educes a complex system wherein each planet is seen as a particular 'mode' endowed with a specific characteristic, and related to one particular Sense, or a metal, a perfume, or a plant, for example. It is more important, however, to grasp the connexion of each planet with a given virtue or tendency: thus, the Sun is related to the will and to activity, the Moon to imagination and the world of forms, Mars to action and destruction, Mercury to intuition and movement, Jupiter to good judgement and direction, Venus to love and relationships, Saturn to endurance and reserve. However, the fundamental tendencies of these qualities are sometimes negative and sometimes positive. Ely Star suggests the following arrangement, in accordance with the principles of evolution and spiritualization: Sun—potential good, Moon—potential evil, Mercury—duality and, consequently, free will, Venus—objective good, Mars—objective evil, Jupiter—subjective good, Saturn—subjective evil. The planets are thus divided into two zones, one luminous and the other dark, both of them necessary to the cycle of existence; these zones correspond to the clear and dark sections respectively of the Chinese symbol of universal flux—the *Yang-Yin* (54). Mertens-Stienon has studied the planetary powers in their theogonic aspect, proceeding from the outside inward, so that the most distant becomes the oldest and the most 'primitive' of the gods: Uranus engenders Saturn (celestial space creates time), and the reign of Saturn is succeeded by the constructive order of Jupiter; next comes the offspring of Jupiter—Mars (the active principle), Venus (the passive) and Mercury (the neutral) (40). From the symbolic point of view, this evolutive series draws the inquirer inwards, concentrating itself within the human spirit, since the spirit is the microcosm which reflects the macrocosmic universe. The importance of the planetary archetypes is apparent in the persistent influence of Graeco-Roman mythology, for it was the classic myths that most clearly and forcibly expressed their inner meaning; as Jean Seznec (53) has shown, these myths continued in popularity throughout the Christian culture of the Middle Ages and the Renaissance unopposed by the Church, since it perceived their symbolic and psychological truth. Waldemar Fenn maintains that there are certain prehistoric engravings which contain groups of four and of three component elements and that these drawings correspond to planetary configurations. The popular art of the Nordic races, of course, keeps to this division of the spheres—essential from the psychological viewpoint—into two groups: an inner group of three factors and an outer one of four. Given the equation of the planets with the seven Directions of Space (as we have previously outlined), then the inner group (disposed along the vertical axis) would comprise the series of Sun-Mercury-Moon, while the outer, equivalent to the cardinal points, relates to Venus-Mars-Jupiter-Saturn. This suggests that, as components of the human spirit, the three central ingredients have more importance and greater influence than the outer four, since the latter concern the square and the symbolism of situation and limitation (as with the tetramorphs), whereas the former constitute the very psychic dynamism of the ternary order, comprehending the active, the passive and the neuter.

Plants An image of life, expressive of the manifestation of the cosmos and of the birth of forms. Aquatic plants, in particular, are symbolic of the 'nascent' character of life. In India, cosmic images are depicted as emerging from the lotus flower (17). At the same time, man, conscious that biologically he was related to the animals, could not but be aware that his upright posture was more closely related to that of the tree, the shrub and the very grass, than to the horizontal posture of all animals (other than the celestial birds). Thus, whereas totemism drew up relationships between man and certain animals, the astrobiological era was characterized by frequent connexions and equations between mythic beings and plants. In particular, lives which had come to a violent end were supposed to carry on a metamorphosed existence in vegetable form. Osiris, Attis, Adonis, to name only a few deities, are closely related to plants. Another aspect of plant-symbolism is the annual cycle, in consequence of which they sometimes symbolize the mystery of death and resurrection (17). The fertility of the fields affords the most powerful image of cosmic, material and spiritual fecundity.

Playing-cards The entire pack of playing-cards is symbolic in origin. It finds its fullest expression in the twenty-two major enigmas of the Tarot pack (each card representing an integral allegory which is, up to a certain point, complete in itself), followed by the fifty-six lesser enigmas. The latter comprise fourteen figures in each of the four suits: gold—equivalent to diamonds (made up of circles, disks and wheels), clubs (truncheons and sceptres), spades (swords) and cups—equivalent to hearts. The gold symbolizes the material forces; the club or staff the power of command; the cup or chalice varies somewhat in significance but generally concerns the receptacle as such: the chalice or the chest, for instance; the sword is an emblem, in this particular instance, of discrimination between error and justice. The number inscribed on each card implies the symbolism pertaining to that particular number, *see* TAROT.

Pleiades   The constellation of the Pleiades comprises the central group in sidereal symbolism. Both Hebrew and Hindu traditions see in these stars the image of the septenary as applied to space, to sound and to action (40).

Plough   Symbol of fertilization. In an Aryan legend, Rama, the hero, marries Sita (the furrow). Because the earth is female in nature, ploughing is a symbol of the union of the male and the female principle. The former Chinese custom of ceremonial plough-ing by the emperor at the beginning of his reign is connected with this symbolism (33).

Point   The point signifies unity, the Origin and the Centre. It also represents the principles of manifestation and emanation, and hence in some mandalas the centre is not actually shown but must be imagined by the initiate. There are two kinds of point to be considered: that which has no magnitude and is symbolic of creative virtue, and that which—as suggested by Raymond Lull in his *Nova Geometria*—has the smallest conceivable or practicable magnitude and is a symbol of the principle of manifestation. Moses of Leon defined the nature of the original Point as follows: 'This degree is the sum total of all subsequent mirrors, that is, of all external aspects related to this one degree. They proceed therefrom because of the mystery of the point, which is in itself an occult degree emanating from the mystery of the pure and awe-inspiring ether. The first degree of all is absolutely occult, that is, not manifest, and cannot be attained' (25). This explains why the Centre—identical with the mystic point of Moses of Leon—is usually represented as a hole.

Pole   The mystic 'Centre', or the 'unvarying mean', is the fixed point which all symbolic traditions concur in designating as the 'pole', since the rotation of the earth takes place around it (28). On the other hand, the pole is also identified with the zenith. In ancient China, it was represented by the hole in the centre of the jade disk known as *Pi* (7). The 'unvarying mean' is, nevertheless, the cause of all change. The Chinese *Book of Changes* shows that the continuous metamorphoses of matter are generated by the great pole—a Oneness located far beyond all duality, beyond all occurence, and equated with the 'unmoved mover' of Aristotle (58). This contradiction between the immobile and the cause of all movement was expressed metaphorically by the alchemists in the saying: 'At the pole lies the heart of Mercury, which is true fire' (32).

Pomegranate The Greeks believed that the pomegranate sprang from the blood of Dionysos. There are similar beliefs linking anemones with Adonis and violets with Attis (21). But the predominating significance of the pomegranate, arising from its shape and internal structure rather than from its colour, is the reconciliation of the multiple and diverse within apparent unity. Hence, in the Bible, for example, it appears as a symbol of the Oneness of the universe (37). It is also symbolic of fecundity.

Poplar In addition to the general symbolism attached to trees, wood and vegetable life, the poplar has a special allegorical significance connected with the fact that the two sides of the poplar leaf are of a different shade of green. Thus, it becomes the tree of life, bright green on the side of water (moon) and a darker green on the side of fire (sun) (50). The poplar also has a place within the general range of bipolar symbols (positive-negative) (32).

Potion Generally a love-potion, frequently mentioned in Roman antiquity, where it is said, for example, that the poet Lucretius' madness was caused by a potion. It appears with still greater frequency in mediaeval legends and is related to the Celtic *geis*, according to Jean Marx (*Nouvelles Recherches sur la littérature Arthurienne*). A potion symbolizes love's ill-fortune. Whoever drinks it can no longer observe the feudal laws, nor the duties incumbent on his position, and can even be driven to death by this plight, as exemplified by Tristan.

Potne Theron This is the name given by the Greeks to compositions depicting the figure of a man between two animals; they were much used in ancient and mediaeval art (for example, the harp of Ur in Mesopotamia; the capital at Estany; Cappadocian seals, or Sumerian ivories). Sometimes this feature attached itself to legendary or historic figures: Gilgamesh in Mesopotamia, or Daniel and the lions in the Christian, Biblical tradition. But, for the Greeks, this composition was a symbol of the union of man with nature, or of the equilibrium of forces necessary to bring this union about. Now, in the view of Shekotov, the Russian art critic, 'the symmetrical disposition of figures around a single centre denotes, both in an artistic context and in religious or profane ceremonies, the idea of triumph'.

Power The symbolism of power has been subjected to an extensive study by Percy Ernst Schramm in his *Herrschaftszeichen und Staatssymbolik* (Stuttgart, 1954). Power, as a symbol, represents irradiating force, but it is only latterly that it has acquired this significance, for in totemistic and primitive times it was generally understood more in the sense of an image of the forces of nature (and of the animal world in particular) than as an expression of abstract or temporal dominion. Hence, the principal attributes of a superior power are simply magnified versions of totemic emblems or of adornments derived from them, such as necklaces of teeth and claws, hides, head-dresses, horns, and various kinds of standards exhibiting these objects. It was probably with the dawning of the solar cult that the diadem—the original form of the crown—came to be adopted as another attribute of power. The immediate effect of the assumption of power upon the body and the attitude of mind is to confer impassivity, indifference—either real or affected—and serenity and, equally, a tendency to 'swell with pride'. Hence the fascination of the hieratic gesture and its use on solemn occasions. Dynamic movements such as stretching out the arms or nodding or turning the head may also be executed in a rhythm suggestive of hieratic strength and calm. Ancient art gave expression to a basically similar attitude towards the powers of the world. Height above ground-level, and the situation of a particular symbolic element at the centre of a symmetrical pattern—the Greek *Potne Theron* for instance—are further illustrations of power-symbolism, deriving from the symbolisms of level and of the 'Centre'. Differentiated expressions of power give rise to the king, the priest and the military leader, each one characterized by his respective attributes. The synthesis of power is denoted by ternary symbols such as the triple crown. Certain other symbols embracing the threefold power, such as the trident, are generally reckoned to pertain to the infernal regions, but this has come about rather through the influence of traditional, mythological ideas than by true symbolic logic. Magic power—a corrupt form of religious power—is symbolized by the wand and sometimes by the sword. There are also certain other objects linked with the idea of power, but they are attributes or instruments rather than symbols proper.

Of great interest is the complex symbolic system behind the emblems of the Egyptian pharaoh. The double crown denotes Upper and Lower Egypt, but it also expresses the ideas of the masculine and feminine principles, and of heaven and earth. Sceptres —straight (the lash) and curved (the crook)—are probably attributes of cattle-raising and of agriculture respectively; yet at the same time they denote the straight path (or the solar, diurnal, logical course) and the crooked path (the lunar, nocturnal and intuitive). The Uraeus beyond doubt symbolizes the sublimated serpent—raised, that is to say, in height (the *kundalini*), so as to become a symbol of strength transformed into spirit or an aspect of power. In itself, the idea of power embraces the notions of extreme self-awareness and integrity, defensive concentration of forces, appropriation and domination of the environment, and effulgence. Hence, to take these ideas in turn, the symbols of power are names, seals, marks, standards and signs; masks, helmets, head-dresses, swords and shields; sceptres, crowns, *pallia* and palaces; and effulgence is expressed by gold and precious stones. Domination also finds expression in such forms of the quaternary as four-headed sceptres, *hermae* or thrones alluding to the cardinal points. The crown, in its most highly developed form, embraces the diadem or circle and the hemisphere or image of the vault of heavens; and sometimes it denotes the four points of the compass—or suggests them by means of four bands which rise up from the diadem to meet higher up, in the middle, surmounted by another symbolic motif. The idea of royalty is, of course, linked with sun-symbolism, and therefore the animals associated with it are such as the eagle and the lion, and on occasion the dragon. Once Christianity had become the official religion of the Roman Empire, various Christian symbols of sublimation accrue to the symbolism of power, notably the crucifix and the fleur-de-lis. The latter symbol is found in Byzantium, whence it reached Central Europe, Germany, France and the Western world by the 1st millennium A.D.

Precinct All images to do with the precinct—an enclosure, a walled garden, a city, a square, a castle, a *patio*—correspond to the idea of the *temenos*, or a sacred and circumscribed space which is guarded and defended because it constitutes a spiritual entity. Such images as this may also symbolize the life of the individual and in particular the inner life of his thoughts (32). It will be recognized that a square or a circle is the tactical formation commonly adopted as a means of defence in a critical situation against a more powerful adversary. This in itself would suffice to explain the meaning of the mandala, or any one of the innumerable symbols that are based upon the notion of the precinct or the protection of a given space, identified with the self. Circular dances, such as the maypole dance, or the *sardana* of Catalonia; or the prehistoric stone-circles (sometimes known as cromlechs); or emblems featuring fences or people formed in a circle—all carry this same symbolic meaning, this same notion of self-protection, as Adama van Scheltema has noted in *Documents* VII (Paris, 1930) in connexion with the *Centre féminin sacré*.

Prester John The realm of the fabulous Prester John, like certain other mythic 'lands', is, in fact, a symbol of the supreme, spiritual 'centre' (28).

Prime Matter This represents the basic stage out of which grew the alchemic process with its quest for the transmutation of gold, that is, for perfect and definitive sublimation, or the consolidation of the spirit itself. The alchemists gave a host of names to this unidentified prime matter: quicksilver, lead, salt, sulphur, water, air, fire, earth, blood, *lapis*, poison, spirit, sky, dew, shade, mother, sea, moon, dragon, chaos, microcosm, etc. The *Rosarium* terms it 'root of itself', and elsewhere it is named 'earth of paradise'. This explains why prime matter was thought to come from the mountain where distinctions are still unknown and where all things are one, neither distinguished nor distinguishable (32). It is also regarded as associated with the unconscious.

Prince   The prince, or the son of the king, is a rejuvenated form of the paternal king, as the nascent sun is a rejuvenation of the dying sun. The prince often figures as the hero in legends; his great virtue is intuition and it is by no means rare for him to possess the powers of a demiurge (32).

Procession   This word, expressive of the idea of marching, finds its truest expression in the liturgical procession. Davy points out that it takes its meaning from the idea of a pilgrimage and indicates the need for constant progress unfettered by earthly things, although making progressive use of them. The idea of the procession is also reminiscent of the Exodus of Israel and of the desert-crossing (14). As Schneider has noted, the movements of claustral processions imply a symbolism related to space-time: the hymns which are sung last the length of the procession; the return to the cloister is equivalent to the passage of a year by virtue of the correspondence of the four sides with the cardinal points and the seasons. But, speaking more generally, every procession is a rite which gives substance to the concept of the cycle and passage of time, as is proved by the fact of its returning to the point of departure. Various symbolic and allegorical figures are attached to it: the Chinese dragons, for instance, or the Roman eagles (since a military march-past is a form of procession). Christianity has incorporated some early aspects of the symbol into its rites; for example, there is a book upon St. Macarius that contains some allegorical chariots with all the principal symbolic animals drawing them, from the bear and the rhinoceros to the unicorn and the phoenix. Those festivals which have incorporated elements of folklore have likewise assimilated the symbolic implications of folk art. From prehistoric times, giants, carnival grotesques, dwarfs, dragons, vipers, lions, oxen, have all figured in processions. The famous *tarasque*[1] of Tarascon, has been seen as the Great Whore of Babylon. The eagle may correspond to St. John; the viper and the dragon allude to the legend of St. George. According to esoteric thought, giants,

[1] The figure of a huge serpent or dragon carried in Corpus Christi processions.—*Translator*

dwarfs, salamanders and nymphs are elemental spirits pertaining respectively to air, earth, fire and water. To carry them in procession is to display man's dominion over them, for although they are borne in triumph, they are really exhibited as captives; and it was in this sense that the Romans incorporated them into their grand march-past at the end of a campaign.

Professions Schneider has noted the sober and artisan character of mystic thought, with its belief that an individual's profession or calling is what basically determines his mythic and cosmic situation. This is not to invalidate common-sense ways of thinking, but to substantiate them by rooting them firmly in the plane of transcendence. Were we to envisage an ideal landscape with a valley, a mountain with its corresponding cave, and the sea, we would find that the sea is the haunt of seamen and fishermen, the valley corresponds to labourers and gardeners, the mountain-side to shepherds, the cave to blacksmiths and perhaps also to potters, and the mountain-peak to the ascetic and the lofty-minded sages. Schneider suggests that, by analogy, the mountain is also the dwelling-place of warriors, miners, doctors and martyrs (50, 51). In order to determine the appropriate grade of each profession it is necessary only to apply the laws of the symbolism of level. If the symbolic significance of any profession lies in the translation of its practical aspects to the realm of the spiritual or the psychological, the sailor's calling symbolizes the coming to grips with the unconscious and with the passions, or the struggle at the level of the chaotic. The fisherman draws symbolic tokens out of the deeps. The farmer is in close contact with fecund nature and contributes with his labours to the fertility of the soil. The gardener fulfils the same function on a higher spiritual and intellectual plane, for the garden is a symbol of the soul, and he works upon his garden in order to improve it. Blacksmiths and potters are creators of forms, masters of matter. The miners' work is analogous to that of fishermen, since they extract what is valuable from one of the Elements. The ascetic and the sage direct the pattern of life, virtually without action. Doctors purify existence and combat what is harmful. The martyr suffers and triumphs over life by his sacrifice. Other callings related to the demiurge are those of the weaver and the spinner (who spin and sever the threads of existence). There were certain professions which, about the 4th millennium before our era, characterized the period of the profoundest development in man. As Berthelot has observed, the devising of the calendar, the development of metallurgy and the production of the first of the alloys (bronze), seem to have been the causes of the change from primitive to civilized cultures (in Mesopotamia and Egypt in the first place). Berthelot has also drawn an interesting parallel between the development of certain cults and the corresponding growth of the professions which determined and demanded them as the level of civilization rose. The hunters, fishermen and weavers of the Palaeolithic Age limited their cults to the animals which provided them with their subsistence; the shepherd and seafarer of Neolithic and early historical times based their cults upon the moon and the stars, which were their means of orientation; the blacksmith, metallurgist and early chemist, with whom the era of recorded history opens, exalted fire in their cults, since it played a decisive part in their work. And finally, the agricultural worker, or the prevalence of his conception of the world, ensured the predominance of the solar cult, since the sun is the creator of the cycle of the year and of the seasons. In the above observations, then, we have attempted to show how men's callings are graduated from the most primitive to the most recent, with their corresponding symbolism (7). The caste-system may also be related to this.

Prometheus The Prometheus myth, according to Piobb, is an illustration of sublimation—by virtue of the family resemblance between the vulture and the eagle—which confirms the alchemic relationship between the volatile and the fixed principles. At the same time, suffering (like that of Prometheus) corresponds to sublimation because of its association with the colour red—the third colour in the alchemic *Magnum Opus*, coming after black and white. The rescue of Prometheus by Hercules expresses the efficacy of the process of sublimation, and its outcome (48).

Promised Land, The The Promised Land—the Holy Land— was, for the alchemists, with their concept of the three worlds as 'states' and of landscapes as 'expressions', the 'final stage of an experiment'. Where, within the order of time, peace and perfection is the goal, within the order of space it becomes the Promised Land, whether it is Canaan for the Jews wandering in the desert, or Ithaca for Ulysses sailing the seas (57). The Israelites identified their spiritual 'Centre' with Mount Sion, known to them as the 'heart of the world'. Dante described Jerusalem as the 'pole of the spirit' (28).

Pumpkin or **Gourd, Double** A Chinese emblem of Li T'ieh-kuai, the second of the Eight Immortals. Like the hour-glass, twin drums, St. Andrew's cross or the letter X, it is a symbol of the link between the two worlds—the upper and the lower—and of the principle of inversion regulating the ordered pattern of events of cosmic phenomena, that is, night and day, life and death, infamy and sublimity, sorrow and joy. Li T'ieh-kuai was, in effect, a mythic figure whose essential characteristic was his ability to leave his body and visit heaven. He was also symbolized by a column of smoke (5). But this symbol of the twin pumpkin is very far from being limited to the Far East; it was also common in the West. Among other representations, the frontispiece of Book II of Maier's work on alchemy, *Symbola*

Aureae Mensae (1617) shows us the twin pumpkin in the form of two amphorae, with the top one up-ended. The surprising thing is that this image also incorporates the above-mentioned symbol of the column of smoke joining the interior of the lower amphora with the upper; in this case there is not just a single column, but a ring of smoke circulating between the mouths of the two amphorae.

Pun   Schneider (50) has summed up one of the most profound of all symbolic questions with his remark that 'to create a poetic pun is to jump over or annihilate the distance between two logical or spatial elements—to place under one yoke two elements which are naturally discrete'. This is the explanation too of the mystic sense of modern poetry derived from Rimbaud and Reverdy. In the words of the latter: 'The image is a pure creation of the spirit. It is born not of a comparison, but of the reconciliation of two more or less distinct realities. The more distant and apt the two realities so reconciled, the stronger will be the image, and the greater emotive force and poetic reality will it possess'—symbolic reality, we would rather say. In consequence, what is equivocal tends towards the orgiastic disruption of the 'given order' to make way for the 'new order'. Hence the fact that 'the art of equivocal phrases' always expresses, in a cultural sense, the need to invert one style in order to attain the opposite (as, for instance, from the Gothic to the Renaissance, or from 19th-century realism to the formalist style of the 20th century).

Putrefaction   The alchemic symbolism of *putrefactio*, with its graphic representation as black crows, skeletons, skulls and other funereal signs, embraces the concept of life renewed—like the zodiacal sign of Pisces. Hence it has been said that it signifies 'rebirth of matter after death and the disintegration of the residue' (57). From the psychological point of view, putrefaction is the destruction of the intellectual impediments in the way of the evolution of the spirit. Certain rites and folkloristic customs seem to be derived from the alchemic concept; at least, they appear in a similar symbolism. Thus in Corella (Navarre), the Good Friday procession is headed by a skeleton which, in ancient times, had bunches of grapes hanging from its back. This conveys the idea of the new life, which arises from *putrefactio*, and which was in reality already present in the Orphic mysteries and in all beliefs in the value of sacrifice as the generator of new forces.

Pyramid   There is an apparent contradiction in the symbolism of the pyramid. In the first place, in megalithic culture and in European folklores which have preserved its memory, it is symbolic of the earth in its maternal aspect. Pyramids with Christmas decorations and lights, moreover, express the twofold idea of death and immortality, both associated with the Great Mother. But this concerns the pyramid only in so far as it is a hollow mountain, the dwelling of ancestors and an earth-monument. The pyramid of stone, of regular geometrical shape, corresponds to fire, at any rate in the Far East (4). Marc Saunier has suggested the right approach to a more precise understanding of the problem. He regards the pyramid as a synthesis of different forms, each with its own significance. The base is square and represents the earth. The apex is the starting-point and the finishing-point of all things —the mystic 'Centre' (Nicholas of Cusa, in his disquisitions, concurs with this interpretation). Joining the apex to the base are the triangular-shaped faces of the pyramid, symbolizing fire, divine revelation and the threefold principle of creation. In consequence, the pyramid is seen as a symbol expressing the whole of the work of creation in its three essential aspects (49).

Quadriga   A variant of the square (q.v.). It carries the inherent symbolism of the quaternary, here implied in the four horses drawing the chariot. With this in mind, Dio Chrysostom worked out the following analogies: the charioteer corresponds to the Pantokrator and the chariot to the halo (indicating two different levels of the manifest world through the intersection of the circles of heaven and earth); and the four horses relate to the four Elements and the tetramorphs. The symbolic relationship of the horses with the Elements is the key to the following passage: 'The first horse is very fleet. His coat is shining and bears the signs of the planets and the constellations. The second horse is slower and is lit up on only one side. The third goes slower still and the fourth twists round and round. But there comes a time when the hot breath of the first sets fire to the mane of the second, and the third drowns the fourth with his sweat.' The four horses correspond to fire, air, water and earth respectively, beginning with the most energetic of the Elements and ending with the most material or *lento*. The quadriga, then, becomes a symbol of the universe of space-time (31).

Quaternary   The quaternary bears the same relationship to the number-series as does the tetramorph on the mystic plane; if they are not identical they are certainly related or analogous. It is based, of course, upon the number four. In the words of Plato: 'The ternary is the number pertaining to the idea; the quaternary is the number connected with the realization of the idea.' Hence within the septuple pattern of space, the ternary is situated on the vertical line because it is associated with the vertical division into three worlds on three levels, whereas the quaternary is located on the surface, that is, on the intermediate of the three planes, or, in other words, it is situated in the world of phenomena. The quaternary, then, corresponds to earth, to the material pattern of life; and the number three to moral and spiritual dynamism. The human anatomy confirms this concept of the number four. The spatial or surface-symbolism of the number four is described by the Renaissance writer, Cartari, in *Les Images des dieux des anciens*: 'The square figures representing Mercury, possessing only a head and a phallus, signified that the sun is the lord of the world, the sower of all things; furthermore, the four sides of the square represented what the four-stringed sistrum portrayed as an attribute of Mercury, that is, the four regions of the world, or, in other words, the four seasons. . . .' (32). There is a clear connexion between these 'herms' and the Indian figures of Brahma with four faces (60), corresponding to the four Kumaras (who were four angels in Persian tradition), related to the four so-called 'royal' stars (Aldebaran, Antares, Regulus and Fomalhaut) and represented by the four fixed signs of the Zodiac, in turn related to the tetramorphs. Another obvious connexion is the symbol of the four rivers of paradise which rise at the foot of the Tree of Life (or the world-axis) (40). This fourfold orientation conforms with the cardinal points which, according to the Zohar, correspond to the four Elements (9) and to all quaternary forms. The most interesting of these correspondences are these: East corresponding to spring, air, infancy, dawn and the crescent moon; South, to summer, fire, youth, midday and full moon; West, to autumn, water, middle-age, evening and the waning moon; North, to winter, earth, old age, night and the new moon. As is the case with symbols based upon seven (the week or the planets, for example) or upon twelve (the year or the Zodiac), analogies with the symbolism for four may extend to cover every possible process in life (55). The Elements correspond to the so-called elemental beings as follows: Air—sylphs and giants; fire—salamanders; water—undines and mermaids; earth—gnomes and dwarfs. Gaston Bachelard considers that the four temperaments are related to the Elements (1), in which case the pattern of correspondences might be seen as follows: Air linked with the sanguinary; fire with the nervous; water with the lymphatic; earth with the bilious (55). Bachelard, in his psychoanalytic work upon the significance of the Elements, studies the significant way in which dynamic images are related with a particular Element, such as the image of fire in Hoffmann, water in Edgar Allan Poe, air in Nietzsche. To return to the question. of the cardinal points, there is not complete accord about which of them—West or North—is the most negative, but there is complete agreement that the East is the luminous source of the spirit (14, 31, 48). In China, the Emperor once used to perform a strange rite whereby he identified himself with the annual course of the sun, embracing also the points of the compass. This he did by living in one quarter of his square-shaped palace at a time, depending upon the season and the compass-point corresponding to that season (in accordance with the pattern we have just mentioned) (7). The mystic animals corresponding to the cardinal points are: East, blue dragon; South, red bird; West, white tiger; North, black tortoise (6). But in the Western world, according to Schneider, these animals become: East (or the morning)—lion; South (or midday)—eagle; West (or the evening)—peacock; North (or the night)—ox (50). The importance of the number four is borne out statistically: the square is the shape most frequently used by man, or, where necessary, the rectangle. According to a Hindu belief—comparable with the Platonic—completeness has four angles and is supported on four feet (60). Jung has shown profound interest in the symbolism of the quaternary, and upon its basis he has built up the pattern of the human psyche as one endowed with four functions: sensing, intuiting, feeling and thinking. These four functions he relates to the four ends of a cross, postulating that the three placed respectively at the left, the right and the top are conscious, while the fourth is unconscious (or repressed). But the placing of the functions varies according to the individual personality (34). These four functions cluster around the essential component of volition or judgement, just as the tetramorphs are ranged around the Pantokrator. Jung adds that the principal components—the archetypes—of the human being are disposed similarly in quaternary order; they are: the anima, shadow, ego and personality forming around the *Selbst* or 'the God within' (32). The phases of the alchemic process may also be placed in quaternary order, from lowest to highest: black, white, red, gold. Diel's 'life-urges' may be similarly ordered, for although Diel mentions only three (conservation, reproduction and spiritualization or evolution) this is because the hidden function, in this case, is thanatism.

Quinary This is a group of five elements. It is represented formally by the pentagon and the five-pointed star, and also by the square together with its central point. Traditionally, the number five symbolizes man after the fall, but, once applied to this order of earthly things, it signifies health and love (44). Esoteric thinking sees this, not as the effect but, in fact, as the cause of man's five extremities with the number five inscribed also on each hand and foot (54). This association of the number five with the human figure, common during the Romanesque period, is found all over the world, from England to the Far East. Agrippa of

Nettesheim depicted the image of man with arms and legs apart and related to the pentagram. Many amulets and talismans are based upon the number five, not only because of the associated ideas of the human figure, health (or physical integrity) and love, but because the quinary is symbolic of the whole of the material world (denoted by the quaternary) plus the centre or quintessence. In Morocco, for example, to protect oneself against the evil eye one repeats the phrase *hamsa fi ainek* ('five in your eye'). Certain Islamic rites and concepts were patterned after the quinary: there are five religious duties, five keys to secret knowledge, five daily prayers and a solemn oath is repeated five times (12). For the Chinese, five is the most important of all the numbers. The quinary, in sum, represents the natural rhythm of life, the order of the cosmos. The following groups (among others) are based upon the quinary 'model': the five planets (Mercury, Venus, Mars, Jupiter, Saturn); the five elemental forms (metal, vegetable, water, fire, earth); the five colours (white, black, blue, red, yellow); the five musical timbres (of bronze, stone, silk, wood and clay); the five essential landscapes (of mountains and woods, rivers and lakes, hills, fertile plains, springs and swamps) (13). In the Near East and in the West the number five has been used solely as an expression of the human figure as a whole, and of eroticism; here the predominant model-numbers have been four and seven, and it is according to these numbers that the cosmic components of the universe and of man have been ordered.

Radiance   Bachelard (3) has suggested that there is an interesting connexion between radiance, the human glance and starlight. In itself, a brightness or radiance is always felt to be supernatural, like a message standing out clearly against a negative or neutral background. Brightness is, of course, related to fire and to daylight both in their positive and in their destructive aspects.

Rags and Tatters   They are symbolic of wounds and gashes in the soul. More precise meanings are derived from the actual garment which is in tatters.

Rahab   This priestess symbolizes primordial chaos mastered by God in the beginning of time, comparable with Tiamat vanquished by Marduk in Chaldean tradition (7). She represents the essential idea of all cosmogonies.

Rain   Rain has a primary and obvious symbolism as a fertilizing agent, and is related to the general symbolism of life (26) and water.

Apart from this, but for the same reason, it signifies purification, not only because of the value of water as the 'universal substance'—as the mediating agent between the non-formal or gaseous and the formal or solid, an aspect which is common to all symbolic traditions (29) —but also because of the fact that rainwater falls from heaven (7). Hence it is also cognate with light. This explains why, in many mythologies, rain is regarded as a symbol of the 'spiritual influences' of heaven descending upon earth (28). In alchemy, rain symbolizes condensation or albification—further proof that, for the alchemists, water and light were of the same symbolic family.

Rats The rat occurs in association with infirmity and death. It was an evil-doing deity of the plague in Egypt and China (35). The mouse, in mediaeval symbolism, is associated with the devil (20). A phallic implication has been superimposed upon it, but only in so far as it is dangerous or repugnant.

Rectangle Of all geometric forms, the most rational, the most secure and regular; this is explained empirically by the fact that, at all times and in all places, it has been the shape favoured by man when preparing any space or object for immediate use in life: house, room, table, bed, for example. The square implies tense domination born of an abstract longing for power, whereas the circle avoids all earthly associations by virtue of its celestial symbolism. Less regular shapes than the rectangle, such as the trapezium or the trapezoid, are abnormal or dolorous forms, expressive of suffering and inner irregularity (42).

Red Sea In alchemic symbolism 'crossing the Red Sea' is symbolic of the most dangerous part of an undertaking or of a stage in a man's life. To leave Egypt for the Promised Land implies the act of crossing this sea bloodied with wounds and sacrifice; hence the crossing is a symbol of spiritual evolution (57) and also of death seen as the threshold between the worlds of matter and of the spirit. The man who sacrifices himself, in a sense dies.

Reefs Reefs and shoals were, in antiquity, the object of religious awe and were personified as giants and aquatic monsters (8). Sandbanks and even islands were looked upon in the same way. Here we can see the great myth of regression or petrifaction (that is, stagnation of the spiritual flow of evolution) which the ancient mind considered the worst of all crimes. Hence, in the *Odyssey*, reefs, islands, complete with their enchantress (Calypso or Circe), and quicksands, are all symbols of every kind of enchantment and obstruction of destiny.

Regard or **Glance** To regard some object, or simply to see it, is traditionally identified with acquaintance or awareness (and also with the possession of knowledge or simply with possession) (26). On the other hand, the glance is symbolically comparable with the teeth in representing the defensive barrier put up by the individual against the world round him—the towers and the city wall, respectively, of the 'city within'.

Reins   Reins enter into the symbolism of the chariot and of horses. Since the chariot is symbolic of the body and horses signify the forces of life, the reins bespeak the relationship between the soul and the body—the nerves and willpower. To cut the reins is equivalent, symbolically, to dying (38).

Relief   The depth of a relief, in general corresponding to the vividness of the forms depicted rather than to their intensity, is connected with the ideas of truth and material reality. A relief which is lacking in force symbolizes futility, falsity, equivocation and utter lack of persuasive power or of attractive 'values' of any kind. An intensely expressive relief, on the other hand, denotes the powerful surge of an emotion or of an idea in all its nascent power.

Return   The return home, or the return to the material home or to the motherland or birthplace, is symbolic of death, not in the sense of total destruction but of reintegration of the spirit into the Spirit. As the Chinese thinker Lieh-tzŭ observed, 'when the soul leaves the form, both are restored to their true essence, and that is why they are said to have returned home' (58).

Rhomb   According to Hentze (*cit.* Eliade, 17), the rhomb is emblematic of the female sexual organ. This would seem to confirm the Greek definition of the rhomb as an instrument of magic which, when brandished, was supposed to excite and inflame the passions of men (8)—an analogous and related idea, fetishist in character.

Ribbons   Ribbons knotted together to form a circle (worn by Romans as a kind of diadem in the same way as they wore garlands of flowers) are symbols of immortality by virtue of their circular shape. They also carry a heroic significance, like all crowns or garlands, for the very act of 'crowning' an undertaking fulfilled is so called because of the symbolic relationship between the crown and the concept of absolute fulfilment.

Ring   Like every closed circle, the ring is a symbol of continuity and wholeness. This is why (like the bracelet) it has been used both as a symbol of marriage and of the eternally repeated time-cycle. Sometimes it occurs in animal form, as a snake or an eel biting its tail (Ouroboros); sometimes as a pure geometrical form (8, 20, 32). It is interesting to note that, in some legends, the ring is regarded as the only remaining link of a chain. Thus, it is told that when Jupiter allowed Hercules to rescue Prometheus, it was on condition that the latter should thereafter wear an iron ring, set with a piece of rock from the Caucasus, as a symbol of submission to his punishment (8). Another type of ring is found in the circle of flames surrounding the dancing Shiva as he performs the cosmic dance; this flame-ring can be related to the Zodiac. Like the Zodiac and the Ouroboros of the Gnostics, it has an active and a passive half (evolution, involution), and stands for the life-cycle of both the universe and each individual being: the circular dance of nature in eternal process of creation and destruction. At the same time, the light radiated by the ring of flames symbolizes eternal wisdom and transcendental illumination (60).

Rite   In essence, every rite symbolizes and reproduces creation (17). Hence, rites are connected with the symbolism of ornaments (38). The slow-moving ritual, characteristic of all ceremonies, is closely bound up with the rhythm of the astral movements (3). At the same time, every rite is a meeting, that is, a confluence of forces and patterns; the significance of rites stems from the accumulated power of these forces when blended harmoniously one with the other.

River   An ambivalent symbol since it corresponds to the creative power both of nature and of time. On the one hand it signifies fertility and the progressive irrigation of the soil; and on the other hand it stands for the irreversible passage of time and, in consequence, for a sense of loss and oblivion (8, 60).

Rock   The Chinese attribute to the rock a symbolism denoting permanence, solidity and integrity (5), and this may be taken as generally valid. Like the stone, it is held in many traditions to be the dwelling-place of a god. As a Caucasian tradition has it: 'In the beginning, the world was covered with water. The great creator-god then dwelt inside a rock' (35). It seems, then, that man intuitively regards stones (as in the myth of Deucalion) and rocks as the source of human life, while the soil (inferior because more disintegrated) is the mother of vegetable and animal life. A mystic significance is attributed to this mineral, arising from the sound it makes when struck and because of its unity—that is, its solidity and cohesion.

Room   A symbol of individuality—of private thoughts. The windows symbolize the possibility of understanding and of passing through to the external and the beyond, and are also an illustration of any idea of communication. Hence, a closed room lacking windows may be symbolic of virginity, according to Frazer, and also of other kinds of non-communication. Many rites involving the enclosure-image are performed to mark the reaching of puberty, all over the world. The legend about Danae, shut up by her father in a bronze tower, pertains to this particular symbolism. There is a Siberian legend concerning a 'dark house of iron' which is also relevant to it (21). We might also mention the 'vase with a lid', one of the eight emblems of good luck in Chinese Buddhism, and a symbol of wholeness, of the idea with no 'exit', or, in other words, of supreme intelligence triumphant over birth and death (signified respectively by the doors and windows of the room) (5). This explains why the hermetically sealed room may possibly be a variant form of the 'vase with a lid'.

Rope Like the chain, it is a general symbol for binding and connexion. Knotted cord, in Egyptian hieroglyphics, signifies a man's name. Since the knot is a symbol for the individual's existence, there are various hieroglyphic signs related to the name of a person in the shape of a knot or a bow or a belt or a crown and so on. The seal has the same significance (19). The silver cord in Vedic teaching has a significance which goes still deeper: it expresses the sacred, inner path which binds the outer consciousness of man (his intellect) with his spiritual essence (the 'centre' or 'silver palace') (38).

Rose The single rose is, in essence, a symbol of completion, of consummate achievement and perfection. Hence, accruing to it are all those ideas associated with these qualities: the mystic Centre, the heart (14), the garden of Eros, the paradise of Dante (4), the beloved (31), the emblem of Venus (8) and so on. More precise symbolic meanings are derived from the colour and number of its petals. The relationship of the white rose to the red is in accordance with the relationship between the two colours as defined in alchemy (q.v.). The blue rose is symbolic of the impossible. The golden rose is a symbol of absolute achievement. When the rose is round in shape, it corresponds in significance to the mandala. The seven-petalled rose alludes to the septenary pattern (that is, the seven Directions of Space, the seven days of the week, the seven planets, the seven degrees of perfection). It is in this sense that it appears in emblem DCCXXIII of the *Ars Symbolica* of Bosch and in the *Summum Bonum* of Robert Fludd (32). The eight-petalled rose symbolizes regeneration (46).

Rotation For Roux, in *Les Druides* (Paris, 1961), rotation (the dynamic determining of circumference in rites or in art) generates a magic force, particularly of a defensive order, since it marks out a sacred precinct—the circle—which calls for the projection of the self. For Blavatsky, David's dance round the Ark, like that of the Sabean star-worshippers, was a circular dance or at least a dance that followed a closed curve.

Round Table The Round Table is equated, by its shape, with the Chinese disk of jade, *Pi*, which represents the sky. The appearance of the Grail in the centre of the table completes the symbolism, for the concave shape of the sacred chalice corresponds to the central hole in the Chinese *Pi*. The twelve knights are related to—but not identical with—the signs of the Zodiac, expressing in particular a parallel tendency, the struggle for the triumph and the establishment of 'paradise regained', or, in other words, of the 'unvarying mean'.

The tasks allotted to the knights implied the perfection of the circle of the sun, and involved succouring the weaker sex, the chastisement of tyrants, the liberation of the bewitched, the outwitting of giants, and the destruction of all evil men and noxious animals (4); and this programme was but the prelude to the establishment of the reign of the 'Centre'. Similar institutions are the 'round council' of the Dalai Lama (consisting of the twelve great *Namshans*) and the Twelve Peers of France. The model which is composed of twelve parts is the most important of all (the next being the ternary division, and then the quaternary and septenary) since it is equated with the circle and, in consequence, with the idea of totality (which is at times also expressed by the number ten). It was for this reason that the Etruscan state was divided into twelve parts and Romulus created twelve lictors (28). The evil that afflicted the Round Table, through the love of Queen Guinevere for Lancelot and the frailties of other knights, was sufficient cause for the failure of the community of knights to achieve their mystic ends; only Sir Galahad of the pure heart could come near to fulfilment once he had been granted the divine gifts of the shield and the sword.

Rudder   In ancient representations of ships, the rudder frequently plays an important part as an allegory expressive of the ideas of safety and the steering of a straight course. It figures with the same significance in mediaeval and Renaissance emblems.

Ruins   The symbolic sense of ruins is self-evident and derived directly from the literal sense: they signify desolation and life defunct. They are tantamount to sentiments, ideas or bonds which are no longer animated by the breath of life but which nevertheless persist shorn of any use or function relevant to thought and existence, but saturated with the past and redolent with a sense of the destruction of its reality wrought by the passage of time. Ruins are symbolically equivalent to biological mutilation.

Sacrifice   The central idea of cosmogonies is that of 'the primordial sacrifice'. Inverting the concept, we can deduce that there is no creation without sacrifice. To sacrifice what is esteemed is to sacrifice oneself, and the spiritual energy thereby acquired is proportional to the importance of what is lost. All forms of suffering can be sacrificial, if fully and wholeheartedly sought and accepted. The physical and negative signs—of mutilation, chastise-

ment, self-abasement and severe penalties or tribulations—are all
symbolic of the obverse tendencies in the spiritual order. This is
why the majority of legends and folktales, stories of heroes, saints
and exceptional men commonly tell not only of suffering but also
of strange situations of inferiority such as that so vividly illustrated
in the story of Cinderella. (*See illustration* p. 103.)

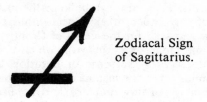

Zodiacal Sign
of Sagittarius.

Sagittarius According to Subba Rao, this is a cosmic symbol
expressive of the complete man—he who is at once animal, spiritual
and worthy of his divine origin. Man thus constitutes a link between
heaven and earth, implying a state of tension which finds its symbolic
expression in the arc (or rainbow). Sagittarius, the Centaur, or the
Archer signify this triple nature of the symbol; the horse
symbolizes the instinctive organism, the human part denotes the
three higher principles embracing the monad as expressed by the
arrow. In the Babylonian epic of Gilgamesh, Sagittarius is
represented by 'scorpion-men' who are 'no more than two-thirds
divine' (40).

Sails In Egyptian hieroglyphs, a determinative sign symbolizing
the wind, the creative breath and the spur to action (19). It
corresponds to the Element of air. In some mediaeval emblems it
appears as an allegory of the Holy Spirit (4).

Salamander A mythological fire-spirit, a kind of lizard which
was supposed to inhabit the Element of fire (57, 8). In graphic
symbolism, and also in alchemy, the salamander signifies fire—
which in fact constitutes its general significance.

Salvation In numerous legends and stories, and in many myths,
situations are recounted in which 'salvation' should occur and frequently does occur. Obviously, this adventure is a profanation of the
avatar of the soul on its return journey after its 'fall' from the paradisiac state. The salvation *par excellence* is that occasioned by the
Passion of the Lord. However, an association between the ideas of
sacrifice and salvation is found in many religions.

Sandals, Winged An attribute of Mercury, and a symbol of
'loftiness' of spirit in Greek mythology, with the same significance
as Pegasus. Perseus put on winged sandals in order to slay Medusa
the Gorgon (15).

Sarcophagus Symbolic of the feminine principle and, at the same time, of the earth as the beginning and end of material life. Its significance corresponds to that of the receptacle, the amphora and the boat (9). Hence, in alchemy, it is known as the 'philosophical egg' (or the vessel of transmutation).

Saturn Saturn symbolizes time which, with its ravenous appetite for life, devours all its creations, whether they are beings, things, ideas or sentiments. He is also symbolic of the insufficiency, in the mystic sense, of any order of existence within the plane of the temporal, or the necessity for the 'reign of Cronos' to be succeeded by another cosmic mode of existence in which time has no place. Time brings restlessness—the sense of duration lasting from the moment of stimulus up to the instant of satisfaction. Hence, Saturn is symbolic of activity, of slow, implacable dynamism, of realization and communication (15); and this is why he is said to have 'devoured his children' (32) and why he is related to the Ouroboros (or the

Saturn (from *Poeticon astronomicon*, Venice, 1485).

serpent which bites its own tail). Other attributes of his are the oar (standing for navigation and progress in things temporal), the hour-glass and the scythe (8). In the scythe we can detect a double meaning: first, its function of cutting, parallel to and corroborating the symbolism of devouring; and, secondly, its curved shape, which invariably corresponds to the feminine principle. This is why the alchemists, masters in the spiritual science of symbolism, named Saturn '*Mercurius senex*': given the androgynous character of Mercury, Saturn takes on the same characteristic ambiguity of gender and sex, and is related to the earth, the sarcophagus and putrefaction, as well as to the colour black. Mertens Stienon suggests that Saturn is, in every case, a symbol of the law of limitation which gives shape to life, or the localised expression in time and space of the universal life (40).

Saturnalia A characteristic of ancient mythology is the idea that each reign must give way to another, even on the plane of the divine; it was an idea which was inextricably bound up with the notion of life as continuity and succession, and of sacrifice as the sole source of re-creation. The successive cosmic reigns of Uranus, Saturn and Jupiter provided a model for earthly government, for the 'ritual assassination of the king' at certain astral conjunctions or at the end of certain periods, and later for the displacement of this bloody ceremony by its simulacra. In Rome, the Saturnalia was the most outstanding example of such sacrifice and simulacra. Frazer notes that it was a general practice in ancient Italy to elect a man to play the part of Saturn and enjoy all the prerogatives of the god for a while before dying either by his own hand or by sacrifice. The principal figure in the Carnival festival is a burlesque image and a direct successor of the old king of the Saturnalia. The 'King of the Bean', the mediaeval 'Bishop of Fools', the 'Abbot of Unreason' and the 'Lord of Misrule' are all personifications of one and the same thing and may well stem from a common source. In every case they are symbolic of the ideas of duration and sacrifice, whereby, by means of inversion and transformation, the brevity and intensity of life may be contrasted with its vulgar mediocrity (21). The Carnival itself is, in its brevity, a symbol of this desire to concentrate into a given period of time all the possibilities of existence, apart from the fact that, in its orgiastic sense, it is an invocation of primordial chaos and a desperate quest for the 'way out of time'.

Scales This instrument, of Chaldaean origin (7), is the mystic symbol of justice, that is, of the equivalence and equation of guilt and punishment. In emblems, marks and allegories it is often depicted inside a circle crowned by a fleur-de-lis, a star, a cross or a dove (4). In its most common form, that is, two equal scales balanced symmetrically on either side of a central pivot, it has a secondary meaning—subservient to the above—which is, to a certain extent, similar to other symbolic bilateral images, such as the double-bladed axe, the Tree of Life, trees of the Sephiroth, etc. The deepest significance of the balance derives from the zodiacal archetype of Libra, related to 'immanent justice', or the idea that all guilt automatically unleashes the very forces that bring self-destruction and punishment (40).

Scales (of the Fish) On the one hand, they signify protection and defence. On the other, water and the nether world. And also, by extension, the previous persisting into the subsequent, the inferior into the superior. The story of the Apostles (Acts ix, 18) tells how, when Paul was called by the voice of God, there fell from his eyes 'as it had been scales' (50). The scaly pattern on the lower parts of some beings such as mermaids, mermen and Baphomet of the Knights Templar serves to emphasize their association with level-symbolism, expressing in visual form the cosmic (or moral) inferiority of what, from the viewpoint of vertical 'height', appears below.

Scars Certain elements of reality which are not in themselves symbols, or which have not *yet* been analysed for symbolic significance, nevertheless evidently possess such significance. This is sometimes brought to light by the conjunction of several separate events. The author once dreamed of an unknown damsel (*anima*) whose beautiful face was marked by scars and burns which in no way disfigured her features. Milton says that Satan's face 'deep scars of thunder had intrenched'. Lacroix, in *Rostros de la Fe*, states that 'it is certain that the stigmata of original damnation can sometimes be read in the beautiful faces of these coveted objects'. Moral imperfections, and sufferings (are they one and the same?) are, therefore, symbolized by the wounds and scars caused by fire and sword.

Sceptre Related to the magic wand, the club, the thunderbolt and the phallus, as well as to Thor's hammer. The symbolism of all these falls within the general group of signs and emblems of fertility (31), but it could be linked also to that of the 'world-axis'. In allegories containing the sceptre, the form, colour and material of the object all play their part in enriching the basic symbolism. One of the most common representations of a sceptre terminates in a fleur-de-lis, which is a symbol of light and purification.

Scissors Like the cross, a symbol of 'conjunction' (51); but it is also an attribute of the mystic spinners who cut the thread of life of mortal Man. It is, then, an ambivalent symbol expressive of both creation and destruction, birth and death.

Scorpio The eighth sign of the Zodiac. It corresponds to that period of the span of man's life which lies under the threat of death (that is, the 'fall'). It is also related with the sexual function (40). In the Middle Ages the scorpion makes its appearance in Christian art as an emblem of treachery and as a symbol for the Jew (20). In the symbolism of megaliths it is the antithesis of the bee whose honey succours Man. Finally, its symbolism is equivalent to that of the hangman (51).

Zodiacal sign of Scorpio.

Scythe   An attribute of Saturn and, in general, linked with allegories of death; it is also associated with Attis and the priests of Cybele, in which case the allusion is to self-mutilation (8). In some images of these deities it is not a large agricultural scythe that is portrayed but a small dagger curved in shape and called *harpe*. Broadly speaking, all curved weapons are lunar and feminine symbols, whereas straight ones are masculine and solar. Straightness signifies penetration and forcefulness, curves suggest the means to an end and passivity. For this reason, the *harpe* has been linked with the 'indirect way', that is, with the secret path which leads to the beyond. According to Diel, the scythe is also symbolic of the harvest—of renewed hopes for rebirth. Hence, like Pisces in the Zodiac, the scythe-symbol incorporates the ambiguity of the beginning as the end, and vice versa (15). Both these senses—of mutilation and of hope—are, despite their contradictory nature, related to the idea of sacrifice inherent in all images of weapons.

Sea   The symbolic significance of the sea corresponds to that of the 'Lower Ocean'—the waters in flux, the transitional and mediating agent between the non-formal (air and gases) and the formal (earth and solids) and, by analogy, between life and death. The waters of the oceans are thus seen not only as the source of life but also as its goal. 'To return to the sea' is 'to return to the mother', that is, to die.

Seal   Like other marks or brands, the seal is a sign of ownership and individuality—of differentiation. And, in the form of a seal of beeswax or sealing-wax, it is symbolic of virginity, of narrowmindedness and of repression.

Seal of Solomon   This consists of two triangles superimposed and interlaced so as to form a six-pointed star. Wirth terms it the 'star of the microcosm', or a sign of the spiritual potential of the individual who can endlessly deny himself. In reality it is a symbol of the human soul as a 'conjunction' of consciousness and the unconscious, signified by the intermingling of the triangle (denoting fire) and the inverted triangle (water) (59). Both of these are, according to alchemic theory, subject to the principle of the immaterial, called Azoth by the philosophers, and represented in the

Seal of Solomon by a central point which is not actually portrayed but which has to be seen in the imagination alone, as in some of the mandalas of India and Tibet.

Seasons, The They consist of the four 'phases' of the sun's orbit and hence correspond to the phases of the moon as well as to the four stages of a man's life. The Greeks represented the seasons by the figures of four women: Spring was depicted wearing a floral crown and standing beside a shrub in blossom; Summer, with a crown of ears of corn, bearing a sheaf in one hand and a sickle in the other; Autumn carries bunches of grapes and a basket full of fruit; Winter, bare-headed, beside leafless trees. They have also been represented by the figures of animals: Spring as a sheep, Summer as a dragon, Autumn as a hare, Winter as a salamander (8). The four-part division of the seasons enables them to be related also to the points of the compass and to the tetramorphs.

Sea-urchin Called 'serpent's egg' in Celtic tradition, it is one of the symbols for the life-force (26) and the primordial seed.

Secret All secrets symbolize the power of the supernatural, and this explains their disquieting effect upon most human beings. Jung is emphatic about this, pointing out that, for the same reason, it is very helpful for the individual so affected to unburden himself of his secrets (31). On the other hand, the ability to master this state of tension within oneself confers an awareness of unfailing superiority —a sensation which is common in individuals who live outside the law and in spies and privy counsellors to kings and magnates. This same notion supplies part of the basic attraction of esoteric thought and of all forms of Hermetic science in literature and art.

Seed Symbolic of latent, non-manifest forces, or of the mysterious potentialities the presence of which, sometimes unsuspected, is the justification for hope. These potentialities also symbolize the mystic Centre—the non-apparent point which is the irradiating origin of every branch and shoot of the great Tree of the World (26).

Sefiroth The sum of the ten sefirah, or emanations of God, according to the Cabbala (which, in itself, constitutes a mystical and symbolic explanation of the Creation). The sefirah are: Crown, Wisdom, Understanding, Mercy, Justice, Beauty, Firmness, Splendour, Victory, and Kingdom or Shekhinah. There have been attempts to identify these aspects of the divine power with the mythological deities which, even in the days of the Roman Empire, were already symbols for the Stoics, the Neo-Pythagoreans and the Neoplatonists. The most important books of historical investigation into the Cabbala (whose principal work, the *Zohar*, was written in Spain during the 13th century by Moisés de Léon) are those of Gershom G. Scholem, Professor at the University of Jerusalem. In another sense, the syntheses of A.-D. Grad are interesting.

Septenary This is an order composed of seven elements. Ultimately, it is founded upon the seven Directions of Space: two opposite directions for each dimension, plus the centre. This spatial order of six dynamic elements, plus one which is static, is projected into the week as a model of the septenary in the passage of time. Three is, in many cultures, the number pertaining to heaven (since it constitutes the vertical order of the three-dimensional spatial cross) and four is associated with the earth (because of the four directions—comparable with the cardinal points—of the two horizontal dimensions). Hence, seven is the number expressing the sum of heaven and earth (as twelve is the expression of their multiplicative possibilities) (22). In religion, the septenary is expressed or alluded to by means of ternaries such as the three theological virtues plus the quaternary of the cardinal virtues; the septenary of the capital sins (59), in particular, is seen in traditional symbolist theory as deriving from the influence of—or analogy with—the spiritual principles of the seven planets, or the ancient mythological deities. In the heavens, seven finds particular expression in the constellation of the Pleiades, the daughters of Atlas (six of whom are visible and one hidden) (9). Seven, with its characteristic quality of synthesis, is regarded as a symbol of the transformation and integration of all hierarchical orders as a whole (32); hence there are seven notes in the diatonic scale, seven colours in the rainbow, and seven planetary spheres together with their seven planets. Sometimes it is taken as being split into—or alternatively as the union of—the numbers two and five (the Sun and Moon; and Mercury, Venus, Mars, Jupiter and Saturn), or three and four (the Sun, Moon and Mercury; and Venus, Mars, Jupiter and Saturn). Seven is represented graphically by the joining of the triangle and the square, the triangle being either superimposed upon or inscribed within the square. This septenary pattern is often employed in extensive architectural layouts, for it has a quality of the mandala about it, comparable with the notion of 'squaring the circle'. It would be impossible to name, even in brief or in sum, all the innumerable applications of the septenary, or the ways in which this cosmic 'model' figures in myths, legends, folktales and dreams, or in historical events, works of art, and so on. At times the seven-scheme takes on a complex symbolism—the planetary gods in their evil guise, or the days of the week conceived in terms of spiritual peril (in the configuration of the seven-headed dragon); and sometimes it gives expression to the reigning celestial order (as with the seven-branched candelabra in the Temple of Solomon. Schneider notes that, in the Scottish sword-dance, St. George conquers the dragon in the company of seven saints (the seven-heads theme inverted in order to ensure victory) (51). It was from its use as a symbol for the complete musical scale (as in Orpheus' lyre) that the number seven came to acquire such widespread application: there were seven Hesperides, seven kings who attacked Thebes and seven who defended it, seven sons and seven daughters of Niobe (38); and Plato conceived of a celestial siren singing in each of the seven spheres, and these 'seven Sirens of the Spheres' correspond to the seven virgins in Cinderella (4) and the seven fairies of legend and folklore (one each for each Direction of space and time). For Loeffler, these fairies correspond to the seven *Lipiki* of Hindu esoteric thought, that is, the spirits relative to each plane of the human consciousness: sensation, emotion, reflective intelligence, intuition, spirituality, will and intimations of the divine (38). Hence the esoteric conclusion that the human being is composed of seven spheres after the pattern of the heavens. The Jewish Cabbala provides a link between the mythological deities, in so far as they are creative and beneficient, and the seven celestial hierarchies: the Sun—the angel of light—Michael; the Moon—the angel of hope and dreams—Gabriel; Mercury—the civilizing angel—Raphael; Venus—the angel of love —Anael; Mars—the angel of destruction—Samael; Jupiter—the administering angel—Zachariel; Saturn—the angel of solicitude—Oriphiel. Lévi has drawn a number of parallels based on the septenary, exactly corresponding to certain elements on all planes of the cosmos. To quote only the emblems which he attributes to particular deities: the Sun—a serpent with a lion's head; the Moon —a globe divided into two half-moons; Mercury—the Hermetic caduceus; Venus—the lingam; Mars—a dragon biting the hilt of a sword; Jupiter—a flaming pentagram in the claws of an eagle; Saturn—an aged man with a scythe (37). It is not too difficult to grasp the significance of numbers based on the septenary. The vast majority of symbols containing seven elements all over the world originate from the celestial prototype of the seven spheres. Cola Alberich refers to a number of examples of the number seven appearing as a characteristic feature of tattoos and amulets. He quotes Hippocrates, for example: 'The number seven, because of its occult virtues, tends to bring all things into being: it is the dispenser of life and the source of all change—for the moon itself changes its phase every seven days. This number influences all sublime beings.' And Cola Alberich comments that 'combs with seven points were magic symbols in Susa; among the Chinese, the "fox with seven tails" is the evil genius; the saints and sages have "seven holes" in their heart; the animal spirits are seven in number; there are seven fairies of seven colours; on the seventh day of the seventh month, great popular festivals were held all over China, and the most favoured of amulets is the lotus with seven leaves. In Tibet, there are seven emblems of Buddha. . . . In the sacred pyramids of Mocha, on the

Peruvian coast, the *guaca* (Indian tomb) of the sun has seven steps. In Islam, the number seven enjoys great popularity: there are seven heavens, seven earths, seven seas; pilgrims walk seven times round the temple of Mecca; there are seven days of ill-omen; man is composed of seven substances; seven is the number of the foods gathered from the fields. . . .' (12).

Seriality Serial order dèrives from the separate existence of a certain number of elements in discontinuity, disclosing minor differences when opposed to or contrasted with other orders or scales. Serial orders are, then, composed of the differentiation of one entity, or the diversification of what is unitary or the unification of what is relatively diverse. Hence we should distinguish in any given series: (*a*) the *limits* or poles of the series; (*b*) a limited number of *elements* included in the series by virtue of their ability to fall into place between the two poles; (*c*) an inner *graduation* which obtains between two or more of these elements. This graduated scale expresses the relationship between the qualitative and the quantitative (that is, the potentiality of either to be transformed into the other) as exemplified by the vibratory phenomena of the notes of the musical scale and the colours of the spectrum. The arrangement of a series in time is equivalent to defining or constituting a *process*, and this process will be evolutive if it is ascending, and regressive if it is descending or recurring.

Serpent (or **Snake**) If all symbols are really functions and signs of things imbued with energy, then the serpent or snake is, by analogy, symbolic of energy itself—of force pure and simple; hence its ambivalence and multivalencies. Another reason for its great variety of symbolic meaning derives from the consideration that these meanings may relate either to the serpent as a whole or to any of its major characteristics—for example, to its sinuous movements, its common association with the tree and its formal analogy with the roots and branches of the tree, the way it sheds its skin, its

Serpent (after an Inca image).

threatening tongue, the undulating pattern of its body, its hiss, its resemblance to a ligament, its method of attacking its victims by coiling itself round them, and so on. Still another explanation lies in its varying habitat: there are snakes which inhabit woods, others which thrive in the desert, aquatic serpents and those that lurk in lakes and ponds, wells and springs. In India, snake cults or cults of the spirit of the snake are connected with the symbolism of the waters of the sea. Snakes are guardians of the springs of life and of immortality, and also of those superior riches of the spirit that are symbolized by hidden treasure (17). As regards the West, Bayley has suggested that the snake, since its sinuous shape is similar to that of waves, may be a symbol of the wisdom of the deeps (4) and of the great mysteries. Yet, in their multiplicity and as creatures of the desert, snakes are forces of destruction, afflicting all those who have succeeded in crossing the Red Sea and leaving Egypt (57); in this sense, they are connected with the 'temptations' facing those who have overcome the limitations of matter and have entered into the realm of the 'dryness' of the spirit. This explains why Blavatsky can say that, physically, the snake symbolizes the seduction of strength by matter (as Jason by Medea, Hercules by Omphale, Adam by Eve), thereby providing us with a palpable illustration of the workings of the process of involution; and of how the inferior can lurk within the superior, or the previous within the subsequent (9). This is borne out by Diel, for whom the snake is symbolic not of personal sin but of the principle of evil inherent in all worldly things. The same idea is incorporated into the Nordic myth about the serpent of Midgard (15). There is a clear connexion between the snake and the feminine principle. Eliade observes that Gresmann (*Mytische Reste in der Paradieserzahlung*, in *Archiv f. Rel.* X, 345) regarded Eve as an archaic Phoenician goddess of the underworld who is personified in the serpent (although a better interpretation would be to identify it with the allegorical figure of Lilith, the enemy and temptress of Eve). In support of this, Eliade points to the numerous Mediterranean deities who are represented carrying a snake in one or both of their hands (for example, the Greek Artemis, Hecate, Persephone), and he relates these to the finely sculpted Cretan priestesses in gold or ivory, and to mythic figures with snakes for hair (Medusa the Gorgon, or the Erinyes). He goes on to mention that in Central Europe there is a belief that hairs pulled out from the head of a woman under the influence of the moon will be turned into snakes (17). The serpent (or snake) was very common in Egypt; the hieroglyph which corresponds phonetically to the letter Z is a representation of the movement of the snake. Like the sign of the slug, or horned snake (phonetically equivalent to F), this hieroglyph refers to primigenial and cosmic forces. Generally speaking, the names of the goddesses are determined by signs representing the snake—which is tantamount to saying that it is because of Woman that the spirit has fallen into matter and evil. The snake is also used, as are other reptiles, to refer to the primordial—the most primitive strata of life. In the *Book of the Dead* (XVII), the reptiles are the first to acclaim Ra when he appears above the surface of the waters of Nou (or Nu or

Nun). The demonic implications of the serpent are exemplified in Tuat, whose evil spirits are portrayed as snakes; however, these— like the vanquished dragon—may also take on a beneficent form as forces which have been mastered, controlled, sublimated and utilized for the superior purposes of the psyche and the development of mankind, and in this sense they correspond to the goddesses Nekhebit and Uadjit (or Buto). They also become an Uraeus—the same thing happens in the symbolism of the Kundalini—constituting the most precious ornament of the royal diadem (19).

As we have said, it is the basic characteristics of the snake which have determined its symbolic significances. To quote Teillard's definition of the snake, it is: 'An animal endowed with magnetic force. Because it sheds its skin, it symbolizes resurrection. Because of its sinuous movement' (and also because its coils are capable of strangling) 'it signifies strength. Because of its viciousness, it represents the evil side of nature' (56). Its ability to shed its skin greatly impressed ancient writers: Philo of Alexandria believed that when the snake shakes off its skin it likewise shakes off its old age, that it can both kill and cure and that it is therefore the symbol and attribute of the aggressive powers, positive and negative, which rule the world. (This is a Gnostic and Manichean idea of Persian provenance.) He decided finally that it is the 'most spiritual of animals'. Jung has pointed out that the Gnostics related it to the spinal cord and the spinal marrow, an excellent image of the way the unconscious expresses itself suddenly and unexpectedly with its peremptory and terrible incursions (31). He adds that, psychologically, the snake is a symptom of anguish expressive of abnormal stirrings in the unconscious, that is, of a reactivation of its destructive potentiality. This is directly comparable to the significance of the serpent of Midgard in Norse mythology. In the *Völuspa* it is proclaimed that the deluge will commence when the serpent awakens to destroy the universe (31). For Zimmer, the serpent is the life-force which determines birth and rebirth and hence it is connected with the Wheel of Life. The legend of Buddha tells how the serpent wound itself round his body seven times (as in the effigies of the Mithraic Cronos), but, since it could not crush him, it turned into a youth bowing low before Gautama (60).

The connexion of the snake with the wheel is expressed in graphic form in the Gnostic symbol of the Ouroboros, or serpent biting its own tail; half of this mythic being is dark and the other half light (as in the Chinese *Yang-Yin* symbol), which clearly illustrates the essential ambivalence of the snake in that it pertains to both aspects of the cycle (the active and the passive, the affirmative and the negative, the constructive and the destructive). Wirth comments that the 'ancient serpent is the prop of the world, providing it with both materials and energy, unfold ing as reason and imagination, and also as a force of the darkness' (59). The snake was an important symbol for the Gnostics, and especially for the so-called Naassene sect (from *naas*—snake). Hippolytus, criticizing this doctrine, asserted that the snake was said to live in all objects and in all beings. This brings us to the Yoga concept of the Kundalini or the snake as an image of inner strength. Kundalini is represented symbolically as a snake coiled up upon itself in the form of a ring (*kundala*) (29), in that subtle part of the organism corresponding to the lower extremity of the spinal column; this, at any rate, is the case with the ordinary man. But, as a result of exercises directed towards his spiritualization—Hatha Yoga, for instance—the snake uncoils and stretches up through wheels (*chakras*) corresponding to the various plexuses of the body until it reaches the area of the forehead corresponding to the third eye of Shiva. It is then, according to Hindu belief, that man recovers his sense of the eternal (28). The symbolism here probably relates to an ascending force, rising up, that is, from the area governed by the sexual organ up to the realm of thought—an interpretation which it is also possible to justify by simple reference to the symbolism of level, taking the heart as central. In other words, the symbol denotes 'sublimation of the personality' (Avalon, *The Serpent Power*). Jung has noted that the custom of representing transformation and renovation of figures of snakes constitutes a well-documented archetype; and he suggests that the Egyptian Uraeus is the visible expression of the Kundalini on a higher plane (32). There are also various rites which accord with this concept of progressive elevation. The progress through the six *chakras*—there is in fact a seventh, but it is unnamed and (like the central point of certain mandala-like patterns) is not represented visually—may be regarded as analogous to climbing up the terraces of the *ziggurat* or mounting the steps pertaining to the seven metals in the Mithraic ritual (11). Apart from the circular (and cosmic) position it tends to take up, and the quality of completeness which this implies, the snake is frequently related to other symbols. The most common of these is the tree, which, being unitary, may be said to correspond to the masculine principle, in which case the ophidian would represent the feminine. The tree and the serpent are, in mythology, prefigurations of Adam and Eve. Furthermore, by analogy, we also have here a situation of symbolic Entanglement—the snake curled round the tree (or round the staff of Aesculapius)—and a symbolic image of moral dualism. Diel, who tends to favour this kind of interpretation, suggests that the snake coiled round the staff or club of the god of medicine recalls the basic, Biblical symbol of the Tree of Life encircled by the snake and signifying the principle of evil; the pattern here points to the close relationship between life and corruption as the source of all evil. Diel goes on to suggest that it is this subversion of the spirit that brings about the death of the soul, and that this is what medicine must, in the first place, set out to combat (15).

Now, the opposite to the encircling (or triumphant) snake is the crucified snake, as it is to be found among the figures included in *Abraham le Juif* (Paris, Bibl. Nat. Ms. Fr. 14765, of the 16th century) (32). This figure of the reptile nailed to a cross—or the chthonian and feminine principle vanquished by the spirit—is also represented mythically by the victory of eagle over serpent. Heinrich Zimmer recalls that, in the *Iliad*, an eagle appears to the Greeks, carrying a wounded snake in its claws. The seer Calchas saw this as an omen portending the triumph of the Greeks (the masculine and patriarchal order of the Aryans subduing the predominantly feminine and matriarchal principle of Asia) (60). Since all struggle is a form of 'conjunction' and therefore of love, it is hardly surprising that man should have created a synthesis of opposing powers—heaven and earth—in the image of the 'plumed serpent', the most notable symbol of pre-Columbian America. This serpent has feathers on its head, in its tail and sometimes on its body. Quetzalcoatl is another androgynous symbol of this kind (41). The symmetrical placing of two serpents, as in the caduceus of Mercury, is indicative of an equilibrium of forces, of the counterbalancing of the cowed serpent (or sublimated power) by the untamed serpent, so representing good balanced by evil, health by sickness. As Jung has shrewdly observed, this much-used image is an adumbration of homoeopathy—a cure effected by what caused the ailment. The serpent therefore becomes the source of the healing of the wound caused by the serpent. This is why it could serve as a symbol of St. John the Evangelist (32) and appear in association with a chalice.

The different forms which the serpent may take are not numerous. The sea-serpent seems simply to emphasize the integration of the symbolism of the unconscious with that of the abyss (9). If it has more than one head, this merely serves to add to the basic symbolism, the extra significance corresponding to the particular number of heads it is given. The dragon or the serpent with seven heads occurs often in legends, myths and folktales simply because seven represents multiplication of unity and locates the reptile among the essential orders of the cosmos. The seven-headed serpent partakes of the symbolism of the seven Directions of Space, the seven days of the week, and the seven planetary gods, and has a bearing upon the seven sins (9). The three-headed serpent refers to the three principles of the active, the passive and the neutral. In alchemy, the winged serpent represents the volatile principle, and the wingless the fixed principle. The crucified serpent denotes the fixation of the volatile

and also sublimation (as in the Prometheus myth). Alchemists also
saw in the serpent an illustration of 'the feminine in Man' or his
'humid essence', relating the reptile to Mercury (57) as the androgynous god who—like Shiva—was doubtless endowed with a tendency
towards both good and evil (an aspect also portrayed by the Gnostics
in their twin serpents called *Agathodaemon* and *Kakodaemon*) (9).
There are also serpents of unusual aspect—the snake with a sheep's
head, for instance, in reliefs on certain Gallo-Roman sepulchres. In
view of the favourable symbolic sense of the sheep (connected with
Aries, spring, initiation and fire), this adaptation implies a degree of
spiritualization (16). Finally, according to Schneider, the sacrificed
serpent is the symbolic equivalent of the swan's neck and of the
swan itself (and it is by the swan that the hero is wafted heavenwards,
plucking away upon his harp) (50). That is to say, the sacrifice of
the serpent (as a life-force) makes it possible to accept death grate-
fully (like the swan) and to soar up to higher regions. Father Heras
has suggested that the snake is symbolic of fertility and destruction
and that it is in this sense that it appears on the menhir of Kernuz
(Finistère). It appears in opposition to the arrow in the effigy of the
horned god of Cerdeña (with another head on top alluding to the
symbolism of the Gemini).

Sexes, The   Plato, in *Timaeus*, speaks of the sexes as 'living', as
if in some way they were independent of the beings to which they
pertain. This is visually symbolized by the ventral faces given to
some of the fabulous mediaeval figures, as well as by the paws added
to the heads of the *gryces*, deriving from ancient Carthaginian and
Gnostic images. Now, orthodox Freudians have reduced the great
majority of objects, depending upon whether their predominant
characteristic is that of the container or the contained, to either
feminine or masculine sexual implications; but there is nothing new
in this, for implicit in the ancient Chinese *Yang-Yin* symbol is the
notion of a classification whereby all things fall within a system
which locates the genders at opposite poles, corresponding to the
duality of the sexes. We must not overlook that the sexes may
symbolize spiritual principles; consciousness and the unconscious,
heaven and earth, fire and water. The sexual *conjunctio* is the most
graphic and impressive of all images expressive of the idea of union,
and hence alchemists used it to represent initiatory truths which
transcend the laws of biology, as Jung has demonstrated, particularly
in *Psychology of the Transference*.

Shadow   As the Sun is the light of the spirit, so shadow is the
negative 'double' of the body, or the image of its evil and base side.
Among primitive peoples, the notion that the shadow is the *alter ego*
or soul is firmly established; it is also reflected in the folklore and
literature of some advanced cultures (35). As Frazer has noted, the

primitive often regards his shadow, or his reflection in water or in a mirror, as his soul or as a vital part of himself (21). 'Shadow' is the term given by Jung to the primitive and instinctive side of the individual.

Shape (or **Form**) Certain branches of science, such as the Psychology of Form, Isomorphism and Morphology, have arrived at conclusions which coincide with those of traditional symbolism. The most comprehensive and valid definition of the significance of form is that which appears in the legendary *Tabula Smaragdina*: 'What is above is like what is below', which Goethe confirmed and bettered by adding: 'What is within'—the idea—'is also without'—form. Hence, Paul Guillaume has been able to declare that 'the terms of shape, structure and organization pertain not only to the language of biology (that is, forms) but also to psychology (that is, thought or ideas) . . .' and that 'isomorphism, propounding a theory of form which revives the ancient tradition of parallelism (or magic analogy), refuses to draw a dividing line between spirit and time'. This

 The circle and the triangle are basic symbols.

observation is rounded off with the observation that 'shapes correspond, in our perception and thought, to comparable forms in the nervous processes'; hence, what is circular is equivalent both to the circle and to the cyclic, and the square is identical with things quaternary and also with the number four (50), so that form takes its place as the 'intermediary between spirit and matter' (57). In the broadest sense, then, we may conclude that a preference for regular shapes indicates 'regulated' or well-ordered sentiments, whereas irregular forms suggest 'unregulated' sentiments. Oval shapes are related to things biomorphic; cubes with the artificial and the constructional; simple shapes with what is straightforward; and complex shapes with what is complicated. The same applies to rhythms, structures and compositions. There are other general principles too, such as that which equates symmetry with equilibrium and with the static; asymmetry with dynamism; absolute regularity and, likewise, absolute irregularity with chaos, in so far as they are. both expressions of the undifferentiated: differentiation is brought about by ritual, that is, by the organization of regularized irregularity. Examples of morphological analyses may be taken over and applied to the symbolic; to take one example: in the phenomenon of growth, the circular or irradiating form signifies, in symbolic terms, the regular force of diffusion, the existence of a centre as the 'Origin', and a uniform pattern of resistance. These laws are equally true of the spirit. Forms which, within a given system or group, are different one from the other may be ordered in a series or in a scale (or within orders of analogies and correspondences). So, the trapezium, the rectangle, the square, the circle represent a series which progresses from irregularity to regularity, a series which could equally well apply to moral evolution. Jung touches upon this question, commenting that the square, as the minimal composite number (symbolizing a situation), represents the pluralist or inner state of the man who is not yet at one with himself. And yet the square is superior to the trapezium, just as the trapezium is superior to the trapezoid. The octagon is the 'intervening figure' (or the intermediary) between the square and the circle. It is unnecessary to emphasize that the meaning of a symbol varies from plane to plane, notably on the psychological and cosmic planes. So, for example, from the psychological point of view, the triangle, in its natural position with the apex uppermost, when placed between the square and the circle, is expressive of communication. But, objectively speaking, these three figures symbolize the relationship (represented by the triangle) between earth (the square) and heaven (the circle, the wheel, or rose-window); this explains why these are the essential symbols of so many Cistercian and Gothic façades. Another law to be taken into account is that forms explain objects, and objects forms; that is to say, the symbolic meaning of a being or figure is usually confirmed and emphasized by the significance of its shape, the converse also being true. Gothic spires are related to the pyramid, therefore the pyramid is related to Gothic spires. In India, geometric forms have the following cosmic implications: The sphere is associated with the ether or heaven; the crescent with air; the pyramid, fire; the cube, earth (4). The analysis of the symbolism of geometric shapes has been carried to excess by some writers—Piobb among them. Star, for example, proposes the following correspondences: the sphere, intellectual life, pure thought, and abstraction; the cone, a synthesis of all other shapes and a symbol for psychic wholeness; the cylinder, material thoughts and the mechanistic intellect (55). In general, flat shapes have a more spiritual character than shapes with bulk, but the latter are linked more closely with the macrocosmos. It is unnecessary to emphasize that, in the symbolism of shape—even when three-dimensional—the diagrammatic cross-section or ground-plan is of the essence. Thus, to take the cathedral as an example, the figure of the cross, that is, of the ground-plan, takes precedence over the temple/mountain symbolism deriving from the irregularly ascending pyramid-shape without neutralizing its effect. Another factor of importance is number-symbolism: for example, two towers, over and above the inherent symbolism of towers, of prisms and cylinders, embrace a meaning which springs from their duality. For this reason, most religious edifices shun the number two (since it implies conflict) and turn to the number three (implying resolution, quite apart from the fact that it is the image of the Trinity), and the two bell-towers of the façade are completed by the cimborrio above the transept. The circle and the square stand for limitlessness and limitation respectively.

Sheaf In Egyptian hieroglyphics, a determinative sign defining the concept of limitation (19).

Sheaf (or **Bundle**) Eliade points out that the Latin *fascis* (sheaf or bundle) and *fascia* (band, sash, or bandage) are related to *fascinum* (fascination or evil-doing); they are words which fall within the vast symbolic group composed of bindings, knots, bows, plaits, ropes and cords, all of which allude to 'being tied to' existence (18). But this is to explain only the negative side of the symbol. Like most symbols, it tends to ambivalence, and in the positive sense, the sheaf symbolizes unification, integration and strength.

Shekhinah This is not a symbol but a Cabbalistic sefirah. It represents the feminine aspect of the Supreme Being, i.e., to quote Jungian terminology, his *anima*, of which all such souls as the young woman, the stranger, the beloved, are mirrors. The never-ending search for the *ideal* through a multiplicity of women must represent the search for the Shekhinah, either through the images of the *anima* or simply through women's powers of carnal seduction which, according to the Book of Henoch, even tempted some of the angels themselves. The rejection of the woman—as exemplified by Hamlet's spurning of Ophelia—might, in such a context, represent a longing to return to the angelic state, to escape from the merely human condition by an opposite route to that of *conjunctio*. Gershom G. Scholem, in *On the Kabbalah and its Symbolism* (London, 1965), says that the Shekhinah may contain aspects which are negative, occult and destructive, and this leads one by another path to the Hindu trinity, in which Siva (or Shiva) symbolizes the destructive side of the deity. It should not be forgotten that, in this case, destruction is only concerned with the phenomenic side of beings, and, in reality, it is transformation, renovation and rebirth.

Shell One of the eight emblems of good luck in Chinese Buddhism, found in allegories about royalty, and also a sign for a prosperous journey (5). This favourable implication is the result of the shell's association with water, the source of fertility. According to Eliade, shells are also related to the moon and to Woman. Pearl-symbolism also is very closely linked with the shell. The mythic birth of Aphrodite from a shell is of obvious relevance (18). In Schneider's view, the shell is the mystic symbol of the prosperity of one generation rising out of the death of the preceding generation (5). In all probability, its favourable meaning is—as in the case of the well and the bottle—a consequence of the thirsty traveller or pilgrim linking the shell in his mind with the presence of water; this would explain its significance in mediaeval allegories.

Shepherd   The title given to the lunar god Tammuz (or Thammuz) as the shepherd of the 'flocks' of the stars. According to Krappe, this idea is closely bound up with the passion of Tammuz (as Adonis) for Aphrodite (or Ishtar), because of the relationship between the phases of the moon and dismemberment (35). The shepherd is also the conductor of souls to the Land of the Dead—the psychopomp, and a symbol of supreme power, since flocks are representative of the cosmic forces.

Shield   The symbolic significance of the shield amounts to a simple transposition of its defensive function to the spiritual plane. The fact that coats-of-arms were generally emblazoned upon shields yields an additional meaning which may be interpreted as implying that the knight defends himself by displaying his identity and invoking it in the hour of peril.

Ship   On coins, a ship ploughing through the seas is emblematic of joy and happiness (8). But the most profound significance of navigation is that implied by Pompey the Great in his remark: 'Living is not necessary, but navigation is.' By this he meant that existence is split up into two fundamental structures: living, which he understood as living for or in oneself, and sailing or navigating, by which he understood living in order to transcend—or what Nietzsche from his pessimistic angle called 'living in order to disappear'. The *Odyssey* is, basically, nothing but a navigation-myth in the sense of victory over the two essential perils of all sailing: destruction (or the triumph of the ocean—corresponding to the unconscious) and withdrawal (regression or stagnation). Yet Homer reserves the end of the periplus of Odysseus for a triumphant but affectionate 'return' to his wife, his hearth and home. This is a mystic idea analogous to the mystery of the 'fall' of the soul into the material plane of existence (by the process of involution) and to the necessity of its returning to the starting-point (evolution)—a mystery which has been expounded by Platonic idealism and by Plotinus in particular. This law of the returning soul corresponds to the belief in the concept of a 'closed' universe (like that of the Eternal Return) or the conception of all phenomena as a cyclic organization. Navigation, as envisaged in any philosophy of the absolute, would deny even the hero his triumphant return to the homeland and would make of him a perpetual explorer of oceans, under endless skies. But to come back to the symbolism of the ship, every vessel corresponds to a constellation (48). The ship-symbol has been related to the holy island, in so far as both are differentiated from the amorphous and hostile sea. If the waters of the oceans are symbolic of the unconscious, they also can allude to the dull roar of the outside world. The notion that it is essential first to learn to sail the sea of the passions in order to reach the Mountain of Salvation is the same as the idea mentioned earlier in connexion with the perils of exploring the oceans. For this reason Guénon suggests that 'the attainment of the Great Peace is depicted in the form of sailing the seas'; hence, in Christian symbolism, the ship represents the Church (28). Some of the less clearly defined aspects of the symbolism of the ship—comparable here with the small boat and the carriage—are related to symbols of the human body and of all physical bodies or vehicles; in addition to this, there is a cosmic implication deriving from the age-old comparison between the sun and the moon on the one hand, and, on the other, two ships floating upon the celestial ocean. The solar ship frequently appears on Egyptian monuments. In Assyrian art, too, ships shaped like cups are clearly solar in character; this cup-shape narrows down still further the scope of the meaning (35). Another meaning, sometimes quite independent of the foregoing, derives not so much from the idea of the ship as such but rather from the notion of sailing; this is the symbolism of the Ship-of-Death. Hence, many primitive peoples place ships on the end of a pole or on the roof of a house. On occasion, it is the roof itself (of the temple or house) which is made to resemble a ship. Always the implication is the desire to transcend existence—to travel through space to the other worlds. All these forms, then, represent the axis valley-mountain, or the symbolism of verticality and the idea of height. An obvious association here is with all the symbols for the world-axis. The mast in the centre of the vessel gives expression to the idea of the Cosmic Tree incorporated within the symbolism of the Ship-of-Death or 'Ship of Transcendence' (50).

Ship of Fools This symbol is fairly common in mediaeval iconography and is related to the Biblical 'foolish virgins'. It expresses the idea of 'sailing' as an end in itself, as opposed to the true sense of 'sailing', which is transition, evolution and salvation, or safe arrival at the haven. Hence, illustrations of *stultifera navis* usually showed a naked woman, a wine-glass and other allusions to terrestrial desires. The Ship of Fools is, then, a parallel symbol to that of the Accursed Hunter.

Shoes According to Swedenborg, shoes symbolize the 'lowly nature', in the sense both of the humble and the despicable (4). Shoes are also a symbol of the female sex organ and may have this implication in the story of Cinderella. For the ancients, they were a sign denoting liberty.

Sieve In the Egyptian system of hieroglyphs, the sign representing a cribble or sieve symbolizes the means of selecting the particular forces needed to reach a required synthesis. The deepest significance of this symbol alludes—like all alchemic experiments—to work carried out upon oneself. The concepts here involved fall within the ambit of the Greek maxim 'know thyself', but the criterion is concerned more with action than with speculation (19). To sieve is to purify and to perfect, to garner the useful, and to discard the useless.

Sigma The S-shape, both vertical and horizontal, together with all its derived forms known generically in the art of ornamentation as scrolls, symbolize relationship and movement or the underlying rhythm of apparently continuous motion. As Ortiz has noted, sigmoid signs, like the spiral, have been utilized as symbols of the wind, but they are more properly related to the whirlwind or whirlpool. The double, symmetrical spiral (like the Ionic volute) may, according to a suggestion of Breuil, be a stylized image of the bull's horns. The curved swastika is composed of two intersecting sigmas (41). A different, wider and deeper implication of the sigma (closely connected, however, with the symbolism of the whirlwind and the hurricane as a synthesis of the Elements and as the supreme cosmic 'moment') is afforded by Schneider's suggestion that the sigma, especially in its vertical position, is a representation of the stream winding its way down the mountain-side and so constituting a characteristic symbol of the valley-mountain axis (or earth-heaven, or, in other words, the *hieros gamos*). He further suggests that this S-shape seems to be formed by one waning moon plus another waxing: the symbols for the two alternating phases of the evolutive and involutive processes which govern the sacrificial relationship of earth and heaven. He believes that this is the explanation of the frequency of the sigma in primitive ornamentation (50).

Sign According to Raymond Lull, 'meaning is the revelation of secrets through the sign', a thesis which puts the emphasis upon the sign as a fact, as a reality. On the other hand, for Stanislas de Guaita (*Essais de Sciences maudites*, II, Paris, 1915) the sign is the 'point of reference needed by the will (or conscience) in projecting itself towards a predetermined goal'. The sign, then, is the concrete form, the symptom, of an invisible, an inner reality and, at the same time, the means whereby the mind is reminded of that reality. Determination and meaning are immanent in the sign. The occult theory of 'signatures' conceives everything that exists as a sign and holds that everything has a feasible 'reading' (the shape of a tree, the position of three or more rocks on a plain, the colour of some eyes, marks

XVII. **Hero.** Archetypal image of the Archangel triumphant over the Adversary (15th-century painting).

XVIII. **Horse.** Celtic candelabra incorporating symbolic horse and solar wheel. (Museo Arqueológico Nacional, Madrid).

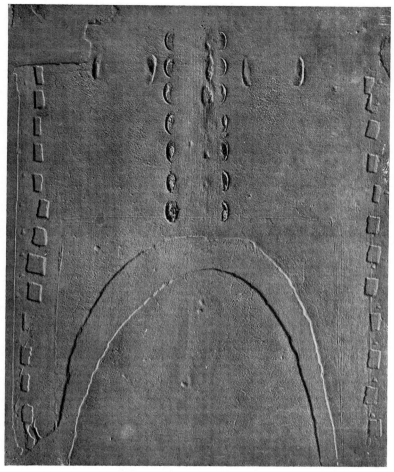

XIX. Antonio Tapies. A painting (1958) that illustrates the *imago ignota.*

XX. **Lamb.** Door to the sanctuary of the church of San Plácido (Madrid), by Claudio Coello.

XXI. **Libra** and other signs of the Zodiac—a 15th-century mural by
Fernando Gallego, Salamanca University.

XXII. Night Sea Crossing. Ship and whale, as symbols at once related and opposed—Gothic miniature.

XXIII. **Siren** in its most characteristic form of 'bird-woman'—relief in Barcelona cathedral.

XXIV. The number two is an essential element in the symbolism of the twin-tailed siren. (From a Roman painting).

XXV. **Sphinx.** Greek, 5th century B.C.

XXVI. **Steps.** Jacob's dream (after an old engraving).

XXVII. **Supporter.** 'Wild Men' are the commonest type of heraldic
supporters—College of San Gregorio, Valladolid.

XXVIII. **Tetramorphs** surrounding the mandorla of the Pantokrator—
Romanesque painting, San Isidoro de León.

XXIX. **Tree and Serpent.** In this Roman composition the two symbols are associated with the story of Adam and Eve.

XXX. **Virgo.** The sixth sign of the Zodiac. Part of a 15th-century mural by Fernando Gallego in Salamanca University.

XXXI. **Window.** Detail of a painting by Pedro Berruguete (*c.* 1500), with symbolic vase with lilies.

XXXII. **Year.** Circular representation of the signs of the Zodiac, corresponding to the year's labours (from a medieval miniature).

made by natural forces on a natural or artificial terrain, the structure of a landscape, the pattern of a constellation, etc.). Auguste Rodin, a realist who was always hovering on the borders of symbolism, in his *Conversations* collected by Paul Gsell, places all art within this realm of occult meaning, with the words: 'lines and shades are for us nothing more than the signs of a hidden reality. Beyond the surface, our gaze plunges into the spirit'. The painter Gustave Moreau expressed himself in similar terms when referring to 'the evocation of thought by line, arabesque and plastic means'. In the present century, Max Ernst and Dubuffet, among other artists, have explained their pictorial and graphic experiments as an immersion in the psychic projected onto the material. At the same time, C. G. Jung gives a similar explanation of the quest of the alchemists.

Twin-tailed siren (15th century).

Siren   A symbolic figure which usually takes one of two main forms: as a bird-woman or as a fish-woman. The sirens in Greek mythology were supposed to be daughters of the river Achelous by the nymph Calliope; and Ceres turned them into birds. They inhabited mountainous places. Legend attributed to them a song of such sweetness they could entice the wayfarer, only to devour him. Latterly, the myth arose of sirens with fish-tails whose haunts were rocky islands and cliffs and who behaved in the same manner as did their sisters inhabiting the Element of air. The siren-myth is one of the most indestructible of all myths; among some marine peoples it has persisted even into the present day (8). Material concerning these sirens is to be found in Aristotle, Pliny, Ovid, Hyginus, the *Physiologus* (2nd century A.D.) and mediaeval bestiaries. Dating from before the 10th century are the two-tailed sirens on the tympanum of the chapel of St. Michael d'Aiguilhe at Le Puy, and the siren-birds at Saint-Benoît-sur-Loire. These and the French viper-fairies—as exemplified by Melusina in particular—are complex figures and we are not satisfied that a merely literal interpretation is the right one. They may well be representations of the inferior forces in woman, or of woman as the inferior, as in the case of lamias; or they could also be symbolic of the corrupt imagination enticed towards base ends or towards the primitive strata of life; or of the torment of desire leading to self-destruction, for their abnormal bodies cannot satisfy the passions that are aroused by their enchanting music and by their beauty of face 'and bosom. It seems that they are largely symbols of the 'temptations' scattered along the path of life (or of symbolic navigation) impeding the evolution of the spirit by bewitchment, beguiling it into remaining on the magic island; or, in other words, causing its premature death. The twin-tailed siren (a fine example of which may be seen on a capital in the apse of San Cugat monastery) can be explained psychologically as a simple amalgamation: the two legs of woman applied to the single 'tail of the fish giving the twin-tail of the woman-fish; but it may also be interpreted symbolically by reference to the profound significance of the Gemini. It seems to us that the twin tail is an infernal replica of the classical attitude of adoration in which both arms are raised—an attitude characteristic, for example, of the Cretan statuettes of priestesses. Given that the sea is the lower abyss and an image of the unconscious, then the twin fish-tail, pertaining to the sea, must express a duality (or conflict) within the watery deeps. Wirth maintains that the siren is quite simply a symbol of woman, and that woman is a true incarnation of the spirit of the earth, as opposed to the man, who is the son of heaven. He expresses his concept of transmigration as follows: 'Life entices the souls of those deprived of it. Why does the other world not retain once and for all those spiritual entities that aspire towards reincarnation? The daughters of men ensnare the sons of heaven with their beauty, dragging them irresistibly down. The spell thus cast is attributed to the siren whose song so captivates the listener that he falls into the ocean' (of the lower waters and of nascent forms) 'teeming with multitudinous life. This temptress owes her powers to the changing forms governed by the moon, the crescent of which shines upon her forehead' (59) (Plates XXIII and XXIV).

Skeleton In the majority of allegories and emblems it is the personification of death. In alchemy it is a symbol of the colour black and of the putrefaction or 'disjunction' of the component elements.

Skin Skin is associated with the ideas of birth and rebirth. In the Egyptian system of hieroglyphs there is a determinative sign comprising three skins knotted together, signifying 'to be born'; it comes into the composition of words such as 'to engender', 'to bring up', 'child', 'to form'. The amulet which the Egyptians used to present to the newly-born comprised, like the hieroglyph, three animal pelts which were attached to a solar globe. The number of the skins here refers to the essentially threefold nature of the human being—the body, the soul and the spirit—while the globe denotes his incorporation into the All. The symbolism of skin is borne out by the rite known as 'the passage through the skin' which pharaohs and priests used to carry out in order to rejuvenate themselves; this rite was later replaced by a simulacrum, and then latterly it became just a panther's tail which kings wore knotted round their waist. This notion that an individual may assume the characteristics of an animal, with its totemic implications, also comes into skin-symbolism (19). There is a basic analogy here with the sacrificial rite once practised by the priests of pre-Columbian Mexico in which human victims were clad in skins; similarly with the wearing of skins by the bearers of the *signum* in Roman legions.

Skull Broadly speaking, it is an emblem of the mortality of man, as in the literary examples of Hamlet and Faust. However, like the snail's shell, it is in truth 'what survives' of the living being once its body has been destroyed. It therefore comes to acquire significance as a receptacle for life and for thought, it is with this symbolic meaning that it figures in books on alchemy, where it is represented as the receptacle used in the processes of transmutation (32). A great many forms of superstition, ritual and—indeed—of cannibalism, are derived from this idea.

Sleeping Beauty On the one hand she may be regarded as a symbol of the anima in the Jungian sense. On the other she symbolizes, rather than the unconscious proper, the ancestral images which lie dormant in the unconscious, waiting to be stimulated into action. As Loeffler points out, in fairy-tales and legends princesses lie dreaming in their palaces, like memories and intuitions deep down in our unconscious. The princesses in their palaces, though not always asleep, are invariably outside the world of action, so that every sleeping, or otherwise secluded, princess stands for a passive potential (38).

Slug The sign denoting the slug—sometimes also interpreted as a small snake—symbolizes the male seed, the Origin of life, the silent tendency of darkness to move towards light; this concept is well expressed in Chapter 17 of the Book of the Dead (19).

Smoke The antithesis of mud, since mud combines the Elements of earth and water, whereas smoke corresponds to air and fire. There are some folklore traditions which attribute a beneficent power to smoke, which is supposed to possess the magic ability to ward off the misfortunes that beset men, animals and plants (21). On the other hand, the column of smoke is a symbol of the valley-mountain antithesis, that is, of the relationship between earth and heaven, pointing out the path through fire to salvation (17). According to Geber, the alchemist, smoke symbolizes the soul leaving the body.

Snail   In Egyptian hieroglyphics the snail is associated with the action of the microcosmic spiral upon matter (19). Modern scientific research in morphology tends to verify this intuition, not only in this particular case but also in all cases where the spiral scheme appears in nature.

Sophia   Woman as *anima* (the soul of man) and as spiritual guide. According to the Gnostic Ptolemaeus, in his *Letter to Flora*, Sophia is the intermediary between the soul of the world (the demiurge) and ideas (pleroma) or plenitude, a mass of aeons opposed to the world of phenomena. For the 17th-century mystics Jakob Böhme and Georg Gichtel, Sophia, the divine virgin, was originally found in 'primordial man' (see Eliade, *Méphistophélès et l'androgyne*, Paris, 1962). She abandoned him, and man cannot be saved until he finds her again. This idea, which is related to the Persian idea of the loved one (Daena), was taken up by the Catharists; it also colours romantic thought (as in Novalis, Hölderlin, Poe, Wagner). A brutally figurative allegory of the idea is furnished by the Greek myth of Athene born from the head of Zeus (i.e. the virgin = thought).

Sorcerer   Like the giant and the magician, he is a personification of the Terrible Father, of the 'evil demiurge' of the Gnostics, prefigured in Saturn (31).

Sound   In India, the sound of Krishna's flute is the magical cause of the birth of the world. The pre-Hellenic maternal goddesses are depicted holding lyres, and with the same significance (56). There are other traditional doctrines which hold that sound was the first of all things to be created, and that which gave rise to all others, commencing with light, or, alternatively, with air and fire. An instance of this is the lament quoted in the *Poimandres* of Hermes Trismegistos (31).

Space   In a manner of speaking, space is an intermediate zone between the cosmos and chaos. Taken as the realm of all that is possible, it is chaotic; regarded as the region in which all forms and structures have their existence, it is cosmic. Space soon came to be associated with time, and this association proved one of the ways of coming to grips with the recalcitrant nature of space. Another—and the most important—was the concept of space as a three-part organization based upon its three dimensions. Each dimension has two possible directions of movement, implying the possibility of two poles or two contexts. To the six points achieved in this way, there was added a seventh: the centre; and space thus became a logical structure. The symbolisms of level and of orientation were finally.

brought to bear in order to complete the exegesis. The three dimensions of space are illustrated by means of a three-dimensional cross, whose arms are oriented along these six spatial directions, made up of the four points of the compass plus the two points of the zenith and the nadir. According to René Guénon, this symbolism—because of its structural character—is identical with that of the Sacred Palace (or the inner palace) of the Cabala, located at the centre-point from which the six directions radiate. In the three-dimensional cross, the zenith and the nadir correspond to the top and the bottom, the front and back to East and West, the right and left to the South and North. The upright axis is the polar axis, the North-South axis is the solstitial line, the East-West the equinoctial. The significance of the vertical or level-symbolism concerns the analogy between the high and the good, the low and the inferior. The Hindu doctrine of the three *gunas*—*sattva* (height, superiority), *rajas* (intermediate zone of the world of appearances, or ambivalence) and *tamas* (inferiority, or darkness)—is in itself sufficient to explain the meaning of the symbolism of level up and down the vertical axis. It is, in consequence, the intermediate plane of the four-directional cross (that which incorporates the cardinal points and which implies the square) which represents the world of appearances. Taking next the East-West axis, traditional orientation-symbolism associates the East—being the point of sunrise—with spiritual illumination; and the West—the point where the sun sets—with death and darkness. Passing next to the North-South axis, there is no one definite interpretation. In many oriental cultures, the zenith coincides with the mystic 'Hole' through which transition and transcendence are effected, that is, the path from the world of manifestation (spatial and temporal) to that of eternity. But it has also been identified with the centre of the three-dimensional cross, taken as the heart of space. Reduced to two dimensions—those of the contrasting horizontal and vertical arms—the cross comes to represent harmony between extension (associated with width) and exaltation (with height). The horizontal arm concerns the implications of a given gradation or moment in an individual's existence, and the vertical pertains to moral elevation (25). William of Saint-Thierry, describing the seven gradations of the soul, observes that it ascends these steps in order to reach the celestial life (14). If we seek an interpretation which will justify the four points of the horizontal plane's being reduced to two (the left and right), we can find a basis for it in Jung's assertion that the rear part coincides with the unconscious and the front with the manifest or consciousness; and since the left also can be equated with the unconscious and the right with consciousness, the rear then becomes equivalent to the left and the front to the right (32). Other equivalents are: left side with the past, the sinister, the repressed, involution, the abnormal and the illegitimate; the right side with the future, the felicitous, openness, evolution, the normal and the legitimate (42). In all this, there is an apparent contradiction with the corresponding number-symbolisms: Paneth observes that, in most cultures, the uneven numbers are considered to be masculine and the even numbers to be feminine. Since the left side is the *zone of origin* and the right that of the *outcome*, the corresponding number-symbolisms would seem to be one (the uneven or masculine number) for the left side (that is, the past) and two (the even or feminine number) for the right side (the subsequent or outcome). The solution is to be found in the fact that the number one (unity) never corresponds to the plane of the manifest world or to spatial reality: it is the symbol of the centre, but not in the sense of occupying any situation in space which might imply a sequel. Hence we must conclude that two is the number corresponding to the left side and three is that related to the right. Guénon explains the way in which the cosmic order conforms with all this in a lucid exposition of the relevant Hindu doctrines to the effect that the right hand zone is the solar region; the left-hand the lunar. 'In the aspect of this symbolism which refers to the temporal condition, the Sun and the right eye correspond to the future, the Moon and the left eye to the past; the frontal eye corresponds to the present which, from the point of view of the manifested, is but an imperceptible moment, comparable to the geometrical point without dimensions in the spatial order; that is why a single look from the third eye destroys all manifestation (which is expressed symbolically by saying that it reduces everything to ashes), and that is also why it is not represented by any bodily organ; but when one rises above this contingent point of view, the present is seen to contain all reality (just as the point carries within itself all the possibilities of space), and when succession is transmuted into simultaneity, all things abide in the "eternal present", so that the apparent destruction is truly a "transformation"' (26). Now, the seven aspects that define space have been regarded as the origin of all septenary groups, and in particular of the seven planets, the seven colours and the seven kinds of landscape (50). Hence Luc Benoist can assert that the Christian Church, by building on earth a mighty, three-dimensional cross of stone, has created for the entire world the co-ordinate lines of a supernatural geometry. Benoist then quotes Clement of Alexandria as saying that the six directions of space symbolize—or are equivalent to—the simultaneous and eternal presence of the six days of the Creation, and that the seventh day (of rest) signifies the return to the centre and the beginning (6). Once the cosmic sense of spatial symbolism has been demonstrated, it is simple to deduce its psychological applications. And once the static laws have been determined, it is easy to grasp the dynamic implications, always bearing in mind the symbolism of orientation. Here, we must point out that the swastika—a solar and polar symbol—implies a movement from right to left, like the apparent movement of the sun; and that Clotho—one of the Parcae—spins her 'wheel of destiny' in the same direction, that is, the opposite way to existence, so destroying it. Right-handedness is characteristic of all symbols of natural life (28); hence, in the Egyptian system of hieroglyphs, to enter is to go towards the right and to go out is to go towards the left (19); orienting these hieroglyphs, we have the right corresponding with the rise and the left with the setting of the sun. Similarly, the right side takes on an extra implication of birth and life, while the left side acquires an association with death (17). Another consequence, apparent in allegories and emblems, is that the right side corresponds to the higher virtues— if one may put it that way—such as compassion, and the left side to justice. All of the above conclusions are logical deductions drawn from the study of oriental tradition, supported by the findings of experimental psychology. But they are conclusions which have also been verified by anthropologists and sociologists in their studies of the habits of diverse peoples. Ania Teillard, for example, has collated a mass of facts; she quotes J. J. Bachofen as asserting (in his *Mutterrecht und Urreligion und Grabersymbolik der Alten*) that, in the important and very common equation 'right hand=masculinity', the left hand harbours magic powers and the right hand the force of reason, and also that in matriarchal societies one always finds the idea of superiority attributed to the left side, and conversely. To turn to the left is to look back upon the past, the unconscious, implying introversion; to turn to the right is to look upon the outside world, implying action and extraversion. At the same time, ethnologists are agreed that during the first stage of any period of sun-worship, the right side becomes pre-eminent, whereas in lunar cults it is the left side which prevails (56). In paintings, reliefs and other artistic creations of man, the left side is characterized by a more vivid projection of the self (that is, by identification) and the right side is more extravert.

Spark An image of the spiritual principle which gives birth to each individual, related also to the Cabbalistic (emanatist) concept of souls scattering from the centre outwards into the world in the form of sparks (32). For Jung, it is therefore a symbol of the heavenly father.

Sparrowhawk Like the eagle, this bird was consecrated to the sun by the Egyptians, the Greeks and Romans, who attributed to it all the powers associated with the sun (8).

Sphinx A fabulous being composed of several parts of the human being and four of various animals. The sphinx at Thebes had the head and breasts of a woman, the body of a bull or dog, the claws of a lion, the tail of a dragon and the wings of a bird (8). Being the supreme embodiment of the enigma, the sphinx keeps watch over an ultimate meaning which must remain for ever beyond the understanding of man. Jung sees in it a synthesis of the 'Terrible Mother', a symbol which has left its mark on mythology as well (31). The mask of the sphinx pertains to the mother-image and also to nature-symbolism; but beneath the mask lie the implications of the myth of multiplicity or of the enigmatic fragmentation of the cosmos. According to esoteric tradition, the Gizeh sphinx is a synthesis of all the science of the past. It is shown contemplating the rising sun and seems to embrace both heaven and earth in its meaning. It is, of course, a symbol which unites, in the midst of the heterogeneity of existence, the four Elements (corresponding to the tetramorphs) with the quintessence or the spirit (signified by the human part of the figure) (49) (Plate XXV).

Spider   The spider is a symbol with three distinct meanings; sometimes they merge or overlap, sometimes one or the other predominates. The three meanings are derived from: (i) the creative power of the spider, as exemplified in the weaving of its web; (ii) the spider's aggressiveness; and (iii) the spider's web as a spiral net converging towards a central point. The spider sitting in its web is a symbol of the centre of the world, and is hence regarded in India as Maya, the eternal weaver of the web of illusion (32). The spider's destructive powers are also connected with its significance as a symbol of the world of phenomena. As Schneider points out, spiders, in their ceaseless weaving and killing—building and destroying—symbolize the ceaseless alternation of forces on which the stability of the universe depends. For this reason, the symbolism of the spider goes deep, signifying, as it does, that 'continuous sacrifice' which is the means of man's continual transmutation throughout the course of his life. Even death itself merely winds up the thread of an old life in order to spin a new one (51). The spider is a lunar animal because the moon (owing to its passive character, in the sense that it merely *reflects* light, and because of its waxing and waning phases, taking these in the positive and negative sense) is related to the world of phenomena, and, on the psychic level, to the imagination. Thus the moon, since it holds sway over the whole phenomenal world (for all phenomenal forms are subject to growth and death), weaves the thread of each man's destiny. Accordingly, the moon is depicted as a gigantic spider in many myths (17).

Spindle or **Bobbin**   The spindle and the distaff, and likewise the act of sewing, are symbols of life and the temporal; they are therefore related to the moon, a symbol expressing the transitoriness of life or all that goes in phases. Hence, deities incorporating the characteristics of the moon, the earth or vegetation usually have the spindle or the distaff as attributes; this is the case with Ishtar, Atargatis, etc. (17). Schneider supports this with his definition of the spindle as a symbol of the *Magna Mater* who is sewing with it inside a mountain of stone or on top of the Tree of the World. In shape, the spindle is a mandorla and so acquires the symbolism of two intersecting circles which stand for heaven and earth, that is, of the sacrifice which renews the generating force of the universe. All spindle-shaped symbols signify the broad idea of mutual sacrifice and the power of inversion (50).

Spinning Spinning—like singing—is equivalent to bringing forth and fostering life. Hence Schneider's comment 'unhappy is the poor spinner who leaves her skeins (that is, her offspring) to dry on the river-bank and finds them gone' (51). The Parcae, like fairies, are spinners. Likewise, a host of figures of legend and folklore.

Spiral A schematic image of the evolution of the universe. It is also a classical form symbolizing the orbit of the moon (50), and a symbol for growth, related to the Golden Number (32), arising (so Housay maintains) out of the concept of the rotation of the earth. In the Egyptian system of hieroglyphs the spiral—corresponding to the Hebrew *vau*—denotes cosmic forms in motion, or the relationship between unity and multiplicity. Of especial importance in relation to the spiral are bonds and serpents. The spiral is essentially macrocosmic (19). The above ideas have been expressed in mythic form as follows: 'From out of the unfathomable deeps there arose a circle shaped in spirals. . . . Coiled up within the spirals, lies a snake, a symbol of wisdom and eternity' (9). Now, the spiral can be found in three main forms: expanding (as in the nebula), contracting (like the whirlwind or whirlpool) or ossified (like the snail's shell). In the first case it is an active sun-symbol, in the second and third cases it is a negative moon-symbol (17). Nevertheless, most theorists, including Eliade, are agreed that the symbolism of the spiral is fairly complex and of doubtful origin. Its relationship with lunar animals and with water has been provisionally admitted (18). Going right back to the most ancient traditions, we find the distinction being made between the creative spiral (rising in a clockwise direction, and attributed to Pallas Athene) and the destructive spiral like a whirlwind (which twirls round to the left, and is an attribute of Poseidon) (51). As we have seen, the spiral (like the snake or serpent and the Kundalini force of Tantrist doctrine) can also represent the potential centre as in the example of the spider's web. Be that as it may, the spiral is certainly one of the essential motifs of the symbolism of ornamental art all over the world, either in the simple form of a curve curling up from a given point, or in the shape of scrolls, or sigmas, etc. Parkin observes in his *Prehistoric Art* that 'no ornamental motif seems to have been more attractive than the spiral'. Ortiz (41) suggests that, from a semantic point of view, the spiral is an emblem of atmospheric phenomena and of the hurricane in particular; but the fact is that the hurricane in its turn is a symbol of secession from the creative (as well as destructive) functions of the universe, that is, of the suspension of the provisional but pacific order of the universe. He also points to the connexion between breathing and the creative breath of life. He goes on to suggest that the volute in ancient cultures was a spiral form symbolizing the breath and the spirit. It is for this reason that the Egyptian god Thoth is represented with a large spiral on his head. Finally, by virtue of its significance in connexion with creation, with movement and progressive development, the spiral is an attribute of power, found in the sceptre of the Egyptian pharaoh, in the *lituus* of Roman augurs and in the present-day walking-stick. In addition to the above, it is also possible that the spiral may symbolize the relationship between the circle and the centre. For the spiral is associated with the idea of the dance, and especially with primitive dances of healing and incantation, when the pattern of movement develops as a spiral curve. Such spiral movements (closely related to the pattern of the mandala and to the spiral form that appears so frequently in art from the Mesolithic Age onwards—particularly in France, Ireland and England) may be regarded as figures intended to induce a state of ecstasy and to enable man to escape from the material world and to enter the beyond, through the 'hole' symbolized by the mystic Centre. Striking examples of such spirals are those of Gravinias (Morbihan), New Grange (Leinster), Carnwath (Scotland) and Castle Archdall (Ulster).

Spiral, Double The double spiral represents the completion of the sigmoid line, and the ability of the sigmoid line to express the intercommunication between two opposing principles is clearly shown in the Chinese *Yang-Yin* symbol. Two double spirals intersecting form the swastika with curved arms, a motif which is fairly common although not so frequent as the arrangement of a series of double spirals in a continuous rhythm. It has been suggested that this motif first appeared in Danubian culture, whence it spread outwards to the north and south of Europe and across Asia to the Far East. Whereas the architectural meander of straight lines and right angles is a symbol of earth, the double spiral is closely linked with water. Given that water is the Element of transition, transformation and regeneration, the double spiral is capable of fully representing its symbolic significance. Hence, it is of common occurrence in the Cretan and other markedly marine cultures. From a cosmic point of view, the double spiral may be regarded as the flattened projection of the two halves of the egg of the world, or of the primordial hermaphrodite separated into two halves, or of the Upper and Lower Waters (8). Hence, together with the St. Andrew's cross, and the drum shaped rather like an hour-glass, it constitutes a symbol of Inversion and of the relationship between opposites (6, 50).

Spur The spur is a symbol of active force. It is attached to the heel like the wings of Mercury, and protects the legendary Achilles' heel. The spur of gold, together with the belt, symbolized, in the Middle Ages, the 'defensive' (or moral) virtues of the knight.

Square The square, as the expression of the quaternity, is a symbol of the combination and regulation of four different elements. Hence, it corresponds to the symbolism of the number four and to all four-part divisions of any process whatsoever. Psychologically, its form gives the impression of firmness and stability, and this explains its frequent use in symbols of organization and construction. For Jung, the four-part division of movements and forms is of greater value than the three-part. Whether or not this is so, what is certain is that, as against the dynamism of the odd numbers and their related geometric forms (such as: three, five, the triangle or the pentagon), the even numbers and forms (for example: four, six, eight, the square, the hexagon, the octagon) are characterized by the qualities of stability, firmness and definition. Hence, ternary symbolism tends to illustrate activity and dynamism (or pure spirit), whereas the quaternary alludes predominantly to things material (or the merely rational intellect). The four Elements, the four seasons, the four stages of Man's life, and specially the four points of the compass, are all sources of the order and the stability of the world. This does not contradict the feminine character which Chinese, Hindu and other traditions ascribe to the square, since it corresponds to the earth, in contrast to the masculine character of the circle (and the triangle) (32). In Egyptian hieroglyphs the square signifies achievement and the square-shaped spiral denotes constructive, materialized energy (19). However, the square resting upon one of its corners acquires a dynamic sense which is quite new, implying a change in its fundamental symbolism: during the Romanesque period, it was used as a symbol of the sun, comparable with the circle (51).

Squaring the Circle The ancient Mesopotamians used to place a circle between two squares in order to find out its area. And the idea of equating the circle with the square also grew out of the concept of the rotating square. But our concern is not with the mathematical but the symbolic problem. 'Squaring the circle', like the *lapis* or the *aurum philosophicum,* was one of the preoccupations of the alchemists; but whereas the latter two were symbols of the quest for the evolutive goal of the spirit, the former problem concerned the equating of the two great cosmic symbols of heaven (or the circle) and earth (or the square). It is to do, then, with the union of two opposites; not juxtaposition as in the *coniunctio* of the two arms of the cross, for example, but the equation and cancelling out of two components in a higher synthesis. The square was seen to correspond to the four Elements. The aim of 'squaring the circle', then (which strictly ought to be called 'circling the square'), was to obtain unity in the material world (as well as in the spiritual life) over and above the differences and obstacles (the static order) of the number four and the four-cornered square. We have already suggested that the rotated square was reckoned an important part of this project, and Heinrich Khunrath comments in his *Von hylealischen Chaos*: 'By means of circumrotation or circulatory revolution, the quaternary is restored to purest simplicity and innocence' (32). Another means of getting an *ersatz* 'squaring' was to superimpose two squares, inscribing a circle within them, in such a way as to form an octagon. The octagon can indeed be considered, in both a geometric and a symbolic sense, as the intermediary form between the square and the circle. For this reason it never symbolized the *opus* itself (that is, the mystic consummation of the synthesis of opposites), but it did stand for the path indicated by things quaternary (such as the earth, the feminine element, matter or reason) towards the circle (representing perfection, eternity and spirit). That is why many mediaeval baptisteries, fonts and cupolas are octagonal in shape.

Staff   The staff has a double symbolism, as a support and as an instrument of punishment. As regards the first, Frazer notes that the ancient Egyptians held a festival after the Autumn Solstice which they called the 'Nativity of the Sun-Stick', because they supposed that, as the day grew shorter and the sunlight weaker, the sun needed a stick for support (21). Dalí has revived the mythic staff in the form of crutches, which are a recurrent theme in his paintings. The use of staff-symbolism, both among the ancient Egyptians and in a modern artist such as Dalí, exemplifies an elementary principle of symbolism: the correlation and interchangeability of the material and spiritual aspects of a given situation. As a weapon it is symbolically identical with the club, the royal weapon (15) (Oedipus kills Laius, whom he does not know to be his father, with a blow of his staff).

Stag   Its symbolic meaning is linked with that of the Tree of Life, because of the resemblance of its antlers to branches. It is also a symbol of the cycles of regeneration and growth, as Henri-Charles Puech has observed. The stag, in several cultures of Asia and pre-Columbian America, came to be thought of as a symbol of regeneration because of the way its antlers are renewed. Like the eagle and the lion, it is the secular enemy of the serpent, which shows that, symbolically, it was viewed favourably; it is closely related to heaven and light, whereas the serpent is associated with night and subterranean life (18). Hence, in the Milky Way, on both sides of the Bridge of Death and Resurrection are figures of eagles, stags and horses acting as mediators between heaven and earth (50). In the West, during the Middle Ages, the way of solitude and purity was often symbolized by the stag, which actually appears in some emblems with a crucifix between its horns (thus providing the last link in the chain of relationships: tree/cross/horns) (4). It has also been considered as a symbol of elevation (20). The Greeks and Romans perceived certain 'mystical' gifts in the stag, which they exaggerated through psychic projection. One of these supposed gifts was the ability instinctively to recognize medicinal plants, which is what lies behind the assertion in ancient bestiaries that 'the stag can recognize the dictamnus plant'. His prestige is in part a consequence of his appearance: his beauty, grace, agility (46). Because of his rôle as messenger of the gods, the stag may be considered as the antithesis of the he-goat.

Stains   The symbolism of blots or stains—like that of the wall-flakings which so impressed Piero de Cosimo and Leonardo da Vinci—is a combination of the symbolisms pertaining to the shapes of these stains and their texture or material. A related symbol is that of clouds, in so far as both clouds and blots suggest imaginary shapes which, by analogy, may be identified with other shapes. Proof of this has been afforded by the Rorschach test. These blots or stains are often associated with the passage of time, in which case they allude to ideas of the transitory and death. At the same time, stains and areas of discoloration or imperfection of all kinds may also be explained by reference to the symbolism of the abnormal, for, according to the alchemists, such 'infirmities' in objects or materials actually constitute 'prime matter', the basis for the creation of philosophical gold (equated with spiritual evolution). As the *Rosarium Philosophorum* says: 'Our gold is not common gold. You, nevertheless, have asked about the green assuming that the mineral is a leprous body because of the green which grows in it. It is for this reason that I tell you that what is perfect in the mineral is solely this green, because very soon it will be transformed by our craft into the truest gold.' Relevant to this is Nietzsche's remark, in *Thus Spake Zarathustra*, that 'Out of the lowest the highest reaches its peak' (32).

Star   As a light shining in the darkness, the star is a symbol of the spirit. Bayley has pointed out, however, that the star very rarely carries a single meaning—it nearly always alludes to multiplicity. In which case it stands for the forces of the spirit struggling against the forces of darkness. This is a meaning which has been incorporated into emblematic art all over the world (4). For this reason, 'identification with the star' is possible only to the chosen few. Jung recalls the Mithraic saying: 'I am a star which goes with thee and shines out of the depths' (31). Now, individual stars are often seen in graphic symbolism. Their meaning frequently depends upon their shape, the number of points, the manner of their arrangement, and their

Five-pointed and six-pointed stars.

colour (if any). The 'flaming star' is a symbol of the mystic Centre—of the force of the universe in expansion (4). The five-pointed star is the most common. As far back as in the days of Egyptian hieroglyphics it signified 'rising upwards towards the point of origin', and formed part of such words as 'to bring up', 'to educate', 'the teacher', etc. (19). The inverted five-pointed star is a symbol of the infernal as used in black magic (37).

Stars   Being nocturnal, their symbolism is associated with that of night; they are also linked with the idea of multiplicity (or with disintegration) because they appear in clusters, and with order and destiny because of their disposition and location (according to Horapollo Niliacus).

Stars, The   The seventeenth enigma of the Tarot, depicting an allegorical image of a naked girl kneeling down beside a pool, as, from a golden jar, she pours a life-giving liquid into the still waters. In her left hand she holds a silver jar from which she pours fresh water on to the dry earth, encouraging the growth of the vegetation—signified most often by a sprig of acacia and a rose in full bloom, an emblem of immortality and of love. Above this figure are a bright star and several lesser ones. The ultimate meaning of this symbol seems to be expressive of intercommunication of the different worlds, or the vitalization by the celestial luminaries of liquids contained in certain vessels, and implying, furthermore, the transference of these celestial characteristics to the purely material Elements of earth and water. For this reason, Oswald Wirth concludes that this enigma represents the soul uniting spirit with matter (59).

State of Mind   The symbolist idea that the different worlds are so many different states of being (crystallized into different orders of matter and form with their corresponding, expressive characteristics), and that they can be systematized, in their diversity, within a scale or series, after the manner of the regular figures of geometry, colours or sounds, can equally well be taken the other way round. In which case, the states of being, which, from the psychological point of view, are represented as corresponding emotional states, that is, as varying 'states of mind' (comparable with the emotional expressions peculiar to each one of the musical modes: severe, ecstatic, anguished, enthusiastic, active, erotic, melancholic)—these states of being, then, come to be represented as certain definite kinds of landscape, in which the additional symbolisms of level, of symmetry, of light and colour, all play a definite part.

State of Preservation A symbol whose meaning is almost literal, or analogous to the physical, by simple transference of the physical characteristics of a thing on to the spiritual and psychological plane. So, for example, fracture symbolizes fragmentation, disintegration and mutilation on the spiritual level; wear stands for weariness of spirit, poor health and a worn-out sentiment or idea; corrosion for destruction, infirmity and suffering. We have here the age-old concept of the parallel between the physical and the psychic worlds, an idea which gave rise to the alchemists' postulate that a series of operations upon matter must have repercussions upon the spirit— and indeed this was true by virtue of the force of their *intention*. Nevertheless, one must guard against accepting the above symbological interpretation as the only possible one, for it is a very generalized conclusion; there are, in fact, other symbolic meanings, sometimes, in particular cases, of greater importance than this, deriving from the agent which is bringing it about. The action of each of the Elements, for instance, always imparts a strong flavour of its own symbolic character. Fire, water or earth, if they burn or soak an object, or cause it to putrefy, in addition to altering its physical identity and changing its state also inject into it some part of their own mode of behaviour.

Steed A symbol of the animal in man, that is, of the force of the instincts. As a riding-mount, it is also a symbol of the body. That is why most mythological figures, quite apart from their other attributes, are linked with one particular mount (Wotan mounted on Sleipnir, Ahuramazda on Angramainyu, Mithras on the bull, Men on a horse with human feet, Freyr on the boar with bristles of gold) (31). The arrangement of the symbol is like that of the centaur, but the hierarchical order is reversed: whereas the centaur stands for the superior force of the instincts (or even for intuition, a gift attributed by some primitive peoples to animals in general and to the horse in particular), the steed in itself symbolizes control of baser forces. In India, the mount is seen as *vahana* (materialization). The pedestal plays a similar rôle, its shape always being symbolic. In this way, the goddess Padmâ, for example, is associated with the lotus (60).

Steel According to Evola in *La tradizione ermetica*, steel denotes the transcendent toughness of the principle of the all-conquering spirit.

Steps This is a symbol which is very common in iconography all over the world. It embraces the following essential ideas: ascension, gradation, and communication between different, vertical levels. In the Egyptian system of hieroglyphs, steps constitute a determinative sign which defines the act of ascending; it forms part of one of the appellations of Osiris, who is invoked as 'he who stands at the top of the steps'. Ascending, then, can be understood both in a material and in an evolutive and spiritual sense. Usually, the actual number of steps involved in the symbol is of symbolic significance. In Egyptian images, the number tends to be nine: the triple ternary which symbolizes the gods of the ennead who, together with Osiris, make up the symbolic number ten which stands for the completed cycle or the return to unity (19). A great many Egyptian tombs have yielded up amulets in the shape of ladders. The Book of the Dead says: 'My steps are now in position so that I may see the gods.' Eliade has pointed out parallel images, such as the following: Among many primitive peoples, mythic ascension is indicated by means of a rope, a stake, a tree or a mountain (symbolizing the world-axis). Or, according to an Oceanian myth, the hero reaches heaven by means of the fantastic hyperbole of a chain of arrows. And in Islamic tradition, Mohammed saw a ladder which the just climbed up to reach God (17). To refer again to primitive belief, Schneider observes that in order to 'reach' the mountain of Mars and reap its benefits, one must ascend the ladder of one's forebears —suggesting a biological and historical source for the mystic symbol of the ladder. Hence steps are also one of the most notable symbols in ancestral rites (50). Images specifically connected with the steps are the mountain, and architectural structures incorporating steps, such as the Egyptian pyramid of Sakkara, the Mesopotamian ziggurats, or the teocallis of America of pre-Columbian days; we have then a synthesis of two symbols—that of the 'temple-mountain' and that of the steps—signifying that the entire cosmos is the path of ascension towards the spirit. In Mithraism, the ceremonial steps were seven in number, each step being made of a different metal (as was each different plane of the ziggurat in a figurative sense). According to Celsus, the first step was of lead (corresponding to Saturn). The general correspondence with the planets is self-evident. Now, this idea of gradual ascent was taken up particularly by the alchemists from the latter part of the Middle Ages onwards; they identified it sometimes with the phases of the transmutation process. In Stephan Michelspacher's work *Die Cabala, Spiegel der Kunst und Natur* (1654), the following graded scale is given: Calcination, Sublimation, Solution, Putrefaction, Distillation, Coagulation, Tincture, leading to a kind of shrine inside a mountain (32). According to the Zohar, the ladder which Jacob is said to have seen in his dreams had seventy-two rungs and its top disappeared into the clouds (39). Broadly speaking, in emblems and allegories throughout the Middle Ages, it is the ascending (affirmative) aspect of the steps which predominates, emphasized by the signs and symbols clustering round the ladder. Bayley points out that many steps are surmounted by a cross, the figure of an angel, a star or a fleur-de-lis (4) located on the border itself. In Romanesque art, and generally in the thought characteristic of the period, the steps are the symbol of the 'relationship between the worlds' (14, 20), but it must not be forgotten that, within the spatial symbolism of level, there are not two grades indicating two different worlds (the terrestrial or intermediary and the celestial or upper) but three (through the addition of a third: the infernal or lower world). This is why Eliade (for reasons of psychology as well) states that the steps are a vivid image of 'breaking through' the levels of existence in order to open up the way from one world to another, establishing a relationship between heaven, earth and hell (or between virtue, passivity and sin). Hence, steps located beneath the level of the earth are always a symbol for an opening into the infernal regions. In Bettini's *Libro del monte santo di Dio* (Florence, 1477), steps are shown superimposed upon a mountain; to emphasize the parallel—and indeed identical—symbolism of the mountain and the ladder, the former is portrayed as if it were terraced and the terraces are shown to be the rungs of the ladder. On these rungs are the names of the virtues: Humility, Prudence, Temperance, Fortitude, Justice, Awe, Mercy, Science, Counsel, Understanding and Wisdom. The steps are portrayed as if chained to the mountainside. On the peak of the mountain is a mandorla formed of angels with Christ in the centre. (Plate XXVI).

Stick   A material symbol of the valley-mountain axis, comparable with steps, the cross and the artificial stake. The post has the same symbolic sense, largely because it stands erect. A burnt stick represents death and wisdom (50).

Stone   Stone is a symbol of being, of cohesion and harmonious reconciliation with self. The hardness and durability of stone have always impressed men, suggesting to them the antithesis to biological things subject to the laws of change, decay and death, as well as the antithesis to dust, sand and stone splinters, as aspects of disintegration. The stone when whole symbolized unity and strength; when shattered it signified dismemberment, psychic disintegration, infirmity, death and annihilation. Stones fallen from heaven served to explain the origin of life. In volcanic eruptions, air turned to fire, fire became 'water' and 'water' changed to stone; hence stone constitutes the first solid form of the creative rhythm (51)—the sculpture of essential movement, and the petrified music of creation (50). The mythic and religious significance is only one step removed from this basic symbolic sense, a step which was taken by the immense majority of peoples during the animistic era. Meteorites, in particular, came in for worship; the most celebrated are the Kaaba meteorite in Mecca and the Black Stone of Pessinus, an aniconic image of the Phrygian Great Mother taken to Rome during the last of the Punic Wars (17). Here is a description of the Mohammedans' stone, taken from Marques-Rivière: 'Inside the Kaaba, which is nothing more than a dark hall, there are three columns holding up the roof which has a number of silver and gold lamps hanging down from it. The floor is of marble tiles. In the eastern corner, some five feet above floor-level, not far from the door, is the famous black stone (al hadjar alaswad) sealed off, composed of three great sections. . . . In colour it is reddish black with red and yellow patches; in appearance it recalls lava or basalt' (39). Among the stones venerated by the ancients, we must not overlook the Greek omphaloi; Guénon maintains that they are really bethels, a word derived from the Hebrew Beith-El (or the House of God), related to the biblical 'And this stone which I have set for a pillar, shall be God's House' (Genesis xxviii, 22), even though its sense is magic and not architectonic (28). There are numerous legends dealing with stones: the so-called Abadir which Saturn devoured, mistaking it for Jupiter; or the stones of Deucalion and Pyrrha; or those in the myth of Medusa the Gorgon (6); or that which contained Mithras until his birth (11). There are other stones in folktales, but these seem to be invested with rather more modest powers: the Lapis lineus, for example, as it was called by the Romans, which was supposed to be able to prophesy by changing its colour; or the Irish stone Lia-Fail, associated with coronations (8). As for the philosophers' stone in alchemy, it represents the 'conjunction' of opposites, or the integration of the conscious self with the feminine or unconscious side (or in other words, the fixing of volatile elements); it is, then, a symbol of the All (33). As Jung rightly says, the alchemists approached their task obliquely—they did not seek the divine in matter but tried to 'produce' it by means of a lengthy process of purification and transmutation (32). According to Evola, the touchstone is symbolic of the body, since it is 'fixed', as opposed to the 'wandering' characteristic of thought, the spirits and desires. But only the resuscitated body—in which 'two will be one'—can correspond to the philosophers' stone. Evola points out that, for the alchemist, 'between eternal birth, reintegration, and the discovery of the philosophers' stone, there is no difference whatsoever'.

Stone-Circle   Often called a 'cromlech', and popularly known as 'the giant's circle'. Diodorus Siculus had in mind the great stone-circle of Stonehenge when he referred to the existence, on an island off Gaul 'as big as Sicily', of 'the circular temple of Apollo' where the Hyperboreans sang the praises of god-the-sun. The sun-symbolism connected with the stone-circle is obvious (16). It also partakes of circle-symbolism (that is, of the cyclic process, Oneness and perfection), of disk-symbolism (representing the sun), and of stone-symbolism (or, in the eyes of most primitive peoples, theophany—a manifestation of the divine which they associated with fertility-cults). Often standing in the midst of the circle of monoliths is the 'hyrmensul' or sun-stone.

Stork   This bird, dedicated to Juno by the Romans, was a symbol of filial piety. It is also an emblem of the traveller (8). In the allegory of 'Great Wisdom', two storks are shown facing each other and flying within a circle formed by the figure of a snake (4).

Storm   The myth of the creative storm (or creative intercourse between the Elements) is universal: among the Nordic peoples it appears in connexion with Thor, in Assyrio-Babylonian mythology with Bel, in the Germanic with Donar, in the Greek with Zeus, among the Slavs with Peroun, and so on (38). The storm, like everything else that occurs in heaven or descends therefrom, has a sacred quality about it.

Stranger   In myths, legends, folktales and in literature as a whole, the 'stranger' is frequently 'the one destined to replace' the reigning power in a country or locality. He stands for the possibility of unseen change, for the future made present, or for mutation in general. Frazer tells us how Lityerses, a son of King Midas, was wont to challenge people to a reaping match, and if he vanquished them he used to thrash them; but one day he met with a stranger who, proving himself to be a stronger reaper, slew him (21).

Strength   The eleventh enigma of the Tarot pack. The image shows a queen who, without apparent effort, overcomes a lion, holding his jaws wide open. The allusion to the Zodiac is clear enough—Leo vanquished by Virgo—and the subject finds its mythological counterpart in Hercules overcome by Omphale. Wirth points to a highly interesting detail in the allegory: the queen does not slay the lion, but clasps it to her bosom having stunned it with her club, signifying that one must not despise the inferior, but master it and put it to good use. There is an echo here of the alchemists' belief that what is base must not—and indeed cannot—be destroyed, it must be transmuted into what is superior. In the affirmative sense, this enigma symbolizes the triumph of intelligence over brutality; in the negative, it denotes insensibility and fury (59).

String (or Cord)   All types of string, cord or rope are forms of binding, and this forms the basis of their symbolic meaning. It is what lies behind the sacred cord worn by all high-caste Hindus. The *Jâbâla-Upanishad* makes it clear that the sacred cord is the external symbol of the *Sûtrâtma*, or the spiritual thread binding together all things in existence, as the thread of a necklace binds together all the pearls (60). This is an idea of such clarity that expressions of it are to be found everywhere. The cords worn by soldiers and by officials, sashes and bows, braid and stripes, are all nothing but emblems of cohesion and binding, although in a form referring to a particular social status. In our view, this and no other is the significance of the neck-tie, despite the Freudian tendency to interpret it as a phallic symbol.

Struggles between Animals   Animals symbolize different stages of instinct and can therefore be placed along an ideal vertical axis (for example, in ascending order: bear, lion, eagle). Accordingly, a struggle between different animals—between a lion and a griffin, a serpent and an eagle, an eagle and a lion, etc.—represents the struggle between widely-differing instinctive inclinations. The victory of a winged animal over a wingless one is always a positive symbol, comparable to sublimation. The struggle of an eagle with a lion involves a vector of lesser intensity than that between an eagle and a serpent, because the distance separating the latter pair is greater. The struggle between real and fabulous animals may represent the conflict between realistic instincts or tendencies and fanciful or misleading ones. But this must be decided by the context, for it may also represent a reduction in the power of the imagination (that is, in the creative fantasy), to the benefit of material, direct and realistic activity.

Styx, The   A subterranean spring or lake in Greek mythology —corresponding to the underground sea in Egyptian belief— which the sun crosses every night. By analogy, therefore, the lower waters of the Styx pertain to death, just as every sunrise points to resurrection (8).

Subterranean Chambers   Symbolic of the body's inside, the viscera. Verne's 'journey to the centre of the earth', through caves, passages and wells, is a return to the maternal body, to the earth.

Sulphur   Symbolic of the desire for positive action, and of vital heat (57). In the complex symbolism of alchemy, sulphur represents one of the stages of the evolution of matter (and of the psyche). According to René Alleau, the various stages, from the lowest to the highest, can be classified as follows: prior elements, denoting the inherent possibilities of the cosmos, or of man; prime matter, or the elementary organization of inherent possibilities, equivalent perhaps to the unconscious, or the instincts; mercury, or the first purification, feelings, imagination, the dominant female principle; sulphur, or more profound purification, reason and intuition, the male principle; and the Great Work, or transcendence.

Sun In theogony, the Sun represents the moment (surpassing all others in the succession of celestial dynasties) when the heroic principle shines at its brightest. Thus, after Uranus, Saturn and Jupiter, comes Helios Apollo. On occasion, the Sun appears as the direct son and heir of the god of heaven, and Krappe notes that he inherits one of the most notable and moral of the attributes of this deity: he sees all and, in consequence, knows all. In India, as Sûrya, it is the eye of Varuna; in Persia, it is the eye of Ahuramazda; in Greece, as Helios, the eye of Zeus (or of Uranus); in Egypt it is the eye of Ra, and in Islam, of Allah (35). With his 'youthful' and filial characteristic, the Sun is associated with the hero, as opposed to the father, who connotes the heavens, although the two (sun and sky) are sometimes equated. Hence, the weapon of heaven is the net (the pattern of the stars) or the power of binding; while the hero is armed with the sword (symbolically associated with fire). And it is for this reason that heroes are promoted to solar eminence and even identified with the Sun itself. In a given period of history and at a certain cultural level, the solar cult is the predominant if not the only one. Frazer, however, as Eliade has noted, brought out the divergencies of the solar elements in the sacred rites of Africa, of Australia and Oceania as a whole, and of North and South America. The cult of the Sun reached an advanced stage of development only in the New World, and—most advanced of all—in Mexico and Peru. Eliade concludes that, since these were the only countries in pre-Columbian America to evolve a viable political system, it may be concluded that there is a parallel between predominantly solar cults and 'historical' forms of human existence. We must not overlook the fact that Rome, the most powerful political force of Antiquity, and the originator of the historical sense, upheld solar hierophany, which, during the Empire, dominated all other cults in the form of Mithraic ritual (17). An heroic and courageous force, creative and guiding—this is the core of solar symbolism; it may actually come to constitute a religion complete in itself, as is shown by the 'heresy' of Ikhnaton in the 18th dynasty of Egypt; here the hymns to the sun are, setting aside their profound lyrical interest, expressions of theories about the beneficent activity of the king of astral bodies. The sun on the horizon had long served the Egyptians of the Ancient Empire as a means of defining 'brightness' or 'splendour'. They were also forcibly struck by the analogy between the daily disappearance of the Sun and the winter solstice (19). At

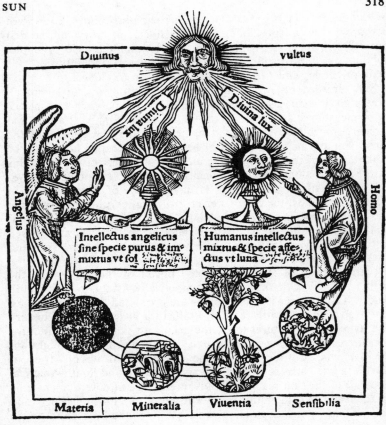

The Sun and the Moon, symbols of the active and the passive
principles of the universe as 'Intellectus angelicus' and 'Humanus
intellectus' respectively. (Engraving from Bovillus, *De Intellectu*,
Paris, 1510.)

the same time, there was, for the primitive, astrobiological mind, an
essential connexion between the Sun and Moon, analogous to that
between heaven and earth. It is well known that, for the vast majority
of peoples, the sky is symbolic of the active principle (related to the
masculine sex and to the spirit), while the earth symbolizes the
passive principle (cognate with the feminine sex and with matter);
these equations, nevertheless, are occasionally transposed. And the
same thing happens with the Sun and Moon: solar 'passion', so to
speak, with its heroic and fierce character, clearly had to be
assimilated to the masculine principle, and the pale and delicate

nature of lunar light, with its connexion with the waters of the ocean (and the rhythm of woman), obviously had to be classified as feminine. These equations are certainly not constant; but the exceptions do not invalidate the essential truth of this symbolism. Even physically speaking, the Moon merely fulfils the passive rôle of reflecting the light which the Sun actively diffuses. Many primitive tribes hold that the eyes of heaven are the Sun and the Moon located on either side of the 'world-axis', and there are prehistoric drawings and engravings which may be interpreted after this fashion. Eliade notes that, for the Pigmies and Bushmen, the sun is the eye of the supreme god. The Samoyeds see the Sun and the Moon as the eyes of heaven, the Sun being the good eye, and the Moon the evil eye (one can see here an unequivocal instance of the symbolism of dualism expanded by the assimilation of that of moral polarity). The idea of the invincible character of the sun is reinforced by the belief that whereas the Moon must suffer fragmentation (since it wanes) before it can reach its monthly stage of three-day disappearance, the Sun does not need to die in order to descend into hell; it can reach the ocean or the lake of the Lower Waters and cross it without being dissolved. Hence, the death of the Sun necessarily implies the idea of resurrection and actually comes to be regarded as a death which is not a true death. For this reason, too, ancestor-worship is associated with the cult of the sun, in order to offer the symbolic promise of protection and salvation. Megalithic monuments are based upon the amalgamation of these two cults (17). Thus, the broadest and most authentic interpretation sees the sun as the cosmic *reductio* of the masculine force, and the Moon of the feminine (49). This implies that the active faculties (of reflexion, good judgement or will power) are solar, while the passive qualities (imagination, sentiment and perception) are feminine, with intuition possibly androgynous (26). The 'correspondences' of the Sun are chiefly gold, among the metals, and, of the colours, yellow. Alchemists regarded it as 'gold prepared for the work' or 'philosophical sulphur', as opposed to the Moon and mercury (the metal), which is lunar (57). Another alchemic concept, that of the *Sol in homine* (or the invisible essence of the celestial Sun which nourishes the inborn fire of Man) (57), is an early pointer to the way the astral body has latterly been interpreted by psychoanalysts, narrowing its meaning down to that of heat or energy, equivalent to the fire of life and the libido. Hence Jung's point that the Sun is, in truth, a symbol of the source of life and of the ultimate wholeness of man (32). But here there is probably some inexactitude, for totality is in fact uniquely symbolized by the 'conjunction' of the Sun and the Moon, as king and queen, brother and sister (32). In some folklore-traditions, the urge to allude in some way to the supreme good, which, by definition, is incapable of definition, is met by the saying 'to join the Sun and the Moon'.

Now, having established the principal terms of solar symbolism—as an heroic image (*Sol invictus*, *Sol salutis*, *Sol iustitiae*) (14), as the divine eye, the active principle and the source of life and energy—let us come back to the dualism of the Sun as regards its hidden passage—its 'Night Sea-Crossing'—symbolic of immanence (like the colour black) and also of sin, occultation and expiation. In the *Rigveda*—Eliade reminds us—the Sun is ambivalent: on the one hand it is 'resplendent' and on the other it is 'black' or invisible, in which case it is associated with chthonian and funereal animals such as the horse and the serpent (17). Alchemists took up this image of the *Sol niger* to symbolize 'prime matter', or the unconscious in its base, 'unworked' state. In other words, the Sun is then at the nadir, in the depths out of which it must, slowly and painfully, ascend towards its zenith. This inevitable ascent does not relate to its daily journey, although this is used as an image, and hence it is symbolized by the transmutation of prime matter into gold, passing through the white and red stages, like the Sun itself in its orbit. Of undoubted interest, as an indication of the intensity of man's attitude towards the Sun, is the reference by Tacitus and Strabo to the 'sound' made by the Sun as it rises in the East and drowns in the oceans of the West. The sudden disappearance of the Sun below the horizon is related to the sudden death of heroes such as Samson, Hercules and Siegfried (35).

Sun, The   The nineteenth enigma of the Tarot pack. The allegory shows the disk of the astral king surrounded by alternating straight and flamelike rays, golden and red, symbolizing the twofold activity of the Sun in giving out warmth and light. Beneath the Sun, from which a golden spray is falling, are a young couple in a green field, and in the background there is a wall. This couple symbolize the Gemini under the beneficial influence of spiritual light. The Sun is the astral body of immutable constancy, and hence it reveals the reality of things—not their changing aspects as the Moon does. It is related to purification and tribulation, the sole purpose of which is to render transparent the opaque crust of the senses so that they may perceive the higher truths. But the Sun, apart from providing light and heat, is the source of supreme riches, and this is symbolized, in the allegory, by the golden drops which, as in the myth of Danae, rain down upon the human couple. On the positive side, this enigma symbolizes glory, spirituality and illumination. On the negative side, it stands for vanity or an idealism incompatible with reality (59).

Sun-shade   A solar symbol, an emblem of authority and dignity, and one of the eight allegories of good fortune in Chinese Buddhism

(5). It incorporates the symbolic concepts of irradiation and protection.

Superiority In certain Babylonian rites, the *hieros gamos* was represented by an act of erotic consummation between a priestess of Ishtar and a slave, who was afterwards put to death. This was not an act of cruelty, but the inevitable consequence which attended the act of the slave, as the shadow pursues the body. For if he had been left alive, the remainder of his existence would have been a living death, since he had experienced contact with the Superior. The same may be said of Lazarus; and this is the meaning of the myth of Semele, consumed by the fiery radiance of Jupiter whom she sought to see in all his true and essential glory. The superior destroys—burns up—the inferior. But, for this very reason, the recipient of any such token of the supra-normal who is not destroyed by the gift but proves himself capable of retaining it, establishes thereby his own (comparable) superiority. Hence, anything of value surpassing the ordinary and the commonplace is a sign of special favour and a symbol of absolute transcendence. He who dares to desire the superior, thereby invites comparison with it; if he succeeds in entering into the domain of this superiority and withstands it, then he is invested with it, but should he prove unworthy then he must needs be destroyed. Every limiting situation, every extreme trial—such as placing one's hand in boiling water, for instance—denotes this same idea. The knight conquered and devoured by the dragon is thereby proved inferior. Only the knight capable of vanquishing the dragon is worthy to confront it. Aspiring to the hand of the 'princess' is another expression of the same idea. As Plato observes in the *Republic*: 'All great things are fraught with danger.'

Coat of arms with supporters in
the form of Wild Men.

Supporters In heraldic or decorative compositions, human, animal or fabulous beings that support the coat of arms or the central figure or element. These supporters, nearly always two in

number, one on either side, symbolize those base forces which, once
hostile and aggressive, have been obliged to become the servants and
defenders of the central element, symbolizing the victorious power
(Plate XXVII).

Swallow A bird sacred to Isis and to Venus (8), and an allegory
of spring. The poet Bécquer makes use of this symbol to convey
the pathos and the inexorable nature of time, drawing analogies
with other symbols.

Swan A symbol of great complexity. The dedication of the swan
to Apollo, as the god of music, arose out of the mythic belief that it
would sing sweetly when on the point of death (8). The red swan is a
symbol of the sun (2). But almost all meanings are concerned with
the white swan, sacred to Venus, which is why Bachelard suggests
that in poetry and literature it is an image of naked woman, of chaste
nudity and immaculate whiteness. But Bachelard finds an even
deeper significance: hermaphroditism, since in its movement and
certainly in its long phallic neck it is masculine yet in its rounded,
silky body it is feminine. In sum, then, the swan always points to
the complete satisfaction of a desire, the swan-song being a particular
allusion to desire which brings about its own death (2). This
ambivalent significance of the swan was also well known to the
alchemists, who compared it with 'philosophical Mercury' (57), the
mystic Centre and the union of opposites, an interpretation entirely
in accord with its archetypal implications (56). Now, in Schneider's
view, the swan, by virtue of its relationship with the harp and the
sacrificial serpent, also pertains to the funeral-pyre, because the
essential symbols of the mystic journey to the other world (apart
from the death-ship) are the swan and the harp. This would afford
another explanation of the mysterious song of the dying swan. The
swan also has a bearing upon the peacock, although the situation is
reversed. The swan/harp relationship, corresponding to the axis
water/fire, denotes melancholy and passion, self-sacrifice, and the
way of tragic art and martyrdom. Conversely the peacock/lute
relationship, linked with earth/air, is possibly a representation of
logical thought (50). As Jacques de Morgan has shown in *L'Humanité
préhistorique*, if it was the horse that pulled the Sun-god's chariot by
day, it was the swan that hauled his bark over the waters by night.
The relevance to this myth of the Lohengrin legend is self-evident.

Swastika This graphic symbol is to be found in almost every
ancient and primitive cult all over the world—in Christian catacombs,
in Britain, Ireland, Mycenae and Gascony; among the Etruscans,
the Hindus, the Celts and the Germanic peoples; in central Asia
as well as in pre-Columbian America. The implications of the
swastika are very wide, for it is a synthesis of two symbols of
independent force: the (Greek) cross with arms of equal length and

the cross with four arms appearing to rotate in the same direction. The tetraskelion, or swastika with four arms at right angles, is also called the *gammadion* because it can be formed by joining up four gamma letters. According to Ludwig Müller, the swastika, during the Iron Age, represented the supreme deity (39). For Mackenzie, it is associated with agriculture and with the points of the compass. Colley March sees the swastika as a specific sign denoting rotation about an axis. There are in fact two swastikas: the right-handed *Swastika* and the left-handed *Swavastika* (41). The shape of the swastika has been interpreted as a solar wheel with rays and feet sketched in at the extremities (56). By the Middle Ages, the most general interpretation was that it symbolized movement and the power of the sun (14); but, at the same time, it was seen as an obvious symbol of the quaternary, in the particular sense of the 'configuration of a movement split up into four parts', related to the poles and the four cardinal directions (16). The latter view is one held by René Guénon, for whom the swastika is the 'sign of the pole'. Since it is widely accepted that the pole and the zenith coincide with the mystic Centre, it follows, then, that the swastika would signify the action of the Origin upon the universe (25). Schneider has suggested a very different meaning: that the swastika is the symbol of the succession of the generations, and that the hooks on the ends of its arms are the ships of life, or, put another way, the different stages of life (51).

Sword The sword is in essence composed of a blade and a guard; it is therefore a symbol of 'conjunction', especially when, in the Middle Ages, it takes on the form of a cross. Among many primitive peoples it was the object of much veneration. The Scythians used to make an annual sacrifice of several horses to the blade of a sword, which they conceived as a god of war. Similarly, the Romans believed that iron, because of its association with Mars, was capable of warding off evil spirits (8). The belief still persists in Scotland (21). Founders of cities, in the ancient *Che-King* tales of China, wear swords (7). As a religious symbol, it is still in use as part of the ceremonial dress of oriental bishops. Its primary symbolic meaning, however, is of a wound and the power to wound, and hence of liberty and strength. Schneider has shown that, in megalithic culture, the sword is the counterpart of the distaff, which is the feminine symbol of the continuity of life. The sword and the distaff symbolize, respectively, death and fertility—the two opposites which constitute the basic symbolism of the mountain (Schneider suggests that in the animal world the equivalents are the phallic fish and the frog) (50). Furthermore, given the cosmic sense of sacrifice (that is, the inversion of the implied realities of the terrestrial and the celestial orders), the sword is then seen as a symbol of physical extermination and psychic decision (60), as well as of the spirit and the word of God, the latter being a particularly common symbol during the Middle Ages (4). In this connexion, Bayley draws attention to the interesting relationship between the English words *sword* and *word*. There can be no doubt that there is a sociological factor in sword-symbolism, since the sword is an instrument proper to the knight, who is the defender of the forces of light against the forces of darkness. But the fact is that in rites at the dawning of history and in folklore even today, the sword plays a similar spiritual rôle, with the magic power to fight off the dark powers personified in the 'malevolent dead', which is why it always figures in apotropaic dances. When it appears in association with fire and flames—which correspond to it in shape and resplendence—it symbolizes purification. Schneider bears this out with his comment that whereas purification goes with fire and the sword, punishment goes with the lash and the club (51). In alchemy, the sword is a symbol for purifying fire. The golden sword—Chrysaor in Greek mythology—is a symbol for supreme spiritualization (15). The Western type of sword, with its straight blade, is, by virtue of its shape, a solar and masculine symbol. The Oriental sword, being curved, is lunar and feminine. Here one must recall the general meaning of weapons, which is the antithesis of the monster. The sword, because of its implication of 'physical extermination', must be a symbol of spiritual evolution, just as the tree is of involution; that is, the tree stands for the development of life within matter and activity. This dualism between the spirit on the one hand and life on the other was resolved by Ludwig Klages, for his part, by opting for life, but Novalis has well expressed the contrary opinion with his observation that 'life is an infirmity of the spirit'. It is a duality which is well illustrated by the opposing characteristics of wood (which is feminine) and metal. If the tree corresponds to the process of proliferation, then the sword represents the inverse. At least Conrad Dinckmut's *Seelen Wurzgarten* (Ulm, 1483), like many other similar works, has a 15th-century illustration of Christ with a branch or a tree on the left side of his face, whereas symmetrically opposite there is a sword. This association of the sword with the tree is of great antiquity: we ourselves have seen a prehistoric Germanic relief depicting two figures, one being feminine and bearing a branch, the other masculine, with a sword. One may also see here an allegory of War and Peace; certainly the mediaeval illustration may allude to the olive branch, but there is nothing of this in the Germanic relief. Evola maintains that the sword is related to Mars, but with additional vertical—and horizontal—symbolisms, alluding, that is, to life and death. It is also linked with steel as a symbol of the transcendent toughness of the all-conquering

325

SYMBOLISM, PHONETIC

spirit. To quote from Emilio Sobejano, *Swords of Spain*, in *Arte Español*, XXI (1956): 'Among the Germanic races, as Livy observed, the sword was at no time very common; on the contrary, it served as a symbol befitting high command and the loftiest rank; one only has to think of the dignity and pomp which characterized the institution of the *Comes Spatharius*, created by the Emperor Gordian the Younger around the year 247. . . . The sword is almost exclusively the prerogative of high dignitaries. There is an Arabic tradition to the effect that it was the Hebrews who invented the sword, and that the place where it was first made—a tragic sign of how the idea first came into the world—was mount Casium, on the outskirts of Damascus, which was to become famous throughout Islam on account of its steel, and where, according to the ancient belief, Cain slew his brother. There, by an accident of fate, settled the first artificers of the newly invented weapon.' The sword of fire bears testimony to the intrinsic relationship between the symbols of the sword, steel (or iron), Mars and fire, all of which have a 'common rhythm'. On the other hand, it emphasizes the heat of the flame and the coldness of the bare metal; hence, the sword of fire is a symbol implying an ambivalent synthesis, like the volcano (*gelat et ardet*), and also a symbol of the weapon which severs Paradise (the realm of the fire of love) from earth (the world of affliction).

Sword, Broken Because the sword symbolizes spiritual aggression or a hero's courage, the broken sword is a symbol of those qualities being in a state of destruction. Nevertheless, like the 'buried sword', it is more likely to appear in mediaeval legends as an inheritance which has to be reconquered by personal valour. Thus, as a youth, Siegfried discovers the pieces of the sword Balmunga, which Odin was said to have given to his father Siegmund. Mime, the blacksmith, was unable to reforge it, but Siegfried succeeds in doing so. In the epic entitled 'Gawain-poems' in the Arthurian cycle (Jean Marx, *Nouvelles Recherches sur la littérature Arthurienne*, Paris, 1965), Gawain is given a broken sword which he is unable to repair completely, symbolizing his inability to penetrate to the 'centre' of his undertaking.

Sybil A figure of antiquity, which reappears in mediaeval literature and iconography, symbolizing the intuiting of higher truths and prophetic powers.

Symbolism, Phonetic When, about 1870, Rimbaud wrote his famous sonnet on the vowels, assimilating each one to a colour, he doubtless yielded to a presentiment rather than to a true intuition and formulated a possibility rather than a certitude: A (black), E (white), I (red), U (green), O (blue). The idea of placing vowels into correspondence with colours is essential to the penetration of the symbolism of phonemes (syllables), but the identifications proposed by Rimbaud do not appear correct to us. Also, as the critics have pointed out, he defines, for example, the U by a line in which the I predominates. But there is another feat in the sonnet in question, and that is its boldness in altering the apparently sacred order of the vowels: A, E, I, O, U.

Anybody who has penetrated the world of symbolism will know that the theory of 'correspondences' is one of its corner-stones. This theory postulates that one phenomenon alone takes place and that its appearances are resonances of the same thing on different planes of reality (sounds, colours, letters, planets in the solar system, mythological gods, prime metals, etc.). In Marius Schneider's books—especially in *El origen musical de los animales-símbolos en la mitología y escultura antiguas*, as the very title indicates—he based his entire symbolic system on sounds. He proposes correspondences which may appear strange, arbitrary and fantastic to one who has not delved deeply into the analyses of this eminent ethnologist, professor at Cologne University and student *in situ* of African symbolic thought. He goes so far as to identify musical intervals with types of landscape (a major fifth = fountain, pool, marsh, etc.). He suggests a symbolism of the vowels which seems correct. In general, he classifies them in two groups: A, O (affirmative vowels) and U, I (negative, dissolvent vowels). The E would seem to occupy an intermediate position. Taking into account the fact that the scales of many systems have seven elements (for example, the directions of space, the days of the week, the planetary gods, the colours, the notes of the diatonic scale, etc.), one must form a group of seven vowels (which, indeed, do exist in many languages) in order to establish exact correspondences. But before indicating what these relationships might be, let us transcribe the definition of the term 'symbolic correspondence' as found in Schneider's work. For him, 'such correspondences are based on the idea of the indissoluble unity of the universe in which each phenomenon has its own particular cosmic position and receives its mystical meaning through the plane which it occupies in the world and through the analogous relationship which it maintains with a specific "corresponding" element, which may be a heavenly body, a colour, a substance, an element of nature, an animal, a part of the human body, an era in human life, etc.' According to Schneider, this symbolist philosophy flourished during the Megalithic period and then spread throughout most of the world, even including Indonesia. It appears that in many languages which do not belong to the same 'family', there are still to be found phonemes which have exactly the same or a similar meaning, and which must be derived from the language–universal concept of both that period and the one immediately preceding it. Gustav Zollinger, in *Tau oder Tau-t-an*, explains this point and makes some interesting connexions. Working from the opposite side, that of the symbolism of letters as signs, Alfred Kallir, in *Sign and Design*, also reaches similar conclusions.

If we arranged a series of seven vowels according to the logic of symbolism, we would have the scale: A, O, OE, E, I, Ü, and U, which corresponds perfectly to the series of colours: Red, orange, yellow, green, blue, indigo and violet; and to the diatonic scale of C minor: C, D, E flat, F, G, A flat, B. The reason why this scale has to be minor and not major is that in this way the distances between the intervals correspond better to the 'distances' separating the colours and the sounds. The meaning of each vowel is easy to find in accordance with the meaning of the corresponding colour and musical sound. From the very start, we may see the perfect correspondence between the warm colours (red, orange and yellow) and the affirmative sounds (A, O, and OE, or AE), while the correspondence of the E, as the intermediate sound between the affirmative and the dissolutive groups, with green, the transitional tone between the warm and cold colours, is unquestionable.

The organization of consonants within a similar system is difficult. Apart from the lucubrations of the Cabbala, and the definitions of the symbolism of letters to be found within it, it is extremely difficult to find other sources from which to derive such a system. But there are a few facts which have been proved as certain: for example, Schneider and other authors of treatises on symbolism point out the opposition between the M and the N (fecundating, maternal waters, and the dissolvent waters of the Nothingness), the contrast between the F and the T (affirmation and sacrifice), and between the B and the Z (body or house and lightning). This last contrast appears in the sixteenth enigma of the Tarot (The Tower Struck by Lightning). Thus, it may be seen that, if one eliminates from the consonants all those which repeat sounds, and arranges them in two scales (each one of them is the middle of the whole series inverted), one meets these correspondences of opposites face to face. Thus the first half is: B, D, F, G, K, L, M, and the second half: N, P, R, S, T, X, Z, each scale consisting of seven consonants, which give the following symbolic oppositions: B–Z, D–X, F–T, G–S, K–R, L–P, and M–N. Provisionally, as the symbolism of the letter as a sign has already been studied (by Kallir and other authors), this knowledge should be applied and then, when one knows the symbolism of one consonant, one knows that of its opposite number (its antithesis). Then, one only has to confirm this symbolism by the sound impression in order to attribute it to the letter as a phoneme. Once the symbolism of the vowels and consonants has been established, they can be placed in relation in order to analyse the meaning of different syllables or words. The consonants to be omitted are the following: W (= U), Y (= I), J (= G), Q (= K) and H.

All this may seem superficial, artificial, or, worse still, useless. But nothing in investigation is useless, and even the most superficial is important in a field which no one has explored in detail as yet. We only wish that this type of linguistic and literary analysis might have the necessary repercussion so that one day we may establish a basis of authentic phonetic symbolism—in which many linguists believe, but without passing judgement on the substance.

Symmetry   This is equivalent to achievement, crowning triumph and supreme equipoise (as in the caduceus, the reliefs of Naksh-i-rustam, and in heraldic shields).

Tarot Pack, The   Present-day psychology has confirmed the conclusions of Eliphas Lévi, Marc Haven and Oswald Wirth that the Tarot cards comprise an image (comparable to that encountered in dreams) of the path of initiation (56). At the same time, Jung's view, coinciding with the secular, intuitive approach to the Tarot enigmas, recognizes the portrayal of two different, but complementary, struggles in the life of man: (*a*) the struggle against others (the solar way) which he pursues through his social position and calling; and (*b*) against himself (the lunar way), involving the process of individuation. These two ways correspond to reflexion and intuition—to practical reason and pure reason. A person of lunar temperament first creates, then studies and verifies what he already knew; the man of solar temperament studies first and then produces. These two approaches also correspond, up to a point, to the concepts of introversion (which is lunar) and extraversion (which is solar)—or to contemplation and action (34). The complete pack of cards, known by the name of *Tarocco*, is made up of 22 major enigmas, with images that together comprise a synthesis and, up to a point, an entity; and 56 minor images, incorporating 14 figures in four series: gold—corresponding to the English 'diamonds'— bearing figures of circles, disks and wheels; clubs (maces and sceptres); swords ('spades') and goblets ('hearts'). The gold suit symbolizes the material forces, the club the power of command, the goblet sacrifice, and the sword, discernment and the meting out of justice. The 22 major cards correspond to the letters of the Hebrew alphabet. Included in each of the suits of the minor cards are the King, the Dame (Queen), the Knight (Horse) and the Knave (Jack) (48). These suits have been equated with the powers that reign on earth and, in consequence, with the controlling or higher professions, as follows: government with clubs; the military career with spades (swords); the priesthood with goblets; intellectual activity with gold —for all forms of treasure are always symbolic of the riches of the spirit and the mind (54). According to Saunier, the images of the major enigmas derive from the symbolic paintings in the Egyptian Books of Thoth-Hermes, representing the knowledge of the universe (49). However, Oswald Wirth, whose interpretations of the symbolism of the Tarot we shall, in the main, follow, points out that archaeology has never unearthed the least trace of anything that might conceivably be an Egyptian, Arabic or Graeco-Arabic Tarot pack. But he indicates that the Cabala must have been well known to the authors of the Tarot, because they fixed the number of major enigmas at 22, which is the same as the number of letters in the Hebrew alphabet, every one of them pregnant with symbolism, and the same, also, as the number of the *teraphim*, the hieroglyphs used by the Hebrews in divination. Wirth, arguing from the fact that Italy was undeniably the first country to develop playing-cards, maintains that these allegorical images grew up in that country. The earliest representation known to us of the major enigmas dates from 1392. To quote Eliphas Lévi: 'The Tarot is a monumental and singular work, simple and strong as the architecture of the pyramids, and, in consequence, as durable; it is a book which is the sum of all the sciences and whose infinite permutations are capable of solving all problems; a book which informs by making one think; it is perhaps the greatest masterpiece of the human mind, and certainly one of the most beautiful things handed down by Antiquity.' The 22 mysteries are: I, The Minstrel; II, The Archpriestess; III, The Empress; IV, The Emperor; V, The Archpriest; VI, The Lover; VII, The Chariot; VIII, Justice; IX, The Hermit; X, The Wheel of Fortune; XI, Strength; XII, The Hanged Man; XIII, Death; XIV, Temperance; XV, The Devil; XVI, The Tower Struck by Lightning; XVII, The Stars; XVIII, The Moon; XIX, The Sun; XX, The Judgement; XXI, The World; XXII or 0, The Fool. The cards from I to XI comprise the solar way—active, conscious, reflective and autonomous. Cards XII to XXII denote the lunar way—passive, unconscious, intuitive and 'possessed'. We cannot here explain the relationships which can be drawn, or the patterns of meanings which can be derived from these relationships, without going beyond the bounds of strict symbolism; an examination of the particular meaning of each card will be found under its appropriate heading. Nevertheless, we will quote the broadest meanings of these 22 enigmas suggested by Eliphas Lévi: I signifies The Being, the spirit, creation; II, sanctuary, the law, knowledge, woman, the mother, the church; III, the Word, fecundity, generation in all three worlds; IV, the door, initiation, power, the cubic stone or its base; V, information, proof, philosophy and religion; VI, enmeshment, union, antagonism, equilibrium, combination; VII, the weapon, the sword, triumph and majesty; VIII, the scales, attraction and repulsion, the path or way, promise and threat; IX, good, morality, wisdom; X, manifestation, fecundity, the paternal sceptre; XI, the hand in the act of taking and sustaining; XII, an example, teaching, a public lesson; XIII, domination and strength, rebirth, creation and destruction; XIV, the seasons, the flux and flow of life, always different yet always the same; XV, magic, eloquence, commerce, mystery; XVI, sudden subversion, weakness; XVII, effusion of thought, the moral influence of the idea upon forms, immortality; XVIII, the Elements, the visible world, reflected light, material forms, symbolism; XIX, the head, the summit, the prince of heaven; XX, vegetation, the generative virtues of the soil; XXI, the senses, the vehicle, the body, transitory life; XXII, the microcosm, the sum of All-in-All. Each of these images comprises a fusion of certain ideas relative to the outer and inner worlds, disposed according to the forms and patterns of the mind. The intention is to create, by means of these images, an order more comprehensive even than that comprising the twelve divisions of the Zodiac, and to design a wheel which would embody all the archetypal potentialities of the existence and evolution of mankind.

Our aim has been simply to sketch in an idea of how the Tarot pack functions as a symbolic instrument. In order to grasp the full range of its significance, it is necessary to study not only the basic commentaries written upon it but also the cards themselves, observing all the combinations and implications—a field so vast as to constitute a special branch of symbolism as wide-ranging as that of dreams.

Tattooing Tattooing and ornamentation may be regarded as falling within one generic symbolic group, for both are expressions of cosmic activity. But since tattoos are applied to the body, other important meanings accrue to it—sacrifice, the mystical and magical. E. Gobert, in *Notes sur les tatouages des indigènes Tunisiens*, suggests that tattooing is connected with the Arabic proverb 'blood has flowed, the danger has passed'. Since sacrifice has the power to store up latent forces which later may be made use of, each sacrifice tends to invert a given situation. A mystic purpose lies at the root of the mark or sign of identification: he who brands himself seeks to display his allegiance to that which is signified by the mark. (Lovers' marks carved on tree-trunks, and initials and heart-shapes pricked out on the skin, are clear illustrations of this.) In the last analysis, the attitude of allegiance is reversed: the sign is expected to 'reciprocate' this display of sacrifice and subservience on the part of the individual who has so marked himself; and this is the magic property of the tattoo as a defensive talisman. Apart from these three meanings of the tattoo, ethnologists have noted two others: it may serve as a sign designating sex, tribe and social status (*v.* Robert Lowie's *Cultural Anthropology*), in which case it is simply a profane version of the mystic symbolism; and, also, as a personal adornment. This latter purpose seems to us over-simplified, but we cannot go into the matter here. In particular, tattooing is a 'rite of entry' or of initiation which alludes to the turning-points in the span of a man's life and in the development of his personality. Cola has pointed out that some of the most ancient monuments of pre-history, in particular those of Egypt, suggest that tattooing was practised in ancient times, for the priestess of the goddess Hathor displayed three lines on her lower belly. He also enumerates the principal techniques of tattooing: incision, stitching, wounding by cutting or burning, and pseudo-tattoos or paintings on the face or body (in which case the motives are the same although the effect is transitory). Among primitive races, the principal forms of tattoos are as follows: stripes, dots, combinations of both, or numbers expressed through either, chains, knots and rosettes, crosses, stars, triangles, rhombs, circles, combinations of any two or more of these, and also, highly stylized anthropomorphic figures either complete or fragmentary (just the limbs), etc. Cola also notes that tattoos have been used in imitative magic. For instance: the tattooed figure of a scorpion is credited with the power of warding off the actual scorpion's sting; and the image of a bull is a guarantee of numerous progeny (12).

Zodiacal sign of Taurus.

Taurus The second sign of the Zodiac expresses the evolutionary force of Aries—that is, the spring-time pugnacity of the ram—in an intensified form. It also denotes the functions of fecundation and creation in both aspects, victorious and sacrificial—related, that is, to the primordial sacrifice; an example of this is the myth of Mithras, 'for out of his body grow all the plants and herbs that adorn the earth with verdure, and from his seed spring all the animal species' (Cumont, *Les Mystères de Mithra*). This basic idea of the bull as the force which animates forms of all kinds is deeply rooted in a great many myths. At the same time, the fact that the sign of Taurus corresponds to the number two relates it to the principle of duality composed of the masculine (*Viraj*, or *Yang*) and the feminine (*Vac*, or *Yin*). There is also a morphological relationship between the bull, on account of its head and horns, and the waxing and waning aspects of the moon, which is further evidence of the bull's symbolic function of invigoration, at least in the sublunary sphere. The sign of Taurus governs the throat and voice, and is in turn dominated by Venus (40).

Teeth According to Allendy, teeth are the primigenial weapons of attack, and an expression of activity. Loss of one's teeth, then, signifies fear of castration or of complete failure in life, or inhibition (56); it represents an attitude which is the inversion of that of the Primitive, who, according to the findings of anthropology, commonly adorned himself with the teeth and claws of conquered animals. Some interpretations underline the significance of teeth in respect of the sexual aspect of energy. But of greater importance is the Gnostic concept—for which we are indebted to Leisegang's *Die Gnosis*—in which the teeth constitute the battlements, the wall and the fortifications of the inner man, from the material or energetic point of view, just as the eyes and the glance are the defence of the spirit. This explains the negative symbolism of the loss or fracture of the teeth.

Temperance The fourteenth enigma of the Tarot pack, this card contains the image of a winged being, clad in a red tunic and a cloak with a lining of greenish-blue, who is pouring water out of a silver vessel into a golden one. In itself, this hermaphroditic—or gynandrous—figure has a favourable significance, since it is expressive of the *coniunctio oppositorum*. The act of pouring denotes the transformation of water as it passes from the lunar order (of silver) to the solar order (of gold), that is, from the world of transient forms and of feeling to the world of fixed forms and of reason; the water here is that of the 'Upper Ocean'—or vital fluid. This enigma suggests universal life, and ceaseless circulation through formation, regeneration and purification (59).

Temple The word 'temple' derives from the root *tem*—'to divide'. Etruscan soothsayers made a division of the heavens by means of two straight lines intersecting at a point directly above the head, the point of intersection being a projection of the notion of the 'Centre', and the lines representing the two 'directions' of the plane; the north-south line was called *cardo* and the east-west *decumanus*. Phenomena were interpreted according to their situation within this division of space. Hence, the earthly temple is seen as an image of the celestial temple and its basic structure is determined by considerations of order and orientation (7). The temple affords a particular and additional meaning to the generic symbolism of architectonic structures. Broadly speaking, it is the mystic significance of the 'Centre' which prevails; the temple and, in particular, the altar, being identified with the symbol of the mountain-top as the focal point of the intersection of the two worlds of heaven and earth. Solomon's temple, according to Philo and Flavius Josephus, was a figurative representation of the cosmos, and its interior was disposed accordingly: the incense table signified thanksgiving; the seven-branched candelabra stood for the seven planetary heavens; the holy table represented the terrestrial order. In addition to this, the twelve loaves of bread corresponded to the twelve months of the year. The Ark of the Covenant symbolizes the intelligibles (14). Romanesque, Gothic and Renaissance architects, each in their own way, sought to imitate this superior archetype. For example, between 1596 and 1604, imaginary reconstructions of the Temple of Solomon appeared in various works published in Rome and based upon holy writ, and the illustrations they contained deeply influenced the architects of the period. Another fundamental significance of the temple derives from its being a synthesis of the various symbols for the world-axis, such as the hollow mountain, steps and the sacrificial mountain-peak mentioned above. In certain astrobiological cultures the temple or altar is in fact built upon an artificial mountain—the *teocalli* of Mexico is an example. A more advanced concept can be seen in the architectural portrayal of those essential elements of the inner pattern of the universe founded upon the numbers three, seven, ten and twelve in particular. Seven is basic to the representation of the planets and their derived symbolisms, and hence the Mesopotamian temple-mountains—or *ziggurats*—were constructed after the fashion of a seven-terraced pyramid. Each of the terraces was dedicate to a particular planet. The Babylonian *ziggurat* known as *Etemenanki* ('the house of the seven directions of heaven and earth') was built of crude bricks overlaid with others that had been fired. A tablet in the Louvre records that in plan it measured 2,200 feet long by 1,200 wide. The first level was black in colour and dedicated to Saturn, the second orange-coloured and sacred to Jupiter, the third red and consecrated to Mars, the fourth golden and sacred to the Sun, the fifth yellow (to Venus), the sixth blue (to Mercury), the seventh silver (to the Moon) (39). This order is not always observed, for sometimes the Moon is situated in the sixth heaven and the Sun in the seventh (17). Berthelot, however, suggests that the *ziggurat* not only embraces the mystic aspects of the Mountain and the Centre (by virtue of its mass and situation) and of Steps (because of its shape), but also constitutes an image of paradise, since vegetation appears to flourish on its terraces (7). The origins of this type of structure are Sumerian (7), and examples are to be found in Egypt, India, China and pre-Columbian America. Eliade, in confirming this, adds that the climb to the top of the Mesopotamian or of the Hindu temple-mountain was equivalent to an ecstatic journey to the 'Centre' of

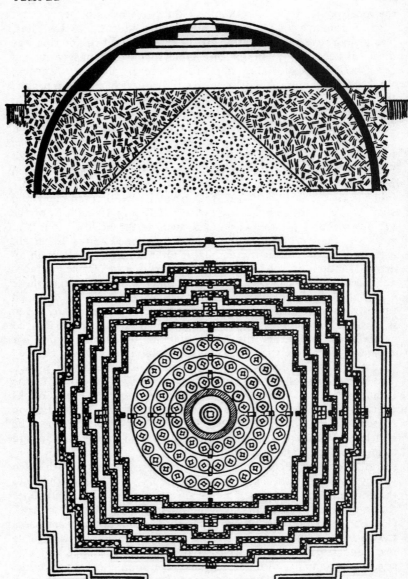

Borobudur temple.
Elevation and ground-plan, illustrating the mandala pattern.

the world; once the traveller has reached the topmost terrace, he breaks free from the laws of level, transcends profane space and enters a region of purity (18). It is hardly necessary to observe that climbing mountains implies ultimately the same mystic tendency, as can be seen in the fact that mountain heights are the chosen abode of the recluse. And the favourable symbolic significance of the goat derives solely from his predilection for heights. Another important example of the temple-mountain, a product of Hindu culture, comes from Indo-China—the temple of Borobudur built in the centre of the island of Java in the 8th century of our era. Basically it consists of four levels of square-shaped galleries, with four more circular platforms on top surmounted by an enclosed belvedere. In form, then, it is similar to the Egyptian *ziggurat*, or, in the Khmer language, a *Phnom*, signifying a temple-mountain comparable with Meru, the Hindu Olympus. Four flights of steps up the centre of each pyramid face lead directly from the base to the top. It would appear that the profoundest meaning attached to this temple is of a supernatural character. Its name—Borobudur—signifies 'the seat of secret revelation'. All graduated edifices such as steps concern the symbolism of discontinuous spiritual evolution, that is, the separate but progressive stages of evolution (6). At the same time, the ground-plan of the Borobudur temple is diagrammatically a true *yantra*, and its various square and round-shaped levels constitute a mandala related to the symbolism of 'squaring the circle' (6). The symbolic structure of the Greek temple is fundamentally the same as that of the lake-dwelling: that is, it symbolizes the intercommunication between the Three Worlds—the Lower (represented by the water and the piles on the one hand and earth and the subterranean part on the other), the Terrestrial (the base and columns) and the Upper (suggested by the pediment). Christian cathedrals are related less to the macrocosm than to the microcosm, the human figure being depicted in terms of the apse (representing the head), the cross and transepts (the arms), the nave and side aisles (the body) and the altar (the heart). In the Gothic temple, the upward sweep, the vital rôle of the vertical axis—and indeed the structure as a whole—embrace the idea of the temple-mountain with its implied synthesis of the symbolism of both macrocosm and microcosm. According to Schneider, the two towers usually placed at the western face correspond to the twin-peaked 'mountain of Mars' in primitive megalithic cultures (and linked with the Gemini myth), while the cimborrio over the transept is expressive of a higher synthesis, an image of heaven. Both the synthesis and the crux of the matter are established by Gershom G. Scholem, in *Les Origines de la Kabbale* (Paris, 1966). He recalls that God lives in his reason or that God is the absolute Reason and logos of the world, and that the temple 'is the house' or abode of God, and thus identifies *temple* with *reason*.

Tent In the Egyptian system of hieroglyphs this is a determinative sign relating to that division of the soul which is known as 'body of glory' and which surrounds the spirit like a tent (19). Deriving from this hieroglyph is the broad symbolic meaning of the tent as something which 'envelops'. In our view, this symbolism is closely connected with the symbolisms of weaving and of clothes. For the Greeks, the physical world—and space itself—were 'the vestments of the gods', or, in other words, comparable with the tent as something which envelops and hides them from sight. To tear aside the temple-veil, or to rend one's garments, represents a desperate attempt to achieve, by force of analogy, the tearing aside of the veil that enshrouds the mystery of the other world. Berthelot suggests two other symbolic meanings of the tent: one related to its function as a nomadic dwelling, and the other arising from the mystic significance of the desert (7).

Ternary The ternary system is created by the emergence of a third (latent) element which so modifies the binary situation as to impart to it a dynamic equilibrium. As Jung has observed, Plotinus with his characteristic combination of philosophical precision and poetic allusiveness compared Oneness (the creative principle) with light, intellect with the sun, and the world-soul with the moon. Unity is split internally into three 'moments'—the active, the passive and the union or outcome of these two (31). Undoubtedly, the vital, human significance of the number three and the ternary embraces the multi-secular origins of biological evolution. The existence of two (father and mother) must almost inevitably be followed by three (the son) (42). As Lao-Tse says: 'One engenders two, two engenders three, three engenders all things' (58). Hence three has the power to resolve the conflict posed by dualism; it is also the harmonic resolution of the impact of unity upon duality. It symbolizes the creation of spirit out of matter, of the active out of the passive (55). Besides the triangle, there are a number of symbols relevant to the ternary, since, in a sense, it may be said to be the 'inner structure of unity'. Hence, many infernal beings that are base counterparts of the ternary are three-headed like Cerberus or Hecate, or else wield three-pronged weapons such as the trident. The notion of the 'three suns'—the East, the zenith and the West—is related to this symbolism and, according to Dontenville, the form of the tripod is derived from it. If the number four has been found the most fitting 'model' to symbolize exterior or situational quantitative values, three has proved itself the number attached to the interior or vertical order of things. Hence, disposed in accordance with the essential points pertaining to the symbolism of level—the high, the middle and the low—it comes to be related to the 'Three Worlds' (the celestial, terrestrial and infernal), in turn closely connected with the three-part division of man into spirit (the impalpable or the mind), the soul (sentiments) and body (the instincts), and with the moral categories of the good, the indifferent and the bad. There are some writers who analyse the ternary structure of man in terms of intuition (or moral light), thought (intellectual light) and instinct (animal light) (54). Also corresponding to this division, modified by the influence of a particular ruling force, are the well-known stages of mystic perfection: the unitive, illuminative and purgative; in alchemy these stages are symbolized by the colours red, white and black. In Hindu thought the three levels are termed *sattva* (the highest state or that of the predominance of the spirit), *rajas* (the intermediate, dynamic and transforming state) and *tamas* (the instinctive or inferior state). Eliade suggests that the image of the three levels as three cosmic divisions carved out by moral precepts and diffused by human thought is very ancient, for it is present among the pigmies of the Semang tribe in Malaya and among other races at the very earliest stage of cultural development (18). In Ireland this idea is symbolized by a three-storied tower (4). For Diel, the essential functions of man are three in number: conservation, reproduction and spiritualization, and the deformation or perversion of these three functions is represented by the three traditional 'enemies' of the soul—the world, the flesh and the devil, in turn representing the inversion of the three theological Virtues. Guénon, dealing with the 'three worlds' described by Dante in the *Commedia*, suggests the following interesting ternary correspondences: *Sattva*, *rajas* and *tamas* related respectively to the sky, the atmosphere and the earth's surface or interior; to the future, the present and the past; and to the superconscious, the conscious and the unconscious (27).

Tetrachord According to Schneider, the tetrachord *do*, *re*, *mi*, *fa* may be regarded in the mystic sense as the mediator between heaven and earth; while the tetrachord *sol*, *la*, *ti*, *do* could be taken to represent the divine order. The common note—*do*—relates the symbol to the eagle (of the tetramorphs) (50).

Tetramorphs This is an illustration of the quaternary principle, linked with the concept of situation (just as the ternary is connected with that of activity) and with the intuitive sense of spatial order. It is to the Christian etramorphs, with their synthesis of the four symbols of the Evangelists, that we are bound to look for the purest and truest expression of this ancient and universal idea. Megalithic culture, possibly reflecting some obscure tradition of remote antiquity, was given to expressing the struggle of the gods against the monsters that, from the beginnings of creation, sought to devour the sun. When they formed the cosmos out of chaos, the gods, in order to safeguard what they had created, placed the lion on the celestial mountain and posted four archers (at the Cardinal Points) to ensure that none might disrupt the cosmic order (50). This proves that the four Cardinal Points, besides representing the extremities of the four horizontal Directions of Space (which, since they pertain to the earth as the zone of manifestation, denote the superficial and the tangible, whereas the nadir and the zenith relate to heaven), may also denote autonomous, spatial zones, as worlds in themselves. This idea is expressed in graphic symbolism by those forms of crosses whose four limbs are rounded (to imply circular motion) or hammer-headed. These personified, autonomous zones may take on a beneficent or a malign character. As a defence against the latter influence stand the four archers already mentioned. In the tetramorphs, the beneficent aspects of the spatial 'order' are all equidistant from the 'Centre'. Schneider relates the animals of the tetramorph to the notes of the tetrachord. The relatively common habit of dividing a country into four provinces implies the same basic idea. Ireland used to be called the 'Island of the Four Kings', these Kings corresponding to four regions, with a fifth in the centre where the High King reigned, like the Pantokrator among the four symbols. This analogy vividly expresses the strength and cohesion of a spatial order derived intuitively, according to Jung, from spiritual and psychological principles and modelled either upon three or upon four depending upon whether those principles pertain to the notions of activity and inner structure or to passivity and situation. This pattern is completed by the number five: four plus the central point, sometimes denoted by a circle or almond-shaped mandorla; or else by the number seven: four outside and three inside. This scheme finds expression in a great many monuments designed upon the basis of a square, walled-in space with three towers in the centre—the Escorial, for instance. Before coming back to the Christian tetramorphs, let us consider some comments of Schneider about the quaternary order in China: 'In the *Ta-tai-li*, the philosopher Tsêng-tse distinguished, as was the custom, four animals destined for the service of a saint; two of these animals (those covered with hair and feathers) proceed from *Yin* (the feminine and passive principle) and two others are depicted bearing a hide, a cuirass or scales.' In this way they clearly reflect the four Elements (with the 'Centre' corresponding to the quintessence, or the spirit) —air, fire, water and earth. Another four-part grouping of animals is to be found in Sumerian art, composed of a lion, an eagle and a peacock mounted on the back of an ox. *The Book of the Dead*, on the other hand, mentions a group of three beings with the heads of animals and a fourth being with a long-eared human head (like the heads in some Romanesque paintings). Likewise, Ezekiel's vision contains the lion, the eagle, the ox and man. Oriental iconography must have had a great influence upon Ezekiel's vision—and Egyptian images must have been specially influential. The four mystic beings in Christian tradition are usually the lion, the eagle, the ox and the (winged) man. A 4th-century mosaic in the apse of Santa Pudenziana in Rome groups them in pairs on either side of the crucifix. Biblical illustrations do not always follow the order laid down in the holy writ. St. Jerome suggested the following correspondences: the lion corresponding to resurrection, the eagle to ascension, the man to incarnation, the ox to passion. By comparing the four-part grouping of ancient Mesopotamia (of the lion, the eagle, the ox and the peacock) with that of Ezekiel (the lion, eagle, ox and man), we arrive at the equation peacock=Man' (50). According to Chochod, the equivalent Chinese animals afford the following correspondences: the dragon corresponding to the lion, the unicorn to the bull, the turtle to Man, the phoenix to the eagle (13). The spatial arrangement set out in Ezekiel (i, 10) is: the lion on the right with the man above him, the ox on the left and, above him, the eagle (50). Applying the principles of spatial symbolism, whereby, psychologically speaking, the superior is always a sublimation of the inferior, and the right side invariably appertains to the consciousness while the left side concerns the unconscious, we arrive at the conclusion that the winged man is the sublimation of the lion and the eagle of the ox. In esoteric thought the four beings can be interpreted symbologically as follows: the eagle is air, intelligence and action; the lion is fire, strength and movement; the ox is earth, labour, forbearance and sacrifice; and the winged man is an angel symbolizing the intuitive knowledge of truth. According to Lévi, certain 'disciples of Socrates' substituted the cock for the eagle; the horse for the lion; the sheep for the ox (the latter substitution being explained by the proximity of the two zodiacal signs of Aries and Taurus, while that of the cock for the eagle would follow from the aerial character of both animals) (37, 59). Correspondences such as these, we repeat, are not identical relationships but analogies— that is, close affinities, or relationships between component elements of separate 'series', resulting from their analogous situation within the series. Consequently, all the various meanings attributed to the tetramorphs help to suggest the range of their allusions, as well as the complex mechanism governing the pattern of their properties. In Christian symbolism, the symbolic associations of the four Evangelists (as the archers defending truth and the order of Christ —the 'Centre') are: Matthew, the winged man; Mark, the lion; Luke, the ox; John, the eagle (49) (Plate XXVIII).

Texture   The symbolism of texture has received scant attention nor has it even been recognized as a problem. But certain trends of contemporary art indicate that the material quality of a work of art, or the relationship between the apparent surface—space—and the surface proper—the inter-relationship of points in space—is once again being accorded that recognition it formerly enjoyed in ornamental and even in figurative art. We may see in texture two essential component elements: one that produces a pattern of lateral concurrences and one which, so to speak, thrusts upwards. The first—the lateral—factor gives rise to features which are sometimes pre-formal—nascent, symbolic forms only to be glimpsed after careful study, related to the paradoxical 'informal forms' (symbolic blots, klexographies, paper-transfers, and so on), to the so-called 'buried symbolism' of some works of art—which has been seen as a kind of infra-configuration produced by the play of light and shade, by the brush-strokes or by the background patterns— and associated also with the symbolism of composition in so far as this creates an effect of perspective. But texture proper is determined by the quality and thickness of the impasto, of the material, and by the structure of this material as it is understood in mineralogy, producing textures which are caked or fibrillar or pearlitic or porous or cellular, and so on. Broadly speaking, textures may be divided into the hard and smooth and the soft and porous. Since the impression of smoothness (or continuity) is increased in proportion to the distance from which it is viewed, all smooth textures may be regarded as symbolic of remoteness and, by analogy, of cold colours. Conversely, porous textures symbolize nearness and warm colours, expressing a greater degree of inner dynamism in the material and in the corresponding tactile sensation. More detailed conclusions than the above could be educed only after a closer study of the problem of texture.

Theatre An image of the world of phenomena, for both the theatre and the world are 'stages'. Guénon has noted that the theatre is not limited to representing the terrestrial world alone: in the Middle Ages it stood for both this world and the next. The author symbolizes the demiurge; the actors stand in relation to their parts as the Jungian *Selbst* stands to the personality (29).

Theogony According to Diel, the successive reigns of Uranus, Saturn and Jupiter express the progressive stages of the mind, equivalent to unconscious, conscious and superconscious (15). Primeval Neptune, as the ancient Uranian god (associated with the Upper Waters), also symbolized the unconscious, like all aged kings and like the sea-king himself, standing, that is, both for the historical aspect of the unconscious—man's ancestral memory—and for its cosmic aspect, or the latent seeds of thought which did not burgeon until the reign of Saturn (signifying time and, consequently, man as an existential being). By superconsciousness is meant intuition of the supernatural and recognition of the celestial sphere.

Thighs In the Egyptian system of hieroglyphs they express strength (19), a significance which corresponds exactly to their function as the dynamic support of the body. This symbolism was preserved by the Cabala, laying special emphasis upon the firmness and majesty of the thighs.

Thirst Symbolized by the dragon, and denoting the blind appetite for life, according to Evola.

Thorn The thorn of the acacia, in particular, was regarded by the Egyptians as an emblem of the mother-goddess Neith. It is also related to the world-axis, and therefore to the cross (4). The thorn on the rose-bush helps to emphasize the counterpoise or 'conjunction' between thesis and antithesis, that is, between the ideas of existence and non-existence, ecstasy and anguish, pleasure and pain; this again is related to the symbolism of the cross. The crown of thorns adds to the basic symbolism of the thorn the evil characteristics of all things multiple and also the cosmic symbolism of the circle (by virtue of the shape of the crown).

Thread According to the Zohar, thread is one of the most ancient of symbols (like hair). It denotes the essential connexion between any of the different planes—the spiritual, the biological, social, etc. (38).

Threshold A symbol of transition and transcendence. In architectural symbolism, the threshold is always given a special significance by the elaboration and enrichment of its structure by means of porches, perrons, porticoes, triumphal arches, battlements, etc., or by symbolic ornamentation of the kind which, in the West, finds its finest expression in the Christian cathedral with its sculpted mullions, jambs, archivolts, lintels and tympana. Hence the function of the threshold is clearly to symbolize both the reconciliation and the separation of the two worlds of the profane and the sacred. In the East, the function of protecting and warning is effected by the 'keepers of the threshold'—dragons and effigies of gods or spirits. The Roman god Janus also denoted this dualism characteristic of the threshold, which can be related analogically to all other forms of duality (6). Hence the tendency to speak of the threshold between waking and sleeping.

Throne In Asiatic symbolism, the throne stands midway between the mountain and palace on the one hand and the head-dress on the other, for they are all rhythmic variants of one and the same morphological family that symbolize—or, rather, allude to—the 'Centre'. They are also signs expressive of synthesis, stability and unity (37). In the Egyptian system of hieroglyphs, the throne is a determinative sign embracing the concepts of support, exaltation, equilibrium and security (19).

Thule This mythic realm derives its name from *Tula*—or the

'Peerless Land'—which Guénon considers more ancient than *Paradêsha*. It is found in many languages from Russia to Central America. In Sanskrit, *Tulâ* signifies 'scales' and is related to the zodiacal sign of Libra. But there is an ancient Chinese tradition which suggests that the antique 'scales' were related to the Great Bear. This would seem to point to the conclusion that Thule is identical with the polar region, that is, with the 'Centre' *par excellence*. Thule has also been called the 'white island'—identical with the 'white mountain'—or the symbol for the world, as well as with the Blessed Islands of Western tradition. Guénon has also mentioned that whiteness, in relation to topographical features, is always an allusion to these paradisiac isles which man has lost and to which he returns again and again in his legends and folktales. Guénon adds that Latin *albus* (white) corresponds to the Hebrew *Lebanah*, signifying the moon, and points to the examples of Albania, Albion and Alba Longa as places signifying 'whiteness'. The equation of island with mountain is explained by him by the fact that both express ideas of stability, superiority and of refuge from prevailing mediocrity. The island, rising unscathed in the midst of the swirling ocean (representing the outer world—the 'sea of the passions'), corresponds to the biological symbol of the mountain, as the 'mount of salvation' which towers above the transient 'stream of forms' (28).

Thunderbolt The thunderbolt (or lightning) is celestial fire as an active force, terrible and dynamic. The thunderbolt of Parabrahman, the fire-ether of the Greeks, is a symbol of the supreme, creative power. Jupiter possesses this attribute by way of emphasizing his demiurgic nature. At the same time, the flash of lightning is related to dawn and illumination. Because of these parallels, lightning is connected with the first sign of the Zodiac, symbolic of the spring-principle and of the initial stage of every cycle (40). The thunderbolt is held to be an emblem of sovereignty. The winged thunderbolt expresses the ideas of power and speed (8). Jupiter's three thunderbolts symbolize chance, destiny and providence—the forces that mould the future (8). In the majority of religions we find that the godhead is hidden from man's gaze, and then suddenly the lightning-flash reveals him momentarily in all his active might. This image of the Logos piercing the darkness is universal (9). The *vajra*, the Tibetan symbol for both 'thunderbolt' and 'diamond', is also connected with the world-axis (22); but, if the cross or crucifix, the steps and the sacrificial stake, are all symbols of man's longing for the higher world, the thunderbolt expresses the inverse: the action of the higher upon the lower, It is also related to the glance from the third eye of Shiva (or Siva), the destroyer of all material forms.

Tiger Two interpretations of the tiger have been offered which are easily reconciled: 'It is associated with Dionysos, and is a symbol of wrath and cruelty' (8); 'In China, it is symbolic of darkness and of the new moon' (17). For darkness is always identical with the darkness of the soul, and corresponds to that state which the Hindus term *tamas* and which falls within the general symbolism of level, and also denotes the unbridled expression of the base powers of the instincts. Now, in China the tiger seems to play a rôle comparable with that of the lion in African and Western cultures: both animals —like the dragon—take on two different characters—as the wild beast and as the tamed animal. This is what lies behind the tiger as an allegorical expression of strength and valour in the service of righteousness. Five mythic tigers together constitute a symbol which is invested with the same meaning as the tetramorphs in Christian tradition, in so far as they are the defenders of the spatial order against the forces of chaos. The Red Tiger reigns in the south, his season being summer and his Element fire; the Black Tiger reigns in the north—winter is his season, and his Element water; the Blue Tiger reigns in the East, in the spring and amidst vegetation; the White Tiger predominates in the west, in autumn and among the metals; and, finally, the Yellow Tiger (solar in colour) inhabits the earth and reigns supreme over all the other tigers. This Yellow Tiger is located in the 'Centre', as the Emperor was situated in the heart of China and as China lies at the centre of the world (13). This quaternary division plus the centre as the fifth Element is, as Jung has shown, of archetypal significance in the symbolism of situation. When the tiger appears in association with other animals, his symbolic significance varies according to the relative status of the animals within the hierarchy: for instance, the tiger struggling with a reptile stands for the superior principle, but the converse applies if it is locked in combat with a lion or a winged being.

Time Berthelot has noted that the time-pattern usually follows from the division of space, and this applies most particularly to the week (7). It was indeed the awareness of the seven Directions of Space (that is, two for each of the three dimensions plus the centre) that gave rise to the projection of the septenary order into time. Sunday—the Day of Rest—corresponds to the centre and, since all centres are linked with the 'Centre' or the Divine Source, it is therefore sacred in character. The idea of rest is expressive of the notion of the immobility of the 'Centre', whereas the other six Directions are dynamic in character. At the same time, the 'Centre' of space and time also retains a spiritual significance. As Elkin has said, 'It must not be thought that the mythic era is now past: it is also the present and the future, as much a state as a period.' Corresponding, in the strictest sense, to this zone within the circle, the 'Centre', is spacelessness and timelessness, or the non-formal, or, in short, the 'mystic nothingness' which, in oriental thought, is the hole in the Chinese disk of jade called *Pi*, representing heaven. As Eliade notes, *in illo tempore* everything was possible—species and forms were not fixed but 'fluid'. He goes on to point out that a return to this state implies the cessation of time (17). The idea that time—the week—derives from the space-pattern ought strictly to be discarded in favour of the notion that both time and space are the outcome of one and the same principle.

Titans They signify the wild and untamable forces of primeval Nature (15). The astrobiological and mythic mind—rightly—found it impossible to accept the idea that there was no intermediate stage between the state of chaos and the creation of a cosmic order by man-the-conqueror-of-darkness. Antediluvian monsters and pre-Cromagnon Man were intuited as fabulous animals, Titans, giants and Cyclops, who struggled initially with the gods, and eventually suffered defeat at the hands of the hero—the representative of the 'true man', *not, that is, of the 'mass man' but of the individual who stands out as the mark of the progressive evolution of the species and of the spirit.* In the psychology of the individual this myth still persists in the shape of monsters and of certain other base beings that allude to the 'shadows'—the 'dark' or inferior side. The beginning of Calderón's play *Life is a Dream* is symbolic in this way: the cave stands for the unconscious; the imprisoned Cyprian lamenting his loss of liberty represents the 'dark side' of the dramatist—his baser part—mastered and rendered powerless by the sound judgement and will-power of his 'conscious side' schooled in intellectual and moral disciplines.

Toad The inverse and infernal aspect of the frog-symbol; that is to say, the symbolic significance is the same though in a negative sense. Or, as the traditional language of esoteric thought puts it: 'There are also certain animals whose mission it is to break up the astral light by a process of absorption peculiar to them. There is something fascinating about their gaze: they are the toad and the basilisk.'

Tomb Symbolic of the body as matter (57), of transformation and of the unconscious (56). It is also sometimes a maternal and feminine symbol of a generic kind.

Torch Identified with the sun (14), it is the symbol of purification through illumination. It was the weapon wielded by Hercules against the hydra of Lerna; its fire cauterizes wounds. It occurs in many allegories as the emblem of truth (15).

Tower In the Egyptian system of hieroglyphs, the tower is a determinative sign denoting height or the act of rising above the common level in life or society (19). Basically, then, the tower is symbolic of ascent. During the Middle Ages, towers and belfries held the significance of watch-towers, but also, by the simple application of the symbolism of level (whereby material height implies spiritual elevation), they expressed the same symbolism as the ladder— linking earth and heaven. The tower-symbol, given that it is enclosed and walled-in, is emblematic of the Virgin Mary, as can be seen in a great many allegorical designs and litanies (14). Since the idea of elevation or ascent, implicit in the tower, connotes transformation and evolution, the athanor (the alchemists' furnace) was given the shape of a tower to signify inversely that the metamorphosis of matter implied a process of ascension. Another symbol usually mentioned in this connexion is the bronze tower in which Danae, the mother of Perseus, was imprisoned (48). Finally we would point to the analogy between the tower and man: for just as the tree is closer to the human figure than are the horizontal forms of animals, so, too, is the tower the only structural form distinguished by verticality: windows at the topmost level, almost always large in size, correspond to the eyes and the mind of man. It is in this sense that the Tower of Babel acquired special symbolic point as a wild enterprise bringing disaster and mental disorder (31). And, for the same reason, the sixteenth enigma of the Tarot denotes catastrophe by the image of a tower struck by lightning. However, it is possible to discover a dual tendency in the symbolism of the tower. Its upward impulse may be accompanied by a deepening movement; the greater the height, the deeper the foundations. Nietzsche talked of descent during ascent. Nerval (in *Aurélia*, to be precise) refers to the symbolism of the tower and says: 'I found myself in a tower, whose foundations were sunk so deep into the earth and whose top was so lofty, reaching up like a spire into the sky, that my whole existence already seemed bound to be consumed in climbing up and down it.'

Tower Struck by Lightning The sixteenth enigma of the Tarot pack, this card is an allegory showing a tower half-destroyed by a flash of lightning which strikes the top (symbolically equivalent to the head). This tower should be identified with the first of the two columns known as Jachin and Boaz, that is, as a symbol of individual power and life. To emphasize that the structure is an image of the living human being, the bricks are flesh-coloured. Pieces of the tower that have fallen away are shown to have struck, first, a king and, secondly, the architect of the tower. The evil implications of the allegory are connected with Scorpio, and allude to the dangerous consequences of over-confidence—or the sin of pride, with its related symbolism of the Tower of Babel. Megalomania, the wild pursuit of fanciful ideas, and small-mindedness form the context of this symbol (59).

Toys Toys are symbols of temptation. According to Diel, this is the meaning when, in Greek mythology, the Titans offer toys to the infant Dionysos (15). A similar trial confronted Achilles when he was given a choice of jewels and valuables, among them a sword, which the hero chose without hesitation.

Trapezium This geometric`form unites the shape of the ox's head with that of the primitive stone axe. It is a symbol of sacrifice (50), and also of irregularity or abnormality since geometric figures must, by analogy, express notions of degrees of perfection depending upon how regular are their shapes. The scale of regularity would run as follows: circle, square, trapezium, trapezoid.

Treasure Treasure represents a sublimated form of the symbolism of the colour gold, a solar attribute, as opposed to gold as coins, which signifies exaltation of and corruption by earthly desires (15). In myths, legends and folktales, the treasure is usually found in a cave; there is a double image here embracing the idea of the cave, as the mother-image or the unconscious, containing 'the elusive treasure'. This is an allusion to one of the fundamental mysteries of life (31)—to nothing less than the mystic 'Centre' within the spirit of man, which Jung has dubbed the *Selbst*, to distinguish it from the mere 'ego'. The trials and tribulations that attend the quest for treasure may, up to a point, be equated with the experiments of the alchemists in their pursuit of transmutation (32). Jung maintains that the treasure which the hero wins only after painful effort is nothing less than himself reborn in the cave in which introversion or regression has confined him. The hero, in so far as he remains bound to the mother-principle, is himself the dragon, but in so far as he is reborn of the mother, he is the conqueror of the dragon (and therefore of his former self) (31). In truth, all striving and all suffering are steps along the path of moral progress. And it is possible to equate the one with the other, for as Eliphas Lévi—rightly, in our view—asserts, 'to suffer is to strive'. The truth of his remark is borne out by Rorschach's discovery that colour and movement are expressions respectively of feeling and of activity, denoting quantities that are analogous and yet opposed, as it were the two 'balance-pans' of the psyche. But it is only when born of conscious choice that work and suffering contribute to progress in its profoundest sense of self-awareness, virtue and superiority.

The dragon in the cave may also represent the sevenfold malignity of the seven planets (as the seven deadly sins), whereas the hero's weapons are the god-given powers which make victory possible. Gold coins, however, and all other derived concepts such as, for example, a bulging wallet, symbolize 'treasure easily come by' (that is, earthly desires, the sensual pleasures, love in so far as it is selfish love) and in consequence 'easily lost'.

Tree The tree is one of the most essential of traditional symbols. Very often the symbolic tree is of no particular genus, although some peoples have singled out one species as exemplifying *par excellence*

347

the generic qualities. Thus, the oak was sacred to the Celts; the ash to the Scandinavian peoples; the lime-tree in Germany; the fig-tree in India. Mythological associations between gods and trees are extremely frequent: so, Attis and the pine; Osiris and the cedar; Jupiter and the oak; Apollo and the laurel, etc. They express a kind of 'elective correspondence' (26, 17). In its most general sense, the symbolism of the tree denotes the life of the cosmos: its consistence, growth, proliferation, generative and regenerative processes. It stands for inexhaustible life, and is therefore equivalent to a symbol of immortality. According to Eliade, the concept of 'life without death' stands, ontologically speaking, for 'absolute reality' and, consequently, the tree becomes a symbol of this absolute reality, that is, of the centre of the world. Because a tree has a long, vertical shape, the centre-of-the-world symbolism is expressed in terms of a world-axis (17). The tree, with its roots underground and its branches rising to the sky, symbolizes an upward trend (3) and is therefore related to other symbols, such as the ladder and the mountain, which stand for the general relationship between the 'three worlds' (the lower world: the underworld, hell; the middle world: earth; the upper world: heaven). Christian symbolism—and especially Romanesque art—is fully aware of the primary significance of the tree as an axis linking different worlds (14). According to Rabanus Maurus, however, in his *Allegoriae in Sacram Scripturam* (46), it also symbolizes human nature (which follows from the equation of the macrocosm with the microcosm). The tree also corresponds to the Cross of Redemption and the Cross is often depicted, in Christian iconography, as the Tree of Life (17). It is, of course, the vertical arm of the Cross which is identified with the tree, and hence with the 'world-axis'. The world-axis symbolism (which goes back to pre-Neolithic times) has a further symbolic implication: that of the central point in the cosmos. Clearly, the tree (or the cross) can only be the axis linking the three worlds if it stands in the centre of the cosmos they constitute. It is interesting to note that the three worlds of tree-symbolism reflect the three main portions of the structure of the tree: roots, trunk and foliage. Within the general significance of the tree as world-axis and as a symbol of the inexhaustible life-process (growth and development), different mythologies and folklores distinguish three or four different shades of meaning. Some of these are merely aspects of the basic symbolism, but others are of a subtlety which gives further enrichment to the symbol. At the most primitive level, there are the 'Tree of Life' and the 'Tree of Death' (35), rather than, as in later stages, the cosmic tree and the tree of the knowledge of Good and Evil; but the two trees are merely two different representations of the same idea. The *arbor vitae* is found frequently, in a variety of forms, in Eastern art. The—

apparently purely decorative—motif of *hom* (the central tree), placed between two fabulous beings or two animals facing each other, is a theme of Mesopotamian origin, brought both to the West and to the Far East by Persians, Arabs and Byzantines (6). In Romanesque decoration it is the labyrinthine foliage of the Tree of Life which receives most emphasis (the symbolic meaning remaining unchanged, but with the addition of the theme of Entanglement) (46). An important point in connexion with the 'cosmic tree' symbol is that it often appears upside down, with its roots in heaven and its foliage on earth; here, the natural symbolism based on the analogy with actual trees has been displaced by a meaning expressing the idea of involution, as derived from the doctrines of emanation: namely, that every process of physical growth is a spiritual *opus* in reverse. Thus, Blavatsky says: 'In the beginning, its roots were generated in Heaven, and grew out of the Rootless Root of all-being. . . . Its trunk grew and developed, crossing the plains of Pleroma, it shot out crossways its luxuriant branches, first on the plane of hardly differentiated matter, and then downward till they touched the terrestrial plane. Thus . . . (it) is said to grow with its roots above and its branches below' (9). This concept is already found in the Upanishads, where it is said that the branches of the tree are: ether, air, fire, water and earth. In the Zohar of Hebrew tradition it is also stated that 'the Tree of Life spreads downwards from above, and is entirely bathed in the light of the sun'. Dante, too, portrays the pattern of the celestial spheres as the foliage of a tree whose roots (i.e. origin) spread upwards (Uranus). In other traditions, on the other hand, no such inversion occurs, and this symbolic aspect gives way to the symbolism of vertical upward growth. In Nordic mythology, the cosmic tree, called Yggdrasil, sends its roots down into the very core of the earth, where hell lies (*Völuspâ*, 19; *Grimnismâl*, 31) (17).

We can next consider the two-tree symbolism in the Bible. In Paradise there were the Tree of Life and the tree of the knowledge of good and evil. Both were centrally placed in the Garden of Eden. In this connexion, Schneider says (50): 'Why does God not mention the Tree of Life to Adam? Is it because it was a second tree of knowledge or is it because it was hidden from the sight of Adam until he came to recognize it with his new-found knowledge of good and evil—of wisdom? We prefer the latter hypothesis. The Tree of Life, once discovered, can confer immortality; but to discover it is not easy. It is "hidden", like the herb of immortality which Gilgamesh seeks at the bottom of the sea, or is guarded by monsters, like the golden apples of the Hesperides. The two trees occur more frequently than might be expected. At the East gate of the Babylonian heaven, for instance, there grew the Tree of Truth and the Tree of Life.' The doubling of the tree does not modify the symbol's fundamental significance, but it does add further symbolic implications connected with the dual nature of the Gemini: the tree, under the influence of the symbolism of the number two, then reflects the parallel worlds of living and knowing (the Tree of Life and the Tree of Knowledge). As is often the case with symbols, many more specialized meanings have been developed on the basis of the general tree-symbolism already outlined. Here are a few: firstly, the triple tree. According to Schneider, the Tree of Life, when it rises no higher than the mountain of Mars (the world of phenomena) is regarded as a pillar supporting heaven. It is made up of three roots and three trunks—or rather one central trunk with two large boughs corresponding to the two peaks of the mountain of Mars (the two faces of Janus). Here the central trunk or axis unifies the dualism expressed in the two-tree symbolism. In its lunar aspect, it is the Tree of Life and emphasizes the moon's identification with the realm of phenomena; in its solar aspect it relates to knowledge and death (which, in symbolism, are often associated). In iconography, the Tree of Life (or the lunar side of a double or triple tree) is depicted in bloom; the tree of death or knowledge (or the solar side of a double or triple tree) is dry, and shows signs of fire (50). Psychology has interpreted this symbolic duality in sexual terms, Jung affirming that the tree has a symbolic, bisexual nature, as can also be seen in the fact that, in Latin, the endings of the names of trees are masculine even though their gender is feminine (31). This *conjunctio* confirms the unifying significance of the cosmic tree. Other symbols are often brought into association with the tree, sometimes by analogy with real situations, sometimes through the juxtaposition of psychic images and projections. The resulting composite symbolism is, of course, richer and more complex, but also more specific, and consequently less spontaneous and of less scope. The tree is frequently related to the rock or the mountain on which it grows. On the other hand, the Tree of Life, as found in the celestial Jerusalem, bears twelve fruits, or sun-shapes (symbols of the Zodiac, perhaps). In many images, the sun, the moon and the stars are associated with the tree, thus stressing its cosmic and astral character. In India we find a triple tree, with three suns, the image of the Trimurti; and in China a tree with the twelve suns of the Zodiac (25). In alchemy, a tree with moons denotes the lunar *opus* (the Lesser Work) and the tree with suns the solar *opus* (the Great Work). The tree with the signs of the seven planets (or metals) stands for prime matter (protohyle), from which all differentiations emerge. Again, in alchemy, the Tree of Knowledge is called *arbor philosophica* (a symbol of evolution, or of the growth of an idea, a vocation or a force). 'To plant the philosophers' tree' is tantamount to stimulating the creative imagination

(32). Another interesting symbol is that of the 'sea-tree' or coral, related to the mythic sea king. The fountain, the dragon and the snake are also frequently related to the tree. Symbol LVII of Bosch's *Ars Symbolica* shows the dragon beside the tree of the Hesperides. As regards the symbolism of levels, it is possible to establish a vertical scale of analogies: dragons and snakes (primal forces) are associated with the roots; the lion, the unicorn, the stag and other animals expressing the ideas of elevation, aggression and penetration, correspond to the trunk; and birds and heavenly bodies are brought into relation with the foliage. Colour correspondences, are: roots/black; trunk/white; foliage/red. The snake coiled round the tree introduces another symbol, that of the spiral. The tree as world-axis is surrounded by the sequence of cycles which characterizes the revealed world. This is an interpretation applicable to the serpent watching at the foot of the tree on which the Golden Fleece is suspended (25). Endless instances could be quoted of such associations of symbols, full of psychological implications. Another typical combination of symbols, extremely frequent in folktales, is that of the 'singing tree'. In the *Passio S. Perpetuae XI* (Cambridge, 1891) we read that St. Saturius, a martyr alongside St. Perpetua, dreamed on the eve of his martyrdom 'that, having shed his mortal flesh, he was carried eastward by four angels. Going up a gentle slope, they reached a spot bathed in the most beautiful light: it was Paradise opening before us', he adds, 'like a garden, with trees bearing roses and many other flower-blooms; trees tall as cypresses, singing the while' (46). The sacrificial stake, the harp-lyre, the ship-of-death and the drum are all symbols derived from the tree seen as the path leading to the other world (50) (Plate XXIX). Gershom G. Scholem, in *Les Origines de la Kabbale*, speaks of the symbolism of the tree in connexion with hierarchical, vertical structures (such as the 'sefirothic tree' of the Cabbala, a theme that we cannot develop here). He asks himself whether the 'tree of Porphyry', which was a widespread symbol during the Middle Ages, was of a similar nature. In any case, it is reminiscent of the *Arbor elementalis* of Raymond Lull (1295), whose trunk symbolizes the primordial *substance* of Creation, or *hyle*, and whose branches and leaves represent its nine *accidents*. The figure ten has the same connotation as in the sefiroth, the 'sum of all the real which can be determined by numbers'.

Trees and Flowers   In Chinese symbology, they usually symbolize longevity and fertility. Predominantly popular are the bamboo, the cherry-tree and the pine, called 'the three friends' because all three are evergreen. In painting they frequently appear together (2).

Triangle   The geometric image of the ternary and, in the symbolism of numbers, equivalent to the number three. In its highest sense it concerns the Trinity. In its normal position with the apex uppermost it also symbolizes fire and the aspiration of all things towards the higher, unity—the urge to escape from extension (signified by the base) into non-extension (the apex) or towards the Origin or the Irradiating Point. Nicholas of Cusa said of the triangle that, truncated (without its apex), it served the alchemists as a symbol of air; inverted (with apex pointing downwards) it symbolizes water; and inverted but with the tip cut off, it symbolizes earth. Two complete triangles, one in the normal position and one inverted—representing, respectively, fire and water—superimposed so as to form a six-pointed star (called Solomon's seal), constitute a symbol of the human soul. A triangle surmounted by horns was the Carthaginian symbol for Tanit (or Tanith) (12).

Trident Various interpretations of the trident or three-pointed spear have been advanced, ranging from Eliade's suggestion that originally it was a representation of the teeth of sea-monsters (17), to Diel's explanation which we will discuss below. It is an attribute of Neptune and of Satan. According to Bayley, it is a corrupt form of· the cross (4), adapted, that is, in such a way as to suggest a vicious character. More precisely, every instrument, object or being having three members or parts where one would normally suffice realizes a trebling of its symbolic force or potentiality (8). This is born out by Zimmer's comment that the trident denotes threefold hostility. The third point might well correspond to the third eye of Shiva (or Siva) the Destroyer, since the trident is also an attribute of this god. The fact that the trident was the weapon of the Roman *retiarius* is highly significant, for the net which he also used relates him to the Uranian deity, whereas the sword wielded by the *mirmillo* gladiator suggests the heroic, solar son. Hence, the trident, in the hands of the *retiarius*, would seem to be an attribute of archaic, paternal power opposed to the unique heroism of the solar son. Diel, with his moralist approach, carries the negative implication of the trident to its logical conclusion, suggesting that it symbolizes triple sin, corresponding to the perversion of the three 'vital urges' of nutrition or preservation (transformed into possession, property and authority); reproduction (lust); and spiritualization or evolution (which, in its negative aspect, becomes vanity). Hence it is an attribute of the god of the unconscious and of sin—Neptune, whose realm is the haunt of monsters and base forms of life. The triple character of the trident is an 'infernal replica of the Trinity', comparable with the three heads of Cerberus or of triform Hecate (17). On the other hand, a favour-able interpretation has also been ascribed to the trident; Charles Ploix, in *La Nature et les dieux*, associates it with the wand used in water-divining (2), although this interpretation seems to rest on somewhat dubious grounds. According to Father Heras, the trident was, in the proto-Indian era, an attribute of god.

Triform A second name of Hecate, who, with her three heads, presided, according to Servius, over birth, life and death (representing the past, the present and the future). This is a teratological application of the principle of triplicity or triunity (8). Similar in significance is the *Trimurti* (embracing creation, preservation and destruction) formed by Brahma, Vishnu and Shiva (60). Triform symbolism conforms to the general symbolism of ternary forms, in its depiction of power as holiness, science and armed might, in turn clearly corresponding to the spirit, the intellect and vitality (28).

Triple Enclosure A schematic pattern of various forms (three squares or concentric circles, combinations of both or combinations with polygons) which, according to Louis Charbonneau-Lassay in *L'Ésotérisme de quelques symboles géométriques chrétiens*, symbolizes the ternary or triple make-up of man: body, soul, spirit; or of the world: physical universe, intelligible or intellectual universe, spiritual or transcendental universe. This symbol, in the form of squares, has been found engraved on some stelae such as that of Suèvres (Orléannais, France), dating back roughly to the Druidic or Gallo-Roman period. Similar symbols have been found engraved in bone, attributed to the Merovingian period, and in the *graffiti* of the Knights Templars in the castle of Chinon (1308). The reverse of English coins in the 14th and 15th centuries and the obverse of Castilian 'anagram' coins are triple enclosures in pattern and perhaps in significance.

Triple enclosure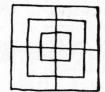

Tripod Dontenville regards this as a solar symbol, not because it has a circular top but because of the three supports which can be said to correspond to the three solar 'moments'—the rising, the zenith and the setting (16). The symbolic figure of the triskeles—three legs joined together to form a kind of swastika—is similar in meaning according to Dontenville (16), but Ortiz holds that it is expressive of 'swift movement' (41).

Triumph The symbols of triumph are related to those of power. In addition, there are elements of exhibition and exaltation; and thereby they become connected with the symbols of verticality, ascension and radiance, and with the solar symbols (crown, palm, gold, purple, chariot, white horses, stepped temples). It was probably the Romans who created the most perfect form of triumphal symbolism for the glorification of their *imperatores* and Caesars. The standards of the legions and cohorts, with an eagle or a phoenix on the point of a lance, are themselves another example of triumphal symbols.

Trumpet Since it is a metal instrument, it corresponds to the Elements of fire and water and also to the twin-peaked Mountain of Mars. Metallic instruments pertain to nobles and warriors, whereas wooden instruments, from their associations with the valley, are more properly related to the common folk and to shepherds (50). The trumpet symbolizes the yearning for fame and glory (8). On the other hand, the horn, because of its shape, is connected with the symbolism of the animal-horn (50).

Tunic Whereas the cloak symbolizes the outer bounds of the personality or the 'mask' which envelops the Jungian *Selbst*, the tunic may denote the self or the soul, that is, the zone in most direct contact with the spirit. An individual clothed in an orange-coloured tunic is 'afire', since orange is the colour symbolizing fire and passion. The tunic of Nessus, which was the cause of Hercules' death by burning, was of this same colour. Holes in the tunic (or a suit), or tatters, are equivalent to scars and symbolic of the wounds in the soul. Concerning the orange-coloured tunic, Zimmer relates that in India this was the garment in which criminals were clothed when condemned to death for terrible crimes (60).

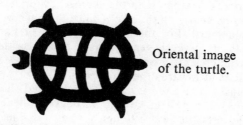

Oriental image of the turtle.

Turtle The turtle has a variety of meanings, all of which are organically related. In the Far East its significance is cosmic in implication. As Chochod has observed: 'The primordial turtle has a shell that is rounded on the top to represent heaven, and square underneath to represent the earth' (13). To the Negroes of Nigeria it suggests the female sex organ (12) and it is in fact taken as an emblem of lubricity. In alchemy it was symbolic of the '*massa confusa*' (32). These disparate senses have, nevertheless, one thing in common: in every case, the turtle is a symbol of material existence and not of any aspect of transcendence, for even where it is a combination of square and circle it alludes to the forms of the manifest world and not to the creative forces, nor to the Origin, still less to the irradiating Centre. In view of its slowness, it might be said to symbolize natural evolution as opposed to spiritual evolution which is rapid or discontinuous to a degree. The turtle is also an emblem of longevity. An engraving in the *Hypnerotomachia Poliphili* (p. 79) depicts a woman holding a pair of outspread wings in one hand and a turtle in the other. The counterbalancing of one with the other would suggest that the turtle is the inversion of the wings; that is, that since the wings signify elevation of the spirit, the turtle would denote the fixed element of alchemy although only in its negative aspect. In short, then, it would stand for turgidity, involution, obscurity, slowness, stagnation and highly concentrated materialism, etc. Perhaps this is the explanation of the turtles in Moreau's painting of *Orpheus* with their disquieting negativeness.

Turtle Dove   A symbol of fidelity and of affection among human beings (8). It is to be found in many allegories and is sometimes confused with the dove.

Twelve   Strictly, of all the numbers, twelve is the broadest in scope, for the Tarot formulas are such that they contain two groups of eleven and four of fourteen, but the components of these numbers have no archetypal significance. Given that the two essential proto-types of quantity are the numbers three and four (signifying respectively dynamism or inner spirituality, and stability or outer activity), it can be argued that their sum and their multiplication give the two numbers which are next in importance: seven and twelve. The latter corresponds to the geometrical dodecagon; but it may also be associated with the circle, since their symbolic meaning is practically identical. For this reason, systems or patterns based upon the circle or the cycle tend to have twelve as the end-limit. Even when structures are made up of less than twelve elements at first, they later tend towards the superior number of twelve, as, for example, in music, where the seven-note modal scale has developed into the twelve-note system of the Arnold Schoenberg school. Other examples are: the twelve hours on the clock-face; the twelve months of the year; the twelve major gods of many mythologies, as a kind of amplification of the seven planets; and the markings of the wind-rose (corresponding to Eurus, Solanus, Notus, Auster, Africus, Euroauster, Zephyrus, Stannus, Ireieus, Boreas, Aquilo, Volturnus). All these examples, then, prove the existence of an order founded upon patterns of twelve, which can be split up either into the 'inner' three-part division of the 'outer' or circumstantial pattern of four, or else into the 'outer' four-part division of the 'inner' and actual pattern of three. For the Vedic Indians, the twelve middle days of winter (from Christmas to Epiphany) were an image and a replica of the entire year; and a similar tradition exists in China (17). In our view, the symbolism of the Zodiac lies at the root of all these systems based upon the number twelve, that is, the idea that the four Elements may appear in three different ways (levels or grades), giving twelve divisions. It is for these reasons that Saint-Yves draws the sociological conclusion that, among groups of human beings in the line of symbolic tradition, 'the circle which comes highest and nearest to the mysterious centre, consists of twelve divisions representing the supreme initiation (the faculties, the virtues and knowledge) and corresponding, among other things, to the Zodiac'. Guénon (who quotes the above) adds that the twelve-formula is to be found in the 'circular council' of the Dalai Lama, and (quite apart from the twelve apostles) in the legendary knights of the Round Table and the historical Twelve Peers of France. Similarly, the Etruscan state was subdivided into twelve minor states; and Romulus created twelve lictors (28).

Twilight (or **Half-light**) The half-light of morning or evening is a symbol of dichotomy, representing the dividing-line which at once joins and separates a pair of opposites. Frazer relates an Indian legend which embodies a curious mythic stratagem: 'Indra swore to the demon Namuci that he would slay him neither by day nor by night. . . . But he killed him in the morning-twilight' (21). Half-light is characterized by lack of definition and ambivalence, and is therefore closely related to the space-symbolism of the Hanged Man or of any object suspended between heaven and earth. Evening-light is associated with the West, symbolizing the location of death. Dontenville suggests that it is, therefore, not by chance that Perseus goes westward in his quest for the Gorgon's head. And the same may be said of Hercules in his journey to the garden of the Hesperides, since the place and the time of sunset imply the end of one cycle (corresponding to the zodiacal sign of Pisces) and the beginning of another. According to legend, Merlin buried the sun in Mount Tombe. King Arthur fell mortally wounded in the West, and there he was healed by Morgana the Fairy (a name deriving from *Morgen* —morning) (16).

Twins In representations of the *sacrificium mithriacum*, the two dadophori, Cautes and Cautopates, are very frequently shown, one with his torch pointing upwards and the other with his turned downwards: the one is alight, the other extinguished. Cumont considers that they symbolize life and death. Sometimes one dadophorus has the head of a bull and the other that of a scorpion, confirming Cumont's conclusion. They also signify the two essential aspects of the sun: its alternate appearance and disappearance— day and night (31). A careful study of Primitive traditions and of the mythologies of the more advanced cultures has enabled us to draw the conclusion that most of them incorporate the symbol of the twins, such as the Vedic Asvins (or Ashwins), Mitra and Varuna, Liber and Libera, Romulus and Remus, Isis and Osiris, Apollo and Artemis, Castor and Pollux, Amphion and Zethus, or

Arion and Orion. On some occasions the addition of a third figure (brother or sister) permits of further associations, as, for example, Castor and Helen, or Osiris and Set. They are always mythic beings born of an immortal father and a mortal mother. The respective characteristics of their parents—expressed in landscape-symbolism by the dualism of the mountain (representing heaven) and the valley or water (representing earth)—are not fused in their offspring, but discrete. Thus, one brother may be a fierce hunter, another a peaceful shepherd (50). In sum, these beings are usually beneficent deities (17). Through the influence of totemism or of animalistic symbolism, they appear fairly often in the symbolic guise of animals: as birds (35)—the myth of oviparous human birth is a parallel manifestation of this; or as lions (that is, the wild lion and the tame lion, or day and night) (4); or as horses, one white or chestnut, the other black. The twin Indian Ashwins (or Asvins) are depicted in this latter form, one in light and the other in darkness, as if the chariot they draw is ever running along the borderline of dusk. But most commonly one of the twins signifies the eternal side of man, his inheritance from his celestial father (as a reflection of the *hieros gamos*), or, in short, his soul, and the other twin indicates the mortal side (40). However, they also symbolize the counterbalancing principles of good and evil, and hence the twins are portrayed as mortal enemies. This is what lies behind the Egyptian myth of Osiris and Set and the Persian myth of Ahuramazda and Angra-mainyu (or Ahriman) as well as the Iroquois myth of Hawneyn and Hanegoasegeh and the Slav myth of Bielbog and Chernobog (or Zcernoboch) (the 'white god' and the 'black god') (35). Since the life-principle is usually allied with evil, the principle of good has to fall back upon ascetic spirituality; it follows then, that, in order to achieve immortality, it is essential to accept the maxim 'Deny thyself'. In India, such duality is precisely exemplified in the two names of *Atman* (or individual soul) and *Brahman* (world-soul); up to a point, they are pantheistic in tendency. Friedrich Nietzsche exactly described the mystic message implied in this partial negation necessary for the salvation of the spiritual essence of Man, with his advice: 'Cast into the abyss that which lies most heavily upon you. Let man forget. . . . Divine is the art of forgetting. If you would raise yourself—if you yourself would dwell among the heights, cast into the sea that which lies most heavily upon you'; yet Nietzsche, as a Westerner, does not succeed in escaping from self.

Twisted Shapes These fall within the broad group of symbolic abnormalities, in so far as they deviate from the norm in shape and significance (where, for example, the normal shape is straight or curved).

U

Umbrella This symbol is invariably related to the sun-shade, which is a solar emblem of the monarchs of certain peoples. But its mechanism has tended to lend it a phallic significance. It is a father-symbol for this reason and because of its implications of protection and of mourning (42).

Undines Water-nymphs, or undines, are symbolically the inverse of sirens: in the latter, the fishy part of their body refers to the relationship between the waters (and the moon) and woman; with undines, it is the feminine—or perilous—nature of the waters which is symbolized. Krappe notes that these nymphs are usually wicked in so far as they represent the treacherousness of rivers, lakes and torrents.

Unicorn Symbolic of chastity and also an emblem of the sword or of the word of God (20, 4). Tradition commonly presents it as a white horse with a single horn sprouting from its forehead, but according to esoteric belief it has a white body, a red head and blue eyes. Legend has it that it is tireless when pursued yet falls meekly to the ground when it is approached by a virgin (59). This seems to suggest that it is symbolic of sublimated sex. In China, the animal known as Ch'i-lin is identified by some writers with the unicorn, whereas there are others who dispute this because it has two horns. It is an attribute of high-ranking army officers and an emblem of uprightness and high birth. Its skin is of five colours—red, yellow, blue, white and black; its cry is like the sound of bells. In legend it is reputed to live for a thousand years and to be the noblest of animals (5). Jung, in his work on the relationships between psychology and alchemy, has studied a great many aspects of this fabulous animal, concluding that, broadly speaking, it has no one definite symbolic character but rather many different variants embracing single-horned animals, both real and fabulous, such as the sword-fish or certain types of dragon. He notes that the unicorn is at times transmuted into a white dove, offering the explanation that on the one hand it is related to primordial monsters while on the other it represents the virile, pure and penetrating force of the *spiritus mercurialis*. He quotes the remark of Honorius of Autun in his *Speculum de Mysteriis Ecclesiae*, as follows: 'The very fierce animal with only one horn is called unicorn. In order to catch it, a virgin is put in a field; the animal then comes to her and is caught, because it lies down in her lap. Christ is represented by this animal, and his invincible strength by its horn. He, who lay down in the womb of the Virgin, has been caught by the hunters; that is to say, he was found in human shape by those who loved him.' However, in Antiquity the unicorn appears on occasion with certain evil characteristics. The *Physiologus Graecus* comments that it is 'an animal fleet of foot, single-horned and harbouring ill will towards men'. As Jung has observed, the Church does not recognize this negative side of the unicorn. On the other hand, the alchemists made use of its ambivalent implications in order to symbolize the *Monstrum Hermaphroditum*. The universality of this symbolic being, non-existent in nature, is indeed surprising; it is, for instance, in the Vedas. Regarding its iconography, of special interest are the 15th-century tapestries in the Cluny Museum in Paris, with their illustrations of *La Dame à la Licorne* (32).

Urn A symbol of containment which, like all such symbols, corresponds to the world of things feminine. The urn of gold or silver, associated with a white lily, is the favourite emblem of the Virgin in religious iconography. The urn with a lid is one of the eight emblems of good luck in Chinese Buddhism, and signifies Oneness, or that state of supreme intelligence which triumphs over birth and death (5).

Utensils Generally speaking, their symbolic significance amounts to a simple transference to the spiritual plane of their practical and utilitarian function (56). Secondary implications are prompted by the particular shape, material and colour of the utensil.

V

Valley Within the symbolism of landscapes, the valley, which, because it is low-lying, is considered to lie at the level of the sea, represents a neutral zone apt for the development of all creation and for all material progress in the world of manifestation. Its characteristic fertility stands in contrast to the nature of the desert (symbolically a place of purification), of the ocean (which represents the Origin of life but which, in relation to man's existence, is sterile), and of the mountain (the region characterized by snows and the ascetic, contemplative life, or by intellectual illumination). In short, the valley is symbolic of life itself and is the mystic abode of shepherd and priest (51).

Vase In the Egyptian system of hieroglyphs, this is a determinative sign corresponding to Nu (or Nun or Nou), the god of repose,

immanence and acceptance (19), The 'full vase' is associated with
the Plant of Life and is an emblem of fertility (17). The golden vase
or pot filled with white lilies is the common emblem of the
Virgin Mary.

Vault According to Leo Frobenius, in prehistoric and protohistoric thinking, every vault represents the union of the sky-god
with the earth-goddess. The separation of the two deities created the
void (22).

Vegetation Vegetation, in all its forms, has two main implications: firstly, pertaining to its annual cycle, whence its symbolism
of death and resurrection following the pattern of winter and
spring; and, secondly, that of its abundance, giving rise to its
significance in connexion with fertility and fecundity. Vegetation
rites are celebrated in many different regions, and on dates ranging
from Carnival (Shrove-tide) to the feast of St. John (24th June) (17).
In every case, the aim is to encourage the cosmic forces to continue
to bring about the annual regeneration of life.

Vehicles The various ancient and modern vehicles are corruptions
of the essential symbol of the chariot. Those that possess some
individual characteristics are connected with existence itself; those
that are generic in character pertain to the collective life (56).
According to Jung, the particular type of vehicle that appears
relates to the individual's characteristic movement—whether lively
or slow, regular or irregular—or the character of his inner life or
his mind, or whether his ideas are his own or borrowed, and so on
(32). Every vehicle is an expression of the body (including the mind
and thought) or, in other words, of the spirit in its existential aspect.
Thus, from the symbolic point of view, to see in the imagination, or
in dreams, a chariot or a car on fire has the same significance as the
vision of a man in an orange-coloured tunic (since orange is the
colour of fire).

Veil In addition to partaking of the generic symbolism of
fabrics, the veil signifies the concealment of certain aspects of truth
or of the deity. Guénon draws attention to the double meaning of
the verb 'to reveal' ('re-veil'), which may mean either to pull back
the veil or to cover again with a veil. The Bible tells us that when
Moses came down from mount Sinai 'the skin of his face shone' so
that he had to cover his face with a veil while he spoke with the
people because they were unable to look upon his shining face
(Exodus xxxiv, 29-35) (28).

Venus The planet Venus is, in alchemy, related to the goddess
of love and also to copper. In astrology, it is associated with the
Moon in particular and with Mars. Its spiritual significance has two
aspects: that of spiritual love and that of mere sexual attraction,
so that some writers have come to regard its true symbolic significance as physical and mechanical in character.

Verbs   Every verb denotes an action, a passion or an operation, and its symbolism is a direct consequence of the transference of this material sense to the spiritual plane. For example, to take food is symbolic of receiving spiritual or intellectual nourishment; to kill is to eradicate a given being from the mind; to travel is to move, by exercise of the imagination and awareness, away from one world and towards another; and so on.

Verticality   Since all symbolism is, in essence, dynamic, the idea of verticality is closely related to upward movement, which, by analogy with the symbolism of space and with moral concepts, corresponds symbolically to the tendency towards spiritualization (dealt with in connexion with the symbolism of Levels—q.v.). Symbolic theory attaches such importance to the level or height of a given figure (in relation to the norm) that it can even define the significance of this form or being solely by reference to its vertical 'height'. Bachelard corroborates this and even goes so far as to say that 'it is impossible to ignore the vertical axis in expressing moral values' (3).

Vessel   In the Egyptian system of hieroglyphs, a determinative sign corresponding to the idea of receptacles in general. It is a symbol whose immediate significance is that of the context in which the intermingling of forces takes place, giving rise to the material world. From this sense arises a secondary symbolism—that of the female matrix (19).

Victory   The crown as an expression of fulfilment, and the palm in the sense of elevation and exaltation, are the two outward attributes of victory. When Victory is personified as a winged figure, the allusion is to its spiritual worth. Whether, as in the Mithraic mysteries, the victory is over the bull, or whether it is over the dragon or some other such monster, as in the exploits of Hercules, Perseus, Bellerophon and St. George, the significance of the act of conquering lies in the disarming of the adversary and his subjugation to the will of the victor. In addition to the objective and cosmic sense of victory, there is also a psychological implication: confrontation with another force presupposes resemblance, and therefore the conquered force is the very inferiority of the conqueror himself.

Vine   Just as the grape has an ambivalent symbolism, pertaining to sacrifice and to fecundity, so wine frequently appears as a symbol both of youth and of eternal life. In the earliest times, the supreme ideogram of life was a vine-leaf. According to Eliade, the Mother-Goddess was known by the Primitives as 'The Goddess of the Vines', representing the unfailing source of natural creation (17).

Virgo   The sixth sign of the Zodiac. For the Egyptians it was identical with Isis. Since it is governed by Mercury and corresponds to the number six, it is symbolic of hermaphroditism, or that state which is characterized by dual—positive and negative—forces. Hence Virgo is sometimes depicted with the symbol of the soul or the Seal of Solomon (two triangles, representing fire and water,

Zodiacal sign
of Virgo.

superimposed and intersecting to form a six-pointed star) (40). In mythology and in religions generally, this symbol is always associated with the birth of a god or a demigod, as the supreme expression of the dynamic consciousness (52) (Plate XXX).

Volcano   In mythology, the volcano is invested with antithetical powers: on the one hand there is the extraordinary fertility of the volcanic earth in such regions as Naples, California or Japan; but on the other hand the destructive fire of the volcano is linked with the idea of evil. This accounts for the variety of ideas associated with the volcano. For the Persians, for instance, it was quite simply the Great Adversary, Ahriman, who, in the form of a huge dragon or serpent, was shackled (as in the comparable myth of Prometheus) to mount Demâvand, the volcano of Elburz, there to await the Day of Judgement (35). The volcano is symbolic not only of the primary force of nature and of the fire of life (representing creation and destruction) (4), but also of the original 'site' of the 'descent' of the Elements—involution, that is to say; here, in the bowels of the volcano, the Elements of air, fire, water and earth are intermingled and transformed (50). Hence it becomes feasible to relate the volcano to Shiva, the god of creation and destruction. As a psychological symbol, the volcano represents the passions which, according to Beaudoin, become the sole source of our spiritual energy once we have managed to master and transform them. An examination of the 30th symbol of the *Ars Symbolica* of Bosch in relation to the legendary motto *Gelat et ardet*, points to the conclusion that there is a profound significance of the volcano touching upon the *coincidentia oppositorum*. Another important sense of the volcano arises from its peculiar characteristic whereby a long period of latent, enclosed and occult labour is followed by a sudden and terrible eruption. By analogy between this process and many other similar processes in the lives of individuals and social groups, the word 'volcano' has come to be used as an image of this dual tendency of tension and distension (31).

Vulcan   Vulcan, as a symbol, is related to the smith who has his forge in the mountain-cave, and hence to the demiurge. Indeed, the ancients explained volcanoes by reference to underground forges and supernatural smiths. The cult of the Hephaestia festival was connected with the volcanic activity of the Aegean islands (35). But Vulcan, the demiurge, is characterized by negative qualities as ascribed to him by the Gnostics and the doctrine of Mani. He is lame and this is symbolic of his weak or corrupt soul. According to Diel, he bears a family relationship to the Christian devil. His deformity was a consequence of his defiance of Jupiter—the spirit—who punished him by hurling him down from mount Olympus. Diel also suggests that Vulcan, Icarus and Prometheus are symbolic of the intellect—understood almost in its technical and 'merely human' sense—in open rebellion against the spirit (15).

Vulture In Egyptian hieroglyphs, the sign of the vulture—like the wavy line which is the sign for water—stands for the idea of the Mother (19). According to Jung, the 'mother'-symbolism of the Egyptian vulture is probably derived from its necrophagous habits (31). It was believed that the vulture, because it fed upon corpses, was related to Mother Nature (and to death). The Parsees place their dead in specially built towers so that vultures will consume them, believing that this facilitates rebirth (56). A sublimation of this meaning—mythic rather than symbolic in nature—is found in India, where the vulture is the symbol of the tutelary spirits which watch over the individual in lieu of the parents, denoting abnegation and spiritual counsel (38).

Wall Its significance is diverse, depending upon which of its different characteristics is taken as fundamental. In the Egyptian system of hieroglyphs, the wall is a determinative sign conveying the idea of 'rising above the common level' (19); clearly the predominant sense here is that of its height. A wall enclosing a space is the 'wall of lamentations', symbolic of the sensation of the world as a 'cavern'—of the doctrine of immanentism or the metaphysical notion of the impossibility of reaching the outside. It expresses the ideas of impotence, delay, resistance, or a limiting situation. Now, the wall seen from within as an enclosure has a secondary implication of protection which, according to its function and the attitude of the individual, may even be taken as its principal meaning. Psychoanalysts frequently regard it in this light and hence have classified it as a mother-symbol, comparable with the town and the house or home (56). Bayley sums up the two essential features of the wall as follows: Like the house, it is a mystic symbol representing the feminine element of mankind. This enables us to understand the (otherwise absurd) assertion of the Shulamite in the *Song of Songs*: 'I am a wall'. At the same time, this image has another term of comparison, that of matter as opposed to spirit (4). It should be noted that the symbolism in the latter case remains unchanged, since matter corresponds to the passive or feminine principle, and spirit to the active or masculine.

Wallowing Rolling on the ground, and especially wallowing in mud or swamp, form part of primitive therapy all over the world. The custom also figures in some rites involving rain or fertility, and is also to be found in magic practices where a man is required to roll on the ground in order to rise up again transformed into a wolf (51). The myth of Antaeus is connected with this belief. In all this, the supposition is that contact with the earth instigates certain latent possibilities either in the cosmos or in the individual or his spirit. The desire to be cured, or for metamorphosis or rain, corresponds to the general longing for 'Inversion'—the upsetting of a given order so that it may be replaced by its opposite. To roll on the ground is, then, one of those sacrificial acts that are supposed to encourage or facilitate inversion, a change in circumstances or in the broad stream of life.

Wand, Magic Alongside the 'technical' symbolism implied by its material or its colour, its significance derives from the magic power attributed to it, which in turn derives from the concept of every stick or wand as a straight line, embodying implications of direction and intensity. Derived, or related, forms are the royal sceptre, the marshal's baton, the battle-club, the mayor's staff and the conductor's baton (48).

Wandering Jew The legend of Ahasuerus, the Wandering Jew, is believed to be of Western origin. Underlying it is the symbolic idea of the man who cannot die, or who, after his apparent death (King don Rodrigo, or don Sebastian, or King Arthur, for example) appears again. The tradition can be related also to that of the Eternal Youth—the oriental Jadir. In Jung's opinion they are but one symbol alluding to the imperishable side of Man, such as in the myth of the Dioscuri or the Gemini (31).

War In a cosmic sense, every war concerns the struggle of light against darkness—of good against evil. In mythology, there are copious examples of such struggles between the powers of light and the forces of darkness: Jupiter's combat with the Titans, Thor versus the giants, Gilgamesh and other heroes versus monsters (4). The particular field of action is symbolic of the plane of reality on which the action takes place. In Islamic tradition, material war is merely the 'little holy war', whereas the 'great Holy War' is that which liberates man from the enemies within. The more just the war, the more faithful the image of it. Guénon specifically states that the only justification for war is the reducing of multiplicity to unity—disorder to order. In this way, war can be seen as the means of reinstating the original order, or as a kind of 'sacrifice' which echoes the cosmogonic sacrifice. Exactly the same applies to the psychic plane: Man must seek to achieve inner unity in his actions, in his thoughts, and also between his actions and his thoughts. Unity of purpose is symbolized by ritual orientation, in which the terrestrial 'centres' (the North star, or the East) become visual images of the one true 'Centre' (25).

Warriors They symbolize forebears, or the latent forces within the personality ready to come to the aid of the consciousness. If the warriors are hostile, then they signify antagonistic forces, but still within the framework of the personality. This symbolism is similar to that of the four archers who defend the cardinal points; the 'spaces' rendered independent of the 'centre' are illustrations of the forces which may rise up, as it were, against the integrity of the individual. Defenders and attackers then become, respectively, forces for and against the personality.

Water In Egyptian hieroglyphs, the symbol for water is a wavy line with small sharp crests, representing the water's surface. The same sign, when tripled, symbolizes a volume of water, that is, the primaeval ocean and prime matter. According to hermetic tradition, the god Nu was the substance from which the gods of the first ennead emerged (19). The Chinese consider water as the specific abode of the dragon, because all life comes from the waters (13). In the Vedas, water is referred to as *mâtritamâh* (the most maternal) because, in the beginning, everything was like a sea without light. In India, this element is generally regarded as the preserver of life, circulating throughout the whole of nature, in the form of rain, sap, milk and blood. Limitless and immortal, the waters are the beginning and the end of all things on earth (60). Although water is, in appearance, formless, ancient cultures made a distinction between 'upper waters' and 'lower waters'. The former correspond to the potential or what is still possible, the latter to what is actual or already created (26). In a general sense, the concept of 'water' stands, of course, for all liquid matter. Moreover, the primaeval waters, the image of prime matter, also contained all solid bodies before they acquired form and rigidity. For this reason, the alchemists gave the name of 'water' to quicksilver in its first stage of transmutation and, by analogy, also to the 'fluid body' of Man (57). This 'fluid body' is interpreted by modern psychology as a symbol of the unconscious, that is, of the non-formal, dynamic, motivating, female side of the personality. The projection of the mother-*imago* into the waters endows them with various numinous properties characteristic of the mother (31). A secondary meaning of this symbolism is found in the identification of water with intuitive wisdom. In the cosmogony of the Mesopotamian peoples, the abyss of water was regarded as a symbol of the unfathomable, impersonal Wisdom. An ancient Irish god was called Domnu, which means 'marine depth'. In prehistoric times the word for abyss seems to have been used exclusively to denote that which was unfathomable and mysterious (4). The waters, in short, symbolize the universal congress of potentialities, the *fons et origo*, which precedes all form and all creation. Immersion in water signifies a return to the pre-formal state, with a sense of death and annihilation on the one hand, but of rebirth and regeneration on the other, since immersion intensifies the life-force. The symbolism of baptism, which is closely linked to that of water, has been expounded by St. John Chrysostom (*Homil. in Joh.*, XXV, 2): 'It represents death and interment, life and resurrection. . . . When we plunge our head beneath water, as in a sepulchre, the old man becomes completely immersed and buried. When we leave the water, the new man suddenly appears' (18). The ambiguity of this quotation is only on the surface: in this particular aspect of the general symbolism of water, death affects only Man-in-nature while the rebirth is that of spiritual man. On the cosmic level, the equivalent of immersion is the flood, which causes all forms to dissolve and return to a fluid state, thus liberating the elements which will later be recombined in new cosmic patterns. The qualities of transparency and depth, often associated with water, go far towards explaining the veneration of the ancients for this element which, like earth, was a female principle. The Babylonians called it 'the home of wisdom'. Oannes, the mythical being who brings culture to mankind, is portrayed as half man and half fish (17). Moreover, in dreams, birth is usually expressed through water-imagery (*v.* Freud, *Introduction to Psycho-Analysis*). The expressions 'risen from the waves' and 'saved from the waters' symbolize fertility, and are metaphorical images of childbirth. On the other hand, water is, of all the elements, the most clearly transitional, between fire and air (the ethereal elements) and earth (the solid element). By analogy, water stands as a mediator between life and death, with a two-way positive and negative flow of creation and destruction. The Charon and Ophelia myths symbolize the last voyage. Death was the first mariner. 'Transparent depth', apart from other meanings, stands in particular for the communicating link between the surface and the abyss. It can therefore be said that water conjoins these two images (2). Gaston Bachelard points to many different characteristics of water, and derives from them many secondary symbolic meanings which enrich the fundamental meaning we have described. These secondary meanings are not so much a set of strict symbols, as a kind of language expressing the transmutations of this ever-flowing element. Bachelard enumerates clear water, spring water, running water, stagnant water, dead water, fresh and salt water, reflecting water, purifying water, deep water, stormy water. Whether we take water as a symbol of the collective or of the personal unconscious, or else as an element of mediation and dissolution, it is obvious that this symbolism is an expression of the vital potential of the psyche, of the struggles of the psychic depths to find a way of formulating a clear message comprehensible to the consciousness. On the other hand, secondary symbolisms are derived from associated objects such as water-containers, and also from the ways in which water is used: ablutions, baths, holy water, etc. There is also a very important spatial symbolism connected with the 'level' of the waters, denoting a correlation between actual physical level and absolute moral level. It is for this reason that the Buddha, in his Assapuram sermon, was able to regard the mountain-lake—whose transparent waters reveal, at the bottom, sand, shells, snails and fishes—as the path of redemption. This lake obviously corresponds to a fundamental aspect of the 'Upper Waters'. Clouds are another aspect of the 'Upper Waters'. In *Le Transformationi* of Ludovico Dolce, we find a mystic figure looking into the unruffled surface of a pond, in contrast with the accursed hunter, always in restless pursuit of his prey, implying the symbolic contrast between contemplative activity—the *sattva* state of Yoga—and blind outward activity—the *rajas* state. Finally, the upper and lower waters communicate reciprocally through the process of rain (involution) and evaporation (evolution). Here, fire intervenes to modify water: the sun (spirit) causes sea water to evaporate (i.e. it sublimates life). Water is condensed in clouds and returns to earth in the form of life-giving rain, which is invested with twofold virtues: it is water, and it comes from heaven (15). Lao-Tse paid considerable attention to this cyclic process of meteorology, which is at one and the same time physical and spiritual, observing that: 'Water never rests, neither by day nor by night. When flowing above, it causes rain and dew. When flowing below, it forms streams and rivers. Water is outstanding in doing good. If a dam is raised against it, it stops. If way is made for it, it flows along that path. Hence it is said that it does not struggle. And yet it has no equal in destroying that which is strong and hard' (13). When water stands revealed in its destructive aspects, in the course of cataclysmic events, its symbolism does not change, but is merely subordinated to the dominant symbolism of the storm. Similarly, in those contexts where the flowing nature of water is emphasized, as in the contention of Heraclitus that 'You cannot step twice into the same river; for fresh waters are ever flowing in upon you.' Here the reference is not to water-symbolism as such, but to the idea of the irreversible flow along a given ·path. To quote Evola, in *La tradizione ermetica*: 'Without divine water, nothing exists, according to Zosimus. On the other hand, among the symbols of the female principle are included those which figure as origins of the waters (mother, life), such as: Mother Earth, Mother of the Waters, Stone, Cave, House of the Mother, Night, House of Depth, House of Force, House of Wisdom, Forest, etc. One should not be misled by the word "divine". Water symbolizes terrestrial and natural life, never metaphysical life.'

Water-Maidens   These are mythic beings in Hispanic folklore, diminutive figures with a star in their forehead, shimmering, straw-coloured bodies and golden locks. On the fingers of their right hand they wear white rings and on the left wrist a gold band with black stripes. Legend has it that yellow flowers spring up in their footprints, bringing happiness to the person who finds them (10). These endearing creatures exactly illustrate the functioning of symbolic mechanism: the antithesis of black and white reflects the theme of symbolic inversion; and gold is an emblem of power. In short, these water-maidens are endowed with the power to stir up and invert the order of things, bringing happiness to the wretched—that is, to everyone.

Waves   There is a Chinese tradition that the waves are the abode of dragons, and that they are also symbolic of purity (5). The apparent contradiction here arises from the fact that the ocean swell offers two different aspects: because of their rhythmic undulations they are reminiscent of dragons, and by virtue of their white foam they suggest purity. There is thus no question of dual tendencies here—only juxtaposition.

Weapons   Within the general symbolism of the hero's struggle, his weapons are, in a way, the counterpart of the monsters he has to fight. Just as there are different kinds of monsters, so there are different kinds of weapons. Hence, the weapon used in mythic combat has a deep and specific significance: it defines both the hero and the enemy whom he is trying to destroy. Since, in a purely psychological interpretation of the symbol, the enemy is simply the forces threatening the hero from within, the weapon becomes a genuine representation of a state of conflict. (The wings of Icarus, the sword of Perseus, the club of Hercules, the staff of Oedipus, Neptune's trident, Hades and Satan) (15). Jung summarizes this by saying that 'weapons are an expression of the will directed towards a certain end' (56). Paul, giving advice on how the Christian should meet the enemy, says, in the Epistle to the Ephesians (vi, 10-17):

'Finally, my brethren, be strong in the Lord, and in the power of his might. Put on the whole armour of God, that ye may be able to stand against the wiles of the devil. For we wrestle not against flesh and blood, but against principalities, against powers, against the rulers of the darkness of this world, against spiritual wickedness in high places. Wherefore take unto you the whole armour of God, that ye may be able to withstand in the evil day, and, having done all, to stand. Stand therefore, having your loins girt about with truth, and having on the breastplate of righteousness; and your feet shod with the preparation of the gospel of peace; above all, taking the shield of faith, wherewith ye shall be able to quench all the fiery darts of the wicked. And take the helmet of salvation, and the sword of the Spirit, which is the word of God' (46). According to St. Ephraem, the allegorical interpretation of Paul's symbolism is as follows: the helmet—hope; the girding of the loins—charity; shoes —humility; the shield—cross; the bow—prayer; the sword—the word of God (46). Diel's interpretation of the symbolism of weapons also stresses their moral significance; he observes that, with 'the weapons lent by the deity'—it will be recalled that in myths, mediaeval legends and folklore weapons are often miraculously given to the hero—man must struggle against the urge of his irrational desires, against the beguiling monster, thus serving the higher aims of the spirit and of the species. Arms therefore symbolize the powers and functions of sublimation and spiritualization, in contrast to monsters, which stand for the baser forces (15). This is why myths and legends stress the almost autonomous power of the weapons, attributes and objects belonging to heroes, saints and demigods, such as Roland's oliphant, Thor's hammer and the rod of Moses (4). In addition to this general significance, the symbolism of some arms is enriched by the associations of the Element to which they pertain. Thus, the bolas of South American Indians and *gauchos*, and the sling, have associations with the air; the spear, with earth; the sword, with fire; the trident, with the watery deeps (41). Further connotations follow on from certain groupings of arms in connexion with status or character: the sceptre, the mace, the staff and the whip are attributes of royalty; the spear, the dagger and the sword are the weapons of the knight; the knife and the poniard are secret weapons and, to a certain extent, base; the thunderbolt and the net are the arms of the Uranian gods, and so on. A comparison between the different symbolic grades of arms and the Jungian archetypes would give the following correlations: Shadow (knife, dagger), Anima (spear), Mana (mace or club, net, whip), Self (sword). On the basis of this correlation, Schneider states (50) that the combat of spear against sword is that of earth against heaven. On the other hand, a further specific meaning pertains to the sword as the 'weapon of salvation', in connexion with medicinal rites (51) and with ceremonies more exalted in implication. Crushing weapons, such as the club, stand for destruction rather than victory (15).

Weaving The act of weaving represents, basically, creation and life, and particularly the latter in so far as it denotes accumulation and multiplication or growth. In this sense it was known, and put to magic and religious use, in Egypt and the pre-Columbian cultures of Peru (40). Beigbeder recalls that weaving was an attribute of the Parcae, and also of the Virgin in Byzantine iconography. The weaving symbol is universal, and of prehistoric origin.

Week The pattern of the week is related to that of the seven Directions of Space: two days are associated with each of the three dimensions, while the centre, as the 'unvarying mean' or the image of the Aristotelian 'unmoved mover', corresponds to the day of rest. The fact that this space-time prototype, founded upon the number seven, embraced also the planetary spheres and the principal deities of each pantheon, can be seen in the way each of the planets (including the sun and the moon) gave its name to one of the weekdays. As a consequence of this influence of the planetary gods (comparable in their negative aspect with the seven deadly sins), the seven-headed monster of myth, legend and folklore also refers to the dangers of temptation growing day by day as the week progresses.

Well In Christian symbolism the well falls within the group of ideas associated with the concept of life as a pilgrimage, and signifies salvation (4). The well of refreshing and purifying water is symbolic of sublime aspirations, or of the 'silver cord' which attaches man to the function of the Centre. Demeter and other deities were shown standing beside a well (15). But this symbol is found not only in the higher cultures of Antiquity but also among the primitives. Schneider has noted that, in the medicinal rites of peoples at the animistic level, the centre of the scene is taken up by a lake or well in whose water the sick wash their hands, breast and head. At the water's edge, reeds grow and shells are to be found, and both are signs of the waters of salvation (51). In particular, the act of drawing water from a well is—like fishing—symbolic of drawing out and upwards the numinous contents of the deeps (31). To look into the waters of a lake or well is tantamount to the mystic attitude of contemplation. Finally, the well is also a symbol of the soul, and an attribute of things feminine (32).

West For the Egyptians and the Greeks, the West—where the sun sets—is where the kingdom of the spirits is to be. St. Jerome sites the devil here. The East symbolizes the kingdom of Christ and the West the kingdom of the devil (the death of the sun). In the High Middle Ages, the Nordic peoples located the poisoned sea of destruction and the abyss in the West.

Wetness Although its value may be positive on the plane of natural life, it has an entirely negative effect on spiritual life. Dryness and heat correspond to the predominance of fire, the active element; but wetness corresponds to that of water, the element of passivity and dissolution.

Whale Symbolic of the world, the body and the grave (20), and also regarded as an essential symbol of containing (and concealing). Rabanus Maurus (*Operum*, III, *Allegoriae in Sacram Scripturam*) lays particular stress on this aspect (46). Nowadays, however, the whale seems to have acquired more independence as a symbolic equivalent of the mystic mandorla, or the area of intersection of the circles of heaven and earth, comprising and embracing the opposites of existence (51).

Wheel This is a symbol, wide in scope, much used in the ornamental arts and in architecture, complex and enclosing several layers of meaning. Some of the disagreement about its symbolic sense may be due to confusion of the disk (which is immobile) with the wheel (which rotates). There is, however, no objection to the fusion of the two symbols with a view to reconciling the two ideas of the disk and the wheel. One of the elementary forms of wheel-symbolism consists of the sun as a wheel, and of ornamental wheels as solar emblems (14). As Krappe has pointed out, the concept of the sun as a wheel was one of the most widespread notions of antiquity. The idea of the sun as a two-wheeled chariot is only at one remove from this. These same ideas can be found among the Aryans and also among the Semites (35). Given the symbolic significance of the sun as a source of light (standing for intelligence) and of spiritual illumination, it is easy to understand why the Buddhist doctrine of the solar wheel has been so widely admired (31). 'Catherine-wheels', and the 'wheel of fire' rolled down the hillside in popular festivals of the summer-solstice; and the mediaeval processions in which wheels were mounted on boats or carts, as well as the torture-on-the-wheel; and such traditions as the 'Wheel of Fortune' or the 'Wheel of the Year', all point to a deeply rooted solar or zodiacal symbolism. The function of the wheel-of-fire was, in essence, to 'stimulate' the sun in its activity and to ward off winter and death (17). It is, therefore, a symbolic synthesis of the activity of cosmic forces and the passage of time (57). There is, it must be admitted, a discrepancy between the interpretation of those who see the wheel particularly as a solar symbol, and those who relate it to the symbolism of the pole (although basically both allude to the mystery of the rotational tendency of all cyclic processes). The swastika, being an intermediate sign between the cross and the wheel, is similarly regarded by some as a solar and by others as a polar sign. Guénon tends towards the latter hypothesis

(28). But, in any case, the allusion is, in the last resort, to the splitting up of the world-order into two essentially different factors: rotary movement and immobility—or the perimeter of the wheel and its still centre, an image of the Aristotelian 'unmoved mover'. This becomes an obsessive theme in mythic thinking, and in alchemy it takes the form of the contrast between the volatile (moving and therefore transitory) and the fixed. The dual structure of the wheel is usually indicated by characteristic patterns which tend to confine geometric ornamentation—either stylized or figurative—to the periphery, while the round, empty space in the middle is either left vacant, or a single symbol is inscribed therein—a triangle, for instance, or a sacred figure. Guénon notes that the Celtic wheel-symbol persisted into the Middle Ages, and adds that the ornamental *oculi* of Romanesque churches and the rose-windows of Gothic architecture are versions of this wheel. He also shows that there is an indubitable connexion between the wheel and such emblematic flowers as the rose (in the West) and the lotus (in the East) (28)—in other words, figures patterned after the mandala. The rim of the wheel is divided into sectors illustrating phases in the passage of time. In alchemy, there are numerous symbolic representations of the wheel, denoting the circulatory process: the ascending period is shown on one side, the descending on the other. These alchemic stages are also represented as birds soaring heavenwards or swooping down to earth, denoting sublimation and condensation, in turn corresponding to evolution and involution, or spiritual progress and regression (32). The 'Wheel of Law, Truth and Life' is one of the eight emblems of good luck in Chinese Buddhism. It illustrates the way of escape from the illusory world (of rotation) and from illusions, and the way towards the 'Centre' (5). The wheel which is divided up into sectors by radii drawn from its outer perimeter to the circumference of an inner circle, is a graphic symbol sometimes seen in water-marks of mediaeval times over a plant-stem located between the horns of an ox (symbolizing sacrifice); Bayley opines that this wheel represents the 'communion of saints', or the reunion of the faithful in the mystic Centre (4). René Guénon says, in relation to Taoist doctrine, that the chosen one, the sage, invisible at the centre of the wheel, moves it without himself participating in the movement and without having to bestir himself in any way. He quotes, among others, the following Taoist passages: 'The sage is he who has attained the central point of the Wheel and remains bound to the "Unvarying Mean", in indissoluble union with the Origin, partaking of its immutability and imitating its non-acting activity'; 'He who has reached the highest degree of emptiness, will be secure in repose. To return to the root is to enter into the state of repose', that is, to throw off the bonds of things transitory and contingent (25).

Wheel of Fortune, The   The tenth enigma of the Tarot pack. It is an allegory which turns upon the general symbolism of the wheel. Based upon the symbolism of the number two, it expresses the equilibrium of the contrary forces of contraction and expansion— the principle of polarity. The wheel is set in motion by a handle— fateful because it is irreversible—and it is floating on a figurative representation of the ocean of chaos, supported by the masts of two boats which are joined one to the other; in each boat there is a snake, symbolizing the two principles of the active and the passive. The ascending half of this wheel has an effigy of Hermanubis and his caduceus, while the descending portion displays a Typhon-like monster with its trident; the two halves symbolize respectively the constructive and destructive forces of existence, the first figure being related to the constellation of Canis, and the second to Capricorn (denoting, within the symbolism of the Zodiac, the principle of dissolution initiated in Pisces). Above the wheel, this allegorical card has a motionless sphinx, alluding to the mystery of all things and the intermingling of the disparate (59).

Whip   The symbolism of the whip is a mixture of that of the knot or bow and that of the sceptre, both of them signs for domination, mastery and superiority. It expresses the idea of punishment, like the truncheon and the club—counterbalanced by the sword as a symbol of purification—and also the power to encircle and over-whelm (51). In Egypt, the lash, because of its morphological associa-tion with lightning, was the attribute of *Min*, the god of the wind, and, in general, of certain deities reigning over storms (41). The Dioscuri carried whips; and bronze whips figured in the cult of Zeus in Dodona (35). The Egyptian Pharaohs used the whip as an emblem of power. The Romans used to hang their whips in their triumphal chariots (8). Logically, the whip ought also to be related to rites of flagellation (or fecundity) (8). It is, furthermore, an attribute of the 'Terrible Mother' (31).

Whirlwind   Characterized by spiral or helicoid movement, this symbol expresses the dynamism of the three-dimensional cross— that is, of space itself. It is, therefore, symbolic of universal evolution.

Whistling   Whistling is, to follow Jung, like clacking the tongue in so far as both are archaic ways of calling to and attracting the attention of theriomorphic deities—or totemic or deified animals (31). This explains the social taboo upon whistling.

Wild Man   The image of the Wild Man or savage, covered only with a loin-cloth, or a garment of leaves or skins, is a common one in the folklore of almost every country. It is related to, but not identical with, such mythic beings as the 'snowman', the ogre, giants, etc. In heraldry, the image takes the form of the supporter of an escutcheon, when its significance becomes analogous to that

373 WINDOW

of the animals that normally fulfil this function—that is, they express, by virtue of their bilateral symmetry, the counterbalancing of base forces, while sustaining certain spiritual and sublimating elements (the heraldic symbols themselves). Sometimes one finds Wild Women of similar aspect and similar significance. Frazer has described some folklore customs which are unquestionably related to this fabulous woman. Some regions of Germany, during Whitsuntide, hold a festival called 'the Expulsion of the Wild Man', in which the part of the savage is played by a youth, covered in leaves and moss, who hides in the woods. The others then begin a chase which ends with his figurative death. Next day they make a stretcher and place on it a straw puppet resembling the Wild Man. This they carry in procession to a lake where the executioner throws it into the water (21). In Bohemia, the 'king' makes his appearance clothed in grass and flowers. The Wild Man seems to coincide with the 'Scapegoat' in the ritual assassination of the king. Jung suggests that this myth symbolizes the primitive or baser part of the personality, or the unconscious in its perilous and regressive aspect, which he has termed the 'shadow' (56). It is also connected with fabulous islands such as the island of St. Brendan or the land of Prester John.

Wind The wind is air in its active and violent aspects, and is held to be the primary Element by virtue of its connexion with the creative breath or exhalation. Jung recalls that in Arabic (and paralleled by the Hebrew) the word *ruh* signifies both 'breath' and 'spirit' (31). At the height of its activity, the wind gives rise to the hurricane (a synthesis and 'conjunction' of the four Elements), which is credited with the power of fecundation and regeneration. It was taken up in this sense by the alchemists, as can be seen for example in Jamsthaler's *Viatorium Spagyricum* (Frankfort, 1625) (31). The winds were numbered and brought into correspondence with the cardinal points and the signs of the Zodiac, so as to bring out their cosmic significance. In Egypt and Greece the wind was reckoned to possess certain evil powers; but for the Greeks, this menacing implication, which they associated with Typhon, was reversed from that moment when the fleet of Xerxes was destroyed by a tempest (41).

Window Since it consists of an aperture, the window expresses the ideas of penetration, of possibility and of distance, and because it is square in shape, its implications are rational and terrestrial. It is also symbolic of consciousness (32), especially when it is located at the top of a tower, by analogy with the head of the human figure. Divided windows carry a secondary significance, which may at times even be the predominant sense, deriving from the number of openings or lights and from the inter-relationships between the relevant number-symbolism and the general symbolism of the window (Plate XXXI).

Wine   An ambivalent symbol like the god Dionysos himself. On the one hand wine, and red wine in particular, symbolizes blood and sacrifice; on the other, it signifies youth and eternal life, like that divine intoxication of the soul hymned by Greek and Persian poets which enables man to partake, for a fleeting moment, of the mode of being attributed to the gods (17).

Wine-skin   An attribute of the satyr and of Silenus. In Greek, the phrase 'to untie the wine-skin' meant to indulge in Venusian delights (8). The phrase itself is suggestive of the lingam in the conjunction of a masculine, phallic element (the feet of the goat) and a feminine element (the skin as a receptacle). This idea was taken up by Christians who linked it with the idea of sin, and the wine-skin thereby came to symbolize evil-mindedness or a heavy conscience. Pinedo has pointed out that the wine-skin carried by various figures in Romanesque designs—such as that on the *Porta Speciosa* of the sanctuary at Estibaliz—bears precisely this meaning, and he quotes the Psalms in support: 'He gathereth the waters of the sea together as in a wine-skin[1]: he layeth up the depth in storehouses' (Psalms xxxiii, 7) (46). Analogous in significance are the haversack, the shepherd's pouch, and also the horn-pipe and the bladder of the buffoon (though, because of his sacrificial character, the buffoon alludes to the sins of others).

Wings   In the more general sense, wings symbolize spirituality, imagination, thought. The Greeks portrayed love and victory as winged figures, and some deities, such as Athena, Artemis and Aphrodite were at first—though not later—also depicted with wings. According to Plato, wings are a symbol of intelligence, which is why some fabulous animals are winged, depicting the sublimation of those symbolic qualities usually ascribed to each animal. Pelops' horses, and Pegasus, as well as Ceres' snakes, have this attribute. Wings are also found on certain objects such as heroes' helmets, the caduceus and the thunderbolt in the cult of Jupiter (8). It follows that the form and nature of the wings express the spiritual qualities of the symbol. Thus, the wings of night-animals express a perverted imagination, and Icarus' wax wings stand for functional insufficiency (15). In Christian symbolism it is said that wings are simply the light of the sun of justice, which always illuminates the mind of the righteous. Since wings also signify mobility, this meaning combines with that of enlightenment to express the possibility of 'progress in enlightenment' or spiritual evolution (46). In

---

[1] The English Authorised version reads: 'He gathereth the waters of the sea together as *an heap* . . .' The Septuagint gives 'wine-skin'.—*Translator.*

alchemy, wings are always associated with the higher, active, male principle; animals without wings are related to the passive female principle (33). It should also be recalled that, since the foot is regarded as a symbol of the soul (15), the wings on the heels of some deities, especially Mercury, stand for the power of spiritual elevation comparable in essence with cosmic evolution. Jules Duhem, in his thesis on the history of flight, remarks that, in Tibet, 'Buddhist saints travel through the air wearing a special kind of shoes known as "light feet"' (3).

Withdrawal Every withdrawal, retreat or concealment—like the moon and like sleep—symbolizes that period of life before and after its involution as matter, that is, before and after the manifest life of appearances.

Wolf Symbolic of valour among the Romans and the Egyptians. It also appears as a guardian in a great many monuments (8). In Nordic mythology we are told of a monstrous wolf, Fenris, that would destroy iron chains and shackles and was eventually shut up in the bowels of the earth. It was also said that, with the twilight of the gods—the end of the world—the monster would break out of this prison too, and would devour the sun. Here, then, the wolf appears as a symbol of the principle of evil, within a pattern of ideas which is unquestionably related to the Gnostic cosmogony. Nordic mythology presupposes that cosmic order is possible only through the temporary shackling of the chaotic and destructive potential of the universe—a potential which (through the process of Symbolic Inversion—q.v.) must triumph in the end. The myth is also connected with all other concepts of the final annihilation of the world, whether by water or by fire.

Woman In anthropology, woman corresponds to the passive principle of nature. She has three basic aspects: first, as a siren, lamia or monstrous being who enchants, diverts and entices men away from the path of evolution; second, as the mother, or *Magna mater* (the motherland, the city or mother-nature) related in turn to the formless aspect of the waters and of the unconscious; and third, as the unknown damsel, the beloved or the anima in Jungian psychology. In his *Symbols of Transformation*, Jung maintains that the ancients saw Woman as either Eve, Helen, Sophia or Mary (corresponding to the impulsive, the emotional, the intellectual, and the moral) (33). One of the purest and all-embracing archetypes of Woman as anima is Beatrice in Dante's *Commedia* (32). All allegories based upon the personification of Woman invariably retain all the implications of the three basic aspects mentioned above. Of great interest are those symbols in which the Woman appears in association with the figure of an animal—for example, the swan-woman in Celtic and Germanic mythology, related to the woman with the hoof of a goat in Hispanic folklore. In both cases the woman disappears once her maternal mission has been completed and, similarly, the virgin *qua* virgin 'dies' in order to give way to the matron (31). In iconography it is common to find parts of the female figure combined with that of a lion. The Egyptian goddess Sekhmet, characterized by her destructiveness, had the body of a woman and the head (and therefore the mind) of a lion. Conversely, a figure with a lion's body and a woman's head appears in the *Hieroglyphica* of Valeriano as an emblem of the hetaira (39). The inclusion of feminine, morphological elements in the composition of traditional symbols such as the sphinx always alludes to a background of nature overlaid with the projection of a concept or of an entire complex of cosmic intuitions. In consequence, the Woman is an archetypal image of great complexity in which the decisive factor may be the superimposed symbolic aspects—for example, the superior aspects of Woman as Sophia or Mary determine her function as a personification of science or of supreme virtue; and when presented as an image of the anima, she is superior to the man because she is a reflection of the loftiest and purest qualities of the man. In her baser forms as Eve or as Helen—the instinctive and emotional aspects—Woman is on a lower level than the man. It is here, perhaps, that she appears at her most characteristic—a temptress, the *Ewig Weibliche*, who drags everything down with her, and a symbol comparable with the volatile principle in alchemy, signifying all that is transitory, inconsistent, unfaithful and dissembling. See also *The Loved One* and *Sophia*.

Woman, Dead The image, vision or dream of a dead young woman in her tomb, is a direct symbol of the death of the *anima*. The French legend of Queen Blanche, quoted by Gérard de Sède in *Les Templiers sont parmi nous* (Paris, 1962), tells of this. Sède, in this context, links the names of Isis, a legendary Yse of the Knights Templars, and Yseult or Isolde. Georg Gichtel, a disciple of Jakob Böhme, refers to this symbol of the dead maiden or queen (dead in fact or in appearance, that is to say, sleeping, as in the well-known fairy tale) as one that relates 'to the corruption of the shining Paradisiac body' (cf. Evola, *La Tradizione ermetica*, Bari, 1948).

Wood A mother-symbol (31). Burnt wood signifies wisdom and death (50). The magic and fertilizing propensities of the wood burnt in sacrificial rites are supposed to be transmitted to the ashes and the charcoal. Cremation is regarded as a return to the 'seed'-state; this has given rise to many rites and folklore customs, related in turn to fire-symbolism (17).

World Symbolically, the world is the realm in which a state of existence is unfolded (25), comprising many component parts adhering together. Used in the plural, the term pertains, in a sense, to space-symbolism, but the 'worlds' are really only different modes of the spirit (26). The explanation of the cosmic and moral significance of the three worlds (the infernal, the terrestrial and the celestial) is to be sought in the symbolism of level. The inferior must not always be equated with the subterranean, for, in megalithic cultures, the latter was usually located high up, or in the hollow interior of mountains (conceived as the dwelling-place of the dead). Guénon has pointed out that references to the 'subterranean world' are found in a large number of cultural traditions, in which the 'cult of the cavern' or cave is linked with that of the 'centre'. One must also bear in mind the equation of the cavern with the cave of the heart, the latter being considered as the Centre of being or the Egg of the World (28).

World, The   The twenty-first enigma of the Tarot pack. The fact that the series consists of ternaries and septenaries is further proof that the number 21 implies a synthesis, or the totality of the manifest world, that is, the world of space as a reflection of permanent creative activity. This idea is represented in the allegorical image of this playing-card by a young girl running with two small sticks inside a garland which is surrounded by the cosmic quaternary or tetramorphs. The sticks are symbolic of polarization inducing the rotational motion of all things in the entire cosmos. According to Wirth, this girl also represents major Fortune, whereas minor Fortune corresponds to the tenth card of the Tarot. The quaternary is connected with the Elements, and the garland with the cosmic process (59).

World-image   The host of possibilities opened up by the very word 'world', points to the great number of symbolic images capable of reflecting its multiple aspects. All the great symbols are really images of the world: The septenary, for example, in the form of candelabra with seven branches, reflecting the arrangement of the planets; and bilateral symmetry as, for example, in the caduceus of Mercury, is the image of the world in so far as it is an equilibrium of hostile forces; and all forms of wheel symbols, such as the Zodiac, mandalas, or the Tarot pack, correspond to the world in so far as it appears as a cycle or succession of changes. But the essence of the world is the conflict between time and eternity, matter and spirit, or the conjunction of opposites which yet remain separate on the plane of existence—a conflict, that is, between continuity and discontinuity, usually conveyed by means of images reconciling the square with the circle, sometimes simply by 'squaring the circle' as in alchemic practice, and sometimes by multiplying one of the component elements by four, as in the oriental pentacle of Laos. The arrangement of the tetramorphs as a spiritual quaternary, keeping the centre as an image of the Origin (that is, heaven) which is counterbalanced by the world of manifestation, is sometimes represented as a city with four towers and four gates, always with an image of paramount significance in the centre (32). Frobenius recounts the history of a group of interesting symbols of this kind bearing upon the ritual cups or chalices of Ethiopia (inspired in the ceramics of Susa) in the fourth millenary before our era. In the middle of these cups there is a cross or some other symbol either of the swastika or of the damero type; this may be a representation of earth, for on the edges there is a motif sketched in, which might be an image of water. An African cup from Benin has a sea-serpent in the same position; here the symbol may be related to the dragon biting his own tail as in the Gnostic *Ouroboros*. A wooden disc from Morka shows an image of the sun in the centre, then a double chain suggesting the ocean, and finally an outer corona divided into four parts to accord with the four cardinal points (corresponding in turn with the seasons and the four Elements). But Frobenius also speaks of three-dimensional images of the world. He relates how, in 1910, he happened to be in the Yoruba (West Africa), where he made his way to the holy city of Ife, and there, in a place sacred to the god Ejar, he found an object like a kind of platform with a cone at each of its four corners and another larger one in the centre, surmounted by a cup or chalice. The central cone is the Mountain of the World (the mystic mandorla); and the four others correspond to the cardinal points. He notes the relationship between this image and certain thrones with five supports (22). Quite apart from the pictorial images of the Pantokrator and the tetramorphs, which are comparable to the above, Christianity too has an example of the same kind of pattern, depicted three-dimensionally, in the baptismal font at Estibaliz. Pinedo describes it as follows: The base is a heavy column, with four smaller ones close to it (analogous with the Centre and the four cardinal points); above it, a lotus flower is shown opening its corolla (a symbol of the world made manifest, and of nativity). Above this corolla, there is a colonnade with arches on which are inscribed other smaller, trefoiled .arches. In the spaces there are diverse symbolic beings (connoting the plane of cosmic life, that is, of existence). Above the arches, there is a pattern representing the battlements of the celestial Jerusalem—paradise regained (46). As a symbol of the world, then, in all its fundamental aspects, this image is the most artistic, the most exact and complete known to us.

World Soul This concept is related ideologically to that of the Great Mother and to that of the moon as a source of change and transmutation. It has certain negative characteristics, e.g. a tendency to divide and multiply—which is the essential prerequisite for all creative and reproductive processes (31). Only in literature is the

World Soul a single whole, and it is then equivalent to the 'mystic void' of Hindu and Hebrew traditions.

Worm Jung defines the worm as a libidinal figure which kills instead of giving life (31). This comes from its underground associations, its base characteristics, its connexion with death and with the biological stages of dissolution and the primary. Thus, it is death which the worm symbolizes—but death which is relative from the point of view of what is superior or organized; basically, like the snake, it denotes crawling, knotted energy.

Woven Fabric The phrase 'the web of life' is an eloquent expression of the symbolism of woven fabric which is not only concerned with ideas of binding and increase through the blending of two elements (the warp and the woof—the passive and the active), nor is it merely equivalent to creation; rather does it denote the mystic apprehension of the world of phenomena as a kind of veil which hides the true and the profound from sight. As Porphyry observed: 'The ancients called the heavens "a veil" because, in a sense, they are the garments of the gods.' And as Plato said: 'The one and only Demiurge commands the secondary demiurges'— that is, the mythological gods—'to bind the immortal to the mortal in a symbolic fabric'. In addition to the symbolism of weaving, this idea embraces that of the Gemini (signifying the dual composition of all things in existence, one part being immortal and the other mortal). Plutarch observed that weaving was invented by Isis with the assistance of her sister Nephthys (40). The legend of the 'Web of Penelope' is related to this. Guénon sees the warp and woof as equivalent to the horizontal and vertical limbs of the cosmic cross, where the upright represents the various states of being and the horizontal the degree of development reached by these states. He also mentions that the two lines of the loom can be identified with the masculine and the feminine principles, and that this is why, in the *Upanishads*, the Supreme Brahma is designated 'He upon whom the worlds are woven as warp and woof'. At the same time, the alternation of life and death, condensation and dissolution, the predominance of *Yang* or of *Yin*, are, for the Taoists, like the alternating 'waves' of thread in the weave of the fabric (25). Apart from this essential symbolism, a fabric has further symbolic meanings deriving from its colour, form and function (where applicable). Piobb, with particular reference to Scotch tartans, has pointed out that certain types of fabric are characterized by patterns with an esoteric purport (48). Ornamental designs have the same symbolic significance whether they appear in a fabric, or are engraved on a stone or painted in a miniature (see *Graphics*). The veil, as an elemental form of weaving and as clothing, is symbolic of 'wrapping', that is, of matter. The seven veils in Salome's dance, or in the myth of Ishtar, correspond to the seven planetary spheres and their respective influences.

Yang-Yin   A Chinese symbol of the dual distribution of forces, comprising the active or masculine principle (*Yang*) and the passive or feminine principle (*Yin*). It takes the form of a circle bisected by a sigmoid line, and the two parts so formed are invested with a dynamic tendency which would be wanting if the division were by a diameter. The light half represents the *Yang* force and the dark half denotes *Yin*; however, each half includes an arc cut out of the middle of the opposing half, to symbolize that every mode must contain within it the germ of its antithesis. Guénon considers that the Yang-Yin is a helicoidal symbol, that is, that it is a section of the universal whirlwind which brings opposites together and engenders perpetual motion, metamorphosis and continuity in situations characterized by contradiction. The entrance to and exit from this movement lie outside the movement itself, in the same way that birth and death stand apart from the life of the individual in so far as it is conscious and self-determined. The vertical axis through the centre of the Yang-Yin constitutes the 'unvarying mean' or, in other words, the mystic 'Centre' where there is no rotation, no restlessness, no impulse, nor any suffering of any kind. It corresponds to the central zone of the Wheel of Transformations in Hindu symbolism, and the centre or the way out of the labyrinth in Egyptian and western symbolism. It is also expressive of the two counterbalancing tendencies of evolution and involution (25).

Year   More than a symbol, the year is, as it were, the prototype of all cyclic processes (the day, the span of human life, the rise and fall of a culture, the cosmic cycle, etc.). All cycles are composed of an ascending and a descending phase, i.e. evolution and involution; sometimes, cycles are also subdivided into three or, more frequently, four phases (seasons of the year, ages of man). The overall division of the cyclic process, however, need not necessarily be symmetrical. Thus, in a cycle composed of twelve units, such as the year (or the wheel of the Zodiac), the ascending and descending phases can be taken either as 6 plus 6 (symmetrical division) or 8 plus 4 (asymmetrical division). The former is a more geometrical, the latter a more empirical division. The year is usually represented by the figure of an old man in a circle, with two or three outer rings containing such items as: the names of the months, the cycle of work appropriate to each month, the signs of the Zodiac and so on. Often the circle of the year is, in its turn, enclosed in a square the corners of which are occupied by four figures personifying the four seasons. The tapestry of the Creation, in Gerona cathedral, is a famous example. Two interesting points in connexion with the annual cycle are: (i) in Chinese tradition, the cycle is divided into two equal parts, corresponding respectively to darkness/death, and light/life; (ii) there was a primitive belief that every man undergoes a process of regeneration every year, from December to June, symbolizing death and resurrection (51) (Plate XXXII).

Yoke Like the sheaf or bunch, the yoke is a symbol of union and discipline; but by virtue of its association with the ox, it is also symbolic of sacrifice (50).

Yoni Like the mandorla, the Yoni is the gateway, or the zone of interpenetration wherein two circles intersect. Indians, in order to ensure regeneration, make an image of the Yoni in gold, and pass through it (21).

Youth and Old Man These two figures personify the rising and the setting sun. Another similar idea is that which considers each sun as the offspring of its predecessor; this provides us with an explanation of the great number of solar gods born of other sun-gods (35). In addition to this system of 'continuous connexion', or of circular links, the Old Man is always the father (the master, tradition, contemplation, the celestial sovereign, justice), while the Youth is the son (the governed, subversion, intuition, the hero, boldness). The counterbalancing formula of Youth-Old Man loses its equipoise once the Youth is a mature man and the Old Man decrepit, because the latter then becomes infantile and asexual.

Z

Zenith The zenith is a symbol which can be synonymous with that of the central hole in the Chinese heaven known as *Pi*, as well as with that of the peak of the mountain-temple, or the pyramid, or the sacrificial stake, or the pillar of the world (18). It is the point through which mystics believe their thoughts may pass out of space into non-space, out of time into timelessness. Hence, the importance of the formal likeness of this symbol with that of the hole.

Zodiac One of the most widespread of symbols, despite its complexity. In almost every land and age its characteristics are the same—the circular form, the twelve subdivisions with their corre-

sponding signs and their relationship with the seven planets. The
Mesopotamian cultures, Egypt, Judea, Persia, India, Tibet, China,
America, Islam, Greece and Northern Europe—all were acquainted
with zodiacal symbolism. The name of this circular 'form' comes from
zoe (life) and *diakos* (wheel); and the basic element of this 'wheel of
life' is found in the Ouroboros (the snake biting its own tail),
symbolizing the *Aion* (duration). The general significance of the
Zodiac concerns the process by which 'primordial energy, once
fecundated, passes from the potential to the virtual, from unity to
multiplicity, from spirit to matter, from the non-formal world to
the world of forms', and then returns along the same path (52).
This accords with the teaching of oriental ontology, which holds
that the life of the universe is split into two opposing yet complementary phases: involution (or materialization) and evolution (or
spiritualization). Applying this belief to the Zodiac, the first six
signs (from Aries to Virgo) come to represent involution, while the
other six (from Libra to Pisces) relate to evolution. This pattern
refers not only to the evolution of the cosmos in the broadest sense,
but also to specific phases of this process as well as to any given
period in the development of the manifest world as such (for
example, a period in history, the lifetime of a race or of an individual,
the period of the world's existence, the time taken in carrying out a
task) (52). As evidence of the great antiquity of this symbol, we
would point to the zodiacal signs in the rock-paintings in the Cueva
de Arce (at the Laguna de la Janda, Cadiz), the celestial maps in
the stone-engravings at Eira d'os Mouros (in Galicia), and the
sculpting of the cromlech at Alvão (in Portugal), not to speak of
the numerous other examples of the same kind of thing: but there
is no conclusive evidence of the existence of a truly systematic
understanding of Zodiacal symbolism before the time of king
Sargon of Agade (2750 B.C.), who was known to possess a work of
astrology containing forecasts of the eclipses of the sun. From the
time of Hammurabi (2000 B.C.) man's study of the heavens began
to assume a more scientific character. But the Zodiac, and the
characteristic signs as we know them today, cannot, in the opinion
of Berthelot, be traced back farther than the tablet of Cambyses
(6th century B.C.); this, however, does not invalidate the theory
that the separate elements that contributed to the symbolic pattern
of the Zodiac as a whole were of much greater antiquity than this.
For example, the mystic twelvefold vision of the world; and
the symbol of the ram associated with the mythic Ram and with
the Primitive cult of the sun; and also the Gemini. Marc Saunier
has commented, in connexion with the twelve-part division of the
Zodiac, that spreading into our solar world from an unknowable
unknown, through the twelve luminous doors of the Zodiac, it

becomes concentrated into the form of the sun whence it radiates
outwards to the seven planetary spheres which refract its unity in
the gamut of sounds, rhythms and colours (49). As Jung notes,
according to Manichean belief the demiurge builds a cosmic wheel,
related to the *rota* and the *opus circulatorium* of alchemy and
identical in that it signifies sublimation (31). It is almost unnecessary
to point out that this form of motion, rotation on the vertical
plane—descending and ascending—echoes the Platonic theories of
the soul's 'fall' into material existence and its need to find salvation
by returning along the same path. The most important and definitive
adaptations of the zodiacal cycle—for other variants arise by
analogy—are, first, that which equates the twelve signs with monthly
periods, and the complete cycle with the year (commencing with
March—with the spring), and, secondly, that corresponding to the
great cycle (lasting 25,920 years) of the precession of the equinoxes,
whereby, every 2160 years, the equinox withdraws by the space of
one sign (thirty degrees). The fact that the figures which make up
the zodiacal pattern are mostly animals has prompted Schneider to
suggest that the constellations may owe their curious names to an
earlier religion of totemistic origin, whose basic features were
subsequently applied to the heavens through the process of
catasterism (50). Piobb has observed that the Zodiac, besides being
a process, may also be understood as a circuit and that its twelve-
part division springs from the way in which the quantitative becomes
qualitative (in vibrations, sounds or colours) and hence the ecliptic
is a zone of energy differing in potential between its entrance (Aries)
and its exit (Pisces). He also notes that, if one wishes to grasp the
ancient conceptions, one must regard the Zodiac as a totality
comprising twelve ideographs which, in sum, epitomize the
dodecagon (48). It is clear that every twelve-part scheme alludes to
the zodiacal pattern. The signs (q.v. under separate headings) are
as follows: Aries, Taurus, Gemini, Cancer, Leo, Virgo, Libra,
Scorpio, Sagittarius, Capricorn, Aquarius, Pisces (40). According to
Senard, these twelve signs are derived from the four Elements
combined with the three modes or *gunas* (levels) known as *sattva*,
rajas and *tamas* (corresponding, firstly, to a situation—or level—of
superiority or of essence; secondly, to an intermediate or transitional
situation: and, thirdly, to the level of the inferior and material).
But we cannot here go into Senard's theory of the signs of the
Zodiac, beyond noting, briefly, the meanings that he attributes to
each of them: Aries he interprets as the urge to create and transform:
Taurus as undifferentiated magnetism; the Gemini as creative
synthesis, or imagination; Cancer as gestation and birth; Leo as
individuation, will; Virgo as intelligence; Libra as equilibrium;
Scorpio as histolysis; Sagittarius as coordination and synthesis;

Capricorn as ascesis; Aquarius as illumination; and Pisces as mystic fusion (52). Mertens-Stienon founds his study of the Zodiac upon an article by the Hindu T. Subba Rao, published in October 1881 and translated into French for *Le Lotus bleu* in 1937, drawing also upon the work of Blavatsky and Dupuis (the latter favouring an almost exclusively astronomical interpretation of the myths). Mertens Stienon, then, divides the zodiacal signs into three quaternaries, although in our view a better division would be the inverse of this—four ternaries, forming a triunity for each of the seasons of the year (as well as for the cardinal points). He supports the view that the Zodiac may serve to symbolize and analyse the phases of each and every cycle, together with the evolutive stages which it embraces. He distinguishes between the astronomical Zodiac (the constellations) and the intellectual Zodiac (symbols), affirming that it was the constellations that took their names from the symbols. For instance, since, in Egyptian times, so much importance was attached to the symbolic bull and ram, this was why, astronomically speaking, these figures came to mark the vernal equinoxes which, in our era, coincide with Pisces. He shows that the apparent orbit of the sun through the twelve divisions corresponds to twelve degrees or stages in the action of the active principle upon the passive. These stages are denoted in mythology by the avatars of the creator-god—by his metamorphoses and manifestations. The precise symbolism of each sign springs from: (*a*) the number it bears in the series of twelve signs: (*b*) its situation within the series as a whole; (*c*) its situation within each of the four ternaries; (*d*) its symbolic figure; (*e*) the ideas related to this figure; and (*f*) the concomitant planetary symbolism. In the symbolism of the Zodiac one can sense the resolve to create, as in the Tarot pack, an all-embracing archetypal pattern—a kind of figurative model to serve as a comprehensive definition of each and every existential possibility in the macrocosm and the microcosm. As is the case with other symbolic forms, zodiacal symbolism is the product of the *serial* intellection of the universe, arising out of the belief that all things occupy positions and situations in space-time which are limited and typical, and implying, not determinism, but belief in the 'system of destinies', that is to say, the theory that certain antecedents must cause certain consequences and that any given situation must have ramifications that are neither replaceable nor arbitrary. Regarding the application of the Zodiac to the cycle of human existence in the concrete sense, there are certain obvious affinities with symbols pertaining to medicinal rites, as Schneider has shown. It is to Jorge Quintana, and his *El gobierno teocrático de Mohenjo-Daro* (Ampurias, IV), that we owe our knowledge of an octonary zodiac dating from the proto-Indian period of the third millennium before our era. This zodiac is composed of the following signs: *edu* (the ram), *yal* (the harp), *nand* (the crab), *amma* (the mother), *tuk* (the scales), *kani* (the dart), *kuda* (the pitcher) and *min* (the fish). There are obvious parallels between most of these signs and those of the dodecanarian Zodiac. The supreme god of the proto-Indians was equated with the sun, crossing, in his procession through the constellations, the corresponding degrees of the Zodiac, whence he derives his title of 'god of the eight forms'.

Zone Every zone or area of space holds a symbolic significance deriving from its level on the vertical axis and its situation in relation to the cardinal points. In the broadest sense, zone may, by analogy, be equated with degree or mode. The colours are really only zones of the spectrum, and, by this token, any arrangement of zones is susceptible of interpretation as a serial whole.

BIBLIOGRAPHY OF PRINCIPAL SOURCES

BACHELARD, GASTON. *La Psychanalyse du feu*. Paris, 1938 (1).
— *L'Eau et les Rêves*. Paris, 1942 (2).
— *L'Air et les Songes*. Paris, 1943 (3).
BAYLEY, HAROLD. *The Lost Language of Symbolism*. London, 1912 (repr. 1951) (4).
BEAUMONT, A. *Symbolism in Decorative Chinese Art*. New York, 1949 (5).
BENOIST, Luc. *Art du monde*. Paris, 1941 (6).
BERTHELOT, René. *La pensée de l'Asie et l'astrobiologie*. Paris, 1949 (7).
B. G. P. *Diccionario universal de la mitología*. Barcelona, 1835 (8).
BLAVATSKY, H. P. *The Secret Doctrine*. London, 1888 (9).
CARO BAROJA, Julio. *Algunos mitos españoles*. Madrid, 1941 (10).
CEPOLLARO, A. *Il rituale mitriaco*. Rome, 1954 (11).
COLA, J. *Tatuajes y amuletos marroquíes*. Madrid, 1949 (12).
CHOCHOD, Louis. *Occultisme et magie en Extrême-Orient*. Paris, 1945 (13).
DAVY, M.-M. *Essai sur la Symbolique Romane*. Paris, 1955 (14).
DIEL, Pail. *Le Symbolisme dans la mythologie grecque*. Paris, 1952 (15).
DONTENVILLE, Henri. *La Mythologie française*. Paris, 1948 (16).
ELIADE, Mircea. *Tratado de historia de las religiones*. Madrid, 1954 (17).
— *Images et Symboles*. Paris, 1952 (18).
ENEL. *La langue sacrée*. Paris, 1932 (19).
FERGUSON, George W. *Signs and Symbols in Christian Art*. New York, 1954 (20).
FRAZER, Sir James G. *The Golden Bough*. London, 1911–15 (21).
FROBENIUS, Leo. *Histoire de la civilisation africaine*. Paris, 1952 (22).
FROMM, Erich. *The Forgotten Language*. London, 1952 (23).
GHYKA, Matila. *Philosophie et mystique du nombre*. Paris, 1952 (24)
GUÉNON, René. *Le Symbolisme de la croix*. Paris, 1931 (25).
— *Man and his Becoming according to the Vedānta*. London, 1945 (26).
— *L'Esotérisme de Dante*. Paris, 1949 (27)
— *Le Roi du monde*. Paris, 1950 (28).
— *Aperçu sur l'Initiation*. Paris (29).
JACOBI, Jolan de. *The Psychology of C. G. Jung*. London, 1951 (30).
JUNG, C. G. *Symbols of Transformation* (Collected Works, 5). London, 1956 (31).
— *Psychology and Alchemy* (Collected Works, 12). London, 1953 (32).
— 'Psychology of the Transference'. In *The Practice of Psychotherapy* (Collected Works, 16). London, 1954 (33).
— 'The Relations between the Ego and the Unconscious'. In: *Two Essays on Analytical Psychology* (Collected Works, 7). London, 1953 (34).
KRAPPE, A. H. *La Genèse des mythes*. Paris, 1952 (35).
LEHNER, Ernst. *Symbols, Signs and Signets*. Cleveland, 1950 (36).
LÉVI, Éliphas. *Les Mystères de la Kabbale*. Paris, 1920 (37).
LOEFFLER-DELACHAUX, M. *Le Symbolisme des contes de Fées*. Paris, 1949 (38).
MARQUÈS RIVIÈRE, J. *Amulettes, talismans et pantacles*. Paris, 1950 (39).
MERTENS STIENON, M. *L'Occultisme du zodiaque*. Paris, 1939 (40).
ORITZ, Fernando. *El Huracán*. Mexico, 1947 (41).
PANETH, L. *La Symbolique des nombres dans l'Inconscient*. Paris, 1953 (42).
PAPUS. *Traité méthodique de science occulte*. Paris, 1891 (43).
— *La Science des nombres*. Paris, 1934 (44).
— *Initiation astrologique*. Paris, 1919 (45).
PINEDO, Ramiro de. *El Simbolismo en la escultura medieval española*. Madrid, 1930 (46).

PIOBB, P. V. *Formulaire de l'haute magie.* Paris, 1937 (47).
— *Clef universelle des sciences secrètes.* Paris, 1950 (48).
SAUNIER, Marc. *La Légende des symboles, philosophiques, religieux et maçonniques.* 2nd edn. Paris, 1911 (49).
SCHNEIDER, Marius. *El origen musical de los animales-símbolos en la mitología y la escultura antiguas.* Barcelona, 1946 (50).
— *La danza de espadas y la tarantela.* Barcelona, 1948 (51).
SENARD, M. *Le Zodiaque.* Lausanne, 1948 (51).
SEZNEC, Jean. *The Survival of the Pagan Gods.* New York, 1953 (53).
STAR, Ély. *Les Mystères de l'Etre.* Paris, 1902 (54).
— *Les Mystères du verbe.* Paris, 1908 (55).
TEILLARD, Ania. *Il Simbolismo dei Sogni.* Milan, 1951 (56).
TESTI, Gino. *Dizionario di Alchimia e di Chimica antiquaria.* Rome, 1950 (57).
WILHELM, Richard. *Lao Tse und der Taoismus.* Stuttgart, 1925 (58).
WIRTH, Oswald. *Le Tarot des imagiers du Moyen Age.* Paris, 1927 (59).
ZIMMER, Heinrich. *Myths and Symbols in Indian Art and Civilization.* New York, 1946 (60).
ZOLLINGER, Gustav. *Tau oder Tau-T'an, und das Rätsel der sprachlichen und menschlichen Einheit.* Berne, 1952 (61).

ADDITIONAL BIBLIOGRAPHY

ADAM, Leonhard. *Nordwestamerikanische Indianerkunst*. Berlin, 1923.

ADRIAN, P. G. *Réflexions sur l'univers sonore*. Paris, 1955.

AELIANUS, Claudius. *De Natura Animalium*. Jena, 1832.

AGRIPPA, H. C. *Opera*. Lyon, XVI century.

ALBERT, M. *Le culte de Castor et Pollux en Italie*. Paris, 1883.

ALCAZAR, Luis. *Vestigatio arcani sensus in Apocalypsi*. Antwerp, 1619.

ALCIATI, Andrea, *Emblemata*. Paris, 1580.

ALLBERRY, Charles. *Symbole von Tod und Wiedergeburt im Manichäismus*. Eranos Jahrbuch 1939. Zurich, 1940.

— *Allegorien und Embleme*. Vienna, 1900.

ALLEAU, René. *Aspects de l'alchimie traditionnelle*. Paris, 1952.

— *De la Nature des symboles*. Paris, 1958.

ALLEN, Emory A. *The Prehistoric World or Vanished Races*. Cincinnati, 1885.

ALLEN, J. R. *Early Christian symbolism in Great Britain and Ireland before the XIII century*. London, 1877.

ALLEN, Maude Rex, *Japanese Art Motives*. Chicago, 1917.

ALLENDY, — *Le Symbolisme des nombres*. Paris, 1948.

AMADES, Joan. *Mitología megalítica*. Ampurias III. Barcelona, 1941.

AMMAN, Jost. *Beschreibung aller Stände*. Frankfurt, 1568.

ANDRAE, R. *Ethnographische Parallelen, Neue Folge*. Leipzig, 1889.

ANDRAE, Walter. *Die ionische Säule, Bauform oder Symbol?* Berlin, 1933.

ANTONIADI, E. M. *L'Astronomie des prêtres égyptiens*. Paris, 1936.

ARATUS, Paulus. *Emblemas sacras y profanas, seguidas de un discurso . . .* Rome, 1589.

Archeological Institute of America. *Mythology of all Races*. Boston, 1925-32.

Ars memorandi or *rationarium evangelistarum*. (With verses by Petrus de Rosenheim.) Pforzheim, 1502.

ARTEMIDORUS DALDIANUS. *Onirocriticon libri V*. Leipzig, 1864.

ARTIN, YAKOUB. *Contribution à l'étude du blason en Orient*. London, 1902.

AUBER, C. A. *Histoire et théorie du symbolisme religieux*. Paris, 1884.

— *Histoire du symbolisme religieux avant et depuis le Christianisme*. Paris, 1844.

BACHELARD, Gaston. *Lautréamont*. Paris, 1939.

BACHOFEN, J. J. *Der Mythus von Orient und Occident*. Munich, 1926.

— *Mutterrecht und Urreligion*. Leipzig, 1927.

BALTRUSAITIS, Jurgis. *Art sumérien, art roman*. Paris, 1934.

— *Le Moyen Age fantastique*. Paris, 1955.

BARBERINO, Francesco. *Memorie Imprese e Ritrati*. Bologna, 1672.

BARBIER DE MONTAULT. *Traité d'iconographie chrétienne*. Paris, 1890.

BARRETT. *Lives of the alchemystical philosophers with a catalogue of books in occult chemistry*. London, 1815.

BAUER, A. *Chemie und Alchemie in Österreich bis zum beginnenden XIX. Jahrhundert*. Vienna, 1883.

BEARD, Daniel C. *The American Boy's Book of Signs, Signals and Symbols*. Philadelphia and London, 1918.

BECQ DE FOUQUIÈRES. *Les Jeux des anciens*. Paris, 1873.

BEDA. *Opera*. Cologne, 1612.

BEIGBEDER. *La Symbolique*. Paris, 1957.

BELL, Eric Temple. *La Magie des Nombres*. Paris, 1952.

BERCHEM, Egon von. *Die Wappenbücher des Deutschen Mittel-Alters.* Basel, 1928.
BERGER, E. H. *Mythische Kosmographie der Griechen.* Leipzig, 1904.
BERJEAU, J. Ph. *Early Dutch, German and English Printer's Marks.* London, 1866.
BERNOULLI, R. 'Spiritual Development as Reflected in Alchemy', etc. In *Spiritual Disciplines* (Papers from the Eranos Yearbooks, 4). New York and London, 1960.
BERTHELOT, P. E. M. *Introduction à l'étude de la chimie des anciens et du Moyen-Age.* Paris, 1889.
— *Les Origines de l'Alchemie.* Paris, 1885.
BERTHELOT, P. E. M., and RUELLE, C. E. *Collection des anciens alchimistes grecs.* Paris, 1887–88.
BIDEZ, J., and CUMONT, F. *Les Mages hellénisés.* Paris, 1938.
BIENKOWSKI, P. *Les Celtes dans les arts mineurs gréco-romains.* Cracow, 1928.
BIRINGUCCIO, Vannoccio. *De la Pirotechnia.* Venice, 1540.
BOCCACCIO. *Genealogia deorum gentilium.* Venice, 1472.
BOCCHIO, Achille. *Symbolicarum quaestionum de universo genere.* Bologna, 1555.
BOCHART, S. *Hierozoicon, sive bipertitum opus de Animalibus S. Scripturae.* London, 1663.
BOISSAER, Jean-Jacques. *Emblematum Liber.* Frankfurt, 1593.
BONGUS, P. *De mystica numerorum significatio.* Venice, 1585.
BORGES Y GUERRERO. *Manual de zoología fantástica.* Mexico, 1957.
BORNEMANN, S. *Die Allegorie in Kunst Wissenschaft und Kirche.* Freibrug im Breisgau, 1899.
BORNITUS, Jacobus. *Emblemata ethico-politica.* Mainz, 1669.
BOWES, James Lord. *Japanese Marks and Seals.* London, 1882.
BOWRA, C. M. *The Heritage of Symbolism.* London, 1943.
BRANT, Sebastian. *Stultifera Navis.* Basle, 1497.
BRÉAL, M. *Semantics.* London, 1900.
BRETON, André. *Cahiers G. L. M. 7.* Paris, 1938.
— *L'Amour fou.* Paris, 1937.
BRIFFAULT, Robert. *The Mothers.* London and New York, 1927.
BRILLANT, M. *Les Mystères d'Eleusis.* Paris, 1920.
BRIQUET, Charles Moïse. *Les Filigranes.* Paris, 1907.
BRUCK ANGERMUNT, Jacobus. *Emblemata politica.* Cologne, 1618.
BRUNE, Johan de. *Emblemata of Zinnewerck.* Amsterdam, 1624.
BRYANT, Jacob. *Analysis of Ancient Mythology.* London, 1807.
BUDGE, E. A. Wallis. *Amulets and Superstitions.* London, 1930.
— *Egyptian Magic.* London, 1899.
BUHLER, Karl. *Ausdruckstheorie.* Jena, 1933.
BULARD, Marcel. *Le Scorpion symbole du peuple juif.* Paris, 1935.
BUREN, E. Douglas van. *Symbols of the Gods in Mesopotamian Art.* Analecta Orientalia. Rome, 1945.
BURNOUF, E. *Le Vase sacré et ce qu'il contient* . . . Paris, 1896.
BURTON, William, and Hobson, R. L. *Handbook of Marks on Pottery and Porcelain.* London, 1909.
CADET DE GASSICOURT and ROURE DE PAULIN. *L'Hermétisme dans l'art héraldique.* Paris, 1907.
CAILLIET, E. *Symbolisme et âmes primitives.* Paris, 1936.
CALLET, Ch. *Le Mystère du langage.* Paris, 1928.
CAMBRIEL, L. P. F. *Cours de philosophie hermétique ou d'alchimie.* Paris, 1843.
CAMERARIUS, Joachinus. *Symbolorum et emblematum centuriae.* Mainz, 1668.
CAMILLI, Camillo. *Imprese illustri di diversi* . . . (with illustrations by Girolamo Porro). Venice, 1586.
CAPUA, Johannes de. *Hortus Sanitatis.* Mainz, 1491.

CARTARI, Vincenzo. *Le Imagine dei Dei degli Antichi*. Venice, 1625.
CARTER, D. *The Symbol of the Beast*. New York, 1957.
CARUS, Paul. *Chinese Philosophy*. Chicago, 1898.
— *The Soul of Man*. London, 1891.
— *The History of the Devil*. London, 1900.
CASANOVA, Ludovicus. *Hieroglyphicorum*. Lyon, 1626.
CASSIRER, Ernst. *Antropología filosófica*. Mexico, 1951.
— *Idee und Gestalt*. Berlin, 1921.
CASTELLANOS DE LOSADA, Basilio Sebastián. *Compendio del sistema alegórico y diccionario manual de la iconología universal*. Madrid, 1850.
CAUSSINO, Nicolao. *Symbolica aegyptiorum sapientia*. Paris, 1647.
CHAFFERS, William. *The Collector's Hand Book of Marks and Monograms on Pottery and Porcelain*. London, 1898.
CHAIGNET, A. E. *Pythagore et la philosophie pythagoricienne*. Paris, 1873.
CHARBONNEAU-LASSAY, L. *Le Bestiaire du Christ*. Brussels, 1940.
— *L'Ésotérisme de quelques symboles géométriques chrétiens*. Paris, 1960.
CHARLES, E. *Roger Bacon. Sa vie, ses ouvrages, ses doctrines*. Paris, 1861.
CHASSANG, A. *Le merveilleux dans l'Antiquité*. Paris, 1862.
CHRISTIAN. *Histoire de la Magie*. Paris, 1863.
CHOMPRE, P. *Dictionnaire abregé de la fable*. Paris, 1727.
CIRLOT, J. E. *El Ojo en la Mitología, su simbolismo*. Barcelona, 1954.
— *Hacia una cienca de los símbolos*. In « Sumario », VIII, 22. Barcelona, 1952.
COBARRUBIAS Y HOROZCO, Sebastián de. *Emblemas morales*. Madrid, 1610 and 1951.
COLONNA, E. *Materiae Signa*. New York, 1888.
COLONNA, Francesco. *Hypnerotomachia Poliphili*. Venice, 1499.
COLLUM, V. C. C. *The Tressée Iron-Age Megalithic Monument*. London, 1935.
CONTENAU, G. *La Magie chez les assyriens et les babyloniens*. Paris, 1947.
COOK, A. B. *Zeus, a Study of Ancient Religion*. London, 1914–40.
COOMARASWAMY, A. *Elements of Buddhist Iconography*. Cambridge, Mass., 1935.
— 'Symbolism of the Dome.' *Indian Hist. Quart.* XIV, 1, 1935.
— 'The Inverted Tree.' *Quart. Journ. Myth. Soc. Bangalore*, XXIX, 2, 1938.
CORBIN, Henry. *Terre céleste et corps de résurrection*. Paris, 1960.
CORDUERO, Moise. *Le Palmier de Déborah*. Mantua, 1623.
— *Le Jardin des Grenades*. Cracow.
COURT DE GEBELIN, A. *Monde primitif*. Paris, 1773–82.
CREUZER, Frédéric. *Les Religions de l'Antiquité considérées principalement dans leurs formes symboliques et mythologiques*. Paris, 1825.
CRUVEILHIER, J. *Paracelse, sa vie et sa doctrine*. Paris, 1842.
CUMONT, Franz. *L'Aigle funéraire des Syriens et l'apothéose des empereurs*. Paris, 1910.
— *Les Mystères de Mithra*. Brussels, 1900.
— *Recherches sur le symbolisme funéraire des Romains*. Paris, 1942.
— *Textes et monuments illustrés rélatifs aux mystères de Mithra*, 1896–99.
CYLIANI. *Hermès dévoilé*. Paris, 1832.
DAMMARTIN. *Traité sur l'origine des caractères alphabétiques*. Paris, 1839.
DANIÉLOU, Jean. *Les Symboles chrétiens primitifs*. Paris, 1961.
DANZEL, Th. W. *Symbole, Daemonen und Heilige Türme*. Hamburg, 1930.
DARMSTAEDTER, E. *Der babylonisch-assyrisch Lasurstein*. In 'Studien zur Geschichte der Chimie'. Berlin, 1937.
DAVID, Madeleine V. *Le Débat sur les écritures et l'hiéroglyphe aux XVII et XVIII siècles*. Paris, 1965.
DEBIDOUR, V.-H. *Le Bestiaire sculpté en France*. Paris, 1961.
De DAT, Giuiliano. *Il secondo cantare dell'India*. Rome, 1494.
DELAAGE. *La Science du vrai*. Paris, 1882.

DELALAIN, P. *Inventaire des Marques Typographiques.* Paris, 1866.
DELATTE, A. *Hergarius.* Liège, 1938.
DELEHAYE, Hippolyte. *Légendes hagiographiques.* Brussels, 1905.
DELLA PORTA, G. Battista. *Fisionomia dell'Uomo.* Padua, 1627.
DEONNA, E. *Quelques réflexions sur le symbolisme.* Rev. Hist. Rel. Paris, 1924.
DIERBACH, J. H. *Flore mythologique* . . . Dijon, 1867.
DIGBY, G. W. *Meaning and symbol.* London, 1955.
DINET, P. *Cinq livres des hiéroglyphiques.* Paris, 1614.
DIONYSIUS, pseudo-. *Divine Names,* etc., tr. C. E. Rolt. London, 1920.
— *The Celestial Hierarchies.* London, 1935.
DOBERER, Kurt Karl. *The Goldmakers.* London, 1948.
DORE, Henri. *Researches into Chinese Superstition.* Shanghai, 1914.
DUCHAUSSOY, Jacques. *Le Bestiaire divin ou le symbolique des animaux.* Paris, 1958.
ELEAZAR, Rabbi Abraham. *Uraltes Chymisches Werck.* Leipzig, 1760.
ELIADE, Mircea. *Méphistophélès et l'Androgyne.* Paris, 1962.
— *Myths, Dreams and Mysteries.* London, 1960.
ELLIS, Havelock. *The World of Dreams.* London, 1924.
EMERSON, Ellen Russel. *Indian Myths.* Boston, 1884.
ENDRES, F. C. *Mystik und Magie der Zahlen.* Zurich, 1951.
ENGELBRECHT, A. *Hephaestion von Theben und sein astrologisches Compendium.* Vienna, 1887.
Eranos-Jahrbuch. Zurich.
EVOLA, G. C. *La Tradizione Ermetica.* Bari, 1931.
FABRE D'OLIVET. *The Hebraic Tongue Restored.* New York, 1921.
— *La Musique expliquée.* Paris, 1928.
FAIR Publishing Company. *A Century of Texas Cattle Brands.* Forth Worth, 1936.
FAULHABER and REMMELIN. *Wortrechnung.* Nuremberg, 1914.
FAULMANN, Karl. *Das Buch der Schrift.* Vienna, 1878.
FAYE, E. de. *Les Apocalypses Juives.* Paris, 1892.
FENN, Waldemar. *Gráfica prehistórica de España y el origen de la cultura europea.* Mahon, 1950.
FERRANDO ROIG. *Simbología cristiana.* Barcelona, 1958.
FERRERO, Guglielmo. *I Simboli in rapporto alla storia e filosofia del diritto.* Turin, 1893.
FIGUIER, G. *L'Alchimie et les Alchimistes.* Paris, 1856.
FINGESTEN, Peter. 'Spirituality, Mysticism and non-objective'. In *The Journal,* XXI-I. New York, 1961.
FISSER. *Le symbole littéraire.* Paris.
FLAMEL, Hortensius. *Le Livre rouge: Résumé du magisme, des sciences occultes et de la philosophie hermétique.* Paris, 1842.
FRAENGER, Wilhelm. *Altdeutsches Bilderbuch.* Leipzig, 1930.
FRANCISCUS DE HOLLANDIA. *De Aetatibus Mundi Imagines,* 1545.
FRANCK, Adolphe. *Darstellung und Deutung der Allegorien.* Hamburg, 1880.
— *La Kabbale.* Paris, 1843.
— *Paracelse et l'alchimie au XVI siècle,* 1857.
FRANKFORT, H. *Cylinder Seals.* London, 1939.
FREEMAN, Rosemary. *English Emblem Books.* London, 1948.
FRIEDENSBURG, Ferdinand. *Symbolik der Mittelaltermünzer.* Berlin, 1913.
FRIEDMANN, Hermann. *Wissenschaft und Symbol.* Munich, 1948.
— *Symbolism in the Dura Synagogue.* New York, 1963.
FREUD, Sigmund. *The Interpretation of Dreams* (Standard Edition of *Works,* vols. 4–5). London, 1953.
FROBENIUS, Leo. *Das Zeitalter des Sonnengottes.* Berlin, 1904.
FUENTE LA PEÑA, Antonio de. *El Ente dilucidado.* Madrid, 1677.

GAILLARD, Louis. *Croix et Swastika en Chine.* Shanghai, 1893.
GATTEFOSSÉ, R. M. *Les Sages écritures.* Lyon, 1945.
— 'Métaphysique préhistorique.' *Bull. Soc. Préhist. Maroc,* 1934.
GEBER. *Works.* Trans. Richard Russell. London, 1928.
GERLACH, Martin, *Allegorien und Embleme.* Vienna, 1900.
— *Allégories et Emblèmes.* Vienna, 1882.
GESSMANN, G. W. *Die Geheimsymbole der Chemie und Medizin des Mittelalters.* Graz, 1899.
GIARDA, Christoforus. *Icones symbolicae.* Milan, 1628.
GIEHLOW, Karl. *Die Hieroglyphenkunde des Humanismus in der Allegorie der Renaissance, besonders der Ehrenpforte Kaisers Maximilian I.* Vienna, 1915.
GIOVIO, Paolo (Paulus Jovius), *Dialogi,* 1562.
GISBERT, Combaz. *L'évolution du stûpa en Asie: les symbolismes du stûpa.* Mélanges chinois et boudhiques. Brussels, 1933.
GISSEY, Odo de. *Les Emblesmes et Devises du Roy, des Princes . . .* Paris, 1657.
GOBLET D'ALVIELLA. *La migration des Symboles.* Paris, 1891.
GOLDSMITH, Elizabeth Edwards. *Ancient Pagan Symbols.* London, 1929.
— *Life Symbols as Related to Sex Symbolism.* London, 1924.
— *Sacred Symbols in Art.* London, 1912.
GOODENOUGH, E. R. *Jewish symbols in the greco-roman period.* New York, 1953–54.
— Symbolism in the Dura Synagogue. New York, 1963.
GOULIANOF. *Essai sur les hiéroglyphes d'Horapollon.* Paris, 1827.
GOULD, Charles. *Mythical Monsters.* London, 1886.
GRANDVILLE. *Les Fleurs animées.* Paris, 1874.
GRAVELOT and COCHIN. *Iconologie par Figures.* Paris, *c.* 1789.
GREEN, Henry. *Andrea and his Books of Emblems.* London, 1872.
GREINER, R. H. *Polynesian Decorative Designs.* Honolulu, 1922.
GRILLOT DE GIVRY, Emile Angelo. *Witchcraft, Magic and Alchemy.* Boston, 1931.
GROLLIER, Charles de. *Résumé Alphabétique des Marques de Porcelaine.* Paris, 1927.
GROSSLEY, Robert. *A Great Revelation.* London, 1899.
GRUEL, Léon. *Recherches sur les Origines des Marques Anciennes qui se rencontrent dans l'Art et dans l'Industrie du XVe au XIXe siècle. Part Rapport au Chiffre Quatre.* Paris, 1926.
GUBERNATIS, Angelo de. *La Mythologie des plantes.* Paris, 1878.
GUÉNON, René. *Symboles fondamentaux de la science sacrée.* Paris, 1962.
GÜNTER, H. *Psychologie de la Légende.* Paris, 1954.
GUILLAUME, Paul. *La Psychologie de la Forme.* Paris, 1937.
HAATAN, Abel. *Traité d'Astrologie judiciaire.* Paris, 1895.
HARLESS, G. C. A. *Jacob Böhme und die alchymisten.* Berlin, 1870.
HARTLAUB, G. F. *Der Stein der Weisen.* Munich, 1959.
— *Zauber der Spiegels.* Munich, 1951.
HAUTECOEUR, Louis. *Mystique et architecture. Symbolisme du cercle et de la coupole.* Paris, 1954.
HECK, Johan Georg. *Iconographic Encyclopaedia of Science, Literature and Art.* London–New York, 1851.
HEITZ, Paul. *Basler Büchermarken bis zum Anfang des 17. Jahrhunderts.* Strasburg. 1895.
— *Elsässische Buchermarken bis Anfang des 18. Jahrhunderts.* Strasburg, 1892.
HELLPACH, Willy. *Geopsyche* Stuttgart, 1950.
HENSELING, Robert. *Das all und wir.* Berlin, 1936.
HENTZE, Carl. *Mythes et Symboles lunaires.* Antwerp, 1932.
HERAS, P. E. *¿ Quiénes eran los Druidas?* Ampurias. Barcelona, 1949.

HERMES TRISMEGISTOS. *The Divine Pymander.* London, 1923.
— *Oeuvres.* Paris, 1945.
HEWSON, William. *Illustrations of Tracts on the Greek-Egyptian Sun-Dial.* London, 1870.
— *The Hebrew and Greek Scriptures.* London, 1870.
HILD, J. A. *Etude sur les démons dans la littérature et la religion des Grecs.* Paris, 1881.
HINKS, Roger. *Myth and Allegory in Ancient Art.* London, 1939.
HIRTH, Georg, Muther and Richard. *Meisterholzschnitte aus Vier Jahrhunderten.* Munich, 1893.
HOEFER. *Histoire de la Chimie depuis les temps les plus reculés jusqu'à notre époque.* Paris, 1842–43.
HOMEYER, Karl Gustav. *Die Haus- und Hof-Marken.* Berlin, 1870.
HOPPER, F. *Medieval Number Symbolism.* New York, 1938.
HORAPOLLO. *The Hieroglyphics.* New York, 1950.
HORNUNG, Clarence Pearson. *Handbook of Designs and Devices.* New York, 1946.
HOROZCO Y COBARRUBIAS, Juan de. *Emblemas morales.* Segovia, 1589 and 1604.
HOWELL, James. *The Parly of Beasts; or Morphandra Queen of the Inchanted Island.* London, 1660.
HOYOS SÁINZ, Luis de. *Manual de Folklore.* Madrid, 1947.
HROZNY, B. (Fr.) *Symbola ad studia Orientis . . .* Prague, 1949.
HUBAUX, J. and LEROY, M. *Le Mythe du Phénix dans les littératures grecque et latine.* Liège, 1939.
HUBER, M. *Die Wanderlegende von den Siebenschläfern.* Leipzig, 1910.
HUMBERT, J. *Mythologie grecque et romaine.* Paris, 1901.
HUNTER, Dard. *Papermaking Through Eighteen Centuries.* New York, 1930.
IAMBLICHUS. *On the Mysteries of the Egyptians.* London, 1895.
— *Des Mystères.* Paris, 1895.
IBERICO, Mariano. *El sentimiento de la vida cósmica.* Buenos Aires, 1946.
JACKSON, J. W. *Shells as evidence of the migration of early culture.* Manchester, 1917.
JACQUEMAR. *La pierre philosophale et la phlogistique.* Paris, 1876.
JEAN, M., and MEZEL, A. *Maldoror.* Paris, 1947.
JUNG, C. G. See WILHELM, Richard, and JUNG, C. G.
—, and KERENY, I. *Introduction to a Science of Mythology.* London, 1951.
— *Mysterium Coniunctionis.* London, 1963.
— (with Joseph L. Henderson, Marie-Louise von Franz, Aniela Jaffe). *Man and His Symbols.* London, 1963.
JUNIUS, Adrianus. *Emblemata.* Antwerp, 1565.
KALLIR, Alfred. *The Victory of V.* London, 1958.
— *Sign and Design.* London, 1961.
KARLGREN, B. 'Some fecundity symbols in Ancient China.' *Bull. Mus. Far East,* No. 2, Stockholm, 1930.
KARST, J. *Mythologie arméno-caucasienne et hétito-asiatique.* Strasburg, 1948.
KATZ, David. *Gestalt Psychology.* London, 1951.
KENDRICK, T. D. *Anglo-Saxon Art.* London, 1938.
KERVYN DE LETTENHOVE. *Le Toison d'or.* Brussels, 1907.
KHUNRATH, H. *Amphitheatrum Sapientiae aeternae solius verae Cabalae, Mageiae, Alchemiae, Cabalisticum . . .* Hanau, 1609.
KING, Charles William. *The Gnostics and their remains, ancient and mediaeval.* London, 1864.
KINGSLAND, W. *The Esoteric Basis of Christianity.* London, 1893.
KIRCHER, A. *Aedipus aegyptiacus hoc est universalis hieroglyphicae veterum doctrinae instauratio.* Rome, 1652.

KIRCHGÄSSNER, Alfons. *La Puissance des Signes.* Paris, 1962.

KOCH, Rudolf. *The Book of Signs.* London, 1930.

KOPP, H. *Die alchemie in alterer und neuerer Zeit.* Heidelberg, 1886.

KOTANY, Heishichi. *Japanese Family Crests.* Kyoto, 1915.

KÜHN, Herbert. *The Rock Pictures of Europe.* Translated by Alan Houghton Brodrick. London, 1956.

KÜNSTLE, Karl. *Ikonographie der christlichen Kunst.* Freiburg im Breisgau, 1926–28.

KUNZ, Georg Frederick. *The Magic of Jewels and Charms.* London, 1915.

KUNZ, G. F. and STEVENSON, C. H. *The Book of the Pearl.* London, 1908.

KURTH, Willi. *The Complete Woodcuts of Albrecht Dürer.* London, 1927.

KUTSCHMANN, Th. *Geschichte der Deutschen Illustration.* Goslar, 1900.

LAARSS, Richard Hummel. *Das Buch der Amulette und Talismane.* Leipzig, 1923.

LAJARD, F. *Recherches sur le culte du cyprès piramidal . . .* Paris, 1854.

— *Recherches sur le culte public et les mystères de Mithra en Orient et en Occident.* Paris, 1867.

LANG, A. *Myth, Ritual and Religion.* London, 1887.

LANGE, R. *Japanische Wappen.* Berlin, 1903.

L'ANGLOIS, P. *Discours des hiéroglyphes . . .* Paris, 1584.

LANOÈ-VILLÈNE. *Le Livre des Symboles.* Paris, 1921.

LANZONI, Francesco. *Genesi, Svolgimento e Tramonto delle Leggende storiche.* Rome, 1925.

LAUFER, B. *Jade. A study in Chinese archaeology and religion.* Chicago, 1912.

— *The Diamond. A study in Chinese and hellenistic Folk-Lore.* Chicago, 1915.

LAYARD, John. *The Lady of the Hare.* London, 1944.

LEBRUN DE VIRLOY. *Notice sur l'accroissement de la matière métallique.* Paris, 1888.

LEDESMA, Alfonso de. *Epigramas y hieroglyphicos,* 1623.

LEE, Gordon Ambrose. *Some Notes on Japanese Heraldry.* London, 1909.

LEISEGANG, Hans. 'The Mystery of the Serpent.' In *The Mysteries* (Papers from the Eranos Yearbooks, 2). New York and London, 1955.

— *La Gnose.* Paris, 1951.

LE VOILE D'ISIS. *Les Gemmes.* Paris.

LÉVY-BRÜHL, Lucien. *L'expérience mystique et les symboles chez les primitifs.* Paris, 1938.

LIBAVIUS, Andreas. *Alchymia . . . Recognita Emendata et Aucta.* Frankfurt, 1606.

LINNAEUS. *Systema Naturae, sive Regna trib Naturae systematice proposita per classes, ordines, genera et species.* Leyden, 1735.

LIPFFERT, Klementine. *Symbol-Fibel.* Kassel, 1955.

LITTLE Gem Brand Book Company. *Little Gem Brand Book.* Kansas City, 1900.

LOEFFLER-DELACHAU. *Le Symbolisme des contes de Fées.* Paris, 1949.

LOISY, A. *Les mythes babiloniens et les premiers chapitres de la Genèse.* Paris, 1901.

LÜDY, Fritz. *Alchemistiche und Chemische Zeichen.* Berlin, 1929.

LULL, Raymond. *De Auditu Kabbalistico, sive ad omnes scientias introductorium.* Strasburg, 1651.

MAACK, Ferd. *Die heilige Mathesis.* Leipzig, 1924.

MAASS, E. *Orpheus.* Munich, 1895.

MACCIO, Paolo. *Emblemata . . .* Bologna, 1628.

MADHIHASSAN, Dr. S. 'Über enige Symbole der Alchemie'. In *Die Pharmazeutische Industrie,* 24, 41–45. Aulendorf i. Württ., 1962.

— 'Ouroboros as the earlier symbol of the Greek Alchemie'. In *Igbal.* Lahore, 1961.

MAHNKE, Dietrich. *Unendliche Sphäre und Allmittelpunkt.* Halle, 1937.

MALLINGER, J. *Les secrets ésotériques dans Plutarque.* Paris, 1946.

MARMOL, F. de. *Dictionnaire des Filigranes*. Namur, 1900.
MARNEFFE, Alphonse de. *Les Combinaisons de la Croix et du Triangle Divin dans les Blasons et les Marques de Marchands*. Charleroi, 1939.
MARTINO, P. *Parnasse et Symbolisme*. Paris, 1954.
MAURY, A. *Croyances et légendes de l'antiquité*. Paris, 1863.
McCLATCHIE, Thomas R. H. *Japanese Heraldry*. Yokohama, 1877.
MEINER, Annemarie. *Das Deutsche Signet*. Leipzig, 1922.
MENARD, L. *Hermès Trismégiste*. Paris, 1867.
MENARD, René. *La mythologie dans l'Art ancien et moderne*. Paris, 1878.
MENDO, Andrés. *Principe . . . en emblemas*. León de Francia, 1662.
MENDOZA, Carlos. *La Leyenda de las plantas*. Barcelona, 1889.
MENESTRIER, François. *La philosophie des images énigmatiques*. Lyon, 1694.
MERTENS STIENON, M. *Space and the Cross*. London, 1935.
— *Studies in Symbolism*. London, 1933.
MICHELET, J. *Origines du droit français cherchés dans les symboles et formules du droit universal*. Paris, 1900.
MONEROT, Jules. *La poésie moderne et le Sacré*. Paris, 1945.
MOREAU, J. *La construction de l'idéalisme platonicien*. Paris, 1939.
MORGAN, L. H. *Ancient Society*. New York, 1877.
MORTILLET, Gabriel de. *Le signe de la croix avant le Christianisme*. Paris, 1866.
MUELLER, Niklas. *Glauben, Wissen und Kunst der Alten Hindus*. Mainz, 1822.
MUNSCH, René H. *L'Ecriture et son dessin*. Paris, 1948.
MUTHER, Richard. *Die Deutsche Bücherillustration der Gothik und Frührenaissance (1460–1530)*. Munich, 1884.
MYLIUS, Joannes Daniel. *Philosophia Reformata*. Frankfurt, 1622.
NAGLER, Georg Caspar. *Die Monogrammisten*. Munich, 1858–79.
NANYO, Kyokai. *Family Crests*. Tokyo, 1940.
NAVILLE, E. *La religion des anciens égyptiens*. Paris, 1907.
NENTER, *Bericht von der alchymie*. Nuremberg, 1727.
NICOLAI, Johannis. *Tractatus de Siglis Veterum*. Lyon, 1703.
NINCK, Martin. *Die Bedeutung des Wassers im Kult und Leben der Alten, Eine symbolgeschichtliche Untersuchung*. Philogus (Leipzig), 1921.
NOOT, Jan Van der. *XII Boeken Olympiados*. Antwerp, 1579.
NOTT, Stanley Charles. *Chinese Culture in the Arts*. New York, 1946.
NÚÑEZ DE CEPEDA, Francisco. *Emblemas sacros*. León, 1682.
NUTT, Alfred. *Studies on the Legend of the Holy Grail*. London, 1888.
OBERMAIER, Hugo. *Fossil Man in Spain*. New York, 1924.
OGDEN, C. K., and RICHARDS, I. A. *The Meaning of Meaning*. London, 1923.
OKADA, Yazuru. *Japanese Family Crests*. Tokyo, 1941.
ONIANS, R. B. *The Origins of European Thought*. London, 1954.
OPPEL, Karl. *Das alte Wunderland der Pyramiden*. Leipzig, 1868.
ORIN, J. M. H. *Le plan divin dévoilé*. Paris, 1890.
ORTIGUES, Edmond. *Le Discours et le symbole*. Paris, 1962.
PALLADINUS, Jacobus, of Teramo. *Belial*. Heilbronn, 1448.
PALLISER, Fanny Bury. *Historic Devices, Badges and War Cries*. London, 1870.
PANOFSKY, Erwin. *Hercules am Scheidewege*. Leipzig, 1930.
— *Meaning in the Visual Arts*. New York, 1955.
PANOFSKY, E. and D. *Pandora's Box*. London, 1956.
PAPUS. *Initiation astrologique*. Paris, 1919.
PARRINDER, Geoffrey. *West African Religions*. London, 1949.
PASSERI, G. B. *Thesaurus Gemmarum Antiquarum*. Florence, 1750.
PATRICK, S. *Parable of the Pilgrim*. London, 1665.
PAVITT, William Thomas and Kate. *The Book of Talismans, Amulets and Zodiacal Gems*. London, 1914.
PELADAN, J. *Les idées et les formes*. Paris, 1901.

PERRY, W. J. *The Children of the Sun.* London, 1923.
PERYT SHOU. *Symbolik und magische Zahlentheorie.* Berlin, 1923.
PETRASANTA, Silvestro. *De symbolis heroicis.* Antwerp, 1635.
PICARD, C. *Les origines du polythéisme hellénique.* Paris, 1931.
PICINELLI, D. Filippo. *Mondo Simbolico ampliato.* Venice, 1670.
POISSON, Albert. *Nicolas Flamel.* Paris, 1893.
— *Roger Bacon, Lettre sur les prodiges de la nature et de l'art.* Paris, 1893.
— *Théories et Symboles des Alchimistes.* Paris, 1891.
PORTAL, F. *Des Couleurs symboliques.* Paris, 1837.
POUCHET, F. A. *Histoire des sciences naturelles au moyen âge,* etc. Paris, 1853.
PRAMPOLINI, Giacomo. *La mitologia nella vita del popolo.* Milan, 1937–38.
QUINTANA VIVES, Jorge. *Aportaciones a la interpretación de la escritura protoindia.* Madrid, 1946.
— *El gobierno teocrático de Mohenjo-Daro,* Ampurias, IV. Barcelona, 1942.
RADIN, Paul. *The Road of Life and Death.* New York.
REGNAUD, P. *Le Rig-Véda et les origines de la mythologie indo-européenne.* Paris, 1892.
REINACH, S. *Cultes, mythes et religions,* Paris, 1908–23.
REINER Imre. *Das Buch der Werkzeichen.* St. Gallen, 1945.
RENOUARD, Ph. *Les marques typographiques Parisiennes des XVᵉ et XVIᵉ siècles.* Paris, 1928.
REPULLÉS, E. *El simbolismo en la arquitectura cristiana.* Madrid, 1898.
RIPA, Cesare. *Iconologia, or Moral Emblems.* London, 1709.
RISCO, Vicente. *Mitología cristiana.* Madrid, 1963.
— 'Fieras de romance'. In *Revista de Dialectología y tradiciones populares.* Tomo XIV. Madrid, 1958.
RIS-PAQUOT, Oscar Edmond. *Dictionnaire encyclopédique des marques et monogrammes.* Paris, 1893.
ROBERTS, W. *Printer's Marks.* London, 1892.
ROBSON, Thomas. *The British Herald.* Sunderland, 1830.
ROSENHEIM, Petrus de. *Ars Memorandi, or Rationarium Evangelistarum.* Pforzheim 1507.
ROUGIER, L. *L'origine astronomique de la croyance pythagoricienne en l'immortalité céleste des âmes.* Cairo, 1933.
ROUSSEAU, René-Lucien. *Les Couleurs.* Paris, 1959.
RUSCELLI, Girolamo. *Le imprese illustri.* Venice, 1572.
RUTH-SOMMER, Hermann. *Alte Musikinstrumente.* Berlin, 1916.
SAAVEDRA FAJARDO, Diego de. *Idea de un príncipe . . . empresas,* 1640.
SABATHIER. *L'Ombre idéale de la sagesse universelle.* Paris, 1679.
SABBE, Maurice. *Le Symbolisme des marques typographiques.* Antwerp, 1932.
SAINTYVES, P. *Les saints successeurs des dieux.* Paris, 1907.
— 'Pierres magiques.' *Corpus de folklore Préh.* II, 1934.
SAMBUCUS, Joannes. *Emblemata cum aliquot nummis antiqui operis.* Antwerp, 1564.
SAN MARTE. *Neue Mitteilungen aus dem Gebiete historisch-antiquarischer Forschungen,* II.
SAULCY, F. Caignart de. *Histoire de l'Art judaïque tirée des textes sacrés et profanes.* Paris, 1858.
SAXL, KLIBANSKY and PANOFSKY. *Saturn and Melancholy.* London, 1964.
SAYCE and MARCH. 'Polynesian Ornament; a Mythography or a symbolism of Origin and Descent.' *Journ. Anthrop. Inst.,* 1893, XII.
SCHELTEMA, Frederik Adama van. *Die Kunst des Abendlandes.* Stuttgart, 1950.
SCHWAB, Gustav. *Gods and Heroes.* London, 1947.
SCHEDEL, Hartmann. *Liber Chronicorum.* Nuremberg, 1493.
SCHEIL, V. *Esagil ou le temple de Mardouk à Babylone.* Paris, 1913.

SCHEFFER, T. von. *Hellenistiche Mysterien und Orakel.* Stuttgart, 1940.
SCHENCK, Georg. *Monstrorum Historia memorabilis.* Frankfurt, 1609.
SCHMIDT, Albert M. *La Littérature Symboliste.* Paris, 1947.
SCHMIEDER, K. C. *Geschichte der Alchemie.* Halle, 1832.
SCHOLEM, G. G. *Major Trends in Jewish Mysticism.* London, 1955.
SCHUILER CAMMANN. *Cosmic Symbolism of the Dragon Robes of the Ch'ing Dynasty.* In Art and Thought.
SCHWALLER DE LUBICZ, R.-A. *Propos sur Ésotérisme et Symbole.* Paris, 1960.
SCOTT, Thomas. *Philomythie or Philomythologie.* London, 1616.
SELIGMANN, Kurt. *Mirror of Magic.* New York, 1948.
SILBERER, Herbert. *Problems of Mysticism and its Symbolism.* New York and London, 1917.
SILVESTRE, L. C. *Marques Typographiques.* Paris, 1867.
SIMPSON, William. *The Buddhist Praying-wheel.* London, 1896.
SIMROCK, K. *Traces of a Hidden Tradition in Mediaeval Mysticism.* London, 1900.
SKEAT, Walter W. 'Snakestones and stone thunderbolts as subject for systematic investigation.' *Folklore,* 1912, XXIII.
SMITH, William Robertson. *Lectures on the religion of the Semites.* London, 1927.
SOLÓRZANO PEREIRA, Ioannes. *Emblemata . . .* Madrid, 1651.
SOTO, Hernando de. *Emblemas moralizados,* 1599.
SOUSA DE MACEDO, Antonio de. *Eva y Ave o Maria triunfante.* Murcia, 1882.
SPENCER, Herbert. *Principles of Sociology,* 1876–96.
STAFFORD, Thomas Albert. *Christian Symbolism in the Evangelical Churches.* New York-Nashville, 1942.
STEKEL, W. *Dichtung und Neurose.* Wiesbaden, 1909.
— *The Interpretation of Dreams.* New York, 1943.
— *Technique of Analytical Psychotherapy.* London, 1939.
STROEHL, Hugo Gerard, *Blumen und Blüten in der Japanischen Heraldik.* Vienna, 1907.
— *Heraldischer Atlas.* Stuttgart, 1899.
— *Imitationsfiguren in der Japanischen Heraldik.* Berlin, 1910.
— *Nihon Moncho, Japanisches Wappenbuch.* Vienna, 1906.
Symbollon. Basle.
TACCHI VENTURI, P. *Storia delle religioni.* Turin, 1934–36.
THOMPSON, Tommy. *The A.B.C. of Our Alphabet.* London-New York, 1942.
THOMSON, Thomas. *History of chemistry.* London, 1930.
THURNWALD, R. 'Das Symbol in Lichte der Völkerkunde.' *Zeitschrift f. Aesthetik u. allgem. Kuntswiss,* XXI.
TIFFEREAU, C. T. *Les métaux sont des corps composés.* Paris, 1855.
TONDELLI, Leone. *Gnostici.* Turin, 1950.
TOPSELL, Edward. *The History of Four-footed Beasts and Serpents; Describing at Large their True and Lively Figure, their Several Names, Conditions, Kinds, Virtues . . .* London, 1658.
TORMO, Elías. *El simbolismo en el arte.* Madrid, 1902.
TRITHEIM, J. *Polygraphie et universelle escriture cabalistique.* Paris, 1561.
TSUDA, Noritake. *Handbook of Japanese Art.* Tokyo, 1935.
TYLOR, Edward. *Anthropology.* London, 1881.
— *Primitive culture; Researches into the Development of Mythology, Philosophy, Religion, Language, Art and Custom.* London, 1871.
TYPOTIUS, Jacobus. *Symbola varia diversorum principum.* Arnheim, 1679.
ULMANN, Paul. *La Croix de Saint-André dans la sculpture romane, bas-reliefs mithraïques et doctrines albigeoises.* Paris, 1947.
ULSTADT, Philipp. *Coelum Philosophorum, seu De Secretis Naturae.* Paris, 1544.
URBAN, Wilbur Marshall. *Language and Reality.* London, 1939.
VAGANAY, L. *Le problème eschatologique dans le IVe livre d'Esdras.* Paris, 1906.

VALERIANO, Giampietro. *Hieroglyphica*. Basel, 1556.
VILLAVA, Juan Francisco de. *Empresas espirituales*. Baeza, 1613.
VILLIERS, Elizabeth. *The Mascot Book*. New York and London, 1923.
VINYCOMB, John. *Fictitious and Symbolic Creatures in Art*. London, 1906.
VOLKMANN, Ludwig. *Bilderschriften der Renaissance*. Leipzig, 1923.
WAITE, A. E. *The Holy Grail*. London, 1933.
WEBBER, Frederick Roth. *Church Symbolism*. Cleveland, 1927.
WECHSSLER, Edward. *Die Sage vom Heiligen Graal*. 1898.
WESTERHOVIUS, A. H. *Hieroglyphica oder Denkbilder der alten Völker*. Amsterdam, 1741.
WESTON, Jessie L. *Works*.
WILHELM, Richard, and JUNG, C. G. *The Secret of the Golden Flower*. London, 1932.
— *The I Ching*. London, 1970.
WILKINS, John. *Mathematicall Magick*. London, 1680.
WILLIAMS, Charles Alfred Speed. *Outlines of Chinese Symbolism and Art Motives*. Shanghai, 1932.
WILLIAMS, John. *An Essay on the Hieroglyphics of the Ancient Egyptians*. London, 1836.
WINCKELMANN, J. J. *Versuch eine Allegorie*. Leipzig, 1866.
WIRTH, O. *Le Symbolisme hermétique dans ses rapports avec l'alchimie* . . . Paris, 1931.
WOLFF. *Mythologie der Feen und Elfen von Ursprunge dieses Glaubens bis auf neuesten Zeiten*. Weimar, 1828.
WON KENN. *Origine et évolution de l'écriture hiéroglyphique et de l'écriture chinoise*. Paris, 1926.
YAMAGUSHI, H. S. K. *We Japanese*. Miyanoshi-Hakone, 1937.
ZIEBER, Eugène. *Heraldry in America*. Philadelphia, 1895.
ZIMMER, Heinrich. *Kunstform und Yoga im Indischen Kultbild*. Berlin, 1926.
ZIMMERMANN, Werner. *Geheimsinn der Zahlen*. Munich, 1944.
ZYKAN, J. 'Drache und Perle.' *Articus Asiae* VI, 1–2, 1936.

INDEX

Note. Main entries in the dictionary are not included. Cross-references in bold type are to main entries in the dictionary.

Abadir, 314
Abell, Walter, 213-14
abnormality, 11; *see also* jester
abraxas, 2
abyss, 228, 365
acacia, 341
Achelous, 297
Achilles, 77, 111, 307, 345-6
acrobat, 159
Actaeon, 215
activity and passivity, 47
Adam, 135, 188, 286, 288, 348
Adam Kadmon, 118, 198
Adonis, xx, 259, 294
Aelian, 155
Aeneas, 165
aerolite, 164, 240
Aeschylus, 136
Aesculapius, 51, 147, 288
Aesir, 65
Agathodaemon, 290
agriculture, xvii; *see also* **farmer**
Agrippa of Nettesheim, 197, 270-1
Ahasuerus, 363
Ahriman, 1, 65, 104, 178, 356, 361; *see also* Angramainyu
Ahuramazda, 104, 311, 317, 356
Aigremont, Dr. (pseud.), 111
Ain-Soph, 243
air, 102; *see also* wind
Akasha, 15, 18, 152, 256
Alan of Lille, xxii, 227
Alberich (elf king), 58
Alberich, Cola, 2, 284
Alberuni, 64
Albertus Magnus, 10
alchemy, xxvi ff., 1, 83, 171, 255, 264, 314, 337; angel, 9; animals, 12; ascent, 312; ass, 21; birds, 27; chaos, 43; child, 45-6; colours, 55, 56, 60; crow, 71; crown, 72; digestion, 81; dragon, 87; eagle, 92; fire, 105; flowers, 110; globe, 119; heart, 142; hermaphrodite, 147; letters, 183-4; mandalas, 202; Mercury, 207-8; moon, 216; multiplicity, 222; phoenix, 254; serpent, 290; signs, 132; sun, 320; symbols, 132; tree, 349; wheels, 371; wings, 375
Alciate, Andrea, xxiii
Aldebaran, 269
alembic, 247
Alexander the Great, xlv, 148, 173, 192

Algonquins, 139
Alleau, René, xlii, 29, 116, 144, 208, 255, 316
allegory, xl; relation to symbol, xi, xli ff.
Allendy, René, 332
almond tree, 21
alpha and omega, 183
alphabet, 131; Egyptian, 182; Hebrew, 183; moon and, 216
Alvão, 382
Amalthea, 62
Amance, 149
Amazons, 145, 188
ambivalence, 26, 134
Ambrose, St., 19, 250
Amfortas, xxiii, 97, 168
Amon, 102, 175; Amon-Ra, 19
Amphion and Zethus, 355
amphisbaena, 44
Amrita, 43, 113
amulets, 271, 299, 312; hand and, 137; silver, 216
Anael, 284
Anaitis, 214
analogy(ies), xl-xli; and function, xxxix-xl; Jung on, xii, xxxviii-xxxix; of spiritual and material, xvi
anchor, 85
Ancient of Days, 132, 243
androgyne, *see* hermaphrodite
Andromeda, 186
anemone, 261
angel(s), 49, 153, 166; seven, 284
Angramainyu, 104, 311, 356; *see also* Ahriman
anima, 39, 66, 76, 110, 163, 218, 293, 299, 375
animals, in alchemy, 11-12; benevolent, 12; and cardinal points, 270; domestication of, xvii; lunar, 11, 217; man between two, 261; natural and fabulous, 10; oviparous, 247; processions, 12; speaking, 11; symbols, 129-30; tame and wild, 10; in watermarks, 13; and women, 375-6; *see also names of individual species;* tetramorph
ankh, 70-1; *see also* cross, anserated; *nem ankh*
Antaeus, 363
Antares, 269
antimony, 132

972-92

14.95

City and Islington Sixth Form College
283-309 Goswell Road
London
EC1
020 7520 0601

CITY AND ISLINGTON
COLLEGE

SFC✓

This book is due for return on or before the date last stamped below.
You may renew by telephone. Please quote the Barcode No.
May not be renewed if required by another reader.

Fine: 5p per day

21 OCT 2003

07 OCT 2005   11 MAY 2006

11 OCT 2005   06 NOV 2009

18 NOV 2005
14 OCT 2005

26 JAN 2006

22 FEB 2006

THE LEARNING CENTRE
CITY & ISLINGTON COLLEGE
383 HOLLOWAY ROAD
LONDON   N7 0RN

D1338816

location changed
to Marlborough

SA012023

972.92
SHE
3 WEEKS

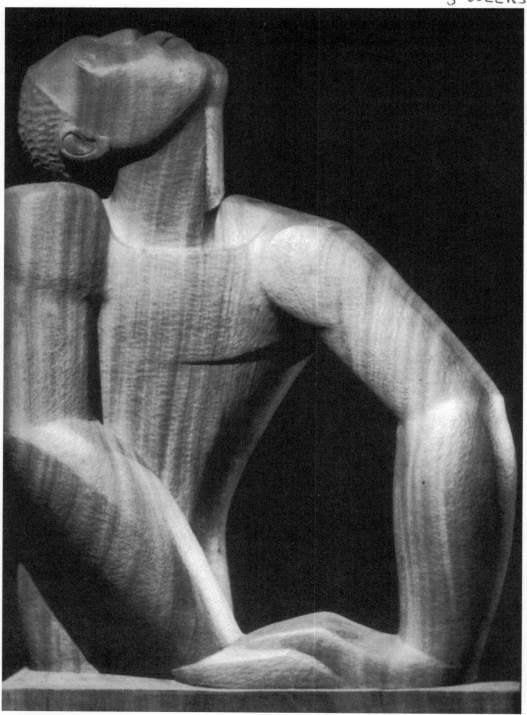

Negro Aroused by Edna Manley, courtesy of the National Gallery of Jamaica

The Story of the Jamaican People

PHILIP SHERLOCK
& HAZEL BENNETT

LIBRARY
ISLINGTON SIXTH FORM CEN
THE LEARNING CENTRE
CITY ANNETTE COLLEGE
383 HOLLOWAY ROAD
LONDON N7 0RN

THE LEARNING CENTRE
CITY & ISLINGTON COLLEGE
383 HOLLOWAY ROAD
LONDON N7 0RN

 IAN RANDLE PUBLISHERS
KINGSTON

MARKUS WIENER PUBLISHERS
PRINCETON

in collaboration with the
Creative Production and Training Centre Ltd, Kingston, Jamaica

LIBRARY
ISLINGTON SIXTH FORM CENTRE
ANNETTE ROAD
LONDON N7 6EX

© Philip Sherlock and Hazel Bennett

First published 1998 by

Ian Randle Publishers Limited
206 Old Hope Road, Box 686
Kingston 6, Jamaica

In collaboration with the Creative Production and
Training Centre Ltd (CPTC), Kingston, Jamaica

ISBN 976-8123-09-5 Cloth
    976-8100-30-3 Paper

A catalogue record for this book is available
from the National Library of Jamaica

and

Markus Wiener Publishers, Inc.
114 Jefferson Road
Princeton, NJ 08540

Library of Congress Cataloging-in-Publication Data
Sherlock, Philip Manderson, Sir.
    The story of the Jamaican People / Philip Sherlock and Hazel
Bennett
Includes bibliographic references and index.
    ISBN 1-55876-145-4 (hc : alk. Paper). — ISBN 1-55876-146-2
(pb : alk. Paper)
    1. Jamaica—History. 1. Bennett, Hazel. 11. Title.
F1881.S5 1997
96.45648 CIP
972.92—dc21   972.92 SHE

Book and cover design by ProDesign Ltd, Red Gal Ring, Kingston

Set in 11/13 Adobe Garamond with Casablanca Antique display

Printed and bound in the USA

Cover painting *Mannings Hill Market* by Alexander Cooper
The Hardingham Collection

This book is dedicated to
the People of Jamaica, the gallant makers of our history;
the Youth of Jamaica in whose hands the nation's future rests; the
Promoters and Custodians of the nation's history.

LIBRARY
ISLINGTON SIXTH FORM CENTRE
ANNETTE ROAD
LONDON N7 6EX

Contents

ACKNOWLEDGEMENTS

The authors acknowledge with gratitude the interest and support of Sir Alister McIntyre, Vice-Chancellor of the University of the West Indies and of Mrs Jean Smith, Director of Special Programmes Division of the Vice-Chancellor's Office.

Special thanks are due to the Creative Production and Training Centre Ltd (CPTC) which gave its sponsorship to the book and to Mr Wycliffe Bennett, the Chairman and Chief Executive Officer, for his invaluable advice and guidance throughout the writing. The CPTC is producing a companion series, ten one-hour documentaries entitled "The Story of the Jamaican People". Developing the parameters for these documentaries inspired the authors to write this book. We thank the Hon. Burchell Whiteman, Minister of Education, Youth and Culture, for his early encouragement.

We acknowledge our indebtedness to the Institute of Jamaica, to Mr Aaron Matalon, Chairman of the Council of the National Gallery of Jamaica, and to the Hon. Rex Nettleford, O.M., who was both guide and inspiration. In addition we are indebted to the University of the West Indies Library, the National Library of Jamaica, the National Gallery of Jamaica and the Jamaica National Heritage Trust for providing access to scarce material.

The authors record with pleasure the help of Miss Luletta King, who typed and retyped the manuscript and continued to smile.

The authors hope that this book will serve as a useful first step towards new approaches to the study of the Jamaican people. The authors take full responsibility for the contents.

We would also like to acknowledge our indebtedness to the following organisations and individuals who also gave permission for the use of the photographs in this publication:

The National Library of Jamaica
The Jamaica Information Service
The Creative Production and Training Centre Ltd
The Jamaica Library Service
The National Gallery of Jamaica
The Jamaica National Heritage Trust
The Institute of Jamaica Publications
The Gleaner Company
The University of the West Indies, Mona, Library
Kingston Publishers
Mr A. D. Scott
Miss Suzanne Issa
Miss Nellie Chin
Mr Cedric McDonald
Mr and Mrs Easton Lee
Mrs Sheila Barnett
Mr Wycliffe Bennett
Mr J. Tyndale-Biscoe
Mr Oliver Cox
Mr Tom Willcockson
Mr. Wallace Campbell

INTRODUCTION

In this book the authors tell the story of the Jamaican people from an African-Jamaican, not a European, point of view.

The story begins in West Africa, with many different African peoples, but chiefly with the Akan, Ashanti, Yorubas, Ibibios and with nations from the region of the Congo.

The Jamaican people have never accepted what was presented to them as the history of Jamaica. The heroes of the British Empire are not their heroes. Their battlefields are in African-America, in Palmares in Brazil, in Accompong, the Great River Valley of Hanover and St James, in Morant Bay, wherever African-American freedom fighters struggled for liberty.

Africa is at the centre of the story. Africa is motherland not only for all African-Jamaicans, but for African-Americans throughout the Americas.

By claiming Africa as the homeland, Jamaicans gain a sense of historical continuity, of identity, of roots. With this perspective they also claim a remarkable heritage of achievement on a hemispheric scale across four centuries, from the beginning of the Atlantic Slave Trade in 1518. African-Jamaicans, not Europeans, built into the story the love of liberty, and a passion for justice and equality–witness Cudjoe, Nanny, Sam Sharpe, Gordon, Bogle, Garvey, Norman Manley and Bustamante.

Africans and their descendants, the African-Jamaican people laid the foundation for a rich national culture by retaining their sense of spiritual values, by creating a vivid creole language, preserving their natural love for drama, music, song, drumming, for laughter, sympathy and wit. They created religious cults and modes of self-expression and developed Jamaica's internal marketing system based, in the early years, on provision grounds on marginal land, and on a network of Sunday markets and higglers.

In the nineteenth century others joined us, partners in the struggle for nationhood, from India, China, Lebanon and Syria, in addition to those who chose to make Jamaica their home when the Spanish colonists left. Loyal Jamaicans, they also treasure their own cultural heritage. They understand the need of the African-Jamaicans to do the same.

This book is a beginning. We hope it will carry further the work already begun by our artists, poets, writers, carvers, sculptors, athletes, reggae musicians, the dub poets, the rastafarians, the scholars, members of the public and private sectors and political parties who are dedicated to building a better Jamaica. A better Jamaica will come if the African-Jamaican people know and treasure their story.

Their history confirms Norman Manley's words, spoken towards the end of his life: "I affirm of Jamaica that we are a great people. Out of the past of fire and suffering and neglect, the human spirit has survived – patient and strong, quick to anger, quick to forgive, lusty and vigorous, but with deep reserves of loyalty and love and a deep capacity for steadiness under stress and for joy in all the things that make life good and blessed."

CHAPTER I

Honour the Ancestors

This history begins with a tribute of loving respect for the Jamaican and West Indian people, achievers of our freedom and independence.

George Lamming sets the opening theme with words from the introductory essay to his novel *In the Castle of My Skin*. He speaks there of his desire to bring,

> this world of men and women from down below to a proper order of attention; to make their reality the supreme concern of the total society.
>
> Along with this desire there was also the writer's recognition that this world, in spite of the long history of deprivation, represented the womb from which he himself had sprung, and the richest collective reservoir of experience on which the creative imagination could draw.
>
> This world of men and women from down below is not simply poor. This world is black and it has a long history at once vital and complex. It is vital because it constitutes the base of labour on which the entire Caribbean society has been built; and it is complex because plantation slave society (the point at which the modern Caribbean began) conspired to smash its ancestral African culture, and to bring about a total alienation of man, the source of labour, from man, the human person.

The story of the Jamaican people includes accounts of the coming of the Jews in the sixteenth century and of the East Indians, Chinese, Syrians and Lebanese in the nineteenth and twentieth centuries. These all became valued partners in the movement towards nationhood and independence. But our story centres on the historical experience of Jamaicans of African origin, who constitute the overwhelming majority of the population. Their ancestors were in Jamaica 150 years before the English arrived and their long struggle for freedom and justice forms an epic chapter in the story of African-America. Their ancestral links are with various West African countries. Africa, not Britain, is their motherland.

Africa is present everywhere in Jamaica. She has been here for five centuries. She walks the dark valleys and sun-baked savannas, the coastal plains and sculptured mountain slopes. She reveals herself in the physical appearance of nine out of every ten Jamaicans, in their body language, everyday talk, in their way with words, their crafts, customs, cults, in their attitudes and modes of self-expression. She is the homeland of a vigorous creative people who, out of a past of fire, exploitation and suffering, preserved a passion for freedom and justice and built these values into the Jamaican way of life.

Britain also is present. She was dominant in Jamaica for three centuries. She is present in churches and schools, in the institutions and forms of law and government. Her presence lingers in old great houses, around broken fortifications and in eighteenth-century sugar ports. Today she lives in her powerful, supple language, an open sesame to one of mankind's great treasuries of literature and to communication with countless millions of people throughout the world.

The Taino is slowly becoming a reality. For long, cassava and tobacco, the hammock and polished stone tools in museums, broken pieces of pottery and worn grinding stones provided proof of his presence in the island before Europe arrived five centuries ago. To most of us the Taino presence remains no more than shapes and shadows seen through a light evening mist, mute witnesses to the demonic force of European colonisation and to the genocide of millions of the indigenous people of the Americas. But recent studies have shown that the Tainos survived longer than was thought. Few though they were, they resisted forced labour and the last survivors established a base in the Dry Harbour Mountains of St Ann and another in the Blue Mountains, probably at Nanny Town. Three important Taino carvings have recently been found and authenticated. The story of the Tainos is woven into the story of the African-Jamaicans, the "old indigenous" melding with those who became the "new indigenous".

Europe brought Africa to the Caribbean early in the sixteenth century. Europe came as victor, dispossessor, exploiter. Africa came as victim, dispossessed, exploited. For five centuries the two shaped Caribbean history, Europe through the sugar-and-slave plantation, colonialism and the doctrine of white superiority, and Africa through the African-Jamaican's rejection of slavery, his triumphant struggle for freedom and justice, his resilience of spirit and his creativity. From the start the story of the Jamaican people is one of a stubborn defiant courage that would not be denied the final triumph.

The greatest agony the imported African slave endured was not physical, terrible though that was, but psychological. He suffered the trauma of being captured or betrayed, of being sold by men of his own race, of being transported in festering slave ships to a strange land, of being bought as a piece of property and of being set to work at new tasks for masters of another race and colour who spoke a strange language. He lived under laws which, in the English-speaking Caribbean and North American colonies, stripped him of the rights of personality and denied him a sense of destiny, of a future. What a catalogue of immeasurable woes and irreparable wrongs! This was in very truth the severest deprivation of all, this surgical severing of the ties with community, with ancestors, with one's history, with one's land.

Even at this distance in time it is painful to recall this Gethsemane agony, to enter, as the Haitian poet Jean Briere does, into the experience of uprooting:

> Together we knew the horror of the slave-ships
> and often like me you feel cramps
> awaking after the murderous centuries
> and feel the old wounds bleed in your flesh.

Briere was addressing Haitian blacks but his words find a home in the hearts of the Jamaican people and of all African-Americans. Their story begins with the African men and women, the ancestors, who came in these slave ships from Africa, and with their positive response to deprivation and penalisation. To grasp the significance of their achievement it is necessary to place their history in the context of plantation America, a vast region that extends from North-East Brazil through Suriname, the Guyanas, the Caribbean to the deep south of the United States. These people, coming though they did from different language groups, from tribes with different cultures, from widely separated kingdoms and empires in Africa, and having been distributed as "pieces of India" throughout this region, were as one in their rejection of slavery. Wherever in the Americas the slave plantation was, there also were the African-American freedom fighters. Their defiance lives on in the American civil rights movement, in the dream of Martin Luther King, in the vision of Marcus Garvey and in the words of African-American writers such as Claude McKay, Langston Hughes and Alain Locke.

This defiance was not a passing mood. It was what

The Ancestor by Edna Manley

Courtesy of the National Gallery of Jamaica

Sam Sharpe said, that he preferred death to slavery. It was what Paul Bogle said: "It is time for us to help ourselves, skin for skin. The iron bar is now broken in this parish . . . War is at us, my black skin. War is at hand."

This central empowering theme of the struggle of the African for liberty, justice and political power gives coherence and purpose to the story of the Jamaican people and links them with other African-Americans.

The struggle took many forms. One was marronage, flight to the forest and mountains and the formation of maroon communities. In a later chapter we will give a more detailed account of the founding of these free autonomous communities in Jamaica by Cudjoe, Nanny and the Trelawny and Portland maroons. There were other African freedom fighters on the plantations, nameless and forgotten men and women who struck a blow for freedom by sabotage, go-slows, damage to property, deliberate misunderstanding of instructions. Without realising it, the Jamaican sugar planter William Beckford paid tribute to them for their success in making slavery unpleasant for the owner: "They were so very capricious, so hardened and provoking that the best tempers may be soured by opposition and be made severe by obstinacy . . . the tricks that are constantly practised by the former, who are worthless and idle, are sufficient to make their superintendents cautious." (Beckford: 1790) These also were among the freedom fighters.

Sam Sharpe, leader of the largest of the many uprisings and rebellions in Jamaica, carried the struggle for freedom and the rejection of slavery further by claiming freedom as a human right and by making the issue one of morality: "The whites had no more right to enslave the blacks than the blacks to enslave the whites."

The struggle did not end with emancipation. The Jamaican people preserved a passion for justice, equality and for a voice in the management of their affairs. In 1865 George William Gordon and Paul Bogle led the demand of the St Thomas peasants for social justice. In the words of Samuel Clarke, at a Kingston Rally in 1865, it was "time for the negro to throw off the yoke and seek your liberty . . . there was one law for the black man and one for the white man". Heroes and martyrs, Gordon and Bogle rejected the doctrine of white supremacy and claimed equality for all before the law.

Up to this point freedom had been achieved, but freedom without an economic base, without social recognition, without the provision of medical and educational services. By 1850 free villages had been established but in ten grim years, from 1855 to 1865, cholera, small pox, floods and drought ravaged Jamaica. The coffin makers and grave diggers were busy. The people endured but they were in great distress. In their affliction a group of St Ann peasants petitioned the Queen for help in 1865. They

would work with heart and hand but they needed land. These m
women, poor and in distress, by sheer courage and determinatic
bringing into existence a black peasantry and an economy based c
holdings. They did not ask for charity but for help in obtaining
reply the Queen gave them a sermon on the virtue of hard work

History vindicated the peasants of St Ann, and with them the ,
people. In 1897 a Royal Commission endorsed the programme the people
and the Baptist missionaries had initiated in the 1830s and that the
petitioners of 1865 had put forward. For the first time in their history the
achievement of the Jamaican people was officially recognised. The Commission reported: "It seems to us that no reform offers so good a prospect
for the permanent welfare in the future of the West Indies as the settlement
of the labouring population on the land as small peasant proprietors as the
only means by which the population can in future be supported."

But the mass of the people had no voice in shaping government policy.
That was shaped by British officials and a legislative council of which only
five of the members were Jamaicans; and these were elected by a small èlite.
There were no African-Jamaicans on the council; and as for the peasants,
heavy taxation and land of poor quality soon led to a fall in the number of
peasant freeholds. It was in this period that the black peasantry turned to
emigration as a solution for perpetual poverty, and left in their thousands
for Panama, Costa Rica and Honduras.

The royal commission's words did not bring any significant improvement in the life of the peasant, as the steady flow of emigrants indicates.
But two highly significant developments were taking place amongst the
Jamaican people. Marcus Garvey challenged them to make freedom a
reality by emancipating themselves from the shackles of white imperialism,
by claiming their African past, by pride in their race and by striving for
political power. His trumpet call, "Up, you mighty race" inspired racial
pride, a sense of purpose and of self-esteem. As George Cumper points out,
"In 1865 the new class which was pressing for recognition and partnership
in the society was the peasantry. In 1938 a similar role was played by the
'proletarian' wage workers." (Cumper: 1954) The anger of the black
peasants and of the black working class boiled over, with eruptions of
violence in 1935 and 1936 in St Vincent, St Lucia, St Kitts and British
Guiana; with riots at the docks in Falmouth and Kingston in May and
October 1935 and with the Frome riot of January 1938. Once more the
Jamaican people became the agents of change. In this period of confrontation and conflict Alexander Bustamànte and Norman Manley began the
transformation of Jamaican society, Bustamante by organising a labour
movement and the Jamaica Labour Party, Norman Manley by leading a
campaign for universal adult suffrage and freedom from colonial domin-

ance and by organising the People's National Party. These two leaders, opponents but never enemies, became the architects of Jamaican independence; and the Jamaican people have demonstrated that people of the African race are as capable as the people of any other race of founding and maintaining democratic systems of government.

These changes began in the minds of grassroots blacks who realised in a natural pragmatic way that, as Sam Sharpe insisted, freedom was a right for which those who wished to be free had to be prepared to die; that freedom was not an end in itself, a static condition, but a never-ending process of preserving and enlarging the gains that had been won.

The people did these things with little government help. The cost in human suffering was heavy. In 1850 a stipendiary magistrate declared that the country had done little or nothing for the blacks. In 1860 an American journalist, William Sewell, described the mortality rate among children as frightful, and pointed out that the government provided, in 1859, the sum of £2,950 for the education of children between the ages of ten and 15. This worked out at one shilling per child for the year. The churches and the teachers, not the government, not the privileged, stood by the people, guiding and counselling them. Short of capital, the people shared their labour by "day for day", "morning digging", by "pardner" or "susu." Their burial scheme societies, lodges and benevolent and friendly societies added fellowship, a measure of social security, and social recognition to their lives.

From the homes of the people, from board houses roofed with cedar shingles or zinc, wattle and daub thatched roof cottages, each set in its yard, each surrounded by fruit trees, mango, avocado, pear, ackee, soursop, star apple, banana, coconut, coffee, each in dry parishes with its square tank or its "kick-and-buck", each with its lean-to kitchen or covered fireplace, from these came many of the primary school teachers, the black clergy, the policemen, the emigrants who went overseas to Panama, Central America, the United States and, in the 1920s, to Cuba. From these yards and from the "eight by ten" rooms of landless tenants came the urban wage-earners who emerged in the 1930s as the Jamaican working class. Theirs was a monumental achievement, but up to the 1920s "Quashie" remained a term of derision for those who so decisively shaped our history.

Our poets, our artists, recorded our story. Edna Manley revealed the strength and meaning of our history in "Negro Aroused", while George Campbell transformed that history into a psalm:

> For the old roads
> Lead to new ones

And our fathers are our sons
And our sons are our fathers.
No part of our past that is not
Part of our memory
No death in our past
That is not resurrection unto us.

We pay honour also to those who cast in their lot with us; to the Portuguese Jews who chose to stay when Isasi and the Spanish colonists left and who, like blacks and browns, were denied civil rights up to 1829; to the East Indians who loved Jamaica and chose to stay after the indenture period although they had been humiliated and unjustly treated; to the Chinese who so often, throughout the country, made it easier for the poor to buy bread and won a place in our affection; to the Syrians and Lebanese who expressed their dedication to Jamaica by public service, industry and philanthropy. For more than a century these have contributed to Jamaica's progress and to the quality and diversity of Jamaican culture. Their devotion to their own homelands and their knowledge of their own history enabled them to enter fully into the effort of African-Jamaicans to move toward self-government and independence. African-Jamaicans have learned much from these fellow citizens about pride in one's history.

In the chapters that follow we discuss the distinguished hertiage of achievement which African-Jamaicans inherited from the people, the makers of our history. We move on from the story of this heritage and the perception of our history as a source of inspiration to Africa the homeland, and then we turn to the great turning point in human history when mankind turned from hunting to agriculture and from a nomadic way of life to a sedentary one.

And in this change we come face-to-face with the pioneers of urban civilisation, with Chinese people in the valley of the Yellow River, with Indians in the Indus River, with people from the Middle East and from the valley of the Nile. In these early chapters we find unexpected, exciting linkages with other heirs to great civilisations and ancient cultures.

CHAPTER 2

On claiming our great heritage

How does the Jamaican see himself or herself? Has he or she developed the self-pride, self-respect, the sense of self-esteem for which Marcus Garvey pleaded and which history justifies?

The second question is linked with the first and with our theme of Africa as the original homeland. What is the Jamaican's world picture of Africa and of the standing of people of African descent in a world that is no longer dominated by white power? Does the African-Jamaican's world vision begin, as Europe affirmed, with barracoons and slave ships leaving a savage, black country, a land where "the heathen in his blindness bows down to wood and stone"?

In our search for the answers we come to a third question which is at the very heart of our subject. Why do Jamaicans avert their eyes from their history, when in all countries the teaching of history is an opportunity to build up a basic nationalism and patriotism in the mind of a child. And in the minds of the people also, for as Norman Manley said, "It is out of your own minds, out of your own faith in yourselves, out of your own conviction about the future of the country that the spirit of national unity and of patriotism will be built." The African-Jamaican people left to their children, and their children's children, a great heritage. The challenge is to use that heritage for building a sense of self-worth and for national unity and achievement.

Richard Hart, in *Blacks in Rebellion*, put the challenge in these words:

> One of the problems confronting the pioneers of the new popular movements was the formidable historical legacy of a widespread lack of racial self-respect.
>
> Garvey's oratory in the late 1920s and early 1930s had struck a responsive chord and the experience of participation in this movement had provided many thousands of people with a founda-

tion for self-assurance. But even so the task of inspiring national self-confidence was a formidable one.

The historical legacy of self-denigration was only partly attributable to the objective circumstances of generations of enslavement and cruel exploitation. It was also the contrived effect of a system of education and indoctrination designed to promote a loyalty to the prevailing imperialism and an acceptance of the domination of whites over blacks.

Many peoples who have been subjected to alien domination have been able to draw strength from their own legends and history. The Jamaican people were at a disadvantage. The imperial power had largely succeeded in erasing from their memory their African cultural heritage. Jamaica had no legends but it did have a history. And there were aspects of that history which, if brought to the people's attention, could provide abundant inspiration for future struggles against oppression.

Africa and Britain provide ennobling examples of ways in which they used history for empowerment. Many African societies see to it that the young learn the genealogies of their descent. As John Mbiti explains this gives "a sense of depth, historical belongingness, a feeling of deep-rootedness and a sense of a sacred obligation to extend the genealogical line".

Also, many African tribes see God as participating in human history. "They do not sever man from his total environment, so that in effect human history is cosmic history . . . God is not divorced from this concept of history; it is His universe, He is active in it and apparent silence may be a feature of his divine activity." (Mbiti: 1970)

African folklore, an important part of African history, emphasises the universality of the human spirit, overcoming the barriers of race: "Are the dreams of other men so different from those of Africans? It is difficult to speak of a black or a white soul. Souls are seen to be the same in their aspirations."

And where can a nobler tradition of freedom and justice be found than in English history, with its dedication to just and ancient fundamental rights and its record of the progressive safeguarding of the folk, the common people, against the tyranny of rulers.

This tradition was deep-rooted, for as Ernest Rhys points out in *The Growth of Political Liberty*, "the islands bred a notable people, already showing a marked bias and stout temper, before any Angle or Saxon had landed. We read in Tacitus that they would bear cheerfully the service of government if they were not ill-treated, for their subjection ran to obedience, but not to servitude."

In later generations rulers such as Alfred the Great and Saxon King Edgar strengthened the tradition of just laws. King Edgar stated: "This is what I will – that Every Man be worthy of folkright, poor and rich alike, and that righteous dooms [judgments] be judged to him." (Rhys: 1921) Alfred, for his part, by insisting that English history should be set down in an English book, ensured that law by law, record by record, the prescriptive right of the folk to safe conduct in their life and work and justice at the hands of their rulers and governors, is asserted and reasserted.

There followed in 1215 the Magna Carta, the great cornerstone of English liberty, which safeguards the tenant, the heir-at-law, the king's labourer and the common man against feudal abuses: "No man is to be put in prison, outlawed, punished or molested, but by the judgment of his equals, or by the law of the land." (Rhys: 1921)

It could have been Osei Tutu of Kumasi speaking, or the West African creators of the great empires of Ghana, Mali and Songhai, which were organised before the formation of states in northern and eastern Europe.

The Britain that cherished this glorious tradition of "folk right" and "folk moot" betrayed that heritage when it became a coloniser and slave master. In contrast, the enslaved Africans proved to be "a notable people of marked bias and stout temper" who rejected European tyranny.

The Africans and the British saw themselves as the makers of their history. Jamaicans have averted their eyes from their past because they know only that of their history which told of the victories of Nelson and Rodney, which portrayed Europe as model, Africa as a land of savages and the African as an inferior sort of human being. African-Jamaicans know deep within themselves that this is not their history. They refuse to accept or to recognise it.

Also, and this distressed them greatly, they have felt ashamed of being the descendants of docile slaves, who accepted enslavement and European domination and never achieved anything, never created anything, had no past of which to be proud, no history that empowered their descendants and gave them a feeling of self-worth.

The existing system of education, having been taken over from the coloniser without fundamental changes, reinforces their self-doubt, their uncertainty about affirming their blackness, their African heritage, their standing in the world.

Outraged at the utter neglect of African history and at the distortions in British colonial history, Marcus Garvey challenged the black majority to "affirm your ancestry, claim your history", but 300 years of that history had been blotted out; and those 300 years contained the distinguished record of black achievement throughout plantation America, a liberating record of African-American triumph.

Poet/singer Jimmy Cliff, took up the protest, accusing the British coloniser in bitter words:

> You stole my history
> Destroyed my culture,
> Cut out my tongue
> So I can't communicate

He protested against the purpose of the coloniser as being the destruction of his self-esteem:

> You mediate
> And separate,
> So myself I should hate

Jimmy Cliff's message was that for three centuries they had lived like people without being certain who they were, people without a past, without a present, with little prospect of a future; the theft was part of a planned assault on the mind of the black majority so that "myself I should hate". George Lamming reinforced Jimmy Cliff's words.

> If people are shaped by the view that they are made into history by some chosen few who are the real makers of history, you stablize the relation of dominant and dominated . . . If we could ever succeed in planting in people, not only the idea but the fact, in their consciousness, that they are the makers of history, then you alter the relationship between them and those who hold them in their hands. (Lamming: 1983)

We come here to the fact that the African-British conflict had two dimensions, one taking the form of liberation wars for freedom and justice, and the other being the even more difficult resistance to the doctrine of white superiority. It is one of the great achievements of Robert Love and Marcus Garvey that when it appeared that Europe and the governing class in Jamaica were on the point of capturing the African mind they turned the tide; and in that critical period the emerging national movement, coupled with the worldwide anti-colonial movement, brought about the defeat of colonialism. But through the system of education the colonial stereotypes and principles survived.

Only by ridding the mind of the colonial stereotypes and of attitudes of dependence, only by seeing that the African-Jamaican people are the makers of their history, can African-Jamaicans find in their historic achievements the inspiration they need for rekindling the national spirit, for building a united Jamaica, and also ways of using the collective intelligence and wisdom of the Jamaican people to meet the imperatives of the twenty-first century.

The basic colonial principles were: the doctrine of the superiority of the white race and the inferiority of the black. Europe was civiliser and Africa was savage. Skin colour was a badge of status, with blackness denoting slave labour and the gradations of colour moving downwards to degradation. These ideas were clearly stated by British intellectuals such as Thomas Carlyle and James Anthony Froude.

In his highly neurotic and unpleasant *Discourse on the Negro Question* and in his later writings Carlyle maintained that "supply and demand . . . have an uphill task of it with such a man [the Negro]. Strong sun supplies self gratis, rich soil in those unpeopled or half-peopled regions, almost gratis; these are his 'supply' and half an hour a day directed upon these will produce pumpkin, which is his demand".

J. A. Froude insisted that "it is as certain as any future event can be that if we give the negroes as a body the political powers which we claim for ourselves, they will use them only to their own injury. They will slide back into their own condition and the chance will be gone of lifting them to the level to which we have no right to say that they are incapable of rising".

Froude said: "Nature has made us unequal, and Acts of Parliament cannot make us equal. Some must lead and some follow, and the question is only one of degree and kind." Should political freedom be forced on this child or on this race, they would be driven back into "the condition from which the slave trade was the beginning of their emancipation". Blacks had not demonstrated any capacity for civilisation except "under European laws, European education and European authority . . . and the old African superstitions lie undisturbed at the bottom of their souls. Give them independence and in a few generations they will peel off such civilisation as they have learnt as easily and as willingly as their coats and trousers".

These were the attitudes of the ruling class. Even the liberal-minded royal commission of 1897 saw "black economic and moral progress as depending on white guidance and control". (Holt: 1992)

Slavery and the slave trade were justified, as Carlyle and Froude indicated, because Europe, as benefactor and civiliser, rescued the African from savagery.

Isaiah Berlin, one of the great British philosophers of our time, has pointed out that in the nineteenth and twentieth centuries European thought has been astonishingly Eurocentric and that even the most radical political thinkers of this period, speaking of the inhabitants of Africa and Asia, have some curiously remote and abstract ideas. They think of Asians and Africans almost exclusively in terms of their treatment by Europeans. "The peoples of Africa and Asia are discussed as wards or as victims of Europeans, but seldom . . . in their own right, as people with histories and cultures of their own, with a past and present and future which must be

understood in terms of their own actual character and circumstances."
(Berlin: 1981)

Eric Williams considered that for the West Indian people: "the most pernicious effect of colonialism . . . for the West Indies has been that many black people have internalised this value system and have come to believe in the deepest recesses of their minds that black is in fact inferior to white".

To this day another product of British racism is the split society, with political and economic control in the hands of a white and brown èlite, and with limited educational opportunities for a large, predominantly African, or African and East Indian underclass, trained to serve as cheap labour: "The whole policy of the colonizer is to keep the native in his primitive state and make him economically dependent."

Already we begin to realise that the Africans, thrown as individuals into a society governed by these principles, must have felt utterly alone. Consider the nature of Jamaican society and the odds appear insuperable.

Jamaican society, mirrored the principles of colonialism and revealed their impact in all its crudity. One of Jamaica's distinguished sociologists, Orlando Patterson, described it as lacking any sense of concern for moral values and for the welfare of the community. Britain created in Jamaica a society that was wholly dedicated to making money by producing sugar, exploiting the land and the African.

> As the island reached its period of greatest prosperity, toward the end of the third decade of the eighteenth century, the wealthiest land-owners, possessing well over three-quarters of the island's property (including slaves) were all absentees, living in great style in Britain, where they married into the petty aristocracy and made up the greatest part of the West India lobby, the most powerful interest group in British politics at that time (Williams: 1944).

Orlando Patterson points out that as a result the core of the white ruling class in Jamaica consisted of the attorneys or agents of the absentee propri-etors, the few resident large-scale owners, and leading echelons of the appointed officers. Unlike the slave systems of the American South or of the Iberian colonies there was here no ruling class who, infused with the pioneer spirit, were committed to the social well-being and cultural devel-opment of their community.

That was not all. In Jamaica England institutionalised violence and legalised injustice by establishing a system of negro jurisprudence which the clerk of the English Committee on the Slave Trade (1789) analysed in these terms:

> The leading idea in the negro system of jurisprudence is that which
> was the first in the minds of those most interested in its formation,

namely that negroes were property, and a species of property that needed a rigorous and vigilant regulation.

To secure the rights of owners and maintain the subordination of negroes seems to have most occupied the attention and excited the solicitude of the different legislatures ... the welfare of these unhappy objects was left to the owner ... The provisions therefore, for the protection and for improving the condition of the negroes make a very small portion of the earlier policy respecting slaves.

In discussing a slave's rights in a court of law, Michael Craton wrote: "Very little measure appears to have been assigned, by any general laws, to the authority of the master in punishing his slaves. It appears that any degree of severity in the way of punishment, though it went even to the life of the slave, was looked upon as an object not deserving public consideration and that even murder was not marked with any very heavy penalty." (Craton: 1976)

Europe created a society that was totally immoral. Legislation made the African slave, male or female, property, a chattel, no longer a person. In so doing, the concept of the family as a basic social unit was destroyed. The white owner exercised the functions of the father as protector, provider, source of authority, counsellor and model. The natural father was downgraded to progenitor and the woman from mother to breeder.

In law, "The young of slaves stand on the same footing as other animals." The master was owner, not the parent. Women "were breeders, animals whose monetary value could be precisely calculated in terms of their ability to multiply their numbers". An absentee proprietor, Monk Lewis, wrote: "The concerns of the family must be to a slave woman matters of very inferior moment compared with the work of her owner. He insists on all the prime of her strength being devoted to his business; it is only after the toils, the indecencies, the insults and miseries of the day spent in the gang that she can think of doing anything to promote the comfort of her household." (Lewis: 1834)

Philip Curtin in *The Atlantic Slave Trade,* states that in the period 1518-1874 about 10 million Africans were brought as slaves to plantation America. Just under 2 million were brought to Jamaica. This book tells how these people made our history: not the British government, the white ruling class, not the powerful, the privileged, but the black majority who had been stripped of all possessions, even of their names and of their status as persons. They and their descendants initiated every movement towards freedom and justice. They built the foundations of nationhood.

The chapters that follow tell the story of the Africans and of their descendants, but we will point here to three of the major achievements of the enslaved Africans and African-Jamaicans. First, we come face-to-face with the greatest achievement of African-Jamaicans and of African-Americans. From the years of their first landings in plantation America, more than a century before the Mayflower arrived in New England, the enslaved Africans set about founding free and independent societies wherever in the Americas. Big Massa had his backyard. The African resistence to enslavement went beyond rejection to creating models of free, just and independent societies. By doing this the African pioneered all the liberation movement of the Americas, with the Palmares Republic, the Suriname Bush Negroes and with the establishment of Haitian Independence in 1807.

This achievement is all the more remarkable because the Africans arrived in America as individuals from different language groups, tribes and kingdoms, who had been removed by force from their kinsfolk, from participation in beliefs, ceremonies, rituals and festivals. They had been severed from their roots, from the security of their tribe and "from the entire group of those who made them aware of their own existence. To be without one of these corporate elements is to be out of the whole picture".

Europe, as explorer, coloniser, slave master brought the African by force to the Americas. She did this with the assistance of some Africans, a fact that many African-Jamaicans find it hard to think of or to accept. But the supreme achievement was that the African-American responded immediately to the challenge of freedom by becoming a liberator and a champion of justice.

African-Jamaicans began the struggle for freedom and justice more than a century before the *Mayflower* arrived and a century-and-a-half before liberty, fraternity and equality became the battle cry of the American War of Independence and of the French Revolution. The African-American struggle for these rights which began early in the sixteenth century and continued up to the time of Martin Luther King, the Alabama bus boycott that began with Rosa Parks, the United States Civil Rights Act (1957), the Unites States Equal Opportunity Act, and a claim for equality that found powerful expression in the Black Power Movement of the 1960s.

The story of the African-Jamaican and African-West Indian people is a significant part of that larger hemispheric struggle. It was global as well as hemispheric, for in the process of time African-West Indians such as Marcus Garvey, George Padmore, C. L. R. James, the Haitian founders of Négritude and its principal exponent Aimé Césaire of Martinique, contributed to the nationalist and liberation movements led by Nnamdi Azikiwe, Kwame Nkrumah and Jomo Kenyatta.

This hemispheric perspective extends across 500 years and reveals the magnitude and significance of the liberation movements which began with scattered, uprooted groups of African fugitives seeking freedom in the forests and mountains of the Americas.

The first Africans to come to the Americas were brought by their masters to Hispaniola in Ovando's fleet in 1502. One of them "escaped to the Indians" soon after arriving. This solitary African's rejection of enslavement set a pattern that was followed by enslaved Africans in Jamaica and throughout plantation America. The word "maroon" is from the Spanish *cimarron*, the name originally given to domestic cattle that had taken to the hills in Hispaniola. It was given also to Indians who had escaped from the lowlands and by the 1530s it referred also to African runaways.

Marronage became a regional movement in which the Africans planted in the slave masters' own backyards visible, tangible reminders of freedom, justice, and independence. Mexico, Colombia, Brazil, the Guyanas, Jamaica, Peru, Haiti, Cuba, the French islands, bear witness to the hemispheric scale of these liberation movements.

In these terms the African-Jamaican heritage ranks with the affirmation of the inalienable rights of man in the American Declaration of Independence and with Abraham Lincoln's declaration at Gettysburg that government was of the people, by the people, for the people.

It was the supreme achievement of the African-American peoples that they transformed slavery into freedom, initiated the longest, most extensive liberation movement in the history of the Americas, and recorded decisive triumphs over European enslavement, colonialism and racial prejudice.

In the process they enriched the cultures of the various countries in which they lived, creating creole languages, a distinguished range of folk cultures and producing world-recognised masterpieces in music, sculpture painting and the dance.

In the history of the Americas three leaders command veneration and evoke profound feelings of gratitude. The three are: white George Washington who defeated the English tyranny and led the North American colonists to independence as citizens of the United States; brown Simón Bolívar, who defeated the Spanish troops and started various independence movements throughout America; and the black ex-slave, Toussaint L'Ouverture, who defeated the armies of Napoleon and took Haiti to independence.

CHAPTER 3

Africa, the original homeland

Marcus Garvey was the first African-Jamaican to make Africa a reality to middle-class and working-class Jamaicans. But many well-educated middle- and upper-class Jamaicans saw both Africa and Garvey through European eyes. This was because

> colonial ideological policy consistently debased Africa as well as peoples and things African. The future, the colonizer claimed, belonged to Europe. Hence colonial subjects were made to identify progress with the ideals of their master. In the process of the formation of Jamaica as a nation the negation of Africa and blackness has been constant. And so has the resistance to it of black people. (Lewis: 1987)

Garvey saw that the reaction of Jamaicans to the name of Africa and to people of African descent defined how Eurocentric they were, how completely they had been transformed into Anglo-Jamaicans. They saw Africa as savage, and Africans as savages. "The image marked the colonial mind, so slavery was portrayed as civilizing." (Lewis: 1987)

Lewis said that in a predominantly black society in the 1920s, as far as Jamaica's leading journalist and novelist, Herbert George DeLisser, was concerned,

> insofar as Jamaica was civilized, it was English . . . DeLisser said that Jamaica bore the indelible impress of English influence and that Jamaicans were proud of their connections with the British empire . . . so when DeLisser came to write Jamaican history through his novels, he portrayed that to be black was to be savage at heart. Paul Bogle, leader of the 1865 rebellion and later a national hero, was described as being a brave man, but underneath the veneer of his religion lay deep the superstitions of the African savage.

The story of the Jamaican people reveals how essential it is to see that history has to do with processes as well as events, with ideas, aspirations, religious beliefs, self-concept, the way in which we see the standing of our nation and people in the world. This means that self-esteem and unquestioning pride in racial ancestry are powerful motivating forces.

The historical experience of the African-Jamaica people shows that only Africa can evoke this response. Garvey emphasised the centrality of Africa, not of Europe, of blackness, not of whiteness, of affirming an African identity, as essential steps to power, and in the first instance, to self-determination. He lamented the fact that in his day West Indians had developed more of the white psychology than of the black outlook, "for the greatest hope lay in the outlook of the Negro toward independence".

In the period 1920-45 some Jamaicans began to see themselves and Africans through African-Jamaican eyes. The change was radical. We have shown how middle- and upper-class Jamaicans saw Africans and the black working class up to the 1920s. In contrast, let us look first at the response of the bush negroes of Suriname who had removed themselves for generations from close contact with colonial authority. From them we move to the first voices of Jamaican nationalism and of the centrality of Africa, this being the generation that followed after the Anglo-Jamaicans. Our purpose in doing this is to show that the story of the African-Jamaican people begins with Africa as the cradle of mankind and as their original homeland. This is why we focus on the story of mankind and not of an empire; and why the perspective includes the emergence of centres of urban civilisation in Mesopotamia, the land between the Tigris and Euphrates; Egypt and the valley of the Nile; the valley of the Indus and the valley of the Yellow River in China. These do not speak of racial superiority. They speak of the basic unity of human beings and of membership in one family, the human race.

We begin with the emotional reaction of the four paramount chiefs of the bush negroes of Suriname when they visited Ghana and Nigeria in 1970. When they arrived in Ghana, Granman Gazon, in vivid imagery, declared that "the same wind that drove us against our will from Africa has now aided us to find our way back". The granman spoke of the emotional shock of returning to their homeland. At their meeting with the Asantahene in Kumasi, each stood close to the ruler of the Ashanti people and addressed him with great emotion. "Granman Aboikoni, trembling with emotion, sang a Kromanti song while kneeling before the Asantahene . . . They declared that finally they had found their true king again. On another occasion Granman Aboikoni concluded with a prayer in Kromanti (a sacred language of the Bush Negroes) in which the Almighty, Nana Kodiapon, is invoked. This caused great emotion for the same Supreme Ruler is invoked in Ghana."

African-Jamaicans share the emotional attachment that Granman Aboikoni and his fellow chiefs felt for their ancestral homeland. They were outraged by Benito Mussolini's attack on Ethiopia. In response, some proudly took the name of Ras Tafari, denounced the white world as Babylon and chose to worship a black god, the emperor, Haile Selassie. In recent years they poured out their love for Africa in the welcome that they gave to Nelson Mandela. Africa provides the sense of racial identity and of self-worth which the white world for so long denied them.

Through the work of Garvey and of the rapidly growing national movement, Jamaica moved to the wonderful daybreak of the late 1930s, when they began to discover themselves. One of the earliest was black Hiram Vaughan of Barbados, who said to the black girl he loved,

> Turn sideways now and let them see
> What loveliness escapes the schools,
> Then turn again and smile and be
> The perfect answer to those fools
> Who only prate of Greece and Rome
> The face that launched a thousand ships
> And such like things but keep tight lips
> For burnished beauty nearer home.

In the same period George Campbell, thought of in Jamaica as the poet of the revolution, in the closing lines of his poem in celebration of Edna Manley's carving, "Negro Aroused", cried:

> the heart shouts, Freedom,
> I lift my face to heaven, awakened,
> Shouting louder, louder,
> With triumph, with a new found strength
> Freedom! We cry only freedom – we were dead when
> Sleeping, now we live! We are aroused.

In his poem "Last Queries" he asks

> Say is my skin beautiful —
> Soft as velvet
> As deep as the blackness of a weeping night . . .

In those electric years of self-discovery and self-emancipation, Victor Stafford Reid wrote one of Jamaica's greatest stories, *New Day*, giving to the English Language new cadences and passionate rhythms. In 1981 Vic Reid said of his historical novels: "The whole reason for my writing is to have the black people proud of themselves, and their history."

Alongside the poets and novelists are two historians, C. L. R. James with *Black Jacobins* and Eric Williams with *Capitalism and Slavery* who revealed in all their starkness the savagery, greed and intellectual dishonesty of European colonialism. History was their abeng, signalling the beginning of the intellectual emancipation of the West Indian people by their own historians. Rupert Lewis and Robert Hill followed with research studies and books that reveal the heroic stature of Marcus Garvey as thinker, black leader and emancipator, who called on African-Jamaicans to take pride in and to cherish the African-Jamaican people, the makers of the history of the Jamaican people who "from the beginning have had to fight their own way up to where they are today. Some have done well but the great majority are almost where they were when they came off the plantations. They are propertyless and almost helpless". (Garvey)

It is for this generation also to claim their great historical heritage and to acknowledge Africa as motherland, as the cradle of mankind and the launching pad for the dispersal of the human beings, the nomadic hunters and food-gathering people who gradually, throughout half-a-million years, established hunting grounds and dwelling places in all the continents save Antarctica.

We begin with Africa because that is where the history of the African people and the human race begins. In contrast, imperial Europe saw the history of the Americas as beginning with the arrival of her pathfinder, Christopher Columbus, in 1492, followed by the colonisation of the New World in the following century. As for the African people, imperial Europe considered that their history began when they came under her rule. This was like saying that the history of the English people begins with the Norman Conquest in 1066.

So, on to Africa, whose political, cultural and racial diversity is bewildering. Our African ancestors came from West Africa, from the region that extends south from Senegambia to Angola. This is only a part of a continent that includes one-tenth of the world's population. These 300 million in number are divided into 50 nations, the majority belonging to about 1,000 tribes, each with its own distinct language, culture and territory. John Mbiti, one of Africa's most distinguished theologians and philosophers, points out that Africa has all the main races of the world and that each group can rightly claim to be African. Ethnologists and anthropologists have classified them broadly as follows: Bushmanoid people with light yellowish skin are found in parts of eastern and southern Africa; caucasoid people, with light to medium brown and pink skin in southern, eastern and northern Africa; mongoloid people whose skin pigmentation ranges from black to brown, yellow and pink; negroid people, black to dark-brown and brown, who are found almost everywhere in Africa; and pygmoid people with light-brown yellowish skins.

Imagine that in order to form an impression of the size and antiquity of

on the trans-Saharan trade. Regularly Arab caravans brought luxury goods, salt, which was a dietary necessity, and firearms and returned to the Mediterranean ports with gold. The power and splendour of the empires of the western Sudan – Ghana, Mali and Songhai – were achieved by the gold trade, for this region supplied Europe with about one-quarter of its requirement. The profits from the trans-Saharah trade, which was facilitated by the introduction of the camel from Arabia into North Africa 1000 BC, enabled these three empires to dominate the political, economic and cultural development of West Africa.

The capture by the Portuguese of the important gold-trading city of Ceuta in Morocco in 1415 was their first major step towards exploring the West African coast to find out if there was any point of entry into the Indian Ocean. Portugal had only recently regained its territory from the Moors. It was a small country with a population of about 70,000 persons, impoverished but bred to battling Atlantic rollers with sturdy fishing-boats. It recognised that it was outside the Mediterranean world, since to travel from Lisbon to Venice took some 40 days. On the other hand, Portugal held a few Atlantic islands, Madeira and the Azores, that had potential as sugar-producers.

Portugal's only prospect of wealth lay in finding a sea route down the African coast to the spice-producing countries of Asia and in developing a trade in gold with West Africa and in sugar with its own plantations in Madeira and the Canary Islands.

The bankers and traders of Genoa were interested. A city of between 60,000 and 80,000 people, it depended entirely on its inhabitants' entrepreneurial skills. They lived by their wits. Genoa "manufactured goods for other people; sent out her shipping, for other people; invested, but in other places. Even in the eighteenth century, only half of Genoese capital remained in the city. The rest, for want of local investment openings, went abroad. The constraints of geography sent it on foreign ventures". (Braudel: 1982) The Genoese are of special interest to us because they were among the first of the European bankers and traders to invest in commodities and in ventures that prepared the way for the Atlantic Age. They had organised Sicilian sugar production and there were Genoese settlements in North Africa, Seville, Lisbon, Bruges and Antwerp. Genoese investors saw that there were profits to be made in Portugal, and soon they were handling some of Lisbon's wholesale and retail trade, although the latter was generally kept in the hands of Portuguese citizens.

Between 1433 and 1482 the Portuguese occupied Madeira (1433), rediscovered the Azores (1430) and discovered the Cape Verde Islands (1455), Fernando Po and São Tome off the coast of Africa (1471). They also built up a profitable trading area on the African coast that supplied ivory, a pepper substitute called malaguetta, gold dust and slaves, the number of which rose from about 1,000 in the 1450s to 3,000 annually in the 1480s. By signing a treaty with Spain in 1479 and building a fort at São Jorge da Mina on the Guinea coast in 1481, Portugal established its monopoly of trade with the western coast of Africa.

The Genoese played a substantial part in this expansion of Portuguese power and of its monopoly of the West African trade. So did the Florentines, but the Genoese were Portugal's chief partners. They promoted the spread of the sugar plantation from the eastern Mediterranean to Sicily, southern Spain (whence sugar moved to Hispaniola), Morocco, the Portuguese Algarve, Madeira and onto the Cape Verde Islands.

Through these efforts Portugal established a profitable, coherent economic zone that included bases for trade along the African coast. At the same time it continued its search for control of the spice trade. Success came when Bartholomew Diaz rounded the Cape of Good Hope in 1488. Ten years later, in 1498, Vasco da Gama returned to Lisbon with the news that Portugal had won the race for the spice trade.

The impact on Alexandria and Venice was disastrous. Braudel reports that in 1504, when the Venetian galleys arrived at Alexandria in Egypt, they found not a single sack of pepper waiting for them.

But Portugal lost an even richer prize. In 1484 the Genoese-born Christopher Columbus put his proposal for a westerly route to the Indies to the King of Portugal and his advisers. Understandably, they rejected the proposal for by then they were sure that the Atlantic led into the Indian ocean and control of the spice trade was within their grasp. What more could Columbus offer than, possibly, a shorter sea route and therefore a less expensive one?

Columbus turned to Spain and in 1492, the Spanish sovereigns, having completed the reconquest of Spain, commissioned him to discover a western pathway to Cathay and the Indies.

Before daybreak on the morning of Friday, 2 August 1492, Columbus ordered his fleet of three ships to weigh anchor and leave the sheltered waters of the Rio Tinto for the Atlantic. Soon the wind filled their sails and the ships came to life with creaking timbers and billowing sails: the *Santa María* of 100 tons, the low, swift sailing *Pinta*, a caravel, and the midget *Niña*. There were 90 men aboard the fleet, most of them from the villages and townships around Cadiz. Columbus made first for the Canary Islands, took water and other supplies aboard and then set out on a westerly course, making for the kingdom of the Great Khan in Asia, which by his reckoning was about 3,000 miles away. By 1 October he had covered that distance but there was no sign of land. The crew grew mutinous for they noted that the winds blew constantly in a westerly direction, always away from home. On 7 October, they saw flocks of birds and in the water the branch of a tree, still green and with berries on it.

Suddenly, at 2 o'clock on the morning of the 12 October, a sailor, Rodrigo, who was on watch on the *Pinta* shouted, "Tierra, Tierra." Ahead appeared something gleaming white. On the orders of Columbus they lay offshore, waiting for daylight. After 31 days at sea, they had arrived at a small island in the Bahamas which was inhabited by Tainos, and which bore the name of Guanahani. Columbus named it San Salvador (Holy Saviour). He was sure that he had come to an island off the coast of Japan. He was sure that gold lay ahead, and pepper, cloves, cinnamon, nutmeg, mace, aloes, ginger, the riches of the world and great glory.

Constructed replicas of the *Niña, Pinta* and *Santa María*

Japan and China were some 10,000 miles away across the Pacific, but to the day of his death in 1506 Columbus believed that he had discovered a sea route to Cathay. He never realised that he had come to the Americas, the western coastlands of the Atlantic Basin, that he had put the old world of the Americas in permanent contact with the older world of Europe and had prepared the way for a shift of power from the Mediterranean to the Atlantic. These things became known when other explorers began to reveal the magnitude of an achievement that he was never able to comprehend.

With Columbus as pathfinder and explorer, Europe entered the Americas. When he landed on Guanahani later that morning, he was greeted by a group of friendly Indians. He wrote in his journal:

> All I saw were youths, none of them more than thirty years of age. They were very well made, with very handsome bodies and very good countenances – they are of the colour of the Canareans, neither black nor white . . . they neither carry nor know anything of arms, for I showed them swords, and they grasped them by the blade and cut themselves through ignorance. They have no iron.

Columbus also noted that they ought to be good servants, and of good skill, for they repeated very quickly all that was said to them.

On that small, sandy island, surrounded by uncomprehending friendly indigenous Americans who had discovered and settled it centuries earlier, Columbus affirmed Europe's mission of conquest, dispossession and enslavement. He lost no time in unfurling the flag of Spain. To the bewildered Tainos he was saying, "This island is no longer yours. Now it belongs to Spain." He followed this up by claiming for Spain, Cuba, Hispaniola and in 1494, Jamaica.

The Tainos, stone-age people, marvelled at the swords the Europeans carried. The shedding of blood when they grasped the blade signified what was to happen. The entry in his journal, "They ought to be good servants, and of good skill," foretold the enslavement of the Taino people. He hoped that a trade in Indian slaves would prove as profitable as the market in African slaves that the Portuguese had already established in Lisbon.

Territory, gold, spices, slaves, the demand for which had driven the Portuguese to storm Ceuta and begin their long exploration of the African coast, had driven Columbus to cross the Atlantic. Market forces had him in their grip. A proud, fiercely ambitious man, he dreamed of wealth and a coat-of-arms, as clauses in his proposal to the Spanish rulers reveal. He proposed:

> Firstly, that your Highness . . . appoint from this date the said Don Cristóbal Colon to be your Admiral in all those islands and mainlands which by his activity and industry shall he discover . . . That of all and every kind of merchandise, whether pearls, precious stones, gold, silver, spices and other objects of merchandise . . . Your Highnesses grant . . . to the said Don Cristóbal, the tenth part of the whole, after deducting all the expenses.
>
> That in all the vessels which may be equipped . . . the said Don Cristóbal Colon may . . . contribute and pay the eighth part of all that may be spent in the equipment, and that likewise he may have and take the eighth part of the profits that may result. (Columbus)

From Guanahani Columbus set out to explore the north cost of Cuba, for although he had completed his voyage, the search for gold had only just begun. Always the question came, "Have you gold?" Columbus found none along the north coast of Cuba. Not until he landed on the northern coast of Hispaniola did he see ornaments made of the precious metal. He left some of his crew behind in a small fortified settlement at La Navidad, with instructions to collect gold, and hurried back to Spain with exhibits and samples of gold and Indians.

In September 1493 Columbus, laden with honours, returned to Hispaniola. He had been made Admiral of the Ocean Sea, and was in command of an armada of 17 vessels. He and his successors had been ennobled and potentially were very wealthy.

This voyage was for settlement. Aboard were 1,400 men, including armed footmen and horsemen, smiths, carpenters, "all kinds of pulse or grain and corn, as well for food as to sow; besides vines, plants and seeds . . . and sundry kinds of artillery and iron tools . . . as bows, arrows, cross-bows, broadswords, pikes, hammers, nails, saws, axes". (Martyr)

At Gomera in the Canaries the fleet had taken aboard,

> goats and ewes and eight sows . . . From these eight sows have multi-
> plied all the pigs which to this day have been and are in the Indies,
> which have been and are numbered and this was the seed from which
> all that there is here of things of Castile has [sic] sprung, whether pigs
> and seeds of orange, limes and melons and all kinds of vegetables.
> Horses, sheep, cattle, vines, wheat barley, rye, citrus; and from
> Hispaniola many of them spread and grew. (Las Casas: 1875)

This *armada* was followed in 1502 by an even larger one of 30 ships and 2,500 people under the command of Nicolas de Ovando. They were sent to reinforce the 300 or so surviving from the earlier settlement. There were in the fleet a few African slaves who accompanied their masters from Spain. Soon after arriving, one of the Africans escaped to the Indians in the mountainous interior, and so became the first African maroon in the Americas.

In this early period of the Spanish settlement of Hispaniola, one of the more enterprising and better-off settlers, Gonzalo de Velosa, started Hispaniola's sugar industry:

> Now sugar is one of the richest crops to be found in any province or
> Kingdom of this world and on this island there is so much and it is
> so good although it was so recently introduced and has been followed
> for such a short time . . . Every one was blind until Bachelor Gonzalo
> de Velosa, at his own cost and investing everything he had and with
> great personal effort, brought workmen expert in sugar to this island,
> and built a horse-powered mill and first made sugar in this island; he
> alone deserves thanks as the principal inventor of this rich industry.
> (Oviedo)

The *armadas* under Columbus and Ovando marked the beginning of a global redistribution of races, cultures, languages, technology, animals and plants which continues to this day. The sugar cane, citrus, and people – Europeans, Africans, East Indians, Jews, Lebanese and Syrians – are constant reminders that West Indians are imported people in a largely imported environment. The roots of the West Indian community are to be found across the Atlantic, in the Old World. There also most of the useful plants and all the domestic animals had their origin. Many of the social institutions, religious beliefs, languages, various skills and technologies travelled with Old World people to the Caribbean and to mainland America. In consequence, Africa, Asia and Europe give historical continuity to the story of the various racial and cultural groups that make up the West Indian community.

The movement we have described should be seen as a redistribution, or transplanting, and not as a complete severance. The story of the African-Jamaican people begins in West Africa, whereas the recorded history of the West Indian community begins with an abrupt event, the arrival of Columbus in the Caribbean.

Unseen, in silence, mankind's constant and feared companions also crossed the Atlantic. Smallpox, typhoid, influenza and measles decimated the New World populations and in exchange syphilis, endemic among the Tainos, journeyed to Spain and raged with extraordinary virulence among Spanish armies fighting in North Italy.

This redistribution began at the dictates of money and of imperial ambitions, which caused the land-enclosed Mediterranean to give way to the Atlantic and Venice, Genoa and Florence to give way to Lisbon, Antwerp, Amsterdam, London, Paris, all financial and banking centres that had direct contact with the Americas.

We turn from these global movements to Hispaniola, where enslavement and savagery wiped out the Tainos in less than a century. Columbus, Nicolas de Ovando and Juan de Esquivel led the way.

Columbus, a great explorer and sea-commander, knew that he had enemies among the colonists. Many regarded him as a foreigner, the son of a Genoese artisan, tricked out with an empty title and a new coat of arms. Socially, in Spain's rigid hierarchy, he was an upstart. Only by discovering a source of gold and other precious metals could he consolidate his standing with the Spanish sovereigns. Following their instructions, he set out from Hispaniola to explore the south coast of Cuba and, from there, went on to Yamaye (Jamaica) where, according to the Tainos, gold was plentiful. His greedy, questing eyes found no evidence of gold in Jamaica. Greatly disappointed, Columbus returned to Hispaniola empty-handed, only to find that the dissatisfied and angry colonists were sending a stream of complaints to Spain.

Frustrated and insecure, Columbus decided to pacify the colonists by supplying them with Taino slaves and to prove that Hispaniola was a source of wealth by sending Tainos to Spain for sale as slaves. He sent a detachment of armed colonists into the countryside to hunt down the Tainos with horses and fierce dogs. The colonists brought in some 1,500 captives. The Torres fleet of three caravels returned to Spain that autumn with 500 of these captives who were to be put up for sale. About 600 were claimed by the colonists. An eyewitness, Michele de Cuneo, reported that the remaining 400, "Many of them with infants at the breast, in order better to escape us, since they were afraid we would turn to catch them again, left their infants anywhere on the ground and started to flee like desperate people, and some fled our settlement of Isabella for seven or eight days beyond the mountains and across huge rivers."

Two hundred of the Indians died before the Torres fleet reached Spain. Their bodies were thrown into the sea. Half of the survivors were sick when they disembarked in Cadiz. Cuneo's comment was "they are not working people, and they very much fear cold, nor have they long life". Queen Isabella ordered that the pitiful remnant should be sent back to their homes. The hope Columbus had cherished of a profitable trade in Taino slaves came to nothing.

Under Ovando and his successors Hispaniola became the stage on which the first tragic act in the destruction of many millions of the indigenous American people was played out. Even at this distance in time the story is one of horror and heartbreak. In a long and shameful catalogue of savagery, one of the most horrifying was the invitation to 80 Taino *caciques* to assemble for a meeting in a building, where Ovando's soldiers tied them to the wooden posts supporting the roof. The building was then set on fire and they were burnt to death. Anacaona, wife of the chief *cacique,* Caonabo, was then taken to Santo Domingo and hanged for plotting against the Spaniards. Architect of the massacre was Juan de Esquivel who later became the first Spanish governor of Jamaica.

Many of the Tainos were soon wiped out, some by imported diseases, others by forced labour in the mines and yet others by starvation, for they had little time to devote to tilling their food plots. "I sometimes came upon dead bodies on my way," wrote Las Casas, "and upon others who were gasping and moaning in their death agony, repeating hungry, hungry." It is thought that there were 300,000 Tainos in Hispaniola when the Spaniards first arrived in 1492. There were only 60,000 in 1508. By 1512 the number was down to 20,000. Oviedo, the Spanish historian, doubted if there were 500 left in 1548. In 1586, when Francis Drake sacked the city of Santo Domingo, he reported that there were no Indians left in the island.

While the Tainos of the islands were being enslaved and destroyed, the Europeans subjected the American Indians of the mainland to forced labour and enslavement. In Braudel's words, "America, lacking population, could only become something if man was shackled to the task: serfdom and slavery, those ancient forms of bondage, appeared once more . . . The everlasting problem in this boundless landscape was consequently a shortage of labour." (Braudel: 1982)

In the search for labour, Europe as conqueror ravaged the indigenous people. Diseases brought in from Europe and Africa, added their destructive force to that of the conqueror and coloniser. In many regions

> the indigenous population collapsed on this first impact of the white
> conquests, . . . Central Mexico, which once had some 25 million
> inhabitants, was reduced, it is estimated, to a residual population of

one million. The same abysmal demographic collapse occurred in the island of Hispaniola, in the Yucatan, in Central America and later in Colombia . . . The word genocide is not too strong to describe what happened to the American Indians or the black people of Africa, but it is worth noting that white men did not survive entirely unscathed and were sometimes lucky·to escape at all. (Braudel: 1982)

Eric Williams, in his seminal work *Capitalism and Slavery* showed how one form of enslavement followed another. White enslavement followed on Indian enslavement, followed by the system of English and French bond servants, who were virtually slaves, but for a limited period of five or seven years.

> Their lot barely differed from that of the Africans who were now beginning to arrive. In England and in France every trick was tried to meet the demand for bond servants. Misleading advertisements were coupled with violence. From Western England after Monmouth's rebellion, hundreds of rebels were transported to Barbados. In France, press gangs would swoop down on certain districts of Paris. Men, women and children were kidnapped into emigration in Bristol, or heavy criminal sentences were passed to increase the number of volunteers.

Wherever the European colonisers went they pressed ahead with great cruelty in their relentless search for labour. How was it that they were so insensitive to human suffering and killed other human beings so easily?

In Spain centuries of fighting against the Moors, with raids in which no quarter was given, and centuries of grinding poverty had produced a tough, ruthless people, as events in Hispaniola showed. But violence prevailed in many other parts of Europe as well as in Spain. In his work *Of Arms and Men*, O'Connell points out:

> ultimately it was the inhumanity which Europeans applied to themselves which caused the period from 1562 to 1648 in Western European history to be such a horrific one. Just why it is that predation and technology were turned inward with such wilful malevolence is hard to pin down . . .pressures created by fundamental economic, cultural and spiritual change played a significant role.

In his historical analysis of weapons in Western culture, O'Connell suggests a definite relationship between "the drive for transnational dominion, the promiscuous use of weaponry and very brutal and costly wars". He paints a nightmare picture of northern Europe, in which a massive increase of firepower and the pressure upon local food supplies "turned the armies of the day into rapacious, ill-disciplined swarms . . . For eighty years these armed bands were destined to stagger about the Nether-lands, France and Germany destroying all before them . . . a contemporary might well have wondered if northern Europe had not taken up killing largely for its own sake".

Using the military technology at their command, the *conquistadores*, Hernando Cortés, Francisco Pizarro and those who followed in their footsteps quickly overwhelmed the stone-age people who opposed them with spears tipped with shell, bone or, as in Mexico, with obsidian. Horses and hunting dogs, animals they had never known, terrified the Indians. But more than anything else, "it was the gun which paralysed them. There were reports of Aztec warriors fainting at the sound of cannon . . . firearms served to epitomise the conquistadores military advantage, imparting to it a magical quality which made resistance so much more manifestly hopeless." (O'Connell: 1989)

Within a few years after Cortés conquered Mexico and Pizarro subdued the Incas, American silver, gold and precious metals began to flow from Panama and Vera Cruz, by way of Havana, to Cadiz, to supplement the royal income by about one-quarter to one-third of the amount squeezed out of the heavily burdened 6 million inhabitants of Castile. Many of these were impoverished peasants.

> Even the development of agriculture was retarded by the privileges of the Mesta, the famous guild of sheep owners whose stock were permitted to graze widely over the Kingdom, with Spain's population growing in the first half of the sixteenth century . . . The flood of precious metals from the Indies, it was said, were to Spain as water on a roof – it poured on and then was drained away . . . While the coloniser ravaged the Americas, Spain's rulers used the loot they plundered to ravage large parts of Europe in 140 years of warfare, to the point where Spain herself, exhausted and drained of energy, fell into a decline and became but a shadow of her former self. (Kennedy: 1987)

The voyages of exploration and the conquest we have described mark the beginning of Western Europe's rise to world dominance, but there were few signs of this ascendancy in the Europe of the early 16th century. In the decade of the 1520s when Cortés was conquering Mexico, Europe was an embattled continent, internally a confusion of warring principali-ties and powers, with Ottoman galleons raiding Italian ports and with the armies of the Ottoman Turks thrusting north from Constantinople, which they had captured in 1453, towards Budapest and Vienna.

The European of that period thought of China under the Ming dynasty, which emerged in 1368 and held power for four centuries, as being the world's leading centre of civilisation. In that period, "The most striking feature of Chinese civilization must be its technological precocity." Printing with moveable type had appeared some two centuries earlier. "There were great libraries, paper money was in circulation, the flow of commerce had increased, markets had multiplied and a large iron industry had been established which produced about 125,000 tons a year, more than the British iron output in the early stages of the Industrial Revolution seven centuries later." Gunpowder and cannon were in use and had helped the Chinese to defeat their Mongol rulers in the fourteenth century.

Ming China was also active overseas. Under this dynasty the Chinese greatly extended overseas exploration, invented the magnetic compass, traded with the Indies and the Pacific islands, developed a prosperous coastal trade, maintained an army of one million men and in 1420 – a navy of 1,350 combat vessels,

> including 400 large floating fortresses and 250 ships for long-range cruising. In addition there were many privately managed vessels that traded with Korea, South-East Asia, Japan and even as far as East Africa. Among the most famous voyages in history are the seven long-distance voyages made by Admiral Cheng Ho between 1405 and 1433, that involved hundreds of ships and tens of thousands of men.
>
> It must be noted, however, that the Chinese apparently never plundered nor murdered – unlike the Portuguese, Dutch and other European invaders of the Indian Ocean. According to the Confucian code, warfare itself was a deplorable activity and armed forces were made necessary only by the fear of barbarian attacks or internal revolts. (Kennedy: 1987)

Gradually, under the Ming dynasty, burdened and paralysed by a conservative bureaucracy, China became a country turned in upon itself. But in the fourteenth and fifteenth centuries, through a combination of the Confucian code of ethics and significant technological advances, this non-white nation set an example of humane civilised behaviour that is in sharp contrast with the record of Europe as coloniser and also at home, a record that compelled an eyewitness, Hugo Grotius, the Dutch legal philosopher, to declare: "I saw prevailing throughout Europe a licence in making war of which even barbarous nations would have been ashamed."

CHAPTER 7

Spanish Jamaica

On his second voyage to the Americas Columbus charted a more southerly route, and ended up in the Eastern Caribbean, where he spent several weeks exploring the islands before reaching Hispaniola in September 1493. He found La Navidad, the fort he had built to accommodate 39 men left behind from the shipwrecked *Santa Maria*, in ruins, and all its inhabitants dead. It turned out that some of the men had been killed by the natives in retaliation for stealing and violating their women; others had died at the hands of their own comrades and the remainder had succumbed to various illnesses.

The overriding ambition of these early explorers was to acquire great personal fortunes at any cost, and having fulfilled their dream, to return home to Europe to live out their days in comfort. But the game of life is not always played out as men would wish. The majority of those who followed Columbus' dream over the next 200 years, found early graves in the Americas and comparatively few ever saw their native land again.

With La Navidad destroyed, Columbus was forced to locate another site and it took him several months to do this and to lay out the town. It was not until the following April, 1494, when the town of Isabella was beginning to take shape that Columbus resumed his charting of the surrounding seas. On the afternoon of 5 May, 1494, after 11 days at sea, his three vessels, the *Pinta*, the *San Juan* and the *Cardera* came in sight of towering blue-green mountains. It was the island of *Yamaye* (Jamaica), which he had first learned about in January 1493.

Taino eyes followed the strange vessels as they slowly made their way in a westerly direction along the island's north coast, and when towards evening they turned towards shore, at a place which Columbus later named Santa Gloria, native warriors leapt into action to protect their territory. But they were powerless to alter fate. The prophecy that one day strangers would come amongst them covered with garments and armed with thunders and lightnings of heaven was about to be fulfilled.

The tragic encounter of those Taino warriors at Santa Gloria, near St Ann's Bay, and Rio Bueno (misnamed Puerto Bueno), as they faced gunpowder and steel blades for the first time, is well-documented and need not detain us here. However, it should be remembered that next morning, these trusting and forgiving Tainos fed the ungracious foreigners who had so cruelly wounded and abused them the evening before. Later many took their own lives rather than endure abuse and enslavement at the hands of the European invaders.

So little is recorded about the Jamaican Tainos that we are grateful to Andres Bernaldez for the brief account of the people Columbus met in August 1494, when he skirted the coastline for a second time. Bernaldez was palace curate at Seville in Spain and travelled with Columbus on his second voyage of discovery. He probably heard the story of that visit from the admiral himself.

The Tainos whom Columbus met in their canoes at Cow Bay on the south coast, demonstrated by their behaviour that they belonged to an ordered society. Bernaldez describes the *cacique's* entourage which included his wife, daughter, sons, brothers, attendants, guards and musicians. He describes the head coverings of the men, some made of feathers, some fashioned like a helmet; the facial and body paintings of the group, ornaments of beads and beaten metal worn on their foreheads, ears, necks, waists, arms and feet as well as the elaborate ceremonial dress of some of the attendants. He makes mention of musical instruments being played at the time – two wooden trumpets "well worked with patterns of birds and other objects" fashioned from very dark and delicate wood, and also "a kind of musical instrument which they plucked". As was their practice, the visitors traded worthless curios and trinkets and even broken pieces of glass for Taino ornaments before sailing away.

Nine years passed before Columbus reappeared on Jamaican shores. On this occasion his two badly leaking vessels, with one anchor between them, barely limped to shore at the place he had named Santa Gloria. The natives of Maima and the surrounding villages found no joy at sight of them, and soon became disgruntled when they were called upon to provide regular supplies of food for an additional 140 individuals. Stone-age farming practices could not meet such demands indefinitely. Iron fish hooks traded by the newcomers may have helped somewhat, but the Tainos seemed unable to satisfy the enormous appetites of the Europeans.

While the shipwrecked Spaniards waited to be rescued, they roamed the countryside searching for gold and trading their worthless trinkets and curios for precious food and fish. One chief, called Ameryo, at the village

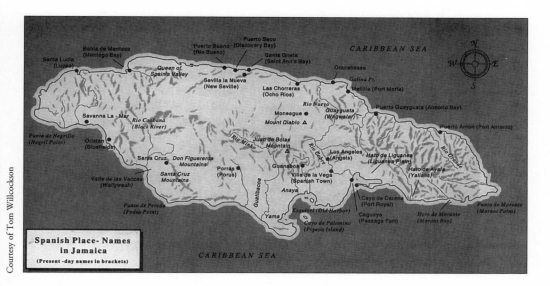

Courtesy of Tom Willcockson

of Ameryo near Morant Point, unaware of the value of his goods, gave one of Columbus' captains, Diego Méndez, a laboriously hand-carved canoe in exchange for a cheap brass basin and a used shirt and coat.

When the Tainos began to show signs of disenchantment Columbus had to find ways of keeping them under control. From books in his possession, he knew that an eclipse of the moon was about to take place. On the appointed day, he gathered some chiefs on the decks of his rotting vessels and then told them that the moon would rise "inflamed and angry" because of their intransigence. At the height of the eclipse he told the terrified natives that if they repented he would ask his god to call off the punishment, and they would see the sign begin to disappear slowly from the heavens. After that terrifying experience, the Tainos reluctantly agreed to continue supplying the Spaniards with food.

Weeks passed and there was no sign of rescue so he decided to send captain Diego Méndez and a small company of men to seek help in Hispaniola, some 170 kilometers to the north. The first attempt failed because of heavy seas. On the second try they succeeded but their shipmates in Jamaica had no way of knowing this. Eight months later there was still no word from them, and concern heightened among the stranded men. It had taken Méndez' crew three days, battling perilous seas and blazing sun, to make the crossing. They had run out of food and drink and one Taino had died from hunger and exhaustion. They eventually reached their destination but experienced great difficulty in trying to contact the governor, Ovando, who had no liking for Columbus. After many weeks they made contact with him but he refused to help.

Weeks turned into months and the men in Jamaica waited in vain for word from Hispaniola. In his despair, Columbus recorded his own worries in the following letter to the Spanish Crown (dated 1503):

> It is visible enough how all methods are made use of to cut the thread which is breaking, for I am in my old age, and loaded with unsupportable pains of the gout and am now languishing and expiring with that and other infirmities among savages, where I have neither medicines for the body, priests nor sacraments for the soul. My men mutinying, my brother, my son, and those that are faithful, sick, starving, and dying. The Indians have abandoned us; and the governor of Santo Domingo, Obando, has sent rather to see if I am dead, than to succor us, or carry me alive hence, for his boat neither delivered a letter nor spoke, or would receive any from us, so I conclude your highness' officers intend here my voyage and life shall end. (Williams: 1963)

Governor Ovando had refused to rescue the shipwrecked men or to offer them supplies and in the end Méndez had to hire a boat and arrange the rescue himself.

The men on the island of Jamaica had by this time lost all hope, and on 2 January, 1504, some of them, led by Captain Francisco Porras and his brother Diego, mutinied. Their attempt to sail for Hispaniola failed because of rough seas. They turned back and in their frustration they wandered across the island wreaking havoc on the native people, before setting up their rebel camp in the village of Maima. There they were eventually defeated by men loyal to Columbus.

During the empty months of waiting, the Spaniards, guided by the native people, are believed to have crossed the densely wooded mountains from the north to the southern plains. The village of Porus, situated where the central mountain range meets the Clarendon plains, is supposed to have been named after the Porras brothers, and the nearby Don Figueroa mountain range, takes its name from Columbus' son. It is almost certain that they were in search of minerals, for it is unlikely that such hardy men would have expended so much energy cutting through dense jungle in search of cassava, which was easily available from villages all along the north shore.

On 28 June, 1504, one year and four days after they had been marooned on Jamaica, Diego Méndez's rescue ship arrived, and on the following day Colombus and the surviving crew of just over 100 men left for Hispaniola. Méndez's dying wish was to have a ship inscribed upon his tombstone and underneath, the word "canoa".

Columbus owned the island of Jamaica on which he was marooned. It was one of the rewards he had received from the Spanish Crown in 1494, but Ferdinand and Isabella quickly regretted this as a rash decision, and not long after took back control of the island. In 1508, two years after Columbus' death, they returned it to his heir, the viceroy, Diego. Shortly after that the Crown once again exerted control. On this occasion it granted permission to two generals, Alonzo de Ojeda and Diego de Nicuesa, to use the island as a provision base for their armies in Central America. Fearing that he was once more about to lose his patrimony, Diego Columbus quickly appointed as governor, Juan de Esquivel, the organiser of the massacre of Anacaona and the other natives at Higuey, and dispatched him with 60 men to "subdue and colonise" the island. Their arrival on 9 December, 1509, sounded the death knell for the Tainos.

The settlers hunted the native people mercilessly, enslaved those they caught and worked them to death on farms and in unproductive mines. Chiefs who resisted were either killed or sold to the other islands to work in mines and to pan for gold in the rivers. Soon the leaderless people gave up the resistance.

Other settlers who came were equally cruel as Bartolomew de Las Casas, who was then living in Hispaniola, reported. According to him the settlers who proceeded to San Juan and to Jamaica had the same aim as that which had governed their presence in Hispaniola, "to add more notorieties and excessively great cruelties, killing, burning, scorching and throwing people to wild dogs and afterwards oppressing and harassing them in the mines and other areas of economic activities". (*History of the Indies*. Book III)

Las Casas' father was a former merchant of Seville who had travelled on the second voyage and took back a Taino slave for his son, Bartholomew. The elder Las Casas returned to Hispaniola and in 1502 Bartholomew joined him there. Together with one Pablo de la Renteria, Bartholomew de Las Casas acquired several large estates (allotments) which they operated under the *encomienda* system. This system allowed colonists to employ native families on their ranches provided they were converted to Roman Catholicism and were treated humanely. The natives were deemed to be the property of the Spanish Crown, and were not to be worked more than necessary; but this was at the discretion of the Spanish settlers. The settlers were not allowed to exchange, sell, gamble or give away the possessions of the natives except for food and alms, without the prior approval of the priests or the island administrator. Nor were the colonists allowed to take away their lands. When a native family died out, the land was to pass over to the Crown. An Indian Sacristan was to be appointed if possible, "to serve in the church and teach the children to read and write until the age of nine, especially the children of the caciques and other important people of the village, and to speak Spanish". It was probably on these instructions that the Dominican friar, Fr Duele opened a school at New Seville. He had travelled on the second voyage, and had come to Jamaica with the first colonists in 1509. The school was short-lived for the friar died in 1511, and nothing more was heard of it.

In that same year Las Casas' conscience was jolted when Dominican friars began attacking the immorality of slavery under the *encomienda* system. The friars questioned the right of one set of individuals to enslave others less fortunate. They further asked if the Indians were not human beings, whether or not they had rational souls, and if the colonists were not bound to love them as they loved themselves. They warned Spanish Christians holding Indian labour under this system that they were in danger of mortal sin.

In 1514, after three years of soul-searching, Las Casas entered the priesthood. His change of heart is supposed to have occurred while he was reading a passage in Ecclesiastes, "stained is the offering of him that sacrificeth from a thing wrongfully gotten . . .". This led him to examine ethical questions such as predetermined "natural capacity" and "higher capacity" which justified the right of those with greater intelligence to rule over those of a "lower natural capacity". Based on his experience in Hispaniola, Las Casas concluded that the native people were being "unjustly" enslaved according to the moral and legal system of Latin Christianity. On the other hand, he felt that the African was "servile by nature" and so was "justly" enslaved.

His conscience was not disturbed when, in 1517, he petitioned the Spanish king for African slaves to replace the dwindling Taino population in the region. The royal contract or *asiento* was prepared and it seemed to have passed through several hands before it was sold to Genoese merchants who were authorised to import 4,000 slaves from West Africa. There is no proof that the shipment ever arrived but it opened the way for the infamous Atlantic Slave Trade – a traffic which resulted in unspeakable atrocities against millions of people from Africa. Slavery was an institution condoned by the Catholic Church, provided the slaves were held by specifically defined "just titles" for some 1,400 years. The "fallible ordinary magisterium", or the instrument which sanctioned this approval, remained in force until 1965, when it was repealed by the Second Vatican Council.

Once it was obvious that Jamaica had no mineral wealth, about half of the original 60 settlers who came with Esquivel left within a year or two to seek their fortunes elsewhere. A number of those who remained set up ranches on the plains of St Elizabeth, Westmoreland, Clarendon, St Catherine, St Thomas-in-the-East and in the vicinity of New Seville. In 1534, when the capital was removed to the St Catherine Plains and renamed Villa de la Vega, it was estimated that only about 20 of the original settlers remained in the old capital.

Pedro de Mazuelo, the Island Treasurer, was the main architect behind the removal of the capital. He owned a sugar estate on the St Catherine Plains, and realised the economic potential of sugar cultivation on flat lands as well as the greater convenience of shipping from the southern ports. The new capital, Villa de la Vega, was conveniently sited near to Mazuelo's estate.

Most settlers had by now given up hope of finding minerals, and had turned to logging and farming – growing cassava, sweet potato, grapes, oranges, cocoa, and rearing cattle, horses, pigs and other domestic animals introduced from Europe. Almost everything flourished including a new industry using cotton which the Spaniards found growing on the island. They found the native people twisting the cotton fibres into ropes, which they then used in the making of hammocks. Governor Esquivel, who went into partnership with the Spanish king to develop commercial farms and ranches, expanded cotton cultivation and in a short while began exporting shirts and hammocks to Cuba and to towns on the Spanish Main. The project was greatly aided by a royal decree that required each individual to possess a hammock.

Jamaica was ideal farming country and quickly acquired the reputation as a supplier of domestic animals and ground provisions to the armies of conquest on the American mainland, as well as to other islands in the region. For instance, in 1514, Las Casas and his partner, Renteria, stocked their new estate in Cuba with animals and cassava from Jamaica, and in 1521, the governor, Francisco de Garay exported 50 cows, 50 yearling calves, 200 sheep, 1,000 pigs and 2,000 *cargas* of cassava to Panama. Annual shipments of cassava were also sent to Cartagena.

Jamaica could have sustained a viable trade in ground provisions, meat products, hardwood and the new-found spice, pimento, had adequate shipping facilities been available, but in those first years, a convoy of only two vessels made the annual trip from Spain to Central America, carrying European foodstuffs and manufactured goods. Rarely did they call at Jamaica although it was en route. On their return journey they usually carried minerals and other valuables plundered on the mainland and were not inclined to fill their holds with bulky and comparatively inexpensive agricultural products from Jamaica. Colonists were therefore forced to purchase necessities such as oil, vinegar, wine and manufactured goods from Cartagena, at exorbitant prices. Martin Vásquez writing to Columbus' heir in June 1556, noted the commercial isolation imposed by the establishment of the convoy system and by state centralisation, which hampered the growth of commercial relationships. Droughts and plagues of locusts also laid waste the farms and severely affected the island's economic prosperity during the early years of the sixteenth century. (Padron: 1952)

Soon after his arrival in December 1509, Esquivel began sending glowing reports of the numbers of natives that had been converted to Christianity, but other accounts of the atrocities taking place also reached Spain and he was charged with misdemeanours, negligence in his administrative duties and indifference to the conversion of the natives. An *audiencia* was ordered to enquire into these charges and Esquivel was recalled in disgrace in 1512. He had spent little more than two years on the island.

Controls had to be instituted at the highest level to stem the decline of the native population, then the main source of labour. In 1511 instructions were issued to the Jeronimite Reform Commission to visit the region, beginning with Hispaniola and Jamaica. They were to take a census of the native populations, note the treatment meted out to them, the numbers under the control of individual settlers and whether or not these settlers were in a position to take proper care of them. A royal decree which was designed to prevent the settlers overworking the natives, stated that neither in San Juan nor in Jamaica should Indians be forced to carry heavy weights. It set out the conditions under which they should be employed in the mines and in households. For instance, each household was limited to not more than six servants, and these were not to be used in the mines. The natives were to receive two-thirds of gold smelted and their share was to be used to pay for the lands, cattle and other expenses incurred in establishing settlements for them. "From what is left the administration was to buy them clothes, shirts, 12 hens and one rooster for each household" and the transactions should be recorded. However, as there was no gold, it is doubtful if the instructions were ever implemented.

Farms were to be bought for the settlers who were appointed to administer the native settlements. They were to be paid a miner's salary in addition to being allowed to mine for themselves. Anyone failing to comply with these instructions would be fined. For a second offence the fine would be doubled. For the third offence it would be tripled and the offender would lose the natives under his control. This may have had a sobering effect for a time, but nothing could halt the decline of the population who were dying off at a rapid rate from European diseases and ill-treatment.

Other regulations were also put in place. The *repartimiento*, introduced by Esquivel, enabled a colonist to apply for, and receive special permission to use the indigenous people for limited periods of time, in such endeavours as planting, reaping, logging and rounding up cattle. Francisco de Garay who became governor in 1514, introduced another set of regulations, the *requerimiento* (the requirement). Under this system colonists were to convert the natives to Christianity. The hope was that they would be "always tractable, would be properly maintained and would live and greatly multiply". Taino slaves were expected to acknowledge the supremacy of the Pope and the Spanish sovereign, but as the majority of them did not understand the language of their captors and had no idea of the significance of these personages, they were deemed to be disobedient and consequently were punished.

Under Spanish supervision, Taino slaves built Jamaica's first Spanish settlement, New Seville. They cleared the primeval forests for farming, hauled timber and probably built the first log cabins occupied by the first colonists, as well as the 25 more substantial houses said to have existed along a one-mile stretch of road in the town. They quarried limestone blocks from a hill one mile away, hauled them to the building sites and carried out most of the heavy construction work. The size of some of the cut stones used in the building of the governor's palace, which was the most imposing stone structure in the town, explains the necessity for the controls.

The Spaniards soon learned to appreciate the excellence of Taino crafts-manship. A Taino *cacique*, baptised and renamed Juan de Medina, and members of his family, were said to have been skilled masons and crafts-men. They are known to have worked on the governor's palace and may also have worked on the elaborate stone church begun in 1525 through the efforts of Peter Martyr, first Spanish abbot of Jamaica. Martyr died in

Courtesy of Jack Tyndale-Biscoe

Aerial photograph of the site of the town of New Seville, left of the town of St Ann's Bay

Sixteenth-century carving from New Seville

1526 before he could take up his appointment but construction continued although at a greatly reduced pace. In 1533 the Spanish king called for an accounting on the church but the following year the capital was transferred, and the church was never finished.

It is believed that native craftsmen carved some of the limestone lintels found on the New Seville site, as they bear distinctive Taino features. These and other carvings found in the old capital are credited as being among the finest of contemporary workmanship in the Americas and on the Iberian Peninsula.

Later in the sixteenth century, an attempt was made to bring the surviving natives together on a reservation, ostensibly to protect them from extinction. However, neither the colonists nor the Tainos supported the move. The colonists feared that they might lose the slaves already in their possession, and only three Tainos seemed to have agreed to the proposal. The project was dropped because trackers claimed that they could not capture the Tainos hiding in the forests.

A physical survey of the island reveals extensive flat, fertile plains to the south of the main mountain ranges which run from east to west, almost all the way across the island. These grassy plains, watered by many rivers, made better farm lands than the steep, wooded hills on the north and the harbours on the south coast were easier to navigate. Those mountain ranges, difficult to traverse except by experienced woodsmen, have through the centuries, provided cover for all who struggled to escape enslavement and imprisonment. The very fertile Guanaboa Vale, securely hidden among the steep almost inaccessible Clarendon hills, have sheltered in turn, Tainos escaping enslavement, freed Spanish slaves and also maroon resistance fighters. In the eighteenth century it protected the maroon leader, Juan de Bolas (Lubolo) and his band of fighters, until they succumbed to the inducements of the English. From these mountains, escaped slaves made nightly raids on the plains below, stealing cattle from the Spanish plantations, and with the coming of the English, weapons and supplies from the sugar plantations.

The cockpit country of Trelawny and St Elizabeth is very close to the savannas of St Elizabeth, Westmoreland and Trelawny. Among these precipitous hills, during the eighteenth and nineteenth centuries, the Trelawny Maroons kept the English at bay for a long time, until their leaders were tricked into submission, and deported. The northern ranges of the Blue Mountains hid the first Taino freedom fighters in their bid to escape enslavement. At Seaman's Valley, Windsor, Moore Town and Comfort Castle on the Portland side of the great Blue Mountain chain, Taino hideouts predate maroon strongholds.

When the Spanish settlers found their labour force depleted they turned to Africa for replacements. Until then the only Africans on the island, were personal household servants of a few settlers. Esquivel had two or three as well as two children, two years of age whom he received as gifts. These servants did not come directly from Africa but from European countries where African slavery was already institutionalised. Then slavery did not carry the stigma which came to be attached to it in the West Indies and in Jamaica, in particular, after the end of the seventeenth century.

Under the Spaniards, slaves who had "converted" to Christianity, could receive sacraments of the Church and were permitted the basic rights of marriage. They could obtain their freedom so long as the proper conditions were met: this meant that they could be freed by their owners or by the State or they could purchase their freedom. The State occasionally rewarded a slave for valour in war by granting him his freedom – a life "full of tranquility". At the time of the transfer of the capital to Villa de la Vega, former slaves were given lands on the edge of town to build their houses and to plant their gardens.

There is no certainty that the first field slaves requested by Las Casas in 1517, or another consignment approved in 1523, ever arrived. On another occasion the Portuguese king was approached to supply 5,000 slaves to the region, of which 300 were earmarked for Jamaica. Women were supposed to be included in the shipment as they were expected to produce children and increase the slave population.

Cheap cane sugar was by then becoming popular in Europe, and Spanish farmers in the Americas were set to take advantage of these new developments, except they lacked the know-how to turn sugar cane juice into sugar crystals. Pedro de Mazuelo was possibly the first Spanish colonist in Jamaica to acquire the necessary expertise. In 1534 he imported 30 Africans from the Canary Islands who may have been knowledgeable in sugar manufacture. He also brought a number of Portuguese indentured servants to his plantation on the southern plains who may also have had similar expertise. Although these Portuguese were not accepted socially by the Spaniards, in time they came to be influential commercial traders and also continued their trading activities under the English.

From time-to-time rumours of gold being found on the island surfaced, but mostly these were without foundation. Gold was the prime motivator for Spanish expansion in the Americas, and as Jamaica lacked this commodity, it was never able to attract large numbers of settlers. The situation was not helped by the local priests who extorted property from dying unmarried colonists, using the fear of eternal damnation to get them to sign over their property to the Church. A royal *audiencia* eventually stopped the practice and made it easier for relatives of deceased persons to take up residence in the island.

Throughout the period of Spanish occupation the island's white population fluctuated between a few hundred and a few thousand souls. At the end of the sixteenth century one report noted 120 "very respectable" Spanish inhabitants on the island. This was probably a fair assessment as at one time the Spanish Crown was obliged to ship 400 destitute individuals from Puerto Rico to boost the local population. The Spanish colonists were in such straitened financial circumstances that they could not accommodate all the newcomers, and Governor Melgajero had to keep 50 of them in his house for a time. The first extant census, undertaken by Abbot Bernardo de Balbuena, in 1611, shows 523 Spaniards, 558 slaves, 107 free blacks, 74 Taino herdsmen, and 75 newcomers. The figures are supported by the fact that in 1635 the military could only muster three companies of 200 men each with the possibility of another 1,000 available in an emergency. In 1643, twelve years before the English invasion, there were four badly under-equipped companies of 500 men each along with a cavalry of mulattoes, free negroes and servants. All they had among them were eight pieces of artillery of which only one was functional. The situation was not much better at the time of the English conquest when the Spanish commander could only find about 120 men to defend Port Caguaya. Settlers living near to Villa de la Vega had been so harassed by French, Dutch and English freebooters over the years, that at first sign of approaching ships they fled to the shelter of the surrounding hills, taking their few possessions with them.

Jamaica's slave population also remained small, probably not more than 1,000 at any one time, because slaves were not only expensive but difficult to acquire. Sometimes years passed before a slaver from Paria or Guinea or Angola called to replenish their supplies and to dispose of their contraband cargo. Money was usually in short supply and the colonists could not always take advantage of the opportunities when they arose. Once a shipment of 150 Africans left behind by a French vessel had to be disposed of by credit. Although payment was accepted in provisions, eleven years later the debt had not been cleared. The problem was compounded by the Spanish Crown and the Columbus heirs haggling over who should receive payment for the slaves. The colonists blamed their financial situation on poor administration, and the loss of their produce to frequent enemy raids.

If Balbuena's 1611 census is to be accepted there were probably not more than about two or three slaves to a farm or ranch. The holdings were not extensive and did not require large numbers of field-hands to maintain them. Farm animals needed little care as they were let loose and left to forage on the open range. Once the fields were prepared and planted it was a matter of weeding occasionally and waiting for the crops to come to maturity. This could take several months as in the case of cassava and plantains, or as long as seven years in the case of cocoa. Master and slave worked at close quarters with each other, and eventually a trust developed between them to the extent that on occasion slaves were allowed to carry arms in defence of the island. Jacinto Sedeño, governor of the island from 1639 to 1640 mentions the use of black divisions and two garrisons comprised of "mulattoes on horseback and free blacks with scimitars".

Spanish trade monopoly continued to restrict Jamaica's economic progress. The colonists could only transport their goods in Spanish ships and as they had no way of knowing when a vessel was likely to call, or whether it would take on goods prepared for shipment, spoilage was heavy. It is said that skins rotted on the docks and logs were attacked by termites.

Hardly any reports appear of runaway slaves in Spanish occupied Jamaica. The maroon phenomenon came about after the capture of the island by the English, as many of the former Spanish slaves elected to hold on to their newly acquired freedom. The fact that in 1655, at the time of the English invasion, some 300 of them remained with Don Cristóbal Arnaldo de Isasi to defend the island against the invaders indicates that their treatment could not have been bad. Former Spanish slaves who had by then established themselves in the mountainous interior, helped to feed the defenders for a time. It was only in the dying years of the war that many of them defected to the enemy and precipitated the final conquest of the island by the English.

With the coming of the English, slavery took on a more evil connotation. Large gangs of African field labourers, herded, degraded, dehumanised, under the lash of their English oppressors, redefined the meaning of slavery. The slave was now chattel, an item that could be disposed of at the whim of his owner.

CHAPTER 8

Two Jamaicas emerge

Black Jamaica began to take shape during the earliest years of Spanish rule. The establishment of the African blood-line began with the small group of Africans who accompanied their masters to Jamaica in 1509, when Juan de Esquivel, the island's first governor, and a party of Spanish colonists moved from Hispaniola to New Seville, on the outskirts of St Ann's Bay, and set about building the island's first capital.

English-speaking white Jamaica began to take shape after the English took Jamaica from the Spaniards in 1655. By that time there were about 1,500 persons of African descent in the island, some of whom were free. At that time the population was of the order of a medium-sized village of about 6,000 people, one-quarter of whom were black. The island was poverty-stricken. The economy was based on hides and lard and the black labour force was small, but even so there are reports of fugitive slaves setting up *palenques* on their own. Edward Long reports in his history: "There had been a Spanish village at Paretty . . . From one or two Negroes they learned that the Blacks had entirely detached themselves from the Spaniards and were resolved to maintain their footing in the island so long as cattle remained for them to kill." (Long: 1774)

On the morning of 10 May 1655, two fishermen searching for turtles off Port Morant saw a large fleet of 38 ships moving toward them from the east. This was no pirate's raid. So large a fleet meant war. The fishermen made for land as quickly as they could and gave the news. Messengers on horseback hurried west along the coast, giving the alarm as they went, until at last they reached the capital city of Villa de la Vega. From vantage points on the Hellshire Hills African eyes kept watch while the fleet dropped anchor off Passage Fort and began to disembark a force of soldiers. There were 8,000-9,000 men aboard, more than the total population of Jamaica.

The Africans and Spaniards who watched the slow landing of men and of cannon knew that this meant conquest and settlement. What could an ailing old governor with five or six cannons and a few hundred, ill-equipped men do against so large a force?

But the fleet had no business being off Passage Fort. It should have been in Santo Domingo, with its commanders, Admiral William Penn and General Robert Venables, in the governor's residence and the army in charge of Hispaniola. Those were the instructions the commanders had been given.

English policy in the 1650s aimed at the creation of a colonial trading system based on mercantilist theory, which was the economic face of imperialism. It was based on the theory of "beggar my neighbour", one nation's loss being another nation's gain. An inflow of gold and silver meant victory, and an unfavourable balance of trade signified defeat. The doctrine decreed with Mosaic zeal and authority that each metropolitan power and its colonies should be firmly cemented into an economic unit, with the colony producing raw materials and the mother-country processing and marketing the product and achieving a favourable balance of trade by tariffs, bounties, monopolies (such as the West Indian sugar monopoly of the eighteenth century) and the use of force.

The English Navigation Ordinance or Act of 1651, for example, prohibited the import of colonial products into England except in English ships and confined the import of European goods into English colonies to English ships or ships of the country where the goods originated. Protestant Holland, the greatest trading nation of that period, protested. Their negotiators were reminded that they (the Dutch) had always forbidden English traders from doing business with the United Provinces. The Navigation Act stated a policy "from which we think it not fit to recede", said the English negotiators.

For 200 years mercantilism set Europeans to the task of killing each other with cold-hearted zest. The memorial tablets on the walls of St Peter's Church in Port Royal and the battlements and cemeteries at English Harbour in Antigua and Brimstone Hill in St Kitts reveal the cost of this theory of empire.

The English-Dutch War of 1652, and Oliver Cromwell's Great Western Design, which was planned in 1653-54, were products of these imperial policies. The Western Design revived the Elizabethan strategy of using sea-power to break the flow of Mexican and Peruvian silver that kept the Spanish armies in the field and to strengthen English trade by cutting the links that held together Spain's overstretched empire.

Francis Drake had been the incarnation of Queen Elizabeth the First's policy and its most brilliant exponent. He was "a driven man dedicated practically from adolescence to wreaking personal havoc on Philip's empire. 'El Draque' became virtually the devil incarnate to Spaniards who plied the seas, intercepting plate ship after plate ship and even further disrupting the staggering Iberian economy. By 1580 not a single bar of Peruvian or Mexican silver safely crossed the Atlantic". (O'Connell: 1989) With plunder of this size Queen Elizabeth could wage war on the cheap.

Drake's slashing raids had been based on local knowledge. His men were efficient and well-disciplined. Cromwell's project was based on inaccurate and prejudiced intelligence. Neither Admiral Penn nor General Venables was of the stature of Drake, as the attack on Hispaniola showed.

The fleet set sail from England at the end of 1654. On board were 2,500 men, more than half of whom were conscripts from the slums of London. It reached Barbados in January 1655 and took on 3,000-4,000 persons of similar status. At St Kitts, Nevis and Montserrat it enlisted another 1,200 men. These West Indian conscripts were mostly indentured labourers and time-expired individuals, who were landless, or debtors trying to escape from their creditors.

The following contemporary account gives a fair description of the recruits: "Certainly these Islanders must be the very scum of scums, mere dregs of corruption, and such upon whose endeavors it was impossible to expect a blessing." (Bridenbaugh: 1972)

On 14 April the fleet arrived off the coast about 30 miles from Santo Domingo, the capital of Hispaniola. The ships were too small to carry adequate supplies of food and water for long periods and by the time the vessels reached the Caribbean the 2,500 enlisted men from Europe had consumed most of the provisions. Supplies of corn and cassava for the army of 7,000 men who were on their way to Santo Domingo were difficult to obtain. The men suffered from thirst, dysentery, fever and hunger. They bore no resemblance to a fighting force.

The landing in Hispaniola was a disastrous failure. "All that saves it from our utter contempt is the nearly inspired element of farce that informed every moment of it . . . In Hispaniola, attacked by a detachment of Spanish Lancers, General Venables hides behind a tree, emerging after the fight to accuse his troops of cowardice." (Hearne: 1965)

Jamaica was the consolation prize. Afraid to face Cromwell's displeasure, the commanders turned their attention to that poorly defended island.

It was well-known that the governor, Don Juan Ramírez de Arellano, was old and ill. The islanders were weary of defending themselves against intruders. The Maestro de Campo, Don Francisco de Proenza, had only five iron cannons and 180 poorly armed men to defend the port and the town of Villa de la Vega and the surrounding countryside. The capital fell within a day or two. The only spoils the English found were cured cow-hides which the slaves used to cover the earthen floors of their houses. These were later sold in New England.

According to the terms of capitulation which Governor Ramírez de Arellano signed, the Spaniards were to leave the island by 23 May. Although greatly outnumbered they had no intention of complying. Some moved their families and their belongings west to Pereda (Pedro Plains), while others made their way up the Rio Minho Valley to a stronghold at Los Virmejales (Veramahollis) where their African allies kept them supplied with meat and ground provisions. Realising that they had been tricked, the English intensified their attack and some of the Spaniards capitulated. On 1 July 1655 seventy of them, including women and children, carrying only their personal belongings, sailed from Caguaya for Campeche on the *Spanish Main*. In the weeks following, others who had taken refuge at Los Virmejales also made their way to the north coast and thence to Cuba.

Spanish resistance continued, however. For five years, with assistance from some African bands, the Spanish leader Arnaldo Isasi held out. A brave man, he was virtually abandoned by Spain and by his nearest neighbours, Cuba and Mexico. The aid that was sent was too little and too late. He was forced to capitulate in 1660. Our major concern is not with departing Isasi and his bedraggled companions but with the three bands of maroons that remained in Jamaica and with the early years of English settlement. The African guerrillas were divided into three bands. One was stationed in the hills above Guanaboa Vale with Juan de Bolas (Lubolo) as their leader. A second band was stationed in the Clarendon hills at Los Virmejales under Juan de Sierras and the third band was probably stationed near Porus. They kept the Spanish defenders supplied with food from extensive provision grounds hidden in deep inaccessible valleys in the St Catherine and Clarendon hills and they frequently descended to the plains in search of meat and weapons.

Not all the Africans chose to assist Isasi. Some acted on their own. It is very likely that those who allied themselves with Isasi served under their own leaders.

The English soon learned to respect the Africans, whether they were acting on their own or not. Two English commanders, Admiral Goodson and Major General Robert Sedgwick, reported on 24 January 1656: "The Negroes . . . live by themselves in several parties, and near our quarters, and do very often, as our men go into the woods to seek provisions, destroy and kill them with their lances. We now and then find one or two of our men killed, stripped and naked, and these rogues begin to be bold, our English rarely, or seldom killing any of them."

In March Sedgwick reported: "The Spaniard is not considerable, but of the Blacks there are many, who are like to prove as thorns and pricks in our side." Some months later he wrote that "in two days more than forty of our soldiers were cut off by the Negroes".

After the English defeated the reinforcements who came from Cuba and Mexico, it became clear that Isasi and his men were heading for defeat. Juan de Bolas went over to the English with about 150 followers who were based in the Clarendon mountains. This signalled the end. Some months later, after being defeated in a surprise attack led by Juan de Bolas, Isasi surrendered.

Two months after the surrender, Isasi and his men left for Cuba in two boats they had built. The party consisted of 68 Spaniards and eight Africans. There are two versions of why 36 persons were left in Jamaica. One version claims that after the boats were completed it was found that there was not sufficient room for all. The other version states that 36 Jewish traders chose to continue as residents in Jamaica under English rule.

In 1661 Edward D'Oyley, who had been military governor of Jamaica and had transformed the survivors of the mob that landed in 1655 into a fighting force, and who was serving for some months as civil governor, was instructed "to give such encouragement as securely you may wish to such negroes and others as shall submit to live peaceably under his majesty's obedience and in due submission to the government of the island". Governor, Sir Charles Lyttleton, who had been Lord Windsor's deputy, who assumed duties in 1663, was instructed to carry out the following orders: "that Juan Luyola and the rest of the negroes of his Palenque, on account of their submission and services to the English, shall have grants of land and enjoy all the liberties and privileges of Englishmen . . . that Luyola be colonel of the black regiment of militia, and he and others appointed magistrates over the negroes to decide all cases except those of life and death". A grant of 30 acres was made to each of the men. The majority of the free blacks did not approve of the alliance with the English and some of his companions cut Juan de Bolas to pieces. The *palenque* south of Cave Valley, on the Virmejales, rejected offers of permanent peace. In 1670 rewards were offered for the heads of Juan de Sierras and his men. As Hart points out, this may have been linked with the deaths of a number of white men in Clarendon.

The Africans of Spanish Jamaica had established the resistance pattern of fugitive slaves based on *palenques*, their strongholds of freedom. The English conquest of Jamaica did not mean the conquest of these free Africans nor the destruction of their *palenques*. Long's statement makes it clear that the last of the Spaniards to withdraw from Jamaica left about 30 of their Negro slaves behind, who secreted themselves in the mountains and afterwards entered into alliance with the other "unsubdued banditti". It is a tribute to the Africans that Long, the planter-historian, saw them as unsubdued banditti. To us these unsubdued banditti were following the tradition set by maroons in Brazil, Mexico and Colombia. Their *palenques*

FORT RUPERT

Bridewell Prison?

Palisadoes

School

Society of the
Artillery of
Jamaica

Court House?

St. Paul's Church

White's Line

Marshallsea Prison?

FORT CARLISLE

King's House

Herb & Fruit Market (High St.)

Wherry Bridge

Fish Market

Cope's alley

Water Lane

Waterman's Wharf

Bird's alley

Smith's alley

State Storehouses

Sea Lane and
Common landing place

King's Wharf and
Storehouses

Catt and

N

E 60400

N 37800

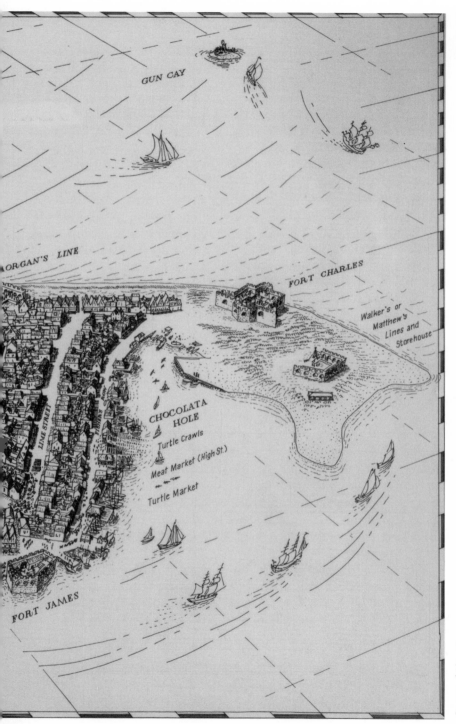

GUN CAY

MORGAN'S LINE

FORT CHARLES

Walker's or
Matthew's
Lines and
Storehouse

CHOCOLATA
HOLE

Turtle Crawls

LINE STREET

Meat Market (High St.)

Turtle Market

FORT JAMES

Courtesy of Oliver Cox

Two Jamaicas emerge   83

symbolise the implanting by Africans of the concepts of freedom and racial equality in plantation America.

With the establishment of civil government in 1663, English Jamaica set itself to the tasks of attracting settlers and strengthening its defences. A Spanish diplomat put into vivid words the threat that English Jamaica posed to Spain: it was "a dagger pointed at Spain's soft underbelly". Cromwell recognised that a very important strategic position had been gained. He went to war with Spain rather than give it up. At first, settlement was slow. Officers and men of the conquering army received grants of land to plant and settle, chiefly in the fertile well-watered Rio Minho Valley, but many died and few succeeded. Admiral Blake, by destroying the Spanish navy off the Canary Islands in 1657, had greatly weakened Spain's ability to mount a counter-attack, but even so the English knew that there was no time to be lost in making Jamaica secure against attack.

Edward D'Oyley, soldier that he was, hit on the quickest solution. He tried to attach the buccaneer stronghold of Tortuga to his government, but the French element there was too strong. The English buccaneers, outnumbered in Tortuga, began to make their headquarters in Port Royal. To do this on any scale, and openly, needed a governor who at the very least would close an eye to what was happening. At first King Charles II sought to secure trade with Spain by agreement and appointed Thomas Modyford, a seasoned Barbadian sugar planter, to be governor of Jamaica, in the hope that he would be able to persuade Spain to agree to trade. The Spaniards, however, doubted whether Modyford could suppress the buccaneers. In 1665 the English government, facing the possibility of war with Holland and possibly France, desperately needed fighting men in the Caribbean. The only striking force available consisted of the buccaneers. Modyford was authorised to grant commissions of "reprisal" to buccaneer captains, it being understood that the plunder they secured would be their pay for services rendered. Once again the old battle-cry was sounded, "No peace beyond the Line". The buccaneers would be a striking force at sea and would cost embattled England, fully engaged with the Dutch and French, no money.

The flaw in the plan was that the buccaneers would only fight where there was chance of booty, and rich booty at that. They proved unreliable against the Dutch and French forces in the eastern Caribbean, where Antigua and Montserrat fell to the French, but they were brilliantly, brutally successful against the Spanish, with whom England was normally at peace.

The buccaneers made their first big raid under a Dutchman, Edward Mansfield or Mansvelt. They attacked and sacked Grenada in Central America and returned with a great store of booty. They then raided Cuba.

Following on this, Henry Morgan became their leader. In 1668 he sacked the town of Puerto Bello. He returned to Port Royal with 250,000 pieces-of-eight, goods and munitions.

There followed a catalogue of successes, including the capture of three Spanish treasure ships off Maracaibo, and Morgan's crowning exploit, a march across the Isthmus of Panama and the sacking of the city. Ten bloodthirsty years of rapine were brought to an end in 1670, when, by the Treaty of Madrid, England and Spain agreed to abstain from pillage and revoke all letters of reprisal. By this treaty Spain for the first time agreed: "the most serene King of Great Britain – shall have and shall hold – all the lands and regions – situated in the West Indies or in any part of America which the said King of Great Britain and his subjects happen to have and hold at the moment." (Article 7 of the Treaty of Madrid) (Padron)

It took time to put a check to piracy and buccaneering, but by 1685 public opinion, even in Jamaica, had swung against both. The West Indian interest in England and merchants in the West Indies were determined to force a trade. As if to mark the end of an age, Henry Morgan, and General George Monk, first Duke of Albemarle, the last governor who countenanced the old ruffian, died in 1688. Four years later old Port Royal, in its time the wickedest city in the world, the Babylon of the West, was plunged beneath the waves by the great earthquake of 1692. "A punishment for their sins," the pious said.

With Morgan and the buccaneers as shield and sword, Jamaica had come safely through the early years of settlement, but at first few settlers came despite the government's generous offers of land. Some of the early settlers were officers who had served with the army of occupation. These included Colonels Samuel Barry, Philip Ward and Henry Archbould, Major Richard Hope and Major Thomas Ballard. The three names Hope, Barry and Ballard are preserved as Jamaican place-names.

Many of the earliest settlers found early graves, not fortunes. The first 1,600 to take up the offer of land came from Nevis in 1656, with Governor Luke Stokes as their leader. Within a year they were followed by some 250 others, mostly women, from Bermuda. They were given lands at St Thomas-in-the-East, some of which had been Spanish farms, but within a few months of their arrival two-thirds of the Nevis settlers had been wiped out by yellow fever and dysentery.

On 25 March 1656, a proclamation read in New England offered settlers "sufficient proportion of land to them and their slaves for ever, near some good harbour in the said land; Protection (by God's blessing) from all enemies; a share of all the Horses, cattle and other beaves, wild and tame upon the place freely, together with other privileges and Immunities". Persons born in the island of English parentage were deemed "to be free denizens of England" and would henceforth enjoy all the benefits, privileges and advantages of Englishmen born in England.

Settlers also came from Suriname. They were English exiles to Barbados who had migrated there. When the war broke out between the English and the Dutch they moved to Jamaica. They settled at Suriname Quarters (Ackendown) then in the parish of St Elizabeth, but now a part of the parish of Westmoreland. They brought with them the knowledge of sugar manufacture, and some became successful sugar producers.

The critical questions were the status of the settler, the most profitable crop and the availability of labour. The status of settlers was defined in a proclamation issued by Lord Windsor, who succeeded D'Oyley as governor in December 1661. This conferred privileges on free-born subjects of England born out of wedlock in Jamaica. The proclamation was publicised in Barbados even before Lord Windsor reached Jamaica, to allow persons from the other islands to benefit from the new law and from the generous land grants available there. African-Jamaican children born out of wedlock to Englishmen were excluded and the bastardy law ensured that their right to inheritance was severely limited. It remained in force until the twentieth century when it was removed from the statute books. Only then could African-Jamaican children born out of wedlock enjoy the same rights as children born to married couples in Jamaica.

Lord Windsor was also authorised "to grant 30 acres for every servant transported thither and at the end of indenture of four years, 30 acres for each servant". This assured every bond servant of property at the end of his period of indenture. Windsor was encouraged to establish trade with foreigners and was also authorised to ratify former land grants to planters. He used his authority to enrich himself and his associates, amongst them Thomas Lynch, Richard Hope, Henry Archbould and William Beeston. They received huge land grants, totalling somewhere about one-half the size of the parish of St Andrew, including large parts of the Liguanea Plains and extending north to Hope Bay.

The island was administered by the governor and a council of 12 men; a House of Assembly with 30 or more elected representatives; and a local council of justices and vestry in each parish. All representatives were selected from among local white freeholders and paid officials.

The council of 12 was nominated by the Colonial Office in England on the recommendation of the governor. It was both an advisory and an executive body, dealing with matters such as the jurisdiction of civil courts, law and order and the framing of acts and ordinances in keeping with English law. In time it became the Upper House of the Legislature.

The first elected Assembly met on 20 January, 1664 at St Jago de la Vega, the representatives having been "fairly chosen in the several quarters of the island". Its size was flexible and could change according to the council's determination. In the 1670s it had 30 members and in the mid-nineteenth century there were as many as 47. Seats were allocated to a parish depending on its prosperity and on the influence of certain residents. Elections were sometimes rigged to enable individuals to obtain seats.

Jamaica had representative government on a tightly limited franchise. It had the power to pass laws but these had to be approved by the Crown within two years of the date of enactment. At times the Assembly pushed its powers to the limit and there were occasions when the English government wished to restrict its authority. Finally, in 1677, on the advice of the Lords of Trade and Plantations, the Crown decided to cancel the Assembly's power to pass laws. Henceforward laws were to be passed in England and then sent to Jamaica for ratification. As in Ireland, they could be debated but not changed. The English colonists strongly objected to being degraded to the level of Irishmen.

The Earl of Carlisle brought the first of these laws to the island in 1678. The Assembly rejected them all, claiming their rights as Englishmen. The members declared: "Nothing invites people more to settle and remove their families and stock into this remote part of the world, than the assurance they have had of being governed in such manner as that none of their rights would be lost so long as they were within the dominions of the kingdom of England." (Journals of the Assembly of Jamaica) Carlisle tried repeatedly to reach an agreement with the Assembly but failed. The members insisted on keeping the rights to which as Englishmen they were entitled. After months of arguing, the leaders of the resistance, Chief Justice Samuel Long and Colonel William Beeston, were arrested on charges of treason and sent to England for trial. Long's persuasive argument before the King in council, defending the rights and privileges of members of the Assembly as Englishmen, led the council to cancel the instructions. The Jamaica Assembly continued to frame its own laws until it surrendered that power to the Crown in 1865.

The authority delegated to the Assembly in the seventeenth century gave it the power of life and death over the people of African origin. In time, it gave rise to the passing of some of the most stringent slave laws in human history. By law, the African slave was defined as a chattel, a piece of property, with few basic rights.

The term representative government applied only to male white Jamaicans with clearly defined property qualifications. All others were excluded: women, Jews, free brown and black Jamaicans and all the slaves. As far as the Africans were concerned, white representative government meant tyranny.

CHAPTER 9

Profits versus human rights

The decade of the 1680s is a convenient vantage point from which to observe unregulated capitalism at work. We watch the triumph of a small group of large landholders, who began the transformation of Jamaica into a sugar-and-slave plantation manned by enslaved Africans.

In the early years of English settlement cocoa was the favoured crop, not sugar cane. Some colonists had established cocoa walks because they required only a small labour force and modest holdings of land which yielded a profit. In 1672, Richard Blome, in his *Description of the Island of Jamaica*, based on the notes of Governor Sir Thomas Lynch, spoke of cocoa as:

> The principal and most beneficial commodity of the isle by reason of the aptness of the ground to produce and bear it above other places, here being at present above 60 cocoa-walks besides abundance of young walks which are growing up and still more aplanting, so that in time it will become the only noted place for the commodity in the world, which is so much made use of by us and other Nations but in far greater measure by the Spaniards who alone are enough to take the product of the isle, so that there is no fear that it will become a drug and lye upon the hands of the Planter.

There were other products such as indigo and tobacco, as well as hides in great quantity, dye woods, salt, tortoise shell from the "great store of Tortoises" that were taken along the coast, ginger, "better in this isle than in many of the Caribee Islands", and pimento "very Aromatical and of a curious gusto, having the mixed taste of diverse spices", growing in great quantity wild in the mountains. The Spaniards, noted Blome, esteemed it highly and exported it as a choice crop.

In the period from 1675 the settlers turned from cocoa and other crops that could be handled with modest resources to sugar, which demanded capital and a large labour force.

The changeover from smallholdings manned by white indentured servants and a relatively small number of African slaves to large sugar estates manned by gangs of enslaved African labour was revolutionary. It led to the development of the New World plantation, "a combination of African labour, European technology and management, Asiatic and American plants, European animal husbandry and American soil and climate". (Sheridan: 1970) Success had followed the establishment by the Portuguese of the first plantations in Madeira, then in the islands of Principe and São Tome in 1470 and 1472, and finally in North-East Brazil.

But Portugal had gained too many victories. Her enemies attacked her, among them the Dutch, the most relentless of all. With great enthusiasm they set about stripping the Portuguese of their conquests in the Far East, off the western coast of Africa and in Brazil. The four corners of the world shook with the noise of their cannon and their notes of credit. A small country, Holland was described by an observer in 1738 as a land floating in water, a field that is flooded for three parts of the year.

> But, proceeding with great skill, the Dutch built up a fleet the equivalent of all other European fleets put together, and pursuing a policy of toleration, welcomed international financiers and banking houses, the Jews foremost among them. They dominated the trade of Europe and built ships cheaper than anyone else at the famous shipyards at Saardam near Amsterdam, which, provided they were given two months notice, could turn out a warship ready for rigging every week for the rest of the year. Add to this the fact that in Holland, whatever the branch of activity, credit was abundant, easy to come by and cheap . . . The country became the major European market for second hand ships, and since manpower was scarce, foreign seamen volunteered or were pressed into service. (Braudel: 1982)

It was in character, then, that when Barbadian settlers faced disaster in 1635-36 because they had lost the tobacco market to Virginia, the Dutch, traders to the world, were at hand with advice and credit. It was they who pioneered the establishment of a sugar industry in the Caribbean. The Portuguese might have done so, had they not been busy evicting the Dutch from Brazil; in any case they were not anxious to sell their trade secrets to the British. It suited the Dutch, on the other hand, to encourage the production of any West Indian crop that could be sold in Europe; so, when the Barbadians lost their market for tobacco in England,

> Some of the most industrious men, having gotten plants (of sugar cane) from Fernambock, a place in Brazil, and made tryall of them at the Barbados, and finding them to grow, they planted more and more so . . . they were worth the while to set up a very small ingenio

. . . They did not know how to place the plants, the right placing of their furnaces, the true way of covering their rollers with plates . . . But about the time I left the Island, which was in 1650, they were much better'd. (Ligon: 1657)

The imperatives of sugar soon became clear. Ligon listed them as:

500 acres of land with a faire dwelling house and Ingenio in a room 400 feet square, a boyling house, filling house, cisterns and still-house, with a curing house 100 feet long and 40 feet broad, with stables and smith's forge and room to lay provisions of corns and Bonavist beans. Houses for Negroes and Indian slaves, with 96 Negroes and 3 Indian women with their children, 28 Christians, 45 cattle for work, 8 milch cows, a dozen horses and mares and 11 Asinigoes (asses). In this plantation of 500 acres, there was employed for sugar something more than 200 acres, about 80 acres for pasture, 120 for wood, about 20 for Cotton Wool, 70 acres for provisions, viz. Corns, Potatoes, Plantains, Cassava and Bonavist; some few acres of which were for fruit, Viz. Pines, Plantains, Millions, Bananas, Goaves, Water Millions, Orange and Lemons. Thomas Modyford, who later became Governor of Jamaica, paid £7,000 for his half-share of the plantation. Eight years earlier the whole estate was worth only £400. (Ligon: 1657)

In the 1630s there had been 11,000 white smallholders in Barbados, all planting crops on a scale suited to a farmer with a short pocket. Many of them had come from England, where they sold themselves for five years as bondservants, in the hope of a grant of land. Now no land was available.

Whereas divers People have been transported from England to my island of Barbados in America, and have there remained a long time as servants, in great labour for the profits of other persons, upon whose account they were first consigned thither, expecting that their faithful service according to the covenants agreed upon at their first entrance there to make some advantages to themselves by settling of plantations for their own use; but . . . the land is now so taken up as there is not any to be had but at great rates, too high for the purchase of poor servants. (Earl of Carlisle)

The rich bought out the poor. About 750 large estates squeezed out the 11,000 smallholdings. Thousands of displaced settlers made their way to Jamaica and the Carolinas. The green tide of sugar cane and the black tide of Africans swept all before them. A visitor reported:

If you go to Barbados, you shall see a flourishing island, and many able men. I believe they have bought this year no less than a thousand Negroes, and the more they buy, the better able they are to buy, for in a year and half they will earn (with God's blessing) as much as they cost . . . A man that will settle there must look to procure servants, which if you could get out of England, for 6 or 8, or 9 years time, only paying their passages, or at the most but some small above, it would do very well, for so thereby you shall be able to do something upon a plantation, and in short time be able, with good husbandry, to procure Negroes (the life of this place) out of the increase of your own plantation. (Downing: 1645)

The writer echoed what Spanish colonists had reported earlier; that it was certain the Indies could not be maintained without negroes, because the lack of Indians had made it necessary to supplement them with negroes, as it was impossible to obtain Spaniards or creoles who were willing to do that kind of work.

Those who, like Colonel James Drax, had money to invest in land, livestock, factory and a labour force, made fortunes: "His beginning was founded upon a stock not exceeding £333 Sterling and has raised his fortune to such a height that he would not look towards England till he were able to purchase an estate of ten thousand pound land yearly." As for Colonel Modyford, "he had taken a resolution to himself not to set his face for England till he made his voyage and employment there worth him a hundred thousand pounds sterling; and all by this sugar plant." (Ligon: 1657)

Colonel Modyford had seen the plantation transform Barbados into a wealth-creating island. By 1666 it had increased its wealth sevenfold. African slaves had increased in number from 6,000 in 1643 to 20,000 in

Drax Hall Estate

1655, to 40,000 in 1668 and to 64,000 in 1672. By the end of the century, in 1698, there were 18 black slaves to every white man.

Modyford recognised that lack of land had put a limit to the prosperity of Barbados. Jamaica had more fertile land and fewer people; in 1677 there were only 9,000 whites and just over 9,000 blacks. In 1672, probably at Modyford's urging, the Assembly passed an act which allowed the earliest settlers to take out patents for as much land as they could plant in five years; but, lamented Governor Beeston, "Few people come."

In Jamaica the sugar plantation began its swift conquest in two belts along the south coast, one running west from Holland Point, Hordley and Bath through Lyssons to eastern areas of the Liguanea Plain where the Hope River provided water and power; the other on the fertile plains of South Clarendon. Describing land-use patterns in this period, Higman refers also to "smaller pockets along the Black River, the interior lowlands of St Catherine (St John's Precinct) and coastal St Mary in the north. Maps of Jamaica published in the first half of the eighteenth century suggest that this pattern was maintained throughout the period". (Higman: 1976)

Increased production seemed to do no more than whet the European appetite for sugar. Between 1740 and 1790 the plantations marched along the north coast, through Llandovery, Rose Hall and Tryall, and southward on to the Westmorland Plain by way of Friendship and the Roaring River and Williamsfield Estates. Soon heavy wagons drawn by cattle were moving from the estates to sugar ports, to Rio Bueno, Falmouth, Lucea and Savanna-la-Mar. "The number of sugar mills operating in the island increased from 57 in 1670 to 419 in 1739 and 1,061 in 1786. In the northern parish of St James, however, the number increased from 20 to 115 between 1745 and 1774. Between 1792 and 1799 some 84 new sugar estates were established, more than half of them in St Ann, Trelawny and St James." (Higman: 1976)

Today's landscape and the skin colour of most Jamaicans testify to the plantation's radical transforming power throughout the region. A traveller flying down the archipelago sees yesterday's change drawn out on the landscape, a spreading checker-board of sea-green fields and of brown stubble, the characteristic combination of field and factory dramatising the fact that sugar cane is a crop and that sugar is an industrial product, and occasional fields of ground provisions huddled on marginal hillsides. When he lands at Basseterre, St Johns, Bridgetown, Kingston or Montego Bay, he finds himself in the presence of Africa, and recognises that the landscape tells but a part of the story.

The shift from smallholdings to estate, from white serfs to black slaves, was brought about by the implanting of "an absolutely unprecedented

social, economic and political institution and by no means simply an inno-
vation in the organisation of agriculture". (Mintz: 1974) The Brazilian
scholar, Gilberto Freyre, pointed out that to travel through the Deep
South of the United States, the Guyanas and North-East Brazil, is to pass
through a region in which the social configuration was moulded by the
sugar-and-slave plantation, the characteristic features being racial intermingling, monoculture and large landholdings.

As the estates spread, so the African presence grew. Philip Curtin's
census of the Atlantic Slave Trade shows the link between the plantation,
an instrument or unit of production, and the African, the agent of production, the worker whose muscle power, stamina and intelligence enriched
Europe; and the inflow of Africans was on so large a scale and lasted for so
long that it transformed the older English colonies of Barbados, St Kitts,
Antigua and Jamaica into predominantly black colonies.

In Jamaica in 1739 there were 99,000 Africans and 10,000 whites. The
net import of Africans into Jamaica between 1655 and 1807 was 747,506.
George Roberts lists the white population of the island in 1787 as 25,000
and the slave population as 210,894, a continuing ratio of around one
white to ten blacks.

The annual import of Africans saved the African-Jamaicans from extinction because of the high mortality rate due to overwork. The chilling fact was
bluntly stated by Richard Sheridan, that the Africans were brought to the
West Indies to form new plantations, to increase the labour force of existing
plantations and to replace workers who died or became superannuated.

> It is evident that few plantations could remain productive for long
> without imports for replacement. It is paradoxical that high profits
> were not necessarily incompatible with high mortality; not a few
> contemporaries pointed out, as did Lord Brougham, that so long as a
> slave market exists, men find their profit in working out a certain
> number of their slaves, and supplying the blacks by purchase, rather
> than by breeding. Slavery, as a profitable institution, thus depended
> on the constant recruitment of cheap labour by importation from
> Africa. (Sheridan: 1970)

Cuba in this period had a flourishing industry based on tobacco planters
with small holdings. As a result the demographic history of Cuba differed
markedly from that of the plantation islands. Early in the eighteenth
century, when the sugar plantation was absorbing the cocoa-walks in
Jamaica, tobacco was introduced into Cuba. Smallholdings of tobacco
flourished alongside the sugar industry which had been introduced
between 1590 and 1600, but which had been handicapped by lack of
markets and difficulties in importing equipment and slaves. It suffered

from the economic strait-jacket into which the laws of the Indies had forced Cuba, which "cut Cuba off completely from foreign trade and limited its traffic with Spain to the single port of Seville, to which the Spanish colonies of the New World were limited by only one expedition a year". (Guerra y Sanchez: 1964) This rigid control held back the expansion of the sugar industry for two centuries and "guaranteed that Cuban society would have a gradual internal growth based on a white population that owned and tilled its native soil." So limited a sugar industry could not threaten the infant tobacco industry. Indeed, as Guerra y Sanchez indicates, tobacco, being of excellent quality, flourished and the tobacco smallholdings contributed to the break-up of the vast cattle ranches.

In the very century in which the number of Cuban tobacco smallholdings was increasing and a white Cuban yeomanry was becoming significantly important in standing and numbers, control of large areas of Jamaica was passing into the hands of a relatively small number of owners. Barry Higman, in *Jamaica Surveyed*, points out that in 1670, just before the rise of the plantations, 724 proprietors held an average of 261 acres of patented land in the settled areas. Only seven per cent of them owned 1,000 acres or more. About three-quarters of a century later the average holding stood at 1,045 acres; 29 per cent owned 1,000 acres and four per cent held over 5,000 acres. Schemes for increasing the number of small landholders came to little and "the system of great estates employing large gangs of slaves under the supervision of small numbers of whites spread to engulf the entire island by the late eighteenth century". Cuba's turn came in the nineteenth century. We will return to her in the period of the emergence of a black yeomanry in Jamaica.

White Jamaica became from this period an absentee society that "drained the island of the very people it needed for leadership in all aspects of life". (Patterson: 1969) In consequence we watch the growth of a society that was utterly immoral, inefficient and lacking in any sense of social responsibility. In 1720 the rector of Kingston reported to the bishop of London that there were not six families in the island which could be described as gentlemen: "They have no maxims of Church or State but what are absolutely anarchic."

This was the society into which the African was pitchforked. The shock was traumatic not only because he was now the property of another human being but because of the nature of white Jamaican society. From whatever nation or tribe he came, he had been nurtured in a deeply religious society with a well-understood code of ethics and system of justice and of community obligations.

We seek guidance in this subject from one of Africa's leading theologians and philosophers, John Mbiti:

Because traditional religions permeate all the departments of life, there is no formal distinction between the sacred and the secular, between the religious and non-religious, between the spiritual and the material areas of life. Wherever the African is, there is the religion: he carries it to the fields where he is sowing seeds or harvesting a new crop he takes it with him to the beer party or to attend a funeral ceremony; and if he is educated, he takes religion with him to the examination room at school or in the University; if he is a politican he takes it to parliament.

Traditional religions are not primarily for the individual, but for his community of which he is part. Chapters of African religions are written everwhere in the the life of the community, and in traditional society there are no irreligious people. To be human is to belong to the whole community, and to do so involves participating in the beliefs, ceremonies, rituals and festivals of that community. A person cannot detach himself from the religion of his group, for to do so is to be severed from his roots, his foundation, his context of security, his kinship and the entire group of those who make him aware of his own existence. To be without one of these corporate elements of life is to be out of the whole picture. Therefore, to be without religion amounts to a self-excommunication from the entire society, and African peoples do not know how to exist without religion. (Mbiti: 1970)

We point to the African background because Europeans justified the slave trade as saving the African from savagery and moving him nearer to civilisation. The historic fact is that the European record of the conquest and settlement of the Americas is one of savagery, of the legalisation of injustice, of the most barbarous punishments and, in the English-speaking Caribbean, gross immorality.

In Jamaican society:

For the non-white and particularly the non-free, the legal system was a grim travesty. Traditional British law either completely neglected or, in the few cases where it obliquely touched on the topic, very clumsily handled the problem of slavery or other forms of unfreedom. The local masters preferred it that way. They made little attempt at formulating a slave code until the last quarter of the eighteenth century and when they did it was largely as an anti-abolitionist propaganda tactic . . . .

For the nine-tenths of Jamaicans who made up the slave population, the master was the law. In him rested the power of life and death. Occassionlly a white person might have had to pay a fine for murdering his slave, but in the majority of such cases no legal action could be taken even to inflict the mildest penalty since a negro could not give evidence against any white person. (Patterson: 1969)

The Africans were not Christians but their gods and ethical values were a very precious part of daily life, as Mbiti emphasises. Many traditional African societies thought of God as omniscient (knowing all things), almighty and present everywhere. He is the watcher of everything, the great eye, the sun, the all-powerful.

The Zulu, a warlike people, think of him as "he who bends down . . . even majesties". The Gikuyu see him as always having been in existence, as one who never dies.

> No father nor mother nor wife nor children;
> He is all alone.
> He is neither a child nor an old man
> He is the same today as he was yesterday.

A traditional pygmy hymn describes him as spirit.

> In the beginning was God,
> Today is God
> Tommorrow will be God
> Who can make an image of God?
> He has no body,
> He is a word which comes out of your mouth
> That word, it is no more,
> It is past, and still it lives.
> So is God.

God governs the universe and the life of mankind. His will is immutable and man generally has to invoke it or accept it . Some, such as the Nuer people, believe that God is always right, that "God evens things out." The Akan give him the title of creator, originator, inventor; rain is the most widely acknowledged token of God's providence. He is known as the rain giver or water giver.

These examples indicate that the African could not conceive of an utterly irreligious society, nor of one so unjust as plantation society. To them justice was one of the attributes of God, who was ruler and master: "The notion of God as Judge also strengthens traditional ethical sanctions which in turn uphold community solidarity. When praying during a crisis the Azande declare to God that they have not stolen nor coveted other people's goods and they address him as the one who "settles the differences between us who are men." The Nuer believe that God is the Guardian of the traditions. (Mbiti: 1970)

Furthermore, the physical and the spiritual were seen as two dimensions of one and the same universe, and the African experienced this religious universe through acts of worship, sacrifices and offerings, prayers, innovations, blessings and salutations. Also, and this prevails throughout black America, music, singing and dancing run deep into the innermost parts of African peoples and many things come to the surface under musical inspiration which otherwise may not be readily revealed.

John Mbiti notes that in Africa he found the collection and study of religious songs very scanty, and yet this is another rich area where one expects to find repositories of traditional beliefs; ideas, wisdom, feeling. The Negro spirituals of the deep south and the Jamaica spirituals that Olive Lewin collected, shepherdesses and preachers from Moses Baker and George Lisle through Daddy Sharpe and Paul Bogle to Bedward represent a remarkable continuity of a powerful religious tradition.

We close with some African prayers that convey a sense of the reality and presence of God and of direct and easy access to him.

Thus, on becoming pregnant a Bachwa woman cooks food and takes portions of it to the forest, where she offers them to God, saying "God, from whom I have received this child, take Thou and eat."

The Bambuti pygmies in the event of a thunderstorm, pray "Grandfather, Great Father, let matters go well with me, for I am going into the forest." If they are already in the forest they pray, saying "Father, Thy children are afraid; and behold, we shall die."

The Nuer people "like to pray at any time because they like to speak to God when they are happy". A typical prayer runs:

> Our Father, it is Thy universe, it is
> Thy will, let us be at peace, let the
> Soul of thy people be cool; Thou art
> Our Father, remove all evil from our path.

The concept of God as father and judge and the images revealed in the prayers are, as Carl Jung pointed out, "always related to the primordial images of the collective unconscious. These images are really balancing or compensating factors which correspond with the problems life presents in actuality. This is not to be marvelled at since these images are deposits representing the accumulated experience of thousands of years of struggle for adaptation and existence".

The West African people belonged to different language groups, communities and tribes, but they shared certain basic cultural similarities, such as a strong sense of community, a powerful attachment to the land, a concern for children as the "buds of expectation and hope" as well as for the ancestors, for personal dignity and a respect for the tribal leaders and for the freedom enjoyed within the boundaries of tribal obligations. These are all a part of the rich religious heritage of the West African people and they explain the immediate, widespread and long-sustained struggle of the dispersed African-Amercian people for freedom.

CHAPTER 10

The beginning of the African diaspora

The African's deep longing for his country and his anger at the injustices he suffered find expression in one of the oldest Jamaican folk songs:

> If me want for to go in a Ebo
> Me can't go there!
> Since dem tief me from a Guinea
> Me can't go there.

> If me wan't for go in a Congo
> Me can't go there!
> Since dem tief me from my tatta
> Me can't go there!

Other work-songs run:

> Guinea corn I long to turn you,
> Guinea corn I long to eat you.

> Two man a road, Cromanty boy
> Two man a road, fight for you lady.

The names Iboland, Guinea, Congo, Cromanty (Coromanti) lead us back to West Africa, whence came the ancestors of most African-Jamaicans and to Kormantine, the port on the Gold Coast (Ghana) from which many of them were shipped.

The words that we use everyday confirm the origins of the folk songs, especially the names of plants, foods, utensils, spirits; afu (yam) yampee, bissy (kola nut), ackra (cakes) fufu (yam cooked and pounded), susumba, ockra, duckunu, gingy (fly), senseh (fowl), bankra (basket), abeng, nyam (eat), bufu-bufu (clumsy) and tata (father). Some forms of expression have parallels in West Africa. The Twi language, for example, has only three parts of speech, nouns, pronouns and verbs, which often do duty as adjectives, prepositions, and the like. We have parallel forms in, for instance, "duck picney"; and the prepositions "here" and "there" sometimes become "dis end" or "dat end", in "ah nebba walk dat end".

As Cassidy points out, the English part of the vocabulary of Jamaica talk is overwhelmingly the largest, but of non-British influences the African is the largest and most profound; it appears not only in the vocabulary but also in pronunciation and grammar. More than half of the Africanisms identified appear to be from the Twi language which is spoken by the Ashanti, Akwapim, Fante and Akyem. It was along the stretch of coast from Takorida to Lagos, formerly the Gold Coast, that "the Europeans built the greatest concentration of fortifications anywhere on the African coast – drawn by the gold trade to the interior and the existence of a series of rocky points with moderately safe landing beaches on the lee side or by an occasional lagoon or river mouth where lighters could load and unload in security." (Curtin: 1969)

The map shows the chief trading areas on the West African coast. Starting from the north they were modern Senegambia (Senegal and Gambia); modern Sierra Leone, which included the coastal region of Guinea-Conakry, Guinea-Bissau and a small part of Liberia; the Windward Coast which included the modern Ivory Coast and Liberia; the Gold Coast, or present-day Ghana; the Bight of Benin including today's

States of West Africa

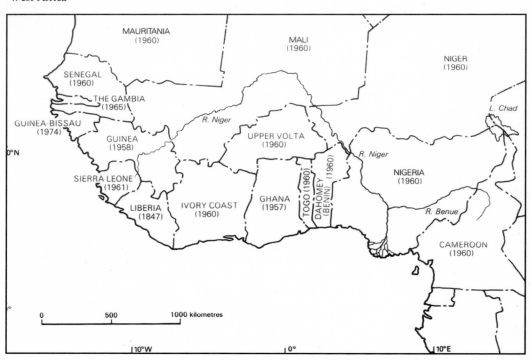

THE STORY OF THE JAMAICAN PEOPLE

Togo and Benin; the Bight of Biafra which included the Niger Delta and the mouths of the Cross and Duala Rivers, bounded by the Benin River on the west and Cape Lopez, and from Cape Lopez south to the Orange River, the area known as Angola (Central Africa). On the Indian Ocean side the trading areas ran from the Cape of Good Hope to Cape Delgado, including the island of Madagascar.

So large is the region, and so many were the trading areas, that African-Americans can claim many and different ancestral homelands. African-Brazilians have their closest ties with Angola, African-Americans of South Carolina with Angola and the Bight of Benin and African-Americans of Virginia with Senegambia and the Bight of Biafra.

Jamaica's closest ties are with Ghana and the Akan-Ashanti people, with the Yoruba, Ibo and Ibibio of Nigeria and the Niger Delta, and with some tribes of Central Africa. Between 1751 and 1790 while only about a quarter of the total English slaves delivered in the New World went to Jamaica, about 80 per cent of these came from the Gold Coast. (Curtin: 1969)

If we were to travel north from Takorida or Accra, we would pass through three distinct vegetation zones before coming to Timbuctu or Gao on the southern borders of the Sahara. First there is a green belt of tropical rain forest some 200 miles wide; then the forest gives way to savanna grass-land, but not cropped grass as in the pastures of St Ann, Trelawny, Manchester; but, giant grass that stands from 6-10 feet tall and reaches 50 feet on the savanna of Guinea. Finally we come to the Sahel, "the shore of the desert", arid country inhabited by the pastoral nomad Fulani. North of the Sudan lies the world's largest desert, the Sahara, which is traversed by ancient camel routes that linked powerful trading cities such as Timbuctu, Gao and Jenne with Tangiers, Algiers, Tunis and Tripoli on the coast of the Mediterranean.

Imagine that we are at Takorida, a seaport of Ghana. We are about to set out on a journey through Ghana and Nigeria, the ancestral homelands of African-Jamaicans and of most West African people, among them the Ashanti, Ewe, Fon, Egba Oyo, Ibo and Ibibio and Yoruba. It is a journey through a landscape, but more importantly, it is a journey back across four centuries, to the early days of the arrival of the Portugese and the beginning of the Atlantic Slave Trade.

It is a painful journey to make, one full of suffering and agony, but it is a journey that all African-Americans should make in their minds if they wish to understand the magnitude of the African-Americans' achievement, if they seek to discover the significance of the African heritage, and if they wish to liberate themselves fully from the self-doubts and ambiguities engendered by enslavement, colonialism and racial discrimination.

At the heart of the story of the African-Jamaican and the African-American is the fact that deep within him, nurtured by his experience and culture, there was "an irreducible core of free, creative, spontaneous human nature, of some elementary sense of identity, dignity and worth" (Hausheer: 1982) that empowered him to resist, and eventually to defeat, those who sought to transform him, a person, into a useful tool, a slave. The African-Jamaican and African-American liberation wars are an inspiring part of the rejection of that attempt at dominance, but not the whole of it. It is a mark of Marcus Garvey's greatness that he saw that total liberation involved recognising the centrality of Africa and the significance of the African heritage.

Our imaginary journey becomes, then, a search for roots, for that sense of historical continuity which in turn nurtures a sense of identity and of worth. In our journey we will bear in mind that human beings are "defined precisely by their possession of an inner life, of purposes and ideals, and of a vision or conception, however hazy or implicitly, of who they are, where they came from, and what they are at. Indeed, it is just their possession of an inner life in this sense that distinguishes them from animals and natural objects". (Hausheer: 1982)

Our guides and companions are two West Indians who lived and worked in West Africa: the historian Walter Rodney and the poet-historian Edward Kamau Brathwaite.

Walter Rodney, for a time professor of history at the University of Dar-es-Salaam in Tanzania, opens our eyes to the impact of the Atlantic Slave Trade on African social and political life and helps us to understand how it came about that Africans captured and sold Africans to the slave-traders.

> Europeans obtained slaves in Africa, on the one hand, by stimulating a demand for the manufactured goods they had to offer, and, on the other hand, by exploiting the tribal and religious divisions and the incipient class contradictions within African society . . . In general, however, it seems clear that the prospects of profit from the slave trade became so attractive that old rivalries were either revived or smoothed over, according to which was the most profitable.
>
> It is equally important to assess the manner in which slave-raiding affected people of different social levels within the hierarchical society of West Africa. For the vast majority it brought insecurity and fear, whether or not they were lucky enough to escape sale into slavery, because the slave trade meant violence in the form of skirmishes, ambushes and kidnapping – often carried out by professional man-hunters under the supervision of the ruling elites.

Walter Rodney draws our attention also to the fact that many members of the ruling class, who traditionally were responsible for maintaining stability and guaranteeing order, went into "partnerships of exploitation" with the Europeans. As time passed, for one reason or another the old ruling classes were replaced by a new class of men, sometimes drawn from within local society as in the Niger Delta, sometimes from the ranks of professional slave traders of part European origin: African-Portuguese, African-English, African-Brazilian. What mattered was "the skill and devotion with which they served the capitalist system".

The Atlantic Slave Trade corrupted many of the ruling classes of West Africa and corrupted West African society at the lower levels by increasing the number of servile societies. "Fulas of the Futa-Djalon and the Nike of Eastern Nigeria still kept a large labour force in conditions of bondage."

With Walter Rodney's analysis in mind, we turn to Edward Kamau Brathwaite, who in his trilogy *Rights of Passage*, *Masks* and *Islands* travels from the Americas to West Africa, claims his heritage and then returns. In *Masks* the poet tells of his journey from Takorida, one of the seaports of Ghana, to his birthplace. Knowing how deeply religious the African is, the poet begins with prayers to the ancestors, Nana Firimpong, and to the Akan goddess of the earth, Asase Yaa.

> Nana Firimpong
> once you were here,
> hoed the earth
> and left it for me
> green rich ready
> with yam shoots, the
> tuberous smooth of cassava
> Asase Yaa,
> You, Mother of Earth
> on whose soil
> I have placed my tools
> on whose soil
> I will hope
> I will hope

After the prayers we come to the Akan ritual, the making of the drum, with the two curved sticks of the drummer, the gourds and the rattles; and throughout the poem Akan rites and rhythms transport us out of the culture of Europe into that of the Akan people. The beat of the talking drums

> Kon kon kon kon
> Kun kun kun kun

is followed by the great orchestral burst of a mmenson, an orchestra of seven elephant tusk horns used on state occasions to relate history.

> Summon now the Kings of the forest
> horn of the elephant,
> mournful call of the elephant,
> Summon the emirs, Kings of the desert,
> horses caparisoned, beaten gold bent;
> archers and cries, porcupine
> arrows, bows bent;
> recount now the gains the losses,
> Agades, Sokota, El Hassen dead in his tent,
> the silks and the brasses

To the steady haunting beat of the talking drums Africa appears before us and we witness the long desert migrations from the western Sudan to the Volta, and:

> the mouth of great rivers
> that smile, of forests
> where farms may be broken;
> deep lakes in those forests
> and plains where our cattle
> may graze

In a dramatic transition from this richly tapestried background the poet, today's African-American, seeks his birthplace and his kinsmen. He lands at Takorida where, first as in St Ann and Manchester, the green struggles through the red earth.

> Mammies crowded with cloths,
> flowered and laughed;
> white teeth
> smooth voices like pebbles
> moved by the sea of their language.
> Akwaaba they smiled
> meaning welcome . . .
> You who have come
> back a stranger
> after three hundred years

The mammies give him a stool on which to sit, water to wash his hands, food to eat:

> Here is plantain
> here palm oil
> red, staining the fingers,

good for the heat
for the sweat,
and they ask "Do you remember?"

He searches in vain for his kinsfolk:

tossed my net
but the net caught
no fish
I dipped a wish
but the well
was dry

Nightmare memories buried deep in the mind begin to stir. Korabra, the signal drum often played at funerals, beats out its message "go and come back" and

Back
through Elmina,
white granite stone
stalking the sun
light, the dungeon unbars
the whips of the slavers
see the tears
of my daughters . . .
My scattered
clan, young
-est kinsmen,
fever's dirge
in their wounds,
rested here;
Then limped on
down to their dungeon.

What flaws in the ancestors, what flaws in himself, brought about this enslavement? Osei Tutu, founder of the Ashanti nation, enters to shouts of praise, Osee Yei, Osee Yei. He asks:

When the worm's knife cuts
the throat of a tree, what will happen?
It will die
When a cancer has eaten the guts
of a man, what will surely happen?
He will die
My people, that is the condition of our
country today

it is sick at heart, to its bitter clay
we cannot heal it or hold it together
from curses
because we do not believe in it

In that moment of self-discovery, from the compound where his mother
buried his birth cord under gravel, the poet asks:

why did the god's
stool you gave us,
Anokye,
not save us from pride,
foreign tribes' bibles,
the Christian god's hunger
eating the good of our tree

With self-discovery, with the claiming of the African birthright, comes
a sense of identity. The self-doubts engendered by enslavement fall away.
Revitalised by his renewed identification with Africa, the poet sings of the
coming of dawn and the symbol of life:

As the cock
now cries in the early dawn
so slowly slowly
ever so slowly
I will rise
and stand on my feet
akoko bob opa
(the cock crows in the early dawn)
akoko tua bon
(the cock rises and crows)
I am learning
Let me succeed.

Making our African pilgrimage, we need to look more closely at our
African kinsfolk and ancestors. We begin with the three ancient empires of
Ghana, Mali and Songhai. "There can be no doubt that throughout the
period under discussion (the tenth century to the time of the Moroccan
invasion of 1591) the dominating political, economic and cultural initia-
tives and influences stemmed from these three great empires. There seems
no question in fact that the empires of Ghana, Mali and Songhai rank
among the highest achievements of Negro Africans in history." (Fage:
1969)

Ancient Ghana, a kingdom of the early Sudan (from which the Gold
Coast took its name after independence in 1957) had its beginnings

among the Soninke people, hunters and food-gatherers from a period a thousand years or more BC. "Somewhat about 300 B.C. an increasing population, the demands of food-production and attacks by Libyco-Berbers led the Soninke to elect their first King." (Wallace and Hinds) The Soninke were fighting people, so they were able to gain control of the trans-Saharan trade, from which they gained a substantial revenue. Furthermore, technologically they were a jump ahead of their neighbours, for in their wars they used iron technology, spears and arrows tipped with iron. In addition, they deployed the horse, as cavalry, as well as foot-soldiers in their army. Nor was their revenue limited to their share of the trans-Saharan trade, for to the south, within easy reach, were the agricultural and gold-bearing lands of the Upper Niger and the Senegal rivers. By the tenth century AD the empire of Ghana had expanded and was widely known and respected in other parts of Africa and in the Middle East. This was a century or more before William the Norman conquered the English and possibly two centuries before Tainos began their migration from the basin of the Orinoco to the Caribbean archipelago. Two of the trades that brought Ancient Ghana glory, slaves and gold, belong to an even earlier period when Carthaginians, Greeks and Romans were engaged in commerce along the North African coast. A Greek merchant from Alexandria, Cosmas, who became a monk, wrote in AD 525 a vivid description of the "silent trade", the gold trade. His account, one of the classics of African history, engenders in us a sense of the mystery and antiquity of the African people and links us with the Queen of Sheba who brought to Solomon bars of ebony, spices and gold.

Every other year the king of Axum on the Red Sea sent agents south across the desert to bargain for gold.

> They take along with them to the mining district oxen, lumps of salt and iron, stop at a certain spot, make an encampment which they protect with a hedge of thorns, slaughter the oxen, cut the meat in pieces and lay the meat, lumps of salt and the iron on the hedge. Then come natives bringing gold in nuggets like peas, and lay one or two or more of these upon what pleases them . . . and then they retire to some distance off. Then the owner of the meat approaches, and if he is satisfied he takes the gold away and upon seeing that, the owner comes and takes the flesh or the salt or the iron. If however he is not satisfied he leaves the gold, when the native, seeing that he has not taken it, comes and either puts down more gold or takes up what he had laid down and goes away . . . The space of six months is taken up with this trading expedition . . . In going they march very slowly, chiefly because of the cattle, but in returning they quicken their pace lest on the way they should be overtaken by winter and its rains.

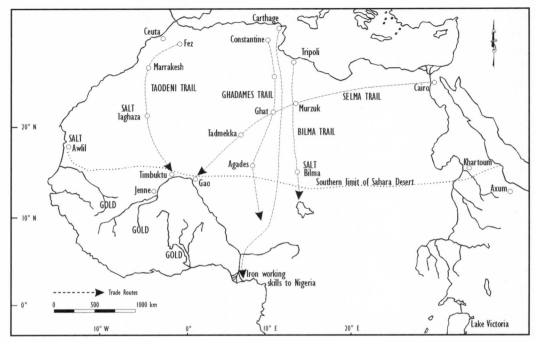

Trans-Saharan
trading routes,
tenth to
eighteenth
centuries

Another legend tells how Arab traders with goods and salt met the
ancient Ghanian people, who guided them to special trading spots,
signalled the opening of the market by beating large drums and then
followed the procedure described by Cosmas.

The trade in gold and in slaves brought wealth and power to the Ghana,
but in 1076 the empire was overrun by the Almoravids, a Berber Muslim
dynasty that ruled Morocco and Muslim Spain and founded Marrakesh as
the capital of their powerful empire. They dominated the caravan routes in
the Sahara and, after a period of steady decline, the empire of Ghana fell
apart.

The empire of Mali, which took over control of the area from Ghana,
held sway over the important Niger-Timbuctu trade route, which also cut
across trade routes that ran northwards from Ghana, where the Mande
opened new gold mines about the middle of the fourteenth century. The
Mali empire added to its wealth by levying tribute from other clans and
their villages.

Although Mali had conquered the Songhai people, whose kingdom was
on the banks of the Niger, between Gao and Dendi, the latter never
accepted defeat. Their opportunity for revenge came when succession
disputes destroyed the unity of the empire of Mali. Between 1494 and
1528 two Songhai rulers, Sonni Ali and Askia Muhammed, established an

empire as extensive as Mali's had been, with a powerful army and with full access to the profitable trans-Saharan trade. But after Askia Muhammed's death in 1528 Songhai, like Mali, was torn apart by succession disputes. In 1591 invaders from Morocco regained control of the salt mines of the Sahara and severely disrupted the trading system on which the Mali empire depended. Broken by internal disputes, it was unable to beat back an expeditionary force from Morocco which captured its three principal cities, Gao, Jenne and Timbuctu in 1591. These, and other royal pilgrimages to Mecca,

> might suggest that their purpose was primarily to further political and economic relations with North Africa. They certainly had this effect. They led, for instance to the transmission of regular embassies across the Sahara; to the establishment of hostels for Sudanese students in Cairo; to the coming of the Sudanic courts of men like, Es-Saheli (who is said to have built mosques and palaces at Timbuctu and Gao) and of other less well remembered advisers, technicians, clerics, jurists and simple adventurers: and they certainly led to an increase in trans-Saharan trade, particularly with Egypt. (Fage: 1969)

But these empires were not Islamic creations; although there was a degree of Islamization in all three empires. Whether we look at Ghana, Mali or Songhai, "these empires were in origin pagan creations which, once they had become established found a degree of Islamization convenient for reasons of State . . . But in its origin, the empire building process would seem to have been fundamentally a pagan reaction to the development of North African trade". (Fage: 1969)

The wealth and splendour of these three empires echo across the centuries in the accounts of Arab scholars and explorers. Most dazzling of all were the glittering pilgrimages to Mecca of the Mansa Musa of Mali in 1324 and of Askia Muhammed of Songhai in 1495-97.

Powerful empires emerged also in other parts of Africa. In 1484, when Portugese explorers reached a point south of the estuary of the Congo (Zaire) River they found the impressive empire of the Congo. South of the Congo there were several Bantu-speaking states and to the east well-organised kingdoms based on modern Zimbabwe; and in the region to the south-east of Salisbury (now Harare), was the famous empire of Mwenemutapa.

This widespread emergence of great kingdoms and empires called for a range of administrative skills and for sophisticated procedures by which a system of checks and balances put limits on the power of the supreme ruler. It called also for sensitivity and creativity in managing extensive commercial undertakings and training large armies that included cavalry.

In the Sudan, where the Muslims were dominant, systems of education and religious centres were established. Timbuctu, Jenne and Gao, for example, were internationally recognised centres of culture as well as powerful commercial cities.

Famous though they were, the ancient empires of Ghana, Mali and Songhai do not stir our emotions as deeply as do the names of the people who lived in the forest belt and the savanna south of the Niger, the Akan-Ashanti people, the Yoruba, the Ibo, as well as the names of kingdoms such as Oyo and Benin, homes of the glorious terracottas and bronzes of Ibo and Benin that are supreme examples of human artistic creativity.

Akan-Ashanti people moved into the forest belt in the region north of Accra in the eleventh and twelfth centuries AD and established small scattered communities and trades with the savanna kingdoms of the north. To the south of them, along the coast, lived small clans and states that owed allegiance to the forest dwellers. It was with these small clans that the Europeans first traded.

Toward the end of the seventeenth century, in the years when Jamaica was turning from cocoa-walks to sugar plantations, the Ashanti came under pressure from the Denkyira people, who were supplying the Europeans with slaves. Two remarkable leaders, the warrior-statesman Osei Tutu, and a priest, Okampo Anokye, saw that the only hope for the Ashanti lay in unity. First, Osei Tutu led the united Ashanti to victory over their neighbours. Then Anokye provided them with a powerful symbol of national unity, the golden stool. He took three cuttings of the kumnini tree and planted one each at Kwaman, Juaben and Kumawa. Those at Juaben and Kumawa grew. This was taken as a sign that Osei Tutu was the leader chosen by the gods, and from that day Kwaman became Kumasi, the name meaning "under the Kumnini tree".

Soon after this a great gathering was held at Kumasi. There Anokye brought down from the sky, with darkness and thunder, a wooden stool adorned with gold, which floated to the earth and alighted gently on Osei Tutu's knees. The stool, declared Anokye, contained the spirit of the whole Ashanti nation. In this way Anokye impressed on the divided Ashanti clans the fact that they were a nation, united by a religious bond of which the golden stool was the symbol. This was the origin of the Sika Agua Kofi (Friday's golden stool) of the Ashanti.

The rulers of the Ashanti showed great skill in fostering the sentiment of national unity among the various Akan-speaking groups. They forbade them to promote their individual loyalties while the king, Osei Tutu, the Asantahene or king, took care to build up an army in which the recruits, who were drawn from the various groups, were trained together. The Asantahene, or king, governed with the help of a well-run bureaucracy

Above, an Ashanti gold mask
and *below*, a Benin bronze

Shango, the Yoruba god of
thunder

headed by a confederacy council. He derived his authority from the golden stool, and the office was hereditary, but he did not have absolute authority. The chief decision-making body within the government was an executive council or inner cabinet.

The Yoruba also developed a highly centralised political system in this period. The process began with the emergence, in the middle of the seventeenth century, of Oyo as the dominant power of Yorubaland. It drew much of its strength from the fact that it commanded the caravan routes which linked the Guinea Coast with the trans-Saharan trade routes and so was able to impose fees on caravans and merchants passing through. It also became a slave-dealing state. The revenue it obtained from these sources enabled Oyo to build a powerful army that included cavalry and that was in part equipped with guns bought from the Europeans. By the year 1700 the empire of Oyo dominated most of Nigeria west of the Niger as well as part of Benin.

Like the Ashanti, the office of *alafin* (king) was hereditary but a system of checks and balances put limits on to his authority. He was assisted by the *oyo mesi*, a council of notables, which was headed by a prime minister who was also the high priest and controlled all the religious groups in Yorubaland except Sango and Ita. The army was controlled by the *oyo mesi*, not the *alafin*.

The Yoruba, who today number some 12 million people and form one of the largest African societies, are not a single tribe but groups of diverse people who are bound together by cultural and political ties.

> We have in the Yoruba an ancient people moving southward from the savanna into the forest. Immigrant groups and conquerors from without and inter-kingdom wars from within have all contributed to produce a kaleidoscopic pattern of cultures and structure that seem to defy classification into three or four basic types . . . yet there is a cultural uniformity among the various Yoruba groups that clearly differentiates them from their neighbours. Common language, dress, symbolism in chieftaincy and ritual unite them. (Lloyd: 1965)

The Yoruba are history-focussed people. At major festivals the achievements of the past are recited, so that generation after generation draws strength and cohesion from their knowledge of their history, as well as from the unifying influence of their towns. The Yoruba have always lived in towns, and they look down on those people who are without towns or kings. However, the towns are not industrial centres; they grow out of the countryside.

> A typical Yoruba town has 70% of its adult men engaged in farming and 10% each as craftsmen and traders. The smaller subordinate

towns of a kingdom usually have a slightly lower proportion of crafts-
men and traders than has the metropolitan town. The farmlands of
Ibadan extend for twenty miles from the town; those of a smaller
town say of 20,000 inhabitants, probably four or five miles. When
the farm is so far from the town compound, a small hamlet is built at
the farm . . . The farm population commutes between town and
farm. (Lloyd: 1965)

But with over 50 different kingdoms in Yorubaland what is true of
Ibadan and Abeokuta may not apply to other towns, such as Ijebu Ode
and Ondo.

In contrast with Jamaica, Yorubaland is almost wholly given up to
peasant farming. There are no large-scale economic units. About three out
of every four adult men are farmers, the others become traders, blacksmiths, woodcarvers, and the like.

For women the traditional crafts are pottery, spinning, dyeing and
weaving on a vertical loom. Unlike most African societies, the women do
no farm work. They trade in foodstuffs and in cloth, the men in meat-
buying and in buying export crops such as cocoa and palm-oil kernels.

The markets are a joy and a perpetual surprise because of their size;
sometimes there are as many as a thousand sellers, most of them women,
for most of the marketing is in their hands and it may be a full-time
occupation from which they may become independently wealthy.

East of Yorubaland, in eastern Nigeria, lies Iboland, a large region that
extends from Lokoju, where the Benue River branches eastwards from the
Niger, to the Cross River which empties into the Atlantic at Old Calabar,
and from the swamp lands where the first yams are harvested and the crop
is reaped by the end of August, the time of the New Yam Festival. The
period of waiting from mid-May to August is the season of famine. The
season between the end of August and mid-October is rain-time. The yam
harvest continues up to mid-October, and in this period most of the
women's small crops are harvested. From mid-October to February is the
season of ceremonials and rest from farm work. During this period the
bush on land that has been rested is cut and burned in preparation for
cultivation, or heap-time.

Like the Yoruba, the Ibo are not a single people, but are made up of 200
or more groups that total more that 7 million people; but they differ
markedly in many respects. The Yoruba religion has an elaborate hierarchy
of gods, with Olorun (the owner of the sky) as the supreme god, with
Shango the god of thunder and Ogun, the god of iron and war among
them. The Ibo recognise forces or powers at work, but have no supreme
god or hierarchies of gods; instead, there is a multitude of good and evil
spirits, the most powerful of which have special shrines (orishas). The

contrast extends to the ways in which political unity is secured. The Yoruba have a complex centralised kingdom and the Ibo have a close-knit kinship system that recognises descent from the mother as well as from the father and a network of associations that consult and take decisions together. Furthermore, whereas the Yoruba people are town-dwellers, the various Ibo societies live in dispersed village communities.

In order to understand the values that underlie Ibo society and the goals the Ibo people set themselves, let us look at an Ibo writer's revealing portrait of himself and his people.

> Once a young man has attained the age of reason, his parents become strict with him. He is taught the value of a busy life. Every youth, even the son of the richest man of his community, must acquire the lifelong taste of manual work. You very rarely find an Ibo man or woman begging for alms. An Ibo prefers to die than to be idle. Even the lame and crippled work for their existence. The blind find themselves work in their communities. This pride enhances the prestige of an Ibo wherever he goes . . .
>
> The Ibo looks proud because he is bred in a free atmosphere where everyone is another's equal. He hates to depend on anyone for his life needs. He does not mind if others look proud. He has much to be proud of in his land. Nature has provided for him. He is strong and able to work or fight. He is well formed. He is generally happy in his society where no ruler overrides his conscience. He likes to advance and he is quick to learn. He likes to give rather than take. (Udeagu: 1960)

From these West African nations came the men and women who left us a priceless heritage of courage and achievement. Their West African background of self-respect and self-confidence equipped the women for leadership. Many West African countries "held and still hold a high opinion of women and especially of the mother. Among such nations the most vital event of a woman's life is bearing a child . . . For without the great gift of children, the family, the tribe, the nation will die. The mother and the child are both precious". (Mathurin-Mair:1986)

The West African woman was leader as well as mother. Many of these societies have a matrilineal form of inheritance, by which property is passed on through the female members. The tribal history of the ancient kingdom of Kongo or of the Ashanti tells of women who were leaders of their nation, such as the old mother of the tribe, Mpemba Nzinga, who founded the kingdom of Kongo, and the queen mother of the Ashanti whose stool was for long superior to the king's, or the women of the royal household of Dahomey who exercised enormous influence because they were in charge of the nation's taxes. As Mathurin points out, when African men and women entered the Caribbean "they were already educated and steeped in their national culture. The culture contained among much else a tradition of warrior nations and a history of proud and respected women. This sort of heritage produced rebels and ensured that there would always be women among the rebels".

CHAPTER 11

The Atlantic Slave Trade

Slavery, or trading in persons, is as old as man. It was not limited to one race or one class of people. It was not for blacks only. Slavery recognised no colour bar. In the view of the ancients it was a law of nature to which all human beings were subject. Europe, Asia and Africa all contained slave-taking and slaveholding societies. There were internal and external slave markets centuries before an Atlantic Slave Trade came into existence. The slaves – men, women and children – were of many races and colours. Celts, Nubians, Africans, Numidians and Gauls were all to be found in the slave markets of the Old World, throughout the Mediterranean, the Black Sea region, the Middle East, India and the Far East.

Originally the term "Slav" denoted a member of the largest linguistic and ethnic European group, which included Slovaks, Serbs, Croats, Bulgars, Ukrainians, Russians and Byelorussians. In the twelfth century the Germans drove the Slavs east of the River Elbe, destroying many and enslaving others. The word "slave", which is identical with the racial name, means one who is the property of, and entirely subject to another person, whether by capture, purchase or birth. Slavery, which existed amongst both primitive and advanced peoples, is the most extreme form of lack of freedom, other forms being subjection, servanthood and serfdom.

An African scholar, Mbaye Gueye, has pointed out, as have others, that the slave trade was a very ancient practice in Africa, but that before foreign intervention it was carried out on a fairly small scale. It was chiefly a means of reintegrating into society individuals who had been cut off from their families following a war or some other catastrophe.

> The African ideal is that of a community existence based on power-ful family ties with a view to a well-ordered, secure life . . . In these conditions a man on his own formerly had no chance of survival. Enslaving people whom natural or other disasters had cast adrift was a useful means of providing them with a social framework . . . Those

could remember. In August 1800 a transport ship, the *Asia*, took most of the 550 survivors to Sierra Leone where they settled.

General Walpole rejected the Assembly's offer of 500 guineas to purchase a sword: "As the House has thought fit not to accede to the agreement entered into between me and the Trelawny maroons, and as their opinion of that treaty stands on their minutes very different to my conception of it, I am compelled to decline the offer."

Angry at having been made an instrument to dupe and entrap the maroons, Walpole atttempted to have the matter reviewed in England. He obtained a seat in parliament and there moved a resolution seeking for an examination of the treaty negotiations, but he failed to win sufficient support.

The Earl of Balcarres had no hesitation about accepting the Assembly's offer of 700 guineas to purchase a ceremonial sword.

CHAPTER 14

The sugar estate: Bastion of white power

Contemplating a ruined great house, Derek Walcott, West Indian Nobel Prize laureate, painted in vivid language the beauty of the setting, "green lawn, broken by low walls of stone dipped to the rivulet", and against that tranquillity he placed the brutality and transience of imperial power.

> I thought next
> Of men like Hawkins, Walter Raleigh,
> Drake
> Ancestral murderers and poets;
>
> The names spoke of great victories and of Africans whose lives
>   paid for those victories,
>
> Ablaze with rage I thought
> Some slave is rotting in that
> manorial lake . . .

Throughout his poems and plays Walcott interprets and illuminates the West Indian historical experience and reveals that his own search for a sense of complete creative selfhood reflects every West Indian's need to claim his roots and his heritage. Kamau Braithwate (on whose work we drew heavily in the chapter on the West African Homeland), opens the eyes of West Indians to the centrality of Africa as mother and as an indispensable resource of spirituality.

Throughout this book we call on the creative artists of Jamaica and of the West Indies. We affirm that the story of the people of Jamaica cannot be told without their participation. They are our griots, bards, minstrels, storytellers, interpreters, historians, prophets. Their artifacts are found in the historical experience of the Jamaican and West Indian people, in the culture and way of life of the folk, in the necessities of the shanty towns and country homes, in deep-buried memories of their roots, of colonialism and of social change. Through their gift for entering into the inner world of West Indians, of understanding their purposes, ideals, sense of personal dignity and creativity, they add precious insights to our understanding of ourselves. We will find that the creative artists, especially the poets, including those who write in the vernacular, and the novelists, add insight, depth and texture to our story.

Today the sugar estate is one of the great mainstays of the Jamaican economy, a provider of commodities for export and of public service to the nation. Many of the great houses that survive are of elegance and charm, with high-quality joinery and woodwork; they settle into the landscape with an air of distinction. They are among Jamaica's historical treasures. The modern plantation systems in the islands and in many parts of plantation America are efficient units of production and their earnings contribute to national development. The labour force is protected by labour unions and industrial relations in line with developed countries. Worthy Park, Frome, Innswood, New Yarmouth and other sugar estates contribute to Jamaica's economic and social well-being. In many cases the estates serve smaller cane farmers as well as the large suppliers and they also receive substantial investments from overseas.

The plantation we are considering was very different. Its labour force was made up of slaves brought in from Africa under conditions of great cruelty. Each slave was required to remain within the boundaries of the estate to which he was assigned. Political representation and religious instruction were closed to him. He was almost wholly at the mercy of the master or his representative. His skin colour, black, branded him as inferior. He was the victim in a detestable system of apartheid. Every aspect of the plantation represented conflict: black slave and white master, slave quarters and great house, provision ground and plantation, outlawed religions, cults and established church, justice for whites and legally instituted injustice for blacks, chattel status for blacks and civil rights for whites, restricted movement for blacks and freedom of movement for whites, pickney gangs for blacks and schools for whites, the "bongo image" against the "busha image", yard-talk and English, slave and freeman. Conflict was the characteristic feature.

The sugar estates spread along the north coast from Agualta Vale in St Mary, west to Tryall in Hanover and south to the plains of Westmoreland. They prospered, but drought often plagued the southern belt. As Charles Leslie, a visitor to the island in 1740 wrote, "Liguanea is quite dry and fine sugar-works that used to produce many hundred hogsheads of sugar are now turned into cattle penns. This likewise is the fate of the parishes of St Catherine's, St Dorothy's and Vere which once were the choicest and richest spots in the whole Island but are now good for little but to raise cattle." (Leslie: 1739)

Even in these high-technology days King Sugar is an imperious ruler. He was much more so when the only sources of power were wind, water and animals. The requirements for making good sugar were good soil, level land for the crop, ease of access, convenience of distance from the shipping place and a stream running through the premises. Layout was important. The principal objectives were a central location for the works and an overall symmetry in the ordering of buildings and crops. An important component of the industry was that the cost of transporting the cane to the mill, especially when the load of cane was moved by ox-carts or asses, should be kept to the minimum. Another critical question was the source of power. Animal power was slow and costly; watermills called for aqueducts and a reliable source of supply, windmills had to be on hilltops or exposed sites. In the late eighteenth century steam power, most efficient of all, became available, but called for new roads and buildings.

Barry Higman in his book, *Jamaica Surveyed*, has brought together a valuable collection of surveyor's drawings of a number of Jamaican sugar estates, pens and coffee plantations, with clear, historical and descriptive case studies that identify important characteristics. He notes:

> Within tropical America, the dominance of the large slave plantation was nowhere greater than in Jamaica. Around 1830, for example, 36 per cent of Jamaican slaves lived in units of more than 200, compared to 5 per cent in the sugar-producing regions of Louisiana and a mere 1 per cent in Bahia. Roughly 60 per cent of slaves in Louisiana and Bahia belonged to holdings of less than 50, whereas only 25 per cent of Jamaica's slaves were in such units. Within the British Caribbean only Tobago, St Vincent and Antigua matched the concentration of slaves in very large plantations found in Jamaica. The French and Spanish colonies always possessed a relatively substantial small holder class and even St Domingue and Cuba in their short-lived climax periods as slave societies failed to approach the Jamaica pattern.
>
> Further, in spite of the much larger slave population of the United States, there were only 312 plantations of 200 or more slaves in 1860 compared with 393 in Jamaica in 1832. Although the large plantation typified the relations of production in the slave societies of Brazil and the United States, the plantation itself remained something of a myth, most slaves living outside its physical context. In Jamaica myth and reality converged.

The figures for plantation expansion are impressive. Periodic droughts notwithstanding, the number of sugar-works or mills increased rapidly in

Montpelier Estate,
St James

the period 1670-1800. Between 1670 and 1739 the number increased from 57 to 419, and stood at 1,061 in 1786. The north coast expansion was spectacular. There were only 20 mills in St James in 1745, but 30 years later, in 1774, there were 115. In the seven years between 1792 and 1799 some 84 new estates were established in the island, more than one-half of them being in St Ann, Trelawny and St James. By 1804 the north coast had as many mills as the south coast.

Hope, Papine and Mona Estates were three estates of more than 1,000 acres each, which had three different owners and date back to the early years of English rule. Major Roger Hope, who served under General Venables, founded Hope Estate in the 1660s. The estate passed to the Elletson family by Hope's daughter's marriage to Chief Justice Elletson. Lady Nugent, wife of the governor of Jamaica, visited the Papine and Hope estates in October 1801. She described the Papine estate as being beautiful, with a fine walk of bamboo supported by a coconut tree at every 12 feet; breadfruit trees in great perfection; jackfruit trees with fruit like huge pumpkins hanging from the trunks, being too heavy for the limbs. The situation of the house was bad, for it was shut out from the seabreeze by the Long Mountain. The owner, Mr Hutchinson, who served an enormous breakfast of all sorts of meats and fruits, "was a quiet, awkward Scotchman and so overcome by the honour we have done him that it is quite distressing to see the poor man".

The sugar estate: Bastion of white power   153

Lady Nugent went on to the Hope Estate:

> Driving through a cane-piece as it is called, a negro man running
> before us to open the gates . . . It is said to be an old estate . . . As you
> enter the gates, there is a long range of negro houses, like thatched
> cottages, and a row of coconut trees and clumps of cotton-trees. The
> sugar-house and all the buildings are thought to be more than usually
> good. The overseer, a civil, vulgar [common] Scotch officer on half-
> pay did the honours to us. I went to the overseer's house [and] talked
> to the black women who told me all their histories. The overseer's
> chere'amie, [sweetheart] and no man here is without one, is a tall
> black woman, polished and shining, well-made. She showed me her
> three yellow children and said with some ostentation she should soon
> have another . . . [Lady Nugent described the husband as] a Scotch
> Sultan, who is about fifty, clumsy, ill-made and dirty. He had a
> dingy, sallow brown complexion, and only two yellow discoloured
> tusks, by way of teeth. However, they say he is a good overseer, . . .
> almost all the agents, attorneys, merchants and shopkeepers are of
> that country [Scotland] and really do deserve to thrive in this, they
> are so industrious . . . I should mention there is an excellent hospital
> on this estate which is called a hot-house where the blackies appear
> perfectly comfortable.

The three estate owners, beset by drought, wisely joined together to
meet the cost of supplying water from the Hope River. At first, they used
cattle to turn the mills but that was slow and unproductive. They built
water works, starting "from a dam near the northern boundary of Hope
estate. The water passed through a series of ground-level masonry gutters,
solid and arched brickwork aqueducts and underground channels for a
distance of 2 miles, turning the mill wheels on Hope, Papine and Mona in
its course". (Higman: 1988)

The reservoir was at the northern boundary of Papine Estate. From this,
Higman records that Papine supplied water to Up Park Camp under
contract to the value of £630 in the early 1850s and to the Lord Bishop of
Jamaica at £27. The water from the Papine reservoir (passed) through the
cane fields and provision grounds of that estate, rising to 12 feet in an
aqueduct at Papine works, then underground . . . to emerge at the flood gate
and rise again into another aqueduct before reaching Mona works. Hope
Estate abandoned sugar cultivation in the 1840s, selling its water rights to
the Kingston and Liguanea Water Company. (Higman: 1976) Papine
continued to make sugar until the 1880s and Mona until 1914 when it was
the only estate in St Andrew. Sections of the aqueduct remain in the Hope
Gardens and on the grounds of the University of the West Indies.

From these struggling estates we move to Drax Hall in St Ann, founded in 1669 by William Drax, an English planter from Barbados.

Whereas Mona, Papine and Hope experienced water shortages, Drax Hall was concerned with milling efficiency and making the best use of the typical north coast topography of a ribbon of plain and sharply rising hills. Travellers who take the coastal main road today from St Ann's Bay to Ocho Rios will find that it forms the dividing line between the flat land where 40 or more cane-pieces once flourished and the steeply sloping hills where pimento trees still grow.

In 1715 Charles Drax sold 1,000 acres of the estate to Peter Beckford, probably the richest Jamaican planter of the time. At his death he owned nine sugar plantations and was part-owner of seven others, nine cattle pens and a mansion in Spanish Town. His second son, William, inherited a large part of his father's estate and by 1754 owned more than 22,000 acres. In 1762 he bought the remainder of Drax Hall in a manner, reported some, "that excited the indignation of every honest man who became acquainted with the transaction". William found Jamaica too small for his energies and wealth. He became an absentee proprietor, starting off as a London merchant, shipowner and alderman. He was elected Lord Mayor of London twice. The estate was sold to John H. Pink in 1821. The calamitous fall in sugar prices notwithstanding, William Sewell, who purchased Drax Hall after its listing as an encumbered estate in 1863, produced sugar through the 1880s, then changed over to bananas and cattle and finally to copra and limes.

The Negro village is of special interest because of data found there when nine of the house sites were excavated. The houses were made of locally available materials, marl, rough limestone cobbles, bricks. "Three distinct rooms were identified, one with limestone block flooring, the middle room with marl cobble flooring, and the third with soil only." The data supports the view that West African housing patterns and construction practices contributed to the techniques employed in African-Jamaican building. Perhaps the most significant of all was the house-yard layout, with yard space provided within a garden area, where decisions were made, family quarrels took place as in a play, friends entertained and all the family conversed together. (Higman: 1988)

One of the exciting discoveries was a small bent piece of sheet metal. It was being cleaned when it was identified as an oil lamp similar to those which are still in use in Ghana. It was bent at each of the four corners, with one corner folded over itself. A wick was placed in the metal fold. The lamp could provide illumination for hours.

In the kitchen area found behind each house at Drax Hall, the archae-ologists discovered many utensils found in food preparation: grinding stones, pieces of iron cooking pots, yabba fragments and a fireplace or hearth demarcated by several stones which, as in West African practice, were put around the fire to support the round bottom earthenware yabbas. (Armstrong: 1990)

Part of the yard area served as a garden plot. A survey of remnant vegetation growing at the site yielded 124 identifiable species. Over half (64) had known ethno-botanical uses in Jamaica, such as goatweed and susumba for colds and flu, ackee, guava, soursop. Ackee trees were found not only at Drax Hall but at all six sites in the preliminary survey. Perhaps clusters of ackee trees provide indications of the sites of slave villages.

Those conducting the survey at Drax Hall concluded that the archaeological data confirmed the presence of house-yard living areas which "provided a clear picture of an emerging culture within the slave settlement. This local expression of the emerging African-Jamaican culture system incorporates both continuity and change . . . It was created by the slaves in spite of the oppressive economic and political institution of slavery".

There were about 300 African slaves on the Drax Hall estate in the 1750s, with a small number of whites, ranging from manager and supervisors to skilled artisans. There were no Jamaicans. They were all exiles: the whites were homesick and often quarrelsome, surrounded by much larger groups of resentful slaves given to mocking the master or the slave driver, singing:

> It's time for man go home
> It's time for man an' it's time for beas'
>
> Time for man go home
> Da bird in de bush bawl qua qua
> Time for man go home
> Buckra bring ol' iron to break a man down,
> time for man go home,
> De monkey a bush bawl qua, qua, qua
> Time for man go home.

No one belonged or wished to belong. The name "Jamaica" was no more than a label. The impression of a place without homes and settlements was deepened by the fact that, as John Dennes wrote to the Earl of Wilmington (1718):

> The island may be divided into eight parts, four of which is good arable land, two other pasturage (or what is call savanna) which is uninhabitable, but the four parts that is good land tis not because people will not or do not care to go and settle there, but because the land is engrost by a few rich men there and in England, who have run

out vast tracts & obtained patents for them, but having so much are not able to settle them.

An example was the Modyford family. Sir Thomas Modyford, at one time lieutenant governor of the island, his two sons and his brother owned among them 21,218 acres in eight parishes. Governor Lynch also noted in 1683 that 3,000 patents had been issued for 1,080,000 acres. One hundred years later, when much of this land still lay undeveloped the local Assembly resisted attempts by the Colonial Office to withhold the patents because according to them "it would strike at the very existence of property". In 1739 Leslie claimed that two-thirds of the island was still uninhabited. Some 30 years later the situation had not changed.

This much we have learned from our visits, that the West Indian sugar-and-slave plantation brought into existence a special kind of society "created for sugar; Jamaican customs and culture were fashioned by sugar; sugar, for two hundred years, was the only reason behind Jamaica's existence as a centre for human habitation". (Hearne: 1965)

During those two centuries two other types of holdings were developed, the pens and the provision grounds. The sugar estate, pen and coffee mountain and the provision ground each marched to its own music, its

Crop Time
by Albert Huie

Courtesy of the National Gallery of Jamaica

The sugar estate: Bastion of white power

own lifestyle fashioned by the purpose that brought it into being, a technology and methods that sustained it, a changing rhythm of its own dictated by the seasons for breeding, weeding, nurturing, harvesting. The influence of the leader of the supervisors and labour force, the seasons bringing rain or drought, the changing mood of the landscape all stamped their impress on each place, yet held them inescapably within general confines of their own.

William Beckford captured the surge of energy on a sugar estate at crop time. He described how every object about the plantation, but especially around the buildings, appears at this time of year to be alive; and "the beating of the coppers, the clanking of the iron, the drivings of the logs, the wedging of the gudgeons, the repetition of the hammers, and the hooping of the puncheons are the cheerful precursors of the approaching crop".

The driving purpose was to produce sugar for export to Britain. African slaves, British managers, overseers, bookkeepers and the creditors advancing money in London and Liverpool all marched to the beat of sugar. The tempo rose to a fury of activity in crop-time. Unlike Beckford, Lady Nugent was overcome by the demonic energy and the supremacy of the machine:

> At each cauldron in the boiling-house was a man with a large skimmer upon a long pole, calling constantly to those below, attending the fire, to throw on more trash, for if the heat relaxes in the least all the sugar in the cauldron is spoiled. Then there were several negroes employed in putting the sugar into the hogsheads. I asked the overseer how often his people were removed. He said every twelve hours; but how dreadful to think of their standing twelve hours over a boiling cauldron and doing the same thing, and he owned to me that sometimes they did fall asleep, and get their poor fingers into the mill, and with a hatchet nearby always ready to sever the whole limb, as the only means of saving the poor sufferer's life I would not have a sugar estate for the world.

An estate boiling house

Beckford and Maria Nugent pictured more than a system of production process. They pictured a totally servile society. John Hearne's description is of compelling force: "There was nothing in West Indian plantation slavery, granted the fortuitous differences of colour, to distinguish it, say, from the pitiless exploitation of slaves in the Athenian silver mines or on the Roman estates. Expect for one factor: its total nature. Society in the ancient world, as in the American South, had always enough free citizens to think the thoughts, establish the customs, generate the moral climate that only flourish in liberty." (Hearne: 1965) But within a few years of Henry Morgan, who was no source of redemption, Jamaica was a slave society in which the slaves heavily outnumbered the free. Personal advantage, not the public good, was what counted; the exploitation of woman, man, land, not responsible conduct; profits, not morality; a society totally corrupted by its perception of nine-tenths of the total population as property, as an inferior form of human being.

The result was a society from which those whites who could afford to do so, fled. Higman notes that by 1775 about 30 per cent of the island's sugar estates were in the hands of absentees, many of whom were descendants of early settlers who returned to Britain after establishing their fortunes. The number of absentees rose after the decline in the plantation economy forced many to surrender their mortgaged properties to metropolitan merchants and bankers, beginning a trend to corporate ownership. By the time of emancipation 80 percent of the sugar estates were owned by absentees. (Higman: 1988) White planter society was steadily deteriorating to the point where it reached moral bankruptcy in 1865.

Free blacks and coloureds resided mostly in towns where many worked as shop assistants, servants, porters, and women worked as milliners and small shopkeepers selling preserves and provisions. A few even owned one or two slaves who took the goods for sale into the estates. Some, by dint of hard work, acquired wealth but they still could not gain acceptance from the whites. If, for instance, whites and non-whites attended a theatrical performance the two groups entered through separate doors and sat in different seats. Sometimes different performances were put on for the two groups. The same discrimination existed in churches where pews were reserved for whites while coloureds and blacks sat in the gallery.

They were barred from the legislature, from serving on the jury and from giving evidence against whites. Most of the offenders against blacks and coloureds were white, and the blacks and coloureds could not expect justice in the courts.

Nor was whiteness a bond between rich white, with big house, coach and horses, fine saddles and riding horse and a "walking bakra". No disgrace was considered so great "as that of a white man being seen walking on foot when away from his home; only such as have forfeited their character and were destitute would have been found in such a situation, so 'walking bakra' a name synonymous to beggar, coupled with that of vagabond." (Marly: 1828)

The plantocracy and all white owners of property, being heavily outnumbered by the blacks, kept legislative power in their hands and erected a protective wall of legislation around themselves. White landowners dominated both houses of the Legislature and the Vestry. At all times the disparity between the numbers of blacks and whites was great. In 1778 there were 18,420 whites to 205,000 blacks. At about this time coloureds, outnumbered whites by three to one. The whites felt their position threatened and to ensure that the free blacks and coloureds would not be socially or financially independent, made it a criminal offence in 1711 for them to hold public office, to work as supervisors on estates, or to engage in any activity that allowed them a measure of independence. In the following year, they were debarred from acting as navigators or from driving carriages for hire. However, by the mid seventeenth century the shortage of headmen was such that managers ignored this law, and when charged gladly paid the fines and continued to use the blacks and coloureds.

At one time, persons who had been freed or who had purchased their freedom but did not own land and at least 10 slaves were required to wear a badge with a blue cross on the right shoulder. This law was however not rigorously enforced and by 1790 it had been allowed to lapse.

All free persons were compelled to register in a parish and had to appear before a magistrate in order to obtain their certificate of freedom. Every conceivable stumbling block was put in their way to deprive them of their dignity. In 1733, legislation allowed a brown man and his family the same rights as a white man born of English ancestors but it usually required the brown man to marry a white person if his children were to inherit this status.

Even more oppressive was the plantocracy's deliberate use of the law to pervert justice and to leave the slave defenceless. One of the most shocking instances dates back to the year 1748 when the Jamaica Assembly rejected a bill that would have prohibited the mutilation or dismembering of slaves by their owners without the consent of a magistrate. Slavery was both cruel and arbitrary, and even humane owners were not likely to sacrifice an iota of authority over a slave since this would mean reducing authority over his property.

We have looked at the plantation in its physical setting, sometimes of tender, charming beauty, and we have considered briefly the purposes and ethos of the plantation, seeking in vain for signs of some civilizing influences.

The resident planter-attorneys were the real rulers of island society; they filled the public bodies – not only the nominated councils, but also the elected oligarchic assemblies. In the British colonies, planters also filled, in effect, most of the public offices, for though the more important officials were appointed by letters-patent in England, the actual work was commonly done by deputies in the islands who were remunerated by fees and who paid a rent to the principals. Office, like land, was thus a form of property, often owned by absentees. (Parry and Sherlock: 1958)

Each estate appeared to be a world in itself, self-sufficient with its own labour force in residence from skilled artisans to field gang, its own hospital, water-supply, its warehouse, cattle, mules, horses, its own drays and source of fuel. In reality, however, each slave plantation was a wealth-creating machine serving the rich, tied to finance houses and banks in London, Bristol, Liverpool; and linked through them with the Atlantic Trade System within which both the Plantation Trade – whether it be tobacco, sugar or cotton – and the Slave Trade operated. Just as the French colonies were a part of France so, as Edmund Burke declared, "the whole of the import and export trade revolved and circulated in the United Kingdom and was, so far as it affected profit, in the nature of a home trade as if the several countries of America and Ireland were all pieced on to Cornwall". Burke failed to see that Britain itself and Western Europe were functioning parts of an Atlantic trading system in which as Joseph Inikori, points out, the buying and selling of slaves to the Americas benefitted Europe by stimulating considerable mercantile skills, expert financing, improved shipbuilding, the production of new types of goods, an expanding market in the slave-producing regions of tropical Africa. "The creative responses of the economies of Atlantic Europe to the requirements of this function (the slave trade) formed an important part of the development in those economies." Inikori points to studies of the British economy for the period 1750-1807 when Britain dominated the buying and selling of slaves to the Americas and the demand for insurance cover led to the development of marine insurance in Britain as well to the expansion of credit facilities and banking. Further, it increased shipbuilding to meet the demand for ships; "between 1791 and 1807 about 15 per cent of all tonnage built in Britain was destined for the Guinea trade, about 95 per cent of which went into the shipping of slaves". Manufacturing also benefitted and expanded.

As we point to ways in which the West Indian sugar trade and African labour produced the wealth that financed the Industrial Revolution, it is appropriate to acknowledge the pioneering work of two West Indian scholars. C. L. R. James and Eric Williams. Williams "points repeatedly to the causal links between the slavery, near slavery, serfdom, quasi wage-earning in the New World and the rise of capitalism in Old Europe. The essence of mercantilism, he concludes, was slavery". Inikori shows how Britain, through its activities in the slave trade, benefitted not only from a growth of world trade in this period but in this most important aspect, that "the critical developments and the technological developments of the period were all called forth and made economic by the practical problems of production for an extended world market"; (Inikori: 1979) or, as a British economist points out, "Colonial trade introduced to English industry the quite new possibility of exporting in great quantities other than woollen goods to markets where there was no question of the exchange of manufactures for other manufactures. The process of industrialization in England from the second quarter of the eighteenth century was to an important extent a response to colonial demands for rails, axes, buckets, coaches, clocks saddles . . . and a thousand other things."

The pens and "coffee mountains" diversified Jamaica's system of large holdings without weakening the power of the plantocracy or the structure of slavery. They enshrined slavery. In contrast, the "Negro grounds", "Negro houses", and slowly growing "Negro marketing system" based on a chain of Sunday markets symbolise the cradle of freedom.

CHAPTER 15

Pens, provision grounds and higglers

The word "pen" derives from the Old English "penn", the name for to a small enclosure for sheep and other animals. In Middle English, "pennen" meant "to shut in", "pen in", "bolt in", with the Old English variants, "penn" meaning a "pin" or "peg", and the verbs "to pin", "to pin in", "to unpin". Early English colonists of the period 1660-90, finding Jamaica stocked with wild cattle, often spoke of "penning" those they caught.

In Jamaica the word was used early on to denote an enclosure for animals and also a farm or gentleman's estate. A law passed by the Jamaican legislature in 1695 decreed: "All owners of Neat cattle cows shall keep one white man at each Pen, and two white men at every Pen where-unto belongs above 200 Head of Cattle." We read also of "breeding pens" and "lowland pens". In 1801 Lady Nugent wrote of driving to "Lord B's Penn". By then "pen" meant a cattle farm or enclosure and also any country estate or gentleman's estate. For example, "at these pens or country houses, and on the land adjoining, they breed plenty of hogs, sheep, goats and poultry" (Marsden: 1788); or "his pen produces a super-abundance of maize and guinea corn". Others write of "these beautiful parklike estates called pens". (Cassidy, LePage: 1967) The English writer Anthony Trollope, who visited Jamaica in 1860, said: "Hardly any Europeans, or even white creoles, live in the town. They have country seats, pens as they call them, at some little distance." There was even a "penn punch", which consisted mainly of brandy and cherry brandy.

The names of the few surviving pens, such as Bamboo Pen, should be preserved and not forgotten as Admiral's Pen, Liguanea Pen, Rollington Pen have been. How wise and pleasing it would have been to have preserved two or three of the "little grass penns with good houses on them" that were dispersed about Half Way Tree, "and a small grass penn stocked with sheep and goats".

Another word taken from the farmers and peasants of England into Jamaica talk is "ground", with its Jamaican equivalent "grung". The word "ground" was commonly used in the dialects of South-West England and in parts of southern Scotland to mean "a field or piece of cultivated land". In Jamaica "grung" denotes a smallholding cultivated by the owner, as in "mi a go mi grung now", or as in the folktale, "Bredda Puss was a tie up him food fe leff him grung goh home." (Cassidy, LePage: 1967) On every slave plantation there was a portion of land called "Negro grounds", out of which each slave was allotted a portion to cultivate. In Jamaica-talk a cultivator today often speaks with affection and pride of "going grung", which he may describe with a smile as "mi piece of rockstone", for the "grung" may indeed consist very largely of saucers of red earth in between razor-edged rocks. Sometimes the word "mountain" was used for "grung" as well as in connection with crops, as in "coffee mountain". Lord Adam Gordon, in *Travels in America and the West Indies (1764-65)*, told how he "attended him also to his farm (Pen) and to his Mountain which is cool and pleasant".

A record of a conversation in St Ann in 1957 ran:

> "Where is Uncle Charles now?"
> "Ah mounten".
> "Doing what?"
> "Gone dig food".
> "What does he do with the food?"
> "Cook a mounten" (Cassidy, Le Page: 1967)

The pens and coffee mountains greatly expanded and diversified Jamaica's system of agriculture based on large holdings and committed to using African slaves and to protecting white power. We will visit Goshen, one of the largest pens, Union in St Ann, Montrose in St Mary, which was owned by Simon Taylor, Jamaica's wealthiest planter and largest slave holder, Salt Pond Hut and finally Vineyard, where we will observe the seasoning of the overseer Thomas Thistlewood. We will find that in Jamaica a pen was not always a small enclosure but was often a fairly large property.

The sugar plantation produced for export whereas the pen supplied the demands of the local market. Their programmes were not dictated by a monoculture, but moved to different rhythms, meeting the needs of a variety of animals, planning the care of pastures, picking the purple pimento berries at the proper time, sending cattle to distant markets, dispatching logwood chips to the port of shipment, selling grass and cordage to an urban market, buying worn-out cattle from an estate to fatten and butcher for local consumption.

Goshen Pen, at the foot of the Don Figueroa Mountains, situated between Horse Savanna and Bull Savanna, was famous for its livestock. In the days of carriages, buggies, kittareens and horse riding, customers often bought their ponies and mares from Goshen Pen.

In 1780 Goshen comprised 3,917 acres, including 12 pieces in guinea grass and 12 pieces in common grass. South of the pastures were a number of buildings, a dwelling house and garden circled by stables, a coach house, store houses, offices, a well, a sheep pen and further to the south slave houses, shown as 36 squares set out in regular lines. Scattered through the pastures were several wells and natural wells. The chance introduction of guinea grass in 1744 had greatly enriched Goshen and other pens through-out the island. A bag of the seeds had been given to George Ellis, twice chief Justice of Jamaica, as feed for some rare West African birds by the captain of a slave ship. The birds died shortly after and the seeds were thrown away in a field where they flourished. It was soon noticed that the cattle enjoyed the strange grass and, in the process of time, many penkeepers planted it.

"Fifty years later, at the time of emancipation, Goshen and Long Hill Pen had a combined population of 420 slaves. The total number of taxable livestock on the pens in 1832 was 1744, making the enterprise a very extensive one." (Higman: 1988)

Union Pen was in St Ann, about five miles inland from the north coast and near the border with St Mary. At the time of its survey in around 1825 it covered 1,130 acres, including 803 acres in guinea grass and 204 acres in wood and "Negro grounds". The pimento was concentrated close to the dwelling house and its barbecues, which were on a central hilltop that overlooked the slave houses. The proprietor was a coloured man, Benjamin Scott Moncrieffe, who belonged to a wealthy, educated family which had applied for special rights under slavery and had been welcomed in white society before abolition. His son Peter became a barrister and sat in the Assembly in the 1840s. Benjamin Moncrieffe also owned neighbouring Friendship and acquired Eltham and Benham Spring Estates. Union sold working cattle and fat cattle as well as pimento. Moncrieffe also tried to make money at the races at the popular courses of the day at Drax Hall, Montego Bay, Spanish Town and Kingston. His personal accounts show that he took with him some slaves as grooms, domestic servants and occasionally as jockeys. He paid his jockeys when they won and gave his "boys" allowances to cover living expenses and sometimes money to place bets. His total race meeting expenses in 1828 came to £110.14.3. He was lucky, for he won "the Free Prize by St Ann's beating Watt's Eclipse and Davis' Superior £100", and "£133.6.8 by St Ann's beating Watt's Eclipse, Davis Superior and Doctor Roper's Vanity over the Montego Bay course". In 1829, in Clarendon "Romp fell while running well".

Montrose in St Mary was a pen developed by a wealthy planter, Simon Taylor, to supply one of his sugar estates, Llanrumney, also in St Mary. Burrowfield Pen in St Thomas served his two sugar estates in that parish, Lyssons and Holland. He also owned Haughton Court in Hanover and Prospect, now Vale Royal. Montrose and Burrowfield Pens were not tied to trading only with the Taylor estates but were free to trade with others also.

Simon Taylor (1740-1813), was, we are told,

> in the habit of accumulating money, so as to make his nephew and heir . . . one of the most wealthy subjects of His Majesty. In strong opposition to Government at present and violent in his language against the King's Ministers for their conduct toward Jamaica. He has most extraordinary manners and lives principally with overseers of estates and masters of merchant vessels; but he has had an excellent education [he went to Eton], is well-informed and is a warm friend to those he takes by the hand. He is also very hospitable but is said to be most inveterate in his dislikes. (Nugent: 1939)

It was said that Taylor exercised greater influence in Jamaica, and for a longer period, than any other individual.

Lady Nugent, who charmed him into a measure of civility, wrote

> I cannot here avoid mentioning that Mr. Taylor is an old bachelor and detests the society of women . . . A little mulatto girl was sent into the drawing room to amuse me. She was a sickly delicate child, with straight light-brown hair, and very black eyes. Mr. T appeared very

anxious for me to dismiss her, and in the evening the house keeper told me she was his own daughter and that he had a numerous family, some almost on every one of his estates. (Nugent: 1939)

On 20 August 1802, the Lt Governor, George Nugent, had reported to the Colonial Office that Taylor,

a rich proprietor in Jamaica, who by a misrepresentation to the members of the House of Assembly, was the principal cause of their refusing to grant any further supplies to His Majesty for the Maintenance of the Military Establishment, (having stated to them that it was in contemplation in England to lay an additional Tax of 20's [20 shillings] on sugars and which he attempted to prove that the Planters cannot support any additional Burthens. (Nugent: 1939)

The real author of that report was supposed to be the West India merchant George Hibbert.

Salt Pond Hut was at the other end of the social scale from the gracious pens of the merchant-planters of Kingston, such as Prospect, with its long avenue of yokewood trees, 120 sheep and lambs to crop the grass and charm the guests, a few cows to supply milk, five mules and some horses for riding and for drawing a variety of chaises. Salt Pond Hut made money. The plan showed a property of 1,413 acres, a section of it running from Spanish Town to Passage Fort and Dawkins, Salt Pond Hut and another section along the Rio Cobre to where it met the Salt River. It contained 162 acres of Scots grass, a rough variety that grew on brackish land, and 78 acres of mangroves suitable for planting Scots grass.

Every day bundles of Scots grass were sent into Kingston, usually by sea, along with cordwood, corn and a few cattle, mules, horses and asses. The income from the sales for 1811 was £14,342, which was more than the historian Edward Long estimated that a typical sugar estate earned. The plan, drawn by John Fullarton in 1808, noted: "The place marked near Passage Fort shows the situation of several huts made by free negroes being a trespass on the property."

Vineyard Pen in Westmoreland, between Black River and Lacovia, was where Florentius Vassall appointed Thomas Thistlewood overseer in 1750. They fell out in the course of the year, and in 1751 Thistlewood went to Egypt Pen beyond Savanna-la-Mar where he remained until 1767, when he bought a small property of 160 acres between Egypt and Kirkpatrick Pen and established himself as the leading horticulturist in western Jamaica. He died in 1786.

Before coming to Jamaica Thistlewood had travelled to India, Brazil and western Europe. He kept a diary throughout his adult life. He knew nothing about managing slaves or a pen, or about Jamaican planter society, and as Douglas Hall observes in his edition of *Diary of a Westmoreland Planter*, these papers "are unique and provide a veritable treasure house of information on life and labour in slave-day Westmoreland . . . Thistlewood recorded events as they occurred but very seldom did he attempt to interpret or explain his or any other's actions." The diaries enable us to watch the encounter between a white stranger, totally inexperienced as an overseer, and a group of African slaves who became his teachers and companions, for he had little opportunity to mingle with other whites or to learn from other white overseers.

Vineyard Pen was over 1,000 acres but much of it was in swamp, through which a track led to the Vineyard barcadier or jetty, where supplies were loaded on to canoes or larger craft to save heavy carriage on the deeply rutted roadways.

Vineyard carried some cattle, horses, mules, asses, sheep, goats, pigs, ducks, turkeys and fowls; it produced timber, mostly mahogany and logwood, and a variety of trees and crops in the garden, as well as in the slaves provision grounds. Thistlewood lost no time in making some improvements: "the fattening pasture is about 23 acres, the plantain walk about 11½ or 12 . . . .The Negroes new cleared ground about 8 acres. The common road leading from my house to the stile into the corn ground is about 1,568 yards". He increased the cultivation of foodstuffs and the corn walk became a plantain walk which in January 1751 carried about 1,800 plantain trees. The slaves possibly had about 1,800 plantain trees also.

The housing for the penkeeper and slaves was modest. Thistlewood had cracks in the walls of his house mended. "When mud walls are sufficiently dry and very much cracked in this country, they mix water, soft cow dung and wood ashes with a small quantity of fire mould, till it be as scarce to run out of the hand. With this they rub the walls once or twice over, and it will fill and cover all the cracks."(Hall: 1989)

It is probable that the slaves lived in houses like the one Thistlewood built for his mistress Marina before he left Vineyard. It was of wattle and plaster, thatched, with two connecting rooms, one 9 feet by 7 feet, the other 6½ feet by 7 feet. The larger had a single door leading out.

From the time of his arrival Thistlewood became involved in chronicling the seasons:

> In St Elizabeth (above us) the rain, or season, that comes in July, August, September is called the great spring, and the corn that is gathered about Christmas, the year corn. The rain that comes in March, April, May, the crab rain from the great density of land crabs which then run at night – and the crop of corn which is gathered in July, the parrakeet corn, because they then abound.

As Hall points out,

> The emphasis on land for food production reflected the hard conditions of cultivation in south St Elizabeth and the small possibility of finding supplementary supplies for neighbouring properties. Here provision grounds apparently provided no marketable surpluses moving from neighbouring estates to Vineyard or vice-versa, and there is, remarkably, no mention whatever of the existence in the area of a slave-supplies Sunday Market. (Hall: 1959)

Thistlewood had to learn to eat what the slaves ate; not the 26 capons, one young roast cock, 20 laying hens, three maiden pullets, 16 young fowls, one laying duck, two squabs, one musk melon, 19 sweetsops, that he sent by road on 12 December to the Vassalls.

> He made intriguing discoveries: "On 10 July 1750 have boiled goats milk (which is very rich) every morning to breakfast; eat some Docono, made of plantain, very good (17 July 1750); at dinner had pepper pot of callaloo and prickly pear with some ochro. Had for supper hominy, it eats like cracked oatmeal pretty much, made of Indian corn beat and cracked; had some Cayya boiled for dinner to my beef.

This may refer to a condiment made of "Cayan pepper", or, less likely, to a preparation of a healing weed now called "strong back" or to a type of root crop similar to eddo which is called taya.

There were 42 slaves when Thistlewood took up his duties as overseer in July 1750. The diaries show that 13 of them were "new", that is, recently acquired. They included Accubah, a Coromanti, a field slave who had been given a new hoe. About two months earlier she had been whipped, with Mary and Mr Banton's Will, for having helped the boy to escape custody on the night of Wednesday 10 October; Betty or Accramah, a new Negro, a Coromanti . . . Christie or Gesse, a new negro field worker, a Congo; Cynthia or Naccuma, a Bambarah Negro, "what the Coromantees call Crappah or Temme donko being brought into this country young; Deborah or Binda, new, a Congo who at first worked in the field; Jenny or Cragua, a new negro; Marina or Worree, new, a Congo," Thistlewood's mistress up to the end of his year at Vineyard. He asked Dick to build a house for her. Mary or Adomah, new, a Congo who had been housed with Charles, but in May 1751 her provision ground was separated from his "as they can't agree and he uses her very ill".(Hall: 1988)

Attention was given to the provision grounds. In addition to the old and new grounds Thistlewood developed the Negro cleaned ground, bushed and cleaned by the slaves, each of whom received at least 100 square feet. It was tough going, but, as a slave informed Thistlewood, "There were tricks in the trade for if the hands blister by hard work, piss upon them and it will harden them."

They worked at these tasks and received their separate allocations. Thoughts of the homeland must have come to the new slaves; memories of the men going about the traditional African tasks of clearing the fields that had lain fallow with bush and making yam heaps, with women and boys helping; men planting the yams and after sprouting tying the vines to the poles to keep them off the soil; the women hoeing and weeding the fields of yams and, after the men had harvested them, carrying them to the yam barn with high wooden racks built on the edge of the village. This background of tradition, the inherited skills of generations of West African farmers and the accustomed crops, the corn, yams, plantains, beans, peas, made the provision grounds a part of Africa, the only places in Jamaica where Africans were free to make their own decisions, reap their own crops and enter into the money economy by selling the livestock and vegetables they produced.

> The word "higgler" came from England to Jamaica; it is rarely used there, whereas it is in common use in Jamaica to denote a seller of any kind of small produce or goods; formerly an itinerant peddler, now also one who brings produce into a market to sell. (Cassidy, LePage: 1967) The word "higgler" is related to the English "to hack" and "to haggle", to argue with a vendor. "Haggle" has the variant "higgle". A higgler forms the link between the isolated small farmers and the market, usually a woman of the neighbourhood or a nearby area, who walks and buys produce to take to the market. Some country higglers spread their goods in the market and sell directly to house buyers, and others sell to town higglers, town residents who rent stalls in the markets where they buy at wholesale and sell at retail. (Katzin: 1959)

The expert higgler at Vineyard Pen was Phibbah. Other slaves, Joan a washerwoman for example, kept and sold pigs and poultry as well as produce. Phibbah, however, deserves special mention. A woman of great reliability and dignity and not afraid to speak her mind, she seems to have engaged in business and to have accumulated property of her own. On 6 August 1750 she bought a sow from Simon for 3 cobbs and a boar piggy for a crown. She paid for them with a pistole (then equal to one pound, three shillings and nine pence Jamaica currency). She was a trader in the tradition of the West African women. Sometimes, usually once a month, she, with Scipio as escort, went out on the road. They went out, for instance, on Wednesday 17 April 1751 and returned to Vineyard on Monday 22 April. Financed by the pen, Phibbah had sold 58 yards of "garlix" and 9 yards of "across bar" cloth at 7 beads a yard and 44 yards of "check" at 5 beads a yard. She brought home 689 beads or twenty-one pounds ten shillings and sevenpence half-penny in Jamaica currency. After a later trip on which she apparently had had some difficulty, Thistlewood gave her a note: "Gave Phibbah, a ticket that she may not be molested, thus Vineyard Pen. June 5, 1751. The Bearers hereof, (a Negro man and woman named Scipio and Phibbah in company) belong to the Vineyard Penn and are the property of Florentius Vassall Esquire by whose orders they go out with cloth to sell, which is certified by me, Thomas Thistlewood." (Hall: 1989)

The Sunday market was the selling place for produce from the provision ground and for stock reared by the slaves, a good fat farrow for example of small pigs, milch goats, kids, capons, pullets, bananas, sweet potatoes, peas, corns, avocado pears, yams and twisted tobacco.

For the plantation the provision ground was a necessity. Feeding the growing army of slaves was a priority. No provision ground, no salted fish, meant no sugarcane fields, no sugar trade. Bryan Edwards argued that it was better to export sugar and import food because one acre of his canefield would buy more Indian corn than could be raised on five times that area of land and pay the freight as well. Ground provision had to be grown, and in quantity. Hungry belly walked the land and thousands died when war or hurricane disrupted the food supply.

The English Government enlarged the local supplies by importing food plants. Taro a root brought to the Americas by the Portuguese proved to be a valuable supplement. So, in Jamaica especially, was the ackee, brought in from West Africa in 1776 to be combined with salted codfish. The mango, an Asiatic tree, added flavour and invaluable vitamins to a heavy diet of starch. The breadfruit entered in the 1790s but was fed only to pigs for its first 50 years. Then Jamaicans discovered what they had been missing in the "yellow heart". Other life-savers included the "red afu" (a dark yellow yam) and the "white afu" (a pale yellow), the mozella, "Madam sit-down" (a Portland yam with a big round bottom) and the St Vincent yam, called "come here fe help we" because it gives an early crop and stays in the earth for a long time without going bad. With these were various versions of the taro or coco known as hog-taya, or eddo. Sir Hans Sloane wrote in 1725: "Tayas or Eddos are eaten in Jamaica, and cause a heat in the throat, called commonly there scratching the throat, and this when well-boiled." Among other varieties are the purple coco and the delicious commander coco. Its other names are "leff man" and "leff back" because it does not disintegrate in the pot.

These names illustrate how the provision ground and the yard gave rise to folk names rich in laughter and sparkle, such as: "scissors tail" for a variety of sweet potato with split leaves; "full pot" for another variety that swells and fills the pot; "tie-leaf" and "blue-drawers" for the ducknu, wrapped in plantation or banana leaf and boiled or baked. In the process the leaf turns bluish green.

The male and female cultivators through the provision grounds and the rural and urban higglers through the chain of Sunday markets on which an internal marketing system was based, worked without access to education and risk-financing and established a system of smallholder agriculture complementary to the large plantations. The system was West African in origin, as this account shows:

> The Yoruba enjoy trading and huge markets with over a thousand sellers are a common sight. Yoruba traders are conspicuous as far afield as Accra and Abidjan, Bamako and Duagadogou. The nineteenth century travellers reported meeting large caravans of traders passing from one region of Nigeria to another; today the collection of export crop and the distribution of goods imported by sea are both important. There is also an extensive trade in local foodstuffs.
>
> The marketing process is complex. One woman visits a farmer on his land and buys a headload of yams; she sells these to a second woman in a small rural market. Then at a larger rural market – held every four days – the latter sells to a woman wholesaler from the town, who later resells to women who will sit in the town's night market (among the Oyo) and sell to the consumers. In a similar manner, imported goods travel from the warehouse of the expatriate firm to the rural consumer. Most four or eight day markets are held in cycles, the women visiting each in turn. (Lloyd: 1965)

In Jamaican towns there was a sharper sexual division of work than in the country parts where both women and men were cultivators. In the ports the men were artisans, seamen, coopers, butchers, fishermen, droghers and the like. Some of the women were in domestic service as cooks, nannies and washerwomen, but they dominated marketing and they became a powerful force, as we can see by looking at early nineteenth-century Kingston, where in 1817 there were 17,798 slaves, 9,865 of them females. Of a total slave-holding population of 3,499 slave holders, 1,957 were female. Female slaveholders owned a total of 5,900 female slaves.

The picture was similar in other urban centres in Jamaica. For 26 towns in Jamaica for the years 1829-32 there was a ratio of 83.29 males to 100 females. The closest to that of Kingston in favour of females was 90.2: 100 for the parish of Vere. There were also more Africans than creoles in the urban slave population, the figures for 1817 (ten years after the abolition of the slave trade), being 9,147 compared with 8,651 creoles. It is estimated that 66 per cent of all urban slaves worked as domestics in Kingston, and that many female slaves were involved almost exclusively in higglering and hawking goods about the streets, generally for the profit of the mistress.

Whatever they marketed, the urban slaves generally enjoyed a fairly independent existence and were always responsible for dealings in cash or kind. "The seller was involved in a series of commercial transactions which could not be directly controlled by the owner and which provided experience of a way of life separate from the slave condition." (Higman: 1988)

The world of the higgler was a hard one, for the authorities disliked their marketing activities. Street vendors were frequently apprehended and fined. Newspapers carried regular reports on penalties imposed: "two negroes . . . fined in the mitigated penalty on ten shillings, five pence each for hawking and peddling goods through the street".

As marketing activities increased, the authorities were constantly engaged in regulating public markets and providing new facilities. In 1817 the Kingston Common Council proposed "suppressing the irregular

Slave higglers

marketplace on the parade for provisions and goods coming in from the country for sale". (Simmonds: 1987)

Slaves travelled over land and by sea to markets and estates to sell their goods. The authorities in Spanish Town complained bitterly in 1822 about the streets being greatly infested by a set of hawkers and peddlers from Kingston to "the great injury of the trading part of the community and in the very eye of the police". Kingston Harbour had its market canoes, which were not always safe. In March 1819 several women and children drowned when a market canoe going from Passage Fort to Port Royal upset. Four slaves travelling by market canoe from Port Henderson were more fortunate. When their market canoe overturned in a sudden squall, sailors from the Sapphire man-of-war rescued them. Their provisions went to the bottom.

Phibbah, Scipio and Dick of Vineyard Pen and throughout the generations, other higglers, peddlars and itinerant traders prepared the economic foundations for a society of free smallholders. Today's higglers and peddlars keep us alive with the islandwide food distribution system that the early higglers established, and enrich our lives with their concept of a market as a "gathering place for kinsfolk, district folk, the whole community; around market, school and church the life of the whole district revolved".

Higglering calls for a range of skills. Along with the counting and change-making, they must develop what they call profit-making techniques.

> This involves the ability to acquire steady customers, buy high quality produce, to barter, stand ground, to judge one type of customer from the next. The higgler must also learn to keep track of her money, to distinguish between money which is overhead and that which is profit. She must acquire the skill of offering a little extra in order to attract and maintain a steady customer, yet at the same time not give away all her profit. She must acquire the skill to maintain a delicate balance in this area. (Durant-Gonzales: 1976)

The first task in the markets is to establish one's own spot: "Once space is acquired, each higgler maintains her spot week in and week out. It becomes her business address, the place with which she is identified and at which she is easily located by customers and friends. Miss Addy is a street higgler who sells from the sidewalk and says that her location is always reserved for her. Over an eight-month period, I observed her and 50 other street higglers selling from the same sidewalk location.

I was told by higglers that market space is maintained through a system of mutual recognition which is based on the higgler establishing the fact that she is there each week. If her space is occupied upon her arrival, says Miss Addy, "The women just 'small up' [make room]." In the event that a woman is coming to market for the first time, the policy is that the other higglers 'small up' and make room for the additional person. One veteran of 25 years in the higglering business explained: "We all have to sell, and all the women know and understand and accept this. For each of us must make a living." (Durant-Gonzales: 1976)

An urgent priority is to establish staunch customers, which is based on unspoken loyalties between higgler and customer. In her study Durant-Gonzales describes the relationship as defined by Miss Addy, who told how "A customer would come together well". In the words of another higgler, "If my staunch customers buy yams from me each week, I must have yams for these customers. Even if I am not selling yams, I will buy them from another higgler just so that my staunch customers get them." (Durant-Gonzales: 1976)

During slavery while higglers and male peddlars were building an economic foundation that was bonded together by common loyalties, they were building stable family units in response to the plantation system of moral degradation. In these various ways the African-Jamaicans of the plantation grounds, the male and female traders, the higglers laying claim to market space through their efforts to better themselves, chiselled away at the base of plantation slavery and modified the whole system by establishing rights through custom and usage.

They added an even more significant achievement by their response to the destruction of the traditional African codes governing family relationships and the kinship system. The functions of the natural father as protector, provider, counsellor and model were usurped by the slaveholder who sexually exploited the women, using them as breeders of slaves. The Africans, barred from the religous rites of the church and denied Christian marriage, responded by establishing basic family units through common-law unions. Through this response to the marginalisation of the natural father and the degradation of motherhood they maintained a form of social structure that reflected moral and ethical principles and satisfied fundamental human needs. For this the white slave-holding society with brazen hypocrisy branded them as immoral, but our poets, George Campbell among them, remind us of the significance of what they achieved.

> No degradation resented by our fathers
> That is not glory unto us.
> No suffering of our ancestors
> That is not part of our Emancipation.

CHAPTER 16

Into a new age

The liberation struggles of the 18th century did not weaken the sugar-and-slave plantation. They did not diminish the trade in African labour. The great house appeared as formidable a symbol of white power as it ever had been. The slave ships sailed into Kingston harbour as frequently as they had always done. Sugar was doing well. In the 25 years from 1751 to 1775 Jamaica imported 172,500 Africans compared with 128,000 in the preceding quarter of a century. In spite of the fact that they were known as leaders of rebellions, 39 per cent came from the Gold Coast.

For the Jamaican sugar planter the skies were clear. The mills would continue grinding, the slaves continue working, the money continue flowing. It appeared that nothing would weaken the basic principles that slavery was a necessity and that one human being had the right to buy another. No one in his senses would have predicted that in 1776 the North American colonies would declare their independence from England, that the French Revolution would break out in 1788, that the Napoleonic wars would tear Europe apart between 1795 and 1815, and that steam power, industrialisation, science and technology would begin to displace the humanities as the foundation of civilisation in the 1780s.

The slaves watched and registered change in their minds. They were illiterate, but illiteracy is not a synonym for stupidity. The planters and overseers often made the mistake of underestimating the intelligence of the slave, his capacity for understanding, his skill in behaving as if he were indeed a "bungo" or simpleton.

The white planters and merchants, like the ancient Romans, who usually called their slaves, "little one" or "boy", and considered themselves infinitely superior to these "overgrown children", looked with contempt on the private lives of the blacks and on their intellectual ability. It was safe to discuss the rights of man in their presence for they certainly were unable to understand. The planters should have remembered that during the 1730s plantation slaves had established efficient information networks with the maroons.

Often the informers of the slaves were the great house people themselves. Baron de Wimpffen, who visited St Domingue in 1790, at a time when the rights of man and liberty were fashionable table talk, expressed alarm at the behaviour of the whites. "Surrounded by mulattoes and negroes, they indulge themselves in the most imprudent discussions on liberty etc. To discuss the 'Rights of Man' before such people, what is it but to teach them that power dwells with strength, and strength with numbers."

We turn at this point from the Jamaica sugar plantations to Europe and search the decade of the 1760s for the signs of radical change, some at that time no larger than the outline of a man's hand against a distant sky, some no more than the publication of a book, the announcement of an invention. Nothing seemed powerful enough to fracture the structure of mercantilism, the rigidities of a feudal class structure based on the rights of the propertied and the obligations of labouring classes and serfs.

The signs were to be found in the preaching of an obscure Anglican priest, John Wesley, in the ideas and reasoning of two philosophers, François-Marie Voltaire and Jean-Jacques Rousseau, in the reflections of Adam Smith, a Scottish professor of philosophy at Cambridge, in his *Wealth of Nations*, in the experiments of a Scottish engineer, James Watts, about ways of harnessing steam power, and in James Hargreaves' use of technology to produce the spinning jenny, all reminders that ideas are more powerful than an army with banners.

We will also consider ways in which the Evangelical Movement and the Enlightenment touched and changed the world of the African-Jamaican on his remote plantation, destroyed slavery and the West India sugar monopoly in England, and established white-black alliances based on religious conviction and the acceptance of the principle of human rights. We will refer also to the scientific and technological advances of the age, the emergence of an English working class and their involvement in the passing of the Act of Emancipation.

The Evangelical Movement was a response to the preaching of John Wesley. In May 1738 Wesley "felt his heart grow strangely warm within him" at a meeting with Moravian Brethren in London, and in that moment of conversion received from God an assurance of salvation through faith in Christ alone. Up to the time of his death in 1791 John Wesley, with his brother Charles, and for years with the help also of his friend George Whitfield, delivered this message of personal salvation to the people of England, usually at crowded open-air meetings.

John Wesley's passionate message and the hymns written by Charles, such as "Hark, hark my Soul", "Jesu, lover of my Soul" and any of the 6,000 hymns he wrote, brought England to its knees in prayer. His message reached the poor, the outcast.

> Outcasts of men to you I call,
> Harlots and publicans and thieves.
> He spreads His arms to embrace you all,
> Sinners alone His grace receives.
> No need for him the righteous have,
> He came the lost to seek and save.

So widespread and so fervent was the religious revival that by the 1790s the old dissenting churches, such as the Baptists, were having their own religious revival. The Baptists founded a missionary society in 1792. The London Missionary Society was founded in 1795 and the British and Foreign Bible Society in 1803.

The revival also inspired a reform movement within the Church of England, which up to then had been somnolent and complacent. Among the reformists was William Wilberforce. But slavery had not yet become a moral issue. Granville Sharp, a terrier of a little man who never let go, made it so. Sharp took up the case of a slave, James Somersett, whose master lived in England. Somersett fell ill and was turned adrift by his master. With Sharp's help he recovered. On his recovery his master claimed him. Sharp resisted the claim. The case finally went before Lord Mansfield, Chief Justice of England, who on 22 July 1772 decided: "The

Early Moravian church and mission school

state of slavery is of such a nature that it is incapable of being introduced on any reasons, moral or political, but only by positive law . . . It's so odious that nothing can be suffered to support it, but positive law. Whatever inconveniences, therefore, may follow from a decision, I cannot say this case is approved by the law of England and therefore the black must be discharged."

As a result of this ruling all 10,000 of the slaves held in England at the time gained their freedom. Encouraged by the ruling, the abolitionists intensified their efforts. The Quakers formed an anti-slavery society and were joined, among others, by Granville Sharp, Thomas Clarkson and James Ramsay, a clergyman who had been in the West Indies for 19 years and spoke with great feeling about the cruelty of slavery. In 1784, Wilberforce was converted and became a member of the Saints, the name given to a group of god-fearing English abolitionists. Having read Clarkson's book attacking the slave trade, Wilberforce decided to devote his life to destroying the system.

Wilberforce, Clarkson and Sharp made a gifted team. Clarkson was a brilliant publicist and mobiliser of public opinion, Sharpe was known for his bristling tenacity, Wilberforce for his charm, eloquence, gifts of leadership, popularity and dedication. Of course they had limitations. William Hazlitt, the English essayist, pointed to the lack of a coherent philosophy of benevolence in one who protected property and saw poverty as due to laziness, and he mocked at "the gentry, Mr. Wilberforce and the Prince Regent and all those who governed . . . by no other principle than truth and no other wish than the good of mankind! This puff will not take with us! We are old birds and not to be caught with chaff."

The fact is that Wilberforce committed his talents, time and strength to persuading parliament to abolish the slave trade. Napoleon got in the way but Wilberforce pressed on, and for the first time in their history the African-Jamaicans discovered that they had allies and friends in the world of white power.

Among the first were the Moravian missionaries who started work in Jamaica in 1754 at the invitation of two absentee proprietors, William Foster and Joseph Barham. They gave 300 acres of land at Bogue in St Elizabeth for a mission station. They accepted the system of slavery and kept slaves but they showed kindness to the slaves. Malaria, yellow fever and dysentery struck down the missionaries. Jamaicans remember these Moravian missionaries, and those who followed them and founded Bethlehem College at a later date.

In 1787 members of the Clapham Sect used their political influence to found the first English colony in Africa by organising and financing a company to establish Sierra Leone as a home for freed slaves. Then, in 1788, one of the abolitionists, Bolben, horrified at the conditions he had seen on a slave ship in the Thames, introduced a bill in parliament to limit the number of slaves that ships might carry in proportion to their tonnage.

Public interest was mounting. Anti-slavery pamphlets maintained the pressure. So did the celebrated potter, Josiah Wedgwood, whose cameo of a negro pleading for freedom, the chains hanging from his wrists and fettered legs, caught public attention. Anti-slavery groups were organised. Hundreds of petitions were sent to the House of Commons, the first time that this form of large-scale public pressure had been tried. A motion was passed in the House for the abolition of the slave trade in four years. The four years became 14. In that period, when the Napoleonic wars demanded the full attention of the government and the planters staged counter-attack after counter-attack, Wilberforce stuck to his task. Year after year he grimly moved his resolution for the abolition of the slave trade. In 1805 the Commons passed the bill but the Lords deferred it. At last in 1807 the bill was passed and on 1 January 1808 the Act for the Abolition of the Slave Trade came into force.

This victory told the West Indian planters that the forces of change were working against them despite a declaration by the Legislature of the Leeward Islands "that no power shall endeavour to deprive us of obtaining slaves from Africa". No mouse ever roared more loudly.

The Evangelical Movement exerted a powerful influence in Jamaica through two black preachers, George Isle and Moses Baker. Towards the end of the War of Independence in 1782, a number of loyalist families moved from the United States with their slaves to Canada, the Bahamas and Jamaica. Among those who came to Jamaica were two black ex-slaves, George Lisle and Moses Baker, who founded there the native Baptist Church. George Lisle's preaching attracted large numbers of people, and the government prosecuted him for uttering seditious words. The charge failed but he was thrown into prison on a trumped-up charge of debt. Moses Baker, and Lisle after his release, continued their ministry and built up a large following.

Lisle and Baker hold a place of honour in the story of the Jamaican people. They did two things that neither the Moravians nor the English Baptist and Methodist missionaries who came after them, could have done. They planted the seed of an indigenous evangelical movement amongst the people, blending the Christian message with traditional African modes of worship, including spirit possession dancing, the clapping of hands and swaying of the body. Like Africans, African-Jamaicans are deeply religious. No aspect of their story is more important than their religion, folk beliefs, native churches. It cries out for closer and

Pens, provision grounds and higglers

THE STORY OF THE JAMAICAN PEOPLE

fuller study by our own and other scholars, especially African theologians and philosophers. The work of George Simpson and of other recent writers on religious movements indicate how much more needs to be undertaken, and urgently. Such efforts are beyond the scope of this book but we would be at fault if we did not indicate the importance of the missionary work done by these two black Baptist preachers, through whom the Evangelical Movement first touched African-Jamaicans. The Moravians had set an example of religious brotherhood, but Lisle and Baker established a religious movement through itinerant preachers, "daddys" or deacons, and warners, men and women who felt called "to go through the villages and fields for to warn them".

This use of assistant preachers was in itself a significant development. It was a "ranking" of the slaves by blacks and not by white owners, masters, overseers; an appointment of slaves by the preachers to guide, counsel and convert, not to act as drivers whose symbol of authority was the whip. Their symbol was a sacred book that contained messages of brotherhood and love. Through their preaching George Lisle and Moses Baker defined the mission of the Christian church in Jamaica and gave it a system of organisation based on small chapels and deacons. They brought within the reach of the people two books that soon became the treasured library of the African-Jamaican people, the Bible and a Hymn Book. Baker himself was prosecuted, early in his ministry, for quoting from this hymn in his sermon:

> Shall we go on in Sin
> Because Thy grace abounds,
> Or crucify my Lord again
> And open all His Wounds?
> We will be slaves no more
> Since Christ has made us free,
> Has nailed our tyrants to the cross
> And bought our liberty.

Driven by this vision, teams of "daddys" and preachers were active amongst the enslaved. Some who were not licensed became itinerant preachers. Adam, for example, was a creole runaway slave: "a fisherman by trade, much pitted in the face with the small pox, short and well-made, and will attempt to pass for free; being a great smatterer in religious topics, has been lately converted by Parson Lisle, and is always preaching or praying; he was seen on board a ship this morning, going to Old Habour, and no doubt will sail out with her when she is completely loaded".

Lisle and Baker were Baptists. So were most of the English missionaries, Knibb, Burchell, Phillipo and others who enter our story in the following chapter. The term "dissenters" covers many diverse groups but we use it here for two of the oldest, the Quakers and the Baptists, both of whom were committed to the principles of self-government with a great measure of local autonomy for each congregation, in contrast to the established Church of England with its principle of centralised authority. Lisle and Baker were committed to these principles of greater autonomy for the local churches so there was no basic conflict between them and the English Baptists over church organisation.

The English Baptists had no problem, for example, in appointing slaves as deacons. Indeed, they could not have carried out their work without them. The black missionaries prepared the way for the Europeans in the matter of church organisation, and by ministering directly to the African-Jamaicans, they established typical Baptist linkages between working-class people and their church. Further, Lisle and Baker, because they had experienced slavery, passed on a tradition of passionate concern for the enslaved and for the mass of the people and the tradition of a church where African-Jamaicans were at home and participated both in managing its religious affairs and also in maintaining the principles of freedom, equality, brotherhood. In maintaining this tradition William Knibb and his colleagues were indispensable, but the first steps were taken by Lisle and Baker and carried on by Baptist churches and also of the religious and revivalist churches of George William Gordon, Paul Bogle, the prophet Alexander Bedward and the Rastafarians.

Nor should we forget that the African-Jamaicans, without allies, had done a great deal to modify slavery, to lay the foundations of a free society with a substantial infrastructure for food production and internal trading. The forces of change began to touch their lives in the years when they were reaching the limits of what was possible. Without powerful allies it would have been difficult for them to achieve more than they did. The Evangelical Movement exerted a powerful influence which, strengthened by the Enlightenment, became a liberating force.

The Evangelical Movement quickened conscience whereas the Enlightenment quickened minds and drove men to storm the barricades of tyranny. Each was a transforming force, but historical forces do not operate in isolation. Each reinforces the other. We are looking at an age in which they combined to spawn revolutions and counter-revolutions, collisions between working class and propertied class, noble and serf; and, in the world of ideas, an often brutal collision between patriotism and liberty, between the natural rights of man to political representation and the power of "men of riches, men of estates, to make man a perpetual slave"; a world of conflict between "levellers" who the leveller Colonel Rainsborough declared, "the poorest he that is in England hath a life to live as the greatest he . . . every man that is to live under a government ought first by his own consent to put himself under that government . . . I should doubt whether he was an Englishman or no, that should doubt of these things" (Woodhouse: 1951) and on the other hand a vision of the mass of the English people as inferior, depraved, degraded. As the Duchess of Buckingham firmly assured the Countess of Huntington, the Methodist doctrines were "most repulsive and strongly tinctured with impertinence and disrespect toward their superiors in perpetually endeavouring to level all ranks and to do away with all distinctions. It is monstrous to be told you have a heart as sinful as the common wretches that crawl on the earth". (E. P. Thompson: 1963). The lesson for us is that the confrontation took place in the stinking courts and alleys of London and of Paris and also in the slave plantations of the Caribbean. The great moulding forces of this period, whether generated by appeals to conscience, to intellect or by technological advance, make it abundantly clear that the story of the Jamaican people is both an essential part of the story of African-Americans and in many ways has parallels with the European working class.

The Enlightenment broke into the Caribbean with hurricane force. Rousseau and Voltaire were not cloistered European philosophers remote from us. They stoked a revolution in New England in 1776, another in Paris in 1788, yet another in St Domingue, in 1792. Their teachings may even have influenced the second Maroon War in St James in 1795. It is time to turn to them.

The Enlightenment emerged as a major trend, a widespread intellectual awakening, in the decade of the 1760s. The most prominent leaders were Voltaire and Rousseau. In his *Social Contract* published in 1762, Rousseau argued that, by an implied contract, the State is bound to guarantee the rights and liberties of the subject. He maintained that "natural man" was essentially good but was corrupted by the introduction of property, science and culture. His views on the rights of man strongly influenced leaders of the American War of Independence, such as Thomas Jefferson and Benjamin Franklin; leaders of the French Revolution, including Robespierre; leaders of the Romantic Movement in Europe and German philosophers such as Kant and Goethe. In 1763 Voltaire's play *Saul* attacked sections of the Old Testament and then, in 1764, his *Pocket Philosophical Dictionary*, denounced oppression, untruth and dogma.

The words of these two philosophers sounded throughout Western Europe and the American colonies. Voltaire's words were trumpet calls: "Faith consists in believing when it is beyond the power of reason to believe. It is not enough for a thing to be possible for it to be believed", or again, "I disapprove of what you say but I will defend to the death your right to say it," (attributed to Voltaire) and "If God did not exist it would be necessary to invent him." So did Rousseau's powerful "Man was born free and everywhere he is in chains," and his warning that "The strongest is never strong enough to be always the master, unless he transforms his strength into rights, and obedience into duty" and "Nature never deceives us, it is always we who deceive ourselves."

Freedom, the rights of man, equality and brotherhood became realities. Thomas Jefferson, in drafting the American Declaration of Independence wrote: "We hold these truths to be self-evident, that all men are created equal, that they are endowed by their creator with inherent and inalienable rights, that among these are life, liberty and the pursuit of happiness." The Enlightenment fashioned the battle cries for the French Revolution with the words "Liberty, fraternity, equality".

The first great explosion took place in Paris on 14 July 1789 when a Paris mob stormed and took the Bastille, a prison fortress and symbol of royal tyranny in the centre of the city. Simon Schama in his work on the French Revolution describes the explosion. "The bringing together of political patriotism and social unrest – anger with hunger – this was (to borrow the revolutionaries' favourite electrical image) like the meeting of two live wires. At their touch a brilliant incandescence of light and heat occurred. Just what and who would be consumed in the illumination was hard to make out."

There were years of debate in western Europe – and especially in France – about the rights of man. In the French Caribbean colonies the white colonists, landowners and slave owners loudly demanded liberty, meaning the right to run the colony as they wished, as well as to deny liberty to the mulattoes and to the blacks. In Paris the Friends of the Blacks, a society recently formed on the pattern of the English anti-slavery society, campaigned on behalf of the mulattoes.

The all-white colonial assemblies in St Domingue, Martinique and Guadeloupe sent six representatives to the French National Assembly, which under intense pressure in its decree of 15 May provided that mulattoes born of free persons, if qualified in other respects, should have the right to vote for the provincial and colonial assemblies which had been established four years earlier. The St Domingue planters reacted with cries of "Secede" just as Jamaican planters were to do some 20 years later.

The white colonists refused to obey the decree. The mulattoes in St Domingue demanded their rights. Some took up arms. The ruling whites executed Oge, one of the mulatto leaders, by breaking him on the wheel. As a result, revolutionary opinion in France turned against the planters.

The white colonists were determined to keep political power in their hands. They were adamant that they would not share it with the mulattoes, for, as one of their leaders declared, "The mulattoes themselves are but pawns in a larger game. For once our slaves suspect that there is a power other than their masters . . . if once they see that the mulattoes have successfully invoked this power and by its aid have become our equals – then France must renounce all hope of preserving her colonies."

While the white colonists tried to bar the gate and the mulattoes struggled to break though, the slaves were active with nocturnal rituals and oath-taking. In August 1791, drums, discreet but insistent, dominated the night, speaking from secret places in the dark forest to the Africans on the plantations of the great northern plain.

Desperate, determined Africans gathered in the forest in a circle around their leader, a Jamaican called Boukman, while the throbbing of the drums increased, keeping time with their quickening heartbeats. They drank a blood oath, swearing to be loyal to each other, and then Boukman invoked the ancestors:

> The god who created the sun which gives us light, who rouses the waves and rules the storm, though hidden in the clouds, he watches us. He sees all that the white man does. The god of the white man inspires him with crime, but our god calls upon us to do good works. Our god who is good to us orders us to revenge our wrongs. He will direct our arms and aid us. Throw away the symbol of the god of the whites who has so often caused us to weep, and listen to the voice of liberty, which speaks in the hearts of us all. (Gordon: 1983)

Following on this period of preparation, they rose in arms. Within a few weeks the Great Houses were smoking ruins, the cane fields smouldering stubble.

St Domingue was soon a shambles. Everywhere "big whites" and "small whites", royalists and revolutionaries, mulattoes and blacks, free men and slaves fought and plundered in shifting alliances and confusion. Not until September 1792 did a French revolutionary army reach St Domingue, charged with orders to enforce the rule of liberty, equality and fraternity. Faced with royalist resistance, the commander, Leger Felicite Sonthonax, associated himself with the blacks, who with his backing sacked the town of Cap Français. That August Sonthonax proclaimed a conditional emancipation which was confirmed in 1794 by the French National Assembly. It declared: "Negro slavery in all colonies to be abolished, consequently all men, without distinction of colour, living in the colonies are French citizens and shall enjoy the rights guaranteed by the constitution." The action taken by Sonthonax alienated the browns, many of whom were slave owners. The surviving whites in the north fled, some to the United States and others to Cuba, Puerto Rico, where the west coast town of Mayaguez retains its French characteristics to this day, Trinidad, the eastern Caribbean and to Jamaica.

The names of black leaders now emerged, among them Boukman, Henri Christophe from St Kitts, Jean Jacques Dessalines (who was African-born) and Toussaint.

In 1793 England and Spain, both of whom were at war with revolutionary France, sent expeditions to invade St Domingue. The English force under General Maitland took Port-au-Prince. They were defeated by yellow fever, force of numbers and the military skill of Pierre-Dominique Toussaint.

Jean Jacques
Dessalines

THE STORY OF THE JAMAICAN PEOPLE

In Jamaica Lord Balcarres was convinced that the outbreak of the maroon war of 1795 was inspired by the example of the French islands and by French revolutionary agents, although this was never proved. The effect, however was that the government of Jamaica refused to send reinforcements to General Maitland. The troops which arrived from England were fresh and unseasoned, and the final outcome of the expedition to St Domingue was never in doubt.

Toussaint L'Ouverture had been a slave on a Haitian estate in the north. He took little part in the 1791 uprising but on the outbreak of war with Spain he entered the Spanish service as a royalist mercenary, and built up a very effective force of about 4,000 men. In 1795, alarmed at the progress of the English and at the prospect of the restoration of slavery that an English victory would bring about, he deserted with his troops from the Spanish army and offered his services to the battered French republican army. By 1798 he had so worn down the English that General Maitland was glad to withdraw his forces in return for an amnesty to his Haitian partisans and for a commercial treaty. In signing this agreement Toussaint acted like an independent head of state. He was so, indeed, in

Toussaint L' Ouverture

St Domingue. He, more than any other black leader, held the loyalty of the people and of his troops. Abroad, he enjoyed the respect and friendship of John Adams, the president of the United States. This had enabled him to get from the United States the ships and supplies he needed to combat the English.

After expelling the English, Toussaint subdued the mulattoes under Pierre de Rigaud in the west in 1800, a year of terrible carnage in which about 10,000 mulattoes – men, women, children – were killed. In 1801, in defiance of Napoleon's orders, he took control of Spanish Santo Domingo. Napoleon, however, had plans for rebuilding the French colonial system in America, basing it on Louisiana, with St Domingue as the outer fortress. The first step was to reduce Toussaint to obedience. He sent out a strong force under General Charles Victor Emanuel Leclerc, who succeeded, at great cost. Toussaint's chief supporters, Jean Jacques Dessalines and Henri Christophe, and their followers, joined the French. The French kidnapped Toussaint, took him to France and imprisoned him in the fortress of Joux near the Swiss border. The French regained control but yellow fever, that terrible enemy, was destroying their army.

Leclerc's prestige with Dessalines, Christophe, Maurepas and other rebel leaders was high. Then news came from Guadeloupe that Napoleon's General Antoine Richepanse, who had regained control of the island, had reintroduced slavery. Thousands of Haitians sprang to arms once more. They felt certain that Leclerc had orders from Napoleon to reintroduce slavery in Haiti. Some recalled Toussaint's warning to Napoleon when the government of France was changed to a Directorate in 1795, that if the French tried to reimpose slavery they would expose themselves to total ruin and the colony to inevitable destruction. "Do they think", he had asked indignantly, "that the men who have been able to enjoy the blessing of liberty will calmly see it snatched away?"

Toussaint was dead, but Dessalines, Christophe, Maurepas and the other Haitian leaders knew that under Napoleon the French were a foreign enemy. The Haitians knew that Leclerc's army had been greatly weakened. It was no longer the formidable force it had been. All their supplies had to be bought at high prices and brought in. Leclerc had reported to Napoleon that he was: "master of the North but almost all of it had been burnt and I can expect no resources from it. The rebels were still masters of a part of the West and they had burnt the positions they no longer held; for the present he could expect no supplies from there". At this critical time in November 1802 yellow fever claimed Leclerc.

In Europe, Napoleon broke the Treaty of Amiens in 1803, resumed the war, gave up his plans for an American empire and abandoned his forces in St Domingue. Leclerc's successor surrendered to the English in 1803, and Dessalines started a campaign of extermination against all surviving whites in Haiti. Just before the treaty was signed in 1800 in which France abandoned its claim to St Domingue, Dessalines and Christophe declared: "Restored to our former dignity, we have won back our rights and we swear never to let them be destroyed by any power on earth."

The old Taino name, Haiti, land of mountains, was restored to what had been the colony of St Domingue, and in 1804 Dessalines was declared Emperor of Haiti. On his assassination in 1806 he was succeeded by Christophe.

Thinking over the events we have described, and the impact of the two forces of change that we have identified, these differences become clear: the Evangelical Movement, largely rooted in the Protestant world, contributed significantly to social change in Jamaica but not in Haiti; the people of colour in Haiti suffered the same civil disabilities as those in Jamaica, but their political and social aspirations were opposed by a much larger body of resident whites, both rich and middle class, than in Jamaica, where the mulattoes were essentially conservative. They shared the "terrified consciousness" of the whites for the blacks.

The Enlightenment reinforced the anti-slavery movement in England, but it did not provide Jamaican browns with a battle cry. The Evangelical Movement was concerned with religious principles and man's conversion. The Enlightenment dealt with the principles of government and the rights of man. Each movement exercised a powerful influence in the Caribbean, one through the work of Lisle and Baker in Jamaica, the other through the Friends of the Blacks and the Black Jacobins in Haiti. We turn now to African-Jamaicans in this period: to their capacity for response to change and the impact of science, technology and the Industrial Revolution on them.

In the decade of the 1760s, when Voltaire and Rousseau were challenging tyranny and generating revolution, a few obscure scientists and technicians were taking the first steps towards mankind's first global revolution. In 1765 James Watt invented a separate condenser, then moved on to make the first steam engine, which put steam power at the service of mankind, made possible the mechanisation of the British textile and mining industries and transformed transport by land and sea. Four years later, in France, an artillery officer, Nicolas Cugnet, road-tested his steam-driven gun carriage, regarded as the first mechanically propelled vehicle. By 1770 the first steps in mechanising the cotton industry were pioneered by James Hargreaves with his spinning jenny.

Edmund Cartwright followed in 1785 with a power loom and a few years later two American inventors introduced power-driven cotton spinning. Eli Whitney's cotton-gin of 1793 marked a decisive step towards a massive increase in English cotton production. Land and water transport soon felt the impact of steam power: Robert Fulton with the first steam-boat, *Clermont*, on the Hudson River (1807), Henry Bell's *Comet* on the Clyde (1812) and George Stevenson's *Rocket* (1829), the first successful steam locomotive.

When we look at these inventions and the mechanisation of English industry over the period 1790-1830, we are also witnessing the formation of the English working class. It is appropriate to bear in mind the judge-ment of an English historian: "the changing productive relations and working conditions of the Industrial Revolution were imposed not upon raw material but upon the free-born Englishman . . . The factory hand or stockinger was also the inheritor of Bunyan, of remembered village rights, of notions of equality before the law, of craft traditions". Nor was slavery imposed upon raw material, but upon the freeborn African who had been nurtured in communities with ethical codes and well-developed forms of social organisation that respected the human being. They also inherited notions of individual rights, justice and liberty. These were a part of the African birthright, to be fought for and defended to the death.

CHAPTER 17

Challenge and response, 1760-1830

Liberating forces from Europe swept across the flourishing sugar islands of the Caribbean, spreading dismay and panic through white Jamaica, ravaging St Domingue with invading armies, with rebellious bands of African slaves bent on freedom, desperate mulattoes and white planters broken and in flight from a land that was yesterday's pride. The foundations and structures of French imperial power crumbled before the assaults of Toussaint and Dessalines. Meanwhile, Bryan Edwards, the historian of the Jamaican plantocracy, lamented that the devouring forces of subversion were abroad and the horizons were red with the flames of revolution.

In Jamaica the slaves were establishing hillside chapels under the leadership of their own black deacons. The field-workers in their songs mocked the white managers and overseers.

> One, two, three
> All de same
> Black, white, brown
> All de same,
> All de same.
> One, two three

We ask ourselves how it was that planter society in Jamaica was so resistant to change, so monumentally stolid, and how was it that enslaved blacks were able to respond to change, even though the 1780s and 1790s were decades of hardship and disaster.

Five hurricanes devastated Jamaica between 1780 and 1786, and the American War of Independence sharply reduced the flow of food and plantation supplies from the North American colonies to the West Indies. During the years 1780-81 Barbados was on the point of starvation. Malnutrition and physical hardships cut her slave population from 68,500 in 1773 to 54,500 in 1783. Famine threatened Jamaica. Antigua lost 1,000 slaves in 1778, Montserrat nearly 1,200, Nevis and St Kitts 300-400 each. So severe was the shortage of food in the 1780s that the West India interest and the English Government went searching for new food plants. The Jamaica House of Assembly resolved that every encouragement should be given to cultivating yams, eddos, maize, plantains and such exotics as nutmeg, cloves, cinnamon and coffee. The exploratory voyages of Captains James Cook and Louis Antoine de Bougainville to the South-East Pacific in the eighteenth century and the later voyages of William Bligh augmented the West Indian food supply.

The import of food plants, especially breadfruit, from the newly discovered islands of the South-East Pacific began in the last three decades of the eighteenth century. Jamaican planter society still remained set in its attitudes, incapable of a positive response to the challenges of the age. One reason was that the sugar plantation remained the prime source of Jamaica's life and wealth.

> The society created by sugar was rigid, base and greedy. It consumed life, energy and thought, and manured the industrial revolution of England with the profits from its labour. (Hearne: 1965)

Sugar was tenacious. Once a mill and boiling house had been established, land bought and planted in cane, slaves acquired and trained, there was no breaking its grip. The estate had to go on producing sugar. But the cause went deeper. The paralysing factor was white racism. Racism split the population into two segments, and colour prejudice fragmented it. The mulattoes were firmly told by the House of Assembly in November 1813: "The free people of colour in this island have no right or claim whatever to political power, or to interfere in the administration of the Government as by law established in the Governor, Council and Assembly."

Throughout the British colonies, peopled largely by non-whites, the colonial ideologies were racist. As Anthony Maingot observes:

> The majority of English scholars, for instance, steadfastly held to two fundamental tenets; first, that Teutonic, and especially Anglo-Saxon, races were superior in all respects; and secondly that inferiority could only be ameliorated through tutelage to the former. The French, Dutch, Belgian, Italian, Germans all shared this racial vision.

Since there were only a few white women in Jamaica, white males mated with black women and mulattoes became an important component of the population. There are no reliable figures of the racial mixture of the population of Jamaica in the period before emancipation, but the census taken in 1844 showed a total population of 377,433, made up of 293,128 (77.7 per cent) black, 68,529 (18.1 per cent) brown and 15,776 (4.2 per cent) white.

The whites remained completely dominant, holding all political and economic power. The group was split apart by class distinctions but united by race. Their superiority was institutionalised in law as well as in social terms. Below them came the "free coloured", who often owned property, including slaves, and pressed in season and out for civil rights. They aimed at entry into the white world. The base of the pyramid was black, and consisted of three-quarters of the population of the island.

These figures demonstrate that the sociocultural history of Jamaica was the history of an attempt by Europeans to contain a people more numerous than themselves, phenotypically different, whom they feared but whose labour they wished to keep available for economic exploitation. They indicate too that it is the history of the resistance of Africans to strategies of control and the Africans' anger at the system's tenacity that brought change about.

The deep fear the whites had of the blacks, their "terrified consciousness", caused chiefly by the great difference in numbers between them and the black slaves drove them to barbaric reprisals after black uprisings; for instance, it threw Lord Balcarres and the planter class into a panic over Haiti. It explains the heavy emphasis placed on law and order by the plantocracy and the colonial governments and their quick resort to violence as a means of enforcing authority. Plantation Jamaica was a garrison society, committed to the production of one major commodity, sugar, for export to the protected market in Britain, as an integral part of the mercantile system. It was dedicated also to maintaining white superiority by a closed system of representative government and by maintaining and protecting the system of slavery and making money from sugar. It was incapable of change.

In contrast, the African-Jamaicans somehow found within themselves the obstinate strength to reject, and to continue to reject, slavery. They did so by marronage, sabotage and sporadic outbursts of violence, as well as by acquiring the language, skills and knowledge of their white "masters".

In this response, we detect a process that was deliberate and selective: rejecting the system and yet adjusting to it and using it for their own betterment. This was a finely tuned sensing of the possible, of how to use the provision ground and traditional trading skills of the African-Jamaican women to establish a domestic market in produce and livestock.

It would have been a remarkable achievement for any people anywhere. It becomes a miracle when we realise that the African-Jamaican's lifespan under slavery averaged little more than seven years. Yet the dynamics of the society had its origins in them and brought a Jamaican culture into being.

The mortality rate was extremely high among children under four-years-of-age who died of epidemic diseases and ignorance. Monk Lewis, an absentee slave-owner, in his journal of his visit to Jamaica, tells of a woman, "a tender mother who had borne ten children and now has but one alive; another, at present in the hospital, has borne seven and but one has lived to puberty. So heedless and inattentive are the best-intentioned mothers and so subject in this climate are the infants to dangerous complaints. The locked jaw (tetanus) is the common and most fateful one, so fatal indeed that the midwife (the grandee) told me the other day: "Oh massa, till nine days over, we no hope of them." Alongside these there were others who declared that "They preferred to see their own children dead rather than be obliged to witness their daily punishment."

Recently arrived slaves also had a high mortality rate. Their period of seasoning extended over two or three years. For example, at Worthy Park Estate where the records were carefully kept and health care was good, between March 1792 and late 1793, of the 181 Africans bought, one-quarter died, the majority from dysentery and yaws. Environmental diseases, smallpox, fevers, lack of the will to live soon struck them down. Add to disease the tendency of some planters to overwork the slaves during the period of seasoning and so causing their death.

Whence did our ancestors, the African-Jamaican woman, man, child in threadbare osnaburg clothing, draw the strength to lay the foundations of our nation by their insistence not only on freedom but also on justice, and to create that rich unique Jamaican seed-bed of culture, our folk lore, from which come the tunes and music, the rock-steady and reggae that carry the name of Jamaica around the world?

The poets, like the griots of the West African people, lead us to some answers. Derek Walcott does this in a poem in which he describes the absence of history, tradition, ruins. He writes, "I saw the figures of ancient almond trees in a grove past Rampanalgas on the north coast (Trinidad) in a group of dead uprooted ancestors."

Lorna Goodison reminds us that our history is both chronicle and chronology, synthesis and analysis, poetry and archaeology, art and science, compilation of data and intuition. We also have tried to see our history "not as a march of ideologies but as a human event of complicated and often tragic outcomes". We have tried to understand how the enslaved people revealed their inner selves through the mechanisms they developed, through the language they bequeathed to us, the culture they created, a culture rich in its own right. The very names that the people gave to places tell of their moods, hopes and fears.

> I love so the names of this place,
> how they spring brilliant like "roses . . .
> Stonehenge . . . Sevens, Duppy Gate, Wait a Bit,

Wild Horses, Tan and See, Time and Patience,
Unity. It is Holy here, Mount Moses
dew falls upon Mount Nebo, south of Jordan,
Mount Nebo . . .
Paradise is found here, from Pisgah
we look out
and Wait a Bit, Wild Horses, Tan and See,
Time and Patience . . .

(Sherlock)

The landscapes with their picture names remind us of the African gift for animating phrases. The names and the language disclose "a visible history". Land of Look Behind takes us into an impenetrable region of razor-edged limestone pinnacles, hidden caves, tangled withes; Starve Gut Bay confronts us with famine, the country bus becomes Gaiety or Western Pride; a fisherman's boat becomes "In God we Trust".

The African-Jamaican was not a solo performer in this process of adaptation and of fashioning a Jamaican culture and a history. The environment played its part, the soil and the climate dictating planting time, crop time and crop-over; drought and hurricane imposed their timetable; the moon defined the best times for planting. The plantation moulded the way of life and laid out the daily routine, while the sugar cane combined with the seasons to set the calendar; northers, generated in the Arctic, spread the chills and fevers that killed so many, and hurricanes spawned off the West African coast flooded the Portland valleys and drove sailing ships ashore.

The other participant was the European, the coloniser, who imposed his laws based on the overriding importance of property instead of the human being; his religion with its division of human affairs into sacred and secular, compared with the African whose religion "accompanies the individual from long before his birth to long after his physical death"; and his language, one of mankind's most powerful and flexible means of communication. It served the colonisers' primary purposes of giving instructions, doing business and indoctrinating others in European superiority and African depravity; but it also provided the African with a base for creating his own language, Jamaica talk.

They did this without the inspiration of psalmists and prophets, knowing only that they had to find ways of communicating, of fashioning a new language quickly, and they did. There was no Jamaica talk in 1700 but by 1800 the folk had "an English learned incompletely with a strong infusion of African influence", a vigorous, vivid language made up of "preservations, borrowings, new formations, transferred meanings, and special preferences, the two chief components being English of various kinds and African".

Africa contributed more than vocabulary. It provided ways of forming new words or plurals by repetition, as in "wass wass" meaning plenty of wasps, or "fool fool" for foolish, as well as our way of speaking with the whole body, of using sounds as exclamation marks or full stops.

The proverbs are sparkling nuggets of sunshine. They take us into the inner world of the ancestors, where they record in a sentence years of experience, evaluations, warnings. Their ancestors, not having mastered the art of writing, passed on their experience and wisdom in their proverbs, the wise sayings of the dark. Their eyes are Yoruba, Ibo, Ewe, Efik, Fon; but they had made the Middle Passage, worked as plantation slaves and absorbed the lessons of their new condition. The proverbs of the homeland are polite, elegantly embroidered, tactful, poetic, as in the riddle:

> We call the dead, they answer,
> We call the living, they do not answer.
> The dry leaves on the earth are dead, crackle when trodden on,
>   whereas green leaves, the living, make no sound when we step
>   on them.

The Yoruba and the West Indians delight in irony, but West Africans speak from a more stable, more secure society, in which throughout the generations the elders have spoken with authority, knowing that "When we divide the meat, the gall must get its share."

The African-Jamaican's historical experience is that some get all the gall. His proverbs are as witty, as ironic. The sense of the comic is as keen, but there are sombre moods also, an inaccessible loneliness, the menace of lightning hidden in a cloud. The plantation taught him that "Poor man never vex" because he dare not show his anger; "Man you can't beat, you have fe call him fren." Let the overseers remember that "Time longer dan rope" and "Every day you goad donkey, one day him will kick you." "Not everybody who kin dem teet [smiles] wid you is fren." Let the blacks beware of those who carry tales: "When six yeye meet, story done"; and "De dog dat carry bone come will carry bone go." Never forget that "White man yeye burn neger (Negro)" and "When black man tief, him tief half a bit (five cents), when backra tief, him tief whole estate." Above all, be tactful: "Do not be seen counting the toes of a man who has only nine." Never overestimate your power: "The river carries away an elderly person who does not know his own weight." Always be on your guard: "Not because cow don't have tongue him don't talk". Remember that "You never tek popgun kill alligator," and beware how you mock at the elders: "Little pig ask him mumma (mother) say what mek you mout"so long an' she say 'Never mind, me pickney, the same thing that mek fe mi mout long will make fe you long too.'"

The Ashanti handed down to us brilliant folktales about the trickster Anansi, the spider-man, as the hare is the chief character in the Yoruba folk tales and the tortoise in the stories of the Ibo people.

As in the West African stories Anansi is "craven" (greedy), and, being small and weak, he wins by guile, not by strength. It is Anansi "who mek wasp sting, who mek dog belly come hollow, who mek Jackass bray".

The Anansi stories belong to "evening time", the work-songs or "jamma" to sun hot time, when field work becomes tedious, as in yam time, when in Hanover "to tek out yam without Jamma" was impossible. "The song itself may not be poetical, but the charm lies in the tune, the voice of the "bomma" (the leader) and the rhythmic swing of the workers." One of the oldest of the work-songs is among several recorded in the 1790s by J. B. Moreton. "Jamma, is certainly African and must have been in use for a long time . . . Bomma is very likely African, meaning either to shout, sing out or join together – as this leading singer leads the group. When Bomma wants to end the song he shouts "Black Water" or "Bog Walk".

Songs recorded by J. B. Moreton and Monk Lewis include references to slavery, being stolen from Guinea and having to face the cruelties and restrictions of plantation slavery. "This," observes Orlando Patterson, "is in marked contrast to the American slave songs where there are surprisingly few references to servitude." Lewis records a song entitled "We very well off", sung by the blacks. The reference to the cruelty they can expect from the overseer after the owner's departure comes out in the second verse.

> Hey ho day! neger now quite eeri [hearty]
> For once me see massa – hey-ho-day
> When massa go me no care a dammee
> For how dem usy me hey-ho-day

The ring games and dancing songs tell of ways in which our African ancestors amused themselves. Some of the earliest recordings of these songs, by Sloane in his *Natural History of Jamaica* (1680), show that songs were being sung in African languages. He recorded tunes from Angola, Pawpaw and "Koromanti".

It is as if the ancestors stepped out of the eighteenth century to whisper their proverbs and songs to us, and to take us into that inner world of dreams, hopes and prayers where they gained relief from the plantation horrors. One song is about a planter who ordered that an elderly ill slave should be carried to a lonely gully on the estate, and abandoned there, but "bring back the frock and board".

> Take him to the Gully! Take him to the Gully!
> But bring back the frock and board,

"Oh massa! massa! me no deadee yet",
Take him to the Gully. Take him to the Gully
Carry him along!

We feel at home with the songs and the music, the proverbs, the stories, for deep down they are ours, and we can see how the ancestors, by fashioning them out of their African memories and their plantation experiences, prepared the way for our poets and musicians. The mood is the same here.

I was down in the valley for a very
long time
But I never get weary yet . . .
I was walking on the shore and
they took me in the ship
And they throw me overboard
And I swam right out of the belly of the whale
And I never get weary yet . . .

(Toots Hibbert)

Sun a shine but things nuh bright,
Doah pot a bwile, bickle nuh nuff,
River flood but water scarce yah,
Rain a fall but dutty tough

(Louise Bennett)

The dances and the masquerade are treasures. The juncunoo, which links "music and dance, mime and symbol" is an early traditional dance form of African descent that still survives in Jamaica.

The mask has a central place in African religions, and it may be that juncunoo, a masquerade form, and myal, a possession-healing form of religion, were closely allied in their early forms in Jamaica, as they are allied in the two powerful male secret societies of West Africa, Poro and Egungun. The juncunoo moved through three phases in Jamaica. The first was the early years of introduction and adaptation, and this was followed in the 1770s by the addition of a European feature, the set girls. The third stage came after emancipation and it was this masquerade which shows the British influence most clearly.

The capacity for response was in itself complex, for the African slaves came from different tribes, spoke different languages and worshipped different gods. Also, as Patterson reminds us, if we were to examine the slave society at any given time we would find a basic division between the communities of the African-born and the Jamaican-born slaves. The unifying forces were blackness and the passion for freedom. It remains true, however, that most of the slaves imported into Jamaica came from the same culture area, and "underlying the great regional or tribal differences . . . there is a very wide substratum of basic ideas that persists in the rituals, myths, and folk tales of West African peoples." (Forde: 1954)

This African-rooted, African-inspired body of folk culture, was the African-Jamaicans' response to uprooting and alienation during the century after emancipation, when society felt the full force of colonialism. There was no other link, no other "indigenous form of self-expression", no other source from which to nourish the sense of African identity. Neither brutality nor hardship broke their spirit. They preserved through three centuries of exploitation an unquenchable vitality and an equally remarkable ability to "tek bad someting mek laugh".

Denigrated as "ole nayga music" and "black neyga foolishness", the folk kept their tunes, their stories and masquerade until Marcus Garvey and the Rastafarians drove home the fact that "the Western black man's attitude to Africa, whether he knows it or not, is at bottom his attitude to himself". It is in the exciting vitality of today's culture that we find a demonstration of the capacity of the African-Jamaicans of the eighteenth century to respond positively to penalisation and indoctrination. The folklore is the living memorial which the people fashioned as their answer to the castles and ruins, their source of healing, recognition of each other as shipmates on the long voyage to nationhood.

CHAPTER 18

The primacy of freedom

The nineteenth century dawned to the cannonade and battle cries of the Napoleonic war (1802-15), to the flames and carnage of the Haitian revolution and, in Jamaica, to terrifying rumours that slaves brought from St Domingue by fugitive French planters were planning an uprising. More than 1,000 were transported. There followed conspiracies in Kingston in 1803, and in 1808 a mutiny of 50 African Chambas and Coromantis in the West India Regiment at Fort Augusta.

For more than 100 years African-Jamaicans had battled for survival and freedom. Towards the end of that harsh, difficult century they had felt the impact of a new age, heard of talk in England about a law to abolish the slave trade, seen Haiti become an independent black and free republic, talked secretly under cover of night about the rights of man, discussed messages from Jacobin agents. Then, in 1807, word came that William Wilberforce and his followers had at last won their long battle for the abolition of the slave trade. Many concluded that this meant the abolition of slavery.

Earlier liberation wars had centred on the maroons or on plantations in specific parishes. Now freedom for all African-Jamaicans seemed a possibility. The Jamaica born blacks were in the majority. All spoke a Jamaican dialect, shared the same creole culture, the same desire for freedom and through their folk language communicated fully with each other.

Work songs recorded in this period reflect a change of mood a more open mockery of backra, a growing distrust of him, more frequent references to freedom, an increasing restiveness. There is the steady rhythm of the provision-ground in some work songs; others mocked at backra's frailty and told of the early coming of freedom.

> New-come backra
> He get sick

He tek fever
He be die
He be die
New come backra
He be die,

Another folk song that dates back to the early 1800s speaks of freedom as if it were already here.

Talla ly li oh
Freedom ah come oh!
Talla ly li oh
Here we dig, here we hoe.
Talla ly li oh
Slavery ah gone oh,
Talla ly li oh
Here we dig, here we hoe.
King George me ah go
Here we dig, here we hoe, . . .
Me nuh work no more,
Massa, he ah go
Freedom ah come oh
Talla ly li oh
Here we dig, here we hoe.

The revolutionary songs were the Christian hymns, some of which were introduced by the black Baptist missionaries, others by the white missionaries. They met the deep need of African-West Indians for musical forms of religious expression, set a wholly new valuation on the human being and portrayed the close continuing spiritual bond with the father of all mankind. The militant mood of some hymns relieved their frustration.

We will be slaves no more
Since Christ has made us free,

The new chapels resounded to the hymns of the Evangelical Revival, such as Charles Wesley's:

Hide me, O My Saviour hide
Till the storm of life is past,
Safe into the haven guide,
O receive my soul at last
Soldiers of Christ arise
And put your armour on.

The hymns touched the imagination of the folk who (as Olive Lewin has shown us) composed songs that are rich in feeling in the mood of such

Jamaican intuitive painters of the mid-twentieth century as Kapo (Mallica Reynolds) and Everald Brown.

> Moses saw the fire burning,
> Moses saw the fire burning
> Moses saw the fire burning over there,
>
> Shining light
> Shining light
> Shining light in the wilderness
> over there, over there

Yet closer to the intuitives of Jamaica and the primitives of Haiti are early folk spirituals, such as that which tells of a synod in heaven, with God asking:

> Who will go and die for Adam?
> Who will go and die for Adam?
>   I will go
>   I will go
> When the question was asked in heaven
> There was half an hour silence
> There was half an hour silence,
> Who will go and die for Adam?
>   I will go
>   I will go.

The people in a very African way felt the closeness of the spirit world as a direct, not a mystical, experience, and spoke of immediate and personal contact with a God of dreams and visions.

The hymn book and the Bible added a new dimension to the drab agony of an osnaburg or crocus bag world, from which the vivid colours and drama of tribal Africa had been drained. We have seen how the African-Jamaicans met the challenge of alienation and deprivation by creating dance forms, songs and the drama of the masquerade. To these were now added the grand imagery of the Bible, unforgettable pictures of the armies of the oppressor swept away by the waters of the Red Sea; David with his sling-shot victorious over Goliath; Daniel in the lion's den; a bush that burned but was not consumed, a valley of dry bones resurrected in Ezekiel's vision, divine messages delivered through dreams, visions, a whirlwind and a still small voice. The impact on the African-Jamaican was profound. He found hope in the presence of the missionaries, strength and spiritual comfort in the message of salvation which they brought, in the hymns and in the Bible, both of which enriched his imagination and deepened his aesthetic experience.

As we have seen, the English missionaries came by invitation. George Lisle had been converted by a Baptist preacher in Savannah, Georgia, so it was natural that as a loyalist refugee he should turn to the recently founded Baptist Missionary Society in London for help. In 1791 he wrote to the secretary, Dr John Rippon saying: "We have purchased a piece of land at the East end of Kingston containing three acres for the sum of £146. currency and on it we have begun to build a meeting house. We have raised the brick wall eight feet high and intend to have a gallery." Lisle made his living by farming and moving goods with a wagon and team of horses, but he got into debt over the chapel and was imprisoned for three years and five months. In this difficult time the rector of the Kingston Parish Church helped him. As soon as he was free, he resumed his work. Of the slaves who were members he wrote: "Out of so small a sum (as their gifts) we cannot expect anything that can be of service from them. If we did it would soon bring scandal upon religion."

The missionary pioneer in western Jamaica was Moses Baker, who was born in New York and was a barber by trade. When the English evacuated New York in 1783 he left with his wife and child and came to Kingston as a loyalist refugee. In 1788 he was employed by Mr Winn, a planter, to instruct the slaves on his estate. His missionary work progressed and in 1813 Baker appealed to the Baptist Missionary Society in London for help. The society responded by sending out the first missionary, John Rowe, in 1814. In 1815, when other English missionaries were beginning to arrive, slave discontent broke into rebellion. Around Christmas some slaves at Lyndhurst property in St Elizabeth got together with a black from St Domingue and a brown preacher and began to plan a rebellion. They met at night and sang a freedom song which the brown preacher taught them:

> Oh me good friend Mr. Wilberforce
> make we free
> God Almighty thank ye, God
> Almighty thank ye,
> God Almighty mek we free.
> Backra in this country no mek
> we free,
> What Negro for to do? What
> Negro for to do?
> Take force by force! Take force by force!

The freedom fighters elected a "King of the Eboes" and two captains who were to serve under him. However, information was laid against them and the authorities took action. One of the captains escaped to the woods but the "King" and the other leaders were seized and executed. The governor, the Duke of Manchester, reported:

At a trial held in the Parish of St Elizabeth, it appeared in evidence that nightly meetings had been held on the property . . . That the object of their meeting was to impress the slaves generally with a belief that Mr. Wilberforce was to be their deliverer, and that if the white inhabitants did not make them free, they ought to make themselves free . . . It further appeared in the evidence that these slaves have been taught that there was no necessity of being christened by the clergyman of the Parish, for that they had permission to be baptised by a Negro preacher belonging to Earl Balcarres, and the Negroes so baptised ever after paid a part of what they possessed to the head Preacher whom they call the Bishop. (Hart: 1985)

The freedom song reveals powerful forces at work among the slaves, who were skilled in reading the mind of "that trickified man", backra. They knew that Britain had abolished the slave trade. The arrival of the British missionaries was proof that they had friends in the white world. The drumbeats of revolution grew more insistent, and many took seriously the words of the king of the Eboes at his execution, that he left behind enough of his countrymen to carry out his plans and to revenge his death.

In 1816 African-West Indians underlined their demand for freedom. In that year the first of the last three great liberty uprisings in the West Indies took place in Barbados without prior consultation with slaves elsewhere. The outbreak revealed an awareness of the erosion of planter power, a belief that freedom was near at hand and a distrust of negotiation. The words of Nanny Grigg, one of the rebels, set the mood: "they were all damn fools to work, that she would not, as freedom they were sure to get . . . the Negroes were to be freed on Easter morning and the only way to get it was to fight for it, otherwise they would not get it". Nanny Grigg's message was the same as the brown priest's song: "Take force by force!" She stands amongst the leaders of the freedom-fighters, representative of the African-West Indian fighting women, brief, blunt and as resolute as Nanny of Jamaica and her Nanny Town people, firm as an old mahogany tree with its roots deep in the earth.

In 1823 in Demerara (Guyana) the largest slave rebellion in that country's history took place under the leadership of Tacky. At Le Resouvenir Estate the slaves rose, demanded immediate emancipation and very nearly seized control of the country.

The plan said Colonel Leaky, in evidence before a government inquiry into the causes of the rising, was to remain quiet on the estate and not to work. We were desirous that no injury

William
Wilberforce

should be done to any of the whites, so that no complaint might be made against them. The governor of Demerara, in a despatch to the Colonial Office, said that the slaves demanded unconditional emancipation.

> They declared that the Act for the amelioration of slavery by abolishing the flogging of females and carrying whips was no comfort to them. God made them of the same flesh and blood as the whites. They were tired of being slaves to them, they should be free, and they would not work any more. I assured them if by peaceful conduct they deserved His Majesty's favour they would find their lot substantially though gradually improved, but they declared they would be free.

The missionary John Smith was thrown into prison and died while awaiting execution. The words he wrote to the London Missionary Society deserve to be widely known.

> Under my persecutions and afflictions it affords me no small consolation that the Directors cherish the assurance of my entire innocence. The instructions I received from the Society I always endeavoured to act upon. I have endeavoured from the beginning to discharge my duty faithfully. In doing so I have met with the utmost unceasing opposition and reproach. But so far have these things been from shaking my confidence in the goodness of the cause in which I was engaged, that if I were at liberty, and my health restored, I would again proclaim all my days the glad tidings of Salvation amidst similar opposition, but of this I see no prospect. The Lord's hand is heavy upon me. I can still praise his name.

The Demerara freedom fighters took the line that Daddy Sharpe was to take some eight years later in Jamaica: no violence to whites and immediate freedom because there was no moral justification for slavery. In contrast, the Barbados planters in 1823 followed the example of the Demerara counterparts in their treatment of the martyr John Smith. They forced William Shrewsbury, a Methodist missionary, to leave the island, the charge being that he had urged the slaves to take their freedom by force. "The slaves are as much disregarded and neglected as if they possessed no immortal souls", he reported to his missionary society.

The year of the Demerara rebellion was marked in Jamaica by increasing tension and frequent reports of conspiracies and plots. The parish of Hanover, for example, "was thrown into a state of excitement, though treachery once more baffled the designs of the conspirators". The governor reported that those who were planning rebellion were fully impressed with the belief that they were entitled to their freedom and that one of the leaders had said that the war had only begun. He was right; and it is at this point that we turn to the only friends that African-Jamaicans had in Jamaica, the newly arrived white missionaries.

The missionaries had been instructed by their societies to adapt to the existing order, to concentrate on preaching the gospel, saving souls and inculcating moral values. In their early years they followed a cautious course, but, as Edward Brathwaite so dramatically portrayed, their presence was a challenge to slavery and an affirmation of brotherhood with the slaves:

> At once novel levels of equality appear – both here and in heaven. The evangelical missionaries not only eroded estate boundaries with their 'circuits' or 'districts', but to convert they had to get down off the horse, traditional symbol of superiority, and walk from door to door like modern-day political campaigners. For the first time, then, the slave was looking at a white man eyeball to eyeball, face to face, mouth to ear, hallelujah. And the congregations that were formed were not only exempt from (or rather, eroded) the curfew laws, but were holds in a ship bound for Zion which didn't clank with chains; though since slavery was a sin, many masters might be destined – not unhappily – for somewhere else.
>
> And there was their own religion also, transformed by the Middle Passage, it is true; but still their own. And Deacon/Daddy in his distant chapel had to call on dream and vision, had to shout out locomotion, if the people of his passion were to know him, love him, let him lead them. Mask, Myal, Memory of Mackandal. Sharpe laid 'pagan' oaths upon the Holy Bible. They could have spoken in tongues like kongo kumina; like cowhead jankonnu. The leadership of liberation of the slave was only possible when all the elements of his culture could be raised, utilized and used. (Braithwaite: 1971)

The Christian doctrines of the fatherhood of God, the brotherhood of all human beings, the call to personal salvation, the valuation of the human soul as precious beyond price in the sight of God, these were revolutionary concepts in the world of the sugar-and-slave plantation. So was learning to read and write, especially when the Bible was the book of instruction. So were the methods of religious instruction, especially the class meetings and the tradition of self-government in church affairs. These built habits of consultation and of leadership. The Baptist missionaries were bred in the political tradition of the Dissenters, of the notion of being freeborn Englishmen, "the inheritors of Bunyan, of remembered village rights, of notions of equality before the law and of the folk as the creators of political traditions". They revived in the minds of the African-Jamaicans memories of their own communal traditions, of tribal values, rights, obligations. And most explosive of all was the value placed by God on the individual human being compared with the £30 or £40 of the slave market. The missionary's behaviour said far more than he realised.

Further, and wholly unrecognised by the missionaries, yet of profound importance, was the fact that the concepts of eternity, of a future judgment, of a paradise in the future, were wholly new to the African-Jamaican. In John Mbiti's words,

> The linear concept of time in western thought, with an indefinite past, present and infinite future is practically foreign to African thinking. The future is virtually absent, because events which lie in it have not taken place, they have not been realised, and cannot, therefore, constitute time. Actual time is what is present and what is past. It moves 'backward' rather than forward and people set their minds not on future things, but chiefly on what has taken place. (Mbiti: 1970)

The memory of Africa had faded, but the plantation regime had not totally implanted the European concept of time. Mervyn Alleyne has pointed out that to this day, "the folk's concept of time is defined in terms of the events that are taking place or have taken place. It is not an imposed mathematical formula; it is a phenomenal event." This concept of time being determined by the events and by individual participation in them explains why Vic Reid, in his historical novel *New Day*, makes Joseph Campbell, the narrator of the story, say "They do not know what we have seen, for no place has been found in their English history books for the fire that burnt us in sixty-five". This recognition of the need to participate in past events explains the importance of the griots in the African tribe, leading the Africans, through their ancestors, to claim and participate in their past; it reveals the power of shrines in the lives of all people and it explains why today's Jamaican needs to claim his heritage and so make it a part of his present.

In these circumstances talk about the abolition of slavery at some vague period in the future made no sense. Neither present conditions nor the traditional concept of time gave it any validity. Freedom now was the demand.

After 1823 the missionaries became more militant than they had been, and even more so with the arrival of William Knibb in 1824. His brother had come in 1814 and had succumbed to disease a few months after his arrival. Knibb was asked by the missionary society if he would replace his brother. He consulted his sick mother, who said that he would be no son of hers if he failed to answer the call. He had not been long in the island before he confessed to a "burning hatred of slavery which was glutted with crimes against God and man". He was anxious to secure for the slaves the

William Knibb

few rights they had in law and in letters to Britain he urged greater speed and urgency to end the system of slavery.

The missionaries counted heavily on the support of the English Abolition Society, which had been inactive since securing the abolition of slavery in 1807. Joseph Sturge, Quaker and abolitionist, explained: "It was not until 1823 that Mr. Buxton submitted to the House of Commons the first resolution ever moved in that Assembly that brought in question, and then only in a very cautious form, the lawfulness of negro slavery." Thomas Fowell Buxton was one of a group of abolitionists who played an important part in getting the British Government to pass legislation to ameliorate the condition of the slaves in the West Indies and eventually to pass the abolition law. After referring to the Napoleonic war and its terrible drain on British time and energy, Sturge continued:

> Nor does it appear that the excellent men who laboured so long and so successfully to put the traffic in men under the ban of law . . . ever contemplated speedy emancipation as a thing either practicable or safe. By degrees, however, attention began to be directed more and more to the conditions of the slaves by men such as Wilberforce, Brougham, Lushington, Denman, Whitemore, William Smith, and above all [Thomas Fowell] Buxton, whose vigilance nothing escaped.

In 1823 the abolitionists formed a Society for the Gradual Abolition of Slavery, and agreed to launch a parliamentary campaign to that end. William Wilberforce wrote his appeal on behalf of the slaves, rebutting the argument of some planters who claimed that the West Indian slaves were better off than the British peasant as far as feeding, clothing and lodging were concerned. Wilberforce countered:

> Are these the only claims, are these the chief privileges of a rational and immortal being? Is the consciousness of personal independence nothing? Are self-possession and self-government nothing? Is it of no account that our persons are violated by any private authority, and that the whip is placed only in the hands of the public executioner? Are all the charities of the heart, which arise out of domestic relations, to be considered as nothing, and I may add, all their security too among men who are free agents and not vendible chattels, liable perpetually to be torn from their dearest connections and sent into a perpetual exile?

Some slaves could read. They knew of the appeal by Wilberforce and of the campaign against slavery. Certainly they learned about the Society's decision in 1830 to press for immediate emancipation. Wilberforce and Buxton had not been in favour of this decision but once it was taken they threw their full weight behind it.

Forces generated by the Industrial Revolution were strengthening the anti-slavery trends. They brought new groupings into existence, among them new industrial interests, hostile to the West India monopoly of the British sugar market. New economic thinking, stimulated by Adam Smith's *Wealth of Nations*, was raising questions about the efficiency of slave labour and of the West India sugar planters. The West India interest found itself being forced from a central position of power to the periphery.

Joseph Sturge

In Britain the West India Committee of Planters and Merchants fought a bitter rearguard action. Led by Lord Chandos, Lord Seaford and the recently appointed agent for Jamaica, William Burge, a virulent opponent of the missionaries, the committee sought to win public support by emphasising the importance of the West Indian sugar-producing colonies to Britain and the need to protect slavery as an institution created by law. They denounced the preaching of the missionaries as subversive, especially the Baptists, who consistently and provocatively taught the equality of all men in the sight of God, and assured the slaves that the time had come for all men to be free. They declared that emancipation would strike a dangerous blow at the fundamental principle of the sanctity of property. The committee warned that to set the blacks free would be, as a correspondent to the *Times* put it, "to let loose so many wild beasts. Immediate emancipation would destroy not only their masters but the slaves themselves".

The planters, both absentees and locals, saw themselves as patriotic Englishmen who had rejected suggestions from the North American colonists to join them in their war of independence. With the abolition of the slave trade, which they had strongly opposed, they realised that they were losing ground.

Hurt and angry, the whites in Jamaica grew desperate. The House of Assembly rejected the British parliament's proposals for purging slavery of its cruellest features, and in February 1831 reduced from three to two the number of days' holiday the slaves were entitled at Christmas. The planters angrily denounced the British Government around their dining tables and in their newspapers. At public meetings in many parishes they abused the British Government for planning to deprive them of their property, for delivering them "over to the enemies of our country", for throwing them "as a prey before misguided savages". The hurricane signals were out.

When we put these two decades of mounting African-West Indian discontent alongside developments in Britain, we observe an unexpected concordance of events and extraordinary linkages between the African-West Indian enslaved workers and the emerging British working class, themselves virtually enslaved factory hands and coal mine-workers; for the African slave trade and African-West Indian slaves produced much of the wealth that financed the Industrial Revolution.

The calendar is revealing. In the West Indies there were slave uprisings in Westmoreland and St Elizabeth in 1815, a rebellion in Barbados in 1816, another in Demerara in 1823, yet another in Jamaica in 1832. In Britain there was the Luddite crisis in 1811-13, when mobs rampaged through Lancashire smashing machines in a protest against industrialisation; in 1817 the Pentridge rising of miners; in 1819 the Peterloo massacre, when armed militia men charged a mob of working folk; the Ten-Hour Movement and trade union activities of the 1820s, and in 1831-32 a revolutionary crisis over the reform bill. (Thompson: 1963)

The inventors, technologists and scientists towards the end of the eighteenth century put steam power at the service of mankind, pioneered the mechanisation of British industry, spread William Blake's "dark satanic mills" and factories through Lancashire and Yorkshire. This led to unregulated industrial growth and the emergence of an English working class. Their condition in this period throws light on the conditions of African-West Indians. English social reformers, such as Richard Oastler recognised this, when they attacked the mill-owners for their savage exploitation of the workers. "You are more Tyranical, more Hypocritical than the slave drivers of the West Indies." The "big gang" and "pickney gang" had counterparts in:

> The little infants and their parents taken from their beds in all kinds
> of weather . . . the miserable pittance of food chiefly composed of
> water gruel and oatcake broken into it, together with a few potatoes
> and a bit of bacon or fat for dinner, and if late a few minutes a quarter
> of a day is stopped in wages. The negro slave in the West Indies has
> probably a little breeze of air to fan him. The English spinner slave
> locked up in factories eight stories high, has no relaxation till the
> ponderous engine stops. (Thompson: 1963)

Few accounts of child labour in this period are more affecting than the account, quoted by E. P. Thompson, of a boy whom the minister of religion had recently interred who had been found standing asleep with his arms full of wool and had been beaten awake. This day he had worked seventeen hours; he was carried home by his father, was unable to eat his supper, awoke at 4. a.m. the next morning and asked his brothers if they could see the lights of the mill as he was afraid of being late, and then died. No wonder that Thompson considering the "pickeny gangs" of the British industrial revolution, commented:

> The exploitation of little children on this scale and with this intensity, was one of the most shameful events in our history: at the centre of our story stands the human being. The enslaved African, the English mill-workers and coal-miners of the period of unregulated industrialization the indentured East Indian Labourer. The basic relationship had to do with economics, with the owner or employer who had access to capital and the worker whose capital lay in his strength and intelligence. Market forces have no special sanctity.
>
> The differences between the emerging English working class and the African-Jamaicans are as revealing as are parallels. In the Caribbean the basic conflict was between white-owner black-labour; in Britain of the 1800-1830's, white-master white-labour. The determining factor is economic, not racial: capitalist-labour; money-hands. In the Caribbean the shortage of labour led to forced labour, the sequence being American Indian, white indentured servant, African forced labour. In Britain there was no shortage of rural poor. Where the relationship between capitalist and worker was not regulated it became one of conflict and bitter hostility. In 1832 it was defined by Sam Sharpe: 'had rather die than be a slave'. In Britain it was defined in 1834 by sanctioning the transportation of Dorchester labourers for forming a trade union, and in the same year by a Leeds stuff-weaver, William Rider: 'The war-cry of the masters has not only been sounded, but the havoc of war; war against freedom; war against opinion; war against justice; and war without justifying cause.' (Thompson: 1963)

The white factory worker of this period was also "a hand", a tool, and in consequence his major disputes were about wages and working conditions, by the potters against the truck system, by the building workers for direct cooperative action and by all groups of workers for the right to form trade unions. The African-West Indian's priority was freedom. The exploited white hands, through their experience in the mines and factories, through study of Tom Paine's *Rights of Man*, and their advocacy of the infant Chartist Movement, understood the nature of the support the abolitionists needed.

CHAPTER 19

Rebellion and emancipation

The Western Liberation Uprising of 1832, which marks the climax of the African-Jamaicans' struggle against slavery, and the British parliament's Act of Emancipation of 1833, belong together. The uprising was not an isolated event. The works of leading scholars of slave resistance in the West Indies enable us to identify its four basic stages. The series of liberation movements began with escapes and struggles during the period of forced recruitment in Africa and the Middle Passage, moved through the rooting of the slave plantation in the Americas (1500-1700) to the 50 years (1750-1800) of total dependence on slave labour, to a final period of crisis in the plantation economy and of the general growth in Britain of anti-slavery sentiment (1800-34).

This long conflict was an African response affirming the right of man to freedom in which, finally, the African prevailed. In this final phase, although the Western Liberation Uprising failed in its immediate objective, it succeeded in achieving its primary goal of emancipation.

Who would have imagined that the rebel leaders swinging from the gallows in Montego Bay during that agonising May of 1832 were to become the honoured dead of a predominantly African-Jamaican people or that their leader, Sam Sharpe, would be revered as one of the heroes and creators of the nation?

The Western Liberation Uprising differed from earlier uprisings, such as that of Tacky's Coromantis recently arrived from Africa and that of the King of the Eboes with his small band of plantation slaves, in that more than 20,000 African-Jamaicans were involved. The call was to slaves everywhere, not a call to arms but a call to withdraw their labour, and it was issued to people who were determined to win their freedom.

Kamau Brathwaite emphasises that "western Jamaica was, by the early years of the 19th century, psycho-culturally prepared for revolution against the plantation system". (Brathwaite: 1971) From the late 1820s Sam Sharpe had been talking of strike: of locking down all plantations.

There was also man-and woman-power. In the western part of the island (St James, Trelawny, St Elizabeth, Hanover, Westmoreland) some 30 per cent of all the colony's slaves were concentrated, that is 106,000 out of more than 310,000. Of this 106,000 between 18,000 and 40,000 were involved in the revolt; among them were urban blacks and coloureds, and free black women, two of whom were executed for their part in the rebellion. (Brathwaite: 1971)

The leaders formed the élite of the labour force, men who had exercised as much authority as a slave could exercise, some of them deacons of the Baptist Church, literate, aware of events in Britain, and especially of the work of the abolitionists.

Sam Sharpe planned and led the rebellion. He was born in Montego Bay, worked there as a domestic slave, and was a deacon of Thomas Burchell's church. He also built up a following of his own among the Native Baptists.

Of medium height, with a fine sinewy frame and a broad, high forehead, Samuel, or Daddy Sharpe was an outstanding leader who impressed all whom he met with his sincerity, intellectual grasp, oratorical power and personal magnetism. His eyes were unforgettable, with a brilliance that was almost dazzling. The Methodist missionary Henry Bleby, who visited him while he was in prison, spoke of his power as a speaker and leader.

> I heard him two or three times deliver a brief extemporaneous address to his fellow prisoners on religious topics . . . and I was amazed at the power and freedom with which he spoke and at the effect which was produced upon his auditory. He appeared to have the feelings and passions of his hearers completely at his command and when I listened to him once, I ceased to be surprised at what Gardner had told me, that when Sharpe spoke to him and others on the subject of slavery, he Gardner was wrought up almost to a state of madness. (Bleby: 1868)

The blacks believed all that Daddy Sharpe told them because he had been born and brought up in Montego Bay, could read and was a trusted leader of Thomas Burchell's church, "and the negroes considered that what Sharpe told them when he came to the mountains must be true, as it came from the church".

One of Daddy Sharpe's followers was Edward Hylton who told how, while at Mountain Spring, he received a message from Sharpe asking him to come to a meeting at Johnson's house on Retrieve Estate in St James.

The gathering at Retrieve took the form of a prayer meeting but Sharpe, William Johnson, who became one of the leaders in the rebellion, Hylton and a few others stayed on. After a while Sharpe spoke to them in a low, soft tone so that his voice would not be heard outside. According to Hylton, he kept them spellbound while he spoke of the evils and injustice of slavery, "asserted the right of all human beings to freedom and declared, on the authority of the Bible, that the white man had no more right to hold the blacks in bondage than the blacks had to enslave the whites". (Bleby: 1868)

Then came these vital words.

> Because the King had made them free, or was resolved upon doing it, the whites and Grignon [of the militia] were holding secret meetings with the doors shut at the house of Mr. Watt of Montego Bay, and had determined to kill all the black men, and save all the women and children, and keep them in slavery; and if the black men did not stand up for themselves and take their freedom, the whites would then put them out at the muzzle of their guns and shoot them like pigeons. (Bleby: 1868)

The meeting continued far into the night. Sharpe outlined the plan of operation. They bound themselves by oath not to work after Christmas as slaves but to assert their claim to freedom and to be faithful to each other. If backra would pay them, they would work as before. If any attempt was made to force them to work as slaves, they would fight for their freedom. They took the oath and kissed the Bible.

Sharpe campaigned actively. "We must all agree to set down after Christmas. We must not trouble anybody and raise no rebellion. We did not swear to burn anywhere or to fight." But realist as well as visionary, he knew that the planters, so intransigent, so angry, might not be willing to negotiate. He knew that they might use force. If they did, the slaves would use force. His "set down" movement was like Gandhi's *satyagraha* (holding to the truth) campaign of civil disobedience through non-violent resistance to unjust laws, but, said Sharpe, if need be, force would be met with force. The first act was to be "the sitting down, the laying down of tools, not swords, on Tuesday after Christmas, and the negotiation thereafter of a wage". (Brathwaite: 1971) William Knibb stressed that point in his testimony to parliament. "There was no design of leaving the property, but they intended what would be called in England a turn-out, till they were promised remuneration for their labour, and the price they had fixed was 2/6 a day." Bleby stated that he had the opportunity of ascertaining the fact beyond doubt, that the destruction of property formed no part of the plan of the original conspirators; and that life was not to be sacrificed, except in self-defence.

Painting by Barington Watson, Wycliffe Bennett Collection

Sam Sharpe

There were contingency plans: "the burning plan, the land a flaming telegraph; trash houses, wood roofs, plantation flooring, stairways, jalousies and shutters and the long waiting miles of sugar-cane, conjoint with the paramilitary operation of Gardner and Dove: Black regiment, drill, rank, uniform, chains of command, redoubts, rendezvous, flash-points, fortifications, escape routes." (Brathwaite: 1971)

Robert Gardner, Thomas Dove and Sharpe's other "officers" were untrained men, but a British officer who fought against them said it was astonishing what sagacity had been displayed by them in the selection of their positions. They invariably availed themselves of such as commanded a full view of the hostile approaches and a secure but concealed retreat for themselves, with a supply of water and ground-provisions, always constructing impediments to each entrance. In addition to being on a hill, the headquarters was within gunshot of the roads to Montego Bay, to Black River, Barnyside. "And in the last resort, scattered riots, retreat into the forests and mountains, maroon tactics." (Brathwaite: 1971)

The date set for the withdrawal of labour was Tuesday, 28 December. On that day the Christmas holidays would come to an end, the slaves would not resume work and negotiations would begin. Incidents at Salt Spring Estate on 15 December led the Montego Bay magistrates on 19 December to order the commanding officer of the militia to send a company of the 22nd Regiment to the bay. The authorities were on the alert.

Crisp, clear mornings, night skies brilliant with stars, the Pleiades, Sirius, Orion and Venus near the moon, make this a season of magical beauty. An army officer, Bernard Martin Senior, who served with the British in putting down the revolt, remarked:

> At this period of the year the scenery cannot be surpassed, being so diversified by the various hues of the different crops. The bright yellow of the ripened sugar cane, forming a fine contrast with the deep green of the Indian corn, just beginning to spear, which tint is again carried by an occasional luxuriant pasture of Guinea grass. Now and then an occasional avenue of coconut trees . . . a noble pile of buildings, surrounded at some trifling distance with innumerable neat-looking houses, inhabited by the negroes.

Tension was high. The missionaries urged patience. On 27 December William Knibb, visiting Moses Baker's chapel at Crooked Spring, now Salter's Hill, tried to persuade the slaves that rumours about freedom having been granted were untrue, but his words were received with evident dissatisfaction by many of the slaves present, several of whom left the chapel offended. Others remarked: "The man . . . must be mad to tell them such things." (Bleby: 1868)

That same evening the Presbyterian missionary Hope Waddell bade his congregation "Be patient". He was at one with them in desiring their freedom but it could come only in a peaceful way, by the efforts of their friends in Britain. But "time longer than rope and time run out", was what the people thought.

On the evening of 28 December, Hope Waddell, returning to his station at Cornwall, near Montego Bay, found the congregation dispersing in fright. The only answer that could be got was

> "Palmyra on fire." It was not an ordinary estate fire. It was the pre-concerted signal that . . . the struggle for freedom had begun. It was the response to "Kensington on fire" . . . the one hoisted the flaming flag of liberty and the other saluted it, calling on all between and around to follow their example . . . Scarcely had night closed in, when the sky toward the interior was illuminated by unwanted glares as fires rose here and there in rapid succession. (Waddell: 1970).

The editor of the *Cornwall Courier* wrote at 11 o'clock that night from his office in Falmouth: "The whole sky in the South West is illuminated. From our office we at the moment perceive five distinct fires."

Waddell and Samuel Barrett, owner of Cornwall, took their message from Cornwall to Spots Valley which belonged to an absentee proprietor. There the case was different.

> They listened to Mr. Barrett reading the proclamation issued by Sir Willoughby Cotton till it spoke of their returning to work, when they all lifted up their voices and overwhelmed him with clamour. 'We have worked enough already, and will work no more. The life we live is too bad; it is the life of a dog. We don't be slaves no more; we flog no more. We free now . . . no more slaves again.' (Waddell: 1970)

"In the space of five minutes after the pre-concerted signal was made, fifteen enormous fires were seen in different directions around this once charming scene; and then it was but too plain that the work of devastation had commenced in its most horrific form. The conch shell was heard to blow in every quarter, accompanied by huzzas and shouts of exultation from the infatuated slaves." (Senior: 1978)

The voices of the exultant slaves echo across the generations through the shouts of a lonely slave, a black Paul Revere, with a blazing torch, racing through the night shouting, "No watchman now! no watchman now! nigger man . . . burn the house, burn backra house! Brimstone come . . . bring fire, and burn massa house!"

Whispered across the years, we hear Joseph Williams, a former slave of Mr Tharpe of Hampton Estate in St James, who told his granddaughter,

Beatrice Williams, about slavery and about the night at Mr Tharpe's great house, when

> De white people dem a play dem . . . ah hear say dem have a billiard table deh . . . and when dem a bun down di house . . . black people knock fire pon dem house. Mi hear seh wen Missa Tharpe come him say him doan mind di house wa burn, like the billiard table . . . for it was class. Kensington . . . an dem lick fire pan backra house again (laugh) . . . Is big fire a night you know . . . but dem no have no wisdom . . . because the man wha deh afar, him can see ina di light . . . When backra see dem im fire gun afta dem . . . bow! Shoot afta dem! Dem run, bwoy. (Brodber: 1983)

Exaltation echoes through the voices, exaltation, a sense of freedom, a feeling or release, of liberation.

On 29 December 1831 Montego Bay was in a panic with rumours that the rebel slaves were going to set the town ablaze every night. Pandemonium reigned. The townspeople took comfort from the arrival on New Year's Day of a party of marines from Port Royal on the *HMS Sparrowhawk* and General Sir Willoughby Cotton, commander of British forces in Jamaica. The commodore of the fleet stationed at Port Royal disembarked from the *HMS Blanche* a day later with 300 soldiers and 16 artillery men with two field-pieces and rockets. The general reported that he "had relieved apprehension and quieted the feeling of alarm" in the bay, "but the eastern part of Hanover and the whole of the northern portion of St James are in open revolt and almost the whole of the estates destroyed, and the negroes gone boldly away".

In Trelawny, Custos James McDonald reported to the governor that many of the slaves in the parish were at that moment in a state of rebellion and that nine-tenths of the slave population had that morning refused to turn out to work.

Westmoreland and St Elizabeth were involved. The editor of the *Cornwall Courier* reported that the parishes of Westmoreland and St James had for some days been in a state of considerable excitement, with rumours of intended insurrection among the slave population. The Westmoreland Regiment had been on duty since Monday morning. In this western third of Jamaica there were about 106,000 slaves, most of them attached to the sugar estates and cattle pens, but there were a number of slaves in the urban areas also, in elegant Falmouth with its Georgian buildings and sugar-loading wharves; in Montego Bay, in the busy sugar port of Lucea, in Savanna-la-Mar and Black River. The harbours were busy with sloops and schooners trading with Spanish America.

Jamaica's long central watershed begins at Holland Point in the east and continues westwards across the full length of the island to Dolphin Head and Negril. The watershed defines the course of the rivers, sending the Jones and Y. S. Rivers south through Lacovia to join the Black River, while the Great River Valley runs north to empty its waters into the sea just west of Montego Bay. Along its course are those names which figure in the Western Liberation Uprising of 1831-32: Marchmont, Lapland, Catadupa, Retrieve, Cambridge, Greenwich, Hazelymph, Seven Rivers, Montpelier, Copse and Lethe. This watershed and the two river systems dictated the shape and fate of the enterprise.

The first round went to two bands made up of about 500 badly armed, inadequately trained men, who challenged the St James militia under Colonel W. S. Grignon, planter and plantation attorney (known as "Little Breeches"). The colonel reported that the company of the St James Regiment most positively refused to remain at the post. He retreated the whole body to Montego Bay, thus enabling the freedom fighters to cut the road from Montego Bay to Savanna-la-Mar, but they lost their two leaders, Johnson and Alexander Campbell. Johnson was killed "so near the white people that they could not carry him away", and Campbell "died in the morning – we made a rough coffin and buried him. Gardner read the funeral service over him".

For a brief period the freedom fighters held the initiative, and there were reports of activity along the Great River into St Elizabeth. In early January the tide began to turn under pressure from the St Elizabeth and Westmoreland militia regiments and the British soldiers. General Cotton was steadily augmenting his forces with marines and 100 additional soldiers from Kingston, but he also made sure that a large force was held ready in Kingston to deal with any discontent there or elsewhere; and he called on the Accompong maroons to cover the Great River area from Chesterfield to Duckett Spring.

The African-Jamaicans were not skilled in guerrilla warfare. Only a small number of them had firearms or were trained to use them. Most were armed with cutlasses, sharpened sticks and wooden clubs. With these they fought bravely, attacking armed militia men and soldiers. The torch was their most effective weapon. Breaking up into small groups, they established bases in the forests and moved frequently

Attack on Montpelier Estate during the "Baptist War"

from place-to-place. In late February the governor, Somerset Lowry, Earl of Belmore, reported to his council-of-war in Spanish Town that the rebels had been driven into the fastness of the country and that their forces were greatly diminished; but they remained a threat, and he was forced to continue martial law for another 30 days. In the words of the *Royal Gazette*, 21-28 January 1832:

> We had hoped that by the early arrival of the Commander of the forces in St James, with the overwhelming disposable force of Regulars and Militia under his command, the Rebels, would long ere this have been captured or killed. Such we lament to say is not the case. The Rebels have had breathing space allowed them; of this they have availed themselves most amply, and they are now much better organized than they could possibly have been at the commencement of the insurrection.

This assessment was inaccurate. The end was in sight, notwithstanding the courage of the freedom fighters. General Cotton's forces bottled them up in the Great River Valley, closing the northern exit at Roundhill and the mouth of the Great River, taking control of Montpelier and the Great River Barracks and pushing the Black Regiment on to Belvedere and Greenwich. By 26 January the freedom fighters had been forced to break up into small bands and take refuge in the forests. At the end of March Sam Sharpe gave himself up, joining Robert Gardner, Linton, Thomas Dove, Dehaney and other leaders in prison in Montego Bay.

But the spirit of the slaves was not broken. The Anglican rector in Westmoreland, who spoke to some of those taken prisoner, was convinced that the rebellion would break out again, not only from the causes which had occasioned the late one, but also because the blacks believed the king had given them freedom. Even more telling is this passage from a letter written by J. B. Suicke, a white resident, on 23 May, the day of Sam Sharpe's execution: "The question will not be left to the arbitrament of a long angry discussion between the government and the planter. The slave himself has been taught that there is a third party and that party himself. He knows his strength and will assert his claim to freedom. Even at this moment, unawed by the late failure, he discusses the question with a fixed determination." (Suicke: 1832)

The freedom fighters had demonstrated also, by means of the torch, how vulnerable the sugar plantation was. Through the five western parishes and far away in eastern Portland, where discontent had erupted, burnt-out sugar works, estate buildings and ravaged cane-pieces testified that "the rebels, though defeated, had destroyed an appreciable part of the material basis of their enslavement. They had succeeded in making slavery an insupportably expensive system to maintain." (Hart: 1985)

The people had responded to Sam Sharpe's call in large numbers. Between 25,000 and 40,000 withdrew their labour from the estates. These freedom fighters, and they were numerous, by so massive a response and by sacrifice made emancipation an act of necessity, not of philanthropy.

Joseph Williams speaks of white reprisals against the backs. He tells how "dem haffi live a . . . tek long thatch an mek house . . . ena bush". He refers to the suffering, "Di black people meet it. If me even come an' see dem a do a white man anyting me nah talk, no man, I don't business wid it, I couldn't business wid it. The ole generation pay for it . . . Lawd, them meet it! Dem meet it."

Some liberal whites were outraged at the reprisals on the slaves and the attacks on the missionaries. Joseph Williams tells of Mr Tharpe, owner of several properties in Trelawny:

> im always work wid dem slave dem . . . and him kinda have sympathy
> wid dem . . . One day when him [a fugitive] came out of the bush to
> find something – You know you have you pickney dem – you haffi
> go look something gie dem . . . him come out, dem ketch him an
> anoder man a go along . . . an dem shoot di first one so, Bam . . .
> There was Missa Tharpe . . . drive up same time and seh 'What? I
> wont have that, No, loose him down, loose him. Shoot none of my
> slaves.' Granpa seh dem loose him an' him live a hundred years.
> (Brodber: 1983)

Mr Tharpe's reference to "old slaves" suggests that the incident which took place in the hard time after the 1832 rebellion had been crushed. The freedom fighters engaged in a widespread destruction of property in protest against a barbaric system of forced labour, but they did not go on a crusade against white people. The records of the parishes that were involved show that 14 whites and three of their brown allies were killed, and that at least three of the whites were soldiers. As a Presbyterian missionary wrote, "Had the masters, when they got the upper hand, been as forbearing, as tender of their slaves' lives as their slaves had been of theirs, it would have been to their lasting honour and to the permanent advantage of the colony." Through their courts martial and their civil courts the plantocracy and the military instituted a reign of terror, with summary trials, savage floggings and hangings. About 750 slaves and 14 free persons were convicted for alleged participation in the rebellion and of that number 580 were executed. Fouteen whites and three browns were killed and 12 whites and three browns wounded. The occupations of those convicted provide an illustration of how widely based the uprising was. The field slaves were in the majority but a high percentage of the participants possessed mechanical and other skills. Most significant of all was the involvement of a large number of drivers.

A white backlash followed. The old formula, "Teach them a lesson" was the cry of those who had seen their property destroyed, their labour force broken up. Mingled with anger was fear of the black majority. Resentment took several forms: floggings and executions under a show of legality, personal attacks on missionaries, an organised campaign to expel them from Jamaica. A few liberal Jamaicans were outraged by these excesses. Mr Roby, Collector of Customs in Montego Bay, and Samuel Barrett, Speaker of the House of Assembly, wrote to William Knibb expressing deep disgust at the way in which he and Thomas Burchell had been treated. These were in the minority.

The white backlash took the form of an uprising organised by the Colonial Church Union which was formed by estate owners and Anglican ministers of religion at a meeting in the Anglican rectory at St Ann's Bay, on 26 January 1832. The rector, the Rev. William Bridges, was present. The union resolved "to present a general petition to the Legislature for the expulsion of all sectarian missionaries, and to prevent the dissemination of any religious doctrines at variance with those of the English and Scottish Churches". Members then set about destroying nonconformist chapels. Rev. Henry Bleby's chapel in Falmouth was destroyed. He was tarred and feathered. Some Moravians were affected, but the Baptists bore the brunt of the attack. Before the governor could take steps to stop this unlawful action, 11 Baptist churches had been destroyed, including those at Salters Hill, Falmouth, Montego Bay, Rio Bueno, Brown's Town, Lucea and St Ann's Bay.

The Baptist missionaries took up the challenge. At a meeting in Spanish Town they decided to send William Knibb to Britain to tell the British people what had happened and to affirm that the Jamaican slaves had a right to religious instruction and to worship God.

News of the Western Liberation Uprising reached the British government on 19 February 1832. The despatch from Lord Belmore, governor of Jamaica, was published in full in the *London Extraordinary Gazette* on 22 February and the struggle for West Indian freedom moved from the cane-fields and towns of Jamaica to Britain, to the British parliament and people.

This took place during a period of great crisis in Britain over the reform of parliament and the extension of the franchise to a much larger number of people. Reform was the top priority. The Whigs had been given a handsome majority over the Tories in the 1831 general election so that they might extend the franchise. The Tories, however, had a majority in the House of Lords and they were holding up the Reform Bill.

By blocking the bill the Lords ignited popular discontent. A mob sacked Nottingham Castle. Extensive riots devastated Derby and Bristol. The military was called out to prevent the colliers from burning aristocratic properties. On Guy Fawkes night (5 November, 1831) the Bishops who had voted against the Reform Bill were burnt in effigy, coal pits were set on fire and gas pipes cut. The industrialists, fearing that the sabotage would spread, pressed the government to resolve the deadlock. Working men organised political unions and started military drilling. The underlying threat of civil war receded when the political process recommenced in December; but the Reform Bill had yet to be carried.

In 1830 the Abolitionist Society decided to press for immediate emancipation. There was little chance that the emancipation of African slaves in remote West Indian islands would receive priority at a time when popular discontent over wider political representation for the British people was strong and deep. The Whigs were committed to the principle of protecting property rights. How at such a time could they give priority to setting free the West Indian labour force, the property of English owners? By following the calendar of events and bearing in mind a picture of Britain itself torn apart by dissensions and riots, we come to recognise Thomas Fowell Buxton's superb qualities of leadership. We see also how by its size and by the extent of the destruction Sam Sharpe's demand for immediate emancipation put the Jamaican issue on the front burner alongside parliamentary reform. The Colonial Church Union, by its fanatical behaviour, destroyed the case of the West Indian planters while the victims of their attack, the missionaries, helped the Abolitionists to transform their case into a national cause, a cause that had to do with freedom of conscience, and not only with property. Freedom of conscience was an issue which England itself had settled during the Reformation.

Thomas
Fowell Buxton

As soon as news of the rebellion was received, the West India interests immediately strengthened their propaganda campaign, denounced the "incendiary preachers", emphasised the importance of the sugar colonies to Britain, highlighted the savagery of the slaves and inveighed against the lunacy of "letting loose so many wild beasts". These statements improved their public standing. Buxton counter attacked on 7 March when he declared in the House of Commons: "If the question respecting the West Indies was not speedily settled it would settle itself in an alarming way (i.e., by further rebellions) and the only way it could be settled was by extinction of slavery."

On 23 March William Burge returned to the attack. In a debate in the House of Commons, he charged that disturbances in the West Indies were always a result of discussions about reform and amelioration in the House of Commons. Buxton rebutted the charge, declared that the planters were responsible for the rebellion and pointed to the white insurrection in which the planters had publicly advertised their intention of seceding to the United States.

Two weeks after the debate, on 1 April, Lord Belmore's report on the white insurrection was published in Britain. It described in detail the attacks on chapels and on the missionaries. The burnt-out cane fields had signalled an attack on property while the burnt-out nonconformist chapels signalled an attack on the right of dissent and freedom of conscience. The talk about secession and open defiance of the law by the Colonial Church Union shocked many who had been wavering in their support of the anti-slavery campaign. The tide of public opinion began to turn against the planters.

On 12 May, in the midst of the crisis, the Abolitionists held their annual meeting and called on their supporters for even greater effort. Pointing to massive national support, Buxton urged immediate action. The committee passed a resolution calling on the government to emancipate the slaves without delay. Heartened by the growing swell of public support, Buxton lifted the meeting to a moment of greatness with the closing passage of his address:

> When we look at the career of affliction of our brother man . . .
> When we view him entering this life by the desert track of bondage
> . . . and see him consigned to a premature and unregarded grave,
> having died in slavery . . . there can be but one feeling in my heart,
> one expression on my lips: 'Great God, how long is this inequity to
> continue?' (Buxton: 1832)

The political crisis came to a head in the middle of May 1832. On 12 May the king refused the request of the Whigs that he appoint a number of peers so as to give them the necessary majority in the House of Lords which would allow them to outvote the opposition. The Whigs resigned. The King recalled Wellington. For ten days Britain was on the brink of revolution. The popular slogan was "Stop the Duke – Go for Gold." The Whigs returned to power on 19 May, the Lords accepted the Reform Bill and the king signed it on 7 June.

While these things were happening, public support for the abolition of slavery was growing. During May missionaries from Jamaica arrived, amongst them the formidable William Knibb, who told the committee of the Baptist Missionary Society: "But if it be necessary I will take them [my wife and children] by the hand and walk barefoot through the Kingdom, but I will make known to the Christians of England what their brethren in Jamaica are suffering." Some members hesitated at making slavery the central issue but finally all who heard him decided to give their support. He began his campaign at the annual missionary meeting at Spitalfield's Chapel in London, where he declared, "Whatever the consequence I will speak. I will not rest day or night until I see slavery destroyed root and branch," and he pointed to the story of the anti-slavery campaign as "a wonderful evidence of the force and influence of the truth when brought home to the heart and conscience of a Christian nation".

Never before had the case against slavery been presented so forcibly to the British people by white men who had spent some years in Jamaica, ministering to African-Jamaicans, observing the plantation system from within, acquainting themselves with the slave laws and learning how great were the powers of the owner.

Buxton lost no time. Public opinion was behind him. His instinct told him to act now. Against the advice of his closest advisers, Dr Stephen Lushington among them, in the interval between the return of the Whigs to power and the king's signing of the Reform Bill, Buxton proposed a Motion in the House of Commons for a Commons Commission of Enquiry into Slavery to counterbalance the pro-slavery Lords Committee. He framed the resolution in such a way as to commit the Whigs to immediate emancipation. They could hardly refuse, but they actively tried to avoid the commitment Buxton sought.

Ministers of government and members of the Whig Party pressured Buxton to withdraw the motion. "It was like a continual tooth-drawing the whole evening," he said. But he stood firm. In his speech to the Commons he declared that "a war against people struggling for their rights would be the falsest position in which it was possible for England to be placed".

Buxton's motion was defeated by 136 to 90, but the size of his minority impressed the government and heartened the society for a nationwide drive. It made good use of the evidence of persecution which the white insurrection provided. The evidence was fully documented by the governor of Jamaica's May despatch as well as by the missionaries.

The British parliament passed the Act of Emancipation on 28 August 1833. It came into effect on 1 August 1834. Brathwaite's analysis of the voting on the bill reveals how effective the campaigning had been. It demonstrated that 70 per cent of the minority votes came from English and Welsh boroughs with large dissenting congregations, just the constituency the abolitionists had been aiming at.

Throughout the islands jubilation prevailed at the news of freedom. On 31 July 1834, at a great gathering at Knibb's church in Falmouth, at midnight the cry went up, "The monster is dead, the monster is dying", and some of the hated symbols of slavery were buried.

The old slave Joseph Williams tells of the celebrations and the burial of the hated whip and chain in his account to his granddaughter.

> (Female): Him say ef you ever hear bout slavery? Yes, dem tell me about slavery, tell me about Parson Knibb and Parson Burgess [Burchell]. Parson Knibb and Parson Burgess? Yes. A Him go to h'England ask fi freedom fi Jamaica. A so freedom come yah. Mi fader did tell me about dat dem parson. . . . Sorry fi de people dem, dem go to England and ask di Queen – di King or di Queen – fi gie dem freedom in Jamaica.(Brodber: 1983)

For nearly 130 years, from 1834 to 1962, the official version of the emancipation struggle was in substance the story of the old slave, Joseph Williams. The Western Liberation Uprising was defeat and disaster, to be forgotten, rubbed out as though it had never been. Sam Sharpe, Linton, Robert Gardner, the others who were executed, mouldered in their shallow unmarked graves. Year after year, throughout Jamaica, on 1 August, Jamaicans – and children particularly – celebrated the British gift of freedom and sang: "Rule Britannia, Britannia rule the waves/Britons never, never, never shall be slaves." This was also the story as seen through the eyes of British officials and educators.

These are not the facts. Through the uprising of 1831-32 Sam Sharpe and the other freedom fighters reset the timetable for freedom. It is a story of missionaries who struggled for emancipation and then spent themselves in developing a system of education. It is a story of British abolitionists, Buxton and William Wilberforce pre-eminent among them; and it is the story of British dissenters, Christian working folk whose support was vital in making abolition a national movement.

Samuel Sharpe, Thomas Dove, Linton, Dehaney and the rest claimed freedom and the right to rebel against a system that denied them freedom. They saw themselves as free men. This is the message Sam Sharpe burnt into the minds of his followers, that he "had rather die than be a slave". This is what Patrick Ellis meant when on 6 February 1832 finding himself surrounded by soldiers, he stepped forward, uncovered his breast and cried out, "I am ready, give me your volley. Fire, for I will never again be a slave." This is what the hundreds of freedom fighters meant by the way they faced death.

They paid the price. In justice to them the price exacted should be known. Trial was a summary affair. By far the greater number were executed "In many instances, . . . criminals were condemned during the morning and executed between two and four o'clock". (Senior: 1969) Of

106 slaves tried in St James, 99 were convicted, six executed, one pardoned and two dismissed. Of the 99 convicted, 84 were sentenced to death. In Hanover, 96 of the 138 convicted were sentenced to death; in Westmoreland, 33 of the 64 convicted were sentenced to death. Other punishments in St James included one sentence of 500 lashes, one of 300 lashes with life imprisonment, one of 200 lashes with six months' imprisonment, and so the dreadful story of barbarity went. (Hart: 1985)

It was a searing picture of a society in which property was put before the human being and violence was the first resort in maintaining authority.

Sam Sharpe learned of the executions while in prison. He himself was tried at Montego Bay on 19 April. He was publicly hanged there on 23 May 1832. At no time did his courage, his nobility of spirit shine more brightly than on the day of his execution. Henry Bleby reports that he seemed to be unmoved by the near approach of death. He addressed the assembled crowd in a clear, unfaltering voice, admitted that he had broken the laws of the country and declared that he depended for salvation upon the Redeemer who shed his blood for sinners upon Calvary. Sharpe's reference to the crucifixion of Jesus by the Roman authorities was significant. Relating the event to his own execution could not have escaped his audience. (Hart: 1985) Sharpe declared that the missionaries had nothing whatever to do with the uprising. This meant that he took full responsibility. Then in Bleby's words, in a few moments "the executioner had done his work and the noble-minded originator of this unhappy revolt had ceased to exist".

But he did not die in vain. Bleby's judgement was:

> The revolt failed of accomplishing the immediate purpose of its author, yet by it, a further wound was dealt to slavery which accelerated its destruction for it demonstrated to the imperial legislature that among the Negroes themselves, the spirit of freedom had been so widely diffused as to render it most perilous to postpone the settlement of the most important question of emancipation to a later period. (Bleby: 1868)

Daddy Sharpe was the leader, strong yet modest, deeply religious and compassionate, heroic in character and in life's daily testings. In the following poem he speaks of his encounter to the Jamaican people.

> I love the strong and fighting things,
> and I do miss the belly laugh at evening time,
> and talk and singing with my brothers them
> at night time on the mountain top.
> And now the darkness fall upon them all
> on Thomas Dove, and Gardner and on William James

from Ducketts; and on Johnson from Retrieve,
and on Dehaney who did tell them straight
he know they have determined he must hang
so hang him then and he will take with him
whatever things he knows,
and will not sign confession.
Them all have gone. How I to stay?
Them all be dead. How I to live?

Sherlock

CHAPTER 20

A home of their own

The Act of Emancipation (1833) set in motion forces of radical social change that confronted Jamaica's white governing class – the plantocracy – and her newly-freed African-Jamaicans with challenges that could not be ignored.

The critical question was the same for the governing class and the African-Jamaican labour force – could either or both find a way of laying the foundations of a free and just society?

The answers lie in the history of the period 1838, when full freedom came into effect, and 1865. We begin with the year 1831 when the Jamaica House of Assembly removed the civil disabilities under which some free Jamaicans had laboured for these reflect the racist and vicious character of white plantation society.

In 1831, three years before Emancipation a law was passed which conferred on black and coloured people "of free condition" the right to vote provided they met the necessary property qualifications. They were entitled to "have and enjoy all the rights, privileges, immunities, etc." as if they were "descended from white ancestors". The power of the ballot was a privilege until then exercised only by the white minority. The free people moved from being faceless exiles to becoming citizens, albeit of limited status.

The 1831 Act declared that "whereas it is expedient to grant additional privileges to coloured and black persons of free condition . . . it is hereby enacted and ordained . . . that all such persons of free condition, whether lawfully manumised or being the free-born subjects of His Majesty shall from the first day of August next be permitted to vote at any election for any person to serve in the assemblies of the island provided he possesses an estate to freehold or a house . . . of the annual value of one hundred pounds . . . or shall possess an estate of freehold in land and premises . . .

in such parish where such election shall be held, of the actual annual value of fifty pounds." (*Laws of Jamaica* 1831)

In claiming his rights under the law, George William Gordon declared in the House of Assembly in November 1863, "I stand here tonight as one of the sons of free Jamaica. I claim all the ancient privileges and rights granted to us by Magna Carta and the Bill of Rights."

Slavery, racism and the plantation had up to that time shaped the social and economic structure of West Indian societies, with the exception of British Honduras whose economy had been sustained by logging rather than by the sugar-and-slave plantation.

The Act of Emancipation set in motion the most significant and far-reaching social and economic revolution in the history of Jamaica and of the other countries of the Commonwealth Caribbean. It mandated that in the first instance large numbers of individuals were no longer slaves but neither were they free citizens. They were "apprenticed labourers". Full freedom was granted in 1838 but full and free citizenship was still a long way off.

The decisive section of the Act decreed that "whereas divers persons are held in slavery within divers of His Majesty's colonies and it is just and expedient that all such persons should be manumitted and set free and that all reasonable compensation should be made to the persons hitherto entitled to the services of such slaves for the loss which they will incur . . . be it therefore enacted that from the first day of August, one thousand eight hundred and thirty four, all persons who have been duly registered as slaves shall by force and virtue of this act . . . become and be apprenticed labourers . . ." (Abolition of Slavery Act 1833)

Slave owners in Jamaica received compensation from the British Government amounting to £6,616,927 for the inconvenience and loss they were expected to suffer when they no longer controlled the forced labour which had been the mainstay of their opulent lifestyles. The emancipated people, ten times in number to the plantation owners and the other white employees, received no compensation, no guidance, no training to enable them to rearrange their lives independent of the oppressive slave-plantation system.

For the duration of the apprenticeship period the employers (the former masters) were required to supply this new labour force "with such food, clothing, lodging, medicine, medical attendance . . . as by any law now in force in the colony". The governor was required to appoint Justices of the Peace and Special Magistrates to maintain law and order and to protect the interests of the apprentices but they generally sided with the planters. This led to many abuses and as a result the apprenticeship period was terminated in 1838, two years before it was due to end.

Emancipation struck at the heart of the system of slavery by introducing the payment of wages to labourers. Under slavery, planters had operated with little working capital. They did not pay wages except to overseers and their kind, and they cut the outlay on food to a minimum by letting the workers grow much of what they required. They sold their sugar through agents in Britain who in turn purchased supplies required on the plantation and advanced working capital in lean years.

These arrangements suited the agents admirably because they could collect interest on the moneys loaned by insisting that all the debtors' sugar should pass through their hands. The price of Jamaica sugar was therefore fixed after taking all these factors into consideration.

Jamaica planters faced strong competition from European beet sugar, and from Mauritius, Brazil, Puerto Rico, Fiji and Cuba, countries continuing to rely on slave labour. They either had to improve efficiency through controlled expenditure and use new, improved equipment: ploughs, harrows, steam engines to turn the mills, or go bankrupt. Now wages for the workers had to be paid in reasonable time and this created cash flow problems. The planters required more working capital than formerly, and many were still in debt to their London agents although much of the compensation money had gone to repay debts, mortgages and sub-mortgages.

While all of this was taking place the price of sugar continued to decline, mainly because of inefficient management practices. The price had risen for a while when the Haitian revolution put Jamaica's chief competitor, St Domingue, out of business but cheap sugar from Cuba was rapidly becoming a threat.

Emancipation scene, Spanish Town

Planters blamed emancipation for their economic woes although the slide in production had started many years earlier. By 1775 about 30 per cent of estates in the island were already in the hands of absentee owners. In most instances the overseers and attorneys in charge were more interested in feathering their own nests than in seeing to the economic welfare of their employers. A further decline in the economy after 1790 forced many planters to surrender their mortgaged properties to metropolitan merchants and bankers thereby beginning a trend towards corporate ownership. (Higman: 1976)

Between 1805 and 1850 the market price of sugar fell repeatedly: by 25 per cent between 1805 and 1825, by another 25 per cent between 1825 and 1835, and again by another 25 per cent between 1835 and 1850. (Sewell: 1968) At the time of emancipation, 80 per cent of the sugar estates were owned by absentees while approximately 75 per cent of coffee plantations and roughly 85 per cent of pens continued to be operated by proprietors resident in the island.

The final blow came between 1846 and 1854 when, in order to meet the demand for cheap food to feed her rapidly increasing population, Britain removed the preferential tariff on West Indian sugar and opened

News of emancipation being read

THE STORY OF THE JAMAICAN PEOPLE

the market to international competition. Once 24,895 tons of foreign sugar entered Britain in 1846 at a lower tariff rating than had been set previously, British and West Indian financial houses collapsed. Merchant houses, which in the past had financed the planting of sugar crops also lost their investments on failed wheat and potato crops in Britain and on over-speculation in other industrial ventures. In 1847 13 West India houses which had been founded to meet the urgent need for capital in the islands went into bankruptcy. These included the Planters Bank in Jamaica and the West India Bank in Barbados.

The Jamaica sugar industry was almost wiped out. Planters were forced to sell their crops on the open market, often at a loss. Production fell by more than 50 per cent from 71,000 tons in 1832 to 25,000 tons in 1852. The inbond price of sugar in Britain which had been £49 per ton in 1840, dropped to £23 in 1846. Many of the already struggling sugar and coffee plantations were partly or wholly abandoned and the price of property plummeted. On some estates the wage bill was cut by as much as a half or two-thirds, to the detriment of the labourers.

Added to this, natural disasters struck. Between 1850 and 1851 the island was ravaged by cholera, smallpox and drought. About 32,000 persons died leaving the already dwindling labour force sadly depleted. One Scottish doctor in the island took advantage of the depressed conditions to purchase 50 plantations, and later became exceedingly wealthy from banana and coconuts.

Planter society had never been free. It had always been in bondage to the sugar-and-slave plantation. Just as the slave carried on his body the marks of servitude, whites – resident owners, managers, overseers – carried in their minds the tensions and anxieties generated by living in a garrison society dominated by fear and also by feelings of betrayal and abandonment by Britain.

The hysteria that gripped whites in Montego Bay at the outbreak of the Western Liberation Uprising, the viciousness and scale of white reprisals against blacks and against white missionaries which followed in 1832, the enactment of punitive laws to enforce subjugation which remained in place up to the time of the Morant Bay Uprising in 1865 – these all signalled the decline and fall of the planter oligarchy.

From this withering plantation society we turn to the African-Jamaicans who, in the face of planter hostility following emancipation, were laying the foundations of the Jamaican nation. In these early years are to be found the source of empowerment and ennoblement that came from the defeat of the planter's attempt at coercion, refusal to be bound to the estates at less than subsistence wage, efforts to make emancipation meaningful and to triumph over what appeared to be insuperable obstacles. Few whites understood the implications of the changes taking place and therefore the need to reorganise their operations and ease the transition process.

First, we will give an account of planter coercion and exploitation in the apprenticeship period and the creation of an African-Jamaican yeomanry. In the chapter that follows we will describe in some detail the people's rejection of planter domination by means of political monopoly and by coercive legislation.

Many former slaves turned peasants, built their own homes, formed new communities and determined, however humble their circumstance and no matter how difficult the struggle, to remain outside of the inflexible plantation system.

The only Jamaican planter to grant full freedom to his field hands in 1834, thereby attempting to save them from further victimisation, was the Marquis of Sligo. He was possibly influenced by his Antiguan colleagues who declared full freedom in 1834, knowing that the only source of employment on that island was on the plantations and that the emancipated people would therefore still be under their control.

In Jamaica, however, "Many masters in their bitterness of heart, vented their wrath upon their unfortunate labourers . . . within a period of two years 60,000 apprentices received a total of a quarter of a million lashes and 50,000 other punishments by tread-mill, chain-gang work, or some other device . . ." (D. F.Walker: 1930)

The following account demonstrates the useless waste of human energy, loss of valuable time, and numerous atrocities meted out to some unfortunate apprentices. The narrator, an apprentice from Penshurst Estate, knowing that he was to be brought before the visiting magistrate the following day, hid from work. Finally after about seven weeks he was caught and taken by the Captain of Police at St Ann's.

> I met him on the road; he took me and put me in dungeon at Carlton; was kept there from Wednesday until Friday morning, then policeman came and took me to Brown's Town, and put me in Cage till next day; then Mr Rawlinson [the magistrate] had me handcuffed and sent me to Penshurst, and put me in dungeon for ten days before he try me . . . Then he sentenced me to St Ann's Bay Workhouse, for nine days, to get fifteen lashes in going in; to dance the treadmill morning and evening, and work in the penal gang; and after I come back from punishment, I must lock up every night in dungeon till he visit the property again, and I have to pay fifty days out of my own time for the time I been runaway.

At the workhouse he was given fifteen lashes with the cat-o-nine tails and chained by the neck to another man. Next morning he was put on the treadmill along with others. The treadmill ground the cornmeal which fed the prisoners. He was not flogged because he quickly learned how "to catch the step by next day but they flog all the rest that could not step the mill, flogged them most dreadful." (Lalla & D'Costa: 1990)

The apprentice, Williams, also described in detail the brutality of the punishments meted out to other unfortunate victims. From the viewpoint of today it should be noted that the orders of the magistrates were carried out by fellow blacks in the name of justice.

Full freedom in 1838 left the former slaves destitute. All they thought they owned or were accustomed to having, even their English names, belonged to someone else. The Emancipation Act had provided that they should continue to live on the estates and receive the same food, clothing, medicine and medical attention for the duration of their apprenticeship. They were then to be allowed three months grace to continue living in their huts and to come to some arrangement with their former masters. There was some confusion over the interpretation of the specific clause that permitted them to continue to live in their huts but the Jamaica Attorney General ruled in favour of the planters. If they remained on the plantation they should pay rent for their dwellings. Immediately almost every planter began issuing notices to their former slaves requiring them to pay about one-third of their weekly wages in rent or quit the premises. The average wage was about three shillings a week. Those who failed to pay could be evicted on one week's notice, and if they failed to leave at the end of the time they could be arrested and imprisoned. The former slaves and their families found themselves destitute, without food or shelter or means of livelihood, "turned adrift and exposed to great misery and distress".

Emancipation gave them the right to free movement; the right to choose where and when they wished to work, but without a basic education and training many were compelled to remain on the plantation as field hands and tenants-at-will under conditions determined by the landlord, and for wages set by him. It was not sufficient to be legally free from slavery; they had to be free from unjust bonds, free to lead normal, healthy lives of their own choosing.

The rent they paid in a year could have purchased at least an acre of land and turned them into smallholders with some limited degree of independence. The planters believed that because the labourers could earn more by weekly work on the estates, they would prefer to stay. They also believed that, in keeping with African tradition, the labourers would be reluctant to move away from the houses in which they were born, their provision grounds and the graves of their ancestors which served as shrines. Above all there was nowhere for them to go. But they underestimated the will of the majority who went to great lengths to preserve their newly gained freedom.

The labour force decreased considerably but the planters thought that this was only temporary.

They squatted on Crown lands in the mountains or on abandoned estates, rented or leased marginal lands from individuals strapped for cash, and in some instances managed to purchase small plots on which they built modest cottages, from which they could not be evicted on the whim of an individual. Only the most destitute without any option became tenants on the estates.

When the planters realised that the labourers did not wish to work for them, they resorted to legislation which maintained their white monopoly and made life intolerable for the African-Jamaicans. For instance, anyone found carrying produce without a written permit could be arrested on the assumption that the goods had been stolen. The Trespass Act permitted the shooting of small stock: goats, sheep, pigs, which were generally owned by smallholders, but horses and cows from the plantations were exempt. To aggravate the situation further, when these animals destroyed the peasants' provision grounds there was no compensation.

In the Grange Hill area of Westmoreland at about this time, the Rev. Henry Clarke expressed his distress at the spite and vindictiveness of landlords who constantly relocated workers' cottages to prevent them from taking advantage of permanent crops such as breadfruit and coconuts which they had planted. "Every village of the estates in this district, of five thousand inhabitants, has been moved within the last ten years; and as the people have to pull down and rebuild their cottages at their own expense, they have got into the way of erecting miserable little huts, in which the poor things are compelled to live, like pigs in a sty." The tenants refused to maintain these flimsy huts because of the uncertainty of their conditions of tenure.

The average wage was sixpence a day with the use of cottage and provision grounds and some missionaries, especially William Knibb, urged the people not to accept such extortionist arrangements. Some misguided ones took this as a signal not to work and began wandering about the countryside fully believing that Queen Victoria had freed them from labour of every kind, and would supply them with food and provisions from England for the rest of their lives. Rumours spread rapidly that they had also been granted free lands and that the planters had bribed some authorities and missionaries to rob them of their rights. They therefore refused to pay rent and by so doing placed themselves at the mercy of landlords only too anxious to evict them from their cottages and provision grounds.

The only real assistance the former slaves received came from some missionaries who obtained loans from their English friends, and then used the money to purchase small acreages which they then subdivided into

small lots for sale to their church congregations. They frequently had to use friends to carry out such transactions as the lands would not have been made available otherwise. Pride of ownership gave the people the self-confidence they badly needed, but the extremely small lots could not support the purchasers and their families by the only method they knew, which was agriculture.

Sligoville, the first free village, founded by the Rev. James Phillippo, below

In 1835 through the efforts of the Rev. James Phillippo the first free village was established at Sligoville in the hills above Spanish Town. He sub-divided 25 acres into one- and two-acre lots and sold them. They were quickly taken up and in June 1838, two months before full freedom was declared the first lot was fully paid for by Henry Lunan, a headman and former slave from an adjoining property.

In one of his letters to a friend asking for a loan, the Rev. Knibb emphasised,

> Should any of our members, as I know they will, be the victims of treachers, scorn or trickery, they may have a home . . . While the land owners have all the land they can, and they will, and they do daily oppress the people by demanding abominable high rents for their houses. In many cases though the house is no better than a hog-sty. I have seen demands of eight shillings and fourpence per week rent at the same time only one shilling and eightpence per day for wages, so that a man must work five days to pay for his house and grounds.

A home of their own   237

Knibb noted that the people were not asking for charity, they were paying back their loans and would continue to do so.

Some estates charged rentals as high as eight shillings and fourpence per week, and some out of spite refused employment to these tenants. The emancipated people who entered into financial transactions without the help of the missionaries often fell victim to unscrupulous landlords and attorneys who cheated them openly. Some were issued false documents; others received valid receipts but discovered later that these were not sufficient proof of ownership and so lost their investment. Few held proper deeds.

Petty tradesmen and artisans such as carpenters, masons, shoemakers and fishermen began migrating to the towns, especially to Kingston and Spanish Town, where they soon found that life was more difficult than on the plantation. They found that it was not easy to obtain employment. They lived in squalid conditions often as many as nine and ten to a room. They were among the first victims of epidemics.

At emancipation owners had been directed to make reasonable time and opportunity for labourers to be given religious and educational instruction. Missionaries in the field were also advised to engage themselves actively in this exercise.

Government's policy of restricting the amount of Crown lands available to the former slaves and of keeping vast tracts in the hands of a few, ensured that agriculture could not become a viable option for the masses. But the peasants tried to find ways of circumventing these restrictions. In some instances, they obtained grazing rights or the right to gather wood for fuel or to plant their provision grounds. The landowner in return received a share of the smallholder's profits. In addition he sometimes transported and marketed the produce for a fee which was not always in the best interest of the small farmer.

When planters stopped ejecting the people and began paying fairer wages production improved. Those who charged excessive rents, including charging rent for each member of the family and demanding payment in cash or working it out in days on the estate, found that they were short of labour. Some deliberately offered irregular employment believing that by increasing the hardships the labourers would be forced to work harder and the planter would benefit. But this only alienated the labour force further.

The authorities disapproved of the efforts of the missionaries to assist the peasants to establish communities and to educate themselves. They felt there was no need for the former slaves to aspire to become more than field hands. Nevertheless, in spite of strong resistance from both the planters and the authorities, the settlements of the smallholders in time grew into organised communities with the assistance of the missionaries.

Knibb possibly did more than anyone else to develop the free villages. He raised about £10,000 and with this he acquired at least three estates, including Birmingham and Kettering not far from Falmouth, divided them into small lots and resold them to the former slaves. Joseph Sturge, the English Quaker, who with another Quaker, Harvey, had been sent by the Anti-Slavery Society to report on the workings of the apprenticeship system, in one instance loaned £400 to purchase part of Mt Ablyla (also called Standfast) Estate. One hundred families were settled there. He also bought the freedom of James Williams, the apprentice from Penshurst, (whose story appears above), and took him to England.

The missionaries designed the layout of the ideal village but because of the steepness of the terrain and the lack of access roads the original plan could not always be implemented. Most villages could be reached only by narrow bridle paths; water had to be fetched from springs and gullies some distance away, and proper sanitary facilities were often unheard of. The following is a description of what the typical village was expected to be like:

> The villages are laid out in regular order, being divided into lots more or less intersected by roads or streets. The plots are usually in the form of an oblong square. The cottage is situated at an equal distance from each side of the allotment, and at about eight or ten feet, more or less, from the public thoroughfare. The piece of ground in the front is, in some instances, cultivated in the style of a European garden: displaying rose bushes, and other flowering shrubs among the choicer vegetables and fruits of the country, heterogeneously inter-mixed. (Phillippo: 1843)

Retreat Pen near Manchioneal is one of those villages laid out using the plan. It had 41 half-acre lots, more or less.

In contrast to the dilapidated plantation huts they once lived in, the peasants constructed modest dwellings often of Spanish wall or board which they cut from forest trees; roofs were shingled with wood or thatched with palm leaves. Some had wooden floors. A typical cottage consisted of two or three rooms – one or two bedrooms and a living room or hall which was sometimes converted into sleeping quarters as the family outgrew the bedroom space.

A few concerned persons of influence on the island called upon the government to assist with the development of the villages but their appeals fell on deaf ears. Lyndon H. Evelyn, Deputy Receiver General and Public Treasurer at Savanna-la-Mar recommended that the villages should be modeled on the English Agricultural Village plan, having a chapel and minister, "as religion held great attraction for the masses". He also called for schools, "as education was wholesome training for the young and held happy memories". He recommended that there should be houses and provision grounds for the elderly and that merchants and skilled workers should involve themselves in village activities. Smallholders were to be encouraged to grow export crops such as ginger, arrowroot, pimento, coffee and sugar cane, and so improve their living standard.

The Custos of St Elizabeth suggested that in addition to a church and school there should be a marketplace where African-type entertainment could be encouraged. But this only elicited a negative response from the planters and those in authority. They thought that if the labourers paid exorbitant rents and taxes they would be forced to work harder, production would increase and the planters would benefit.

Where it was possible, the people built a chapel and sometimes a school-house usually under the guidance of a missionary. Walter Dendy, the Baptist missionary, architect, builder and philanthropist who arrived in Jamaica twelve days after the Western Liberation Uprising, was one of them. In time, the government provided teachers and on occasion when they proved unsuccessful the villagers sometimes employed their own teachers. The wives of missionaries taught Bible classes, sewing, fancy work, cookery, music and general reading.

More ambitious adults learnt from their children attending day school, especially as they wanted to learn to read the Bible for themselves. The result was evidenced by a high level of literacy in some villages. Education became the means by which upward mobility was usually achieved. "The spelling book was a powerful factor of Christian enlightenment, and through the schools thousands were daily brought under the direct influence of the Gospel. All the churches took part in this great work of education." (Walker: 1930)

Mico College, which opened in 1836

As the need for more teachers grew missionaries selected young men of promise from among their congregations and instructed them. The training of these adults as class leaders and lay preachers opened opportunities for some of them to become "confidential servants in business houses, subordinate estate managers, governesses and school teachers".

In 1836, through the bequest of Lady Mico, the Mico Institution (Mico College), had been established "for the benefit of African slaves made free and engaged in the work [of teaching]". The educational level of the students was at first low, but the level of performance improved.

Knibb was the first to express the need for the training of local men for the ministry and in 1842, along with James Phillippo and Thomas Burchell, he approached the Baptist Missionary Society in England. A year later, in 1843, Calabar College was opened at Rio Bueno in Trelawny with ten students. They were all older men, very dedicated but mostly illiterate. However, three eventually graduated as ministers and seven as teachers. Under the tutelage of the Rev. Joshua Tinson, they acquired skills in reading, composition and pronunciation as well as some Hebrew and Greek, and "took the gospel of love to their brethren in the villages of the interior". In 1868 Calabar was transferred from Trelawny to Kingston.

Church and school were the centre of village life following the English tradition. "The church choir was a training ground for vocalists; the school provided recitations, the schoolroom was the natural venue for any entertainment except for organ recitals and concerts of sacred music, which were held in the church." (Jacobs: 1973)

Overall, about 19 unprofitable sugar estates were turned into free villages as well as some abandoned coffee plantations in the parishes of St Andrew, St John, Manchester and Metcalfe. Ewart, one of the special stipendiary magistrates assigned to the parish of St Thomas, to administer justice and prevent social and economic disturbance, reported from Morant Bay in October 1840 that three extensive villages had been established on former sugar plantations in the interior of that parish. He observed that the lots ranged in size from one to ten acres and that there were already in place about 300 cottages, "neat and comfortable and surrounded by gardens and provision grounds".

In November of that same year, Richard Chamberlaine, another stipendiary magistrate from the parish, who had been away for two years, remarked on the number of settlements and cottages that had sprung up "right and left" where before had been "bush and jungle". He was pleasantly surprised at the expansion of existing villages, the number of new shops, improved construction methods and the more spacious houses being built. Chamberlaine was a coloured man who later became custos of the parish.

Ten years after emancipation, Knibb reported that there were 23 villages in Trelawny with 1,790 houses; in St Thomas-in-the-Vale, 10 villages with 1,780 houses and in St James 10 villages with 1,000 houses all completed. In several areas, for example in Manchester, in upper Clarendon and St Catherine, among the foothills of the Blue Mountains in Portland and St George, in the Port Royal Mountains of St Andrew, villages developed in spite of the lack of government support.

They were also to be found in other remote areas across the island. Fifteen were at one time located in St Mary, 15 in the Dry Harbour

Mountains of St Ann where the village of Dumbarton consisted of 60 quarter-acre lots. There were also villages at Harmony Hall and Trysee not far from Brown's Town. The Methodists established the village of Epworth, also in St Ann, and well into the twentieth century it remained a "dry" village where alcohol could not be sold. Not many settlements were located near to large estates and small towns. Usually lands in these more advantageous areas were denied the aspiring smallholders.

Eventually about 2,000 such villages were established, allowing many thousands of freed people to become proud owners of homes of their own. Those who could not afford to purchase lands sometimes rented or leased plots and house spots. The house spots were at times so small they could hardly hold the tiny cottages, but their owners wanted homes of their own.

The most spectacular growth of smallholdings occurred immediately after the apprenticeship period. In 1840, two years after full freedom, only about 883 persons owned holdings of under ten acres; five years later, the number had increased to 20,724 and by 1865, at the time of the Morant Bay Uprising, the number stood at about 60,000. The planters were suffering as a result of the movement of workers away from the plantations, since only about one-third of the labourers available at the time of emancipation were then willing to work on the plantations.

Although the Jamaican peasantry could now become involved in the island's administrative affairs the requirements were stringent. They could register to vote if they owned real property worth £6 or paid £30 in rent or paid £3 in direct taxes. By the middle of the century some 20,000 could have met these requirements but under 3,000 registered to vote. The Baptist missionaries began a concerted effort to get small settlers to register and by 1863 in one or two parishes they made up as much as 63 per cent of the voters list. They could not however exert much influence through the electoral process as the property clause required a member of the Assembly to have an annual income of £300, and unencumbered property worth £3,000. Without sympathetic representation there could be no meaningful change.

Although planters and officials thought otherwise, the smallholders were generally industrious people. In 1850, John Candler, an English Quaker, observed that on the whole they performed as much work on the estates as in the days of slavery. He said that no one who had seen them at work in the cane fields, or hoeing coffee on the steep hillsides, or who had travelled among their provision grounds in the mountains, could call them idle. "I have seen them again and again, hundreds and thousands of them, men, women and children, loaded with provisions and fruits, which they carry on their heads, pouring down from the hills to market carrying weights which no European would encounter, and sweating under the heavy toil, yet all labouring cheerfully because they are free." (Olivier: 1933) The redistribution of the population across the interior of the island had a positive impact on the internal economy as trade followed settlement into the interior.

Sewell noted that planters blamed their economic ruin, not on their own inefficiency but on the shortage of labour and the refusal of the labourers to work an eight-hour day. As a stranger he could not answer these charges, but the people whom he had encountered were eager to work, to carry his luggage, to run errands and to offer their assistance for a paltry remuneration. He had never seen so many servants and attendants as in Jamaica. A government clerk had as many servants as a foreign ambassador. "Servants must have under-servants, and agents, sub- agents . . . He sees labour everywhere – on the roads, the streets, the wharves, and it is only upon the plantations that he hears any complaint. Yet even there he detects none of the labor-saving machinery that he has been accustomed to see at home, where labor is really scarce and dear . . ." (Sewell: 1968) The master-slave mentality was still very strong.

The Chief Commissioner of Roads told Sewell that he had 3,000 men in constant employment who worked diligently for five days a week, and marketed and cultivated their grounds on the sixth. They were never idle although stone breaking was harder than plantation work.

The Superintendent of the Rio Grande Copper Mines also told him that for eight years he had never experienced any labour shortage even though the men worked eight hours a day, six days a week. When the mines eventually closed, one sugar estate near Annotto Bay recruited 36 of the miners at thirty-six cents a day. It was three months before they were paid, and then they received only half the amount agreed upon. No wonder the labourers preferred to keep far away from the estates.

The rapid expansion of free villages in the interior enabled some strategically located older villages to grow into prosperous market towns. One observer noted that before emancipation Old Harbour consisted of two taverns, one or two houses, a post office, a pound, a blacksmith's shop operated by a slave, and a jail. Within two years it had become a thriving town through the flourishing marketing activities of the villagers from the interior. There was now a new court-house, many good houses and buildings, ten to twelve small shops, three blacksmith's shops, a tinsmith's shop and police station, in addition to the pound and two taverns from earlier days. It was the scene of a flourishing Saturday Market where all sorts of ground provisions, baked products, meat, poultry as well as items of haberdashery were sold.

Porus, another of these villages, owed its existence to a land speculator, Andrew Drummond, who had purchased 700 acres for £500, divided it into 15- to 25-acre lots and sold the whole at a profit of £1,500. Several individuals either grouped together to purchase a lot, or the lots were subdivided again immediately after purchase. In 1839, not long after the transaction had taken place, another writer noted that some 1,500 residents were located there on half-acre to two-acre lots. The village was ideally situated, within easy reach of plantations in both Clarendon and Manchester but the writer observed that not one villager had gone out to seek employment. They engaged in shared labour, "day for a day", which allowed poor families to complete their projects, whether it be land preparation for planting or house building, without having to pay in cash. The person receiving the assistance would give back the day or days to those who had assisted him and this would continue until the projects were completed.

Another observer mentions the irreproachable conduct and industry of the Porus residents, and the fact that they were little troubled that the land was not particularly productive. (In the twentieth century it was analysed as having a high bauxite content.) Their main goal had been accomplished, they owned a home of their own. After that they could choose where they wished to work.

The composition of the village of Maldon in the hills of St Elizabeth gives some idea of the activities of many villagers. Of the 52 smallholders in the village, one was a teacher, another was a servant, 27 were jobbers: carpenters, masons and some who did task work. Twelve grew provisions for sale, split shingles and engaged in other activities such as cleaning pastures.

This display of self-reliance was not to the planters' liking. At a meeting of landowners and attorneys held in Trelawny in 1858, the planters, frustrated by the fact that they could no longer exploit the labourers as before declared, "The people will never be brought to a stage of continuous labour while they are allowed to possess the large tracts of land now cultivated by them for provision." To subvert their efforts the government had by then begun to import cheap labour from China and India to fill the gap created by the refusal of smallholders to work on the estates. The story of the East Indians and Chinese and how they fared is told in chapter twenty-five.

Education was not encouraged by the authorities who felt that it would give the field-hands political and social ambitions and this would make them unfit for labour. But the more enterprising smallholders wished their children to take advantage of the educational opportunities they had missed. They wanted them to become lawyers, doctors, teachers and rich businessmen even when the basic educational preparation was obviously inadequate. The majority settled for apprenticing the children to tradesmen especially in the towns. Agriculture as a means of earning a livelihood was frowned upon. The elders hoped to spare their children the experiences and drudgery they had endured as plantation labourers but not everyone was so motivated. To some individuals, school was a waste of time. They considered that the children could be more profitably employed working in the fields, doing domestic chores or taking care of their younger siblings. With these ingrained attitudes illiteracy remained a major problem condemning many intelligent young Jamaicans to frustration and poverty.

The industry of the average free village accounts for the rapid development of the internal economy of the island. By 1879, the island was self-sufficient in basic food items. Lucea yam from Hanover was sold in other parishes across the island; yam from Portland was exported to Central America where many Jamaicans had found employment. Almost every village had its own small animal-powered sugar mill and boiling house. About 50 per cent of sugar consumed in the island during this period was produced by these small farmers and sold in the form of "wet" sugar. Village shopkeepers became produce dealers, purchasing exportable crops in small quantities or exchanging them for basic food items. They in turn resold the goods in bulk to exporters in Kingston and other parish towns.

Twenty-five years is a short time in the life of a people. Some African-Jamaicans who had been young at the time of the Sam Sharpe and Western Liberation Uprising were middle-aged at the time of Gordon, Bogle and the Morant Bay Uprising, Yet in that relatively short period of time the African-Jamaicans with help only from the missionaries, and out of their own limited resources, had settled large areas of inland Jamaica and had founded a landed yeomanry with homes of their own.

CHAPTER 21

Towards political liberty

The heroes of a nation embody its cherished values, express its highest purposes, inspire its noblest achievements. They speak to those who will listen and to minds that will understand. They sacrifice their lives even to death to win freedom, justice and political independence for the majority.

Just as Sam Sharpe set African-Jamaicans on the road to freedom, in 1832 George William Gordon and Paul Bogle in 1865 moved them towards political liberty by championing resistance to white minority oppression that divorced morality from the exercise of power.

Gordon and Bogle did not initiate the struggle. That began with the first African slaves to come to the Americas and was continued through the centuries by others who resisted planter coercion and oppression by means of parliamentary control. But by articulating an ideology, Gordon and Bogle (and earlier, Sam Sharpe), transformed a wide-ranging series of protests into a campaign for civil liberty. By giving this campaign moral force as well as ethical sanction they gave it purpose and continuity. They identified the basic concepts of good government for the newly emancipated peasant folk who chose to assert their rights to political liberty and justice guided by religious principles.

The Greeks in the age of Pericles had recognised that in a democracy the administration's function was to favour the many instead of the few. So did the Saxon kings Edgar and Alfred the Great. In Edgar's words, "This is what I will – that Every Man be worthy of folk-right, poor and rich alike, and that righteous dooms be judged to them." In the same spirit Alfred decreed that English history should be truly set down in an English book, "Thus, law by law, record by record the prescriptive right of the folk to safe conduct in their life and work, and to justice at the hands of their rulers and governors, is asserted and re-asserted." (Rhys: 1921)

Governor Eyre and Jamaica's nineteenth-century planter oligarchy disregarded the fact that they, being of English descent, were the inheritors of a long and proud tradition of struggle for political liberty for which their forefathers had died. These were the very rights that the African-Jamaican people were claiming.

The concept of justice as an attribute of God was familiar to the peoples of Africa. Many saw God as king, lord and maker. As ruler and maker he was judge: the one who settled the differences between us who are men. (Mbiti: 1970) The African-Jamaicans inherited West African attitudes and beliefs and expected authority and political justice to be exercised with regard to God's teaching.

Gordon and Bogle became the icons of the great mass of the Jamaican people in the same way that Sam Sharpe had incarnated their consuming desire for freedom. The mission of the two heroes and their martyrdom make Bogle's Stony Gut chapel and the Morant Bay court-house shrines that commemorate the memory of those who chose to enlarge the freedom they had gained, by continuing the struggle of their African ancestors for equality such as they had known in their homelands.

These two leaders, one brown, one black, along with thousands of simple folk, understood no less clearly than the founders of the English nation that the rights of the many had to be protected against the power of the few. Preacher Gordon appealed to the Higher Judge when he accused Governor Eyre of oppression: it was the Lord who would soon pluck his hand out of his bosom and so confound the whole band of oppressors. In St Thomas-in-the-East, where magisterial oppression was worse than in other parishes, Gordon wrote to his friend and estate manager at Rhine: "The Governor is an evil doer: the Lord will plenteously reward him."

A bulletin published for the capture of Bogle at the time of the Morant Bay Uprising described him as: "very black, shiney of skin, heavy marks of smallpox on face, especially on nose, good teeth – large mouth, red thick lips; about five feet eight inches tall, broad shoulders; carries himself indolently, with no whiskers". He was an independent small farmer in the village of Stony Gut where he owned a large piece of land on which he had built his own Native Baptist church.

Bogle's church blended Christian and African beliefs and values with strong religious militancy. "Central to its functioning was a remarkable relationship between Bogle and George William Gordon . . . part political and religious alliance, part friendship, their relationship was founded in resistance." (Holt: 1992)

In their last three or four years, the two men defined the central themes of justice and concern for the "many", which widened into a struggle against the monopoly of political power that was taken up by Robert Love, Sandy Cox and Bain Alves with their trade unions, Marcus Garvey, Norman Manley in his campaign for universal adult suffrage and

Alexander Bustamante in his formation of the labour movement, and led to political independence in 1962.

Gordon was born a slave. The baptismal register at Spanish Town records his birth in December 1815 as the son of a quadroon slave at Cherry Garden Estate, and notes that it had taken place three months earlier. His father was Joseph Gordon, an attorney who had come to Jamaica to manage a number of sugar estates for absentee owners, and had become a property owner himself. The boy was intelligent and industrious and by the age of ten could "read, write and keep accounts". He was manumitted by his father and sent to live with his godfather, James Daley, a businessman of Black River. At age 16 Gordon launched out into the business world by opening a produce-dealer's store in Kingston. It is said that he was assisted by his father and a white woman who loaned him £1,000.

George William Gordon's baptismal entry

Gordon prospered and in time set up his counting-house on Port Royal Street. In 1843 he was reportedly worth £10,000 and could afford to send his three sisters to Europe to be educated. He was engaged in several business ventures and became a large landed proprietor owning estates and other property in several parishes, including two or three estates in St Thomas-in-the-East and Cherry Garden in St Andrew, which he purchased when his father ran into financial difficulty.

Gordon's disquiet at the appallingly poor social conditions then obtaining caused him to draw public attention to a number of issues that needed to be addressed: lack of medical attention for the poor and infirm, the insanitary conditions in prisons and the treatment of prisoners, especially in St Thomas.

In 1844 at age 29 he was elected representative for the parish of St Andrew and continued his battles in the Assembly for one term. He codemned the victimisation of poor blacks and criticised fraud and corruption in high places – forgery, burglary, cattle stealing – and other crimes which went unpunished while the peasants were penalised for petty crimes. As was to be expected, these attacks on the establishment brought him into open conflict with some of his brown colleagues and with other members of the Assembly and the vestries. He failed to gain another seat until 1863 when he was elected to represent the parish of St Thomas-in-the-East.

Gordon's business deals extended to several parishes and this enabled him to serve as justice of the peace in several of them. Because of his unrelenting criticism of the political administration and the social conditions in St Thomas, the custos refused to let him take his seat in the vestry, using the excuse that he was not a practising member of the Church of England. When Gordon would not leave the meeting, the custos had him physically removed. Bogle and other St Thomas small settlers then voted him in as "the people's church warden", but the governor withdrew his commission as justice of the peace and he once again was denied a seat. Gordon took the rector and custos to court and won.

Although he was an untiring political advocate, contrary to popular belief Gordon was not a member of the Town Party, which was then comprised mostly of coloured professionals and businessmen residing mainly in Spanish Town and Kingston. (Robotham: 1981)

In addition to his political activities, Gordon was a man of deep religious conviction. He was christened an Anglican but converted to the Baptist faith and was baptised by the Rev. James Phillippo. He was always on the move, travelling from one church to another, preaching, offering counsel, starting new missions or serving in whatever way he could. In 1860-61 a great religious revival swept the island, and at Christmas 1860 Gordon transferred his allegiance to the Native Baptists and established his own independent Baptist chapels at Bath, at Spring Gardens near Stony Gut and in Kingston. At the same time he continued his association with the Presbyterians and Baptists and other religious organisations.

Paul Bogle, a younger charismatic leader, was also converted at about this time. Gordon ordained Bogle as a deacon in his tabernacle in Kingston in March 1865, after the latter had built his own chapel at Stony Gut in December 1864.

Bogle's letters to his pastor, "elder brother" and friend, Gordon, concerned urgent matters to be addressed: an ethical base for justice, votes to be registered and bakras to be defeated. In one letter he wrote, "We want to see you at our village . . . for we have plans [to] arrange with you. Come up, we beseech you as quick as possible so that we may arrange how the baptism is to go at Spring." A second letter written later that day followed.

> At a meeting held at the Liberal School Society Meeting House at the above named place [Stony Gut] to take into consideration what plans we might adopt to recover your place that is lost in the political world but in the religious one we are assured your progress is great; may God grant it so. Among other plans we resolve to have a hundred tax payers put on [the electoral roll], independent of freeholders, and those who will or can without borrowing from us. (Holt: 1992)

Eric Williams, political leader and historian, sums up the nature of the system that Gordon and Bogle were attempting to reform.

George William
Gordon

Massa had a monopoly of political power in the West Indies which he used shamelessly for his private ends . . . He used this power ruthlessly . . . [Massa] developed the necessary philosophical rationalization of this barbarous system. It was that the workers both African and Indian, were inferior beings, unfit for self-government, permanently destined to a status of perpetual subordination, unable ever to achieve equality with Massa. It was there in all the laws which governed the West Indies for generations, – the laws which denied equality on the grounds of colour . . . the laws which equated political power and the vote with ownership of land, the laws which . . . attempted to ensure that the non-European would never be anything but a worker in the social scale, the improvement of whose standard of living depended, as a British Secretary of State once told the workers in Jamaica in 1865, on their working on Massa's plantation for wages. (Williams: 1981)

The response of Gordon and Bogle and other African-Jamaicans was the rejection of the dominance of a minority of property owners whose attitudes were rooted in the monopoly of political power and racism. Their struggle which culminated in the Morant Bay Uprising marks an important phase in the demand for justice but it did not end there. As in the pre-emancipation period, so in the century that followed, the dynamics of change came from the African-Jamaican people. With sacrifice and determination they finally, in 1945, achieved full political representation through universal adult suffrage and the secret ballot.

In order to appreciate more fully why Gordon and Bogle and countless others worked unremittingly to change the system, we must remind ourselves that the oppressive social and economic conditions had not changed, and look briefly at some of the laws implemented during the period which adversely affected the lives of the masses.

The Master and Servant's Act, which came into force following emancipation, and remained in force after 1842 allowed the planter to reduce wages and provide employment irregularly to the detriment of the labour force. Those dependent on plantation employment never knew when they would be laid off, or when they would be paid. They could be fined for trivial offences, so that sometimes they lost almost all their wages and had nothing left to take home to their families.

The Jamaican peasant was denied cultivable land for rent. He was prevented from utilising abandoned estates. Access to Crown lands was restricted by prices fixed so high "as may place them out of reach of persons without capital". (House of Commons, 14. 600-699) European, Indian and Chinese indentured labour was recruited to deprive Jamaicans of a means of livelihood. "A Jamaican man" writing in the *Liverpool Standard* of 1833 about the European immigration noted that "This would benefit the planters without injury to the negroes: to the former it would give a greater quantity of labourers, consequently a greater competition in the market . . . to the latter it would make the necessity of working greater, consequently, less fear of their relapsing into barbarism."

The Assembly used the ballot to retain its hold on power, and introduced legislation to ensure that the situation would not change. The 1840 Franchise Act which was based on proof of ownership of property was amended to include an hereditaments (inheritance) tax which put the poor small settler at a further

Paul Bogle

disadvantage. In 1851 a literacy clause proposed in the Assembly was defeated by a slim margin of 13 to 11. It would be introduced again some ten years later. Eight coloured representatives voted against the bill. The hereditaments tax no doubt affected the number of voters, as between 1840 and 1852 voter registration declined from 1,800 to 753 in a country with a population of over 400,000. Epidemics of cholera, influenza and smallpox in 1850 and 1851 devastated the population and may also have contributed to the decline. It was now obvious that the voters' roll had to be increased.

Proposed new legislation in 1854, ostensibly to rectify the inadequacies of the earlier election law, also had an underlying motive, to add to the financial burden of the peasant. It was defeated by a narrow margin.

The hereditaments tax which had imposed a charge of twelve shillings, six pence on voters met with so much opposition that it was withdrawn in 1858, but was replaced in the following year by a ten shillings poll tax. In the debates which followed in the Assembly the governor admitted that although there was no great change in the amount taxpayers were being called upon to pay, it would in practice be "a great discouragement of the exercise of the Franchise, by the more numerous and humbler Class of Freeholders, and that it was advocated in Assembly for no other reason". (Holt: 1992) A compromise was reached and a stamp duty of ten shillings was introduced only for those wishing to exercise the franchise. According to Holt, the impact on the £6 freeholders, the peasant voters, was especially crippling. They were now forced to pay an additional sum of money in order to exercise the ballot. Previously this group had made up one-third of the voters' list. By 1860 it was one-sixth of the list, and by 1863, one-eighth. This meant that their ability to choose a representative to their liking was greatly reduced.

Political equality for the masses could only be achieved through their ability to exercise the vote and to this end the Baptists had been campaigning since 1840 to increase their numbers on the electoral roll. They were joined by the Methodists and a number of activists across the island, among them Gordon and Bogle and their Stony Gut associates.

Bogle was influential throughout the St Thomas area and was respected as a political and a religious leader. Along with his brother Moses and an associate James Maclaren, he had worked zealously to get the St Thomas small settlers to meet the requirements that would enable them to register and to vote. Both he and Gordon were in the habit of advancing the tax moneys for financially hard-pressed freeholders. In other parishes other committed individuals were doing the same thing. In a few instances they made dramatic strides, but much more needed to be done. Only 1,903 names appeared on the electoral roll in 1863 out of a population of 450,000, and of that number only 1,457 cast their ballots in 1864. They voted in 47 representatives from 23 constituencies, an average of 31 voters per representative. In such circumstances the voice of the masses was not being heard.

Taxation was also used as a weapon. Plantation owners paid considerably lower duties on imported goods than did the poor. Food and clothing attracted duties sometimes twelve times higher than previously. Andrew H. Lewis, protesting against the state of affairs in the Assembly in 1861 said, "They were taxed on their bread, their salt, their lucifers, their clothes, and everything else they use." The tax on donkeys was more than that on horses. Peasant carts which previously went untaxed were now charged eighteen shillings per year while plantation carts continued to go untaxed. The revenues collected provided services for the benefit of the planters while the needs of the peasants were ignored.

As social conditions deteriorated, financial burdens piled up, living expenses increased and sporadic outbursts of anger and discontent erupted across the island. Some persons, homeless and without employment, resorted to stealing foodstuffs and to picking wild fruit in pastures. They were punished with flogging and imprisonment. Gordon continued to organise public protests.

Toll gates were placed at strategic locations on roads leading to the town of Savanna-la-Mar, which poor people frequently used. For three nights in February 1859 the protestors tore down the toll gates and when they were brought to trial, tensions ran so high that according to one reporter, "The peasantry of the parish assembled in such large numbers, and were in so excited a state, that it was deemed advisable to adjourn [the trial]." Resentment against the system was widespread and the legislation was withdrawn in 1863.

Protests against unfair property laws sometimes united whole communities. This happened at Florence Hall in Trelawny where the villagers kept vigil every night for three months to prevent Theodore Buie from being ejected from the property of which he was part owner. The resistance led to arrests, to a march on the police station at Falmouth, and to burning the wharf in the town. In the end some persons lost their lives and over 120 were punished.

Squatters and legitimate tenants objected to being turned off the lands they were occupying when they refused to pay rents additional to the legally required quitrents they had already paid. Sometimes they obstructed attorneys and surveyors in the course of their duties and threatened them with bodily harm.

Having to provide proof of ownership was another common method used to defraud inexperienced land purchasers who could not produce proper deeds. Gordon urged resistance against some of these oppressive measures. He helped many peasants to acquire lands for free villages, loaned small farmers money to plant economic crops, such as coffee, and then sold the crops for them. It is claimed that he also gave cattle to his supporters so that they could become taxpayers and meet the voting requirements. In the Assembly he urged the extension of the franchise to a wider cross-section of the population and in 1865, when he could make no headway with the local administrators, he took his complaints to the Colonial Office. He was seeking fair representation which meant that the majority, not the few, would have the power to pass laws.

Governor Eyre came under his attack for mismanagement and lack of integrity. He said,

> But when everyday we witness the maladministration of the law by the Lieutenant-Governor, we must speak out. You are endeavouring to suppress public opinion, to pen up the expression of public indignation; but I tell you it will soon burst forth like a flood, and sweep everything before it. There must be a limit to everything: a limit to oppression – a limit to transgression – a limit to illegality. (Gordon)

When challenged and asked if he was speaking of insurrection he replied, "Ay! that will be the result."

News of growing discontent among the masses and the unwillingness of the white minority to compromise reached Britain, and the London secretary of the Baptist Missionary Society, Dr Edward Underhill, undertook to visit the region to obtain first-hand information. His findings, which were published in 1862, confirmed the reports of the harsh social and economic conditions the peasants had been protesting about for a long time.

After two years, nothing having been done to improve the situation, Underhill brought the matter to the attention of his friend Edward Cardwell, acting Secretary-of-State for the Colonies. The letter outlined many irregularities, acts of oppression, unjust tribunals, denial of political rights, declining social conditions and the indifference of the island's administrators to the worsening conditions and the high level of unemployment. Underhill wrote:

> Crime has fearfully increased. The number of prisoners . . . is considerably more than double the average, and nearly all for one crime, larceny. Summonses for petty debts disclose an amount of pecuniary difficulty which has never before been experienced; and applications for parochial and private relief prove that multitudes are suffering from want, little removed from starvation.

He described the nakedness of the poor, which he attributed to the increase in duties and the high cost of cotton cloth. Unemployment was also a major contributing factor.

The Colonial Office forwarded Underhill's letter to Governor Eyre for his comments. In his reply of 2 March, 1865 Eyre claimed that the accusations were exaggerated and distorted; that the problem of poverty was to be blamed on the low moral character of the people and on their willingness to squander money on such things as fancy church clothes. Several members of the legislature supported his claims that the peasants had brought these privations upon themselves by "sheer idleness, a growing dislike to steady industry, and a consequent preference to a dishonest mode of living".

Eyre admitted that social and economic conditions were bad and growing worse, but maintained that laziness was the major problem of the blacks. Eyre had Underhill's letter printed and circulated widely, along with comments from himself.

The island had been affected in 1864 by severe floods, followed by drought, which had destroyed coffee crops and provision grounds and had added to the worsening conditions. The whole island was suffering but the situation in St Thomas appeared to be particularly bad. Poor and inadequate medical facilities, poor housing for the sick and infirm, lack of medical attention for persons awaiting trial, led Gordon to protest to the governor. When he attempted to bring witnesses to confirm his accusations, especially concerning the insanitary conditions at the jail, the local justices refused to hear them because they claimed that their testimony was irrelevant. By then the jail had already been cleaned.

Intolerance and bias in the judicial system also caused Bogle and his associates to organise their own unofficial court system at Manchioneal, Serge Island and other places in the parishes of St Thomas, St David and St Andrew. They selected their own judges, clerks of the peace and police force, issued summonses, tried cases and levied fines. The courts may have been linked to the local churches, so that disobeying the court's authority could mean expulsion from the church. The membership fee was one shilling. (Holt: 1992)

Bogle began training his followers in military drills and apparently contemplated the use of force if necessary to bring down the oppressive system. Underhill's letter became the rallying point for concerned persons both black and white wishing to change the system. The meetings became known as Underhill meetings. Gordon presided over one in Kingston on 3 May, the Spanish Town meeting of 16 May was called by the Honourable Richard Hill, a respected member of the Assembly and a special magistrate and was presided over by "H. Lewis, Esquire", a member of the Assembly for St Catherine.

There was an orchestrated campaign to document the conditions and the reports were sent to the governor to be transmitted to the Colonial Office. The organisers were determined to have their cause heard and were prepared if necessary to send a delegation to Britain. George Price, Custos of St Catherine, actually went to Britain to lay the matter before the Secretary-of-State for the Colonies. On 5 September, on the eve of his departure from the island he was handed a petition signed by 40 persons from St Thomas who complained of short payment of wages and other hardships they were suffering.

At least three parishes also prepared petitions. There was a much publicised one from the people of St Ann, one from the people of St Elizabeth and another from free Africans employed as indentured labourers at Vere in Clarendon. Excerpts from the St Ann petition of April 1865 are quoted below because they set out most vividly the hardships the people faced and their appeal for help.

> We the undersigned of this island beg with submission to inform our Queen that we are in great want at this moment from the bad state of our island. Soon after we became free subjects We could get plenty of work, and well paid, then all the estates was in a flourishing state, but at this moment the most of the estates are thrown up . . . Some of us, after we became free subjects, purchased a little land, some of us a lot, half acre, one acre, and so on, at the rate of £10. and £12. per acre merely as a home.

We have to leave our homes every day when we can get employment, so that we may have means to go to market on Saturdays, by working on an estate or pen. Our little homes, we, having turned up the soil so often, that it becomes useless for provision, by which means we are compelled to rent land from the large proprietors at the rate of two pounds eight shillings per acre for one year, and the rent must be paid in advance. In many instances our provisions are destroyed by cattles; and if the proprietors find the most simple fault, three months' notice is given, and we have to destroy our provisions, at the same time numbers of us having a large family of eleven or twelve children depending on the provisions for subsistence . . . Formerly we could get from one shilling and sixpence per day as labourers, as a carpenter or other tradesmen three shillings to four shillings per day. A job that we formerly would get two pounds for at this moment is only twelve shillings. Three or four of us may take job work and when it is finished in many instances we have to wait for weeks for payment for our work . . . If our Most Gracious Sovereign Lady will be so kind as to get a quantity of land, we will put our hands and heart to work, and cultivate coffee, corn, canes, cotton and tobacco, and other produce. We will also form a company for the purpose, if our Gracious Lady Victoria our Queen will also appoint an agent to receive such produce as we may cultivate and give us means of subsistence while at work . . . We your humble servants will thankfully repay our Sovereign Lady by installments of such produce as we may cultivate. Your humble servants are willing to work so that we may be comfortable . . . If it had not been for the breadfruit and coconut numbers of us would have perished . . . Our difficulties are very great. We have to pay fourpence per yard for cloth of the worst kind. The cloth in general is so high in price that numbers of our people is half naked. If our Gracious Sovereign will be so kind as to grant our request in a few years time our Sovereign Lady Queen Victoria will see the improvement of our island, and the benefit that your humble servants will derive . . . We think that our distress is felt throughout the island and we hope that some of our adjoining neighbours, in other parishes will also state to our Sovereign their distress . . . We, your most humble servants, will as a duty bound ever pray, God bless the Queen.

Of the 108 persons who signed the petition only 26 could write their names. The others marked with an "X".

In spite of this, the government stubbornly refused to acknowledge the seriousness of the situation and the need to redress the grievances.

Cardwell relied on Eyre's advice and his reply of 14 June 1865 showed no compassion. He said that the letter had been laid before the Queen, and that he had been commanded:

> To inform them that the prosperity of the labouring classes as well as of all other classes, depends in Jamaica and in other countries on their working for wages, not uncertainly or capriciously, but steadily and continuously, at the times when their labour is wanted, and for so long as it is wanted; that if they would use this industry, and thereby render the plantations productive. They would enable the planters to pay higher wages for the same hours of work than are received by the best field labourers in the country [Britain] and as the cost of the necessities of life is much less in Jamaica than it is here [in Britain] they would be enabled by adding prudence to industry, to lay by an ample provision for seasons of drought and dearth.

Their own industry and prudence would avail them of the means of prospering, not by any schemes which had been suggested to them by instigators. Her Majesty would regard with interest and satisfaction their advancement through their own merits and efforts.

Eyre had 50,000 copies of the "Queen's Advice" with his own preface printed and distributed throughout the island. It was read from some pulpits, but other preachers refused to comply and returned the parcels unopened. It was posted in all public places but served only to increase the discontent.

Gordon's attacks on the administration did not let up and on 24 March 1865, he drew the Assembly's attention to the reintroduction of the tread-mill, an instrument of torture withdrawn after full freedom. These severi-ties and tortures, he said, were diabolical and were intended to consign the prisoners to an early grave. His pleas fell upon deaf ears.

An Underhill meeting called for 29 July at Morant Bay was postponed because the custos refused to allow the courthouse to be used. On 12 August the custos again refused the use of the courthouse and Gordon presided over the meeting in the open air. The meeting passed resolutions denouncing the government's policy concerning the economic depression, low wages and the use of public funds which the governor had authorised for paying the law suit which Gordon had won.

The meeting resolved to send a deputation to Spanish Town to place the grievances before the governor. Paul Bogle and a group of men includ-ing James Maclaren walked more than 40 miles to Spanish Town with the letter, but Eyre refused to meet them or hear their complaints.

Frustrations were at boiling point and came to a head a few weeks later when a special magistrate whom the people trusted was dismissed. On

Saturday 7 October, while the custos, Baron von Ketelhodt, was presiding over a petty sessions court, spectators were gathered in the square and in the court because they were on the lookout for any miscarriage of justice. After the first case was heard and the fines imposed, James Geohegan, another campaigner, shouted to the defendant, a boy, to pay the fine of four shillings but not the other costs of twelve shillings, six pence, which usually went towards the salaries of the clerks. Two policemen ordered to arrest him were dragged from the steps of the courthouse and beaten. Geohegan and his accomplices escaped and the court adjourned prematurely.

On the following Monday the second case which had been put off from the Saturday before came up for hearing. The defendant, William Miller, was cited for trespassing because he had gone into a pasture to recover his horse which one James Williams had impounded. Williams was demanding that Miller pay for the grazing. The court found Miller guilty of trespass. At that point Bogle and some ten or twelve other onlookers urged him to appeal. The magistrates were irate. They later had 28 warrants prepared, all backdated to Saturday 7 October, giving the impression that the beating of the policemen and the disturbance in the court had all taken place on the same day.

On Tuesday 10 October, six policemen and two rural constables went to Stony Gut to execute the warrants. They attempted to seize Bogle but armed men lying in wait in the chapel rescued him. Then about 350 other supporters emerged from the cane fields and surrounded the police. Three of them were captured and beaten and threatened with death unless they swore upon oath to stop serving the "Bukra", and "Cleave to the Black".

The men for whom the warrants had been issued, including Bogle, agreed to present themselves at Morant Bay on the following day. In the meantime, they despatched a petition to Governor Eyre at Spanish Town, requesting his protection against the "outrageous assault" committed upon them by the policemen at Morant Bay.

News of the disturbances at Morant Bay spread rapidly throughout the eastern parishes and on 11 October sympathisers set out on foot from Manchioneal and from Stony Gut for Morant Bay. Details of what followed are confusing but it seems clear that they were prepared to support Bogle and his companions in whatever way was necessary.

Stony Gut was only about five miles from Morant Bay and some 400 demonstrators from that village reached the town first. They were in a noisy and belligerent mood. They sacked the police station before moving on to the courthouse where the vestry was sitting. The custos, Baron von Ketelhodt, feeling that the situation could have become explosive, had arranged to call out the volunteer militia from Bath. On the approach of the Stony Gut demonstrators he came out on the courthouse steps and began reading the Riot Act. The crowd began advancing towards the courthouse, whereupon the volunteers fired a volley into the crowd. About ten people died. Pandemonium broke loose. The crowd scattered, regrouped and retaliated with sticks, stones, machetes and inadequate fire-power. The custos was hit by a flying object.

They attacked the courthouse, set fire to the schoolhouse and adjoining buildings, and burst open the jail. Fifty-one prisoners escaped and it is said that they later returned to Stony Gut with Bogle and his followers where Bogle held a meeting of thanksgiving for his victory. Members of the vestry and the magistrates took refuge in the schoolhouse and in another house close by until they were driven out by fire. They were then attacked as they fled. Some were shot, others were chopped, and still others beaten to death. A few escaped injury by hiding during the night under hedges and in a latrine. Baron von Ketelhodt, was found dead next day with his head smashed and one of his fingers on his right hand cut off and his ring taken.

The marchers from Manchioneal were intercepted by a contingent of black soldiers from Port Antonio who shot about 160 persons, hanged seven in Manchioneal and shot three others travelling in the opposite direction towards Port Morant.

On 12 October, the day following the riots, Governor Eyre's reply to the petition arrived at Stony Gut. It was signed by his secretary, Edward Jordan. It noted that the governor had received unsavoury news about their activities. It continued:

> Some of you had been guilty of gross outrage and violence, and he [the Governor] warns you that such proceedings cannot be allowed to take place with impunity. His Excellency feels it to be his duty at once to inform you that you are misled by the misrepresentations of evil disposed and designing men and that unless you promptly withdraw from the unlawful attitude which you have assumed, very serious consequences must follow.

By then the situation was out of control. On 13 October martial law was declared. A week of bloody fighting ensued with reprisals on both sides. Some of the protesters, led by Bogle, captured the courthouses at Bath and Morant Bay. Bogle's appeal to the maroons at Hayfield was refused because the maroons had sworn in the 1739 peace treaty signed with the English to assist the government in capturing runaway slaves and in crushing slave revolts. But this was no slave revolt; Bogle and his supporters were free men fighting for justice. On 23 October, the maroons captured Bogle and handed him over to the authorities. The following day he was court-martialled and hanged.

Gordon was nowhere near Morant Bay while all of this was taking place. He was ill and staying at a cousin's house on North Street in Kingston. Nevertheless, some persons declared under oath that he was the chief instigator of the Stony Gut protests. A warrant was issued for his arrest. On learning of this, on 16 October Gordon went to Headquarters House where Commanding General O'Connor lived to give himself up, whereupon he was promptly arrested by Governor Eyre himself, in the presence of the custos of Kingston, Dr Bowerbank. Eyre took him by ship, *The Wolverine*, to Morant Bay, then to Port Antonio and back to Morant Bay, and on 20 October handed him over to the provost marshal, Gordon Ramsay. He was refused legal advice and spiritual consolation and witnesses willing to testify on his behalf were refused a hearing. On Saturday, 21 October he was tried for treason and found guilty; and on Monday, 23 October he was hanged.

The commission's records are filled with accounts of atrocities. Some people were given as many as 100 lashes before they were tried and hanged.

One man, a butcher, claimed that he was forced to flog 49 persons on the day after the riots. When his arm became tired he was given a glass of rum and water to refresh himself. He started flogging at 9 o'clock in the morning and did not stop until 4 o'clock in the afternoon.

In retaliation for the 29 white persons killed and 34 others seriously injured, the homes of all the would-be protesters were burned and their crops destroyed. The official records state 1,000 homes burned, 354 people executed by court martial, 50 shot without trial, 25 shot by the maroons, ten "killed otherwise" and 600 flogged. Commodore McClintock, who helped to quell the uprising, estimated that the loss of life was nearer 1,500. The first set of hangings took place at Port Morant "under the eye of Mr Eyre himself". (Robotham: 1981)

The hangings continued day by day, and so many people were packed in the graves that, as one witness told the Commission, "last night a particularly disagreeable effluvia arose from the graves . . . [and] pervaded the entire town. It was only with the greatest difficulty that one could avoid nausea". (Jamaica Royal Commission: 1866)

Despite these atrocities, Gordon's last letter to his wife displays a quality of nobility and generosity of spirit which remain an inspiration to all generations. He wrote:

> I do not deserve this sentence, for I never advised or took part in any insurrection. All I ever did was to recommend the people who complained to seek redress in a legitimate way . . . Say to all friends an affectionate farewell; and that they must not grieve for me, for I die innocently . . . Comfort your heart. I certainly little expected this. You must do the best you can, and the Lord will help you; and do

Gordon's body being taken down after hanging at Morant Bay.
Painting by Barrington Watson (Wycliffe Bennett Collection)

not be ashamed of the death your poor husband will have suffered
. . . I thought his Excellency would have allowed me a fair trial, if any
charge of sedition or inflammatory language was partly attributable
to me; but I have no power of control. May the Lord be merciful to
him . . . I have been allowed one hour, I wish more time had been
allowed . . . And now may the grace of our Lord Jesus Christ be with
us all. Your truly devoted and now nearly dying husband, G. W.
Gordon. (Olivier: 1933)

CHAPTER 22

The people betrayed and vindicated

Sometimes, in the mist-shrouded Portland and St Thomas valleys, in the sad evenings and in the grieving time in Stony Gut with its burnt-out houses and desecrated chapel, a song born of the killings carries its message through the darkness.

> War down a Monkland
> War down a Morant Bay,
> The Queen never know,
> War oh, war oh,
> War oh, heavy war oh.

In those months Governor Eyre and his supporters in Britain were declaring: "Black insurrection could not be treated in the same way as a white one, because the negro in Jamaica . . . is pestilential . . . a dangerous savage at best." (Holt: 1992)

The debate raged in Britain, where Eyre explained that persons living at a distance, who were unacquainted with the country and with the negro character, were "unable to appreciate the value of all the little incidents or circumstances which to my mind indicated a great and imminent danger". On the basis of those "little incidents or circumstances", magnified by paranoia into a "great and imminent danger" possibly as many as 1,500 innocent people were massacred.

> Soldiers from Newcastle
> came down a Monkland
> With gun an sword
> Fe kill sinner, oh,
> War oh, war oh.

The royal commission enquiring into the Morant Bay Uprising praised Eyre for acting quickly to put down the rebellion, but condemned him for prolonging the period of martial law, for the illegality and injustice of

Gordon's trial and for the barbarous and wanton punishment inflicted upon many people. They decided that the causes of the uprising were the people's demands for land and a breakdown in the system of justice. They did not face the basic issues which Gordon and Bogle had championed and for which they died, the need for a political system that favoured the many and not the few, equality before the law and a system of justice founded on ethical principles.

In Britain, as in Jamaica, most of the upper and middle classes sided with Eyre against Gordon, Bogle and the African-Jamaican people. Most of the British working class were against Eyre. They burned him in effigy in Hyde Park. They were campaigning for the very goals for which Gordon and Bogle died, an administration in favour of the many and an extension of the franchise to reduce the political power of the few. They won their battle in 1867. Three-quarters of a century was to pass before the Jamaican people won their campaign for adult suffrage and self-government.

But Morant Bay marked the beginning, not the end, of Gordon and Bogle's work. It was the planter oligarchy that surrendered the right of self-government which, 200 years earlier, Edward Long and William Beeston had battled for and preserved.

The end of planter rule was an ignoble one. It becomes even more shameful when considered alongside the action of the Barbados House of Assembly. When it was pressured by the Colonial Office in 1876 to surrender its right to self-government and accept Crown colony rule, a coloured member of the Barbados House, Conrad Reeves, urged his colleagues to reject the proposal in these words: "We are not, like some other colonies, afflicted with absenteeism . . . The leading men in this country are persons whose ancestors for generations have lived and died here . . . all classes of the country have the utmost confidence in its institutions." Reeves spoke of his vision for his country: "Here in Barbados all our situations are framed to meet exigencies of a single community, though made up of different classes, and to fit them for the enjoyment of that self-government which is the common right of the entire colony."

In contrast, Governor Eyre, full of self-congratulation and self-righteousness, before leaving for England appealed to the House to abolish itself. He paraded before them the terrifying spectre of black Haiti, appealed to the "fears" of the white and coloured and portrayed patriotism not in terms of country but of a surrender of the democratic principles advocated by Gordon and Bogle.

> It is necessary to bring these facts before you in order to convince you how widely spread and how deeply rooted the spirit of disaffection is; how daring and determined the intention had been, and still is, to

make Jamaica a second Haiti, and how imperative it is upon you, gentlemen, to take such measures as, under God's blessing may avert such a calamity . . . I invite you, gentlemen, to make a great and generous sacrifice for the sake of your country, and in immolating on the altar of patriotism the two branches of the Legislature of which you yourselves are the constituent parts, to hand down to posterity a noble example of self-denial and heroism.

A small group of coloured members opposed Eyre, but they were defeated. Robert Osborn had urged on the governor, Charles Grey, in a debate in May 1853 that responsible government was the way to protect coloured interests: "Do away with the Assembly and the coloured people would sink into the insignificance from which they had risen." Class interests, property rights and security were the factors that counted with most of the members of the Jamaica House of Assembly.

In 1866 Jamaica was made a Crown colony. "Massa" was still there, but the Crown was now in control. The governor was clad in all the panoply of imperial power, a helmet bedecked with plumes and feathers, a ceremonial sword that symbolised armed might. A nominated legislature dramatised the fact that the people had been stripped of the right to self-government. The basic philosophy was the same as that of the planter oligarchy, however, although the imperial mission was stated in other terms: "the direct protection by the Crown of the unrepresented classes, which takes the place of representation". Governors were instructed: "Her Majesty's government has also the right to expect in those to whom such great trusts are committed that they will show themselves able to withstand the pressure of any one class, or idea, or interest, and that they will maintain that calmness and impartiality of judgement which should belong to the governor of an English colony." As for the officials: "The business of all the official members is to consider the interests of the peasantry very closely and, without making themselves exclusively the representatives of those classes, to see that their interests do not suffer."

Governors and officials set worthy examples of professional competence and integrity, and many developed an abiding affection for Jamaica and the Jamaican people. The first governor under the new constitution, Sir John Peter Grant, for example, laid the foundations for the development of an efficient, honest civil service, greatly improved the island's deplorably bad communications and transportation systems and introduced a railway service linking Kingston with Port Antonio and Montego Bay. A few, such as Lord Olivier and Sir Hugh Foot, transformed an official position of limited tenure into a mission on behalf of the Jamaican people. But all were trapped in a system that was based on the doctrine of white superiority and imperial control. The most scathing indictment of Crown colony rule is to be found in the report of the Royal Commission of 1940.

The concept was that of a shepherded dependent people. Its justification lay in the conviction, as the English historian James Anthony Froude emphasised, that blacks had not demonstrated any capacity for civilisation except "under European laws, European education, European authority . . . and the old African superstitions lie undisturbed at the bottom of their souls. Give them independence and in a few generations they will peel off such civilisation as they have learnt as easily and as willingly as their coats and trousers". (Froude: 1887) The central issues remained what they had been under planter rule: property and colour. The Colonial Office spoke in the same terms as the Jamaican plantocracy: "The planters, being the best educated class and most interested in the permanent prosperity of the c[ountry], should have great power controlling the Government and great share in the Government of the island." So administration would continue to favour the whites, for not only were the blacks regarded as being morally deficient, but also in Carlyle's words, they were "born to be servants . . . to the whites." (Olivier: 1933) To govern a country was beyond them.

The gospel of a divinely ordained trusteeship of non-white people by Europeans was soon to be preached with great urgency, for in the closing decades of the nineteenth century and the opening decade of the twentieth century (1870-1917) mankind moved into a global age. The second Industrial Revolution, the rapid rise of the United States to the rank of world power and the spread of European imperialism marked the beginning of this global age.

Forces of change generated or reinforced by these developments touched Jamaican society in significant ways. We will identify related trends which began to manifest themselves in Jamaica from about the 1870s onwards; in order to show the connections, we will turn from the local to the global perspective.

The new age began with Europe's theft of the continent of Africa, an event of the greatest importance for all African-Americans. Between 1880 and 1900, in 20 years, the European powers – Britain, France, Germany, Italy, Belgium, Portugal and Spain – carved up Africa amongst themselves. In those two decades:

> The entire continent had been seized, annexed, fought over and partitioned. Of the forty political units into which it had been divided – often with little more than a ruler and pencil wielded in London, Paris or Berlin – direct European control extended to thirty-six. Only Ethiopia, which had fought off the Italians, and Liberia, with its financial links to the United States, claimed real independence. (*Times Atlas of World History*)

Explanations were offered for this shocking use of armed force. One was that new markets had to be found for the products of the second Industrial Revolution. Another was that colonisation provided Europe with productive new outlets for its many tensions and rivalries. The true driving forces were in fact distrust of each other, greed for power, greed for riches. The whole non-white world was involved. Non-Europeans fought back against this overwhelming imperialism, which "unleashed an anti-colonial reaction throughout Africa and Asia, the extent, intensity and significance of which have rarely been fully appreciated". (*Times Atlas of World History*) Just as the African-Americans waged a liberation campaign for 150 years against enslavement, so non-whites throughout Asia and Africa fought against imperialism. Among them were: the Ethiopians, who decisively defeated the Italians at Adowa in 1896; the uprising of Arab Pasha and his followers in Egypt against the British; the fierce Ashanti wars against the British in West Africa in 1876 and 1878; the Mahdi who captured Khartoum; the Zulu and Matabele, the Herero and Maji-Maji in South West Africa and Tanganyika, who rose in 1904 and 1906 against the Germans. The remarkable feature of this resistance is summarised in words that bear directly on the liberation movement of the Jamaican people, even though the scale was so very much smaller:

> The remarkable fact is the persistence of opposition in spite of disheartening set-backs and harsh repression. None of the powers which had launched the scramble for colonies in 1884 was secure in its possessions; nowhere was the finality of European rule accepted. The tangible achievements of nationalists in this period were negligible; but by keeping the flame of resistance alive, they inaugurated the process which led, a generation later, to the emancipation of the colonial peoples. (*Times Atlas of World History*)

By 1910 the strength of the anti-colonial movement throughout the colonies and also among liberals and intellectuals in Europe itself revealed grave weaknesses in the system. The American historian Barbara Tuchman portrayed this instability in her dramatic description of the funeral procession of Edward VII of Britain in May 1910.

> Nine Kings rode in the funeral . . . the crowd, waiting in hushed and black-clad awe, could not keep back gasps of admiration. In scarlet and blue and green and purple, three by three the sovereigns rode through the palace gates, with plumed helmets, gold braid, crimson sashes, and jewelled orders flashing in the sun. After them came five heirs apparent, forty more imperial or royal highnesses, seven queens . . . Together they represented seventy nations in the greatest assembly of royalty and rank ever gathered in one place and, of its kind, the

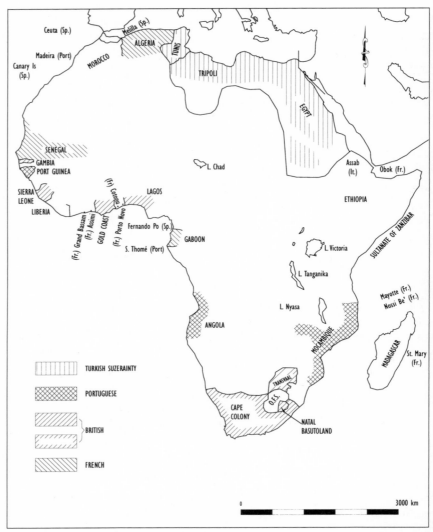

Ceuta (Sp.)
Melilla (Sp.)
ALGERIA
TUNIS
Madeira (Port)
Canary Is (Sp.)
MOROCCO
TRIPOLI
EGYPT
L. Chad
Assab (It.)
Obok (Fr.)
SENEGAL
GAMBIA
PORT GUINEA
SIERRA LEONE
LIBERIA
(Fr.) Colony
LAGOS
ETHIOPIA
(Fr.) Grand Bassam
(Fr.) Assini
GOLD COAST
(Fr.) Porto Novo
Fernando Po (Sp.)
GABOON
S. Thomé (Port)
SULTANATE OF ZANZIBAR
L. Victoria
L Tanganika
Mayotte (Fr.)
Nossi Be' (Fr.)
L Nyasa
MADAGASCAR
St. Mary (Fr.)
ANGOLA
MOÇAMBIQUE
TRANSVAAL
CAPE COLONY
O.F.S.
NATAL
BASUTOLAND

TURKISH SUZERAINTY

PORTUGUESE

BRITISH

FRENCH

0   3000 km

last. The muffled tongue of Big Ben tolled nine of the clock as the
cortege left the palace, but on history's clock it was sunset, and the
sun of the old world was setting in a dying blaze of splendor never to
be seen again. (Tuchman: 1910)

With the European colonisation of Africa, the West Indian colonies
shrank overnight to proportions in keeping with the bankrupt condition
of its sugar industry in the 1880s. In the great days of sugar the islands had
been the darlings of empire. The partitioning of Africa so enlarged the
empire that the West Indian colonies, small and with limited resources,

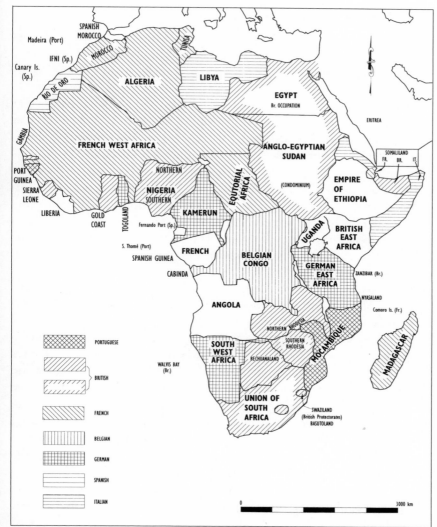

SPANISH MOROCCO

Madeira (Port)

IFNI (Sp.)

Canary Is. (Sp.)

MOROCCO

RIO DE ORO

ALGERIA

LIBYA

TUNISIA

EGYPT
Br. OCCUPATION

ERITREA

GAMBIA

FRENCH WEST AFRICA

ANGLO-EGYPTIAN SUDAN

SOMALILAND
FR. BR. IT.

PORT. GUINEA

SIERRA LEONE

LIBERIA

GOLD COAST

TOGOLAND

NORTHERN

NIGERIA
SOUTHERN

EQUATORIAL AFRICA

(CONDOMINIUM)

EMPIRE OF ETHIOPIA

KAMERUN

Fernando Poo (Sp.)

S. Thomé (Port)

FRENCH

SPANISH GUINEA

CABINDA

BELGIAN CONGO

UGANDA

BRITISH EAST AFRICA

GERMAN EAST AFRICA

ZANZIBAR (Br.)

NYASALAND

Comoro Is. (Fr.)

ANGOLA

NORTHERN RHODESIA

SOUTHERN RHODESIA

MOÇAMBIQUE

MADAGASCAR

SOUTH WEST AFRICA

WALVIS BAY (Br.)

BECHUANALAND

UNION OF SOUTH AFRICA

SWAZILAND
(British Protectorates)
BASUTOLAND

PORTUGUESE

BRITISH

FRENCH

BELGIAN

GERMAN

SPANISH

ITALIAN

0   3000 km

were pushed from a central position to the very limits of the periphery. Their market of some 3 million people was but a fraction of the market provided by Western Nigeria alone. The West India interest, so powerful in the 1750s in the councils of the old empire, so much a part of the English nation, was gravely weakened when France captured the European market with its cheaper beet-sugar. By then it was evident that Cuba, with its vastly larger production of cane-sugar, was destined to dominate the American market. Big Massa, inefficient and over-protected for over-long, bent on cheap labour instead of the use of modern technology, no longer had the credibility he had enjoyed in the eighteenth century.

The people betrayed and vindicated

The world as a whole was characterised at the time by the spread of divisive colonial systems and white power based on the concept of trusteeship. Black Jamaicans began to take pride in their country's development; Robert Love and Marcus Garvey pioneered Jamaica's national and political development.

There were other major developments in the world at large that radically affected Jamaican society. The most important was the formation of a world economy in the period 1870-1914, the chief features being the development of a worldwide system of communications based on telegraphy, railways, steamships, greatly improved road systems and canals, notably the Suez and Panama Canals. The expansion of these communication systems made possible also the growth of world trade in which the United States played an increasingly powerful part through industrial and trading corporations that established a US sphere of influence throughout the Caribbean, with its attendant forms of imperialism and political as well as financial control.

These manifested themselves in 1898, when the sinking of the warship *Maine* in Havana harbour provided the United States with a cause for declaring war on Spain in the course of the Cuban revolution. The United States destroyed a Spanish fleet in the Philippines and invaded Puerto Rico. By the Treaty of Paris, Spain withdrew from Cuba and ceded Puerto Rico, Guam and the Philippines to the United States. This marked the beginning of the Americanisation of the Caribbean Basin. In 1901, led by President Theodore Roosevelt, the United States decided to build the Panama Canal, following this up with buying French shares in the Canal and a treaty with Panama in 1903 that gave the United States perpetual control of the Canal Zone. In such ways Europe's imperialism in the Caribbean influenced the growth of US imperialism.

It is as if we were looking at two maps of the Atlantic Basin, one portraying the physical features, the other showing the sweep of ideologies and technologies. The first represents the continental land masses with their archipelagoes and vast oceanic currents such as the southern and northern equatorial currents that stitch Africa and western Europe to Central and North America, and the Gulf Stream that ties Mexico and the Bahamas to western Europe. We can identify also the giant wind systems, the north-east trade winds that transported Columbus and his ships from the Azores to the Caribbean and the westerlies that took him back by way of the Florida channel. The picture is one of interlocking, interconnected wind systems and ocean currents that facilitated man's movement into an Atlantic Age. The second map shows the ideological and technological currents that moved mankind into the global age and underpinned European and North American dominance.

So vast a background enlarges those communities whose people prove capable of response. From the 1870s African-Jamaicans responded to the challenge of European imperialism and racial discrimination by developing a nationalist movement and by the affirmation of an African identity. They responded to engulfing poverty by grasping the opportunity to initiate an export trade in bananas and by joining the labour force that built the Panama Canal, established the banana plantations in Central America, expanded Cuban sugar production and manned the assembly lines in United States and Canadian industrialised cities.

Towards the end of the century a little black boy, Marcus Garvey who was born in the seaside town of St Ann's Bay, had his first lesson as a schoolboy in racial discrimination and discovered at the same time the world of books.

The Jamaican people, in response to local pressures and global influences, contributed through their labour to the creation of a world system of trade and transport, to the growth of national movements and they demonstrated Africa's creative power which manifested itself in the people's capacity for response to persecution and restriction.

Our first step is to look more closely at the nature and structure of Jamaican society during this period. Our focus is on the distribution of the population, the occupational status and the literacy levels. It is significant that in the nineteenth century only 10 per cent of the black population lived in Kingston and St Andrew; the rest lived in the rural parishes. In contrast, 20.6 per cent of the coloureds and 52.9 per cent of the whites lived in Kingston and St Andrew. This pattern of population distribution follows that of the plantation period and of the years in which inland Jamaica was being settled mainly by black smallholders.

The cluster of schools, churches, professional services, newspapers, government offices and commercial organisations in Kingston gave it a great advantage. St James was not far behind. The black majority who lived in the rural areas were at a disadvantage in respect of education and the health services.

The growth of the working class also throws light on changes in the society. Table 1 below shows how slow the transition was to a completely free economy, and how very small the number of professionals was, especially between 1843 and 1891. On the other hand the increase in the commercial class signifies increasing diversification of enterprises and growing urbanisation.

The literacy figures for the parishes reflect the government's neglect of public education which reached only a small proportion of the population. In mountain villages, where the majority of the people had settled, access was difficult and schools were few and far between. Adults could not afford

Table 1

Year	Professional	Domestic (personal)	Commercial	Agricultural	Industrial	Total
1891	5,900	5,300	8,100	137,600	26,500	183,400
1911	6,800	5,500	13,700	158,400	36,300	220,600
1921	7,100	7,200	13,500	160,300	36,300	224,300
1891	1,100	21,400	2,800	133,700	31,100	190,200
1911	2,400	32,500	6,000	113,100	36,200	190,300
1921	4,300	45,400	7,200	125,400	37,300	219,600

to attend day school and only the more determined attended evening classes two or four nights per week after a strenuous day's work. Most of those who wished to learn to read attended classes once a week, at Sunday schools, where their only reading text was the Bible. Education was not free. Schools collected a small weekly charge for pupils learning to read and an additional sum for those learning to write. It was generally accepted that labourers had no need for literacy.

The very small Negro Education Grant that had been made after emancipation to assist in erecting school buildings ceased after the Morant Bay Uprising. In its place two education grants were made which were based on the average school attendance and on the quality of the annual examination results. This forced teachers to ensure that more children passed the test but it did not necessarily mean improved teaching methods.

Few opportunities existed for upward mobility in society. The people were taught to be "content with that place in life to which God had called them". If their fathers were labourers or cowherds or were engaged in some other menial task, that was as far as they should expect to go. The few who managed to surmount the educational and social hurdles were not allowed to rise to positions of responsibility in the government service. Government departments were headed by white expatriates and all other senior positions were filled by whites or near-whites. It was the policy in the civil service that the few blacks and coloureds employed were not to be promoted above a certain level. In practice, the darker the complexion, the lower the category in which individuals were placed.

Improvement in literacy levels was brought about largely by the Jamaican elementary schoolteacher and the Jamaican trained parson; and it was with these, as well as with the "banana man" and the peasant cultivators, that social change began. The three decades that followed the 1865 uprising witnessed remarkable manifestations of this creative, unquenchable spirit. One manifestation was the founding in 1894 of the Jamaica Union of Teachers (JUT) and in 1895 of the Jamaica Agricultural Society (JAS). "It would indeed be difficult to over-estimate the importance of such professional associations in the pre-independence period when the Crown Colony machine, even modified as it was in 1944, meant practically unmixed official rule by expatriate departmental heads uncurbed by any form of a national will." (Lewis: 1968)

Lewis emphasised that these two organisations acted as focal points in the anti-colonial struggle by initiating the forming of a national will in a variety of ways, by campaigns in defence of teachers' rights against school management boards, the setting up of vocational schools, methods of teacher payment, forming an independent bloc of farming opinion, and formulating Jamaican points of view on a wide range of public issues, including racial discrimination and the "foreign" content of school education with its almost complete disregard for Jamaican history. These early manifestations of a national will indicate the same quality of spirit that the Portland and St Thomas banana cultivators displayed in the 1870s. The Jamaican responses had their origins in diverse groups and took different forms. Gordon and Bogle had symbolised the common interests of educated and illiterate, brown and black. The JUT and the JAS represented the identification of educated professionals with the peasant folk.

Recent studies by Holt, Satchell and other scholars throw light on the sale of private land in the three last decades of the nineteenth century. This enables us to trace the course of land purchases by peasants in the 1870s and to identify the beginnings of a black proletariat in the years that followed. We watch also the beginnings of the banana trade, the growing dominance of the United Fruit Company (UFC), and the flight of black labour from engulfing rural poverty.

In the period 1870-1900 some 2½ million acres of private property in Jamaica changed hands. The peak period for the peasants was the decade of the 1870s, when large numbers bought small parcels of land of 10 acres or less from planters in financial need. The 1880s saw sales to peasants slowing down and sales to people with capital increasing. This trend strengthened in the 1890s. "Although other actors – planters, merchants, and other élites – were coming increasingly to dominate the land market and to engross larger and larger shares of Jamaica's arable land, peasants held their own until the 1890s which, ironically, was precisely the moment that the British and Jamaican governments embraced the promotion of small proprietorships as official policy." (Holt: 1992)

Holt's reference to Jamaican government policy has to do with the reports of two royal commissions, one headed by Crossman in 1885 and the other by Norman in 1897. These reports represented a radical change in the thinking of the British government. Up to this time the sugar plantation had been regarded as the foundation of West Indian prosperity and the planters as the only acceptable advisers on political affairs. As

Arthur Lewis put it, with these two reports, little Quashie, for so long derided and despised, moved to the centre of the stage.

The Crossman Commission indicated this change in colonial policy:

> It is to the possession of provision grounds that the industrious negro turns with the greatest liking, and there now exists in Jamaica a substantial and happily numerous population of the peasant proprietor class, which easily obtains a livelihood by the growth of the minor tropical products of fruit and spices, cocoa and coffee, and so contributes materially to the general prosperity . . . Again, the negroes have found in other ways means of earning money. Public works in Jamaica, such as the construction of railways, provide them with regular pay at home.

The Panama Canal proved a great attraction: "The negro who refuses to work on estates in Jamaica will willingly labour for wages on these other undertakings even when the rate of wages is in reality not higher, but where he imagines himself to be more of a free agent."

These were the first words of vindication and endorsement from the Colonial Office; not sermons about the beauty of industry or the moral muscle developed by hard work, but a tribute to the peasant proprietor.

Ten years later, in 1897, another royal commission was even more enthusiastic about turning its back on the sugar plantation system and endorsing the further development of smallholdings. It urged that the interests of the general public should be safeguarded against those of the sugar producers:

> It must be recollected that the chief outside influences with which the governments of certain colonies have to reckon are the representative of the sugar estates, that these persons are not interested in anything but sugar, that the establishment of any other industry is often detrimental to their interests and that under such conditions it is the special duty of Your Majesty's Government to see that the welfare of the general public is not sacrificed to the interests or supposed interests of a small but influential minority which has special means of enforcing its wishes and bringing its claims to notice. (Norman Commission)

Traditionally, the government and the planters had done everything in their power to block the establishment of smallholdings. Now the Norman Commission endorsed the programme the peasants had pioneered:

> The settlement of the labourer on the land has not as a rule been viewed with favour in the past, by the persons interested in sugar estates. What suited them best was a large supply of labourers,

entirely dependent on being able to find work on the large estates and consequently subject to their control and willing to work at low rates of wages. But it seems to us that no reform offers so good a prospect for permanent welfare in the future of the West Indies as the settlement of the labouring population on the land as small peasant proprietors; and in many places this is the only means by which the population can in future be supported. (Norman Commission)

It was in this period that the trend against peasant smallholders and in favour of large proprietors began to manifest itself. In order to see the development of this trend, we focus now on the rise of the banana trade.

In 1866 a chance meeting took place between a Yankee skipper and a group of peasant cultivators at Oracabessa. The captain, George Bush, was searching for bananas for the growing US fruit market. The trade had started with the sale of some bunches of Cuban bananas in the United States early in the century and had grown to the point where, by 1830, Cuba was exporting some 15,000 stems to Boston. Sea captains went scouting for supplies in other islands. The Oracabessa cultivators supplied Bush with 500 stems and urged him to call in at Port Antonio. There he completed his purchases, returned to Boston and before long was back in Port Antonio where, in 1869, he opened an office as agent for a number of Boston fruit companies. Other shippers included Lorenzo Dow Baker, who soon became the moving spirit in forming the Boston Fruit Company, (later the United Fruit Company).

The conflict that developed involved the African-Jamaican peasant who grew bananas on a smallholding that he either owned or rented, an American corporation that aimed at complete control of the sources of production, the means of transport and distribution in the United States, and the government of Jamaica, which had been urged by two royal commissions to undertake the settlement of the labouring population on the land as peasant proprietors.

Two pioneering sociological studies, *Cuban Counterpoint* by Fernando Ortiz and *My Mother who Fathered Me* by Edith Clarke, guide us to a fuller understanding of the conflict as seen through the eyes of the Jamaican smallholder.

Ortiz illumined Cuban history by contrasting the independent tobacco farmer with his smallholding and the intensive system of sugar agriculture which demands large-scale production. Edith Clarke pointed to the contrast between the smallholders of Orange Grove, an integrated society "in which kinship plays an important part", and Sugar Town, which,

is not so much a social entity as a conglomerate of disparate sections, held together only by a common involvement with the sugar estate .

. . The town's population rose and fell with the sugar-growing seasons as migrant workers flooded in seeking work and out again once jobs grew scarce . . . If lucky enough to be employed, the father went off early to the mill, having washed down bread, or an occasional cornmeal dumpling with bush tea.

Turn to the banana and the coming of the multinational corporation, and we become witnesses to a fundamental transformation in Jamaica's social and economic life between the mid-nineteenth and twentieth centuries. The two central figures in this change were the US corporation organised by Lorenzo Dow Baker and the banana man of whom Claude McKay wrote and whom the poet Evan Jones portrayed:

> Touris, whiteman wipin his face
> Met me in Golden Grove Market place,
> He looked at me ol clothes brown
> with stain
> An soaked right through wid de
> Portlan' rain
> He cas his eye, turn up his nose,
> He says youre a beggar man I
> suppose . . .
> I said, by God an dis big
> right han
> You mus recognise a banana
> man . . .

His great treasure, his source of pride, were in his ten acres of mountain side, his Gros Mitchel and Lacatan bananas, some coconut trees, some hills of yam; and his livestock:

> . . . on dat very same lan'
> Five she-goats an a big black ram.

Bananas, yams, coconuts, goats, gave the banana man the dishes he and his family loved. Boiled green bananas went perfectly with salted fish, with salted mackerel, cod, herring; and how could "run down" be prepared without green bananas? As porridge, as dumpling or as fried ripe banana fritters or as baked ripe bananas served with coconut milk, or as ripe fruit, it kept company throughout the generations with the Jamaican people. When the smallholder looked at a cane-piece he saw "busha", but he saw in his banana walk the money to send his children to school, to clothe and feed his family, to pay his taxes.

The extent to which the banana tree and the stems of bananas were woven into his everyday life can be judged from the list of names it inspired, by its shape and colour. Cassidy listed banana bird, banana borer, banana breeze (meaning one of 40 miles an hour or more, strong enough to blow the tree down), banana chips, banana Cudjoe, banana Katy, banana quit, banana spider, banana yoky, banana fig. Folk beliefs clustered around the tree which, like yams, sweet potatoes and plantains should be planted about five days before the full moon.

Loading bananas at Port Antonio

The fruit, handled with care, was well-suited to large-scale as well as to middle- and small-scale agriculture. The black peasant pioneered the Jamaica banana trade and in so doing contributed also to the development of the Jamaica tourist industry. It was to the Jamaican peasant cultivator also that two royal commissions paid tribute for providing Jamaica with a complementary system of smallholding agriculture and for diversifying the range of export crops. Jamaican society was restructured by bringing into existence a self-supporting peasantry.

These things being so, how was it that the trustee of the people, the governor and his chief officials, heads of the departments of lands, finance, agriculture and trade, did not seek to strengthen his bargaining position with US customers who, at an early stage, showed that they aimed at control?

A part of the problem lay in the nature of Crown colony government, which separated rulers from the ruled by discouraging any form of representative government or of popular participation. This bred attitudes of superiority rooted in race, which blinded them to the relevance of the history of the English working class (in this instance of the English cooperative movement) to the needs of the peasant banana growers. The vindication of the peasantry in the 1880s and 1890s was accompanied by their betrayal.

Production in the 1870s and 1880s was in the hands of smallholders; the fruit came from 2,880 or more smallholdings in Portland. In the last 30 years of the century Port Antonio's banana trade reached one-quarter of the island's total:

> A little sleepy town of 1,305 in 1880, the port was transformed with new wharves, new roads and bridges, and a 37 per cent increase in population. The surge of depositors and savings in its government savings bank suggests both the impact of the fruit trade on the town and the role of the peasant class in the trade. The number of bank

The people betrayed and vindicated   277

depositors and their total savings increased from 238 with £5,000 in 1880 to 778 with £10,155 in 1889 . . . Much of that growth came from small depositors, which suggests a more prosperous peasant class. (Holt: 1992)

In these critical years the government remained blind to Lorenzo Dow Baker's control strategy and to the need of the peasantry for guidance and support. Baker (1840-1908) made his second trip to Jamaica in 1871 when he called in at Port Antonio with a cargo of saltfish, flour and pork. He sold his cargo, took on board some coconuts and 1,450 stems of bananas and returned to Boston where, after a 17-day voyage, he sold the fruit, making a profit of $2,000. Encouraged, he started to devote himself to the banana trade, competing with other shippers such as J. E. Kerr and Company in Montego Bay. Rainfall and temperature made Port Antonio a good base, so in 1880 the L. Baker Company, with Baker as resident manager, opened its doors there. Baker, a shrewd, energetic New Englander, saw the importance of controlling his sources of supply. He lost no time in buying Bog Estate of 1,850 acres, which bordered on the town, at a cost of £1 an acre. Bog, which he renamed Boundbrook, included about one-third of Port Antonio's waterfront, with good port facilities. His next step was to acquire control of a shipping line for, like his competitors J. E. Kerr and Company in Montego Bay, he saw the great advantage that steamships had over sailing ships, since bananas were perishable. Pursuing his strategy of control, and realising that efficient shipping arrangements were vital, he gradually gained control of the carrying trade. This, in turn, gave him control over production.

The other chief source of bananas was Central America. By a series of mergers Baker's company and some other fruit companies formed the Boston Fruit Company, and later merged with Minor Keith's company in Costa Rica to become the United Fruit Company.

In the meantime a British company, Elders, Dempster and Company, on the urging of the Colonial Secretary, Joseph Chamberlain, set up the Imperial Direct Line of banana steamers in 1901 and formed Elders and Fyffes as a fruit and shipping company. But the British company was no match for the experienced and now strongly based United Fruit Company which had gained virtual control of the trade. In 1902 the American company bought 45 per cent of Elders and Fyffes stock, and by 1913 had come to control all the stock. Then, by cutting its freight rates, the United Fruit Company put the Imperial Direct Line out of business.

The Jamaican smallholder was squeezed out. What had happened in the 1650s to the white smallholders of Barbados, when they were bought out by Modyford, Drax and other sugar planters, now happened to the small

Jamaican banana planters. By 1899 most of the sugar estates were going in for the "backwood's nigger business" and were finding it profitable. Between 1895 and 1897 about 2,000 acres of land in the Rio Cobre delta around Spanish Town were in bananas. Peasants found it difficult to add to their holdings and too costly to rent.

The United Fruit Company's control of the trade now enabled it to dictate the price of bananas. Whether growers had contracts or not, the price they received depended on what the buyers judged the quality to be. The small growers were no longer in a position to bargain. Their fruit could be downgraded or rejected without redress. Lord Olivier described the process: "Only those actually acquainted with the manner in which bananas are purchased can appreciate how easily the buyer can convert a contract promising attractive prices into an unprofitable arrangement for the growers by means of heavy rejections and downgrading." (Olivier: 1936)

For the first time in his history the African-Jamaican faced the reality of economic coercion from a non-British source, a US version of corporate imperialism in the form of the United Fruit Company.

Baker summed up his self-image and his methods in his statement that he saw his work in Jamaica as an evangelical mission, and his wealth as an indication from God that he was succeeding in the work to which he had been called. His instructions to his son showed that he saw the peasant suppliers only as units of production: "Tell the people that if they wish to sell their fruit they must bring it down." Also, "Never mind what people say, throw it back on their barrels, let them suffer for it if they will not mind you."

As the company grew in strength and tightened its control, and as the large landholders bought up all available land, the banana man realised that he was confronting an oppressive reincarnation of the slave owner. Banana land was slipping out of his grasp.

The peasants were shrewd, intelligent people who had for generations learned to read bakra's mind. It had not taken them long to learn that Crown colony rule meant that even if they were granted the vote their elected representatives would have no power, since the governor had the right to nominate more members at any time and so outvote them. They knew that Crown colony rule had resulted in taxes falling more heavily on the poor than on the rich. They realised that the political process now meant less to them than it had done in the days when Gordon and Bogle built them into a voting bloc. It was all a pretence, a masquerade in which Pitchy Patchy would never rise above the role of Pitchy Patchy.

While land was available, there had been hope of change, but the grass-roots people saw that under a government whose laws equated political power and the vote with ownership of land, and which attempted to ensure that the black would never be anything but a worker in the social scale, he would never have full freedom. Once again the African-Jamaican demonstrated, as he had done in the western Jamaica and Morant Bay Uprisings, that the dynamics of social change rested with the mass of the people.

That response took three forms, each a total rejection of corporate economic coercion and monopoly of land ownership. The favoured response was emigration. As George Roberts points out, the dominant feature of the period 1881-1921 was a net outward movement. This increased with each decade and attained considerable dimensions (77,000 persons) during the decade 1911-21 when the total net outward movement was nearly 146,000 or about 3,600 a year. Some 46,000 went to the United States, 45,000 to Panama, at least 20,000 to Cuba and some 43,000 to other areas, including Costa Rica. (Roberts: 1957)

Another response was the beginning, although small in the period 1881-1911, of a movement from the rural areas to Kingston, which became the capital city in 1872. The city had been enlarged in 1867, when its boundaries were extended to include Smith Village, Hannah Town and Fletcher's Land, at the time parts of St Andrew. A major movement of people to Kingston and St Andrew took place in the 1920s but the trend had become obvious already in the 1880s. An 1880 report on the island's juvenile population noted that there was a tendency for the rural population to move to Kingston in search of work. This tendency underscored the emergence of a Jamaican proletariat, which became a significant political force by the 1930s.

These responses were, in the course of time, to reinforce and enlarge the third major development, which was of primary importance, namely the growth of political consciousness and the formulation of Jamaican political objectives. This continued with Robert Love and Marcus Garvey and provided the cohesive, generative force that found expression in a national movement and in early efforts to organise trade unions.

CHAPTER 23

Robert Love points the way

We have seen how the Jamaican peasantry over the 30 years following the introduction of Crown colony government succeeded in achieving some measure of financial independence through agricultural pursuits and how, just as the colonial government was beginning to acknowledge their industry, although not their right to political equality, they were once more subjected to foreign capitalist domination and brought to a state of near economic slavery. Sugar had fallen on bad times, accounting for only 18 per cent of the island's exports in 1897, but the United Fruit Company and the banana plantations were flourishing and applying economic pressure on the workforce. The peasantry was under siege.

Some were coerced into selling their small acreages to people anxious to get into the banana trade. Others unable to pay their mortgages and meet outstanding debts lost their lands in official seizures. Many frustrated, landless, homeless and unemployed began to leave the rural countryside for the towns in search of a better life but unable to find suitable employment they ended up in overcrowded slums and expressed their disaffection by resorting to violence. Others joined the recruiting lines to Central America, and even when the news coming back from the Canal Zone was of disease, repression and frustration, the migration continued. There were also the thousands of field labourers who, after completing the reaping and replanting exercises on the banana and sugar plantations, faced the long "dead season" when there was no employment, "and starvation roamed the land".

The island continued to suffer from regressive taxation. High customs duties had been introduced after emancipation, ostensibly to make up the revenue lost by the downturn in the economy, and brought in far more than was required. Duties were levied not on manufactured goods but on consumer goods: on the basic necessities such as corn, flour, rice, salted fish and meat, which were needed mainly by the labouring class. Revenues collected for the year 1845 illustrate this. Import revenues came to 65 per cent, or £186,085; the rest was made up of £77,440 from land tax and £6,121 from stock traded. It was a pattern that remained in place for the next 60 years. Jamaicans bought their foodstuffs dear and sold their produce cheap. Taxation fell heavily on the poor.

Governor Musgrave's paper delivered to the Colonial Institute in London in 1880 noted that the great mass of consumers who furnished this revenue were not labourers on sugar estates but small settlers and peasants. C. S. Salmon, writing about the situation in *Depression in the West Indies*, 1884, concluded that a great injustice had been done to the islands; that they had been handed over, as it were, to a powerful corporation, and that the consequences of this monopoly were to be seen in underdevelopment and stagnation.

The voice of conscience raised on behalf of the faceless masses after emancipation had been suppressed in 1866 and was not to be heard again until the last decade of the century. With the introduction of Crown colony government, political control was passed to the governor. He was advised by a council of six government officials and three elected from among the local plantocracy. These appointees, all white, held office at his discretion and were reluctant to intervene on behalf of the African-Jamaican majority lest they offend their patron and forfeit their privilege.

The Jamaican upper class had willingly surrendered the island's constitution in 1866, and now found that they had also lost their political influence. It would take years of struggle on the road back to political representation, black empowerment and eventually political independence. Late in 1883, in the face of local and international pressure, the Colonial Office announced as a moderate step in advance the reintroduction of limited elected representation.

At the general elections in May 1884, nine representatives were elected and to these the governor added six officials, heads of government departments, appointed by the governor to the Legislative Council. The representatives had limited authority as the governor held in reserve four other appointments which he could utilise as he saw fit, and he also had the power of veto. If the representatives voted unanimously on an issue the governor could overrule them on grounds of paramount importance or by deploying "the official majority", that is, by simply increasing the number of ex-officio members to ten. In W. Adolphe Roberts' words, "The period was to be uneventful . . . and apathetic politically . . . . The island settled down to a version of feudalism that succeeded in being a mild copy of the old order, without its sporadic wealth, without its turmoil. Socially the Negro was 'kept in his place'." (Roberts: 1955)

This may have been the generally accepted impression, but the facts are otherwise. The petty bourgeoisie – successful smallholders, teachers, parsons, low-level civil servants and clerks – were frustrated by their exclusion from mainstream politics and began to mobilise the black electorate. They set about identifying and recruiting persons having the necessary property and educational qualifications to add their names to the electoral roll. The 1884 electoral roll showed the following registrations: 98 Indians, 1,001 Europeans, 2,578 mulattoes, 3,766 "Africans", making a total of 7,443 out of a possible 15,000 eligible to register but with active recruiting, among the African-Jamaicans, the numbers grew to 42,266 in 1889.

Whites were greatly outnumbered and this rekindled fears about the power of the natives. A literacy clause was introduced into the Franchise Act to prevent those unable to read and write from exercising the ballot. At the next elections in 1893, this effectively excluded almost half the number of voters. In the past illiterate electors had cast their ballots with the assistance of literate people. The beleaguered masses were now more frustrated than ever and desperately needed articulate leadership to challenge their exploitation and press for social reform.

Dr Robert Love, the black Bahamian anti-colonialist who had visited the island for a few weeks in 1889 while on his way to Haiti returned a year later to make Jamaica his home. Having lived in Panama and Central America, Love was only too familiar with the unfair trading practices of large companies such as the United Fruit Company. He empathised with the Jamaicans in their efforts to gain black empowerment and rid themselves of exploitation.

Robert Love

The most urgent issue was to increase black representation in the Legislative Council. In 1890 there were no blacks in the Council, although a few had managed to win seats on parochial boards. Although the successful voter registration campaign had taken place in 1889, the year before Love settled in Jamaica, he was in time to witness the panic of the whites and the introduction of the restrictive literacy clause.

The campaign to increase the black vote intensified with his participation. He and his associates compiled lists of suitably qualified black persons to counter the propaganda that black candidates were not available to run for elections. Love began to take the limelight by publicly supporting the call for greater representation in the government, for social reform and for black participation in the administrative life of the country.

He was born possibly in 1839, not far from the

town of Nassau where Africans, found aboard slave ships after the abolition of the slave trade in 1807, were liberated by the British navy and
allowed to establish free communities. When he was still a small boy, his
mother, sister and aunts had been abducted and brought to Jamaica as
slaves. Whether or not Love ever managed to make contact with any of
them later is not certain.

He grew up in the Anglican church in Nassau, received a basic education (including Greek and Latin) and became a deacon in the church. Not
one to accept opinions without question, Love apparently had serious
differences with the church leadership, then migrated to the United States
where he completed his religious studies in the South and where, from
time-to-time, he was embroiled in controversy.

Haiti, the first black country in the world to throw off the colonial yolk,
was then in the midst of its liberation struggles and Love, caught up in the
euphoria of race pride, offered his services. He trained as a medical doctor
because he felt that in this way he could contribute meaningfully to the
black liberation cause. He first went as a missionary, then accepted an
appointment with the Haitian army in 1881 as a medical doctor but his
stay in the republic was shortlived. Within two years he had become so
involved in the politics of the country that he supported a palace coup led
by the party in opposition and was exiled. From Haiti he apparently went
to Panama where he lived for some time before deciding to make Jamaica
his home.

Love adjusted to the Jamaican way of life without difficulty, especially
as he was still a British subject. Ironically, on his arrival in the island the
establishment press of the day, assuming that he was white, described him
as an Englishman and practising physician. In those days no ordinary black
man became a professional.

Many people were expressing progressive ideas similar to his own at the
time. Some were to influence the formulation of the Fabian socialist
philosophy which was "to guarantee to the dependencies the institutions
of liberty, the social health and material prosperity on which their struggle
depends . . . constructive reform [of] social and economic policies, civil
liberty, local government, preventive medicine, nutrition, mass education,
literacy, free association, co-operative organization, trade unionism, political representation". (Jones: 1945) Love and his associates campaigned for
the issues set out in the Fabian socialist philosophy, which included greater
black empowerment, fair employment practices, equal opportunity for
blacks in the civil service and other public institutions.

Love first attracted public attention in 1893, when he delivered a lecture
on Toussaint L'Ouverture and the Haitian situation at the Conversorium
School on Church Street in Kingston. Contributions from the lecture

went to a worthy cause, the Wesley Chapel Fund. Love was not a prepossessing man but he was an electrifying speaker. The lecture was so well-received that he was invited to repeat it in Kingston and in Spanish Town. Not only was he highly educated, he was articulate. When *The Daily Gleaner* refused to publish his letters on these issues, Love decided to start his own weekly newspaper, *The Jamaica Advocate*, in December 1894. Through his medical practice he could finance this small weekly newspaper which became the voice of the underprivileged.

For the upcoming 1893 general elections, Love and his companions campaigned vigorously but only four coloured men, Charles Campbell, Richard Hill Jackson, George Steibel and J. T. Palache, a Kingston solicitor of mixed Jewish descent, presented themselves as candidates, and only one, Palache, gained a seat. However, the number of black and coloured representatives grew until by the middle of the 1930s they formed the majority in the legislature. But full political control did not come until Jamaica attained independence from Britain in 1962.

Love appreciated the problems of the working-class people in his adopted country, for he had been subjected to his share of discrimination during his early years in the Bahamas and also in the Jim Crow South of the United States. In the republic of Haiti he had witnessed black men in authority oppress their black fellowmen. Change could only come when it was recognised that there was no difference between people of different skin tones.

According to Richard Hart, Love was perhaps the first leader to challenge publicly the assumption that blackness and inferiority were synonymous. He said that anything a white man could do he, the black man, could do as well. His dedication to improving the Jamaican condition earned him a place in W. Adolphe Roberts' *Six Great Jamaicans*.

As an anti-colonialist, Love believed that the primary goal of any black country ought to be self-rule. However, bearing in mind his American and Haitian experiences, he rationalised that possibly "the best hope for black people lay within the British legal and political system". If the Jamaican masses were to take their rightful place within the British political system, they had to resist colonial oppression and strive for self-rule.

Through the pages of *The Jamaica Advocate* blacks were encouraged to assert their equality, express their political views, educate themselves and develop self-esteem and pride in their African heritage. At no time did Love give any thought to severing the British ties.

Love also called for blacks to be appointed to public office as justices of the peace and as members of government boards and commissions. His motto was: "Everything for the people; everything by the people; and nothing without the people."

Until Jamaica could achieve self-rule the best compromise was to adopt the French parliamentary system with representatives from the colonies sitting in the parliament in Paris. He suggested that the British should do the same, but the proposal was never entertained.

The establishment continued to spread rumours that black people were indifferent to politics and that there were no suitable black candidates available. The apparent indifference of the people lay not so much in their lack of interest in assuming responsibility but in their inability to fulfil the high property and financial requirements for political office. They faced severe economic hardships with a declining economy and resultant social pressures, together with job competition with Indian indentured labour. In the 1880s many were left homeless, starving and naked. Natural disasters in succeeding years had also destroyed their provision grounds and many were left penniless. Restrictions placed on employment and advancement of blacks in the police force, the military and the civil service thwarted the ambition of the masses. Top posts in these agencies were filled by whites and near-whites, and blacks could only gain employment in low-paying jobs. The only way to change the system was to keep hammering at the weaknesses and Love persisted in his attacks, writing in the press and speaking from public platforms.

He was branded a racist but he never identified solely with colour, declaring publicly that "complexioned distinctions should be buried in the idea of nationality". Love threw his weight behind anyone, white or black, whom he felt would further his progressive ideals. W. B. Hannan, a white candidate to the legislative council for Clarendon and one of the free thinkers of the day, received his support. Hannan was an Englishman and member of a group of socialists whose ideas had contributed to the establishment of the Fabian Society in 1884. Love and Hannan called for administrative reform and in *The Jamaica Advocate* they attacked the plantation system which they felt "kept the labourer dependent, poor, ignorant, unclean, contemptible and miserable".

In 1894 Love and his colleagues organised the People's Convention, which he claimed was to celebrate "in a sympathetic and useful manner the sixtieth anniversary of the abolition of slavery". It became an annual event at which social issues such as popular education, land distribution, voter registration, taxation and citisenship were discussed and recommendations for improvements made. He hoped that one day blacks would enjoy political recognition just as other white British citizens did, and that through the convention a black nationalist leader with "an attachment to the soil" would emerge whose influence would spread internationally.

Few amendments of any significance had been made to the tax law since 1865 and the law introduced in 1890 continued to favour the few at the expense of the many. In some instances it allowed owners of 1,000 acres and more to pay one pound, sixteen shillings and eight pence annually, or one farthing per acre, while owners of five-acre lots (the small £6 voter) paid two shillings per year. Taxes on draft animals and on drays, wagons and carts remained high. The peasant paid three shillings, six pence for each donkey and six shillings for each cart, wagon, or dray wheel. Higher taxes were imposed on cottages with floorings, so many persons were forced to remove them to avoid the higher rate. Customs duties were fashioned from the same pattern, favouring the wealthy and penalising the poor.

In challenging the system, Love and his colleagues advocated a single tax structure based upon land tax instead of indirect taxes such as customs duties. It was clear that unless blacks could gain the majority in the legislature where they could formulate policy there would be no meaningful change. Love openly advocated self-rule and called upon the public to support his campaign.

His friend and political advocate, Whitfinch, in supporting the call for self-rule, wrote in *The Jamaica Advocate*: "In order to occupy a place of respect among the people's of the earth, it is absolutely necessary that we be entrusted with that which is our birthright, Self-Government. We do not ask a favour, No! we ask for the restoration to us of STOLEN PROPERTY."

As regards fairer political representation under the existing crown colony system, Love recommended one representative for each of the 14 parishes instead of nine for the whole island. The Colonial Office eventually adopted the recommendation, in 1895, but with many reservations, because "the number of black and brown men or even of Kingston Jews and lawyers in the Council" would adversely affect their efforts to attract white investors, and the election of such persons, including "newspaper editors of a low type" would be "unreasonable and very troublesome".

Local newspapers, which were largely supportive of the *status quo*, kept insinuating that "dangerous men were active in Jamaica". Love was their prime target as they feared that if he joined forces with the better educated and more influential brown middle class, the country could rise up in revolt and become another Haiti. As in the case of Governor Eyre, these fears were born of racism.

In order to erase the popular belief that blacks were not interested in politics or would make unsuitable candidates, Love and his associates continued to publicise lists of persons with suitable educational and financial qualifications who might be willing to come forward. They also encouraged local communities to seek out black candidates and support them. On one of their lists, the 21 names included three teachers, two solicitors in Kingston, eight clergymen and eight other individuals.

In *The Jamaica Advocate* of 12 December 1895 Love wrote, "Let the Negroes look around them in their own parish for a representative Negro, gather round him, help him, send him to the Legislative Council." But he cautioned that skin colour was not to be an overriding factor, neither were they to accept candidates blindly or be influenced by their financial status. On two occasions in *The Jamaica Advocate* of May 1895 the following notice appeared, "Don't neglect this. If you wish your country to be better you must help to make it better. Your vote is your power." He also said, "The ballot is our one great weapon of offence and defence. Every Negro who has the vote has the power to help himself." The 1896 elections recorded the highest voter turnout up to that time.

The show of black candidates was, however, disappointing. Only two came forward. They were Josiah Smicle from St Thomas and Alexander Dixon from Santa Cruz in St Elizabeth. They were the first black men since Edward Vickers, a Kingston landlord (1847) and Charles Price, a builder (1849), to win seats in the Assembly. Dixon had appeared on one of Love's lists.

Perhaps because only two men presented themselves, the rumours of black indifference persisted. *The Jamaica Post* newspaper on 6 October 1898 noted with some degree of malice: "We see local elections for board members unattended by a single peasant voter time after time, and when we go among these unsophisticated electors and enquire the reason, it is invariably, 'What good them doing for Black People, Sir?' " This was in spite of the fact that there were black and coloured men already serving on parochial boards.

In 1899 the governor of the day invoked the "official majority clause" to ensure that the elected representatives in the Council could not outvote any proposal with which he was not in favour. No other governor had ever sought to invoke that power before. Love and his supporters challenged the decision and led a series of political protests for several months running.

Conservative elements in the society that were uncomfortable with having elected representatives in the legislature had begun to make representations to have the Jamaica Constitution revert to crown colony status. This retrograde step would have brought further economic and social distress to unfortunate poor blacks, thousands of whom, after more than half a century, were still landless and disenfranchised. Love helped to organise a delegation to Britain to argue against the proposed change.

He kept up his campaign for black representation in local and national councils, offering himself as a candidate and winning a seat in the Kingston City Council in 1898 and 1903, and in the Legislative Council in 1906.

Vassal Calder, a local white planter from St Elizabeth, who was appointed to the Legislative Council spitefully attacked him and his equally caustic response shows how deep the prejudices were on both sides. Calder said, "Dr. Love must remember that his ancestors were my ancestors' slaves, and as such he could never be my equal. He is aggrieved because my ancestors rescued him from the bonds of thraldom and deprived him of the privilege of being King of the Congo . . . enjoying the epicureal and conjugal orgies and the sacrificial pleasures of his ancestral home in Africa." Love replied:

> The men who released my ancestors were not the men who enslaved them. The men who enslaved my ancestors were the Blackbeards and the Morgans, a type of Calder; the men who released them were the Wilberforces and the Granville Sharpes, a different type altogether. After all, slavery is but a preying of the strong upon the weak and all nations have undergone the ordeal in their time, including Calder's nation. The shame is not on the slaves but on the tyrant . . . Mr. Calder boasts that he can trace his ancestry back two hundred years. What of that? I can go back to Adam. When he said that had I not been removed from Africa I would be sitting on the Congo throne I verily believe that, and since "Authority is authority where'er it's to be found" as King of the Congo I would be the equal of the King of England. Calder would have had to approach both of us with due deference which subjects show to royalty. (Sherlock: 1980)

In spite of the fact that thousands of desperately poor people were living under difficult conditions, and were either unemployed or earning extremely low wages, Love did not support confrontationist action. Yet he responded to the call from the Kingston dock workers, when out of desperation they went on strike for four days in 1895, after their efforts to negotiate a pay increase had failed. Love saw this action as a "new departure" in social protest and used it to develop a workable strategy through the formation of labour clubs.

He recognised that a sufficiently large number of people could come together and exert pressure on employers to their own benefit. He also saw that institutions using cooperative methods to obtain financing could assist industrious individuals to "expand their influence in public life and . . . advance their status".

Love conceived of group-based institutions which would reinforce the type of economic and social independence he believed would generate the resources necessary to enable the less fortunate in the society to "expand their influence in public life and . . . advance their status". He put his ideas into practice by forming the Jamaica Advocate Cooperative Association to take over the newspaper when he could no longer run operations.

Love saw Friendly societies as organisations providing healthy social interaction and a modicum of financial stability for the very poor. He founded the Sparks Lodge and became its first master. He had learnt from experience that educational attainment was essential to the achievement of social goals, and so he kept motivating ambitious young people to acquire the necessary education that would help them to fulfil their goals.

Love was not a teacher, but he became an honorary member of the Jamaica Union of Teachers which was formed in 1894. The 1882 Royal Commission had criticised the lack of efficiency in the schools and noted that the increase in simple literacy by no means corresponded with the increase in the number of pupils at school. The Lumb Commission of 1897 criticised the standard of teaching and recommended a 10 per cent retrenchment in the already low elementary school budget. Education was placed on the agenda of the 1898 People's Convention but there was not much that the representatives could do.

In 1905 the Lumb Commission's recommendations "to reduce salaries of all teachers, trained and untrained, good, bad and indifferent alike" as well as to decrease aid for the first- and second-class schools by another 10 per cent were put into effect. The elementary school budget for the whole island was £52,605. After 1865 teachers had been paid by results, mainly in the Three Rs and had apparently become skilled in qualifying for the allowance without any significant improvement in the performance of the students. The report noted that "the curriculum was extensive and the teaching superficial". Education expenditure had risen sixfold between 1861 and 1881 to £23,400, while enrolment (including whites and coloureds) had only doubled to 231,268. At the same time the number of illiterates had doubled.

Out of a black adult population of some 250,000 at that time, it is estimated that only about 22,000, less than 10 per cent, could read and write. The Colonial Office was not prepared to increase the expenditure further.

Love championed the teachers' cause, in the press and on the platform, especially the economic hardships they were enduring as a result of the reduction in their already low salaries.

He had great praise for black women who served as models in their society and were at the centre of family life. In encouraging them to improve their education and become better leaders, he observed that it was by their leadership that the black race would succeed. He also encouraged the education of black girls as he believed that the black race could not rise above the level of its womanhood. He felt that they needed to be protected against the abuse of bookkeepers on sugar estates. Black children also needed to be protected from unfair treatment at school because of the colour of their skin.

When the public holidays legislation was being introduced, Love advocated its extension to include "cooks, housemaids, footmen and field labourers".

Black empowerment could only come with greater black participation in political, economic and administrative life. His hope lay in the spread of Pan-Africanism, because this movement had an obligation to spread black consciousness throughout the diaspora and even to Africa.

The first Pan-African Conference was held in London in 1900 and although Love did not attend, he published the conference proceedings in full in *The Jamaica Advocate*. Pan-Africanism emphasises the richness and diversity of African cultures, and inculcates feelings of self-worth and self-determination among peoples of African descent. For the first time hundreds of African-Jamaicans were exposed to its philosophy and understood the purpose of the movement. Within a month of the publication of the proceedings, more than 500 individuals from across the island joined the Jamaica branch of the association. The mission of the Jamaica branch, as he saw it, was to take the Pan-African message throughout the region, to the United States and as far as Africa.

Love, more than anyone else, influenced the direction Marcus Garvey was to take in championing black consciousness, anti-colonialism and Pan-Africanism. In acknowledging his debt to Love in 1920, Garvey declared, "Much of my early education in race consciousness is from Dr. Love. One cannot read his *Jamaica Advocate* without getting race consciousness." (*The Daily Gleaner:* 1930)

Many of the prejudices Love challenged and the causes he fought for still remained unresolved at the end of his life. His black, literate, middle-class audience never managed to reach out sufficiently to the masses.

Love died on 21 November 1914. He had become seriously ill in 1906 and in 1910 gave up active politics. Garvey's mission was to develop the political strategy conceived of and started by Love, and to take the message of race consciousness into the international arena.

CHAPTER 24

Marcus Mosiah Garvey, 1887-1940

Marcus Garvey remains a vitalising, inspiring force today. He touches Jamaicans closely because he raises questions of race and social commitment with which they still have to come to terms. His message is as relevant now as it was in the 1920s and 1930s, when he formed the People's Political Party. As an independent and predominantly black nation, Jamaicans now have the power to reach decisions on issues he raised.

A study of his life and times shows that he has been urging us to assume a larger role in the scheme of things. He has deepened and enriched our knowledge of ourselves, of our past and our potential as a society. We become aware, also, of a prophet, a man who throughout his life lived his message; and did so through triumph and disaster, in the face of derision and oppression, of imprisonment and of rejection. From the beginning he was driven by a passionate concern for the African-Jamaican people, and indeed for all peoples of African origin throughout the world.

He reminded African-Americans of their background of slavery and of having been let loose in the world without a cent in their pockets or land to settle on that they could call their own. From the beginning they had to fight their own way up to where they are today. Some had done well but the great majority remained propertyless and almost helpless. If they were to improve themselves they had to focus on personal success.

In revering Marcus Garvey as a national hero, Jamaicans pay tribute also to a leader who pioneered a role for Africa and Africans in world affairs. His vision was of black united nations governed by black leaders.

Garvey had a profound respect for books, education and scholarship. He was a philosopher as well as a man of action, a thinker who arrived at his conclusions by analysing the West Indian experience. He grew up in Jamaican colonial society at a time when, as Rupert Lewis points out:

Colonial ideological policy consistently debased Africa as well as people and things African. The future, the coloniser claimed, belonged to Europe. Hence colonial subjects were made to identify progress with the ideals of their master. In the process of the formation of Jamaica as a nation the negation of Africa and blackness has been constant. And so has the resistance to [this negation] by black people. (Lewis: 1987)

The Jamaican people identify with Garvey as one who built their self-esteem, challenged them to affirm their racial identity and reunited them with Africa as homeland. That this should be so is a measure of the cultural and social revolution that has been taking place in Jamaica. This revolution is radically changing the Jamaican self-image to one of assertiveness and racial equality. It has projected Jamaica onto the world stage politically and has moved increasing numbers of black people into leadership roles in their country.

By examining some of his major statements and reflecting on his method of reaching conclusions, we come to understand the magnitude of Garvey's achievement and the quality of his mind. We need to do this because those in the centres of white power and influence in Jamaica, in the United States and Europe saw Garvey as a formidable threat and used all the means in their power, the law included, to obstruct and vilify him. They projected the image of a black racist subversive, a rabble-rouser, a confidence man and trickster.

The Jamaican upper and middle classes of the 1920s rejected his challenge "to formulate a program of racial preservation and to develop a settled racial outlook". In them the terrified consciousness of the sugar-and-slave plantocracy period still lingered. Some kept their distance, not because they disagreed with Garvey's philosophy, but because they feared victimisation if they were seen to be supporting the challenge to the status quo.

In the words of a Jamaican peasant, Marcus Garvey was "not a usual man". Born and schooled in rural Jamaica, he became by his own effort a scholar who understood that nations make, and are made by, their history. He was an educator and an exceptionally gifted communicator of ideas. His richly stored mind linked the particular with the universal, the past with the present, the local or national with the global. To read even a few of his statements and reflections is to encounter a mind that illumines the Jamaican historical experience. In his analysis of colonial society in the 1920s, for example, he demonstrates his methods of basing conclusions on observation and analysis. Writing to the president of the Tuskegee Institute in Alabama in 1916, he said that the Jamaicans were not as racially conscious as the American black because they lived under a common system of sociological hypocrisy. (Hill) He observed:

> We have no open race prejudice here, and we do not openly antagonise one another. The extremes here are between white and black . . . The black people here form the economic asset of the country, they number 6 to 1 of colored and white combined and without them in labour or general industry the country would go bankrupt . . . The black people have had seventy-eight years of Emancipation but all during that time they have never produced a leader of their own, hence they have never been led to think racially but in common with the destinies of the other people with whom they mix as fellow citizens.

Garvey noted the increase of race consciousness 22 years later, in 1938:

> The West Indians generally, have developed more of the white psychology than of black outlook; but gradually, in some of the islands, the consciousness of race is dawning upon the people which may develop, to place the competent Negroes there in the right frame of mind to be of service when needed. There is much hope for the West Indies as for anywhere else in the outlook of the Negro toward nationalisation and independence.

Garvey's advocacy of a Jamaican national spirit and his critical appraisal of those blacks who regarded England as the mother country were a continuation of the work of Dr Love and his associates who laboured at the end of the nineteenth century to improve the racial consciousness and social conditions of the Jamaican working classes. Love encouraged them to unite, to form themselves into unions and organisations and elect representatives to the legislative council who would be concerned with their welfare. He knew that Jamaica's long overdue political awakening had to come from within, not from without.

Garvey was one of the few of his time who understood how seriously the inner world of the African had been damaged, and in some instances destroyed, by the experience of enslavement combined with alienation; by a transfer of authority and by total immersion in a wholly materialistic society.

George Lamming, in eloquent moving words, describes the outcome:

> The result was a fractured consciousness, a deep split in its sensibility which now raised difficult problems of language and values; the whole issue of cultural allegiance between the imposed norms of White Power represented by a small numerical minority and the fragmented memory of the African masses: between White instruction

and Black imagination. The totalitarian demands of White supremacy in a British colony, the psychological injury inflicted by the
sacred rule that all forms of social status would be determined by
degrees of skin complexion; the ambiguities among Blacks themselves
about the credibility of their own spiritual history . . . Could the
outlines of a national consciousness be charted and affirmed out of all
this disparateness? And if that consciousness could be affirmed, what
were its true ancestral roots, its most authentic cultural base?
(Lamming: 1988)

Lamming's analysis, written long after Garvey's death, underscores
why Garvey challenged African-Jamaicans and indeed all persons of
African descent to set themselves the task of building a racial as well as a
national consciousness, to liberate themselves from colonialism, to build
self-esteem and race-pride. These were, and remain, the imperatives of
decolonisation. Garvey had the capacity for penetrating beyond process to
inner causes and needs and he went beyond anti-colonialism to advocate
a programme of decolonization. (Lewis: 1987)

The irony is that Garvey probably learned the importance of racial
pride, self-esteem and a settled racial outlook from books he used in
elementary school, readers written for English children that built pride
in the English way of life, in the English landscape, in the heroes of
England, in its victories and achievements. With his love of reading and
elocution, young Garvey learned the importance of racial pride from
authors who glorified English achievements; from William Shakespeare's
"This England never did and never shall/Lie at the proud foot of a
conqueror"; or from John Milton's vision of "a mighty and puissant
nation rousing herself like a strong man after sleep and shaking her
invincible locks".

Garvey grew to understand that the key to racial harmony lay in the
open acceptance of racial differences and respect for them. He advocated
racial consciousness but attacked and rejected racial discrimination of
any kind. Race consciousness and a sense of self-worth are important
elements in national development. They are essential for self-respect, for
as Isaiah Berlin emphasised in his essay on nationalism, "To be made an
object of contempt, amused condescension, or patronizing reliance by
proud, successful neighbours is one of the most traumatic experiences
that individuals or societies can suffer." (Berlin: 1981)

Pomp and circumstance are as essential elements in the culture of blacks
as they are for people of all other races. In the same way that other nations
establish their hierarchy of honours, awards and titles, so Garvey established his own system of honours for his Universal Negro Improvement

Association (UNIA): honours such as Earl of the Congo, Viscount of the Niger, Baron Zambezi and Knight of the Nile. In this regard he brooked no condescension.

He was a universalist, concerned with the Africans of the diaspora and of the African continent. He saw racial consciousness as an active and independent program of upliftment. As a result, he never descended to the level of the apostles of white superiority. His vision was Pan-Caribbean, Pan-American, Pan-African.

Two very different groups of Jamaicans have broadened and deepened our understanding of Marcus Garvey. The Rastafarians have consistently given Africa the central place that belongs to a homeland, affirmed their Africanness and revered Garvey. Alongside them stand scholars such as Robert Hill and Rupert Lewis who, on the basis of rigorous academic scholarship, have shown the significance and importance of Garvey's work and of Garvey as a world leader.

Garvey was born on 17 August 1887, in the small rural town of St Ann's Bay. He was christened Malcus Mosiah but early assumed the name of Marcus. At St Ann's Bay he spent his formative years under the influence of two self-educated men, his father, Malcus Mosiah Garvey, and his godfather, Alfred E. Borrowes. From them young Marcus learned certain positive attitudes which guided his life. He was an avid reader and developed a passion for learning. He always carried a pocket dictionary from which he learnt three or four words each day and as a result built up a phenomenal vocabulary. This he utilised to the fullest extent as a public speaker and orator, and as a writer and newspaper editor.

His exposure to a wide range of subjects in his father's and godfather's book collections developed his enquiring mind and an interest in social issues. On his return to Jamaica from the United States at the end of 1927 he owned one of the finest libraries in the island. His collection included works on science, history, African history, religion and art and was consulted by a number of prominent persons in Kingston.

Garvey's first exposure to race prejudice was as a child and it obviously left a deep hurt and possibly more than any other single experience, helped to frame his philosophy on race consciousness. He used to play with a white girl, the daughter of the Methodist minister in the town, until the day came when she was told by her mother that she could no longer associate with Marcus because he was black.

The skills acquired in his godfather's printery equipped him to earn a living wherever he went. Most important of all, he understood the power of the press and never failed to use it to mobilise people of African descent and to lead them to a clearer understanding and appreciation of their black heritage.

Robert Love was one of Garvey's mentors and gave him elocution lessons when he moved to Kingston. From Love, Garvey also learnt much about pride in race and challenging colonialist prejudices. The young man from St Ann's Bay was all the time refining his ideas on racial consciousness. His involvement in the printers' strike in 1908 and his championing of these underpaid workers seemed a natural thing to do, although it cost him his job with the P. A. Benjamin Company, a firm of manufacturing chemists. At that time they were also publishing a small advertising sheet, *The Commercial Messenger*, on which Garvey may have worked. While with the company Garvey made his first venture into publishing. He began *Garvey's Watchman* but this small journal apparently ran for only three issues.

Garvey became a regular contributor to the local newspapers and often addressed social issues affecting the working classes, but the establishment press of the day, as they had done to Love earlier, did not always approve of his radical views and did not always publish his letters.

Garvey began seriously improving his oratorical skills by visiting different churches and observing their preachers; he practised reading aloud, entered and organised elocution contests, and took advantage of every opportunity to appear on public platforms. A contemporary remembers his first visit to the East Queen Street Literary and Debating Society.

> The chairman gave him permission to speak during the "open" half-hour on the topic under debate and as would be expected, this strange awkward looking young man, not so long ago from the country, made us all sit up and listen. (Murray: 1969)

The anti-colonialist National Club of Jamaica attracted him and he soon became a regular speaker at their public forums. Eventually he was elected the club's secretary. The founder was Sandy Cox, a Kingston barrister who had been discriminated against in the Civil Service and was strongly anti-colonialist. Cox advocated that the only way that coloured and black people in Jamaica could better their condition was to unite with other members of the black race in all parts of the world. The club attracted some prominent persons of like views, but after a time it became primarily a platform for Cox, the politicians H. A. L. Simpson and Alexander Dixon, whom Love had supported in his political bid to get into the House of Representatives, and also Marcus Garvey. Eventually out of frustration and disappointment Cox emigrated to the USA. Referring to that period of his life, some 17 years later, Garvey noted: "The people were [then] not sufficiently racially conscious to appreciate a racial movement because they lived under a common system of social hypocrisy that deprived them of that very racial consciousness." (*Black Man*: 1933)

Garvey began reaching out to local artisans, rural peasant farmers, labourers searching for recognition and self-assurance. He awakened in them national consciousness and urged them to shake off their economic oppression. But his vision could not be contained within the confines of the Jamaican society and in 1909 he set out for Central America where thousands of African-West Indians were employed on the Panama Canal and on banana and sugar plantations in Costa Rica.

There Garvey found employment as a timekeeper on one of the United Fruit Company's banana plantations and this gave him first-hand knowledge of the poor working conditions of Jamaican labourers employed there. He was moved to protest to the British Consul in Port Limon on their behalf but his representation was ignored. In his determination to create greater social awareness among the suffering masses in the region and throughout the diaspora, he next took his message to Bocas del Toro, Colón, Nicaragua, Honduras, Colombia and Venezuela and in 1912 he left for Britain in the hope of reaching a still wider audience. There he came under the influence of the Egyptian, Duse Mohammed Ali, whose magazines *Africa Times* and *Orient Review*, discussed Egyptian affairs as well as conditions of Africans under the imperialist powers. From this experience Garvey learned a great deal about African politics. For a short time while working on the docks of London, he attempted to improve his education by attending part-time classes at Birbeck College which had been established by London University to serve working-class students without formal qualifications.

Garvey in Costa Rica

It was during that year in Britain that Garvey developed and crystalised his idea of one great international organisation of black people, educated, financially independent, having pride in race; black people who would take their place as equals on the world stage. Later he explained his vision in these words: "I saw before me even as I do now, a new world of black men, not peons, serfs, dogs and slaves but a nation of sturdy men making their impress upon civilization and causing a new light to dawn upon the human race." (Lewis: 1987)

Garvey returned to Jamaica in July 1914, and on 1 August, emancipation day, he launched the Universal Negro Improvement and Conservation Association and the African Communities League, later referred to as the Universal Negro Improvement Association (UNIA). At first, persons approached the movement cautiously as they were not sufficiently aware of what he was trying to do, and were afraid to speak out on controversial issues.

"Membership was scanty, and hearing was half-hearted. Most people here regarded the young man as an empty dreamer. But he persisted." (Murray: 1969)

The general objectives of the UNIA which were set out in 1914 remained Garvey's guiding principles to the end of his days. They were to encourage material success through individual effort; encourage educational attainment, race consciousness and racial pride. The stated aim was "One God! One aim! One destiny!" The UNIA was also:

> To reclaim the fallen of the race; administer to and assist the needy; assist in civilizing the backward tribes of Africa; strengthen the imperialism of inde-pendent African states . . . establish educational institutions [Universities, Colleges and Secondary Schools] for the further intellectual improvement and cultural awareness of the boys and girls of the race; to develop world-wide commercial and industrial intercourse. (Cronin: 1962)

In 1920 Garvey explained what strengthened his resolve to carry out his dream:

> Just at that time other races were engaged in seeing their cause through – the Jew through their Zionist Movement and the Irish through their Irish Movement – and I decided that, cost what it might, I would make this a favourable time to see the Negro interest through. (Hill: 1987)

The UNIA disseminated Garvey's ideas of African nationalism, and anti-imperialism through political, ethical and practical instructions and provided its membership with opportunities for literary, artistic and creative expression.

Garvey was inspired by Booker T. Washington's achievements at the Tuskegee Institute in Alabama, and began planning a similar facility in Jamaica which he hoped would provide opportunities for the advancement of intelligent, ambitious black people. Dr Washington invited Garvey to Tuskegee and planned to visit Jamaica, but he died in 1915 before the visits could materialise. Washington's successor, Major Robert R. Moton, along with Dr W. E. DuBois, Pan-Africanist editor of *Crisis*, the journal of the National Association for the Advancement of Colored People (NAACP), visited Jamaica for two days in 1916. However, the First World War was then in progress and the British government, perceiving Garvey as a threat to colonial stability, advised Dr Moton not to contact this trouble-maker. (Murray: 1969) Garvey was determined to meet him, and did so at a reception in his honour organised by the Jamaica Union of Teachers at the Mico College. Nothing meaningful resulted from the encounter.

Impatient to get his educational institution off the ground, Garvey decided to seek financial assistance overseas. In 1916 he set out on what was to have been a five-month tour of the West Indies and the United States, but it became instead an eleven year odyssey. The Jamaica Institute he envisaged never materialised.

Garvey continued to refine much of his political ideology and his concepts of self-actualisation. He launched the first American branch of the UNIA in February 1918 in New York and by the 1920's UNIA enterprises were employing more than 1,000 persons in Harlem, New York, and surrounding communities. The movement was also attracting worldwide attention as a black political force.

Garvey gave his first public lecture on Jamaica in Harlem on 9 May, 1916, shortly after his arrival in the United States. It was not well-received because with his unusual appearance and strange accent he seemed out of place in the American environment. His timing was, however, right because the Harlem Renaissance was becoming popular: black intellectuals in the United States and from other countries were then expressing their radical opinions in publications and speeches on the sidewalks of Harlem.

Among these so-called "new negroes" were: Herbert H. Harrison, the well-known black lecturer; A. Philip Randolph, member of the Sleeping Car Porters Association and editor of *The Messenger*; Dr W. E. B. DuBois of the NAACP, and the Jamaicans, W. A. Domingo and Claude McKay. They had all experienced racism and were caught up in the excitement of the Bolshevik revolution and the teachings of Lenin and Trotsky. McKay and others would later denounce communism when they realised that the communist ideals of the citizens' voluntary fulfilment of their duties and their participation in the affairs of society did not replace the state or create a truly classless society.

They crusaded for liberty and equality in American society and challenged their fellow blacks to throw off the yoke of white supremacy. They encouraged them to learn more about their African heritage and "the positive, rich, material content of their Africanity". Their publications challenged social inequality and the injustices meted out to Africans throughout the world and in their homeland as a result of colonial exploitation. Thousands of once prosperous and self-sufficient African people were now starving because great numbers of them had been coerced into abandoning their traditional ways of life to work instead on plantations of cotton, cocoa and groundnut for the European market, while others were being forced to work in miserable conditions in unsafe mines underground from which they received little economic benefit.

Garvey helped to keep the African issue alive as he challenged the falsehoods and misrepresentations of African history spread abroad by

European colonisers. He reached out to American blacks who during the First World War had misguidedly left their farms in the South to work under wretched conditions in factories in the North. Black American soldiers returning from the war also found that during their absence discrimination had grown worse, and that promises of equality and opportunity made by the President of the United States were not being fulfilled. Garvey brought the veterans hope and promoted financial enterprises which it was hoped would provide them with an alternative to a dependency on government largess.

Within four or five years the UNIA became both one of the largest Pan-Africanist movements and the largest international movement of black peoples on the African continent and in the countries of the diaspora. At its peak it is estimated that there were 1,700 groups in 40 countries with 4 million members. The largest concentration was in Harlem.

Garvey was so committed to the use of the printing press as a means of disseminating his message of black upliftment that wherever he went he started publishing ventures even though they were never successful. Henry Rogowski, publisher of the socialist paper, *New York Call,* assisted him with the necessary credit to start the *Negro World,* which first appeared on 17 August 1918, seven months after the inauguration of the New York branch of the UNIA. W. A. Domingo was its first editor and served for a year. He introduced Garvey to the writings of Edward W. Blyden, the West Indian from St Thomas, in the Virgin Islands, who had migrated to West Africa in the 1850s and had become a revered African scholar. Blyden's *Christianity, Islam, and the Negro Race* profoundly influenced Garvey.

In formulating the New York manifesto of the UNIA, Garvey was influenced by Booker T. Washington's body-of-conduct-of-life philosophy. The UNIA emphasised discipline, self-education and a strict code of behaviour. Members learned the UNIA catechism, songs and poetry, attended political and religious instruction and listened to Garvey preach his gospel of success. He motivated them to take pride in self and in race and to develop self-confidence. The same philosophy of moral and intellectual improvement and self-discipline pervaded the movement in Jamaica. The UNIA organised training cells to reinforce the organisation's ideology and paramilitary training for the special guard, the African Legion, which was assigned to protect UNIA officials on ceremonial occasions and was expected to respond to any eventuality in Africa. Members of the Black Cross Nurses Auxiliary received training in elementary nursing care to enable them to minister to the poor and needy. The Universal African Motor Corps, a women's group, received driving instruction and training in motor mechanics.

Wherever he went, Garvey imbued blacks with pride in self and in race, and strengthened their self-esteem. A report in the Baltimore paper, the *African-American* dated 13 December 1918, in highlighting the international aspect of his mission, noted: "In addition to forming a league for political and social improvement of the Negro's condition in this country, the aim is to establish in Africa a strong Negro nation, which could command respect for the Negro, who resides in white countries." (Hill: 1987)

Garvey promoted "nationalist agitation against imperialism" primarily through the *Negro World* which ran from January 1918-1933 and was distributed worldwide as well as through the numbers of other short-lived publications which he edited from time-to-time. In places with a high rate of illiteracy, one copy of the *Negro World* generally served several persons at a time. Jomo Kenyatta, is reputed to have told C. L. R. James that Kenyan nationalists, unable to read would gather round a copy of the paper and listen to articles being read over and over. It was banned at different times in almost every colonial country in Central America, the West Indies and Africa.

In addition to articles on race consciousness, the *Negro World* carried articles by other black intellectuals in French and Spanish aimed at non-English speaking peoples of the region. Subscribers were encouraged to send comments and many came from all over the world. The newspaper's front page editorial by Garvey, was always addressed to the "Fellowmen of the Negro Race". At its peak the paper had a circulation of 50,000 but it may even have reached 200,000 briefly.

Garvey's encouragement of black resistance to discrimination and exploitation, as well as his support of Mahatma Ghandi's and Eamon de Valera's Indian and Irish nationalist activities brought him into conflict with imperialist governments. In 1919 the United States Department of Justice, under J. Edgar Hoover, assigned special agents to monitor his activities, and an attempt was made upon his life that year. Efforts were also made to keep him out of the United States by denying him a re-entry visa in 1921. Garveyism influenced many young African freedom fighters. The Kikuyu employed one of Garvey's "bishops" to train young people and from these schools the Kenyan resistance movement, the Mau Mau, grew.

Garvey never lost sight of the movement's international goal. After his deportation to Jamaica at the end of 1927, he continued to write for the *Negro World* in New York, telegraphing in his front-page editorials every week. These continued to emphathise with the struggles of other colonial nations.

Each UNIA branch was independent of the parent organisation, and had its own Liberty Hall headquarters. The UNIA's flag of red, black and

Marcus Garvey

Marcus Mosiah Garvey, 1887-1940

green denoted "red for the blood of the race nobly shed in the past and dedicated to the future; black for pride in colour of the skin; green for a promise of a better life in Africa". (Cronin: 1955)

From the business section of the movement, the Negro Factories Corporation, grew a number of cooperative enterprises which included groceries, a restaurant, a steam laundry, a tailoring and dressmaking shop and a publishing house in the United States. In all cases, however, management was weak and the businesses under-capitalised. They were also undermined by American bureaucracy, although they were never at any time a threat to the American economy.

Garvey organised the first International Convention of the UNIA in August 1920, at Madison Square Gardens in New York. The commencement date was significantly set for 1 August, emancipation day. The convention led off with three religious services and a parade of 2,000 delegates from 25 countries and four continents. Knowing that they were under surveillance from the Federal Bureau of Investigation, the group marched in silence to the strains of the UNIA band and choristers. The members of the African Legion, 200 Black Cross nurses, the Black Eagle flying corps and members of the Juvenile Auxiliary were all attired in uniform. Officers of the African Legion in their dark blue military-style dress and dress swords created a stir, and strengthened rumours that Garveyites were preparing to overthrow the colonial powers.

Some 25,000 persons gathered on the following day at Madison Square Gardens to hear Garvey's challenge to the black race. In his wide-ranging address he said, "We are the descendants of a suffering people; we are the descendants of a people determined to suffer no longer . . . We shall raise the banner of democracy in Africa or 400 million of us will report to God the reason why . . . We pledge our blood to the battlefield of Africa where we will fight for true liberty, democracy and the brotherhood of man." (Edwards: 1967) He urged the gathering and millions of other Africans to

Garvey and the UNIA reviewing a convention parade in 1924

claim Africa for themselves. "It will be a terrible day when the blacks draw the sword to fight for their liberty. I call upon the 400,000,000 blacks to give the blood you have shed for the white man to make Africa a republic for the Negro." (Hill: 1987)

The Declaration of Rights of the Negro Peoples of the World, presented at the convention, protested against the oppressive conditions under which black people continued to labour. It set out 54 demands for black nationalism, political and judicial equality, racial self-determination and a free Africa governed by black people. established titles and distinctions for officers of the movement. Garvey w. declared Provisional President of Africa and President General and Administrator of the UNIA. His official title was His Highness the Potentate. (Edwards: 1967)

In 1921 Garvey returned to the West Indies for what was planned as a brief visit but it took him four months to obtain the re-entry permit to the United States. Thereafter, his militant stance seems to have become more conciliatory, although in that same year he condemned organisers of the Second Pan-African Congress for attempting to amalgamate opposite races, remarking that it was "a crime against nature". He also questioned the hope of achieving social equality in the United States, because it was a white man's country in which the Negro was physically outnumbered and would ultimately lose out.

The Second International Convention held in 1921 was less impressive than the first, possibly because of rumours about the mismanagement of the Black Star Line, his shipping company. But Garvey concentrated upon the African situation and expressed his hope for "a free and redeemed Africa". He hoped to establish a settlement of skilled black persons in Liberia, the "land of opportunity", where black Americans and West Indians would contribute their skills to the development of a great African republic. Several discussions on the matter followed with the Liberian authorities about possible sites for future settlements. Then in 1925 the Liberian government, obviously under pressure from the United States and other outside influences, repudiated the agreement. It issued a statement to the effect that it was "irrevocably opposed both in principle and in fact to the incendiary policy of the UNIA headed by Garvey". (Lewis: 1968)

Garvey had in the meantime purchased and shipped equipment to Liberia to be used to establish a lumber company. The machinery was seized by the Liberian customs and was eventually sold for a fraction of its true value to pay the customs duty.

The Liberian project which came to be known as the "Back to Africa Movement" was not looked on with favour by imperialists and by many black colonials who interpreted it to mean the repatriation of all colonial blacks to Africa. These opponents claimed that Garvey intended to overthrow the imperialist masters who were in fear of their colonial economies collapsing. Garvey later explained that he had not expected all Negroes to leave America and the West Indies for Africa. He only wished to contribute to the building of an independent black nation.

One of Garvey's most ambitious dreams was the formation of a steamship company the Black Star Line. This company was to be owned and operated by black people, in the same way that a white steamship

Garvey makes a farewell address before his deportation from the US in 1927

company was owned and managed by white people. He hoped to build up a fleet of five ships between June and October 1919, "to trade in the interests of the Negro race" and to link coloured peoples of the world in commercial and industrial endeavours. Caribbean and African merchants had been having difficulty getting shipping space on the British Elder Dempster line and it was hoped that the Black Star Line would ease the problem.

The company financed by US$5 shares, sold only to blacks netted about US$750,000. No one was permitted to purchase more than 200 shares. Unfortunately, neither Garvey nor any of his close associates knew anything about finance or the shipping business. They put too great faith in untrustworthy dealers and unreliable crew members, both black and white. Proper records were not always kept and official procedures were often ignored. The first three vessels negotiated for were old and fit only for the scrap heap. They ended up as liabilities, leaving the company to face a deficit of around US$476,000. By 1922 the Black Star Line Shipping Company was bankrupt.

The United States attorney general's office had warned Garvey that it was illegal to sell shares by post for a company that had not yet been properly incorporated. Garvey ignored the warnings and ran foul of the law. Eventually in January 1922 he and three other company officials were indicted on charges of commercial fraud. The charges noted that the company had knowingly used "fraudulent representations" and "deceptive artifices" to sell stocks through the mail and had advertised and sold space on a mythical vessel. (Cronin: 1955) Garvey was indicted on 12 counts, fined US$1,000, held without bail for three months and after an unsuccessful appeal was sentenced to a term of five years in an Atlanta jail. The three other men, referred to as "conspirators", were not charged.

At the trial he defended himself for most of the time and this did not help his case as his often belligerent manner and gerrymandering lost him public sympathy. He appealed the sentence, lost the appeal and was imprisoned in an Atlanta jail on 3 February 1925. Many, especially those who wished to see this black upstart put in his place, thought that he had received his just deserts, but others felt that he had been unfairly treated. The *New York Evening Bulletin*, a white daily, noted on 12 February 1925: "He did many strange things, it is true, but he performed many fine acts, too . . . Had the man been given half a fair deal, his financial schemes might have been successful and he might have been able to avoid the unfortunate disasters which led him into the courts and brought punishment upon him".

The *Buffalo Evening Times* of 24 February, 1925, wrote: "There is still something that is not pleasant about this whole business." It questioned the fairness of the judgment and noted that in the past white men charged with similar offences had received much lighter sentences.

The colonial governments, challenged by Garvey's militancy, were relieved at the news of his imprisonment, but they could not shake his determination or his optimism. His commitment to the establishment of a black shipping line was so fixed that not even the difficulties experienced in the earlier failed attempts could deter him. In 1924, while his appeal was pending, Garvey became involved once again in another shipping company, the Black Cross Navigation and Trading Company, registered in New Jersey. It negotiated for the purchase of a ship in somewhat better condition than the first three and his supporters, anxious to see a black shipping company become a reality, were enthusiastic.

After many delays, this ship, the *General Goethals*, which Garvey had planned to rechristen the *Booker T. Washington*, set out on a voyage round the Caribbean carrying passengers and cargo. Emonei Carter, secretary general of the UNIA was sent along on the voyage to sell stocks at each port of call to raise funds to meet expenses. The vessel reached Kingston on 10 February 1925, but Carter could nor raise sufficient money and the ship was tied up in port for a month until its debts were liquidated. It then sailed for Colón, Panama and spent another month there for lack of funds before it was cleared. It was supposed to have sailed for New York via Kingston but there is no certainty that it ever returned to New York. Garvey was then in prison, the image of the organisation had been badly tarnished and it was difficult to get financial support.

Garvey's dream of establishing a black university was realised if only for a short time when Liberty University was opened in the state of Virginia in September 1926. It too was badly affected by the problems of the UNIA and after three years it closed for lack of financial support.

After the UNIA petitioned President Coolidge in 1927, Garvey's prison term was commuted to two and a half years. He was released in early December 1927, taken to New Orleans and deported to Jamaica. To his second wife Amy Jacques fell the task of clearing up his financial affairs, selling his Harlem property and shipping his possessions home. The reception he received on his arrival in the island on 10 December 1927, was heartening and fuelled his optimism. Cheering crowds greeted him at the docks and thousands lined the streets to watch him pass by. *The Daily Gleaner*, 12 December 1927 reported his arrival as follows:

A short statue attired in a drab suit and wearing a Panama hat was on the second deck. It was Marcus Garvey the idol of the coloured people and his identity could not be mistaken . . . Deafening cheers were raised and remarks heard on all sides in the huge crowd showed the high esteem in which he is held by the ordinary people of this country.

The Ward Theatre which seats approximately 1,000, could not accommodate the gathering which attended the reception in his honour.

At home in Jamaica he organised training courses and cultural activities for adults and children, organised street corner meetings in Kingston and travelled to rural parishes, taking his message of black nationalism to all who would listen and read. Convinced of the Messianic nature of his mission, in 1928 he visited UNIA branches in Central America in the hope of revitalising the movement and he also visited Europe for a short time. Between 1929 and 1931 he published the *Blackman* first as a daily and later as a weekly newspaper. This was followed by the evening daily the *New Jamaican*, from July 1932 to September 1933 and then the *Black Man* magazine which began late in 1933. Where the Negro was concerned, he said, there were no national boundaries, nor would he give up the struggle until Africa was free.

In 1922 the UNIA through Garvey had proposed to the League of Nations that it should take over the former German colonies in Africa, but this was blocked by a ruling which stipulated that petitions could only be considered from existing governments. In 1928 the UNIA presented another petition in which it recommended that the entire regions of West Africa should be incorporated into a commonwealth of black nations under the government of black men. It also condemned the multinational company, Firestone, for its stranglehold on Liberia, the United States for its occupation of Haiti and the American Fruit Company for its undue influence in Central America.

Garvey was also devoting his energies to building up a sense of national pride in Jamaica. Edelweiss Park, an old house and property at Cross Roads in the Corporate Area of Kingston and St Andrew, which he purchased in 1929, became a centre for spiritual upliftment, self-improvement, political indoctrination and purposeful recreation.

Political and religious instruction formed part of the weekly programme, and was intended "to combat ignorance and narrow-mindedness among the masses". Thousands thronged to hear Garvey speak on Sunday nights and young and old journeyed from far off rural places, just to get a glimpse of the man who carried the message of inspiration and anti-colonial solidarity. At these meetings they were given a better understanding of their role in society and the confidence to challenge economic and social oppression. For five years Edelweiss Park gave them the will to achieve but in 1934 it had to be sold for debt.

Garvey decided to enter local politics and in 1929 formed the People's Political Party. It had mass support and fielded three candidates for the 1930 general elections. However as it turned out, many supporters could not meet the necessary voter registration requirements and the party could not command sufficient votes to win a seat. The People's Political Party was the first of what Garvey hoped would have been a number of political parties in the Caribbean championing the cause of the faceless masses.

The party manifesto advocated constitutional change to secure Jamaican representation in the British parliament so that the people might achieve a greater measure of self-government. It called for significant social and economic reform: minimum wage legislation, promotion of native industries, land reform and compulsory improvement of urban areas and public housing; the establishment of a Jamaican university, a polytechnic, a national opera house, and a school for domestic science. It also recommended the building of a town hall in Kingston, the establishment of a legal aid department to assist poor people in the courts as well as legislation to protect voters against those who would seek to manipulate the political process unfairly.

The manifesto also proposed that there should be a law to impeach and imprison judges who, in defiance of British justice and constitutional rights entered into underhand agreements with lawyers and others to deprive ordinary individuals of their rights in the courts. When Garvey elaborated on this particular clause at a public meeting he was charged with contempt of court, sentenced to three months in jail, and fined £100. While serving the sentence he won a seat in the local elections for the Allman Town Division of the Kingston and St Andrew Corporation but the Corporation declared his seat vacant. However, when a by-election was called to fill the vacancy, Garvey was re-elected unopposed. He had by then served his prison term.

Garvey's advocacy of social reform gave the Kingston dock workers the courage to demand better wages and working conditions in May 1929. When they were ignored some 500 of them walked off the job leaving 15,000 stems of bananas on the docks. All they were asking for was four shillings, two pence for loading 100 stems of bananas, instead of the one shilling, nine pence which is what they were receiving. They were also demanding double time on Sundays. Because Garvey was their spokesman he incurred the wrath of the powerful United Fruit Company, which saw the possibility of its profits being eroded.

Discontent was also spreading on the sugar plantations where workers were facing the same social and economic pressures. Their obvious complaints could no longer be ignored and in February 1930 a royal commission headed by Sir Sidney Olivier was appointed to enquire into the situation. Testifying before the commission, Garvey drew attention to the exploitation of the workers and recommended that wage guidelines and set hours of work should be instituted as well as legislation to prevent the exploitation of children in the workplace. He called for health and accident insurance for people working in the banana and sugar industries and attacked the KSAC for paying too low wages.

Garvey's pleadings went unheeded but he continued to call for social change and warned that if conditions were not improved the oppressed would rise up in rebellion. Seven years later, in 1938 as he had predicted, violence erupted on the Westmoreland sugar plantations. Only then did the authorities begin to address better housing and fair employment.

The Sixth International Convention of the UNIA in Kingston in August 1929, emphasised international outreach and revitalisation of the UNIA. Representatives were invited from all social organisations in the island, including churches, benevolent societies and lodges. On this occasion overseas delegates came from the United States, Central America, Cuba and the Bahamas. The Carib International Association from Guatemala was refused entry and one delegate spoke on behalf of Nigeria.

The convention discussed international issues affecting the conditions of black people. It recommended that the political arm of the movement should be revived and given a new mandate to secure the enfranchisement of the black American population; that the UNIA should engage in large-scale agricultural enterprises in the West Indies, Africa and the United States; and that negro consuls should be located in centres of large black populations. The matter of proper black representation at the League of Nations in Geneva was raised but because of the expense involved it was abandoned. In spite of past difficulties with failed shipping ventures, it was recommended that the Steamship Company should be revived and renamed the African Steam Navigation Company, but that was not to be.

Because education for blacks was so inadequate, the convention urged that a school building programme should be instituted, especially in isolated communities with predominantly black populations. Departments to oversee health and public education were also to be instituted. A target of $600,000,000 was set for the establishment of three Negro universities in the West Indies, West Africa and America. Daily newspapers were to be strategically established in several European capitals, in West Africa, Cape Town and in important West Indian islands so that they could shape sentiment in favour of the entire Negro race. 1 October was designated Health Day, when emphasis would be placed on personal hygiene and sanitation of the surroundings.

Among the social activities arranged during the convention was a debate between Garvey and Otto Huiswood, a representative of the American Negro Labour Congress. The topic was cooperation between black and white workers. Garvey's emphasis on racial solidarity and self-preservation as the first law of nature received overwhelming support from the audience.

On the closing night, 22 August, there was a re-enactment of the court life of Ancient Africa before some 10,000 persons at Edelweiss Park.

> The high dignitaries of the UNIA, accompanied by their bejewelled ladies, appeared resplendent in their rich robes of state, while the officers of the African Legion fairly dazzled the excited black multitude with their dapper uniforms, shiny Sam Brown belts, and gleaming swords . . . As the President General of the UNIA and Provisional President of Africa passed between lines of erect legionnaires holding aloft drawn swords, the vast assemblage gave a mighty roar of greeting. Accompanied by his wife and the High Potentate of the Association, Garvey made his way to a lavishly decorated stage where he informed his audience that they were but celebrating what had gone before in the noble court of Ethiopia, the grandeur of past ages. (Cronin: 1955)

One regrettable occurrence at the convention was the split in the UNIA between the Jamaican and the American representatives. Garvey accused some members of the movement of dishonesty and disloyalty over the failed shipping company and the events which led to his imprisonment. He and some of those loyal to him preferred to start a new organisation but Henrietta Vinton Davis and some of the other Americans did not agree. This dissension lost the UNIA much public support.

The African nations were by this time awakening to the importance of unification and in that same year the National Congress of Black West Africa was convened in Lagos, Nigeria. Jamaica was not represented but Garvey published J. B. Danquah's seminal address to the conference in the *Blackman* and so subscribers were kept abreast of this important international happening.

Garvey continued to broaden the perspective of his audiences at both local and international levels. Edelweiss Park became the mecca for cultural events in Jamaica. One music competition is described thus by a contemporary.

> Over 2,000 listeners were packed on the ground floor and in the galleries . . . Contestants were classified into solos, duets, quartets and choral ensembles. All the items offered were serious, rather than popular music. They included selections from Haydn, Tchaikovsky, Arditi, Eli, Handel; offerings which ordinarily would hardly appeal to the musically unsophisticated. At the beginning Garvey described how polite society here and abroad behaved at concerts, and asked the listeners to show the same polite and encouraging behaviour to the contestants. Throughout the long programme . . . there was polite, considerate and appreciative reception by the large mixed audience. (Mills: 1969)

By including classical music Garvey was demonstrating that there was no difference between black and white people, and that poor people were just as capable of appreciating the finer things of life. His audiences understood his message and responded appropriately.

In the *Negro World* of 26 June 1931, Garvey pointed out the need for a code of ethics for black children which should be no different from that for white children. He said that in the same way that white children had a philosophy, a set creed to guide their lives, so black children needed a similar code. (Hill: 1987)

The Seventh International Convention of the Negro Peoples of the World was convened in Kingston on 1 August 1934, the centenary of the abolition of slavery. Garvey had by then softened his political stance from militancy to popular mobilisation and compromise. At the convention he said, "Others are learning that they cannot gain much today by being too aggressive; we have to be more compromising than other peoples. It is because of our peculiar position – a position that we have invited upon ourselves." (Hill: 1987)

A five-year plan stressed the international aspects of the movement and reiterated some of the recommendations from the Sixth Convention dealing with the development of shipping, manufacturing, mining, agriculture and other industries in the West Indies, Central and South America and Africa. It approved the adoption of a standard African language, discouraged nonconformist religions and cults with passing reference to the Rastafarians. It condemned birth control.

The UNIA had by now lost much of its earlier dynamism and the Jamaican colonial administration added to the pressure by attempting to enforce a US$30,000 judgment handed down against the old UNIA in a New York court. Creditors auctioned the Kingston headquarters, Liberty Hall, at 76 King Street, although it was later restored to the organisation. They levied on Garvey's printing press and office equipment, and other items. These adversities broke the organisation financially, but not Garvey's fighting spirit, or his vision of a mighty black race, triumphant.

He did not give up his vision of a vigorous UNIA with international outreach and continued to prepare UNIA officers for leadership roles. He continued to write the front-page editorial of the weekly *Negro World* in New York and maintained contact with UNIA branches in the West Indies, Central America and Canada, confident that black nations would eventually take their rightful place in the world.

In 1935, in the face of financial and political adversities, Marcus Garvey decided to emigrate to Britain where he would be nearer the centre of world influence. For the next five years he maintained his international associations and worked steadfastly for the political unification of the black race. He lectured regularly on black nationalism, attended UNIA conferences in St Kitts, in other West Indian islands and in Canada. He continued to publish the *Black Man* journal but at six pence per copy and a small circulation, the journal was not viable. It ceased publication in 1939.

After attending a UNIA conference in Toronto in 1936, Garvey decided to open a School of African Philosophy in Toronto with lessons prepared in London. The main objective was to train blacks for world leadership in the UNIA. The course started in 1937, and was available "only to Negroes". Applicants were expected to have a high school education. Of the nine students who enrolled, eight graduated. Two years later a second correspondence course was offered in London at a cost of US$25. The advertisements named Garvey as principal. He had hoped to attract 1,000 students but only 11 registered. They came from the United States,

Nigeria, Uganda, Cape Province and South Africa. The training course had its greatest influence upon the Africans. Most of them were later involved in the liberation of their countries.

The university and technical institute which Garvey had envisaged for Jamaica materialised after his death. The University College of the West Indies was established in 1948, and the College of Arts, Science and Technology, in 1958. Social and educational programmes such as public high schools in rural areas, legal aid clinics and the beautification of public parks were all instituted after the island attained political independence in 1962. Poor health drained Garvey's energies in England, and in January 1940 he suffered a stroke. He died six months later on 10 June, in straitened circumstances.

In spite of his many frustrations and reversals of fortune, Garvey accomplished what no other black leader had done before. He created an international awareness of the right of the black race to coexist with other peoples of the world as equals. He awakened race consciousness and race pride in millions of working-class blacks in Africa as well as in the diaspora. He taught them to respect their own worth and to demand their rights as human beings.

Shortly before his death in 1940, the *Boston Guardian* wrote: "Already his name is legend, from Harlem to Zanzibar". The African, Mazilinko, pointed to his Messianic role when he said, "After all is said and done, Africans have the same confidence in Marcus Garvey which the Israelites had in Moses". (Hill: 1987) He fought for freedom, justice and equality and remains a source of inspiration to all popular movements for black people and to all who would aspire to lead the black race.

Twenty-four years after his death, in 1964, the Government of Jamaica honoured his name by declaring him Jamaica's first National Hero. His remains were brought from England and interred at the National Heroes Park. Even a quarter of a century after his death the controversy generated by the government's action revealed that a substantial core of middle-class Jamaicans still were not comfortable with Garvey's message of decolonisation and physical return of black people to Africa. It was left to a handful of liberal journalists to convince their fellow-countrymen that "Garvey's greatness lay in the massive psychological warfare that he deployed to wipe out the inherited inferiority complex and the facelessness of the Negro in a white world". (Lewis: 1968)

Marcus Garvey's grave at National Heroes Park

Time, the judge, has gradually adjusted the balance. In 1983 the polls ranked Jamaica's national heroes as follows: Bustamante 37 per cent, Bogle 19 per cent, Garvey 15 per cent, Manley 14 per cent. By 1987 Garvey had soared to 56 per cent, Bustamante was at

20 per cent, Manley 16 per cent and Bogle 5 per cent. A January 1988 survey showed that 88 per cent of those polled agreed that Garvey's life and work should be taught in all schools.

Throughout his crowded, often difficult and tempestuous life, Marcus Garvey was above all, a champion of blacks, the one who fought fearlessly for their rights. As a young man, he lost his job at the Benjamin Company for supporting a strike of underpaid employees; at the beginning of his career as a race leader, he protested to the British consul in Port Limon about the victimisation of black banana workers by the American Fruit Company. Throughout his life he championed the cause of people of African origin worldwide, and more than any other African-American leader, he attacked the European partitioning of Africa. To this day African leaders pay tribute to him.

The statue in honour of Garvey erected at the St Ann Parish Library

In 1939, the year before his death, he expressed his vision of a liberated Africa. He saw it as "a country of the future. Her inhabitants, her everything tend toward an Africa of the natives, where they will rise to govern as other men are governing". (*Black Man*: 1939) That dream of black supremacy, at first slow in realisation, has taken on momentum with the dismantling of apartheid in South Africa in April 1994, through the exercise of the ballot by black South Africans for the first time, and the appointment of the first black president in that nation's history.

Today, more than ever before, Jamaicans honour Garvey as a black world leader and as a great national hero who gave his life to guarding over and protecting the rights of blacks.

CHAPTER 25

Building a new society: People from India, China and the Middle East

The accepted forms of Jamaica's institutional and social life are of European derivation, but African ways are commonly observable. On the one hand Europe provides a model for government, religion, law, property, education and language. On the other, there are African survivals in social customs, eating habits, the role of women in the family, in cooperative efforts for planting and reaping crops, in practices related to death and burial, in magical rites, in African words and phrases, tone and flavour of speech. There are African drum-beats and rhythms every-where and growing evidence that Africa is now the central force in Jamaica's great cultural movement. We have also seen that under European domination the attitude of the ruling minority was one of exploitation and repression to others of whatever race. Cheap labour was required to work the plantations whether that labour was provided by slaves from Africa or by indentured servants from Europe or Asia. The main difference between the slave and the indentured servant was that one was condemned to perpetual bondage whereas the other was freed after serving a specified period.

The Jews were among the first ethnic groups to settle in the island. They were brought as indentured servants in the early sixteenth century because of their skills in sugar manufacturing. Sugar led to the establishment of the plantation society which required vast capital and an unlimited supply of labour. After serving out their apprenticeship the Jews became traders, selling local dyewoods and other products to the Spanish mainland, and importing wines and European goods for the Jamaican and West Indian trade. Their business dealings continued under the English and helped to lay the foundations for the island's internal and external trade.

The English found it expedient to grant the Jews freedom of worship. Their presence was needed to maintain the statutory ratio between the white minority and the overwhelming black majority. The Jewish community has remained numerically small but their influence in trade and in the professions has been considerable.

Deficiency in the white population had always been a concern under the plantation system. Consequent upon emancipation the government and the white ruling class were faced with the possibility of a drastic reduction of labour supply and with the fact that being so greatly outnumbered by the black population, they could face extinction.

The need for adequate supplies of cheap labour to replace those who had begun to move away from the plantation, and also the need to maintain the ratio between blacks and whites led, in the first instance, to the importation of white indentured servants from Germany, Scotland, England and Ireland. Beginning in 1834, some 450 Europeans were recruited to establish villages in the mountainous interior. The Germans who were the first to arrive were expected "to introduce new methods of cultivation and to have in general a favourable influence on the Negro worker". They were given material and financial assistance in the hope that they would settle down as small farmers. Others were allocated in twos to the plantations where they were employed mainly as artisans on coffee plantations and cattle pens. A few were employed in the police force.

Mention has already been made of one German community that has survived into the twentieth century but generally the project was not successful. In all about 4,100 Europeans, hoping to escape famine and other hardships at home, came during an eleven-year period, between 1834 and 1845, in spite of strong discouragement. Anti-emigration groups such as "the friends of humanity" and local missionaries, including William Knibb, claimed that the climate was unhealthy, planters were cruel and the emigrants would be reduced to a state of near slavery.

The Europeans at first loved the climate and the easy lifestyle, but enthusiasm soon waned when they were faced with having to perform manual labour. They had signed a civil contract but found that a breach could land them in jail with a fourteen-day sentence. Many left the plantations for the city. A few, assisted by benefactors, migrated to the United States, and yellow fever and other tropical diseases reduced the numbers of those remaining. Of 127 persons who arrived early in 1841, only 24 were still with their original employers at the end of 1842.

The Jamaican Government's request to the Colonial Secretary in London to recruit Africans was not received favourably, because it was feared that this could be viewed as another form of African enslavement. Nevertheless, between 1841 and 1867, 10,000 Africans were recruited mainly from St Helena, Sierra Leone and adjoining coastal areas. Many of them had been liberated from slave ships by the British navy. As mentioned earlier, in the period leading up to and following the Morant Bay Uprising, several of these African labourers joined the African-Jamaicans in their struggles for social improvements.

Having failed to attract adequate numbers of cheap labour from Europe, North America and Africa, the government turned to India and China. Indian labour had already been tried in Mauritius and seemed to be successful. It was therefore thought that Jamaica and the other sugar producing British West Indian colonies could benefit similarly. Indian immigrants were however treated with great disrespect. They were paid lower than the African-Jamaican workers, and were therefore relegated to the bottom of the Jamaican society. Because their form of dress, lifestyle and language were unfamiliar to African-Jamaicans, they were singled out for ridicule and were often referred to as "slave coolies".

The Indian Government took care to protect those who had signed up for the indentured labour programme. It monitored recruitment, stipulated conditions under which the recruits should be employed, set the period of indenture, laid down guidelines for their transportation and repatriation, and appointed a Protector of Immigrants to see to their welfare in the country of destination. In Jamaica the Protector of Immigrants was not an Indian national. He was appointed by the Assembly and, as was to be expected, apparently showed more concern for the interests of the employers than for the welfare of the Indian labourers.

No emigrant contracted for service could be taken on board a vessel if he did not have in his possession a government permit. Theoretically, this permit was issued only after the emigrants and the contractor had appeared in person before a magistrate, and the details of the contract explained to the emigrants. The problem was, however, that the contract was in English and the vast majority of the recruits could not speak or understand English. Thousands of illiterate unsuspecting persons lured by rumours of prosperity and a better life in the West Indies, put their thumb marks to documents they did not understand. By so doing they signed away their independence for a fixed number of years. At first contracts were for one year, then they were set at two years and afterwards for five years.

Recruiting depots were opened in Madras and Calcutta and agents were paid up to £7 for every recruit. This sum was less than one-third the amount paid for European indentured labour. A few higher caste and better educated Indians joined the emigrants to Jamaica. They found, however, that on arrival they were treated as common labourers.

In 1845, the first 261 East Indians landed at Old Harbour Bay. There were 200 men and 28 women, mainly between the ages of 20 and 29 years, as well as 33 children under the age of 12. Another 1,851 arrived in 1846 and 2,439 in 1847. After that the Indian Government suspended immigration for the next 11 years while it re-examined this form of contractual labour. The immigration programme resumed in 1859 and continued regularly until the First World War when reduction in available shipping space halted the programme and it was eventually terminated.

Re-enactment of the East Indian arrival 150 years later, 1995

On arrival in Jamaica the Indians were distributed in groups of 20 and 40 to plantations contracting for their service. They went mainly to the parishes of St Thomas, Portland, St Mary, Westmoreland and Clarendon. They were transported in mule-drawn carts and later, after the introduction of the railway, in overcrowded freight cars without seats. They were taken to the nearest railway station, then had to walk the rest of the journey to the plantation. The conditions of their indenture were almost as debasing as slavery.

Little thought was given to their personal welfare. They were herded into dingy, overcrowded barracks, without proper flooring, often with no water supply or sanitary conveniences. A barrack of three or four small rooms accommodated several individuals or families in each room without respect for privacy. The detached kitchen, the crudest of broken down huts, usually served the occupants of more than one room. If the labourers worked "with only ordinary exertion" for the required five and a half or six days a week, they were paid one shilling a day and slightly more if they worked "with extraordinary exertion".

On arrival each immigrant was provided with a suit of clothing, agricultural implements and cooking utensils, at their employer's expense. The only deduction from their wages was two shillings and six pence for their

Indentured workers are taken to estates on dray carts

weekly rations of rice, flour, dried fish or goat's flesh, peas and seasonings. Children were supplied with half rations at one shilling and threepence per week. Employers were instructed to pay them weekly, and not to treat them harshly. They were to receive quarterly checks by a doctor, and if they became ill they were to be taken to the nearest hospital for treatment.

These labourers kept poor health and suffered from tropical diseases such as malaria, yaws, and hookworm. Malaria was at that time incurable but could be prevented by administering regular doses of quinine. Employers were encouraged to supply them with the drug but this was not always done.

In order to ensure that employers received the maximum benefit from their labour, the Indians were confined to the plantation and could not leave the precincts unless they obtained a permit to do so. This applied even when they were on their annual two-week vacation leave. Like the Europeans, if they failed to work because of ill-health or for any other reason, or if they left their place of employment without permission, they could be fined or face a jail sentence.

On completion of their contract, they were issued with a certificate of freedom which enabled them to move freely about the country. However, they could not apply for their return passage until two years after the contract had expired. In addition, they had to have lived in the country for a total of ten years before they could be repatriated.

A ship was chartered periodically to transport the repatriates. However, by the time it arrived there were usually more passengers than could be accommodated. The healthier individuals were therefore left behind with the expectation that they would continue to work on the plantations. Those with families were required to pay the fares of the other family members. If they could not, they were forced to remain in the country.

In an attempt to reduce the numbers applying for repatriation, the law was amended so that after 1903 time-expired Indians had to apply for this facility within two years of completing the contract or forfeit their claim. Contracts could be renewed for one year, but these "second term coolies" were treated as if they were first-term labourers. Very few took up the option.

Their inability to understand and speak English placed them at an even greater disadvantage. Indian names were transposed at will by officials and many an individual ended up in Jamaica with a different name from the one he had been assigned at birth.

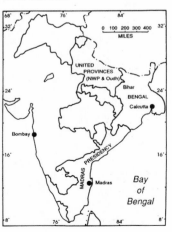

Recruitment areas in India

The first Indian labourers had come mainly from Northern India. Later others came from Uttar Pradesh, Bihar, the Central Provinces, Punjab and the North West Frontiers. Most may have been illiterate, but their cultural traditions and established religions predated Christianity and other Western cultures by three or four thousand years. In India magnificent temples intricately decorated with sculptures, paintings and precious stones dominate the countryside and dictate an ordered way of living. The people commemorate their social customs, their myths and legends in song and dance especially on occasions such as marriages, births, deaths and changing of the seasons. Most Westerners were ignorant of these traditions and employers unfamiliar with them described the Indians as heathens.

No thought was given to accommodating their customs and beliefs. Indeed, non-Christian religions were outlawed and devout Hindus and Muslims were forced to congregate whenever and wherever was convenient. Some met by the riverside where they went to bathe and wash their clothes on weekends. Others kept little shrines in their homes where they could.

The Jamaican Government refused to recognise non-Christian marriages. The Indians were obliged to perform Christian ceremonies in addition to celebrating their traditional marriages or stigmatise their children as "bastards" who were unprotected under the Inheritance Law. It was not until 1957, more than 110 years after the first East Indians arrived, that the law was amended to permit non-Christian marriages.

Deliberate efforts were made by Christian religious organisations to convert them to Christianity. They coerced them into Christian marriages although they knew that the participants were often not Christians. They persuaded them to give up their children for adoption, or place them in orphanages with the excuse that the children would have better opportunities in the Jamaican society. In spite of these efforts, some Indian traditions survived. These include arranged marriages, the celebration of certain traditional festivals and community administration by the Council of Five (*panchayat*).

> In spite of modifications in the family system the words "family" and "relatives" have not lost their magic or magnetism in arousing traditional loyalties and emotions. The feeling of closeness between parents and children, brothers, sisters, cousins and uncles, and the concern for each other's welfare still exist. The elders may not be able to dictate, yet feel responsible for the welfare of younger ones."
> (Mansingh & Mansingh: 1976)

About 80 per cent of the Indian immigrants were Hindus and many of the rest were Muslims. Religious practices precluded Hindus from eating pork, chicken or fish and Muslims from eating beef. These dietary habits helped to set the Indians apart, so did the deliberate segregation of Indian and African-Jamaican dwellings by employers afraid of African-Jamaican influences upon the Indians. The Indians were treated by the African-Jamaican with the same prejudice and suspicion as the slaves had been treated by their white masters. The more successful they were at their tasks, the more they were resented by their fellow workers who saw them as threatening their livelihood.

For the most part the Indians were poor and knew nothing of the land the problems of the land to which they came. Their highly developed cultures and fixed caste systems, in which skin pigmentation and type of employment determined social status, caused the Indians to view the darker complexioned African-Jamaicans as socially inferior. They referred to them disparagingly as *kafari* or infidel. Even into the twentieth century some Indians refused to allow their children to attend the same schools with black children.

In 1938, almost 100 years after the arrival of the first East Indians, a survey revealed that on the major sugar estates living conditions were still cramped and unhealthy. Only one in every eight barracks was supplied with water from either pipes or wells; 38 per cent had no provision at all and about half took their water from rivers and ponds. Even when the river was some distance away, women had to trudge back and forth carrying pails of water and laundry.

Provision had been made for persons who so desired to commute the unexpired portion of their contract. They were required to repay, in cash, one-fifth of the sum outstanding, depending on the number of years or portion of a year remaining. They could also be released from the contract if the individual was suffering from some permanent disability or infirmity and the employer had requested his release. The indigent person could then be sent to hospital or be repatriated if and when shipping space was available.

Not all those who commuted their contract or completed the time returned to India. Between 1910 and 1911, for example, only one-fifth of the number eligible chose repatriation and overall only about one-third were repatriated. The others remained in the island.

Repatriation was not encouraged by either the Jamaican or the Indian Governments. The Jamaican Government found difficulty in paying all the return passages, and also saw repatriation as depleting the labour force. Contracting plantations assisted with the cost of the return fares but the sums collected were often insufficient. Also, many more Indians sought repatriation than was expected and ships were reluctant to take returning passengers from Jamaica because of the high death rate at sea.

The Indian Government claimed that too many returned as invalids and destitutes and had become a financial burden on the government. Often those returning had lived for such a long time away from their homeland that their relatives could not be located, and they had lost touch with their culture and traditions. They had become strangers in their own land. The Jamaican Government was only too pleased with the Indian Government's attitude as it saved the cost of the return fares.

Beginning in 1873, time-expired Indians were encouraged to remain in the island with the offer of a bounty in lieu of passage. They could choose to take either £12 in cash or 10 acres of land. Hindrances were also placed in their way to prevent them from taking advantage of the return passage and the compensation. For instance, one man married to a Jamaican-born

Indian woman was denied passage for his wife because she was a "foreigner".

Crown lands selected for allocation were usually to be found in the mountainous interior, infertile, of marginal value, and often without proper water supply. If the time-expired Indians refused to accept these allotments, the lands reverted to the Crown and they had to find lands of their own choosing, at their own expense. On rare occasions, as happened in Hayes, Clarendon, some succeeded in having basic infrastructure installed before they would accept the lands. In 1879, the land grant incentive was withdrawn, and in 1906 land grant in lieu of repatriation was discontinued. Those wishing to return to India now had to pay part of their return fare as well as purchase warm clothing and blankets for the journey.

In the 1880s when economic conditions in the island were at a low level because of the continued fall in sugar prices, thousands of rural unemployed, having no other means of earning a living, began the great trek to Central America in search of employment and better wages. They worked on the Panama Railroad and on the Panama Canal project. Others, including the Indians forsook the plantations hoping to find employment in the towns mainly in Kingston, but work was equally difficult to come by as there were no industries to absorb them.

Some Indians with skills practised their trade as jewellers, fishermen, barbers and the like. Others established themselves in villages as shopkeepers, first with a few basic items needed by the community; then as the

An Indian family in Golden Vale Plantation in 1896

business prospered they added additional services supplying dry goods and hardware. Beginning in the twentieth century, increasing numbers continued the migration to the towns, especially to Kingston and St Andrew, where they found it difficult to compete with the African-Jamaicans for the scarce jobs. They were forced to turn to what they knew best, agriculture. They became market gardeners.

They huddled together in shacks on the outskirts of the city, without amenities – light, water, roads or sanitary conveniences. They rented small plots of land, half-an-acre and less, planted vegetables and sold them from door to door in residential areas of the city. They managed to eke out a living and at the same time provided a valuable service to housewives who learned to eat healthier by including in their diet, the fresh vegetables supplied by the Indians.

The government, conscious that the growing worldwide depression, which began in the late 1920s, would have an even more disastrous impact on the already battered Jamaican economy, discouraged rural migration and the practice of market gardening. In 1931 a law was passed prohibiting the sale of items from door to door. The hope was that the market gardeners would be forced to return to the plantations and so help to save what was left of the sugar and banana industries. In response to public protest this law was amended to permit the sale of poultry, game, fruit and ground provisions to continue, but restriction on the sale of vegetables, which was almost entirely an Indian monopoly was not removed until 1945.

A few industrious Indians went into rice planting, the growing of vegetables and other crops on a large scale. Rice was the crop of preference but suitable lands were difficult to come by. They were to be had mainly on the plains of Westmoreland, where rundown sugar lands were selectively leased only to those willing to work three or four days a week on the plantation. However, successive years of drought and hurricane during the late 1890s brought the sugar planters to the brink of ruin, and they were obliged to lease more lands for rice planting. The arrangements were deliberately kept loose. Price per acre varied, so did conditions under which the lands were made available, and as soon as conditions began to return to normal and the sugar industry showed signs of reviving, owners took over the leased lands and put them once again into sugar cane cultivation. The acreage in rice was drastically reduced and an industry which could have been productive was stifled. Experiences such as these caused Indians to lose faith in Jamaican institutions and Jamaican justice. They bypassed the normal banking systems, preferring to entrust their savings and valuables to the care of some reliable member of the Indian community.

After the takeover of the rice lands, more displaced and unemployed

Indians joined the trek to the towns in search of employment. They added to the rapid urbanisation of Kingston, and lands once available for market gardening grew scarce and more expensive. Productive market gardens gave way to slums and housing projects. The already poor East Indian gardeners became poorer. The East Indian Progressive Society which was formed to protect their welfare, appealed to the government to make lands available in the Molynes Road, Waltham Park and Four Miles areas of St Andrew. However, the government, preferring to see the Indians back on the estates, declared that these lands were too expensive and advised the Indians to apply to land settlement schemes in the rural areas.

Economic conditions did not improve as sugar prices fell even lower in the face of worldwide recession beginning in 1929, and banana production was reduced as banana fields were rapidly wiped out by the Panama and leaf spot diseases. Sugar and banana were the only two major industries employing large numbers of persons. Independent small farmers in the rural communities were also suffering as they were losing more and more of their banana crops to disease.

Money became a scarce commodity. The labouring classes especially in Kingston faced starvation and the government was forced to institute relief work to avert a crisis. There were too few jobs for the numbers seeking employment and as a result, the jobless African-Jamaicans unwilling to share the few jobs, turned their hostility on the East Indian minority. They were forced out of the queues and Government Relief Programme selectors refused to employ them claiming that they were not capable of doing anything other than agricultural work. Those who remained on the banana plantations were employed for only two days a week throughout a whole crop season.

The Second World War caused severe restrictions of imported goods and this encouraged some Indians to enter into large scale rice cultivation once again. However, as soon as the war ended, they were once more forced out of business by the importation of cheaper foreign rice and the termination of their leases by landowners hoping for improvement in the sugar industry. The Indians found difficulty acquiring lands for purchase. Of 17,318 East Indians owning approximately 11,600 acres in 1926, two high caste Indians owned 4,037 acres. The remaining 7,563 acres had to be shared for the rest of the Indian population: an average of less than half-an-acre per person.

Striking aspects of Indian contribution to Jamaican culture are in the festivals and in jewellery. African-Jamaicans participate in the *hosay* and *divali* festivals although few fully understand their symbolism. The *hosay* is a Muslim celebration re-enacting the war between two brothers, sons of Mohammed, their death and burial. It stretches over nine nights of

A *hosay taj*

mourning. The sword fight and replica of the tomb of the slain brothers are central to the festival activities, the processions and the dances. Where there are significant numbers of East Indians, for example, in the parish of Clarendon, African-Jamaicans have helped to keep the *hosay* festival tradition alive. They build the *taj*, the replica of the tomb, perform the sword dances and participate in other activities. The dances associated with the festival have lost much of their significance and in recent years have begun to evolve into a western-style dance.

Divali is a Hindu celebration which takes place usually in late October or early November, on the darkest night of the year. It is associated with the reaping of grain and celebrates in song and dance, the victory of good over evil. It also celebrates the return of Prince Rama after 14 years of exile. At the time of *divali* houses are cleaned, everywhere is brightly lit and everyone is in good spirits.

Elements of Indian dress have been incorporated into the jonkunoo dance, adapted from African dance forms and performed usually at Christmas time. Indian jewellery has significantly influenced the Jamaican jewellery trade, especially the style of bangles which are sometimes referred to as slave bangles.

The recruitment of indentured labour to work in foreign countries was never popular in India. The Indian Government had from 1875 opposed the scheme because of the oppression of the Indians in the Caribbean. Faced with mounting opposition, the British Colonial Office put an end to the programme in 1917, in spite of pressure from colonial governments

Celebrating
Satnarine pujah

THE STORY OF THE JAMAICAN PEOPLE

to continue the traffic. Lack of transportation during the First World War was also a contributory factor, as three of the six ships normally engaged in transporting the labourers were commandeered for war service. The last set of Indians to be brought to Jamaica arrived in 1914. The last repatriates left in 1929 and legal repatriation ended in 1930.

Over a period of 70 years, more than 36,400 East Indians were brought to Jamaica and approximately one-third returned to their homeland. The estimated number of Indians living in Jamaica today is about 70,000, double the number who came under the indenture programme. The majority are still engaged in agricultural pursuits although in recent years some have moved into business and commerce and the professions.

The Chinese also constitute a separate racial group "which serves as a cushion between whites and blacks". Compared with the East Indians, their numbers are small and of little or no political significance. They were first brought to the island as indentured labourers between 1854 and the 1880s. The first Chinese to the West had been brought to work in the gold mines of California in 1848. Two years later, another group of workers was brought to Panama to help with the construction of the Panama Railroad, but they fared badly in the equatorial forests and mosquito infested swamps through which the railroad passed. Large numbers died from malaria and other diseases, from starvation and from physical abuse.

They insisted on leaving the country and in 1854, after some negotiation, 472 were sent to Jamaica in exchange for Jamaican labour. These Chinese were in such poor physical shape that most of them died within a short while. The government then brought in approximately 328 from Hong Kong but again the losses were high. Of a total of 800 from Panama and Hong Kong only 200 were still alive at the end of eight months. This possibly gave rise to the rumour that Chinese men were weak, and were therefore counted "two for one". Between 1864 and 1870, an additional 200 were also brought from Trinidad and British Guiana. They were apparently in better condition than those who had come earlier.

Chinese labourers were given three-year contracts which included the repatriation clause. They were housed in the same stifling, insanitary conditions, in overcrowded barracks as the Indians were allotted. They carried out the same menial tasks as other field labourers, worked for the same low wages of one shilling six pence a day, six days a week.

They protested about the long working hours and some Chinese labourers in St Thomas took strike action and refused to work the twelve-hour day. The time was reduced to nine hours per day. This is one of the earliest recorded strikes in Jamaica. As harsh as their conditions were, most Chinese served out their period of indenture although a few deserted to the towns.

They found openings in rural villages, set themselves up as grocers and at one time had almost complete monopoly of rural grocery shops so much so that the phrase used to describe a grocery store was "Chinese shop". This was a significant contribution to opening up the interior of the island and also to providing a vital service to villagers, at first bringing them basic necessities and as time passed, a wider range of goods. The average rural dweller was poor and usually had no fixed income. The Chinese shopkeeper accommodated his customers with credit, by selling in small quantities and by barter. A customer could barter a few pounds of ginger, pimento, annatto, coffee or other economic crop which would be weighed, valued, and the equivalent in groceries exchanged. Any balance due to the customer was paid in cash. From time-to-time the shopkeeper would also lend small sums of money to a client, with the assurance that the debt would be repaid in due course.

During the 1880s when the departure of African-Jamaican and East Indian labour from the plantation appeared to pose a threat to production, the Jamaican Government turned once again to Hong Kong for more cheap labour. News had by then spread of the success of some of the earlier Chinese immigrants. Some 680 farm labourers, lured by prospects of prosperity took up the offer. Not all of them were indentured labourers. Some borrowed the passage money, and relatives in Jamaica sent for others.

They set out from Macao on the South China coast and, after ten weeks at sea, arrived in Jamaica on 12 July 1884. Their wooden vessel, driven partly by steam and partly by sail, was so badly battered in a typhoon that it had to be abandoned at the first Canadian port of call and the passengers transferred to another vessel to continue their onward journey to Jamaica. Among them were 501 men and 105 women, 84 boys and girls including three babies born at sea. There were also on board a translator and a herbal doctor. The ship was provisioned with familiar Chinese foodstuffs: salted eggs, salted vegetables, rice, cooking oil, vinegar, soybean sauce, fowls, pigs and other livestock as well as medicines. (Lee: 1957)

Their first experience in Jamaica was most disheartening. On disembarkation they were taken to the Spanish Town prison and kept there under armed guard until they were shipped out in mule carts to the various plantations which had contracted for them. They were treated with the same distrust and faced the same discrimination which earlier Chinese and Indian labourers had experienced.

Most of them were Hakka people, farmers from Kwang Tung province in South East China with a climate similar to that of Jamaica. In Jamaica they found familiar medicinal herbs, fruits and vegetables which included sugar cane, bananas, plantains and dasheen. They had all come with one goal in mind, to acquire wealth and return to build China.

Once they had fulfilled the contract they left the estates and sought employment with their sponsors and with other established members of the Chinese community. They were prepared to perform menial tasks until they could acquire a sufficient amount of money to set themselves up in business. Some obtained small loans; others received their start from "fwee chen", the equivalent of the African-Jamaican "partner money" or "susu". "Fwee chen" required each participant to contribute an agreed amount regularly, whether it was weekly or monthly. When it was an individual's time to be paid, he or she received the draw for that week and this continued until all participants were re-paid.

In 1888, some 800 other immigrants arrived from Hong Kong. By then Jamaica was becoming a popular destination for Chinese immigrants. No doubt with prodding from the local business community, fearful that the Chinese were taking over the retail grocery trade, the government, in 1905, began to restrict their entry to the island. Immigrants then had to apply for registration with the immigration authorities, be recommended by some member of the local Chinese community who had to give an undertaking that they would not become a burden on the society and guarantee their good conduct. An official permit was then issued which the immigrant had to produce on arrival.

There was no Chinese consular representation on the island and the immigrants had little recourse in law. Their only official contact and source of appeal was through the Chinese Embassy in London, and it took a very long time for them to get action. They therefore established their own social institutions which are still in operation today. The Chinese Benevolent Association offers humanitarian and social services; the Chinese Sanitarium takes care of the sick, and an old folks home provides for the aged and indigent.

During the latter part of the nineteenth century and the early years of the twentieth century, a halfway house was established in Panama where prospective immigrants to Jamaica could await clearance. They could wait for as long as five years and more. Sometimes the permit was not forthcoming as unscrupulous agents, having taken money from sponsors in China and in Jamaica had no intention of troubling themselves any further. Those stranded in Panama could not return home or they would lose face. Some took the only honourable way out and committed suicide.

In 1910, the immigration law, as it affected Chinese and persons from the Middle East, was further amended. It required them to deposit £30 on arrival, which was returnable after one month. They were also required to demonstrate written and spoken familiarity with at least 50 words in either English or French or Spanish, as well as undergo a physical examination.

The literacy requirement was not always rigidly enforced and at times immigrants were admitted who could only sign their names in English.

Up to 1894, it was illegal for Chinese nationals to leave their country. But those who came to Jamaica were prepared to take the risk, in the hope that they could amass sufficient wealth and return to China with dignity. They were discouraged by relatives at home from acquiring property in Jamaica lest they be tempted to settle permanently in the island. They therefore rented land instead of purchasing it. Not many, however, worked the land although they were originally farmers.

Because of the language difficulty, some Chinese were cheated in land transactions just as the Indians were and they were made to believe that it was the government that had taken their land away. They lost faith in the official institutions and just as the Indians did, they selected a reliable Chinese shopkeeper to serve as banker.

As soon as they could they branched out into new business ventures, into laundries and restaurants and bakeries in addition to the usual retail and wholesale grocery trade. Though few in number, they have contributed significantly to Jamaica's commercial and industrial growth. They became general importers and distributors of rice, saltfish, saltmeats, flour and cornmeal and made these commodities staples in the Jamaican diet.

In the early years, because of ignorance of Chinese dress, African-Jamaicans referred disparagingly to the black, silk outfits worn by the Chinese as "oil-skin". When the thrifty Chinese turned flour bags into suits, they were criticised. They were disparaged and insulted by the local village bullies who thought that they did not understand what was being said. Jamaicans were suspicious of Chinese customs relating to death as they did not understand the Chinese traditions and the philosophy that only those who gave life should first look on or touch the dead. No one else was allowed to view the body until all the rituals were completed.

The myth about Chinese men being weak was attributed to the amount of rice they ate. The truth was that the Chinese ate much larger quantities of vegetables and meats and had a much more varied diet than the average

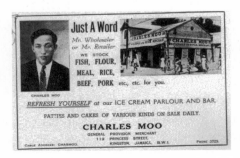

Jamaican. Mixed marriages were frowned upon by both sides and even today are accepted with some reservation. If anything unfortunate happens in such a marriage, the Chinese relatives tend to blame the bad luck on the fact that it was interracial. Children born to Jamaican and Chinese parents are "not quite good enough". Chinese mockingly refer to them as "half Chinese" or "eleven o'clock children": "not quite there, not quite twelve o'clock".

Gradually these prejudices have faded as African-Jamaicans developed familiarity with some of the Chinese customs and the Chinese have adapted to some Jamaican lifestyles. Their economic success has caused some African-Jamaicans to envy their good fortune without appreciating the amount of hard work that has gone into their endeavours. During the 1930s riots, the disaffected in the Jamaican society vented their envy and frustrations on the more successful members of minority groups, especially the Chinese. Their business places were frequently robbed and in extreme cases, owners were murdered.

One member of the Chinese community expressed it this way:

Chinese Free Mason Society participating in Jamaica's Tercentenary Celebrations, 1955

The reason for the apparent discrim-ination is not racial but economic, because these small concerns are profitable only when operated on a family basis. These concerns pay no salaries and money is withdrawn only for the necessities of operation and living expenses. Consequently, the meagre profits accumulate and the capital grows until it is suffi-ciently large to provide a good standard of living for the operators. (*The Star*, 8 August, 1936)

For a long time the colonial government continued to discriminate against the minority groups by introducing laws restricting daily opening hours of business places, compelling them to curtail their operations although the businesses were operated by family members and were therefore not affected by the law. Chinese and Jews were singled out for additional taxation. Chinese, whether new arrivals or returning residents, were required to pay an additional head tax of £5 although other foreigners were exempt.

Nevertheless, the rate of new arrivals kept increasing. In a 70-year period (1854-1924), 4,000 Chinese emigrated to Jamaica. In the next six years (1925-30), an additional 2,000 arrived. Compared with the African-Jamaican population and even with the number of Indians, the figure was relatively small but the Jamaican Government, facing economic pressures of the depression years with thousands of unemployed having no prospects of jobs in the immediate future, decided to close its doors to Chinese immigrants. After 7 January 1931, only children under 14-years-of-age were allowed in on a student permit. Returning Chinese residents were required to produce a re-entry permit which had to be obtained prior to departure. Restrictions were tightened further in 1940 when only diplomats, tourists and students with permits were allowed entry. Sometime later limited quotas were granted for wives, children and parents. Jamaican-born Chinese had to show proof of birth.

A school solely financed and operated by the Chinese and established in the latter part of the nineteenth century which prepared Chinese children for a prolonged stay in China, was excluded from government financial assistance although Christian denominational schools all qualified for grants.

Chinese immigrants were mainly farmers but only a few appear to have gone into farming. However, when foreign trade was restricted during the Second World War, some turned to rice cultivation but abandoned the rice fields as soon as the war ended, because of government policy to allow the importation of cheaper rice in competition with the locally grown product.

The Chinese custom of using fireworks to celebrate special occasions became a favourite Jamaican attraction, especially at Christmas time. It was however banned in the middle of this century when elements in the society began using it for antisocial purposes. In more recent times Chinese celebratory dances such as the lion dance have been included among the annual National Festival events. This is one area of the creative arts which demonstrates the integration process.

Chinese industry and their disciplined approach to work, their care and nurturing of children and the emphasis they place on education and on family life, set examples for the Jamaican society. The tradition of the extended family in Chinese culture parallels that in African cultures. So is respect for age whether it be to a member of the immediate family, or to an outsider. In these ways the Chinese have helped to preserve such values in the Jamaican society.

A much smaller number of immigrants from the Middle East have also made their contribution to the building of the Jamaican nation. In the early years of the twentieth century, some Jews, Lebanese and others from the Middle East began arriving. We will recall that Jews helped to finance Columbus' expedition to the West; a few had come with the first Spanish explorers to Jamaica, and others had been brought as indentured servants to help establish the sugar industry in the sixteenth century. Since the beginning of the sixteenth century there has always been a Jewish community in Jamaica.

Religion has been a bond. Although non-Christian religions were not tolerated for a very long time in this predominantly Christian society, the Jews were allowed to establish their own places of worship. They, like other minority groups, faced discrimination but they had early established control over the Jamaican economy and because of their financial strength they could not be ignored. Over the centuries small numbers have come and joined the already established merchant class. They have prospered and in times of crisis have often come to the rescue of the insolvent plantation owners.

Elias Issa, (back row, centre, a Lebanese who migrated to Jamaica in 1894), with his family

Building a new society: People from India, China and the Middle East

The more recent arrivals from the Middle East left their homes in Palestine and Lebanon, then part of the former country of Syria, to escape political and religious discrimination and to seek a better way of life in a new country. In the redistribution of power after the First World War, Syria was carved up politically. The new geographical and political boundaries, some of them under European "protection", uprooted generations of settled people and bred animosity among communities which normally had lived together in peace for centuries.

Jamaica became a stopover point for many en route to the land of opportunity, the United States. Others encouraged by success stories of relatives and friends on the island, chose to remain. They did not come as indentured servants; this was "chain" migration where prospective migrants learn of opportunities, are provided with transportation and have initial accommodation and employment arranged by means of primary social relationships with previous migrants. (Nicholls: 1956) A few came by accident. Having bought passage on a westward bound ship, often from Marseilles, they disembarked whenever the ship reached what they considered might be a suitable destination. Sometimes that place happened to be Jamaica. Many were farmers, some were professionals but in the beginning they were prepared to take any form of employment.

Some Lebanese, (often referred to as Syrians) at first went into banana production but found difficulty breaking the entrenched cartel of the fruit companies. They therefore followed members of the older Jewish community and became merchants and traders. One of the easiest ways of getting started was to become a pedlar. The future pedlar would identify an area, survey the possibilities, obtain a loan from one of the more established members of the "Syrian" community, acquire a modest amount of merchandise that was likely to find acceptance in the area, then sell his wares of cloth and household items from door to door. As business improved, the pedlar would acquire a donkey to transport the goods, then later upgrade his status with a buggy and still later to a motor vehicle. Householders greatly appreciated this convenience although their choice was limited. The fact that they could purchase the goods at home and pay in small instalments made the arrangement even more attractive. Eventually when a pedlar amassed sufficient money, he opened a small dry goods shop and gave up travelling on the road.

Because of European interest in the Middle East, the immigrants from Palestine and Lebanon were usually familiar with some European language, particularly French or English. They therefore did not have the same difficulty in communicating as the Indians and Chinese before them.

They were thrifty, worked hard, and where they could, paid periodic visits to their homeland to ensure that their children retained the culture and language of their ancestors. The Second World War disrupted this practice. Fewer individuals were able to share this experience, and so the younger generation became more rapidly integrated into the Jamaican society.

Whereas African family structures were seriously eroded over 300 years of British rule, the later immigrants from India, China and the Middle East were not subject to such a long and intensive period of deculturisation. As a result they have retained more of their original cultural values while at the same time integrating into the Jamaican society. They have retained religious rites and festivals and art forms which have enriched the emerging Jamaican nation while the Rastafarians were displacing Babylon.

CHAPTER 26

Day da light, oh

There are mountain-top times in the Jamaica story when "day da light" and sunrise comes, as if we were standing on the peak on a clear dawn when:

> The innocence of daybreak revealed the island like a cut beryl set in a glassy sea. The sharp ranges were of precious stone. The white clouds were intense drifts of the pure cold atmosphere. The rivers lay veiled in motionless slumber like opal serpents. Port Antonio shone in the ring of its harbour like a snowy lily in an azure jug. And far away to the north-east the thin lake line of Cuba was steady against the paler blue of sky and sea. (Pringle)

The Jamaican finds his story in the landscape; the lake line of Cuba and the harbour of Port Antonio summon up ancestral memories of a separating sea, of slave ships and perpetual exile; the mountain ranges tell of places of refuge for blacks in search of freedom; the plantations on the coastal plains speak of having been for 300 years the battlefields of Africa's conflict with Europe; of blacks stripped of the rights of ownership, of rights to the labour of their bodies or to the possession of their own children, of blacks in conflict with whites who had everything; a political monopoly, control of the legislature, the guardianship and protection of Britain.

The struggle lasted for just over 300 years, from 1655 to 1962. It covers four phases. At the end of the first phase, in 1739, England recognised the right of two bands of maroons to freedom and independence. A century later, in 1834, the second phase ended when Britain passed the Act of Emancipation by which all slaves in the British empire were set free.

But the conflict was far from over. The blacks soon found that slavery did not die in 1834 and that full freedom did not come in 1838. The complete mastery of one man over another was no longer legal, but the economic mastery of the estate owners over landless free blacks still

THE STORY OF THE JAMAICAN PEOPLE

prevailed, the mastery of the educated over the illiterate, of the white and the brown over the black. The third phase came to its climax with the Morant Bay Uprising in 1865.

In that year the character of the conflict changed. The objectives sharpened: the right of the black labour force to a better way of life, their right to representative government and to racial equality. This claim made with increasing urgency by Robert Love and by Marcus Garvey in the first quarter of the twentieth century transformed a riot at Frome in 1938 into a critical turning-point in a cultural and political revolution that swept the Jamaican people to independence in 1962, when white authority transferred the seals and symbols of power to duly constituted black authority. The empowering forces were race consciousness and an emerging nationalism.

Neville Dawes in his *Prolegomena to Caribbean Literature*, spoke of this aspect of Garvey's work: "There is one element in the African's experience of the New World that does not seem to have been given much attention and that is his attitudes, changing attitudes, to Africa as Mother and to the African continent. I consider this to be vital to an understanding of what is going on in the Caribbean not simply in the creation of literature but in the general area of culture and cultural development."

Dawes spoke of various changes in our attitude to Africa.

> The first phase was one of pure plangency, one of the pure bereavement of the child dispossessed of its mother – the cry echoed on the shores of Hwyidah, perhaps in the Ewe language, as the slave ships, full of Africans who had been tricked aboard, pulled away to the dark sea-journey. Our brothers and sisters have gone, the dirge said. On what shore will they land? The second phase was characterised by the gradually darkening memory of Mother Africa, as my forefathers of the Diaspora began to learn new ways of necessity.

At the third phase, the process of colonisation became Europe's battle for control of the African-Jamaican's mind. Dawes pictured it; at this point the real Mother Africa was almost dead in the mind of the diaspora and the colonisation of the African in the Western world was almost complete. At this point Africa became "the fully dark continent of cannibals and snakes and powerful juju and not as a source of democratic forms of society of justice of the realistic understanding of the divine".

In this setting Garvey's trumpet-call to racial pride and an affirmation of racial identity set African-Jamaicans to the task of reclaiming their identity and their heritage. The national movement and the cultural revolution initiated by Garvey were the revolutionary forces that released Jamaicans from colonialism.

The process began in the mind, with self-discovery and self-liberation. It was often painful and distressing. We who belong to later generations need to enter for a moment into the inner world of two of our griots, Claude McKay and Una Marson, in order to understand the significance of this affirmation of a racial identity and the recognition that the basic heritage of the African-Jamaican people is African.

Claude McKay was from the James Hill area in North Clarendon, with its glorious landscape, its superb view of the Bull Head Mountain and its independent country folk, amongst whom he grew up, the son of a small farmer. He described rural Jamaican society in *Banana Bottom*, which was published in New York in 1933, but which pictured rural Jamaica in the early 1900s. For a brief period McKay served as a policeman in Kingston and then emigrated to the United States where he became a leading figure in a distinguished group of black American writers during the Harlem renaissance. Una Marson was a black middle-class Jamaican whose *Heights and Depths* and *The Moth and the Star,* established her as Jamaica's outstanding woman poet of the 1920s and 1930s.

McKay and Una Marson write as Jamaicans with anguish and triumph about Africa as mother country and African-Jamaicans as kinsfolk. Before journeying with them through that experience let us remind ourselves that our own conflict is a part of the larger story of African-Americans, our island struggle of Africa against Europe, black against white, a part of a story hemispheric in scale and unbroken in sequence from the 1520s, when black maroons took to the mountains of Hispaniola. Further, just as the creative dynamic in Jamaican history came from the African and not from the European so throughout plantation America "all along it was the people who had African slave forbears and had suffered the anguish of the early plantations, who were giving the new Caribbean society cultural shape and purpose as they once brought, through their labour, economic significance and prominence to the sugar-producing region". (Nettleford: 1978) We bear in mind also Rex Nettleford's warning that:

> It is a mistake to sacrifice in all this the specificity of racial cultural concerns which are self-evident in every single territory of the Caribbean. Not only have the vast majority in places like Jamaica been the survivors of an oppressive system, they are still being the survivors of a global conspiracy to keep the Black in his place, whatever his demonstrated potential as a creative resourceful being. (Nettleford: 1978)

We will spend time in the company of McKay and Una Marson because their message remains relevant. Their work, their suffering, their confirmation of racial identity, of historic achievement, their example of intellectual integrity, enable us as their successors and kinsfolk "to chart our own courses along universal paths to freedom and dignity for the people".

McKay's *Banana Bottom* stated the African-Jamaican position. It is Jamaica's first self-portrait and the first classic in Jamaican and West Indian prose. The author holds a place of honour in our history for he led the way in creating a Jamaican literature that draws its inspiration from the African-Jamaican historical experience. He wrote as eyewitness, novelist, chronicler and interpreter, realist and visionary. McKay introduced us also to an elderly Englishman, Walter Jekyll, who is Squire Gensir in the story. Jekyll taught him that the folklore of the Jamaican people is:

> Your spiritual link between you and your ancestral origin . . . My mind is richer because I know your folk-lore. This man was the first to enter into the simple life of the island negroes and proclaim significance and beauty in their transplanted African folk tales and in the words and music of their native dialect. Before him it had generally been said the Negroes were inartistic. But he had found artistry where others saw nothing . . . wherever the imprints of nature and humanity were to be found, there also were the seeds of creative life.

Models of greatness were absent from that colonial society. The past was forbidden. Africa was taboo. A black minister, the Rev. Lambert, in *Banana Bottom* urged his predominantly black congregation to reject Africa, for "there are no people so addicted to sorcery (Obeah) as we negroes. The continent we came over from is cursed and abandoned of God because of magic. We brought along the curse from there . . . Give up our ancient God of darkness. Throw the jungle out of your hearts and forget Africa".

Self-rejection was the doctrine the Euro-African preached. Self-fulfilment was to be found in Europe. In consequence there were neither heroes nor any unifying memory of great achievements in Jamaican society. "Greatness could not exist in the backwoods. Nor anywhere in the colony. To them and to all the islanders greatness was a foreign thing. The biggest man in the colony was the governor. But not even the most ignorant peasant thought him great."

Banana Bottom is novel and allegory. The central character, Bita, is a symbol of the African-Jamaican seeking for and assenting her African identity in a colonial society. It is also a shattering indictment of a colonial system of education based on the principle of black inferiority: "Too bad she should have been taken and educated

Claude McKay

above her station," Busha Glengley said of Bita, and "Anyway, look out about teaching them wrong ideas. They may use them against us some day . . . Yes, us, of the white race . . ."

Bita, who had been grievously wronged in her childhood, symbolises the uprooted African-Jamaican, who somehow preserves that unsurrendering element of personality that manifested itself in the long series of liberation struggles. Although educated in Britain, she remained African:

> Let me tell you right now that a white person is just like any other human being to me. I thank God that although I was brought up and educated among white people I have never wanted to be anything but myself. I take pride in being coloured and different, just as an intelligent white person does in being white. I can't imagine anything more tragic than people torturing themselves to be different from their natural unchangeable selves.

Bita knew that in Jamaican society colour dictated standing. She took this into account without passion or anger:

> What could a cultivated Negro girl from the country hope for better than a parson. Marrying a good parson was a step higher than marrying a schoolmaster. If she had happened to be born a light brown or yellow girl she might, with her training, easily get away with a man of a similar complexion . . . but she was in the black and dark-brown group and there were no prospects of her breaking into the intimate social circles of the smart light-brown and yellow group.

In the end, Bita moved from living with the missionaries who had adopted, reared and educated her, and went back to her own father and his peasant home. "She had grown out of that soil, his own soil, and had gone abroad only for polishing. Her choosing of her own will to return there filled him with pride, so strong was his affection for the land."

The symbolism of Bita's return was highlighted by a brown-black controversy that raged at the time over a switch in civil service requirements; "Some of the strongest support for the change had come from a group of black men, most of whom had near-white or white wives and light-coloured children; among these was a black clergyman with a large family of freckled reddishly-coloured children." McKay derided the idea that civil service posts should be given to peasant youths fresh from the huts who possessed no background but were clever enough to pass the examinations. There were in *Banana Bottom* aged white-headed blacks who remembered that "the honorable and reverend black legislator had not even had the benefit of a hut as background but that the roof over his head had been the trash-house of the sugar-cane plantation and his bed the trash-heap".

Una Marson, (centre) at the BBC

Bita carried her affirmation of identity and of kinship with other African-Jamaicans further by marrying one of them, the drayman, Jubban. The browns and whites saw her as "only a nigger gal", but "she was proud of being a Negro girl. And no sneer, no sarcasm, no banal ridicule of a ridiculous world could destroy her confidence and pride in herself and make her feel ashamed of that fine body that was the temple of her high spirit".

Bita moves against a richly tapestried background of African-Jamaican people; a gregarious, often raucous yard and village society with its own art forms and cults which it preserved against the preachings of the church and the hostility of the powerful. Just as African-Jamaicans finally achieved freedom and justice by their own long-sustained efforts, so throughout rural Jamaica the African-Jamaican people drew on their African cultural heritage. They were a part of a deeply segmented society but culturally they belonged to Africa. McKay emphasised this by showing that it was Africa that called most powerfully to British-educated Bita. At the market Bita,

> mingled in the crowd, responsive to the colour, the swell and press of it. It gave her the sensation of a reservoir of familiar kindred humanity into which she had descended for baptism. She had never had that big moving feeling as a girl . . . if she had never gone abroad for a period so long . . . she might never have had the experience . . .

Accents and rhythms, movements and colours, nuances that might have passed unnoticed if she had never gone away were now revealed to her in all their striking detail.

Bita loved the harvest festival, Sunday school, picnic, a tea meeting at Kojo Jeems yard where she delighted in "dancing down the barrier between high breeding and common pleasures under her light-stamping feet until she was one with the crowd". She could easily understand the pungent perfume of the pimento exciting love with the pickers up to their necks in it, squatting upon the leaves with stems and berries in their hands, which dominated the atmosphere with their odour; and the old-time revival with a thin little black woman with a bright bandana upon her head, beating a drum and followed by other women and a few men all bearing supple-jacks and singing

> Rolling, rolling, rolling down
> Ages rolling, rolling ages
> Rolling along for a golden crown
> Silver shoes and silver clothes . . .

Then the dancing began. These bodies poised straight in religious ecstasy and dancing vertically up and down while others transformed themselves into curious whirling shapes, seemed filled with an ardent nearly-forgotten spirit, something ancestral recaptured in the emotional fervour, evoking in her memories of pictures of savage rites, tribal dancing with splendid swaying plumes, and the brandishing of the supple-jacks struck her as symbolic of raised and clashing spears . . . Magnetised by the spell of it, Bita was drawn nearer and nearer into the inner circle until with a shriek she fell down.

When Bita had recovered her senses under the mimosas where she had been taken, she was at a loss to explain what had happened to her. She remembered experiencing an overwhelming mesmeric feeling and a sensation of becoming a different person in a strange place and suddenly there was lacuna and she was conscious of nothing more.

Herein lies the message of *Banana Bottom*, with its portrayal of the great cultural achievement of the disenfranchised mass of the African-Jamaican people, who in their pulsating, gregarious way responded to Africa, preserved their tradition of open spaces, and dance, drumming, songs, proverbs, riddles, spirituals, kumina, myal and other cults, and the yard, road, village, their theatre, where they developed an indigenous Jamaican culture.

Even where the forms or phrases were copied from the great house, even where European-style dances and rituals were taken over, something African was retained. The spirituality that existed before the missionaries came had its source in Africa, in ancestral memories of communication with God or the gods at any time and in any place, all a natural part of the African way of life.

Looking, then, at the folk culture and the African way of life, we learn respect for the inner thoughts of the African, whose concepts of the individual human being and of the child, stand in sharp contrast to white plantation society's example of social irresponsibility and sexual promiscuity. These are embodied in McKay's Marse Arthur, with his "healthy pink face, betraying not the slightest sign of mind, restless eyes and fleshy mouth, known for his amorous embodiment of social irresponsibility". In opposition to this, we have the African concept of a child:

> In African societies, the birth of a child is a process which begins long before the child's arrival in the world and continues long thereafter. It is not just a single event . . . Nature brings the child into the world, but society creates the child into a social being, a corporate person. For it is the community which must protect the child, feed it, bring it up, educate it and in many other ways incorporate it into the wider community. Children are the buds of society and every birth is the arrival of 'spring' when life shoots out and the community thrives. (Mbiti: 1970)

We continue in the company of Claude McKay as the outstanding Jamaican poet of his generation. He and Una Marson rooted Jamaican literature in the Jamaican experience in a way that had not been done before. He stripped away the hypocrisies with which Jamaicans of that period habitually shrouded the colour bar and race hatred. By portraying his own experience he revealed the crippling effects of self-contempt, self-doubt, self-rejection, the haunting uncertainties and anxieties caused by a feeling of inadequacy. At a critical moment in our history his works set Jamaicans on the road to self-liberation, to the discovery of a country that was theirs, of a nation and race that were theirs.

Angry at racial separatism and colour discrimination and "a social system characterized by strongly entrenched class-colour differences", McKay pictured the contrast between Backra's world and Quashie's world, to which he belonged:

> You tase petater an' you say it sweet
> But you no know how hard we wuk fe it . . .
> De sun hot like when ketch a town;
> Shade tree look temptin, yet we caan' lie down . . .
> You see petater tear up groun', you run

McKay felt the contrast deeply. He rebelled against Backra's view of the picturesque peasant life.

Watch how dem tourist like fe look
Out 'pon me little daughter,
Wheneber fe her tu'n to cook
Or fetch a pan of water:
De sight look gay;
Dat is one way,
But I can tell you say,
'Nuff rock'tone in de sea, yet none
But those 'pon lan' know 'bouten sun.

McKay's inner conflict worsened when as a policeman he had to enforce the laws of the white world against people of his race. The conflict became an agony when he had to witness the flogging of a black prisoner.

I dared not look at him,
My eyes with tears were dim,
My spirit filled with hate
Of Man's depravity,
I hurried through the gate.

But he could not separate himself from the system he served by hurrying through the gate. He returned – to comfort the prisoner and affirm his brotherhood with him. Then, making his exit from his country to America, he came face-to-face with racial hostility, symbolised in the White House:

Your door is shut against my tightened face,
And I am sharp as steel with discontent,
But I possess the courage and the grace
To bear my anger proudly and unbent . . .
Oh, I must search for wisdom every hour,
Deep in my wrathful bosom sore and raw,
And find in it the superhuman power
To hold me to the letter of your law!
Oh, I must keep my heart inviolate
Against the potent poison of your hate.

As Lloyd Brown points out in his study of Claude McKay's work, the poet was searching for a distinctive identity that harmonised West Indian folk culture and his African heritage with "the countervailing weight of a Western heritage". Reflecting on McKay's experience, we see that there were two emancipation struggles, one from physical bondage in 1834 and the other an emancipation of the spirit, towards which Claude McKay and Una Marson were striving.

Una Marson, like Claude McKay, has an important place in the story of the Jamaican people, a story that goes beyond a recital of battles won, beyond a catalogue of political events. It penetrates into the ways in which black and brown Jamaicans see themselves, other Jamaicans and their world. She is important as a poet whose works "were concerned, to a considerable degree, with the situation and identity of the Jamaican woman . . . the sexual perspectives of the woman are integrated with the cultural and racial themes which she clearly shares with Claude McKay". (Brown)

There is the personal agony of frustration, of the prisoned pain of conflicts engendered by colour prejudice and self-rejection.

> Rest then my heart, thou knowest but too well
> How strong and fierce relentless winds can blow.
> For hearts do not upon the wild rocks break
> They only know deep hurt and ache on ache.

She turned from the theme of the picturesque, exotic tropics to the experience of an African-Jamaican woman.

> We who see through the hypocrisy . . .
> feel the blood of black and white alike
> Course through our veins as our strong heritage
> Must range ourselves to build the younger race.

But the realities of self-rejection tormented her.

> I like me black face
> And me kinky hair
> I like me black face
> And me kinky hair
> But nobody loves dem,
> I don't think its fair
> Now I'se going press me hair
> And bleach me skin
> I'se gwine press me hair
> And bleach me skin
> What won't a gal go
> Some kind of man to win.
> Your mama does love you
> And you colour is high.

Our time spent with Claude McKay and Una Marson opens up the inner dimensions of the story of the African-Jamaican people. In a white-dominated society in which blackness was despised, educated Claude McKay denounced the potent poison of race hatred, and Una Marson affirmed her liking for her black face and kinky hair. In them we see the movement towards a Jamaican culture, beginning with an affirmation of racial identity.

CHAPTER 27

The birth of a national consciousness, 1920-44

The final conflict between African-Jamaica and Britain began in the 1920s at the bidding of Quashie, the most underrated character in Jamaica's history, and of Marcus Garvey, the most feared and derided black leader of his time.

So decisive, so far-reaching were the results of this conflict that we refer to it here as the Jamaican revolution. It brought about the enfranchisement of all adult Jamaicans, set the feet of the people on the path to independence, speeded up the rapid growth of racial and national consciousness, the emergence of a Jamaican culture, the development of ties with Africa and the modernisation of the Jamaican economy.

Early in the 1920s the rural unemployed began to lay siege to the outworks and lower bastions of the citadel of Euro-Jamaican power in Kingston and lower St Andrew. So it comes about that the African-Jamaican peasant stands with Garvey, Alexander Bustamante and Norman Manley as heroes of that final conflict which began with the start of urbanisation (1920s) intensified during the Garvey years (1927-35), reached a decisive turning-point in the Frome years (1938-44) and moved into the period of consolidation and development in the period 1944-62.

The first phase of the revolution began early in the 1920s when the rural unemployed began to move to Kingston and lower St Andrew, the only places in the island where there was the remotest chance of finding work. By doing this they set in motion the process of urbanisation which, being so all-embracing, functioned as catalyst, incubator of ideas and generator of social discontent. By the time that Garvey returned to Jamaica in December 1927 a proletariat had begun to emerge.

In this chapter we focus on the urbanisation of Kingston and St Andrew in the years 1920-44 with indications of ways in which urbanisation contributed to fundamental social change. The chapters that follow focus on the political and socio-economic aspects of the revolution, the leaders of which were Alexander Bustamante and Norman Manley, and on the period of consolidation that followed the climactic years 1938-44. The final chapter gives an account of the extraordinary upsurge of creativity that followed the emergence of racial and national consciousness in the 1930s. These aspects belong together, are interdependent and interact upon each other.

The great ennobling themes of the story of the Jamaican people come together in this period of revolutionary ferment. The long struggle of the mass of the people for betterment and for freedom from economic oppression, the 1832 uprising for liberty and for human rights, brown George William Gordon's alliance with black Paul Bogle in the Morant Bay rejection of serfdom, find their champions in Garvey and later in Bustamante and Manley.

By treating the revolution in this way, by seeing that it grew out of the struggle of the mass of the Jamaican people for a better life, and out of the vision of Jamaican leaders, we link past generations with our own in an empowering experience of achievement.

So powerful a force as urbanisation calls for fuller consideration. It has been defined as the process and effects of gathering people in cities and towns. The concept covers urban expansion in area and population and the resulting changes in land use, ways of life, landscape and the geographical and occupational distribution of people. Of course urbanisation was not a uniquely Jamaican phenomenon. "The unprecedented scale and speed of urbanization in the 20th century – the majority of mankind will soon be living in urban places – has brought a host of urgent needs . . . and has made it a major concern of our time." (*Dictionary of Modern Thought*: 1977)

Linked with the process are the words "proletariat" and "bourgeois", which came into current use in the early twentieth century. It was Karl Marx who, in the opening passage of his *Communist Manifesto* (1848) drew attention to the message of conflict which these words conveyed: "The history of human society, past and slave, patrician and plebeian, lord and serf . . . the bourgeois age . . . has simplified class antagonisms . . . society is splitting into two great hostile classes . . . bourgeois and proletariat."

Marx was often more specific, using terms such as "wage labourers", "factory hands", the "working class". The word "proletariat" nevertheless became an important concept in the communist literature of the 1920s. In earlier times, such as the fifteenth and sixteenth centuries, "proletariat" had referred simply to landless men whose only means of livelihood was selling their labour. In our time it conveys also a suggestion of class conflict.

The word "bourgeois" was used in Europe in the Middle Ages to denote one who was neither a peasant nor a lord. Later it was applied to the master or employer in relation to the worker, with the result that gradually it became synonymous with the middle class. Since the nineteenth century the word has been used to express two contradictory judgments. Marx went on to say in the passage quoted above that the bourgeoisie historically had played "a most revolutionary part . . . .The bourgeoisie cannot exist without constantly revolutionizing the instruments of production . . . and with them the whole relations of society". Opposed to this judgement is that which portrayed the bourgeois or middle class as avaricious, mean and reactionary. Whereas "economic and political historians tend to see the bourgeois class as tearing up the roots of traditional society and its fixed ways, cultural historians . . . have tended to write from an aristocratic point of view and to decry the breakdown of standards when all culture becomes a commodity". (*Dictionary of Modern Thought*: 1977)

We turn now from the concept of urbanisation to the process, its scale and the numbers involved, and then we place it in the Jamaican historical context, for although the process is at work in all developing and developed countries, it is shaped in each country by that nation's history, needs and way of life.

In the preceding chapter we saw that between 1880 and 1920 more than 146,000 Jamaicans, practically all from rural Jamaica, moved overseas in search of employment. Emigration was their response to poverty at home.

In Jamaica, although the First World War (1914-18) had brought higher prices for sugar and had increased a demand for logwood to replace the German synthetic dyes, conditions had worsened. The entry of the United States into the war had reduced the demand for bananas. Four hurricanes in the period 1911-21 had ravaged the banana plantations. These disasters had been followed by the Spanish influenza epidemic of 1918, which caused heavy loss of life, inflicted great suffering on the rural poor and deepened the widespread gloom and the general feeling of despair.

But hope remained. In 1920 Cuban sugar was selling on the New York market for 22 cents per lb. Jobs were still available in the United States and in Cuba.

Then the blow fell, removing all hope. The great depression set in. By 1929 the price of Cuban sugar was down to one cent per lb on the New York market. Word spread throughout rural Jamaica that "no entry" signs were up in Panama, Honduras, Costa Rica, Cuba and the United States. No jobs were available. The "pull-factor", a demand for Jamaican labour, no longer operated. Cuban cane fields were no longer the mecca they had been for Jamaicans. Lengthening bread lines in the industrial cities of the United States and closed factories told of rising unemployment. New restrictions on immigration to the United States and other countries reversed the inflow of Jamaican labour, so that it became a return flow from the host country to the home country. In Jamaica in the late 1920s the picture was bleak. More people came than went, fewer babies died, more people lived longer, sugar prices were down, banana trees were dying from the Panama and leaf spot diseases.

By the early 1930s the situation was desperate in Jamaica and throughout the West Indies. In the words of Arthur Lewis, "It is generally agreed that bad conditions which have ruled in recent years are a major predisposing factor (to economic distress). The prices of the principal West Indian exports were on the average almost halved between 1928 and 1933 and workers were forced to submit to drastic wage cuts, increased taxation and unemployment." Even in relatively prosperous Trinidad, there was a steady drift of unemployed workers from the plantations to the towns.

In Jamaica the rural unemployed responded to the no-entry barriers overseas and aggravated poverty at home by initiating a transfer of population from rural to urban Jamaica. L. Broom in a 1951 study noted that the most significant trend in the present-day Caribbean was the urbanisation of agricultural populations and the progressive concentration of people in the major city. They did this without the inducement of industrial development in the city. Their target was the island's major urban areas, Kingston and St Andrew. There were four currents, the two major ones being the northern and the southern currents and the two minor ones representing additions to Kingston and St Andrew from Portland and St Thomas:

Southern current	35,000
Northern current	27,500
Portland current	4,200
St Thomas current	2,300

The heaviest flow, made up of 37,300 people, came from the southern parishes. (Roberts: 1957)

The figures provide evidence of increasing economic instability in these years. The general restlessness of the rural population also indicated this. About one-fifth of the total population, 90,200 males and 108,900 females, moved from one parish to another in that period. Suburban St Andrew became the favoured location for about 47,500 persons. Of this number 11,300 were from Kingston, which "emphasises the shrinking importance of Kingston as a residential area". (Roberts: 1957) This general movement of people led to the growth of other urban centres in the island. As Roberts points out, "The parishes showing appreciable gains from neighbouring parishes were St James, St Catherine, St Thomas and Clarendon. St James was the chief beneficiary, through the pull exerted by the expanding Montego Bay area which, ever since the 1920's, had been displacing Port Antonio as the chief centre of the tourist industry." (Roberts: 1957)

This large movement of male and female unemployed workers from every part of Jamaica to Kingston and St Andrew gave rise to a proletariat that grew in numbers year by year. At the same time jobless veterans were returning from the First World War, bitter at the racial insults they had suffered at the hands of those for whose countries they had fought. Greatly shocked and hurt at the scant welcome given to them, many joined the ranks of the disaffected. Later in the 1920s, thousands of immigrants returning from the United States were dismayed at the conditions they found in Jamaica. Many were strong anti-imperialists, and others were active nationalists, sympathetic to racist and radical movements. This strong inflow of disaffected, educated, unemployed people from Europe and the United States reinforced the ranks of both the proletariat and the radical bourgeoisie, whose leaders were drawn from the Jamaica Union of Teachers, the Jamaica Agricultural Society, followers of Sandy Cox, Bain Alves and Garvey. They injected into a sector of the middle class that revolutionary force of which Marx wrote. They were reinforced by the anti-colonialists and the nationalists of the 1930s and 1940s, among them such pioneers as W. A. Domingo, W. Adolphe Roberts, O. T. Fairclough, H. P. Jacobs and Ken and Frank Hill. They made the political education of the people one of their chief objectives.

By 1930 it had become clear that by initiating and accelerating the urbanisation process, the powerless, landless, jobless African-Jamaican people had yet again started another social and political revolution. There were now groupings at work in the society that had not been there in the times of Sam Sharpe, George William Gordon and the banana smallholders of the 1880s and 1890s. Two of the most significant were the easily inflamed proletariat in Kingston and St Andrew, with their linkages to other new urban areas, and a radical sector of the bourgeoisie committed to a nationalist, African-Jamaican ideology.

In those years urbanisation began to transform the Liguanea landscape and emphasised the concept of Jamaica as being two societies. The contrasts stood out large and bold, without cover-up, all in the open air: the Jamaica of the black and poor, of Trench Town, Dungle, Back O' Wall, and on the surrounding hills the Jamaica of the rich and powerful white and brown minority.

This landscape mirror brought Jamaicans face-to-face with the reality that M. G. Smith, Jamaican scholar and poet, analysed in his *Plural Society*. His theoretical analysis was invaluable in opening Jamaican eyes to the need for understanding and taking measures to solve their gravest problems, massive black unemployment and a deeply divided society. It was confirmed by one of Jamaica's first and finest novelists, Roger Mais, who told in *Brother Man*, of entering into the slum culture, a divided and split world, the division not being just a question of colour, nor yet of rich and poor, but also "of differences that involved widely different acceptances and rejections of values, that involved different interpretations of reality, that involved the use of identical words to express different concepts and understandings . . . that other world to which the majority belong". (Manley: 1966)

A Rastafarian poet, Sam Brown, pointed to the lightning hidden in the hurricane cloud.

> Some young desperates look to the hills,
>   see the seat of their distress,
> They see the dwellers of the hills as them
>   that do oppress . . .
> Men, women and children stark naked,
>   lunatics of wants, reformatory.
> Executives in horseless chariots
> Sometimes pass through
>   hold their noses,
> Hapless poor look with vengeful
>   eyes, for them no bed of roses . . .

The executives in horseless chariots, holding their noses in disgust, were passing through a world that they had brought into being. The young desperates, the naked and afflicted, had built the shacks and slums, but the massive rural unemployment that had driven them from the rural to the urban areas of Jamaica was a result of economic and social policies adopted by the colonial government in alliance with a white-brown upper class.

The League of Coloured People in London, which had been founded by a black Jamaican, Dr Harold Moody, and which had a future Nobel Prize winner, W. Arthur Lewis, as one of its members, made this point in its analysis of the 1945 Report of the Royal Commission under Lord Moyne. The league held the predominantly white political leadership responsible for existing conditions and stated bluntly that many of the Royal Commission's proposals for welfare and development had been made for years but had been blocked by the local ruling classes who held a political monopoly and who were backed by the system of Crown colony rule. Lewis in particular emphasised that until radical political and constitutional changes had been made there would be no end to agitation and little prospect of development.

The poet's image of "the dwellers of the hills as them that do oppress" captured in a few words the harsh penalisation endured by African-Jamaicans. It brought to mind Gordon's attack on Eyre and the white magistracy for oppressing the peasantry, the complaint of the St Ann peasants about oppressive estate owners, the heavy emigration of rural unemployed between 1911 and 1921, and Garvey's blunt assertion in 1938 that the African-Jamaican people had no reason for patriotism to Britain since it had done nothing for them.

In substance the Moyne Commission's report was an indictment of Crown colony rule. It confirmed the charges made by Garvey, the League of Coloured People and Arthur Lewis. Through the policies they followed, the government and the upper-middle class discouraged industrialisation and manufacturing, used systems of taxation that burdened the poor and eased the prosperous, denied educational opportunity to the lower class, the blacks, and created a type of caste system that kept blacks at the base of the social pyramid. These measures, designed to retain a low-cost black labour force, burdened the available land with too many people and increased rural unemployment. Crown colony and upper-class rule created the urban slums.

To test the validity of this statement we turn to a comprehensive study of Kingston, Colin Clarke's *Kingston, Urban Change and Reform*, which covers the period 1692-1962. Clarke's findings reveal that during the week ending 12 December 1942 one-fifth (21 per cent) of black wage-earners in Jamaica were unemployed. Underlying and reflecting this poverty was their poor educational level. A large number of the black population of Kingston and St Andrew was illiterate. The black:

> was caught in a vicious circle in buying a secondary education for his children and keeping them at school for regular intervals . . . In 1943 fewer than 2.5 percent of the blacks in Kingston had received or were receiving secondary education . . . coloured men had achieved much greater success than blacks in obtaining white collar jobs in the civil service and the professions and in acquiring artisan and technical skills. (Clarke: 1962)

The figures for the island showed that almost 60 per cent of black wage-earners earned less than ten shillings per week, and the greater part of the population in Kingston remained desperately poor.

The link with educational opportunity was clear. "The social system was largely regulated by the educational institutions of the colony.

Consequently, the financially well-entrenched white minority could easily dominate the social and economic scene, while insisting that a free society existed without a legal basis for racial discrimination." (Clarke: 1962)

Clarke found that the burden of the caste system fell heavily on the blacks in the period 1820-1943. By the end of the nineteenth century some were filling minor posts in public departments and others were qualifying as physicians, solicitors, barristers, teachers, journalists and nurses, but the greater proportion in Kingston were employed in semi-skilled trades, in unskilled labouring jobs or in domestic service: "Although the white bias of the society and inferiority complex of the Negro were inherited from slavery both features became a continuing part of the social system in Kingston." The statistics show that in the 1930s unemployment had become characteristic of the labour situation. This critical condition was aggravated by an educational system that barred the way to vertical mobility and neglected even those areas for which it was supposed to fit the people: craftsmanship and the mechanical trades.

The Europeans defended colonial rule as being the trusteeship of an inferior race by a superior one, and it maintained that black poverty was proof of that inferiority. Their doctrine manifested itself in Eurocentricity, which so distorted their vision of mankind that they saw all other races and cultures as inferior. Isaiah Berlin, for example, points out that in the nineteenth and twentieth centuries even the most imaginative and radical political thinkers saw Asians and Africans almost exclusively in terms of their treatment by Europeans.

> Imperialists, benevolent paternalists, liberals, socialists discussed the people of Africa and Asia either as wards or as victims of Europeans, but seldom, if ever, in their own right, as people with histories and cultures of their own; with a past and present and future which must be understood in terms of their own actual character and circumstances, even if the existence of such indigenous cultures is acknowledged . . . it tends to be largely ignored. (Berlin: 1981)

In consequence, as late as the 1930s upper- and middle-class Jamaicans, white, coloured and black, having been educated in schools which nurtured Eurocentricity, were Jamaican by residence, British in attitudes and values and very British in their contempt for Africans and other African-Jamaicans. Eurocentricity was pathological, a first phase of that racial and national fanaticism called Fascism, that made Benito Mussolini invade Ethiopia and under the evil name of Nazism drove Adolf Hitler to exterminate some 6 million Jews and to plunge the world into a war that wiped out some 50 million men, women and children worldwide. Religious, racial and national fanaticisms, through holy wars, the slave trade, genocide, the holocaust and the Second World War were the great scourges of mankind and remain the most shameful chapters in the history of the world.

Racial and colour discrimination created the two Jamaicas described by Richard Sheridan as well as by M. G. Smith and Madeleine Kerr, from whom we quote below. Their message is as relevant for independent Jamaica as it was for Jamaica the colony.

Smith described the traditional cultural differences between the upper and middle strata of Jamaican society and the lowest stratum. He stressed that the moral axioms and values of the upper and middle strata were very different from those of the lower class: "Materialism provides the formative principle or reference point in the value system of the intermediate section, spiritual as well as secular values reflecting these principles." (Smith: 1974)

Kerr, as a social psychologist, was more concerned with ways in which social values and structures inhibited development. Her conclusion was that in the Jamaican society of the 1940s it was extremely difficult (indeed virtually impossible) for a Jamaican to move upwards from the lowest stratum. The value systems and class structure hindered acculturation.

> The fact that people are trying to adjust to a pattern which in itself is an economic impossibility, the fact that children are brought up to adjust to a family situation in which the mother is basically the most important person yet the father has to be respected as if he were; the fact that a coloured man knows that he will have more difficulty than his white neighbour in reaching posts of responsibility; the fact that whiteness was identified with 'good' and 'desirable' and 'black' with 'bad' and 'undesirable'; the fact that the majority of people know that it is unlikely that they will spend their lives at anything more than subsistence level, all these cause the most far-reaching psychological reactions. (Kerr: 1963)

Fifty years have passed since Kerr's work and her findings show that great progress has been made in changing the image of "blackness" as well as in transferring political and economic power from Europeans to Jamaicans. But as long as the landscape reflects two deeply divided societies, as long as it remains true that the value systems and educational system hinder acculturation, so long will the findings of Smith and Kerr deserve study. Indeed, the rise of a counter culture based on drugs and on murder as a purchaseable commodity makes some of their findings more relevant now than they were in the 1940s.

We turn at this point from the social scientists and enter the shanty town world of the 1930s and 1940s. Two remarkable street singers of the

1930s, Slim and Sam, are our guides. They respond with deep understanding and sympathy, with a defiant wry humour and self-mockery, to the grim challenges of desperate urban poverty, chronic unemployment, colour discrimination and political disenfranchisement.

Keeping company with Slim and Sam, we enter a vigorous, violent world, bawdy, full of "ginnals", of the young scuffling for a meal, a place of rascality and heroism, of cruelty and tenderness. All the characters in folklore, the Anansi stories, proverbs, the folk vocabulary, flourished in the merciless sunshine of West Kingston, among them the "cubbitch" man, Mr Cramouchin, deceitful and sly, who brought hard times to all.

Slim and Sam

> Annotto can't sell, the price is unfair
> Pimento a blossom an' drop
> Hard time, hard time
> Hard time a carry the day.
> For they won't put Cramouchin away.

Close beside him walked Mr Geechy, the stingy man with the "tight han", domineering "trong-eye Joe" and the "boasify" lady who "shake up dem hip". The vices were greed, selfishness, covetousness, stinginess, while the fault-finding "fenky-fenky" customer and the clumsy, stupid "buffootoo boy" were objects of derision. The dramatic characters of the great markets of West Africa moved besides these, the formidable women traders who show "dat dem no peaw-peaw, dat what dem say is law; the trickify Anansi-man or sam-fie man and the boisterous 'trong-mout' male trader selling livestock and jackass rope".

Through this raucous, clamorous world moved the folk-singers poking fun at the returned immigrant from Panama.

> Colon man dah come.
> And de brass chain dah lick him belly
> Bam bam bam, . . .
> You ask him for de time an' him
> look upon de sun;

Hard times brought laments from the market traders.

> Carry me ackee go a Linstead Market,
> Not a quattie wut sell
> Everybody come feel up, feel up
> Not a quattie wut sell

The two ballad singers, tall, "mauger" Slim who sang first voice and short, stout guitarist Sam, told in one of their favorite songs how:

> Up Constant Spring road dis time
> Right a number one-sixty-nine
> A gang a coolie duppy combine
> Fi stone Isaac
> Run Isaac, run fi you life
> Run Isaac, run wid you wife
> You gi de duppy dem food an ting
> Di more you give dem di more dem sing
> Di more you give dem di more dem sing,
> So tek you body from Constant Spring
> An' run Isaac

Slim and Sam sang of "duppy power" in a world in which every night peopled the countryside with duppies, rolling calves and a headless woman carrying a baby on her right shoulder and every day brought unemployment.

> A went to Sandy Gully fe go get a bite
> Dem set dung me name and a feel alright
> De very day a start to work di man dem strike . . .
> If I had a gun a would a hang myself,
> If I could a swim I would a shoot myself,
> If a had a rope a would a drown myself,
> Waai.

Though Slim and Sam could lighten the passing hour, they could not banish the reality that Sam Brown portrayed, the brutalising experience of ghetto life for all who endured it.

> Tin can houses, old and young, meangy
> dogs, rats, inhuman stench,
> Unthinkable conditions that cause the
> stoutest heart to wrench
> Tracks and little lanes like human
> veins, emancipated people . . .

Slim and Sam's self-mockery and Sam Brown's anger were protests against the enfeebling impotence of the poor, their paralysing powerlessness, their helplessness. But saddest of all was the general blindness of the rich and powerful to the condition of both urban and rural poor. It was little wonder that the Royal Commission commented that the general insanitary environment gave rise to malaria, worm infestation and bowel disease, tuberculosis and other diseases. It also went beyond a listing of diseases brought on by insanitary conditions and condemned the levels of the health services and of the housing of the people as grossly inadequate, the status of women as wholly unsatisfactory, and declared that the children were the most exploited of all West Indian people. The Commission spoke in scathing terms of British colonial society. It regretted the absence of those factors and traditions which elsewhere make for social cohesiveness and a sense of membership of a community. "The whole West Indies are practically devoid of all the multifarious institutions, official and unofficial, which characterize British public life and bring a very large proportion of the population into some living contact with the problems of social importance." (West Indies Royal Commission [1938-39]: 1945)

The Commission was looking at the product of very nearly three centuries of British rule. During that period the moulding forces had been utterly divisive and the upper classes had established a tradition of social irresponsibility. Their policies had created the slums and their racial prejudices had blinded them to the needs of all but themselves. Their Eurocentricity had hindered the growth of anything like a sentiment of national unity, for "the European mind failed to apply the idea of equality – so much at the centre of European liberalism – to the subject Caribbean peoples. There is hardly a single outstanding mind in the history of that liberalism which felt able to accept the Negro as the equal of the white person." (Lewis: 1968)

Had the Royal Commission known where to look they would have found the network of associations for which they were searching in the lowest stratum of the society in the neglected black rural communities clustered around church and school. There they would have found the folk organisations, the friendly societies, the lodges and burial scheme societies, the leaders' meetings, class meetings, prayer meetings, the informal labour-sharing morning diggings, the day-for-day groups, the informal saving unions known as "susu" and "partner", the folk-leaders and counsellors that included parson, teacher, village druggist, Aunt Eliza, Tata Joe, Busha Tom, Cousin Mattie, key figures in islandwide networks for counselling, guidance, comfort, father-figures, mother-figures for the people and their children.

Looking back across the post-emancipation century, 1830-1929, we see that, inspired by the churches, by their parsons and teachers, the African-Jamaican labouring folk created the social and economic linkages and associations that encouraged social cohesion and built a tradition of social responsibility, of caring, of brotherhood and sisterhood. Here were to be found a unique blending of Christian and West African religious concepts, a sense of family as involving also kinsfolk and community, of authority as being rooted in morality and not in the use of force, of religion permeating all the departments of life, of human beings as living in a religious universe in which natural phenomena are associated with God. The formative principle was religious, not political; and it was religion in the form of Christianity, with its central message of love. To Eurocentricity and the assertion of authority through violence, the common people offered the alternative of caring and of fellowship.

Whoever knew that impoverished rural community in the late 1920s cannot forget the common pot of the tenement yard shared with migrants from other villages. Or who, brought up in a country district, can forget the sight of four men carrying on their shoulders a homemade stretcher with two bamboo trees as the two poles, and on the stretcher a woman or child, setting out on ten miles of unpaved country road from Glengoffe to the hospital at Linstead. Listening to them and their accompanying friends singing "Abide with me, fast falls the eventide" and "Jesu, Lover of My Soul", or listening to Bedward's shepherds and shepherdesses singing of Zion on their way to the healing waters of the Hope River, was to understand the reality of religion to the Jamaican folk. The churches, the parsons and the teachers, by implanting the Christian message of love, reinforced the memories of African tribal life with its tradition of social responsibility.

"The African influence is strongest in Revival, which is more than 200 years old and includes two traditions, Revival Zion and Pukumina. Women play a leading part as members, healers, preachers. In religion there is a deep tradition of women serving as healers . . . in our religious tradition women serve in virtually all capacities, evangelists, missionaries, deacons, ushers, secretaries. If women as a group were to withdraw their membership all churches would cease to function as viable social entities . . . Women play a major role in the maintenance of values shaped by religion." (Chevannes: 1995)

Chevannes refers to a very significant feature of Revival, which is that there is no dichotomy between this world and the next.

> Among the European religions the next life is seen as that world where everything that is not right will be rectified . . . However, in the Jamaican tradition God's justice, His regard and love are made manifest in this life. Such beliefs make religion a potent force in the drive of the people for self-improvement and upward mobility. As the leading social force in religion women are therefore the leading force in self-improvement.

The women African- and Euro-Jamaicans leaders pioneered the way for the women's movement that developed in the 1930s and 1940s. The demographic setting is provided by George Roberts. His analysis reveals the distance the women had travelled from the immediate post-emancipation period when 80 per cent of all gainfully occupied women were in agriculture. This proportion declined slowly, standing at 64 per cent in 1921 and 47 per cent in 1943: "It is the large scale withdrawal of females after 1921 that has in the main resulted in the great reduction in the numbers of persons engaged in agriculture." (Roberts: 1957) Between 1921 and 1943 the number of females in agriculture declined from 125,400 to 45,600. Roberts points out that changing definitions of employment may explain some of the reduction but that this diminishing dependence of females on agriculture as work in this period appeared also in other West Indian populations. This reduction in female employment marked a break with slave society in which "every adult was potentially a work unit". Another important feature was the growth in the proportion of women in domestic service, but most significant of all was the increase in the number of women in commercial occupations. This grew from 2,800 in 1891 to 51,200 in 1943, the increase "being consistent with diversification of enterprises, growth of service occupations attendant on enhanced urbanization and improving standards of living". (Roberts: 1957)

The increase in the number of women in domestic service in the urban area was itself a sign of trouble, being an indication, as Arthur Lewis has pointed out, that there were more women competing for a limited number of jobs. And urbanisation did not screen poverty behind the picturesque. It stripped away the easy phrases about a "happy smiling people". It showed poverty and joblessnes for what they were, stark and ugly, and by the 1930s some educated middle- and upper-class Jamaicans began to respond to what they saw.

That fact was in itself significant, for there were no mother-figures, no female symbols of compassion in plantation great house society. These were to be found among the African-Jamaican labour force, among the slave nurses, the higglers and traders and common-law wives. Plantation society marginalised and degraded all its women, black, white and coloured.

For this reason it was especially significant that in this period in response to the evidence of increasing unemployment among women and widespread suffering amongst children, a redoubtable group of concerned women leaders emerged. Some had come into prominence as members of the Jamaica Union of Teachers, others as public-spirited upper-class citizens, yet others as writers, feminists, champions of the rights of children. They included Mary Morris Knibb, Amy Bailey, May Farquharson (Miss Amy and Miss May), Edith Dalton James, Ethlyn

Rhodd, Marjory Stewart, Edris Allan (later Lady Allan), Lilly Mae Burke, Gladys Longbridge (later Lady Bustamante), Una Marson and Carmen Lusan. These were among the women pioneers who led the way in establishing a tradition of social concern. By reaching out beyond the dividing lines of colour, race and class they charted a worthy and indispensable role for women in Jamaican society. The women leaders of the 1920s and 1930s, black, brown, white, African-Jamaicans and Euro-Jamaicans, set about putting an end to the marginalisation of women in Jamaican society. These women understood that it was their task to invest womanhood with its proper meaning and dignity.

Another indicator of increasing concern for the welfare and advancement of the African-Jamaican people was the founding in 1936 of the Jamaica Welfare Ltd. Arising out of a discussion between Norman Manley and the president of the United Fruit Company, Samuel Zemurray, the company established a fund to be used for the welfare of the people of Jamaica, with emphasis on the rural people. Manley was to form a competent board and report annually. The board was free to plan as it thought best. Zemurray was of Armenian peasant stock. He had begun his working life peddling bananas on the New Orleans wharves. It may be that he was struck by Manley's account of the plight of the Jamaican peasantry. The funds provided by the company were used to finance the work of Jamaica Welfare Ltd, Jamaica's first community development non-government organisation, founded in 1936. An account of the work is given in *Working Together for Development,* edited by Norman Girvan, which documents Jamaica's rich experience in grass-roots development from the late 1930s to the 1960s. The book represents a major contribution to the social history of Jamaica. The philosophic concept that governed the work of Jamaica Welfare was that development is a process which begins with "the unfolding of what is in the germ" (dictionary defintion), and leads to the release of the creative potential in an individual, a community, a nation.

Within ten years of its foundation, Jamaica Welfare had become a model for developing countries in Africa and Latin America. In that period international agencies began recruiting from it as consultants and as officers leaders such as Thom Girvan, Eddie Burke, Arthur Carney, Chester Dowdy, Marjory Stewart and Sybil Francis.

The three guiding principles were: to enable people to make the best use of the opportunities that exist or that they can create, for betterment; the creation of a dynamic for action by inspiring desire, hope, self-confidence; and to keep the action moving by a combination of planned activities leading to the constant regeneration of energy at the start. These tasks can only be carried out through education, "not the education of books but education related to living problems and derived from the action taken to solve them." (Manley: 1971)

The affirmation of racial identity, the emergence of women as advocates of social responsibility and the formulation of a Jamaican theory of social development based on an analysis of the historical experience of the people and their needs, signified a rejection of colonial dependence and a movement towards self-government.

Central to the process was the liberating force of a discovery of personal and racial identity. This force manifested itself in political, economic and cultural developments. The change began within the Jamaican society a decade or more before the British Government announced its policy of self-government and colonial development. A Jamaican theory of social development and its methodology influenced British colonial development and welfare policy in the 1940s.

CHAPTER 28

The founders of the nation:
Marcus Garvey, Alexander Bustamante,
Norman Manley

The founders of the Jamaican nation are Marcus Garvey, Alexander Bustamante and Norman Manley. They belong to the same period in history, were country-bred, lower-middle class and working class. Marcus Garvey was black, Manley and Bustamante were coloured. Each was a leader in his own right, and each contributed in his own unique way to the creation of the Jamaican nation. Their vision of the Jamaican people still shapes our way of life. The work of each is incomplete when isolated from the work of the other two. Though Garvey was senior, the three belong together, not as a team, but each as a leader of heroic quality, whose special contribution expressed his deepest convictions.

Garvey's liberating call to African-Jamaicans was to an affirmation of racial identity, to racial pride, self-worth and to claiming their African heritage. History has vindicated him. He broke new ground by founding a political party to contest the Jamaica election of 1930 and by publishing a political programme. His election message was not forgotten: "My opponents say I am against white and fair-skinned people. This is not so. I am against the class system here which keeps the poor man down, and the poor mostly black people. It is only natural therefore that their interest should be nearest and dearest to my heart . . . Let us all work together as fellow-Jamaicans and ring in the changes for a new Jamaica."

To the liberating force of Garvey's insistence on racial consciousness and on an African identity Manley added the empowering force of a feeling of national unity. He declared:

No amount of economic good will make our people a real unity. All efforts will be wasted unless the masses of the people are steadily taken along the path in which they will feel more and more that this place is their home, that it is their destiny . . . (Manley: 1971)

Manley's work was made possible by Garvey, who gave to blackness a new dynamic personality, animated the great majority of the people with hope and confidence, kindled their interest in changing their condition through organised political activity, insisted on self-help and intellectual effort as a foundation for progress, and pointed the Jamaican away from his isolation to a larger brotherhood that linked Africa and the Americas. Paying tribute to him ten years after his death, the editor of *The Daily Gleaner* wrote: "It would be true to say of Jamaica, and to a lesser extent of the other British West Indies, that national consciousness received its main stimulus from the movement associated with the still revered Marcus Garvey." Manley spoke to many whose ears had been unstopped by Garvey, whose eyes had been opened by him, whose faith in their future and in their country had been kindled by him.

To these liberating messages Alexander Bustamante added a direct and powerful call to the great mass of the African-Jamaican people, for a better life here in a country where they were the majority, but from whose society they had been excluded. The three messages covered the primary requirements for transforming the colony, Jamaica, into both nation and homeland. To ideology Bustamante added a visual image of compassion, of shepherd and provider, qualities that John Dunkley, the first leading intuitive painter of modern Jamaica, portrayed in one of his best-known paintings. Bustamante contributed to the ideologies of racial and of

The Shepherd by John Dunkley

national consciousness the compassionate feeling of a leader for his people. Jamaica was singularly fortunate in its founding fathers, each one speaking in his own way with a prophetic assurance and authority, as when Garvey, receiving news of his defeat at the polls in 1930, declared, "The voters (not the people) have turned back the clock of progress for another ten years, but party system is well established in your minds and it will come, it is bound to come." (Edwards: 1962)

A Caribbean-wide revolution entered into an explosive phase in 1933, when Fulgencio Batista and the Cuban army drove the dictator Machado from Cuba. There followed strikes and disorders in Puerto Rico's sugar-belt. In 1935 sugar workers in

Courtesy Wallace Campbell Collection

St Kitts led by Robert Bradshaw struck for higher wages. Disorder broke out and some of the strikers were killed. In the same year workers in British Guiana rioted and set fire to canefields. Tension mounted in St Vincent where a workingmen's association was formed to demand land and a new constitution. In St Lucia coal carriers went on strike. Also in 1935 a fiery Grenadian, Uriah "Buzz" Butler, led a march of unemployed into Port-of-Spain, formed a militant Workers' Home Rule Party and, in 1937, called a strike in the oil-fields. Two oil wells were set ablaze. Two of a party of policemen were killed when they attempted to arrest Butler. In Barbados a follower of Butler's from Trinidad, Clement Payne, attracted large crowds with his attacks on the government and his demand for trade unions. A showdown followed. The governor ordered that Payne be deported. He was taken before the court, tried and ordered to be deported, but a young Barbadian lawyer, Grantley Adams, won an appeal against the verdict. He was deported, nevertheless. The people rioted. Fourteen were killed and 59 wounded.

In Jamaica Alexander Bustamante and A. G. S. Coombs formed the Jamaica Workers' and Tradesmen's Union in 1934 and started holding mass meetings protesting against low wages and working-class poverty. Crowds gathered in the streets demanding work. Bustamante and Coombs led marches. From time-to-time the police broke up crowds of unemployed, and Jamaica learned something about the destabilising power of an angry unemployed proletariat.

Bustamante, originally Alexander Clarke, was born in Hanover on 24 February 1884. He left the island when he was about 20, returned in 1934 at the age of 50 and settled in Kingston. Tall, thin, with a striking face and a great shock of hair, dramatic in speech and appearance, Bustamante took the centre of the stage wherever he went. He was greatly disturbed at the poverty in Kingston, the ineffectiveness of the Legislative Council and the lack of concern amongst the employers. He wrote trenchant letters to *The Daily Gleaner* and, always a man of action, led street marches and protest demonstrations. To *The Daily Gleaner's* criticism of the demonstrations he replied, "Hungry men and women and children have a right to call attention to their condition and to ask of people fulfilment of promises made to them so long as they do so without using violence." To someone asking in the columns of *The Daily Gleaner*, "Who is Bustamante?" he replied, "Bustamante is a lonely fighter." Thus he stamped his image on the minds of the people. He conjured up vivid pictures, for example, the prospect of having the supine Legislative Council in power for another three years was like having an elephant on its back with its trunk full of water; or, in Jamaica the rich man had his stomach growing out day after day until it ripened while the stomachs of the poor were shrunken like loofahs.

Unemployment was widespread among the rural folk in these years, but a glimmer of hope came with the building of a large sugar factory at Frome in Westmoreland, where the West Indies Sugar Company (WISCO) had acquired control of 30,000 acres of fertile land. The British firm of Tate and Lyle, which had a controlling interest in WISCO, also owned the island's other major sugar producing complex, Monymusk in Vere.

Reports of high wages attracted thousands of unemployed to Frome. Their presence aggravated an already tense situation caused by wage deductions and inefficiencies in the pay office. On 1 May 1938 the workers struck, police were rushed in, rioting broke out, four people were shot by the police, some 15 were wounded and 105 were arrested for rioting. Three weeks later violence broke out in Kingston; on 21 May dock workers went on strike and the mob brought Kingston to a standstill.

On 23 May, Manley, the island's most brilliant lawyer, was in Savanna-la-Mar, attending an official inquiry into the Frome riots, when news reached him of rioting in Kingston. He hurried back to the city that afternoon. Kingston was strangely still.

> Everywhere was shut up. The crowds had seen to that, and soldiers moved around, passing at street corners knots of silent, sullen people waiting in an ugly frame of mind. I did not at all like what I saw . . . I heard that there was trouble at the fire brigade headquarters . . . He and his faithful friend of those days, St. William Grant, had been arrested . . . When I heard that they were to strike that afternoon and that Bustamante had gone there to address them. I went home deeply persuaded by all I saw and feared that with Bustamante arrested and all workers in the Corporate Area [city] on strike we were in for a serious time and that violence, disorder and bloodshed would be the final result. (Edwards: 1967)

That evening and far into the night Manley and his wife Edna, confronted with this grim tangle of despair, discussed the situation.

The following morning he told the governor of his intention to put aside his legal work for the time being and offer his assistance to any group

of workers who had grievances and wished him to negotiate on their behalf. The governor welcomed his intervention. William Seivright, who later became mayor of Kingston, offered his support. A group of women workers sought his help. Then, later in the day, a critical meeting took place. A delegation from the waterfront called on him.

> The men knew exactly what they wanted both as to straight time work and as to overtime. They had a straight position for which they were fighting and had been offered very little on their demand. But over and above all that, there was an intervening problem. They insisted that they had struck without any advice from Bustamante. As they explained, he had intervened on their behalf and told them what the employers were prepared to do but had been careful to say that he was not advising them to strike . . . they were certain that Bustamante had been arrested because they had struck and they told me that they had no intention of going back to work unless Bustamante was released from jail. (Manley: 1938)

The governor then appointed a conciliation committee, accepting Manley's advice about members. The shippers agreed to grant the demand of the wharf workers for increased day pay but would not budge on night time. Eventually, under pressure from the conciliation committee, the shipping association agreed to all Manley's terms, thinking these would eliminate the demand for Bustamante's release. The stand Manley took determined the course of events and made this a point of confluence of the workers' protests with the anti-colonial movement.

Courtesy of Kingston Publishers

Alexander
Bustamante
makes a final
address before
leading the
historic protest
march

They expected me to agree with their view. I did not. I told them
bluntly that I would not be responsible for what happened to the
Corporate Area if the week-end passed and Bustamante was still in
jail. There were, I said, active plans to start a graver level of trouble.
True, I said, the fire brigade issue had been settled by me but there
were plans to start on Sunday a scale and range of fires that would
leave the brigade helpless . . . I spoke strongly. I had it in mind that
only pressure from the committee could make the Governor change
his mind. I did not advise them . . . The move had to come from
within the body itself. (Manley: 1938)

The mayor of Kingston, Dr Oswald Anderson, made an emotional
appeal to the committee to save the city of Kingston, which urged the
governor to release Bustamante. The governor agreed. Bustamante and St
William Grant were released on bail.

In the weeks that followed the island was rent apart by widespread
turmoil and labour unrest. Bustamante and Manley travelled throughout
the country urging calm and promising their support. By the time quiet
was restored, eight lives had been lost, 32 people had been wounded and
another 139 injured, and some 400 imprisoned for rioting. There followed
the Orde Brown Inquiry into labour conditions and the appointment of
the West India Royal Commission with Lord Moyne as chairman.
Bustamante and Manley were now recognised as national leaders committed to building a new modern Jamaica. Bustamante forged ahead with
developing the Bustamante Industrial Trade Union while Manley

announced at the end of May 1938 that he had accepted the invitation of a delegation led by O. T. Fairclough to form a national political party. The immediate aim was to set about organising a party committed to self-government.

Alexander Bustamante was among those present at the historic meeting of 1938. He was by then the acknowledged leader of the Jamaican working class, their leader in the way that Garvey had been in the late 1920s. He politicised the great mass of the people and through the Bustamante Industrial Trade Union organised them into a formidable force which soon won the respect of employers and of the public. So by 1940, through the leadership of these two men, organised labour and a political party had become powerful realities.

Manley's words at the launching of the People's National Party in 1938 indicate the strength that the national movement had gathered during the 1930s: "Anyone looking at the past ten years will realise that we in this country have been more and more concentrating upon our own affairs. We have thought more of Jamaica, spoken more about Jamaica, breathed more of the atmosphere of Jamaica than ever before." He spoke of the dawn of the feeling among Jamaicans that Jamaica should be their country. "There is a tremendous difference between living in a place and belonging to it and feeling that your own life and your destiny is irrevocably bound up in the life and destiny of that place. Radical change was under way."

These events were overtaken by the Second World War which began in 1939. When the war ended, only the United States, whose money and industries had through land-lease, sustained and augmented the war economies of her allies, seemed the immediate and real victor. Anti-Semitism and the doctrine of a superior Aryan race had been rejected.

The British Government understood this. They saw that the concepts of empire and of the trusteeship of a superior race were dead. They knew that in the war young West Indians were flying and dying with their own pilots, that West Indians were serving in France and were with Field-Marshal Montgomery at El Alamein; that black and coloured West Indians were working in the munitions factories in the Midlands. A new spirit of understanding replaced the old colonial relationship. Jamaicans recall that even when the Battle of Britain was at its fiercest, Britain met the Jamaican representation for the introduction of universal adult suffrage, and granted self-government by reforming the constitution in 1944. It went further and signalled the end of the colonial policy of economic exploitation by adopting a policy of colonial development and welfare, by setting up a colonial development fund of £10 million in 1942, when the country was virtually bankrupt, and by doubling that amount in 1945 to £20 million.

But it remains a question whether the demand for self-government having been met, the period of tutelage need have been spread over as long a period as 18 years. What was granted was diluted self-government in doses graduated to suit the imperial interests. This was further evidence of the extent to which the colonial system of education bred a lack of self-confidence among blacks in their own ability to manage their affairs and confirmed among whites the sense of superiority in their dealings with colonial peoples. This persistence of a colonial mentality explains why Garvey continually appealed to history and pressed for a system of education that included higher education. Many of those who had the vote opposed the demand for universal adult suffrage, and proposed instead the introduction of a literacy test.

The central issue went beyond administrative efficiency to the restructuring of Jamaican society and the full liberation, through education and knowledge, of the Jamaican working class. Garvey foresaw that.

It is for this reason that in the closing paragraphs of this chapter we now return to Marcus Garvey, to Africa and to the African heritage, and to Garvey's insistence on blacks of every class having the opportunity to develop to the full their intellectual ability. Culture, self-liberation and self-discipline were essential parts of his message.

In the 1920s when the revolution began, the black Jamaican man, heavily burdened with a tradition of discrimination and trapped in a society still dominated by the white-based values of the sugar-plantation system, stood in need of a vision and a voice. So did the black man of the United States, who began to discover after the First World War that the American dream was not dreamed for him, that the American promise had not been made for him. So also did the black man of the European colonies of Africa, who was beginning to perceive that the right of self-determination, the great slogan of that war, did not apply to him.

The African-Jamaican, in common with blacks throughout the world was in desperate need of a voice and a vision. Marcus Garvey became the voice and, like a prophet, communicated the vision. He generated within blacks the will to free themselves and to fit themselves, intellectually and through self-discipline, to play a part in history that would earn respect for Africa, their own people and for Jamaica, the land of their birth, their homeland.

CHAPTER 29

From colony to nation:
Political progress and economic growth

For more than three centuries we have travelled with the African-Jamaican people as they struggled towards freedom. Only occasionally did we come to gentler country and green pastures; always mountains lay ahead and there were rivers to cross. For the first time, however, in 1944, all the Jamaican people became involved in making the decisions, setting the directions and implementing them.

With the granting of a new constitution on 20 November 1944 the Jamaican people took the first steps towards independence. They had always chosen the difficult road no matter where it led, to Accompong and the Land of Look Behind, to Nanny Town and to the mountains in St Thomas that looked down on Paul Bogle's chapel. The coastal plains were still backra's property.

Jamaica's first general election took place on 14 December 1944, soon after the granting of the new constitution. The People's National Party (PNP) and the more recently formed Jamaica Labour Party (JLP) contested it. Alexander Bustamante had broken with the PNP in 1942 and founded the JLP in 1943. In Norman Manley's words:

> There came the time when Sir Alexander made what history may come to regard as his greatest contribution to democracy in Jamaica, and this was the formation and creation – for it really was an act of creation – of the Jamaica Labour Party which led to the establishment of the two-party system in Jamaica . . . It is said that when God was creating the world, God said "Let there be light" and there was light. And when Sir Alexander was creating the Jamaica Labour Party, Sir Alexander said 'Let there be a Jamaica Labour Party', and there was a Jamaica Labour Party. (Nettleford: 1971)

Time has confirmed Norman Manley's judgment that by creating a second party this man, his cousin, "Originally by nature and temperament autocratic, who had very strong and firm opinions of his own, was able to grow in a democratic world and to contribute to it because he was able to face the fact that, having said, 'Let there be a party' and there was a party, it had to become an organised body." (Nettleford: 1971)

The JLP swept the board with 25 elected members as against the PNP's five and two independents. Norman Manley lost to a relatively unknown Dr Edward Fagan, so strong was Busta's gravitational pull. Manley took defeat like the democrat that he was. When the news reached him in the Half Way Tree Court House that he had lost to Dr Fagan, he said, "Vox Populi, Vox Dei, the people have spoken. Moses never saw the promised land." With the assistance of Ivan Lloyd of St Ann, who led the opposition in the House, he built the PNP into a formidable opposition party. He gained his seat in the second general election which took place in 1949.

Before carrying our story any further, we turn to the people themselves. "I cast my vote at a polling station in one of the poorer suburbs of Kingston. As clearly as though it were yesterday and not more than half a century ago, I saw a friend, old Ebenezer Brown, a small cultivator, coming towards me, his black wrinkled face gleaming with pride and happiness. He greeted me by holding out the forefinger of his right hand which had been dipped in a scarlet dye to show that he had voted. 'I feel big,' he said, 'and now all we is one.'"

Africa remains at the centre of our story. Ebenezer Brown, as deep-rooted in the Jamaican soil, as tough and gnarled as the lignum vitae tree that sheltered his yard, symbolised the majority of the Jamaican people, all of them laden with buried memories of the terrible plantation years and of tribal relationships, of the presence of the ancestors, of a hierarchy of rulers whose business it was to protect and be the fathers of the people. The ancestral sense of self-worth and tribal fellowship had been grievously damaged by the psychosocial controls of the sugar-and-slave plantation but, by exercising the right to vote, Ebenezer had affirmed his personal worth and his membership of the Jamaican community. How would he fare during the crowded years that led to independence?

We will continue our journey with Jamaicans like old Ebenezer during these tumultuous years of early nationhood in our attempt to join him in his inner world. Pandit Nehru of India used to explode at nonsense about the idealisation of the simple peasant life. "I have almost a horror of it . . . what is there in the man with the hoe to idealise over? Crushed and exploited for innumerable generations, he is only little removed from the animals that keep him company."

Nehru was attacking the class view of the peasant. So as to keep close to the people, we interweave events with reflection, chronology with leaps from one generation to another, believing with historians such as John Plum and Simon Schama that history should be synthesis as well as analysis, chronicle as well as text; and having learned also that throughout our history the enslaving forces have come from those in power and liberation from the peasantry.

Nor is the phrase "laden with Africa" used lightly. Africa lived on in religious concepts, traditional codes about family relationships, kinsfolk, family spirits, ethical values, modes of expression, physical gestures, and it lived on also in deep-buried memories, frustrations and anger carried over from two centuries of plantation life into our own time.

Society, as in plantation times, fell into three classes, differentiated by race, colour, education and means. The upper class of whites with a discreet sprinkling of light browns, and a middle class of propertied browns, on the basis of a limited franchise, exercised a political monopoly and buttressed the governor who, as the Crown's representative, ruled the colony. The lower class, predominantly black and dark brown, mostly illiterate or with some elementary schooling, formed an exploited, controlled labour force, underpaid, despised, whose only means of change lay in occasional outbursts of violence.

In the period 1938-62, Jamaica moved from the colonial condition to full and sovereign nationhood. Unemployed peasants, by riots at Frome, the unemployed proletariat by islandwide disorders expressed through a group of nationalists drawn from the middle and lower classes, and a group of disaffected trade unionists, set the forces of radical change in motion. At the same time a combination of educated, politically motivated, African-Jamaicans, black and brown, by organised political action ensured that the violent protests of 1938 would be translated into political progress and economic growth. We watch in these often tumultuous years a transfer of political power from a predominantly white-brown minority to a predominantly black majority and we watch also with growing excitement and wonder the release of an astonishing and unexpected creativity that commanded international attention and respect.

In this chapter we tell the story of that release of creative energy in the fashioning of a constitution that began as a tepid Colonial Office version of "embryo ministers", then advanced to full internal self-government and finally to sovereignty as a nation in 1962. In the same period we move from a rejection of a Colonial Office economic dominance in 1944 to the development of a diversified and vastly more productive economy.

The first phase of the movement towards self-government and independence included the launching of the PNP in 1938, the PNP's campaign for universal adult suffrage and self-government, Alexander Bustamante's founding of the Bustamante Industrial Trade Union (1943) and then of the JLP. In this first phase Bustamante concentrated on organising labour as a political force. He was not yet convinced of the need for self-government.

The start was difficult. It took the constant pressure of Norman Manley and the PNP to keep universal adult suffrage and self-government on the Colonial Office agenda. They did this with the support of the Jamaica Progressive League in New York and of Sir Stafford Cripps, Creech Jones and other members of the Fabian Colonial Bureau in Britain. When, following the 1938 riots, the Moyne Commission's proposals were tabled, the Rev. Ethelred Brown of the Jamaica Progressive League in New York found them so unsatisfactory that he exploded, scattering brimstone and ashes upon the governor in Kingston and the Secretary of State in London.

As a result of this increasing pressure from within Jamaica, the United States and Britain, the British Government in 1944 granted a constitution which provided for universal adult suffrage and an elected majority in the legislature. It provided for a legislature made up of an elected House of Representatives and a Legislative Council which included official and unofficial members, and an executive council under the governor as chairman, with three officials, two nominated members who were not officials and five ministers from the House of Representatives. Creech Jones, a leading member of the British Labour Party, regretted that Jamaica would still be answerable to the Colonial Office. This meant, he pointed out, that Jamaicans would not learn the practical work of government.

The first five years (1944-49) were a charade. Ministers had to report on various departments but were not responsible for seeing that action was taken by them. They had no executive responsibilities for the departments. The constitution provided for "partnership" between the governor and official members and the "ministers", but not for a ministerial system. In his presidential address of 1945 to the PNP, Manley emphasised that the greatest defect of the constitution was that in their [the Colonial Office's] efforts to play safe they gave great power but they failed to give a corresponding responsibility. "The house can pass any resolution and nobody can stop them." But in the executive council the governor had the casting vote and so "When it suits him the leader of the majority party comes in the House and says 'I am only half government – in fact I am not government at all . . .' and you can't pin them with any responsibility at all." (Nettleford: 1971)

The two fundamental changes had been made, however: the granting of universal adult suffrage and an elected majority in the legislature. These were great cornerstones for the erection of a democratic system of government. The second phase began with Manley's motion in the legislature, in cooperation with the JLP government, for the introduction of a ministerial system. In 1953 the amended constitution increased the number of House of Representative members in the Executive Council to eight. This gave them a majority over official and nominated members, so that ministers now had the responsibility for carrying out decisions reached in the House. Under the new system Alexander Bustamante became Jamaica's first chief minister. He was succeeded by Norman Manley in 1955, when the PNP won the general election for the first time.

Constitutionally, the next advance in self-government came in 1957 when the Executive Council, over which the governor presided, gave way to a Cabinet, at that time called the Council of Ministers, over which the chief minister presided. The Council was made up of eight members from the House of Representatives and two or three from the Legislative Council, these being appointed by the governor on the nomination of the chief minister. Officials were no longer members of the government.

In 1958 Jamaica became an independent country in all internal matters, with only bills relating to defence and international affairs being reserved for the Queen. The governor's veto powers were retained but could be exercised only on the advice of the Cabinet. A Minister of Home Affairs took over matters formerly dealt with by the Colonial Secretary and, in some measure, by the Attorney-General.

Throughout their history the black majority had learned to judge the upper- and middle-class people by their actions and conduct, not by their words. Reports of constitutional change became reality only when they saw that where backra alone had walked, blacks and browns now walked. The people saw social change painted in skin colour, black and brown ministers of government walking through King's House as of right, and receiving the salutes of white soldiers. In 1957 they hailed Florizel Glasspole's educational reforms that gave their children greater access to secondary education. They greeted with affection and acclamation, as their own, a new generation of political leaders, black, brown, white, among them Donald Sangster, Noel Nethersole, Hugh Shearer, Robert Lightbourne and Clifford Campbell. They gained an understanding of democratic principles from the way in which their two leaders behaved, the respect they showed for each other and from the way in which each accepted defeat at the polls, Manley in 1944 and 1961, Bustamante in 1955 and in 1959. From the conduct of these two leaders they learned the underlying principles of two-party government, that differences of opinion did not have to mean hatred and vindictiveness, that Busta could invite a political opponent to have a drink and swinging to the vernacular would say with a laugh, "You is only a damn PNP." Manley for his part could declare to the

Bustamante and Manley, cousins and friendly political rivals

annual conference of the PNP in 1961: "On matters where I am consulting with the Opposition, I think it is right that I should treat them with the greatest respect and discuss no details until I have discussed details with them." (Nettleford: 1971) In 1964 he declared to another annual conference, "I will be no party to inciting people to physical violence as a means of progress in this country." (Nettleford: 1971)

Bustamante and Manley, by example and by words, demonstrated their full acceptance of the two-party system, "in a general way the foundations of their society, so that neither consciously desires or intends or will be forced to destroy the other". Furthermore, he emphasised that the opposition's great role is "to preserve democratic procedures and fundamental human rights; in a word, to protect society from the excesses and corruptions of power that will always be found wherever power finally resides". The central change in the introduction of Crown colony government in 1865 had been that it transferred power from a white minority to the crown; in 1944 there was set in motion the transfer of those powers from the Crown to the whole society in 1962. Manley, in his moving tribute to Busta in 1968, in a characteristic spirit of fair play and with a profound respect for history, said:

Jamaica was fortunate in throwing up among its leaders one man, Sir Alexander, who gave confidence to the masses of this country, who won their affection and love to the most extraordinary degree and their loyalty and who proved afterwards by the whole course of his life that he had accepted the responsibilities of that time, and grown in stature with them as the years passed. And in considering Sir Alexander's rightful claims to the growth of democracy in Jamaica, I think that is the first thing to be said. (Nettleford: 1971)

We see the years 1927-62 as a period when the three great founders of the nation, Garvey, who left Jamaica in 1935, and later Bustamante and Manley, by word and example, taught that:

Democracy means recognition of the rights of others. Democracy means equality of opportunity for all in education, in the public service, and in private employment . . . Democracy means the protection of the weak against the strong.

Democracy means the obligation of the minority to recognise the right of the majority. Democracy means the responsibility of the government to its citizens, the protection of the citizens from the exercise of arbitrary power and the violation of human freedoms and individual rights. Democracy means freedom of worship for all and the subordination of the right of any one race to the overriding right of the human race. Democracy means freedom of expression and assembly of organization. (Williams: 1981)

These words were spoken by another great West Indian nation-builder, Eric Williams, in his Independence Day speech as prime minister of Trinidad and Tobago on 31 August 1962. The Jamaican people, by their voting record, by their support of the trade unions and by their demand for greater educational opportunity, showed that they greatly valued the vote and the two-party system. But they also regarded bread and jobs as basic issues. Crown colony rule had doomed the mass of the people to poverty and unemployment. What change would self-government bring?

That the British government should have taken these two critical decisions at this time deserves special notice, because the Second World War was then at its fiercest. Although poverty and government neglect had caused great distress amongst West Indians and although the demand for self-government was pressed with vigour, the debate was conducted with great respect and consideration on both sides, without racial or class rancour, and certainly without hatred. In the West Indies and in Africa, Britain won both affection and respect from her former colonists in these years of the triumph of the various national movements.

In the 1940s, also, international developments and the general climate of opinion were helpful to countries which, like Jamaica, were moving towards independence. Many of the major institutions of the United Nations, for example, were established at this time: the Food and Agriculture Organisation in Rome in 1945, the International Monetary Fund and the International Bank for Reconstruction and Development in the same year, and UNESCO and the International Labour Organisation in 1946.

Even during the havoc and gloom of the Second World War, green shoots of hope and brightening skies moved mankind to start building again, and to do so with the needs of non-industrialised nations in mind. Even a brief sample list of some of the chief events that took place in the five or six years following the grant of self-government to Jamaica indicates the beginning of a new age: the winding up of the old League of Nations in 1946 and the meeting of the United Nations General Assembly in London and then in New York, which became its permanent headquarters; the establishment of a General Agreement on Tariffs and Trade in Geneva by 23 countries (1947); President Harry Truman of the United States' call for a programme of technical aid to underdeveloped countries (1949); and the production of electricity by atomic energy (1951).

Events such as these strengthened the feeling amongst Jamaicans that they were entering an age of which interconnectedness and interdependence were the chief features. Small islands were no longer remote or wholly on their own. Science and technology, now the foundation of civilisation, were transforming our globe into an electronic village in which technology transfer and the dissemination of new knowledge could be used to help bridge the gap between rich and poor, developed and underdeveloped.

In this new age the trained human intelligence was recognised as being a nation's most precious asset. The social scientists, and especially the economists, sociologists and anthropologists transformed attitudes and influenced government policies in the way that Adam Smith's *Wealth of Nations* had done in the eight-eenth century. Our own Arthur Lewis, who wrote a seminal work, *The Theory of Economic Growth*, in the 1950s, noted the role of culture in impeding or furthering economic growth. Gunnar Myrdal's fuller treatment of this subject in his study of poverty amongst the peoples of South-East Asia, John Kenneth Galbraith's work *The Nature of Human Poverty* and John Maynard Keynes' work in economics helped to shape the thinking of the industrialised nations, especially in such areas as international aid, the internationalisation of trade, modernisation and the role of governments in promoting industrialisation and restructuring developing societies.

In such a world the key-word was "development" and the development of human resources was the top priority. International and national funding agencies made funds and training available. In these critical years the Jamaican people moved along the road from dependence to full internal self-government, their tutor being Norman Manley. Like Garvey and Eric Williams, he believed passionately that the ultimate powers of society should rest with the people and that – to echo Thomas Jefferson – if we think them not informed enough to exercise their powers with discretion, the remedy is not to take their powers from them but to inform their discretion with education.

Garvey did this throughout his life, instructing blacks in the history of Africa and in the need for social change through a representative, organised political system. Eric Williams pointed with justifiable pride to his programme of political education based on the "University" of Woodford Square, where he sought "to open the door behind which our dynamic energies are at present confined". Manley's testament is the body of speeches edited by Rex Nettleford under the title *Manley and the New Jamaica*. These four leaders, two of them Jamaican, in the first quarter of a century of West Indian nationhood provided the West Indian people with a theory of West Indian (or indeed Caribbean) political philosophy, which was rooted in the West Indian historical experience and aimed at the intellectual and spiritual liberation of the West Indian people. They rejected the Eurocentric mode of thinking, and "accepted the principle of parliamentary democracy and of belief in the essential importance and value of the individual man". (Nettleford: 1971)

We have taken account of global trends which favoured the efforts of poor countries to develop their natural and human resources, and indeed regarded such efforts as conditions for social and economic assistance, and we have referred to the creation of a West Indian system of political philosophy as a West Indian counterpart to constitutional advance. Hitherto, the primary consideration had been the best interests of the British empire. The changes in decision-making, in the guiding principles, constitutional goals and economic development were defined by Jamaicans. This explains why these years are so vital in our history.

When Bustamante and the JLP came to power and Ivan Lloyd and the PNP elected members took their places in the House, they all knew that they were on test as representatives of all the people, all the unemployed, the squatters and the vacant-eyed youth. They had to create bread and jobs. It was for these that Bustamante had marched through the streets of Kingston. The governor also knew that he would be held responsible if social discontent erupted, for under the 1944 constitution he, and not the ministers, was ruler.

In 1944 he set up an economic policy committee under a British economist, F. C. Benham. It turned out to be like consulting Queen Victoria. The committee laid it down that Jamaica should not use tariff protection to encourage local manufacturing. Benham advised that Jamaica's future lay in agriculture and in providing a market for British manufactured goods. But the development economists of the period, the West Indian Arthur Lewis among them, urged that countries like Jamaica, with surplus labour, a small home market, limited natural resources, too many people on the overburdened land, had no choice but to manufacture for export, to use tariffs for protection and to attract overseas investors by tax incentives. Trade was to include manufactured goods as well as agricultural products and raw materials.

Next door Puerto Rico was setting an example. The leader of the Populares, Muñoz Marín, who had campaigned in the 1930s under the promise "Land and bread", confronted by slum-ridden cities and rural distress, had worked out an agreement with the United States for Puerto Rico to be granted the status of Commonwealth in free association with the United States, and so had opened the way for emigration and for industrialisation through a planned programme of economic growth.

In Jamaica unemployment and rising social tension were also warnings that there was no time to lose. In 1945 Norman Manley said: "There is on the part of the masses, standing on one side of the dividing gulf, a deep resentment and urge to end and change it all. On the other side are the privileged few. These cannot escape the fear that secretly haunts them." Bustamante, an expert in sensing social tension, in breaking with colonial tradition, lost no time and moved ahead with the development of natural resources and the use of incentive legislation to encourage industrialisation.

Suddenly rays of sunshine broke through the dark clouds. The rumour spread that bauxite had been found in Jamaica. The incredulous Jamaican peasant shook his head and proclaimed his suspicion of backra, that trickified man: "Dem did know something long time", "Dem did know long time but didn't want fe share it", and "Ah nuh so it go. Dem a play dem tricks. You see dem too trickify."

But it was true. Jamaicans were sitting on a fortune, bauxite, red earth, which changed its name to alumina hydrate as it was purged of its redness and moved up the social scale to whiteness, and then to the summit and so gleaming a metal that not even whiteness could attain to it.

It was true, and every small upland farmer began to look at his patch of red earth and recalculate its worth. In 1868 a government geologist had found that Jamaica's red earth was largely a mixture of iron and alumina, but 19 years were to pass before the commercial development of the metal aluminium began in France and the United States, and another 50 years passed before Jamaica's bauxite attracted overseas attention. The demand soared for a light, strong, pliable metal for aeroplanes and for prefabricated, strong yet light, metal shutters, cookery ware and furniture of a hundred types. The demand was for the strongest, most pliable, most durable of them all, aluminium. So the world broke in on Jamaica, to buy its bauxite.

In 1942 a Jewish Kingston merchant and St Ann penkeeper, Alfred D'Costa, had some of the red earth on his property near Claremont analysed because it was so infertile. Bauxite was found to be present. A survey of Jamaica's bauxite reserves followed and soon afterwards negotiations began between the government and Canadian (Alcan) and United States companies (Reynolds and Kaiser). The 1942 estimate of 5 million tons was revised after more extensive surveys to between 500 million and 600 million tons. In the 1950s the three companies were extracting more than 5 million tons a year and Jamaica had become one of the world's major producers of bauxite. In 1957 the original agreement between the government and the companies was modified, with the result that the revenue paid on bauxite that had been mined increased tenfold, from a total of £352,000 per year to £3,700,000 in 1960-61.

Jamaica learned much from the bauxite companies, who from the beginning set an example of good citizenship. It could easily have been otherwise, for Jamaicans love their upland pastures and the sight of bulldozers tearing up the grass dramatised, often in a painful way, the extractive nature of the industry. In addition, these areas were often those most suitable for cattle rearing. Agricultural land is in short supply in Jamaica, as the process of urbanisation and the frequent waves of emigration show. By law the bauxite companies were required to keep agriculturally productive land in production until it was needed for mining, and to restore the mined-out land as far as possible to its original level of agricultural productivity. In response, the companies increased and improved the herds of cattle and gave particular attention to afforestation. Further, by skilled and sympathetic programmes of industrial relations and of community development, with special attention to education, and by ensuring that employment was open to qualified Jamaicans, men and women, at all levels, the bauxite companies eliminated racial discrimination in the industry and contributed both to the building of self-esteem and of a sense of national unity.

Jamaica's red earth from her upland pastures and her gleaming beaches of white sand became in the 1950s two of her chief money-earners. Dust-covered rust-coloured containers loaded the earth onto ships bound for the United States and freight cars laden with alumina hydrate loaded ships

Courtesy of Jack Tyndale-Biscoe

Aerial photo-
graph of bauxite
installation,
Discovery Bay

bound for Canada, while some of the largest cruise ships in the world discharged their passengers at Ocho Rios and Montego Bay, already the two major centres of tourism on the north coast.

Montego Bay was the pace-setter. In the 1930s Doctor's Cave had been nothing more than a gracious curve of sand leading to a small, friendly cave, popular with the local people because the water was so buoyant, with a constant, pleasantly warm temperature all year round. Doctors recommended the safe, healing waters; and after the Second World War, when tourism became a global industry, Doctor's Cave began to attract the wealthy and achy.

In the early 1950s, with Abe Issa as chairman of the Jamaican Tourist Board, Jamaica set out to woo the tourists, and under his leadership and that of John Pringle, both gifted entrepreneurs, tourism became one of Jamaica's most important sources of revenue. In 1950 just under 75,000 tourists came to Jamaica. Three years later the arrivals had trebled. Between 1950 and 1954 the revenue from tourism almost doubled, rising from very nearly £3 million to £5,750,000.

There were losses. Jamaicans felt squeezed off their own beaches. In response, in 1955 the government established the Beach Control Authority with powers to declare any beach a public recreational beach. There was concern that coloured and black Jamaicans might be unwelcome in north-coast hotels. Generally, it was cash, not colour, that made a difference. All in all, good sense prevailed and in the 1950s tourism became a vital industry.

Aerial photograph of Ocho Rios

Courtesy of Jack Tyndale-Biscoe

Bauxite and tourism would ease, but could not solve, the problem of unemployment. Driven by intensifying social discontent, encouraged by the urging of the economists and by the example of Puerto Rico, the government decided to move ahead with a programme designed to create new jobs by encouraging manufacturing and industrialisation. In 1944 the Textiles Industry Law and the Hotel Law were enacted, followed by the Pioneer Industry Law in 1949, described as "the fountain head of subsequent industrial development", because, like the Puerto Rican model, it applied to any industry that qualified as a "pioneer", and not to one particular industry. The purpose was to encourage local entrepreneurs to become manufacturers. This was followed in 1952 by the creation of the Industrial Development Corporation, "to stimulate, facilitate and undertake the development of industry". The drive for industrialisation gained strength with the passing of these laws, and with the recruitment of a black Jamaican entrepreneur, Robert Lightbourne, who had established himself in Birmingham, England. He returned to Jamaica to direct the Industrial Development Corporation.

Manley welcomed the foundation of the Industrial Development Corporation, which had indeed been on the PNP's agenda: "We who welcomed this part of a series of essential measures for the beginning of a planned economy have done so because we recognize that without measures of this sort we cannot attempt to solve the problem which grows greater year by year."

After the PNP took office in 1955 the government supplemented earlier legislation with the Industrial Incentives Law of 1956 which, along with the Export Industries Law of the same year, sought to make Jamaica a major manufacturing centre by granting tax concessions during a "holiday period". The law was designed to attract foreign investors who already had foreign outlets for their goods in countries within easy reach of Jamaica, by granting tax concessions on initial imports of machinery and all imports of raw materials and fuel. The finished products were exempt from duty, but they all had to be exported.

Planned social and economic growth required the modernisation of the Civil Service, and its transformation from a Eurocentred law-and-order civil service ornamented with ceremonial swords and helmets into an innovative, creative public service of bright young Jamaicans eager to develop their country's natural resources, to build a strong economy and a united nation. The new group included leaders such as Egerton Richardson, John Mordecai, G. Arthur Brown, Don and Gladstone Mills. Working hand-in-hand with these was an English development planner, George Cadbury. Dedication to Jamaica and the Jamaican people was the motivating force. Whatever the political party in power, Jamaica was the cause to serve. The creative energy of young, trained Jamaicans working harmoniously and loyally with the political leaders and the appreciation the politicians showed for their advice, explain the extraordinary record of the 1950s in transforming Jamaica into a dynamic, patriotic self-governing community. They worked with the political leaders to create a range of specialised agencies and organisations such as the Industrial Development Corporation, the Agricultural Development Corporation (already mentioned), the Bank of Jamaica, the Central Planning Agency, the Central Bureau of Statistics and the Jamaica Broadcasting Corporation. This was the silent revolution which enabled Jamaica to develop a range of successful programmes for economic growth and to perform the monumental task of meeting the multiplying demands of an expanding and greatly diversified economy.

This drive for industrialisation and manufacturing, directed alternatively by the JLP and the PNP, was the single most important economic initiative of these years of extraordinary achievement.

Instead of recounting the events in order, we will treat the programmes as a case-study, for these years have much to teach us about the development process, social change, the liberating power of affirming a racial identity and about the persistence of colonial stereotypes.

We begin with the historical significance of the programmes. For the first time in their history of struggle, black Jamaicans joined in the process of electing their representatives, and for the first time the elected representatives of all the Jamaican people made employment, bread and jobs their major concern. By setting this priority the first elected government of all the people rejected the colonial imperatives and set a Jamaican agenda. They broke the stranglehold of the planter class on political power. For the first time the government of Jamaica stopped being a struggle between planter interests and a British governor, and became a democratic exercise in selecting political and social goals.

For the first time also, the Jamaican legislature examined the experience of another Caribbean society in order to learn from it. It is one of the ironies of our history that Jamaicans emerging from British colonial rule turned to Puerto Rico, which as a Spanish stronghold, had repulsed Francis Drake's attempt at landing in the seventeenth century. La Fortaleza, once the seat of the Spanish governor, became the residence of the American governor, Rexford Tugwell, one of Franklin Roosevelt's New-Dealers. The political leader of Puerto Rico, Muñoz Marín, was leading his people's struggle against the very poverty and degradation with which Bustamante, Manley and African-Jamaicans were struggling. The Puerto Rican techniques for encouraging industrialisation were reflected in the Jamaican legislation, and contributed to the success that attended Jamaica's effort.

For the first time in their history the Jamaican people experienced the exhilarating effect of achievements and of growing confidence. The government by its sense of purpose and increasing competence soon won the support of leaders of the private sector such as the Hannas, Issas, Matalons. Carl Stone draws attention to this growing sense of direction and of achievement in an important analysis of this period.

> Between 1944 and the mid-1950's this policy perspective on economic strategies changed radically as elected politicians came into full control of domestic economic policy. Greater self confidence was infused into the business class as the political system was democratized. Urban merchant interests took on the challenge of shifting from being commission agents of manufacturing companies to creating a local manufacturing sector with state support and protection.

Writing with reference to the expansion of industry between 1956 and 1967, and to the parallel expansion in bauxite, tourism and other services, he noted the consequent rise of

> a vibrant, new and increasingly wealthy and influential entrepreneurial class. The political directorate treated the interests of the new entrepreneurs as equal to the interests of the economy as a whole as the country's economic future seemed hinged on their continued

expansion. They had easy access to the corridors of power . . . They effectively replaced the planters as the dominant owning interests after the earlier decline in plantation agriculture in the first two decades of the twentieth century.

The record of economic growth for the period 1945-60 is impressive by any standards. Between 1954 and 1960, the sale of electricity to industry doubled to 50 million kilowatts. Between 1943 and 1960 national income per head at current prices grew from £32.50 to £128, while gross domestic product increased from £70 million in 1950 to £230 million in 1960. This rate of growth was exceeded only by two other countries, Puerto Rico and Japan.

This extraordinary achievement had a minus sign attached to it. The gap between the general mass of the people and the new entrepreneurs widened. Edward Seaga voiced the general concern when, as one of the leading young politicians of the 1960s, he pointed out that the "haves were getting richer and the have-nots were getting poorer". A week later Bustamante declared that Jamaicans were sitting on the brink of a volcano.

The figures did indeed point to serious social dislocation. Clarke's analysis showed that "despite the economic changes which had taken place the pattern of employment in Kingston in 1960 remained basically similar to that in 1943" (Clarke: 1973); and Volker's study indicated that "manufacturing concerns with ten or more workers employed only 17,000 persons in Kingston in 1960 . . . and race and colour were important outward symbols of the social situation".

It was a time of growing anger among the urban poor. Alongside Carl Stone's portrayal of the wealthy entrepreneurs we place Simpson's description of the rural poor arriving in Kingston.

> Everyday young people arrived from country districts; many of them gravitate to West Kingston . . . Some men come with the hope of finding work, fewer girls than men arrived, some to work as domestic servants, others to become prostitutes or scuffle for a living. Many of the incoming men fell into the practice of "living around", of gambling and stealing, and if they had no friends, money or relatives they had to "live hard", to cotch, or start squatting or living on the dungle, all these being signs of extreme population pressure and over-crowding.

By 1960, during the period of economic growth, more than one-half of all unemployed Jamaicans were residing in the Corporate Area, and overcrowding increased, with the result that "although some rehousing had been effected in these areas, in general they were characterized by popula-tion increase and social stagnation . . . By 1960, therefore, the distinction between the slums and the better areas was as marked as, if not more marked than, it had been in 1943. Gross population densities at the two dates support this contention." (Clarke: 1975)

Norman Manley described the problem in anguished terms: "And what do we do? We have to move from an economy wholly dependent on agriculture; we have to answer the people hammering on the door for bread; we have to find more jobs, to take more people off the land, to open more schools, to generate more capital, and we remain wholly dependent on external markets."

Equally disturbing was the insidious disease of class-blindness which focused judgement only on what was happening within one's class and made it appear to be universal. Even Norman Manley, the most scrupulously fair of men, fell victim to this form of selective blindness when he described West Indian society, and Jamaican society in particular, as "made up of people drawn from all over the world, predominantly Negro or of mixed blood, but also with large numbers of others, and nowhere in the world has more progress been made in developing a non-racial society in which colour is not significant". (Nettleford: 1971) But in this very period Negro racist organisations in Kingston were becoming increasingly belligerent.

As Clarke reports, some Rastafarians vilified the brown population in particular, describing them as mulattoes, quadroons and spittoons; and there was a group which cried out during their meetings, "Manley is Pharaoh! Pharaoh, let my people go." And they used to chant "He layeth me down to sleep on hard benches, he leadeth me by the still factories." (Clarke: 1975)

Many Jamaicans had hoped in the 1950s for a lessening of social tension and, most pressing of all, for a coming together of the "two Jamaicas" in preparation for the setting up of the Federation of the West Indies. They were grievously disappointed to find that the rapid growth of the economy had widened the cleavage and added to the anger of the have-nots.

Things had gone otherwise in Puerto Rico. Slums had been cleared, income levels lifted, high rates of economic growth achieved and social tensions eased. The difference lay in the fact that whereas Jamaica concentrated on economic growth through incentive legislation, Puerto Rico made this a part of a larger programme for social change. The University of Puerto Rico, which had been revitalised and modernised, was entrusted with the task of becoming a vigorous centre of education and research and of developing a profound sense of unity in the Puerto Rican people. The school system was strengthened with an efficient network of technical and vocational schools, and a number of reorganised second-unit schools enriched the Puerto Rican children's knowledge of their physical and cultural environment. As in the American tradition, every effort was made to increase social mobility through equality of educational opportunity. The result was that social cohesion was strengthened and a sense of unity enforced by the impressive rate of economic growth.

Here we come to a major cause of the dislocating impact of Jamaica's industrialisation drive of the 1950s. The goals, values, methods, outlook of Jamaica's system of education remained colonial and generated split loyalties. Evan Jones' description of one of the most prestigious of Jamaica's schools in 1940 reveals how, in the period we are considering, while the Puerto Ricans were striving to develop through education a deep sense of unity in the Puerto Rican people, and while Jamaica's nationalists were campaigning for national unity, Jamaica secondary education was rooting the country's élite children in Europe. The greatest and most debilitating split in society was not that which was reflected in the urban landscape, but that which revealed split loyalties. The educational system was the chief barrier to social development.

It was years later, in 1958, that Jamaica's ministry of education referred to the general criticism of the secondary schools for their lack of concern about Jamaica and lack of knowledge about its people.

As for primary education, the colonial administrators and the ruling élites had one set of objectives, that of maintaining the *status quo*, while the people sent their children to school "with the intention of changing their socio-economic position, that is, changing the *status quo*. This cross-purpose is the source of dysfunctionality in the Jamaican educational system." (Miller: 1989) As late as 1989 Miller pointed out: "In a real sense the ideas that have informed educational developments in independent Jamaica have been those that were formulated by the colonial administration in the 1940's." As a result, while Jamaicans were driving ahead with industrial development, their system of education was weakening, their efforts splitting the society culturally as well as economically.

Puerto Rico and Jamaica, in contrasting ways, drove home the lesson that development involves political, social and economic factors, that it centres on the human being and is "an unfolding of what is in the germ", a release of creative potential.

It remains for Jamaican society to recognise the centrality of Africa, and to translate Sheikh Anta Diop's message into a system of education. As he said, "The Negro must be able to grasp the continuity of his nation's history and to draw from it the moral support he needs to recover his place in the civilised world."

The teachers are the heroes in our account of Jamaica's colonial system of education which endured for some years after independence. "Teacher" was one of the heroic community builders, along with the country parson, the village nurse and "Doc" the druggist. These by their dedicated leadership, made the school a way of escape from rural poverty.

CHAPTER 30

Culture and nationhood

Division, separation: these were the key words during the three centuries of British rule. Always, decade after decade, from 1655 to 1940, there were two groupings of people in Jamaica, "two Jamaicas" separated by race, colour and political power.

There were no overarching loyalties, no collective memories, no sense of a community that for long had shared the same soil. For Africans the plantation was a place from which to escape. There was no common creed, no common language, no common culture. The term "Jamaica" was little more than a label, a name on a map. There were Africa and Europe; and Europe, the dominant power, dedicated itself to maintaining difference, not to nurturing unity.

The badges were stark, unequivocal, irreversible. "White" meant "good" and "black" meant "bad", although the African experience was that Europe meant guns, slave ships and the Middle Passage for hundreds and thousands and indeed, in total, for 10 million African men and women.

"White" meant "good" and "black" meant "bad", even though Governor Eyre was never charged with the murder of George William Gordon, nor the Colonial Office charged with using an unfair system of taxation to compel the African-Jamaican to bear the tax burden, nor for using legislative power to safeguard the political power of the white and brown minority.

The British Crown was the only symbol of unity. For the upper and middle classes it represented protection and the preservation of privilege. For the working class it meant persistent poverty. The chief dividing factor was race, but Euro-Jamaica masked this fact with a ritual of pretence. There was a carefully preserved picture of a multiracial society in which "racial issues tend to be avoided in political discourses. No one who is progressive talks about racial consciousness. Class consciousness is acceptable, either from the standpoint of radical politics or as a reflection of social mobility. In Jamaican history since Garvey the only sector to consistently challenge the false multi-racialism has been the Rastafarians". (Lewis: 1987)

The picture presented by traditional historians is of a colony united under British rule, moving gradually in the 1940s towards self-government and finally to independence. In reality, the divisions and differences were so many, so deep, that in recent years scholars such as the Jamaican sociologist M. G. Smith described it as a plural society. Up to the 1920s there was little sentiment of national unity and little that could be described as a Jamaican culture. How could it have been otherwise when for two centuries and up to the abolition of the slave trade freshly arrived Africans were separated from each other and distributed to different plantations? Or when many Euro-Jamaicans saw Britain as home and Jamaica as a place of exile?

Jamaica's nationhood, then, did not grow out of memories of an earlier tribal unity. Its social heritage reflects its history of racial and colour discrimination. Its educational system was designed to perpetuate social and economic differences. If we define culture as the social heritage of a community, the total body of material artefacts, the mental and spiritual artefacts (systems, ideas, beliefs) and the distinctive forms of behaviour, then up to the 1930s the colony's social heritage could not exercise a powerful cohesive force because it was itself split.

To a Jamaican what happened in the 1930s and 1940s is nothing short of a miracle, for the political revolution described in the preceding chapters was attended by a powerful surge of creative energy that impelled Jamaicans of all classes to think of Jamaica as "my country" and of Jamaicans of all colours as "my people".

Norman Manley made this point when he launched the People's National Party.

> Anyone looking back on the past ten years (1928-1938) will realise that we in this country have been more and more concentrating upon our own affairs. We have thought more of Jamaica, spoken more about Jamaica, breathed more of the atmosphere of Jamaica than we can recall before in this country. And it has been symptomatic of the existence of an increasing number of organisations in all classes of the community . . . and most marked in the growth of opinion among the young men of this country, of the dawn of the feeling that this should be their home and their country . . . There is a tremendous difference between living in a place and belonging to it and feeling that your own life and your destiny is [sic] irrevocably bound up in the life and destiny of that place. (Nettleford: 1971)

Marcus Garvey had challenged the people to claim the African heritage and to cherish self-esteem and nationalist Jamaica was rejecting imperial domination. With one touch of creative intensity, generated by self-discovery and self-emancipation, the desert flowered.

The change came as silently, as magically as spring comes in upland Jamaica, with its delicate greens and the glowing purple of new leaves on the pimento trees, and on the Liguanea Plain with the tender translucent green of the lignum vitae trees. The impulse came from the people's discovery of their identity and this was accompanied by a surge of creative energy unparalleled in their history. Animated by these creative forces, Jamaicans brought into being a literature, an art movement and wide-ranging activities in sports and athletics, the whole comprising a burgeoning, distinctive culture.

The extraordinary achievements in athletics, sport and in diverse cultural movements, including Rastafarianism and the women's movement, brought the two Jamaicas nearer together. After considering the cultural revolution in sport, athletics and the creative arts, we will reflect on the role of education and culture in making nationhood the meaningful reality that it should be.

Our story of cultural achievement is one that inspires pride and confidence in all Jamaicans. African-Jamaica's first breakthrough in one area of British supremacy came in 1930 when young George Headley, not yet 21 years of age, "completed his fourth century in four tests, with a record West Indian Test score of 223 in the first test ever played at Sabina [Park]". (Carnegie: 1996) The time came when the British cricketing world rose to its feet to acclaim George Headley's entry into the world of cricket's immortals with a century at Lord's in each innings of the match. The famous West Indian tour in England in 1950, with two of the world's great spin bowlers, Alfred Valentine and Sonny Ramadhin, and three of the world's great batsmen, Everton Weekes, Frank Worrell and Clyde Walcott, further demonstrated that West Indian cricket had achieved world levels.

Herb McKenley

By 1950 Herb McKenley had also announced the entry of Jamaica into world athletics. In 1947 McKenley had managed to:

> set the first time-measured world record by a Jamaican, or any other English-speaking West Indian, for that matter. In 1948 he set another world-record for the quarter-mile of 46 seconds

Arthur Wint

flat, and ran 45.9 for the metric equivalent 400 metres, feats that had been set down as impossible barriers by experts in the sport years before. In that same year he was beaten for the Olympic 400 meters title by his countryman, Arthur Wint . . . The two gave Jamaica the first ever such triumph in the entire history of the Olympic games over athletes from the United States of America (USA) in a male sprint event. (Carnegie: 1996)

Another of the pace-setters in athletics was Keith Gardner, gold medalist in the hurdles in the Commonwealth Games of 1954 and 1958. These triumphs, coming as they did in this period of nat-ional awakening, in competition with the rest of the world, were of pro-found importance. By winning instant worldwide recognition in competition with people of all races and cultures, they lifted Jamaica's self-esteem, opened the eyes of Jamaicans to the potential of all Jamaican youth and shattered the myth about black inferiority.

By great good fortune, through the foresight of a British governor of the Crown colony period, Sir Anthony Musgrave, Jamaica had the institu-tional underpinnings for nurturing and extending a cultural revolution, the Institute of Jamaica and the National Gallery. They are reminders not only of Sir Anthony Musgrave, who established the Institute for the encouragement of literature, science and art, but also of an Englishman, Frank Cundall, who almost single-handedly built up the West India Reference Library into one of the finest collections of its kind in the Americas, and of scientists such as Sawkins and, in more recent times, Bernard Lewis, who built up the Natural History Museum with its price-less collection of Jamaica's fauna and flora. In the 50 years between the founding of the institute and the revolution of the 1930s, the institute was the only agency in Jamaica dedicated to studying and preserving the country's political and natural history and encouraging an interest in indigenous Jamaica.

Institute of Jamaica

In the 1930s the institute became both catalyst and activator for Jamaica's burgeoning art movement. It brought together young Trelawny-bred Albert Huie, mature master-barber John Dunkley back from his travels in Central America, Edna Manley who was London-trained in the cubist style, realist-romantic Ralph Campbell, lonely Henry Daley and the questioning social satirist Carl Abrahams, all individualists working on their own with absolute certitude as if they had been tutored in five centuries of an artistic tradition. Edna Manley had returned to Jamaica with her husband Norman in 1922, and had produced her first piece of sculpture, "The Beadsellers", a year later. She then spent ten years grappling with the technical problems of carving in mahogany in the place of stone, and learning how to create an authentic Jamaican icongraphy out of the body gestures, arms akimbo, vital dancing bodies and defiant heads of Jamaicans. Soon, groups of Jamaican sculptors, painters, poets were busy portraying the historical experience of the African-Jamaican people. Where will one find a more powerful, more moving portrayal of a poor, elderly black woman than in Albert Huie's "Woman in the Sun", a more African and Jamaican interpretation of revivalism than in Carl Abrahams' "Backyard", urban squalor more disturbing than in the darkness of David Pottinger's "Street Scene" or find more intensely African carvings than David Miller's "Rasta Man" and "Mask"?

Albert Huie

Edna Manley's "Negro Aroused", and Dunkley's portrayal of what the negro protest was about, marked the beginning of the Jamaican art movement. The carvings, "Negro Aroused", "Young Negro", "The Diggers", "caught the inner spirit of our people and flung their rapidly rising resentment of the stagnant colonial order into a vivid appropriate sculptural form". (Smith: 1974) David Boxer enlarged the theme: "With their powerful insistent rhythms which frame the essential leitmotif of the head turned back, straining upward towards a vision, or downward in suppressed anger . . . [they] have truly become the icons of that period of our history, a period when the black Jamaican was indeed aroused, ready for a new social order, demanding his place in the sun." (Boxer: 1989)

Edna Manley

A significant concordance of events highlights these years 1937 and 1938, the period of proletariat unrest in Kingston, of the Frome riots, the period also of Edna Manley's first exhibition of sculpture (1937), and the emergence of Albert Huie, Carl Abrahams and John Dunkley, three of Jamaica's great painters. They felt, experienced, portrayed the emotions, desperation, frustrations, hopes, visions of the people. Edna Manley's "Negro Aroused" and John Dunkley's dark-grey landscapes of never-ending roads, a

world with neither dawn nor noonday, its landscape of truncated trees, of soul-yearnings and dreams, Carl Abrahams' "Last Supper", were all memory and prophecy, effort and vision, self-discovery and racial affirmation, pain and triumph. The great collection of the National Gallery of Jamaica presents a moving, often apocalyptic, always uplifting portrait of the Jamaican people during this period. Carl Abrahams, Karl Parboosingh, Alvin Marriott, the revivalist preacher Mallica Reynolds, known as "Kapo", Sydney McLaren and Cecil Baugh, the potter, are among the honoured names of the men and women who in one generation told the story of the Jamaican people in vivid splendid works of art.

John Dunkley

The message went deep. It was Africa confronting Europe with a deeply religious sense of the world and of man's relationship with God, which we find especially in the work of the "intuitive painters", members of "a whole

Kapo

undercurrent of untutored art in Jamaica that could not be ignored as the isolated primitives which critical opinion has made them out to be". (Boxer: 1989) The work of Kapo, for example, commanded international attention and admiration. In Boxer's words, Kapo's first important painting (1947) was:

An image of Christ, a black Christ seated on the shore of the Sea of Galilee. Shortly afterwards he abandoned painting and produced between 1948 and 1967 a remarkable collection of works that have few equals among Jamaican, indeed Caribbean, carvers in wood. The inspiration for these carvings came out of Revivalism: the works are imbued with the movement, the rhythms, the whole intense emotionalism of this religion that is at once African and Christian. (Boxer: 1989)

Ralph Campbell

Alongside the artists of this period moved the poets and novelists, George Campbell, Vic Reid, Roger Mais, John Hearne and Andrew Salkey, who joined their fellow West Indians of the period, George Lamming, Vidia Naipaul, Jan Carew, Edgar Mittelholzer, Arthur Seymour and others in founding a West Indian literature that was soon recognised as a significant contribution to world literature.

The range of artistic achievement was wide. It brought together educated middle-class, white Edna Manley, working-class African-Jamaicans, all meeting as Jamaicans, all driven by the urge to portray the land and the Jamaican experience.

The range of achievement extended to setting and implementing national goals, to areas of scholarship and scientific research on the one hand, and, on the other, it included the founders of a messianic group that came to be called Rastafarians. It was Sir Herbert McDonald's vision and his insistence on building a national stadium and sports arena that made it possible for Jamaica to host the Central American and Caribbean Games in 1962, the British Empire and Commonwealth Games in 1966, thus also providing the country with a venue for accommodating national events of great size.

Vic Reid

Of the scholars and scientists, Thomas Philip Lecky deserves special mention. Early in the 1920s he entered the Farm School, where he became so interested in livestock and so skillful in dealing with cattle that his fellow-students called him "Cow Bredda". Determined to breed a special kind of cattle suited to Jamaican conditions, he became Livestock Officer at Hope, equipped himself by studying at the Universities of McGill, Toronto and Edinburgh, continued his experiments over many years and at last, in the 1950s, established a new breed of cattle, the Jamaica Hope, an animal slightly bigger than a Jersey that yielded a good supply of milk and beef. Lecky did with cattle what J. R. Bovell did in Barbados by propagating new and better varieties of sugar cane and what J. B. Sutherland did for Jamaica by breeding the Lacatan variety of banana.

T. P. Lecky

The Rastafarians draw their inspiration chiefly from the Bible – the Old Testament especially – and an American publication, *The Sixth and Seventh Books of Moses*. Their story brings together despised black men in Back O' Wall, the Emperor Haile Selassie and a worldwide musical explosion that featured Bob Marley.

Rex Nettleford reminds us that the Rastafarian Movement was yet another form of the African-Jamaican's protest against a society in which:

> The sounds and pressure of poverty continued to be underlined in clear colour, the Jamaican of unmistakably African descent decidedly relegated to the base of the society. All the responses known to Jamaican history were invoked by the Rastafarian . . . For in Rastafarianism are to be found such old responses as psychological withdrawal, black nationalism, apocalyptic exultation and denunciation tied to a bold assertion of a redemptive ethic as aid to liberation and relief from suffering. (Nettleford: 1973)

In 1930 Ras Tafari, great-grandson of King Saheka Selassie of Shoa, was crowned Negus of Ethiopia in St George's Cathedral, Addis Ababa. The young king took the name Haile Selassie (Might of the Trinity), as well as other titles, King of Kings and the Lion of Judah, which put him in the legendary line of descent from King Solomon.

Many followers of Marcus Garvey saw this as a revelation from God. Some recalled that years earlier, just before leaving for the United States, Garvey was reported to have said, "Look to Africa for the crowning of a Black King. He shall be the Redeemer." The words "came echoing like the voice of God. Possessed by the spirit of this new development, many Jamaicans now saw the coronation as a fulfillment of biblical prophesy and Haile Selassie as the Messiah of African redemption". (Barrett: 1977)

Garvey thought and dreamed Ethiopia. The "Universal Ethiopian Anthem" began with the words "Ethiopia, thou land of our fathers", and he never wearied of declaring:

> We negroes believe in the God of Ethiopia, the Everlasting God –
> God the Son, God the Holy Ghost, the one God of all ages. This is
> the God in whom we believe but we shall worship him through the
> spectacles of Ethiopia; and, as Scripture foretold, Ethiopia shall once
> more stretch forth its hands to God.

Garvey's message lived on after him. He is for many Rastafarians a great prophet, and for some none other than John the Baptist incarnate: "There can be no doubt that Garvey's Back to Africa Movement set the stage for the rise of Rastafarianism." This was the glory that filled the mind of Leonard Howell, who had served in the Ashanti war of 1896, had learned several African languages and had returned to Jamaica some time after the coronation, convinced that Haile Selassie was the messiah of the black people. He began his ministry amid the slums of West Kingston. He was joined later by three other preachers, Joseph Hibbert, Robert Hinds and Archibald Dunkley. They built up a small but faithful membership.

Somehow the name "Ras Tafari" and not "Haile Selassie" came to be adopted, "Ras" being in Amharic a title equivalent to the English "Duke" and "Tafari" being the king's family name. His name, Haile Selassie, is used in their ritual, in prayers and songs. The name "Jah", which is also reverenced, is probably a shortened form of "Jehovah".

By 1933 Howell and his followers were ready with their redemptive message of Haile Selassie as the Supreme Being and only ruler of black people. The question is not whether or not they were right in their belief. This is what they believed and in the strength of that belief they placed Africa at the centre of Jamaican concerns.

The year 1935 was one of great distress for the Rastafarians, for it saw Mussolini's brutal, unprovoked attack on Ethiopia. Jamaicans in general were angered at this assault, and they welcomed the founding in New York two years later of the Ethiopian World Foundation to work for the unity and solidarity of the black people of the world. By 1938 several local groups were established in Jamaica.

In the meantime, the Rastafarians held together and began to grow in numbers, despite harassment and hardship. Leonard Howell and some hundreds of his followers settled a derelict and desolate estate, Pinnacle, near Sligoville. The police raided Pinnacle in 1941 and arrested a number of Rastafarians. During those difficult years the Brethren developed their community-style of living, proclaimed their identity by wearing dreadlocks and solidified the movement notwithstanding police harassment. Some time before his death, other leaders succeeded Howell.

Confrontation, not flight to the hills, became the mood. In March 1958, for the first time in local history, members of the Rastafarian cult were having what they called a "Universal Convention" at their headquarters, the Coptic Theocratic Temple in Kingston Pen. Hundreds of Rastafarians, men and women, attended the convention. On 24 March, reported the *Star*,

> The City Kingston was 'captured' near dawn on Saturday by some 300 . . . men of the Rastafarian cult along with their women and children. About 3:30 a.m. early market goers saw members of the Rastafarian Movement gathered in the centre of Victoria Park, with towering poles atop of which fluttered black flags and red banners, and loudly proclaiming that they had captured the city . . . When the police moved toward them a leader of the group with his hands uplifted issued a warning to the police: 'Touch not the Lord's anointed' . . . the police finally moved them.

Later that year Old King's House in Spanish Town was "captured" in the name of the Negus of Ethiopia. The police replied by enforcing the Jamaica Dangerous Drugs Law, arresting members of the cult, shaving their heads and generally harassing them. A sociologist of the University of the West Indies urged in the press that "the aspiration of a social group are not to be disregarded by an attitude of angry contempt for its personal and private habits . . . For in the long run the type of Prince Emanuel [a Rastafarian leader] may have more to do with the West Indies future than the type of Lord Hailes" [former Governor-General of the West Indies].

In 1959 the Rev. Claudius Henry, another messianic leader, was charged with planning a military takeover of Jamaica. He was convicted of treason and sent to prison for six years. Claudius Henry's son Ronald and a small band of guerrilla fighters were later captured in the Red Hills in an operation in which two British soldiers were killed. The rebels were sentenced to death. There is no evidence that the Rastafarians were linked with Claudius Henry.

At this point some of the leading Rastafarian brethren, disturbed at the turn events had taken, and at the harm that Henry's rebellious acts had done to their cause, asked the university to enquire into their doctrines, grievances and conduct, and to report on them to the government. The Nettleford-Smith-Augier report, undertaken and completed in a month, marks a turning point in the history of Rastafarianism. "The study not only revealed the socio-economic conditions of the movement to the general public, but also, for the first time, articulated the history and doctrine of the movement." The report found that the great majority of Rastafari brethren are peaceful citizens who do not believe in violence. Rastafarian doctrine is radical in the broad sense that it is against the oppression of the black race, much of which derives from the existing economic structure.

The report highlighted the social cleavages in Jamaican society, many of which were caused by the colonial system of education. Upper-class Jamaicans, and many in the middle class, being products of the secondary schools, looked at the black working class through European eyes. The report reminds us that cultural development requires not only institutional underpinning such as the Institute of Jamaica, the national stadium and the arena provided, but also the support of scholarship, analysis and research. It draws strength from both vision and intellectual rigour. By 1960 the young University of the West Indies was beginning to contribute to the cultural movement through active, talented groups, such as the University Singers, University Players and highly gifted students such as Slade Hopkinson, future Nobel Prize winner Derek Walcott, Rex Nettleford and Archie Hudson Phillips. Alongside these were the scholars of the recently founded Institute of Social and Economic Research, the Institute of Education and the faculties of the Social Sciences, the Arts, Natural Sciences and Medicine. A number of young scholars were already making their mark, among them M. G. Smith, Norman Girvan, Alister McIntyre, Elsa Goveia, not scholars in isolation but men and women involved in West Indian research and in nation-building. With them were visiting scholars such as the Jamaican, Fred Cassidy, whose *Jamaica Talk* and *A Dictionary of the Jamaican Language*, written jointly with Robert Le Page, demonstrated the historical and aesthetic value of the folk-language. Sociological and economic research revealed how British colonial policy lived on in the educational system and being divisive hindered it from becoming a unifying force.

The second phase of the Rastafarian movement began in the 1960s, when along with the women's movement it became a transforming cultural force. At this point we will pause to join the young Jamaican nation in its celebration of independence and in its welcome to two royal visitors.

In July 1962, from Holland Point to Negril, from Old Harbour Bay to

Port Maria, Jamaicans made ready to celebrate their achievement of independence. Black, green and gold: these are the strong vibrant colours of Jamaica's flag, black for Africa, an affirmation of racial identity; green, a token of ever-springing hope; gold for the sun's life-giving energy.

At midnight on 5 August 1962 the Union Jack was lowered, the flag of Jamaica was raised officially for the first time and the words of Jamaica's national anthem echoed through the streets and across the fields, not a battle cry like the *Marseillaise* but the prayer of a small, newly independent nation for guidance and protection for themselves and for "Jamaica, land we love".

> Eternal Father, bless our Land,
> Guide us with Thy Mighty hand
> Keep us free from evil powers
> Be our guide through countless hours
> Through our leaders great defender
> Grant us wisdom from above.

On 6 August 1962, at the first session of Jamaica's parliament, the constitutional documents were handed to the prime minister, Alexander Bustamante, by Princess Margaret who, on behalf of the Queen, wished the new nation well. It was a solemn occasion. With that act Jamaica moved from the protection of the British Crown and stood alone, shaper of her own future.

The most moving ceremony was the lowering of the Union Jack and the hoisting of the black, green and gold flag in the national stadium at midnight. Next morning at the ceremony in Gordon House, Norman Manley in a brief speech, gave depth to the occasion when he reminded the nation:

> We here today stand surrounded by an unseen host of witnesses, the men who in the past and through all our history strove to keep alight the torch of freedom in this country. No one will name them today but this house is in very deed their memorial and they are with us in spirit in these great days and they too moved through the door which opened into our new future only one day ago.
>
> And what of the future? We have come to independence prepared and ready to shoulder our new responsibilities and united I believe in one single hope that we may make our small country a safe and happy home for all our people. (Nettleford: 1971)

"For all our people": that was the test and the challenge. The cultural revolution pointed the way to go. So did a second royal visit, that of Haile Selassie, which took place for four days from 21 April 1966. Princess Margaret's visit signified the withdrawal of Britain. The visit by the

Emperor of Ethiopia underscored Africa's role in the Caribbean and revealed that the contacts with the true motherland had been kept open by the ancestors.

> Their souls shuttle
> still the secret paths of ocean
> connecting us still, the current unbroken
> the circuits kept open. (Chamberlin: 1993)

Haile Selassie went to Trinidad at the invitation of the Prime Minister, Eric Williams, and continued on to Jamaica at the invitation of a group of African nationalists, among them Dr M. B. Douglas, who wrote:

> There were no less than 100,000 people at the airport to meet him. The Rastafarians numbered at least 10,000. As soon as the plane had come to a stop, the Rastafarians responded with a roar of joy and surged out on the tarmac, each one pushing to get a touch of the plane. When the Emperor saw the people, the Rastafarian flags, the cheering and singing, he wept.
>
> The crowd was so thick around the plane that the Emperor was unable to get out for close to thirty minutes . . . Then the crowd followed instructions to make way and the Emperor got into a car and rode off to King's House, but by this time all the official plans for the welcome ceremony had been cancelled.
>
> The Rastafarians were not interested in protocol . . . their explanation was "This is our day: This is our God. It is him we come to see. It is we who welcome him."

The Rastafarian papers told how for the first time Rastafari brethren were officially invited to King's House: "Glory be to the visit of Emperor Haile Selassie. Although we were born here, the privilege was never granted to us until April 21, 1966. The Rases were there, the aristocrats were there . . . It took Ras Tafari in person to occasion the reality 'that all men were created equal'. And, declared another, 'The emperor's coming lifted us from the dust and caused us to sit with princes of this country.'" (Barrett: 1977)

Haile Selassie is said to have given some of the brethren instructions not to seek to emigrate to Ethiopia until they had liberated the people of Jamaica and that the day of his arrival should be celebrated each year. Following on these instructions the Rastafarians began to adjust to Jamaica as home. In so doing they set in motion a wave of new industries, the most remarkable and important being music, especially the Rastafari drumbeat originated by Count Ossie, in the early years a member of the movement.

Rastafarian musicians and singers, "Toots" Hibbert among them, ventured into world markets with their tunes and songs. By 1968 Hibbert's "Do the Reggae" was taking the market. Within a year or two Bob Marley was making reggae the world's favourite beat. His performances were intensely moving:

> A spasm of frenzied joy greeted Bob Marley as he jumped, spun, and shook his dreadlocks in front of the audience. With raised hands, in true Rastafarian style, he psyched his audience with his familiar yell, "Yeah". The audience responded "Yeah". Then reverently he . . . with bowed head and drooping dreadlocks, invoked the god of Rastafarianism, "Jah" and . . . concluded the invocation with the chant "One Lord, and One God in Mount Zion. (Barrett: 1977)

Leonard Barrett described Reggae as "Africa, Jamaica, soul, nature, sorrow, hate and love all mingled together. It sprang from the hearts of Africa's children in 'Babylon' – Jamaica. It is liminal music that sings of oppression in exile, a longing for home, or for a place to feel at home." Marley stamped his personality on reggae until the sound became identified with the Rastafarian movement. Reggae music, now a multimillion dollar business, derives from that unique sect whose music is an inseparable and expressive ingredient. (Barrett: 1977)

In this period also the Rastafarian "dub" poet, joined the other Jamaican writers of the 1960s and 1970s. The term "dub poetry" was promoted early in 1979 by Oku Onuora (the former Orlando Wong), to identify work then being presented . . . by Oku himself, Michael Smith and Noel Walcott. "The dub poem," Oku said, "is not merely putting a piece of poem pon a reggae rhythm; it is a poem that has a built-in reggae rhythm (so to speak) backing, one can distinctly hear the reggae rhythm coming out on the poem." (Morris) One of the earliest of these poets was Jimmy Cliff, with defiant songs that are social commentary and angry protest.

> And I keep on fighting for the things
>   I want
> Though I know that when you're dead
>   you can't
> But I'd rather be a 'free man' in the grave
> Than living as a puppet or a slave.

To this group of poets belong also Peter Tosh, Mutabaruka and Michael Smith with their vivid images of the lonely Rastafarian attacking oppressive "Babylon".

I an I alone
Ah trod tru' creation,
Babylon on I right,
Babylon on I left
Babylon in front of I
an Babylon behind I
an I an I alone in de middle
like a Goliat wid a sling shot.

The message was the same as that which the working-class women of the Sistren Theatre Collective were delivering in the 1970s, for they also added important new dimensions to the cultural revolution movement by making drama and literature a passionate protest, a lightning flash revelation of the searing effects of social injustice.

Throughout our story, whether it had to do with economic growth, industrialisation or the demand of an oppressed group for social change, we have identified the colonial system of education as a major impediment to social and cultural development. The story of the working-class Jamaican women confirms this conclusion. For example, in education the role of women in Jamaican history is totally ignored. Nowhere do we see more clearly than in *Lionheart Gal*, the destructive effect of a system of education that marginalised the human being and inculcated the acceptance of circumscribed horizons. *Lionheart Gal*, a collection of the life stories of 13 working-class and two middle-class Jamaican women, has to do with the period between 1940 and 1980. The passage quoted below is from "My Own Two Hand". These stories, as the editor points out, "attest to the fact that, when women select their own creative organizational forms, they begin to build a base from which they do transform their own lives. But this transformation is only secure in so far as it is guaranteed by the power relations in the whole society". (Sistren with H. Ford Smith: 1986) Sistren and the women's movement challenge the structure and value systems of traditional Jamaican society. They also reveal the inner lives of many Jamaican women, their loneliness, the intolerable mental strain that results from a lack of stable family life and of regular employment, and the degradation of labour. The women who speak here like the Rastafarians, and like the liberation fighters of earlier generations, are leaders against oppression. They display the strength of will, the leadership, the refusal to accept defeat that are at the heart of the history of the Jamaican people.

Baldwin help me to di building, but a me head it. Sometime when me an him quarrel, him no go. Ah haffi go myself, mix di mortar and put di block. Ah haffi help myself and do di work. When me an' him no quarrel, him go and structure di work an' do it.

Di house is made of wood and concrete. It is not like one a dem lickle concrete box dat dem have nowadays for poor people to live in. It is not big. So it fit right against di mountin side. It have plenty window to let in light and air. We plant up di land around it, so we have banana and odder fruit and vegetable.

Building di house mek me feel proud of meself for me never wait pon no man fi do it. If Baldwin say him cyaan do something me find anodder way out, but me nah siddung an wait pon him. Me tek me own decision and me stick to it. Baldwin and me have an understanding. Him know dat nowadays me tek me own initiative and depend pon meself and tru dat, him haffi respect me. (Sistren with H. Ford Smith: 1986)

Another selection from *Lionheart Gal* reveals the same strength, the same belief that "without a reality we shall emerge from captivity", the same struggle against a hostile social environment, the same loneliness and the same ennobling spirit.

The gap between the two Jamaicas remains wide, but there were times when great events brought both groups together so that they thought in terms of Jamaica, and of being Jamaicans and even West Indians. In cricket our bowlers, batsmen and wicketkeepers revealed the cohesive national power of great achievement. So did our distinguished male and female athletes, among them Donald Quarrie, the first male sprinter from any country to make five Olympics and gain a medal in each of the five; and in the decade of the 1980s the women athletes came into their own. For the first time they outperformed or equalled the men. Among them were Grace Jackson and Merlene Ottey, the sprint queen. Merlene won a gold medal in the World Championships at Stuttgart in 1993 and confirmed her claim as one of the world's great female short-distance runners.

Merlene Ottey

Her achievement bound all Jamaicans together in pride and in rejoicing. Nationhood was no longer a cold, remote concept. Our athletes transformed it into the warm relationship of kinsfolk. To this decade of the 1980s also belong three boxers, Trevor Berbick, Lloyd Honeygan and the remarkable Mike McCallum, who in 1986 held three world titles in boxing at the same time.

World-class achievements such as these provide Jamaicans with their own models of performance and achievement. The story would have been remarkable if it had been in one or two areas of activity only, such as sports and athletics, but it covers a wide cultural spectrum including painting, sculpture, literature, music and dance. The achievements derived from the great mass of the people, who were drawing on their creative gifts, setting new standards, breaching the old barriers of colour and race. The story of this cultural movement is told in *Jamaica in Independence*, edited by Rex Nettleford, who refers to the continuity of effort made possible by the understanding and support of political leaders such as Norman Manley, Edward Seaga and Michael Manley, as well as by the strength of voluntary associations that, like tributaries, enlarged the main stream.

Voluntary organisations reinforced the ongoing work of the educational authorities and the Institute of Jamaica and Jamaica Welfare Ltd (now the Jamaica Social Development Commission), to foster a spirit of self-help and self-esteem in rural areas. The 1920s and 1930s witnessed the development of competition among the performing arts with the founding of the Poetry League of Jamaica (1923), the Musical Society of Jamaica (1926) and the Jamaica Arts Society (1937). The Little Theatre Movement (LTM) came into existence in 1941, the Jamaica Library Service in 1949 and the National Dance Theatre Company of Jamaica (NDTC) in 1962. Henry and Greta Fowler, founders of the LTM, established the annual national pantomime which is now over 50-years-old.

Rex Nettleford

NDTC

The NDTC, founded by Rex Nettleford and Eddie Thomas, has become a company of international repute.

In 1955 the work of the Jamaica Welfare Ltd in the country parts, received a special boost when Louise Bennett, a young charismatic woman, recently returned from drama school in England, joined the staff. She was at one with the heart and soul of the Jamaican people, and a comic muse inspired her poetry, music and song. Wherever she went she established an immediate rapport with the people. Miss Lou's use of the dialect on stage, platform and in print, has helped the Jamaican dialect to gain acceptance at all levels of society. Her work as folklorist, writer and commedienne has established her as perhaps the most authentically Jamaican of all performing artists of her generation.

Louise Bennett
Coverly

The year 1955 also witnessed the staging of the first Jamaica National Festival of Arts. It was islandwide and year-long, and formed part of the celebrations to mark the tercentenary of the association of Jamaica with Britain. It was the fact of being a national festival that made the observance national as distinct from being colonial. The task of mounting the festival was given to a young civil servant, Wycliffe Bennett, who had proposed the idea. The festival discovered and displayed artistic talent which was distributed randomly in the society. It came at the right time and helped develop a conscience for ideal beauty among the people.

A second festival was held in 1958. Then, in April 1963, Edward Seaga, Minister of Development and Welfare, put the festival on a permanent footing. It became an annual event on "the creativity of the nation – a national stage where Jamaicans from all walks of life would have the opportunity to create their own brand of artistic expression, reflecting their life history and their life styles". (Seaga)

Nettleford noted: "Jamaica stands out among newly independent, third world countries in its efforts to provide for itself an institutional structure for cultural development in independence . . . The contact with the young . . . was guaranteed by pulling together in 1965 under the umbrella of . . . the Festival Commission, [which was] broadened in concept in the 1970's to become the Jamaica Cultural Development Commission (JCDC)." (Nettleford: 1978) JCDC's extensive programmes of training were developed along with national contests in song, dance, speech and drama. Leaders in the movement included Wycliffe Bennett and Hugh Nash.

Barrington Watson

The years saw also an impressive broadening and deepening of artistic activity among a new generation of painters, sculptors and potters such as Barrington Watson, Eugene Hyde, Osmond Watson, Gloria Escoffery, Judy MacMillan, Colin Garland, Christopher Gonzales, Fitzroy Harrack, Alexander Cooper, Karl Craig and Cecil Baugh's outstanding successors Gene Pearson and Norma Harrack. The story is the same in the dance, in the plays of Trevor Rhone, in the works of women writers such as Lorna Goodison and Olive Senior. In these decades of the 1970s and 1980s, the cultural movement changed in mood, leaving behind the early fervour of self-discovery and the anger at anti-colonialism and turning to the essential task of interpreting and claiming as a matter of right the experience of the Jamaican people. Lorna Goodison's work reveals this new mood of identification.

So does Pam Mordecai's anthology *From Our Yard*, which reflects the very significant developments taking place in Jamaican society. The press and the media helped to bring this change about. Through radio and TV the journalists and broadcasters have brought Jamaicans into closer, more personal contact with each other. The talk shows, "Public Eye" among them, are building on strong foundations laid by the journalists, commentators, analysts and editors of the longer established print media. Among the print journalists of great influence were Theodore Sealy, Ulric Sommonds, L. D. "Strebor" Roberts, Jack Anderson, Aimee Webster-DeLisser, Evon Blake, Vic Reid, John Maxwell, Hector Bernard, J. C. Proute, Morris Cargill and Peter Abrahams. The talk-show hosts and presenters on radio and television have included Lindy Delapenha, Ronnie Thwaites, Barbara Gloudon, Wilmot Perkins and Dennis Hall. These introduced a greater degree of transparency and accountability into Jamaican public life and conduct. This daily frank interchange of views gives life to democracy and independence. In a young nation with so long a history of racial, economic and political division, this daily continuing discussion has reinforced the opportunities for giving meaning to the concept of nationhood.

Islandwide networks of minibus operators and transistor radios have, in Carl Stone's words, "laid the base for the emergence of genuinely national public opinion among the majority classes although a certain level of parish and country regionalism still persists in the western end of the island".

The private sector has also played an increasingly important role by modernising the nation's industrial and commercial sector and by bringing the business community out of the parochialism of the colonial period by developing a network of global contacts and by setting an example of civil responsibility.

The change in attitude between the expatriate business leadership of the 1930s and that of the post-independence period is striking. Jamaican industrialists, manufacturers, entrepreneurs, financiers and professional groups have established a tradition of public philanthropy by setting up charitable foundations, taking a close interest in cultural activities, in promoting athletics, sport, games, scholarly and literary undertakings, as well as through the service clubs with their encouragement of self-help and of sensitivity to community needs. Their support of the University of the West Indies, of the College of Arts, Science and Technology (University of Technology), of schools, of teaching and research programmes has been of major importance in strengthening social cohesion and increasing educational and economic opportunity. Furthermore, by advice and by their specialised knowledge and expertise, they influence the development of a harmonious relationship between the public and private sectors.

A rapidly growing proletariat, a more sophisticated and consumer-oriented public demands more goods and services; an increasingly large group puts economic betterment first and foremost. The task of nation-building was formidable. Norman Manley minced no words about that when he called for the development of a national spirit and of a system of education that would strengthen the nation. He declared: "You have got to make up your minds as to whether you believe that this country can aim at the great adventure of being fit for achieving self-government . . . This country can only become worthwhile if all the discordant and disunited elements in it can be knitted into a new unity and that can only be brought about by the development of a national spirit." (Nettleford: 1971)

The appeal was made to the teachers of Jamaica in 1939. Norman Manley asked them, "Have we ever in Jamaica inculcated in the children in our schools a spirit which believes that the Jamaican is a fine person?

That he is a laudable person? That the Jamaican has a great future before him?" (Nettleford: 1971)

The questions were asked more than half-a-century ago. Their continuing relevance compels us to look critically at the Jamaican system of education. Our guide is one of Jamaica's best-known educators, Errol Miller. In his essay, "Educational Development in Independent Jamaica", Miller pointed out:

> The most fundamental change to date has been in the size of the system. The educational system is now bigger than it ever was in the colonial period . . . there is evidence that educational standards have improved since independence . . . not only has the educational system expanded in the Independence period but expansion has been accompanied with qualitative improvements as well. Not only has more been produced but at a better standard. (Miller: 1989)

He pointed out, however, that in certain vital areas the colonial patterns continued of prejudice against primary students, anglicisation, devaluation of the achievements of teachers, students and schools, and a sense of cross-purpose in the expectations of the providers and the participants.

A devastating section follows:

> In a real sense the ideas that have informed educational developments in independent Jamaica have been those that were formulated by the colonial administration in the 1940's. Very little new thinking has taken place. B. H. Easter (expatriate Director of Education in the

Prime Ministers of Jamaica since Independence, from left to right: Alexander Bustamante (1962–67); Donald Sangster (Feb. 1967–April 1967); Hugh Shearer (1967– 72); Michael Manley (1972-80, 1989–92); Edward Seaga (1980– 89); P. J. Patterson (1992–)

early 1940's) still directs Jamaican education. This probably explains why what has been accomplished has not differed much from the objectives that guided educational provision in the colonial past.

The racist assumptions and divisive notions remained embedded in the system of education, because up to the 1940s, even those of us who were nationalists knew only the imperialist ver-sion of Jamaica's history. Without realising it, we looked at our society through British eyes because we had at the time no intellectual focus of our own.

Today the first step is for the nation to recognise that the existing deep social cleavages and antagonisms can only be resolved by strengthening the sense of national unity. This calls for the fundamental educational reform of which Errol Miller spoke. By projecting Eurocentric values and attitudes, the existing system of education weakens Jamaica's drive for economic growth, reinforces the traditional social cleavages, erodes the African-Jamaican's sense of a racial identity, denies Africa her place of centrality as motherland, denigrates the historic African-Jamaican achieve-ments of the defeat of slavery and of the white planter oligarchy, and leaves the significance of the national symbols in doubt. National symbols generate powerful emotional and creative forces, but they do not permit of ambiguity.

The immediate challenge is for African-Jamaicans to claim their past with its record of heroic uprisings against European oppression, to claim their African heritage and to draw on today's achievements as a source of empowerment. It is out of our deep feeling about Jamaica and the Jamaican people that a better, happier Jamaica will come, out of our own faith in ourselves and our country, out of our own conviction about its future, out of our own minds, out of our own will.

The guiding principles for revitalising the Jamaican nation and making the educational system a source of inspiration begin with the affirmation that Jamaica is predominantly a black nation whose ancestral motherland is West Africa. The only way to destroy the psychosocial controls instituted by European imperialism is to set the historical record straight. This is the self-liberation of which Garvey spoke. Once this has been accomplished, the nation will find a perennial source of strength in its past.

The nation must enlist the help of its visionaries and achievers – be they poets, sculptors, athletes, priests and clergymen, business men, politicians – in order to make Jamaica's record known to its people. Achievement is infectious. Development is a state of mind. Let the walls of every school in Jamaica carry visual reminders of our great heritage, with portraits of the national heroes and other pathfinders.

The private sector of Jamaica, corporations, foundations and service clubs, have played a role in enriching the quality of Jamaican life and in building self-esteem. They have established a tradition of memorialising historic achievements by commissioning artists to create murals that give a feeling of completeness to their finest buildings. By their generous support of sports and athletics they have opened up opportunities for achieving international and world records. This knitting together of commercial, industrial and manufacturing organisations with the interests and advancement of the Jamaican people is a significant indicator of the growing strength of nationhood.

Religion remains at the centre of national life. Church and school, parson and teacher, working with their church leaders, continue to build into the social fabric a tradition of democratic self-government which they began when colonial rule was authoritarian. In addition they enuniciate the principle that power should always be based on morality. They strengthen the trends toward self-help and voluntarism that provide the folk with the labour and capital they need in times of emergency. Through the outreach work of all the religious bodies, the sacrificial service of the ghetto priests and sisters, and through a network of religious societies and clubs, the various religious bodies continue to shape the life of Jamaica.

In this period of crisis Jamaica depends more than she has ever done on the intellectual and moral quality of her people, on their wisdom and patriotism. The times call for a renewing and deepening of religious commitment as well as for greater intellectual effort. In consequence, educational reform should give high priority to inculcating ethical principles and moral values.

Yesterday reminds us that our West African ancestors were captives in small crowded ships on a lonely ocean. "Shipmates" was the word that held them together and gave them hope. Today, we and all mankind are shipmates on a small spaceship – fragile, destructible, planet earth. The onward-rushing third millennium beckons us to greatness of vision in transforming our two Jamaicas into a united, vibrant nation fitted by its record of cultural achievement to contribute significantly to the unity and happiness of our shipmates.

Select Bibliography

Abolition of Slavery Act, 1833. Will. IV. Cap. LXXIII.

Abrahams, Peter "The blacks", in *African Treasury* ed. by Langston Hughes, (New York: Pyramid Books, 1969).

Anti-Slavery Reporter, 2 May 1859.

Armstrong, Douglas V. *The old village and the great house: An archaeological and historical examination of Drax Hall Plantation, St. Anns Bay, Jamaica*, (Urbana: University of Illinois Press, 1990).

Atkins "A Voyage to Guinea, 1735", in *Caribbean generations: A CXC history source book*, ed. by Shirley Gordon, (Kingston: Longman Caribbean, 1986).

Baugh, Edward "Sometimes in the middle of the story", in *Come Back to me my Language*, ed. by J. E. Chamberlain, (University of Illinois Press, 1993).

Barrett, Leonard *The Rastafarians: the dreadlocks of Jamaica,* (Kingston: Heinemann & Sangster's Bookstores Ltd, 1977).

Beckford, George *Persistent Poverty: Underdevelopment in plantation economies of the third world*, (London: Oxford University Press, 1972).

Beckford, William *A Descriptive Account of the Island of Jamaica* 2 vols, (London, 1790).

Bell, K. N. & Morrell, W. P. Slavery and the Plantation System. Select Documents on British Colonial Policy 1830-1860, mimeo.

Berlin, I. *Against the Current: Essay on the History of Ideas*, (Oxford: Clarendon Press, 1981).

Bernáldez, Andrés *Historia de los Reyes Católicos, Don Fernando y Doña Isabel* 2 vols, (Seville, 1870).

Black, C. V. *A New History of Jamaica* (Kingston: William Collins Sangster Jamaica Ltd, 1973).

Blanchard, P. *Democracy and Empire in the Caribbean*, (New York, 1947).

Bleby, Henry *Death Struggles of Slavery* . . . 2nd edn, (London, 1868).

Blome, Richard *Description of the Island of Jamaica*, (London: T. Milbourne, 1672).

Boxer, David *Edna Manley, Sculptor*, (Kingston: National Gallery of Jamaica & Norman Manley Foundation, 1989).

Bradford, Ernle *Christopher Columbus*, (New York: Viking Press, 1973).

Brathwaithe, Edward *The Development of Creole Society in Jamaica, 1770-1820*, (Oxford: Clarendon Press, 1971).

—— *Masks*, (Oxford University Press, 1968).

Braudel, Fernand *Civilization and Capitalism, 15th to 18th Century* 3 vols, (New York: Harper & Row, 1982-84).

Bridenbaugh, Carl & Roberta *No Peace Beyond the Line*, (New York: Oxford University Press, 1972).

Brodber, Erna "Oral Sources and . . . Social History . . .", *Jamaica Journal* 16:4 (1983).

Bryan, Patrick *Leisure and Class in Late Nineteenth Century Jamaica*, (Kingston: Department of History, University of the West Indies, 1987).

Buxton, Thomas F. Meeting of Abolitionists, 12 May 1832.

Callendar of State Papers, HMSO 1663.

Campbell, George *First Poems,* (London: Garland Publishers, 1981).

Campbell, Mavis *The Dynamics of Change in a Slave Society; a sociopolitical history of the free coloured of Jamaica, 1800-1865*, (New Jersey: Associated Universities Press, 1976).

Carlyle, Thomas "Occasional Discources on the Negro Question", *Frazer's Magazine* (1849).

Carmichael, A. C. *Domestic Manners and Social Conditions of the White, Coloured and Negro Population of the West Indies* 2 vols, (London: Whittaker, Treacher Company, 1883).

Carnegie, James *Great Jamaican Olympians*, (Kingston Publishers, 1996).

Caseate, Frank *Jamaica Talk*, (London: Macmillan, 1961).

Caseate, F. & LePage, R. B *Dictionary of Jamaican English*, (Cambridge University Press, 1967).

Chamerlain, J. E. *Come Back to me my Language*, (University of Illinois Press, 1993).

Chevannes, Barry *Rastafari: Roots and Ideology*, (Kingston: The Press, 1995).

Child, Joshua *A New Discourse of Trade . . .*, (London: J. Hodges etc., 1740).

Clarke, Colin *Kingston, Jamaica: Urban Development and Social Change 1692-1962*, (Berkley: California Press, 1975).

Clarke, Edith *My Mother who Fathered me*, (London: Allen & Unwin, 1957).

Clarkson, Thomas *The History of the Rise, Progress and Accomplishment of the Abolition of the African Slave Trade* 2 vols, (London Reese & Orme, 1808).

Colón, Don Pedro *The Petition of Don Pedro Colón de Portugal y Castro, Duke of Veragua and la Vega, Marquis of Jamaica to Her Royal Highness Mariana of Austria, Queen Regent of Charles II of Spain, for the Island of Jamaica 1672*, (Mill Press, 1992).

Cox, Oliver *Upgrading and Renewing a Historic City: Port Royal, Jamaica*, (Kingston: Jamaica National Heritage Trust, 1984).

Craton, Michael *Slavery, Abolition and Emancipation: black slaves and the British Empire*, (London: Longman, 1976).

Cronon, Edmund D. *Marcus Garvey: Black Moses*, (University of Wisconsin Press, 1955).

Cumper, George "Labour Demand and Supply in Jamaican Sugar Industry 1830-1950", *Social & Economic Studies* 2:4 (1954).

Cundall, Frank & Pietersz, J. *Jamaica Under the Spaniards*, (Kingston: Institute of Jamaica, 1919).

Curtin, Philip D. *The Atlantic Slave Trade*, (University of Wisconsin Press, 1969).

—— *Two Jamaicas*, (Harvard University Press, 1955).

Dallas, R. C. *History of the Maroons*, (London: Longman & Reese, 1803; Frank Cass 1968).

da Veiga Pinta, Francoise & Carreira, A. "Portuguese participation in the slave trade . . ." in *African Slave Trade from the Fifteenth to the Nineteenth Century*, (Paris: UNESCO, 1979).

Davidson, David "Negro Slave Control and Resistance in Colonial Mexico, 1519-1650" in *Maroon Societies: rebel slave communities in the Americas,* (Garden City, New York: Anchor Press, 1973).

Dawes, Neville *Prolegomena to Caribbean Literature,* (Kingston: Institute of Jamaica for the African Caribbean Institute, 1977).

Dennes, Jona Letter to Spencer Compton 14 August 1683, (Spencer Compton Papers, 1675-1765).

Dictionary of Modern Thought, (New York: Harper & Row, 1977).

Diop, C. A. *The African Origin of Civilization: Myth or Reality,* (Westport: Lawrence Hill, 1974).

Downing, G. Letter to his Cousin. 1645.

Durant-Gonzales, Victoria *The Role and Status of Rural Jamaican Women: Higglering and Mothering.* (Ann Arbor: UCLA Microfilms, 1976).

Eden, R. *The History of Trauayle in the West and East Indies: The first book of the Decades of the Ocean Written by Peter Martyr of Angieria Milenoes, Counfaylour to the Bishop of Rome Leo X,* (London, 1577).

Edwards, A. *Marcus Garvey 1887-1940,* (London: New Beacon Publications, 1967).

Edwards, Bryan *The History, Civil and Commercial, of the British Colonies in the West Indies* 2 vols, (London: J. Stockdale, 1793).

Edwards, Paul ed. *Equiano's Travels 1789,* (London: Heinemann, 1967).

Espiñoza, Antonio V. *Compendio y Descripción de las Indias Occidentáles . . .,* (Washington, 1948).

Esquemeling, John *The Buccaneers of America,* (Amsterdam, 1678).

Fage, J. D. *A History of West Africa,* (London: CUP, 1969).

Forde, C. Daryll *Introduction to African Worlds,* (Oxford University Press, 1954).

Froude, James A. *The English in the West Indies,* (London: Lingmans, Green & Co, 1887).

Gibbs, J. ed. *Peoples of Africa,* Abridged, (New York: Holt, Rinehart & Winston, 1978).

Girvan, Norman *Working Together for Development,* (Kingston: Institute of Jamaica, 1993).

Gordon, Shirley ed. *Caribbean Generations,* (Kingston: Longmans Caribbean, 1986).

Great Britain. *Jamaica. Royal Commission 1866,* Report.

Guerra y Sánchez, J. M. *Historia de la Nación Cubana* 10 vols (Havana, 1952).

—— *Sugar and Society in the Caribbean,* (New Haven: Yale University Press, 1964).

Hall, Douglas. *Free Jamaica, 1838-1865: An Economic History,* (New Haven: Yale University Press, 1959).

—— "Diary of a Westmoreland Planter", *Jamaica Journal* 21:3; 21:4 (1988); 22:1 (1989).

Hamilton, D. L. "Simon Benning, Pewterer of Port Royal", in *Test-aided Archaeology,* ed. by B. J. Little (Boca Raton: CRCP,1992).

Haring, C. H. *The Spanish Empire in America,* (New York: Harcourt, Brace and World, 1963).

—— *Blacks in Bondage,* vol 1 (Kingston: Insitutue of Social and Economic Research, University of the West Indies, 1985).

Hart, Richard *Slaves who Abolished Slavery* vol 2 *Blacks in Rebellion* (Kingston: Social & Economic Research, University of the West Indies, 1985).

Hart, Ansell *The Life of George William Gordon,* (Kingston: Institute of Jamaica, 1972).

Hausheer, R. "Introduction", in *Against the Current: essays in the history of Ideas* ed. by Isaiah Berlin, (Penguin Books, 1982).

Hearne, John "Landscape with faces", in *Ian Fleming Introduces Jamaica*, (Kingston: Sangster's Bookstores, 1965).

Heuman, Gad J. *Between Black and White: Race, Politics and the Free Coloureds in Jamaica 1792-1865*, (Westport: Greenwood Press, 1981).

Hickeringill, Edmund *Jamaica Viewed, with all its ports, harbours ...*, (London, Pr. for John Williams 1661).

Higman, B. W. *Jamaica Surveyed*, (Kingston: Institute of Jamaica, 1988).

—— *Slave Population and Economy in Jamaica 1807-1834*, (Cambridge University Press, 1976).

Hill, R. A. ed. *The Marcus Garvey and Universal Negro Improvement Association Papers* 10 vols, (UCLA Press, 1983-85).

—— *Marcus Garvey: Life and Lessons*, (UCLA Press, 1987).

Hinden, Rita *Fabian Colonial Essays*, (London: Allen & Unwin, 1945).

Holt, T. C. *The Problem of Freedom: Race, Labour, and Politics in 1832-1938*, (Kingston: Ian Randle Publishers, 1992).

Holzberg, C. S. *Minorities and Power in a Black Society. The Jewish Community of Jamaica*, (Maryland: N. S. Publishing Co, 1987).

Hughes, Langston ed. *An African Treasury*, (New York: Crown Publishers, 1960).

Ikake, Ibrahim in *The African Slave Trade from the Fifteenth to the Nineteenth Century*, (Paris: UNESCO, 1979).

Inikori, Joseph "The Atlantic Slave Trade", in *The African Slave Trade from the Fifteenth to the Nineteenth Century*, (Paris: UNESCO, 1979).

Jacobs, H. P. *Sixty Years of Change 1806-1866*, (Kingston: Institute of Jamaica, 1973).

Jamaica Government. Laws of Jamaica 1831.

Jamaica. Royal Commission. Minutes of Evidence . . . 1866.

Jefferson, O. *The Post War Development of Jamaica*, (Kingston: Institute of Social & Economic Research, 1972).

Jones, A. Creech *Fabian Colonial Essays*, (London: Allen & Unwin, 1945).

Journals of the Assembly of Jamaica 1664/5. St. Jago de la Vega . . ., (A. Aikman, 1811).

Katzin, M. F. "Higglers of Jamaica". Ph.D. Thesis, University of the West Indies, Mona 1959.

Kennedy, Paul *The Rise and fall of the Great Powers . . . from 1500-2000*, (New York: Random House, 1987).

Kerr, Madeleine *Personality and Conflict in Jamaica*, (London & Kingston: Collins, 1963).

King, in *Maroon Societies: Rebel Slave Communities in the Americas*, (Johns Hopkins University Press, 1979).

Knibb, William *Address at Spitalfields Chapel*, (London, 1832).

—— Jamaica. Speech . . . before the Baptist Missionary Society in Exeter Hall, 28 April 1842.

Knight, R. A. L. *William Knibb, Missionary and Emancipator*, (London: Carey Press, 1948).

—— *Liberty and Progress: A short history of the Baptists of Jamaica*, (Kingston: The Gleaner Company, 1938).

Kopytoff, B. K. "The Maroons of Jamaica" Ph.D. Thesis, University of the West Indies, Mona, 1974.

Krawath, Fred F. *Christopher Columbus, Cosmographer. A history of metrology, Geodesy, Geography and Exploration from Antiquity to the Columbian Era*, (California: Landmark Enterprises, 1987).

Lalla, B. & D'Costa, J. Language in Exile, (University of Alabama Press, 1990).

Lamming, George *In the Castle of my Skin*, (New York: Collier Books, 1983).

Las Casas, Bartolomew *History of the Indies Bk. III. 1559*, (Madrid, 1875).

Latrobe, J. C. *Negro Education in Jamaica, 1837*, (Ordered by the House of Commons, 1838).

Leslie, Charles *A New and Exact Account of Jamaica ...*, (Edinburgh: R. Fleming, 1739).

Levy, Jacqueline "The Economic role of the Chinese in Jamaica. The Grocery Retail Trade", *Jamaica Historical Review* XV (1986).

Lewis, Gordon *The Growth of the Modern West Indies*, (London: Modern Reader Paperbacks, 1968).

Lewis, M. G. *Journal of a West India Proprietor*, (London: Murray, 1834).

Lewis, Rupert *Marcus Garvey: Anti-Colonial Champion*, (London: Karia Publishing, 1987).

Lewis, R, & P. Bryan eds *Garvey: his Work and Impact*, (Kingston: Institute of Social and Economic Research & Department of Extra-Mural Studies, University of the West Indies, 1988).

Ligon, Richard *True and Exact History of the Island of Barbados . . .*, (London, 1657).

Lloyd, P. C. "The Yoruba of Nigeria", in *Peoples of Africa*, ed. by James L Gibbs (New York: Holt, Rhinehart and Winston, 1965).

Long, Edward *The History of Jamaica . . .*, (London: T. Lowndes, 1774).

Lumsden, Joyce "Robert Love and Jamaican Politics", Ph.D. Thesis, University of the West Indies, Mona 1987.

Mair-Mathurin, Lucille "Women Field Workers in Jamaica during Slavery", Elsa Goveia Memorial Lecture, Mona, 1986.

—— "A Historical Study of women in Jamaica from 1655-1844" Ph.D. Thesis, University of the West Indies, Mona, 1974.

—— *The Rebel Woman in the British West Indies During Slavery*, (Kingston: Institute of Jamaica for the Afro-Caribbean Institute of Jamaica, 1975).

Manley, Norman "Foreword", in *Three Novels of Roger Mais*, (London: Jonathan Cape, 1966).

Mannix, D. *Black Cargoes: A History of the Atlantic Slave Trade 1518-1865*, (London: Longmans, 1962).

Mansingh, L. & Mansingh, A. "Indian Heritage in Jamaica", *Jamaica Journal* 10: 2, 3, 4 (1976).

Marsala, V. J. *Sir John Peter Grant ... 1866-1874*, (Kingston: Institute of Jamaica, 1972).

Marsden, Peter *An Account of the Island of Jamaica*, (Newcastle, 1788).

Mayes, Philip *Port Royal Jamaica. Excavations 1969-1970*, (Kingston: Jamaica National Trust Commission, 1972).

Mbiti, John S. *Concepts of God in Africa*, (London: SPCK 1970).

McKay, Claude *Banana Bottom*, (New York: Harper & Row, 1961).

—— *The Dialect Poetry of Claude McKay*, (New York: Books for Libraries Press, 1972).

Miller, Errol "Educational Development in Independent Jamaica", in *Independence Essays on the Early Years*, (Kingston; London: Heinemann Publishers & James Currey Ltd, 1989).

Mintz, Sidney *Caribbean Transformations*, (Chicago: Aldine Press Co, 1974).

Morrissey, M. *Slave Women in the New World*, (University of Kansas Press, 1989).

Murray, R. N. ed. *J. J. Mills, His own Account of his life and Times Jamaica*, (Kingston: Collins & Sangster's 1969).

Nettleford, Rex *Caribbean Cultural Identity: The case of Jamaica*, (Kingston: Institute of Jamaica, 1978).

—— *Manley and the New Jamaica,* (London: William Clowes & Sons, 1971).

—— ed. *Manley in the New Jamaica. Selected Speeches & Writings 1938-1939,* (London: Longman Caribbean, 1971).

New York Times, 16 January 1992

Nicholls, David "The Syrians of Jamaica", *The Jamaican Historical Review* XV (1986).

Nugent, George Report to Colonial Office 20 February 1802.

Nugent, Maria *Lady Nugent's Journal,* (Kingston: Institute of Jamaica, 1939).

O'Connell, R. L. *Of Arms and Men . . .,* (New York: Oxford University Press, 1989).

Ogilvie, D. L. *History of the Parish of Trelawny,* (Kingston, 1954).

Oldmixon, John *The British Empire in America,* (London, Printed for John Nicholson . . . 1708).

Olivier, S. Lord *Jamaica the Blessed Island London,:* (Fisher & Faber Ltd, 1936).

—— *The Myth of Governor Eyre,* (London: Hogarth Press, 1933).

Olsen, Fred *On the Trail of the Arawaks,* (University of Oklahoma Press, 1974).

Padrón, Moráles *Spanish Jamaica,* (1952).

Parboosingh, I. S. "An Indo-Jamaican Beginning . . .", *Jamaica Journal* 18:2 (1985).

Parrent, J. M. & Parrent, M. B. Columbus Caravels Archaeological Project . . ., Report 1993, mimeo.

Parry, J. H. & Sherlock, P. M. *Short History of the West Indies,* (London: Macmilllan, 1987).

Patterson, H. O. *The Sociology of Slavery: An analysis of the origins, development and structure of Negro slavery in Jamaica,* (N. J. Rutherford; Fairleigh: Dickenson University Press, 1969).

Pawson, M. & Buisseret, D. *Port Royal, Jamaica,* (Oxford University Press, 1975).

Phillippo, J. M. *Jamaica: Its Past and Present State,* (London, 1843).

Polianyi, K. The *Great Transformation* (New York & Toronto: Farrar and Rinehart, 1944)

Price, Richard. ed. *Maroon Societies: Rebel Slave Communities in the Americas,* (New York: Doubleday, 1973).

Rhys, Ernest *The Growth of Political Liberty.* (London: Everyman's Library, 1921)

Roberts, G. W. *The Population of Jamaica,* (Cambridge University Press, 1957).

Roberts, W. A. *Jamaica: the Portrait of an Island,* (New York: Coward-McCann, 1955).

—— *Six Great Jamaicans,* (Kingston: Pioneer Press, 1951).

Robotham, Don *"The Notorious Riot" The Socio-Economic and Political Bases of Paul Bogle's Revolt,* Kingston: Institute of Social and Economic Research, No. 28, 1981 University of the West Indies.

Roland, J. G. ed. *Africa. An Anthology of African History,* (1974).

—— ed. *Africa, the Heritage and Challenge,* (Pace Coll.: Fawcett Publications, 1974).

Rossiter, C. *The First American Revolution,* (New York: Harvest Books, Harcourt Brace, 1956).

Roughley, T. *The Jamaica Planter's Guide . . .,* (London: Longman, Hurst, Reese, Orme & Brown, 1823).

Rouse, Irving *The Tainos: Rise and Decline of the People who Greeted Columbus,* (New Haven: Yale University Press, 1992).

The Royal Gazette, 21-28 January 1832.

Russell, Horace "The Missionary Outreach of the West Indian Church to West Africa in the Nineteenth Century With Particular Reference to the Baptists", Ph.D. Thesis Oxford University, 1972.

Ryman, Cheryl "Jonkonnu a neo-African Form", *Jamaica Journal* 17:1 & 17:2 (1984).

Satchell, V. *The Jamaican Peasantry 1866-1900*, (Kingston: Department of History, University of the West Indies, 1983.

—— *From Plots to Plantations: land transactions in Jamaica, 1866-1900*, (Kingston: Institute of Social and Economic Research, University of the West Indies, 1990).

Schama, Simon *Citizens*, (London: Penguin, 1989).

Sedeno, Jacinto *Description of Jamaica*, (Santa Domingo: Archive de Indias, n.d.) (Government of Jamaica 1639-40).

Senior, B. M. *Jamaica, as it was, as it is, and as it may be . . . also an Authentic Narrative of the Negro Insurrection in 1831*, (New York: Negro Universities Press, 1969).

Senior, Olive "The Panama Railway", *Jamaica Journal* 44 (1980).

—— "The Colon People. Part I", *Jamaica Journal* 11:3 (1977).

—— "The Colon People. Part II", *Jamaica Journal* 42 (1978).

Sewell, William G. *The Ordeal of Free Labour in the British West Indies*, (New York: Economic Classics, 1968).

Shepherd, Verene *Transcients to Settlers: The Experience of Indians in Jamaica, 1845-1950*, (Peepal Tree Publications, 1994).

—— "Transcients to Citizens: The Development of a settled East Indian Community", *Jamaica Journal* 18:3 (1985).

Sheridan, Richard *The Development of the Plantations to 1750*, (Caribbean Universities Press, 1970).

Sherlock, Philip *Norman Manley, a Biography*, (London: Macmillan, 1980).

Simmonds, Lorna "Slave Higglering in Jamaica 1780-1834", *Jamaica Journal* 20:1(1987).

Sistren, with H. Ford Smith *Lionheart Gal*, (London: The Women's Press, 1986).

Sloane, Hans *A Voyage to the islands, Madera, Barbados, Nieves, S. Christopher and Jamaica with the Natural History of the Herbs and Trees . . .* 2 vols, (London, 1707).

Smith, John (Demerara). Letter to the London Missionary Society, 1823.

Smith, M. G. *The Plural Society in the British West Indies*, (Kingston: Sangster's Bookstores, 1974).

Smith, M. G., Augier, Roy, Nettleford, Rex *The Rastafari Movement in Kingston Jamaica*, (Kingston: Institute of Economic and Social Research, University College of the West Indies, 1960).

Sohal, H. S. "The East Indian Indentureship System in Jamaica 1845-1917" Ph.D. Thesis, University of Waterloo, 1979.

The Spencer Compton Papers, 1675-1765.

The Star Newspaper, 8 August 1936.

Stedman, T. G. in *Maroon Societies: Rebel Slave Communities in the Americas,* (Baltimore Johns Hopkins University Press, 1973).

Stewart, John *An Account of Jamaica and its inhabitants,* (London: Longman, Nurse, Reese & Orme, 1808).

Suicke, J. B. Letter to the Earl of Belmore, 25 May 1832

Thompson, E. P. *Making of the English Working Class,* (London: Gollanz, 1963).

Times Atlas of World History, (London, 1984).

Trollope, A. *The West Indies and the Spanish Maine,* (London: Chapman & Hall; Frank Cass, 1968).

Tuchman, B. *The Proud Tower,* (New York: Macmillan, 1966).

Udeagu, Onyenaekeya *An African Treasury,* (New York: Crown Onyenaekeya Publishers, 1960).

Underhill, E. B. *The Tragedy of Morant Bay . . .,* (London: Alexander & Shapherd, 1895).

Waddell, Hope *Twenty-Nine Years in the West Indies and Central Africa . . . 1829-1858,* (London: Nelson, 1863).

Walker, D. F. *The Call of the West Indies,* (London: Cargate P. 1930).

Wallace, & Hinds *Our West African Heritage,* (Kingston: African Caribbean Institute of Jamaica, 1989).

Ward, W. E. F. *History of Ghana,* (New York: Praeger, 1963).

West Indies Royal Commission Report, HMSO, 1884).

West Indies Royal Commission 1938-1939, HMSO, 1945.

West India Royal Commission, Report. 1897, HMSO.

West Indies Sugar Commission 1929-1930 Report 2 vols HMSO, 1930.

Westphal, A. *The Breaking of the Dawn or Moravian Work in Jamaica, 1754-1904,* (Belfast, 1904).

Williams, *Eric Capitalism and Slavery,* (University of North Carolina Press, 1944).

—— *Documents of West Indian History 1492-1655,* (Port-of-Spain: PNM Publishing Co. 1963).

—— *Forged from the Love of Liberty: Selected Speeches of Dr. Eric Williams.* (Port-of-Spain: Longman Caribbean, 1981).

Woodhouse, A. S. P. *Puritanism and Liberty,* (Chicago University Press, 1951).

Wynter, Sylvia "Bernardo de Balbuena . . . 1562-1627", *Jamaica Journal* 3:3; 3:4 (1969); 4:1; 4:3 (1970).

Yin, Lee Tom, ed. *The Chinese in Jamaica,* (Kingston: 1963).

Index of Names

Abraham, 36, 37-38
Abrahams, Carl, 392
Abrahams, Peter: on tribal society, 28, 29
Accompong, 136
Allan, Edris, 360
Alves, Bain, 247
Archbould, Henry, 85, 86
Azikiwe, Nnamdi, 15

Bailey, Amy, 359
Baker, Lorenzo Dow: and Boston Fruit Company, 275; strategy of, 278; views of, 279
Baker, Moses, 39, 203; significance of, work of, 180-181, 182
Balcarres, earl of, 145-149
Ballard, Thomas, 85
Barham, Joseph, 179
Barrett, Samuel, 217, 222
Barry, Samuel, 85
Baugh, Cecil, 394
Beckford, Peter, 155
Beckford, William, 4, 158; quoted, 32
Beeston, William, 86, 87
Benham, F. C., 379
Bennett, Louise: and Jamaican dialect, 405
Bennett, Wycliffe, 405
Berbick, Trevor, 403

Berlin, Isaiah: on Eurocentricity, 12-13
Bernáldez, Andres, 64
Bleby, Henry, 213; on execution of Sam Sharpe, 227
Bligh, William: and West Indian food supply, 192
Blome, Richard: *Description of the Island of Jamaica*, 88
Bogle, Paul, 4, 246; capture of, 259; as deacon, 249; description of, 247; hanging of, 259; and military training of followers, 255; stature of, 252; and unofficial court system, 255; and walk to Spanish Town, 257
Bolas, Juan de, 73, 81
Bolívar, Simón, 16
Borrowes, Alfred, 296
Bougainville, Captain Antoine de, 192
Boukman, 185, 186
Brathwaite, Edward Kamau: poems of, 102, 103-106
Bridges, Rev. William, 222
Briere, Jean: quoted, 3
Brown, Rev. Ethelred, 373
Brown, Everald, 202
Brown, G. Arthur, 383
Brown, Sam: on social conditions in Kingston, 351, 356

Buie, Theodore, 253
Burchell, Thomas, 241
Burke, Eddie, 360
Burke, Edmund, 161
Burke, Lilly Mae, 360
Bustamante, Alexander: activities of, 364, 366-367; as chief minister, 374; and Jamaica Labour Party, 5; and Jamaica Workers' and Tradesmen's Union, 364; and labour movement, 5-6, 248, 363, 368; Norman Manley on, 375-376; release of, 367
Bustamante, Lady Gladys, 360
Buxton, Thomas Fowell, 208

Cadbury, George, 383
Calder, Vassal: and criticism of Robert Love, 288-289
Campbell, Charles, 285
Campbell, George: quoted, 6-7, 19
Campbell, Ralph, 392
Candler, John: on industry of the peasants, 242-243
Cardwell, Edward, 254
Carlyle, Thomas: *Discourse on the Negro Question*, 12
Carney, Arthur, 360
Cartwright, Edmund, 189
Césaire, Aimé, 15

Chamberlaine, Richard, 241
Christophe, Henri, 186, 188
Clarke, Colin: *Kingston, Urban Change and Reform*, 352-353
Clarke, Edith: *My Mother Who Fathered Me*, 275
Clarke, Rev. Henry, 236
Clarke, Samuel, 4
Clarkson, Thomas, 179
Cliff, Jimmy: quoted, 401
Columbus, Christopher, 20; arrival of, in the Bahamas, 55; arrival of, in Hispaniola, 63; encounter with Tainos in Jamaica, 64-67; first encounter with Indians, 55; and settlement of the Indies, 56-57; voyages of, 54-57
Columbus, Diego, 67
Cook, Captain James, 192
Coombs, A. G. S.: and Jamaica Workers' and Tradesmen's Union, 364
Cortés, Hernando, 61
Cox, Sandy, 247; and National Club of Jamaica, 297
Craskell, Thomas, 145
Craton, Michael: on slave punishment, 14
Cromwell, Oliver: and Western Design, 78, 84
Cubah ("Queen of Kingston"), 144
Cudjoe, 4, 136, 137; peace treaty of, 140-141
Cuffy, 136
Cugnet, Nicolas, 189
Cumper, George, 5
Cundall, Frank, 392
Cuneo, Michele de, 58
Curtin, Philip: and census of African slave trade, 93; *The Atlantic Slave Trade*, 14

Daley, Henry, 392
Daley, James, 248
Danquah, J. B., 312
Davis, Henrietta Vinton, 312
Dawes, Neville: *Prolegomena to*

Caribbean Literature, 337; on attitudes to Africa, 337
D'Costa, Alfred: and bauxite, 380
Dehaney, 39
DeLisser, H. G.: and perceptions of Africa, 17
Dendy, Walter, 240
Dessalines, Jean Jacques, 186, 188; assassination of, 189; as emperor of Haiti, 189
Diaz, Bartholomew, 54
Diop, Birago: quoted, 27
Dixon, Alexander, 288, 297
Dom Alfonso, 120
Domingo, W. A., 300, 350
Dove, Thomas, 39, 216, 220
Dowdy, Chester, 360
D'Oyley, Edward, 81, 84
Drake, Francis, 78-79
Drax, Charles, 155
Drax, James, 91
Drax, William, 155
Drummond, Andrew, 243-244
DuBois, W. E., 299, 300
Dunkley, Archibald, 396
Dunkley, John, 363, 392
Edward VII: funeral of, 267-268
Edwards, Bryan: and perception of Africans, 31
Ellis, George, 165
Equiano, Olaudah: account of enslavement of, 123-124, 125-126
Esquivel, Juan de, 59, 67; conduct of, 70
Evelyn, Linden H., 239
Eyre, Governor Edward: and call for abolition of Jamaican Assembly, 264-265; Gordon's attack on, 253

Fairclough, O. T., 350; and formation of People's National Party, 368
Farquharson, May, 359
Foot, Sir Hugh, 265
Foster, William, 179
Francis, Sybil, 360

Froude, J. A.: on civilising mission of Europeans, 266; quoted, 12

Gama, Vasco da, 54
Garay, Francisco de, 69, 70
Gardner, Robert, 216, 220
Garvey, Amy Jacques, 307
Garvey, Marcus, 3, 11, 247; achievements of, 314-315; activities of, in Jamaica, 308-313; and advocacy of social change, 310; on Africa, 17, 18; on black history, 10; and the *Black Man*, 308; in Central America, 298; challenge of, to the peasantry, 5; death of, 314; debate with Otto Huiswood, 311; and decolonisation, 295; deportation of, 307; efforts to intimidate, 302; and Harlem Renaissance, 300; impact of, 292-293; influence of Robert Love on, 291, 297; life of, 296-302, 304-314; and local elections, 310; migration of, to Britain, 313; and the *New Jamaican*, 308; and People's Political Party, 309; as publisher, 301; on race consciousness among Jamaicans, 294-296, 362; research on, 20; return to Jamaica, 307-308; and School of African Philosophy, 313-314; trial and imprisonment of, 306-307; as universalist, 296
Girvan, Norman: *Working Together for Development*, 360
Girvan, Thom, 360
Goodison, Lorna, 406; on history, 194
Gordon, George William, 4, 246; attack on Governor Eyre, 253; and efforts to encourage voting, 253; hanging of, 260; letter to his wife, 260, 262; life of, 248-249; religious conviction of, 249

Gordon, Joseph, 248
Grant, Governor Sir John Peter: work of, 265
Grant, St William: release of, 367
Guthrie, Colonel: and negotiations with Cudjoe, 140

Hannan, W. B., 286
Hargreaves, James, 177, 189
Hart, Richard: *Blacks in Rebellion*, quoted, 8-9
Harvey, Thomas, 239
Hazlitt, William, 179
Headley, George: record of, 391
Hearne, John, 158-159
Henry, Rev. Claudius, 397
Hibbert, George, 167
Hibbert, Joseph, 396
Higman, Barry, 31; *Jamaica Surveyed*, 152
Hill, Frank, 350
Hill, Ken, 350
Hill, Richard: and Underhill meetings, 255
Hill, Robert: and research on Garvey, 20, 296
Hinds, Robert, 396
Honeygan, Lloyd, 403
Hope, Richard, 86
Hope, Roger, 85, 153
Howell, Leonard, 396
Hughes, Langston, 3
Huie, Albert, 392
Huiswood, Otto: debate between Garvey and, 311
Hylton, Edward, 213

Inikori, Joseph: *The Slave Trade and the Atlantic Economies*, 124-125; on capitalism and slavery, 161
Issa, Abe: and tourism promotion, 381
Jackson, Grace, 403
Jackson, Richard Hill, 285
Jacobs, H. P., 350
James, C. L. R., 15, 161; *Black Jacobins*, 19

James, Edith Dalton, 359
James, John, 145
James, Captain Montague, 146
Jefferson, Thomas: and the American Declaration of Independence, 184
Johnny, 136
Johnson, 39
Johnson, William, 214
Jordon, Edward, 259

Kapo, 202, 394
Kenyatta, Jomo, 15; influence of Garveyism on, 302; and the Mau Mau, 28-29;
Kerr, Madeleine: on society and personality development, 354
Ketelhodt, Baron von, 258; death of, 259
King, Johannes, 130-131
King, Martin Luther, 3, 15
Kishee, 136
Knibb, Mary Morris, 359
Knibb, William, 216, 224-225, 236; arrival of, in Jamaica, 207-208; and development of free villages, 239; testimony of, regarding Western Uprising, 214

Lamming, George: on black consciousness, 294-295; *In the Castle of my Skin*, quoted, 1; quoted, 11
La Renteria, Pablo de, 67
Las Casas, Bartolome de, 67-68
Lascelles, Daniel, 31
Lecky, T. P.: and livestock development, 395
LeClerc, General Charles, 188
Leslie, Charles, 151-152
Lewis, Bernard, 392
Lewis, M. G. "Monk": on death of children in Jamaica, 193-194; on slave family, 14
Lewis, Rupert: and research on Garvey, 20, 296
Lewis, W. Arthur: on social conditions in the West Indies, 351-352; *Theory of Economic*

Growth, 377; on West Indian economic policy, 379
Lincoln, Abraham, 16
Lightbourne, Robert: and industrialisation programme, 382
Linton, 39
Lisle, George, 39, 203; significance of work of, 180-181, 182
Locke, Alain, 3
Long, Edward, 77, 167
Long, Samuel, 30, 87
Longbridge, Gladys. *See* Bustamante, Lady Gladys
L'Ouverture, Toussaint, 16; role of, in St Domingue revolution, 187-188
Love, Robert, 247; anti-colonial views of, 285; career of, 283-285; contribution of, to national movement, 11; death of, 291; influence of, on Marcus Garvey, 291; in Kingston City Council, 288; in Legislative Council, 288; and People's Convention, 286; on political representation, 287; and support of black representation in government, 283; and support for Pan-Africanism, 291; on tax structure, 287
Lowry, Somerset (Earl of Belmore), 220
Lunan, Henry: and payment for lot, 237
Lusan, Carmen, 360
Lynch, Thomas, 86
Lyttleton, Sir Charles, 81

Maclaren, James, 252; and walk to Spanish Town, 257
Mais, Roger: *Brother Man*, 351
Manikongo Garcia, 121
Manley, Edna: first exhibition of, 393; and Jamaican art movement, 392-393; "Negro Aroused" of, 6

Manley, Norman: on Bustamante, 375-376; and campaign for universal adult suffrage, 5-6, 247; in dock workers dispute, 1938, 365-367; on national unity, 8, 362-363; and People's National Party, 6, 368; quoted, xii

Marley, Bob, 395, 401

Marriott, Alvin, 394

Marson, Una: in Jamaican cultural revolution, 338, 344-345; and social concern, 360; women in the work of, 345

Martyr, Peter, 71-72

Mazuelo, Pedro de: and sugar making, 74

Mbiti, John, 20; on African concept of time, 207

McCallum, Michael, 403

McDonald, Sir Herbert, 395

McKay, Claude, 3; *Banana Bottom*, 338, 339-344; on banana, 276; and Harlem Renaissance, 300; in Jamaican cultural revolution, 338

McKenley, Herb, 391-392

Medina, Juan de, 71

Mico, Lady: and Mico Institution, 240

Miller, David, 393

Miller, Errol: on education system, 408

Mills, Don, 383

Mills, Gladstone, 383

Modyford, Thomas, 84, 157

Moncrieffe, Benjamin Scott, 166

Moncrieffe, Peter, 166

Monk, George, 85

Moody, Harold, 351

Mordecai, John, 383

Morgan, Henry, 85

Moses, 36, 38-39

Moton, Major Robert, 299

Musgrave, Sir Anthony, 392

Mutabaruka, 401

Nanny, 4, 137

Nanny Grigg, 204

Nettleford, Rex: *Jamaica in Independence*, 404; *Manley and the New Jamaica*, 378; and NDTC, 405

Nkrumah, Kwame, 15

Nugent, George, 167

Nugent, Lady Maria, 153, 154, 158, 166

Nzinga, Queen, 121

Oge, 184

Olivier, Lord, 265

Onuora, Oku: and dub poetry, 401

Ortiz, Fernando: *Cuban Counterpoint*, 275

Osei Tutu: and Ashanti political development, 110, 112

Ottey, Merlene, 403

Ovando, Nicolas de, 57

Padmore, George, 15

Palache, J. T., 285

Parboosingh, Karl, 394

Parks, Rosa, 15

Patterson, Orlando: on colonialism, 13

Penn, Admiral William, 78

Phibbah, 170

Phillippo, Rev. James, 249; and establishment of free villages, 237

Pink, John H., 155

Pizarro, Francisco, 61

Porras, Francisco, 66

Pottinger, David, 393

Price, Charles, 288

Pringle, John: and tourism promotion, 380

Quao, 136

Quarrie, Donald, 403

"Queen's Advice", 257

Ramsay, James, 179

Reid, V. S.: *New Day*, 19, 207

Reynolds, Mallica. *See* Kapo

Rhodd, Ethlyn, 359

Rhone, Trevor, 406

Richardson, Egerton, 383

Rigaud, Pierre de, 188

Roberts, George, 280

Roberts, W. Adolphe, 282, 350; *Six Great Jamaicans*, 285

Rodney, Walter, 102-103

Rousseau, Jean-Jacques, 177; influence of, 183-184

Rowe, John, 203

Sargon: of Kish, 36

Seaga, Edward: and festival of arts, 405-406; on social classes, 385

Sedeño, Jacinto, 75

Selassie, Haile, 19; visit of, to Jamaica, 399, 400

Senior, Olive, 406

Sewell, William, 6

Sharp, Granville, 178-179

Sharpe, Sam, 4, 39, 128; and campaign for strike, 214; execution of, 227; role of, in Western Liberation Uprising, 213-214, 226; significance of, 212-213; surrender of, 220

Simpson, H. A. L., 297

Sligo, marquis of: and freeing of slaves, 234

Slim and Sam: and social commentary, 355-356

Smicle, Josiah, 288

Smith, Adam, 177

Smith, John: imprisonment of, 205

Smith, M. G.: on cultural differences in Jamaica, 354; *Plural Society*, 351

Smith, Michael, 401

Somersett, James, 178

Sonthonax, Leger Felicite, 185

Stedman, T. G.: on maroon warfare in Suriname, 130-132

Steibel, George, 285

Stewart, Margery, 360

Stokes, Luke, 85

Stone, Carl: on industrialisation in Jamaica, 384-385

General Index

Aboukir: Taino artefacts near, 44
Abolition of the Slave Trade Act (1807), 180
Absenteeism: of Jamaican proprietors, 94, 159; and ownership of office, 160-161
Africa: artistic tradition of, 22; as cradle of mankind, 22; effect of partitioning of, 268-269; folklore of, 9; impact of slave trade on life in, 102-103; iron-working in, in antiquity, 22; Jamaican perceptions of, 17-18; Marcus Garvey on, 17; partitioning of, 266-267; place of, in civilisation, 20-24; religion in, 26-27; retentions of, in Jamaica, 2, 316; tribal society in, 28, 29; tribes of, 24, 26; and use of history, 9; visit of Bush Negro chiefs to, 18; white perceptions of history of, 20
African Communities League, 298
African society: features of, 26-29
Africans: and concept of justice, 247; and creation of democratic society in the Americas, 41; enslavement of, by Spanish, 73; and injustice of plantation society, 94-95; in Jamaica, at time of British conquest, 77;

and kinship, 28; in liberation movements in plantation America, 15-16, 81, 84; mortality rate of, 93; music and, 97; and prayer, 26-27; recruitment of, 317-318; and religion, 94-97; and resistance to English invaders, 80; and slavery, 116-118
Agriculture: stigma attached to, 245
Akan-Ashanti people, 110, 112; characteristics of, 134; and the slave trade, 133-134
Aluminium: development of, in Jamaica, 379-380
Anansi: in West African tradition, 197
Anti-colonial movement, 267; in Jamaica, 272
Anti-slavery society: public interest in, 180; work of, 179-180
Apprentices: treatment of, 234-235
Apprenticeship: system of, 230
Aqueduct: at Mona and Hope Estates, 154
Arawakan: as language of the Caribs and Tainos, 43
Art movement: growth of Jamaican, 392-394; new generation of artists in, 406
Asia: and colonisation of New World, 42

Assembly. *See* House of Assembly
Atlantic Age: explained, 51-52; Genoa and, 53, 54
Atlantic Slave Trade, Philip Curtin, 14
Aztecs: and geometry, 43; and mathematics, 43; and zero concept, 43

Back to Africa movement, 305
Bahamas, the: arrival of Columbus in, 55
Bamboo Pen, 163
Banana: export of, 271; Lacatan variety, 395; in life of the peasant, 276-277; in Port Antonio, 277-278; rise in trade, in Jamaica, 275-279
Banana Bottom, Claude McKay, 338, 339-344; message of, 342-343; significance of, 339
Bank of Jamaica, 383
Baptist Church: native, 180
Baptist Missionary Society, 39; arrival of, in Jamaica, 203; founding of, 178
Barbados: slave uprisings in, 204; transformation of, by sugar manufacturing, 91-92
Bauxite: in Jamaica, 379-380
Beach Control Authority, 381
Benham Spring, 166
Bible, the: and African-Jamaicans, 39

Birmingham, 239
Black Cross Navigation and Trading Company: establishment of, 307
Black electorate: mobilisation of, 283
Black Jacobins, 189
Black Jacobins, C.L.R. James, 19
Black Power movement, 15
Black proletariat: beginnings of, 273, 280; growth of, in Kingston and St Andrew, 350
Black Star Line: formation of, 305-306
Blackman, the, 308; folding of, 313
Blacks: challenge to, 409-411; disparity in number between whites and, 160; occupations of, in Kingston, 353; and perception of self determination, 369
Bluefish Caves, Yukon: archaeological finds at, 42
Bog Estate: renaming of, 278
Boston Guardian: tribute of, to Garvey, 314
Boston Fruit Company: formation of, 275; merged, 278
Boundbrook, 278
Boxing: Jamaicans in, 403
Brazil: maroon settlement in, 129
Britain: retentions of, in Jamaica, 2; and use of history, 9-10
British and Foreign Bible Society, 178
Brother Man, Roger Mais, 351
Buccaneers: activities of, 84-85; at Port Royal, 84
Burrowfield Pen, 166
Bush Negroes: of Suriname, 15, 130-132; visit of chiefs of, to Africa, 18. *See also* Maroons
Bustamante Industrial Trade Union: formation of, 367

Cabinet: institution of, in government system, 374

Calabar College: and training of ministers, 241
Cape of Good Hope, 54
Capitalism and Slavery, Eric Williams, 19
Caribbean Basin: americanisation of, 270
Caribs: settlement of, 43
Carpenter's Mountain, Manchester: Taino artefacts in, 44
Carrion Crow Hill, 139
Carvings: of the Tainos, 2
Cassava: export of, by Spanish, 69
Catholic Church: and slavery, 68
Census: of 1611, 74, 75; of African slave trade, 93
Central Bureau of Statistics, 383
Central Planning Agency, 383
Chapels: destruction of, 222
Chartist Movement, 211
Cherry Garden Estate, 248
Children: mortality rate of, in Jamaica, 193-194; skills training for, 244-245
China: civilisation of, 61-62
Chinese: attitude of black Jamaicans toward, 331; immigration of, to Jamaica, 327, 328; in Jamaica, 7; as labourers, 327; occupations of, 330; in retail trade, 328, 330; and riots in the 1930s, 331; savings scheme of, 329; traditional values of, 332-333
Christianity: conversion of Indians to, 70, 71
Church, Spanish: building of, 71-72
Church of England: reform movement in, 178
Civil disabilities: removal of, in Jamaica, 229-230
Civil Rights Act (US), 15
Civil service: modernisation of, 383
Clapham Sect: and establishment

of Sierra Leone, 179-180
Class: composition of the Jamaican ruling, 13; consciousness of, in Jamaica, 389-390; gap among social, 386; insensitivity to, in Jamaica, 386;
Cocoa: cultivation of, by early settlers, 88
Codex Montezuma, 43
College of Arts, Science and Technology, 314
Colonial Church Union, 223; formation of, 222
Colonial development fund: establishment of, 368
Colonialism: beginning of, in Jamaica, 30; culture and release from, 337-338; effect of, on the Caribbean, 10-14, 32; Eric Williams on, 13; Orlando Patterson on, 13
Colour: gradations of, 12; prejudice, in Jamaica, 192; and social change, 374
Communication: developments worldwide, 270
Community organisation: of the peasantry, 357
Compensation: for slave owners, 230
Constitution: criticism of 1944, 373; granting of, in 1944, 370
Co-operation: methods of, among black Jamaicans, 6
Cornwall Courier, 217, 218
Coromanti people: characteristics of, 134; role of, in struggle for freedom, 142-144
Cotterwoods, 139
Cotton industry: development of, 189
Court system: organised by Bogle, 255
Craftsmanship: of the Tainos, 71, 72
Cricket: performance of West Indians in, 391
Crooked Spring, 216

Crop time: on estates, 158
Crown colony government: basis of, 265-266; criticism of, 352; and education of Jamaicans, 32; introduction of, in Jamaica, 264, 265; nature of, 277; political control under, 282
Crown lands: restrictions on ownership of, 238
Cuba: decline of sugar in, 348-349
Cuban Counterpoint, Fernando Ortiz, 275
Culture: differences in, in Jamaica, 354; formation of Jamaican, 194-199, 391; in pre-1920s Jamaica, 390; and release from colonialism, 337-338; women and, 402
Cumina, 39

Day-for-day, 244
Deans Valley, 136
Declaration of Independence, American, 16
Declaration of the Rights of the Negro Peoples of the World: at UNIA convention, 304-305
Decolonisation: Garvey and, 295
Demerara: slave rebellion in, in 1823, 204-205
Democracy: Eric Williams on, 376; meaning of, 376
Democratic society: Africans and creation of, in the Americas, 41
Depression: in post World War I period, 348
Description of the Island of Jamaica, Richard Blome, 88
Development: in post World War II period, 378
Discourse on the Negro Question, Thomas Carlyle, 12
Disease: in the New World, 58, 59-60; in urban Jamaica, 356-357
Divali, 325, 326

Dock workers: influence of Garvey on, 310
Don Figueroa Mountains, 66
Drax Hall, St Ann: artefacts at, 155-156; horse racing at, 166; negro village at, 155-156
Dub poetry, 401
Dye woods, 88

Earthquake: at Port Royal, 85
East Indian Progressive Society, 325
East Indians: culture of, 320; end of immigration of, 326-327; festivals of, 325-326; in Hayes, Clarendon, 323; in Jamaica, 7; living conditions of, 319, 324; and market gardens, 324-325; marriage of, 321; occupations of, 323-324; recruitment methods for, 318-319; and relations with African-Jamaicans, 321; repatriation of, 320, 322; retentions, 325-326; treatment of, in Jamaica, 318, 319-321; and urban drift, 323
Economic conditions: of black peasantry, 4-5; in the 1860s, 254; response of Jamaicans to, 271; transformation of, of peasants, 276
Economic growth: in Jamaica, between 1945 and 1960
Economic policy: Arthur Lewis on, 379; of England, in 1650s, 78, committee to advise on, in Jamaica, 379
Economy, internal: development of, in post-emancipation period, 245
Edelweiss Park: and cultural activities, 309, 312
Education: criticism of Jamaican system of, 387; Crown colony government and, 32; effect of colonial system of, 369; Errol Miller on, 408; grants for, 272; and mobility of the

peasantry, 240; need for reforms in, 409; reforms to facilitate secondary, 374; system of, and attitude to African heritage, 10; women and, 402
Egypt: and Ethiopia, 40; growth of, 22
Egypt Pen, 167
Elders, Dempster and Company: in the banana trade, 278
Elections: first general, 370-371; second general, 371; turnout at, in 1896
Eltham, 166
Emancipation: levels of, 344
Emancipation Act (1833), 212; passage of, 225; significance of, 230; terms of, 230, 235
Emigration: the peasantry and, 5, 280; return to Jamaica of emigrants, 350
Empire-building: death of concept of, 368; effects of, in Africa, 109-110; establishment of pattern of, 36-37
Empowerment: history and, 9
Encomienda system, 67, 68
English Committee on the Slave Trade, 13
English: economic policy of the, 1650s, 78; landing of, in Jamaica, 77-78
Enlightenment: effect of, on the Caribbean, 183-184
Environment: adaptation to, by slaves, 195
Equal Opportunity Act (US), 15
Ethiopia: and Egypt, 40
Ethiopian World Federation: formation of, 396
Eurocentricity: of middle-class Jamaicans, 353-354
Europe: and world dominance, 61
Evangelical movement, 177; indigenous, 180-181
Export trade: development of banana, 271

Ex-slaves: and land ownership, 236-238; treatment of, by planters, 235-238

Fabian Society: establishment of, 286
Family: of Africans, 335; concept of, under slavery, 14; of Middle Eastern immigrants, 335
Farming: in Spanish Jamaica, 69
Federation: in the West Indies, 386
Festival of arts: Edward Seaga and, 405; staging of national, 405; Wycliffe Bennett and, 405
Festivals: of East Indians, 325-326
Firestone: in Liberia, 309
Fletcher's Land, 280
Florence Hall: protest at, 253
Folk songs: of Jamaica, 99
Folk tales: origin of, 197
Food: shortage of, in the late eighteenth century, 191-192; William Bligh and, 192
Food and Agriculture Organisation, 377
Franchise Act: literacy clause in, 283; requirements of, 251
Free blacks: in plantation society, 159
Free coloureds: in plantation society, 159
Free persons: registration of, 160
Free villages: chapels in, 240; establishment of, 237; layout of, 239-240; spread of, 241-242
Freedom: maroons and, 141-142; Sunday market and, 162; as theme in history, 128
Freedom fighters: in the Americas, 3-4
French Revolution, 184
Friendly societies: Robert Love on, 290
Friends of the Blacks, 184

Friendship, 166
Frome: riots in, 365
Fulani, 24

Genoa: and the Atlantic Age, 53, 54
Geometry: and the Incas and Aztecs, 43
Germans: settlement of, in Jamaica, 317
Ghana: and connection to Jamaica, 101; history of, 106-108
Ginger, 88
Global Age, 270
Goshen Pen: described, 165
Government: constitutional reform, in 1944; of Jamaica, in mid seventeenth century, 86, 87; representative, in Jamaica, 87, 282
Government policy: shaping of, 5
Great houses: in Jamaica, 151
Griot: in African society, 207
"Ground": meaning of, 164
Guanaboa Vale, 80
Guerrilla warfare: maroons and, 132
Guinea grass: introduction of, 165
Guys Town, 139

Haiti: independence of, 15; revolution in, 184-189
Hammocks: in Spanish Jamaica, 69
Hannah Town, 280
Harlem Renaissance: Garvey and, 300; Claude McKay and, 300
Haughton Court, 166
Hayes, Clarendon: East Indians in, 323
Hereditaments tax, 251
Hides, 88
Higglering: features of, 174-175
Higglers: slave, 170; urban slaves as, 173; and West African trading tradition, 170-171

Hispaniola: arrival of Columbus at, 63; sugar industry in, 57
Historians: perspective of, 51
History: African use of, 9; British colonial, and self-perception of Jamaicans, 10-11; British use of, 9-10; Derek Walcott on, 194; and empowerment, 9-10; Jamaican attitude to, 10; Lorna Goodison on, 194; white perceptions of African, 20
Holland, 166
Hope Estate, 153; aqueduct at, 154; described, 154
Hope River: and water supply, 154
Horse racing: at Drax Hall, 166
Hosay: celebration, 325-326
House of Assembly: establishment of, in Jamaica, 86, 87; first meeting of, 86, 87; power of, 251; response of Barbadian, to Crown colony rule, 264; on slavery, 209
Hymns: role of, in life of slaves, 201-202

Ibo people, 24, 110; values of, 114
Immigration: from China, 327; from Europe, 317; from India, 318; from the Middle East, 333-334
Immigration law: amendments to, 329-330; and literacy, 330
Imperialism, 78; fight against, by non-whites, 267; growth of US, 270; spread of, 266
In the Castle of my Skin, George Lamming: quoted, 1
Incas: empire of, 42-43; and geometry, 43; and mathematics, 43
Indenture system: slavery and, compared, 127; on sugar plantations, 317
Independence celebrations: in Jamaica, 398-399

Indigo, 88
Industrial Development Corporation: purpose of, 382
Industrial promotion: legislation for 382-383
Industrial Revolution: and anti-slavery trend, 209; financing of, 161-162; second, 266
Industrialisation: adoption of Puerto Rican strategies, 384; legislation to encourage, in Jamaica, 379; in Puerto Rico, 379; in the West Indies, 379
Institute of Jamaica: role of, 392
International Bank for Recon-struction and Development, 377
International Labour Organ-isation, 377
International Monetary Fund, 377
Islam: spread of, into Africa, 24
Iron: use of, in ancient Africa, 22

Jamaica Advocate: of Robert Love, 285, 286
Jamaica Advocate Co-operative Association: formation of, 289
Jamaica Agricultural Society: in anti-colonial struggle, 272-273, 350
Jamaica Broadcasting Corporation, 383
Jamaica Cultural Development Commission, 406
Jamaica Hope: development of, 395
Jamaica in Independence, Rex Nettleford, 404
Jamaica Labour Party: Bustamante and, 5; founding of, 370
Jamaica Library Service, 404
Jamaica Post: on 1896 election, 288
Jamaica Progressive League: and fight for self-government, 373
Jamaica Surveyed, Barry Higman, 152
Jamaica talk: development of, 195-196

Jamaica Tourist Board, 381
Jamaica Union of Teachers (JUT): in anti-colonial struggle, 272-273, 350
Jamaica Welfare Ltd: founding of, 360; guiding principles of, 360-361; as model for development, 360
Jamaica Workers' and Tradesmen's Union: formation of, 364
Jamaicans: attitude of, to history, 10; black Jamaicans, and attitude to Chinese, 332; in building of Panama Canal, 271; and migration, 271; and relations with East Indians, 321-322; response of, to social and economic conditions, 271
Jeronimite Reform Commission: on treatment of Indians, 70
Jews: in Jamaica, 7; early contri-butions of, 316-317
John Canoe: development of, 198
Journalists: and development of the media in Jamaica, 406
Juncunoo. *See* John Canoe
Justice: concept of, and Africans, 247

Kettering, 239
Kingston: establishment of, 135; riots in, 365; slums in, 386; unemployment in, 385; urbanisation of, 346-347, 349
Kingston and Liguanea Water Company, 154
Kingston, Urban Change and Reform, Colin Clarke: on conditions of working class, 352-353
Kinship: Africans and, 28
Kirkpatrick Pen, 167
Kongo: and Portuguese slave trade, 120-121
Koromante. *See* Coromanti
Kumina. *See* Cumina
Kung bushmen, 26

L. Baker Company: opening of, 278
La Navidad (fort), 63
Labour: division of, in slave society, 172; and plantation economy, 91
Labour conditions: Orde Brown inquiry into, in 1938, 367
Labour movement: Bustamante and organisation of, 5-6
Labour unrest: in the West Indies in the 1930s, 364
Lamp: found at Drax Hall, 155
Land grants: to early settlers, 85, 86
Land ownership: Chinese and, 330; during the seventeenth and eighteenth centuries, 156-157; by East Indians, 325; ex-slaves and, 236-238; in the late nineteenth century, 273; and political power, 279-280
Language: development of Jamaica talk, 195-196; influence of African, on Jamaican speech, 99-100
League of Coloured People: on social conditions in the West Indies, 351-352
Lebanese: in Jamaica, 7; occupa-tions of, in Jamaica, 334
Legislation: and discrimination against minorities, 332; for industrial promotion, 382-383
Legislative council: appointments to, 282; black representation in, 283; composition of Jamaican, 5
Liberation movements: in planta-tion America, 15-16
Liberia: plans for, 305
Liberty Hall, 302; sale of, 313
Liberty University: opening of, 307
Lionheart Gal, Sistren Theatre Collective, 402-403
Literacy: and black Jamaicans, 290; and Franchise Act, 283; in late nineteenth-century

Jamaica, 271-273; and universal adult suffrage, 369
Literature: West Indian, 394
Little Theatre Movement, 404
Living conditions: of migrant ex-slaves, 238
Llanrumney, 166
London Missionary Society, 178
Long Hill Pen, 165
Los Virmejales, 80
Lothagm Hill, Kenya: archaeological find at, 22
Lucky Valley Estate, Clarendon: described, 30-31
Lumb Commission: of 1897, on teaching standards, 290; of 1905, 290
Lyndhurst, St Elizabeth: planning of rebellion at, 203-204
Lyssons, 166

Magna Carta, 10
Magnetic compass: invention of, 62
Maldon, 244
Mali: empire of, 108-109
Man: survival and development of early, 34-35
Manley and the New Jamaica, Rex Nettleford, 378
Market canoes: in Kingston Harbour, 174
Market gardening: by East Indians, 324-325; prohibition of, 324
Marketing system: of blacks, 162; West African origin of internal, 172
Markets: regulation of, 173-174. *See also* Sunday market
Marriage: of Chinese, 330; of East Indians, 321
Maroon, 4, 16; first African to become, in Jamaica, 57; phenomenon of, 75
Maroon settlements: in the Americas, 129; in Mexico, 129-130; in Suriname, 130-131

Maroon wars: first, 135, 138-142; second, 145-149; terms of treaty to end first, 140-141
Maroons: and capture of Paul Bogle, 259; and freedom, 141-142; and guerrilla warfare, 132; Leeward, 134; methods of warfare of, 137-138; organisation of, 136-137; transportation of, of Trelawny Town, 148-149; Windward, 136. *See also* Bush negroes
Marronage, 4, 16, 129
Master and Servant's Act: effect of on peasants, 250
Mathematics: and Incas and Aztecs, 43
Mayas: empire of, 42
Mentality: master/slave, in post-emancipation period, 243
Mercantilism: and slavery, 161
Mercantilist theory, 78
Mexico: maroon government of Yanga in, 129-130
Mico Institution: establishment of, 240
Middle East: immigrants from, 333-334
Ming dynasty, 61-62
Missionaries: role of, in anti-slavery movement, 206, 226
Mona Estate, 153; aqueduct at, 154
Montego Bay: tourism in, 381
Montrose, 166
Morant Bay Rebellion: course of, 258-260; enquiry into, 263-264; events leading up to, 254, 255-258; repercussions of, 260; response to, in Britain, 264
Moravians: and missionary work in Jamaica, 179
Mortality rate: of Africans, 93; of children in Jamaica, 193-194; of slaves, 123, 194
"Mountain": meaning of, 164
Moyne Commission: and criticism of Crown colony

rule, 352; findings of, 357; report of, 351, 352
Mulattoes: in Jamaica, 192
Music: Africans and, 97; folk song, 99; Rastafarians and development of Jamaican, 400-402
Musical Society of Jamaica, 404
My Mother Who Fathered Me, Edith Clarke, 275
Myalism, 39

Nanny Town, 136, 139
National Club of Jamaica, 297
National Dance Theatre Company of Jamaica (NDTC), 404, 405
National development: race consciousness and, 295
National Gallery of Jamaica, 392, 394
National Heroes: public opinion of, 314-315
Nationalism: emergence of, in Jamaica, 19-20, 271, 337; growth of, 346; Norman Manley and, 362-363
Navigation Act (1651): of England, 78
Negro Education Grant: termination of, 272
Negro Factories Corporation, 304
Negro People's of the World: convention of, 312-313
Negro World, 301, 302; Kenyatta on, 302
New Day, V. S. Reid, 19, 207
New Jamaican, 308
New Seville: building of, 71; school at, 67-68
New World: disease in the, 58, 59-60; early colonisation of, 42

Obi, 39
Occupations: of blacks in Kingston, 353; of Chinese, 328, 330; of East Indians,

Ring games: in Jamaica, 197
Rio Grande Copper Mines, 243
Riots: at Frome, 365; in Kingston, 365; in Jamaica in the 1930s, 5; in the West Indies, in the 1930s, 5
Rock carvings: and African artistic tradition, 22
Royal Commission: of 1885, 273; of 1897, 5, 12, 273; of, 1897, and endorsement of small holdings, 274-275; of 1930, 310; and enquiry into Morant Bay Rebellion, 263-264; of 1938-39, 351-352, 357. See also Moyne Commission

St Ann, parish of: petition of residents of, on conditions in Jamaica, 255-256
St Domingue: revolution in, 184-189
St Helena: recruitment of Africans from, 318
St Thomas, parish of: conditions in, 254, 255
Salt Pond Hut, 167
Salter's Hill, 216
São Tome: colonisation of, 119
Savings schemes: of Chinese, 329
School of African Philosophy: establishment of, 313-314
Science and technology, 377
Self-government: granting of, to Jamaica, 368, 373
Shango, 39
Sierra Leone: establishment of, 179-180; recruitment of Africans from, 318
Sistren Theatre Collective: Lionheart Gal, 402-403
Six Great Jamaicans, W. Adolphe Roberts, 285
Skills training: for children of ex-slaves, 244-245
Slave revolts: in Barbados, 204; in Demerara, 204; in Jamaica, late seventeenth century, 134-

135, 143-144; women in, 144
Slave trade: abolition of, 180; Atlantic, 118-127; census of, 93; described, 121-122; impact of, on African life, 102-103; Portugal and African, 118-121
Slave village: culture within, 156; described, 31, 32
Slavery: Africans and, 116-118; Catholic Church and, 68; Christianity and, 118; distinction between African and Atlantic, 118; under English, 76; and indenture system compared, 127; Jamaican House of Assembly on, 209; and mercantilism, 161; West India Committee support for, 209
Slaves: and British working class, compared, 210-211; capture and sale of, 121-127; compensation of owners, 230; freeing of, in England, 179; and knowledge of anti-slavery campaign, 208-209; mortality rate of, 123, 194; mutilation of, 160; numbers brought to the New World, 124-125; punishment of, 14; seasoning of, 126; and struggle for freedom, 3-4; Tainos as, 58-59; treatment of, 122-124; in urban areas, 172-173
Sligoville: establishment of, 237
Small holdings: in the banana trade, 275, 278-279; endorsement of, by Norman Commission, 274-275
Smith Village, 280
Social conditions: in the 1860s, 254; response of Jamaicans to, 271; transformation of, of peasants, 276
Social development: impact of Jamaican theory of, 361
Social Development Commission, 404
Social mobility: lack of opportunities for, 272

Social structure: of Jamaica in the 1930s, 372; of plantation society in Jamaica, 193
Society for the Gradual Abolition of Slavery: work of, 208
Songhai: empire of, 109
Songs: of slaves, 197
Sparks Lodge: founding of, 290
Sport: and myth of black inferiority, 392
Squatters, 253
Stamp duty, 251
Steam power: impact of, on industry, 190
Stereotyping: survival of colonial, 11, 12
Story of the Jamaican People, the: perspective of, xi-xii
Strike: Sam Sharpe and campaign for, 214
Sugar: introduction of large-scale production of, 88-90; major areas of production of, in Jamaica, 92; making of, in Spanish Jamaica, 74; price of, 231; and prosperity, 91; removal of tariff on West Indian, 232-233; and transformation of Barbados, 91-92
Sugar industry: decline of, in Cuba, 348-349; decline of, in Jamaica, 231-233; and financing of Industrial Revolution, 161-162; start of, in Hispaniola, 57
Sugar plantation: difference between pen and, 164; dominance of, in Jamaica, 152-153, 156; extent of, in Jamaica, 151-152; and generation of European wealth, 161-162; ownership of, 232
Sunday market, 171; and freedom, 162. See also Markets
Suriname: account of maroon warfare in, 130-132; settlers from, in Jamaica, 86
Suriname Quarters, 86
Syrians: in Jamaica, 7

THE LEARNING CENTRE
CITY & ISLINGTON COLLEGE
383 HOLLOWAY ROAD
LONDON N7 0RN